STATE OF NEW YORK

# FOURTH REPORT

OF THE

# FACTORY INVESTIGATING COMMISSION

1915

VOLUME III

STATISTICAL TABLES

TRANSMITTED TO THE LEGISLATURE FEBRUARY 15, 1915

ALBANY
J. B. LYON COMPANY, PRINTERS
1915

STATE OF NEW YORK

No. 43

# IN SENATE

FEBRUARY 15, 1915

# FOURTH REPORT

OF THE

## New York State Factory Investigating Commission

February 15, 1915

ROBERT F. WAGNER
*Chairman*

ALFRED E. SMITH
*Vice-Chairman*

CHARLES M. HAMILTON
EDWARD D. JACKSON
CYRUS W. PHILLIPS
SIMON BRENTANO
MARY E. DREIER
SAMUEL GOMPERS
LAURENCE M. D. McGUIRE

FRANK A. TIERNEY
*Secretary*

ABRAM I. ELKUS
*Chief Counsel*

BERNARD L. SHIENTAG
*Assistant Counsel*

HOWARD B. WOOLSTON
*Director of Wage Investigation*

ALBERT H. N. BARON
*Assistant Director*

# APPENDIX V

## STATISTICAL TABLES

SUPPLEMENTARY TO REPORT OF GENERAL WAGE INVESTIGATION

## STATISTICAL TABLES

The following statistical appendix is in the nature of a supplement to the main portion of the wage report, and contains detailed statistics with reference to the industries investigated by the Commission.

It presents for convenient reference, a series of tables showing in detail the distribution by localities and divisions of the industries investigated, and affords a basis for direct comparison.

The subjects dealt with in the tables are set forth in the following list:

| *Table Series* | *Subject* |
|---|---|
| I. | Number of employees according to age groups, by locality and sex. |
| II. | Number and per cent. of all employees according to nativity, by locality. |
| III. | Number of employees earning specified weekly rates, by locality and sex. |
| IV. | Number of employees classified according to actual weekly earnings, by locality and sex. |
| V. | Number of employees earning specified weekly rates, by age groups and sex. |
| VI. | Number of employees classified according to actual weekly earnings, by age groups and sex. |
| VII. | Number and per cent. of employees, by sex, according to occupation and nativity. |
| VIII. | Number and per cent. of employees earning specified weekly rates according to occupation and sex. |
| IX. | Number and per cent. of employees classified according to actual weekly earnings by occupation and sex. |
| X. | Number and per cent. of employees classified according to actual weekly earnings, by conjugal condition and sex. |
| XI. | Number and per cent. of employees classified according to actual weekly earnings, by nativity and sex. |
| XII. | Number of employees, for each sex, classified according to actual weekly earnings, by the number of years in the trade. |
| XIII. | Number of employees, for each sex, classified according to actual weekly earnings, by the number of years with the firm. |
| XIV. | Number of employees, for each sex, in the main occupations of specified departments in department stores, earning specified weekly rates. |

XV. Number of employees earning specified weekly rates, by department and sex, in neighborhood and five and ten cent stores.

XVI. Number of employees classified according to actual weekly earnings, by department and sex, in neighborhood and five and ten cent stores.

XVII. Number of employees classified by age groups, by department and sex.

XVIII. Number and per cent. of all employees in each department according to actual weekly earnings — shirts, confectionery and paper box industries.

XIX. Number and per cent. of employees according to average actual weekly earnings, by occupation and sex.

XX. Number and per cent. of all employees working 43 weeks or more, according to actual annual earnings, by occupation and sex.

## KEY TO CODE NUMBERS USED IN THE INDEX OF STATISTICAL TABLES

For convenience in reference all tables in this section are numbered consecutively from 1 to 365 in arabic numerals.

Roman numerals are used to show the various table forms. Correlations of the same items have in every case the same Roman numerals. Thus, Table V is, for all industries and all localities, a table showing the distribution according to weekly rates by age groups.

The other symbols used are given in the following classification:

A. Mercantile establishments.
- 1. Department stores.
  - a. Stock and sales.
  - b. Office.
  - c. Shipping and delivery.
  - d. Manufacturing.
  - e. Plant.
- 2. Neighborhood stores.
  - a, b, c, d, and e the same as above.
- 3. Five and ten-cent stores.
  - a, b, c, d, and e the same as above.

B. Men's shirt industry.
- a. Factory workers.
- b. Office force.
- c. Shipping and delivery.
- e. Plant.

(For New York City only
- 1. Negligee shirts.
- 2. Working shirts).

C. Paper box industry.
- a, b, c, and e as above.

D. Confectionery industry.
- a, b, c, and e as above.

(For New York City only
- 1. Wholesale factories.
- 2. Wholesale factories having a retail outlet).

# LIST OF TABLES

## NEW YORK STATE

### MERCANTILE ESTABLISHMENTS



### DEPARTMENT STORES — STOCK AND SALES

#### NEW YORK STATE



### DEPARTMENT STORES — OFFICE

#### NEW YORK STATE

## DEPARTMENT STORES — OFFICE (*continued*)

### New York State



## DEPARTMENT STORES — SHIPPING AND DELIVERY

### NEW YORK STATE



## DEPARTMENT STORES — MANUFACTURING

### NEW YORK STATE

DEPARTMENT STORES — PLANT

NEW YORK STATE



NEIGHBORHOOD STORES — STOCK AND SALES

NEW YORK STATE



NEIGHBORHOOD STORES — OFFICE

NEW YORK STATE

NEIGHBORHOOD STORES — OFFICE (*continued*)

New York State



NEIGHBORHOOD STORES — SHIPPING AND DELIVERY, MANUFACTURING, PLANT

NEW YORK STATE



FIVE-AND TEN-CENT STORES — STOCK AND SALES

NEW YORK STATE



FIVE-AND TEN-CENT STORES — OFFICE, SHIPPING AND DELIVERY, PLANT

NEW YORK STATE



THE MEN'S SHIRT INDUSTRY — ALL EMPLOYEES

NEW YORK STATE

### THE MEN'S SHIRT INDUSTRY — FACTORY WORKERS

New York State



### THE PAPER BOX INDUSTRY — ALL EMPLOYEES

New York State



### THE PAPER BOX INDUSTRY — FACTORY WORKERS

New York State

### THE PAPER BOX INDUSTRY — FACTORY WORKERS (*continued*)

New York State



### THE CONFECTIONERY INDUSTRY — ALL EMPLOYEES

NEW YORK STATE



### THE CONFECTIONERY INDUSTRY — FACTORY WORKERS

NEW YORK STATE



### OFFICE FORCE — MEN'S SHIRT, CONFECTIONERY, AND PAPER BOX INDUSTRIES

NEW YORK STATE

OFFICE FORCE — MEN'S SHIRT, CONFECTIONERY, AND PAPER BOX INDUSTRIES (*continued*)

New York State



SHIPPING AND DELIVERY — MEN'S SHIRTS, CONFECTIONERY AND PAPER BOX INDUSTRIES

NEW YORK STATE



PLANT — MEN'S SHIRT, CONFECTIONERY, AND PAPER BOX INDUSTRIES

NEW YORK STATE

## NEW YORK STATE, EXCLUSIVE OF NEW YORK CITY

### DEPARTMENT STORES — STOCK AND SALES



### DEPARTMENT STORES — OFFICE

NEW YORK STATE EXCLUSIVE OF NEW YORK CITY



### DEPARTMENT STORES — SHIPPING AND DELIVERY

NEW YORK STATE EXCLUSIVE OF NEW YORK CITY



### DEPARTMENT STORES — MANUFACTURING

NEW YORK STATE EXCLUSIVE OF NEW YORK CITY

## DEPARTMENT STORES — PLANT

NEW YORK STATE EXCLUSIVE OF NEW YORK CITY



## FIVE- AND TEN-CENT STORES — STOCK AND SALES

NEW YORK STATE EXCLUSIVE OF NEW YORK CITY



## FIVE- AND TEN-CENT STORES — OFFICE, SHIPPING AND DELIVERY, PLANT

NEW YORK STATE EXCLUSIVE OF NEW YORK CITY



## THE MEN'S SHIRT INDUSTRY — FACTORY WORKERS

NEW YORK STATE EXCLUSIVE OF NEW YORK CITY



## THE PAPER BOX INDUSTRY — FACTORY WORKERS

NEW YORK STATE EXCLUSIVE OF NEW YORK CITY

## THE CONFECTIONERY INDUSTRY — FACTORY WORKERS

### NEW YORK STATE EXCLUSIVE OF NEW YORK CITY



## NEW YORK CITY

### DEPARTMENT STORES — STOCK AND SALES



### DEPARTMENT STORES — OFFICE

#### NEW YORK CITY



### DEPARTMENT STORES — SHIPPING AND DELIVERY

#### NEW YORK CITY



### DEPARTMENT STORES — MANUFACTURING

#### NEW YORK CITY

### DEPARTMENT STORES — PLANT

NEW YORK CITY



### NEIGHBORHOOD STORES — STOCK AND SALES

NEW YORK CITY



### NEIGHBORHOOD STORES — OFFICE

NEW YORK CITY



### NEIGHBORHOOD STORES — SHIPPING AND DELIVERY, MANUFACTURING, PLANT

NEW YORK CITY



### FIVE- AND TEN-CENT STORES — STOCK AND SALES

NEW YORK CITY



### FIVE- AND TEN-CENT STORES — OFFICE, SHIPPING AND DELIVERY, PLANT

NEW YORK CITY

### THE MEN'S SHIRT INDUSTRY — FACTORY WORKERS

NEW YORK CITY



### THE MEN'S SHIRT INDUSTRY — FACTORY WORKERS, NEGLIGEE SHIRTS

NEW YORK CITY



### THE MEN'S SHIRT INDUSTRY — FACTORY WORKERS, WORKING SHIRTS

NEW YORK CITY



### THE PAPER BOX INDUSTRY — FACTORY WORKERS

NEW YORK CITY



### THE CONFECTIONERY INDUSTRY — FACTORY WORKERS

NEW YORK CITY

THE CONFECTIONERY INDUSTRY — WHOLESALE CANDY, FACTORY WORKERS

New York City



WHOLESALE CANDY FACTORIES WITH RETAIL OUTLET—FACTORY WORKERS

New York City



BUFFALO

DEPARTMENT STORES — STOCK AND SALES



DEPARTMENT STORES — OFFICE

Buffalo



DEPARTMENT STORES — SHIPPING AND DELIVERY

Buffalo



DEPARTMENT STORES — MANUFACTURING

Buffalo

DEPARTMENT STORES — PLANT



NEIGHBORHOOD STORES — STOCK AND SALES



NEIGHBORHOOD STORES — OFFICE, SHIPPING AND DELIVERY, MANUFACTURING, PLANT



THE PAPER BOX INDUSTRY — FACTORY WORKERS



THE CONFECTIONERY INDUSTRY — FACTORY WORKERS



ROCHESTER

DEPARTMENT STORES — STOCK AND SALES

DEPARTMENT STORES — OFFICE, SHIPPING AND DELIVERY, MANUFACTURING, PLANT

SYRACUSE



ALBANY

DEPARTMENT STORES — STOCK AND SALES



DEPARTMENT STORES — OFFICE, SHIPPING AND DELIVERY, MANUFACTURING, PLANT

ALBANY



THE MEN'S SHIRT INDUSTRY — FACTORY WORKERS

ALBANY



SCHENECTADY

DEPARTMENT STORES — STOCK AND SALES

DEPARTMENT STORES — OFFICE, SHIPPING AND DELIVERY, MANUFACTURING, PLANT

SCHENECTADY



UTICA

DEPARTMENT STORES — STOCK AND SALES



DEPARTMENT STORES — OFFICE, SHIPPING AND DELIVERY, MANUFACTURING, PLANT

UTICA



TROY

DEPARTMENT STORES — STOCK AND SALES



DEPARTMENT STORES — OFFICE, SHIPPING AND DELIVERY, MANUFACTURING, PLANT

TROY

## THE MEN'S SHIRT INDUSTRY — FACTORY WORKERS

### TROY



## THE PAPER BOX INDUSTRY — FACTORY WORKERS

### TROY

1. TABLE I, A

NEW YORK STATE

**MERCANTILE ESTABLISHMENTS**

NUMBER OF EMPLOYEES ACCORDING TO AGE GROUPS, BY LOCALITY AND SEX

| LOCALITY | Sex | AGE GROUPS IN YEARS | | | | | | | | | | | |
|---|---|---|---|---|---|---|---|---|---|---|---|---|---|
| | | Total | 14–15 | 16–17 | 18–20 | 21–24 | 25–29 | 30–34 | 35–39 | 40–44 | 45–54 | 55–64 | 65 and over | Not reported |
| New York City | Male | 16,136 | 406 | 860 | 1,927 | 2,440 | 2,289 | 1,933 | 1,821 | 1,390 | 2,076 | 696 | 146 | 152 |
| | Female | 22,479 | 1,153 | 2,853 | 4,856 | 4,930 | 3,348 | 1,736 | 1,405 | 706 | 490 | 75 | 16 | 911 |
| Buffalo | Male | 1,774 | 133 | 174 | 148 | 250 | 218 | 207 | 149 | 144 | 211 | 103 | 25 | 12 |
| | Female | 3,145 | 111 | 333 | 746 | 747 | 507 | 276 | 204 | 91 | 84 | 9 | 1 | 39 |
| Rochester | Male | 954 | 55 | 47 | 82 | 150 | 164 | 124 | 86 | 66 | 103 | 57 | 11 | 9 |
| | Female | 1,916 | 117 | 186 | 331 | 379 | 309 | 197 | 152 | 79 | 96 | 23 | ...... | 47 |
| Syracuse | Male | 461 | 28 | 30 | 32 | 55 | 58 | 52 | 48 | 37 | 68 | 40 | 10 | 3 |
| | Female | 1,136 | 54 | 137 | 258 | 218 | 151 | 96 | 74 | 35 | 48 | 10 | 4 | 51 |
| Albany | Male | 320 | 18 | 23 | 27 | 43 | 38 | 34 | 30 | 30 | 53 | 16 | 7 | 1 |
| | Female | 639 | 14 | 101 | 132 | 118 | 105 | 51 | 49 | 30 | 18 | 8 | ...... | 13 |
| Utica | Male | 295 | 16 | 24 | 38 | 21 | 40 | 24 | 40 | 27 | 14 | 19 | 4 | 1 |
| | Female | 555 | 18 | 91 | 110 | 111 | 70 | 43 | 51 | 25 | 26 | 2 | ...... | 8 |
| Troy | Male | 332 | 10 | 40 | 27 | 25 | 27 | 40 | 30 | 26 | 69 | 29 | 7 | 2 |
| | Female | 490 | 27 | 81 | 85 | 96 | 64 | 33 | 39 | 19 | 22 | 6 | 3 | 15 |
| Schenectady | Male | 175 | 4 | 11 | 17 | 20 | 33 | 20 | 17 | 20 | 21 | 9 | 2 | 1 |
| | Female | 434 | 3 | 73 | 101 | 72 | 64 | 44 | 32 | 19 | 22 | 1 | ...... | 3 |
| Other cities and towns | Male | 295 | 6 | 30 | 38 | 40 | 43 | 27 | 19 | 27 | 33 | 19 | 9 | 4 |
| | Female | 852 | 6 | 68 | 171 | 163 | 131 | 92 | 66 | 44 | 46 | 16 | 1 | 48 |
| State | Male | 20,742 | 676 | 1,239 | 2,336 | 3,044 | 2,910 | 2,461 | 2,240 | 1,767 | 2,675 | 988 | 221 | 185 |
| | Female | 31,646 | 1,503 | 3,923 | 6,790 | 6,834 | 4,749 | 2,568 | 2,072 | 1,048 | 852 | 150 | 25 | 1,132 |
| Cumulative per cent. for the State | Male | 100 | 3.27 | 9.29 | 20.65 | 35.45 | 49.66 | 61.66 | 72.53 | 81.13 | 94.13 | 98.94 | 100 | ...... |
| | Female | 100 | 4.99 | 17.82 | 40.15 | 62.58 | 78.15 | 86.62 | 93.42 | 96.79 | 99.58 | 99.92 | 100 | ...... |

NEW YORK STATE

**MERCANTILE ESTABLISHMENTS**

2. TABLE II, A

NUMBER AND PER CENT. OF ALL EMPLOYEES ACCORDING TO NATIVITY, BY LOCALITY

| Locality | Distribution of native and foreign born | | | | | | | | Distribution of foreign born according to country of birth | | | | | | | |
|---|---|---|---|---|---|---|---|---|---|---|---|---|---|---|---|---|
| | Total | | Not given | | Native | | Foreign | | Ireland | | Germany | | England | | Russia | |
| | No. | Per cent. | No. | Per cent. | No. | Per cent. | No. | Per cent. | No. | Per cent. | No. | Per cent. | No. | Per cent. | No. | Per cent. |
| New York City | 38,615 | 100 | 291 | .7 | 29,680 | 77.1 | 8,644 | 22.2 | 2,912 | 33.8 | 1,026 | 11.84 | 891 | 10.29 | 794 | 9.17 |
| Buffalo | 4,919 | 100 | 24 | .49 | 4,197 | 85.3 | 698 | 14.21 | 59 | 8.5 | 151 | 21.6 | 91 | 13.1 | 27 | 3.9 |
| Rochester | 2,870 | 100 | 13 | .45 | 2,355 | 82.15 | 502 | 17.5 | 60 | 11.9 | 49 | 9.8 | 115 | 22.9 | 17 | 3.4 |
| Syracuse | 1,597 | 100 | 7 | .44 | 1,407 | 88.1 | 183 | 11.46 | 33 | 18. | 24 | 13.1 | 20 | 10.9 | 29 | 15.9 |
| Albany | 959 | 100 | 9 | .94 | 882 | 92. | 68 | 7.06 | 12 | 17.63 | 14 | 20.6 | 11 | 16.2 | 13 | 19.1 |
| Utica | 850 | 100 | 7 | .82 | 760 | 89.4 | 83 | 9.78 | 10 | 12.2 | 9 | 10.8 | 16 | 19.2 | ...... | .... |
| Troy | 822 | 100 | 7 | .8 | 754 | 91.8 | 61 | 7.4 | 17 | 28. | 11 | 18 | 7 | 11.5 | ...... | .... |
| Schenectady | 609 | 100 | 3 | .49 | 549 | 90.2 | 57 | 9.31 | 5 | 8.7 | 11 | 19.3 | 9 | 15.8 | 4 | 7.2 |
| Other cities and towns | 1,147 | 100 | 17 | 1.6 | 1,052 | 91.6 | 78 | 6.8 | 10 | 12.6 | ...... | .... | 21 | 27. | ...... | .... |
| State | 52,388 | 100 | 378 | .72 | 41,636 | 79.54 | 10,374 | 19.74 | 3,118 | 30. | 1,295 | 12.40 | 1.181 | 11.7 | 8.84 | 8.5 |

NEW YORK STATE

**MERCANTILE EATABLISHMENTS**

2. TABLE II, A — (*concluded*)

NUMBER AND PER CENT. OF ALL EMPLOYEES ACCORDING TO NATIVITY, BY LOCALITY

| Locality | Distribution of foreign born according to country of birth (*concluded*) | | | | | | | | | | | | | | | |
|---|---|---|---|---|---|---|---|---|---|---|---|---|---|---|---|---|
| | Canada | | Italy | | Austria | | Scotland | | Hungary | | West Indies | | Wales | | All other* | |
| | No. | Per cent. | No. | Per cent. | No. | Per cent. | No. | Per cent. | No. | Per cent. | No. | Per cent. | No. | Per cent. | No. | Per cent. |
| New York City | 314 | 3.63 | 621 | 7.17 | 468 | 5.42 | 328 | 3.78 | 192 | 2.22 | 154 | 1.77 | ...... | .... | 944 | 10.91 |
| Buffalo | 211 | 30.2 | 21 | 3. | ...... | .... | 68 | 9.7 | ...... | .... | ...... | .... | ...... | .... | 70 | 10 |
| Rochester | 145 | 28.9 | 33 | 6.6 | ...... | .... | 23 | 4.6 | ...... | .... | ...... | .... | ...... | .... | 60 | 17.9 |
| Syracuse | 34 | 18.6 | 11 | 6. | ...... | .... | 19 | 10.4 | ...... | .... | ...... | .... | ...... | .... | 13 | 7.1 |
| Albany | 2 | 2.92 | ...... | .... | ...... | .... | 5 | 7.35 | ...... | .... | ...... | .... | ...... | .... | 11 | 16.2 |
| Utica | 8 | 9.6 | ...... | .... | ...... | .... | 2 | 2.4 | ...... | .... | ...... | .... | 23 | 27.6 | 15 | 18.2 |
| Troy | 16 | 26.2 | ...... | .... | ...... | .... | 4 | 6.5 | ...... | .... | ...... | .... | ...... | .... | 6 | 9.8 |
| Schenectady | 9 | 15.8 | ...... | .... | ...... | .... | 5 | 8.7 | ...... | .... | ...... | .... | ...... | .... | 14 | 24.5 |
| Other cities and towns | 29 | 37.2 | ...... | .... | ...... | .... | 7 | 9. | ...... | .... | ...... | .... | ...... | .... | 11 | 14.2 |
| State | 768 | 7.4 | 686 | 6.6 | 468 | 4.5 | 461 | 4.43 | 192 | 1.83 | 154 | 1.44 | 23 | .2 | 1,144 | 11. |

* Includes for each locality countries representing less than 1 per cent. of the total foreign born employees in the industry in that locality.

NEW YORK STATE
MERCANTILE ESTABLISHMENTS

3. TABLE III, A

NUMBER OF EMPLOYEES EARNING SPECIFIED WEEKLY RATES, BY LOCALITY AND SEX

| WEEKLY RATES IN DOLLARS | NEW YORK CITY | | | BUFFALO | | ROCHESTER | | SYRACUSE | | ALBANY | | UTICA | | WEEKLY RATES IN DOLLARS |
|---|---|---|---|---|---|---|---|---|---|---|---|---|---|---|
| | Male | Female | Not reported | Male | Female | Male | Female | Male | Female | Male | Female | Male | Female | |
| Under $3 00...... | ...... | 6 | 14 | ...... | 8 | ...... | 9 | 1 | 35 | 6 | 12 | ...... | 1 | .....Under $3 00 |
| $3 00– 3 49...... | 21 | 273 | 169 | 20 | 87 | ...... | 4 | 8 | 53 | 3 | 20 | 1 | 4 | .....$3 00– 3 49 |
| 3 50– 3 99...... | 41 | 680 | 279 | 24 | 103 | 12 | 92 | 9 | 23 | 6 | 35 | 10 | 13 | ......3 50– 3 99 |
| 4 00– 4 49...... | 352 | 1,603 | 1,042 | 74 | 120 | 32 | 73 | 11 | 64 | 4 | 10 | 10 | 57 | ......4 00– 4 49 |
| 4 50– 4 99...... | 99 | 850 | 465 | 12 | 73 | 5 | 37 | 3 | 65 | 14 | 35 | 5 | 15 | ......4 50– 4 99 |
| 5 00– 5 49...... | 395 | 1,622 | 953 | 134 | 322 | 22 | 134 | 14 | 125 | 7 | 156 | 7 | 75 | ......5 00– 5 49 |
| 5 50– 5 99...... | 49 | 492 | 215 | 6 | 69 | 3 | 21 | 1 | 15 | ...... | 14 | 1 | 13 | ......5 50– 5 99 |
| 6 00– 6 49...... | 491 | 2,719 | 2,165 | 47 | 822 | 19 | 256 | 10 | 146 | 9 | 126 | 8 | 81 | ......6 00– 6 49 |
| 6 50– 6 99...... | 40 | 395 | 117 | 4 | 62 | ...... | 31 | 1 | 9 | ...... | 7 | ...... | ...... | ......6 50– 6 99 |
| 7 00– 7 49...... | 468 | 2,924 | 1,912 | 38 | 480 | 18 | 343 | 8 | 103 | 11 | 80 | 12 | 55 | ......7 00– 7 49 |
| 7 50– 7 99...... | 245 | 225 | 275 | 6 | 55 | 3 | 35 | 1 | 12 | ...... | 1 | 1 | 4 | ......7 50– 7 99 |
| 8 00– 8 99...... | 821 | 2,648 | 1,499 | 43 | 332 | 28 | 281 | 12 | 123 | 14 | 51 | 11 | 86 | ......8 00– 8 99 |
| 9 00– 9 99...... | 556 | 1,758 | 864 | 49 | 148 | 35 | 176 | 9 | 81 | 14 | 21 | 9 | 37 | ......9 00– 9 99 |
| 10 00–10 99...... | 1,234 | 1,707 | 1,477 | 108 | 192 | 87 | 126 | 28 | 69 | 17 | 23 | 20 | 42 | .....10 00–10 99 |
| 11 00–11 99...... | 635 | 696 | 545 | 54 | 30 | 26 | 46 | 15 | 34 | 8 | 3 | 5 | 8 | .....11 00–11 99 |
| 12 00–12 99...... | 2,108 | 1,186 | 1,569 | 292 | 105 | 189 | 113 | 65 | 59 | 29 | 26 | 46 | 30 | .....12 00–12 99 |
| 13 00–13 99...... | 637 | 316 | 369 | 65 | 23 | 75 | 25 | 14 | 15 | 8 | 1 | 12 | 2 | .....13 00–13 99 |
| 14 00–14 99...... | 1,056 | 504 | 467 | 115 | 33 | 60 | 23 | 31 | 17 | 22 | 1 | 12 | 4 | .....14 00–14 99 |
| 15 00–15 99...... | 1,724 | 489 | 866 | 239 | 42 | 117 | 41 | 46 | 29 | 29 | 6 | 30 | 9 | .....15 00–15 99 |
| 16 00–17 99...... | 1,185 | 367 | 511 | 160 | 11 | 73 | 15 | 34 | 13 | 34 | 3 | 17 | 4 | .....16 00–17 99 |
| 18 00–19 99...... | 1,001 | 302 | 431 | 120 | 12 | 53 | 11 | 26 | 10 | 19 | 2 | 15 | 2 | .....18 00–19 99 |
| 20 00–24 99...... | 1,358 | 319 | 475 | 92 | 9 | 64 | 10 | 47 | 8 | 33 | 4 | 31 | 3 | .....20 00–24 99 |
| 25 00–29 99...... | 672 | 148 | 287 | 37 | 2 | 12 | 7 | 20 | 6 | 14 | 1 | 16 | 6 | .....25 00–29 99 |
| 30 00–34 99...... | 322 | 51 | 70 | 13 | 2 | 3 | 2 | 20 | 2 | 6 | 1 | 5 | 1 | .....30 00–34 99 |
| 35 00–39 99...... | 122 | 30 | 49 | 6 | 1 | 4 | 3 | 8 | 2 | 6 | ...... | 2 | ...... | .....35 00–39 99 |
| 40 00 and over.... | 236 | 56 | 121 | 8 | 1 | 10 | 1 | 14 | 7 | 7 | ...... | 4 | ...... | ...40 00 and over |
| Not reported..... | 168 | 35 | 143 | 8 | 1 | 4 | 1 | 5 | 7 | ...... | ...... | 4 | 3 | .....Not reported |
| Total........ | 16,036 | 22,401 | 17,349 | 1,774 | 3,145 | 954 | 1,916 | 461 | 1,132 | 320 | 639 | 294 | 555 | .......Total |

NEW YORK STATE
MERCANTILE ESTABLISHMENTS

3. TABLE III, A — (*concluded*) NUMBER OF EMPLOYEES EARNING SPECIFIED WEEKLY RATES, BY LOCALITY AND SEX

| WEEKLY RATES IN DOLLARS | TROY | | SCHENECTADY | | OTHER CITIES AND TOWNS | | STATE | | | CUMULATIVE PER CENT. FOR STATE | | WEEKLY RATES IN DOLLARS |
|---|---|---|---|---|---|---|---|---|---|---|---|---|
| | Male | Female | Male | Female | Male | Female | Male | Female | Not reported | Male | Female | |
| Under $3 00 | 1 | ...... | 2 | 3 | ........ | 1 | 10 | 75 | 14 | .05 | .24 | Under $3 00 |
| $3 00– 3 49 | 7 | 47 | 2 | 31 | 1 | 8 | 63 | 527 | 169 | .37 | 1.91 | $3 00– 3 49 |
| 3 50– 3 99 | 2 | 7 | 2 | 10 | 1 | 13 | 107 | 976 | 279 | .91 | 5.00 | 3 50– 3 99 |
| 4 00– 4 49 | 17 | 15 | 2 | 27 | 4 | 45 | 506 | 2,014 | 1,042 | 3.39 | 11.38 | 4 00– 4 99 |
| 4 50– 4 99 | 7 | 20 | ........ | 33 | 2 | 23 | 147 | 1,151 | 465 | 4.11 | 15.04 | 4 50– 4 99 |
| 5 00– 5 49 | 12 | 24 | 4 | 61 | 12 | 82 | 607 | 2,601 | 953 | 7.09 | 23.30 | 5 00– 5 49 |
| 5 50– 5 99 | 2 | 8 | ........ | 1 | ........ | 8 | 62 | 641 | 215 | 7.39 | 25.33 | 5 50– 5 99 |
| 6 00– 6 49 | 6 | 53 | 6 | 39 | 17 | 137 | 613 | 4,379 | 2,165 | 10.38 | 39.19 | 6 00– 6 49 |
| 6 50– 6 99 | ...... | 2 | ........ | 1 | 1 | 6 | 46 | 513 | 117 | 10.61 | 40.81 | 6 50– 6 99 |
| 7 00– 7 49 | 12 | 55 | 6 | 43 | 9 | 90 | 582 | 4,173 | 1,912 | 13.47 | 54.06 | 7 00– 7 49 |
| 7 50– 7 99 | 2 | 41 | ........ | 6 | 1 | 18 | 259 | 397 | 275 | 14.74 | 55.32 | 7 50– 7 99 |
| 8 00– 8 99 | 10 | 56 | 2 | 47 | 18 | 100 | 959 | 3,724 | 1,499 | 19.43 | 67.15 | 8 00– 8 99 |
| 9 00– 9 99 | 10 | 38 | 4 | 36 | 11 | 84 | 697 | 2,379 | 864 | 22.87 | 74.71 | 9 00– 9 99 |
| 10 00–10 99 | 17 | 43 | 9 | 21 | 26 | 83 | 1,546 | 2,306 | 1,477 | 30.43 | 82.07 | 10 00–10 99 |
| 11 00–11 99 | 5 | 6 | 6 | 11 | 9 | 10 | 763 | 844 | 545 | 34.17 | 84.75 | 11 00–11 99 |
| 12 00–12 99 | 29 | 21 | 14 | 21 | 26 | 48 | 2,798 | 1,609 | 1,569 | 47.81 | 89.85 | 12 00–12 99 |
| 13 00–13 99 | 14 | 6 | 4 | 1 | 15 | 10 | 844 | 399 | 369 | 51.94 | 91.12 | 13 00–13 99 |
| 14 00–14 99 | 17 | 17 | 17 | 7 | 17 | 8 | 1,347 | 614 | 467 | 58.53 | 93.07 | 14 00–14 99 |
| 15 00–15 99 | 31 | 8 | 15 | 13 | 23 | 18 | 2,254 | 655 | 866 | 69.50 | 95.15 | 15 00–15 99 |
| 16 00–17 99 | 32 | 8 | 13 | 8 | 16 | 11 | 1,564 | 440 | 511 | 77.15 | 96.54 | 16 00–17 99 |
| 18 00–19 99 | 31 | 1 | 19 | 4 | 28 | 10 | 1,312 | 354 | 431 | 83.58 | 97.66 | 18 00–19 99 |
| 20 00–24 99 | 37 | 5 | 17 | 2 | 27 | 11 | 1,706 | 371 | 475 | 91.93 | 98.84 | 20 00–24 99 |
| 25 00–29 99 | 16 | 1 | 14 | 2 | 22 | 5 | 823 | 178 | 287 | 95.95 | 99.41 | 25 00–29 99 |
| 30 00–34 99 | 9 | 1 | 6 | 3 | 5 | 2 | 389 | 65 | 70 | 97.83 | 99.67 | 30 00–34 99 |
| 45 00–39 99 | 4 | ...... | 5 | 1 | 1 | 2 | 158 | 39 | 49 | 98.60 | 99.79 | 35 00–39 99 |
| 30 00 and over | 2 | ...... | 5 | 1 | 1 | ........ | 287 | 66 | 121 | 100.00 | 100.00 | 40 00 and over |
| Not reported | ...... | 7 | ........ | 1 | 2 | 19 | 191 | 74 | 143 | ........ | ........ | Not reported |
| Total | 332 | 490 | 174 | 434 | 295 | 852 | 20,640 | 31,564 | 17,349 | ........ | ........ | Total |

NEW YORK STATE

**MERCANTILE ESTABLISHMENTS**

4. TABLE IV, A

NUMBER OF EMPLOYEES ACCORDING TO ACTUAL WEEKLY EARNINGS, BY LOCALITY AND SEX

| ACTUAL WEEKLY EARNINGS IN DOLLARS | NEW YORK CITY | | | BUFFALO | | ROCHESTER | | SYRACUSE | | ALBANY | | ACTUAL WEEKLY EARNINGS IN DOLLARS |
|---|---|---|---|---|---|---|---|---|---|---|---|---|
| | Male | Female | Not reported | Male | Female | Male | Female | Male | Female | Male | Female | |
| Under $3 00 | 104 | 323 | 1,344 | 9 | 75 | 3 | 30 | 5 | 60 | 7 | 20 | Under $3 00 |
| $3 00– 3 49 | 62 | 443 | 480 | 24 | 91 | 6 | 15 | 9 | 61 | 3 | 22 | $3 00– 3 49 |
| 3 50– 3 99 | 64 | 710 | 447 | 30 | 110 | 10 | 91 | 8 | 37 | 6 | 39 | 3 50– 3 99 |
| 4 00– 4 49 | 322 | 1,626 | 1,049 | 73 | 160 | 31 | 91 | 11 | 76 | 4 | 17 | 4 00– 4 49 |
| 4 50– 4 99 | 123 | 824 | 541 | 16 | 95 | 7 | 55 | 4 | 54 | 15 | 40 | 4 50– 4 99 |
| 5 00– 5 49 | 391 | 1,414 | 908 | 125 | 364 | 20 | 148 | 13 | 115 | 6 | 129 | 5 00– 5 49 |
| 5 50– 5 99 | 111 | 783 | 492 | 6 | 107 | 3 | 65 | 1 | 33 | ...... | 34 | 5 50– 5 99 |
| 6 00– 6 49 | 468 | 2,134 | 1,442 | 49 | 646 | 22 | 233 | 10 | 131 | 10 | 115 | 6 00– 6 49 |
| 6 50– 6 99 | 128 | 772 | 423 | 7 | 104 | 2 | 53 | 4 | 15 | 1 | 13 | 6 50– 6 99 |
| 7 00– 7 49 | 429 | 2,261 | 1,272 | 37 | 399 | 17 | 288 | 9 | 95 | 10 | 65 | 7 00– 7 49 |
| 7 50– 7 99 | 309 | 625 | 402 | 8 | 88 | 3 | 44 | 1 | 14 | 3 | 5 | 7 50– 7 99 |
| 8 00– 8 99 | 755 | 2,504 | 1,222 | 46 | 312 | 33 | 257 | 13 | 111 | 14 | 54 | 8 00– 8 99 |
| 9 00– 9 99 | 557 | 1,816 | 763 | 48 | 146 | 34 | 157 | 8 | 82 | 16 | 18 | 9 00– 9 99 |
| 10 00–10 99 | 1,103 | 1,592 | 1,229 | 116 | 172 | 81 | 109 | 30 | 67 | 12 | 22 | 10 00–10 99 |
| 11 00–11 99 | 748 | 825 | 594 | 57 | 43 | 41 | 47 | 22 | 37 | 9 | 4 | 11 00–11 99 |
| 12 00–12 99 | 1,812 | 1,037 | 1,197 | 275 | 89 | 166 | 91 | 58 | 47 | 28 | 14 | 12 00–12 99 |
| 13 00–13 99 | 737 | 421 | 418 | 64 | 25 | 73 | 30 | 14 | 14 | 8 | 3 | 13 00–13 99 |
| 14 00–14 99 | 1,092 | 518 | 509 | 101 | 35 | 64 | 25 | 28 | 15 | 19 | 5 | 14 00–14 99 |
| 15 00–15 99 | 1,450 | 485 | 650 | 228 | 40 | 110 | 36 | 45 | 23 | 30 | 6 | 15 00–15 99 |
| 16 00–17 99 | 1,313 | 418 | 493 | 155 | 16 | 78 | 13 | 35 | 14 | 34 | 5 | 16 00–17 99 |
| 18 00–19 99 | 1,049 | 299 | 403 | 122 | 11 | 50 | 12 | 25 | 10 | 19 | 2 | 18 00–19 99 |
| 20 00–24 99 | 1,491 | 329 | 488 | 105 | 9 | 67 | 10 | 47 | 9 | 33 | 4 | 20 00–24 99 |
| 25 00–29 99 | 748 | 146 | 282 | 43 | 2 | 14 | 6 | 19 | 5 | 14 | 1 | 25 00–29 99 |
| 30 00–34 99 | 334 | 46 | 82 | 14 | 2 | 3 | 2 | 20 | 2 | 6 | 1 | 30 00–34 99 |
| 35 00–39 99 | 149 | 29 | 62 | 6 | 1 | 4 | 3 | 8 | 2 | 6 | ...... | 35 00–39 99 |
| 40 00 and over | 262 | 56 | 123 | 8 | 1 | 9 | 1 | 13 | 7 | 7 | ...... | 40 00 and over |
| Not reported | 25 | 43 | 190 | 2 | 2 | 3 | 4 | 1 | ...... | ...... | 1 | Not reported |
| Total | 16,136 | 22,479 | 17,505 | 1,774 | 3,145 | 954 | 1,916 | 461 | 1,136 | 320 | 639 | Total |

NEW YORK STATE

**MERCANTILE ESTABLISHMENTS**

4. TABLE IV, A — (*concluded*) NUMBER OF EMPLOYEES ACCORDING TO ACTUAL WEEKLY EARNINGS, BY LOCALITY AND SEX

| ACTUAL WEEKLY EARNINGS IN DOLLARS | UTICA | | TROY | | SCHENECTADY | | OTHER CITIES AND TOWNS | | STATE | | | CUMULATIVE PER CENT. FOR STATE | | ACTUAL WEEKLY EARNINGS IN DOLLARS |
|---|---|---|---|---|---|---|---|---|---|---|---|---|---|---|
| | Male | Female | Male | Female | Male | Female | Male | Female | Male | Female | Not reported | Male | Female | |
| Under $3 00...... | ...... | 5 | 4 | 18 | 4 | 15 | 2 | 12 | 138 | 558 | 1,344 | .66 | 1.77 | .....Under $3 00 |
| $3 00– 3 49...... | 4 | 10 | 7 | 38 | 3 | 31 | 1 | 15 | 119 | 726 | 480 | 1.23 | 4.08 | .....$3 00– 3 49 |
| 3 50– 3 99...... | 10 | 24 | 4 | 12 | 3 | 13 | 2 | 27 | 137 | 1,063 | 447 | 1.89 | 7.45 | ......3 50– 3 99 |
| 4 00– 4 49...... | 8 | 50 | 16 | 17 | 1 | 26 | 2 | 46 | 468 | 2,109 | 1,049 | 4.15 | 14.13 | ......4 00– 4 49 |
| 4 50– 4 99...... | 5 | 21 | 6 | 20 | ...... | 29 | 3 | 30 | 179 | 1,168 | 541 | 5.01 | 17.83 | ......4 50– 4 99 |
| 5 00– 5 49...... | 8 | 51 | 11 | 17 | 2 | 52 | 11 | 68 | 587 | 2,358 | 908 | 7.85 | 25.29 | ......5 00– 5 49 |
| 5 50– 5 99...... | 3 | 22 | 3 | 25 | 2 | 6 | 1 | 14 | 130 | 1,089 | 492 | 8.48 | 28.74 | ......5 50– 5 99 |
| 6 00– 6 49...... | 9 | 67 | 5 | 50 | 5 | 39 | 14 | 115 | 592 | 3,530 | 1,442 | 11.33 | 40.14 | ......6 00– 6 49 |
| 6 50– 6 99...... | ...... | 15 | 1 | 14 | ...... | 5 | 2 | 6 | 145 | 997 | 423 | 12.03 | 43.30 | ......6 50– 6 99 |
| 7 00– 7 49...... | 12 | 55 | 11 | 52 | 3 | 42 | 5 | 80 | 533 | 3,337 | 1,272 | 14.60 | 53.88 | ......7 00– 7 49 |
| 7 50– 7 99...... | 2 | 8 | 1 | 31 | 3 | 9 | 3 | 16 | 333 | 840 | 402 | 16.22 | 56.44 | ......7 50– 7 99 |
| 8 00– 8 99...... | 10 | 72 | 12 | 53 | 2 | 44 | 15 | 85 | 900 | 3,492 | 1,222 | 20.56 | 67.49 | ......8 00– 8 99 |
| 9 00– 9 99...... | 9 | 39 | 11 | 38 | 2 | 32 | 10 | 69 | 695 | 2,397 | 763 | 23.91 | 75.09 | ......9 00– 9 99 |
| 10 00–10 99...... | 17 | 45 | 16 | 33 | 11 | 19 | 23 | 71 | 1,409 | 2,130 | 1,229 | 30.73 | 81.84 | .....10 00–10 99 |
| 11 00–11 99...... | 8 | 12 | 9 | 5 | 7 | 10 | 7 | 10 | 908 | 993 | 594 | 35.12 | 84.98 | .....11 00–11 99 |
| 12 00–12 99...... | 41 | 27 | 27 | 21 | 13 | 20 | 22 | 43 | 2,442 | 1,389 | 1,197 | 46.93 | 89.38 | .....12 00–12 99 |
| 13 00–13 99...... | 14 | 6 | 12 | 8 | 5 | 1 | 14 | 9 | 941 | 517 | 418 | 51.48 | 91.02 | .....13 00–13 99 |
| 14 00–14 99...... | 13 | 4 | 16 | 17 | 17 | 7 | 11 | 7 | 1,361 | 633 | 509 | 58.06 | 93.04 | .....14 00–14 99 |
| 15 00–15 99...... | 30 | 7 | 31 | 5 | 14 | 13 | 23 | 17 | 1,961 | 632 | 650 | 67.56 | 95.06 | .....15 00–15 99 |
| 16 00–17 99...... | 17 | 3 | 28 | 9 | 14 | 9 | 11 | 12 | 1,685 | 499 | 493 | 75.69 | 96.64 | .....16 00–17 99 |
| 18 00–19 99...... | 15 | 3 | 33 | 1 | 18 | 3 | 26 | 6 | 1,357 | 347 | 403 | 82.36 | 97.74 | .....18 00–19 99 |
| 20 00–24 99...... | 30 | 3 | 36 | 4 | 18 | 2 | 23 | 8 | 1,850 | 378 | 488 | 91.30 | 98.94 | .....20 00–24 99 |
| 25 00–29 99...... | 17 | 4 | 16 | 1 | 11 | 2 | 22 | 4 | 904 | 171 | 282 | 95.66 | 99.48 | .....25 00–29 99 |
| 30 00–34 99...... | 5 | 1 | 10 | 1 | 6 | 3 | 4 | 2 | 402 | 60 | 82 | 97.60 | 99.67 | .....30 00–34 99 |
| 35 00–39 99...... | 3 | ...... | 3 | ...... | 5 | 1 | 1 | 2 | 185 | 38 | 62 | 98.49 | 99.79 | .....35 00–39 99 |
| 40 00 and over.... | 5 | ...... | 2 | ...... | 5 | 1 | 1 | ...... | 312 | 66 | 123 | 100.00 | 100.00 | ...40 00 and over |
| Not reported..... | ...... | 1 | 1 | ...... | 1 | ...... | 36 | 78 | 69 | 129 | 190 | ...... | ...... | .....Not reported |
| Total........ | 295 | 555 | 332 | 490 | 175 | 434 | 295 | 852 | 20,742 | 31,646 | 17,505 | ...... | ...... | .......Total |

NEW YORK STATE

**DEPARTMENT STORES**

5. TABLE V, A, 1. Number of Employees Earning Specified Weekly Rates, by Age Groups and Sex

| Weekly Rates in Dollars | Age Groups in Years | | | | | | | | | | | | | | Weekly Rates in Dollars |
|---|---|---|---|---|---|---|---|---|---|---|---|---|---|---|---|
| | 14–15 | | 16–17 | | 18–20 | | 21–24 | | 25–29 | | 30–34 | | 35–39 | | |
| | Male | Female | Male | Female | Male | Female | Male | Female | Male | Female | Male | Female | Male | Female | |
| Less than $3 00 | 9 | 43 | .... | 18 | ...... | 5 | ...... | 1 | ...... | 1 | ...... | ...... | ...... | 1 | Less than $3 00 |
| $3 00–$3 49... | 39 | 248 | 12 | 155 | 1 | 21 | ...... | 18 | ...... | 17 | ...... | 14 | ...... | 12 | ...$3 00– 3 49 |
| 3 50– 3 99... | 77 | 504 | 16 | 300 | 3 | 44 | 1 | 9 | ...... | 5 | 1 | 2 | ...... | 6 | ... 3 50– 3 99 |
| 4 00– 4 49... | 295 | 458 | 110 | 845 | 13 | 233 | 14 | 72 | 10 | 86 | 11 | 41 | 7 | 24 | ... 4 00– 4 49 |
| 4 50– 4 99... | 59 | 92 | 70 | 379 | 3 | 210 | 2 | 37 | 1 | 44 | ...... | 38 | 2 | 30 | ... 4 50– 4 99 |
| 5 00– 5 49... | 124 | 76 | 282 | 701 | 65 | 795 | 18 | 190 | 14 | 88 | 11 | 45 | 4 | 33 | ... 5 00– 5 49 |
| 5 50 –5 99... | 8 | 11 | 30 | 93 | 12 | 161 | 2 | 48 | ...... | 21 | ...... | 9 | ...... | ...... | ... 5 50– 5 99 |
| 6 00– 6 49... | 21 | 17 | 280 | 461 | 169 | 1,633 | 27 | 818 | 15 | 292 | 6 | 119 | 3 | 86 | ... 6 00– 6 49 |
| 6 50– 6 99... | .... | 7 | 14 | 30 | 22 | 160 | 4 | 71 | 2 | 21 | 1 | 10 | ...... | 4 | ... 6 50– 6 99 |
| 7 00– 7 49... | 4 | 5 | 125 | 133 | 290 | 1,159 | 56 | 1,212 | 13 | 542 | 13 | 263 | 10 | 183 | ... 7 00– 7 49 |
| 7 50– 7 99... | 2 | 1 | 38 | 6 | 166 | 62 | 36 | 101 | 3 | 45 | 3 | 20 | ...... | 24 | ... 7 50– 7 99 |
| 8 00 –8 99... | 1 | 6 | 97 | 51 | 509 | 619 | 152 | 1,293 | 43 | 641 | 28 | 270 | 12 | 221 | ... 8 00– 8 99 |
| 9 00– 9 99... | 1 | ...... | 14 | 17 | 283 | 253 | 178 | 714 | 61 | 523 | 26 | 238 | 21 | 186 | ... 9 00– 9 99 |
| 10 00–10 99... | .... | ...... | 12 | 8 | 265 | 143 | 412 | 621 | 216 | 580 | 124 | 276 | 94 | 211 | ...10 00–10 99 |
| 11 00–11 99... | .... | ...... | 5 | 3 | 75 | 33 | 198 | 219 | 127 | 272 | 55 | 114 | 59 | 77 | ...11 00–11 99 |
| 12 00–12 99... | .... | ...... | 3 | 1 | 146 | 55 | 610 | 275 | 450 | 448 | 310 | 300 | 277 | 208 | ...12 00–12 99 |
| 13 00–13 99... | .... | ...... | 2 | 1 | 34 | ...... | 191 | 62 | 160 | 110 | 104 | 76 | 78 | 62 | ...13 00–13 99 |
| 14 00–14 99... | .... | ...... | .... | 1 | 22 | 16 | 207 | 69 | 246 | 163 | 194 | 113 | 167 | 112 | ...14 00–14 99 |
| 15 00–15 99... | .... | ...... | 2 | 4 | 53 | 3 | 402 | 68 | 486 | 166 | 333 | 127 | 286 | 118 | ...15 00–15 99 |
| 16 00–17 99... | .... | ...... | .... | 2 | 11 | 4 | 120 | 21 | 308 | 95 | 271 | 107 | 233 | 89 | ...16 00–17 99 |
| 18 00–19 99... | .... | ...... | .... | 1 | 6 | 3 | 80 | 24 | 219 | 88 | 254 | 80 | 202 | 85 | ...18 00–19 99 |
| 20 00–24 99... | .... | ...... | .... | ...... | 2 | 1 | 60 | 13 | 241 | 72 | 301 | 84 | 298 | 92 | ...20 00–24 99 |
| 25 00–29 99... | .... | ...... | .... | ...... | 1 | 1 | 8 | 2 | 76 | 25 | 129 | 42 | 163 | 47 | ...25 00–29 99 |
| 30 00–34 99... | .... | ...... | .... | ...... | ...... | 2 | 2 | ...... | 20 | 11 | 62 | 11 | 79 | 14 | ...30 00–34 99 |
| 35 00–39 99... | .... | ...... | .... | ...... | ...... | 1 | 2 | ...... | 7 | 3 | 22 | 8 | 17 | 14 | ...35 00–39 99 |
| 40 00 and over. | .... | ...... | .... | ...... | 1 | 1 | 2 | 1 | 8 | 7 | 37 | 14 | 71 | 14 | .40 00 and over |
| Not reported... | 2 | 2 | 2 | 2 | 13 | 3 | 20 | 6 | 21 | 4 | 33 | 6 | 34 | 3 | ...Not reported |
| Total..... | 642 | 1,470 | 1,114 | 3,212 | 2,165 | 5,621 | 2,804 | 5,965 | 2,747 | 4,370 | 2,329 | 2,427 | 2,117 | 1,956 | .....Total |

NEW YORK STATE
DEPARTMENT STORES

5. TABLE V, A, 1 — (*concluded*) Number of Employees Earning Specified Weekly Rates, by Age Groups and Sex

| Weekly Rates in Dollars | Age Groups in Years: 40–44 | | 45–54 | | 55–64 | | 65 and over | | Not reported | | Total | | Cumulative per cent. of total | | Weekly Rates in Dollars |
|---|---|---|---|---|---|---|---|---|---|---|---|---|---|---|---|
| | Male | Female | Male | Female | Male | Female | Male | Female | Male | Female | Male | Female | Male | Female | |
| Less than $3 00 | .... | ...... | .... | ...... | ...... | ...... | ...... | ...... | 1 | ...... | 10 | 69 | .05 | .24 | Less than $3 00 |
| $3 00–$3 49... | .... | 5 | .... | 2 | ...... | ...... | ...... | ...... | 3 | ...... | 55 | 492 | .34 | 2.01 | ...$3 00– 3 49 |
| 3 50– 3 99... | 1 | ...... | .... | ...... | ...... | ...... | ...... | ...... | ...... | 24 | 99 | 894 | .85 | 5.2 | ... 3 50– 3 99 |
| 4 00– 4 49... | 11 | 9 | 11 | 6 | 3 | 1 | ...... | ...... | 3 | 22 | 488 | 1,797 | 3.49 | 11.6 | ... 4 00– 4 49 |
| 4 50– 4 99... | .... | 15 | .... | 13 | ...... | 2 | ...... | ...... | 2 | 14 | 139 | 874 | 4.12 | 14.8 | ... 4 50– 4 99 |
| 5 00– 5 49... | 2 | 18 | 5 | 19 | 1 | 2 | ...... | ...... | 4 | 32 | 530 | 1,999 | 6.88 | 21.9 | ... 5 00– 5 49 |
| 5 50– 5 99... | .... | 3 | .... | 4 | 1 | 2 | ...... | ...... | 1 | 90 | 54 | 442 | 7.16 | 23.5 | ... 5 50– 5 99 |
| 6 00– 6 49... | 3 | 60 | 6 | 75 | 1 | 14 | 1 | 3 | 3 | 79 | 535 | 3,657 | 9.95 | 36.5 | ... 6 00– 6 49 |
| 6 50– 6 99... | .... | 4 | .... | 1 | ...... | ...... | ...... | ...... | ...... | 89 | 43 | 397 | 10.17 | 37.8 | ... 6 50– 6 99 |
| 7 00– 7 49... | 4 | 115 | 7 | 96 | 8 | 19 | 5 | 6 | 5 | 76 | 540 | 3,809 | 12.98 | 51.6 | ... 7 00– 7 49 |
| 7 50– 7 99... | 1 | 18 | .... | 29 | ...... | 5 | ...... | 1 | 3 | 34 | 252 | 346 | 14.32 | 52.9 | ... 7 50– 7 99 |
| 8 00– 8 99... | 10 | 109 | 12 | 104 | 15 | 27 | 6 | 3 | 17 | 103 | 902 | 3,447 | 19.0 | 65.2 | ... 8 00– 8 99 |
| 9 00– 9 99... | 10 | 87 | 27 | 72 | 11 | 11 | 7 | 4 | 11 | 111 | 650 | 2,216 | 22.3 | 74.7 | ... 9 00– 9 99 |
| 10 00–10 99... | 70 | 99 | 117 | 98 | 77 | 20 | 24 | 2 | 13 | 102 | 1,424 | 2,160 | 29.8 | 80.8 | ...10 00–10 99 |
| 11 00–11 99... | 49 | 35 | 87 | 15 | 39 | 3 | 7 | ...... | 10 | 43 | 711 | 814 | 33.4 | 83.8 | ...11 00–11 99 |
| 12 00–12 99... | 215 | 107 | 363 | 75 | 174 | 13 | 39 | 3 | 21 | 58 | 2,608 | 1,543 | 47.1 | 89.2 | ...12 00–12 99 |
| 13 00–13 99... | 64 | 19 | 97 | 18 | 41 | 1 | 8 | 1 | 2 | 26 | 781 | 376 | 51.0 | 90.6 | ...13 00–13 99 |
| 14 00–14 99... | 111 | 39 | 198 | 30 | 79 | 5 | 23 | ...... | 11 | 36 | 1,258 | 584 | 57.7 | 92.7 | ...14 00–14 99 |
| 15 00–15 99... | 171 | 62 | 275 | 42 | 94 | 2 | 20 | ...... | 20 | 41 | 2,142 | 633 | 68.8 | 94.8 | ...15 00–15 99 |
| 16 00–17 99... | 177 | 47 | 260 | 30 | 85 | 3 | 15 | ...... | 8 | 32 | 1,488 | 430 | 76.8 | 96.2 | ...16 00–17 99 |
| 18 00–19 99... | 157 | 26 | 251 | 13 | 69 | 2 | 14 | ...... | 10 | 24 | 1,262 | 346 | 83.2 | 97.4 | ...18 00–19 99 |
| 20 00–24 99... | 270 | 45 | 358 | 23 | 105 | 2 | 10 | 1 | 14 | 31 | 1,659 | 364 | 91.8 | 98.7 | ...20 00–24 99 |
| 25 00–29 99... | 161 | 24 | 188 | 17 | 56 | 4 | 10 | ...... | 5 | 14 | 797 | 176 | 96.0 | 99.2 | ...25 00–29 99 |
| 30 00–34 99... | 72 | 15 | 100 | 4 | 32 | ...... | 3 | ...... | 4 | 7 | 374 | 64 | 98.0 | 99.5 | ...30 00–34 99 |
| 35 00–39 99... | 31 | 8 | 47 | 2 | 17 | ...... | 4 | ...... | 2 | 3 | 149 | 39 | 98.6 | 99.6 | ...35 00–39 99 |
| 40 00 and over. | 56 | 8 | 83 | 8 | 16 | 1 | 5 | ...... | 1 | 12 | 280 | 66 | 100.0 | 100.0 | .40 00 and over |
| Not reported... | 13 | 7 | 30 | 4 | 12 | ...... | 3 | ...... | 2 | 1 | 185 | 38 | ...... | ...... | ...Not reported |
| Total..... | 1,659 | 984 | 2,522 | 800 | 936 | 139 | 204 | 24 | 176 | 1,104 | 19,415 | 28,072 | ...... | ...... | .....Total |

NEW YORK STATE

**DEPARTMENT STORES**

6. TABLE VI, A, 1 — NUMBER OF EMPLOYEES ACCORDING TO ACTUAL WEEKLY EARNINGS, BY AGE GROUPS AND SEX

| Actual Weekly Earnings in Dollars | Age Groups in Years | | | | | | | | | | | | | | Actual Weekly Earnings in Dollars |
|---|---|---|---|---|---|---|---|---|---|---|---|---|---|---|---|
| | 14–15 | | 16–17 | | 18–20 | | 21–24 | | 25–29 | | 30–34 | | 35–39 | | |
| | Male | Female | Male | Female | Male | Female | Male | Female | Male | Female | Male | Female | Male | Female | |
| Less than $3 00 | 35 | 130 | 19 | 99 | 24 | 83 | 12 | 54 | 10 | 42 | 5 | 16 | 2 | 19 | Less than $3 00 |
| $3 00–$3 49... | 50 | 247 | 26 | 207 | 7 | 62 | 6 | 39 | 7 | 31 | 1 | 21 | 3 | 16 | ...$3 00– 3 49 |
| 3 50– 3 99... | 80 | 385 | 24 | 354 | 7 | 86 | 4 | 34 | 1 | 22 | 3 | 16 | 1 | 12 | ....3 50– 3 99 |
| 4 00– 4 49... | 270 | 504 | 107 | 779 | 23 | 270 | 2 | 95 | 7 | 100 | 12 | 43 | 7 | 23 | ....4 00– 4 49 |
| 4 50– 4 99... | 57 | 81 | 81 | 361 | 16 | 242 | 4 | 56 | 3 | 62 | ...... | 31 | 3 | 31 | ....4 50– 4 99 |
| 5 00– 5 49... | 116 | 69 | 264 | 595 | 62 | 701 | 20 | 229 | 16 | 105 | 14 | 60 | 4 | 42 | ....5 00– 5 49 |
| 5 50– 5 99... | 8 | 12 | 42 | 123 | 42 | 342 | 11 | 169 | 6 | 81 | 5 | 32 | 2 | 23 | ....5 50– 5 99 |
| 6 00– 6 49... | 16 | 17 | 251 | 399 | 157 | 1,259 | 33 | 665 | 25 | 221 | 12 | 114 | 7 | 73 | ....6 00– 6 49 |
| 6 50– 6 99... | 1 | 8 | 27 | 47 | 61 | 316 | 17 | 228 | 9 | 93 | 2 | 40 | 4 | 31 | ....6 50– 6 99 |
| 7 00– 7 49... | 4 | 4 | 109 | 135 | 267 | 946 | 56 | 933 | 11 | 430 | 13 | 196 | 11 | 143 | ....7 00– 7 49 |
| 7 50– 7 99... | 2 | 2 | 41 | 15 | 194 | 163 | 46 | 264 | 10 | 105 | 7 | 53 | 3 | 47 | ....7 50– 7 99 |
| 8 00– 8 99... | 1 | 6 | 80 | 52 | 424 | 600 | 167 | 1,152 | 52 | 605 | 34 | 254 | 20 | 198 | ....8 00– 8 99 |
| 9 00– 9 99... | 1 | 1 | 15 | 17 | 249 | 265 | 188 | 704 | 68 | 513 | 32 | 243 | 23 | 180 | ....9 00– 9 99 |
| 10 00–10 99... | .... | ...... | 12 | 8 | 246 | 144 | 390 | 573 | 199 | 526 | 112 | 248 | 86 | 195 | ...10 00–10 99 |
| 11 00–11 99... | .... | ...... | 5 | 3 | 100 | 37 | 234 | 233 | 144 | 298 | 78 | 137 | 77 | 96 | ...11 00–11 99 |
| 12 00–12 99... | .... | 1 | 4 | 3 | 130 | 52 | 512 | 244 | 395 | 372 | 267 | 239 | 241 | 168 | ...12 00–12 99 |
| 13 00–13 99... | .... | ...... | 2 | ...... | 46 | 5 | 235 | 82 | 180 | 137 | 103 | 92 | 78 | 75 | ...13 00–13 99 |
| 14 00–14 99... | .... | ...... | .... | 2 | 31 | 17 | 225 | 71 | 245 | 170 | 193 | 111 | 171 | 117 | ...14 00–14 99 |
| 15 00–15 99... | .... | ...... | 2 | 3 | 47 | 2 | 329 | 56 | 406 | 152 | 291 | 129 | 248 | 112 | ...15 00–15 99 |
| 16 00–17 99... | .... | ...... | .... | 1 | 13 | 6 | 147 | 23 | 324 | 116 | 289 | 111 | 254 | 106 | ...16 00–17 99 |
| 18 00–19 99... | .... | ...... | .... | 1 | 6 | 2 | 82 | 26 | 228 | 81 | 243 | 79 | 211 | 78 | ...18 00–19 99 |
| 20 00–24 99... | .... | ...... | .... | 1 | 4 | 2 | 68 | 17 | 261 | 66 | 342 | 89 | 321 | 91 | ...20 00–24 99 |
| 25 00–29 99... | .... | ...... | .... | ...... | 1 | 1 | 12 | 3 | 97 | 23 | 145 | 39 | 171 | 44 | ...25 00–29 99 |
| 30 00–34 99... | .... | ...... | .... | ...... | ...... | 2 | 4 | ...... | 31 | 9 | 69 | 11 | 83 | 13 | ...30 00–34 99 |
| 35 00–39 99... | .... | ...... | .... | ...... | ...... | 1 | ...... | ...... | 11 | 3 | 27 | 8 | 26 | 13 | ...35 00–39 99 |
| 40 00 and over. | .... | ...... | .... | ...... | 1 | 1 | 1 | 1 | 13 | 7 | 39 | 13 | 76 | 14 | .40 00 and over |
| Not reported... | 1 | 3 | 3 | 7 | 8 | 21 | 8 | 15 | 7 | 17 | 7 | 11 | 4 | 12 | ...Not reported |
| Total..... | 642 | 1,470 | 1,114 | 3,212 | 2,166 | 5,628 | 2,813 | 5,971 | 2,766 | 4,387 | 2,345 | 2,436 | 2,137 | 1,972 | .....Total |

NEW YORK STATE

DEPARTMENT STORES

6. TABLE VI, A, 1 — (*concluded*) NUMBER OF EMPLOYEES ACCORDING TO ACTUAL WEEKLY EARNINGS, BY AGE GROUPS AND SEX

| Actual Weekly Earnings in Dollars | Age Group in Years: 40–44 | | 45–54 | | 55–64 | | 65 and over | | Not reported | | Total | | Cumulative per cent. of total | | Actual Weekly Earnings in Dollars |
|---|---|---|---|---|---|---|---|---|---|---|---|---|---|---|---|
| | Male | Female | Male | Female | Male | Female | Male | Female | Male | Female | Male | Female | Male | Female | |
| Less than $3 00 | 6 | 4 | 4 | 2 | 2 | 2 | ...... | ...... | 5 | 4 | 124 | 455 | .64 | 1.62 | Less than $3 00 |
| 3 00–$3 49... | 1 | 11 | 1 | 5 | 1 | 1 | ...... | ...... | 3 | 2 | 106 | 642 | 1.08 | 3.92 | ...$3 00– 3 49 |
| 3 50– 3 99... | 1 | 6 | 2 | 4 | 1 | ...... | ...... | ...... | 1 | 22 | 125 | 941 | 1.83 | 7.25 | ....3 50– 3 99 |
| 4 00– 4 49... | 6 | 10 | 8 | 8 | 5 | 2 | ...... | ...... | 3 | 19 | 450 | 1,853 | 4.15 | 13.9 | ....4 00– 4 49 |
| 4 50– 4 99... | 1 | 9 | 1 | 14 | ...... | 3 | 1 | ...... | 3 | 7 | 170 | 897 | 5.0 | 17.1 | ....4 50– 4 99 |
| 5 00– 5 49... | 2 | 23 | 9 | 29 | ...... | 5 | ...... | ...... | 3 | 13 | 510 | 1,871 | 7.6 | 23.8 | ....5 00– 5 49 |
| 5 50– 5 99... | .... | 10 | 1 | 20 | 1 | 3 | ...... | 1 | 1 | 12 | 119 | 828 | 8.2 | 26.7 | ....5 50– 5 99 |
| 6 00– 6 49... | 5 | 65 | 11 | 69 | 2 | 13 | 1 | 4 | 3 | 39 | 523 | 2,938 | 10.9 | 37.2 | ....6 00– 6 49 |
| 6 50– 6 99... | 3 | 9 | 4 | 10 | 3 | 2 | 2 | 1 | 1 | 42 | 134 | 827 | 11.6 | 40.2 | ....6 50– 6 99 |
| 7 00– 7 49... | 6 | 102 | 10 | 74 | 8 | 16 | 3 | 3 | 5 | 61 | 503 | 3,043 | 14.2 | 51.0 | ....7 00– 7 49 |
| 7 50– 7 99... | 1 | 27 | 3 | 30 | 3 | 7 | 1 | 1 | 6 | 38 | 317 | 752 | 15.8 | 53.6 | ....7 50– 7 99 |
| 8 00– 8 99... | 13 | 105 | 18 | 103 | 16 | 22 | 5 | 5 | 15 | 135 | 845 | 3,237 | 20.2 | 65.5 | ....8 00– 8 99 |
| 9 00– 9 99... | 12 | 83 | 32 | 70 | 15 | 9 | 8 | 3 | 8 | 147 | 651 | 2,235 | 23.5 | 73.4 | ....9 00– 9 99 |
| 10 00–10 99... | 62 | 86 | 105 | 94 | 66 | 17 | 23 | 1 | 9 | 116 | 1,310 | 2,008 | 30.2 | 80.5 | ...10 00–10 99 |
| 11 00–11 99... | 59 | 40 | 94 | 18 | 34 | 4 | 9 | 1 | 6 | 74 | 840 | 946 | 34.5 | 84.0 | ...11 00–11 99 |
| 12 00–12 99... | 194 | 92 | 321 | 57 | 158 | 14 | 37 | 2 | 20 | 89 | 2,279 | 1,333 | 46.3 | 88.5 | ...12 00–12 99 |
| 13 00–13 99... | 69 | 23 | 102 | 26 | 44 | 1 | 8 | 1 | 5 | 42 | 872 | 484 | 50.7 | 90.6 | ...13 00–13 99 |
| 14 00–14 99... | 104 | 38 | 202 | 24 | 88 | 5 | 20 | ...... | 12 | 49 | 1,291 | 604 | 57.5 | 92.5 | ...14 00–14 99 |
| 15 00–15 99... | 152 | 57 | 274 | 39 | 81 | 2 | 16 | ...... | 18 | 55 | 1,864 | 607 | 67.0 | 94.6 | ...15 00–15 99 |
| 16 00–17 99... | 191 | 49 | 249 | 32 | 97 | 3 | 17 | ...... | 8 | 39 | 1,589 | 486 | 75.0 | 96.2 | ...16 00–17 99 |
| 18 00–19 99... | 158 | 26 | 265 | 14 | 73 | 2 | 15 | ...... | 12 | 29 | 1,293 | 338 | 81.7 | 97.5 | ...18 00–19 99 |
| 20 00–24 99... | 289 | 50 | 374 | 24 | 108 | 2 | 11 | 1 | 18 | 28 | 1,796 | 371 | 91.0 | 99.0 | ...20 00–24 99 |
| 25 00–29 99... | 167 | 27 | 202 | 15 | 60 | 4 | 10 | ...... | 5 | 13 | 870 | 169 | 95.5 | 99.5 | ...25 00–29 99 |
| 30 00–34 99... | 69 | 13 | 93 | 4 | 31 | ...... | 3 | ...... | 4 | 7 | 387 | 59 | 97.3 | 99.6 | ...30 00–34 99 |
| 35 00–39 99... | 34 | 8 | 55 | 2 | 16 | ...... | 5 | ...... | 2 | 3 | 176 | 38 | 98.6 | 99.7 | ...35 00–39 99 |
| 40 00 and over. | 61 | 9 | 88 | 8 | 20 | 1 | 5 | ...... | 1 | 12 | 305 | 66 | 100.0 | 100.0 | .40 00 and over |
| Not reported... | 10 | 12 | 10 | 15 | 6 | 4 | 4 | ...... | ...... | 8 | 68 | 125 | ...... | ...... | ...Not reported |
| Total..... | 1,676 | 994 | 2,538 | 810 | 939 | 144 | 204 | 24 | 177 | 1,105 | 19,517 | 28,153 | ...... | ...... | .....Total |

7. TABLE V, A, 2

## NEW YORK STATE
## NEIGHBORHOOD STORES

NUMBER OF EMPLOYEES EARNING SPECIFIED WEEKLY RATES, BY AGE GROUPS AND SEX

| WEEKLY RATES IN DOLLARS | AGE GROUPS IN YEARS | | | | | | | | | | | | | | WEEKLY RATES IN DOLLARS |
|---|---|---|---|---|---|---|---|---|---|---|---|---|---|---|---|
| | 14–15 | | 16–17 | | 18–20 | | 21–24 | | 25–29 | | 30–34 | | 35–39 | | |
| | Male | Female | Male | Female | Male | Female | Male | Female | Male | Female | Male | Female | Male | Female | |
| Less than $3 00 | ... | 2 | ... | 3 | ... | ... | ... | ... | ... | ... | ... | ... | ... | ... | Less than $3 00 |
| $3 00–$3 49 | | 6 | 1 | 20 | ... | 2 | ... | 2 | ... | 1 | ... | 1 | ... | ... | $3 00– 3 49 |
| 3 50– 3 99 | 3 | 7 | 3 | 59 | ... | 5 | ... | ... | ... | ... | ... | 1 | ... | ... | 3 50– 3 99 |
| 4 00– 4 49 | 5 | 5 | 11 | 120 | 1 | 31 | ... | 3 | ... | ... | ... | 2 | ... | ... | 4 00– 4 49 |
| 4 50– 4 99 | 1 | 2 | 6 | 52 | ... | 42 | ... | 6 | ... | ... | ... | ... | ... | ... | 4 50– 4 99 |
| 5 00– 5 49 | 5 | ... | 43 | 65 | 18 | 134 | 2 | 33 | 1 | 7 | ... | 2 | ... | 3 | 5 00– 5 49 |
| 5 50– 5 99 | 1 | ... | ... | 13 | 2 | 63 | 2 | 18 | ... | 4 | ... | ... | ... | ... | 5 50– 5 99 |
| 6 00– 6 49 | 1 | ... | 25 | 21 | 28 | 155 | 7 | 111 | 1 | 38 | ... | 9 | ... | 12 | 6 00– 6 49 |
| 6 50– 6 99 | 1 | ... | 1 | ... | 1 | 15 | ... | 24 | ... | 6 | ... | ... | ... | 4 | 6 50– 6 99 |
| 7 00– 7 49 | ... | ... | 1 | 5 | 19 | 92 | 4 | 103 | 2 | 37 | ... | 12 | ... | 6 | 7 00– 7 49 |
| 7 50– 7 99 | ... | ... | ... | ... | 1 | 5 | 1 | 15 | ... | 3 | ... | ... | ... | 2 | 7 50– 7 99 |
| 8 00– 8 99 | ... | ... | 4 | 1 | 15 | 37 | 12 | 100 | 2 | 45 | 3 | 14 | 1 | 17 | 8 00– 8 99 |
| 9 00– 9 99 | ... | ... | ... | 2 | 9 | 12 | 5 | 58 | 2 | 38 | ... | 17 | 2 | 7 | 9 00– 9 99 |
| 10 00–10 99 | ... | ... | ... | ... | 14 | 6 | 29 | 34 | 11 | 33 | 6 | 16 | 3 | 18 | 10 00–10 99 |
| 11 00–11 99 | ... | ... | ... | ... | 2 | ... | 10 | 7 | 3 | 7 | ... | 4 | 3 | 1 | 11 00–11 99 |
| 12 00–12 99 | ... | ... | ... | ... | 9 | 2 | 36 | 19 | 25 | 17 | 15 | 7 | 13 | 6 | 12 00–12 99 |
| 13 00–13 99 | ... | ... | ... | ... | ... | ... | 10 | 3 | 6 | 4 | 10 | 3 | 6 | 1 | 13 00–13 99 |
| 14 00–14 99 | ... | ... | ... | ... | 2 | 1 | 8 | 2 | 12 | 8 | 13 | 4 | 11 | 4 | 14 00–14 99 |
| 15 00–15 99 | ... | ... | ... | ... | ... | ... | 14 | 2 | 10 | 9 | 14 | 4 | 14 | ... | 15 00–15 99 |
| 16 00–17 99 | ... | ... | 1 | ... | ... | ... | 7 | 2 | 13 | 3 | 14 | 2 | 10 | ... | 16 00–17 99 |
| 18 00–19 99 | ... | ... | ... | ... | ... | ... | 2 | 1 | 6 | ... | 1 | 2 | 12 | 2 | 18 00–19 99 |
| 20 00–24 99 | ... | ... | ... | ... | ... | ... | 2 | 2 | 6 | 1 | 8 | 1 | 8 | 1 | 20 00–24 99 |
| 25 00–29 99 | ... | ... | ... | ... | ... | ... | 1 | 1 | 5 | ... | 6 | ... | 8 | 1 | 25 00–29 99 |
| 30 00–34 99 | ... | ... | ... | ... | ... | ... | 1 | ... | 1 | ... | ... | 1 | 3 | ... | 30 00–34 99 |
| 35 00–39 99 | ... | ... | ... | ... | ... | ... | 1 | ... | 2 | ... | 2 | ... | ... | ... | 35 00–39 99 |
| 40 00 and over | ... | ... | ... | ... | ... | ... | 1 | ... | ... | ... | 3 | ... | ... | ... | 40 00 and over |
| Not reported | ... | ... | ... | 1 | 1 | ... | ... | ... | ... | ... | ... | ... | ... | ... | Not reported |
| Total | 22 | 22 | 96 | 362 | 122 | 602 | 155 | 546 | 108 | 261 | 95 | 102 | 94 | 85 | Total |

NEW YORK STATE

**NEIGHBORHOOD STORES**

7. **TABLE V, A, 2 — (*concluded*)** NUMBER OF EMPLOYEES EARNING SPECIFIED WEEKLY RATES, BY AGE GROUPS AND SEX

| WEEKLY RATES IN DOLLARS | AGE GROUPS IN YEARS: 40–44 | | 45–54 | | 55–64 | | 65 AND OVER | NOT REPORTED | | TOTAL | | CUMULATIVE PER CENT. OF TOTAL | | WEEKLY RATES IN DOLLARS |
|---|---|---|---|---|---|---|---|---|---|---|---|---|---|---|
| | Male | Female | Male | Female | Male | Female | Male | Male | Female | Male | Female | Male | Female | |
| Less than $3 00 | ...... | ...... | ...... | ...... | ...... | ...... | ...... | ...... | ...... | ...... | 5 | ...... | .24 | Less than $3 00 |
| $3 00–$3 49 | ...... | ...... | ...... | ...... | ...... | ...... | ...... | ...... | 1 | 6 | 33 | .62 | 1.83 | $3 00– 3 49 |
| 3 50– 3 99 | ...... | ...... | ...... | ...... | ...... | ...... | ...... | 1 | ...... | 7 | 72 | 1.34 | 5.28 | 3 50– 3 99 |
| 4 00– 4 49 | ...... | ...... | ...... | ...... | ...... | ...... | ...... | ...... | ...... | 17 | 161 | 3.08 | 13.00 | 4 00– 4 49 |
| 4 50– 4 99 | ...... | ...... | ...... | ...... | ...... | ...... | ...... | ...... | ...... | 7 | 102 | 3.8 | 17.89 | 4 50– 4 99 |
| 5 00– 5 49 | ...... | ...... | ...... | 4 | ...... | ...... | ...... | 1 | 1 | 70 | 249 | 10.99 | 29.83 | 5 00– 5 49 |
| 5 50– 5 99 | ...... | 1 | ...... | ...... | ...... | ...... | ...... | ...... | ...... | 5 | 99 | 11.5 | 34.49 | 5 50– 5 99 |
| 6 00– 6 49 | ...... | 5 | ...... | 2 | ...... | ...... | ...... | ...... | ...... | 62 | 353 | 17.85 | 51.42 | 6 00– 6 49 |
| 6 50– 6 99 | ...... | 2 | ...... | 1 | ...... | 1 | ...... | ...... | ...... | 3 | 53 | 18.16 | 53.97 | 6 50– 6 99 |
| 7 00– 7 49 | ...... | 5 | ...... | 3 | ...... | 1 | ...... | 1 | 5 | 27 | 269 | 20.92 | 66.89 | 7 00– 7 49 |
| 7 50– 7 99 | ...... | 3 | 1 | 1 | ...... | ...... | 1 | 1 | ...... | 5 | 29 | 21.43 | 68.29 | 7 50– 7 99 |
| 8 00– 8 99 | ...... | 8 | ...... | 6 | 1 | 1 | ...... | ...... | 1 | 38 | 230 | 25.33 | 79.31 | 8 00– 8 99 |
| 9 00– 9 99 | 1 | 4 | 1 | 4 | 1 | ...... | 1 | ...... | 1 | 22 | 143 | 27.59 | 86.18 | 9 00– 9 99 |
| 10 00–10 99 | ...... | 7 | 5 | 3 | 9 | ...... | 1 | 1 | 2 | 79 | 119 | 35.69 | 91.89 | 10 00–10 99 |
| 11 00–11 99 | 2 | ...... | 8 | ...... | 3 | ...... | 1 | 1 | 1 | 33 | 20 | 39.07 | 92.85 | 11 00–11 99 |
| 12 00–12 99 | 20 | 2 | 27 | 1 | 13 | 1 | 2 | 1 | 1 | 161 | 56 | 55.59 | 95.54 | 12 00–12 99 |
| 13 00–13 99 | 7 | 3 | 9 | 2 | 2 | ...... | 1 | ...... | 4 | 51 | 20 | 60.83 | 96.50 | 13 00–13 99 |
| 14 00–14 99 | 4 | 3 | 15 | 3 | 2 | ...... | 2 | 2 | 4 | 71 | 29 | 68.12 | 97.90 | 14 00–14 99 |
| 15 00–15 99 | 13 | 1 | 24 | ...... | 3 | ...... | 2 | ...... | 2 | 94 | 18 | 77.77 | 98.76 | 15 00–15 99 |
| 16 00–17 99 | 8 | 1 | 11 | ...... | 3 | ...... | 2 | 1 | 1 | 70 | 9 | 84.96 | 99.19 | 16 00–17 99 |
| 18 00–19 99 | 9 | ...... | 7 | 1 | 4 | ...... | 3 | 1 | 1 | 45 | 7 | 89.56 | 99.52 | 18 00–19 99 |
| 20 00–24 99 | 7 | 1 | 11 | ...... | 3 | 1 | ...... | ...... | ...... | 45 | 7 | 94.16 | 99.85 | 20 00–24 99 |
| 25 00–29 99 | 3 | ...... | 2 | ...... | 1 | ...... | ...... | ...... | ...... | 26 | 2 | 96.82 | 99.95 | 25 00–29 99 |
| 30 00–34 99 | 4 | ...... | 4 | ...... | ...... | ...... | ...... | 2 | ...... | 15 | 1 | 98.36 | 100.00 | 30 00–34 99 |
| 35 00–39 99 | 3 | ...... | 1 | ...... | ...... | ...... | ...... | ...... | ...... | 9 | ...... | 99.28 | ...... | 35 00–39 99 |
| 40 00 and over | 3 | ...... | ...... | ...... | ...... | ...... | ...... | ...... | ...... | 7 | ...... | 100.00 | ...... | 40 00 and over |
| Not reported | ...... | ...... | ...... | ...... | ...... | ...... | ...... | ...... | ...... | 1 | 1 | ...... | ...... | Not reported |
| Total | 84 | 46 | 126 | 31 | 45 | 5 | 16 | 13 | 25 | 976 | 2,087 | ...... | ...... | Total |

NEW YORK STATE

NEIGHBORHOOD STORES

8. TABLE VI, A, 2 — NUMBER OF EMPLOYEES CLASSIFIED ACCORDING TO ACTUAL WEEKLY EARNINGS, BY AGE GROUPS AND SEX

| ACTUAL WEEKLY EARNINGS IN DOLLARS | AGE GROUPS IN YEARS | | | | | | | | | | | | | | ACTUAL WEEKLY EARNINGS IN DOLLARS |
|---|---|---|---|---|---|---|---|---|---|---|---|---|---|---|---|
| | 14–15 | | 16–17 | | 18–20 | | 21–24 | | 25–29 | | 30–34 | | 35–39 | | |
| | Male | Female | Male | Female | Male | Female | Male | Female | Male | Female | Male | Female | Male | Female | |
| Less than $3 00 | 1 | 2 | 3 | 24 | 5 | 11 | 1 | 8 | 1 | 3 | | 2 | 2 | 2 | Less than $3 00 |
| $3 00–$3 49 | 4 | 7 | 4 | 31 | 2 | 14 | 1 | 3 | | 2 | | 1 | | | $3 00– 3 49 |
| 3 50– 3 99 | 3 | 6 | 3 | 62 | 1 | 10 | | 2 | | 1 | | 2 | | | 3 50– 3 99 |
| 4 00– 4 49 | 5 | 5 | 10 | 103 | 1 | 38 | 1 | 11 | | | | 2 | 1 | 2 | 4 00– 4 49 |
| 4 50– 4 99 | 1 | 2 | 6 | 53 | | 42 | | 8 | | 4 | | | | | 4 50– 4 99 |
| 5 00– 5 49 | 5 | | 40 | 52 | 18 | 124 | 2 | 33 | 2 | 8 | | 3 | | 2 | 5 00– 5 49 |
| 5 50– 5 99 | 1 | | | 12 | 3 | 64 | 2 | 23 | | 5 | | | | 2 | 5 50– 5 99 |
| 6 00– 6 49 | 1 | | 22 | 19 | 22 | 137 | 6 | 96 | 2 | 33 | | 8 | | 12 | 6 00– 6 49 |
| 6 50– 6 99 | 1 | | 1 | | 2 | 20 | 2 | 25 | | 12 | | 1 | 1 | 3 | 6 50– 6 99 |
| 7 00– 7 49 | | | 2 | 3 | 18 | 77 | 3 | 85 | 2 | 24 | | 11 | | 5 | 7 00– 7 49 |
| 7 50– 7 99 | | | | | 3 | 6 | 1 | 28 | | 11 | | 1 | | 2 | 7 50– 7 99 |
| 8 00– 8 99 | | | 3 | 1 | 13 | 36 | 10 | 88 | 2 | 41 | 3 | 12 | 1 | 16 | 8 00– 8 99 |
| 9 00– 9 99 | | | | 1 | 7 | 11 | 6 | 61 | | 32 | | 17 | 2 | 6 | 9 00– 9 99 |
| 10 00–10 99 | | | 1 | | 14 | 8 | 24 | 29 | 14 | 32 | 6 | 11 | 3 | 17 | 10 00–10 99 |
| 11 00–11 99 | | | | | 2 | | 11 | 10 | 4 | 11 | 1 | 3 | 3 | 4 | 11 00–11 99 |
| 12 00–12 99 | | | | | 9 | 2 | 36 | 18 | 17 | 13 | 14 | 6 | 9 | 3 | 12 00–12 99 |
| 13 00–13 99 | | | | | | | 9 | 5 | 8 | 6 | 12 | 5 | 4 | 1 | 13 00–13 99 |
| 14 00–14 99 | | | | | 2 | | 7 | 3 | 9 | 8 | 9 | 5 | 8 | 4 | 14 00–14 99 |
| 15 00–15 99 | | | | | | 1 | 11 | 3 | 11 | 9 | 13 | 5 | 9 | | 15 00–15 99 |
| 16 00–17 99 | | | 1 | | | | 10 | 3 | 13 | 4 | 12 | 2 | 15 | | 16 00–17 99 |
| 18 00–19 99 | | | | | | | 4 | 1 | 7 | 1 | 4 | 2 | 14 | 2 | 18 00–19 99 |
| 20 00–24 99 | | | | | | | 4 | 2 | 7 | 1 | 8 | 1 | 10 | 1 | 20 00–24 99 |
| 25 00–29 99 | | | | | | | 1 | 1 | 6 | | 8 | | 9 | 1 | 25 00–29 99 |
| 30 00–34 99 | | | | | | | 1 | | 1 | | | 1 | 3 | | 30 00–34 99 |
| 35 00–39 99 | | | | | | | 1 | | 2 | | 2 | | | | 35 00–39 99 |
| 40 00 and over | | | | | | | 1 | | | | 3 | | | | 40 00 and over |
| Not reported | | | | 1 | | 1 | | | | | | 1 | | | Not reported |
| Total | 22 | 22 | 96 | 362 | 122 | 602 | 155 | 546 | 108 | 261 | 95 | 102 | 94 | 85 | Total |

NEW YORK STATE

**NEIGHBORHOOD STORES**

8. TABLE VI, A, 2 — *(concluded)* NUMBER OF EMPLOYEES CLASSIFIED ACCORDING TO ACTUAL WEEKLY EARNINGS, BY AGE GROUPS AND SEX

| Actual Weekly Earnings in Dollars | Age Group in Years | | | | | | | | | | | | | Actual Weekly Earnings in Dollars |
|---|---|---|---|---|---|---|---|---|---|---|---|---|---|---|
| | 40–44 | | 45–54 | | 55–64 | | 65 and over | Not reported | | Total | | Accumulative per cent. of total | | |
| | Male | Female | Male | Female | Male | Female | Male | Male | Female | Male | Female | Male | Female | |
| Less than $3 00... | ...... | 1 | ...... | ...... | ...... | ...... | ...... | ...... | 1 | 13 | 54 | 1.33 | 2.59 | ..Less than $3 00 |
| $3 00–$3 49...... | ...... | ...... | ...... | ...... | ...... | ...... | ...... | ...... | ...... | 11 | 58 | 2.46 | 5.37 | .....$3 00– 3 49 |
| 3 50– 3 99...... | ...... | ...... | ...... | ...... | ...... | ...... | ...... | 1 | ...... | 8 | 83 | 3.28 | 9.35 | ......3 50– 3 99 |
| 4 00– 4 49...... | ...... | ...... | ...... | ...... | ...... | ...... | ...... | ...... | ...... | 18 | 161 | 5.13 | 17.06 | ......4 00– 4 49 |
| 4 50– 4 99...... | ...... | 1 | ...... | ...... | ...... | ...... | ...... | ...... | ...... | 7 | 110 | 5.85 | 22.32 | ......4 50– 4 99 |
| 5 00– 5 49...... | 2 | ...... | ...... | 4 | ...... | ...... | ...... | 1 | 1 | 70 | 227 | 13.03 | 33.20 | ......5 00– 5 49 |
| 5 50– 5 99...... | ...... | 2 | ...... | ...... | ...... | ...... | ...... | ...... | ...... | 6 | 108 | 13.65 | 38.38 | ......5 50– 5 99 |
| 6 00– 6 49...... | ...... | 6 | 1 | 2 | ...... | ...... | ...... | ...... | ...... | 54 | 313 | 19.20 | 53.46 | ......6 00– 6 49 |
| 6 50– 6 99...... | 1 | 2 | ...... | 1 | ...... | 1 | ...... | ...... | ...... | 8 | 65 | 20.02 | 56.58 | ......6 50– 6 99 |
| 7 00– 7 49...... | ...... | 5 | ...... | 6 | ...... | 1 | ...... | 1 | 3 | 26 | 220 | 22.69 | 67.11 | ......7 00– 7 49 |
| 7 50– 7 99...... | ...... | 1 | 1 | ...... | ...... | ...... | 1 | 1 | 2 | 7 | 51 | 23.41 | 69.55 | ......7 50– 7 99 |
| 8 00– 8 99...... | ...... | 6 | ...... | 5 | 3 | 1 | ...... | ...... | 1 | 35 | 207 | 27.01 | 79.47 | ......8 00– 8 99 |
| 9 00– 9 99...... | 1 | 4 | 1 | 5 | 2 | ...... | 1 | 1 | 3 | 21 | 140 | 29.17 | 86.18 | ......9 00– 9 99 |
| 10 00–10 99...... | 1 | 3 | 5 | 3 | 7 | ...... | ...... | ...... | 1 | 75 | 104 | 36.87 | 91.17 | .....10 00–10 99 |
| 11 00–11 99...... | 3 | 1 | 7 | ...... | 4 | ...... | 2 | 1 | 1 | 38 | 30 | 40.77 | 92.61 | .....11 00–11 99 |
| 12 00–12 99...... | 15 | 4 | 24 | ...... | 9 | 1 | 2 | 1 | 3 | 136 | 50 | 54.72 | 95.01 | .....12 00–12 99 |
| 13 00–13 99...... | 8 | 4 | 10 | 3 | 3 | ...... | 1 | ...... | 2 | 55 | 26 | 60.27 | 96.26 | .....13 0C–13 99 |
| 14 00–14 99...... | 1 | 3 | 15 | 1 | 1 | ...... | 1 | 2 | 4 | 55 | 28 | 65.82 | 97.60 | .....14 00–14 99 |
| 15 00–15 99...... | 10 | 1 | 18 | ...... | 3 | ...... | 2 | ...... | 2 | 77 | 21 | 73.72 | 98.61 | .....15 00–15 99 |
| 16 00–17 99...... | 11 | 1 | 12 | ...... | 5 | ...... | 2 | 1 | 1 | 82 | 11 | 82.12 | 99.14 | .....16 00–17 99 |
| 18 00–19 99...... | 8 | ...... | 11 | 1 | 4 | ...... | 4 | 1 | 1 | 57 | 8 | 87.97 | 99.52 | .....18 00–19 99 |
| 20 00–24 99...... | 9 | 1 | 11 | ...... | 3 | 1 | ...... | ...... | ...... | 52 | 7 | 93.32 | 99.85 | .....20 00–24 99 |
| 25 00–29 99...... | 4 | ...... | 5 | ...... | 1 | ...... | ...... | ...... | ...... | 34 | 2 | 96.82 | 99.95 | .....25 00–29 99 |
| 30 00–34 99...... | 4 | ...... | 4 | ...... | ...... | ...... | ...... | 2 | ...... | 15 | 1 | 98.36 | 100.00 | .....30 00–34 99 |
| 35 00–39 99...... | 3 | ...... | 1 | ...... | ...... | ...... | ...... | ...... | ...... | 9 | ...... | 99.28 | ...... | .....35 00–39 99 |
| 40 00 and over.... | 3 | ...... | ...... | ...... | ...... | ...... | ...... | ...... | ...... | 7 | ...... | 100.00 | ...... | ...40 00 and over |
| Not reported...... | ...... | ...... | ...... | ...... | ...... | ...... | ...... | ...... | ...... | ...... | 3 | ...... | ...... | .....Not reported |
| Total........ | 84 | 46 | 126 | 31 | 45 | 5 | 16 | 13 | 26 | 976 | 2,088 | ...... | ...... | .......Total |

9. TABLE V, A, 3

NEW YORK STATE

**FIVE AND TEN CENT STORES**

NUMBER OF EMPLOYEES EARNING SPECIFIED WEEKLY RATES, BY AGE GROUPS AND SEX

| WEEKLY RATES IN DOLLARS | AGE GROUPS IN YEARS | | | | | | | | | | | | | | WEEKLY RATES IN DOLLARS |
|---|---|---|---|---|---|---|---|---|---|---|---|---|---|---|---|
| | 14–15 | | 16–17 | | 18–20 | | 21–24 | | 25–29 | | 30–34 | | 35–39 | | |
| | Male | Female | Male | Female | Male | Female | Male | Female | Male | Female | Male | Female | Male | Female | |
| Less than $3 00 | .... | ...... | .... | 1 | ...... | ...... | ...... | ...... | ...... | ...... | ...... | ...... | ...... | ...... | Less than $3 00 |
| $3 00-$3 49... | 1 | ...... | 1 | 2 | ...... | ...... | ...... | ...... | ...... | ...... | ...... | ...... | ...... | ...... | ...$3 00- 3 49 |
| 3 50- 3 99... | .... | ...... | 1 | 8 | ...... | 1 | ...... | ...... | ...... | ...... | ...... | ...... | ...... | ...... | ....3 50- 3 99 |
| 4 00- 4 49... | 1 | 1 | .... | 23 | ...... | 23 | ...... | 3 | ...... | 1 | ...... | 1 | ...... | 2 | ....4 00- 4 49 |
| 4 50- 4 99... | 1 | 1 | .... | 84 | ...... | 58 | ...... | 23 | ...... | 7 | ...... | 1 | ...... | 1 | ....4 50- 4 99 |
| 5 00- 5 49... | 3 | 6 | 4 | 130 | ...... | 141 | ...... | 49 | ...... | 17 | ...... | 7 | ...... | 2 | ....5 00- 5 49 |
| 5 50- 5 99... | 2 | 1 | 1 | 28 | ...... | 46 | ...... | 19 | ...... | 6 | ...... | ...... | ...... | ...... | ....5 50- 5 99 |
| 6 00- 6 49... | 2 | ...... | 8 | 53 | 6 | 188 | ...... | 86 | ...... | 25 | ...... | 9 | ...... | 3 | ....6 00- 6 49 |
| 6 50- 6 99... | .... | ...... | .... | 3 | ...... | 24 | ...... | 26 | ...... | 7 | ...... | ...... | ...... | 1 | ....6 50- 6 99 |
| 7 00- 7 49... | .... | ...... | 4 | 5 | 7 | 36 | 3 | 36 | ...... | 7 | ...... | 4 | ...... | ...... | ....7 00- 7 49 |
| 7 50- 7 99... | .... | ...... | 1 | 1 | 1 | 4 | ...... | 11 | ...... | 3 | ...... | ...... | ...... | ...... | ....7 50- 7 99 |
| 8 00- 8 99... | .... | ...... | 2 | 1 | 10 | 12 | 3 | 22 | 2 | 8 | ...... | 1 | 1 | 2 | ....8 00- 8 99 |
| 9 00- 9 99... | .... | ...... | 2 | ...... | 10 | 5 | 6 | 10 | 2 | 2 | 2 | 3 | ...... | ...... | ....9 00- 9 99 |
| 10 00-10 99... | .... | ...... | 1 | 1 | 11 | 6 | 19 | 11 | 2 | 8 | 3 | ...... | 3 | 1 | ...10 00-10 99 |
| 11 00-11 99... | .... | ...... | 1 | 1 | ...... | 2 | 10 | 5 | 3 | 2 | 4 | ...... | ...... | ...... | ...11 00-11 99 |
| 12 00-12 99... | .... | ...... | .... | ...... | 3 | 1 | 12 | 4 | 8 | 3 | 2 | 1 | 1 | 1 | ...12 00-12 99 |
| 13 00-13 99... | .... | ...... | .... | ...... | ...... | ...... | 5 | 2 | 2 | 1 | 2 | ...... | 1 | ...... | ...13 00-13 99 |
| 14 00-14 99... | .... | ...... | .... | ...... | ...... | ...... | 7 | ...... | 5 | 1 | 2 | ...... | 1 | ...... | ...14 00-14 99 |
| 15 00-15 99... | .... | ...... | .... | ...... | ...... | 1 | 8 | 1 | 5 | 1 | 1 | ...... | 1 | 1 | ...15 00-15 99 |
| 16 00-17 99... | .... | ...... | .... | ...... | ...... | ...... | 1 | ...... | 1 | ...... | 3 | 1 | ...... | ...... | ...16 00-17 99 |
| 18 00-19 99... | .... | ...... | .... | ...... | ...... | ...... | 1 | ...... | 2 | ...... | 1 | 1 | ...... | ...... | ...18 00-19 99 |
| 20 00-24 99... | .... | ...... | .... | ...... | ...... | ...... | ...... | ...... | 2 | ...... | ...... | ...... | ...... | ...... | ...20 00-24 99 |
| 25 00-29 99... | .... | ...... | .... | ...... | ...... | ...... | ...... | ...... | ...... | ...... | ...... | ...... | ...... | ...... | ...25 00-29 99 |
| 30 00-34 99... | .... | ...... | .... | ...... | ...... | ...... | ...... | ...... | ...... | ...... | ...... | ...... | ...... | ...... | ...30 00-34 99 |
| 35 00-39 99... | .... | ...... | .... | ...... | ...... | ...... | ...... | ...... | ...... | ...... | ...... | ...... | ...... | ...... | ...35 00-39 99 |
| 40 00 and over. | .... | ...... | .... | ...... | ...... | ...... | ...... | ...... | ...... | ...... | ...... | ...... | ...... | ...... | .40 00 and over |
| Not reported... | 1 | ...... | 3 | 8 | ...... | 12 | ...... | 9 | 1 | 2 | ...... | 1 | ...... | 1 | ...Not reported |
| Total.... | 11 | 9 | 29 | 349 | 48 | 560 | 75 | 317 | 35 | 101 | 20 | 30 | 8 | 15 | .....Total |

NEW YORK STATE

**FIVE AND TEN CENT STORES**

9. TABLE V, A, 3 — (*concluded*) NUMBER OF EMPLOYEES EARNING SPECIFIED WEEKLY RATES, BY AGE GROUPS AND SEX

| WEEKLY RATES IN DOLLARS | AGE GROUPS IN YEARS | | | | | | | | | | | | | | | | WEEKLY RATES IN DOLLARS |
|---|---|---|---|---|---|---|---|---|---|---|---|---|---|---|---|---|---|
| | 40–44 | | 45–54 | | 55–64 | | 65 AND OVER | NOT REPORTED | | TOTAL | | CUMULATIVE PER CENT. OF TOTAL | | | |
| | Male | Female | Male | Female | Male | Female | Female | Male | Female | Male | Female | Male | Female | |
| Less than $3 00 | | | | | | | | | | | 1 | | .07 | Less than $3 00 |
| $3 00–$3 49 | | | | | | | | | | 2 | 2 | .8 | .22 | $3 00– 3 49 |
| 3 50– 3 99 | | | | | | 1 | | | | 1 | 10 | 1.2 | .95 | 3 50– 3 99 |
| 4 00– 4 49 | | | | 2 | | | | | | 1 | 56 | 1.6 | 5.03 | 4 00– 4 49 |
| 4 50– 4 99 | | | | | | | | | | 1 | 175 | 2.0 | 17.8 | 4 50– 4 99 |
| 5 00– 5 49 | | | | | | | 1 | | | 7 | 353 | 4.9 | 43.7 | 5 00– 5 49 |
| 5 50– 5 99 | | | | | | | | | | 3 | 100 | 6.1 | 51 | 5 50– 5 99 |
| 6 00– 6 49 | | 2 | | 2 | | | | | 1 | 16 | 369 | 12.7 | 77.7 | 6 00– 6 49 |
| 6 50– 6 99 | | 1 | | 1 | | | | | | | 63 | | 82.5 | 6 50– 6 99 |
| 7 00– 7 49 | | 4 | | 3 | | | | 1 | | 15 | 95 | 18.8 | 89.5 | 7 00– 7 49 |
| 7 50– 7 99 | | | | 3 | | | | | | 2 | 22 | 19.7 | 91.0 | 7 50– 7 99 |
| 8 00– 8 99 | | 1 | 1 | | | | | | | 19 | 47 | 27.5 | 94.3 | 8 00– 8 99 |
| 9 00– 9 99 | 1 | | 1 | | 1 | | | | | 25 | 20 | 37.5 | 95.7 | 9 00– 9 99 |
| 10 00–10 99 | | | 2 | | 1 | | | | | 43 | 27 | 50.3 | 97.7 | 10 00–10 99 |
| 11 00–11 99 | | | | | 1 | | | | | 19 | 10 | 63.2 | 98.5 | 11 00–11 99 |
| 12 00–12 99 | 2 | | 1 | | | | | | | 29 | 10 | 75.0 | 99.2 | 12 00–12 99 |
| 13 00–13 99 | | | 1 | | 1 | | | | | 12 | 3 | 80.0 | 99 4 | 13 00–13 99 |
| 14 00–14 99 | 1 | | 2 | | | | | | | 18 | 1 | 87.3 | 99.5 | 14 00–14 99 |
| 15 00–15 99 | 1 | | 2 | | | | | | | 18 | 4 | 94.7 | 99.8 | 15 00–15 99 |
| 16 00–17 99 | 1 | | | | | | | | | 6 | 1 | 97.3 | 99.9 | 16 00–17 99 |
| 18 00–19 99 | | | 1 | | | | | | | 5 | 1 | 99.2 | 100.0 | 18 00–19 99 |
| 20 00–24 99 | | | | | | | | | | 2 | | 100.0 | | 20 00–24 99 |
| 25 00–29 99 | | | | | | | | | | | | | | 25 00–29 99 |
| 30 00–34 99 | | | | | | | | | | | | | | 30 00–34 99 |
| 35 00–39 99 | | | | | | | | | | | | | | 35 00–39 99 |
| 40 00 and over | | | | | | | | | | | | | | 40 00 and over |
| Not reported | | | | | | | | | 2 | 5 | 35 | | | Not reported |
| Total | 6 | 8 | 11 | 11 | 4 | 1 | 1 | 1 | 3 | 249 | 1,405 | | | Total |

NEW YORK STATE

**FIVE AND TEN CENT STORES**

10. TABLE VI, A, 3 — NUMBER OF EMPLOYEES CLASSIFIED ACCORDING TO ACTUAL WEEKLY EARNINGS BY AGE GROUPS AND SEX

| ACTUAL WEEKLY EARNINGS IN DOLLARS | AGE GROUPS IN YEARS | | | | | | | | | | | | | | ACTUAL WEEKLY EARNINGS IN DOLLARS |
|---|---|---|---|---|---|---|---|---|---|---|---|---|---|---|---|
| | 14–15 | | 16–17 | | 18–20 | | 21–24 | | 25–29 | | 30–34 | | 35–39 | | |
| | Male | Female | Male | Female | Male | Female | Male | Female | Male | Female | Male | Female | Male | Female | |
| Less than $3 00 | 1 | 2 | .... | 15 | ...... | 16 | ...... | 11 | ...... | 3 | ...... | 1 | ...... | 1 | Less than $3 00 |
| $3 00–$3 49... | .... | 1 | 1 | 7 | ...... | 14 | 1 | 4 | ...... | ...... | ...... | ...... | ...... | ...... | ...$3 00– 3 49 |
| 3 50– 3 99... | 1 | 1 | 3 | 13 | ...... | 13 | ...... | 7 | ...... | 2 | ...... | 1 | ...... | ...... | ....3 50– 3 99 |
| 4 00– 4 49... | .... | ...... | .... | 34 | ...... | 40 | ...... | 10 | ...... | 5 | ...... | 2 | ...... | 2 | ....4 00– 4 49 |
| 4 50– 4 99... | 2 | ...... | .... | 77 | ...... | 49 | ...... | 23 | ...... | 8 | ...... | 2 | ...... | 1 | ....4 50– 4 99 |
| 5 00– 5 49... | 2 | 4 | 4 | 93 | 1 | 111 | ...... | 35 | ...... | 10 | ...... | 5 | ...... | 1 | ....5 00– 5 49 |
| 5 50– 5 99... | 3 | 1 | 1 | 47 | 1 | 63 | ...... | 27 | ...... | 9 | ...... | ...... | ...... | 2 | ....5 50– 5 99 |
| 6 00– 6 49... | 2 | ...... | 8 | 46 | 5 | 143 | ...... | 59 | ...... | 20 | ...... | 6 | ...... | 3 | ....6 00– 6 49 |
| 6 50– 6 99... | .... | ...... | 3 | 8 | ...... | 44 | ...... | 38 | ...... | 8 | ...... | 3 | ...... | ...... | ....6 50– 6 99 |
| 7 00– 7 49... | .... | ...... | .... | 6 | 3 | 31 | 1 | 31 | ...... | 4 | ...... | ...... | ...... | ...... | ....7 00– 7 49 |
| 7 50– 7 99... | .... | ...... | 2 | ...... | 4 | 8 | 2 | 14 | ...... | 7 | ...... | 3 | ...... | ...... | ....7 50– 7 99 |
| 8 00– 8 99... | .... | ...... | 2 | 1 | 10 | 12 | 4 | 24 | 2 | 7 | ...... | 1 | 1 | 2 | ....8 00– 8 99 |
| 9 00– 9 99... | .... | ...... | 1 | ...... | 10 | 6 | 6 | 11 | 2 | 3 | 1 | 2 | ...... | ...... | ....9 00– 9 99 |
| 10 00–10 99... | .... | ...... | 1 | 1 | 8 | 4 | 11 | 9 | 1 | 3 | ...... | 1 | 1 | ...... | ...10 00–10 99 |
| 11 00–11 99... | .... | ...... | 2 | 1 | 3 | 4 | 11 | 6 | 3 | 5 | 7 | ...... | 2 | 1 | ...11 00–11 99 |
| 12 00–12 99... | .... | ...... | .... | ...... | 3 | 1 | 12 | 4 | 8 | 1 | 1 | ...... | 1 | ...... | ...12 00–12 99 |
| 13 00–13 99... | .... | ...... | .... | ...... | ...... | ...... | 8 | 1 | 2 | 4 | 1 | 1 | ...... | 1 | ...13 00–13 99 |
| 14 00–14 99... | .... | ...... | .... | ...... | ...... | ...... | 6 | 1 | 4 | ...... | 3 | ...... | ...... | ...... | ...14 00–14 99 |
| 15 00–15 99... | .... | ...... | .... | ...... | ...... | 1 | 10 | ...... | 5 | 2 | 2 | ...... | 1 | 1 | ...15 00–15 99 |
| 16 00–17 99... | .... | ...... | .... | ...... | ...... | ...... | 1 | 1 | 4 | ...... | 4 | 1 | 1 | ...... | ...16 00–17 99 |
| 18 00–19 99... | .... | ...... | .... | ...... | ...... | ...... | 2 | ...... | 2 | ...... | 1 | 1 | 1 | ...... | ...18 00–19 99 |
| 20 00–24 99... | .... | ...... | .... | ...... | ...... | ...... | ...... | ...... | 2 | ...... | ...... | ...... | ...... | ...... | ...20 00–24 99 |
| 25 00–29 99... | .... | ...... | .... | ...... | ...... | ...... | ...... | ...... | ...... | ...... | ...... | ...... | ...... | ...... | ...25 00–29 99 |
| Not reported... | .... | ...... | 1 | ...... | ...... | ...... | ...... | 1 | ...... | ...... | ...... | ...... | ...... | ...... | ...Not reported |
| Total..... | 11 | 9 | 29 | 349 | 48 | 560 | 75 | 317 | 35 | 101 | 20 | 30 | 8 | 15 | .....Total |

NEW YORK STATE

**FIVE AND TEN CENT STORES**

10. TABLE VI, A, 3 — (*concluded*) NUMBER OF EMPLOYEES CLASSIFIED ACCORDING TO ACTUAL WEEKLY EARNINGS BY AGE GROUPS AND SEX

| ACTUAL WEEKLY EARNINGS IN DOLLARS | AGE GROUPS IN YEARS | | | | | | | | | | | | | | ACTUAL WEEKLY EARNINGS IN DOLLARS |
|---|---|---|---|---|---|---|---|---|---|---|---|---|---|---|---|
| | 40–44 | | 45–54 | | 55–64 | | 65 AND OVER | | NOT REPORTED | | TOTAL | | CUMULATIVE PER CENT. OF TOTAL | | |
| | Male | Female | Male | Female | Male | Female | Male | Female | Male | Female | Male | Female | Male | Female | |
| Less than $3 00 | .... | ...... | .... | ...... | ...... | ...... | ...... | ...... | ...... | ...... | 1 | 49 | .4 | 3.5 | Less than $3 00 |
| $3 00– 3 49... | .... | ...... | .... | ...... | ...... | ...... | ...... | ...... | ...... | ...... | 2 | 26 | 1.2 | 5.3 | ...$3 00– 3 49 |
| 3 50– 3 99... | .... | ...... | .... | ...... | ...... | 1 | ...... | ...... | ...... | 1 | 4 | 39 | 2.8 | 8.1 | ....3 50– 3 99 |
| 4 00– 4 49... | .... | ...... | .... | 2 | ...... | ...... | ...... | ...... | ...... | ...... | ...... | 95 | ...... | 14.9 | ....4 00– 4 49 |
| 4 50– 4 99... | .... | ...... | .... | ...... | ...... | ...... | ...... | ...... | ...... | 1 | 2 | 161 | 3.6 | 26.4 | ....4 50– 4 99 |
| 5 00– 5 49... | .... | ...... | .... | 1 | ...... | ...... | ...... | ...... | ...... | ...... | 7 | 260 | 6.4 | 45.0 | ....5 00– 5 49 |
| 5 50– 5 99... | .... | 1 | .... | 2 | ...... | ...... | ...... | 1 | ...... | ...... | 5 | 153 | 8.5 | 55.8 | ....5 50– 5 99 |
| 6 00– 6 49... | .... | 1 | .... | ...... | ...... | ...... | ...... | ...... | ...... | 1 | 15 | 279 | 14.5 | 75.6 | ....6 00– 6 49 |
| 6 50– 6 99... | .... | 3 | .... | 1 | ...... | ...... | ...... | ...... | ...... | ...... | 3 | 105 | 15.7 | 83.0 | ....6 50– 6 99 |
| 7 00– 7 49... | .... | ...... | .... | 2 | ...... | ...... | ...... | ...... | ...... | ...... | 4 | 74 | 17.4 | 88.4 | ....7 00– 7 49 |
| 7 50– 7 99... | .... | 2 | .... | 3 | ...... | ...... | ...... | ...... | 1 | ...... | 9 | 37 | 25.0 | 91.0 | ....7 50– 7 99 |
| 8 00– 8 99... | .... | 1 | 1 | ...... | ...... | ...... | ...... | ...... | ...... | ...... | 20 | 48 | 29.0 | 94.2 | ....8 00– 8 99 |
| 9 00– 9 99... | 1 | ...... | 1 | ...... | 1 | ...... | ...... | ...... | ...... | ...... | 23 | 22 | 38.2 | 96.0 | ....9 00– 9 99 |
| 10 00–10 99... | .... | ...... | 1 | ...... | ...... | ...... | 1 | ...... | ...... | ...... | 24 | 18 | 48.0 | 97.2 | ...10 00–10 99 |
| 11 00–11 99... | .... | ...... | 1 | ...... | 1 | ...... | ...... | ...... | ...... | ...... | 30 | 17 | 60.0 | 98.5 | ...11 00–11 99 |
| 12 00–12 99... | 1 | ...... | .... | ...... | 1 | ...... | ...... | ...... | ...... | ...... | 27 | 6 | 71.0 | 99.0 | ...12 00–12 99 |
| 13 00–13 99... | 1 | ...... | 2 | ...... | ...... | ...... | ...... | ...... | ...... | ...... | 14 | 7 | 76.5 | 99.5 | ...13 00–13 99 |
| 14 00–14 99... | .... | ...... | 1 | ...... | 1 | ...... | ...... | ...... | ...... | ...... | 15 | 1 | 82.7 | 99.6 | ...14 00–14 99 |
| 15 00–15 99... | 1 | ...... | 1 | ...... | ...... | ...... | ...... | ...... | ...... | ...... | 20 | 4 | 90.7 | 99.8 | ...15 00–15 99 |
| 16 00–17 99... | 2 | ...... | 2 | ...... | ...... | ...... | ...... | ...... | ...... | ...... | 14 | 2 | 96.4 | 99.9 | ...16 00–17 99 |
| 18 00–19 99... | .... | ...... | 1 | ...... | ...... | ...... | ...... | ...... | ...... | ...... | 7 | 1 | 99.0 | 100.0 | ...18 00–19 99 |
| 20 00–24 99... | .... | ...... | .... | ...... | ...... | ...... | ...... | ...... | ...... | ...... | 2 | ...... | 100.0 | ...... | ..20 00–24 99 |
| 25 00–29 99... | .... | ...... | .... | ...... | ...... | ...... | ...... | ...... | ...... | ...... | ...... | ...... | ...... | ...... | ..25 00–29 99 |
| Not reported... | .... | ...... | .... | ...... | ...... | ...... | ...... | ...... | ...... | ...... | 1 | 1 | ...... | ...... | ...Not reported |
| Total..... | 6 | 8 | 11 | 11 | 4 | 1 | 1 | 1 | 1 | 3 | 249 | 1,405 | ...... | ...... | .....Total |

11. TABLE VII, A, 1, a

NEW YORK STATE

**DEPARTMENT STORES — STOCK AND SALES**

Number and Per Cent. of Employees According to Occupation by Nativity

| Nativity | Occupation | | | | | | | | | | | | | | | | | |
|---|---|---|---|---|---|---|---|---|---|---|---|---|---|---|---|---|---|---|
| | Total | | Superintendents | | Buyers | | Assistant buyers, head of stock | | Receiving and stock clerks | | Stock people | | Floor managers | | Sales people | | Messengers, wrappers, errand boys | |
| | Male | Female | Male | Female | Male | Female | Male | Female | Male | Female | Male | Female | Male | Female | Male | Female | Male | Female |
| Native | 5,580 | 15,948 | 24 | ...... | 116 | 55 | 241 | 434 | 535 | 653 | 561 | 885 | 460 | 47 | 2,918 | 11,552 | 725 | 2,322 |
| Foreign | 2,189 | 1,897 | 6 | ...... | 38 | 5 | 72 | 55 | 174 | 62 | 233 | 77 | 166 | 7 | 1,331 | 1,457 | 169 | 234 |
| Not reported | 53 | 131 | 1 | ...... | .... | 2 | 2 | 3 | 2 | 4 | 12 | 6 | 5 | 1 | 24 | 90 | 7 | 25 |
| Total | 7,822 | 17,976 | 31 | ...... | 154 | 62 | 315 | 492 | 711 | 719 | 806 | 968 | 631 | 55 | 4,273 | 13,099 | 901 | 2,581 |
| Per cent. of total | 100.00 | 100.00 | .4 | ...... | 2.0 | .3 | 4.0 | 2.7 | 9.1 | 4.0 | 10.3 | 5.4 | 8.1 | .3 | 54.6 | 73.0 | 11.5 | 14.3 |

NEW YORK STATE

DEPARTMENT STORES — STOCK AND SALES

12. TABLE V, A, 1, a NUMBER AND PER CENT. OF EMPLOYEES, BY SEX, EARNING SPECIFIED WEEKLY RATES ACCORDING TO AGE GROUPS

| WEEKLY RATES IN DOLLARS | AGE GROUPS IN YEARS | | | | | | | | | | | | | | WEEKLY RATES IN DOLLARS |
|---|---|---|---|---|---|---|---|---|---|---|---|---|---|---|---|
| | 14–15 | | 16–17 | | 18–20 | | 21–24 | | 25–29 | | 30–34 | | 35–39 | | |
| | Male | Female | Male | Female | Male | Female | Male | Female | Male | Female | Male | Female | Male | Female | |
| Less than $3 00 | 5 | 40 | .... | 1 | ...... | 1 | ...... | ...... | ...... | 1 | ...... | ...... | ...... | ...... | Less than $3 00 |
| $3 00– 3 49... | 38 | 220 | 9 | 113 | ...... | 9 | ...... | 1 | ...... | 1 | ...... | 1 | ...... | ...... | ...$3 00– 3 49 |
| 3 50– 3 99... | 59 | 424 | 11 | 238 | 2 | 25 | ...... | 3 | ...... | ...... | ...... | ...... | ...... | ...... | ... 3 50– 3 99 |
| 4 00– 4 49... | 226 | 366 | 76 | 670 | 11 | 159 | 5 | 14 | 5 | 2 | 4 | 1 | 2 | ...... | ... 4 00– 4 49 |
| 4 50– 4 99... | 38 | 72 | 38 | 268 | 1 | 155 | 2 | 27 | 1 | 22 | ...... | 15 | ...... | 18 | ... 4 50– 4 99 |
| 5 00– 5 49... | 67 | 51 | 129 | 412 | 25 | 477 | 2 | 107 | 1 | 38 | 4 | 17 | 1 | 6 | ... 5 00– 5 49 |
| 5 50– 5 99... | 4 | 8 | 13 | 41 | 2 | 85 | 1 | 30 | ...... | 18 | ...... | 5 | ...... | ...... | ... 5 50– 5 99 |
| 6 00– 6 49... | 11 | 7 | 152 | 240 | 90 | 984 | 10 | 547 | 2 | 184 | 2 | 71 | ...... | 41 | ... 6 00– 6 49 |
| 6 50– 6 99... | .... | 5 | 8 | 11 | 7 | 71 | 4 | 45 | 2 | 16 | ...... | 8 | ...... | 2 | ... 6 50– 6 99 |
| 7 00– 7 49... | 2 | 1 | 60 | 59 | 147 | 690 | 21 | 850 | 4 | 418 | 5 | 195 | ...... | 121 | ... 7 00– 7 49 |
| 7 50– 7 99... | 1 | 1 | 3 | 4 | 11 | 35 | 2 | 64 | ...... | 34 | ...... | 9 | ...... | 9 | ... 7 50– 7 99 |
| 8 00– 8 99... | .... | 2 | 33 | 17 | 174 | 348 | 47 | 874 | 10 | 499 | 9 | 216 | 4 | 164 | ... 8 00– 8 99 |
| 9 00– 9 99... | 1 | ...... | 4 | 3 | 97 | 107 | 66 | 450 | 12 | 394 | 6 | 169 | 2 | 128 | ... 9 00– 9 99 |
| 10 00–10 99... | .... | ...... | 4 | 1 | 98 | 57 | 164 | 372 | 63 | 412 | 26 | 205 | 19 | 151 | ...10 00–10 99 |
| 11 00–11 99... | .... | ...... | 1 | ...... | 21 | 18 | 62 | 121 | 32 | 170 | 11 | 87 | 11 | 49 | ...11 00–11 99 |
| 12 00–12 99... | .... | ...... | 2 | 1 | 52 | 25 | 251 | 168 | 153 | 309 | 97 | 226 | 67 | 147 | ...12 00–12 99 |
| 13 00–13 99... | .... | ...... | .... | 1 | 4 | ...... | 42 | 27 | 47 | 60 | 25 | 52 | 13 | 37 | ...13 00–13 99 |
| 14 00–14 99... | .... | ...... | .... | ...... | 5 | 5 | 95 | 41 | 114 | 99 | 75 | 79 | 52 | 75 | ...14 00–14 99 |
| 15 00–15 99... | .... | ...... | 1 | 2 | 2 | ...... | 98 | 33 | 181 | 107 | 123 | 93 | 113 | 84 | ...15 00–15 99 |
| 16 00–17 99... | .... | ...... | .... | 2 | 2 | 2 | 43 | 13 | 117 | 62 | 110 | 69 | 71 | 61 | ...16 00–17 99 |
| 18 00–19 99... | .... | ...... | .... | ...... | 5 | 2 | 28 | 8 | 100 | 59 | 131 | 51 | 93 | 63 | ...18 00–19 99 |
| 20 00–24 99... | .... | ...... | .... | ...... | ...... | ...... | 23 | 8 | 128 | 43 | 162 | 59 | 168 | 59 | ...20 00–24 99 |
| 25 00–29 99... | .... | ...... | .... | ...... | ...... | ...... | 1 | ...... | 42 | 17 | 73 | 21 | 99 | 31 | ...25 00–29 99 |
| 30 00–34 99... | .... | ...... | .... | ...... | ...... | 1 | ...... | ...... | 10 | 9 | 30 | 7 | 42 | 11 | ...30 00–34 99 |
| 35 00–39 99... | .... | ...... | .... | ...... | ...... | 1 | ...... | ...... | 2 | 1 | 8 | 6 | 10 | 9 | ...35 00–39 99 |
| 40 00 and over. | .... | ...... | .... | ...... | ...... | ...... | ...... | ...... | 3 | 3 | 16 | 6 | 41 | 8 | .40 00 and over |
| Not reported... | .... | 1 | 2 | 1 | 4 | 3 | 6 | 1 | 8 | 1 | 4 | 1 | 15 | 1 | ...Not reported |
| Total..... | 452 | 1,198 | 546 | 2,085 | 760 | 3,260 | 973 | 3,804 | 1,037 | 2,969 | 921 | 1,669 | 824 | 1,275 | .....Total |

12. TABLE V, A, 1, a — (*concluded*)

NEW YORK STATE

**DEPARTMENT STORES — STOCK AND SALES**

Number and Per Cent. of Employees, by Sex, Earning Specified Weekly Rates According to Age Groups

| Weekly Rates in Dollars | Age Groups in Years: 40–44 | | 45–54 | | 55–64 | | 65 and over | | Not reported | | Total | | Cumulative per cent. of total | | Weekly Rates in Dollars |
|---|---|---|---|---|---|---|---|---|---|---|---|---|---|---|---|
| | Male | Female | Male | Female | Male | Female | Male | Female | Male | Female | Male | Female | Male | Female | |
| Less than $3 00 | .... | ...... | .... | ...... | ...... | ...... | ...... | ...... | 1 | ...... | 6 | 43 | .08 | .24 | Less than $3 00 |
| $3 00–$3 49... | .... | ...... | .... | ...... | ...... | ...... | ...... | ...... | 2 | ...... | 49 | 345 | .71 | 2.2 | ...$3 00– 3 49 |
| 3 50– 3 99... | 1 | ...... | .... | ...... | ...... | ...... | ...... | ...... | ...... | 18 | 73 | 708 | 1.65 | 6.1 | ... 3 50– 3 99 |
| 4 00– 4 49... | 6 | 1 | 5 | ...... | 1 | ...... | ...... | ...... | 3 | 17 | 344 | 1,230 | 6.1 | 13.0 | ... 4 00– 4 49 |
| 4 50– 4 99... | .... | 8 | .... | 6 | ...... | ...... | ...... | ...... | 2 | 13 | 83 | 604 | 7.2 | 16.3 | ... 4 50– 4 99 |
| 5 00– 5 49... | .... | 4 | .... | 3 | 1 | ...... | ...... | ...... | 2 | 27 | 232 | 1,142 | 10.2 | 22.7 | ... 5 00– 5 49 |
| 5 50– 5 99... | .... | 2 | .... | ...... | ...... | ...... | ...... | ...... | ...... | 86 | 20 | 275 | 10.4 | 24.2 | ... 5 50– 5 99 |
| 6 00– 6 49... | .... | 22 | 1 | 19 | 1 | 1 | 1 | ...... | ...... | 67 | 270 | 2,183 | 13.9 | 36.3 | ... 6 00– 6 49 |
| 6 50– 6 99... | .... | 4 | .... | ...... | ...... | ...... | ...... | ...... | ...... | 79 | 21 | 241 | 14.2 | 37.7 | ... 6 50– 6 99 |
| 7 00– 7 49... | 1 | 63 | 3 | 40 | 5 | 2 | 2 | 2 | 2 | 49 | 252 | 2,490 | 17.4 | 51.7 | ... 7 00– 7 49 |
| 7 50– 7 99... | .... | 3 | .... | 3 | ...... | ...... | ...... | ...... | ...... | 24 | 17 | 186 | 17.7 | 52.5 | ... 7 50– 7 99 |
| 8 00– 8 99... | 5 | 64 | 8 | 55 | 11 | 7 | 4 | 1 | 6 | 72 | 311 | 2,319 | 21.6 | 66.5 | ... 8 00– 8 99 |
| 9 00– 9 99... | 5 | 46 | 10 | 30 | ...... | 1 | ...... | ...... | 4 | 79 | 207 | 1,397 | 24.3 | 73.3 | ... 9 00– 9 99 |
| 10 00–10 99... | 11 | 57 | 20 | 40 | 16 | 8 | 4 | 1 | 5 | 58 | 430 | 1,362 | 29.8 | 81.0 | ...10 00–10 99 |
| 11 00–11 99... | 6 | 25 | 7 | 3 | 6 | 1 | 1 | ...... | 7 | 21 | 165 | 495 | 32.0 | 83.7 | ...11 00–11 99 |
| 12 00–12 99... | 47 | 73 | 74 | 42 | 32 | 2 | 10 | ...... | 8 | 32 | 793 | 1,025 | 42.2 | 89.3 | ...12 00–12 99 |
| 13 00–13 99... | 16 | 14 | 24 | 8 | 6 | ...... | 5 | ...... | 1 | 16 | 183 | 215 | 44.5 | 90.5 | ...13 00–13 99 |
| 14 00–14 99... | 33 | 26 | 62 | 8 | 27 | 1 | 8 | ...... | 4 | 16 | 475 | 350 | 50.8 | 92.5 | ...14 00–14 99 |
| 15 00–15 99... | 79 | 43 | 125 | 24 | 46 | ...... | 11 | ...... | 7 | 20 | 786 | 406 | 61.0 | 95.0 | ...15 00–15 99 |
| 16 00–17 99... | 67 | 33 | 115 | 20 | 37 | 1 | 11 | ...... | 6 | 24 | 579 | 287 | 68.2 | 96.5 | ...16 00–17 99 |
| 18 00–19 99... | 84 | 18 | 128 | 12 | 28 | 1 | 8 | ...... | 5 | 14 | 610 | 228 | 76.2 | 97.7 | ...18 00–19 99 |
| 20 00–24 99... | 158 | 25 | 211 | 10 | 72 | 1 | 7 | 1 | 6 | 20 | 935 | 226 | 88.2 | 98.7 | ...20 00–24 99 |
| 25 00–29 99... | 97 | 11 | 130 | 12 | 37 | ...... | 7 | ...... | ...... | 10 | 486 | 102 | 94.5 | 99.5 | ...25 00–29 99 |
| 30 00–34 99... | 44 | 5 | 53 | 4 | 17 | ...... | 3 | ...... | 1 | 6 | 200 | 43 | 97.2 | 99.7 | ...30 00–34 99 |
| 35 00–39 99... | 16 | 5 | 28 | 2 | 9 | ...... | 3 | ...... | 1 | 2 | 77 | 26 | 98.2 | 99.8 | ...35 00–39 99 |
| 40 00 and over. | 32 | 4 | 46 | 4 | 10 | 1 | 4 | ...... | 1 | 8 | 153 | 34 | 100.0 | 100.0 | 40 00 and over |
| Not reported... | 3 | ...... | 11 | ...... | 7 | ...... | 2 | ...... | ...... | 1 | 62 | 10 | ...... | ...... | ...Not reported |
| Total..... | 711 | 556 | 1,061 | 345 | 369 | 27 | 91 | 5 | 74 | 779 | 7,819 | 17,972 | ...... | ...... | .....Total |

13. TABLE VIII, A, 1, a

NEW YORK STATE

**DEPARTMENT STORES — STOCK AND SALES**

Number and Per Cent. of Employees Earning Specified Weekly Rates According to Occupation and Sex

| Weekly Rates in Dollars | Occupation: Superintendents | Buyers | | Assistant Buyers and Heads of Stock | | Receiving and Stock Clerks | | Stock People | | Floor Managers | | Sales People | | Errand Boys, Messengers and Wrappers | | Total | | Cumulative Per Cent. of Total | | Weekly Rates in Dollars |
|---|---|---|---|---|---|---|---|---|---|---|---|---|---|---|---|---|---|---|---|---|
| | Male | Male | Female | Male | Female | Male | Female | Male | Female | Male | Female | Male | Female | Male | Female | Male | Female | Male | Female | |
| Less than $3 00 | | | | | | 1 | | 1 | 3 | | | | 3 | 4 | 37 | 6 | 43 | .08 | .24 | Less than $3 00 |
| $3 00–$3 49 | | | | | | 1 | 16 | 2 | 21 | | | 1 | 17 | 45 | 291 | 49 | 345 | .71 | 2.2 | $3 00– 3 49 |
| 3 50– 3 99 | | | | | | 2 | 42 | 8 | 106 | | | 1 | 40 | 62 | 520 | 73 | 708 | 1.65 | 6.1 | 3 50– 3 99 |
| 4 00– 4 49 | | | | | | 7 | 70 | 47 | 153 | | | 10 | 173 | 280 | 834 | 344 | 1,230 | 6.1 | 13. | 4 00– 4 49 |
| 4 50– 4 99 | | | | | | 6 | 61 | 22 | 103 | | | 1 | 204 | 54 | 236 | 83 | 604 | 7.2 | 16.3 | 4 50– 4 99 |
| 5 00– 5 49 | | | | | 1 | 17 | 121 | 101 | 233 | | 1 | 13 | 493 | 101 | 293 | 232 | 1,142 | 10.2 | 22.7 | 5 00– 5 49 |
| 5 50– 5 99 | | | | | 1 | 3 | 13 | 4 | 32 | | | 1 | 190 | 12 | 39 | 20 | 275 | 10.4 | 24.2 | 5 50– 5 99 |
| 6 00– 6 49 | | | | | 3 | 53 | 115 | 114 | 122 | | | 40 | 1,800 | 63 | 143 | 270 | 2,183 | 13.9 | 36.3 | 6 00– 6 49 |
| 6 50– 6 99 | | | | | | 2 | 5 | 6 | 15 | | | 5 | 168 | 8 | 53 | 21 | 241 | 14.2 | 37.7 | 6 50– 6 99 |
| 7 00– 7 49 | | | | | 9 | 44 | 81 | 79 | 61 | 1 | | 56 | 2,282 | 72 | 57 | 252 | 2,490 | 17.4 | 51.7 | 7 00– 7 49 |
| 7 50– 7 99 | | | | 1 | 2 | 2 | 8 | 6 | 8 | | 2 | 4 | 150 | 4 | 16 | 17 | 186 | 17.7 | 52.5 | 7 50– 7 99 |
| 8 00– 8 99 | | | 1 | 3 | 19 | 68 | 52 | 57 | 38 | | 3 | 94 | 2,161 | 89 | 45 | 311 | 2,319 | 21.6 | 66.5 | 8 00– 8 99 |
| 9 00– 9 99 | | | | 1 | 37 | 42 | 42 | 33 | 26 | | 16 | 96 | 1,272 | 35 | 4 | 207 | 1,397 | 24.3 | 73.3 | 9 00– 9 99 |
| 10 00–10 99 | | 1 | 3 | 5 | 38 | 73 | 29 | 79 | 14 | 1 | 8 | 237 | 1,266 | 34 | 4 | 430 | 1,362 | 29.8 | 81. | 10 00–10 99 |
| 11 00–11 99 | | | 2 | 1 | 30 | 49 | 15 | 28 | 14 | | 5 | 83 | 427 | 4 | 2 | 165 | 495 | 32. | 83.7 | 11 00–11 99 |
| 12 00–12 99 | | 3 | 2 | 9 | 54 | 128 | 14 | 105 | 14 | 5 | 5 | 525 | 934 | 18 | 2 | 793 | 1,025 | 42.2 | 89.3 | 12 00–12 99 |
| 13 00–13 99 | | | | 4 | 14 | 41 | 6 | 17 | 3 | | 3 | 118 | 188 | 3 | 1 | 183 | 215 | 44.5 | 90.5 | 13 00–13 99 |
| 14 00–14 99 | | | 1 | 12 | 37 | 55 | 11 | 27 | | 5 | | 373 | 299 | 3 | 2 | 475 | 350 | 50.8 | 92.5 | 14 00–14 99 |
| 15 00–15 99 | 1 | 3 | 5 | 21 | 50 | 37 | 5 | 24 | | 25 | 1 | 671 | 345 | 4 | | 786 | 406 | 61. | 95. | 15 00–15 99 |
| 16 00–17 99 | 1 | 8 | 3 | 29 | 36 | 31 | 7 | 22 | | 33 | 4 | 454 | 237 | 1 | | 579 | 287 | 68.2 | 96.5 | 16 00–17 99 |
| 18 00–19 99 | | 5 | | 40 | 43 | 20 | 3 | 9 | | 68 | 3 | 467 | 179 | 1 | | 610 | 228 | 76.2 | 97.7 | 18 00–19 99 |
| 20 00–24 99 | 5 | 14 | 7 | 67 | 49 | 17 | 2 | 7 | 1 | 200 | 3 | 625 | 164 | | | 935 | 226 | 88.2 | 98.7 | 20 00–24 99 |
| 25 00–29 99 | 9 | 24 | 10 | 57 | 37 | 6 | | 3 | | 172 | 1 | 215 | 54 | | | 486 | 102 | 94.5 | 99.5 | 25 00–29 99 |
| 30 00–34 99 | 4 | 26 | 9 | 32 | 15 | 2 | | 2 | | 68 | | 66 | 19 | | | 200 | 43 | 97.2 | 99.7 | 30 00–34 99 |
| 35 00–39 99 | 2 | 10 | 5 | 10 | 11 | 3 | | 1 | | 31 | | 20 | 10 | | | 77 | 26 | 98.2 | 99.8 | 35 00–39 99 |
| 40 00 and over | 9 | 60 | 14 | 21 | 6 | 1 | | 1 | | 20 | | 41 | 14 | | | 153 | 34 | 100.00 | 100.00 | 40 00 and over |
| Not reported | | | | 2 | | | | 1 | | 2 | | 55 | 9 | 2 | 1 | 62 | 10 | | | Not reported |
| Total | 31 | 154 | 62 | 315 | 492 | 711 | 718 | 806 | 967 | 631 | 55 | 4,272 | 13,098 | 899 | 2,580 | 7,819 | 17,972 | | | Total |

14. TABLE VI, A, 1, a

NEW YORK STATE

DEPARTMENT STORES — STOCK AND SALES

NUMBER AND PER CENT. OF EMPLOYEES CLASSIFIED ACCORDING TO ACTUAL WEEKLY EARNINGS, BY AGE GROUPS AND SEX

| Actual Weekly Earnings in Dollars | Age Groups in Years: 14–15 | | 16–17 | | 18–20 | | 21–24 | | 25–29 | | 30–34 | | 35–39 | | Actual Weekly Earnings in Dollars |
|---|---|---|---|---|---|---|---|---|---|---|---|---|---|---|---|
| | Male | Female | Male | Female | Male | Female | Male | Female | Male | Female | Male | Female | Male | Female | |
| Less than $3 00 | 25 | 114 | 15 | 65 | 6 | 50 | 5 | 38 | 5 | 28 | 1 | 10 | ...... | 8 | Less than $3 00 |
| $3 00–$3 49... | 44 | 220 | 19 | 154 | 2 | 37 | 2 | 12 | 1 | 6 | ...... | 3 | 2 | 1 | ...$3 00– 3 49 |
| 3 50– 3 99... | 61 | 307 | 16 | 268 | 4 | 52 | 2 | 19 | ...... | 10 | 1 | 6 | ...... | 4 | ... 3 50– 3 99 |
| 4 00– 4 99... | 204 | 417 | 67 | 608 | 15 | 187 | 1 | 32 | ...... | 15 | 1 | 9 | 2 | 3 | ... 4 00– 4 49 |
| 4 50– 4 99... | 37 | 66 | 44 | 240 | 9 | 136 | 3 | 30 | 1 | 25 | ...... | 13 | 1 | 11 | ... 4 50– 4 99 |
| 5 00– 5 49... | 63 | 46 | 116 | 349 | 23 | 408 | 6 | 135 | 1 | 55 | 3 | 31 | ...... | 15 | ... 5 00– 5 49 |
| 5 50– 5 99... | 4 | 7 | 21 | 61 | 18 | 181 | 4 | 100 | 2 | 54 | 2 | 17 | ...... | 11 | ... 5 50– 5 99 |
| 6 00– 6 49... | 9 | 8 | 134 | 199 | 74 | 720 | 11 | 446 | 8 | 149 | 3 | 69 | 1 | 39 | ... 6 00– 6 49 |
| 6 50– 6 99... | .... | 5 | 16 | 24 | 26 | 202 | 4 | 160 | 1 | 71 | ...... | 31 | ...... | 18 | ... 6 50– 6 99 |
| 7 00– 7 49... | 2 | 1 | 47 | 72 | 125 | 550 | 22 | 628 | 4 | 328 | 4 | 141 | ...... | 94 | ... 7 00– 7 49 |
| 7 50– 7 99... | 1 | 1 | 5 | 10 | 21 | 121 | 6 | 187 | 3 | 83 | 1 | 36 | ...... | 28 | ... 7 50– 7 99 |
| 8 00– 8 99... | .... | 3 | 29 | 20 | 159 | 349 | 54 | 762 | 12 | 458 | 10 | 202 | 6 | 148 | ... 8 00– 8 99 |
| 9 00– 9 99... | 1 | ...... | 6 | 4 | 82 | 127 | 78 | 446 | 15 | 367 | 8 | 179 | 3 | 124 | ... 9 00– 9 99 |
| 10 00–10 99... | .... | ...... | 3 | 1 | 89 | 69 | 146 | 359 | 63 | 368 | 24 | 175 | 15 | 133 | ...10 00–10 99 |
| 11 00–11 99... | .... | ...... | 1 | ...... | 32 | 19 | 78 | 136 | 50 | 195 | 24 | 101 | 13 | 60 | ...11 00–11 99 |
| 12 00–12 99... | .... | 1 | 3 | 1 | 45 | 25 | 191 | 149 | 120 | 247 | 79 | 179 | 59 | 112 | ...12 00–12 99 |
| 13 00–13 99... | .... | ...... | .... | ...... | 8 | 5 | 66 | 51 | 59 | 86 | 26 | 62 | 16 | 47 | ...13 00–13 99 |
| 14 00–14 99... | .... | 1 | .... | 1 | 7 | 4 | 89 | 42 | 99 | 109 | 65 | 80 | 47 | 82 | ...14 00–14 99 |
| 15 00–15 99... | .... | ...... | 1 | 1 | 4 | 1 | 86 | 28 | 142 | 97 | 109 | 92 | 88 | 81 | ...15 00–15 99 |
| 16 00–17 99... | .... | ...... | .... | 1 | 3 | 3 | 50 | 12 | 123 | 83 | 105 | 74 | 78 | 77 | ...16 00–17 99 |
| 18 00–19 99... | .... | ...... | .... | ...... | 3 | 1 | 34 | 10 | 105 | 58 | 124 | 51 | 104 | 56 | ...18 00–19 99 |
| 20 00–24 99... | .... | ...... | .... | 1 | 2 | 1 | 29 | 12 | 138 | 37 | 184 | 61 | 179 | 59 | ...20 00–24 99 |
| 25 00–29 99... | .... | ...... | .... | ...... | ...... | ...... | 1 | 1 | 56 | 16 | 81 | 21 | 103 | 29 | ...25 00–29 99 |
| 30 00–34 99... | .... | ...... | .... | ...... | ...... | 1 | ...... | ...... | 19 | 7 | 34 | 6 | 46 | 11 | ...30 00–34 99 |
| 35 00–39 99... | .... | ...... | .... | ...... | ...... | 1 | ...... | ...... | 4 | 1 | 10 | 6 | 18 | 8 | ...35 00–39 99 |
| 40 00 and over. | .... | ...... | .... | ...... | ...... | ...... | ...... | ...... | 4 | 3 | 17 | 6 | 43 | 8 | .40 00 and over |
| Not reported... | 1 | 2 | 3 | 5 | 5 | 12 | 5 | 9 | 3 | 14 | 5 | 9 | 1 | 8 | ...Not reported |
| Total..... | 452 | 1,199 | 546 | 2,085 | 762 | 3,262 | 973 | 3,804 | 1,038 | 2,970 | 921 | 1,670 | 825 | 1,275 | .....Total |

NEW YORK STATE

**14. TABLE VI, A, 1, a — (concluded)** **DEPARTMENT STORES — STOCK AND SALES**

NUMBER AND PER CENT. OF EMPLOYEES CLASSIFIED ACCORDING TO ACTUAL WEEKLY EARNINGS, BY AGE GROUPS AND SEX

| ACTUAL WEEKLY EARNINGS IN DOLLARS | AGE GROUPS IN YEARS | | | | | | | | | | | | | | | | ACTUAL WEEKLY EARNINGS IN DOLLARS |
|---|---|---|---|---|---|---|---|---|---|---|---|---|---|---|---|---|---|
| | 40–44 | | 45–54 | | 55–64 | | 65 AND OVER | | NOT REPORTED | | TOTAL | | CUMULATIVE PER CENT. OF TOTAL | | | | |
| | Male | Female | Male | Female | Male | Female | Male | Female | Male | Female | Male | Female | Male | Female | | | |
| Less than $3 00 | 2 | 2 | 1 | ...... | 1 | 1 | ...... | ...... | ...... | 2 | 61 | 318 | .78 | 1.78 | Less than $3 00 |
| $3 00–$3 49... | 1 | 3 | .... | ...... | ...... | ...... | ...... | ...... | 1 | 2 | 72 | 438 | 1.71 | 4.21 | ...$3 00– 3 49 |
| 3 50– 3 99... | 1 | 3 | .... | 1 | ...... | ...... | ...... | ...... | 1 | 14 | 86 | 684 | 2.81 | 8.05 | ... 3 50– 3 99 |
| 4 00– 4 49... | .... | 2 | 2 | 1 | 1 | ...... | ...... | ...... | 2 | 16 | 295 | 1,290 | 6.60 | 15.26 | ... 4 00– 4 49 |
| 4 50– 4 99... | .... | 3 | 1 | 4 | ...... | ...... | ...... | ...... | 2 | 6 | 98 | 534 | 7.85 | 18.25 | ... 4 50– 4 99 |
| 5 00– 5 49... | 1 | 8 | 1 | 12 | ...... | 1 | ...... | ...... | 2 | 5 | 216 | 1,065 | 10.60 | 24.2 | ... 5 00– 5 49 |
| 5 50– 5 99... | .... | 6 | .... | 7 | ...... | ...... | ...... | ...... | ...... | 7 | 51 | 451 | 11.28 | 26.8 | ... 5 50– 5 99 |
| 6 00– 6 49... | 1 | 23 | 3 | 17 | 1 | 1 | 1 | 1 | ...... | 27 | 246 | 1,699 | 14.42 | 36.2 | ... 6 00– 6 49 |
| 6 50– 6 99... | .... | 3 | 2 | 1 | 1 | ...... | 2 | ...... | ...... | 31 | 52 | 546 | 15.1 | 39.3 | ... 6 50– 6 99 |
| 7 00– 7 49... | 1 | 56 | 4 | 28 | 6 | 2 | 1 | 1 | 2 | 29 | 218 | 1,930 | 17.9 | 50.1 | ... 7 00– 7 49 |
| 7 50– 7 99... | 1 | 8 | .... | 7 | 2 | ...... | 1 | ...... | 2 | 29 | 43 | 510 | 18.5 | 53.0 | ... 7 50– 7 99 |
| 8 00– 8 99... | 5 | 58 | 9 | 53 | 11 | 4 | 3 | 1 | 3 | 105 | 301 | 2,163 | 22.4 | 65.0 | ... 8 00– 8 99 |
| 9 00– 9 99... | 6 | 44 | 14 | 28 | 2 | 1 | 1 | ...... | 2 | 114 | 218 | 1,434 | 25.1 | 73.1 | ... 9 00– 9 99 |
| 10 00–10 99... | 14 | 53 | 18 | 34 | 13 | 5 | 4 | ...... | 3 | 79 | 392 | 1,276 | 30.2 | 80.2 | ...10 00–10 99 |
| 11 00–11 99... | 7 | 26 | 10 | 7 | 4 | 2 | 3 | 1 | 2 | 51 | 224 | 598 | 33.0 | 83.5 | ...11 00–11 99 |
| 12 00–12 99... | 40 | 63 | 59 | 29 | 28 | 3 | 10 | ...... | 6 | 63 | 640 | 872 | 41.2 | 88.4 | ...12 00–12 99 |
| 13 00–13 99... | 13 | 16 | 30 | 13 | 7 | ...... | 4 | ...... | 3 | 29 | 232 | 309 | 44.2 | 90.2 | ...13 00–13 99 |
| 14 00–14 99... | 28 | 25 | 62 | 8 | 31 | 1 | 6 | ...... | 7 | 33 | 441 | 386 | 49.8 | 92.3 | ...14 00–14 99 |
| 15 00–15 99... | 60 | 38 | 108 | 22 | 35 | ...... | 7 | ...... | 6 | 38 | 646 | 398 | 58.2 | 94.5 | ...15 00–15 99 |
| 16 00–17 99... | 75 | 36 | 105 | 20 | 42 | 1 | 13 | ...... | 7 | 30 | 601 | 337 | 65.9 | 95.8 | ...16 00–17 99 |
| 18 00–19 99... | 85 | 19 | 134 | 13 | 30 | 1 | 9 | ...... | 7 | 21 | 635 | 230 | 74.1 | 97.7 | ...18 00–19 99 |
| 20 00–24 99... | 168 | 29 | 222 | 9 | 74 | 1 | 7 | 1 | 7 | 17 | 1,010 | 228 | 87.0 | 98.0 | ...20 00–24 99 |
| 25 00–29 99... | 104 | 14 | 136 | 12 | 41 | ...... | 8 | ...... | 1 | 8 | 531 | 101 | 93.8 | 99.5 | ...25 00–29 99 |
| 30 00–34 99... | 44 | 4 | 60 | 4 | 19 | ...... | 3 | ...... | 1 | 6 | 226 | 39 | 96.6 | 99.8 | ...30 00–34 99 |
| 35 00–39 99... | 16 | 5 | 29 | 2 | 8 | ...... | 3 | ...... | 1 | 2 | 89 | 25 | 97.9 | 99.9 | ...35 00–39 99 |
| 40 00 and over. | 34 | 4 | 46 | 4 | 10 | 1 | 4 | ...... | 1 | 8 | 159 | 34 | 100.0 | 100.0 | .40 00 and over |
| Not reported... | 6 | 5 | 5 | 9 | 2 | 2 | 1 | ...... | 2 | 6 | 39 | 81 | ...... | ...... | ...Not reported |
| Total..... | 713 | 556 | 1,061 | 345 | 369 | 27 | 91 | 5 | 71 | 778 | 7,822 | 17,976 | ...... | ...... | .....Total |

15. TABLE IX, A, 1, a

NEW YORK STATE

**DEPARTMENT STORES — STOCK AND SALES**

NUMBER AND PER CENT. OF EMPLOYEES CLASSIFIED ACCORDING TO ACTUAL WEEKLY EARNINGS, BY OCCUPATION AND SEX

| ACTUAL WEEKLY EARNINGS IN DOLLARS | OCCUPATION | | | | | | | | | | | | | | | | | | | | ACTUAL WEEKLY EARNINGS IN DOLLARS |
|---|---|---|---|---|---|---|---|---|---|---|---|---|---|---|---|---|---|---|---|---|---|
| | SUPERINTENDENTS | BUYERS | | ASSISTANT BUYERS AND HEADS OF STOCK | | RECEIVING AND STOCK CLERKS | | STOCK PEOPLE | | FLOOR MANAGERS | | SALES PEOPLE | | MESSENGERS, WRAPPERS, ERRAND BOYS | | TOTAL | | CUMULATIVE PER CENT. OF TOTAL | | |
| | Male | Male | Female | Male | Female | Male | Female | Male | Female | Male | Female | Male | Female | Male | Female | Male | Female | Male | Female | |
| Less than $3 00 | | | 1 | | 3 | 6 | 6 | 12 | 25 | | | 12 | 133 | 31 | 150 | 61 | 318 | .78 | 1.78 | Less than $3 00 |
| $3 00–$3 49 | | | | | | 1 | 22 | 7 | 33 | | | 7 | 53 | 57 | 330 | 72 | 438 | 1.71 | 4.21 | $3 00– 3 49 |
| 3 50– 3 99 | | | | 1 | | 5 | 44 | 10 | 118 | | | 3 | 93 | 67 | 429 | 86 | 684 | 2.81 | 8.05 | 3 50– 3 99 |
| 4 00– 4 49 | | | | | 1 | 4 | 74 | 44 | 172 | 2 | | 7 | 201 | 238 | 842 | 295 | 1,290 | 6.60 | 15.26 | 4 00– 4 49 |
| 4 50– 4 99 | | | | | 1 | 8 | 63 | 31 | 93 | 1 | | 3 | 156 | 55 | 221 | 98 | 534 | 7.85 | 18.25 | 4 50– 4 99 |
| 5 00– 5 49 | | | 1 | | 1 | 17 | 110 | 93 | 196 | | 1 | 16 | 493 | 90 | 263 | 216 | 1,065 | 10.6 | 24.2 | 5 00– 5 49 |
| 5 50– 5 99 | | | | | | 12 | 27 | 17 | 41 | | | 6 | 335 | 16 | 48 | 51 | 451 | 11.28 | 26.8 | 5 50– 5 99 |
| 6 00– 6 49 | | | | | 3 | 44 | 93 | 98 | 106 | 1 | | 42 | 1,377 | 61 | 120 | 246 | 1,699 | 14.42 | 36.2 | 6 00– 6 49 |
| 6 50– 6 99 | | | | | 5 | 7 | 17 | 10 | 18 | | 1 | 21 | 449 | 14 | 56 | 52 | 546 | 15.1 | 39.3 | 6 50– 6 99 |
| 7 00– 7 49 | | | | 1 | 9 | 39 | 71 | 67 | 53 | | | 53 | 1,747 | 58 | 50 | 218 | 1,930 | 17.9 | 50.1 | 7 00– 7 49 |
| 7 50– 7 99 | | | | 1 | 4 | 5 | 9 | 14 | 12 | | 2 | 12 | 470 | 11 | 12 | 43 | 510 | 18.5 | 53.0 | 7 50– 7 99 |
| 8 00– 8 99 | | | 1 | 1 | 18 | 65 | 53 | 48 | 36 | | 2 | 103 | 2,017 | 84 | 36 | 301 | 2,163 | 22.4 | 65.0 | 8 00– 8 99 |
| 9 00– 9 99 | | | | 2 | 30 | 48 | 37 | 47 | 25 | 3 | 15 | 88 | 1,322 | 30 | 5 | 218 | 1,434 | 25.1 | 73.1 | 9 00– 9 99 |
| 10 00–10 99 | | 1 | 2 | 5 | 42 | 71 | 28 | 63 | 15 | 2 | 9 | 217 | 1,176 | 33 | 4 | 392 | 1,276 | 30.2 | 80.2 | 10 00–10 99 |
| 11 00–11 99 | | | 2 | 1 | 22 | 55 | 16 | 33 | 10 | | 4 | 124 | 541 | 11 | 3 | 224 | 598 | 33.0 | 83.5 | 11 00–11 99 |
| 12 00–12 99 | | 3 | 2 | 8 | 56 | 111 | 13 | 95 | 12 | 4 | 4 | 401 | 784 | 18 | 1 | 640 | 872 | 41.2 | 88.4 | 12 00–12 99 |
| 13 00–13 99 | | | | 6 | 15 | 38 | 6 | 15 | 2 | | 3 | 167 | 282 | 6 | 1 | 232 | 309 | 44.2 | 90.2 | 13 00–13 99 |
| 14 00–14 99 | 1 | | 1 | 12 | 38 | 58 | 11 | 27 | | 5 | | 331 | 334 | 7 | 2 | 441 | 386 | 49.8 | 92.3 | 14 00–14 99 |
| 15 00–15 99 | | 3 | 4 | 18 | 45 | 35 | 5 | 25 | | 24 | 1 | 536 | 343 | 5 | | 646 | 398 | 58.2 | 94.5 | 15 00–15 99 |
| 16 00–17 99 | 1 | 9 | 4 | 25 | 41 | 31 | 7 | 25 | | 36 | 4 | 473 | 281 | 1 | | 601 | 337 | 65.9 | 95.8 | 16 00–17 99 |
| 18 00–19 99 | | 5 | 1 | 35 | 43 | 23 | 3 | 7 | | 70 | 2 | 494 | 181 | 1 | | 635 | 230 | 74.1 | 97.7 | 18 00–19 99 |
| 20 00–24 99 | 5 | 14 | 5 | 71 | 49 | 17 | 1 | 9 | 1 | 195 | 3 | 699 | 169 | | | 1,010 | 228 | 87.0 | 98.0 | 20 00–24 99 |
| 25 00–29 99 | 9 | 23 | 11 | 56 | 34 | 5 | 1 | 4 | | 169 | 1 | 265 | 54 | | | 531 | 101 | 93.8 | 99.5 | 25 00–29 99 |
| 30 00–34 99 | 4 | 27 | 8 | 35 | 14 | 2 | | 1 | | 66 | | 91 | 17 | | | 226 | 39 | 96.6 | 99.8 | 30 00–34 99 |
| 35 00–39 99 | 2 | 9 | 5 | 13 | 11 | 3 | | 1 | | 31 | | 30 | 9 | | | 89 | 25 | 97.9 | 99.9 | 35 00–39 99 |
| 40 00 and over | 9 | 60 | 14 | 22 | 6 | 1 | | 1 | | 20 | | 46 | 14 | | | 159 | 34 | 100.00 | 100.00 | 40 00 and over |
| Not reported | | | | 2 | 1 | | 2 | 2 | | 2 | 2 | 26 | 68 | 7 | 8 | 39 | 81 | | | Not reported |
| Total | 31 | 154 | 62 | 315 | 492 | 711 | 719 | 806 | 968 | 631 | 55 | 4,273 | 13,099 | 901 | 2,581 | 7,822 | 17,976 | | | Total |

16. TABLE X, A, 1, a

NEW YORK STATE

DEPARTMENT STORES — STOCK AND SALES

NUMBER AND PER CENT. OF EMPLOYEES CLASSIFIED ACCORDING TO ACTUAL WEEKLY EARNINGS, BY CONJUGAL CONDITION AND SEX

| ACTUAL WEEKLY EARNINGS IN DOLLARS | CONJUGAL CONDITION | | | | | | | | | | | | ACTUAL WEEKLY EARNINGS IN DOLLARS |
|---|---|---|---|---|---|---|---|---|---|---|---|---|---|
| | SINGLE | | MARRIED | | WIDOWED OR DIVORCED | | NOT REPORTED | | TOTAL | | CUMULATIVE PER CENT. OF TOTAL | | |
| | Male | Female | Male | Female | Male | Female | Male | Female | Male | Female | Male | Female | |
| Less than $3 00 | 54 | 282 | 5 | 24 | 2 | 6 | ...... | 6 | 61 | 318 | .78 | 1.78 | Less than $3 00 |
| $3 00–$3 49 | 66 | 418 | 4 | 8 | ...... | 6 | 2 | 6 | 72 | 438 | 1.71 | 4.21 | $3 00– 3 49 |
| 3 50– 3 99 | 83 | 661 | 3 | 15 | ...... | 4 | ...... | 4 | 86 | 684 | 2.81 | 8.05 | 3 50– 3 99 |
| 4 00– 4 49 | 289 | 1,268 | 4 | 14 | ...... | 4 | 2 | 4 | 295 | 1,290 | 6.60 | 15.26 | 4 00– 4 49 |
| 4 50– 4 99 | 96 | 496 | 1 | 24 | ...... | 11 | 1 | 3 | 98 | 534 | 7.85 | 18.25 | 4 50– 4 99 |
| 5 00– 5 49 | 206 | 990 | 5 | 29 | 2 | 35 | 3 | 11 | 216 | 1,065 | 10.6 | 24.2 | 5 00– 5 49 |
| 5 50– 5 99 | 48 | 388 | 3 | 32 | ...... | 20 | ...... | 11 | 51 | 451 | 11.28 | 26.8 | 5 50– 5 99 |
| 6 00– 6 49 | 232 | 1,547 | 10 | 69 | 2 | 53 | 2 | 30 | 246 | 1,699 | 14.42 | 36.2 | 6 00– 6 49 |
| 6 50– 6 99 | 46 | 477 | 5 | 30 | ...... | 34 | 1 | 5 | 52 | 546 | 15.1 | 39.3 | 6 50– 6 99 |
| 7 00– 7 49 | 198 | 1,618 | 18 | 137 | ...... | 128 | 2 | 47 | 218 | 1,930 | 17.9 | 50.1 | 7 00– 7 49 |
| 7 50– 7 99 | 36 | 421 | 6 | 32 | ...... | 45 | 1 | 12 | 43 | 510 | 18.5 | 53.0 | 7 50– 7 99 |
| 8 00– 8 99 | 271 | 1,814 | 18 | 139 | 8 | 171 | 4 | 39 | 301 | 2,163 | 22.4 | 65.0 | 8 00– 8 99 |
| 9 00– 9 99 | 191 | 1,173 | 19 | 84 | 4 | 134 | 4 | 43 | 218 | 1,434 | 25.1 | 73.1 | 9 00– 9 99 |
| 10 00–10 99 | 296 | 1,026 | 77 | 87 | 5 | 134 | 14 | 29 | 392 | 1,276 | 30.2 | 80.2 | 10 00–10 99 |
| 11 00–11 99 | 171 | 493 | 42 | 31 | 6 | 56 | 5 | 18 | 224 | 598 | 33.0 | 83.5 | 11 00–11 99 |
| 12 00–12 99 | 387 | 699 | 219 | 49 | 19 | 97 | 15 | 27 | 640 | 872 | 41.2 | 88.4 | 12 00–12 99 |
| 13 00–13 99 | 129 | 249 | 88 | 21 | 10 | 27 | 5 | 12 | 232 | 309 | 44.2 | 90.2 | 13 00–13 99 |
| 14 00–14 99 | 204 | 305 | 209 | 23 | 15 | 46 | 13 | 12 | 441 | 386 | 49.8 | 92.3 | 14 00–14 99 |
| 15 00–15 99 | 275 | 283 | 329 | 34 | 25 | 56 | 17 | 25 | 646 | 398 | 58.2 | 94.5 | 15 00–15 99 |
| 16 00–17 99 | 232 | 246 | 334 | 26 | 17 | 48 | 18 | 17 | 601 | 337 | 65.9 | 95.8 | 16 00–17 99 |
| 18 00–19 99 | 204 | 161 | 378 | 19 | 30 | 34 | 23 | 16 | 635 | 230 | 74.1 | 97.7 | 18 00–19 99 |
| 20 00–24 99 | 283 | 158 | 653 | 23 | 41 | 34 | 33 | 13 | 1,010 | 228 | 87.0 | 98.0 | 20 00–24 99 |
| 25 00–29 99 | 90 | 75 | 396 | 8 | 22 | 10 | 23 | 8 | 531 | 101 | 93.8 | 99.5 | 25 00–29 99 |
| 30 00–34 99 | 38 | 31 | 174 | 2 | 8 | 4 | 6 | 2 | 226 | 39 | 96.6 | 99.8 | 30 00–34 99 |
| 35 00–39 99 | 15 | 16 | 68 | 1 | 4 | 6 | 2 | 2 | 89 | 25 | 97.9 | 99.9 | 35 00–39 99 |
| 40 00 and over | 21 | 24 | 124 | 5 | 5 | 3 | 9 | 2 | 159 | 34 | 100.00 | 100.00 | 40 00 and over |
| Not reported | 20 | 63 | 16 | 12 | 1 | 4 | 2 | 2 | 39 | 81 | ...... | ...... | Not reported |
| Total | 4,181 | 15,382 | 3,208 | 978 | 226 | 1,210 | 207 | 406 | 7,822 | 17,976 | ...... | ...... | Total |

NEW YORK STATE

DEPARTMENT STORES — STOCK AND SALES

17. TABLE XI, A, 1, a NUMBER AND PER CENT. OF EMPLOYEES CLASSIFIED ACCORDING TO ACTUAL WEEKLY EARNINGS, BY NATIVITY AND SEX

| ACTUAL WEEKLY EARNINGS IN DOLLARS | NATIVITY | | | | | | | | | | ACTUAL WEEKLY EARNINGS IN DOLLARS |
|---|---|---|---|---|---|---|---|---|---|---|---|
| | NATIVE | | FOREIGN | | NOT REPORTED | | TOTAL | | CUMULATIVE PER CENT. OF TOTAL | | |
| | Male | Female | Male | Female | Male | Female | Male | Female | Male | Female | |
| Less than $3 00 | 45 | 269 | 15 | 48 | 1 | 1 | 61 | 318 | .78 | 1.78 | Less than $3 00 |
| $3 00–$3 49 | 58 | 386 | 12 | 51 | 2 | 1 | 72 | 438 | 1.71 | 4.21 | $3 00– 3 49 |
| 3 50– 3 99 | 80 | 613 | 5 | 66 | 1 | 5 | 86 | 684 | 2.81 | 8.05 | 3 50– 3 99 |
| 4 00– 4 49 | 256 | 1,156 | 35 | 121 | 4 | 13 | 295 | 1,290 | 6.60 | 15.26 | 4 00– 4 49 |
| 4 50– 4 99 | 83 | 486 | 14 | 43 | 1 | 5 | 98 | 534 | 7.85 | 18.25 | 4 50– 4 99 |
| 5 00– 5 49 | 182 | 980 | 31 | 77 | 3 | 8 | 216 | 1,065 | 10.6 | 24.2 | 5 00– 5 49 |
| 5 50– 5 99 | 40 | 404 | 11 | 45 | ........ | 2 | 51 | 451 | 11.28 | 26.8 | 5 50– 5 99 |
| 6 00– 6 49 | 201 | 1,514 | 45 | 171 | ........ | 14 | 246 | 1,699 | 14.42 | 36.2 | 6 00– 6 49 |
| 6 50– 6 99 | 42 | 478 | 10 | 63 | ........ | 5 | 52 | 546 | 15.1 | 39.3 | 6 50– 6 99 |
| 7 00– 7 49 | 176 | 1,715 | 41 | 197 | 1 | 18 | 218 | 1,930 | 17.9 | 50.1 | 7 00– 7 49 |
| 7 50– 7 99 | 33 | 451 | 9 | 54 | 1 | 5 | 43 | 510 | 18.5 | 53.0 | 7 50– 7 99 |
| 8 00– 8 99 | 223 | 1,916 | 75 | 238 | 3 | 9 | 301 | 2,163 | 22.4 | 65.0 | 8 00– 8 99 |
| 9 00– 9 99 | 169 | 1,242 | 48 | 180 | 1 | 12 | 218 | 1,434 | 25.1 | 73.1 | 9 00– 9 99 |
| 10 00–10 99 | 283 | 1,121 | 108 | 148 | 1 | 7 | 392 | 1,276 | 30.2 | 80.2 | 10 00–10 99 |
| 11 00–11 99 | 160 | 532 | 63 | 61 | 1 | 5 | 224 | 598 | 33.0 | 83.5 | 11 00–11 99 |
| 12 00–12 99 | 426 | 756 | 209 | 110 | 5 | 6 | 640 | 872 | 41.2 | 88.4 | 12 00–12 99 |
| 13 00–13 99 | 158 | 275 | 72 | 33 | 2 | 1 | 232 | 309 | 44.2 | 90.2 | 13 00–13 99 |
| 14 00–14 99 | 297 | 345 | 142 | 36 | 2 | 5 | 441 | 386 | 49.8 | 92.3 | 14 00–14 99 |
| 15 00–15 99 | 449 | 350 | 194 | 43 | 3 | 5 | 646 | 398 | 58.2 | 94.5 | 15 00–15 99 |
| 16 00–17 99 | 376 | 302 | 223 | 35 | 2 | ........ | 601 | 337 | 65.9 | 95.8 | 16 00–17 99 |
| 18 00–19 99 | 430 | 204 | 198 | 26 | 7 | ........ | 635 | 230 | 74.1 | 97.7 | 18 00–19 99 |
| 20 00–24 99 | 678 | 201 | 329 | 26 | 3 | 1 | 1,010 | 228 | 87.0 | 98.0 | 20 00–24 99 |
| 25 00–29 99 | 360 | 91 | 169 | 10 | 2 | ........ | 531 | 101 | 93.8 | 99.5 | 25 00–29 99 |
| 30 00–34 99 | 167 | 35 | 56 | 4 | 3 | ........ | 226 | 39 | 96.6 | 99.8 | 30 00–34 99 |
| 35 00–39 99 | 63 | 21 | 25 | 4 | 1 | ........ | 89 | 25 | 97.9 | 99.9 | 35 00–39 99 |
| 40 00 and over | 112 | 30 | 44 | 2 | 3 | 2 | 159 | 34 | 100.00 | 100.00 | 40 00 and over |
| Not reported | 33 | 75 | 6 | 5 | ........ | 1 | 39 | 81 | ........ | ........ | Not reported |
| Total | 5,580 | 15,948 | 2,189 | 1,897 | 53 | 131 | 7,822 | 17,976 | ........ | ........ | Total |

18. TABLE XII, A, 1, a

NEW YORK STATE

**DEPARTMENT STORES — STOCK AND SALES**

NUMBER OF EMPLOYEES FOR EACH SEX CLASSIFIED ACCORDING TO ACTUAL WEEKLY EARNINGS, BY THE NUMBER OF YEARS IN THE TRADE

| Actual Weekly Earnings in Dollars | Years in Trade: Less than 1 | | 1 | | 2 | | 3 | | 4 | | 5 | | 6 | | Actual Weekly Earnings in Dollars |
|---|---|---|---|---|---|---|---|---|---|---|---|---|---|---|---|
| | Male | Female | Male | Female | Male | Female | Male | Female | Male | Female | Male | Female | Male | Female | |
| Less than $3 00 | 36 | 158 | 9 | 62 | 3 | 15 | 5 | 16 | 1 | 14 | 1 | 7 | 1 | 12 | Less than $3 00 |
| $3 00–$3 49... | 51 | 296 | 10 | 81 | 4 | 25 | ...... | 10 | ...... | 6 | 1 | 2 | 1 | 2 | ...$3 00– 3 49 |
| 3 50– 3 99... | 67 | 434 | 14 | 148 | ...... | 47 | 1 | 14 | ...... | 9 | ...... | 5 | ...... | 4 | ... 3 50– 3 99 |
| 4 00– 4 49... | 228 | 726 | 35 | 323 | 18 | 120 | 2 | 50 | ...... | 14 | ...... | 11 | ...... | 9 | ... 4 00– 4 49 |
| 4 50– 4 99... | 39 | 152 | 38 | 182 | 11 | 82 | 6 | 42 | ...... | 18 | ...... | 13 | ...... | 9 | ... 4 50– 4 99 |
| 5 00– 5 49... | 93 | 295 | 71 | 225 | 24 | 196 | 12 | 124 | 4 | 75 | 2 | 38 | 4 | 23 | ... 5 00– 5 49 |
| 5 50– 5 99... | 19 | 64 | 10 | 77 | 11 | 77 | 5 | 60 | 1 | 55 | 2 | 29 | ...... | 24 | ... 5 50– 5 99 |
| 6 00– 6 49... | 120 | 268 | 47 | 276 | 32 | 277 | 14 | 259 | 5 | 200 | 3 | 135 | 1 | 87 | ... 6 00– 6 49 |
| 6 50– 6 99... | 16 | 50 | 10 | 53 | 7 | 70 | 8 | 87 | 3 | 81 | 3 | 44 | ...... | 45 | ... 6 50– 6 99 |
| 7 00– 7 49... | 83 | 172 | 47 | 190 | 33 | 269 | 17 | 263 | 10 | 255 | 5 | 179 | 2 | 144 | ... 7 00– 7 49 |
| 7 50– 7 99... | 6 | 25 | 8 | 38 | 2 | 49 | 5 | 61 | 4 | 76 | 5 | 64 | 5 | 43 | ... 7 50– 7 99 |
| 8 00– 8 99... | 86 | 82 | 49 | 118 | 46 | 167 | 36 | 219 | 23 | 240 | 10 | 239 | 10 | 224 | ... 8 00– 8 99 |
| 9 00– 9 99... | 34 | 30 | 21 | 41 | 34 | 68 | 33 | 104 | 29 | 139 | 16 | 158 | 10 | 139 | ... 9 00– 9 99 |
| 10 00–10 99... | 65 | 24 | 45 | 30 | 34 | 41 | 39 | 79 | 38 | 90 | 36 | 100 | 26 | 88 | ...10 00–10 99 |
| 11 00–11 99... | 18 | 4 | 8 | 7 | 19 | 12 | 22 | 19 | 30 | 34 | 27 | 38 | 16 | 51 | ...11 00–11 99 |
| 12 00–12 99... | 69 | 12 | 22 | 15 | 50 | 23 | 49 | 29 | 42 | 24 | 57 | 43 | 55 | 61 | ...12 00–12 99 |
| 13 00–13 99... | 6 | ...... | 4 | 1 | 10 | 6 | 23 | 4 | 21 | 7 | 19 | 11 | 21 | 13 | ...13 00–13 99 |
| 14 00–14 99... | 8 | 5 | 13 | 3 | 11 | 5 | 18 | 4 | 27 | 11 | 35 | 9 | 20 | 15 | ...14 00–14 99 |
| 15 00–15 99... | 11 | 3 | 15 | 4 | 17 | 10 | 13 | 9 | 25 | 9 | 29 | 13 | 30 | 11 | ...15 00–15 99 |
| 16 00–17 99... | 3 | 2 | 3 | 2 | 8 | 4 | 20 | 4 | 10 | 10 | 24 | 11 | 13 | 12 | ...16 00–17 99 |
| 18 00–19 99... | 7 | 2 | 11 | 1 | 7 | 1 | 10 | 8 | 6 | 6 | 10 | 6 | 14 | 5 | ...18 00–19 99 |
| 20 00–24 99... | 9 | 5 | 5 | 2 | 10 | 2 | 17 | 2 | 11 | 3 | 11 | 6 | 16 | 1 | ...20 00–24 99 |
| 25 00–29 99... | 7 | 1 | 3 | ...... | 3 | 2 | 1 | 3 | 4 | 1 | 4 | ...... | 8 | 1 | ...25 00–29 99 |
| 30 00–34 99... | .... | 2 | 1 | 2 | 2 | ...... | 1 | 1 | 1 | 1 | 1 | ...... | 3 | ...... | ...30 00–34 99 |
| 35 00–39 99... | .... | ...... | 1 | ...... | ...... | ...... | ...... | ...... | ...... | 1 | 1 | ...... | ...... | 1 | ...35 00–39 99 |
| 40 00 and over. | .... | ...... | 2 | ...... | ...... | ...... | ...... | ...... | ...... | ...... | ...... | ...... | ...... | 1 | .40 00 and over |
| Not reported... | 4 | 9 | 1 | 10 | 3 | 9 | 2 | 5 | 2 | 4 | 2 | 3 | 1 | 3 | ...Not reported |
| Total..... | 1,085 | 2,821 | 503 | 1,891 | 399 | 1,577 | 359 | 1,476 | 297 | 1,383 | 304 | 1,164 | 257 | 1,028 | .....Total |

NEW YORK STATE

18. TABLE XII, A, 1, a — (*continued*)

**DEPARTMENT STORES — STOCK AND SALES**

NUMBER OF EMPLOYEES FOR EACH SEX CLASSIFIED ACCORDING TO ACTUAL WEEKLY EARNINGS, BY THE NUMBER OF YEARS IN THE TRADE

| ACTUAL WEEKLY EARNINGS IN DOLLARS | YEARS IN TRADE | | | | | | | | | | | | | | ACTUAL WEEKLY EARNINGS IN DOLLARS |
|---|---|---|---|---|---|---|---|---|---|---|---|---|---|---|---|
| | 7 | | 8 | | 9 | | 10–14 | | 15–19 | | 20–24 | | 25–29 | | |
| | Male | Female | Male | Female | Male | Female | Male | Female | Male | Female | Male | Female | Male | Female | |
| Less than $3 00 | 1 | 3 | .... | 5 | ...... | 6 | 1 | 10 | ...... | 1 | 1 | 2 | ...... | ...... | Less than $3 00 |
| $3 00–$3 49... | .... | 2 | .... | 4 | ...... | ...... | 1 | 2 | 1 | ...... | 1 | 1 | ...... | ...... | ...$3 00– 3 49 |
| 3 50– 3 99... | .... | 5 | 2 | 2 | ...... | 2 | ...... | 2 | 1 | 1 | ...... | ...... | ...... | ...... | ... 3 50– 3 99 |
| 4 00– 4 49... | 1 | 3 | .... | 2 | ...... | 2 | 1 | 4 | 1 | 3 | 1 | ...... | 1 | ...... | ... 4 00– 4 49 |
| 4 50– 4 99... | .... | ...... | .... | 6 | ...... | 4 | 1 | 11 | ...... | 2 | ...... | 1 | ...... | ...... | ... 4 50– 4 99 |
| 5 00– 5 49... | .... | 10 | .... | 16 | 1 | 5 | ...... | 17 | ...... | 9 | ...... | 2 | 1 | 3 | ... 5 00– 5 49 |
| 5 50– 5 99... | .... | 16 | .... | 14 | 1 | 6 | 1 | 14 | 1 | 3 | ...... | 1 | ...... | 1 | ... 5 50– 5 99 |
| 6 00– 6 49... | .... | 54 | .... | 32 | 2 | 21 | 3 | 35 | 4 | 9 | 2 | 3 | 1 | 1 | ... 6 00– 6 49 |
| 6 50– 6 99... | .... | 28 | .... | 25 | ...... | 15 | ...... | 28 | ...... | 5 | ...... | 1 | 1 | 1 | ... 6 50– 6 99 |
| 7 00– 7 49... | 1 | 136 | 2 | 79 | ...... | 33 | 3 | 123 | 3 | 24 | 2 | 12 | 1 | 2 | ... 7 00– 7 49 |
| 7 50– 7 99... | .... | 43 | .... | 31 | ...... | 19 | 2 | 40 | 1 | 8 | 1 | 3 | ...... | 1 | ... 7 50– 7 99 |
| 8 00– 8 99... | 4 | 198 | 2 | 144 | 6 | 120 | 6 | 259 | 4 | 75 | 1 | 26 | 1 | 7 | ... 8 00– 8 99 |
| 9 00– 9 99... | 9 | 142 | 3 | 130 | 5 | 76 | 9 | 251 | 3 | 94 | 1 | 23 | ...... | 11 | ... 9 00– 9 99 |
| 10 00–10 99... | 17 | 130 | 13 | 121 | 12 | 86 | 20 | 311 | 11 | 99 | 11 | 37 | 3 | 13 | ...10 00–10 99 |
| 11 00–11 99... | 8 | 53 | 11 | 63 | 9 | 40 | 25 | 175 | 12 | 64 | 5 | 20 | 5 | 7 | ...11 00–11 99 |
| 12 00–12 99... | 28 | 61 | 37 | 82 | 14 | 63 | 79 | 254 | 40 | 128 | 29 | 43 | 25 | 10 | ...12 00–12 99 |
| 13 00–13 99... | 9 | 22 | 16 | 21 | 8 | 24 | 38 | 107 | 16 | 54 | 12 | 26 | 9 | 9 | ...13 00–13 99 |
| 14 00–14 99... | 29 | 22 | 28 | 29 | 5 | 28 | 78 | 119 | 49 | 76 | 38 | 37 | 25 | 9 | ...14 00–14 99 |
| 15 00–15 99... | 25 | 16 | 30 | 22 | 18 | 20 | 143 | 143 | 84 | 81 | 57 | 38 | 52 | 14 | ...15 00–15 99 |
| 16 00–17 99... | 24 | 8 | 36 | 9 | 22 | 17 | 124 | 105 | 73 | 71 | 61 | 47 | 63 | 21 | ...16 00–17 99 |
| 18 00–19 99... | 20 | 6 | 20 | 11 | 18 | 7 | 121 | 64 | 106 | 50 | 97 | 41 | 67 | 10 | ...18 00–19 99 |
| 20 00–24 99... | 16 | 8 | 34 | 9 | 17 | 11 | 205 | 53 | 170 | 62 | 155 | 37 | 112 | 11 | ...20 00–24 99 |
| 25 00–29 99... | 6 | 1 | 11 | 1 | 12 | 5 | 80 | 32 | 88 | 18 | 104 | 22 | 83 | 8 | ...25 00–29 99 |
| 30 00–34 99... | 3 | ...... | 7 | ...... | 2 | 2 | 35 | 7 | 42 | 9 | 43 | 11 | 21 | 3 | ...30 00–34 99 |
| 35 00–39 99... | 2 | ...... | 1 | ...... | 1 | ...... | 9 | 5 | 13 | 8 | 19 | 7 | 11 | 2 | ...35 00–39 99 |
| 40 00 and over. | 2 | 1 | 1 | ...... | ...... | ...... | 11 | 5 | 34 | 9 | 34 | 9 | 33 | 3 | .40 00 and over |
| Not reported... | 2 | 4 | 2 | 2 | ...... | 3 | 3 | 17 | 4 | 4 | 2 | 3 | 4 | 4 | ...Not reported |
| Total..... | 207 | 972 | 256 | 860 | 153 | 615 | 999 | 2,193 | 761 | 967 | 677 | 453 | 519 | 151 | .....Total |

18. TABLE XII, A, 1, a — (*concluded*)

NEW YORK STATE

DEPARTMENT STORES — STOCK AND SALES

NUMBER OF EMPLOYEES FOR EACH SEX CLASSIFIED ACCORDING TO ACTUAL WEEKLY EARNINGS, BY THE NUMBER OF YEARS IN THE TRADE

| ACTUAL WEEKLY EARNINGS IN DOLLARS | YEARS IN TRADE | | | | | | | | | | | | ACTUAL WEEKLY EARNINGS IN DOLLARS |
|---|---|---|---|---|---|---|---|---|---|---|---|---|---|
| | 30–34 | | 35–44 | | 45 AND OVER | | NOT REPORTED | | TOTAL | | CUMULATIVE PER CENT. OF TOTAL | | |
| | Male | Female | Male | Female | Male | Female | Male | Female | Male | Female | Male | Female | |
| Less than $3 00. | 1 | ....... | 1 | ....... | ....... | ....... | ....... | 7 | 61 | 318 | .78 | 1.78 | Less than $3 00 |
| $3 00–$3 49.... | ....... | ....... | ....... | ....... | ....... | ....... | 2 | 7 | 72 | 438 | 1.71 | 4.21 | ...$3 00– 3 49 |
| 3 50– 3 99.... | ....... | ....... | ....... | ....... | ....... | ....... | 1 | 11 | 86 | 684 | 2.81 | 8.05 | ... 3 50– 3 99 |
| 4 00– 4 49.... | ....... | ....... | ....... | ....... | ....... | ....... | 7 | 23 | 295 | 1,290 | 6.60 | 15.26 | ... 4 00– 4 49 |
| 4 50– 4 99.... | 1 | ....... | ....... | ....... | ....... | ....... | 2 | 12 | 98 | 534 | 7.85 | 18.25 | ... 4 50– 4 99 |
| 5 00– 5 49.... | ....... | ....... | ....... | ....... | ....... | ....... | 4 | 27 | 216 | 1,065 | 10.60 | 24.2 | ... 5 00– 5 49 |
| 5 50– 5 99.... | ....... | ....... | ....... | ....... | ....... | ....... | ....... | 10 | 51 | 451 | 11.28 | 26.8 | ... 5 50– 5 99 |
| 6 00– 6 49.... | 1 | 1 | 1 | ....... | ....... | ....... | 10 | 41 | 246 | 1,699 | 14.42 | 36.2 | ... 6 00– 6 49 |
| 6 50– 6 99.... | 2 | ....... | 1 | ....... | ....... | ....... | 1 | 13 | 52 | 546 | 15.1 | 39.3 | ... 6 50– 6 99 |
| 7 00– 7 49.... | 2 | 3 | ....... | 1 | ....... | ....... | 7 | 45 | 218 | 1,930 | 17.9 | 50.1 | ... 7 00– 7 49 |
| 7 50– 7 99.... | ....... | ....... | 1 | ....... | ....... | ....... | 3 | 9 | 43 | 510 | 18.5 | 53.0 | ... 7 50– 7 99 |
| 8 00– 8 99.... | 1 | 5 | 1 | 2 | ....... | ....... | 15 | 38 | 301 | 2,163 | 22.4 | 65.0 | ... 8 00– 8 99 |
| 9 00– 9 99.... | 2 | 2 | 2 | ....... | 1 | ....... | 6 | 26 | 218 | 1,434 | 25.1 | 73.1 | ... 9 00– 9 99 |
| 10 00–10 99.... | 3 | 1 | 3 | 3 | 1 | ....... | 15 | 23 | 392 | 1,276 | 30.2 | 80.2 | ...10 00–10 99 |
| 11 00–11 99.... | 1 | 1 | 2 | 1 | 2 | ....... | 4 | 9 | 224 | 598 | 33.0 | 83.5 | ...11 00–11 99 |
| 12 00–12 99.... | 12 | 4 | 16 | 2 | 10 | ....... | 6 | 18 | 640 | 872 | 41.2 | 88.4 | ...12 00–12 99 |
| 13 00–13 99 ... | 7 | 1 | 7 | ....... | 3 | ....... | 3 | 3 | 232 | 309 | 44.2 | 90.2 | ...13 00–13 99 |
| 14 00–14 99.... | 23 | 5 | 18 | ....... | 5 | ....... | 11 | 9 | 441 | 386 | 49.8 | 92.3 | ...14 00–14 99 |
| 15 00–15 99.... | 35 | 3 | 38 | ....... | 9 | ....... | 15 | 2 | 646 | 398 | 58.2 | 94.5 | ...15 00–15 99 |
| 16 00–17 99.... | 46 | 5 | 46 | 2 | 12 | 1 | 13 | 6 | 601 | 337 | 65.9 | 95.8 | ...16 00–17 99 |
| 18 00–19 99.... | 55 | 1 | 40 | 4 | 10 | ....... | 16 | 7 | 635 | 230 | 74.1 | 97.7 | ...18 00–19 99 |
| 20 00–24 99.... | 111 | 6 | 85 | 2 | 9 | 1 | 17 | 7 | 1,010 | 228 | 87.0 | 98.0 | ...20 00–24 99 |
| 25 00–29 99.... | 55 | 2 | 40 | 1 | 13 | ....... | 9 | 3 | 531 | 101 | 93.8 | 99.5 | ...25 00–29 99 |
| 30 00–34 99.... | 29 | 1 | 27 | ....... | 6 | ....... | 2 | ....... | 226 | 39 | 96.6 | 99.8 | ...30 00–34 99 |
| 35 00–39 99.... | 15 | 1 | 15 | ....... | 1 | ....... | ....... | ....... | 89 | 25 | 97.9 | 99.9 | ...35 00–39 99 |
| 40 00 and over.. | 22 | 2 | 11 | 1 | 5 | ....... | 4 | 3 | 159 | 34 | 100.0 | 100.0 | .40 00 and over |
| Not reported.... | 5 | ....... | 1 | ....... | ....... | ....... | 1 | 1 | 39 | 81 | ....... | ....... | ...Not reported |
| Total...... | 429 | 44 | 356 | 19 | 87 | 2 | 174 | 360 | 7,822 | 17,976 | ....... | ....... | .....Total |

NEW YORK STATE

19. TABLE XIII, A, 1, a

**DEPARTMENT STORES — STOCK AND SALES**

NUMBER OF EMPLOYEES FOR EACH SEX CLASSIFIED ACCORDING TO ACTUAL WEEKLY EARNINGS, BY THE NUMBER OF YEARS WITH THE FIRM

| Actual Weekly Earnings in Dollars | Years with Firm | | | | | | | | | | | | | | Actual Weekly Earnings in Dollars |
|---|---|---|---|---|---|---|---|---|---|---|---|---|---|---|---|
| | Less than 1 | | 1 | | 2 | | 3 | | 4 | | 5 | | 6 | | |
| | Male | Female | Male | Female | Male | Female | Male | Female | Male | Female | Male | Female | Male | Female | |
| Less than $3 00 | 45 | 233 | 7 | 45 | 1 | 11 | 4 | 10 | ...... | 2 | 1 | ...... | 1 | 4 | Less than $3 00 |
| $3 00–$3 49... | 60 | 335 | 8 | 70 | 3 | 23 | ...... | 3 | ...... | 3 | ...... | 1 | ...... | ...... | ...$3 00– 3 49 |
| 3 50– 3 99... | 74 | 486 | 10 | 140 | ...... | 31 | ...... | 12 | ...... | 6 | ...... | 3 | ...... | 2 | ... 3 50– 3 99 |
| 4 00– 4 49... | 246 | 849 | 34 | 287 | 11 | 93 | 3 | 34 | ...... | 8 | ...... | 2 | 1 | 3 | ... 4 00– 4 49 |
| 4 50– 4 99... | 47 | 224 | 40 | 178 | 6 | 66 | 2 | 32 | ...... | 11 | ...... | 6 | ...... | 4 | ... 4 50– 4 99 |
| 5 00– 5 49... | 114 | 471 | 66 | 249 | 17 | 157 | 10 | 91 | 5 | 39 | ...... | 18 | 1 | 8 | ... 5 00– 5 49 |
| 5 50– 5 99... | 25 | 158 | 11 | 84 | 10 | 82 | 3 | 47 | 2 | 30 | ...... | 16 | ...... | 12 | ... 5 50– 5 99 |
| 6 00– 6 49... | 155 | 668 | 45 | 342 | 24 | 248 | 12 | 159 | 2 | 100 | 1 | 70 | 2 | 36 | ... 6 00– 6 49 |
| 6 50– 6 99... | 22 | 158 | 11 | 89 | 7 | 80 | 7 | 87 | 1 | 52 | 1 | 20 | ...... | 23 | ... 6 50– 6 99 |
| 7 00– 7 49... | 107 | 562 | 50 | 361 | 27 | 308 | 13 | 231 | 8 | 149 | 3 | 94 | 1 | 53 | ... 7 00– 7 49 |
| 7 50– 7 99... | 15 | 115 | 7 | 90 | 3 | 68 | 4 | 69 | 3 | 54 | 4 | 41 | 1 | 17 | ... 7 50– 7 99 |
| 8 00– 8 99... | 135 | 483 | 61 | 323 | 36 | 277 | 28 | 268 | 12 | 218 | 11 | 127 | 5 | 125 | ... 8 00– 8 99 |
| 9 00– 9 99... | 79 | 273 | 32 | 165 | 31 | 157 | 26 | 201 | 17 | 127 | 7 | 94 | 5 | 95 | ... 9 00– 9 99 |
| 10 00–10 99... | 171 | 282 | 64 | 163 | 35 | 127 | 31 | 153 | 16 | 76 | 23 | 68 | 11 | 63 | ...10 00–10 99 |
| 11 00–11 99... | 72 | 78 | 30 | 51 | 35 | 76 | 19 | 84 | 18 | 48 | 13 | 28 | 9 | 29 | ...11 00–11 99 |
| 12 00–12 99... | 234 | 183 | 96 | 91 | 85 | 71 | 52 | 84 | 38 | 49 | 25 | 37 | 16 | 45 | ...12 00–12 99 |
| 13 00–13 99... | 48 | 34 | 31 | 30 | 36 | 23 | 36 | 37 | 19 | 23 | 8 | 17 | 8 | 14 | ...13 00–13 99 |
| 14 00–14 99... | 95 | 44 | 73 | 38 | 60 | 23 | 47 | 41 | 22 | 22 | 18 | 25 | 17 | 12 | ...14 00–14 99 |
| 15 00–15 99... | 174 | 82 | 97 | 39 | 55 | 31 | 61 | 27 | 43 | 20 | 37 | 16 | 29 | 18 | ...15 00–15 99 |
| 16 00–17 99... | 94 | 51 | 68 | 21 | 59 | 23 | 53 | 26 | 50 | 14 | 28 | 17 | 26 | 13 | ...16 00–17 99 |
| 18 00–19 99... | 131 | 40 | 75 | 23 | 57 | 22 | 63 | 12 | 40 | 9 | 26 | 6 | 23 | 12 | ...18 00–19 99 |
| 20 00–24 99... | 206 | 25 | 107 | 25 | 87 | 17 | 90 | 21 | 46 | 11 | 37 | 7 | 38 | 8 | ...20 00–24 99 |
| 25 00–29 99... | 104 | 14 | 38 | 8 | 48 | 6 | 49 | 10 | 17 | 4 | 24 | 4 | 21 | 2 | ...25 00–29 99 |
| 30 00–34 99... | 28 | 6 | 25 | 5 | 20 | 1 | 18 | 4 | 8 | ...... | 12 | 1 | 6 | 2 | ...30 00–34 99 |
| 35 00–39 99... | 12 | 1 | 9 | 2 | 8 | 3 | 11 | 2 | 1 | 1 | 4 | 1 | 3 | 1 | ...35 00–39 99 |
| 40 00 and over. | 12 | 2 | 14 | 3 | 6 | 3 | 7 | 3 | 6 | 1 | 4 | ...... | 2 | 1 | 40 00 and over |
| Not reported.. | 12 | 16 | 2 | 15 | 4 | 13 | 2 | 4 | 2 | 5 | 3 | 3 | 2 | 2 | ..Not reported |
| Total..... | 2,517 | 5,873 | 1,111 | 2,937 | 771 | 2,040 | 651 | 1,752 | 376 | 1,082 | 290 | 722 | 228 | 604 | .....Total |

19. TABLE XIII, A, 1, a — (*continued*)

NEW YORK STATE

**DEPARTMENT STORES — STOCK AND SALES**

NUMBER OF EMPLOYEES FOR EACH SEX CLASSIFIED ACCORDING TO ACTUAL WEEKLY EARNINGS, BY THE NUMBER OF YEARS WITH THE FIRM

| ACTUAL WEEKLY EARNINGS IN DOLLARS | YEARS IN TRADE | | | | | | | | | | | | | | ACTUAL WEEKLY EARNINGS IN DOLLARS |
|---|---|---|---|---|---|---|---|---|---|---|---|---|---|---|---|
| | 7 | | 8 | | 9 | | 10–14 | | 15–19 | | 20–24 | | 25–29 | | |
| | Male | Female | Male | Female | Male | Female | Male | Female | Male | Female | Male | Female | Male | Female | |
| Less than $3 00 | .... | 1 | 1 | 2 | ...... | 1 | ...... | 5 | ...... | 1 | ...... | ...... | ...... | ...... | Less than $3 00 |
| $3 00–$3 49... | .... | ...... | .... | 1 | ...... | ...... | 1 | 1 | ...... | ...... | ...... | ...... | ...... | ...... | ...$3 00– 3 49 |
| 3 50– 3 99... | .... | 2 | 1 | ...... | ...... | ...... | ...... | ...... | 1 | 1 | ...... | ...... | ...... | ...... | ... 3 50– 3 99 |
| 4 00– 4 49... | .... | 3 | .... | 1 | ...... | 1 | ...... | ...... | ...... | 2 | ...... | ...... | ...... | ...... | ... 4 00– 4 49 |
| 4 50– 4 99... | .... | 2 | .... | 1 | ...... | ...... | ...... | 6 | ...... | 1 | ...... | ...... | ...... | ...... | ... 4 50– 4 99 |
| 5 00– 5 49... | .... | 7 | .... | 3 | ...... | 5 | ...... | 8 | 1 | 2 | ...... | ...... | ...... | 1 | ... 5 00– 5 49 |
| 5 50– 5 99... | .... | 6 | .... | 6 | ...... | 1 | ...... | 6 | ...... | 2 | ...... | ...... | ...... | ...... | ... 5 50– 5 99 |
| 6 00– 6 49... | .... | 24 | 1 | 15 | ...... | 6 | 1 | 22 | ...... | 2 | 1 | ...... | 1 | 1 | ... 6 00– 6 49 |
| 6 50– 6 99... | 1 | 14 | .... | 9 | 1 | 4 | ...... | 9 | 1 | ...... | ...... | ...... | ...... | 1 | ... 6 50– 6 99 |
| 7 00– 7 49... | .... | 77 | .... | 29 | 2 | 16 | 6 | 31 | ...... | 7 | ...... | 3 | ...... | 1 | ... 7 00– 7 49 |
| 7 50– 7 99... | .... | 17 | 3 | 13 | 1 | 11 | ...... | 8 | 1 | 3 | ...... | 2 | ...... | ...... | ... 7 50– 7 99 |
| 8 00– 8 99... | 3 | 107 | 3 | 63 | 2 | 46 | 1 | 88 | 1 | 18 | ...... | 6 | ...... | 3 | ... 8 00– 8 99 |
| 9 00– 9 99... | 8 | 86 | 5 | 62 | 2 | 33 | 5 | 93 | 1 | 30 | ...... | 4 | ...... | 3 | ... 9 00– 9 99 |
| 10 00–10 99... | 8 | 80 | 9 | 56 | 5 | 39 | 10 | 122 | 1 | 30 | 2 | 10 | 2 | 5 | ...10 00–10 99 |
| 11 00–11 99... | 5 | 30 | 5 | 43 | 4 | 26 | 6 | 77 | 3 | 13 | 4 | 8 | 1 | 2 | ...11 00–11 99 |
| 12 00–12 99... | 13 | 57 | 12 | 38 | 9 | 22 | 29 | 116 | 13 | 49 | 10 | 19 | 2 | 5 | ...12 00–12 99 |
| 13 00–13 99... | 5 | 17 | 7 | 19 | 3 | 11 | 20 | 57 | 5 | 18 | 3 | 6 | ...... | ...... | ...13 00–13 99 |
| 14 00–14 99... | 16 | 30 | 20 | 24 | 8 | 17 | 36 | 59 | 17 | 31 | 7 | 12 | 2 | 3 | ...14 00–14 99 |
| 15 00–15 99... | 21 | 19 | 19 | 22 | 9 | 11 | 52 | 62 | 19 | 28 | 10 | 12 | 11 | 7 | ...15 00–15 99 |
| 16 00–17 99... | 28 | 15 | 28 | 13 | 22 | 11 | 72 | 56 | 21 | 40 | 17 | 24 | 16 | 5 | ...16 00–17 99 |
| 18 00–19 99... | 26 | 10 | 18 | 4 | 15 | 9 | 72 | 35 | 37 | 26 | 26 | 15 | 16 | 6 | ...18 00–19 99 |
| 20 00–24 99... | 55 | 10 | 34 | 8 | 35 | 9 | 121 | 33 | 69 | 27 | 28 | 19 | 29 | 4 | ...20 00–24 99 |
| 25 00–29 99... | 26 | 6 | 22 | 5 | 16 | 2 | 67 | 19 | 39 | 9 | 23 | 7 | 16 | 3 | ...25 00–29 99 |
| 30 00–34 99... | 9 | 3 | 9 | 1 | 4 | 1 | 27 | 6 | 23 | 4 | 17 | 4 | 5 | 1 | ...30 00–34 99 |
| 35 00–39 99... | 4 | 2 | 5 | 1 | 2 | ...... | 12 | 3 | 6 | 4 | 3 | 4 | 3 | ...... | ...35 00–39 99 |
| 40 00 and over. | 9 | 1 | 6 | 3 | 3 | ...... | 31 | 4 | 25 | 5 | 16 | 6 | 7 | 1 | 40 00 and over |
| Not reported.. | 2 | 3 | 2 | ...... | 1 | 4 | 4 | 11 | 3 | 4 | ...... | ...... | ...... | 1 | ...Not reported |
| Total..... | 239 | 629 | 210 | 442 | 144 | 286 | 573 | 937 | 287 | 357 | 167 | 161 | 111 | 53 | .....Total |

NEW YORK STATE

19. TABLE XIII, A, 1, a.— (*concluded*) DEPARTMENT STORES — STOCK AND SALES

Number of Employees for Each Sex Classified According to Actual Weekly Earnings, by the Number of Years with the Firm

| Actual Weekly Earnings in Dollars | Years in Trade: 30–34 | | 35–44 | | 45 and over | | Not reported | | Total | | Cumulative per cent. of total | | Actual Weekly Earnings in Dollars |
|---|---|---|---|---|---|---|---|---|---|---|---|---|---|
| | Male | Female | Male | Female | Male | Female | Male | Female | Male | Female | Male | Female | |
| Less than $3 00 | | | | | | | 1 | 3 | 61 | 318 | .78 | 1.78 | Less than $3 00 |
| $3 00–$3 49 | | | | | | | | 1 | 72 | 438 | 1.71 | 4.21 | $3 00– 3 49 |
| 3 50– 3 99 | | | | | | | | 1 | 86 | 684 | 2.81 | 8.05 | 3 50– 3 99 |
| 4 00– 4 49 | | | | | | | | 7 | 295 | 1,290 | 6.60 | 15.26 | 4 00– 4 49 |
| 4 50– 4 99 | | | | | | | 3 | 3 | 98 | 534 | 7.85 | 18.25 | 4 50– 4 99 |
| 5 00– 5 49 | | | | | | | 2 | 6 | 216 | 1,065 | 10.60 | 24.2 | 5 00– 5 49 |
| 5 50– 5 99 | | | | | | | | 1 | 51 | 451 | 11.28 | 26.8 | 5 50– 5 99 |
| 6 00– 6 49 | | | | | | | 1 | 6 | 246 | 1,699 | 14.42 | 36.2 | 6 00– 6 49 |
| 6 50– 6 99 | | | | | | | | | 52 | 546 | 15.1 | 39.3 | 6 50– 6 99 |
| 7 00– 7 49 | | 1 | | | | | 1 | 7 | 218 | 1,930 | 17.9 | 50.1 | 7 00– 7 49 |
| 7 50– 7 99 | | | | | | | 1 | 2 | 43 | 510 | 18.5 | 53.0 | 7 50– 7 99 |
| 8 00– 8 99 | | 1 | | 1 | | | 3 | 9 | 301 | 2,163 | 22.4 | 65.0 | 8 00– 8 99 |
| 9 00– 9 99 | | 1 | | | | | | 10 | 218 | 1,434 | 25.1 | 73.1 | 9 00– 9 99 |
| 10 00–10 99 | 2 | | | | | | 2 | 2 | 392 | 1,276 | 30.2 | 80.2 | 10 00–10 99 |
| 11 00–11 99 | | 1 | | 1 | | | | 3 | 224 | 598 | 33.0 | 83.5 | 11 00–11 99 |
| 12 00–12 99 | 1 | 1 | 2 | | | | 3 | 5 | 640 | 872 | 41.2 | 88.4 | 12 00–12 99 |
| 13 00–13 99 | | | | | | | 3 | 3 | 232 | 309 | 44.2 | 90.2 | 13 00–13 99 |
| 14 00–14 99 | 2 | 1 | | | | | 1 | 4 | 441 | 386 | 49.8 | 92.3 | 14 00–14 99 |
| 15 00–15 99 | 1 | 1 | 5 | | | | 3 | 3 | 646 | 398 | 58.2 | 94.5 | 15 00–15 99 |
| 16 00–17 99 | 10 | 3 | 7 | 2 | 2 | 1 | | 2 | 601 | 337 | 65.9 | 95.8 | 16 00–17 99 |
| 18 00–19 99 | 4 | | 3 | 1 | | | 3 | | 635 | 230 | 74.1 | 97.7 | 18 00–19 99 |
| 20 00–24 99 | 10 | 1 | 9 | 1 | 1 | | 8 | 2 | 1,010 | 228 | 87.0 | 98.0 | 20 00–24 99 |
| 25 00–29 99 | 12 | 1 | 3 | | 1 | | 5 | 1 | 531 | 101 | 93.8 | 99.5 | 25 00–29 99 |
| 30 00–34 99 | 8 | | 6 | | | | 1 | | 226 | 39 | 96.6 | 99.8 | 30 00–34 99 |
| 35 00–39 99 | 4 | | 2 | | | | | | 89 | 25 | 97.9 | 99.9 | 35 00–39 99 |
| 40 00 and over | 4 | | 5 | | 2 | | | 1 | 159 | 34 | 100.0 | 100.0 | 40 00 and over |
| Not reported | | | | | | | | | 39 | 81 | | | Not reported |
| Total | 58 | 12 | 42 | 6 | 6 | 1 | 41 | 82 | 7,822 | 17,976 | | | Total |

NEW YORK STATE

**DEPARTMENT STORES — OFFICE**

20. TABLE VII, A, 1, b

NUMBER AND PER CENT. OF EMPLOYEES BY SEX ACCORDING TO OCCUPATION AND NATIVITY

| NATIVITY | OCCUPATION | | | | | | | | | | | |
|---|---|---|---|---|---|---|---|---|---|---|---|---|
| | TOTAL | | SUPERINTENDENTS | | BOOKKEEPERS | | CLERKS | | SECRETARIES | | STENOGRAPHERS | |
| | Male | Female | Male | Female | Male | Female | Male | Female | Male | Female | Male | Female |
| Native | 2,058 | 5,504 | 32 | 5 | 205 | 524 | 1,277 | 2,542 | 4 | 7 | 29 | 503 |
| Foreign | 418 | 485 | 4 | ....... | 50 | 36 | 268 | 211 | ....... | 1 | 1 | 59 |
| Not reported | 13 | 58 | ....... | ....... | 1 | 5 | 8 | 26 | ....... | 1 | ....... | 4 |
| Total | 2,489 | 6,047 | 36 | 5 | 256 | 565 | 1,553 | 2,779 | 4 | 9 | 30 | 566 |
| Per cent. of total | 100.0 | 100.0 | 1.4 | .1 | 10.6 | 9.3 | 62.8 | 45.9 | .16 | .15 | 1.2 | 9.4 |

NEW YORK STATE

**DEPARTMENT STORES — OFFICE**

20. TABLE VII, A, 1, b — (*concluded*)

NUMBER AND PER CENT. OF EMPLOYEES BY SEX ACCORDING TO OCCUPATION AND NATIVITY

| NATIVITY | OCCUPATION | | | | | | | | | | | |
|---|---|---|---|---|---|---|---|---|---|---|---|---|
| | OFFICE BOYS AND GIRLS | | CASHIERS | | TELEPHONE OPERATORS | | AUDITORS | | DETECTIVES | | ADVERTISERS AND WINDOW DRESSERS | |
| | Male | Female | Male | Female | Male | Female | Male | Female | Male | Female | Male | Female |
| Native | 160 | 85 | 84 | 1,034 | 2 | 192 | 53 | 559 | 26 | 31 | 186 | 22 |
| Foreign | 13 | 3 | 13 | 117 | ....... | 7 | 13 | 44 | 5 | 4 | 51 | 3 |
| Not reported | 1 | 1 | ....... | 10 | ....... | 2 | ....... | 8 | ....... | ....... | 3 | 1 |
| Total | 174 | 89 | 97 | 1,161 | 2 | 201 | 66 | 611 | 31 | 35 | 240 | 26 |
| Per cent. of total | 7.0 | 1.5 | 3.9 | 19.1 | .08 | 3.3 | 2.7 | 10.2 | 1.2 | .6 | 9.6 | .45 |

NEW YORK STATE

DEPARTMENT STORES — OFFICE

21. TABLE V, A, 1, b — NUMBER AND PER CENT. OF EMPLOYEES EARNING SPECIFIED WEEKLY RATES, BY AGE GROUPS AND SEX

| WEEKLY RATES IN DOLLARS | AGE GROUPS IN YEARS | | | | | | | | | | | | | | WEEKLY RATES IN DOLLARS |
|---|---|---|---|---|---|---|---|---|---|---|---|---|---|---|---|
| | 14–15 | | 16–17 | | 18–20 | | 21–24 | | 25–29 | | 30–34 | | 35–39 | | |
| | Male | Female | Male | Female | Male | Female | Male | Female | Male | Female | Male | Female | Male | Female | |
| Less than $3 00 | 1 | 1 | .... | ...... | ...... | ...... | ...... | ...... | ...... | ...... | ...... | ...... | ...... | ...... | Less than $3 00 |
| $3 00–$3 49... | 1 | 24 | 2 | 28 | ...... | 2 | ...... | ...... | ...... | ...... | ...... | ...... | ...... | ...... | ...$3 00– 3 49 |
| 3 50– 3 99... | 4 | 76 | 3 | 59 | 1 | 13 | 1 | 2 | ...... | 1 | ...... | ...... | ...... | ...... | ... 3 50– 3 99 |
| 4 00– 4 49... | 49 | 90 | 23 | 146 | 2 | 44 | 9 | 2 | 1 | 1 | 1 | 1 | 1 | ...... | ... 4 00– 4 49 |
| 4 50– 4 99... | 12 | 20 | 16 | 102 | ...... | 50 | ...... | 3 | ...... | 1 | ...... | 1 | ...... | ...... | ... 4 50– 4 99 |
| 5 00– 5 49... | 37 | 24 | 62 | 264 | 8 | 252 | 3 | 36 | 1 | 3 | 1 | 1 | ...... | 1 | ... 5 00– 5 49 |
| 5 50– 5 99... | 4 | 3 | 14 | 49 | 2 | 68 | ...... | 16 | ...... | 1 | ...... | ...... | ...... | ...... | ... 5 50– 5 99 |
| 6 00– 6 49... | 6 | 9 | 55 | 192 | 33 | 552 | 3 | 173 | 3 | 29 | ...... | 6 | ...... | 5 | ... 6 00– 6 49 |
| 6 50– 6 99... | .... | 2 | 4 | 18 | 9 | 85 | ...... | 22 | ...... | 2 | ...... | ...... | ...... | 1 | ... 6 50– 6 99 |
| 7 00– 7 49... | 1 | 3 | 25 | 69 | 40 | 406 | 2 | 290 | 1 | 71 | 1 | 26 | 1 | 10 | ... 7 00– 7 49 |
| 7 50– 7 99... | .... | ...... | 1 | 2 | 4 | 22 | 3 | 30 | ...... | 2 | 1 | ...... | ...... | ...... | ... 7 50– 7 99 |
| 8 00– 8 99... | .... | 4 | 18 | 28 | 73 | 228 | 13 | 346 | 1 | 93 | 2 | 26 | 1 | 11 | ... 8 00– 8 99 |
| 9 00– 9 99... | .... | ...... | 3 | 12 | 58 | 117 | 25 | 199 | 2 | 80 | 1 | 34 | 1 | 10 | ... 9 00– 9 99 |
| 10 00–10 99... | .... | ...... | 3 | 4 | 58 | 77 | 56 | 180 | 21 | 113 | 15 | 27 | 7 | 16 | ...10 00–10 99 |
| 11 00–11 99... | .... | ...... | .... | 2 | 15 | 13 | 29 | 75 | 8 | 61 | 2 | 16 | 1 | 10 | ...11 00–11 99 |
| 12 00–12 99... | .... | ...... | .... | ...... | 26 | 26 | 101 | 67 | 52 | 80 | 26 | 24 | 25 | 17 | ...12 00–12 99 |
| 13 00–13 99... | .... | ...... | .... | ...... | 10 | ...... | 29 | 27 | 16 | 33 | 8 | 13 | 6 | 9 | ...13 00–13 99 |
| 14 00–14 99... | .... | ...... | .... | ...... | 4 | 9 | 25 | 20 | 31 | 38 | 19 | 10 | 16 | 15 | ...14 00–14 99 |
| 15 00–15 99... | .... | ...... | .... | 1 | 6 | 3 | 46 | 25 | 51 | 27 | 29 | 16 | 29 | 10 | ...15 00–15 99 |
| 16 00–17 99... | .... | ...... | .... | ...... | 1 | 1 | 26 | 5 | 46 | 11 | 34 | 10 | 21 | 11 | ...16 00–17 99 |
| 18 00–19 99... | .... | ...... | .... | 1 | ...... | 1 | 21 | 5 | 51 | 15 | 38 | 11 | 25 | 9 | ...18 00–19 99 |
| 20 00–24 99... | .... | ...... | .... | ...... | ...... | 1 | 14 | 1 | 57 | 13 | 49 | 10 | 46 | 8 | ...20 00–24 99 |
| 25 00–29 99... | .... | ...... | .... | ...... | ...... | 1 | 2 | 1 | 22 | 3 | 23 | 4 | 19 | 2 | ...25 00–29 99 |
| 30 00–34 99... | .... | ...... | .... | ...... | ...... | 1 | 1 | ...... | 7 | 1 | 23 | ...... | 21 | 2 | ...30 00–34 99 |
| 35 00–39 99... | .... | ...... | .... | ...... | ...... | ...... | 1 | ...... | 1 | ...... | 7 | ...... | 1 | ...... | ...35 00–39 99 |
| 40 00 and over. | .... | ...... | .... | ...... | 1 | ...... | 2 | ...... | 3 | ...... | 12 | 3 | 19 | ...... | 40 00 and over |
| Not reported... | .... | 1 | .... | 1 | ...... | ...... | ...... | 1 | 1 | ...... | ...... | ...... | 1 | ...... | ...Not reported |
| Total..... | 115 | 257 | 229 | 978 | 351 | 1,972 | 412 | 1,526 | 376 | 679 | 292 | 239 | 241 | 147 | .....Total |

NEW YORK STATE

21. TABLE V, A, 1, b — (*concluded*)

**DEPARTMENT STORES — OFFICE**

NUMBER AND PER CENT. OF EMPLOYEES EARNING SPECIFIED WEEKLY RATES, BY AGE GROUPS AND SEX,

| WEEKLY RATES IN DOLLARS | AGE GROUPS IN YEARS (*concluded*) 40–44 | | 45–54 | | 55–64 | | 65 AND OVER | NOT REPORTED | | TOTAL | | CUMULATIVE PER CENT. OF TOTAL | | WEEKLY RATES IN DOLLARS |
|---|---|---|---|---|---|---|---|---|---|---|---|---|---|---|
| | Male | Female | Male | Female | Male | Female | Male | Male | Female | Male | Female | Male | Female | |
| Less than $3 00 | ...... | ...... | ...... | ...... | ...... | ...... | ...... | ...... | ...... | 1 | 1 | .04 | .02 | Less than $3 00 |
| $3 00–$3 49 | ...... | ...... | ...... | ...... | ...... | ...... | ...... | ...... | ...... | 3 | 54 | .16 | .91 | $3 00– 3 49 |
| 3 50– 3 99 | ...... | ...... | ...... | ...... | ...... | ...... | ...... | ...... | 6 | 9 | 157 | .52 | 3.52 | 3 50– 3 99 |
| 4 00– 4 49 | ...... | ...... | ...... | ...... | ...... | ...... | ...... | ...... | 5 | 86 | 289 | 3.98 | 8.29 | 4 00– 4 49 |
| 4 50– 4 99 | ...... | ...... | ...... | ...... | ...... | ...... | ...... | ...... | 1 | 28 | 178 | 5.11 | 11.25 | 4 50– 4 99 |
| 5 00– 5 49 | ...... | ...... | ...... | 1 | ...... | ...... | ...... | 1 | 4 | 113 | 586 | 9.65 | 20.95 | 5 00– 5 49 |
| 5 50– 5 99 | ...... | ...... | ...... | ...... | 1 | ...... | ...... | ...... | 4 | 21 | 141 | 10.50 | 23.25 | 5 50– 5 99 |
| 6 00– 6 49 | ...... | 1 | ...... | 2 | ...... | ...... | ...... | 2 | 4 | 102 | 973 | 14.60 | 39.40 | 6 00– 6 49 |
| 6 50– 6 99 | ...... | ...... | ...... | ...... | ...... | ...... | ...... | ...... | 9 | 13 | 139 | 15.14 | 41.70 | 6 50– 6 99 |
| 7 00– 7 49 | ...... | 2 | ...... | 3 | ...... | ...... | ...... | ...... | 14 | 71 | 894 | 17.99 | 56.50 | 7 00– 7 49 |
| 7 50– 7 99 | ...... | ...... | ...... | 1 | ...... | ...... | ...... | ...... | 3 | 9 | 60 | 18.38 | 57.50 | 7 50– 7 99 |
| 8 00– 8 99 | ...... | 3 | ...... | 2 | ...... | ...... | ...... | 1 | 14 | 109 | 755 | 22.68 | 70 00 | 8 00– 8 99 |
| 9 00– 9 99 | ...... | 3 | 2 | 1 | ...... | ...... | 1 | ...... | 12 | 93 | 468 | 26.50 | 77.60 | 9 00– 9 99 |
| 10 00–10 99 | 4 | 9 | 8 | 1 | 10 | ...... | 2 | 2 | 21 | 186 | 448 | 33.95 | 85.20 | 10 00–10 99 |
| 11 00–11 99 | 2 | 3 | 7 | ...... | 1 | ...... | ...... | ...... | 16 | 65 | 196 | 36.55 | 88.40 | 11 00–11 99 |
| 12 00–12 99 | 15 | 8 | 28 | 7 | 10 | 2 | 3 | 3 | 13 | 289 | 244 | 48.40 | 92.40 | 12 00–12 99 |
| 13 00–13 99 | 3 | ...... | 3 | 3 | 2 | ...... | 2 | ...... | 5 | 79 | 90 | 51.45 | 94.00 | 13 00–13 99 |
| 14 00–14 99 | 9 | 3 | 14 | 1 | 3 | ...... | 2 | 2 | 7 | 125 | 103 | 56.45 | 95.60 | 14 00–14 99 |
| 15 00–15 99 | 12 | 2 | 19 | 4 | 8 | 1 | 1 | 2 | 7 | 203 | 96 | 64.50 | 97.40 | 15 00–15 99 |
| 16 00–17 99 | 12 | 7 | 13 | 3 | 4 | ...... | ...... | 2 | 1 | 159 | 49 | 71.00 | 98.00 | 16 00–17 99 |
| 18 00–19 99 | 15 | 3 | 28 | ...... | 3 | ...... | 1 | 1 | 5 | 183 | 50 | 78.30 | 98.80 | 18 00–19 99 |
| 20 00–24 99 | 30 | 3 | 32 | 3 | 11 | ...... | ...... | 3 | 3 | 242 | 42 | 88.10 | 99.50 | 20 00–24 99 |
| 25 00–29 99 | 18 | 2 | 12 | 1 | 5 | 2 | 1 | 5 | 1 | 107 | 17 | 92.40 | 99.75 | 25 00–29 99 |
| 30 00–34 99 | 10 | 5 | 16 | ...... | 6 | ...... | ...... | 1 | ...... | 85 | 9 | 95.90 | 99.90 | 30 00–34 99 |
| 35 00–39 99 | 7 | ...... | 7 | ...... | 3 | ...... | 1 | 1 | ...... | 29 | ...... | 97.00 | ...... | 35 00–39 99 |
| 40 00 and over | 14 | ...... | 18 | 1 | 5 | ...... | 1 | ...... | 1 | 75 | 5 | 100.00 | 100.00 | 40 00 and over |
| Not reported | ...... | ...... | ...... | ...... | 2 | ...... | ...... | ...... | ...... | 4 | 3 | ...... | ...... | Not reported |
| Total | 151 | 54 | 207 | 34 | 74 | 5 | 15 | 26 | 156 | 2,489 | 6,047 | ...... | ...... | Total |

NEW YORK STATE

**DEPARTMENT STORES — OFFICE**

32. TABLE VIII, A, 1, b NUMBER AND PER CENT. OF EMPLOYEES EARNING SPECIFIED WEEKLY RATES, BY OCCUPATION AND SEX

| WEEKLY RATES IN DOLLARS | OCCUPATION | | | | | | | | | | | | | | WEEKLY RATES IN DOLLARS |
|---|---|---|---|---|---|---|---|---|---|---|---|---|---|---|---|
| | SUPERINTENDENTS | | BOOKKEEPERS | | CLERKS | | SECRETARIES | | STENOGRAPHERS | | OFFICE BOYS AND GIRLS | | CASHIERS | | |
| | Male | Female | Male | Female | Male | Female | Male | Female | Male | Female | Male | Female | Male | Female | |
| Less than $3 00 | .... | ...... | .... | ...... | 1 | 1 | ...... | ...... | ...... | ...... | ...... | ...... | ...... | ...... | Less than $3 00 |
| $3 00–$3 49... | .... | ...... | .... | 1 | 1 | 25 | ...... | ...... | ...... | ...... | 1 | 5 | 1 | 4 | ...$3 00– 3 49 |
| 3 50– 3 99... | .... | ...... | .... | 1 | 3 | 66 | ...... | ...... | ...... | ...... | 5 | 15 | ...... | 27 | ....3 50– 3 99 |
| 4 00– 4 49... | .... | ...... | .... | ...... | 39 | 138 | ...... | ...... | ...... | 2 | 46 | 18 | 1 | 57 | ....4 00– 4 49 |
| 4 50– 4 99... | .... | ...... | .... | ...... | 7 | 76 | ...... | ...... | ...... | 4 | 21 | 9 | ...... | 34 | ....4 50– 4 99 |
| 5 00– 5 49... | .... | ...... | .... | 12 | 50 | 298 | ...... | ...... | ...... | 17 | 53 | 24 | 1 | 116 | ....5 00– 5 49 |
| 5 50– 5 99... | .... | ...... | 1 | 3 | 8 | 80 | ...... | ...... | ...... | 9 | 11 | 3 | ...... | 22 | ....5 50– 5 99 |
| 6 00– 6 49... | .... | ...... | 1 | 32 | 59 | 462 | ...... | ...... | ...... | 79 | 23 | 10 | 3 | 260 | ....6 00– 6 49 |
| 6 50– 6 99... | .... | ...... | .... | 6 | 9 | 76 | ...... | 1 | ...... | 8 | 3 | ...... | ...... | 34 | ....6 50– 6 99 |
| 7 00– 7 49... | .... | ...... | 2 | 53 | 46 | 381 | ...... | ...... | 4 | 92 | 3 | 3 | 3 | 255 | ....7 00– 7 49 |
| 7 50– 7 99... | .... | ...... | 1 | 3 | 5 | 35 | ...... | ...... | 1 | 3 | ...... | ...... | 1 | 10 | ....7 50– 7 99 |
| 8 00– 8 99... | .... | ...... | 6 | 69 | 76 | 361 | ...... | ...... | 3 | 85 | 4 | 2 | 1 | 149 | ....8 00– 8 99 |
| 9 00– 9 99... | .... | ...... | 8 | 73 | 59 | 238 | ...... | ...... | 5 | 62 | 2 | ...... | 3 | 54 | ....9 00– 9 99 |
| 10 00–10 99... | .... | ...... | 7 | 92 | 149 | 176 | ...... | 1 | 5 | 76 | 1 | ...... | 5 | 61 | ...10 00–10 99 |
| 11 00–11 99... | .... | ...... | 4 | 44 | 54 | 96 | ...... | ...... | ...... | 21 | ...... | ...... | 2 | 22 | ...11 00–11 99 |
| 12 00–12 99... | .... | ...... | 25 | 70 | 235 | 87 | ...... | 3 | 2 | 42 | 1 | ...... | 4 | 19 | ...12 00–12 99 |
| 13 00–13 99... | .... | ...... | 11 | 28 | 55 | 34 | ...... | 1 | 2 | 12 | ...... | ...... | 4 | 10 | ...13 00–13 99 |
| 14 00–14 99... | .... | 1 | 10 | 30 | 103 | 42 | ...... | ...... | ...... | 15 | ...... | ...... | 5 | 9 | ...14 00–14 99 |
| 15 00–15 99... | .... | ...... | 27 | 25 | 136 | 40 | ...... | ...... | 4 | 19 | ...... | ...... | 8 | 4 | ...15 00–15 99 |
| 16 00–17 99... | .... | ...... | 44 | 10 | 90 | 20 | ...... | 1 | ...... | 2 | ...... | ...... | 9 | 6 | ...16 00–17 99 |
| 18 00–19 99... | .... | 2 | 42 | 6 | 88 | 15 | ...... | 2 | 3 | 10 | ...... | ...... | 16 | 2 | ...18 00–19 99 |
| 20 00–24 99... | 2 | 1 | 43 | 4 | 141 | 17 | 1 | ...... | 1 | 7 | ...... | ...... | 18 | 1 | ...20 00–24 99 |
| 25 00–29 99... | 6 | ...... | 12 | 2 | 61 | 8 | 1 | ...... | ...... | ...... | ...... | ...... | 3 | 4 | ...25 00–29 99 |
| 30 00–34 99... | 13 | ...... | 3 | 1 | 39 | 4 | ...... | ...... | ...... | 1 | ...... | ...... | 2 | ...... | ...30 00–34 99 |
| 35 00–39 99... | 1 | ...... | 3 | ...... | 14 | ...... | 2 | ...... | ...... | ...... | ...... | ...... | 3 | ...... | ...35 00–39 99 |
| 40 00 and over. | 14 | 1 | 6 | ...... | 22 | 2 | ...... | ...... | ...... | ...... | ...... | ...... | 4 | ...... | .40 00 and oved |
| Not reported... | .... | ...... | .... | ...... | 3 | 1 | ...... | ...... | ...... | ...... | ...... | ...... | ...... | 1 | ...Not reporter |
| Total..... | 36 | 5 | 256 | 565 | 1,553 | 2,779 | 4 | 9 | 30 | 566 | 174 | 89 | 97 | 1,161 | .....Total |

23. TABLE VIII. A. 1. b — (*concluded*)

NEW YORK STATE

**DEPARTMENT STORES — OFFICE**

NUMBER AND PER CENT. OF EMPLOYEES EARNING SPECIFIED WEEKLY RATES, BY OCCUPATION AND SEX

| WEEKLY RATES IN DOLLARS | OCCUPATION (*concluded*) | | | | | | | | | | | | | | WEEKLY RATES IN DOLLARS |
|---|---|---|---|---|---|---|---|---|---|---|---|---|---|---|---|
| | TELEPHONE OPERATORS | | AUDITORS | | DETECTIVES | | ADVERTISERS AND WINDOW DRESSERS | | TOTAL | | CUMULATIVE PER CENT. OF TOTAL | | | | |
| | Male | Female | Male | Female | Male | Female | Male | Female | Male | Female | Male | Female | | | |
| Less than $3 00 | ...... | ...... | ...... | ...... | ...... | ...... | ...... | ...... | 1 | 1 | .04 | .02 | | | Less than $3 00 |
| $3 00–$3 49 | ...... | 1 | ...... | 18 | ...... | ...... | ...... | ...... | 3 | 54 | .16 | .91 | | | $3 00– 3 49 |
| 3 50– 3 99 | ...... | 1 | ...... | 47 | ...... | ...... | 1 | ...... | 9 | 157 | .52 | 3.52 | | | 3 50– 3 99 |
| 4 00– 4 49 | ...... | 5 | ...... | 69 | ...... | ...... | ...... | ...... | 86 | 289 | 3.98 | 8.29 | | | 4 00– 4 49 |
| 4 50– 4 99 | ...... | 4 | ...... | 51 | ...... | ...... | ...... | ...... | 78 | 178 | 5.11 | 11.25 | | | 4 50– 4 99 |
| 5 00– 5 49 | ...... | 12 | 1 | 107 | ...... | ...... | 8 | ...... | 113 | 586 | 9.65 | 20.95 | | | 5 00– 5 49 |
| 5 50– 5 99 | ...... | 4 | ...... | 20 | ...... | ...... | 1 | ...... | 21 | 141 | 10.50 | 23.25 | | | 5 50– 5 99 |
| 6 00– 6 49 | ...... | 35 | 4 | 93 | ...... | ...... | 12 | 2 | 102 | 973 | 14.60 | 39.40 | | | 6 00– 6 49 |
| 6 50– 6 99 | ...... | 1 | ...... | 13 | ...... | ...... | 1 | ...... | 13 | 139 | 15.14 | 41.70 | | | 6 50– 6 99 |
| 7 00– 7 49 | ...... | 26 | 2 | 82 | 1 | 1 | 10 | 1 | 71 | 894 | 17.99 | 56.50 | | | 7 00– 7 49 |
| 7 50– 7 99 | ...... | 1 | 1 | 8 | ...... | ...... | ...... | ...... | 9 | 60 | 18.38 | 57.50 | | | 7 50– 7 99 |
| 8 00– 8 99 | 1 | 39 | 5 | 49 | ...... | ...... | 13 | 1 | 109 | 755 | 22.68 | 70.00 | | | 8 00– 8 99 |
| 9 00– 9 99 | ...... | 21 | 7 | 19 | ...... | ...... | 9 | 1 | 93 | 468 | 26.50 | 77.60 | | | 9 00– 9 99 |
| 10 00–10 99 | 1 | 22 | 9 | 13 | 2 | 3 | 7 | 4 | 186 | 448 | 33.95 | 85.20 | | | 10 00–10 99 |
| 11 00–11 99 | ...... | 9 | 3 | 2 | 1 | 1 | 1 | 1 | 65 | 196 | 36.55 | 88.40 | | | 11 00–11 99 |
| 12 00–12 99 | ...... | 9 | 9 | 7 | 3 | 4 | 10 | 3 | 289 | 244 | 48.40 | 92.40 | | | 12 00–12 99 |
| 13 00–13 99 | ...... | 1 | 3 | 3 | ...... | ...... | 4 | 1 | 79 | 90 | 51.45 | 94.00 | | | 13 00–13 99 |
| 14 00–14 99 | ...... | 2 | 2 | 2 | 1 | 1 | 4 | 1 | 125 | 103 | 56.45 | 95.60 | | | 14 00–14 99 |
| 15 00–15 99 | ...... | 3 | 2 | 3 | 4 | 1 | 22 | 1 | 203 | 96 | 64.50 | 97.40 | | | 15 00–15 99 |
| 16 00–17 99 | ...... | ...... | 3 | 4 | ...... | 5 | 13 | 1 | 159 | 49 | 71.00 | 98.00 | | | 16 00–17 99 |
| 18 00–19 99 | ...... | 2 | 6 | 1 | 6 | 8 | 22 | 2 | 183 | 50 | 78.30 | 98.80 | | | 18 00–19 99 |
| 20 00–24 99 | ...... | 2 | 1 | ...... | 7 | 9 | 28 | 1 | 242 | 42 | 88.10 | 99.50 | | | 20 00–24 99 |
| 25 00–29 99 | ...... | ...... | 2 | ...... | 1 | 1 | 21 | 2 | 107 | 17 | 92.40 | 99.75 | | | 25 00–29 99 |
| 30 00–34 99 | ...... | ...... | 3 | ...... | 3 | 1 | 22 | 2 | 85 | 9 | 95.90 | 99.90 | | | 30 00–34 99 |
| 35 00–39 99 | ...... | ...... | 1 | ...... | 1 | ...... | 4 | ...... | 20 | ...... | 97.00 | ...... | | | 35 00–39 99 |
| 40 00 and over | ...... | ...... | 2 | ...... | 1 | ...... | 26 | 2 | 75 | 5 | 100.00 | 100.00 | | | 40 00 and over |
| Not reported | ...... | 1 | ...... | ...... | ...... | ...... | 1 | ...... | 4 | 3 | ...... | ...... | | | Not reported |
| Total | 2 | 201 | 66 | 611 | 31 | 35 | 240 | 26 | 2,489 | 6,047 | ...... | ...... | | | Total |

NEW YORK STATE

DEPARTMENT STORES — OFFICE

23. TABLE VI, A, 1, b NUMBER AND PER CENT. OF EMPLOYEES CLASSIFIED ACCORDING TO ACTUAL WEEKLY EARNINGS, BY AGE GROUPS AND SEX

| Actual Weekly Earnings in Dollars | Age Groups in Years | | | | | | | | | | | | | | Actual Weekly Earnings in Dollars |
|---|---|---|---|---|---|---|---|---|---|---|---|---|---|---|---|
| | 14–15 | | 16–17 | | 18–20 | | 21–24 | | 25–29 | | 30–34 | | 35–39 | | |
| | Male | Female | Male | Female | Male | Female | Male | Female | Male | Female | Male | Female | Male | Female | |
| Less than $3 00 | 3 | 14 | 2 | 14 | 1 | 18 | 3 | 6 | 1 | 1 | 1 | ...... | ...... | ...... | Less than $3 00 |
| $3 00–$3 49... | 3 | 22 | 5 | 33 | ...... | 13 | ...... | ...... | 1 | ...... | ...... | 2 | ...... | 1 | ...$3 00– 3 49 |
| 3 50– 3 99... | 7 | 74 | 4 | 78 | ...... | 24 | 1 | 3 | ...... | 1 | ...... | ...... | ...... | ...... | ....3 50– 3 99 |
| 4 00– 4 49... | 46 | 86 | 25 | 150 | ...... | 59 | 1 | 9 | ...... | 5 | 2 | ...... | ...... | ...... | ....4 00– 4 49 |
| 4 50– 4 99... | 11 | 15 | 20 | 113 | 1 | 94 | ...... | 14 | 1 | 4 | ...... | 1 | ...... | 1 | ....4 50– 4 99 |
| 5 00– 5 49... | 34 | 22 | 57 | 225 | 9 | 228 | 2 | 44 | ...... | 4 | 4 | 1 | ...... | ...... | ....5 00– 5 49 |
| 5 50– 5 99... | 4 | 5 | 14 | 57 | 4 | 135 | 1 | 40 | ...... | 6 | 2 | 1 | ...... | ...... | ....5 50– 5 99 |
| 6 00– 6 49... | 5 | 8 | 48 | 171 | 31 | 468 | 5 | 155 | 3 | 27 | ...... | 7 | 1 | 7 | ....6 00– 6 49 |
| 6 50– 6 99... | 1 | 3 | 7 | 22 | 15 | 101 | 2 | 56 | ...... | 11 | ...... | 2 | ...... | 2 | ....6 50– 6 99 |
| 7 00– 7 49... | 1 | 2 | 21 | 61 | 35 | 345 | 2 | 249 | 2 | 62 | 2 | 24 | 1 | 8 | ....7 00– 7 49 |
| 7 50– 7 99... | .... | 1 | 1 | 3 | 8 | 35 | 3 | 60 | ...... | 9 | 1 | 4 | ...... | ...... | ....7 50– 7 99 |
| 8 00– 8 99... | .... | 3 | 19 | 28 | 71 | 210 | 16 | 321 | 3 | 91 | 2 | 24 | 1 | 11 | ....8 00– 8 99 |
| 9 00– 9 99... | .... | 1 | 3 | 11 | 57 | 113 | 30 | 192 | 3 | 88 | 2 | 33 | 2 | 10 | ....9 00– 9 99 |
| 10 00–10 99... | .... | ...... | 3 | 4 | 52 | 67 | 49 | 152 | 14 | 104 | 10 | 25 | 9 | 16 | ...10 00–10 99 |
| 11 00–11 99... | .... | ...... | .... | 2 | 17 | 16 | 35 | 82 | 13 | 58 | 2 | 18 | 3 | 9 | ...11 00–11 99 |
| 12 00–12 99... | .... | ...... | .... | 2 | 24 | 23 | 90 | 62 | 45 | 74 | 21 | 20 | 20 | 16 | ...12 00–12 99 |
| 13 00–13 99... | .... | ...... | .... | ...... | 10 | ...... | 29 | 23 | 21 | 33 | 9 | 13 | 7 | 11 | ...13 00–13 99 |
| 14 00–14 99... | .... | ...... | .... | ...... | 6 | 11 | 28 | 20 | 29 | 36 | 18 | 9 | 12 | 15 | ...14 00–14 99 |
| 15 00–15 99... | .... | ...... | .... | 1 | 7 | 1 | 47 | 20 | 53 | 23 | 29 | 18 | 29 | 8 | ...15 00–15 99 |
| 16 00–17 99... | .... | ...... | .... | ...... | ...... | 2 | 27 | 6 | 41 | 10 | 35 | 11 | 22 | 10 | ...16 00–17 99 |
| 18 00–19 99... | .... | ...... | .... | 1 | ...... | 1 | 19 | 5 | 54 | 13 | 35 | 8 | 20 | 10 | ...18 00–19 99 |
| 20 00–24 99... | .... | ...... | .... | ...... | 1 | 1 | 15 | 1 | 56 | 13 | 53 | 10 | 48 | 7 | ...20 00–24 99 |
| 25 00–29 99... | .... | ...... | .... | ...... | ...... | 1 | 2 | 1 | 23 | 3 | 23 | 4 | 22 | 2 | ...25 00–29 99 |
| 30 00–34 99... | .... | ...... | .... | ...... | ...... | 1 | 2 | ...... | 7 | 1 | 21 | ...... | 22 | 2 | ...30 00–34 99 |
| 35 00–39 99... | .... | ...... | .... | ...... | ...... | ...... | ...... | ...... | 1 | ...... | 8 | ...... | 1 | ...... | ...35 00–39 99 |
| 40 00 and over. | .... | ...... | .... | ...... | 1 | ...... | 1 | ...... | 4 | ...... | 12 | 3 | 20 | ...... | .40 00 and over |
| Not reported... | .... | 1 | .... | 2 | 1 | 5 | 2 | 5 | 1 | 2 | ...... | 1 | 1 | 1 | ...Not reported |
| Total..... | 115 | 257 | 229 | 978 | 351 | 1,972 | 412 | 1,526 | 376 | 679 | 292 | 239 | 241 | 147 | .....Total |

NEW YORK STATE

23. TABLE VI, A, 1, b — (*concluded*)

**DEPARTMENT STORES — OFFICE**

NUMBER AND PER CENT. OF EMPLOYEES CLASSIFIED ACCORDING TO ACTUAL WEEKLY EARNINGS, BY AGE GROUPS AND SEX

| ACTUAL WEEKLY EARNINGS IN DOLLARS | AGE GROUPS IN YEARS (*concluded*) | | | | | | | | | | | | | ACTUAL WEEKLY EARNINGS IN DOLLARS |
|---|---|---|---|---|---|---|---|---|---|---|---|---|---|---|
| | 40–44 | | 45–54 | | 55–64 | | 65 AND OVER | NOT REPORTED | | TOTAL | | CUMULATIVE PER CENT. OF TOTAL | | |
| | Male | Female | Male | Female | Male | Female | Male | Male | Female | Male | Female | Male | Female | |
| Less than $3 00 | ...... | ...... | ...... | ...... | ...... | ...... | ...... | ...... | 2 | 11 | 55 | .44 | .93 | Less than $3 00 |
| $3 00–$3 49 | ...... | ...... | ...... | ...... | ...... | ...... | ...... | ...... | ...... | 9 | 71 | .80 | 2.09 | $3 00– 3 49 |
| 3 50– 3 99 | ...... | ...... | ...... | ...... | ...... | ...... | ...... | ...... | 8 | 12 | 188 | 1.28 | 5.20 | 3 50– 3 99 |
| 4 00– 4 49 | ...... | ...... | ...... | ...... | ...... | ...... | ...... | ...... | 3 | 74 | 312 | 4.25 | 10.40 | 4 00– 4 49 |
| 4 50– 4 99 | ...... | ...... | ...... | ...... | ...... | ...... | ...... | ...... | 1 | 33 | 243 | 5.58 | 14.39 | 4 50– 4 99 |
| 5 00– 5 49 | ...... | ...... | ...... | 1 | ...... | ...... | ...... | 1 | 5 | 107 | 530 | 9.87 | 23.15 | 5 00– 5 49 |
| 5 50– 5 99 | ...... | ...... | ...... | ...... | 1 | ...... | ...... | ...... | 3 | 26 | 247 | 10.91 | 27.25 | 5 50– 5 99 |
| 6 00– 6 49 | ...... | 1 | ...... | 2 | ...... | ...... | ...... | 2 | 6 | 95 | 852 | 14.72 | 41.30 | 6 00– 6 49 |
| 6 50– 6 99 | ...... | ...... | ...... | ...... | ...... | ...... | ...... | ...... | 7 | 25 | 204 | 15.71 | 44.75 | 6 50– 6 99 |
| 7 00– 7 49 | 1 | 2 | ...... | 3 | ...... | ...... | ...... | ...... | 17 | 65 | 773 | 18.33 | 57.25 | 7 00– 7 49 |
| 7 50– 7 99 | ...... | ...... | ...... | 1 | ...... | ...... | ...... | ...... | 4 | 13 | 117 | 18.90 | 59.50 | 7 50– 7 99 |
| 8 00– 8 99 | ...... | 4 | 1 | 2 | ...... | ...... | ...... | 2 | 11 | 115 | 705 | 23.50 | 71.25 | 8 00– 8 99 |
| 9 00– 9 99 | ...... | 4 | 1 | 1 | ...... | ...... | 1 | 1 | 16 | 100 | 469 | 27.60 | 79.00 | 9 00– 9 99 |
| 10 00–10 99 | 1 | 8 | 5 | 1 | 7 | ...... | 2 | 2 | 15 | 154 | 392 | 33.65 | 85.60 | 10 00–10 99 |
| 11 00–11 99 | 3 | 3 | 7 | 1 | ...... | ...... | ...... | ...... | 17 | 80 | 206 | 36.85 | 89.00 | 11 00–11 99 |
| 12 00–12 99 | 14 | 7 | 28 | 6 | 10 | 2 | 3 | 2 | 13 | 257 | 225 | 47.16 | 92.80 | 12 00–12 99 |
| 13 00–13 99 | 5 | 2 | 2 | 3 | 5 | ...... | 2 | ...... | 6 | 90 | 91 | 50.77 | 94.25 | 13 00–13 99 |
| 14 00–14 99 | 7 | 2 | 14 | 1 | 2 | ...... | 2 | 2 | 5 | 120 | 99 | 56.25 | 95.75 | 14 00–14 99 |
| 15 00–15 99 | 14 | 2 | 22 | 4 | 9 | 1 | 1 | 2 | 6 | 213 | 84 | 64.30 | 97.00 | 15 00–15 99 |
| 16 00–17 99 | 12 | 6 | 13 | 3 | 4 | ...... | ...... | 1 | 1 | 155 | 49 | 70.70 | 97.30 | 16 00–17 99 |
| 18 00–19 99 | 12 | 3 | 31 | ...... | 5 | ...... | 1 | 1 | 4 | 178 | 45 | 77.80 | 98.60 | 18 00–19 99 |
| 20 00–24 99 | 34 | 3 | 29 | 4 | 11 | ...... | ...... | 4 | 3 | 251 | 42 | 87.80 | 99.20 | 20 00–24 99 |
| 25 00–29 99 | 18 | 2 | 10 | ...... | 5 | 2 | 1 | 4 | 1 | 108 | 16 | 92.40 | 99.50 | 25 00–29 99 |
| 30 00–34 99 | 8 | 5 | 15 | ...... | 6 | ...... | ...... | 1 | ...... | 82 | 9 | 95.60 | 99.80 | 30 00–34 99 |
| 35 00–39 99 | 8 | ...... | 10 | ...... | 2 | ...... | 1 | 1 | ...... | 32 | ...... | 96.80 | ...... | 35 00–39 99 |
| 40 00 and over | 14 | ...... | 17 | 1 | 6 | ...... | 1 | ...... | 1 | 76 | 5 | 100.00 | 100.00 | 40 00 and over |
| Not reported | ...... | ...... | 2 | ...... | 1 | ...... | ...... | ...... | 1 | 8 | 18 | ...... | ...... | Not reported |
| Total | 151 | 54 | 207 | 34 | 74 | 5 | 15 | 26 | 156 | 2,489 | 6,047 | ...... | ...... | Total |

NEW YORK STATE

**DEPARTMENT STORES — OFFICE**

24. TABLE IX, A, 1, b NUMBER AND PER CENT. OF EMPLOYEES CLASSIFIED ACCORDING TO ACTUAL WEEKLY EARNINGS, BY OCCUPATION AND SEX

| ACTUAL WEEKLY EARNINGS IN DOLLARS | OCCUPATION | | | | | | | | | | | | | | ACTUAL WEEKLY EARNINGS IN DOLLARS |
|---|---|---|---|---|---|---|---|---|---|---|---|---|---|---|---|
| | SUPERINTENDENTS | | BOOKKEEPERS | | CLERKS | | SECRETARIES | | STENOGRAPHERS | | OFFICE BOYS AND GIRLS | | CASHIERS | | |
| | Male | Female | Male | Female | Male | Female | Male | Female | Male | Female | Male | Female | Male | Female | |
| Less than $3 00 | .... | ...... | .... | 1 | 5 | 17 | ...... | ...... | ...... | 2 | 3 | 3 | ...... | 16 | Less than $3 00 |
| $3 00–3 49... | .... | ...... | .... | ...... | 2 | 36 | ...... | ...... | ...... | ...... | 5 | 4 | 1 | 6 | ...$3 00– 3 49 |
| 3 50– 3 99... | .... | ...... | .... | 1 | 2 | 77 | ...... | ...... | ...... | 1 | 9 | 13 | ...... | 35 | ....3 50– 3 99 |
| 4 00– 4 49... | .... | ...... | .... | 1 | 31 | 142 | ...... | ...... | ...... | 2 | 42 | 20 | 1 | 70 | ....4 00– 4 49 |
| 4 50– 4 99... | .... | ...... | .... | 2 | 12 | 109 | ...... | ...... | ...... | 6 | 21 | 10 | ...... | 50 | ....4 50– 4 99 |
| 5 00– 5 49... | .... | ...... | .... | 11 | 49 | 267 | ...... | ...... | ...... | 22 | 49 | 21 | 2 | 119 | ....5 00– 5 49 |
| 5 50– 5 99... | .... | ...... | 1 | 10 | 12 | 126 | ...... | ...... | ...... | 16 | 12 | 4 | ...... | 54 | ....5 50– 5 99 |
| 6 00– 6 49... | .... | ...... | 1 | 34 | 55 | 420 | ...... | ...... | ...... | 74 | 19 | 10 | 3 | 202 | ....6 00– 6 49 |
| 6 50– 6 99... | .... | ...... | .... | 11 | 19 | 103 | ...... | 1 | ...... | 15 | 3 | ...... | ...... | 49 | ....6 50– 6 99 |
| 7 00– 7 49... | .... | ...... | 2 | 44 | 41 | 331 | ...... | ...... | 3 | 83 | 3 | 2 | 3 | 220 | ....7 00– 7 49 |
| 7 50– 7 99... | .... | ...... | 1 | 11 | 7 | 57 | ...... | ...... | ...... | 16 | ...... | ...... | 1 | 18 | ....7 50– 7 99 |
| 8 00– 8 99... | .... | ...... | 5 | 63 | 84 | 340 | ...... | ...... | 5 | 83 | 4 | 2 | 1 | 137 | ....8 00– 8 99 |
| 9 00– 9 99... | .... | ...... | 10 | 80 | 59 | 234 | ...... | ...... | 7 | 63 | 2 | ...... | 4 | 47 | ....9 00– 9 99 |
| 10 00–10 99... | .... | ...... | 8 | 83 | 119 | 153 | ...... | 1 | 3 | 60 | 1 | ...... | 6 | 57 | ...10 00–10 99 |
| 11 00–11 99... | .... | ...... | 5 | 45 | 69 | 101 | ...... | ...... | ...... | 26 | ...... | ...... | 1 | 21 | ...11 00–11 99 |
| 12 00–12 99... | .... | ...... | 25 | 65 | 206 | 82 | ...... | 3 | 2 | 36 | 1 | ...... | 4 | 19 | ...12 00–12 99 |
| 13 00–13 99... | .... | 1 | 12 | 28 | 64 | 36 | ...... | 1 | 2 | 11 | ...... | ...... | 4 | 9 | ...13 00–13 99 |
| 14 00–14 99... | .... | 1 | 9 | 29 | 103 | 39 | ...... | ...... | ...... | 15 | ...... | ...... | 3 | 9 | ...14 00–14 99 |
| 15 00–15 99... | .... | ...... | 26 | 20 | 150 | 37 | ...... | ...... | 5 | 16 | ...... | ...... | 5 | 4 | ...15 00–15 99 |
| 16 00–17 99... | .... | ...... | 36 | 9 | 91 | 19 | ...... | 1 | ...... | 3 | ...... | ...... | 10 | 6 | ...16 00–17 99 |
| 18 00–19 99... | .... | 2 | 43 | 6 | 86 | 16 | ...... | 2 | 2 | 7 | ...... | ...... | 16 | 3 | ...18 00–19 99 |
| 20 00–24 99... | 2 | ...... | 48 | 4 | 142 | 18 | 1 | ...... | 1 | 7 | ...... | ...... | 18 | 1 | ...20 00–24 99 |
| 25 00–29 99... | 6 | ...... | 12 | 2 | 62 | 7 | 1 | ...... | ...... | ...... | ...... | ...... | 3 | 4 | ...25 00–29 99 |
| 30 00–34 99... | 13 | ...... | 3 | 1 | 37 | 4 | ...... | ...... | ...... | 1 | ...... | ...... | 2 | ...... | ...30 00–34 99 |
| 35 00–39 99... | 1 | ...... | 3 | ...... | 18 | ...... | 2 | ...... | ...... | ...... | ...... | ...... | 3 | ...... | ...35 00–39 99 |
| 40 00 and over. | 14 | 1 | 6 | ...... | 21 | 2 | ...... | ...... | ...... | ...... | ...... | ...... | 5 | ...... | .40 00 and over |
| Not reported... | .... | ...... | .... | 4 | 7 | 6 | ...... | ...... | ...... | 1 | ...... | ...... | 1 | 5 | ...Not reported |
| Total..... | 36 | 5 | 256 | 565 | 1,553 | 2,779 | 4 | 9 | 30 | 566 | 174 | 89 | 97 | 1,161 | .....Total |

NEW YORK STATE

24. TABLE IX, A, 1, b — (*concluded*)

**DEPARTMENT STORES — OFFICE**

NUMBER AND PER CENT OF EMPLOYEES CLASSIFIED ACCORDING TO ACTUAL WEEKLY EARNINGS, BY OCCUPATION AND SEX

| WEEKLY RATES IN DOLLARS | OCCUPATION (*concluded*) | | | | | | | | | | | | WEEKLY RATES IN DOLLARS |
|---|---|---|---|---|---|---|---|---|---|---|---|---|---|
| | TELEPHONE OPERATORS | | AUDITORS | | DETECTIVES | | ADVERTISERS AND WINDOW DRESSERS | | TOTAL | | CUMULATIVE PER CENT FOR STATE | | |
| | Male | Female | Male | Female | Male | Female | Male | Female | Male | Female | Male | Female | |
| Less than $3 00 | ...... | 3 | ...... | 13 | 1 | ...... | 2 | ...... | 11 | 55 | .44 | .93 | Less than $3 00 |
| $3 00–$3 49 | ...... | 1 | ...... | 23 | 1 | 1 | ...... | ...... | 9 | 71 | .80 | 2.09 | $3 00– 3 49 |
| 3 50– 3 99 | ...... | 3 | ...... | 58 | ...... | ...... | 1 | ...... | 12 | 188 | 1.28 | 5.20 | 3 50– 3 99 |
| 4 00– 4 49 | ...... | 6 | ...... | 70 | ...... | 1 | ...... | ...... | 74 | 312 | 4.25 | 10.40 | 4 00– 4 49 |
| 4 50– 4 99 | ...... | 2 | ...... | 64 | ...... | ...... | ...... | ...... | 33 | 243 | 5.58 | 14.39 | 4 50– 4 99 |
| 5 00– 5 49 | ...... | 12 | 1 | 78 | ...... | ...... | 6 | ...... | 107 | 530 | 9.87 | 23.15 | 5 00– 5 49 |
| 5 50– 5 99 | ...... | 13 | ...... | 24 | ...... | ...... | 1 | ...... | 26 | 247 | 10.91 | 27.25 | 5 50– 5 99 |
| 6 00– 6 49 | ...... | 30 | 4 | 80 | ...... | ...... | 13 | 2 | 95 | 852 | 14.72 | 41.30 | 6 00– 6 49 |
| 6 50– 6 99 | ...... | 1 | 2 | 24 | ...... | ...... | 1 | ...... | 25 | 204 | 15.71 | 44.75 | 6 50– 6 99 |
| 7 00– 7 49 | ...... | 21 | 2 | 69 | 1 | 1 | 10 | 2 | 65 | 773 | 18.33 | 57.25 | 7 00– 7 49 |
| 7 50– 7 99 | ...... | 3 | 3 | 11 | ...... | ...... | 1 | 1 | 13 | 117 | 18.90 | 59.50 | 7 50– 7 99 |
| 8 00– 8 99 | 1 | 35 | 2 | 45 | ...... | ...... | 13 | ...... | 115 | 705 | 23.50 | 71.25 | 8 00– 8 99 |
| 9 00– 9 99 | 1 | 26 | 8 | 17 | 1 | ...... | 8 | 2 | 100 | 469 | 27.60 | 79.00 | 9 00– 9 99 |
| 10 00–10 99 | ...... | 18 | 8 | 12 | 2 | 4 | 7 | 4 | 154 | 392 | 33.65 | 85.60 | 10 00–10 99 |
| 11 00–11 99 | ...... | 9 | 3 | 3 | ...... | 1 | 2 | ...... | 80 | 206 | 36.85 | 89.00 | 11 00–11 99 |
| 12 00–12 99 | ...... | 6 | 7 | 8 | 3 | 3 | 9 | 3 | 257 | 225 | 47.16 | 92.80 | 12 00–12 99 |
| 13 00–13 99 | ...... | 1 | 3 | 2 | ...... | 1 | 5 | 1 | 90 | 91 | 50.77 | 94.25 | 13 00–13 99 |
| 14 00–14 99 | ...... | 2 | 2 | 2 | ...... | 1 | 3 | 1 | 120 | 99 | 56.25 | 95.75 | 14 00–14 99 |
| 15 00–15 99 | ...... | 3 | 3 | 3 | 2 | 1 | 22 | ...... | 213 | 84 | 64.30 | 97.00 | 15 00–15 99 |
| 16 00–17 99 | ...... | 1 | 2 | 4 | 3 | 5 | 13 | 1 | 155 | 49 | 70.70 | 97.30 | 16 00–17 99 |
| 18 00–19 99 | ...... | 2 | 5 | 1 | 5 | 5 | 21 | 1 | 178 | 45 | 77.80 | 98.60 | 18 00–19 99 |
| 20 00–24 99 | ...... | 2 | 3 | ...... | 6 | 9 | 30 | 1 | 251 | 42 | 87.80 | 99.20 | 20 00–24 99 |
| 25 00–29 99 | ...... | ...... | 2 | ...... | ...... | 1 | 22 | 2 | 108 | 16 | 92.40 | 99.50 | 25 00–29 99 |
| 30 00–34 99 | ...... | ...... | 3 | ...... | 3 | 1 | 21 | 2 | 82 | 9 | 95.60 | 99.80 | 30 00–34 99 |
| 35 00–39 99 | ...... | ...... | 1 | ...... | 1 | ...... | 3 | ...... | 32 | ...... | 96.80 | ...... | 35 00–39 99 |
| 40 00 and over | ...... | ...... | 2 | ...... | 2 | ...... | 26 | 2 | 76 | 5 | 100.00 | 100.00 | 40 00 and over |
| Not reported | ...... | 1 | ...... | ...... | ...... | ...... | ...... | 1 | 8 | 18 | ...... | ...... | Not reported |
| Total | 2 | 201 | 66 | 611 | 31 | 35 | 240 | | 2,489 | 6,047 | ...... | ...... | Total |

NEW YORK STATE

25. TABLE X, A, 1, b

**DEPARTMENT STORES — OFFICE**

NUMBER AND PER CENT OF EMPLOYEES CLASSIFIED ACCORDING TO ACTUAL WEEKLY EARNING, BY CONJUGAL CONDITION AND SEX

| ACTUAL WEEKLY EARNINGS IN DOLLARS | CONJUGAL CONDITION | | | | | | | | | | | | ACTUAL WEEKLY EARNINGS IN DOLLARS |
|---|---|---|---|---|---|---|---|---|---|---|---|---|---|
| | SINGLE | | MARRIED | | WIDOWED OR DIVORCED | | NOT REPORTED | | TOTAL | | CUMULATIVE PER CENT OF TOTAL | | |
| | Male | Female | Male | Female | Male | Female | Male | Female | Male | Female | Male | Female | |
| Less than $3 00 | 9 | 55 | 1 | ...... | 1 | ...... | ...... | ...... | 11 | 55 | .44 | .93 | Less than $3 00 |
| $3 00–$3 49 | 9 | 69 | ...... | 1 | ...... | 1 | ...... | ...... | 9 | 71 | .80 | 2.09 | $3 00– 3 39 |
| 3 50– 3 99 | 12 | 182 | ...... | 1 | ...... | 2 | ...... | 3 | 12 | 188 | 1.28 | 5.20 | 3 50– 3 99 |
| 4 00– 4 49 | 73 | 309 | 1 | 2 | ...... | ...... | ...... | 1 | 74 | 312 | 4.25 | 10.40 | 4 00– 4 49 |
| 4 50– 4 99 | 33 | 237 | ...... | 2 | ...... | 1 | ...... | 3 | 33 | 243 | 5.58 | 14.39 | 4 50– 4 99 |
| 5 00– 5 49 | 101 | 517 | 5 | 5 | ...... | 1 | 1 | 7 | 107 | 530 | 9.87 | 23.15 | 5 00– 5 49 |
| 5 50– 5 99 | 24 | 234 | 2 | 2 | ...... | ...... | ...... | 11 | 26 | 247 | 10.91 | 27.25 | 5 50– 5 99 |
| 6 00– 6 49 | 90 | 821 | 1 | 13 | 1 | 5 | 3 | 13 | 95 | 852 | 14.72 | 41.30 | 6 00– 6 49 |
| 6 50– 6 99 | 25 | 194 | ...... | ...... | ...... | 4 | ...... | 6 | 25 | 204 | 15.71 | 44.75 | 6 50– 6 99 |
| 7 00– 7 49 | 63 | 739 | 2 | 12 | ...... | 10 | ...... | 12 | 65 | 773 | 18.33 | 57.25 | 7 00– 7 49 |
| 7 50– 7 99 | 12 | 111 | ...... | 2 | ...... | ...... | 1 | 4 | 13 | 117 | 18.90 | 59.50 | 7 50– 7 99 |
| 8 00– 8 99 | 105 | 664 | 6 | 12 | ...... | 12 | 4 | 17 | 115 | 705 | 25.50 | 71.25 | 8 00– 8 99 |
| 9 00– 9 99 | 94 | 445 | 5 | 7 | 1 | 11 | ...... | 6 | 100 | 469 | 27.60 | 79.00 | 9 00– 9 99 |
| 10 00–10 99 | 119 | 357 | 22 | 15 | 6 | 8 | 7 | 12 | 154 | 392 | 33.65 | 85.60 | 10 00–10 99 |
| 11 00–11 99 | 60 | 193 | 17 | 1 | ...... | 6 | 3 | 6 | 80 | 206 | 36.85 | 89.00 | 11 00–11 99 |
| 12 00–12 99 | 165 | 198 | 79 | 10 | 6 | 8 | 7 | 9 | 257 | 225 | 47.16 | 92.80 | 12 00–12 99 |
| 13 00–13 99 | 60 | 77 | 27 | 8 | 1 | 2 | 2 | 4 | 90 | 91 | 50.77 | 94.25 | 13 00–13 99 |
| 14 00–14 99 | 64 | 88 | 48 | 4 | 4 | 1 | 4 | 6 | 120 | 99 | 56.25 | 95.75 | 14 00–14 99 |
| 15 00–15 99 | 101 | 72 | 97 | 3 | 8 | 8 | 7 | 1 | 213 | 84 | 64.30 | 97.00 | 15 00–15 99 |
| 16 00–17 99 | 69 | 39 | 80 | 3 | 3 | 6 | 3 | 1 | 155 | 49 | 70.70 | 97.30 | 16 00–17 99 |
| 18 00–19 99 | 72 | 37 | 92 | 3 | 6 | 4 | 8 | 1 | 178 | 45 | 77.80 | 98.60 | 18 00–19 99 |
| 20 00–24 99 | 104 | 30 | 130 | 4 | 6 | 4 | 11 | 4 | 251 | 42 | 87.80 | 99.20 | 20 00–24 99 |
| 25 00–29 99 | 24 | 13 | 81 | 1 | 3 | 1 | ...... | 1 | 108 | 16 | 92.90 | 99.50 | 25 00–29 99 |
| 30 00–34 99 | 17 | 6 | 60 | 2 | 4 | 1 | 1 | ...... | 82 | 9 | 95.60 | 99.80 | 30 00–34 99 |
| 35 00–39 99 | 4 | ...... | 26 | ...... | 2 | ...... | ...... | ...... | 32 | ...... | 96.80 | ...... | 35 00–39 99 |
| 40 00 and over | 12 | 2 | 56 | 2 | 2 | 1 | 6 | ...... | 76 | 5 | 100.00 | 100.00 | 40 00 and over |
| Not reported | 3 | 17 | 3 | ...... | 1 | ...... | 1 | 1 | 8 | 18 | ...... | ...... | Not reported |
| Total | 1,524 | 5,706 | 841 | 115 | 55 | 97 | 69 | 129 | 2,489 | 6,047 | ...... | ...... | Total |

NEW YORK STATE

DEPARTMENT STORES — OFFICE

26. TABLE XI, A, 1, b — NUMBER AND PER CENT OF EMPLOYEES CLASSIFIED ACCORDING TO ACTUAL WEEKLY EARNINGS, BY NATIVITY AND SEX

| ACTUAL WEEKLY EARNINGS IN DOLLARS | NATIVITY | | | | | | | | | | ACTUAL WEEKLY EARNINGS IN DOLLARS |
|---|---|---|---|---|---|---|---|---|---|---|---|
| | NATIVE | | FOREIGN | | NOT REPORTED | | TOTAL | | CUMULATIVE PER CENT OF TOTAL | | |
| | Male | Female | Male | Female | Male | Female | Male | Female | Male | Female | |
| Less than $3 00 | 10 | 52 | 1 | 2 | ........ | 1 | 11 | 55 | .44 | .93 | Less than $3 00 |
| $3 00–$3 49 | 9 | 64 | ........ | 5 | ........ | 2 | 9 | 71 | .80 | 2.09 | $3 00– 3 49 |
| 3 50– 3 99 | 11 | 173 | 1 | 12 | ........ | 3 | 12 | 188 | 1.28 | 5.20 | 3 50– 3 99 |
| 4 00– 4 49 | 63 | 292 | 10 | 18 | 1 | 2 | 74 | 312 | 4.25 | 10.40 | 4 00– 4 49 |
| 4 50– 4 99 | 27 | 224 | 6 | 16 | ........ | 3 | 33 | 243 | 5.58 | 14.39 | 4 50– 4 99 |
| 5 00– 5 49 | 100 | 482 | 6 | 42 | 1 | 6 | 107 | 530 | 9.87 | 23.15 | 5 00– 5 49 |
| 5 50– 5 99 | 22 | 229 | 4 | 16 | ........ | 2 | 86 | 247 | 10.91 | 27.25 | 5 50– 5 99 |
| 6 00– 6 49 | 86 | 777 | 8 | 72 | 1 | 3 | 95 | 852 | 14.72 | 41.30 | 6 00– 6 49 |
| 6 50– 6 99 | 23 | 187 | 2 | 14 | ........ | 3 | 25 | 204 | 15.71 | 44.75 | 6 50– 6 99 |
| 7 00– 7 49 | 53 | 697 | 10 | 63 | 2 | 13 | 65 | 773 | 18.33 | 57.25 | 7 00– 7 49 |
| 7 50– 7 99 | 10 | 106 | 3 | 10 | ........ | 1 | 13 | 117 | 18.90 | 59.50 | 7 50– 7 99 |
| 8 00– 8 99 | 102 | 641 | 13 | 59 | ........ | 5 | 115 | 705 | 23.50 | 71.25 | 8 00– 8 99 |
| 9 00– 9 99 | 83 | 435 | 17 | 29 | ........ | 5 | 100 | 469 | 27.60 | 79.00 | 9 00– 9 99 |
| 10 00–10 99 | 121 | 358 | 32 | 33 | 1 | 1 | 154 | 392 | 33.65 | 85.60 | 10 00–10 99 |
| 11 00–11 99 | 65 | 188 | 15 | 15 | ........ | 3 | 80 | 206 | 36.85 | 89.00 | 11 00–11 99 |
| 12 00–12 99 | 205 | 197 | 51 | 26 | 1 | 2 | 257 | 225 | 47.16 | 92.80 | 12 00–12 99 |
| 13 00–13 99 | 79 | 83 | 11 | 8 | ........ | ........ | 90 | 91 | 50.77 | 94.25 | 13 00–13 99 |
| 14 00–14 99 | 100 | 89 | 19 | 10 | 1 | ........ | 120 | 99 | 56.25 | 95.75 | 14 00–14 99 |
| 15 00–15 99 | 172 | 70 | 39 | 14 | 2 | ........ | 213 | 84 | 64.30 | 97.00 | 15 00–15 99 |
| 16 00–17 99 | 126 | 43 | 28 | 4 | 1 | 2 | 155 | 49 | 70.70 | 97.30 | 16 00–17 99 |
| 18 00–19 99 | 139 | 35 | 39 | 10 | ........ | ........ | 178 | 45 | 77.80 | 98.60 | 18 00–19 99 |
| 20 00–24 99 | 209 | 39 | 41 | 3 | 1 | ........ | 251 | 42 | 87.80 | 99.20 | 20 00–24 99 |
| 25 00–29 99 | 84 | 14 | 24 | 2 | ........ | ........ | 108 | 16 | 92.40 | 99.50 | 25 00–29 99 |
| 30 00–34 99 | 70 | 7 | 12 | 2 | ........ | ........ | 82 | 9 | 95.60 | 99.80 | 30 00–34 99 |
| 35 00–39 99 | 26 | ........ | 5 | ........ | 1 | ........ | 32 | ........ | 96.80 | ........ | 35 00–39 99 |
| 40 00 and over | 57 | 5 | 19 | ........ | ........ | ........ | 76 | 5 | 100.00 | 100.00 | 40 00 and over |
| Not reported | 6 | 17 | 2 | ........ | ........ | 1 | 8 | 18 | ........ | ........ | Not reported |
| Total | 2,058 | 5,504 | 418 | 485 | 13 | 58 | 2,489 | 6,047 | ........ | ........ | Total |

NEW YORK STATE

27. TABLE XII, A, 1, b

**DEPARTMENT STORES — OFFICE**

Number of Employees for Each Sex, Classified According to Actual Weekly Earnings, by the Number of Years in the Trade

| Actual Weekly Earnings in Dollars | Years in Trade: Less than 1 | | 1 | | 2 | | 3 | | 4 | | 5 | | 6 | | Actual Weekly Earnings in Dollars |
|---|---|---|---|---|---|---|---|---|---|---|---|---|---|---|---|
| | Male | Female | Male | Female | Male | Female | Male | Female | Male | Female | Male | Female | Male | Female | |
| Lest than $3 00 | 5 | 30 | 2 | 8 | 1 | 6 | ...... | 2 | 1 | 4 | 1 | 3 | ...... | ...... | Lest than $3 00 |
| $3 00–$3 49... | 5 | 48 | 1 | 11 | 1 | 6 | 1 | ...... | ...... | 1 | 1 | 1 | ...... | ...... | ...$3 00– 3 49 |
| 3 50– 3 99... | 5 | 113 | 4 | 54 | 2 | 9 | ...... | 5 | ...... | ...... | ...... | ...... | ...... | 1 | ... 3 50– 3 99 |
| 4 00– 4 49... | 52 | 134 | 14 | 104 | 4 | 34 | ...... | 15 | ...... | 8 | ...... | 2 | ...... | 1 | ... 4 00– 4 49 |
| 4 50– 4 99... | 11 | 77 | 18 | 66 | 2 | 44 | 1 | 25 | ...... | 11 | ...... | 4 | ...... | 1 | ... 4 50– 4 99 |
| 5 00– 5 49... | 53 | 177 | 35 | 116 | 10 | 88 | 4 | 65 | 1 | 26 | ...... | 17 | 1 | 7 | ... 5 00– 5 49 |
| 5 50– 5 99... | 3 | 39 | 9 | 50 | 9 | 60 | 1 | 39 | ...... | 18 | 1 | 14 | 1 | 1 | ... 5 50– 5 99 |
| 6 00– 6 49... | 33 | 187 | 21 | 155 | 17 | 161 | 9 | 127 | 3 | 77 | 2 | 35 | 4 | 18 | ... 6 00– 6 49 |
| 6 50– 6 99... | 3 | 16 | 6 | 25 | 6 | 16 | 7 | 41 | 2 | 30 | 1 | 17 | ...... | 13 | ... 6 50– 6 99 |
| 7 00– 7 49... | 15 | 85 | 11 | 80 | 17 | 99 | 9 | 121 | 4 | 93 | 4 | 61 | 2 | 48 | ... 7 00– 7 49 |
| 7 50– 7 99... | 1 | 3 | .... | 5 | ...... | 14 | 4 | 14 | 3 | 15 | 3 | 10 | ...... | 22 | ... 7 50– 7 99 |
| 8 00– 8 99... | 18 | 40 | 20 | 38 | 22 | 64 | 22 | 88 | 13 | 81 | 7 | 83 | 6 | 65 | ... 8 00– 8 99 |
| 9 00– 9 99... | 16 | 21 | 7 | 27 | 11 | 36 | 17 | 44 | 17 | 54 | 10 | 41 | 5 | 52 | ... 9 00– 9 99 |
| 10 00–10 99... | 30 | 11 | 21 | 12 | 16 | 27 | 21 | 35 | 9 | 40 | 14 | 30 | 11 | 39 | ...10 00–10 99 |
| 11 00–11 99... | 20 | 2 | 12 | 5 | 4 | 6 | 8 | 15 | 4 | 20 | 4 | 20 | 4 | 13 | ...11 00–11 99 |
| 12 00–12 99... | 44 | 10 | 25 | 4 | 22 | 8 | 30 | 15 | 25 | 21 | 14 | 10 | 15 | 14 | ...12 00–12 99 |
| 13 00–13 99... | 7 | 1 | 6 | ...... | 4 | 3 | 9 | 3 | 15 | 1 | 8 | 2 | 7 | 2 | ...13 00–13 99 |
| 14 00–14 99... | 6 | 2 | 7 | 1 | 9 | 4 | 11 | 5 | 12 | 7 | 12 | 5 | 6 | 5 | ...14 00–14 99 |
| 15 00–15 99... | 12 | 2 | 15 | ...... | 5 | 5 | 8 | 2 | 11 | 1 | 20 | 4 | 17 | 6 | ...15 00–15 99 |
| 16 00–17 99... | 1 | ...... | 3 | ...... | 5 | 2 | 9 | 2 | 6 | 2 | 11 | 2 | 4 | 3 | ...16 00–17 99 |
| 18 00–19 99... | 4 | ...... | 6 | ...... | 3 | 3 | 2 | 3 | 9 | 3 | 7 | 1 | 6 | 1 | ...18 00–19 99 |
| 20 00–24 99... | 7 | ...... | 9 | ...... | 8 | ...... | 1 | 1 | 7 | ...... | 6 | ...... | 8 | 4 | ...20 00–24 99 |
| 25 00–29 99... | 1 | 1 | 3 | ...... | 1 | 1 | 4 | ...... | ...... | ...... | ...... | ...... | 4 | ...... | ...25 00–29 99 |
| 30 00–34 99... | 1 | ...... | .... | ...... | 1 | 1 | 3 | ...... | 1 | ...... | ...... | ...... | 1 | ...... | ...30 00–34 99 |
| 35 00–39 99... | 1 | ...... | .... | ...... | ...... | ...... | 1 | ...... | ...... | ...... | 2 | ...... | ...... | ...... | ...35 00–39 99 |
| 40 00 and over | 1 | ...... | .... | 1 | ...... | 1 | 3 | ...... | 2 | ...... | 3 | ...... | ...... | ...... | 40 00 and over |
| Not reported... | 1 | 3 | .... | 2 | 1 | 2 | 1 | 2 | 1 | 1 | ...... | 2 | ...... | ...... | ...Not reported |
| Total..... | 356 | 1,002 | 255 | 764 | 181 | 700 | 186 | 669 | 146 | 514 | 131 | 364 | 102 | 320 | .....Total |

87. TABLE XII, A, 1, b — (*continued*)

NEW YORK STATE

**DEPARTMENT STORES — OFFICE**

NUMBER OF EMPLOYEES FOR EACH SEX, CLASSIFIED ACCORDING TO ACTUAL WEEKLY EARNINGS, BY THE NUMBER OF YEARS IN THE TRADE

| ACTUAL WEEKLY EARNINGS IN DOLLARS | YEARS IN TRADE (*continued*) | | | | | | | | | | | | | | ACTUAL WEEKLY EARNINGS IN DOLLARS |
|---|---|---|---|---|---|---|---|---|---|---|---|---|---|---|---|
| | 7 | | 8 | | 9 | | 10–14 | | 15–19 | | 20–24 | | 25–29 | | |
| | Male | Female | Male | Female | Male | Female | Male | Female | Male | Female | Male | Female | Male | Female | |
| Less than $3 00 | .... | 2 | .... | ...... | ...... | ...... | ...... | ...... | 1 | ...... | ...... | ...... | ...... | ...... | Lest than $3 00 |
| $3 00–$3 49... | .... | 1 | .... | ...... | ...... | ...... | ...... | 1 | ...... | ...... | ...... | ...... | ...... | ...... | ...$3 00– 3 49 |
| 3 50– 3 99... | .... | 1 | .... | 2 | ...... | ...... | ...... | ...... | ...... | ...... | ...... | ...... | ...... | ...... | ... 3 50– 3 99 |
| 4 00– 4 49... | .... | ...... | .... | 3 | 1 | ...... | 2 | ...... | ...... | ...... | ...... | ...... | ...... | ...... | ... 4 00– 4 49 |
| 4 50– 4 99... | .... | 3 | .... | 2 | ...... | ...... | ...... | 1 | ...... | ...... | ...... | ...... | ...... | ...... | ... 4 50– 4 99 |
| 5 00– 5 49... | .... | 5 | .... | 4 | ...... | ...... | 1 | 2 | 1 | ...... | ...... | ...... | ...... | ...... | ... 5 00– 5 49 |
| 5 50– 5 99... | .... | 3 | .... | 2 | ...... | ...... | ...... | 3 | 1 | ...... | ...... | ...... | ...... | ...... | ... 5 50– 5 99 |
| 6 00– 6 49... | 2 | 15 | .... | 8 | ...... | 5 | 2 | 6 | 1 | 2 | ...... | 1 | ...... | ...... | ... 6 00– 6 49 |
| 6 50– 6 99... | .... | 10 | .... | 4 | ...... | 4 | ...... | 6 | ...... | 3 | ...... | ...... | ...... | ...... | ... 6 50– 6 99 |
| 7 00– 7 49... | .... | 60 | .... | 22 | ...... | 13 | ...... | 33 | 1 | 5 | ...... | 3 | ...... | 1 | ... 7 00– 7 49 |
| 7 50– 7 99... | .... | 11 | .... | 7 | ...... | 3 | 1 | 6 | ...... | 1 | ...... | ...... | ...... | ...... | ... 7 50– 7 99 |
| 8 00– 8 99... | 2 | 68 | 1 | 51 | 1 | 27 | 1 | 58 | ...... | 8 | ...... | 2 | ...... | ...... | ... 8 00– 8 99 |
| 9 00– 9 99... | 5 | 48 | 3 | 37 | 2 | 27 | 2 | 54 | 1 | 9 | 1 | 5 | ...... | 1 | ... 9 00– 9 99 |
| 10 00–10 99... | 8 | 40 | 2 | 31 | 1 | 21 | 8 | 69 | 4 | 8 | 1 | 6 | 2 | 3 | ...10 00–10 99 |
| 11 00–11 99... | 8 | 19 | 2 | 15 | ...... | 16 | 10 | 49 | 1 | 14 | ...... | 5 | ...... | 1 | ...11 00–11 99 |
| 12 00–12 99... | 17 | 15 | 11 | 20 | 7 | 12 | 17 | 63 | 12 | 14 | 2 | 8 | 3 | 3 | ...12 00–12 99 |
| 13 00–13 99... | 4 | 12 | 7 | 10 | 2 | 6 | 8 | 37 | 7 | 9 | 2 | 3 | 3 | 1 | ...13 00–13 99 |
| 14 00–14 99... | 9 | 5 | 4 | 5 | 3 | 6 | 16 | 26 | 7 | 12 | 8 | 7 | 2 | 3 | ...14 00–14 99 |
| 15 00–15 99... | 19 | 8 | 13 | 6 | 5 | 1 | 40 | 29 | 13 | 10 | 13 | 3 | 7 | 1 | ...15 00–15 99 |
| 16 00–17 99... | 9 | 1 | 13 | 1 | 6 | 3 | 39 | 10 | 23 | 8 | 9 | 7 | 8 | 5 | ...16 00–17 99 |
| 18 00–19 99... | 8 | 1 | 7 | 4 | 13 | ...... | 42 | 13 | 23 | 8 | 13 | 3 | 16 | 2 | ...18 00–19 99 |
| 20 00–24 99... | 10 | ...... | 9 | 4 | 8 | 1 | 60 | 17 | 40 | 7 | 33 | 2 | 16 | 2 | ...20 00–24 99 |
| 25 00–29 99... | 2 | ...... | 3 | 1 | 2 | ...... | 31 | 4 | 23 | 5 | 13 | ...... | 9 | 1 | ...25 00–29 99 |
| 30 00–34 99... | 1 | ...... | 2 | ...... | 1 | ...... | 17 | 2 | 15 | 1 | 13 | 2 | 10 | 3 | ...30 00–34 99 |
| 35 00–39 99... | .... | ...... | .... | ...... | ...... | ...... | 3 | ...... | 7 | ...... | 6 | ...... | 3 | ...... | ...35 00–39 99 |
| 40 00 and over | 1 | ...... | 1 | 1 | 1 | ...... | 10 | ...... | 12 | 1 | 9 | ...... | 15 | ...... | 40 00 and over |
| Not reported... | .... | ...... | .... | ...... | ...... | 1 | 2 | 2 | ...... | ...... | ...... | ...... | 1 | 1 | ..Not reported |
| Total..... | 105 | 328 | 78 | 240 | 53 | 146 | 312 | 491 | 193 | 124 | 123 | 57 | 95 | 28 | .....Total |

27. TABLE XII, A, 1, b — *(concluded)*

NEW YORK STATE

**DEPARTMENT STORES — OFFICE**

NUMBER OF EMPLOYEES FOR EACH SEX, CLASSIFIED ACCORDING TO ACTUAL WEEKLY EARNINGS, BY THE NUMBER OF YEARS IN THE TRADE

| ACTUAL WEEKLY EARNINGS IN DOLLARS | YEARS IN TRADE *(concluded)* 30–34 | | 35–44 | | 45 AND OVER | NOT REPORTED | | TOTAL | | CUMULATIVE PER CENT OF TOTAL | | ACTUAL WEEKLY EARNINGS IN DOLLARS |
|---|---|---|---|---|---|---|---|---|---|---|---|---|
| | Male | Female | Male | Female | Male | Male | Female | Male | Female | Male | Female | |
| Less than $3 00 | ...... | ...... | ...... | ...... | ...... | ...... | ...... | 11 | 55 | .44 | .93 | Less than $3 00 |
| $3 00–$3 49 | ...... | ...... | ...... | ...... | ...... | ...... | 2 | 9 | 71 | .80 | 2.09 | $3 00– 3 49 |
| 3 50– 3 99 | ...... | ...... | ...... | ...... | ...... | 1 | 3 | 12 | 188 | 1.28 | 5.20 | 3 50– 3 99 |
| 4 00– 4 49 | ...... | ...... | ...... | ...... | ...... | 1 | 11 | 74 | 312 | 4.25 | 10.40 | 4 00– 4 49 |
| 4 50– 4 99 | ...... | ...... | ...... | ...... | ...... | 1 | 9 | 33 | 243 | 5.58 | 14.39 | 4 50– 4 99 |
| 5 00– 5 49 | ...... | ...... | ...... | ...... | ...... | 1 | 23 | 107 | 530 | 9.87 | 23.15 | 5 00– 5 49 |
| 5 50– 5 99 | ...... | ...... | 1 | ...... | ...... | ...... | 14 | 26 | 247 | 10.91 | 27.25 | 5 50– 5 99 |
| 6 00– 6 49 | ...... | ...... | ...... | ...... | ...... | 1 | 55 | 95 | 852 | 14.72 | 41.30 | 6 00– 6 49 |
| 6 50– 6 99 | ...... | ...... | ...... | ...... | ...... | ...... | 20 | 25 | 204 | 15.71 | 44.75 | 6 50– 6 99 |
| 7 00– 7 49 | ...... | ...... | ...... | ...... | ...... | 2 | 49 | 65 | 773 | 18.33 | 57.25 | 7 00– 7 49 |
| 7 50– 7 99 | ...... | ...... | ...... | ...... | ...... | 1 | 6 | 13 | 117 | 18.90 | 59.50 | 7 50– 7 99 |
| 8 00– 8 99 | ...... | 1 | ...... | ...... | ...... | 2 | 31 | 115 | 705 | 23.50 | 71.25 | 8 00– 8 99 |
| 9 00– 9 99 | ...... | ...... | ...... | ...... | ...... | 3 | 13 | 100 | 469 | 27.60 | 79.00 | 9 00– 9 99 |
| 10 00–10 99 | ...... | 1 | ...... | ...... | ...... | 6 | 19 | 154 | 392 | 33.65 | 85.60 | 10 00–10 99 |
| 11 00–11 99 | ...... | ...... | ...... | ...... | ...... | 3 | 6 | 80 | 206 | 36.85 | 89.00 | 11 00–11 99 |
| 12 00–12 99 | 5 | 1 | 1 | 1 | 1 | 6 | 6 | 257 | 225 | 47.16 | 92.80 | 12 00–12 99 |
| 13 00–13 99 | 1 | ...... | ...... | ...... | ...... | ...... | 1 | 90 | 91 | 50.77 | 94.25 | 13 00–13 99 |
| 14 00–14 99 | 2 | 1 | 2 | ...... | 1 | 3 | 5 | 120 | 99 | 56.25 | 95.75 | 14 00–14 99 |
| 15 00–15 99 | 3 | 1 | 2 | 1 | 1 | 9 | 4 | 213 | 84 | 64.30 | 97.00 | 15 00–15 99 |
| 16 00–17 99 | 3 | 2 | 1 | ...... | 1 | 4 | 1 | 155 | 49 | 70.70 | 97.30 | 16 00–17 99 |
| 18 00–19 99 | 10 | ...... | 4 | ...... | 1 | 4 | 3 | 178 | 45 | 77.80 | 98.60 | 18 00–19 99 |
| 20 00–24 99 | 16 | 2 | 10 | ...... | 1 | 2 | 2 | 251 | 42 | 87.80 | 99.20 | 20 00–24 99 |
| 25 00–29 99 | 4 | 1 | 5 | 1 | 1 | 2 | 1 | 108 | 16 | 92.40 | 99.50 | 25 00–29 99 |
| 30 00–34 99 | 7 | ...... | 6 | ...... | 1 | 2 | ...... | 82 | 9 | 95.60 | 99.80 | 30 00–34 99 |
| 35 00–39 99 | 7 | ...... | 1 | ...... | 1 | ...... | ...... | 32 | ...... | 96.80 | ...... | 35 00–39 99 |
| 40 00 and over | 6 | ...... | 8 | ...... | 3 | 1 | 1 | 76 | 5 | 100.00 | 100.00 | 40 00 and over |
| Not reported | 1 | ...... | ...... | ...... | ...... | ...... | 2 | 8 | 18 | ...... | ...... | Not reported |
| Total | 65 | 10 | 41 | 3 | 12 | 55 | 287 | 2,489 | 6,047 | ...... | ...... | Total |

28. TABLE XIII, A, 1, b

## NEW YORK STATE
## DEPARTMENT STORES — OFFICE

NUMBER OF EMPLOYEES FOR EACH SEX CLASSIFIED ACCORDING TO ACTUAL WEEKLY EARNINGS, BY THE NUMBER OF YEARS WITH THE FIRM

| ACTUAL WEEKLY EARNINGS IN DOLLARS | YEARS WITH FIRM | | | | | | | | | | | | | | ACTUAL WEEKLY EARNINGS IN DOLLARS |
|---|---|---|---|---|---|---|---|---|---|---|---|---|---|---|---|
| | LESS THAN 1 | | 1 | | 2 | | 3 | | 4 | | 5 | | 6 | | |
| | Male | Female | Male | Female | Male | Female | Male | Female | Male | Female | Male | Female | Male | Female | |
| Less than $3 00 | 5 | 37 | 2 | 8 | 1 | 3 | ...... | 2 | 2 | 3 | ...... | 1 | ...... | ...... | Less than $3 00 |
| $3 00–$3 49... | 7 | 51 | 1 | 10 | ...... | 8 | 1 | ...... | ...... | 1 | ...... | ...... | ...... | ...... | ...$3 00– 3 49 |
| 3 50– 3 99... | 7 | 125 | 4 | 49 | 1 | 8 | ...... | 2 | ...... | ...... | ...... | ...... | ...... | 1 | ....3 50– 3 99 |
| 4 00– 4 49... | 55 | 151 | 15 | 103 | 1 | 34 | ...... | 13 | ...... | 5 | ...... | 2 | ...... | 2 | ....4 00– 4 49 |
| 4 50– 4 99... | 15 | 90 | 15 | 71 | 2 | 37 | 1 | 25 | ...... | 12 | ...... | 2 | ...... | 1 | ....4 50– 4 99 |
| 5 00– 5 49... | 61 | 216 | 29 | 124 | 9 | 91 | 3 | 51 | 1 | 16 | ...... | 17 | 2 | 4 | ....5 00– 5 49 |
| 5 50– 5 99... | 6 | 71 | 9 | 52 | 8 | 54 | 1 | 36 | ...... | 19 | 1 | 9 | ...... | 2 | ....5 50– 5 99 |
| 6 00– 6 49... | 41 | 299 | 21 | 166 | 16 | 157 | 7 | 94 | 3 | 60 | ...... | 31 | 4 | 16 | ....6 00– 6 49 |
| 6 50– 6 99... | 5 | 51 | 6 | 33 | 4 | 17 | 7 | 37 | 2 | 23 | 1 | 13 | ...... | 13 | ....6 50– 6 99 |
| 7 00– 7 49... | 18 | 188 | 16 | 121 | 15 | 104 | 8 | 107 | 4 | 69 | 3 | 46 | 1 | 39 | ....7 00– 7 49 |
| 7 50– 7 99... | 3 | 21 | 2 | 9 | 1 | 13 | 3 | 20 | 1 | 10 | 2 | 8 | ...... | 15 | ....7 50– 7 99 |
| 8 00– 8 99... | 40 | 142 | 22 | 93 | 17 | 63 | 12 | 81 | 11 | 74 | 5 | 61 | 3 | 41 | ....8 00– 8 99 |
| 9 00– 9 99... | 31 | 69 | 11 | 61 | 16 | 47 | 6 | 61 | 14 | 38 | 7 | 33 | 2 | 42 | ....9 00– 9 99 |
| 10 00–10 99... | 66 | 58 | 21 | 43 | 15 | 43 | 13 | 50 | 7 | 28 | 8 | 15 | 7 | 27 | ...10 00–10 99 |
| 11 00–11 99... | 38 | 21 | 12 | 15 | 9 | 13 | 5 | 21 | 3 | 19 | 4 | 16 | 2 | 14 | ...11 00–11 99 |
| 12 00–12 99... | 93 | 35 | 38 | 17 | 28 | 20 | 23 | 23 | 22 | 12 | 7 | 5 | 8 | 14 | ...12 00–12 99 |
| 13 00–13 99... | 21 | 8 | 13 | 4 | 8 | 7 | 8 | 9 | 12 | 5 | 5 | 5 | 8 | 5 | ...13 00–13 99 |
| 14 00–14 99... | 25 | 6 | 14 | 6 | 11 | 10 | 12 | 14 | 9 | 3 | 10 | 1 | 5 | 4 | ...14 00–14 99 |
| 15 00–15 99... | 49 | 10 | 35 | 10 | 17 | 5 | 12 | 5 | 9 | 3 | 21 | 4 | 11 | 4 | ...15 00–15 99 |
| 16 00–17 99... | 21 | 3 | 9 | 1 | 12 | 2 | 16 | 2 | 10 | 4 | 13 | 5 | 4 | 3 | ...16 00–17 99 |
| 18 00–19 99... | 27 | 4 | 19 | 4 | 11 | 7 | 8 | 6 | 7 | 1 | 5 | ...... | 4 | ...... | ...18 00–19 99 |
| 20 00–24 99... | 27 | 1 | 14 | 3 | 22 | 4 | 15 | 5 | 9 | ...... | 11 | 1 | 8 | 2 | ...20 00–24 99 |
| 25 00–29 99... | 8 | 2 | 9 | 1 | 7 | ...... | 10 | 1 | 6 | ...... | 5 | 1 | 2 | ...... | ...25 00–29 99 |
| 30 00–34 99... | 7 | 2 | 2 | 2 | 4 | 1 | 6 | ...... | 3 | ...... | 4 | ...... | 2 | ...... | ...30 00–34 99 |
| 35 00–39 99... | 5 | ...... | 1 | ...... | ...... | ...... | 5 | ...... | 1 | ...... | ...... | ...... | 1 | ...... | ...35 00–39 99 |
| 40 00 and over. | 6 | ...... | 4 | 1 | 4 | 2 | 5 | ...... | 4 | ...... | 4 | ...... | 1 | ...... | .40 00 and over |
| Not reported... | 1 | 3 | .... | 3 | 2 | 2 | 1 | 3 | ...... | 3 | ...... | ...... | ...... | 1 | ...Not reported |
| Total..... | 688 | 1,664 | 344 | 1,010 | 241 | 752 | 188 | 668 | 140 | 408 | 116 | 276 | 75 | 250 | .....Total |

NEW YORK STATE

28. TABLE XIII, A, 1, b — *(continued)*

**DEPARTMENT STORES — OFFICE**

NUMBER OF EMPLOYEES FOR EACH SEX CLASSIFIED ACCORDING TO ACTUAL WEEKLY EARNINGS, BY THE NUMBER OF YEARS WITH THE FIRM

| ACTUAL WEEKLY EARNINGS IN DOLLARS | YEARS WITH FIRM *(continued)* | | | | | | | | | | | | | | ACTUAL WEEKLY EARNINGS IN DOLLARS |
|---|---|---|---|---|---|---|---|---|---|---|---|---|---|---|---|
| | 7 | | 8 | | 9 | | 10–14 | | 15–19 | | 20–24 | | 25–29 | | |
| | Male | Female | Male | Female | Male | Female | Male | Female | Male | Female | Male | Female | Male | Female | |
| Less than $3 00 | .... | 1 | .... | .... | .... | .... | .... | .... | .... | .... | .... | .... | .... | .... | Less than $3 00 |
| $3 00–$3 49... | .... | .... | .... | .... | .... | .... | .... | .... | .... | .... | .... | .... | .... | .... | ...$3 00– 3 49 |
| 3 50– 3 99... | .... | 1 | .... | 1 | .... | .... | .... | .... | .... | .... | .... | .... | .... | .... | ....3 50– 3 99 |
| 4 00– 4 49... | .... | .... | .... | 1 | 1 | .... | 2 | .... | .... | .... | .... | .... | .... | .... | ....4 00– 4 49 |
| 4 50– 4 99... | .... | 2 | .... | .... | .... | .... | .... | 2 | .... | .... | .... | .... | .... | .... | ....4 50– 4 99 |
| 5 00– 5 49... | .... | 4 | .... | 3 | .... | .... | .... | 2 | .... | .... | .... | .... | .... | .... | ....5 00– 5 49 |
| 5 50– 5 99... | .... | 1 | .... | 1 | .... | .... | 1 | 1 | .... | .... | .... | .... | .... | .... | ....5 50– 5 99 |
| 6 00– 6 49... | 1 | 11 | .... | 6 | .... | 3 | 1 | 4 | 1 | 2 | .... | .... | .... | .... | ....6 00– 6 49 |
| 6 50– 6 99... | .... | 9 | .... | 2 | .... | 1 | .... | 2 | .... | 2 | .... | .... | .... | .... | ....6 50– 6 99 |
| 7 00– 7 49... | .... | 40 | .... | 18 | .... | 10 | .... | 23 | .... | 4 | .... | 3 | .... | 1 | ....7 00– 7 49 |
| 7 50– 7 99... | .... | 8 | .... | 5 | .... | 1 | 1 | 5 | .... | 1 | .... | .... | .... | .... | ....7 50– 7 99 |
| 8 00– 8 99... | 3 | 41 | 1 | 36 | .... | 18 | 1 | 45 | .... | 7 | .... | .... | .... | .... | ....8 00– 8 99 |
| 9 00– 9 99... | 3 | 32 | 2 | 28 | 4 | 15 | 1 | 34 | 1 | 3 | .... | 3 | .... | .... | ....9 00– 9 99 |
| 10 00–10 99... | 4 | 33 | 2 | 15 | 1 | 20 | 6 | 43 | 2 | 6 | .... | 5 | 1 | 3 | ...10 00–10 99 |
| 11 00–11 99... | 4 | 12 | .... | 7 | .... | 13 | 3 | 39 | .... | 11 | .... | 4 | .... | .... | ...11 00–11 99 |
| 12 00–12 99... | 12 | 13 | 4 | 12 | 3 | 5 | 11 | 49 | 3 | 10 | 1 | 5 | 2 | 2 | ...12 00–12 99 |
| 13 00–13 99... | 5 | 7 | 1 | 7 | 1 | 5 | 5 | 21 | 1 | 6 | .... | 1 | 1 | 1 | ...13 00–13 99 |
| 14 00–14 99... | 6 | 6 | 4 | 8 | 4 | 1 | 12 | 25 | 6 | 8 | 1 | 5 | 1 | 2 | ...14 00–14 99 |
| 15 00–15 99... | 10 | 5 | 6 | 3 | 5 | 1 | 26 | 24 | 6 | 4 | 3 | 3 | 1 | 1 | ...15 00–15 99 |
| 16 00–17 99... | 7 | 1 | 10 | 1 | 7 | 5 | 24 | 7 | 14 | 5 | 5 | 4 | 1 | 5 | ...16 00–17 99 |
| 18 00–19 99... | 8 | 1 | 3 | 1 | 8 | .... | 28 | 9 | 23 | 5 | 13 | 4 | 6 | 2 | ...18 00–19 99 |
| 20 00–24 99... | 14 | .... | 4 | 4 | 4 | 1 | 44 | 11 | 36 | 4 | 26 | 3 | 10 | 1 | ...20 00–24 99 |
| 25 00–29 99... | 4 | .... | 2 | .... | 2 | 1 | 23 | 3 | 15 | 5 | 5 | 1 | 5 | .... | ...25 00–29 99 |
| 30 00–34 99... | 2 | 1 | 4 | .... | 3 | .... | 14 | .... | 14 | .... | 8 | 2 | 5 | 1 | ...30 00–34 99 |
| 35 00–39 99... | .... | .... | 2 | .... | .... | .... | 5 | .... | 4 | .... | 3 | .... | 1 | .... | ...35 00–39 99 |
| 40 00 and over. | 2 | .... | 2 | 1 | 1 | .... | 9 | .... | 12 | 1 | 4 | .... | 10 | .... | .40 00 and over |
| Not reported... | .... | .... | .... | .... | .... | .... | 3 | 1 | .... | .... | .... | .... | 1 | 1 | ...Not reported |
| Total..... | 85 | 229 | 47 | 160 | 44 | 100 | 220 | 350 | 138 | 84 | 69 | 43 | 45 | 21 | .....Total |

NEW YORK STATE

28. TABLE XIII, A, 1, b — (*concluded*) DEPARTMENT STORES — OFFICE

NUMBER OF EMPLOYEES FOR EACH SEX CLASSIFIED ACCORDING TO ACTUAL WEEKLY EARNINGS, BY THE NUMBER OF YEARS WITH THE FIRM

| ACTUAL WEEKLY EARNINGS IN DOLLARS | YEARS WITH FIRM (*concluded*) | | | | | | | | | | | ACTUAL WEEKLY EARNINGS IN DOLLARS |
|---|---|---|---|---|---|---|---|---|---|---|---|---|
| | 30–34 | | 35–44 | | 45 AND OVER | NOT REPORTED | | TOTAL | | CUMULATIVE PER CENT OF TOTAL | | |
| | Male | Female | Male | Female | Male | Male | Female | Male | Female | Male | Female | |
| Less than $3 00 | ....... | ....... | ....... | ....... | ....... | 1 | ....... | 11 | 55 | .44 | .93 | Less than $3 00 |
| $3 00–$3 49 | ....... | ....... | ....... | ....... | ....... | ....... | 1 | 9 | 71 | .80 | 2.09 | $3 00– 3 49 |
| 3 50– 3 99 | ....... | ....... | ....... | ....... | ....... | ....... | 1 | 12 | 188 | 1.28 | 5.20 | 3 50– 3 99 |
| 4 00– 4 49 | ....... | ....... | ....... | ....... | ....... | ....... | 1 | 74 | 312 | 4.25 | 10.40 | 4 00– 4 49 |
| 4 50– 4 99 | ....... | ....... | ....... | ....... | ....... | ....... | 1 | 33 | 243 | 5.58 | 14.39 | 4 50– 4 99 |
| 5 00– 5 49 | ....... | ....... | ....... | ....... | ....... | 2 | 2 | 107 | 530 | 9.87 | 23.15 | 5 00– 5 49 |
| 5 50– 5 99 | ....... | ....... | ....... | ....... | ....... | ....... | 1 | 26 | 247 | 10.91 | 27.25 | 5 50– 5 99 |
| 6 00– 6 49 | ....... | ....... | ....... | ....... | ....... | ....... | 3 | 95 | 852 | 14.72 | 41.30 | 6 00– 6 49 |
| 6 50– 6 99 | ....... | ....... | ....... | ....... | ....... | ....... | 1 | 25 | 204 | 15.71 | 44.75 | 6 50– 6 99 |
| 7 00– 7 49 | ....... | ....... | ....... | ....... | ....... | ....... | ....... | 65 | 773 | 18.33 | 57.25 | 7 00– 7 49 |
| 7 50– 7 99 | ....... | ....... | ....... | ....... | ....... | ....... | 1 | 13 | 117 | 18.90 | 59.50 | 7 50– 7 99 |
| 8 00– 8 99 | ....... | ....... | ....... | ....... | ....... | ....... | 3 | 115 | 705 | 23.50 | 71.25 | 8 00– 8 99 |
| 9 00– 9 99 | ....... | ....... | ....... | ....... | ....... | 2 | 2 | 100 | 469 | 27.60 | 79.00 | 9 00– 9 99 |
| 10 00–10 99 | ....... | 1 | ....... | ....... | ....... | 1 | 2 | 154 | 392 | 33.65 | 85.60 | 10 00–10 99 |
| 11 00–11 99 | ....... | ....... | ....... | ....... | ....... | ....... | 1 | 80 | 206 | 36.85 | 89.00 | 11 00–11 99 |
| 12 00–12 99 | 1 | 1 | ....... | ....... | ....... | 1 | 2 | 257 | 225 | 47.16 | 92.80 | 12 00–12 99 |
| 13 00–13 99 | ....... | ....... | ....... | ....... | ....... | 1 | ....... | 90 | 91 | 50.77 | 94.25 | 13 00–13 99 |
| 14 00–14 99 | ....... | ....... | ....... | ....... | ....... | ....... | ....... | 120 | 99 | 56.25 | 95.75 | 14 00–14 99 |
| 15 00–15 99 | 1 | 1 | ....... | ....... | ....... | 1 | 1 | 213 | 84 | 64.30 | 97.00 | 15 00–15 99 |
| 16 00–17 99 | ....... | 1 | ....... | ....... | ....... | 2 | ....... | 155 | 49 | 70.70 | 97.30 | 16 00–17 99 |
| 18 00–19 99 | 6 | ....... | 1 | ....... | ....... | 1 | 1 | 178 | 45 | 77.80 | 98.60 | 18 00–19 99 |
| 20 00–24 99 | 7 | 1 | ....... | 1 | ....... | ....... | ....... | 251 | 42 | 87.80 | 99.20 | 20 00–24 99 |
| 25 00–29 99 | 4 | 1 | ....... | ....... | ....... | 1 | ....... | 108 | 16 | 92.40 | 99.50 | 25 00–29 99 |
| 30 00–34 99 | 2 | ....... | 1 | ....... | ....... | 1 | ....... | 82 | 9 | 95.60 | 99.80 | 30 00–34 99 |
| 35 00–39 99 | 4 | ....... | ....... | ....... | ....... | ....... | ....... | 32 | ....... | 96.80 | 99.80 | 35 00–39 99 |
| 40 00 and over | 5 | ....... | 2 | ....... | 1 | ....... | ....... | 76 | 5 | 100.00 | 100.00 | 40 00 and over |
| Not reported | ....... | ....... | ....... | ....... | ....... | ....... | 1 | 8 | 18 | ....... | ....... | Not reported |
| Total | 30 | 6 | 4 | 1 | 1 | 14 | 25 | 2,489 | 6,047 | ....... | ....... | Total |

NEW YORK STATE

DEPARTMENT STORES — SHIPPING AND DELIVERY

29. TABLE VII, A, 1, c — Number and Per Cent. of Employees by Sex According to Occupation and Nativity

| Nativity | Occupation | | | | | | | | | | | | | |
|---|---|---|---|---|---|---|---|---|---|---|---|---|---|---|
| | Total | | Foremen and forewomen | | Clerks and routers | | Drivers | Wagon boys and helpers | Chauffeurs | General labor | Packing | | Stablemen | Not reported |
| | Male | Female | Male | Female | Male | Female | Male | Male | Male | Male | Male | Female | Male | Male |
| Native | 3,496 | 54 | 74 | 1 | 431 | 31 | 925 | 1,141 | 274 | 49 | 518 | 22 | 84 | ....... |
| Foreign | 940 | 4 | 21 | ...... | 106 | ...... | 127 | 122 | 37 | 10 | 296 | 4 | 221 | ....... |
| Not reported | 29 | ...... | 1 | ...... | 7 | ...... | 3 | 11 | 3 | ...... | 3 | ...... | ...... | 1 |
| Total | 4,465 | 58 | 96 | 1 | 544 | 31 | 1,055 | 1,274 | 314 | 59 | 817 | 26 | 305 | 1 |
| Per cent. of total | 100.00 | 100.00 | 2.2 | 1.7 | 12.2 | 53.5 | 23.6 | 28.6 | 7.0 | 1.3 | 18.3 | 44.8 | 6.8 | ....... |

NEW YORK STATE

DEPARTMENT STORES — SHIPPING AND DELIVERY

30. TABLE V, A, 1, c — NUMBER AND PER CENT. OF EMPLOYEES EARNING SPECIFIED WEEKLY RATES BY AGE GROUPS AND SEX

| WEEKLY RATES IN DOLLARS | Age Groups in Years | | | | | | | | | | | | | WEEKLY RATES IN DOLLARS |
|---|---|---|---|---|---|---|---|---|---|---|---|---|---|---|
| | 14–15 | 16–17 | | 18–20 | | 21–24 | | 25–29 | | 30–34 | | 35–39 | | |
| | Male | Male | Female | Male | Female | Male | Female | Male | Female | Male | Female | Male | Female | |
| Less than $3 00 | 3 | .... | ...... | .... | ...... | .... | ...... | ...... | ...... | ...... | ...... | ...... | ...... | Less than $3 00 |
| $3 00–$3 49 | ...... | .... | ...... | 1 | ...... | .... | ...... | ...... | ...... | ...... | ...... | ...... | ...... | $3 00–$3 49 |
| 3 50– 3 99 | 13 | 2 | ...... | .... | ...... | .... | ...... | ...... | ...... | ...... | ...... | ...... | ...... | 3 50– 3 99 |
| 4 00– 4 49 | 20 | 7 | 1 | .... | 1 | .... | ...... | ...... | ...... | ...... | ...... | ...... | ...... | 4 00– 4 49 |
| 4 50– 4 99 | 9 | 12 | 1 | .... | ...... | .... | ...... | ...... | ...... | ...... | ...... | ...... | ...... | 4 50– 4 99 |
| 5 00– 5 49 | 18 | 81 | 5 | 11 | 2 | 1 | 1 | ...... | ...... | 1 | ...... | ...... | ...... | 5 00– 5 49 |
| 5 50– 5 99 | ...... | 3 | ...... | 8 | ...... | 1 | ...... | ...... | ...... | ...... | ...... | ...... | ...... | 5 50– 5 99 |
| 6 00– 6 49 | 2 | 59 | 1 | 27 | 5 | 2 | 2 | 1 | 1 | ...... | ...... | ...... | ...... | 6 00– 6 49 |
| 6 50– 6 99 | ...... | 2 | ...... | 5 | ...... | .... | ...... | ...... | ...... | 1 | ...... | ...... | 1 | 6 50– 6 99 |
| 7 00– 7 49 | ...... | 33 | ...... | 80 | 3 | 11 | 1 | 2 | ...... | 1 | ...... | 2 | ...... | 7 00– 7 49 |
| 7 50– 7 99 | 1 | 33 | ...... | 150 | ...... | 28 | ...... | 1 | ...... | ...... | ...... | ...... | ...... | 7 50– 7 99 |
| 8 00– 8 99 | 1 | 43 | 1 | 235 | ...... | 65 | 7 | 11 | 1 | 6 | ...... | 2 | ...... | 8 00– 8 99 |
| 9 00– 9 99 | ...... | 3 | 1 | 104 | ...... | 59 | 4 | 12 | 1 | 5 | 2 | 3 | 1 | 9 00– 9 99 |
| 10 00–10 99 | ...... | 2 | 2 | 80 | ...... | 101 | 1 | 38 | ...... | 24 | 1 | 17 | ...... | 10 00–10 99 |
| 11 00–11 99 | ...... | 4 | ...... | 26 | 1 | 50 | ...... | 21 | ...... | 11 | ...... | 11 | ...... | 11 00–11 99 |
| 12 00–12 99 | ...... | 1 | ...... | 46 | ...... | 150 | ...... | 121 | ...... | 68 | ...... | 84 | ...... | 12 00–12 99 |
| 13 00–13 99 | ...... | 2 | ...... | 13 | ...... | 87 | ...... | 50 | ...... | 43 | ...... | 32 | ...... | 13 00–13 99 |
| 14 00–14 99 | ...... | .... | 1 | 3 | ...... | 57 | ...... | 65 | ...... | 60 | ...... | 48 | ...... | 14 00–14 99 |
| 15 00–15 99 | ...... | 1 | 1 | 36 | ...... | 227 | 1 | 178 | ...... | 111 | ...... | 81 | ...... | 15 00–15 99 |
| 16 00–17 99 | ...... | .... | ...... | 4 | ...... | 38 | ...... | 82 | ...... | 78 | ...... | 79 | ...... | 16 00–17 99 |
| 18 00–19 99 | ...... | .... | ...... | .... | ...... | 12 | ...... | 11 | ...... | 22 | ...... | 30 | ...... | 18 00–19 99 |
| 20 00–24 99 | ...... | .... | ...... | .... | ...... | 3 | ...... | 5 | ...... | 15 | ...... | 17 | ...... | 20 00–24 99 |
| 25 00–29 99 | ...... | .... | ...... | .... | ...... | 2 | ...... | 1 | ...... | 3 | ...... | 10 | ...... | 25 00–29 99 |
| 30 00–34 99 | ...... | .... | ...... | .... | ...... | 1 | ...... | ...... | ...... | 1 | ...... | 1 | ...... | 30 00–34 99 |
| 35 00–39 99 | ...... | .... | ...... | .... | ...... | .... | ...... | 1 | ...... | 1 | ...... | 2 | ...... | 35 00–39 99 |
| 40 00 and over | ...... | .... | ...... | .... | ...... | .... | ...... | ...... | ...... | ...... | 1 | 1 | ...... | 40 00 and over |
| Not reported | 2 | .... | ...... | .... | ...... | 1 | ...... | 1 | ...... | ...... | ...... | 1 | ...... | Not reported |
| Total | 69 | 288 | 14 | 829 | 12 | 896 | 17 | 601 | 3 | 451 | 4 | 421 | 2 | Total |

NEW YORK STATE

30. TABLE V, A, 1, c — (*concluded*)

**DEPARTMENT STORES — SHIPPING AND DELIVERY**

NUMBER AND PER CENT. OF EMPLOYEES EARNING SPECIFIED WEEKLY RATES BY AGE GROUPS AND SEX

| WEEKLY RATES IN DOLLARS | AGE GROUPS IN YEARS | | | | | | | | | | | | WEEKLY RATES IN DOLLARS |
|---|---|---|---|---|---|---|---|---|---|---|---|---|---|
| | 40–44 | | 45–54 | | 55–64 | 65 AND OVER | NOT REPORTED | | TOTAL | | CUMULATIVE PER CENT. FOR TOTAL | | |
| | Male | Female | Male | Female | Male | Male | Male | Female | Male | Female | Male | Female | |
| Less than $3 00 | ....... | ....... | ....... | ....... | ....... | ....... | ....... | ....... | 3 | ....... | .07 | ....... | Less than $3 00 |
| 3 00– 3 49 | ....... | ....... | ....... | ....... | ....... | ....... | ....... | ....... | 1 | ....... | .09 | ....... | $3 00–$3 49 |
| 3 50– 3 99 | ....... | ....... | ....... | ....... | ....... | ....... | ....... | ....... | 15 | ....... | .43 | ....... | 3 50– 3 99 |
| 4 00– 4 49 | ....... | ....... | ....... | ....... | ....... | ....... | ....... | ....... | 27 | 2 | 1.31 | 3.42 | 4 00– 4 49 |
| 4 50– 4 99 | ....... | ....... | ....... | ....... | ....... | ....... | ....... | ....... | 21 | 1 | 1.50 | 5.17 | 4 50– 4 99 |
| 5 00– 5 49 | ....... | ....... | ....... | ....... | ....... | ....... | 1 | ....... | 113 | 8 | 4.03 | 18.98 | 5 00– 5 49 |
| 5 50– 5 99 | ....... | ....... | ....... | ....... | ....... | ....... | 1 | ....... | 13 | ....... | 4.33 | ....... | 5 50– 5 99 |
| 6 00– 6 49 | ....... | ....... | ....... | ....... | ....... | ....... | ....... | ....... | 91 | 9 | 6.45 | 34.44 | 6 00– 6 49 |
| 6 50– 6 99 | ....... | ....... | ....... | ....... | ....... | ....... | ....... | 1 | 8 | 2 | 6.51 | 37.97 | 6 50– 6 99 |
| 7 00– 7 49 | ....... | ....... | ....... | ....... | 1 | 1 | ....... | ....... | 131 | 4 | 9.48 | 44.8 | 7 00– 7 49 |
| 7 50– 7 99 | 1 | 1 | ....... | 1 | ....... | ....... | 3 | 2 | 217 | 4 | 14.34 | 51.7 | 7 50– 7 99 |
| 8 00– 8 99 | 1 | ....... | 3 | ....... | ....... | ....... | 5 | ....... | 372 | 9 | 22.46 | 67.3 | 8 00– 8 99 |
| 9 00– 9 99 | 1 | ....... | 4 | ....... | 2 | ....... | 4 | ....... | 197 | 9 | 27.10 | 82.8 | 9 00– 9 99 |
| 10 00–10 99 | 14 | ....... | 29 | ....... | 8 | 5 | 2 | ....... | 320 | 4 | 34.24 | 89.7 | 10 00–10 99 |
| 11 00–11 99 | 16 | ....... | 25 | ....... | 11 | 2 | 2 | 1 | 179 | 2 | 38.30 | 93.1 | 11 00–11 99 |
| 12 00–12 99 | 59 | ....... | 104 | ....... | 39 | 6 | 3 | ....... | 681 | ....... | 53.6 | ....... | 12 00–12 99 |
| 13 00–13 99 | 28 | ....... | 36 | ....... | 13 | ....... | ....... | ....... | 304 | ....... | 60.3 | ....... | 13 00–13 99 |
| 14 00–14 99 | 42 | ....... | 51 | ....... | 14 | 3 | 2 | ....... | 345 | 1 | 68.2 | 94.8 | 14 00–14 99 |
| 15 00–15 99 | 44 | ....... | 58 | ....... | 11 | 1 | 3 | ....... | 751 | 2 | 85.0 | 98.3 | 15 00–15 99 |
| 16 00–17 99 | 56 | ....... | 67 | ....... | 15 | 1 | ....... | ....... | 420 | ....... | 94.2 | ....... | 16 00–17 99 |
| 18 00–19 99 | 15 | ....... | 22 | ....... | 3 | 1 | 1 | ....... | 117 | ....... | 96.9 | ....... | 18 00–19 99 |
| 20 00–24 99 | 16 | ....... | 15 | ....... | 5 | ....... | 2 | ....... | 78 | ....... | 98.6 | ....... | 20 00–24 99 |
| 25 00–29 99 | 9 | ....... | 2 | ....... | 1 | ....... | ....... | ....... | 28 | ....... | 99.4 | ....... | 25 00–29 99 |
| 30 00–34 99 | 3 | ....... | 5 | ....... | ....... | ....... | ....... | ....... | 11 | ....... | 99.6 | ....... | 30 00–34 99 |
| 35 00–39 99 | 1 | ....... | 2 | ....... | 1 | ....... | ....... | ....... | 8 | ....... | 99.8 | ....... | 35 00–39 99 |
| 40 00 and over | 2 | ....... | 4 | ....... | ....... | ....... | ....... | ....... | 7 | 1 | 100.00 | 100.00 | 40 00 and over |
| Not reported | ....... | ....... | ....... | ....... | ....... | ....... | 2 | ....... | 7 | ....... | ....... | ....... | Not reported |
| Total | 308 | 1 | 427 | 1 | 124 | 20 | 31 | 4 | 4,465 | 58 | ....... | ....... | Total |

NEW YORK STATE

DEPARTMENT STORES — SHIPPING AND DELIVERY

31. TABLE VIII, A, 1, c — NUMBER AND PER CENT. OF EMPLOYEES EARNING SPECIFIED WEEKLY RATES BY OCCUPATION AND SEX

| WEEKLY RATES IN DOLLARS | OCCUPATION: FOREMEN AND FOREWOMEN | | CLERKS AND ROUTERS | | DRIVERS | WAGON BOYS AND HELPERS | CHAUFFEURS | GENERAL LABOR | PACKING | | STABLEMEN | NOT REPORTED | TOTAL | | CUMULATIVE PER CENT. FOR TOTAL | | WEEKLY RATES IN DOLLARS |
|---|---|---|---|---|---|---|---|---|---|---|---|---|---|---|---|---|---|
| | Male | Female | Male | Female | Male | Male | Male | Male | Male | Female | Male | Male | Male | Female | Male | Female | |
| Less than $3 00 | .... | .... | .... | .... | .... | 3 | .... | .... | .... | .... | .... | .... | 3 | .... | .07 | .... | Less than $3 00 |
| $3 00-$3 49 | .... | .... | .... | .... | .... | 1 | .... | .... | .... | .... | .... | .... | 1 | .... | .09 | .... | $3 00- 3 49 |
| 3 50- 3 99 | .... | .... | .... | .... | .... | 15 | .... | .... | .... | .... | .... | .... | 15 | .... | .43 | .... | 3 50- 3 99 |
| 4 00- 4 99 | .... | .... | .... | .... | .... | 27 | .... | .... | .... | 2 | .... | .... | 27 | 2 | 1.31 | 3.42 | 4 00- 4 49 |
| 4 50- 4 99 | .... | .... | .... | 1 | .... | 19 | .... | 1 | 1 | .... | .... | .... | 21 | 1 | 1.50 | 5.17 | 4 50- 4 99 |
| 5 00- 5 49 | .... | .... | 4 | 2 | .... | 102 | .... | 4 | 3 | 6 | .... | .... | 113 | 8 | 4.03 | 18.98 | 5 00- 5 49 |
| 5 50- 5 99 | .... | .... | .... | .... | .... | 1 | .... | 1 | 11 | .... | .... | .... | 13 | .... | 4.33 | .... | 5 50- 5.99 |
| 6 00- 6 49 | .... | .... | 11 | 5 | .... | 76 | .... | 1 | 3 | 4 | .... | .... | 91 | 9 | 6.45 | 34.44 | 6 00- 6 49 |
| 6 50- 6 99 | .... | .... | .... | .... | 1 | 3 | .... | 1 | 3 | 2 | .... | .... | 8 | 2 | 6.51 | 37.97 | 6 50- 6 99 |
| 7 00- 7 49 | .... | .... | 12 | 3 | 4 | 88 | 1 | 1 | 24 | 1 | 1 | .... | 131 | 4 | 9.48 | 44.80 | 7 00- 7 49 |
| 7 50- 7 99 | .... | .... | 3 | .... | 9 | 199 | 1 | 1 | 1 | 4 | 3 | .... | 217 | 4 | 14.34 | 51.70 | 7 50- 7 99 |
| 8 00- 8 99 | .... | .... | 17 | 8 | 7 | 314 | 1 | 6 | 27 | 1 | .... | .... | 372 | 9 | 22.46 | 67.30 | 8 00- 8 99 |
| 9 00- 9 99 | .... | .... | 18 | 8 | 4 | 142 | 1 | 5 | 25 | 1 | 1 | 1 | 197 | 9 | 27.10 | 82.80 | 9 00- 9 99 |
| 10 00-10 99 | .... | .... | 66 | 2 | 29 | 121 | 12 | 1 | 87 | 2 | 4 | .... | 320 | 4 | 34.24 | 89.70 | 10 00-10 99 |
| 11 00-11 99 | .... | .... | 28 | 1 | 19 | 48 | 2 | 5 | 60 | 1 | 17 | .... | 179 | 2 | 38.30 | 93.10 | 11 00-11 99 |
| 12 00-12 99 | 2 | .... | 115 | .... | 88 | 90 | 17 | 21 | 275 | .... | 73 | .... | 681 | .... | 53.60 | .... | 12 00-12 99 |
| 13 00-13 99 | 3 | .... | 43 | .... | 90 | 5 | 10 | 4 | 102 | .... | 47 | .... | 304 | .... | 60.30 | .... | 13 00-13 99 |
| 14 00-14 99 | 6 | .... | 40 | .... | 59 | 4 | 27 | 1 | 105 | 1 | 103 | .... | 345 | 1 | 68.20 | 94.80 | 14 00-14 99 |
| 15 00-15 99 | 4 | .... | 54 | 1 | 515 | 7 | 115 | 5 | 36 | 1 | 15 | .... | 751 | 2 | 85.00 | 98.30 | 15 00-15 99 |
| 16 00-17 99 | 14 | .... | 61 | .... | 202 | 3 | 83 | .... | 36 | .... | 21 | .... | 420 | .... | 94.20 | .... | 16 00-17 99 |
| 18 00-19 99 | 12 | .... | 40 | .... | 19 | 2 | 27 | 1 | 11 | .... | 5 | .... | 117 | .... | 96.90 | .... | 18 00-19 99 |
| 20 00-24 99 | 25 | .... | 22 | .... | 7 | .... | 10 | .... | 6 | .... | 8 | .... | 78 | .... | 98.60 | .... | 20 00-24 99 |
| 25 00-29 99 | 14 | .... | 7 | .... | 1 | .... | 5 | .... | .... | .... | 1 | .... | 28 | .... | 99.40 | .... | 25 00-29 99 |
| 30 00-34 99 | 4 | .... | 3 | .... | .... | .... | 1 | .... | .... | .... | 3 | .... | 11 | .... | 99.60 | .... | 30 00-34 99 |
| 35 00-39 99 | 6 | .... | .... | .... | .... | .... | .... | .... | .... | .... | 2 | .... | 8 | .... | 99.80 | .... | 35 00-39 99 |
| 40 00 and over | 6 | 1 | .... | .... | .... | .... | .... | .... | .... | .... | 1 | .... | 7 | 1 | 100.00 | 100.00 | 40 00 and over |
| Not reported | .... | .... | .... | .... | 1 | 4 | 1 | .... | 1 | .... | .... | .... | 7 | .... | .... | .... | Not reported |
| Total | 96 | 1 | 544 | 31 | 1,055 | 1,274 | 314 | 59 | 817 | 26 | 305 | 1 | 4,465 | 58 | .... | .... | Total |

32. TABLE VI, A, 1, c

NEW YORK STATE

**DEPARTMENT STORES — SHIPPING AND DELIVERY**

NUMBER AND PER CENT. OF EMPLOYEES CLASSIFIED ACCORDING TO ACTUAL WEEKLY EARNINGS BY AGE GROUPS AND SEX

| ACTUAL WEEKLY EARNINGS IN DOLLARS | AGE GROUPS IN YEARS | | | | | | | | | | | | | ACTUAL WEEKLY EARNINGS IN DOLLARS |
|---|---|---|---|---|---|---|---|---|---|---|---|---|---|---|
| | 14–15 | 16–17 | | 18–20 | | 21–24 | | 25–29 | | 30–34 | | 35–39 | | |
| | Male | Male | Female | Male | Female | Male | Female | Male | Female | Male | Female | Male | Female | |
| Less than $3 00 | 6 | 2 | 1 | 12 | ...... | 1 | 1 | 2 | ...... | 2 | ...... | ...... | ...... | Less than $3 00 |
| $3 00–$3 49 | 3 | 1 | 1 | 5 | ...... | 2 | ...... | 2 | ...... | ...... | ...... | ...... | ...... | $3 00– 3 49 |
| 3 50– 3 99 | 11 | 3 | ...... | 3 | ...... | .... | ...... | 1 | ...... | 1 | ...... | ...... | ...... | 3 50– 3 99 |
| 4 00– 4 49 | 20 | 11 | 1 | 6 | 1 | .... | ...... | 1 | ...... | 2 | ...... | 1 | ...... | 4 00– 4 49 |
| 4 50– 4 99 | 9 | 12 | 1 | 4 | ...... | 1 | ...... | ...... | ...... | ...... | ...... | ...... | ...... | 4 50– 4 99 |
| 5 00– 5 49 | 16 | 82 | 3 | 14 | 2 | 2 | 1 | 4 | ...... | 1 | ...... | 1 | ...... | 5 00– 5 49 |
| 5 50– 5 99 | ...... | 7 | ...... | 17 | 2 | 2 | ...... | 2 | ...... | ...... | ...... | ...... | ...... | 5 50– 5 99 |
| 6 00– 6 49 | 2 | 57 | 1 | 33 | 3 | 8 | 3 | 4 | 1 | 3 | ...... | 1 | ...... | 6 00– 6 49 |
| 6 50– 6 99 | ...... | 4 | ...... | 17 | ...... | 6 | ...... | 4 | ...... | 1 | ...... | ...... | 1 | 6 50– 6 99 |
| 7 00– 7 49 | ...... | 35 | ...... | 89 | 3 | 9 | ...... | 2 | ...... | 1 | ...... | 1 | ...... | 7 00– 7 49 |
| 7 50– 7 99 | 1 | 34 | 1 | 163 | ...... | 34 | ...... | 3 | ...... | 2 | 1 | 1 | ...... | 7 50– 7 99 |
| 8 00– 8 99 | 1 | 27 | ...... | 163 | ...... | 69 | 6 | 9 | 1 | 8 | ...... | 4 | ...... | 8 00– 8 99 |
| 9 00– 9 99 | ...... | 4 | 1 | 89 | ...... | 50 | 4 | 13 | 1 | 3 | 1 | 6 | 1 | 9 00– 9 99 |
| 10 00–10 99 | ...... | 2 | 2 | 77 | ...... | 106 | 1 | 40 | ...... | 26 | 1 | 20 | ...... | 10 00–10 99 |
| 11 00–11 99 | ...... | 3 | ...... | 34 | 1 | 66 | ...... | 24 | ...... | 16 | ...... | 20 | ...... | 11 00–11 99 |
| 12 00–12 99 | ...... | 1 | ...... | 45 | ...... | 130 | ...... | 111 | ...... | 62 | ...... | 72 | ...... | 12 00–12 99 |
| 13 00–13 99 | ...... | 2 | ...... | 17 | ...... | 99 | ...... | 53 | ...... | 42 | ...... | 28 | ...... | 13 00–13 99 |
| 14 00–14 99 | ...... | .... | 1 | 9 | ...... | 78 | ...... | 75 | ...... | 62 | ...... | 48 | ...... | 14 00–14 99 |
| 15 00–15 99 | ...... | 1 | 1 | 25 | ...... | 166 | 1 | 139 | ...... | 92 | ...... | 74 | ...... | 15 00–15 99 |
| 16 00–17 99 | ...... | .... | ...... | 4 | ...... | 49 | ...... | 91 | ...... | 83 | ...... | 81 | ...... | 16 00–17 99 |
| 18 00–19 99 | ...... | .... | ...... | 1 | ...... | 10 | ...... | 11 | ...... | 23 | ...... | 31 | ...... | 18 00–19 99 |
| 20 00–24 99 | ...... | .... | ...... | .... | ...... | 2 | ...... | 6 | ...... | 16 | ...... | 16 | ...... | 20 00–24 99 |
| 25 00–29 99 | ...... | .... | ...... | .... | ...... | 4 | ...... | 1 | ...... | 3 | ...... | 11 | ...... | 25 00–29 99 |
| 30 00–34 99 | ...... | .... | ...... | .... | ...... | 1 | ...... | ...... | ...... | 1 | ...... | 1 | ...... | 30 00–34 99 |
| 35 00–39 99 | ...... | .... | ...... | .... | ...... | .... | ...... | 1 | ...... | 1 | ...... | 2 | ...... | 35 00–39 99 |
| 40 00 and over | ...... | .... | ...... | .... | ...... | .... | ...... | ...... | ...... | ...... | 1 | 1 | ...... | 40 00 and over |
| Not reported | ...... | .... | ...... | 2 | ...... | 1 | ...... | 2 | ...... | ...... | ...... | 1 | ...... | Not reported |
| Total | 69 | 288 | 14 | 829 | 12 | 896 | 17 | 601 | 3 | 451 | 4 | 421 | 2 | Total |

32. TABLE VI, A, 1, c — *(concluded)*

NEW YORK STATE

**DEPARTMENT STORES — SHIPPING AND DELIVERY**

NUMBER AND PER CENT. OF EMPLOYEES CLASSIFIED ACCORDING TO ACTUAL WEEKLY EARNINGS BY AGE GROUPS AND SEX

| ACTUAL WEEKLY EARNINGS IN DOLLARS | AGE GROUPS IN YEARS | | | | | | | | | | | | ACTUAL WEEKLY EARNINGS IN DOLLARS |
|---|---|---|---|---|---|---|---|---|---|---|---|---|---|
| | 40–44 | | 45–54 | | 55–64 | | 65 AND OVER | NOT REPORTED | TOTAL | | CUMULATIVE PER CENT OF TOTAL | | |
| | Male | Female | Male | Female | Male | Female | Male | Male | Male | Female | Male | Female | |
| Less than $3 00 | 2 | ....... | 1 | ....... | 1 | ....... | ....... | 3 | 32 | 2 | .72 | 3.44 | Less than $3 00 |
| $3 00–$3 49 | ....... | ....... | ....... | ....... | ....... | ....... | ....... | ....... | 13 | 1 | 1.01 | 5.17 | $3 00–$3 49 |
| 3 50– 3 99 | ....... | ....... | ....... | ....... | ....... | ....... | ....... | ....... | 19 | ....... | 1.43 | ....... | 3 50– 3 99 |
| 4 00– 4 49 | ....... | ....... | ....... | ....... | 1 | ....... | ....... | 1 | 43 | 2 | 2.40 | 8.62 | 4 00– 4 49 |
| 4 50– 4 99 | ....... | ....... | ....... | ....... | ....... | ....... | 1 | ....... | 27 | 1 | 3.0 | 10.33 | 4 50– 4 99 |
| 5 00– 5 49 | ....... | ....... | 3 | ....... | ....... | ....... | ....... | ....... | 123 | 6 | 5.73 | 20.63 | 5 00– 5 49 |
| 5 50– 5 99 | ....... | ....... | ....... | ....... | ....... | ....... | ....... | 1 | 29 | 2 | 6.42 | 24.7 | 5 50– 5 99 |
| 6 00– 6 49 | 1 | ....... | ....... | ....... | ....... | ....... | ....... | ....... | 109 | 8 | 8.86 | 37.85 | 6 00– 6 49 |
| 6 50– 6 99 | 1 | ....... | 2 | ....... | 1 | 1 | ....... | 1 | 37 | 2 | 9.69 | 41.4 | 6 50– 6 99 |
| 7 00– 7 49 | ....... | ....... | 1 | ....... | 1 | ....... | 1 | ....... | 140 | 3 | 12.82 | 46.5 | 7 00– 7 49 |
| 7 50– 7 99 | ....... | 1 | 3 | 1 | 1 | 2 | ....... | 4 | 246 | 6 | 18.38 | 56.9 | 7 50– 7 99 |
| 8 00– 8 99 | 3 | ....... | 5 | ....... | ....... | ....... | 1 | 6 | 296 | 7 | 25.0 | 68.9 | 8 00– 8 99 |
| 9 00– 9 99 | 2 | ....... | 3 | ....... | 2 | ....... | ....... | 2 | 174 | 8 | 28.9 | 82.7 | 9 00– 9 99 |
| 10 00–10 99 | 18 | ....... | 25 | ....... | 8 | ....... | 5 | 1 | 328 | 4 | 36.2 | 89.6 | 10 00–10 99 |
| 11 00–11 99 | 19 | ....... | 26 | ....... | 8 | 1 | 2 | 2 | 220 | 2 | 41.2 | 93.1 | 11.00–11 99 |
| 12 00–12 99 | 50 | ....... | 92 | ....... | 35 | ....... | 4 | 2 | 604 | ....... | 54.7 | ....... | 12 00–12 99 |
| 13 00–13 99 | 28 | ....... | 35 | ....... | 13 | ....... | ....... | ....... | 317 | ....... | 61.8 | ....... | 13 00–13 99 |
| 14 00–14 99 | 40 | ....... | 48 | ....... | 13 | ....... | 3 | 2 | 378 | 1 | 70.3 | 94.8 | 14 00–14 99 |
| 15 00–15 99 | 42 | ....... | 62 | ....... | 11 | ....... | 1 | 3 | 616 | 2 | 84.2 | 98.3 | 15 00–15 99 |
| 16 00–17 99 | 54 | ....... | 66 | ....... | 19 | ....... | 1 | ....... | 448 | ....... | 94.2 | ....... | 16 00–17 99 |
| 18 00–19 99 | 14 | ....... | 23 | ....... | 3 | ....... | 1 | 1 | 118 | ....... | 96.8 | ....... | 18 00–19 99 |
| 20 00–24 99 | 18 | ....... | 18 | ....... | 5 | ....... | ....... | 2 | 83 | ....... | 98.7 | ....... | 20 00–24 99 |
| 25 00–29 99 | 8 | ....... | 2 | ....... | ....... | ....... | ....... | ....... | 29 | ....... | 99.3 | ....... | 25 00–29 99 |
| 30 00–34 99 | 4 | ....... | 5 | ....... | ....... | ....... | ....... | ....... | 12 | ....... | 99.6 | ....... | 30 00–34 99 |
| 35 00–39 99 | 1 | ....... | 2 | ....... | 1 | ....... | ....... | ....... | 8 | ....... | 99.8 | ....... | 35 00–39 99 |
| 40 00 and over | 2 | ....... | 4 | ....... | ....... | ....... | ....... | ....... | 7 | 1 | 100.00 | 100.00 | 40 00 and over |
| Not reported | 1 | ....... | 1 | ....... | 1 | ....... | ....... | ....... | 9 | ....... | ....... | ....... | Not reported |
| Total | 308 | 1 | 427 | 1 | 124 | 4 | 20 | 31 | 4,465 | 58 | ....... | ....... | Total |

33. TABLE IX, A, 1, c

NEW YORK STATE

**DEPARTMENT STORES — SHIPPING AND DELIVERY**

Number and Per Cent. of Employees Classified According to Actual Weekly Earnings, by Occupation and Sex

| Actual Weekly Earnings in Dollars | Occupation: Foremen and Forewomen | | Clerks and Routers | | Drivers | Wagon Boys and Helpers | Chauffeurs | General Labor | Packing | | Stablemen | Not Reported | Total | | Cumulative Per Cent. of Total | | Actual Weekly Earnings in Dollars |
|---|---|---|---|---|---|---|---|---|---|---|---|---|---|---|---|---|---|
| | Male | Female | Male | Female | Male | Male | Male | Male | Male | Female | Male | Male | Male | Female | Male | Female | |
| Less than $3 00 | | | 2 | 1 | 1 | 23 | | 1 | 5 | 1 | | | 32 | 2 | .72 | 3.44 | Less than $3 00 |
| $3 00-$3 49 | | | | | 1 | 10 | 2 | | | 1 | | | 13 | 1 | 1.01 | 5.17 | $3 00- 3 49 |
| 3 50- 3 99 | | | 1 | | | 16 | 1 | | | | 1 | | 19 | | 1.43 | | 3 50- 3 99 |
| 4 00- 4 49 | | | | | | 39 | | | 3 | 2 | 1 | | 43 | 2 | 2.40 | 8.62 | 4 00- 4 49 |
| 4 50- 4 99 | | | | 1 | | 24 | | 1 | 2 | | | | 27 | 1 | 3.00 | 10.33 | 4 50- 4 99 |
| 5 00 5 49 | | | 5 | 2 | 3 | 104 | 1 | 4 | 5 | 4 | 1 | | 123 | 6 | 5.73 | 20.63 | 5 00- 5 49 |
| 5 50- 5 99 | | | 2 | 2 | | 15 | | 1 | 11 | | | | 29 | 2 | 6.42 | 24.70 | 5 50- 5 99 |
| 6 00- 6 49 | | | 12 | 4 | 1 | 89 | | 1 | 6 | 4 | | | 109 | 8 | 8.86 | 37.85 | 6 00- 6 49 |
| 6 50- 6 99 | | | 4 | | 3 | 20 | | 1 | 9 | 2 | | | 37 | 2 | 9.69 | 41.40 | 6 50- 6 99 |
| 7 00- 7 49 | | | 9 | 2 | 6 | 104 | 1 | 1 | 18 | 1 | 1 | | 140 | 3 | 12.82 | 46.50 | 7 00- 7 49 |
| 7 50- 7 99 | | | 4 | 1 | 8 | 220 | 1 | 3 | 6 | 5 | 3 | 1 | 246 | 6 | 18.38 | 56.90 | 7 50- 7 99 |
| 8 00- 8 99 | | | 20 | 7 | 12 | 220 | 3 | 8 | 30 | | 3 | | 296 | 7 | 25.00 | 68.90 | 8 00- 8 99 |
| 9 00- 9 99 | | | 20 | 7 | 6 | 114 | 3 | 5 | 24 | 1 | 2 | | 174 | 8 | 28.90 | 82.70 | 9 00- 9 99 |
| 10 00-10 99 | | | 61 | 2 | 39 | 117 | 19 | 3 | 86 | 2 | 3 | | 328 | 4 | 36.20 | 89.60 | 10 00-10 99 |
| 11 00-11 99 | | | 33 | 1 | 30 | 43 | 8 | 6 | 81 | 1 | 19 | | 220 | 2 | 41.20 | 93.10 | 11 00-11 99 |
| 12 00-12 99 | 2 | | 94 | | 96 | 76 | 24 | 16 | 227 | | 69 | | 604 | | 54.70 | | 12 00-12 99 |
| 13 00-13 99 | 3 | | 47 | | 95 | 17 | 15 | 3 | 94 | | 43 | | 317 | | 61.80 | | 13 00-13 99 |
| 14 00-14 99 | 6 | | 43 | | 95 | 10 | 27 | | 95 | 1 | 102 | | 378 | 1 | 70.30 | 94.80 | 14 00-14 99 |
| 15 00-15 99 | 3 | | 55 | 1 | 392 | 5 | 92 | 4 | 49 | 1 | 16 | | 616 | 2 | 84.20 | 98.30 | 15 00-15 99 |
| 16 00-17 99 | 14 | | 60 | | 235 | 3 | 69 | 1 | 45 | | 21 | | 448 | | 94.20 | | 16 00-17 99 |
| 18 00-19 99 | 11 | | 37 | | 23 | 3 | 26 | | 13 | | 5 | | 118 | | 96.80 | | 18 00-19 99 |
| 20 00-24 99 | 28 | | 25 | | 6 | | 10 | | 6 | | 8 | | 83 | | 98.70 | | 20 00-24 99 |
| 25 00-29 99 | 12 | | 7 | | 1 | | 7 | | 1 | | 1 | | 29 | | 99.30 | | 25 00-29 99 |
| 30 00-34 99 | 5 | | 3 | | 1 | | | | | | 3 | | 12 | | 99.60 | | 30 00-34 99 |
| 35 00-39 99 | 6 | | | | | | | | | | 2 | | 8 | | 99.80 | | 35 00-39 99 |
| 40 00 and over | 6 | 1 | | | | | | | | | 1 | | 7 | 1 | 100.00 | 100.00 | 40 00 and over |
| Not reported | | | | | 1 | 2 | 5 | | 1 | | | | 9 | | | | Not reported |
| Total | 96 | 1 | 544 | 31 | 1,055 | 1,274 | 314 | 59 | 817 | 26 | 305 | 1 | 4,465 | 58 | | | Total |

NEW YORK STATE

34. TABLE X, A, 1, e

**DEPARTMENT STORES — SHIPPING AND DELIVERY**

NUMBER AND PER CENT. OF EMPLOYEES CLASSIFIED ACCORDING TO ACTUAL WEEKLY EARNINGS BY CONJUGAL CONDITION AND SEX

| ACTUAL WEEKLY EARNINGS IN DOLLARS | CONJUGAL CONDITION | | | | | | | | | | | | ACTUAL WEEKLY EARNINGS IN DOLLARS |
|---|---|---|---|---|---|---|---|---|---|---|---|---|---|
| | SINGLE | | MARRIED | | WIDOWED OR DIVORCED | | NOT REPORTED | | TOTAL | | CUMULATIVE PER CENT. FOR TOTAL | | |
| | Male | Female | Male | Female | Male | Female | Male | Female | Male | Female | Male | Female | |
| Less than $3 00. | 26 | 2 | 5 | ....... | ....... | ....... | 1 | ....... | 32 | 2 | .72 | 3.44 | Less than $3 00 |
| $3 00–$3 49.... | 10 | 1 | 3 | ....... | ....... | ....... | ....... | ....... | 13 | 1 | 1.01 | 5.17 | ...$3 00– 3 49 |
| 3 50– 3 99.... | 18 | ....... | 1 | ....... | ....... | ....... | ....... | ....... | 19 | ....... | 1.43 | ....... | ... 3 50– 3 99 |
| 4 00– 4 49.... | 41 | 2 | 2 | ....... | ....... | ....... | ....... | ....... | 43 | 2 | 2.40 | 8.62 | ... 4 00– 4 49 |
| 4 50– 4 99.... | 26 | 1 | 1 | ....... | ....... | ....... | ....... | ....... | 27 | 1 | 3.00 | 10.33 | ... 4 50– 4 99 |
| 5 00– 5 49.... | 112 | 6 | 10 | ....... | 1 | ....... | ....... | ....... | 123 | 6 | 5.73 | 20.63 | ... 5 00– 5 49 |
| 5 50– 5 99.... | 28 | 2 | 1 | ....... | ....... | ....... | ....... | ....... | 29 | 2 | 6.42 | 24.70 | ... 5 50– 5 99 |
| 6 00– 6 49.... | 104 | 8 | 4 | ....... | ....... | ....... | 1 | ....... | 109 | 8 | 8.86 | 37.85 | ... 6 00– 6 49 |
| 6 50– 6 99.... | 32 | 1 | 5 | ....... | ....... | 1 | ....... | ....... | 37 | 2 | 9.69 | 41.40 | ... 6 50– 6 99 |
| 7 00– 7 49.... | 133 | 3 | 5 | ....... | 1 | ....... | 1 | ....... | 140 | 3 | 12.82 | 46.50 | ... 7 00– 7 49 |
| 7 50– 7 99.... | 236 | 4 | 6 | ....... | 1 | 2 | 3 | ....... | 246 | 6 | 18.38 | 56.90 | ... 7 50– 7 99 |
| 8 00– 8 99.... | 266 | 6 | 18 | ....... | 2 | ....... | 10 | 1 | 296 | 7 | 25.00 | 68.90 | ... 8 00– 8 99 |
| 9 00– 9 99.... | 154 | 5 | 17 | 1 | 1 | 1 | 2 | 1 | 174 | 8 | 28.90 | 82.70 | ... 9 00– 9 99 |
| 10 00–10 99.... | 209 | 3 | 109 | ....... | 2 | 1 | 8 | ....... | 328 | 4 | 36.20 | 89.60 | ...10 00–10 99 |
| 11 00–11 99.... | 137 | 2 | 75 | ....... | 5 | ....... | 3 | ....... | 220 | 2 | 41.20 | 93.10 | ...11 00–11 99 |
| 12 00–12 99.... | 273 | ....... | 300 | ....... | 12 | ....... | 19 | ....... | 604 | ....... | 54.70 | ....... | ...12 00–12 99 |
| 13 00–13 99.... | 172 | ....... | 131 | ....... | 9 | ....... | 5 | ....... | 317 | ....... | 61.80 | ....... | ...13 00–13 99 |
| 14 00–14 99.... | 152 | 1 | 201 | ....... | 11 | ....... | 14 | ....... | 378 | 1 | 70.30 | 94.80 | ...14 00–14 99 |
| 15 00–15 99.... | 271 | 1 | 325 | 1 | 7 | ....... | 13 | ....... | 616 | 2 | 84.20 | 98.30 | ...15 00–15 99 |
| 16 00–17 99.... | 128 | ....... | 294 | ....... | 15 | ....... | 11 | ....... | 448 | ....... | 94.20 | ....... | ...16 00–17 99 |
| 18 00–19 99.... | 27 | ....... | 86 | ....... | 4 | ....... | 1 | ....... | 118 | ....... | 96.80 | ....... | ...18 00–19 99 |
| 20 00–24 99.... | 15 | ....... | 58 | ....... | 6 | ....... | 4 | ....... | 83 | ....... | 98.70 | ....... | ...20 00–24 99 |
| 25 00–29 99.... | 5 | ....... | 20 | ....... | 2 | ....... | 2 | ....... | 29 | ....... | 99.30 | ....... | ...25 00–29 99 |
| 30 00–34 99.... | 1 | ....... | 10 | ....... | 1 | ....... | ....... | ....... | 12 | ....... | 99.60 | ....... | ...30 00–34 99 |
| 35 00–39 99.... | ....... | ....... | 8 | ....... | ....... | ....... | ....... | ....... | 8 | ....... | 99.80 | ....... | ...35 00–39 99 |
| 40 00 and over.. | 1 | 1 | 6 | ....... | ....... | ....... | ....... | ....... | 7 | 1 | 100.00 | 100.00 | .40 00 and over |
| Not reported.... | 3 | ....... | 6 | ....... | ....... | ....... | ....... | ....... | 9 | ....... | ....... | ....... | ...Not reported |
| Total....... | 2,580 | 49 | 1,707 | 2 | 80 | 5 | 98 | 2 | 4,465 | 58 | ....... | ....... | .....Total |

35. TABLE XI, A, 1, c

NEW YORK STATE

**DEPARTMENT STORES — SHIPPING AND DELIVERY**

Number and Per Cent. of Employees Classified According to Actual Weekly Earnings by Nativity and Sex

| Actual Weekly Earnings in Dollars | Nativity: Native Male | Native Female | Foreign Male | Foreign Female | Not Reported Male | Not Reported Female | Total Male | Total Female | Cumulative Per Cent. of Total Male | Cumulative Per Cent. of Total Female | Actual Weekly Earnings in Dollars |
|---|---|---|---|---|---|---|---|---|---|---|---|
| Less than $3 00 | 28 | 1 | 4 | 1 | ........ | ........ | 32 | 2 | .72 | 3.44 | Less than $3 00 |
| $3 00–$3 49 | 11 | 1 | 1 | ........ | 1 | ........ | 13 | 1 | 1.01 | 5.17 | $3 00– 3 49 |
| 3 50– 3 99 | 15 | ........ | 3 | ........ | 1 | ........ | 19 | ........ | 1.43 | ........ | 3 50– 3 99 |
| 4 00– 4 49 | 37 | 2 | 6 | ........ | ........ | ........ | 43 | 2 | 2.40 | 8.62 | 4 00– 4 49 |
| 4 50– 4 99 | 27 | 1 | ........ | ........ | ........ | ........ | 27 | 1 | 3.00 | 10.33 | 4 50– 4 99 |
| 5 00– 5 49 | 115 | 6 | 8 | ........ | ........ | ........ | 123 | 6 | 5.73 | 20.63 | 5 00– 5 49 |
| 5 50– 5 99 | 27 | 2 | 2 | ........ | ........ | ........ | 29 | 2 | 6.42 | 24.70 | 5 50– 5 99 |
| 6 00– 6 49 | 96 | 7 | 13 | 1 | ........ | ........ | 109 | 8 | 8.86 | 37.85 | 6 00– 6 49 |
| 6 50– 6 99 | 34 | 2 | 3 | ........ | ........ | ........ | 37 | 2 | 9.69 | 41.40 | 6 50– 6 99 |
| 7 00– 7 49 | 123 | 3 | 15 | ........ | 2 | ........ | 140 | 3 | 12.82 | 46.50 | 7 00– 7 49 |
| 7 50– 7 99 | 221 | 6 | 21 | ........ | 4 | ........ | 246 | 6 | 18.38 | 56.90 | 7 50– 7 99 |
| 8 00– 8 99 | 260 | 7 | 33 | ........ | 3 | ........ | 296 | 7 | 25.00 | 68.90 | 8 00– 8 99 |
| 9 00– 9 99 | 151 | 8 | 19 | ........ | 4 | ........ | 174 | 8 | 28.90 | 82.70 | 9 00– 9 99 |
| 10 00–10 99 | 255 | 3 | 72 | 1 | 1 | ........ | 328 | 4 | 36.20 | 89.60 | 10 00–10 99 |
| 11 00–11 99 | 150 | 2 | 70 | ........ | ........ | ........ | 220 | 2 | 41.20 | 93.10 | 11 00–11 99 |
| 12 00–12 99 | 417 | ........ | 183 | ........ | 4 | ........ | 604 | ........ | 54.70 | ........ | 12 00–12 99 |
| 13 00–13 99 | 212 | ........ | 104 | ........ | 1 | ........ | 317 | ........ | 61.80 | ........ | 13 00–13 99 |
| 14 00–14 99 | 236 | 1 | 140 | ........ | 2 | ........ | 378 | 1 | 70.30 | 94.80 | 14 00–14 99 |
| 15 00–15 99 | 518 | 1 | 95 | 1 | 3 | ........ | 616 | 2 | 84.20 | 98.30 | 15 00–15 99 |
| 16 00–17 99 | 354 | ........ | 94 | ........ | ........ | ........ | 448 | ........ | 94.20 | ........ | 16 00–17 99 |
| 18 00–19 99 | 90 | ........ | 26 | ........ | 2 | ........ | 118 | ........ | 96.80 | ........ | 18 00–19 99 |
| 20 00–24 99 | 66 | ........ | 16 | ........ | 1 | ........ | 83 | ........ | 98.70 | ........ | 20 00–24 99 |
| 25 00–29 99 | 25 | ........ | 4 | ........ | ........ | ........ | 29 | ........ | 99.30 | ........ | 25 00–29 99 |
| 30 00–34 99 | 10 | ........ | 2 | ........ | ........ | ........ | 12 | ........ | 99.60 | ........ | 30 00–34 99 |
| 35 00–39 99 | 6 | ........ | 2 | ........ | ........ | ........ | 8 | ........ | 99.80 | ........ | 35 00–39 99 |
| 40 00 and over | 5 | 1 | 2 | ........ | ........ | ........ | 7 | 1 | 100.00 | 100.00 | 40 00 and over |
| Not reported | 7 | ........ | 2 | ........ | ........ | ........ | 9 | ........ | ........ | ........ | Not reported |
| Total | 3,496 | 54 | 940 | 4 | 29 | ........ | 4,465 | 58 | ........ | ........ | Total |

36. TABLE XII, A, 1, c

NEW YORK STATE

**DEPARTMENT STORES — SHIPPING AND DELIVERY**

Number of Employees for Each Sex Classified According to Actual Weekly Earnings by the Number of Years in the Trade

| Actual Weekly Earnings in Dollars | Years in Trade | | | | | | | | | | | | | | Actual Weekly Earnings in Dollars |
|---|---|---|---|---|---|---|---|---|---|---|---|---|---|---|---|
| | Less than 1 | | 1 | | 2 | | 3 | | 4 | | 5 | | 6 | | |
| | Male | Female | Male | Female | Male | Female | Male | Female | Male | Female | Male | Female | Male | Female | |
| Less than $3 00 | 15 | ...... | 3 | ...... | 3 | 1 | 3 | ...... | 1 | ...... | 3 | ...... | ...... | ...... | Less than $3 00 |
| $3 00–$3 49... | 7 | 1 | 2 | ...... | 1 | ...... | ...... | ...... | 2 | ...... | ...... | ...... | ...... | ...... | ...$3 00– 3 49 |
| 3 50– 3 99... | 15 | ...... | 2 | ...... | ...... | ...... | ...... | ...... | ...... | ...... | ...... | ...... | ...... | ...... | ... 3 50– 3 99 |
| 4 00– 4 49... | 17 | 1 | 15 | ...... | 2 | ...... | 3 | 1 | ...... | ...... | ...... | ...... | ...... | ...... | ... 4 00– 4 49 |
| 4 50– 4 99... | 15 | 1 | 8 | ...... | 2 | ...... | ...... | ...... | 1 | ...... | ...... | ...... | ...... | ...... | ... 4 50– 4 99 |
| 5 00– 5 49... | 49 | 2 | 39 | 1 | 19 | 1 | 6 | 1 | 2 | ...... | ...... | ...... | 1 | ...... | ... 5 00– 5 49 |
| 5 50– 5 99... | 15 | ...... | 6 | ...... | 4 | ...... | 1 | 2 | 1 | ...... | 1 | ...... | ...... | ...... | ... 5 50– 5 99 |
| 6 00– 6 49... | 54 | ...... | 16 | ...... | 12 | 1 | 13 | 2 | 6 | 3 | 2 | 1 | 1 | ...... | ... 6 00– 6 49 |
| 6 50– 6 99... | 9 | ...... | 8 | 1 | 7 | 1 | 4 | ...... | 1 | ...... | 2 | ...... | ...... | ...... | ... 6 50– 6 99 |
| 7 00– 7 49... | 54 | ...... | 28 | ...... | 22 | 2 | 18 | ...... | 8 | ...... | 3 | 1 | ...... | ...... | ... 7 00– 7 49 |
| 7 50– 7 99... | 83 | 1 | 56 | ...... | 32 | ...... | 30 | 1 | 17 | 1 | 11 | ...... | 7 | 1 | ... 7 50– 7 99 |
| 8 00– 8 99... | 100 | ...... | 45 | ...... | 36 | ...... | 50 | 1 | 20 | 1 | 17 | 2 | 6 | 2 | ... 8 00– 8 99 |
| 9 00– 9 99... | 56 | 1 | 33 | 3 | 18 | ...... | 15 | ...... | 18 | ...... | 6 | 1 | 6 | 1 | ... 9 00– 9 99 |
| 10 00–10 99... | 70 | 1 | 41 | ...... | 42 | ...... | 34 | 1 | 22 | ...... | 18 | ...... | 14 | ...... | ...10 00–10 99 |
| 11 00–11 99... | 28 | ...... | 15 | ...... | 24 | ...... | 22 | ...... | 15 | 1 | 21 | ...... | 16 | ...... | ...11 00–11 99 |
| 12 00–12 99... | 59 | ...... | 51 | ...... | 46 | ...... | 60 | ...... | 36 | ...... | 56 | ...... | 31 | ...... | ...12 00–12 99 |
| 13 00–13 99... | 16 | ...... | 13 | ...... | 23 | ...... | 26 | ...... | 19 | ...... | 20 | ...... | 27 | ...... | ...13 00–13 99 |
| 14 00–14 99... | 6 | 1 | 11 | ...... | 13 | ...... | 24 | ...... | 24 | ...... | 27 | ...... | 24 | ...... | ...14 00–14 99 |
| 15 00–15 99... | 15 | ...... | 26 | 1 | 43 | ...... | 31 | ...... | 49 | ...... | 47 | ...... | 31 | ...... | ...15 00–15 99 |
| 16 00–17 99... | 11 | ...... | 8 | ...... | 9 | ...... | 16 | ...... | 13 | ...... | 22 | ...... | 13 | ...... | ...16 00–17 99 |
| 18 00–19 99... | .... | ...... | 2 | ...... | 1 | ...... | 3 | ...... | 5 | ...... | 4 | ...... | 1 | ...... | ...18 00–19 99 |
| 20 00–24 99... | 1 | ...... | .... | ...... | ...... | ...... | 2 | ...... | ...... | ...... | 2 | ...... | 2 | ...... | ...20 00–24 99 |
| 25 00–29 99... | 1 | ...... | .... | ...... | ...... | ...... | 1 | ...... | 1 | ...... | ...... | ...... | 1 | ...... | ...25 00–29 99 |
| 30 00–34 99... | .... | ...... | .... | ...... | 1 | ...... | ...... | ...... | ...... | ...... | ...... | ...... | ...... | ...... | ...30 00–34 99 |
| 35 00–39 99... | .... | ...... | .... | ...... | 1 | ...... | ...... | ...... | ...... | ...... | ...... | ...... | ...... | ...... | ...35 00–39 99 |
| 40 00 and over. | .... | ...... | .... | ...... | ...... | ...... | ...... | ...... | ...... | ...... | ...... | ...... | ...... | ...... | .40 00 and over |
| Not reported... | 1 | ...... | 1 | ...... | 2 | ...... | 1 | ...... | ...... | ...... | 1 | ...... | 1 | ...... | ...Not reported |
| Total..... | 697 | 9 | 429 | 6 | 363 | 6 | 363 | 9 | 261 | 6 | 263 | 5 | 182 | 4 | .....Total |

NEW YORK STATE

36. TABLE XII, A, 1, c — (*continued*) DEPARTMENT STORES — SHIPPING AND DELIVERY

Number of Employees for Each Sex Classified According to Actual Weekly Earnings by the Number of Years in the Trade

| Actual Weekly Earnings in Dollars | Years in Trade | | | | | | | | | | | Actual Weekly Earnings in Dollars |
|---|---|---|---|---|---|---|---|---|---|---|---|---|
| | 7 | | 8 | | 9 | | 10–14 | | 15–19 | | 20–24 | |
| | Male | Female | Male | Female | Male | Female | Male | Female | Male | Female | Male | |
| Less than $3 00 | 1 | ........ | ........ | 1 | ........ | ........ | ........ | ........ | 1 | ........ | ........ | Less than $3 00 |
| $3 00–$3 49... | ........ | ........ | ........ | ........ | ........ | ........ | 1 | ........ | ........ | ........ | ........ | ...$3 00– 3 49 |
| 3 50– 3 99... | ........ | ........ | ........ | ........ | ........ | ........ | 1 | ........ | ........ | ........ | 1 | ... 3 50– 3 99 |
| 4 00– 4 49... | ........ | ........ | ........ | ........ | ........ | ........ | 2 | ........ | 1 | ........ | 1 | ... 4 00– 4 49 |
| 4 50– 4 99... | ........ | ........ | ........ | ........ | ........ | ........ | ........ | ........ | ........ | ........ | ........ | ... 4 50– 4 99 |
| 5 00– 5 49... | 2 | ........ | ........ | ........ | ........ | ........ | 1 | ........ | 1 | ........ | ........ | ... 5 00– 5 49 |
| 5 50– 5 99... | ........ | ........ | ........ | ........ | ........ | ........ | 1 | ........ | ........ | ........ | ........ | ... 5 50– 5 99 |
| 6 00– 6 49... | ........ | 1 | ........ | ........ | ........ | ........ | 1 | ........ | 1 | ........ | ........ | ... 6 00– 6 49 |
| 6 50– 6 99... | ........ | ........ | 1 | ........ | ........ | ........ | 1 | ........ | 1 | ........ | 1 | ... 6 50– 6 99 |
| 7 00– 7 49... | 3 | ........ | ........ | ........ | ........ | ........ | ........ | ........ | 1 | ........ | 1 | ... 7 00– 7 49 |
| 7 50– 7 99... | 1 | 1 | 1 | ........ | 1 | ........ | 3 | ........ | ........ | 1 | 1 | ... 7 50– 7 99 |
| 8 00– 8 99... | 8 | ........ | 2 | ........ | ........ | 1 | 4 | ........ | 3 | ........ | 1 | ... 8 00– 8 99 |
| 9 00– 9 99... | 5 | 2 | 4 | ........ | ........ | ........ | 5 | ........ | 4 | ........ | 1 | ... 9 00– 9 99 |
| 10 00–10 99... | 8 | ........ | 9 | 2 | 8 | ........ | 24 | ........ | 12 | ........ | 13 | ...10 00–10 99 |
| 11 00–11 99... | 18 | ........ | 8 | ........ | 3 | ........ | 16 | 1 | 7 | ........ | 7 | ...11 00–11 99 |
| 12 00–12 99... | 31 | ........ | 31 | ........ | 16 | ........ | 64 | ........ | 36 | ........ | 32 | ...12 00–12 99 |
| 13 00–13 99... | 26 | ........ | 17 | ........ | 8 | ........ | 56 | ........ | 24 | ........ | 16 | ...13 00–13 99 |
| 14 00–14 99... | 27 | ........ | 27 | ........ | 16 | ........ | 61 | ........ | 36 | ........ | 36 | ...14 00–14 99 |
| 15 00–15 99... | 32 | ........ | 43 | 1 | 30 | ........ | 136 | ........ | 50 | ........ | 39 | ...15 00–15 99 |
| 16 00–17 99... | 20 | ........ | 18 | ........ | 19 | ........ | 106 | ........ | 77 | ........ | 60 | ...16 00–17 99 |
| 18 00–19 99... | 2 | ........ | 4 | ........ | 3 | ........ | 18 | ........ | 30 | ........ | 26 | ...18 00–19 99 |
| 20 00–24 99... | 2 | ........ | 4 | ........ | 1 | ........ | 18 | ........ | 14 | ........ | 9 | ...20 00–24 99 |
| 25 00–29 99... | 1 | ........ | ........ | ........ | ........ | ........ | 7 | ........ | 2 | ........ | 7 | ...25 00–29 99 |
| 30 00–34 99... | ........ | ........ | ........ | ........ | ........ | ........ | 4 | ........ | 2 | ........ | 1 | ...30 00–34 99 |
| 35 00–39 99... | ........ | ........ | ........ | ........ | ........ | ........ | 3 | ........ | 1 | ........ | 1 | ...35 00–39 99 |
| 40 00 and over. | ........ | ........ | ........ | ........ | ........ | ........ | ........ | 1 | 2 | ........ | 4 | .40 00 and over |
| Not reported... | ........ | ........ | ........ | ........ | ........ | ........ | 1 | ........ | ........ | ........ | ........ | ...Not reported |
| Total..... | 187 | 4 | 169 | 4 | 105 | 1 | 534 | 2 | 306 | 1 | 258 | .....Total |

NEW YORK STATE

36. TABLE XII, A, 1, e — (*concluded*)

DEPARTMENT STORES — SHIPPING AND DELIVERY

NUMBER OF EMPLOYEES FOR EACH SEX CLASSIFIED ACCORDING TO ACTUAL WEEKLY EARNINGS BY THE NUMBER OF YEARS IN THE TRADE

| ACTUAL WEEKLY EARNINGS IN DOLLARS | YEARS IN TRADE: 25–29 | 30–34 | 35–44 | 45 AND OVER | NOT REPORTED | | TOTAL | | CUMULATIVE PER CENT. OF TOTAL | | ACTUAL WEEKLY EARNINGS IN DOLLARS |
|---|---|---|---|---|---|---|---|---|---|---|---|
| | Male | Male | Male | Male | Male | Female | Male | Female | Male | Female | |
| Less than $3 00 | 1 | ........ | ........ | ........ | 1 | ........ | 32 | 2 | .72 | 3.44 | Less than $3 00 |
| $3 00–$3 49 | ........ | ........ | ........ | ........ | ........ | ........ | 13 | 1 | 1.01 | 5.17 | $3 00– 3 49 |
| 3 50– 3 99 | ........ | ........ | ........ | ........ | ........ | ........ | 19 | ........ | 1.43 | ........ | 3 50– 3 99 |
| 4 00– 4 49 | ........ | ........ | 1 | ........ | 1 | ........ | 43 | 2 | 2.40 | 8.62 | 4 00– 4 49 |
| 4 50– 4 99 | ........ | 1 | ........ | ........ | ........ | ........ | 27 | 1 | 3.00 | 10.33 | 4 50– 4 99 |
| 5 00– 5 49 | ........ | 1 | ........ | ........ | 2 | 1 | 123 | 6 | 5.73 | 20.63 | 5 00– 5 49 |
| 5 50– 5 99 | ........ | ........ | ........ | ........ | ........ | ........ | 29 | 2 | 6.42 | 24.70 | 5 50– 5 99 |
| 6 00– 6 49 | ........ | ........ | ........ | ........ | 3 | ........ | 109 | 8 | 8.86 | 37.85 | 6 00– 6 49 |
| 6 50– 6 99 | ........ | 1 | ........ | ........ | 1 | ........ | 37 | 2 | 9.69 | 41.40 | 6 50– 6 99 |
| 7 00– 7 49 | ........ | ........ | ........ | ........ | 2 | ........ | 140 | 3 | 12.82 | 46.50 | 7 00– 7 49 |
| 7 50– 7 99 | ........ | ........ | ........ | ........ | 3 | ........ | 246 | 6 | 18.38 | 56.90 | 7 50– 7 99 |
| 8 00– 8 99 | 1 | ........ | 1 | ........ | 2 | ........ | 296 | 7 | 25.00 | 68.90 | 8 00– 8 99 |
| 9 00– 9 99 | ........ | ........ | ........ | ........ | 3 | ........ | 174 | 8 | 28.90 | 82.70 | 9 00– 9 99 |
| 10 00–10 99 | 4 | 3 | 1 | ........ | 5 | ........ | 328 | 4 | 36.20 | 89.60 | 10 00–10 99 |
| 11 00–11 99 | 9 | 5 | 2 | 1 | 3 | ........ | 220 | 2 | 41.20 | 93.10 | 11 00–11 99 |
| 12 00–12 99 | 17 | 16 | 12 | 2 | 8 | ........ | 604 | ........ | 54.70 | ........ | 12 00–12 99 |
| 13 00–13 99 | 10 | 8 | 3 | ........ | 5 | ........ | 317 | ........ | 61.80 | ........ | 13 00–13 99 |
| 14 00–14 99 | 21 | 14 | 8 | ........ | 3 | ........ | 378 | 1 | 70.30 | 94.80 | 14 00–14 99 |
| 15 00–15 99 | 19 | 11 | 1 | 1 | 12 | ........ | 616 | 2 | 84.20 | 98.30 | 15 00–15 99 |
| 16 00–17 99 | 37 | 6 | 2 | 2 | 9 | ........ | 448 | ........ | 94.20 | ........ | 16 00–17 99 |
| 18 00–19 99 | 8 | 8 | 2 | ........ | 1 | ........ | 118 | ........ | 96.80 | ........ | 18 00–19 99 |
| 20 00–24 99 | 11 | 13 | 1 | ........ | 3 | ........ | 83 | ........ | 98.70 | ........ | 20 00–24 99 |
| 25 00–29 99 | 5 | 1 | ........ | ........ | 2 | ........ | 29 | ........ | 99.30 | ........ | 25 00–29 99 |
| 30 00–34 99 | 2 | 2 | ........ | ........ | ........ | ........ | 12 | ........ | 99.60 | ........ | 30 00–34 99 |
| 35 00–39 99 | 1 | ........ | 1 | ........ | ........ | ........ | 8 | ........ | 99.80 | ........ | 35 00–39 99 |
| 40 00 and over | ........ | ........ | 1 | ........ | ........ | ........ | 7 | 1 | 100.00 | 100.00 | 40 00 and over |
| Not reported | 1 | ........ | ........ | ........ | ........ | ........ | 9 | ........ | ........ | ........ | Not reported |
| Total | 147 | 90 | 36 | 6 | 69 | 1 | 4,465 | 58 | ........ | ........ | Total |

37. TABLE XIII, A, 1, C

NEW YORK STATE

DEPARTMENT STORES — SHIPPING AND DELIVERY

NUMBER OF EMPLOYEES FOR EACH SEX CLASSIFIED ACCORDING TO ACTUAL WEEKLY EARNINGS, BY THE NUMBER OF YEARS IN THE FIRM

| ACTUAL WEEKLY EARNINGS IN DOLLARS | YEARS IN FIRM | | | | | | | | | | | | | | | | ACTUAL WEEKLY EARNINGS IN DOLLARS |
|---|---|---|---|---|---|---|---|---|---|---|---|---|---|---|---|---|---|
| | LESS THAN 1 | | 1 | | 2 | | 3 | | 4 | | 5 | | 6 | | 7 | | |
| | Male | Female | Male | Female | Male | Female | Male | Female | Male | Female | Male | Female | Male | Female | Male | Female | |
| Less than $3 00 | 18 | 1 | 4 | .... | 2 | 1 | 3 | .... | 1 | .... | 1 | .... | .... | .... | 1 | .... | Less than $3 00 |
| $3 00–$3 49... | 11 | 1 | 1 | .... | .... | .... | .... | .... | 1 | .... | .... | .... | .... | .... | .... | .... | ...$3 00– 3 49 |
| 3 50– 3 99... | 16 | .... | 2 | .... | .... | .... | .... | .... | 1 | .... | .... | .... | .... | .... | .... | .... | ....3 50– 3 99 |
| 4 00– 4 49... | 27 | 1 | 13 | .... | .... | .... | 1 | 1 | .... | .... | .... | .... | .... | .... | .... | .... | ....4 00– 4 49 |
| 4 50– 4 99... | 18 | 1 | 7 | .... | 1 | .... | .... | .... | .... | .... | .... | .... | .... | .... | .... | .... | ....4 50– 4 99 |
| 5 00– 5 49... | 72 | 3 | 32 | 1 | 14 | 2 | 3 | .... | .... | .... | .... | .... | 1 | .... | .... | .... | ....5 00– 5 49 |
| 5 50– 5 99... | 21 | 1 | 3 | .... | 2 | 1 | 1 | .... | 1 | .... | .... | .... | 1 | .... | .... | .... | ....5 50– 5 99 |
| 6 00– 6 49... | 74 | .... | 21 | .... | 8 | 1 | 4 | 2 | .... | 3 | .... | 1 | .... | .... | .... | 1 | ....6 00– 6 49 |
| 6 50– 6 99... | 19 | .... | 8 | 1 | 3 | 1 | 2 | .... | .... | .... | 2 | .... | .... | .... | 2 | .... | ....6 50– 6 99 |
| 7 00– 7 49... | 76 | .... | 30 | .... | 18 | 2 | 11 | .... | 2 | .... | 2 | 1 | .... | .... | .... | .... | ....7 00– 7 49 |
| 7 50– 7 99... | 147 | 1 | 56 | 1 | 18 | .... | 11 | 1 | 5 | 1 | 2 | .... | 3 | 1 | .... | 1 | ....7 50– 7 99 |
| 8 00– 8 99... | 152 | 4 | 52 | .... | 34 | .... | 21 | 1 | 12 | .... | 6 | 1 | 6 | .... | 3 | .... | ....8 00– 8 99 |
| 9 00– 9 99... | 77 | 2 | 38 | 4 | 19 | .... | 12 | 1 | 10 | .... | 4 | 1 | 1 | .... | 1 | .... | ....9 00– 9 99 |
| 10 00–10 99... | 129 | 2 | 55 | .... | 47 | .... | 26 | 2 | 17 | .... | 14 | .... | 4 | .... | 3 | .... | ...10 00–10 99 |
| 11 00–11 99... | 88 | .... | 28 | .... | 36 | .... | 13 | .... | 13 | 1 | 11 | .... | 5 | .... | 7 | .... | ...11 00–11 99 |
| 12 00–12 99... | 193 | .... | 104 | .... | 74 | .... | 71 | .... | 30 | .... | 32 | .... | 16 | .... | 18 | .... | ...12 00–12 99 |
| 13 00–13 99... | 78 | .... | 37 | .... | 39 | .... | 37 | .... | 24 | .... | 17 | .... | 18 | .... | 15 | .... | ...13 00–13 99 |
| 14 00–14 99... | 69 | 1 | 46 | .... | 41 | .... | 38 | .... | 33 | .... | 19 | .... | 18 | .... | 16 | .... | ...14 00–14 99 |
| 15 00–15 99... | 91 | 1 | 79 | .... | 65 | 1 | 55 | .... | 52 | .... | 46 | .... | 30 | .... | 36 | .... | ...15 00–15 99 |
| 16 00–17 99... | 37 | .... | 32 | .... | 20 | .... | 35 | .... | 32 | .... | 28 | .... | 16 | .... | 38 | .... | ...16 00–17 99 |
| 18 00–19 99... | 6 | .... | 5 | .... | 3 | .... | 13 | .... | 4 | .... | 6 | .... | 2 | .... | 2 | .... | ...18 00–19 99 |
| 20 00–24 99... | 3 | .... | 6 | .... | 4 | .... | 2 | .... | 4 | .... | 4 | .... | 2 | .... | 1 | .... | ...20 00–24 99 |
| 25 00–29 99... | 3 | .... | 1 | .... | .... | .... | 2 | .... | 3 | .... | 1 | .... | .... | .... | 3 | .... | ...25 00–29 99 |
| 30 00–34 99... | 1 | .... | 3 | .... | 1 | .... | .... | .... | 1 | .... | .... | .... | .... | .... | .... | .... | ...30 00–34 99 |
| 35 00–39 99... | 1 | .... | .... | .... | 1 | .... | .... | .... | .... | .... | 1 | .... | .... | .... | .... | .... | ...35 00–39 99 |
| 40 00 and over. | .... | .... | 1 | .... | 1 | .... | 1 | .... | .... | 1 | .... | .... | .... | .... | .... | .... | .40 00 and over |
| Not reported... | 2 | .... | 1 | .... | 1 | .... | 1 | .... | 1 | .... | .... | .... | 1 | .... | 1 | .... | ...Not reported |
| Total..... | 1,429 | 19 | 665 | 7 | 452 | 9 | 363 | 8 | 247 | 6 | 196 | 4 | 124 | 1 | 147 | 2 | .....Total |

NEW YORK STATE

37. TABLE XIII, A, 1, C — (*concluded*) **DEPARTMENT STORES — SHIPPING AND DELIVERY**

NUMBER OF EMPLOYEES FOR EACH SEX CLASSIFIED ACCORDING TO ACTUAL WEEKLY EARNINGS, BY THE NUMBER OF YEARS IN THE FIRM

| ACTUAL WEEKLY EARNINGS IN DOLLARS | YEARS IN FIRM (*concluded*) | | | | | | | | | | | TOTAL | | CUMULATIVE PER CENT OF TOTAL | | ACTUAL WEEKLY EARNINGS IN DOLLARS |
|---|---|---|---|---|---|---|---|---|---|---|---|---|---|---|---|---|
| | 8 | 9 | | 10–14 | | 15–19 | 20–24 | 25–29 | 30–34 | 35–44 | NOT REPORTED | | | | | |
| | Male | Male | Female | Male | Female | Male | Male | Male | Male | Male | Male | Male | Female | Male | Female | |
| Less than $3 00 | ..... | ..... | ..... | ..... | ..... | 1. | ..... | ..... | ..... | ..... | 1 | 32 | 2 | .72 | 3.44 | Less than $3 00 |
| $3 00–$3 49... | ..... | ..... | ..... | ..... | ..... | ..... | ..... | ..... | ..... | ..... | ........ | 13 | 1 | 1.01 | 5.17 | ...$3 00– 3 49 |
| 3 50– 3 99... | ..... | ..... | ..... | ..... | ..... | ..... | ..... | ..... | ..... | ..... | ........ | 19 | ..... | 1.43 | ..... | ....3 50– 3 99 |
| 4 00– 4 49... | 2 | ..... | ..... | ..... | ..... | ..... | ..... | ..... | ..... | ..... | ........ | 43 | 2 | 2.40 | 8.62 | ....4 00– 4 49 |
| 4 50– 4 99... | ..... | ..... | ..... | ..... | ..... | 1 | ..... | ..... | ..... | ..... | ........ | 27 | 1 | 3.00 | 10.33 | ....4 50– 4 99 |
| 5 00– 5 49... | ..... | ..... | ..... | ..... | ..... | ..... | ..... | ..... | ..... | ..... | 1 | 123 | 6 | 5.73 | 20.63 | ....5 00– 5 49 |
| 5 50– 5 99... | ..... | ..... | ..... | ..... | ..... | ..... | ..... | ..... | ..... | ..... | ........ | 29 | 2 | 6.42 | 24.70 | ....5 50– 5 99 |
| 6 00– 6 49... | ..... | ..... | ..... | 2 | ..... | ..... | ..... | ..... | ..... | ..... | ........ | 109 | 8 | 8.86 | 37.85 | ....6 00– 6 49 |
| 6 50– 6 99... | ..... | ..... | ..... | ..... | ..... | ..... | ..... | ..... | ..... | ..... | 1 | 37 | 2 | 9.69 | 41.40 | ....6 50– 6 99 |
| 7 00– 7 49... | ..... | ..... | ..... | ..... | ..... | ..... | 1 | ..... | ..... | ..... | ........ | 140 | 3 | 12.82 | 46.50 | ....7 00– 7 49 |
| 7 50– 7 99... | 1 | ..... | ..... | 1 | ..... | ..... | ..... | ..... | ..... | ..... | 2 | 246 | 6 | 18.38 | 56.90 | ....7 50– 7 99 |
| 8 00– 8 99... | ..... | ..... | 1 | 2 | ..... | 2 | ..... | ..... | ..... | 1 | 5 | 296 | 7 | 25.00 | 68.90 | ....8 00– 8 99 |
| 9 00– 9 99... | 1 | 1 | ..... | 2 | ..... | 1 | 1 | ..... | ..... | ..... | 6 | 174 | 8 | 28.90 | 82.70 | ....9 00– 9 99 |
| 10 00–10 99... | 6 | 6 | ..... | 11 | ..... | 6 | 2 | ..... | 1 | ..... | 1 | 328 | 4 | 36.20 | 89.60 | ...10 00–10 99 |
| 11 00–11 99... | 4 | 1 | ..... | 12 | 1 | ..... | 2 | ..... | ..... | ..... | ........ | 220 | 2 | 41.20 | 93.10 | ...11 00–11 99 |
| 12 00–12 99... | 12 | 6 | ..... | 27 | ..... | 11 | 4 | 1 | 2 | ..... | 3 | 604 | ..... | 54.70 | ..... | ...12 00–12 99 |
| 13 00–13 99... | 10 | 5 | ..... | 21 | ..... | 6 | 6 | 2 | 1 | 1 | ........ | 317 | ..... | 61.80 | ..... | ...13 00–13 99 |
| 14 00–14 99... | 19 | 10 | ..... | 43 | ..... | 15 | 7 | 1 | 2 | ..... | 1 | 378 | 1 | 70.30 | 94.80 | ...14 00–14 99 |
| 15 00–15 99... | 35 | 14 | ..... | 68 | ..... | 22 | 13 | 3 | 3 | 1 | 3 | 616 | 2 | 84.20 | 98.30 | ...15 00–15 99 |
| 16 00–17 99... | 29 | 21 | ..... | 89 | ..... | 51 | 12 | 5 | ..... | 2 | 1 | 448 | ..... | 94.20 | ..... | ...16 00–17 99 |
| 18 00–19 99... | 4 | 4 | ..... | 26 | ..... | 26 | 6 | 7 | 2 | 2 | ........ | 118 | ..... | 96.80 | ..... | ...18 00–19 99 |
| 20 00–24 99... | 4 | ..... | ..... | 17 | ..... | 23 | 4 | 2 | 6 | 1 | ........ | 83 | ..... | 98.70 | ..... | ...20 00–24 99 |
| 25 00–29 99... | ..... | ..... | ..... | 5 | ..... | 4 | 5 | 2 | ..... | ..... | ........ | 29 | ..... | 99.30 | ..... | ...25 00–29 99 |
| 30 00–34 99... | ..... | ..... | ..... | 2 | ..... | 1 | 2 | 1 | ..... | ..... | ........ | 12 | ..... | 99.60 | ..... | ...30 00–34 99 |
| 35 00–39 99... | ..... | ..... | ..... | 2 | ..... | 1 | ..... | 1 | ..... | ..... | 1 | 8 | ..... | 99.80 | ..... | ...35 00–39 99 |
| 40 00 and over. | ..... | ..... | ..... | ..... | ..... | 2 | 1 | ..... | 1 | ..... | ........ | 7 | 1 | 100.00 | 100.00 | .40 00 and over |
| Not reported... | ..... | ..... | ..... | ..... | ..... | ..... | ..... | 1 | ..... | ..... | ........ | 9 | ..... | ..... | ..... | ...Not reported |
| Total..... | 127 | 68 | 1 | 330 | 1 | 173 | 66 | 26 | 18 | 8 | 26 | 4,465 | 58 | ..... | ..... | .....Total |

NEW YORK STATE

DEPARTMENT STORES — MANUFACTURING

38. TABLE V, A, 1, d  NUMBER AND PER CENT OF EMPLOYEES EARNING SPECIFIED WEEKLY RATES, BY AGE GROUPS AND SEX

| WEEKLY RATES IN DOLLARS | AGE GROUPS IN YEARS 14–15 | | 16–17 | | 18–20 | | 21–24 | | 25–29 | | 30–34 | | 35–39 | | WEEKLY RATES IN DOLLARS |
|---|---|---|---|---|---|---|---|---|---|---|---|---|---|---|---|
| | Male | Female | Male | Female | Male | Female | Male | Female | Male | Female | Male | Female | Male | Female | |
| Less than $3 00 | .... | 2 | .... | 17 | ...... | 3 | ...... | ...... | ...... | ...... | ...... | ...... | ...... | 1 | Less than $3 00 |
| $3 00–$3 49... | .... | 4 | 1 | 12 | ...... | 6 | ...... | ...... | ...... | ...... | ...... | ...... | ...... | ...... | ...$3 00– 3 49 |
| 3 50– 3 99... | 1 | ...... | .... | 1 | ...... | 2 | ...... | ...... | ...... | ...... | ...... | ...... | ...... | ...... | ... 3 50– 3 99 |
| 4 00– 4 49... | .... | 1 | 2 | 15 | ...... | 12 | ...... | 1 | ...... | ...... | ...... | ...... | ...... | ...... | ... 4 00– 4 49 |
| 4 50– 4 99... | .... | ...... | 1 | 7 | ...... | 1 | ...... | 1 | ...... | ...... | ...... | ...... | ...... | ...... | ... 4 50– 4 99 |
| 5 00– 5 49... | 1 | 1 | 1 | 15 | ...... | 38 | ...... | 8 | ...... | 2 | 1 | ...... | ...... | 1 | ... 5 00– 5 49 |
| 5 50– 5 99... | .... | ...... | .... | 3 | ...... | 7 | ...... | ...... | ...... | 1 | ...... | ...... | ...... | ...... | ... 5 50– 5 99 |
| 6 00– 6 49... | 1 | ...... | 2 | 23 | 1 | 49 | ...... | 26 | 1 | 9 | ...... | 4 | 1 | 8 | ... 6 00– 6 49 |
| 6 50– 6 99... | .... | ...... | .... | 1 | 1 | 4 | ...... | 3 | ...... | ...... | ...... | 1 | ...... | ...... | ... 6 50– 6 99 |
| 7 00– 7 49... | 1 | ...... | 3 | 2 | 3 | 40 | 2 | 45 | 2 | 18 | 1 | 13 | ...... | 20 | ... 7 00– 7 49 |
| 7 50– 7 99... | .... | ...... | .... | ...... | ...... | 4 | ...... | 6 | 1 | 7 | 2 | 4 | ...... | 10 | ... 7 50– 7 99 |
| 8 00– 8 99... | .... | ...... | 1 | 4 | 9 | 34 | 5 | 57 | ...... | 41 | ...... | 18 | ...... | 30 | ... 8 00– 8 99 |
| 9 00– 9 99... | .... | ...... | 1 | 1 | 9 | 28 | 2 | 56 | 2 | 52 | ...... | 30 | ...... | 36 | ... 9 00– 9 99 |
| 10 00–10 99... | .... | ...... | .... | 1 | 5 | 8 | 2 | 64 | 3 | 51 | 1 | 34 | 2 | 35 | ...10 00–10 99 |
| 11 00–11 99... | .... | ...... | .... | 1 | 2 | 1 | 2 | 21 | 2 | 40 | ...... | 9 | 2 | 17 | ...11 00–11 99 |
| 12 00–12 99... | .... | ...... | .... | ...... | 2 | 4 | 24 | 37 | 17 | 53 | 11 | 43 | 9 | 42 | ...12 00–12 99 |
| 13 00–13 99... | .... | ...... | .... | ...... | 3 | ...... | 4 | 8 | 10 | 17 | 6 | 11 | 9 | 15 | ...13 00–13 99 |
| 14 00–14 99... | .... | ...... | .... | ...... | 6 | 2 | 16 | 8 | 21 | 26 | 12 | 22 | 21 | 20 | ...14 00–14 99 |
| 15 00–15 99... | 1 | ...... | .... | ...... | 5 | ...... | 17 | 8 | 30 | 31 | 36 | 18 | 18 | 18 | ...15 00–15 99 |
| 16 00–17 99... | .... | ...... | .... | ...... | 2 | 1 | 5 | 3 | 29 | 21 | 32 | 26 | 31 | 16 | ...16 00–17 99 |
| 18 00–19 99... | .... | ...... | .... | ...... | ...... | ...... | 10 | 11 | 23 | 14 | 35 | 18 | 27 | 12 | ...18 00–19 99 |
| 20 00–24 99... | .... | ...... | .... | ...... | 1 | ...... | 6 | 4 | 20 | 16 | 27 | 14 | 28 | 24 | ...20 00–24 99 |
| 25 00–29 99... | .... | ...... | .... | ...... | 1 | ...... | 2 | 1 | 6 | 5 | 19 | 16 | 24 | 13 | ...25 00–29 99 |
| 30 00–34 99... | .... | ...... | .... | ...... | ...... | ...... | ...... | ...... | 3 | 1 | 4 | 4 | 6 | 1 | ...30 00–34 99 |
| 35 00–39 99... | .... | ...... | .... | ...... | ...... | ...... | ...... | ...... | 2 | 2 | 4 | 2 | 3 | 5 | ...35 00–39 99 |
| 40 00 and over. | .... | ...... | .... | ...... | ...... | 1 | ...... | 1 | 2 | 4 | 7 | 4 | 6 | 6 | .40 00 and over |
| Not reported... | .... | ...... | .... | ...... | 1 | ...... | 1 | 4 | ...... | 3 | 9 | 5 | 7 | 2 | ...Not reported |
| Total..... | 5 | 8 | 12 | 103 | 51 | 245 | 98 | 373 | 174 | 414 | 207 | 296 | 194 | 332 | .....Total |

38. TABLE V, A, 1, d — (*concluded*)

NEW YORK STATE

**DEPARTMENT STORES — MANUFACTURING**

NUMBER AND PER CENT OF EMPLOYEES EARNING SPECIFIED WEEKLY RATES, BY AGE GROUPS AND SEX

| WEEKLY RATES IN DOLLARS | AGE GROUPS IN YEARS — (*concluded*) | | | | | | | | | | | | | | WEEKLY RATES IN DOLLARS |
|---|---|---|---|---|---|---|---|---|---|---|---|---|---|---|---|
| | 40–44 | | 45–54 | | 55–64 | | 65 AND OVER | | NOT REPORTED | | TOTAL | | CUMULATIVE PER CENT OF TOTAL | | |
| | Male | Female | Male | Female | Male | Female | Male | Female | Male | Female | Male | Female | Male | Female | |
| Less than $3 00 | .... | ...... | .... | ...... | ...... | ...... | ...... | ...... | ...... | ...... | ..... | 23 | ...... | .94 | Less than $3 00 |
| $3 00–$3 49... | .... | ...... | .... | ...... | ...... | ...... | ...... | ...... | ...... | ...... | 1 | 22 | .08 | 1.85 | ...$3 00– 3 49 |
| 3 50– 3 99... | .... | ...... | .... | ...... | ...... | ...... | ...... | ...... | ...... | ...... | 1 | 3 | .16 | 1.97 | ... 3 50– 3 99 |
| 4 00– 4 49... | .... | ...... | .... | 1 | ...... | ...... | ...... | ...... | ...... | ...... | 2 | 30 | .33 | 3.20 | ... 4 00– 4 49 |
| 4 50– 4 99... | .... | ...... | .... | ...... | ...... | ...... | ...... | ...... | ...... | ...... | 1 | 9 | .41 | 3.57 | ... 4 50– 4 99 |
| 5 00– 5 49... | .... | ...... | .... | 1 | ...... | ...... | ...... | ...... | ...... | ...... | 3 | 66 | .66 | 6.28 | ... 5 00– 5 49 |
| 5 50– 5 99... | .... | ...... | .... | ...... | ...... | ...... | ...... | ...... | ...... | ...... | ...... | 11 | ...... | 6.73 | ... 5 50– 5 99 |
| 6 00– 6 49... | 1 | 4 | .... | 3 | ...... | 5 | ...... | 1 | 1 | 6 | 8 | 138 | 1.32 | 12.40 | ... 6 00– 6 49 |
| 6 50– 6 99... | .... | ...... | .... | ...... | ...... | ...... | ...... | ...... | ...... | ...... | 1 | 9 | 1.38 | 12.80 | ... 6 50– 6 99 |
| 7 00– 7 49... | 1 | 9 | 1 | 14 | ...... | 4 | ...... | ...... | 1 | 7 | 15 | 172 | 2.60 | 19.80 | ... 7 00– 7 49 |
| 7 50– 7 99... | .... | 7 | .... | 13 | ...... | 4 | ...... | 1 | ...... | 4 | 3 | 60 | 2.85 | 22.30 | ... 7 50– 7 99 |
| 8 00– 8 99... | 1 | 21 | .... | 31 | ...... | 15 | ...... | 2 | ...... | 17 | 16 | 270 | 4.15 | 33.50 | ... 8 00– 8 99 |
| 9 00– 9 99... | .... | 27 | .... | 35 | ...... | 7 | ...... | 3 | ...... | 19 | 14 | 294 | 5.28 | 45.50 | ... 9 00– 9 99 |
| 10 00–10 99... | 1 | 29 | 1 | 48 | 3 | 11 | 1 | 1 | 1 | 22 | 20 | 304 | 6.91 | 57.90 | ...10 00–10 99 |
| 11 00–11 99... | 1 | 6 | 1 | 12 | 1 | 2 | ...... | ...... | 1 | 5 | 12 | 114 | 7.84 | 62.60 | ...11 00–11 99 |
| 12 00–12 99... | 6 | 21 | 11 | 24 | 5 | 7 | 5 | 3 | ...... | 13 | 90 | 247 | 15.20 | 72.80 | ...12 00–12 99 |
| 13 00–13 99... | 6 | 5 | 6 | 7 | 6 | 1 | 1 | 1 | 1 | 4 | 52 | 69 | 19.43 | 75.60 | ...13 00–13 99 |
| 14 00–14 99... | 6 | 10 | 13 | 18 | 9 | 4 | 3 | ...... | 1 | 13 | 108 | 123 | 28.20 | 80.60 | ...14 00–14 99 |
| 15 00–15 99... | 11 | 16 | 29 | 13 | 9 | 1 | 4 | ...... | 3 | 14 | 163 | 119 | 41.50 | 85.60 | ...15 00–15 99 |
| 16 00–17 99... | 19 | 7 | 30 | 6 | 15 | 2 | 2 | ...... | ...... | 7 | 165 | 89 | 54.90 | 89.20 | ...16 00–17 99 |
| 18 00–19 99... | 23 | 5 | 46 | 1 | 23 | 1 | 2 | ...... | 2 | 5 | 191 | 67 | 70.40 | 91.90 | ...18 00–19 99 |
| 20 00–24 99... | 35 | 17 | 48 | 10 | 7 | 1 | 2 | ...... | ...... | 7 | 174 | 93 | 84.60 | 95.70 | ...20 00–24 99 |
| 25 00–29 99... | 21 | 10 | 27 | 4 | 7 | 2 | 1 | ...... | ...... | 3 | 108 | 54 | 93.30 | 98.00 | ...25 00–29 99 |
| 30 00–34 99... | 8 | 5 | 7 | ...... | 4 | ...... | ...... | ...... | 1 | 1 | 33 | 12 | 96.00 | 98.40 | ...30 00–34 99 |
| 35 00–39 99... | 3 | 3 | 5 | ...... | 3 | ...... | ...... | ...... | ...... | 1 | 20 | 13 | 97.60 | 99.00 | ...35 00–39 99 |
| 40 00 and over. | 5 | 3 | 9 | 3 | ...... | ...... | ...... | ...... | ...... | 3 | 29 | 25 | 100.00 | 100.00 | .40 00 and over |
| Not reported... | 5 | 6 | 6 | 4 | 1 | ...... | ...... | ...... | ...... | ...... | 30 | 24 | ...... | ...... | ...Not reported |
| Total....... | 153 | 211 | 240 | 248 | 93 | 67 | 21 | 12 | 12 | 151 | 1,260 | 2,460 | ...... | ...... | .....Total |

39. TABLE VI, A, 1, d

NEW YORK STATE

**DEPARTMENT STORES — MANUFACTURING**

NUMBER AND PER CENT OF EMPLOYEES CLASSIFIED ACCORDING TO ACTUAL WEEKLY EARNINGS, BY AGE AND SEX

| Actual Weekly Earnings in Dollars | Age Groups in Years | | | | | | | | | | | | | | Actual Weekly Earnings in Dollars |
|---|---|---|---|---|---|---|---|---|---|---|---|---|---|---|---|
| | 14–15 | | 16–17 | | 18–20 | | 21–24 | | 25–29 | | 30–34 | | 35–39 | | |
| | Male | Female | Male | Female | Male | Female | Male | Female | Male | Female | Male | Female | Male | Female | |
| Less than $3 00 | 1 | 2 | ... | 18 | ... | 9 | ... | 2 | ... | 2 | ... | 1 | ... | 3 | Less than $3 00 |
| $3 00–$3 49... | ... | 5 | 1 | 15 | ... | 7 | ... | 1 | 1 | 1 | ... | ... | ... | 1 | ...$3 00– 3 49 |
| 3 50– 3 99... | 1 | ... | ... | 5 | ... | 4 | 1 | 1 | ... | ... | ... | 2 | ... | 1 | ... 3 50– 3 99 |
| 4 00– 4 49... | ... | ... | 2 | 10 | ... | 9 | ... | 4 | ... | 3 | ... | ... | 1 | 1 | ... 4 00– 4 49 |
| 4 50– 4 99... | ... | ... | 1 | 7 | ... | 5 | ... | 2 | ... | 3 | ... | ... | ... | 1 | ... 4 50– 4 99 |
| 5 00– 5 49... | 1 | 1 | 1 | 13 | ... | 37 | ... | 11 | ... | 4 | 1 | 1 | ... | 3 | ... 5 00– 5 49 |
| 5 50– 5 99... | ... | ... | ... | 3 | 1 | 12 | ... | 12 | ... | 6 | ... | 2 | ... | 4 | ... 5 50– 5 99 |
| 6 00– 6 49... | ... | ... | 2 | 22 | 1 | 40 | 1 | 21 | 2 | 10 | 2 | 5 | 2 | 8 | ... 6 00– 6 49 |
| 6 50– 6 99... | ... | ... | ... | 1 | 1 | 5 | 1 | 8 | 1 | 8 | ... | ... | 2 | 5 | ... 6 50– 6 99 |
| 7 00– 7 49... | 1 | ... | 2 | 2 | 2 | 36 | 3 | 41 | 2 | 17 | 1 | 12 | ... | 17 | ... 7 00– 7 49 |
| 7 50– 7 99... | ... | ... | ... | 1 | ... | 7 | 1 | 15 | 1 | 11 | 3 | 6 | 1 | 13 | ... 7 50– 7 99 |
| 8 00– 8 99... | ... | ... | 2 | 3 | 11 | 35 | 5 | 54 | 3 | 46 | 3 | 22 | 4 | 28 | ... 8 00– 8 99 |
| 9 00– 9 99... | ... | ... | ... | 1 | 8 | 25 | 3 | 55 | 3 | 49 | ... | 26 | ... | 32 | ... 9 00– 9 99 |
| 10 00–10 99... | ... | ... | ... | 1 | 5 | 6 | 4 | 58 | 1 | 49 | 1 | 36 | 2 | 37 | ...10 00–10 99 |
| 11 00–11 99... | ... | ... | 1 | 1 | 2 | 1 | 3 | 17 | 4 | 43 | 5 | 16 | 8 | 26 | ...11 00–11 99 |
| 12 00–12 99... | 1 | ... | ... | ... | 2 | 4 | 23 | 32 | 20 | 44 | 10 | 34 | 9 | 38 | ...12 00–12 99 |
| 13 00–13 99... | ... | ... | ... | ... | 3 | ... | 8 | 7 | 10 | 18 | 8 | 17 | 11 | 16 | ...13 00–13 99 |
| 14 00–14 99... | ... | ... | ... | ... | 4 | 2 | 12 | 9 | 22 | 25 | 13 | 19 | 23 | 17 | ...14 00–14 99 |
| 15 00–15 99... | ... | ... | ... | ... | 6 | ... | 13 | 6 | 29 | 31 | 32 | 19 | 19 | 18 | ...15 00–15 99 |
| 16 00–17 99... | ... | ... | ... | ... | 3 | 1 | 10 | 5 | 28 | 22 | 41 | 25 | 31 | 18 | ...16 00–17 99 |
| 18 00–19 99... | ... | ... | ... | ... | ... | ... | 10 | 11 | 22 | 10 | 30 | 20 | 28 | 11 | ...18 00–19 99 |
| 20 00–24 99... | ... | ... | ... | ... | 1 | ... | 6 | 4 | 24 | 16 | 33 | 17 | 35 | 24 | ...20 00–24 99 |
| 25 00–29 99... | ... | ... | ... | ... | 1 | ... | 2 | 1 | 6 | 4 | 22 | 14 | 21 | 12 | ...25 00–29 99 |
| 30 00–34 99... | ... | ... | ... | ... | ... | ... | 1 | ... | 5 | 1 | 6 | 5 | 7 | ... | ...30 00–34 99 |
| 35 00–39 99... | ... | ... | ... | ... | ... | ... | ... | ... | 3 | 2 | 4 | 2 | 3 | 5 | ...35 00–39 99 |
| 40 00 and over. | ... | ... | ... | ... | ... | 1 | ... | 1 | 5 | 4 | 7 | 3 | 7 | 6 | .40 00 and over |
| Not reported... | ... | ... | ... | ... | ... | 4 | ... | 1 | 1 | 1 | 1 | 1 | ... | 3 | ..Not reported. |
| Total....... | 5 | 8 | 12 | 103 | 51 | 250 | 107 | 379 | 193 | 430 | 223 | 305 | 214 | 348 | .....Total |

NEW YORK STATE

39. TABLE VI, A, 1, d — (*concluded*)

DEPARTMENT STORES — MANUFACTURING

NUMBER AND PER CENT OF EMPLOYEES CLASSIFIED ACCORDING TO ACTUAL WEEKLY EARNINGS, BY AGE AND SEX

| ACTUAL WEEKLY EARNINGS IN DOLLARS | AGE GROUPS IN YEARS — *concluded* 40–44 | | 45–54 | | 55–64 | | 65 AND OVER | | NOT REPORTED | | TOTAL | | CUMULATIVE PER CENT OF TOTAL | | ACTUAL WEEKLY EARNINGS IN DOLLARS |
|---|---|---|---|---|---|---|---|---|---|---|---|---|---|---|---|
| | Male | Female | Male | Female | Male | Female | Male | Female | Male | Female | Male | Female | Male | Female | |
| Less than $3 00 | 1 | 2 | 1 | 1 | ...... | ...... | ...... | ...... | ...... | ...... | 3 | 40 | .22 | 1.59 | Less than $3 00 |
| $3 00–$3 49... | .... | 1 | 1 | 1 | ...... | 1 | ...... | ...... | ...... | ...... | 3 | 33 | .44 | 2.90 | ...$3 00– 3 49 |
| 3 50– 3 99... | .... | 1 | 1 | ...... | ...... | ...... | ...... | ...... | ...... | ...... | 3 | 14 | .66 | 3.46 | ... 3 50– 3 99 |
| 4 00– 4 49... | .... | ...... | .... | 2 | ...... | 1 | ...... | ...... | ...... | ...... | 3 | 30 | .89 | 4.66 | ... 4 00– 4 49 |
| 4 50– 4 99... | .... | ...... | .... | 1 | ...... | 1 | ...... | ...... | ...... | ...... | 1 | 20 | .96 | 5.45 | ... 4 50– 4 99 |
| 5 00– 5 49... | .... | ...... | .... | 2 | ...... | 1 | ...... | ...... | ...... | 1 | 3 | 74 | 1.18 | 8.40 | ... 5 00– 5 49 |
| 5 50– 5 99... | .... | 2 | .... | 3 | ...... | 1 | ...... | ...... | ...... | 1 | 1 | 46 | 1.25 | 10.23 | ... 5 50– 5 99 |
| 6 00– 6 49... | .... | 9 | 1 | 6 | ...... | 3 | ...... | 1 | 1 | 6 | 12 | 131 | 2.14 | 15.45 | ... 6 00– 6 49 |
| 6 50– 6 99... | 2 | 2 | .... | 4 | 1 | 2 | ...... | ...... | ...... | 2 | 8 | 37 | 2.73 | 16.90 | ... 6 50– 6 99 |
| 7 00– 7 49... | 1 | 8 | 1 | 13 | ...... | 4 | ...... | ...... | 1 | 10 | 14 | 160 | 3.76 | 23.60 | ... 7 00– 7 49 |
| 7 50– 7 99... | .... | 10 | .... | 12 | ...... | 5 | ...... | 1 | ...... | 2 | 6 | 83 | 4.21 | 26.60 | ... 7 50– 7 99 |
| 8 00– 8 99... | 1 | 25 | 1 | 33 | ...... | 13 | ...... | 3 | ...... | 19 | 30 | 281 | 6.42 | 37.80 | ... 8 00– 8 99 |
| 9 00– 9 99... | .... | 25 | .... | 34 | ...... | 6 | ...... | 3 | ...... | 16 | 14 | 272 | 7.46 | 48.60 | ... 9 00– 9 99 |
| 10 00–10 99... | 1 | 21 | 4 | 49 | 4 | 11 | 1 | 1 | 1 | 21 | 24 | 290 | 9.22 | 60.10 | ...10 00–10 99 |
| 11 00–11 99... | 5 | 10 | 3 | 10 | 1 | 2 | ...... | ...... | 2 | 5 | 34 | 131 | 11.75 | 65.30 | ...11 00–11 99 |
| 12 00–12 99... | 9 | 18 | 10 | 10 | 3 | 7 | 5 | 2 | 1 | 13 | 93 | 212 | 18.60 | 73.80 | ...12 00–12 99 |
| 13 00–13 99... | 7 | 5 | 8 | 10 | 6 | 1 | 1 | 1 | 1 | 7 | 63 | 82 | 23.25 | 77.00 | ...13 00–13 99 |
| 14 00–14 99... | 5 | 11 | 15 | 13 | 10 | 4 | 3 | ...... | ...... | 10 | 107 | 110 | 31.10 | 81.40 | ...14 00–14 99 |
| 15 00–15 99... | 13 | 16 | 30 | 12 | 9 | 1 | 4 | ...... | 3 | 11 | 158 | 114 | 42.80 | 86.00 | ...15 00–15 99 |
| 16 00–17 99... | 22 | 7 | 29 | 8 | 15 | 2 | 1 | ...... | ...... | 7 | 180 | 95 | 56.10 | 89.60 | ...16 00–17 99 |
| 18 00–19 99... | 27 | 4 | 46 | 1 | 22 | 1 | 2 | ...... | 2 | 4 | 189 | 62 | 70.00 | 92.20 | ...18 00–19 99 |
| 20 00–24 99... | 36 | 18 | 52 | 11 | 7 | 1 | 2 | ...... | ...... | 7 | 196 | 98 | 84.50 | 96.00 | ...20 00–24 99 |
| 25 00–29 99... | 21 | 10 | 30 | 3 | 7 | 2 | ...... | ...... | ...... | 3 | 110 | 49 | 92.60 | 98.00 | ...25 00–29 99 |
| 30 00–34 99... | 7 | 4 | 7 | ...... | 4 | ...... | ...... | ...... | 1 | 1 | 38 | 11 | 95.40 | 98.40 | ...30 00–34 99 |
| 35 00–39 99... | 4 | 3 | 5 | ...... | 3 | ...... | 1 | ...... | ...... | 1 | 23 | 13 | 97.20 | 99.00 | ...35 00–39 99 |
| 40 00 and over. | 7 | 4 | 10 | 3 | 3 | ...... | ...... | ...... | ...... | 3 | 39 | 25 | 100.00 | 100.00 | .40 00 and over |
| Not reported... | 1 | 5 | 1 | 6 | 1 | 2 | 1 | ...... | ...... | 2 | 6 | 25 | ...... | ...... | ...Not reported |
| Total..... | 170 | 221 | 256 | 258 | 96 | 72 | 21 | 12 | 13 | 152 | 1,361 | 2,538 | ...... | ...... | .....Total |

NEW YORK STATE

40. TABLE X, A, 1, d

**DEPARTMENT STORES — MANUFACTURING**

NUMBER AND PER CENT OF EMPLOYEES CLASSIFIED ACCORDING TO ACTUAL WEEKLY EARNINGS, BY CONJUGAL CONDITION AND SEX

| ACTUAL WEEKLY EARNINGS IN DOLLARS | CONJUGAL CONDITION | | | | | | | | | | | | ACTUAL WEEKLY EARNINGS IN DOLLARS |
|---|---|---|---|---|---|---|---|---|---|---|---|---|---|
| | SINGLE | | MARRIED | | WIDOWED OR DIVORCED | | NOT REPORTED | | TOTAL | | CUMULATIVE PER CENT OF TOTAL | | |
| | Male | Female | Male | Female | Male | Female | Male | Female | Male | Female | Male | Female | |
| Less than $3 00 | 1 | 37 | 2 | 2 | ....... | 1 | ....... | ....... | 3 | 40 | .22 | 1.59 | Less than $3 00 |
| $3 00–$3 49... | 1 | 31 | 2 | 1 | ....... | ....... | ....... | 1 | 3 | 33 | .44 | 2.90 | ....$3 00– 3 49 |
| 3 50– 3 99... | 1 | 11 | 1 | 1 | 1 | 1 | ....... | 1 | 3 | 14 | .66 | 3.46 | .... 3 50– 3 99 |
| 4 00– 4 49... | 2 | 25 | 1 | 2 | ....... | 3 | ....... | ....... | 3 | 30 | .89 | 4.66 | .... 4 00– 4 49 |
| 4 50– 4 99... | 1 | 17 | ....... | 2 | ....... | ....... | ....... | 1 | 1 | 20 | .96 | 5.45 | .... 4 50– 4 99 |
| 5 00– 5 49... | 2 | 69 | 1 | 4 | ....... | ....... | ....... | 1 | 3 | 74 | 1.18 | 8.40 | .... 5 00– 5 49 |
| 5 50– 5 99... | 1 | 38 | ....... | 3 | ....... | 4 | ....... | 1 | 1 | 46 | 1.25 | 10.23 | .... 5 50– 5 99 |
| 6 00– 6 49... | 5 | 111 | 6 | 8 | 1 | 10 | ....... | 2 | 12 | 131 | 2.14 | 15.45 | .... 6 00– 6 49 |
| 6 50– 6 99... | 2 | 28 | 5 | 4 | 1 | 5 | ....... | ....... | 8 | 37 | 2.73 | 16.90 | .... 6 50– 6 99 |
| 7 00– 7 49... | 9 | 136 | 5 | 6 | ....... | 17 | ....... | 1 | 14 | 160 | 3.76 | 23.60 | .... 7 00 - 7 49 |
| 7 50– 7 99... | 6 | 57 | ....... | 10 | ....... | 14 | ....... | 2 | 6 | 83 | 4.21 | 26.60 | .... 7 50– 7 99 |
| 8 00– 8 99... | 16 | 214 | 12 | 22 | 1 | 37 | 1 | 8 | 30 | 281 | 6.42 | 37.80 | .... 8 00– 8 99 |
| 9 00– 9 99... | 12 | 207 | 2 | 19 | ....... | 36 | ....... | 10 | 14 | 272 | 7.46 | 48.60 | .... 9 00– 9 99 |
| 10 00–10 99... | 10 | 207 | 13 | 29 | 1 | 48 | ....... | 6 | 24 | 290 | 9.22 | 60.10 | ....10 00–10 99 |
| 11 00–11 99... | 14 | 110 | 18 | 5 | 1 | 11 | 1 | 5 | 34 | 131 | 11.75 | 65.30 | ....11 00–11 99 |
| 12 00–12 99... | 43 | 153 | 43 | 18 | 2 | 36 | 5 | 5 | 93 | 212 | 18.60 | 73.80 | ....12 00–12 99 |
| 13 00–13 99... | 18 | 62 | 44 | 7 | 1 | 10 | ....... | 3 | 63 | 82 | 23.25 | 77.00 | ....13 00–13 99 |
| 14 00–14 99... | 34 | 85 | 66 | 11 | 6 | 12 | 1 | 2 | 107 | 110 | 31.10 | 81.40 | ....14 00–14 99 |
| 15 00–15 99... | 40 | 85 | 105 | 9 | 10 | 15 | 3 | 5 | 158 | 114 | 42.80 | 86.00 | ....15 00–15 99 |
| 16 00–17 99... | 34 | 69 | 137 | 14 | 6 | 10 | 3 | 2 | 180 | 95 | 56.10 | 89.60 | ....16 00–17 99 |
| 18 00–19 99... | 29 | 50 | 150 | 4 | 7 | 6 | 3 | 2 | 189 | 62 | 70.00 | 92.20 | ....18 00–19 99 |
| 20 00–24 99... | 27 | 76 | 151 | 9 | 10 | 9 | 8 | 4 | 196 | 98 | 84.50 | 96.00 | ....20 00–24 99 |
| 25 00–29 99... | 13 | 41 | 90 | 7 | 3 | 1 | 4 | ....... | 110 | 49 | 92.60 | 98.00 | ....25 00–29 99 |
| 30 00–34 99... | 7 | 9 | 28 | 1 | 2 | 1 | 1 | ....... | 38 | 11 | 95.40 | 98.40 | ....30 00–34 99 |
| 35 00–39 99... | 1 | 8 | 21 | 3 | 1 | 1 | ....... | 1 | 23 | 13 | 97.20 | 99.00 | ....35 00–39 99 |
| 40 00 and over. | 7 | 16 | 31 | 5 | 1 | 1 | ....... | 3 | 39 | 25 | 100.00 | 100.00 | .40 00 and over |
| Not reported... | 2 | 15 | 2 | 6 | 1 | 3 | 1 | 1 | 6 | 25 | ....... | ....... | ....Not reported |
| Total..... | 338 | 1,967 | 936 | 212 | 56 | 292 | 31 | 67 | 1,361 | 2,538 | ....... | ....... | ......Total |

41. TABLE XI, A, 1, d

NEW YORK STATE

**DEPARTMENT STORES — MANUFACTURING**

NUMBER AND PER CENT OF EMPLOYEES CLASSIFIED ACCORDING TO ACTUAL WEEKLY EARNINGS, BY NATIVITY AND SEX

| Actual Weekly Earnings in Dollars | Nativity | | | | | | | | | | Actual Weekly Earnings in Dollars |
|---|---|---|---|---|---|---|---|---|---|---|---|
| | Native | | Foreign | | Not reported | | Total | | Cumulative per cent of total | | |
| | Male | Female | Male | Female | Male | Female | Male | Female | Male | Female | |
| Less than $3 00 | 1 | 35 | 2 | 5 | ........ | ........ | 3 | 40 | .22 | 1.59 | Less than $3 00 |
| $3 00–$3 49 | 1 | 28 | 2 | 5 | ........ | ........ | 3 | 33 | .44 | 2.90 | $3 00– 3 49 |
| 3 50– 3 99 | 2 | 12 | 1 | 2 | ........ | ........ | 3 | 14 | .66 | 3.46 | 3 50– 3 99 |
| 4 00– 4 49 | 1 | 26 | 2 | 4 | ........ | ........ | 3 | 30 | .89 | 4.66 | 4 00– 4 49 |
| 4 50– 4 99 | ........ | 17 | 1 | 3 | ........ | ........ | 1 | 20 | .96 | 5.45 | 4 50– 4 99 |
| 5 00– 5 49 | 2 | 64 | 1 | 10 | ........ | ........ | 3 | 74 | 1.18 | 8.40 | 5 00– 5 49 |
| 5 50– 5 99 | ........ | 40 | 1 | 6 | ........ | ........ | 1 | 46 | 1.25 | 10.23 | 5 50– 5 99 |
| 6 00– 6 49 | 5 | 109 | 7 | 20 | ........ | 2 | 12 | 131 | 2.14 | 15.45 | 6 00– 6 49 |
| 6 50– 6 99 | 1 | 29 | 7 | 8 | ........ | ........ | 8 | 37 | 2.73 | 16.90 | 6 50– 6 99 |
| 7 00– 7 49 | 7 | 132 | 7 | 27 | ........ | 1 | 14 | 160 | 3.76 | 23.60 | 7 00– 7 49 |
| 7 50– 7 99 | 3 | 58 | 3 | 24 | ........ | 1 | 6 | 83 | 4.21 | 26.60 | 7 50– 7 99 |
| 8 00– 8 99 | 15 | 223 | 15 | 54 | ........ | 4 | 30 | 281 | 6.42 | 37.80 | 8 00– 8 99 |
| 9 00– 9 99 | 9 | 213 | 5 | 55 | ........ | 4 | 14 | 272 | 7.46 | 48.60 | 9 00– 9 99 |
| 10 00–10 99 | 8 | 206 | 15 | 81 | 1 | 3 | 24 | 290 | 9.22 | 60.10 | 10 00–10 99 |
| 11 00–11 99 | 11 | 108 | 23 | 23 | ........ | ........ | 34 | 131 | 11.75 | 65.30 | 11 00–11 99 |
| 12 00–12 99 | 38 | 157 | 53 | 54 | 2 | 1 | 93 | 212 | 18.60 | 73.80 | 12 00–12 99 |
| 13 00–13 99 | 19 | 57 | 44 | 23 | ........ | 2 | 63 | 82 | 23.25 | 77.00 | 13 00–13 99 |
| 14 00–14 99 | 45 | 78 | 61 | 32 | 1 | ........ | 107 | 110 | 31.10 | 81.40 | 14 00–14 99 |
| 15 00–15 99 | 79 | 87 | 77 | 27 | 2 | ........ | 158 | 114 | 42.80 | 86.00 | 15 00–15 99 |
| 16 00–17 99 | 89 | 64 | 91 | 30 | ........ | 1 | 180 | 95 | 56.10 | 89.60 | 16 00–17 99 |
| 18 00–19 99 | 96 | 38 | 92 | 23 | 1 | 1 | 189 | 62 | 70.00 | 92.20 | 18 00–19 99 |
| 20 00–24 99 | 101 | 63 | 95 | 33 | ........ | 2 | 196 | 98 | 84.50 | 96.00 | 20 00–24 99 |
| 25 00–29 99 | 52 | 37 | 58 | 12 | ........ | ........ | 110 | 49 | 92.60 | 98.00 | 25 00–29 99 |
| 30 00–34 99 | 18 | 10 | 20 | 1 | ........ | ........ | 38 | 11 | 95.40 | 98.40 | 30 00–34 99 |
| 35 00–39 99 | 13 | 12 | 10 | 1 | ........ | ........ | 23 | 13 | 97.20 | 99.00 | 35 00–39 99 |
| 40 00 and over | 19 | 18 | 20 | 7 | ........ | ........ | 39 | 25 | 100.00 | 100.00 | 40 00 and over |
| Not reported | 3 | 22 | 3 | 2 | ........ | 1 | 6 | 25 | ........ | ........ | Not reported |
| Total | 638 | 1,943 | 716 | 572 | 7 | 23 | 1,361 | 2,538 | ........ | ........ | Total |

NEW YORK STATE

42. TABLE XII, A, 1, d

**DEPARTMENT STORES — MANUFACTURING**

NUMBER OF EMPLOYEES FOR EACH SEX CLASSIFIED ACCORDING TO ACTUAL WEEKLY EARNINGS, BY THE NUMBER OF YEARS IN THE TRADE

| ACTUAL WEEKLY EARNINGS IN DOLLARS | YEARS IN TRADE | | | | | | | | | | | | | | ACTUAL WEEKLY EARNINGS IN DOLLARS |
|---|---|---|---|---|---|---|---|---|---|---|---|---|---|---|---|
| | LESS THAN 1 | | 1 | | 2 | | 3 | | 4 | | 5 | | 6 | | |
| | Male | Female | Male | Female | Male | Female | Male | Female | Male | Female | Male | Female | Male | Female | |
| Less than $3 00 | 1 | 17 | .... | 8 | ...... | 3 | ...... | 4 | ...... | ...... | ...... | ...... | ...... | 1 | Less than $3 00 |
| $3 00–$3 49... | 1 | 13 | .... | 6 | ...... | 7 | ...... | 1 | 1 | 1 | ...... | 1 | ...... | ...... | ...$3 00– 3 49 |
| 3 50– 3 99... | 1 | 3 | .... | 4 | ...... | 2 | ...... | ...... | ...... | ...... | 1 | 2 | ...... | ...... | ... 3 50– 3 99 |
| 4 00– 4 49... | 2 | 2 | .... | 9 | ...... | 7 | ...... | 4 | ...... | 1 | ...... | ...... | ...... | 2 | ... 4 00– 4 49 |
| 4 50– 4 99... | 1 | 5 | .... | 1 | ...... | 4 | ...... | 2 | ...... | 2 | ...... | ...... | ...... | ...... | ... 4 50– 4 99 |
| 5 00– 5 49... | 2 | 8 | .... | 14 | ...... | 15 | ...... | 12 | ...... | 7 | ...... | 2 | ...... | 2 | ... 5 00– 5 49 |
| 5 50– 5 99... | .... | 3 | .... | 2 | ...... | 3 | ...... | 7 | ...... | 3 | 1 | 8 | ...... | 7 | ... 5 50– 5 99 |
| 6 00– 6 49... | 3 | 20 | 1 | 13 | ...... | 19 | 1 | 23 | ...... | 15 | 1 | 7 | 1 | 5 | ... 6 00– 6 49 |
| 6 50– 6 99... | .... | 2 | .... | 2 | ...... | 1 | 1 | 3 | ...... | 3 | ...... | 6 | ...... | 1 | ... 6 50– 6 99 |
| 7 00– 7 49... | .... | 5 | 4 | 8 | 1 | 13 | 1 | 14 | ...... | 20 | 1 | 19 | ...... | 13 | ... 7 00– 7 49 |
| 7 50– 7 99... | .... | ...... | .... | 2 | ...... | 5 | ...... | 5 | 1 | 8 | ...... | 8 | ...... | 3 | ... 7 50– 7 99 |
| 8 00– 8 99... | 5 | 5 | 5 | 7 | 3 | 8 | ...... | 21 | 2 | 29 | 1 | 22 | 1 | 22 | ... 8 00– 8 99 |
| 9 00– 9 99... | 2 | 8 | .... | 8 | 4 | 12 | 2 | 15 | 2 | 26 | 1 | 19 | 1 | 15 | ... 9 00– 9 99 |
| 10 00–10 99... | 2 | 4 | .... | 4 | ...... | 11 | ...... | 13 | 3 | 15 | ...... | 18 | 2 | 23 | ...10 00–10 99 |
| 11 00–11 99... | 1 | ...... | .... | 1 | ...... | 1 | 3 | 3 | 2 | 4 | 2 | 7 | ...... | 10 | ...11 00–11 99 |
| 12 00–12 99... | 6 | 2 | 2 | 3 | 2 | 3 | 6 | 3 | 3 | 2 | 4 | 8 | 7 | 12 | ...12 00–12 99 |
| 13 00–13 99... | .... | ...... | 3 | ...... | 1 | ...... | 2 | 1 | 2 | 1 | 3 | 3 | 4 | 4 | ...13 00–13 99 |
| 14 00–14 99... | .... | ...... | .... | ...... | 5 | ...... | 1 | 1 | 2 | 3 | 5 | 1 | 2 | 1 | ...14 00–14 99 |
| 15 00–15 99... | 1 | ...... | .... | 2 | 4 | ...... | 5 | ...... | 2 | 1 | 5 | 5 | 6 | 4 | ...15 00–15 99 |
| 16 00–17 99... | .... | ...... | .... | ...... | ...... | ...... | 2 | 3 | 4 | 1 | 2 | ...... | 3 | 1 | ...16 00–17 99 |
| 18 00–19 99... | .... | 1 | .... | 1 | 2 | 1 | ...... | ...... | 2 | 1 | 3 | 1 | 3 | 2 | ...18 00–19 99 |
| 20 00–24 99... | .... | ...... | .... | 1 | ...... | 1 | 1 | 1 | 1 | ...... | 1 | 1 | ...... | 2 | ...20 00–24 99 |
| 25 00–29 99... | .... | ...... | .... | ...... | ...... | ...... | ...... | ...... | ...... | ...... | 1 | 1 | ...... | ...... | ...25 00–29 99 |
| 30 00–34 99... | .... | ...... | .... | ...... | ...... | ...... | ...... | ...... | ...... | ...... | ...... | ...... | ...... | ...... | ...30 00–34 99 |
| 35 00–39 99... | .... | ...... | 1 | ...... | ...... | ...... | ...... | ...... | ...... | ...... | ...... | ...... | ...... | ...... | ...35 00–39 99 |
| 40 00 and over. | .... | ...... | .... | 1 | ...... | 1 | ...... | ...... | ...... | ...... | ...... | ...... | ...... | ...... | .40 00 and over |
| Not reported... | .... | 1 | .... | ...... | ...... | 2 | ...... | 2 | ...... | ...... | 1 | 3 | ...... | ...... | ...Not reported |
| Total..... | 28 | 99 | 16 | 97 | 22 | 119 | 25 | 138 | 27 | 143 | 33 | 142 | 30 | 130 | .....Total |

NEW YORK STATE

42. TABLE XII, A, 1, d — (*continued*) DEPARTMENT STORES — MANUFACTURING

NUMBER OF EMPLOYEES FOR EACH SEX CLASSIFIED ACCORDING TO ACTUAL WEEKLY EARNINGS, BY THE NUMBER OF YEARS IN THE TRADE

| ACTUAL WEEKLY EARNINGS IN DOLLARS | YEARS IN TRADE — (*continued*) | | | | | | | | | | | | | | ACTUAL WEEKLY EARNINGS IN DOLLARS |
|---|---|---|---|---|---|---|---|---|---|---|---|---|---|---|---|
| | 7 | | 8 | | 9 | | 10–14 | | 15–19 | | 20–24 | | 25–29 | | |
| | Male | Female | Male | Female | Male | Female | Male | Female | Male | Female | Male | Female | Male | Female | |
| Less than $3 00 | .... | ...... | .... | 1 | ...... | ...... | ...... | 2 | ...... | 1 | ...... | 1 | 1 | ...... | Less than $3 00 |
| $3 00–$3 49... | .... | ...... | .... | 1 | ...... | ...... | ...... | ...... | ...... | ...... | ...... | 1 | ...... | ...... | ...$3 00– 3 49 |
| 3 50– 3 99... | .... | ...... | .... | ...... | 1 | ...... | ...... | 1 | ...... | 1 | ...... | ...... | ...... | ...... | ... 3 50– 3 99 |
| 4 00– 4 49... | .... | 1 | .... | 2 | ...... | ...... | ...... | 1 | 1 | ...... | ...... | ...... | ...... | ...... | ... 4 00– 4 49 |
| 4 50– 4 99... | .... | ...... | .... | ...... | ...... | ...... | ...... | 4 | ...... | 1 | ...... | ...... | ...... | ...... | ... 4 50– 4 99 |
| 5 00– 5 49... | .... | ...... | .... | 2 | ...... | 1 | ...... | 5 | 1 | 2 | ...... | 1 | ...... | ...... | ... 5 00– 5 49 |
| 5 50– 5 99... | .... | 2 | .... | 1 | ...... | 1 | ...... | 5 | ...... | 1 | ...... | 1 | ...... | 1 | ... 5 50– 5 99 |
| 6 00– 6 49... | 1 | 3 | .... | 4 | ...... | ...... | ...... | 10 | 2 | 6 | ...... | 3 | 1 | ...... | ... 6 00– 6 49 |
| 6 50– 6 99... | .... | 2 | .... | 3 | ...... | 3 | 2 | 1 | ...... | 4 | 2 | 2 | 2 | ...... | ... 6 50– 6 99 |
| 7 00– 7 49... | 1 | 15 | 1 | 8 | 1 | 4 | ...... | 17 | 1 | 8 | ...... | 5 | ...... | 6 | ... 7 00– 7 49 |
| 7 50– 7 99... | 2 | 5 | .... | 6 | ...... | 3 | 1 | 14 | 1 | 6 | 1 | 3 | ...... | 4 | ... 7 50– 7 99 |
| 8 00– 8 99... | 1 | 17 | .... | 25 | ...... | 15 | 2 | 50 | 2 | 23 | 6 | 13 | 1 | 8 | ... 8 00– 8 99 |
| 9 00– 9 99... | 1 | 16 | 1 | 26 | ...... | 8 | ...... | 56 | ...... | 20 | ...... | 17 | ...... | 10 | ... 9 00– 9 99 |
| 10 00–10 99... | 1 | 23 | 1 | 15 | 1 | 15 | 1 | 58 | ...... | 37 | 4 | 22 | ...... | 7 | ...10 00–10 99 |
| 11 00–11 99... | 2 | 10 | .... | 6 | ...... | 10 | 4 | 42 | 7 | 19 | 5 | 11 | 3 | ...... | ...11 00–11 99 |
| 12 00–12 99... | 6 | 12 | 7 | 17 | 6 | 9 | 8 | 65 | 7 | 34 | 9 | 23 | 5 | 8 | ...12 00–12 99 |
| 13 00–13 99... | 2 | 3 | 6 | 1 | 2 | 4 | 7 | 31 | 4 | 15 | 8 | 11 | 4 | 3 | ...13 00–13 99 |
| 14 00–14 99... | 5 | 12 | 5 | 6 | 1 | 4 | 24 | 31 | 14 | 23 | 13 | 8 | 9 | 6 | ...14 00–14 99 |
| 15 00–15 99... | 6 | 6 | 10 | 8 | 5 | 4 | 24 | 33 | 24 | 22 | 15 | 15 | 16 | 7 | ...15 00–15 99 |
| 16 00–17 99... | 5 | 1 | 10 | 5 | 6 | 6 | 28 | 36 | 35 | 20 | 25 | 10 | 22 | 3 | ...16 00–17 99 |
| 18 00–19 99... | 5 | 1 | 1 | 2 | 5 | 3 | 28 | 16 | 29 | 15 | 30 | 13 | 29 | ...... | ...18 00–19 99 |
| 20 00–24 99... | 3 | 1 | 5 | 1 | 6 | 2 | 27 | 26 | 29 | 20 | 37 | 26 | 32 | 13 | ...20 00–24 99 |
| 25 00–29 99... | 2 | 1 | 1 | 1 | 2 | ...... | 13 | 11 | 19 | 16 | 26 | 12 | 20 | 4 | ...25 00–29 99 |
| 30 00–34 99... | 1 | ...... | 2 | ...... | ...... | ...... | 3 | 2 | 9 | 6 | 7 | 2 | 10 | 1 | ...30 00–34 99 |
| 35 00–39 99... | .... | ...... | 1 | ...... | ...... | ...... | 3 | 5 | 3 | 5 | 1 | 2 | 4 | 1 | ...35 00–39 99 |
| 40 00 and over. | .... | ...... | .... | ...... | ...... | ...... | 8 | 5 | 7 | 7 | 4 | 4 | 11 | 4 | .40 00 and over |
| Not reported... | .... | ...... | 1 | 1 | ...... | 1 | ...... | 5 | ...... | 3 | ...... | 2 | 2 | 1 | ...Not reported |
| Total..... | 44 | 131 | 52 | 142 | 36 | 93 | 183 | 532 | 195 | 315 | 193 | 208 | 172 | 87 | .....Total |

NEW YCRK STATE

42. TABLE XII, A, 1, d — (*concluded*)

**DEPARTMENT STORES — MANUFACTURING**

NUMBER OF EMPLOYEES FOR EACH SEX CLASSIFIED ACCORDING TO ACTUAL WEEKLY EARNINGS, BY THE NUMBER OF YEARS IN THE TRADE

| ACTUAL WEEKLY EARNINGS IN DOLLARS | YEARS IN TRADE — (*concluded*) | | | | | | | | | | | | ACTUAL WEEKLY EARNINGS IN DOLLARS |
|---|---|---|---|---|---|---|---|---|---|---|---|---|---|
| | 30–34 | | 35–44 | | 45 AND OVER | | NOT REPORTED | | TOTAL | | CUMULATIVE PER CENT OF TOTAL | | |
| | Male | Female | Male | Female | Male | Female | Male | Female | Male | Female | Male | Female | |
| Less than $3 00 | ....... | ....... | ....... | ....... | ....... | ....... | 1 | 2 | 3 | 40 | .22 | 1.59 | Less than $3 00 |
| $3 00–$3 49 | 1 | 2 | ....... | ....... | ....... | ....... | ....... | ....... | 3 | 33 | .44 | 2.90 | $3 00– 3 49 |
| 3 50– 3 99 | ....... | ....... | ....... | ....... | ....... | ....... | ....... | 1 | 3 | 14 | .66 | 3.46 | 3 50– 3 99 |
| 4 00– 4 49 | ....... | ....... | ....... | ....... | ....... | ....... | ....... | 1 | 3 | 30 | .89 | 4.66 | 4 00– 4 49 |
| 4 50– 4 99 | ....... | ....... | ....... | ....... | ....... | ....... | ....... | 1 | 1 | 20 | .96 | 5.45 | 4 50– 4 99 |
| 5 00– 5 49 | ....... | ....... | ....... | 1 | ....... | ....... | ....... | 2 | 3 | 74 | 1.18 | 8.40 | 5 00– 5 49 |
| 5 50– 5 99 | ....... | ....... | ....... | ....... | ....... | ....... | ....... | 1 | 1 | 46 | 1.25 | 10.23 | 5 50– 5 99 |
| 6 00– 6 49 | ....... | 1 | 1 | 1 | ....... | ....... | ....... | 1 | 12 | 131 | 2.14 | 15.45 | 6 00– 6 49 |
| 6 50– 6 99 | ....... | 2 | ....... | ....... | 1 | ....... | ....... | 2 | 8 | 37 | 2.73 | 16.90 | 6 50– 6 99 |
| 7 00– 7 49 | ....... | 1 | 1 | ....... | ....... | ....... | 2 | 4 | 14 | 160 | 3.76 | 23.60 | 7 00– 7 49 |
| 7 50– 7 99 | ....... | 1 | ....... | ....... | ....... | ....... | ....... | 10 | 6 | 83 | 4.21 | 26.60 | 7 50– 7 99 |
| 8 00– 8 99 | 1 | 3 | ....... | 1 | ....... | 2 | ....... | 10 | 30 | 281 | 6.42 | 37.80 | 8 00– 8 99 |
| 9 00– 9 99 | ....... | 9 | ....... | ....... | ....... | ....... | ....... | 7 | 14 | 272 | 7.46 | 48.60 | 9 00– 9 99 |
| 10 00–10 99 | 2 | 5 | 4 | 4 | 1 | 1 | 2 | 15 | 24 | 290 | 9.22 | 60.10 | 10 00–10 99 |
| 11 00–11 99 | ....... | 1 | 2 | 1 | ....... | ....... | 3 | 5 | 34 | 131 | 11.75 | 65.30 | 11 00–11 99 |
| 12 00–12 99 | 3 | 4 | 6 | 1 | 5 | 1 | 1 | 5 | 93 | 212 | 18.60 | 73.80 | 12 00–12 99 |
| 13 00–13 99 | 5 | 1 | 6 | 1 | 3 | ....... | 1 | 3 | 63 | 82 | 23.25 | 77.00 | 13 00–13 99 |
| 14 00–14 99 | 7 | 4 | 5 | 3 | 4 | ....... | 5 | 7 | 107 | 110 | 31.10 | 81.40 | 14 00–14 99 |
| 15 00–15 99 | 14 | 3 | 15 | 1 | 1 | ....... | 5 | 3 | 158 | 114 | 42.80 | 86.00 | 15 00–15 99 |
| 16 00–17 99 | 17 | 4 | 9 | 2 | 5 | ....... | 7 | 3 | 180 | 95 | 56.10 | 89.60 | 16 00–17 99 |
| 18 00–19 99 | 20 | ....... | 25 | 1 | 3 | ....... | 4 | 4 | 189 | 62 | 70.00 | 92.20 | 18 00–19 99 |
| 20 00–24 99 | 32 | 2 | 14 | ....... | 2 | ....... | 6 | 1 | 196 | 98 | 84.50 | 96.00 | 20 00–24 99 |
| 25 00–29 99 | 12 | ....... | 13 | 1 | 1 | ....... | ....... | 2 | 110 | 49 | 92.60 | 98.00 | 25 00–29 99 |
| 30 00–34 99 | ....... | ....... | 5 | ....... | ....... | ....... | 1 | ....... | 38 | 11 | 95.40 | 98.40 | 30 00–34 99 |
| 35 00–39 99 | 1 | ....... | 6 | ....... | ....... | ....... | 3 | ....... | 23 | 13 | 97.20 | 99.00 | 35 00–39 99 |
| 40 00 and over | 3 | ....... | 6 | ....... | ....... | ....... | ....... | 3 | 39 | 25 | 100.00 | 100.00 | 40 00 and over |
| Not reported | ....... | ....... | 1 | ....... | 1 | ....... | ....... | 4 | 6 | 25 | ....... | ....... | Not reported |
| Total | 118 | 43 | 119 | 18 | 27 | 4 | 41 | 97 | 1,361 | 2,538 | ....... | ....... | Total |

43. TABLE XIII. A, 1, d

NEW YORK STATE

**DEPARTMENT STORES — MANUFACTURING**

NUMBER OF EMPLOYEES FOR EACH SEX CLASSIFIED ACCORDIND TO ACTUAL WEEKLY EARNINGS, BY THE NUMBER OF YEARS WITH THE FIRM

| ACTUAL WEEKLY EARNINGS IN DOLLARS | YEARS WITH FIRM | | | | | | | | | | | | | | ACTUAL WEEKLY EARNINGS IN DOLLARS |
|---|---|---|---|---|---|---|---|---|---|---|---|---|---|---|---|
| | LESS THAN 1 | | 1 | | 2 | | 3 | | 4 | | 5 | | 6 | | |
| | Male | Female | Male | Female | Male | Female | Male | Female | Male | Female | Male | Female | Male | Female | |
| Less than $3 00 | 1 | 21 | .... | 6 | ...... | 4 | 1 | 4 | ...... | ...... | ...... | ...... | ...... | 3 | Less than $3 00 |
| $3 00–$3 49... | 2 | 17 | 1 | 7 | ...... | 6 | ...... | 1 | ...... | 1 | ...... | 1 | ...... | ...... | ...$3 00– 3 49 |
| 3 50– 3 99... | 2 | 7 | .... | 5 | ...... | ...... | ...... | ...... | ...... | ...... | 1 | ...... | ...... | ...... | ... 3 50– 3 99 |
| 4 00– 4 49... | 3 | 7 | .... | 6 | ...... | 6 | ...... | 9 | ...... | 1 | ...... | ...... | ...... | ...... | ... 4 00– 4 49 |
| 4 50– 4 99... | 1 | 11 | .... | 1 | ...... | 4 | ...... | 2 | ...... | 2 | ...... | ...... | ...... | ...... | ... 4 50– 4 99 |
| 5 00– 5 49... | 2 | 19 | .... | 20 | ...... | 15 | 1 | 6 | ...... | 5 | ...... | 2 | ...... | ...... | ... 5 00– 5 49 |
| 5 50– 5 99... | .... | 7 | 1 | 7 | ...... | 5 | ...... | 8 | ...... | 1 | ...... | 4 | ...... | 5 | ... 5 50– 5 99 |
| 6 00– 6 49... | 5 | 39 | 2 | 22 | 3 | 23 | ...... | 13 | ...... | 10 | 1 | 6 | ...... | 1 | ... 6 00– 6 49 |
| 6 50– 6 99... | 2 | 9 | .... | 3 | ...... | 3 | 2 | 2 | 1 | 2 | 1 | 6 | ...... | 4 | ... 6 50– 6 99 |
| 7 00– 7 49... | 3 | 23 | 3 | 30 | 2 | 27 | 4 | 15 | ...... | 12 | 1 | 15 | ...... | 7 | ... 7 00– 7 49 |
| 7 50– 7 99... | 2 | 14 | 1 | 13 | ...... | 6 | ...... | 8 | 1 | 8 | 1 | 4 | 1 | 4 | ... 7 50– 7 99 |
| 8 00– 8 99... | 8 | 46 | 9 | 34 | 2 | 25 | 2 | 28 | 2 | 31 | 1 | 24 | 1 | 27 | ... 8 00– 8 99 |
| 9 00– 9 99... | 2 | 54 | 3 | 34 | 3 | 30 | 1 | 26 | 2 | 25 | 1 | 15 | 2 | 16 | ... 9 00– 9 99 |
| 10 00–10 99... | 3 | 46 | 2 | 26 | 3 | 29 | 4 | 21 | 4 | 27 | 2 | 22 | ...... | 23 | ...10 00–10 99 |
| 11 00–11 99... | 10 | 13 | 6 | 13 | 5 | 15 | 2 | 9 | 2 | 11 | ...... | 10 | 1 | 7 | ...11 00–11 99 |
| 12 00–12 99... | 16 | 34 | 23 | 29 | 15 | 19 | 10 | 14 | 10 | 17 | 2 | 12 | 4 | 9 | ...12 00–12 99 |
| 13 00–13 99... | 15 | 7 | 6 | 5 | 11 | 5 | 6 | 8 | 3 | 5 | 4 | 4 | 3 | 6 | ...13 00–13 99 |
| 14 00–14 99... | 17 | 9 | 14 | 14 | 21 | 9 | 10 | 5 | 10 | 5 | 6 | 6 | 3 | 6 | ...14 00–14 99 |
| 15 00–15 99... | 33 | 9 | 20 | 12 | 26 | 7 | 16 | 5 | 6 | 7 | 7 | 10 | 7 | 11 | ...15 00–15 99 |
| 16 00–17 99... | 23 | 7 | 14 | 4 | 23 | 10 | 17 | 11 | 14 | 6 | 10 | 8 | 10 | 7 | ...16 00–17 99 |
| 18 00–19 99... | 37 | 16 | 23 | 6 | 20 | 3 | 15 | 6 | 10 | 2 | 12 | 6 | 7 | ...... | ...18 00–19 99 |
| 20 00–24 99... | 24 | 7 | 18 | 6 | 24 | 5 | 15 | 13 | 14 | 8 | 8 | 1 | 11 | 6 | ...20 00–24 99 |
| 25 00–29 99... | 14 | 2 | 8 | 4 | 11 | 4 | 7 | 4 | 4 | 1 | 6 | 2 | 7 | 2 | ...25 00–29 99 |
| 30 00–34 99... | 5 | 1 | 3 | 1 | 5 | ...... | 3 | 2 | ...... | ...... | 1 | 1 | 3 | ...... | ...30 00–34 99 |
| 35 00–39 99... | 2 | 3 | 1 | ...... | 4 | 1 | 1 | 3 | ...... | ...... | 2 | ...... | 1 | ...... | ...35 00–39 99 |
| 40 00 and over. | 5 | 4 | 3 | 3 | 3 | 1 | 3 | 2 | 3 | 3 | 5 | ...... | 1 | ...... | .40 00 and over |
| Not reported... | .... | 4 | .... | 2 | ...... | 4 | ...... | 5 | ...... | ...... | 2 | 2 | ...... | 1 | ...Not reported |
| Total..... | 237 | 436 | 161 | 313 | 181 | 266 | 120 | 230 | 86 | 190 | 74 | 161 | 62 | 145 | .....Total |

NEW YORK STATE

43. TABLE XIII, A, 1, d — (*continued*)

**DEPARTMENT STORES — MANUFACTURING**

NUMBER OF EMPLOYEES FOR EACH SEX CLASSIFIED ACCORDING TO ACTUAL WEEKLY EARNINGS, BY THE NUMBER OF YEARS WITH THE FIRM

| ACTUAL WEEKLY EARNINGS IN DOLLARS | YEARS WITH FIRM (*continued*) | | | | | | | | | | | | | | ACTUAL WEEKLY EARNINGS IN DOLLARS |
|---|---|---|---|---|---|---|---|---|---|---|---|---|---|---|---|
| | 7 | | 8 | | 9 | | 10–14 | | 15–19 | | 20–24 | | 25–29 | | |
| | Male | Female | Male | Female | Male | Female | Male | Female | Male | Female | Male | Female | Male | Female | |
| Less than $3 00 | .... | .... | .... | .... | .... | 1 | .... | 1 | 1 | .... | .... | .... | .... | .... | Less than $3 00 |
| $3 00–$3 49... | .... | .... | .... | .... | .... | .... | .... | .... | .... | .... | .... | .... | .... | .... | ...$3 00– 3 49 |
| 3 50– 3 99... | .... | .... | .... | .... | .... | .... | .... | .... | .... | 2 | .... | .... | .... | .... | ... 3 50– 3 99 |
| 4 00– 4 49... | .... | .... | .... | .... | .... | .... | .... | 1 | .... | .... | .... | .... | .... | .... | ... 4 00– 4 49 |
| 4 50– 4 99... | .... | .... | .... | .... | .... | .... | .... | .... | .... | .... | .... | .... | .... | .... | ... 4 50– 4 99 |
| 5 00– 5 49... | .... | .... | .... | 2 | .... | .... | .... | 3 | .... | 1 | .... | .... | .... | .... | ... 5 00– 5 49 |
| 5 50– 5 99... | .... | 1 | .... | 2 | .... | .... | .... | 3 | .... | .... | .... | .... | .... | 1 | ... 5 50– 5 99 |
| 6 00– 6 49... | .... | 3 | .... | 5 | 1 | .... | .... | 4 | .... | 2 | .... | 1 | .... | .... | ... 6 00– 6 49 |
| 6 50– 6 99... | 1 | 1 | .... | 1 | .... | 2 | .... | 1 | 1 | 2 | .... | 1 | .... | .... | ... 6 50– 6 99 |
| 7 00– 7 49... | .... | 10 | 1 | 2 | .... | 2 | .... | 6 | .... | 4 | .... | 4 | .... | 2 | ... 7 00– 7 49 |
| 7 50– 7 99... | .... | 3 | .... | 1 | .... | 1 | .... | 13 | .... | 5 | .... | 1 | .... | 1 | ... 7 50– 7 99 |
| 8 00– 8 99... | 1 | 14 | 1 | 11 | 1 | 4 | 2 | 25 | .... | 9 | .... | .... | .... | 1 | ... 8 00– 8 99 |
| 9 00– 9 99... | .... | 17 | .... | 7 | .... | 11 | .... | 19 | .... | 10 | .... | 4 | .... | .... | ... 9 00– 9 99 |
| 10 00–10 99... | 1 | 22 | 1 | 8 | 1 | 9 | 1 | 37 | .... | 9 | .... | 4 | .... | 4 | ...10 00–10 99 |
| 11 00–11 99... | 3 | 10 | .... | 8 | 1 | 8 | 3 | 15 | 1 | 9 | .... | 1 | .... | 1 | ...11 00–11 99 |
| 12 00–12 99... | .... | 13 | 2 | 10 | 3 | 7 | 7 | 22 | 1 | 13 | .... | 8 | .... | 2 | ...12 00–12 99 |
| 13 00–13 99... | 4 | 3 | 4 | 3 | 1 | 4 | 4 | 20 | 1 | 9 | .... | 2 | 1 | 1 | ...13 00–13 99 |
| 14 00–14 99... | 4 | 10 | 6 | 9 | 6 | 2 | 8 | 19 | .... | 11 | 1 | 1 | .... | 1 | ...14 00–14 99 |
| 15 00–15 99... | 6 | 7 | 11 | 3 | 3 | 5 | 13 | 20 | 4 | 10 | 3 | 4 | 2 | 2 | ...15 00–15 99 |
| 16 00–17 99... | 14 | 7 | 9 | 4 | 10 | 3 | 19 | 18 | 8 | 5 | 6 | 2 | 2 | 1 | ...16 00–17 99 |
| 18 00–19 99... | 9 | 2 | 7 | 3 | 10 | 1 | 12 | 9 | 13 | 5 | 4 | 3 | 3 | .... | ...18 00–19 99 |
| 20 00–24 99... | 7 | 1 | 6 | 2 | 4 | 5 | 39 | 19 | 13 | 15 | 5 | 5 | 4 | 4 | ...20 00–24 99 |
| 25 00–29 99... | 6 | 3 | 3 | 5 | 7 | .... | 17 | 8 | 14 | 5 | 3 | 5 | 1 | 3 | ...25 00–29 99 |
| 30 00–34 99... | 4 | .... | 2 | 1 | .... | .... | 5 | 2 | 4 | 3 | 1 | .... | 1 | .... | ...30 00–34 99 |
| 35 00–39 99... | .... | .... | 1 | .... | 1 | .... | 2 | 2 | 5 | 4 | 1 | .... | 2 | .... | ...35 00–39 99 |
| 40 00 and over. | 2 | .... | 3 | 1 | 2 | .... | 5 | 4 | 1 | 1 | 2 | 2 | 1 | 3 | .40 00 and over |
| Not reported... | .... | .... | 1 | 2 | .... | 2 | 2 | 2 | .... | 1 | .... | .... | 1 | .... | ...Not reported |
| Total..... | 62 | 127 | 58 | 90 | 51 | 67 | 139 | 273 | 67 | 135 | 26 | 48 | 18 | 27 | .....Total |

NEW YORK STATE

43. TABLE XIII, A, 1, a — (*concluded*) **DEPARTMENT STORES — MANUFACTURING**

NUMBER OF EMPLOYEES OF EACH SEX CLASSIFIED ACCORDING TO ACTUAL WEEKLY EARNINGS, BY THE NUMBER OF YEARS WITH THE FIRM

| ACTUAL WEEKLY EARNINGS IN DOLLARS | YEARS WITH FIRM (*concluded*) | | | | | | | | | | ACTUAL WEEKLY EARNINGS IN DOLLARS |
|---|---|---|---|---|---|---|---|---|---|---|---|
| | 30–34 | | 35–44 | | NOT REPORTED | | TOTAL | | CUMULATIVE PER CENT OF TOTAL | | |
| | Male | Female | Male | Female | Male | Female | Male | Female | Male | Female | |
| Less than $3 00 | ........ | ........ | ........ | ........ | ........ | ........ | 3 | 40 | .22 | 1.59 | Less than $3 00 |
| $3 00–$3 49 | ........ | ........ | ........ | ........ | ........ | ........ | 3 | 33 | .44 | 2.90 | $3 00– 3 49 |
| 3 50– 3 99 | ........ | ........ | ........ | ........ | ........ | ........ | 3 | 14 | .66 | 3.46 | 3 50– 3 99 |
| 4 00– 4 49 | ........ | ........ | ........ | ........ | ........ | ........ | 3 | 30 | .89 | 4.66 | 4 00– 4 49 |
| 4 50– 4 99 | ........ | ........ | ........ | ........ | ........ | ........ | 1 | 20 | .96 | 5.45 | 4 50– 4 99 |
| 5 00– 5 49 | ........ | ........ | ........ | ........ | ........ | 1 | 3 | 74 | 1.18 | 8.40 | 5 00– 5 49 |
| 5 50– 5 99 | ........ | ........ | ........ | ........ | ........ | 2 | 1 | 46 | 1.25 | 10.23 | 5 50– 5 99 |
| 6 00– 6 49 | ........ | 2 | ........ | ........ | ........ | ........ | 12 | 131 | 2.14 | 15.45 | 6 00– 6 49 |
| 6 50– 6 99 | ........ | ........ | ........ | ........ | ........ | ........ | 8 | 37 | 2.73 | 16.90 | 6 50– 6 99 |
| 7 00– 7 49 | ........ | ........ | ........ | ........ | ........ | 1 | 14 | 160 | 3.76 | 23.60 | 7 00– 7 49 |
| 7 50– 7 99 | ........ | ........ | ........ | ........ | ........ | 1 | 6 | 83 | 4.21 | 26.60 | 7 50– 7 99 |
| 8 00– 8 99 | ........ | 1 | ........ | ........ | ........ | 1 | 30 | 281 | 6.42 | 37.80 | 8 00– 8 99 |
| 9 00– 9 99 | ........ | 3 | ........ | 1 | ........ | ........ | 14 | 272 | 7.46 | 48.60 | 9 00– 9 99 |
| 10 00–10 99 | 2 | ........ | ........ | 1 | ........ | 2 | 24 | 290 | 9.22 | 60.10 | 10 00–10 99 |
| 11 00–11 99 | ........ | ........ | ........ | ........ | ........ | 1 | 34 | 131 | 11.75 | 65.30 | 11 00–11 99 |
| 12 00–12 99 | ........ | 2 | ........ | ........ | ........ | 1 | 93 | 212 | 18.60 | 73.80 | 12 00–12 99 |
| 13 00–13 99 | ........ | ........ | ........ | ........ | ........ | ........ | 63 | 82 | 23.25 | 77.00 | 13 00–13 99 |
| 14 00–14 99 | ........ | 2 | ........ | ........ | 1 | 1 | 107 | 110 | 31.10 | 81.40 | 14 00–14 99 |
| 15 00–15 99 | 1 | 1 | ........ | 1 | ........ | ........ | 158 | 114 | 42.80 | 86.00 | 15 00–15 99 |
| 16 00–17 99 | ........ | 2 | 1 | ........ | ........ | ........ | 180 | 95 | 56.10 | 89.60 | 16 00–17 99 |
| 18 00–19 99 | 6 | ........ | 1 | ........ | ........ | ........ | 189 | 62 | 70.00 | 92.20 | 18 00–19 99 |
| 20 00–24 99 | 3 | ........ | 1 | ........ | ........ | 1 | 196 | 98 | 84.50 | 96.00 | 20 00–24 99 |
| 25 00–29 99 | 2 | ........ | ........ | ........ | ........ | 1 | 110 | 49 | 92.60 | 98.00 | 25 00–29 99 |
| 30 00–34 99 | ........ | ........ | ........ | ........ | 1 | ........ | 38 | 11 | 95.40 | 98.40 | 30 00–34 99 |
| 35 00–39 99 | ........ | ........ | ........ | ........ | ........ | ........ | 23 | 13 | 97.20 | 99.00 | 35 00–39 99 |
| 40 00 and over | ........ | ........ | ........ | ........ | ........ | 1 | 39 | 25 | 100.00 | 100.00 | 40 00 and over |
| Not reported | ........ | ........ | ........ | ........ | ........ | ........ | 6 | 25 | ........ | ........ | Not reported |
| Total | 14 | 13 | 3 | 3 | 2 | 14 | 1,361 | 2,538 | ........ | ........ | Total |

44. TABLE XIV, A, 1, d

NEW YORK STATE

**DEPARTMENT STORES**

NUMBER OF EMPLOYEES FOR EACH SEX IN THE MAIN OPERATIONS IN THE MANUFACTURING DEPARTMENT EARNING SPECIFIED WEEKLY RATES

| WEEKLY RATES IN DOLLARS | OCCUPATION | | | | | | | | | | | | | | | | | | | WEEKLY RATES IN DOLLARS |
|---|---|---|---|---|---|---|---|---|---|---|---|---|---|---|---|---|---|---|---|---|
| | TAILORS | | FITTERS | | SEWING | | FURNITURE FINISHERS | CABINET MAKERS | UPHOLSTERERS | | CARPET LAYERS | ENGRAVING AND JEWELRY REPAIRING | | ALL OTHERS | | TOTAL | | ACCUMULATIVE PER CENT FOR STATE | | |
| | Male | Female | Male | Female | Male | Female | Male | Male | Male | Female | Male | male | Female | Male | Female | Male | Female | Male | Female | |
| Less than $3 00 | .... | .... | .... | .... | .... | 9 | .... | .... | .... | .... | .... | .... | .... | .... | 14 | .... | 23 | .... | .94 | Less than $3 00 |
| $3 00-$3 49... | 1 | .... | .... | .... | .... | 7 | .... | .... | .... | .... | .... | .... | .... | .... | 15 | 1 | 22 | .08 | 1.85 | ...$3 00- 3 49 |
| 3 50- 3 99... | .... | .... | .... | .... | .... | 3 | .... | .... | .... | .... | .... | 1 | .... | .... | .... | 1 | 3 | .16 | 1.97 | ... 3 50- 3 99 |
| 4 00- 4 49... | .... | .... | .... | .... | .... | 13 | .... | .... | .... | .... | .... | .... | .... | 2 | 17 | 2 | 30 | .33 | 3.20 | ... 4 00- 4 49 |
| 4 50- 4 99... | .... | .... | .... | .... | .... | 5 | .... | .... | .... | .... | .... | .... | .... | 1 | 4 | 1 | 9 | .41 | 3.57 | ... 4 50- 4 99 |
| 5 00- 5 49... | .... | .... | .... | 1 | .... | 32 | .... | .... | 1 | .... | .... | .... | .... | 2 | 33 | 3 | 66 | .65 | 6.27 | ... 5 00- 5 49 |
| 5 50- 5 99... | .... | .... | .... | .... | .... | 9 | .... | .... | .... | .... | .... | .... | .... | .... | 2 | .... | 11 | .65 | 6.72 | ... 5 50- 5 99 |
| 6 00- 6 49... | 3 | .... | .... | .... | 1 | 87 | .... | .... | 2 | 1 | .... | 1 | 1 | 1 | 49 | 8 | 138 | 1.30 | 12.38 | ... 6 00- 6 49 |
| 6 50- 6 99... | 1 | .... | .... | .... | .... | 9 | .... | .... | .... | .... | .... | .... | .... | .... | .... | 1 | 9 | 1.38 | 12.75 | ... 6 50- 6 99 |
| 7 00- 7 49... | 4 | 1 | .... | 1 | 3 | 133 | .... | 1 | 1 | .... | .... | 4 | 1 | 2 | 36 | 15 | 172 | 2.60 | 19.80 | ... 7 00- 7 49 |
| 7 50- 7 99... | .... | 1 | .... | 1 | 2 | 58 | .... | .... | .... | .... | .... | .... | .... | 1 | .... | 3 | 60 | 3.85 | 22.26 | ... 7 50- 7 99 |
| 8 00- 8 99... | 3 | 2 | .... | 5 | 1 | 168 | .... | 3 | 5 | .... | 1 | .... | 4 | 3 | 91 | 16 | 270 | 4.15 | 33.33 | ... 8 00- 8 99 |
| 9 00- 9 99... | 1 | 4 | .... | 10 | 2 | 215 | 1 | .... | 4 | 6 | .... | 1 | 1 | 5 | 58 | 14 | 294 | 5.28 | 45.39 | ... 9 00- 9 99 |
| 10 00-10 99... | 5 | 7 | .... | 19 | 1 | 178 | 3 | .... | 1 | 20 | .... | .... | 1 | 10 | 79 | 20 | 304 | 6.92 | 57.85 | ...10 00-10 99 |
| 11 00-11 99... | 7 | 2 | .... | 6 | 1 | 72 | .... | .... | 4 | 6 | .... | .... | .... | .... | 28 | 12 | 114 | 7.88 | 62.52 | ...11 00-11 99 |
| 12 00-12 99... | 18 | 3 | 1 | 35 | 1 | 89 | 12 | 1 | 3 | 12 | 6 | .... | 1 | 48 | 107 | 90 | 247 | 15.20 | 72.62 | ...12 00-12 99 |
| 13 00-13 99... | 18 | 1 | .... | 6 | .... | 42 | 6 | 1 | 1 | 2 | 2 | .... | 1 | 24 | 17 | 52 | 69 | 19.43 | 75.48 | ...13 00-13 99 |
| 14 00-14 99... | 31 | 2 | .... | 21 | 2 | 60 | 8 | 18 | 4 | 2 | 4 | 5 | 3 | 36 | 35 | 108 | 123 | 28.21 | 80.60 | ...14 00-14 99 |
| 15 00-15 99... | 21 | 2 | 1 | 31 | 2 | 45 | 44 | 18 | 9 | .... | 9 | 5 | 2 | 54 | 39 | 163 | 119 | 41.50 | 85.40 | ...15 00-15 99 |
| 16 00-17 99... | 11 | .... | .... | 28 | 4 | 25 | 32 | 24 | 15 | .... | 14 | 19 | 2 | 46 | 34 | 165 | 89 | 54.87 | 89.05 | ...16 00-17 99 |
| 18 00-19 99... | 20 | .... | 1 | 24 | 5 | 26 | 35 | 7 | 28 | .... | 12 | 20 | .... | 63 | 17 | 191 | 67 | 70.41 | 91.80 | ...18 00-19 99 |
| 20 00-24 99... | 21 | 2 | 4 | 34 | 1 | 20 | 13 | 8 | 22 | .... | 33 | 23 | 1 | 49 | 36 | 174 | 93 | 84.55 | 95.61 | ...20 00-24 99 |
| 25 00-29 99... | 18 | 6 | 3 | 18 | 1 | 3 | 1 | 2 | 29 | .... | 26 | 6 | .... | 22 | 27 | 108 | 54 | 93.50 | 97.82 | ...25 00-29 99 |
| 30 00-34 99... | 3 | .... | 4 | 4 | .... | 1 | .... | .... | 9 | .... | 2 | 3 | .... | 12 | 7 | 33 | 12 | 96.00 | 98.31 | ...30 00-34 99 |
| 35 00-39 99... | 1 | .... | .... | 4 | .... | 1 | .... | .... | 2 | .... | .... | 2 | .... | 15 | 8 | 20 | 13 | 97.64 | 98.85 | ...35 00-39 99 |
| 40 00 and over. | 5 | .... | 7 | 7 | .... | 5 | .... | .... | 1 | .... | .... | 10 | .... | 6 | 13 | 29 | 25 | 100.00 | 100.00 | .40 00 and over |
| Not reported.. | 1 | .... | .... | 2 | .... | 4 | .... | .... | .... | .... | .... | .... | .... | 29 | 18 | 30 | 24 | .... | .... | ..Not reported |
| Total..... | 193 | 33 | 21 | 257 | 27 | 1,319 | 155 | 83 | 141 | 49 | 109 | 100 | 18 | 431 | 784 | 1,260 | 2,460 | .... | .... | .....Total |

NEW YORK STATE

**DEPARTMENT STORES — PLANT**

45. TABLE V, A, 1, e — NUMBER AND PER CENT OF EMPLOYEES EARNING SPECIFIED WEEKLY RATES, BY AGE GROUPS AND SEX

| Specified Weekly Rates in Dollars | Age Groups in Years: 14–15 | | 16–17 | | 18–20 | | 21–24 | | 25–29 | | 30–34 | | 35–39 | | Specified Weekly Rates in Dollars |
|---|---|---|---|---|---|---|---|---|---|---|---|---|---|---|---|
| | Male | Female | Male | Female | Male | Female | Male | Female | Male | Female | Male | Female | Male | Female | |
| Less than $3 00 | .... | ...... | .... | ...... | ...... | 1 | ...... | 1 | ...... | ...... | ...... | ...... | ...... | ...... | Less than $3 00 |
| $3 00–$3 49... | .... | ...... | .... | 2 | ...... | 4 | ...... | 17 | ...... | 16 | 1 | 13 | ...... | 12 | ...$3 00– 3 49 |
| 3 50– 3 99... | .... | 4 | .... | 3 | ...... | 4 | ...... | 4 | ...... | 4 | 1 | 2 | ...... | 6 | ... 3 50– 3 99 |
| 4 00– 4 49... | .... | 1 | 2 | 13 | ...... | 17 | ...... | 55 | 4 | 83 | 6 | 39 | 4 | 24 | ... 4 00– 4 49 |
| 4 50– 4 99... | .... | ...... | 3 | 1 | 2 | 4 | ...... | 6 | ...... | 21 | ...... | 22 | 1 | 12 | ... 4 50– 4 99 |
| 5 00– 5 49... | 1 | ...... | 9 | 5 | 21 | 27 | 12 | 38 | 12 | 45 | 4 | 27 | 3 | 25 | ... 5 00– 5 49 |
| 5 50– 5 99... | .... | ...... | .... | ...... | ...... | 1 | ...... | 2 | ...... | 1 | ...... | 4 | ...... | ...... | ... 5 50– 5 99 |
| 6 00– 6 49... | 1 | 1 | 12 | 5 | 18 | 43 | 12 | 70 | 8 | 69 | 4 | 38 | 2 | 32 | ... 6 00– 6 49 |
| 6 50– 6 99... | .... | ...... | .... | ...... | ...... | ...... | ...... | 1 | ...... | 3 | ...... | 1 | ...... | ...... | ... 6 50– 6 99 |
| 7 00– 7 49... | .... | 1 | 4 | 3 | 20 | 20 | 20 | 26 | 4 | 35 | 5 | 29 | 7 | 32 | ... 7 00– 7 49 |
| 7 50– 7 99... | .... | ...... | 1 | ...... | 1 | 1 | 3 | 1 | 1 | 2 | ...... | 7 | ...... | 5 | ... 7 50– 7 99 |
| 8 00– 8 99... | .... | ...... | 2 | 1 | 18 | 9 | 22 | 9 | 21 | 7 | 11 | 10 | 5 | 16 | ... 8 00– 8 99 |
| 9 00– 9 99... | .... | ...... | 3 | ...... | 15 | 1 | 26 | 5 | 33 | 6 | 14 | 3 | 15 | 11 | ... 9 00– 9 99 |
| 10 00–10 99... | .... | ...... | 3 | ...... | 24 | 1 | 89 | 4 | 91 | 4 | 58 | 9 | 49 | 9 | ...10 00–10 99 |
| 11 00–11 99... | .... | ...... | .... | ...... | 11 | ...... | 55 | 2 | 64 | 1 | 31 | 2 | 34 | 1 | ...11 00–11 99 |
| 12 00–12 99... | .... | ...... | .... | ...... | 20 | ...... | 84 | 3 | 107 | 6 | 108 | 7 | 92 | 2 | ...12 00–12 99 |
| 13 00–13 99... | .... | ...... | .... | ...... | 4 | ...... | 29 | ...... | 37 | ...... | 22 | ...... | 18 | 1 | ...13 00–13 99 |
| 14 00–14 99... | .... | ...... | .... | ...... | 4 | ...... | 14 | ...... | 15 | ...... | 28 | 2 | 30 | 2 | ...14 00–14 99 |
| 15 00–15 99... | .... | ...... | .... | ...... | 4 | ...... | 14 | 1 | 46 | 1 | 34 | ...... | 45 | 6 | ...15 00–15 99 |
| 16 00–17 99... | .... | ...... | .... | ...... | 2 | ...... | 8 | ...... | 34 | 1 | 17 | 2 | 31 | 1 | ...16 00–17 99 |
| 18 00–19 99... | .... | ...... | .... | ...... | 1 | ...... | 9 | ...... | 34 | ...... | 28 | ...... | 27 | 1 | ...18 00–19 99 |
| 20 00–24 99... | .... | ...... | .... | ...... | 1 | ...... | 14 | ...... | 31 | ...... | 48 | 1 | 39 | 1 | ...20 00–24 99 |
| 25 00–29 99... | .... | ...... | .... | ...... | ...... | ...... | 1 | ...... | 5 | ...... | 11 | 1 | 11 | 1 | ...25 00–29 99 |
| 30 00–34 99... | .... | ...... | .... | ...... | ...... | ...... | ...... | ...... | ...... | ...... | 4 | ...... | 9 | ...... | ...30 00–34 99 |
| 35 00–39 99... | .... | ...... | .... | ...... | ...... | ...... | 1 | ...... | 1 | ...... | 2 | ...... | 1 | ...... | ...35 00–39 99 |
| 40 00 and over. | .... | ...... | .... | ...... | ...... | ...... | ...... | ...... | ...... | ...... | 2 | ...... | 4 | ...... | .40 00 and over |
| Not reported... | .... | ...... | .... | ...... | 8 | ...... | 12 | ...... | 11 | ...... | 20 | ...... | 10 | ...... | ...Not reported |
| Total..... | 2 | 7 | 39 | 33 | 174 | 133 | 425 | 245 | 559 | 305 | 459 | 219 | 437 | 200 | .....Total |

45. TABLE V, A, 1, e — (*Concluded*)

NEW YORK STATE

**DEPARTMENT STORES — PLANT**

NUMBER AND PER CENT OF EMPLOYEES EARNING SPECIFIED WEEKLY RATES, BY AGE GROUPS AND SEX

| SPECIFIED WEEKLY RATES IN DOLLARS | AGE GROUPS IN YEARS — (*concluded*) 40–44 | | 45–54 | | 55–64 | | 65 AND OVER | | NOT REPORTED | | TOTAL | | CUMULATIVE PER CENT FOR STATE | | SPECIFIED WEEKLY RATES IN DOLLARS |
|---|---|---|---|---|---|---|---|---|---|---|---|---|---|---|---|
| | Male | Female | Male | Female | Male | Female | Male | Female | Male | Female | Male | Female | Male | Female | |
| Less than $3 00 | .... | ...... | .... | ...... | ...... | ...... | ...... | ...... | ...... | ...... | ...... | 2 | ...... | .13 | Less than $3 00 |
| $3 00–$3 49... | .... | 5 | .... | 2 | ...... | ...... | ...... | ...... | ...... | ...... | 1 | 71 | .03 | 4.75 | ...$3 00– 3 49 |
| 3 50– 3 99... | .... | ...... | .... | ...... | ...... | ...... | ...... | ...... | ...... | ...... | 1 | 27 | .06 | 6.52 | ... 3 50– 3 99 |
| 4 00– 4 49... | 5 | 8 | 6 | 5 | 2 | 1 | ...... | ...... | ...... | ...... | 29 | 246 | .94 | 22.52 | ... 4 00– 4 49 |
| 4 50– 4 99... | .... | 7 | .... | 7 | ...... | 2 | ...... | ...... | ...... | ...... | 6 | 82 | 1.12 | 27.85 | ... 4 50– 4 99 |
| 5 00– 5 49... | 2 | 14 | 5 | 14 | ...... | 2 | ...... | ...... | ...... | 1 | 69 | 198 | 3.21 | 40.80 | ... 5 00– 5 49 |
| 5 50– 5 99... | .... | 1 | .... | 4 | ...... | 2 | ...... | ...... | ...... | ...... | ...... | 15 | 3.21 | 41.75 | ... 5 50– 5 99 |
| 6 00– 6 49... | 2 | 33 | 5 | 51 | ...... | 8 | ...... | 2 | ...... | 2 | 64 | 354 | 5.10 | 64.75 | ... 6 00– 6 49 |
| 6 50– 6 99... | .... | ...... | .... | 1 | ...... | ...... | ...... | ...... | ...... | ...... | ...... | 6 | 5.10 | 65.10 | ... 6 50– 6 99 |
| 7 00– 7 49... | 2 | 41 | 3 | 39 | 2 | 13 | 2 | 4 | 2 | 6 | 17 | 249 | 7.30 | 81.40 | ... 7 00– 7 49 |
| 7 50– 7 99... | .... | 7 | .... | 11 | ...... | 1 | ...... | ...... | ...... | 1 | 6 | 36 | 7.48 | 83.70 | ... 7 50– 7 99 |
| 8 00– 8 99... | 3 | 21 | 1 | 16 | 4 | 5 | 2 | ...... | 5 | ...... | 94 | 94 | 10.32 | 89.80 | ... 8 00– 8 99 |
| 9 00– 9 99... | 4 | 11 | 11 | 6 | 9 | 3 | 6 | 1 | 3 | 1 | 139 | 48 | 14.51 | 93.00 | ... 9 00– 9 99 |
| 10 00–10 99... | 40 | 4 | 59 | 9 | 40 | 1 | 12 | ...... | 3 | 1 | 468 | 42 | 28.65 | 95.75 | ...10 00–10 99 |
| 11 00–11 99... | 24 | 1 | 47 | ...... | 20 | ...... | 4 | ...... | ...... | ...... | 290 | 7 | 37.50 | 96.10 | ...11 00–11 99 |
| 12 00–12 99... | 88 | 5 | 146 | 2 | 88 | 2 | 15 | ...... | 7 | ...... | 755 | 27 | 60.50 | 97.70 | ...12 00–12 99 |
| 13 00–13 99... | 11 | ...... | 28 | ...... | 14 | ...... | ...... | ...... | 1 | 1 | 164 | 2 | 65.40 | 97.85 | ...13 00–13 99 |
| 14 00–14 99... | 21 | ...... | 58 | 3 | 26 | ...... | 7 | ...... | 1 | ...... | 204 | 7 | 71.70 | 98.50 | ...14 00–14 99 |
| 15 00–15 99... | 25 | 1 | 44 | 1 | 20 | ...... | 3 | ...... | 4 | ...... | 239 | 10 | 78.90 | 99.10 | ...15 00–15 99 |
| 16 00–17 99... | 23 | ...... | 35 | 1 | 14 | ...... | 1 | ...... | ...... | ...... | 165 | 5 | 84.00 | 99.40 | ...16 00–17 99 |
| 18 00–19 99... | 20 | ...... | 27 | ...... | 12 | ...... | 2 | ...... | 1 | ...... | 161 | 1 | 88.70 | 99.50 | ...18 00–19 99 |
| 20 00–24 99... | 31 | ...... | 52 | ...... | 10 | ...... | 1 | ...... | 3 | 1 | 230 | 3 | 95.55 | 99.72 | ...20 00–24 99 |
| 25 00–29 99... | 16 | 1 | 17 | ...... | 6 | ...... | 1 | ...... | ...... | ...... | 68 | 3 | 97.80 | 99.93 | ...25 00–29 99 |
| 30 00–34 99... | 7 | ...... | 19 | ...... | 5 | ...... | ...... | ...... | 1 | ...... | 45 | ...... | 99.10 | 99.93 | ...30 00–34 99 |
| 35 00–39 99... | 4 | ...... | 5 | ...... | 1 | ...... | ...... | ...... | ...... | ...... | 15 | ...... | 99.50 | 99.93 | ...35 00–39 99 |
| 40 00 and over. | 3 | 1 | 6 | ...... | 1 | ...... | ...... | ...... | ...... | ...... | 16 | 1 | 100.00 | 100.00 | .40 00 and over |
| Not reported... | 5 | 1 | 13 | ...... | 2 | ...... | 1 | ...... | ...... | ...... | 82 | 1 | ...... | ...... | ...Not reported |
| Total..... | 336 | 162 | 587 | 172 | 276 | 40 | 57 | 7 | 31 | 14 | 3,382 | 1,537 | ...... | ...... | .....Total |

46. TABLE VI, A, 1, e

NEW YORK STATE

**DEPARTMENT STORES — PLANT**

NUMBER AND PER CENT OF EMPLOYEES CLASSIFIED ACCORDING TO ACTUAL WEEKLY EARNINGS, BY AGE GROUPS AND SEX

| ACTUAL WEEKLY EARNINGS IN DOLLARS | AGE GROUPS IN YEARS | | | | | | | | | | | | | | ACTUAL WEEKLY EARNINGS IN DOLLARS |
|---|---|---|---|---|---|---|---|---|---|---|---|---|---|---|---|
| | 14–15 | | 16–17 | | 18–20 | | 21–24 | | 25–29 | | 30–34 | | 35–39 | | |
| | Male | Female | Male | Female | Male | Female | Male | Female | Male | Female | Male | Female | Male | Female | |
| Less than $3 00 | .... | ...... | .... | 1 | 5 | 6 | 3 | 7 | 3 | 11 | 2 | 5 | 2 | 8 | Less than $3 00 |
| $3 00–$3 49... | .... | ...... | .... | 4 | ...... | 5 | 2 | 26 | 2 | 24 | 1 | 16 | 2 | 13 | ...$3 00– 3 49 |
| 3 50– 3 99... | .... | 4 | 1 | 4 | ...... | 6 | ...... | 11 | ...... | 11 | 1 | 8 | 1 | 7 | ... 3 50– 3 99 |
| 4 00– 4 49... | .... | 1 | 2 | 10 | 2 | 14 | ...... | 50 | 6 | 77 | 7 | 34 | 3 | 19 | ... 4 00– 4 49 |
| 4 50– 4 99... | .... | ...... | 4 | ...... | 2 | 7 | ...... | 10 | 1 | 30 | ...... | 17 | 2 | 18 | ... 4 50– 4 99 |
| 5 00– 5 49... | 2 | ...... | 8 | 5 | 16 | 26 | 10 | 38 | 11 | 42 | 5 | 27 | 3 | 24 | ... 5 00– 5 49 |
| 5 50– 5 99... | .... | ...... | .... | 2 | 2 | 12 | 4 | 17 | 2 | 15 | 1 | 12 | 2 | 8 | ... 5 50– 5 99 |
| 6 00– 6 49... | .... | 1 | 10 | 6 | 18 | 28 | 8 | 40 | 8 | 34 | 4 | 33 | 2 | 19 | ... 6 00– 6 49 |
| 6 50– 6 99... | .... | ...... | .... | ...... | 2 | 8 | 4 | 4 | 3 | 3 | 1 | 7 | 2 | 5 | ... 6 50– 6 99 |
| 7 00– 7 49... | .... | 1 | 4 | ...... | 16 | 12 | 20 | 15 | 1 | 23 | 5 | 19 | 9 | 24 | ... 7 00– 7 49 |
| 7 50– 7 99... | .... | ...... | 1 | ...... | 2 | ...... | 2 | 2 | 3 | 2 | ...... | 6 | 1 | 6 | ... 7 50– 7 99 |
| 8 00– 8 99... | .... | ...... | 3 | 1 | 20 | 6 | 23 | 9 | 25 | 9 | 11 | 6 | 5 | 11 | ... 8 00– 8 99 |
| 9 00– 9 99... | .... | ...... | 2 | ...... | 13 | ...... | 27 | 7 | 34 | 8 | 19 | 4 | 12 | 13 | ... 9 00– 9 99 |
| 10 00–10 99... | .... | ...... | 4 | ...... | 23 | 2 | 85 | 3 | 81 | 5 | 51 | 11 | 40 | 9 | ...10 00–10 99 |
| 11 00–11 99... | .... | ...... | .... | ...... | 15 | ...... | 52 | 3 | 53 | 2 | 31 | 2 | 33 | 1 | ...11 00–11 99 |
| 12 00–12 99... | .... | ...... | .... | ...... | 14 | ...... | 78 | 1 | 99 | 7 | 95 | 6 | 81 | 2 | ...12 00–12 99 |
| 13 00–13 99... | .... | ...... | .... | ...... | 8 | ...... | 33 | 1 | 37 | ...... | 18 | ...... | 16 | 1 | ...13 00–13 99 |
| 14 00–14 99... | .... | ...... | .... | ...... | 5 | ...... | 18 | ...... | 20 | ...... | 35 | 3 | 41 | 3 | ...14 00–14 99 |
| 15 00–15 99... | .... | ...... | .... | ...... | 5 | ...... | 17 | 1 | 43 | 1 | 29 | ...... | 38 | 5 | ...15 00–15 99 |
| 16 00–17 99... | .... | ...... | .... | ...... | 3 | ...... | 11 | ...... | 41 | 1 | 25 | 1 | 42 | 1 | ...16 00–17 99 |
| 18 00–19 99... | .... | ...... | .... | ...... | 2 | ...... | 9 | ...... | 36 | ...... | 31 | ...... | 28 | 1 | ...18 00–19 99 |
| 20 00–24 99... | .... | ...... | .... | ...... | 1 | ...... | 16 | ...... | 37 | ...... | 56 | 1 | 43 | 1 | ...20 00–24 99 |
| 25 00–29 99... | .... | ...... | .... | ...... | ...... | ...... | 3 | ...... | 11 | ...... | 16 | 1 | 14 | 1 | ...25 00–29 99 |
| 30 00–34 99... | .... | ...... | .... | ...... | ...... | ...... | ...... | ...... | ...... | ...... | 7 | ...... | 7 | ...... | ...30 00–34 99 |
| 35 00–39 99... | .... | ...... | .... | ...... | ...... | ...... | ...... | ...... | 2 | ...... | 4 | ...... | 2 | ...... | ...35 00–39 99 |
| 40 00 and over. | .... | ...... | .... | ...... | ...... | ...... | ...... | ...... | ...... | ...... | 3 | ...... | 5 | ...... | .40 00 and over |
| Not reported... | .... | ...... | .... | ...... | ...... | ...... | ...... | ...... | ...... | ...... | 1 | ...... | 1 | ...... | ...Not reported |
| Total..... | 2 | 7 | 39 | 33 | 174 | 132 | 425 | 245 | 559 | 305 | 459 | 219 | 437 | 200 | .....Total |

NEW YORK STATE

46. TABLE VI, A, 1, e — (*Concluded*) **DEPARTMENT STORES — PLANT**

NUMBER AND PER CENT OF EMPLOYEES CLASSIFIED ACCORDING TO ACTUAL WEEKLY EARNINGS, BY AGE GROUPS AND SEX

| ACTUAL WEEKLY EARNINGS IN DOLLARS | AGE GROUPS IN YEARS — (concluded) | | | | | | | | | | | | | | ACTUAL WEEKLY EARNINGS IN DOLLARS |
|---|---|---|---|---|---|---|---|---|---|---|---|---|---|---|---|
| | 40–44 | | 45–54 | | 55–64 | | 65 AND OVER | | NOT REPORTED | | TOTAL | | CUMULATIVE PER CENT FOR STATE | | |
| | Male | Female | Male | Female | Male | Female | Male | Female | Male | Female | Male | Female | Male | Female | |
| Less than $3 00 | 1 | ...... | 1 | 1 | ...... | 1 | ...... | ...... | ...... | ...... | 17 | 40 | .5 | 2.6 | Less than $3 00 |
| $3 00–$3 49... | 1 | 7 | .... | 4 | 1 | ...... | ...... | ...... | ...... | ...... | 9 | 99 | .8 | 9.1 | ...$3 00– 3 49 |
| 3 50– 3 99... | .... | 2 | 1 | 3 | 1 | ...... | ...... | ...... | ...... | ...... | 5 | 56 | .9 | 12.8 | ... 3 50– 3 99 |
| 4 00– 4 49... | 6 | 8 | 6 | 5 | 3 | 1 | ...... | ...... | ...... | ...... | 35 | 219 | 1.9 | 27.1 | ... 4 00– 4 49 |
| 4 50– 4 99... | 1 | 6 | .... | 9 | ...... | 2 | ...... | ...... | 1 | ...... | 11 | 99 | 2.3 | 33.6 | ... 4 50– 4 99 |
| 5 00– 5 49... | 1 | 15 | 5 | 14 | ...... | 3 | ...... | ...... | ...... | 2 | 61 | 196 | 4.1 | 46.4 | ... 5 00– 5 49 |
| 5 50– 5 99... | .... | 2 | 1 | 10 | ...... | 2 | ...... | 1 | ...... | 1 | 12 | 82 | 4.5 | 51.7 | ... 5 50– 5 99 |
| 6 00– 6 49... | 3 | 32 | 7 | 44 | 1 | 9 | ...... | 2 | ...... | ...... | 61 | 248 | 6.3 | 67.8 | ... 6 00– 6 49 |
| 6 50– 6 99... | .... | 4 | .... | 5 | ...... | ...... | ...... | 1 | ...... | 1 | 12 | 38 | 6.6 | 70.3 | ... 6 50– 6 99 |
| 7 00– 7 49... | 3 | 36 | 4 | 30 | 1 | 10 | 1 | 2 | 2 | 5 | 66 | 177 | 8.6 | 81.8 | ... 7 00– 7 49 |
| 7 50– 7 99... | .... | 8 | .... | 9 | ...... | 2 | ...... | ...... | ...... | 1 | 9 | 36 | 8.9 | 84.1 | ... 7 50– 7 99 |
| 8 00– 8 99... | 4 | 18 | 2 | 15 | 5 | 5 | 1 | 1 | 4 | ...... | 103 | 81 | 11.9 | 89.3 | ... 8 00– 8 99 |
| 9 00– 9 99... | 4 | 10 | 14 | 7 | 11 | 2 | 6 | ...... | 3 | 1 | 145 | 52 | 16.2 | 92.7 | ... 9 00– 9 99 |
| 10 00–10 99... | 28 | 4 | 53 | 10 | 34 | 1 | 11 | ...... | 2 | 1 | 412 | 46 | 28.5 | 95.7 | ...10 00–10 99 |
| 11 00–11 99... | 25 | 1 | 48 | ...... | 21 | ...... | 4 | ...... | ...... | ...... | 282 | 9 | 36.8 | 96.3 | ...11 00–11 99 |
| 12 00–12 99... | 81 | 4 | 132 | 2 | 82 | 2 | 15 | ...... | 8 | ...... | 685 | 24 | 57.2 | 97.9 | ...12 00–12 99 |
| 13 00–13 99... | 16 | ...... | 27 | ...... | 13 | ...... | 1 | ...... | 1 | ...... | 170 | 2 | 62.4 | 98.0 | ...13 00–13 99 |
| 14 00–14 99... | 24 | ...... | 63 | 2 | 32 | ...... | 6 | ...... | 1 | ...... | 245 | 8 | 69.5 | 98.5 | ...14 00–14 99 |
| 15 00–15 99... | 23 | 1 | 52 | 1 | 17 | ...... | 3 | ...... | 4 | ...... | 231 | 9 | 76.3 | 99.1 | ...15 00–15 99 |
| 16 00–17 99... | 28 | ...... | 36 | 1 | 17 | ...... | 2 | ...... | ...... | 1 | 205 | 5 | 82.5 | 99.4 | ...16 00–17 99 |
| 18 00–19 99... | 20 | ...... | 31 | ...... | 13 | ...... | 2 | ...... | 1 | ...... | 173 | 1 | 87.7 | 99.5 | ...18 00–19 99 |
| 20 00–24 99... | 34 | ...... | 53 | ...... | 11 | ...... | 2 | ...... | 3 | 1 | 256 | 3 | 95.0 | 99.7 | ...20 00–24 99 |
| 25 00–29 99... | 16 | 1 | 24 | ...... | 7 | ...... | 1 | ...... | ...... | ...... | 92 | 3 | 98.0 | 99.9 | ...25 00–29 99 |
| 30 00–34 99... | 6 | ...... | 6 | ...... | 2 | ...... | ...... | ...... | 1 | ...... | 29 | ...... | 99.2 | ...... | ...30 00–34 99 |
| 35 00–39 99... | 5 | ...... | 9 | ...... | 2 | ...... | ...... | ...... | ...... | ...... | 24 | ...... | 99.6 | ...... | ...35 00–39 99 |
| 40 00 and over. | 4 | 1 | 11 | ...... | 1 | ...... | ...... | ...... | ...... | ...... | 24 | 1 | 100.0 | 100.0 | .40 00 and over |
| Not reported... | 2 | 2 | 1 | ...... | 1 | ...... | 2 | ...... | ...... | ...... | 8 | 2 | ...... | ...... | ...Not reported |
| Total..... | 336 | 162 | 587 | 172 | 276 | 40 | 57 | 7 | 31 | 14 | 3,382 | 1,536 | ...... | ...... | .....Total |

TABLE X, A, 1, e

NEW YORK STATE

DEPARTMENT STORES — PLANT

NUMBER AND PER CENT OF EMPLOYEES CLASSIFIED ACCORDING TO ACTUAL WEEKLY EARNINGS, BY CONJUGAL CONDITION AND SEX

| Actual Weekly Earnings in Dollars | Conjugal Condition: Single | | Married | | Widowed or Divorced | | Not Reported | | Total | | Cumulative Per Cent of Total | | Actual Weekly Earnings in Dollars |
|---|---|---|---|---|---|---|---|---|---|---|---|---|---|
| | Male | Female | Male | Female | Male | Female | Male | Female | Male | Female | Male | Female | |
| Less than $3 00 | 10 | 16 | 5 | 12 | ....... | 11 | 2 | 1 | 17 | 40 | .5 | 2.6 | Less than $3 00 |
| $3 00–$3 49 | | 41 | 5 | 4 | ....... | 14 | ....... | 2 | 9 | 99 | .8 | 9.1 | $3 00– 3 49 |
| 3 50– 3 99 | 1 | 27 | 4 | 20 | ....... | 8 | ....... | 1 | 5 | 56 | .9 | 12.8 | 3 50– 3 99 |
| 4 00– 4 49 | 15 | 144 | 17 | 39 | 2 | 27 | 1 | 9 | 35 | 219 | 1.9 | 27.1 | 4 00– 4 49 |
| 4 50– 4 99 | 7 | 50 | 4 | 28 | ....... | 21 | ....... | ....... | 11 | 99 | 2.3 | 33.6 | 4 50– 4 99 |
| 5 00– 5 49 | 41 | 114 | 20 | 40 | ....... | 39 | ....... | 3 | 61 | 196 | 4.1 | 46.4 | 5 00– 5 49 |
| 5 50– 5 99 | 9 | 49 | 3 | 18 | ....... | 14 | ....... | 1 | 12 | 82 | 4.5 | 51.7 | 5 50– 5 99 |
| 6 00– 6 49 | 48 | 126 | 8 | 55 | 4 | 64 | 1 | 3 | 61 | 248 | 6.3 | 67.8 | 6 00– 6 49 |
| 6 50– 6 99 | 7 | 13 | 5 | 12 | ....... | 12 | ....... | 1 | 12 | 38 | 6.6 | 70.3 | 6 50– 6 99 |
| 7 00– 7 49 | 40 | 66 | 14 | 39 | 2 | 70 | 10 | 2 | 66 | 177 | 8.6 | 81.8 | 7 00– 7 49 |
| 7 50– 7 99 | 7 | 4 | 2 | 10 | ....... | 21 | ....... | 1 | 9 | 36 | 8.9 | 84.1 | 7 50– 7 99 |
| 8 00– 8 99 | 59 | 35 | 41 | 12 | 3 | 33 | ....... | 1 | 103 | 81 | 11.9 | 89.3 | 8 00– 8 99 |
| 9 00– 9 99 | 70 | 23 | 68 | 13 | 5 | 16 | 2 | ....... | 145 | 52 | 16.2 | 92.7 | 9 00– 9 99 |
| 10 00–10 99 | 171 | 19 | 216 | 10 | 18 | 15 | 7 | 2 | 412 | 46 | 28.5 | 95.7 | 10 00–10 99 |
| 11 00–11 99 | 126 | 7 | 135 | 2 | 15 | ....... | 6 | ....... | 282 | 9 | 36.8 | 96.3 | 11 00–11 99 |
| 12 00–12 99 | 249 | 14 | 397 | 3 | 30 | 7 | 9 | ....... | 685 | 24 | 57.2 | 97.9 | 12 00–12 99 |
| 13 00–13 99 | 80 | 1 | 85 | ....... | 3 | 1 | 2 | ....... | 170 | 2 | 62.4 | 98.0 | 13 00–13 99 |
| 14 00–14 99 | 58 | 4 | 168 | 1 | 13 | 3 | 6 | ....... | 245 | 8 | 69.5 | 98.5 | 14 00–14 99 |
| 15 00–15 99 | 68 | 4 | 143 | 2 | 11 | 3 | 9 | ....... | 231 | 9 | 76.3 | 99.1 | 15 00–15 99 |
| 16 00–17 99 | 52 | 5 | 142 | ....... | 8 | ....... | 3 | ....... | 205 | 5 | 82.5 | 99.4 | 16 00–17 99 |
| 18 00–19 99 | 52 | 1 | 108 | ....... | 7 | ....... | 6 | ....... | 173 | 1 | 87.7 | 99.5 | 18 00–19 99 |
| 20 00–24 99 | 45 | 2 | 200 | ....... | 7 | 1 | 4 | ....... | 256 | 3 | 95.0 | 99.7 | 20 00–24 99 |
| 25 00–29 99 | 13 | 2 | 68 | 1 | 7 | ....... | 4 | ....... | 92 | 3 | 98.0 | 99.9 | 25 00–29 99 |
| 30 00–34 99 | 6 | ....... | 21 | ....... | 1 | ....... | 1 | ....... | 29 | ....... | 99.2 | ....... | 30 00–34 99 |
| 35 00–39 99 | 4 | ....... | 19 | ....... | ....... | ....... | 1 | ....... | 24 | ....... | 99.6 | ....... | 35 00–39 99 |
| 40 00 and over | ....... | 1 | 22 | ....... | ....... | ....... | 2 | ....... | 24 | 1 | 100.0 | 100.0 | 40 00 and over |
| Not reported | ....... | 1 | 6 | 1 | 2 | ....... | ....... | ....... | 8 | 2 | ....... | ....... | Not reported |
| Total | 1,242 | 769 | 1,926 | 360 | 138 | 380 | 76 | 27 | 3,382 | 1,536 | ....... | ....... | Total |

NEW YORK STATE

48. TABLE XI, A, 1, e

**DEPARTMENT STORES — PLANT**

Number and Per Cent of Employees Classified According to Actual Weekly Earnings, by Nativity and Sex

| Actual Weekly Earnings in Dollars | Nativity | | | | | | | | | | Actual Weekly Earnings in Dollars |
|---|---|---|---|---|---|---|---|---|---|---|---|
| | Native | | Foreign | | Not Reported | | Total | | Cumulative Per Cent of Total | | |
| | Male | Female | Male | Female | Male | Female | Male | Female | Male | Female | |
| Less than $3 00 | 10 | 25 | 7 | 15 | ........ | ........ | 17 | 40 | .5 | 2.6 | Less than $3 00 |
| $3 00–$3 49 | 3 | 72 | 6 | 26 | ........ | 1 | 9 | 99 | .8 | 9.1 | $3 00– 3 49 |
| 3 50– 3 99 | 1 | 42 | 4 | 14 | ........ | ........ | 5 | 56 | .9 | 12.8 | 3 50– 3 99 |
| 4 00– 4 49 | 7 | 132 | 28 | 86 | ........ | 1 | 35 | 219 | 1.9 | 27.1 | 4 00– 4 49 |
| 4 50– 4 99 | 6 | 46 | 5 | 52 | ........ | 1 | 11 | 99 | 2.3 | 33.6 | 4 50– 4 99 |
| 5 00– 5 49 | 7 | 131 | 54 | 63 | ........ | 2 | 61 | 196 | 4.1 | 46.4 | 5 00– 5 49 |
| 5 50– 5 99 | 4 | 53 | 8 | 28 | ........ | 1 | 12 | 82 | 4.5 | 51.7 | 5 50– 5 99 |
| 6 00– 6 49 | 23 | 150 | 38 | 94 | ........ | 4 | 61 | 248 | 6.3 | 67.8 | 6 00– 6 49 |
| 6 50– 6 99 | 4 | 23 | 8 | 15 | ........ | ........ | 12 | 38 | 6.6 | 70.3 | 6 50– 6 99 |
| 7 00– 7 49 | 18 | 102 | 45 | 74 | 3 | 1 | 66 | 177 | 8.6 | 81.8 | 7 00– 7 49 |
| 7 50– 7 99 | 4 | 14 | 5 | 22 | ........ | ........ | 9 | 36 | 8.9 | 84.1 | 7 50– 7 99 |
| 8 00– 8 99 | 34 | 49 | 68 | 32 | 1 | ........ | 103 | 81 | 11.9 | 89.3 | 8 00– 8 99 |
| 9 00– 9 99 | 60 | 34 | 84 | 18 | 1 | ........ | 145 | 52 | 16.2 | 92.7 | 9 00– 9 99 |
| 10 00–10 99 | 183 | 29 | 229 | 17 | ........ | ........ | 412 | 46 | 28.5 | 95.7 | 10 00–10 99 |
| 11 00–11 99 | 110 | 7 | 171 | 2 | 1 | ........ | 282 | 9 | 36.8 | 96.3 | 11 00–11 99 |
| 12 00–12 99 | 300 | 20 | 379 | 4 | 6 | ........ | 685 | 24 | 57.2 | 97.9 | 12 00–12 99 |
| 13 00–13 99 | 72 | 1 | 98 | 1 | ........ | ........ | 170 | 2 | 62.4 | 98.0 | 13 00–13 99 |
| 14 00–14 99 | 102 | 5 | 142 | 3 | 1 | ........ | 245 | 8 | 69.5 | 98.5 | 14 00–14 99 |
| 15 00–15 99 | 97 | 6 | 129 | 3 | 5 | ........ | 231 | 9 | 76.3 | 99.1 | 15 00–15 99 |
| 16 00–17 99 | 94 | 5 | 111 | ........ | ........ | ........ | 205 | 5 | 82.5 | 99.4 | 16 00–17 99 |
| 18 00–19 99 | 91 | ........ | 81 | 1 | 1 | ........ | 173 | 1 | 87.7 | 99.5 | 18 00–19 99 |
| 20 00–24 99 | 154 | 2 | 102 | 1 | ........ | ........ | 256 | 3 | 95.0 | 99.7 | 20 00–24 99 |
| 25 00–29 99 | 50 | 2 | 42 | 1 | ........ | ........ | 92 | 3 | 98.0 | 99.9 | 25 00–29 99 |
| 30 00–34 99 | 13 | ........ | 16 | ........ | ........ | ........ | 29 | ........ | 99.2 | ........ | 30 00–34 99 |
| 35 00–39 99 | 18 | ........ | 6 | ........ | ........ | ........ | 24 | ........ | 99.6 | ........ | 35 00–39 99 |
| 40 00 and over | 10 | 1 | 13 | ........ | 1 | ........ | 24 | 1 | 100.0 | 100.0 | 40 00 and over |
| Not reported | 2 | 1 | 5 | 1 | 1 | ........ | 8 | 2 | ........ | ........ | Not reported |
| Total | 1,477 | 952 | 1,884 | 573 | 21 | 11 | 3,382 | 1,536 | ........ | ........ | Total |

49. TABLE XII, A, 1, e

NEW YORK STATE

DEPARTMENT STORES — PLANT

NUMBER OF EMPLOYEES FOR EACH SEX CLASSIFIED ACCORDING TO ACTUAL WEEKLY EARNINGS, BY THE NUMBER OF YEARS IN THE TRADE

| ACTUAL WEEKLY EARNINGS IN DOLLARS | YEARS IN TRADE | | | | | | | | | | | | | | ACTUAL WEEKLY EARNINGS IN DOLLARS |
|---|---|---|---|---|---|---|---|---|---|---|---|---|---|---|---|
| | LESS THAN 1 | | 1 | | 2 | | 3 | | 4 | | 5 | | 6 | | |
| | Male | Female | Male | Female | Male | Female | Male | Female | Male | Female | Male | Female | Male | Female | |
| Less than $3 00 | 5 | 7 | 2 | 4 | 1 | 4 | 1 | 4 | 2 | 3 | 1 | 2 | ...... | ...... | Less than $3 00 |
| $3 00–$3 49... | 4 | 9 | .... | 9 | 2 | 9 | 1 | 10 | ...... | 9 | ...... | 7 | ...... | 8 | ...$3 00– 3 49 |
| 3 50– 3 99... | 1 | 9 | .... | 8 | 1 | 5 | ...... | 7 | 1 | 3 | ...... | 3 | ...... | 4 | ... 3 50– 3 99 |
| 4 00– 4 49... | 3 | 23 | 3 | 18 | ...... | 14 | 1 | 17 | 1 | 23 | 1 | 21 | ...... | 18 | ... 4 00– 4 49 |
| 4 50– 4 99... | 4 | 9 | 1 | 3 | ...... | 6 | 3 | 12 | ...... | 9 | 1 | 12 | ...... | 3 | ... 4 50– 4 99 |
| 5 00– 5 49... | 8 | 45 | 12 | 31 | 9 | 20 | 5 | 10 | 1 | 14 | 1 | 11 | ...... | 6 | ... 5 00– 5 49 |
| 5 50– 5 99... | 2 | 15 | 1 | 6 | 3 | 7 | 2 | 11 | ...... | 8 | 2 | 7 | ...... | 7 | ... 5 50– 5 99 |
| 6 00– 6 49... | 12 | 48 | 15 | 43 | 7 | 24 | 5 | 24 | 5 | 23 | 4 | 17 | ...... | 9 | ... 6 00– 6 49 |
| 6 50– 6 99... | 2 | 5 | 2 | 1 | 1 | 8 | 3 | 3 | 1 | 4 | 1 | 5 | 1 | 2 | ... 6 50– 6 99 |
| 7 00– 7 49... | 19 | 21 | 13 | 23 | 8 | 15 | 8 | 14 | 3 | 14 | 2 | 15 | 2 | 8 | ... 7 00– 7 49 |
| 7 50– 7 99... | 2 | 2 | .... | 2 | 1 | 5 | 2 | 7 | ...... | 4 | 2 | 5 | 1 | 3 | ... 7 50– 7 99 |
| 8 00– 8 99... | 22 | 5 | 18 | 3 | 11 | 8 | 15 | 7 | 11 | 8 | 11 | 7 | 4 | 9 | ... 8 00– 8 99 |
| 9 00– 9 99... | 32 | 2 | 11 | 3 | 19 | 2 | 14 | 4 | 8 | 1 | 8 | 5 | 6 | 5 | ... 9 00– 9 99 |
| 10 00–10 99... | 109 | 2 | 45 | 3 | 42 | 1 | 37 | 7 | 23 | 3 | 19 | 2 | 17 | 3 | ...10 00–10 99 |
| 11 00–11 99... | 51 | 1 | 40 | ...... | 26 | ...... | 29 | 2 | 25 | ...... | 18 | 1 | 14 | 2 | ...11 00–11 99 |
| 12 00–12 99... | 101 | 2 | 86 | 2 | 64 | ...... | 68 | 1 | 38 | ...... | 49 | 1 | 34 | 2 | ...12 00–12 99 |
| 13 00–13 99... | 21 | ...... | 17 | 1 | 13 | ...... | 17 | ...... | 10 | ...... | 11 | ...... | 14 | ...... | ...13 00–13 99 |
| 14 00–14 99... | 14 | ...... | 16 | ...... | 15 | ...... | 18 | 1 | 16 | ...... | 15 | ...... | 14 | 1 | ...14 00–14 99 |
| 15 00–15 99... | 20 | ...... | 9 | ...... | 10 | ...... | 12 | ...... | 14 | 1 | 6 | ...... | 18 | 2 | ...15 00–15 99 |
| 16 00–17 99... | 4 | ...... | 7 | ...... | 8 | ...... | 9 | ...... | 6 | ...... | 11 | ...... | 5 | 3 | ...16 00–17 99 |
| 18 00–19 99... | 2 | ...... | 1 | ...... | 4 | ...... | 6 | ...... | 6 | ...... | 7 | ...... | 8 | ...... | ...18 00–19 99 |
| 20 00–24 99... | 1 | ...... | 2 | ...... | 4 | ...... | 3 | ...... | 6 | 1 | 6 | ...... | 6 | ...... | ...20 00–24 99 |
| 25 00–29 99... | 1 | ...... | 1 | ...... | 1 | ...... | ...... | ...... | 1 | ...... | 1 | 1 | 1 | ...... | ...25 00–29 99 |
| 30 00–34 99... | 1 | ...... | 1 | ...... | 1 | ...... | ...... | ...... | ...... | ...... | ...... | ...... | ...... | ...... | ...30 00–34 99 |
| 35 00–39 99... | .... | ...... | .... | ...... | 1 | ...... | ...... | ...... | ...... | ...... | ...... | ...... | ...... | ...... | ...35 00–39 99 |
| 40 00 and over. | .... | ...... | .... | ...... | ...... | ...... | ...... | ...... | ...... | ...... | ...... | ...... | 1 | ...... | .40 00 and over |
| Not reported... | .... | ...... | .... | ...... | 1 | ...... | ...... | ...... | 1 | ...... | 1 | ...... | 1 | ...... | ...Not reported |
| Total..... | 461 | 205 | 303 | 160 | 253 | 128 | 259 | 141 | 179 | 128 | 178 | 122 | 147 | 94 | .....Total |

NEW YORK STATE

49. TABLE XII, A, 1, e — *(continued)*

**DEPARTMENT STORES — PLANT**

NUMBER OF EMPLOYEES FOR EACH SEX CLASSIFIED ACCORDING TO ACTUAL WEEKLY EARNINGS, BY THE NUMBER OF YEARS IN THE TRADE

| ACTUAL WEEKLY EARNINGS IN DOLLARS | YEARS IN TRADE *(continued)* | | | | | | | | | | | | | | ACTUAL WEEKLY EARNINGS IN DOLLARS |
|---|---|---|---|---|---|---|---|---|---|---|---|---|---|---|---|
| | 7 | | 8 | | 9 | | 10–14 | | 15–19 | | 20–24 | | 25–29 | | |
| | Male | Female | Male | Female | Male | Female | Male | Female | Male | Female | Male | Female | Male | Female | |
| Less than $3 00 | 1 | 2 | .... | 4 | 1 | 1 | 1 | 7 | ...... | 1 | ...... | ...... | ...... | ...... | Less than $3 00 |
| $3 00–$3 49... | .... | 9 | 1 | 5 | ...... | 4 | ...... | 12 | ...... | 4 | 1 | 1 | ...... | ...... | ...$3 00– 3 49 |
| 3 50– 3 99... | .... | 4 | .... | 2 | ...... | 1 | ...... | 8 | ...... | 2 | ...... | ...... | 1 | ...... | ... 3 50– 3 99 |
| 4 00– 4 49... | .... | 20 | 1 | 9 | ...... | 8 | 10 | 30 | 4 | 12 | 5 | 2 | 3 | ...... | ... 4 00– 4 49 |
| 4 50– 4 99... | 1 | 4 | .... | 8 | ...... | 4 | ...... | 18 | 1 | 6 | ...... | 2 | ...... | 1 | ... 4 50– 4 99 |
| 5 00– 5 49... | .... | 10 | 1 | 6 | 1 | 5 | 3 | 25 | ...... | 7 | ...... | 4 | ...... | ...... | ... 5 00– 5 49 |
| 5 50– 5 99... | .... | 3 | .... | 2 | ...... | 2 | 1 | 6 | ...... | 1 | ...... | 1 | ...... | ...... | ... 5 50– 5 99 |
| 6 00– 6 49... | 1 | 5 | 1 | 10 | ...... | 5 | 2 | 17 | 1 | 6 | 1 | 6 | ...... | 2 | ... 6 00– 6 49 |
| 6 50– 6 99... | .... | 1 | 1 | 2 | ...... | ...... | ...... | 4 | ...... | 2 | ...... | 1 | ...... | ...... | ... 6 50– 6 99 |
| 7 00– 7 49... | 2 | 12 | 1 | 8 | ...... | 7 | 4 | 20 | 1 | 6 | ...... | 6 | 1 | 3 | ... 7 00– 7 49 |
| 7 50– 7 99... | .... | 2 | .... | ...... | ...... | ...... | 1 | 4 | ...... | ...... | ...... | ...... | ...... | ...... | ... 7 50– 7 99 |
| 8 00– 8 99... | 3 | 8 | 1 | 6 | ...... | 3 | 1 | 7 | 3 | 4 | 1 | 2 | ...... | 2 | ... 8 00– 8 99 |
| 9 00– 9 99... | 2 | 2 | 5 | 7 | 4 | 5 | 11 | 7 | 5 | 3 | 2 | 3 | 1 | 1 | ... 9 00– 9 99 |
| 10 00–10 99... | 20 | 5 | 20 | ...... | 10 | 3 | 38 | 8 | 14 | 6 | 2 | 1 | 1 | 2 | ...10 00–10 99 |
| 11 00–11 99... | 9 | ...... | 11 | ...... | 4 | 1 | 32 | 1 | 5 | 1 | 5 | ...... | 4 | ...... | ...11 00–11 99 |
| 12 00–12 99... | 30 | ...... | 35 | 3 | 14 | 1 | 65 | 6 | 33 | 6 | 16 | ...... | 8 | ...... | ...12 00–12 99 |
| 13 00–13 99... | 10 | ...... | 11 | ...... | 4 | ...... | 23 | ...... | 8 | 1 | 3 | ...... | 1 | ...... | ...13 00–13 99 |
| 14 00–14 99... | 15 | 2 | 15 | ...... | 9 | ...... | 38 | 2 | 15 | 1 | 15 | 1 | 12 | ...... | ...14 00–14 99 |
| 15 00–15 99... | 12 | ...... | 20 | ...... | 5 | 1 | 36 | 2 | 19 | 3 | 19 | ...... | 14 | ...... | ...15 00–15 99 |
| 16 00–17 99... | 13 | ...... | 8 | ...... | 14 | 1 | 46 | 1 | 30 | ...... | 18 | ...... | 10 | 1 | ...16 00–17 99 |
| 18 00–19 99... | 8 | ...... | 13 | ...... | 4 | ...... | 34 | 1 | 26 | ...... | 14 | ...... | 17 | ...... | ...18 00–19 99 |
| 20 00–24 99... | 11 | 1 | 10 | 1 | 8 | ...... | 60 | ...... | 39 | ...... | 36 | ...... | 24 | ...... | ...20 00–24 99 |
| 25 00–29 99... | 4 | ...... | 2 | ...... | 3 | ...... | 15 | ...... | 13 | 1 | 14 | 1 | 13 | ...... | ...25 00–29 99 |
| 30 00–34 99... | .... | ...... | 1 | ...... | ...... | ...... | 3 | ...... | 8 | ...... | 7 | ...... | 4 | ...... | ...30 00–34 99 |
| 35 00–39 99... | .... | ...... | 1 | ...... | 1 | ...... | 2 | ...... | 6 | ...... | 5 | ...... | 4 | ...... | ...35 00–39 99 |
| 40 00 and over. | 1 | ...... | .... | 1 | ...... | ...... | 3 | ...... | 5 | ...... | 2 | ...... | 3 | ...... | .40 00 and over |
| Not reported... | 1 | ...... | .... | 1 | ...... | ...... | 1 | 1 | 2 | ...... | ...... | ...... | ...... | ...... | ...Not reported |
| Total..... | 144 | 90 | 159 | 75 | 82 | 52 | 430 | 187 | 238 | 73 | 166 | 31 | 121 | 12 | ....Total |

49. TABLE XII, A, 1, e — (*concluded*)

NEW YORK STATE
DEPARTMENT STORES — PLANT

NUMBER OF EMPLOYEES FOR EACH SEX CLASSIFIED ACCORDING TO ACTUAL WEEKLY EARNINGS, BY THE NUMBER OF YEARS IN THE TRADE

| ACTUAL WEEKLY EARNINGS IN DOLLARS | YEARS IN TRADE (*concluded*) 30–34 | | 35–44 | | 45 AND OVER | | NOT REPORTED | | TOTAL | | CUMULATIVE PER CENT. OF TOTAL | | ACTUAL WEEKLY EARNINGS IN DOLLARS |
|---|---|---|---|---|---|---|---|---|---|---|---|---|---|
| | Male | Female | Male | Female | Male | Female | Male | Female | Male | Female | Male | Female | |
| Less than $3 00 | | | 1 | | | | 1 | 1 | 17 | 40 | .5 | 2.6 | Less than $3 00 |
| $3 00–$3 49... | | | | 1 | | | | 2 | 9 | 99 | .8 | 9.1 | ...$3 00– 3 49 |
| 3 50– 3 99... | 1 | | | | | | | | 5 | 56 | .9 | 12.8 | ... 3 50– 3 99 |
| 4 00– 4 49... | 2 | | 1 | | | | | 4 | 35 | 219 | 1.9 | 27.1 | ... 4 00– 4 49 |
| 4 50– 4 99... | | 1 | | 1 | | | | | 11 | 99 | 2.3 | 33.6 | ... 4 50– 4 99 |
| 5 00– 5 49... | | | | | | | | 2 | 61 | 196 | 4.1 | 46.4 | ... 5 00– 5 49 |
| 5 50– 5 99... | | | | | | 1 | 1 | 5 | 12 | 82 | 4.5 | 51.7 | ... 5 50– 5 99 |
| 6 00– 6 49... | 2 | 2 | 1 | 1 | | | 4 | 6 | 61 | 248 | 6.3 | 67.8 | ... 6 00– 6 49 |
| 6 50– 6 99... | | | | | | | | | 12 | 38 | 6.6 | 70.3 | ... 6 50– 6 99 |
| 7 00– 7 49... | | 1 | | | | | 2 | 4 | 66 | 177 | 8.6 | 81.8 | ... 7 00– 7 49 |
| 7 50– 7 99... | | | | | | | | 2 | 9 | 36 | 8.9 | 84.1 | ... 7 50– 7 99 |
| 8 00– 8 99... | | | | | | | 2 | 2 | 103 | 81 | 11.9 | 89.3 | ... 8 00– 8 99 |
| 9 00– 9 99... | 2 | | 2 | | 1 | | 12 | 2 | 145 | 52 | 16.2 | 92.7 | ... 9 00– 9 99 |
| 10 00–10 99... | 1 | | 2 | | 1 | | 11 | | 412 | 46 | 28.5 | 95.7 | ...10 00–10 99 |
| 11 00–11 99... | | | | | | | 9 | | 282 | 9 | 36.8 | 96.3 | ...11 00–11 99 |
| 12 00–12 99... | 9 | | 8 | | 3 | | 24 | | 685 | 24 | 57.2 | 97.9 | ...12 00–12 99 |
| 13 00–13 99... | 3 | | 1 | | | | 3 | | 170 | 2 | 62.4 | 98.0 | ...13 00–13 99 |
| 14 00–14 99... | 3 | | 2 | | 2 | | 11 | | 245 | 8 | 69.5 | 98.5 | ...14 00–14 99 |
| 15 00–15 99... | 5 | | 4 | | 1 | | 7 | | 231 | 9 | 76.3 | 99.1 | ...15 00–15 99 |
| 16 00–17 99... | 3 | | 4 | | | | 9 | | 205 | 5 | 82.5 | 99.4 | ...16 00–17 99 |
| 18 00–19 99... | 5 | | 12 | | 1 | | 5 | | 173 | 1 | 87.7 | 99.5 | ...18 00–19 99 |
| 20 00–24 99... | 23 | | 13 | | 3 | | 1 | | 256 | 3 | 95.0 | 99.7 | ...20 00–24 99 |
| 25 00–29 99... | 12 | | 8 | | 2 | | | | 92 | 3 | 98.0 | 99.9 | ...25 00–29 99 |
| 30 00–34 99... | 1 | | 2 | | | | | | 29 | | 99.2 | | ...30 00–34 99 |
| 35 00–39 99... | 2 | | 1 | | 1 | | | | 24 | | 99.6 | | ...35 00–39 99 |
| 40 00 and over. | 6 | | 2 | | 1 | | | | 24 | 1 | 100.0 | 100.0 | .40 00 and over |
| Not reported... | | | | | | | | | 8 | 2 | | | ...Not reported |
| Total..... | 80 | 4 | 64 | 3 | 16 | 1 | 102 | 30 | 3,382 | 1,536 | | | ....Total |

NEW YORK STATE

50. TABLE XIII, A, 1, e

**DEPARTMENT STORES — PLANT**

Number of Employees for Each Sex Classified According to Actual Weekly Earnings, by the Number of Years with the Firm

| Actual Weekly Earnings in Dollars | Years with Firm: Less than 1 | | 1 | | 2 | | 3 | | 4 | | 5 | | 6 | | Actual Weekly Earnings in Dollars |
|---|---|---|---|---|---|---|---|---|---|---|---|---|---|---|---|
| | Male | Female | Male | Female | Male | Female | Male | Female | Male | Female | Male | Female | Male | Female | |
| Less than $3 00 | 8 | 20 | 2 | 4 | 1 | 6 | 4 | 4 | 1 | ...... | ...... | 2 | ...... | ...... | Less than $3 00 |
| $3 00–$3 49... | 8 | 33 | .... | 18 | 1 | 7 | ...... | 10 | ...... | 10 | ...... | 6 | ...... | 2 | ...$3 00– 3 49 |
| 3 50– 3 99... | 2 | 19 | .... | 14 | 1 | 7 | ...... | 4 | 1 | 2 | ...... | 3 | ...... | 2 | ... 3 50– 3 99 |
| 4 00– 4 49... | 10 | 65 | 2 | 36 | 1 | 24 | 3 | 33 | 2 | 16 | 1 | 9 | 3 | 9 | ... 4 00– 4 49 |
| 4 50– 4 99... | 9 | 28 | .... | 9 | ...... | 10 | 1 | 10 | ...... | 10 | 1 | 10 | ...... | 3 | ... 4 50– 4 99 |
| 5 00– 5 49... | 45 | 68 | 8 | 36 | 5 | 34 | 2 | 11 | ...... | 10 | ...... | 7 | ...... | 6 | ... 5 00– 5 49 |
| 5 50– 5 99... | 5 | 27 | 2 | 10 | 4 | 7 | 1 | 17 | ...... | 10 | ...... | 6 | ...... | 3 | ... 5 50– 5 99 |
| 6 00– 6 49... | 26 | 84 | 17 | 55 | 5 | 21 | 3 | 27 | 2 | 28 | 3 | 7 | ...... | 4 | ... 6 00– 6 49 |
| 6 50– 6 99... | 6 | 13 | 2 | 6 | 1 | 4 | 1 | 6 | 1 | 1 | 1 | 4 | ...... | 1 | ... 6 50– 6 99 |
| 7 00– 7 49... | 37 | 60 | 14 | 34 | 4 | 13 | 3 | 14 | 3 | 16 | ...... | 7 | ...... | 4 | ... 7 00– 7 49 |
| 7 50– 7 99... | 5 | 5 | .... | 5 | 1 | 6 | 2 | 6 | 1 | 5 | ...... | 3 | ...... | 2 | ... 7 50– 7 99 |
| 8 00– 8 99... | 48 | 16 | 25 | 8 | 11 | 10 | 11 | 8 | 2 | 11 | 2 | 2 | 1 | 7 | ... 8 00– 8 99 |
| 9 00– 9 99... | 60 | 9 | 20 | 6 | 20 | 7 | 15 | 3 | 9 | 1 | 2 | 4 | 3 | 2 | ... 9 00– 9 99 |
| 10 00–10 99... | 180 | 5 | 55 | 9 | 33 | 2 | 45 | 7 | 18 | 6 | 13 | 1 | 12 | 2 | ...10 00–10 99 |
| 11 00–11 99... | 101 | ...... | 51 | 2 | 27 | ...... | 18 | 3 | 16 | 1 | 13 | ...... | 8 | ...... | ...11 00–11 99 |
| 12 00–12 99... | 197 | 4 | 116 | 2 | 68 | 2 | 74 | 2 | 39 | 3 | 33 | 2 | 22 | 1 | ...12 00–12 99 |
| 13 00–13 99... | 50 | ...... | 26 | 1 | 17 | ...... | 19 | ...... | 11 | ...... | 3 | ...... | 3 | ...... | ...13 00–13 99 |
| 14 00–14 99... | 36 | ...... | 38 | ...... | 22 | 1 | 25 | 2 | 17 | 2 | 9 | ...... | 20 | 1 | ...14 00–14 99 |
| 15 00–15 99... | 54 | 1 | 26 | 1 | 21 | 2 | 20 | 2 | 18 | 2 | 9 | ...... | 11 | 1 | ...15 00–15 99 |
| 16 00–17 99... | 33 | ...... | 22 | 1 | 22 | 1 | 15 | 1 | 11 | ...... | 12 | 1 | 12 | ...... | ...16 00–17 99 |
| 18 00–19 99... | 37 | ...... | 25 | ...... | 21 | ...... | 20 | ...... | 12 | ...... | 5 | ...... | 8 | ...... | ...18 00–19 99 |
| 20 00–24 99... | 35 | ...... | 39 | ...... | 28 | ...... | 26 | 1 | 13 | 1 | 11 | ...... | 16 | ...... | ...20 00–24 99 |
| 25 00–29 99... | 14 | 1 | 8 | 1 | 7 | ...... | 10 | ...... | 5 | ...... | 6 | ...... | 7 | ...... | ...25 00–29 99 |
| 30 00–34 99... | 7 | ...... | 2 | ...... | 2 | ...... | 2 | ...... | 1 | ...... | 5 | ...... | 1 | ...... | ...30 00–34 99 |
| 35 00–39 99... | .... | ...... | 2 | ...... | 2 | ...... | 3 | ...... | 2 | ...... | 2 | ...... | ...... | ...... | ...35 00–39 99 |
| 40 00 and over. | .... | 1 | 2 | ...... | 2 | ...... | ...... | ...... | 2 | ...... | 1 | ...... | 1 | ...... | .40 00 and over |
| Not reported... | 1 | 1 | .... | ...... | 1 | ...... | 3 | ...... | 1 | 1 | 1 | ...... | 1 | ...... | ...Not reported |
| Total..... | 1,014 | 460 | 504 | 258 | 328 | 164 | 326 | 171 | 188 | 136 | 133 | 74 | 129 | 50 | .....Total |

50. TABLE XIII, A, 1, e — (*continued*)

NEW YORK STATE

**DEPARTMENT STORES — PLANT**

NUMBER OF EMPLOYEES FOR EACH SEX CLASSIFIED ACCORDING TO ACTUAL WEEKLY EARNINGS, BY THE NUMBER OF YEARS WITH THE FIRM

| ACTUAL WEEKLY EARNINGS IN DOLLARS | YEARS WITH FIRM (*continued*) | | | | | | | | | | | | ACTUAL WEEKLY EARNINGS IN DOLLARS |
|---|---|---|---|---|---|---|---|---|---|---|---|---|---|
| | 7 | | 8 | | 9 | | 10–14 | | 15-19 | | 20-24 | | |
| | Male | Female | Male | Female | Male | Female | Male | Female | Male | Female | Male | Female | |
| Less than $3 00 | 1 | ....... | ....... | 1 | ....... | ....... | ....... | 1 | ....... | 1 | ....... | ....... | Less than $3 00 |
| $3 00–$3 49 | ....... | 5 | ....... | 3 | ....... | 1 | ....... | 3 | ....... | 1 | ....... | ....... | $3 00– 3 49 |
| 3 50– 3 99 | ....... | 1 | ....... | ....... | ....... | ....... | ....... | 2 | ....... | 1 | ....... | ....... | 3 50– 3 99 |
| 4 00– 4 49 | 1 | 5 | 4 | 9 | 2 | 3 | 6 | 8 | ....... | ....... | ....... | ....... | 4 00– 4 49 |
| 4 50– 4 99 | ....... | 4 | ....... | 5 | ....... | ....... | ....... | 7 | ....... | 2 | ....... | ....... | 4 50– 4 99 |
| 5 00– 5 49 | ....... | 9 | ....... | 4 | ....... | 2 | ....... | 8 | ....... | ....... | ....... | 1 | 5 00– 5 49 |
| 5 50– 5 99 | ....... | 1 | ....... | ....... | ....... | 1 | ....... | ....... | ....... | ....... | ....... | ....... | 5 50– 5 99 |
| 6 00– 6 49 | 1 | 3 | 1 | 5 | ....... | 4 | 1 | 6 | ....... | 1 | 1 | 1 | 6 00– 6 49 |
| 6 50– 6 99 | ....... | 1 | ....... | 1 | ....... | ....... | ....... | 1 | ....... | ....... | ....... | ....... | 6 50– 6 99 |
| 7 00– 7 49 | 1 | 11 | ....... | 7 | 1 | 3 | 2 | 5 | ....... | 2 | ....... | 1 | 7 00– 7 49 |
| 7 50– 7 99 | ....... | ....... | ....... | ....... | ....... | ....... | ....... | 3 | ....... | ....... | ....... | ....... | 7 50– 7 99 |
| 8 00– 8 99 | ....... | 4 | 1 | 2 | ....... | 2 | ....... | 5 | 2 | 3 | ....... | 2 | 8 00– 8 99 |
| 9 00– 9 99 | 3 | 2 | 4 | 6 | ....... | 2 | 3 | 7 | 3 | 2 | 1 | ....... | 9 00– 9 99 |
| 10 00–10 99 | 15 | 4 | 12 | 2 | 3 | 2 | 17 | 3 | 6 | 2 | 1 | ....... | 10 00–10 99 |
| 11 00–11 99 | 13 | ....... | 8 | 1 | 4 | ....... | 17 | ....... | 3 | 1 | 3 | ....... | 11 00–11 99 |
| 12 00–12 99 | 32 | ....... | 29 | 3 | 9 | ....... | 30 | 3 | 21 | 2 | 4 | ....... | 12 00–12 99 |
| 13 00–13 99 | 10 | ....... | 6 | ....... | 4 | ....... | 14 | 1 | 5 | ....... | 1 | ....... | 13 00–13 99 |
| 14 00–14 99 | 12 | 1 | 11 | ....... | 11 | ....... | 25 | 1 | 6 | ....... | 6 | ....... | 14 00–14 99 |
| 15 00–15 99 | 16 | ....... | 7 | ....... | 6 | ....... | 17 | ....... | 13 | ....... | 5 | ....... | 15 00–15 99 |
| 16 00–17 99 | 13 | ....... | 13 | ....... | 7 | 1 | 25 | ....... | 13 | ....... | 4 | ....... | 16 00–17 99 |
| 18 00–19 99 | 6 | 1 | 4 | ....... | 2 | ....... | 22 | ....... | 8 | ....... | 2 | ....... | 18 00–19 99 |
| 20 00–24 99 | 10 | ....... | 12 | 1 | 13 | ....... | 27 | ....... | 12 | ....... | 9 | ....... | 20 00–24 99 |
| 25 00–29 99 | 4 | 1 | 4 | ....... | 2 | ....... | 10 | ....... | 11 | ....... | 2 | ....... | 25 00–29 99 |
| 30 00–34 99 | 2 | ....... | ....... | ....... | 1 | ....... | 1 | ....... | 2 | ....... | 1 | ....... | 30 00–34 99 |
| 35 00–39 99 | 1 | ....... | 3 | ....... | 2 | ....... | 4 | ....... | 3 | ....... | ....... | ....... | 35 00–39 99 |
| 40 00 and over | 2 | ....... | ....... | ....... | 1 | ....... | 7 | ....... | 6 | ....... | ....... | ....... | 40 00 and over |
| Not reported | ....... | ....... | ....... | ....... | ....... | ....... | ....... | ....... | ....... | ....... | ....... | ....... | Not reported |
| Total | 143 | 53 | 119 | 50 | 68 | 21 | 228 | 64 | 114 | 18 | 40 | 5 | Total |

NEW YORK STATE

50. TABLE XIII, A, 1, e — (*concluded*)

**DEPARTMENT STORES — PLANT**

Number of Employees for Each Sex Classified According to Actual Weekly Earnings, by the Number of Years with the Firm

| Actual Weekly Earnings in Dollars | Years with Firm (*concluded*) | | | | | | | | | | | | Actual Weekly Earnings in Dollars |
|---|---|---|---|---|---|---|---|---|---|---|---|---|---|
| | 25–29 | | 30–34 | | 35–44 | | Not reported | | Total | | Cumulative per cent of total | | |
| | Male | Female | Male | Female | Male | Female | Male | Female | Male | Female | Male | Female | |
| Less than $3 00 | ....... | ....... | ....... | ....... | ....... | ....... | ....... | 1 | 17 | 40 | .5 | 2.6 | Less than $3 00 |
| $3 00–$3 49 | ....... | ....... | ....... | ....... | ....... | ....... | ....... | ....... | 9 | 99 | .8 | 9.1 | $3 00– 3 49 |
| 3 50– 3 99 | 1 | ....... | ....... | ....... | ....... | ....... | ....... | 1 | 5 | 56 | .9 | 12.8 | 3 50– 3 99 |
| 4 00– 4 49 | ....... | ....... | ....... | ....... | ....... | ....... | ....... | 2 | 35 | 219 | 1.9 | 27.1 | 4 00– 4 49 |
| 4 50– 4 99 | ....... | ....... | ....... | ....... | ....... | ....... | ....... | 1 | 11 | 99 | 2.3 | 33.6 | 4 50– 4 99 |
| 5 00– 5 49 | ....... | ....... | ....... | ....... | ....... | ....... | 1 | ....... | 61 | 196 | 4.1 | 46.4 | 5 00– 5 49 |
| 5 50– 5 99 | ....... | ....... | ....... | ....... | ....... | ....... | ....... | ....... | 12 | 82 | 4.5 | 51.7 | 5 00– 5 99 |
| 6 00– 6 49 | ....... | ....... | ....... | ....... | ....... | 1 | 1 | 1 | 61 | 248 | 6.3 | 67.8 | 6 00– 6 49 |
| 6 50– 6 99 | ....... | ....... | ....... | ....... | ....... | ....... | ....... | ....... | 12 | 38 | 6.6 | 70.3 | 6 50– 6 99 |
| 7 00– 7 49 | 1 | ....... | ....... | ....... | ....... | ....... | ....... | ....... | 66 | 177 | 8.6 | 81.8 | 7 00– 7 49 |
| 7 50– 7 99 | ....... | ....... | ....... | ....... | ....... | ....... | ....... | 1 | 9 | 36 | 8.9 | 84.1 | 7 50– 7 99 |
| 8 00– 8 99 | ....... | 1 | ....... | ....... | ....... | ....... | ....... | ....... | 103 | 81 | 11.9 | 89.3 | 8 00– 8 99 |
| 9 00– 9 99 | ....... | 1 | ....... | ....... | 1 | ....... | 1 | ....... | 145 | 52 | 16.2 | 92.7 | 9 00– 9 99 |
| 10 00–10 99 | ....... | 1 | 2 | ....... | ....... | ....... | ....... | ....... | 412 | 46 | 28.5 | 95.7 | 10 00–10 99 |
| 11 00–11 99 | ....... | ....... | ....... | ....... | ....... | ....... | ....... | 1 | 282 | 9 | 36.8 | 96.3 | 11 00–11 99 |
| 12 00–12 99 | 1 | ....... | 3 | ....... | 1 | ....... | 6 | ....... | 285 | 24 | 57.2 | 97.9 | 12 00–12 99 |
| 13 00–13 99 | ....... | ....... | ....... | ....... | ....... | ....... | 1 | ....... | 170 | 2 | 62.4 | 98.0 | 13 00–13 99 |
| 14 00–14 99 | 5 | ....... | 1 | ....... | 1 | ....... | ....... | ....... | 245 | 8 | 69.5 | 98.5 | 14 00–14 99 |
| 15 00–15 99 | 5 | ....... | ....... | ....... | 1 | ....... | 2 | ....... | 231 | 9 | 76.3 | 99.1 | 15 00–15 99 |
| 16 00–17 99 | 1 | ....... | 2 | ....... | ....... | ....... | ....... | ....... | 205 | 5 | 82.5 | 99.4 | 16 00–17 99 |
| 18 00–19 99 | ....... | ....... | 1 | ....... | ....... | ....... | ....... | ....... | 173 | 1 | 87.7 | 99.5 | 18 00–19 99 |
| 20 00–24 99 | 1 | ....... | ....... | ....... | 2 | ....... | 2 | ....... | 256 | 3 | 95.0 | 99.7 | 20 00–24 99 |
| 25 00–29 99 | 1 | ....... | ....... | ....... | 1 | ....... | ....... | ....... | 92 | 3 | 98.0 | 99.9 | 25 00–29 99 |
| 30 00–34 99 | 1 | ....... | 1 | ....... | ....... | ....... | ....... | ....... | 29 | ....... | 99.2 | ....... | 30 00–34 99 |
| 35 00–39 99 | ....... | ....... | ....... | ....... | ....... | ....... | ....... | ....... | 24 | ....... | 99.6 | ....... | 35 00–39 99 |
| 40 00 and over | ....... | ....... | ....... | ....... | ....... | ....... | ....... | ....... | 24 | 1 | 100.0 | 100.0 | 40 00 and over |
| Not reported | ....... | ....... | ....... | ....... | ....... | ....... | ....... | ....... | 8 | 2 | ....... | ....... | Not reported |
| Total | 17 | 3 | 10 | ....... | 7 | 1 | 14 | 8 | 3,382 | 1,536 | ....... | ....... | Total |

51. TABLE XIV, A, 1, e

NEW YORK STATE

**MERCANTILE ESTABLISHMENTS**

NUMBER OF EMPLOYEES FOR EACH SEX IN THE MAIN OCCUPATIONS IN THE PLANT EARNING SPECIFIED WEEKLY RATES — DEPARTMENT STORES

| WEEKLY RATES IN DOLLARS | OCCUPATION | | | | | | | | | | | | | | WEEKLY RATES IN |
|---|---|---|---|---|---|---|---|---|---|---|---|---|---|---|---|
| | ENGINEERS | FIREMEN | ELECTRICIANS | CARPENTERS | ELEVATOR RUNNERS | PIANO TUNERS | PORTERS | MAIDS | WATCHMEN | MANICURISTS | JANITORS | | CLEANERS | | |
| | Male | Male | Male | Male | Male | Male | Male | Female | Male | Female | Male | Female | Male | Female | |
| Less than $3 00 | ...... | ...... | ...... | ...... | ...... | ...... | ...... | ...... | ...... | ...... | .... | ...... | .... | ...... | Less than $3 00 |
| $3 00–$3 49... | ...... | ...... | ...... | ...... | ...... | ...... | ...... | ...... | ...... | ...... | .... | ...... | .... | ...... | ...$3 00– 3 49 |
| 3 50– 3 99... | ...... | ...... | ...... | ...... | ...... | ...... | ...... | ...... | ...... | ...... | .... | ...... | .... | ...... | ... 3 50– 3 99 |
| 4 00– 4 49... | ...... | ...... | ...... | ...... | ...... | ...... | ...... | 4 | ...... | 1 | .... | ...... | 1 | 1 | ... 4 00– 4 49 |
| 4 50– 4 99... | ...... | ...... | ...... | ...... | 2 | ...... | ...... | ...... | ...... | ...... | .... | ...... | .... | ...... | ... 4 50– 4 99 |
| 5 00– 5 49... | ...... | ...... | ...... | ...... | 3 | ...... | 5 | 3 | ...... | ...... | .... | ...... | .... | 3 | ... 5 00– 5 49 |
| 5 50– 5 99... | ...... | ...... | ...... | ...... | ...... | ...... | ...... | ...... | ...... | ...... | .... | ...... | .... | ...... | ... 5 50– 5 99 |
| 6 00– 6 49... | 1 | ...... | 3 | ...... | 6 | ...... | 6 | 33 | ...... | 3 | 1 | 9 | 1 | 40 | ... 6 00– 6 49 |
| 6 50– 6 99... | ...... | ...... | ...... | ...... | ...... | ...... | ...... | 4 | ...... | ...... | .... | ...... | .... | ...... | ... 6 50– 6 99 |
| 7 00– 7 49... | ...... | 2 | ...... | 1 | 6 | ...... | 4 | 6 | 1 | 18 | 2 | 17 | 3 | 67 | ... 7 00– 7 49 |
| 7 50– 7 99... | ...... | ...... | ...... | ...... | 5 | ...... | ...... | ...... | ...... | ...... | 1 | 16 | .... | 13 | ... 7 50– 7 99 |
| 8 00– 8 99... | ...... | 3 | ...... | 1 | 44 | ...... | 18 | 4 | 1 | 5 | .... | 2 | .... | 20 | ... 8 00– 8 99 |
| 9 00– 9 99... | ...... | 1 | 2 | ...... | 43 | ...... | 59 | 3 | 4 | 2 | 3 | 5 | 4 | 15 | ... 9 00– 9 99 |
| 10 00–10 99... | 3 | ...... | 1 | 1 | 164 | 1 | 221 | ...... | 9 | 2 | 32 | 8 | 13 | 3 | ...10 00–10 99 |
| 11 00–11 99... | 1 | 1 | ...... | 1 | 75 | ...... | 99 | ...... | 30 | ...... | 50 | ...... | 5 | ...... | ...11 00–11 99 |
| 12 00–12 99... | 2 | 3 | 12 | 5 | 171 | 2 | 286 | ...... | 107 | ...... | 48 | ...... | 15 | ...... | ...12 00–12 99 |
| 13 00–13 99... | ...... | 4 | 6 | ...... | 62 | ...... | 26 | ...... | 9 | ...... | 30 | ...... | .... | ...... | ...13 00–13 99 |
| 14 00–14 99... | 3 | 12 | 7 | 3 | 22 | 2 | 22 | ...... | 59 | ...... | 18 | ...... | 9 | ...... | ...14 00–14 99 |
| 15 00–15 99... | 7 | 28 | 20 | 11 | 17 | 2 | 26 | ...... | 19 | ...... | 17 | 1 | 4 | ...... | ...15 00–15 99 |
| 16 00–17 99... | 6 | 29 | 18 | 3 | 6 | 3 | 7 | ...... | 17 | ...... | 14 | ...... | 1 | ...... | ...16 00–17 99 |
| 18 00–19 99... | 20 | 14 | 9 | 14 | 1 | 14 | 5 | ...... | 7 | ...... | 2 | ...... | 1 | ...... | ...18 00–19 99 |
| 20 00–24 99... | 49 | 4 | 27 | 20 | 2 | 21 | 8 | ...... | 1 | ...... | 5 | ...... | .... | ...... | ...20 00–24 99 |
| 25 00–29 99... | 15 | ...... | 5 | 27 | 1 | 1 | 2 | ...... | ...... | ...... | .... | ...... | .... | ...... | ...25 00–29 99 |
| 30 00–34 99... | 5 | ...... | 3 | 12 | ...... | ...... | 2 | ...... | 1 | ...... | .... | ...... | .... | ...... | ...30 00–34 99 |
| 35 00–39 99... | 3 | ...... | 2 | 3 | ...... | ...... | 2 | ...... | ...... | ...... | .... | ...... | .... | ...... | ...35 00–39 99 |
| 40 00 and over. | 4 | ...... | 1 | ...... | ...... | ...... | 1 | ...... | ...... | ...... | .... | ...... | .... | ...... | .40 00 and over |
| Not reported... | ...... | ...... | ...... | ...... | ...... | ...... | 2 | ...... | ...... | ...... | .... | ...... | .... | ...... | ...Not reported |
| Total..... | 119 | 101 | 116 | 102 | 630 | 46 | 801 | 57 | 265 | 31 | 223 | 58 | 57 | 162 | .....Total |

NEW YORK STATE

51. TABLE XIV, A, 1, e — (*concluded*) **MERCANTILE ESTABLISHMENTS**

NUMBER OF EMPLOYEES FOR EACH SEX IN THE MAIN OCCUPATIONS IN THE PLANT EARNING SPECIFIED WEEKLY RATES — DEPARTMENT STORES

| WEEKLY RATES IN DOLLARS | OCCUPATION (*concluded*) | | | | | | | | | | | | CUMULATIVE PER CENT FOR STATE | | WEEKLY RATES IN DOLLARS |
|---|---|---|---|---|---|---|---|---|---|---|---|---|---|---|---|
| | COOKS | | WAITERS | | DISHWASHERS | | OMNIBUS | | ALL OTHERS | | TOTAL | | | | |
| | Male | Female | Male | Female | Male | Female | Male | Female | Male | Female | Male | Female | Male | Female | |
| Less than $3 00 | .... | ...... | .... | 1 | ...... | 1 | ...... | ...... | ...... | ...... | ...... | 2 | ...... | .13 | Less than $3 00 |
| $3 00–$3 49... | .... | 1 | .... | 70 | ...... | ...... | ...... | ...... | 1 | ...... | 1 | 71 | .03 | 4.75 | ...$3 00– 3 49 |
| 3 50– 3 99... | 1 | 1 | .... | 21 | ...... | ...... | ...... | ...... | ...... | 5 | 1 | 27 | .06 | 6.52 | ... 3 50– 3 99 |
| 4 00– 4 49... | .... | ...... | 26 | 216 | ...... | 3 | ...... | ...... | 2 | 21 | 29 | 246 | .94 | 22.52 | ... 4 00– 4 49 |
| 4 50– 4 99... | .... | ...... | .... | 70 | ...... | 1 | ...... | ...... | 4 | 11 | 6 | 82 | 1.12 | 27.85 | ... 4 50– 4 99 |
| 5 00– 5 49... | .... | 6 | .... | 148 | 21 | 6 | 21 | ...... | 19 | 31 | 68 | 197 | 3.21 | 40.80 | ... 5 00– 5 49 |
| 5 50– 5 99... | .... | ...... | .... | 11 | ...... | 2 | ...... | ...... | ...... | 2 | ...... | 15 | 3.21 | 41.75 | ... 5 50– 5 99 |
| 6 00– 6 49... | 1 | 16 | 3 | 157 | 4 | 22 | 22 | 3 | 16 | 71 | 64 | 354 | 5.10 | 64.75 | ... 6 00– 6 49 |
| 6 50– 6 99... | .... | ...... | .... | ...... | ...... | ...... | ...... | ...... | ...... | 2 | ...... | 6 | 5.10 | 65.10 | ... 6 50– 6 99 |
| 7 00– 7 49... | 7 | 16 | 1 | 55 | 15 | 3 | 7 | ...... | 22 | 67 | 71 | 249 | 7.30 | 81.40 | ... 7 00– 7 49 |
| 7 50– 7 99... | .... | 1 | .... | ...... | ...... | ...... | ...... | ...... | ...... | 6 | 6 | 36 | 7.48 | 83.70 | ... 7 50– 7 99 |
| 8 00– 8 99... | 2 | 4 | .... | 14 | 4 | 2 | 1 | ...... | 20 | 43 | 94 | 94 | 10.32 | 89.80 | ... 8 00– 8 99 |
| 9 00– 9 99... | 4 | 5 | 1 | 2 | 4 | ...... | ...... | ...... | 14 | 16 | 139 | 48 | 14.51 | 93.00 | ... 9 00– 9 99 |
| 10 00–10 99... | 6 | 10 | 1 | 1 | ...... | ...... | 1 | ...... | 15 | 18 | 468 | 42 | 28.65 | 95.75 | ...10 00–10 99 |
| 11 00–11 99... | 3 | 3 | .... | ...... | ...... | ...... | ...... | ...... | 25 | 4 | 290 | 7 | 37.50 | 96.10 | ...11 00–11 99 |
| 12 00–12 99... | 13 | 4 | .... | 4 | 1 | ...... | 1 | ...... | 89 | 19 | 755 | 27 | 60.50 | 97.70 | ...12 00–12 99 |
| 13 00–13 99... | 6 | ...... | .... | ...... | ...... | ...... | ...... | ...... | 21 | 2 | 164 | 2 | 65.40 | 97.85 | ...13 00–13 99 |
| 14 00–14 99... | 9 | 2 | .... | ...... | ...... | ...... | ...... | ...... | 38 | 5 | 204 | 7 | 71.70 | 98.50 | ...14 00–14 99 |
| 15 00–15 99... | 11 | ...... | .... | ...... | ...... | ...... | ...... | ...... | 77 | 9 | 239 | 10 | 78.90 | 99.10 | ...15 00–15 99 |
| 16 00–17 99... | 11 | 2 | .... | ...... | ...... | ...... | ...... | ...... | 50 | 3 | 165 | 5 | 84.00 | 99.40 | ...16 00–17 99 |
| 18 00–19 99... | 3 | ...... | .... | ...... | ...... | ...... | ...... | ...... | 71 | 1 | 161 | 1 | 88.70 | 99.50 | ...18 00–19 99 |
| 20 00–24 99... | 14 | ...... | 1 | ...... | ...... | ...... | ...... | ...... | 78 | 3 | 230 | 3 | 95.55 | 99.72 | ...20 00–24 99 |
| 25 00–29 99... | 2 | ...... | .... | ...... | ...... | ...... | ...... | ...... | 15 | 3 | 68 | 3 | 97.80 | 99.93 | ...25 00–29 99 |
| 30 00–34 99... | 1 | ...... | .... | ...... | ...... | ...... | ...... | ...... | 21 | ...... | 45 | ...... | 99.10 | 99.93 | ...30 00–34 99 |
| 35 00–39 99... | .... | ...... | .... | ...... | ...... | ...... | ...... | ...... | 5 | ...... | 15 | ...... | 99.50 | 99.93 | ...35 00–39 99 |
| 40 00 and over. | 1 | ...... | .... | ...... | ...... | ...... | ...... | ...... | 9 | 1 | 16 | 1 | 100.00 | 100.00 | .40 00 and over |
| Not reported... | 2 | ...... | .... | ...... | ...... | ...... | ...... | ...... | 78 | 1 | 82 | 1 | ...... | ...... | ...Not reported |
| Total..... | 97 | 71 | 33 | 770 | 49 | 40 | 53 | 3 | 690 | 344 | 3,382 | 1,536 | ...... | ...... | .....Total |

NEW YORK STATE

**NEIGHBORHOOD STORES — STOCK AND SALES**

52. TABLE VII, A, 2, a NUMBER AND PER CENT OF EMPLOYEES BY SEX, ACCORDING TO OCCUPATION AND NATIVITY

| NATIVITY | OCCUPATION | | | | | | | | | | | | | | | | |
|---|---|---|---|---|---|---|---|---|---|---|---|---|---|---|---|---|---|
| | TOTAL | | SUPER-INTEND-ENTS | BUYERS | | ASSISTANT BUYERS AND HEADS OF STOCK | | RECEIVING AND STOCK CLERKS | | STOCK PEOPLE | | FLOOR MANAGERS | | SALES PEOPLE | | MESSENGERS, WRAPPERS, ERRAND BOYS | |
| | Male | Female | Male | Male | Female | Male | Female | Male | Female | Male | Female | Male | Female | Male | Female | Male | Female |
| Native | 298 | 1,435 | 5 | 19 | 20 | 15 | 23 | 28 | 6 | 12 | 18 | 20 | 3 | 175 | 1,246 | 24 | 119 |
| Foreign | 191 | 187 | 3 | 22 | 6 | 7 | 4 | 7 | ..... | 3 | 4 | 10 | ..... | 129 | 156 | 10 | 17 |
| Not reported | 7 | 9 | ..... | 1 | ..... | ..... | 1 | 1 | ..... | ..... | ..... | 1 | ..... | 4 | 7 | ..... | 1 |
| Total | 496 | 1,631 | 8 | 42 | 26 | 22 | 28 | 36 | 6 | 15 | 22 | 31 | 3 | 308 | 1,409 | 34 | 137 |
| Per cent. of total | 100.0 | 100.0 | 1.6 | 8.5 | 1.6 | 4.4 | 1.7 | 7.2 | .37 | 3.2 | 1.35 | 6.2 | .18 | 62.1 | 86.4 | 6.8 | 8.4 |

NEW YORK STATE

**NEIGHBORHOOD STORES — STOCK AND SALES**

53. TABLE V, A, 2, a NUMBER AND PER CENT OF EMPLOYEES EARNING SPECIFIED WEEKLY RATES, BY AGE GROUPS AND SEX

| WEEKLY RATES IN DOLLARS | AGE GROUPS IN YEARS | | | | | | | | | | | | | | WEEKLY RATES IN DOLLARS |
|---|---|---|---|---|---|---|---|---|---|---|---|---|---|---|---|
| | 14–15 | | 16–17 | | 18–20 | | 21–24 | | 25–29 | | 30–34 | | 35–39 | | |
| | Male | Female | Male | Female | Male | Female | Male | Female | Male | Female | Male | Female | Male | Female | |
| Less than $3 00 | .... | 2 | .... | ...... | ...... | ...... | ...... | ...... | ...... | ...... | ...... | ...... | ...... | ...... | Less than $3 00 |
| $3 00–$3 49... | 4 | 6 | 1 | 15 | ...... | 2 | ...... | 1 | ...... | ...... | ...... | ...... | ...... | ...... | ...$3 00– 3 49 |
| 3 50– 3.99... | 2 | 5 | 2 | 42 | ...... | 3 | 1 | ...... | ...... | ...... | ...... | 1 | ...... | ...... | ... 3 50– 3 99 |
| 4 00– 4 49... | 1 | 4 | 5 | 87 | ...... | 23 | ...... | 2 | ...... | ...... | ...... | 2 | ...... | ...... | ... 4 00– 4 49 |
| 4 50– 4 99... | .... | 2 | 3 | 33 | ...... | 31 | ...... | 5 | ...... | ...... | ...... | ...... | ...... | ...... | ... 4 50– 4 99 |
| 5 00– 5 49... | 3 | ...... | 11 | 41 | 3 | 101 | ...... | 28 | 1 | 3 | ...... | 1 | ...... | 2 | ... 5 00– 5 49 |
| 5 50– 5 99... | .... | ...... | .... | 6 | 1 | 45 | 1 | 17 | ...... | 3 | ...... | ...... | ...... | ...... | ... 5 50– 5 99 |
| 6 00– 6 49... | .... | ...... | 9 | 15 | 12 | 128 | 3 | 93 | 1 | 34 | ...... | 9 | ...... | 12 | ... 6 00– 6 49 |
| 6 50– 6 99... | .... | ...... | 1 | ...... | ...... | 14 | ...... | 20 | ...... | 6 | ...... | ...... | ...... | 3 | ... 6 50– 6 99 |
| 7 00– 7 49... | .... | ...... | .... | 3 | 9 | 61 | ...... | 87 | 2 | 35 | ...... | 11 | ...... | 5 | ... 7 00– 7 49 |
| 7 50– 7 99... | .... | ...... | .... | ...... | ...... | 2 | ...... | 11 | ...... | 3 | ...... | ...... | ...... | 1 | ... 7 50– 7 99 |
| 8 00– 8 99... | .... | ...... | 1 | 1 | 7 | 29 | 6 | 90 | ...... | 40 | 1 | 13 | ...... | 14 | ... 8 00– 8 99 |
| 9 00– 9 99... | .... | ...... | .... | 2 | 5 | 7 | 2 | 48 | ...... | 34 | ...... | 17 | ...... | 7 | ... 9 00– 9 99 |
| 10 00–10 99... | .... | ...... | .... | ...... | 4 | 2 | 17 | 28 | 7 | 28 | 2 | 14 | 2 | 17 | ...10 00–10 99 |
| 11 00–11 99... | .... | ...... | .... | ...... | 2 | ...... | 6 | 5 | 2 | 5 | ...... | 3 | 1 | ...... | ...11 00–11 99 |
| 12 00–12 99... | .... | ...... | .... | ...... | 5 | 1 | 17 | 12 | 9 | 16 | 4 | 7 | 6 | 4 | ...12 00–12 99 |
| 13 00–13 99... | .... | ...... | .... | ...... | ...... | ...... | 4 | 2 | 2 | 4 | 4 | 3 | 4 | 1 | ...13 00–13 99 |
| 14 00–14 99... | .... | ...... | .... | ...... | 1 | 1 | 5 | 2 | 8 | 6 | 8 | 3 | 8 | 4 | ...14 00–14 99 |
| 15 00–15 99... | .... | ...... | .... | ...... | ...... | ...... | 10 | 1 | 8 | 5 | 9 | 4 | 11 | ...... | ...15 00–15 99 |
| 16 00–17 99... | .... | ...... | .... | ...... | ...... | ...... | 1 | 1 | 6 | 1 | 10 | 1 | 7 | ...... | ...16 00–17 99 |
| 18 00–19–99... | .... | ...... | .... | ...... | ...... | ...... | 1 | ...... | 3 | ...... | 1 | 2 | 10 | 2 | ...18 00–19 99 |
| 20 00–24 99... | .... | ...... | .... | ...... | ...... | ...... | ...... | ...... | 3 | 1 | 5 | 1 | 6 | ...... | ...20 00–24 99 |
| 25 00–29 99... | .... | ...... | .... | ...... | ...... | ...... | ...... | 1 | 3 | ...... | 3 | ...... | 7 | 1 | ...25 00–29 99 |
| 30 00–34 99... | .... | ...... | .... | ...... | ...... | ...... | 1 | ...... | 1 | ...... | ...... | 1 | 3 | ...... | ...30 00–34 99 |
| 35 00–39 99... | .... | ...... | .... | ...... | ...... | ...... | 1 | ...... | 2 | ...... | 1 | ...... | ...... | ...... | ...35 00–39 99 |
| 40 00 and over. | .... | ...... | .... | ...... | ...... | ...... | 1 | ...... | ...... | ...... | 1 | ...... | ...... | ...... | .40 00 and over |
| Not reported... | .... | ...... | .... | 1 | 1 | ...... | ...... | ...... | ...... | ...... | ...... | ...... | ...... | ...... | ...Not reported |
| Total..... | 10 | 19 | 33 | 246 | 50 | 450 | 77 | 454 | 58 | 224 | 49 | 93 | 65 | 73 | .....Total |

53. TABLE V, A, 2, a — *concluded*

NEW YORK STATE

**NEIGHBORHOOD STORES — STOCK AND SALES**

NUMBER AND PER CENT OF EMPLOYEES EARNING SPECIFIED WEEKLY RATES, BY AGE GROUPS AND SEX

| WEEKLY RATES IN DOLLARS | AGE GROUPS IN YEARS (*concluded*) 40–44 | | 45–54 | | 55–64 | | 65 AND OVER | NOT REPORTED | | TOTAL | | CUMULATIVE PER CENT OF TOTAL | | WEEKLY RATES IN DOLLARS |
|---|---|---|---|---|---|---|---|---|---|---|---|---|---|---|
| | Male | Female | Male | Female | Male | Female | Male | Male | Female | Male | Female | Male | Female | |
| Less than $3 00 | ...... | ...... | ...... | ...... | ...... | ...... | ...... | ...... | ...... | ...... | 2 | ...... | .12 | Less than $3 00 |
| $3 00–$3 49 | ...... | ...... | ...... | ...... | ...... | ...... | ...... | ...... | 1 | 5 | 25 | 1.01 | 1.66 | $3 00–$3 49 |
| 3 50– 3 99 | ...... | ...... | ...... | ...... | ...... | ...... | ...... | ...... | ...... | 5 | 51 | 2.02 | 4.73 | 3 50– 3 99 |
| 4 00– 4 49 | ...... | ...... | ...... | ...... | ...... | ...... | ...... | ...... | ...... | 6 | 118 | 3.24 | 12.06 | 4 00– 4 49 |
| 4 50– 4 99 | ...... | ...... | ...... | ...... | ...... | ...... | ...... | ...... | ...... | 3 | 71 | 3.85 | 16.40 | 4 50– 4 99 |
| 5 00– 5 49 | ...... | ...... | ...... | 2 | ...... | ...... | ...... | ...... | ...... | 18 | 178 | 7.50 | 27.35 | 5 00– 5 49 |
| 5 50– 5 99 | ...... | 1 | ...... | ...... | ...... | ...... | ...... | ...... | ...... | 2 | 72 | 7.90 | 31.80 | 5 50– 5 99 |
| 6 00– 6 49 | ...... | 1 | ...... | 2 | ...... | ...... | ...... | ...... | ...... | 25 | 294 | 12.96 | 49.85 | 6 00– 6 49 |
| 6 50– 6 99 | ...... | 1 | ...... | ...... | ...... | 1 | ...... | ...... | ...... | 1 | 45 | 13.16 | 52.60 | 6 50– 6 99 |
| 7 00– 7 49 | ...... | 2 | ...... | 2 | ...... | ...... | ...... | 1 | 5 | 12 | 211 | 15.60 | 65.50 | 7 00– 7 49 |
| 7 50– 7 99 | ...... | 1 | ...... | ...... | ...... | ...... | ...... | ...... | ...... | ...... | 18 | 15.60 | 66.70 | 7 50– 7 99 |
| 8 00– 8 99 | ...... | 8 | ...... | 5 | ...... | ...... | ...... | ...... | 1 | 15 | 201 | 18.64 | 79.00 | 8 00– 8 99 |
| 9 00– 9 99 | ...... | 4 | 1 | 3 | ...... | ...... | ...... | ...... | ...... | 8 | 122 | 20.25 | 86.50 | 9 00– 9 99 |
| 10 00–10 99 | ...... | 4 | 1 | 2 | 3 | ...... | ...... | 1 | 2 | 37 | 97 | 27.75 | 92.50 | 10 00–10 99 |
| 11 00–11 99 | ...... | ...... | 2 | ...... | 1 | ...... | ...... | 1 | ...... | 15 | 13 | 30.80 | 93.25 | 11 00–11 99 |
| 12 00–12 99 | 6 | 1 | 10 | 1 | 8 | 1 | ...... | 1 | ...... | 66 | 43 | 44.20 | 95.95 | 12 00–12 99 |
| 13 00–13 99 | 2 | 3 | 1 | 2 | 1 | ...... | 1 | ...... | 2 | 19 | 17 | 48.00 | 97.50 | 13 00–13 99 |
| 14 00–14 99 | 3 | 2 | 8 | 1 | ...... | ...... | 2 | 1 | 4 | 44 | 23 | 56.80 | 98.30 | 14 00–14 99 |
| 15 00–15 99 | 9 | 1 | 20 | ...... | 2 | ...... | ...... | ...... | 2 | 69 | 13 | 70.85 | 99.10 | 15 00–15 99 |
| 16 00–17 99 | 5 | ...... | 8 | ...... | 3 | ...... | 1 | 1 | 1 | 42 | 4 | 79.40 | 99.30 | 16 00–17 99 |
| 18 00–19 99 | 6 | ...... | 6 | ...... | 3 | ...... | 3 | ...... | 1 | 33 | 5 | 86.05 | 99.60 | 18 00–19 99 |
| 20 00–24 99 | 5 | ...... | 7 | ...... | 2 | 1 | ...... | ...... | ...... | 28 | 3 | 91.75 | 99.80 | 20 00–24 99 |
| 25 00–29 99 | 2 | ...... | 1 | ...... | ...... | ...... | ...... | ...... | ...... | 16 | 2 | 95.00 | 99.93 | 25 00–29 99 |
| 30 00–34 99 | 3 | ...... | 4 | ...... | ...... | ...... | ...... | 1 | ...... | 13 | 1 | 97.75 | 100.00 | 30 00–34 99 |
| 35 00–39 99 | 2 | ...... | 1 | ...... | ...... | ...... | ...... | ...... | ...... | 7 | ...... | 99.10 | 100.00 | 35 00–39 99 |
| 40 00 and over | 3 | ...... | ...... | ...... | ...... | ...... | ...... | ...... | ...... | 5 | ...... | 100.00 | 100.00 | 40 00 and over |
| Not reported | ...... | ...... | ...... | ...... | ...... | ...... | ...... | ...... | ...... | 1 | 1 | ...... | ...... | Not reported |
| Total | 46 | 29 | 70 | 20 | 23 | 3 | 7 | 7 | 19 | 495 | 1,630 | ...... | ...... | Total |

54. TABLE VIII, A, 2, a

NEW YORK STATE

**NEIGHBORHOOD STORES — STOCK AND SALES**

NUMBER AND PER CENT OF EMPLOYEES EARNING SPECIFIED WEEKLY RATES, BY OCCUPATION AND SEX

| ACTUAL WEEKLY EARNINGS IN DOLLARS | OCCUPATION | | | | | | | | | | | | | | | | | | | | ACTUAL WEEKLY EARNINGS IN DOLLARS |
|---|---|---|---|---|---|---|---|---|---|---|---|---|---|---|---|---|---|---|---|---|---|
| | SUPER-INTEND-ENTS | BUYERS | | ASSISTANT BUYERS AND HEADS OF STOCK | | RECEIVING AND STOCK CLERKS | | STOCK PEOPLE | | FLOOR MANAGERS | | SALES PEOPLE | | MESSENGERS, WRAPPERS, ERRAND BOYS | | TOTAL | | CUMULATIVE PER CENT OF TOTAL | | |
| | Male | Male | Female | Male | Female | Male | Female | Male | Female | Male | Female | Male | Female | Male | Female | Male | Female | Male | Female | |
| Less than $3 00 | | | | | | | | | | | | | | | 2 | | 2 | | .12 | Less than $3 00 |
| $3 00–$3 49 | | | | | | | | | 2 | | | | 4 | 5 | 19 | 5 | 25 | 1.01 | 1.66 | $3 00– 3 49 |
| 3 50– 3 99 | | | | | | | 3 | 1 | | | | | 11 | 4 | 37 | 5 | 51 | 2.02 | 4.73 | 3 50– 3 99 |
| 4 00– 4 49 | | | | | | 1 | | 1 | 4 | | | 1 | 45 | 3 | 69 | 6 | 118 | 3.24 | 12.06 | 4 00– 4 49 |
| 4 50– 4 99 | | | | | | 1 | | 2 | 1 | | | | 64 | | 6 | 3 | 71 | 3.85 | 16.40 | 4 50– 4 99 |
| 5 00– 5 49 | | | | | | 1 | 1 | 3 | 3 | | | 2 | 171 | 12 | 3 | 18 | 178 | 7.50 | 27.35 | 5 00– 5 49 |
| 5 50– 5 99 | | | | | | 1 | | | 1 | | | 1 | 71 | | | 2 | 72 | 7.90 | 31.80 | 5 50– 5 99 |
| 6 00– 6 49 | | | | | 1 | 4 | 1 | 4 | 5 | | | 11 | 287 | 6 | | 25 | 294 | 12.96 | 49.85 | 6 00– 6 49 |
| 6 50– 6 99 | | | | | | | | | 1 | | | 1 | 44 | | | 1 | 45 | 13.16 | 52.60 | 6 50– 6 99 |
| 7 00– 7 49 | | | | | 2 | 5 | | 1 | 1 | | | 5 | 208 | 1 | | 12 | 211 | 15.60 | 65.50 | 7 00– 7 49 |
| 7 50– 7 99 | | | | | 1 | | | | | | | | 17 | | | | 18 | 15.60 | 66.70 | 7 50– 7 99 |
| 8 00– 8 99 | | | 1 | | | 1 | 1 | | 2 | | | 13 | 197 | 1 | | 15 | 201 | 18.64 | 79.00 | 8 00– 8 99 |
| 9 00– 9 99 | | | | | 4 | | | | 1 | | | 8 | 116 | | 1 | 8 | 122 | 20.25 | 86.50 | 9 00– 9 99 |
| 10 00–10 99 | | 1 | 3 | 1 | 5 | 3 | | | | 1 | | 30 | 89 | 1 | | 37 | 97 | 27.75 | 92.50 | 10 00–10 99 |
| 11 00–11 99 | | | | 4 | 2 | 1 | | 1 | | 1 | | 8 | 11 | | | 15 | 13 | 30.80 | 93.25 | 11 00–11 99 |
| 12 00–12 99 | 2 | | 3 | 4 | 4 | 4 | | 1 | | 1 | 1 | 54 | 35 | | | 66 | 43 | 44.20 | 95.95 | 12 00–12 99 |
| 13 00–13 99 | | | 3 | 2 | 3 | 2 | | | 1 | | | 15 | 10 | | | 19 | 17 | 48.00 | 97.50 | 13 00–13 99 |
| 14 00–14 99 | | 1 | 5 | 1 | 2 | 3 | | | | | 1 | 39 | 15 | | | 44 | 23 | 56.80 | 98.30 | 14 00–14 99 |
| 15 00–15 99 | | 2 | 4 | 2 | 2 | 2 | | 1 | | 6 | | 56 | 7 | | | 64 | 13 | 70.85 | 99.10 | 15 00–15 99 |
| 16 00–17 99 | | 3 | | 2 | 1 | 2 | | | | 3 | | 31 | 3 | 1 | | 42 | 4 | 79.40 | 99.30 | 16 00–17 99 |
| 18 00–19 99 | | 2 | 2 | | | 2 | | | | 10 | | 19 | 3 | | | 33 | 5 | 86.05 | 99.60 | 18 00–19 99 |
| 20 00–24 99 | 2 | 6 | 2 | 4 | 1 | 1 | | | | 6 | | 9 | | | | 28 | 3 | 91.75 | 99.80 | 20 00–24 99 |
| 25 00–29 99 | 2 | 8 | 2 | 1 | | 1 | | | | 1 | | 3 | | | | 16 | 2 | 95.00 | 99.93 | 25 00–29 99 |
| 30 00–34 99 | 1 | 8 | 1 | | | 1 | | | | 2 | | 1 | | | | 13 | 1 | 97.75 | 100.00 | 30 00–34 99 |
| 35 00–39 99 | 1 | 6 | | | | | | | | | | | | | | 7 | | 99.10 | | 35–00–39 99 |
| 40 00 and over | | 5 | | | | | | | | | | | | | | 5 | | 100.00 | | 40 00 and over |
| Not reported | | | | | | | | | | | | 1 | 1 | | | 1 | 1 | | | Not reported |
| Total | 8 | 42 | 26 | 21 | 28 | 36 | 6 | 15 | 22 | 31 | 2 | 308 | 1,409 | 34 | 137 | 495 | 1,630 | | | Total |

55. TABLE VI, A, 2, a

NEW YORK STATE

**NEIGHBORHOOD STORES — STOCK AND SALES**

NUMBER AND PER CENT. OF EMPLOYEES CLASSIFIED ACCORDING TO ACTUAL WEEKLY EARNINGS BY AGE GROUPS AND SEX

| ACTUAL WEEKLY EARNINGS IN DOLLARS | AGE GROUPS IN YEARS | | | | | | | | | | | | | | ACTUAL WEEKLY EARNINGS DOLLARS |
|---|---|---|---|---|---|---|---|---|---|---|---|---|---|---|---|
| | 14–15 | | 16–17 | | 18–20 | | 21–24 | | 25–29 | | 30–34 | | 35–39 | | |
| | Male | Female | Male | Female | Male | Female | Male | Female | Male | Female | Male | Female | Male | Female | |
| Less than $3 00 | 1 | 2 | 1 | 18 | 2 | 10 | 1 | 8 | ...... | 3 | ...... | 2 | ...... | 2 | Less than $3 00 |
| $3 00–$3 49... | 3 | 7 | 1 | 21 | 2 | 9 | 1 | 2 | ...... | 1 | ...... | ...... | ...... | ...... | ...$3 00– 3 49 |
| 3 50– 3 99... | 2 | 4 | 2 | 45 | 1 | 7 | 1 | 2 | ...... | 1 | ...... | 2 | ...... | ...... | ... 3 50– 3 99 |
| 4 00– 4 49... | 1 | 4 | 5 | 71 | ...... | 27 | ...... | 9 | ...... | ...... | ...... | 2 | 1 | 2 | ... 4 00– 4 49 |
| 4 50– 4 99... | .... | 2 | 3 | 35 | ...... | 31 | ...... | 7 | ...... | 4 | ...... | ...... | ...... | ...... | ... 4 50– 4 99 |
| 5 00– 5 49... | 3 | ...... | 11 | 35 | 3 | 96 | ...... | 27 | 1 | 3 | ...... | 2 | ...... | 1 | ... 5 00– 5 49 |
| 5 50– 5 99... | .... | ...... | .... | 5 | 1 | 47 | ...... | 20 | ...... | 5 | ...... | ...... | ...... | 2 | ... 5 50– 5 99 |
| 6 00– 6 49... | .... | ...... | 8 | 13 | 10 | 110 | 2 | 80 | 1 | 29 | ...... | 8 | ...... | 11 | ... 6 00– 6 49 |
| 6 50– 6 99... | .... | ...... | 1 | ...... | ...... | 19 | 1 | 20 | ...... | 12 | ...... | 1 | 1 | 2 | ... 6 50– 6 99 |
| 7 00– 7 49... | .... | ...... | .... | 1 | 8 | 49 | ...... | 71 | 2 | 23 | ...... | 10 | ...... | 4 | ... 7 00– 7 49 |
| 7 50– 7 99... | .... | ...... | .... | ...... | 1 | 4 | ...... | 23 | ...... | 10 | ...... | 1 | ...... | 1 | ... 7 50– 7 99 |
| 8 00– 8 99... | .... | ...... | 1 | 1 | 5 | 28 | 5 | 78 | ...... | 35 | 1 | 11 | ...... | 13 | ... 8 00– 8 99 |
| 9 00– 9 99... | .... | ...... | .... | 1 | 4 | 6 | 3 | 53 | ...... | 28 | ...... | 17 | ...... | 6 | ... 9 00– 9 99 |
| 10 00–10 99... | .... | ...... | .... | ...... | 5 | 4 | 13 | 23 | 8 | 28 | 2 | 9 | 2 | 16 | ...10 00–10 99 |
| 11 00–11 99... | .... | ...... | .... | ...... | 2 | ...... | 7 | 8 | 2 | 9 | 1 | 2 | 1 | 2 | ...11 00–11 99 |
| 12 00–12 99... | .... | ...... | .... | ...... | 5 | 1 | 17 | 11 | 4 | 12 | 3 | 6 | 5 | 3 | ...12 00–12 99 |
| 13 00–13 99... | .... | ...... | .... | ...... | ...... | ...... | 3 | 4 | 4 | 6 | 6 | 5 | 2 | 1 | ...13 00–13 99 |
| 14 00–14 99... | .... | ...... | .... | ...... | 1 | ...... | 4 | 3 | 6 | 6 | 4 | 4 | 5 | 4 | ...14 00–14 99 |
| 15 00–15 99... | .... | ...... | .... | ...... | ...... | 1 | 7 | 2 | 8 | 5 | 8 | 5 | 6 | ...... | ...15 00–15 99 |
| 16 00–17 99... | .... | ...... | .... | ...... | ...... | ...... | 4 | 2 | 7 | 2 | 8 | 1 | 11 | ...... | ...16 00–17 99 |
| 18 00–19 99... | .... | ...... | .... | ...... | ...... | ...... | 3 | ...... | 3 | 1 | 4 | 2 | 13 | 2 | ...18 00–19 99 |
| 20 00–24 99... | .... | ...... | .... | ...... | ...... | ...... | 2 | ...... | 5 | 1 | 5 | 1 | 7 | ...... | ...20 00–24 99 |
| 25 00–29 99... | .... | ...... | .... | ...... | ...... | ...... | ...... | 1 | 4 | ...... | 5 | ...... | 8 | 1 | ...25 00–29 99 |
| 30 00–34 99... | .... | ...... | .... | ...... | ...... | ...... | 1 | ...... | 1 | ...... | ...... | 1 | 3 | ...... | ...30 00–34 99 |
| 35 00–39 99... | .... | ...... | .... | ...... | ...... | ...... | 1 | ...... | 2 | ...... | 1 | ...... | ...... | ...... | ...35 00–39 99 |
| 40 00 and over. | .... | ...... | .... | ...... | ...... | ...... | 1 | ...... | ...... | ...... | 1 | ...... | ...... | ...... | .40 00 and over |
| Not reported... | .... | ...... | .... | ...... | ...... | 1 | ...... | ...... | ...... | ...... | ...... | 1 | ...... | ...... | ...Not reported |
| Total..... | 10 | 19 | 33 | 246 | 50 | 450 | 77 | 454 | 58 | 224 | 49 | 93 | 65 | 73 | ....Total |

55. TABLE VI, A, 2, a — *concluded*

NEW YORK STATE

**NEIGHBORHOOD STORES — STOCK AND SALES**

NUMBER AND PER CENT. OF EMPLOYEES CLASSIFIED ACCORDING TO ACTUAL WEEKLY EARNINGS BY AGE GROUPS AND SEX

| ACTUAL WEEKLY EARNINGS IN DOLLARS | AGE GROUPS IN YEARS | | | | | | | | | TOTAL | | CUMULATIVE PER CENT. OF TOTAL | | ACTUAL WEEKLY EARNINGS IN DOLLARS |
|---|---|---|---|---|---|---|---|---|---|---|---|---|---|---|
| | 40–44 | | 45–54 | | 55–64 | | 65 AND OVER | NOT REPORTED | | | | | | |
| | Male | Female | Male | Female | Male | Female | Male | Male | Female | Male | Female | Male | Female | |
| Less than $3 00 | ...... | 1 | ...... | ...... | ...... | ...... | ...... | ...... | 1 | 5 | 47 | 1.01 | 2.88 | Less than $3 00 |
| $3 00–$3 49 | ...... | ...... | ...... | ...... | ...... | ...... | ...... | ...... | ...... | 7 | 40 | 2.42 | 5.35 | $3 00– 3 49 |
| 3 50– 3 99 | ...... | ...... | ...... | ...... | ...... | ...... | ...... | ...... | ...... | 6 | 61 | 3.64 | 9.08 | 3 50– 3 99 |
| 4 00– 4 49 | ...... | ...... | ...... | ...... | ...... | ...... | ...... | ...... | ...... | 7 | 115 | 5.05 | 16.15 | 4 00– 4 49 |
| 4 50– 4 99 | ...... | ...... | ...... | ...... | ...... | ...... | ...... | ...... | ...... | 3 | 79 | 5.66 | 25.00 | 4 50– 4 99 |
| 5 00– 5 49 | 1 | ...... | ...... | 2 | ...... | ...... | ...... | ...... | ...... | 19 | 166 | 9.50 | 31.20 | 5 00– 5 49 |
| 5 50– 5 99 | ...... | 2 | ...... | ...... | ...... | ...... | ...... | ...... | ...... | 1 | 81 | 9.70 | 36.20 | 5 50– 5 99 |
| 6 00– 6 49 | ...... | 1 | ...... | 2 | ...... | ...... | ...... | ...... | ...... | 21 | 254 | 13.94 | 51.80 | 6 00– 6 49 |
| 6 50– 6 99 | 1 | 1 | ...... | ...... | ...... | 1 | ...... | ...... | ...... | 4 | 56 | 14.74 | 55.20 | 6 50– 6 99 |
| 7 00– 7 49 | ...... | 2 | ...... | 3 | ...... | ...... | ...... | 1 | 3 | 11 | 166 | 16.97 | 65.40 | 7 00– 7 49 |
| 7 50– 7 99 | ...... | 1 | ...... | ...... | ...... | ...... | ...... | ...... | 2 | 1 | 42 | 17.17 | 68.00 | 7 50– 7 99 |
| 8 00– 8 99 | ...... | 6 | ...... | 4 | 1 | ...... | ...... | ...... | 1 | 13 | 177 | 19.80 | 78.80 | 8 00– 8 99 |
| 9 00– 9 99 | ...... | 4 | 1 | 4 | ...... | ...... | ...... | 1 | 2 | 9 | 121 | 21.61 | 86.25 | 9 00– 9 99 |
| 10 00–10 99 | ...... | ...... | 1 | 2 | 2 | ...... | ...... | ...... | 1 | 33 | 83 | 28.30 | 91.20 | 10 00–10 99 |
| 11 00–11 99 | ...... | 1 | 2 | ...... | 1 | ...... | ...... | 1 | ...... | 17 | 22 | 31.71 | 92.75 | 11 00–11 99 |
| 12 00–12 99 | 3 | 3 | 6 | ...... | 5 | 1 | ...... | 1 | 1 | 49 | 38 | 41.60 | 95.04 | 12 00–12 99 |
| 13 00–13 99 | 3 | 4 | 3 | 3 | 2 | ...... | 1 | ...... | 1 | 24 | 24 | 46.50 | 96.52 | 13 00–13 99 |
| 14 00–14 99 | 1 | 2 | 9 | ...... | ...... | ...... | 1 | 1 | 3 | 32 | 22 | 52.95 | 97.87 | 14 00–14 99 |
| 15 00–15 99 | 6 | 1 | 13 | ...... | 2 | ...... | ...... | ...... | 2 | 50 | 16 | 63.02 | 98.85 | 15 00–15 99 |
| 16 00–17 99 | 8 | ...... | 11 | ...... | 5 | ...... | 1 | 1 | 1 | 56 | 6 | 74.33 | 99.22 | 16 00–17 99 |
| 18 00–19 99 | 5 | ...... | 8 | ...... | 3 | ...... | 4 | ...... | 1 | 43 | 6 | 83.02 | 99.59 | 18 00–19 99 |
| 20 00–24 99 | 7 | ...... | 8 | ...... | 2 | 1 | ...... | ...... | ...... | 36 | 3 | 90.29 | 99.78 | 20 00–24 99 |
| 25 00–29 99 | 3 | ...... | 3 | ...... | ...... | ...... | ...... | ...... | ...... | 23 | 2 | 94.94 | 99.90 | 25 00–29 99 |
| 30 00–34 99 | 3 | ...... | 4 | ...... | ...... | ...... | ...... | 1 | ...... | 13 | 1 | 97.57 | 100.00 | 30 00–34 99 |
| 35 00–39 99 | 2 | ...... | 1 | ...... | ...... | ...... | ...... | ...... | ...... | 7 | ...... | 98.98 | ...... | 35 00–39 99 |
| 40 00 and over | 3 | ...... | ...... | ...... | ...... | ...... | ...... | ...... | ...... | 5 | ...... | 100.00 | ...... | 40 00 and over |
| Not reported | ...... | ...... | ...... | ...... | ...... | ...... | ...... | ...... | ...... | ...... | 2 | ...... | ...... | Not reported |
| Total | 46 | 29 | 70 | 20 | 23 | 3 | 7 | 7 | 19 | 495 | 1,630 | ...... | ...... | Total |

56. TABLE IX, A, 2, a

NEW YORK STATE

**NEIGHBORHOOD STORES — STOCK AND SALES**

NUMBER AND PER CENT. OF EMPLOYEES CLASSIFIED ACCORDING TO ACTUAL WEEKLY EARNINGS, BY OCCUPATION AND SEX

| ACTUAL WEEKLY EARNINGS IN DOLLARS | OCCUPATION | | | | | | | | | | | | | | | | | | | | ACTUAL WEEKLY EARNINGS IN DOLLARS |
|---|---|---|---|---|---|---|---|---|---|---|---|---|---|---|---|---|---|---|---|---|---|
| | SUPERINTENDENTS | BUYERS | | ASSISTANT BUYERS AND HEADS OF STOCK | | RECEIVING AND STOCK CLERKS | | STOCK PEOPLE | | FLOOR MANAGERS | | SALES PEOPLE | | MESSENGERS, WRAPPERS, ERRAND BOYS | | TOTAL | | CUMULATIVE PER CENT. OF TOTAL | | | |
| | Male | Male | Female | Male | Female | Male | Female | Male | Female | Male | Female | Male | Female | Male | Female | Male | Female | Male | Female | | |
| Less than $3 00 | ...... | .... | ..... | .... | ..... | .... | ..... | 1 | 1 | .... | ..... | 3 | 33 | 1 | 13 | 5 | 47 | 1.01 | 2.88 | Less than $3 00 | |
| $3 00–$3 49.... | ...... | .... | ..... | .... | ..... | .... | ..... | .... | 2 | .... | ..... | 3 | 15 | 4 | 23 | 7 | 40 | 2.42 | 5.35 | ...$3 00– 3 49 | |
| 3 50– 3 99.... | ...... | .... | ..... | .... | ..... | .... | 3 | 1 | 1 | .... | ..... | .... | 20 | 5 | 37 | 6 | 61 | 3.64 | 9.08 | ... 3 50– 3 99 | |
| 4 00– 4 49.... | ...... | .... | ..... | .... | ..... | 1 | ..... | 1 | 5 | .... | ..... | 2 | 54 | 3 | 56 | 7 | 115 | 5.05 | 16.15 | ... 4 00– 4 49 | |
| 4 50– 4 99.... | ...... | .... | ..... | .... | 1 | 1 | ..... | 1 | 2 | .... | ..... | .... | 71 | 1 | 5 | 3 | 79 | 5.66 | 25.00 | ... 4 50– 4 99 | |
| 5 00– 5 49.... | ...... | .... | ..... | .... | ..... | 1 | 1 | 4 | 2 | .... | ..... | 3 | 161 | 11 | 2 | 19 | 166 | 9.50 | 31.20 | ... 5 00– 5 49 | |
| 5 50– 5 99.... | ...... | .... | ..... | .... | ..... | 1 | ..... | .... | 1 | .... | ..... | .... | 80 | .... | ..... | 1 | 81 | 9.70 | 36.20 | ... 5 50– 5 99 | |
| 6 00– 6 49.... | ...... | .... | ..... | .... | 1 | 4 | 1 | 3 | 3 | .... | 1 | 9 | 248 | 5 | ..... | 21 | 254 | 13.94 | 51.80 | ... 6 00– 6 49 | |
| 6 50– 6 99.... | ...... | .... | ..... | .... | 1 | 2 | ..... | .... | 1 | .... | ..... | 2 | 54 | .... | ..... | 4 | 56 | 14.74 | 55.20 | ... 6 50– 6 99 | |
| 7 00– 7 49.... | ...... | .... | ..... | .... | ..... | 5 | ..... | 1 | ..... | .... | 1 | 4 | 165 | 1 | ..... | 11 | 166 | 16.97 | 65.40 | ... 7 00– 7 49 | |
| 7 50– 7 99.... | ...... | .... | ..... | .... | 1 | .... | ..... | .... | ..... | .... | ..... | 1 | 41 | .... | ..... | 1 | 42 | 17.17 | 68.00 | ... 7 50– 7 99 | |
| 8 00– 8 99.... | ...... | .... | 2 | .... | ..... | .... | 1 | .... | 2 | .... | ..... | 12 | 172 | 1 | ..... | 13 | 177 | 19.80 | 78.80 | ... 8 00– 8 99 | |
| 9 00– 9 99.... | ...... | .... | ..... | .... | 6 | 1 | ..... | .... | 1 | .... | ..... | 8 | 113 | .... | 1 | 9 | 121 | 21.61 | 86.25 | ... 9 00– 9 99 | |
| 10 00–10 99.... | ...... | 1 | 3 | 1 | 4 | 3 | ..... | .... | ..... | 1 | ..... | 26 | 76 | 1 | ..... | 33 | 83 | 28.30 | 91.20 | ...10 00–10 99 | |
| 11 00–11 99.... | ...... | .... | ..... | 4 | 1 | 1 | ..... | 1 | ..... | 1 | ..... | 10 | 21 | .... | ..... | 17 | 22 | 31.71 | 92.75 | ...11 00–11 99 | |
| 12 00–12 99.... | 2 | .... | 4 | 4 | 3 | 4 | ..... | 1 | ..... | 1 | ..... | 37 | 31 | .... | ..... | 49 | 38 | 41.60 | 95.04 | ...12 00–12 99 | |
| 13 00–13 99.... | ...... | .... | 3 | 2 | 4 | .... | ..... | .... | 1 | .... | ..... | 22 | 16 | .... | ..... | 24 | 24 | 46.50 | 96.52 | ...13 00–13 99 | |
| 14 00–14 99.... | ...... | 1 | 4 | 1 | 2 | 3 | ..... | .... | ..... | .... | ..... | 27 | 16 | .... | ..... | 32 | 22 | 52.95 | 97.87 | ...14 00–14 99 | |
| 15 00–15 99.... | ...... | 1 | 3 | 1 | 2 | 2 | ..... | 1 | ..... | 6 | ..... | 39 | 11 | .... | ..... | 50 | 16 | 63.02 | 98.85 | ...15 00–15 99 | |
| 16 00–17 99.... | ...... | 3 | ..... | 2 | 1 | 1 | ..... | .... | ..... | 3 | ..... | 46 | 5 | 1 | ..... | 56 | 6 | 74.33 | 99.22 | ...16 00–17 99 | |
| 18 00–19 99.... | ...... | 1 | 2 | .... | ..... | 3 | ..... | .... | ..... | 10 | ..... | 29 | 4 | .... | ..... | 43 | 6 | 83.02 | 99.59 | ...18 00–19 99 | |
| 20 00–24 99.... | 2 | 7 | 2 | 4 | 1 | 1 | ..... | .... | ..... | 6 | ..... | 16 | ..... | .... | ..... | 36 | 3 | 90.29 | 99.78 | ...20 00–24 99 | |
| 25 00–29 99.... | 2 | 9 | 2 | 2 | ..... | 1 | ..... | .... | ..... | 1 | ..... | 8 | ..... | .... | ..... | 23 | 2 | 94.94 | 99.90 | ...25 00–29 99 | |
| 30 00–34 99.... | 1 | 8 | 1 | .... | ..... | 1 | ..... | .... | ..... | 2 | ..... | 1 | ..... | .... | ..... | 13 | 1 | 97.57 | 100.00 | ...30 00–34 99 | |
| 35 00–39 99.... | 1 | 6 | ..... | .... | ..... | .... | ..... | .... | ..... | .... | ..... | .... | ..... | .... | ..... | 7 | ..... | 98.98 | ..... | ...35 00–39 99 | |
| 40 00 and over.. | ...... | 5 | ..... | .... | ..... | .... | ..... | .... | ..... | .... | ..... | .... | ..... | .... | ..... | 5 | ..... | 100.00 | ..... | 40 00 and over | |
| Not reported.... | ...... | .... | ..... | .... | ..... | .... | ..... | .... | ..... | .... | ..... | .... | 2 | .... | ..... | .... | 2 | ..... | ..... | ...Not reported | |
| Total...... | 8 | 42 | 26 | 21 | 28 | 36 | 6 | 15 | 22 | 31 | 2 | 308 | 1409 | 34 | 137 | 495 | 1630 | ..... | ..... | .....Total | |

57. TABLE X, A, 2, a

NEW YORK STATE

**NEIGHBORHOOD STORES — STOCK AND SALES**

Number and Per Cent. of Employees Classified According to Actual Weekly Earnings by Conjugal Condition and Sex

| Actual Weekly Earnings in Dollars | Conjugal Condition: Single | | Married | | Widowed or Divorced | | Not Reported | | Total | | Cumulative Per Cent. of Total | | Actual Weekly Earnings in Dollars |
|---|---|---|---|---|---|---|---|---|---|---|---|---|---|
| | Male | Female | Male | Female | Male | Female | Male | Female | Male | Female | Male | Female | |
| Less than $3 00. | 5 | 41 | ....... | 4 | ....... | 2 | ....... | ....... | 5 | 47 | 1.01 | 2.88 | Less than $3 00 |
| $3 00–$3 49.... | 7 | 38 | ....... | 1 | ....... | ....... | ....... | 1 | 7 | 40 | 2.42 | 5.35 | ...$3 00– 3 49 |
| 3 50– 3 99.... | 6 | 59 | ....... | 2 | ....... | ....... | ....... | ....... | 6 | 61 | 3.64 | 9.08 | ... 3 50– 3 99 |
| 4 00– 4 49.... | 7 | 111 | ....... | 2 | ....... | 1 | ....... | 1 | 7 | 115 | 5.05 | 16.15 | ... 4 00– 4 49 |
| 4 50– 4 99.... | 3 | 74 | ....... | 1 | ....... | 1 | ....... | 3 | 3 | 79 | 5.66 | 25.00 | ... 4 50– 4 99 |
| 5 00– 5 49.... | 18 | 156 | ....... | 5 | 1 | 3 | ....... | 2 | 19 | 166 | 9.50 | 31.20 | ... 5 00– 5 49 |
| 5 50– 5 99.... | 1 | 76 | ....... | 1 | ....... | 3 | ....... | 1 | 1 | 81 | 9.70 | 36.20 | ... 5 50– 5 99 |
| 6 00– 6 49.... | 21 | 224 | ....... | 12 | ....... | 13 | ....... | 5 | 21 | 254 | 13.94 | 51.80 | ... 6 00– 6 49 |
| 6 50– 6 99.... | 2 | 50 | 1 | ....... | ....... | 5 | 1 | 1 | 4 | 56 | 14.74 | 55.20 | ... 6 50– 6 99 |
| 7 00– 7 49.... | 11 | 149 | ....... | 7 | ....... | 9 | ....... | 1 | 11 | 166 | 16.97 | 65.40 | ... 7 00– 7 49 |
| 7 50– 7 99.... | 1 | 37 | ....... | ....... | ....... | 3 | ....... | 2 | 1 | 42 | 17.17 | 68.00 | ... 7 50– 7 99 |
| 8 00– 8 99.... | 13 | 151 | ....... | 11 | ....... | 11 | ....... | 4 | 13 | 177 | 19.80 | 78.80 | ... 8 00– 8 99 |
| 9 00– 9 99.... | 7 | 100 | 1 | 6 | ....... | 12 | 1 | 3 | 9 | 121 | 21.61 | 86.25 | ... 9 00– 9 99 |
| 10 00–10 99.... | 23 | 67 | 8 | 3 | ....... | 10 | 2 | 3 | 33 | 83 | 28.30 | 91.20 | ...10 00–10 99 |
| 11 00–11 99.... | 12 | 18 | 4 | 2 | ....... | 2 | 1 | ....... | 17 | 22 | 31.71 | 92.75 | ...11 00–11 99 |
| 12 00–12 99.... | 27 | 31 | 17 | 2 | 3 | 3 | 2 | 2 | 49 | 38 | 41.60 | 95.04 | ...12 00–12 99 |
| 13 00–13 99.... | 11 | 16 | 11 | 3 | 1 | 5 | 1 | ....... | 24 | 24 | 46.50 | 96.52 | ...13 00–13 99 |
| 14 00–14 99.... | 12 | 18 | 19 | 1 | 1 | 1 | ....... | 2 | 32 | 22 | 52.95 | 97.87 | ...14 00–14 99 |
| 15 00–15 99.... | 18 | 13 | 28 | 2 | 2 | 1 | 2 | ....... | 50 | 16 | 63.02 | 98.85 | ...15 00–15 99 |
| 16 00–17 99.... | 18 | 5 | 33 | ....... | 4 | ....... | 1 | 1 | 56 | 6 | 74.33 | 99.22 | ...16 00–17 99 |
| 18 00–19 99.... | 8 | 5 | 31 | ....... | 2 | ....... | 2 | 1 | 43 | 6 | 83.02 | 99.59 | ...18 00–19 99 |
| 20 00–24 99.... | 14 | 3 | 19 | ....... | 2 | ....... | 1 | ....... | 36 | 3 | 90.29 | 99.78 | ...20 00–24 99 |
| 25 00–29 99.... | 5 | 2 | 16 | ....... | 1 | ....... | 1 | ....... | 23 | 2 | 94.94 | 99.90 | ...25 00–29 99 |
| 30 00–34 99.... | 1 | 1 | 11 | ....... | ....... | ....... | 1 | ....... | 13 | 1 | 97.57 | 100.00 | ...30 00–34 99 |
| 35 00–39 99.... | ....... | ....... | 6 | ....... | ....... | ....... | 1 | ....... | 7 | ....... | 98.98 | ....... | ...35 00–39 99 |
| 40 00 and over. | 3 | ....... | 2 | ....... | ....... | ....... | ....... | ....... | 5 | ....... | 100.00 | ....... | .40 00 and over |
| Not reported.... | ....... | 1 | ....... | ....... | ....... | 1 | ....... | ....... | ....... | 2 | ....... | ....... | ...Not reported |
| Total...... | 254 | 1,446 | 207 | 65 | 17 | 86 | 17 | 33 | 495 | 1,630 | ....... | ....... | .....Total |

NEW YORK STATE

58. TABLE XI, A, 2, a

**NEIGHBORHOOD STORES — STOCK AND SALES**

NUMBER AND PER CENT. OF EMPLOYEES CLASSIFIED ACCORDING TO ACTUAL WEEKLY EARNINGS BY NATIVITY AND SEX

| ACTUAL WEEKLY EARNINGS IN DOLLARS | NATIVITY | | | | | | | | | | ACTUAL WEEKLY EARNINGS IN DOLLARS |
|---|---|---|---|---|---|---|---|---|---|---|---|
| | NATIVE | | FOREIGN | | NOT REPORTED | | TOTAL | | CUMULATIVE PER CENT. OF TOTAL | | |
| | Male | Female | Male | Female | Male | Female | Male | Female | Male | Female | |
| Less than $3 00 | 3 | 41 | 2 | 4 | ........ | 2 | 5 | 47 | 1.01 | 2.88 | Less than $3 00 |
| $3 00–$3 49 | 4 | 35 | 3 | 5 | ........ | ........ | 7 | 40 | 2.42 | 5.35 | $3 00– 3 49 |
| 3 50– 3 99 | 6 | 55 | ........ | 6 | ........ | ........ | 6 | 61 | 3.64 | 9.08 | 3 50– 3 99 |
| 4 00– 4 49 | 5 | 96 | 2 | 19 | ........ | ........ | 7 | 115 | 5.05 | 16.15 | 4 00– 4 49 |
| 4 50– 4 99 | 2 | 72 | 1 | 7 | ........ | ........ | 3 | 79 | 5.66 | 25.00 | 4 50– 4 99 |
| 5 00– 5 49 | 15 | 156 | 4 | 9 | ........ | 1 | 19 | 166 | 9.50 | 31.20 | 5 00– 5 49 |
| 5 50– 5 99 | 1 | 76 | ........ | 4 | ........ | 1 | 1 | 81 | 9.70 | 36.20 | 5 50– 5 99 |
| 6 00– 6 49 | 15 | 228 | 4 | 24 | 2 | 2 | 21 | 254 | 13.94 | 51.80 | 6 00– 6 49 |
| 6 50– 6 99 | 4 | 50 | ........ | 6 | ........ | ........ | 4 | 56 | 14.74 | 55.20 | 6 50– 6 99 |
| 7 00– 7 49 | 7 | 148 | 3 | 18 | 1 | ........ | 11 | 166 | 16.97 | 65.40 | 7 00– 7 49 |
| 7 50– 7 99 | 1 | 36 | ........ | 5 | ........ | 1 | 1 | 42 | 17.17 | 68.00 | 7 50– 7 99 |
| 8 00– 8 99 | 11 | 151 | 2 | 26 | ........ | ........ | 13 | 177 | 19.80 | 78.80 | 8 00– 8 99 |
| 9 00– 9 99 | 6 | 100 | 3 | 21 | ........ | ........ | 9 | 121 | 21.61 | 86.25 | 9 00– 9 99 |
| 10 00–10 99 | 24 | 71 | 9 | 12 | ........ | ........ | 33 | 83 | 28.30 | 91.20 | 10 00–10 99 |
| 11 00–11 99 | 12 | 19 | 5 | 3 | ........ | ........ | 17 | 22 | 31.71 | 92.75 | 11 00–11 99 |
| 12 00–12 99 | 28 | 34 | 21 | 3 | ........ | 1 | 49 | 38 | 41.60 | 95.04 | 12 00–12 99 |
| 13 00–13 99 | 8 | 19 | 16 | 5 | ........ | ........ | 24 | 24 | 46.50 | 96.52 | 13 00–13 99 |
| 14 00–14 99 | 20 | 19 | 11 | 3 | 1 | ........ | 32 | 22 | 52.95 | 97.87 | 14 00–14 99 |
| 15 00–15 99 | 27 | 11 | 22 | 4 | 1 | 1 | 50 | 16 | 63.02 | 98.85 | 15 00–15 99 |
| 16 00–17 99 | 31 | 6 | 24 | ........ | 1 | ........ | 56 | 6 | 74.33 | 99.22 | 16 00–17 99 |
| 18 00–18 99 | 22 | 5 | 21 | 1 | ........ | ........ | 43 | 6 | 83.02 | 99.59 | 18 00–19 99 |
| 20 00–24 99 | 20 | 1 | 16 | 2 | ........ | ........ | 36 | 3 | 90.29 | 99.78 | 20 00–24 99 |
| 25 00–29 99 | 10 | 2 | 13 | ........ | ........ | ........ | 23 | 2 | 94.94 | 99.90 | 25 00–29 99 |
| 30 00–34 99 | 7 | 1 | 5 | ........ | 1 | ........ | 13 | 1 | 97.57 | 100.00 | 30 00–34 99 |
| 35 00–39 99 | 5 | ........ | 2 | ........ | ........ | ........ | 7 | ........ | 98.98 | ........ | 35 00–39 99 |
| 40 00 and over | 3 | ........ | 2 | ........ | ........ | ........ | 5 | ........ | 100.00 | ........ | 40 00 and over |
| Not reported | ........ | 2 | ........ | ........ | ........ | ........ | ........ | 2 | ........ | ........ | Not reported |
| Total | 297 | 1,434 | 191 | 187 | 7 | 9 | 495 | 1,630 | ........ | ........ | Total |

59. TABLE XI, 2, a

NEW YORK STATE

## NEIGHBORHOOD STORES — STOCK AND SALES

NUMBER OF EMPLOYEES FOR EACH SEX CLASSIFIED ACCORDING TO ACTUAL WEEKLY EARNINGS BY THE NUMBER OF YEARS IN THE TRADE

| ACTUAL WEEKLY EARNINGS IN DOLLARS | YEARS IN TRADE | | | | | | | | | | | | | | ACTUAL WEEKLY EARNINGS IN DOLLARS |
|---|---|---|---|---|---|---|---|---|---|---|---|---|---|---|---|
| | LESS THAN 1 | | 1 | | 2 | | 3 | | 4 | | 5 | | 6 | | |
| | Male | Female | Male | Female | Male | Female | Male | Female | Male | Female | Male | Female | Male | Female | |
| Less than $3 00 | 3 | 23 | 6 | 7 | .... | 3 | .... | 3 | 2 | 3 | .... | .... | .... | 1 | Less than $3 00 |
| $3 00– $3 49... | 4 | 31 | .... | 5 | 1 | 2 | 1 | 1 | 1 | .... | .... | .... | .... | 1 | ...$3 00– 3 49 |
| 3 50– 3 99... | 2 | 40 | 2 | 12 | 1 | 2 | .... | .... | .... | .... | .... | .... | .... | .... | ... 3 50– 3 99 |
| 4 00– 4 49... | 3 | 58 | .... | 26 | 2 | 7 | .... | 4 | .... | 5 | .... | 2 | .... | .... | ... 4 00– 4 49 |
| 4 50– 4 99... | 1 | 23 | 2 | 23 | .... | 21 | .... | 2 | .... | 5 | .... | .... | .... | 2 | ... 4 50– 4 99 |
| 5 00– 5 49... | 9 | 42 | 4 | 47 | .... | 30 | .... | 22 | .... | 14 | .... | 2 | .... | 1 | ... 5 00– 5 49 |
| 5 50– 5 99... | 1 | 6 | .... | 10 | .... | 26 | .... | 17 | .... | 6 | .... | 4 | .... | 4 | ... 5 50– 5 99 |
| 6 00– 6 49... | 9 | 31 | 7 | 29 | 1 | 51 | .... | 45 | 1 | 34 | .... | 13 | .... | 25 | ... 6 00– 6 49 |
| 6 50– 6 99... | .... | 1 | 1 | 4 | .... | 6 | 1 | 6 | .... | 7 | 1 | 12 | .... | 10 | ... 6 50– 6 99 |
| 7 00– 7 49... | 4 | 10 | 5 | 8 | 2 | 22 | .... | 21 | .... | 25 | .... | 23 | .... | 11 | ... 7 00– 7 49 |
| 7 50– 7 99... | 1 | 1 | .... | 6 | .... | .... | .... | 1 | .... | 6 | .... | 7 | .... | 6 | ... 7 50– 7 99 |
| 8 00– 8 99... | 3 | 8 | 1 | 10 | 2 | 9 | 3 | 21 | .... | 17 | .... | 20 | .... | 24 | ... 8 00– 8 99 |
| 9 00– 9 99... | 1 | 1 | 1 | 3 | 3 | 3 | 1 | 8 | 1 | 10 | .... | 9 | .... | 15 | ... 9 00– 9 99 |
| 10 00–10 99... | 2 | .... | 2 | 1 | 2 | 2 | 6 | 5 | 3 | 6 | 3 | 6 | 5 | 7 | ...10 00–10 99 |
| 11 00–11 99... | 2 | .... | 3 | .... | 1 | .... | 1 | .... | 1 | 1 | 2 | 2 | .... | 2 | ...11 00–11 99 |
| 12 00–12 99... | 2 | 1 | .... | .... | 3 | .... | 4 | 1 | 4 | 4 | 5 | 4 | 1 | .... | ...12 00–12 99 |
| 13 00–13 99... | .... | .... | .... | .... | .... | 2 | .... | .... | .... | 1 | 1 | 1 | .... | .... | ...13 00–13 99 |
| 14 00–14 99... | .... | .... | .... | .... | 1 | .... | .... | .... | 2 | .... | 3 | .... | 2 | 2 | ...14 00–14 99 |
| 15 00–15 99... | 1 | 1 | .... | .... | 4 | .... | 1 | .... | 3 | .... | 1 | 2 | .... | 1 | ...15 00–15 99 |
| 16 00–17 99... | .... | .... | 2 | .... | .... | .... | .... | .... | 2 | .... | 1 | .... | .... | .... | ...16 00–17 99 |
| 18 00–19 99... | .... | .... | .... | .... | .... | .... | .... | .... | 1 | .... | 5 | .... | .... | .... | ...18 00–19 99 |
| 20 00–24 99... | .... | .... | .... | .... | 1 | .... | .... | .... | .... | .... | .... | .... | 1 | .... | ...20 00–24 99 |
| 25 00–29 99... | .... | .... | 1 | 1 | .... | .... | .... | .... | 1 | .... | 1 | .... | .... | .... | ...25 00–29 99 |
| Not reported... | .... | 2 | .... | .... | .... | .... | .... | .... | .... | .... | .... | .... | .... | .... | ...Not reported |
| Total..... | 48 | 279 | 31 | 191 | 24 | 186 | 18 | 157 | 22 | 144 | 23 | 107 | 9 | 112 | .....Total |

59. TABLE XI, 2, a — (*continued*)

NEW YORK STATE

**NEIGHBORHOOD STORES — STOCK AND SALES**

NUMBER OF EMPLOYEES FOR EACH SEX CLASSIFIED ACCORDING TO ACTUAL WEEKLY EARNINGS BY THE NUMBER OF YEARS IN THE TRADE

| ACTUAL WEEKLY EARNINGS IN DOLLARS | YEARS IN TRADE (*continued*) | | | | | | | | | | | | ACTUAL WEEKLY EARNINGS IN DOLLARS |
|---|---|---|---|---|---|---|---|---|---|---|---|---|---|
| | 7 | | 8 | | 9 | | 10–14 | | 15–19 | | 20–24 | | |
| | Male | Female | Male | Female | Male | Female | Male | Female | Male | Female | Male | Female | |
| Less than $3 00 | ....... | 1 | ....... | ....... | ....... | ....... | ....... | 3 | ....... | 1 | ....... | ....... | Less than $3 00 |
| $3 00–$3 49 | ....... | ....... | ....... | ....... | ....... | ....... | ....... | ....... | ....... | ....... | ....... | ....... | $3 00– 3 49 |
| 3 50– 3 99 | ....... | 1 | 1 | ....... | ....... | 1 | ....... | 1 | ....... | ....... | ....... | ....... | 3 50– 3 99 |
| 4 00– 4 49 | ....... | ....... | ....... | ....... | ....... | ....... | ....... | 3 | 1 | ....... | ....... | ....... | 4 00– 4 49 |
| 4 50– 4 99 | ....... | 1 | ....... | 1 | ....... | 1 | ....... | ....... | ....... | ....... | ....... | ....... | 4 50– 4 99 |
| 5 00– 5 49 | ....... | 3 | ....... | 1 | ....... | 1 | ....... | 1 | 1 | ....... | ....... | ....... | 5 00– 5 49 |
| 5 50– 5 99 | ....... | 1 | ....... | 2 | ....... | 1 | ....... | 2 | ....... | 1 | ....... | ....... | 5 50– 5 99 |
| 6 00– 6 49 | ....... | 5 | ....... | 6 | ....... | 7 | ....... | 4 | ....... | 2 | ....... | 1 | 6 00– 6 49 |
| 6 50– 6 99 | ....... | 1 | ....... | 4 | 1 | 2 | ....... | 2 | ....... | ....... | ....... | ....... | 6 50– 6 99 |
| 7 00– 7 49 | ....... | 10 | ....... | 8 | ....... | 6 | ....... | 12 | ....... | 8 | ....... | ....... | 7 00– 7 49 |
| 7 50– 7 99 | ....... | 2 | ....... | 5 | ....... | 5 | ....... | 3 | ....... | ....... | ....... | ....... | 7 50– 7 99 |
| 8 00– 8 99 | 1 | 16 | ....... | 9 | ....... | 12 | ....... | 20 | ....... | 6 | 2 | 2 | 8 00– 8 99 |
| 9 00– 9 99 | ....... | 13 | ....... | 9 | ....... | 8 | ....... | 28 | ....... | 7 | ....... | 4 | 9 00– 9 99 |
| 10 00–10 99 | ....... | 7 | 1 | 11 | ....... | 5 | 4 | 22 | 2 | 4 | ....... | 5 | 10 00–10 99 |
| 11 00–11 99 | 1 | 5 | 2 | 1 | ....... | 2 | 3 | 8 | ....... | 1 | ....... | ....... | 10 00–11 99 |
| 12 00–12 99 | 5 | 3 | 3 | 2 | ....... | 2 | 4 | 14 | 3 | 3 | 4 | 2 | 12 00–12 99 |
| 13 00–13 99 | 1 | 3 | 1 | 2 | 1 | 1 | 6 | 9 | 3 | ....... | 3 | 2 | 13 00–13 99 |
| 14 00–14 99 | 2 | 1 | 4 | 4 | ....... | 1 | 3 | 6 | 2 | 4 | 3 | 4 | 14 00–14 99 |
| 15 00–15 99 | ....... | ....... | 5 | 1 | 4 | 1 | 7 | 7 | 8 | 3 | 5 | ....... | 15 00–15 99 |
| 16 00–17 99 | 4 | 2 | 4 | ....... | ....... | 1 | 10 | 2 | 6 | ....... | 10 | ....... | 16 00–17 99 |
| 18 00–19 99 | 2 | ....... | 2 | ....... | ....... | ....... | 9 | 2 | 5 | 2 | 4 | 1 | 18 00–19 99 |
| 20 00–24 99 | 1 | ....... | ....... | ....... | 1 | ....... | 7 | ....... | 5 | 2 | 8 | ....... | 20 00–24 99 |
| 25 00–29 99 | ....... | ....... | ....... | ....... | 1 | ....... | 5 | ....... | 5 | 2 | 6 | ....... | 25 00–29 99 |
| 30 00–34 99 | ....... | ....... | 1 | ....... | ....... | ....... | 1 | ....... | 3 | 1 | 2 | ....... | 30 00–34 99 |
| 35 00–39 99 | ....... | ....... | ....... | ....... | ....... | ....... | 2 | ....... | 1 | ....... | ....... | ....... | 35 00–39 99 |
| 40 00 and over | ....... | ....... | ....... | ....... | 1 | ....... | ....... | ....... | 2 | ....... | ....... | ....... | 40 00 and over |
| Not reported | ....... | ....... | ....... | ....... | ....... | ....... | ....... | ....... | ....... | ....... | ....... | ....... | Not reported |
| Total | 17 | 75 | 24 | 66 | 9 | 57 | 61 | 149 | 47 | 47 | 47 | 21 | Total |

STATE OF NEW YORK

59. TABLE XI, 2, a — (*concluded*)

**NEIGHBORHOOD STORES — STOCK AND SALES**

NUMBER OF EMPLOYEES FOR EACH SEX CLASSIFIED ACCORDING TO ACTUAL WEEKLY EARNINGS BY THE NUMBER OF YEARS IN THE TRADE

| ACTUAL WEEKLY EARNINGS IN DOLLARS | YEARS IN TRADE (*concluded*) 25–29 | | 30–34 | | 35–44 | 45 AND OVER | NOT REPORTED | | TOTAL | | CUMULATIVE PER CENT. OF TOTAL | | ACTUAL WEEKLY EARNINGS IN DOLLARS |
|---|---|---|---|---|---|---|---|---|---|---|---|---|---|
| | Male | Female | Male | Female | Male | Male | Male | Female | Male | Female | Male | Female | |
| Less than $3 00 | ....... | ....... | ....... | ....... | ....... | ....... | ....... | 2 | 5 | 47 | 1.01 | 2.88 | Less than $3 00 |
| $3 00–$3 49 | ....... | ....... | ....... | ....... | ....... | ....... | ....... | ....... | 7 | 40 | 2.42 | 5.35 | $3 00– 3 49 |
| 3 50– 3 99 | ....... | ....... | ....... | ....... | ....... | ....... | ....... | 4 | 6 | 61 | 3.64 | 9.08 | 3 50– 3 99 |
| 4 00– 4 49 | ....... | ....... | ....... | ....... | ....... | ....... | 1 | 10 | 7 | 115 | 5.05 | 16.15 | 4 00– 4 49 |
| 4 50– 4 99 | ....... | ....... | ....... | ....... | ....... | ....... | ....... | ....... | 3 | 79 | 5.66 | 25.00 | 4 50– 4 99 |
| 5 00– 5 49 | ....... | ....... | ....... | ....... | ....... | ....... | 5 | 2 | 19 | 166 | 9.50 | 31.20 | 5 00– 5 49 |
| 5 50– 5 99 | ....... | ....... | ....... | ....... | ....... | ....... | ....... | 1 | 1 | 81 | 9.70 | 36.20 | 5 50– 5 99 |
| 6 00– 6 49 | ....... | ....... | ....... | ....... | ....... | ....... | 3 | 1 | 21 | 254 | 13.94 | 51.80 | 6 00– 6 49 |
| 6 50– 6 99 | ....... | ....... | ....... | ....... | ....... | ....... | ....... | 1 | 4 | 56 | 14.74 | 55.20 | 6 50– 6 99 |
| 7 00– 7 49 | ....... | ....... | ....... | ....... | ....... | ....... | ....... | 2 | 11 | 166 | 16.97 | 65.40 | 7 00– 7 49 |
| 7 50– 7 99 | ....... | ....... | ....... | ....... | ....... | ....... | ....... | ....... | 1 | 42 | 17.17 | 68.00 | 7 50– 7 99 |
| 8 00– 8 99 | ....... | ....... | ....... | ....... | ....... | ....... | 1 | 3 | 13 | 177 | 19.80 | 78.80 | 8 00– 8 99 |
| 9 00– 9 99 | ....... | 2 | 1 | ....... | ....... | ....... | 1 | 1 | 9 | 121 | 21.61 | 86.25 | 9 00– 9 99 |
| 10 00–10 99 | ....... | ....... | 1 | 1 | 1 | ....... | 1 | 1 | 33 | 83 | 28.30 | 91.20 | 10 00–10 99 |
| 11 00–11 99 | ....... | ....... | ....... | ....... | ....... | ....... | 1 | ....... | 17 | 22 | 31.71 | 92.75 | 11 00–11 99 |
| 12 00–12 99 | 1 | 1 | 1 | ....... | 5 | 1 | 3 | 1 | 49 | 38 | 41.60 | 95.04 | 12 00–12 99 |
| 13 00–13 99 | 2 | 2 | 4 | ....... | 1 | 1 | ....... | 1 | 24 | 24 | 46.50 | 96.52 | 13 00–13 99 |
| 14 00–14 99 | 5 | ....... | 2 | ....... | 2 | 1 | ....... | ....... | 32 | 22 | 52.95 | 97.87 | 14 00–14 99 |
| 15 00–15 99 | 7 | ....... | 2 | ....... | 2 | ....... | ....... | ....... | 50 | 16 | 63.02 | 98.85 | 15 00–15 99 |
| 16 00–17 99 | 7 | ....... | 2 | ....... | 5 | 1 | 2 | 1 | 56 | 6 | 74.33 | 99.22 | 16 00–17 99 |
| 18 00–19 99 | 8 | ....... | 2 | ....... | 3 | 1 | 1 | 1 | 43 | 6 | 83.02 | 99.59 | 18 00–19 99 |
| 20 00–24 99 | 5 | 1 | 2 | ....... | 4 | ....... | 1 | ....... | 36 | 3 | 90.29 | 99 78 | 20 00–24 99 |
| 25 00–29 99 | 2 | ....... | 1 | ....... | ....... | ....... | ....... | ....... | 23 | 2 | 94.94 | 99.90 | 25 00–29 99 |
| 30 00–34 99 | 4 | ....... | 1 | ....... | 1 | ....... | ....... | ....... | 13 | 1 | 97.57 | 100.00 | 30 00–34 99 |
| 35 00–39 99 | 1 | ....... | 1 | ....... | ....... | ....... | 2 | ....... | 7 | ....... | 98.98 | ....... | 35 00–39 99 |
| 40 00 and over | 2 | ....... | ....... | ....... | ....... | ....... | ....... | ....... | 5 | ....... | 100.00 | ....... | 40 00 and over |
| Not reported | ....... | ....... | ....... | ....... | ....... | ....... | ....... | ....... | ....... | 2 | ....... | ....... | Not reported |
| Total | 44 | 6 | 20 | 1 | 24 | 5 | 22 | 32 | 495 | 1,630 | ....... | ....... | Total |

NEW YORK STATE

60. TABLE XIII, A, 2, a

**NEIGHBORHOOD STORES — STOCK AND SALES**

NUMBER OF EMPLOYEES FOR EACH SEX, CLASSIFIED ACCORDING TO ACTUAL WEEKLY EARNINGS BY THE NUMBER OF YEARS WITH THE FIRM

| ACTUAL WEEKLY EARNINGS IN DOLLARS | YEARS WITH FIRM | | | | | | | | | | | | ACTUAL WEEKLY EARNINGS IN DOLLARS |
|---|---|---|---|---|---|---|---|---|---|---|---|---|---|
| | LESS THAN 1 | | 1 | | 2 | | 3 | | 4 | | 5 | | |
| | Male | Female | Male | Female | Male | Female | Male | Female | Male | Female | Male | Female | |
| Less than $3 00 | 5 | 41 | ...... | 1 | ...... | 3 | ...... | ...... | ...... | 1 | ...... | 1 | Less than $3 00 |
| $3 00–$3 49 | 5 | 34 | ...... | 4 | 1 | 1 | ...... | 1 | ...... | ...... | ...... | ...... | $3 00– 3 49 |
| 3 50– 3 99 | 2 | 51 | 2 | 8 | ...... | 1 | ...... | 1 | 1 | ...... | ...... | ...... | 3 50– 3 99 |
| 4 00– 4 49 | 5 | 91 | ...... | 19 | 2 | 3 | ...... | 1 | ...... | 1 | ...... | ...... | 4 00– 4 49 |
| 4 50– 4 99 | 2 | 44 | 1 | 22 | ...... | 12 | ...... | 1 | ...... | ...... | ...... | ...... | 4 50– 4 99 |
| 5 00– 5 49 | 17 | 81 | 2 | 48 | ...... | 20 | ...... | 13 | ...... | 3 | ...... | ...... | 5 00– 5 49 |
| 5 50– 5 99 | 1 | 25 | ...... | 16 | ...... | 27 | ...... | 5 | ...... | 2 | ...... | 2 | 5 50– 5 99 |
| 6 00– 6 49 | 16 | 120 | 4 | 47 | ...... | 42 | ...... | 23 | 1 | 8 | ...... | 7 | 6 00– 6 49 |
| 6 50– 6 99 | ...... | 18 | 3 | 6 | ...... | 7 | ...... | 5 | ...... | 8 | ...... | 6 | 6 50– 6 99 |
| 7 00– 7 49 | 8 | 62 | 3 | 29 | ...... | 23 | ...... | 15 | ...... | 13 | ...... | 8 | 7 00– 7 49 |
| 7 50– 7 99 | 1 | 8 | ...... | 7 | ...... | 5 | ...... | 3 | ...... | 4 | ...... | 6 | 7 50– 7 99 |
| 8 00– 8 99 | 9 | 54 | 1 | 24 | ...... | 23 | 1 | 24 | 1 | 15 | ...... | 5 | 8 00– 8 99 |
| 9 00– 9 99 | 2 | 26 | 1 | 17 | 4 | 22 | 1 | 13 | ...... | 8 | ...... | 4 | 9 00– 9 99 |
| 10 00–10 99 | 15 | 14 | 3 | 9 | 6 | 15 | 4 | 6 | 1 | 8 | 1 | 6 | 10 00–10 99 |
| 11 00–11 99 | 6 | 3 | 3 | 3 | 2 | 4 | 3 | 2 | 1 | 1 | 1 | 1 | 11 00–11 99 |
| 12 00–12 99 | 23 | 4 | 4 | 2 | 3 | 6 | 4 | 3 | 4 | 5 | 4 | 5 | 12 00–12 99 |
| 13 00–13 99 | 11 | 2 | 2 | 1 | 2 | 4 | 2 | 2 | 2 | ...... | 2 | 1 | 13 00–13 99 |
| 14 00–14 99 | 15 | ...... | 3 | 4 | 3 | 2 | 5 | 4 | 1 | ...... | 2 | ...... | 14 00–14 99 |
| 15 00–15 99 | 21 | 5 | 5 | ...... | 6 | 2 | 4 | ...... | 4 | 1 | 3 | 1 | 15 00–15 99 |
| 16 00–17 99 | 12 | ...... | 7 | ...... | 10 | 1 | 5 | 1 | 1 | 1 | 4 | 1 | 16 00–17 99 |
| 18 00–19 99 | 7 | ...... | 8 | ...... | 2 | ...... | 6 | ...... | 2 | 1 | 2 | 1 | 18 00–19 99 |
| 20 00–24 99 | 6 | ...... | 1 | ...... | 8 | ...... | 3 | ...... | 5 | 1 | 1 | ...... | 20 00–24 99 |
| 25 00–29 99 | 4 | 1 | 2 | ...... | 5 | 1 | 1 | ...... | 3 | ...... | 3 | ...... | 25 00–29 99 |
| 30 00–34 99 | 3 | ...... | 3 | ...... | ...... | ...... | 1 | ...... | ...... | ...... | ...... | ...... | 30 00–34 99 |
| 35 00–39 99 | 1 | ...... | ...... | ...... | 1 | ...... | 1 | ...... | 1 | ...... | 2 | ...... | 35 00–39 99 |
| 40 00 and over | 1 | ...... | ...... | ...... | ...... | ...... | ...... | ...... | ...... | ...... | ...... | ...... | 40 00 and over |
| Not reported | ...... | 2 | ...... | ...... | ...... | ...... | ...... | ...... | ...... | ...... | ...... | ...... | Not reported |
| Total | 198 | 686 | 58 | 267 | 55 | 224 | 41 | 123 | 28 | 81 | 25 | 55 | Total |

NEW YORK STATE

60. TABLE XIII, A, 2, a — (*continued*) **NEIGHBORHOOD STORES — STOCK AND SALES**

NUMBER OF EMPLOYEES FOR EACH SEX, CLASSIFIED ACCORDING TO ACTUAL WEEKLY EARNINGS BY THE NUMBER OF YEARS WITH THE FIRM

| ACTUAL WEEKLY EARNINGS IN DOLLARS | YEARS WITH FIRM | | | | | | | | | | | | ACTUAL WEEKLY EARNINGS IN DOLLARS |
|---|---|---|---|---|---|---|---|---|---|---|---|---|---|
| | 6 | | 7 | | 8 | | 9 | | 10–14 | | 15–19 | | |
| | Male | Female | Male | Female | Male | Female | Male | Female | Male | Female | Male | Female | |
| Less than $3 00 | ...... | ...... | ...... | ...... | ...... | ...... | ...... | ...... | ...... | ...... | ...... | ...... | Less than $3 00 |
| $3 00–$3 49 | ...... | ...... | ...... | ...... | ...... | ...... | ...... | ...... | ...... | ...... | ...... | ...... | $3 00– 3 49 |
| 3 50– 3 99 | ...... | ...... | ...... | ...... | ...... | ...... | ...... | ...... | ...... | ...... | ...... | ...... | 3 50– 3 99 |
| 4 00– 4 49 | ...... | ...... | ...... | ...... | ...... | ...... | ...... | ...... | ...... | ...... | ...... | ...... | 4 00– 4 49 |
| 4 50– 4 99 | ...... | ...... | ...... | ...... | ...... | ...... | ...... | ...... | ...... | ...... | ...... | ...... | 4 50– 4 99 |
| 5 00– 5 49 | ...... | 1 | ...... | ...... | ...... | ...... | ...... | ...... | ...... | ...... | ...... | ...... | 5 00– 5 49 |
| 5 50– 5 99 | ...... | 1 | ...... | ...... | ...... | 1 | ...... | 1 | ...... | 1 | ...... | ...... | 5 50– 5 99 |
| 6 00– 6 49 | ...... | 5 | ...... | 2 | ...... | ...... | ...... | ...... | ...... | ...... | ...... | ...... | 6 00– 6 49 |
| 6 50– 6 99 | ...... | 2 | ...... | 1 | ...... | 2 | 1 | ...... | ...... | 1 | ...... | ...... | 6 50– 6 99 |
| 7 00– 7 49 | ...... | 5 | ...... | 2 | ...... | 1 | ...... | 1 | ...... | 5 | ...... | 1 | 7 00– 7 49 |
| 7 50– 7 99 | ...... | 2 | ...... | 2 | ...... | 4 | ...... | 1 | ...... | ...... | ...... | ...... | 7 50– 7 99 |
| 8 00– 8 99 | ...... | 9 | ...... | 7 | ...... | 1 | ...... | 2 | ...... | 12 | 1 | 1 | 8 00– 8 99 |
| 9 00– 9 99 | ...... | 2 | ...... | 5 | ...... | 5 | ...... | 4 | ...... | 11 | ...... | 2 | 9 00– 9 99 |
| 10 00–10 99 | 1 | 5 | ...... | 4 | 1 | 3 | ...... | 3 | ...... | 8 | ...... | 2 | 10 00–10 99 |
| 11 00–11 99 | ...... | ...... | ...... | 2 | ...... | 1 | ...... | 1 | 1 | 4 | ...... | ...... | 11 00–11 99 |
| 12 00–12 99 | 1 | ...... | 1 | 3 | 2 | 3 | ...... | 1 | 1 | 3 | 1 | 1 | 12 00–12 99 |
| 13 00–13 99 | 1 | 1 | 1 | 3 | ...... | 1 | 1 | 2 | ...... | 6 | ...... | ...... | 13 00–13 99 |
| 14 00–14 99 | ...... | 1 | ...... | 1 | ...... | 4 | ...... | ...... | 1 | 1 | 2 | 3 | 14 00–14 99 |
| 15 00–15 99 | 3 | ...... | ...... | ...... | ...... | ...... | 2 | ...... | 2 | 4 | ...... | 3 | 15 00–15 99 |
| 16 00–17 99 | 1 | ...... | 2 | 1 | 2 | ...... | 3 | ...... | 7 | ...... | 1 | 1 | 16 00–17 99 |
| 18 00–19 99 | 2 | ...... | 2 | ...... | 2 | 1 | 1 | 1 | 2 | ...... | 5 | 1 | 18 00–19 99 |
| 20 00–24 99 | 2 | ...... | 1 | ...... | 1 | ...... | ...... | ...... | 1 | 1 | 4 | 1 | 20 00–24 99 |
| 25 00–29 99 | ...... | ...... | ...... | ...... | 1 | ...... | ...... | ...... | 2 | ...... | 1 | ...... | 25 00–29 99 |
| 30 00–34 99 | ...... | ...... | ...... | ...... | ...... | ...... | 1 | ...... | ...... | 1 | 4 | ...... | 30 00–34 99 |
| 35 00–39 99 | ...... | ...... | ...... | ...... | ...... | ...... | ...... | ...... | 1 | ...... | ...... | ...... | 35 00–39 99 |
| 40 00 and over | 1 | ...... | ...... | ...... | ...... | ...... | 1 | ...... | ...... | ...... | 2 | ...... | 40 00 and over |
| Not reported | ...... | ...... | ...... | ...... | ...... | ...... | ...... | ...... | ...... | ...... | ...... | ...... | Not reported |
| Total | 12 | 34 | 7 | 33 | 9 | 27 | 10 | 17 | 18 | 58 | 21 | 16 | Total |

NEW YORK STATE

60. TABLE XIII, A, 2, a—(*Concluded*)

**NEIGHBORHOOD STORES — STOCK AND SALES**

NUMBER OF EMPLOYEES FOR EACH SEX CLASSIFIED ACCORDING TO ACTUAL WEEKLY EARNINGS BY THE NUMBER OF YEARS WITH THE FIRM

| ACTUAL WEEKLY EARNINGS IN DOLLARS | YEARS WITH FIRM | | | | | | | | | | ACTUAL WEEKLY EARNINGS IN DOLLARS |
|---|---|---|---|---|---|---|---|---|---|---|---|
| | 20-24 | | 25-29 | 30-34 | NOT REPORTED | | TOTAL | | CUMULATIVE PER CENT. OF TOTAL | | |
| | Male | Female | Female | Male | Male | Female | Male | Female | Male | Female | |
| Less than $3 00 | ........ | ........ | ........ | ........ | ........ | ........ | 5 | 47 | 1.01 | 2.88 | Less than $3 00 |
| $3 00-$3 49 | ........ | ........ | ........ | ........ | 1 | ........ | 7 | 40 | 2.42 | 5.35 | $3 00- 3 49 |
| 3 50- 3 99 | ........ | ........ | ........ | ........ | 1 | ........ | 6 | 61 | 3.64 | 9.08 | 3 50- 3 99 |
| 4 00- 4 49 | ........ | ........ | ........ | ........ | ........ | ........ | 7 | 115 | 5.05 | 16.15 | 4 00- 4 49 |
| 4 50- 4 99 | ........ | ........ | ........ | ........ | ........ | ........ | 3 | 79 | 5.66 | 25.00 | 4 50- 4 99 |
| 5 00- 5 49 | ........ | ........ | ........ | ........ | ........ | ........ | 19 | 166 | 9.50 | 31.20 | 5 00- 5 49 |
| 5 50- 5 99 | ........ | ........ | ........ | ........ | ........ | ........ | 1 | 81 | 9.70 | 36.20 | 5 50- 5 99 |
| 6 00- 6 49 | ........ | ........ | ........ | ........ | ........ | ........ | 21 | 254 | 13.94 | 51.80 | 6 00- 6 49 |
| 6 50- 6 99 | ........ | ........ | ........ | ........ | ........ | ........ | 4 | 56 | 14.74 | 55.20 | 6 50- 6 99 |
| 7 00- 7 49 | ........ | ........ | ........ | ........ | ........ | 1 | 11 | 166 | 16.97 | 65.40 | 7 00- 7 49 |
| 7 50- 7 99 | ........ | ........ | ........ | ........ | ........ | ........ | 1 | 42 | 17.17 | 68.00 | 7 50- 7 99 |
| 8 00- 8 99 | ........ | ........ | ........ | ........ | ........ | ........ | 13 | 177 | 19.80 | 78.80 | 8 00- 8 99 |
| 9 00- 9 99 | ........ | ........ | 1 | ........ | 1 | 1 | 9 | 121 | 21.61 | 86.25 | 9 00- 9 99 |
| 10 00-10 99 | ........ | ........ | ........ | ........ | 1 | ........ | 33 | 83 | 28.30 | 91.20 | 10 00-10 99 |
| 11 00-11 99 | ........ | ........ | ........ | ........ | ........ | ........ | 17 | 22 | 31.71 | 92.75 | 11 00-11 99 |
| 12 00-12 99 | ........ | 1 | ........ | ........ | 1 | 1 | 49 | 38 | 41.60 | 95.04 | 12 00-12 99 |
| 13 00-13 99 | ........ | 1 | ........ | ........ | ........ | ........ | 24 | 24 | 46.50 | 96.52 | 13 00-13 99 |
| 14 00-14 99 | ........ | 2 | ........ | ........ | ........ | ........ | 32 | 22 | 52.95 | 97.87 | 14 00-14 99 |
| 15 00-15 99 | ........ | ........ | ........ | ........ | ........ | ........ | 50 | 16 | 63.02 | 98.85 | 15 00-15 99 |
| 16 00-17 99 | 1 | ........ | ........ | ........ | ........ | ........ | 56 | 6 | 74.33 | 99.22 | 16 00-17 99 |
| 18 00-19 99 | 2 | 1 | ........ | ........ | ........ | ........ | 43 | 6 | 83.02 | 99.59 | 18 00-19 99 |
| 20 00-24 99 | 3 | ........ | ........ | ........ | ........ | ........ | 36 | 3 | 90.29 | 99.78 | 20 00-24 99 |
| 25 00-29 99 | 1 | ........ | ........ | ........ | ........ | ........ | 23 | 2 | 94.94 | 99.90 | 25 00-29 99 |
| 30 00-34 99 | ........ | ........ | ........ | 1 | ........ | ........ | 13 | 1 | 97.57 | 100.00 | 30 00-34 99 |
| 35 00-39 99 | ........ | ........ | ........ | ........ | ........ | ........ | 7 | ........ | 98.98 | ........ | 35 00-39 99 |
| 40 00 and over | ........ | ........ | ........ | ........ | ........ | ........ | 5 | ........ | 100.00 | ........ | 40 00 and over |
| Not reported | ........ | ........ | ........ | ........ | ........ | ........ | ........ | 2 | ........ | ........ | Not reported |
| Total | 7 | 5 | 1 | 1 | 5 | 3 | 495 | 1,630 | ........ | ........ | Total |

NEW YORK STATE

**NEIGHBORHOOD STORES — OFFICE**

61. TABLE VII, A, 2, b NUMBER AND PER CENT. OF EMPLOYEES BY SEX ACCORDING TO OCCUPATION AND NATIVITY

| NATIVITY | OCCUPATION | | | | | | | | | | | | | | | | |
|---|---|---|---|---|---|---|---|---|---|---|---|---|---|---|---|---|---|
| | TOTAL | | SUPER-INTEND-ENTS | BOOKKEEPERS | | CLERKS | | STENOG-RAPHERS | | OFFICE BOYS | CASHIERS | | TELE-PHONE OPERA-TORS | AUDI-TORS | DETEC-TIVES | ADVERTISERS AND WINDOW DRESSERS | |
| | Male | Female | Male | Male | Female | Male | Female | Male | Female | Male | Male | Female | Female | Female | Female | Male | Female |
| Native | 49 | 345 | ..... | 6 | 31 | 13 | 80 | 1 | 12 | 1 | 1 | 162 | 9 | 50 | ..... | 27 | 1 |
| Foreign | 20 | 30 | 1 | 1 | 5 | 6 | 5 | .... | 4 | ..... | ..... | 11 | ..... | 3 | 1 | 12 | 1 |
| Not reported | 2 | 3 | ..... | 1 | ..... | 1 | 1 | .... | ..... | ..... | ..... | 2 | ..... | ..... | ..... | ..... | ..... |
| Total | 71 | 378 | 1 | 8 | 36 | 20 | 86 | 1 | 16 | 1 | 1 | 175 | 9 | 53 | 1 | 39 | 2 |
| Per cent. of total | 100.0 | 100.0 | 1.4 | 11.3 | 9.5 | 28.2 | 22.8 | 1.4 | 4.2 | 1.4 | 1.4 | 46.3 | 2.4 | 14.0 | .27 | 54.9 | .53 |

NEW YORK STATE

**NEIGHBORHOOD STORES — OFFICE**

62. TABLE V, A, 2, b NUMBER AND PER CENT. OF EMPLOYEES EARNING SPECIFIED RATES BY AGE GROUPS AND SEX

| WEEKLY RATES IN DOLLARS | AGE GROUPS IN YEARS | | | | | | | | | | | | | WEEKLY RATES IN DOLLARS |
|---|---|---|---|---|---|---|---|---|---|---|---|---|---|---|
| | 14–15 | 16–17 | | 18–20 | | 21–24 | | 25–29 | | 30–34 | | 35–39 | | |
| | Female | Male | Female | Male | Female | Male | Female | Male | Female | Male | Female | Male | Female | |
| Less than $3 00 | ...... | ...... | 1 | ...... | ...... | ...... | ...... | ...... | ...... | ...... | ...... | ...... | ...... | Less than $3 00 |
| $3 00–$3 49 | ...... | ...... | 5 | ...... | ...... | ...... | ...... | ...... | ...... | ...... | ...... | ...... | ...... | $3 00– 3 49 |
| 3 50– 3 99 | 2 | ...... | 16 | ...... | 2 | ...... | ...... | ...... | ...... | ...... | ...... | ...... | ...... | 3 50– 3 99 |
| 4 00– 4 49 | 1 | 1 | 31 | ...... | 8 | ...... | 1 | ...... | ...... | ...... | ...... | ...... | ...... | 4 00– 4 49 |
| 4 50– 4 99 | ...... | ...... | 19 | ...... | 11 | ...... | 1 | ...... | ...... | ...... | ...... | ...... | ...... | 4 50– 4 99 |
| 5 00– 5 49 | ...... | 5 | 22 | 3 | 31 | ...... | 5 | ...... | 2 | ...... | ...... | ...... | ...... | 5 00– 5 49 |
| 5 50– 5 99 | ...... | ...... | 7 | ...... | 16 | ...... | 1 | ...... | 1 | ...... | ...... | ...... | ...... | 5 50– 5 99 |
| 6 00– 6 49 | ...... | 1 | 5 | 1 | 26 | ...... | 16 | ...... | 2 | ...... | ...... | ...... | ...... | 6 00– 6 49 |
| 6 50– 6 99 | ...... | ...... | ...... | ...... | 1 | ...... | 3 | ...... | ...... | ...... | ...... | ...... | ...... | 6 50– 6 99 |
| 7 00– 7 49 | ...... | 1 | 2 | 4 | 30 | 2 | 16 | ...... | 2 | ...... | ...... | ...... | 1 | 7 00– 7 49 |
| 7 50– 7 99 | ...... | ...... | ...... | ...... | 2 | ...... | 4 | ...... | ...... | ...... | ...... | ...... | ...... | 7 50– 7 99 |
| 8 00– 8 99 | ...... | ...... | ...... | 3 | 8 | 1 | 8 | ...... | 4 | ...... | 1 | ...... | 1 | 8 00– 8 49 |
| 9 00– 9 99 | ...... | ...... | ...... | 1 | 4 | ...... | 8 | ...... | 3 | ...... | ...... | 1 | ...... | 9 00– 9 99 |
| 10 00–10 99 | ...... | ...... | ...... | 2 | 2 | 2 | 5 | ...... | 4 | ...... | ...... | ...... | 1 | 10 00–10 99 |
| 11 00–11 99 | ...... | ...... | ...... | ...... | ...... | ...... | 1 | ...... | 2 | ...... | 1 | ...... | ...... | 11 00–11 99 |
| 12 00–12 99 | ...... | ...... | ...... | ...... | 1 | 1 | 7 | ...... | 1 | ...... | ...... | ...... | ...... | 12 00–12 99 |
| 13 00–13 99 | ...... | ...... | ...... | ...... | ...... | ...... | ...... | ...... | ...... | 1 | ...... | 1 | ...... | 13 00–13 99 |
| 14 00–14 99 | ...... | ...... | ...... | 1 | ...... | 2 | ...... | 1 | 2 | 1 | ...... | ...... | ...... | 14 00–14 99 |
| 15 00–15 99 | ...... | ...... | ...... | ...... | ...... | ...... | 1 | ...... | 3 | ...... | ...... | ...... | ...... | 15 00–15 99 |
| 16 00–17 99 | ...... | 1 | ...... | ...... | ...... | 3 | 1 | ...... | 2 | ...... | 1 | ...... | ...... | 16 00–17 99 |
| 18 00–19 99 | ...... | ...... | ...... | ...... | ...... | 1 | 1 | ...... | ...... | ...... | ...... | ...... | ...... | 18 00–19 99 |
| 20 00–24 99 | ...... | ...... | ...... | ...... | ...... | 2 | 1 | 3 | ...... | 2 | ...... | 1 | ...... | 20 00–24 99 |
| 25 00–29 99 | ...... | ...... | ...... | ...... | ...... | 1 | ...... | 2 | ...... | 3 | ...... | ...... | ...... | 25 00–29 99 |
| 35 00–39 99 | ...... | ...... | ...... | ...... | ...... | ...... | ...... | ...... | ...... | 1 | ...... | ...... | ...... | 35 00–39 99 |
| 40 00 and over | ...... | ...... | ...... | ...... | ...... | ...... | ...... | ...... | ...... | 1 | ...... | ...... | ...... | 40 00 and over |
| Total | 3 | 9 | 108 | 15 | 142 | 15 | 80 | 6 | 28 | 9 | 3 | 3 | 3 | Total |

62. TABLE V, A, 2, b — (*concluded*)

NEW YORK STATE

**NEIGHBORHOOD STORES — OFFICE**

NUMBER AND PER CENT. OF EMPLOYEES EARNING SPECIFIED RATES BY AGE GROUPS AND SEX

| WEEKLY RATES IN DOLLARS | AGE GROUPS IN YEARS | | | | | | | | | | | | WEEKLY RATES IN DOLLARS |
|---|---|---|---|---|---|---|---|---|---|---|---|---|---|
| | 40–44 | | 45–54 | | 55–64 | | NOT REPORTED | | TOTAL | | CUMULATIVE PER CENT. OF TOTAL | | |
| | Male | Female | Male | Female | Male | Female | Male | Female | Male | Female | Male | Female | |
| Less than $3 00 | ....... | ....... | ....... | ....... | ....... | ....... | ....... | ....... | ....... | 1 | ....... | 0.26 | Less than $3 00 |
| $3 00–$3 49 | ....... | ....... | ....... | ....... | ....... | ....... | ....... | ....... | ....... | 5 | ....... | 1.59 | ...$3 00– 3 49 |
| 3 50– 3 99 | ....... | ....... | ....... | ....... | ....... | ....... | ....... | ....... | ....... | 20 | ....... | 6.88 | ... 3 50– 3 99 |
| 4 00– 4 49 | ....... | ....... | ....... | ....... | ....... | ....... | ....... | ....... | 1 | 41 | 1.41 | 17.72 | ... 4 00– 4 49 |
| 4 50– 4 99 | ....... | ....... | ....... | ....... | ....... | ....... | ....... | ....... | ....... | 31 | ....... | 25.93 | ... 4 50– 4 99 |
| 5 00– 5 49 | ....... | ....... | ....... | ....... | ....... | ....... | ....... | 1 | 8 | 61 | 12.68 | 42.06 | ... 5 00– 5 49 |
| 5 50– 5 99 | ....... | ....... | ....... | ....... | ....... | ....... | ....... | ....... | ....... | 25 | ....... | 46.68 | ... 5 50– 5 99 |
| 6 00– 6 49 | ....... | ....... | ....... | ....... | ....... | ....... | ....... | ....... | 2 | 49 | 15.49 | 61.64 | ... 6 00– 6 49 |
| 6 50– 6 99 | ....... | ....... | ....... | 1 | ....... | ....... | ....... | ....... | ....... | 5 | ....... | 62.96 | ... 6 50– 6 99 |
| 7 00– 7 49 | ....... | 1 | ....... | ....... | ....... | ....... | ....... | ....... | 7 | 52 | 25.35 | 76.72 | ... 7 00– 7 49 |
| 7 50– 7 99 | ....... | ....... | 1 | 1 | ....... | ....... | ....... | ....... | 1 | 7 | 26.76 | 78.62 | ... 7 50– 7 99 |
| 8 00– 8 99 | ....... | ....... | ....... | ....... | ....... | 1 | ....... | ....... | 4 | 23 | 32.39 | 84.66 | ... 8 00– 8 99 |
| 9 00– 9 99 | ....... | ....... | ....... | ....... | ....... | ....... | ....... | 1 | 2 | 16 | 35.21 | 88.89 | ... 9 00– 9 99 |
| 10 00–10 99 | ....... | ....... | ....... | ....... | ....... | ....... | ....... | ....... | 4 | 12 | 40.85 | 92.06 | ...10 00–10 99 |
| 11 00–11 99 | ....... | ....... | ....... | ....... | ....... | ....... | ....... | 1 | ....... | 5 | ....... | 93.39 | ...11 00–11 99 |
| 12 00–12 99 | ....... | ....... | 1 | ....... | ....... | ....... | ....... | 1 | 2 | 10 | 43 66 | 96.03 | ...12 00–12 99 |
| 13 00–13 99 | ....... | ....... | ....... | ....... | ....... | ....... | ....... | 1 | 2 | 1 | 46.48 | 96.30 | ...13 00–13 99 |
| 14 00–14 99 | ....... | ....... | 1 | ....... | 1 | ....... | ....... | ....... | 7 | 2 | 56.34 | 96.83 | ...14 00–14 99 |
| 15 00–15 99 | ....... | ....... | 1 | ....... | 1 | ....... | ....... | ....... | 2 | 4 | 59.15 | 97.88 | ...15 00–15 99 |
| 16 00–17 99 | 1 | 1 | ....... | ....... | ....... | ....... | ....... | ....... | 5 | 5 | 66.20 | 99.21 | ...16 00–17 99 |
| 18 00–19 99 | 1 | ....... | ....... | ....... | ....... | ....... | 1 | ....... | 3 | 1 | 70.42 | 99.47 | ...18 00–19 99 |
| 20 00–24 99 | ....... | 1 | ....... | ....... | 1 | ....... | ....... | ....... | 9 | 2 | 83.10 | 100.00 | ...20 00–24 99 |
| 25 00–29 99 | 1 | ....... | 1 | ....... | ....... | ....... | ....... | ....... | 8 | ....... | 94.37 | ....... | ...25 00–29 99 |
| 30 00–34 99 | ....... | ....... | ....... | ....... | ....... | ....... | 1 | ....... | 1 | ....... | 95.77 | ....... | ...30 00–34 99 |
| 35 00–39 99 | 1 | ....... | ....... | ....... | ....... | ....... | ....... | ....... | 2 | ....... | 98.59 | ....... | ...35 00–39 99 |
| 40 00 and over | ....... | ....... | ....... | ....... | ....... | ....... | ....... | ....... | 1 | ....... | 100.00 | ....... | 40 00 and over. |
| Total | 4 | 3 | 5 | 2 | 3 | 1 | 2 | 5 | 71 | 378 | ....... | ....... | ....Total |

NEW YORK STATE

**NEIGHBORHOOD STORES — OFFICE**

3. TABLE VIII, A, 2, b — NUMBER AND PER CENT. OF EMPLOYEES EARNING SPECIFIED WEEKLY RATES, BY OCCUPATION AND SEX

| Weekly Rates in Dollars | Superintendents | Bookkeepers | | Clerks | | Stenographers | | Office Boys | Cashiers | | Telephone Operators | Auditors | Detectives | Advertisers and Window Dressers | | Total | | Cumulative Per Cent. of Total | | Weekly Rates in Dollars |
|---|---|---|---|---|---|---|---|---|---|---|---|---|---|---|---|---|---|---|---|---|
| | Male | Male | Female | Male | Female | Male | Female | Male | Male | Female | Female | Female | Female | Male | Female | Male | Female | Male | Female | |
| Less than $3 00 | .... | .... | .... | .... | .... | .... | .... | .... | .... | .... | .... | 1 | .... | .... | .... | .... | 1 | .... | 0.26 | Less than $3 00 |
| $3 00–$3 49... | .... | .... | .... | .... | .... | .... | .... | .... | .... | 2 | .... | 3 | .... | .... | .... | .... | 5 | .... | 1.59 | ...$3 00– 3 49 |
| 3 50– 3 99... | .... | .... | 1 | .... | 7 | .... | .... | .... | .... | 7 | .... | 5 | .... | .... | .... | .... | 20 | .... | 6.88 | ....3 50– 3 99 |
| 4 00– 4 49... | .... | .... | 5 | .... | 10 | .... | .... | 1 | .... | 16 | 1 | 9 | .... | .... | .... | 1 | 41 | 1.41 | 17.72 | ....4 00– 4 49 |
| 4 50– 4 99... | .... | .... | 1 | .... | 9 | .... | .... | .... | .... | 18 | .... | 3 | .... | .... | .... | .... | 31 | .... | 25.93 | ....4 50– 4 99 |
| 5 00– 5 49... | .... | .... | 3 | 2 | 15 | 1 | 1 | .... | .... | 27 | 2 | 13 | .... | 5 | .... | 8 | 61 | 12.68 | 42.06 | ....5 00– 5 49 |
| 5 50– 5 99... | .... | .... | .... | .... | 4 | .... | .... | .... | .... | 17 | 1 | 3 | .... | .... | .... | .... | 25 | .... | 46.68 | ....5 50– 5 99 |
| 6 00– 6 49... | .... | .... | 2 | 1 | 11 | .... | 3 | .... | .... | 27 | 2 | 4 | .... | 1 | .... | 2 | 49 | 15.49 | 61.64 | ....6 00– 6 49 |
| 6 50– 6 99... | .... | .... | .... | .... | .... | .... | .... | .... | .... | 4 | 1 | .... | .... | .... | .... | .... | 5 | .... | 62.96 | ....6 50– 6 99 |
| 7 00– 7 49... | .... | 1 | 5 | 1 | 6 | .... | 3 | .... | 1 | 33 | 1 | 4 | .... | 4 | .... | 7 | 52 | 25.35 | 76.72 | ....7 00– 7 49 |
| 7 50– 7 99... | .... | .... | 1 | 1 | 1 | .... | 1 | .... | .... | 4 | .... | .... | .... | .... | .... | 1 | 7 | 26.76 | 78.62 | ....7 50– 7 99 |
| 8 00– 8 99... | .... | 2 | 1 | .... | 7 | .... | 2 | .... | .... | 10 | .... | 1 | .... | 2 | 2 | 4 | 23 | 32.39 | 84.66 | ....8 00– 8 99 |
| 9 00– 9 99... | .... | .... | 5 | 2 | 6 | .... | 1 | .... | .... | 1 | .... | 3 | .... | .... | .... | 2 | 16 | 35.21 | 88.89 | ....9 00– 9 99 |
| 10 00–10 99... | .... | .... | 5 | 1 | 3 | .... | 1 | .... | .... | 2 | 1 | .... | .... | 3 | .... | 4 | 12 | 40.85 | 92.06 | ...10 00–10 99 |
| 11 00–11 99... | .... | .... | .... | .... | 2 | .... | .... | .... | .... | 2 | .... | 1 | .... | .... | .... | .... | 5 | .... | 93.39 | ...11 00–11 99 |
| 12 00–12 99... | .... | .... | 2 | 2 | 2 | .... | 3 | .... | .... | 1 | .... | 1 | 1 | .... | .... | 2 | 10 | 43.66 | 96.03 | ...12 00–12 99 |
| 13 00–13 99... | .... | .... | .... | 2 | .... | .... | .... | .... | .... | 1 | .... | .... | .... | .... | .... | 2 | 1 | 46.48 | 96.30 | ...13 00–13 99 |
| 14 00–14 99... | .... | 2 | 1 | 5 | .... | .... | .... | .... | .... | 1 | .... | .... | .... | .... | .... | 7 | 2 | 56.34 | 96.83 | ...14 00–14 99 |
| 15 00–15 99... | .... | .... | 1 | 1 | 1 | .... | .... | .... | .... | 1 | .... | 1 | .... | 1 | .... | 2 | 4 | 59.15 | 97.88 | ...15 00–15 99 |
| 16 00–17 99... | .... | 1 | 2 | .... | 2 | .... | .... | .... | .... | .... | .... | 1 | .... | 4 | .... | 5 | 5 | 66.20 | 99.21 | ...16 00–17 99 |
| 18 00–19 99... | .... | .... | 1 | 1 | .... | .... | .... | .... | .... | .... | .... | .... | .... | 2 | .... | 3 | 1 | 70.42 | 99.47 | ...18 00–19 99 |
| 20 00–24 99... | .... | 2 | .... | 1 | .... | .... | 1 | .... | .... | 1 | .... | .... | .... | 6 | .... | 9 | 2 | 83.10 | 100.00 | ...20 00–24 99 |
| 25 00–29 99... | .... | .... | .... | .... | .... | .... | .... | .... | .... | .... | .... | .... | .... | 8 | .... | 8 | .... | 94.37 | .... | ...25 00–29 99 |
| 30 00–34 99... | .... | .... | .... | .... | .... | .... | .... | .... | .... | .... | .... | .... | .... | 1 | .... | 1 | .... | 95.77 | .... | ...30 00–34 99 |
| 35 00–39 99... | 1 | .... | .... | .... | .... | .... | .... | .... | .... | .... | .... | .... | .... | 1 | .... | 2 | .... | 98.59 | .... | ...35 00–39 99 |
| 40 00 and over | .... | .... | .... | .... | .... | .... | .... | .... | .... | .... | .... | .... | .... | 1 | .... | 1 | .... | 100.00 | .... | .40 00 and over |
| Total..... | 1 | 8 | 36 | 20 | 86 | 1 | 16 | 1 | 1 | 175 | 9 | 53 | 1 | 39 | 2 | 71 | 378 | ..... | ..... | .....Total |

64. TABLE VI, A, 2, b

NEW YORK STATE

**NEIGHBORHOOD STORES — OFFICE**

NUMBER AND PER CENT. OF EMPLOYEES CLASSIFIED ACCORDING TO ACTUAL WEEKLY EARNINGS BY AGE GROUPS AND SEX

| ACTUAL WEEKLY EARNINGS IN DOLLARS | AGE GROUPS IN YEARS | | | | | | | | | | | | | ACTUAL WEEKLY EARNINGS IN DOLLARS |
|---|---|---|---|---|---|---|---|---|---|---|---|---|---|---|
| | 14–15 | 16–16 | | 18–20 | | 21–24 | | 25–29 | | 30–34 | | 35–39 | | |
| | Female | Male | Female | Male | Female | Male | Female | Male | Female | Male | Female | Male | Female | |
| Less than $3 00 | ...... | 1 | 4 | ...... | 1 | ...... | ...... | ...... | ...... | ...... | ...... | ...... | ...... | Less than $3 00 |
| $3 00–$3 49 | ...... | ...... | 10 | ...... | 5 | ...... | ...... | ...... | ...... | ...... | ...... | ...... | ...... | $3 00– 3 49 |
| 3 50– 3 99 | 2 | ...... | 16 | ...... | 3 | ...... | ...... | ...... | ...... | ...... | ...... | ...... | ...... | 3 50– 3 99 |
| 4 00– 4 49 | 1 | 1 | 31 | ...... | 11 | ...... | 2 | ...... | ...... | ...... | ...... | ...... | ...... | 4 00– 4 49 |
| 4 50– 4 99 | ...... | ...... | 17 | ...... | 11 | ...... | 1 | ...... | ...... | ...... | ...... | ...... | ...... | 4 50– 4 99 |
| 5 00– 5 49 | ...... | 4 | 15 | 3 | 26 | ...... | 6 | ...... | 2 | ...... | ...... | ...... | ...... | 5 00– 5 49 |
| 5 50– 5 99 | ...... | ...... | 7 | ...... | 16 | 1 | 3 | ...... | ...... | ...... | ...... | ...... | ...... | 5 50– 5 99 |
| 6 00– 6 49 | ...... | ...... | 5 | 1 | 25 | ...... | 15 | 1 | 3 | ...... | ...... | ...... | ...... | 6 00– 6 49 |
| 6 50– 6 99 | ...... | ...... | ...... | ...... | 1 | ...... | 3 | ...... | ...... | ...... | ...... | ...... | ...... | 6 50– 6 99 |
| 7 00– 7 49 | ...... | 2 | 2 | 4 | 27 | 1 | 14 | ...... | 1 | ...... | ...... | ...... | 1 | 7 00– 7 49 |
| 7 50– 7 99 | ...... | ...... | ...... | ...... | 2 | ...... | 5 | ...... | 1 | ...... | ...... | ...... | ...... | 7 50– 7 99 |
| 8 00– 8 99 | ...... | ...... | ...... | 3 | 7 | 1 | 7 | ...... | 4 | ...... | 1 | ...... | 1 | 8 00– 8 99 |
| 9 00– 9 99 | ...... | ...... | ...... | 1 | 3 | ...... | 7 | ...... | 3 | ...... | ...... | 1 | ...... | 9 00– 9 99 |
| 10 00–10 99 | ...... | ...... | ...... | 2 | 3 | 2 | 5 | ...... | 4 | ...... | ...... | ...... | 1 | 10 00–10 99 |
| 11 00–11 99 | ...... | ...... | ...... | ...... | ...... | ...... | 1 | ...... | 2 | ...... | 1 | ...... | ...... | 11 00–11 99 |
| 12 00–12 99 | ...... | ...... | ...... | ...... | 1 | 1 | 7 | ...... | 1 | ...... | ...... | ...... | ...... | 12 00–12 99 |
| 13 00–13 99 | ...... | ...... | ...... | ...... | ...... | ...... | ...... | ...... | ...... | 1 | ...... | 1 | ...... | 13 00–13 99 |
| 14 00–14 99 | ...... | ...... | ...... | 1 | ...... | 2 | ...... | ...... | 2 | 1 | ...... | ...... | ...... | 14 00–14 99 |
| 15 00–15 99 | ...... | ...... | ...... | ...... | ...... | ...... | 1 | ...... | 3 | ...... | ...... | ...... | ...... | 15 00–15 99 |
| 16 00–17 99 | ...... | 1 | ...... | ...... | ...... | 3 | 1 | ...... | 2 | ...... | 1 | ...... | ...... | 16 00–17 99 |
| 18 00–19 99 | ...... | ...... | ...... | ...... | ...... | 1 | 1 | 1 | ...... | ...... | ...... | ...... | ...... | 18 00–19 99 |
| 20 00–24 99 | ...... | ...... | ...... | ...... | ...... | 2 | 1 | 2 | ...... | 2 | ...... | 1 | ...... | 20 00–24 99 |
| 25 00–29 99 | ...... | ...... | ...... | ...... | ...... | 1 | ...... | 2 | ...... | 3 | ...... | ...... | ...... | 25 00–29 99 |
| 35 00–39 99 | ...... | ...... | ...... | ...... | ...... | ...... | ...... | ...... | ...... | 1 | ...... | ...... | ...... | 35 00–39 99 |
| 40 00 and over | ...... | ...... | ...... | ...... | ...... | ...... | ...... | ...... | ...... | 1 | ...... | ...... | ...... | 40 00 and over |
| Not reported | ...... | ...... | 1 | ...... | ...... | ...... | ...... | ...... | ...... | ...... | ...... | ...... | ...... | Not reported |
| Total | 3 | 9 | 108 | 15 | 142 | 15 | 80 | 6 | 28 | 9 | 3 | 3 | 3 | Total |

NEW YORK STATE

64. TABLE VI, A, 2, b — *(concluded)*

**NEIGHBORHOOD STORES — OFFICE**

NUMBER AND PER CENT. OF EMPLOYEES CLASSIFIED ACCORDING TO ACTUAL WEEKLY EARNINGS BY AGE GROUPS AND SEX

| ACTUAL WEEKLY EARNINGS IN DOLLARS | AGE GROUPS IN YEARS | | | | | | | | | | | | ACTUAL WEEKLY EARNINGS IN DOLLARS |
|---|---|---|---|---|---|---|---|---|---|---|---|---|---|
| | 40–44 | | 45–54 | | 55–64 | | NOT REPORTED | | TOTAL | | CUMULATIVE PER CENT. OF TOTAL | | |
| | Male | Female | Male | Female | Male | Female | Male | Female | Male | Female | Male | Female | |
| Less than $3 00 | ...... | ...... | ...... | ...... | ...... | ...... | ...... | ...... | 1 | 5 | 1.41 | 1.33 | Less than $3 00 |
| $3 00–$3 49 | ...... | ...... | ...... | ...... | ...... | ...... | ...... | ...... | ...... | 15 | ...... | 5.30 | ...$3 00– 3 49 |
| 3 50– 3 99 | ...... | ...... | ...... | ...... | ...... | ...... | ...... | ...... | ...... | 21 | ...... | 10.87 | ... 3 50– 3 99 |
| 4 00– 4 49 | ...... | ...... | ...... | ...... | ...... | ...... | ...... | ...... | 1 | 45 | 2.82 | 22.80 | ... 4 00– 4 49 |
| 4 50– 4 99 | ...... | ...... | ...... | ...... | ...... | ...... | ...... | ...... | ...... | 29 | ...... | 30.50 | ... 4 50– 4 99 |
| 5 00– 5 49 | ...... | ...... | ...... | ...... | ...... | ...... | ...... | 1 | 7 | 50 | 12.67 | 43.80 | ... 5 00– 5 49 |
| 5 50– 5 99 | ...... | ...... | ...... | ...... | ...... | ...... | ...... | ...... | 1 | 26 | 14.08 | 50.30 | ... 5 50– 5 99 |
| 6 00– 6 49 | ...... | ...... | ...... | ...... | ...... | ...... | ...... | ...... | 2 | 48 | 16.90 | 63.40 | ... 6 00– 6 49 |
| 6 50– 6 99 | ...... | ...... | ...... | 1 | ...... | ...... | ...... | ...... | ...... | 5 | ...... | 64.70 | ... 6 50– 6 99 |
| 7 00– 7 49 | ...... | 1 | ...... | 1 | ...... | ...... | ...... | ...... | 7 | 47 | 26.76 | 77.20 | ... 7 00– 7 49 |
| 7 50– 7 99 | ...... | ...... | 1 | ...... | ...... | ...... | ...... | ...... | 1 | 8 | 28.17 | 79.30 | ... 7 50– 7 99 |
| 8 00– 8 99 | ...... | ...... | ...... | ...... | ...... | 1 | ...... | ...... | 4 | 21 | 33.80 | 84.80 | ... 8 00– 8 99 |
| 9 00– 9 99 | ...... | ...... | ...... | ...... | ...... | ...... | ...... | 1 | 2 | 14 | 36.62 | 88.60 | ... 9 00– 9 99 |
| 10 00–10 99 | ...... | ...... | ...... | ...... | ...... | ...... | ...... | ...... | 4 | 13 | 42.25 | 92.00 | ...10 00–10 99 |
| 11 00–11 99 | ...... | ...... | ...... | ...... | ...... | ...... | ...... | 1 | ...... | 5 | ...... | 93.40 | ...11 00–11 99 |
| 12 00–12 99 | ...... | ...... | 1 | ...... | ...... | ...... | ...... | 1 | 2 | 10 | 45.07 | 96.00 | ...12 00–12 99 |
| 13 00–13 99 | ...... | ...... | ...... | ...... | ...... | ...... | ...... | 1 | 2 | 1 | 47.89 | 96.30 | ...13 00–13 99 |
| 14 00–14 99 | ...... | ...... | 1 | ...... | 1 | ...... | ...... | ...... | 6 | 2 | 56.34 | 96.80 | ...14 00–14 99 |
| 15 00–15 99 | ...... | ...... | 1 | ...... | 1 | ...... | ...... | ...... | 2 | 4 | 59.15 | 97.90 | ...15 00–15 99 |
| 16 00–17 99 | 1 | 1 | ...... | ...... | ...... | ...... | ...... | ...... | 5 | 5 | 66.20 | 99.20 | ...16 00–17 99 |
| 18 00–19 99 | 1 | ...... | ...... | ...... | ...... | ...... | 1 | ...... | 4 | 1 | 71.83 | 99.50 | ...18 00–19 99 |
| 20 00–24 99 | ...... | 1 | ...... | ...... | 1 | ...... | ...... | ...... | 8 | 2 | 83.10 | 100.00 | ...20 00–24 99 |
| 25 00–29 99 | 1 | ...... | 1 | ...... | ...... | ...... | ...... | ...... | 8 | ...... | 94.34 | ...... | ...25 00–29 99 |
| 30 00–34 99 | ...... | ...... | ...... | ...... | ...... | ...... | 1 | ...... | 1 | ...... | 95.77 | ...... | ...30 00–34 99 |
| 35 00–39 99 | 1 | ...... | ...... | ...... | ...... | ...... | ...... | ...... | 2 | ...... | 98.60 | ...... | ...35 00–39 99 |
| 40 00 and over | ...... | ...... | ...... | ...... | ...... | ...... | ...... | ...... | 1 | ...... | 100.00 | ...... | 40 00 and over |
| Not reported | ...... | ...... | ...... | ...... | ...... | ...... | ...... | ...... | ...... | 1 | ...... | ...... | ...Not reported |
| Total | 4 | 3 | 5 | 2 | 3 | 1 | 2 | 5 | 71 | 378 | ...... | ...... | .....Total |

65. TABLE IX, A, 2, b

NEW YORK STATE

**NEIGHBORHOOD STORES — OFFICE**

Number and Per Cent. of Employees Classified According to Actual Weekly Earnings by Occupation and Sex

| Actual Weekly Earnings in Dollars | Occupation | | | | | | | | | | | | | | | | | | | Actual Weekly Earnings in Dollars |
|---|---|---|---|---|---|---|---|---|---|---|---|---|---|---|---|---|---|---|---|---|
| | Superintendents | Bookkeepers | | Clerks | | Stenographers | | Office Boys | Cashiers | | Telephone Operators | Auditors | Detectives | Advertisers and Window Dressers | | Total | | Cumulative Per Cent. of Total | | |
| | Male | Male | Female | Male | Female | Male | Female | Male | Male | Female | Female | Female | Female | Male | Female | Male | Female | Male | Female | |
| Less than $3 00 | .... | .... | .... | 1 | .... | .... | .... | .... | .... | 4 | .... | 1 | .... | .... | .... | 1 | 5 | 1.41 | 1.33 | Less than $3 00 |
| $3 00–$3 49 | .... | .... | 1 | .... | 3 | .... | 1 | .... | .... | 5 | .... | 5 | .... | .... | .... | .... | 15 | .... | 5.30 | $3 00– 3 49 |
| 3 50– 3 99 | .... | .... | 1 | .... | 5 | .... | .... | .... | .... | 10 | .... | 5 | .... | .... | .... | .... | 21 | .... | 10.87 | 3 50– 3 99 |
| 4 00– 4 49 | .... | .... | 4 | .... | 13 | .... | .... | 1 | .... | 18 | 1 | 9 | .... | .... | .... | 1 | 45 | 2.82 | 22.80 | 4 00– 4 49 |
| 4 50– 4 99 | .... | .... | 1 | .... | 9 | .... | .... | .... | .... | 16 | .... | 3 | .... | .... | .... | .... | 29 | .... | 30.50 | 4 50– 4 99 |
| 5 00– 5 49 | .... | .... | 3 | 1 | 11 | 1 | .... | .... | .... | 23 | 2 | 11 | .... | 5 | .... | 7 | 50 | 12.67 | 43.80 | 5 00– 5 49 |
| 5 50– 5 99 | .... | .... | .... | 1 | 3 | .... | .... | .... | .... | 18 | 2 | 3 | .... | .... | .... | 1 | 26 | 14.08 | 50.30 | 5 50– 5 99 |
| 6 00– 6 49 | .... | .... | 3 | 1 | 13 | .... | 3 | .... | .... | 23 | 2 | 4 | .... | 1 | .... | 2 | 48 | 16.90 | 63.40 | 6 00– 6 49 |
| 6 50– 6 99 | .... | .... | .... | .... | 1 | .... | .... | .... | .... | 4 | .... | .... | .... | .... | .... | .... | 5 | .... | 64.70 | 6 50– 6 99 |
| 7 00– 7 49 | .... | 1 | 5 | .... | 4 | .... | 3 | .... | 1 | 30 | 1 | 4 | .... | 5 | .... | 7 | 47 | 26.76 | 77.20 | 7 00– 7 49 |
| 7 50– 7 99 | .... | .... | 1 | 1 | 1 | .... | 1 | .... | .... | 5 | .... | .... | .... | .... | .... | 1 | 8 | 28.17 | 79.30 | 7 50– 7 99 |
| 8 00– 8 99 | .... | 2 | .... | .... | 7 | .... | 2 | .... | .... | 9 | .... | 1 | .... | 2 | 2 | 4 | 21 | 33.80 | 84.80 | 8 00– 8 99 |
| 9 00– 9 99 | .... | .... | 4 | 2 | 5 | .... | 1 | .... | .... | 1 | .... | 3 | .... | .... | .... | 2 | 14 | 36.62 | 88.60 | 9 00– 9 99 |
| 10 00–10 99 | .... | .... | 6 | 1 | 3 | .... | 1 | .... | .... | 2 | 1 | .... | .... | 3 | .... | 4 | 13 | 42.25 | 92.00 | 10 00–10 99 |
| 11 00–11 99 | .... | .... | .... | .... | 2 | .... | .... | .... | .... | 2 | .... | 1 | .... | .... | .... | .... | 5 | .... | 93.40 | 11 00–11 99 |
| 12 00–12 99 | .... | .... | 2 | 2 | 2 | .... | 3 | .... | .... | 1 | .... | 1 | 1 | .... | .... | 2 | 10 | 45.07 | 96.00 | 12 00–12 99 |
| 13 00–13 99 | .... | .... | .... | 2 | .... | .... | .... | .... | .... | 1 | .... | .... | .... | .... | .... | 2 | 1 | 47.89 | 96.30 | 13 00–13 99 |
| 14 00–14 99 | .... | 2 | 1 | 4 | .... | .... | .... | .... | .... | 1 | .... | .... | .... | .... | .... | 6 | 2 | 56.34 | 96.80 | 14 00–14 99 |
| 15 00–15 99 | .... | .... | 1 | 1 | 1 | .... | .... | .... | .... | 1 | .... | 1 | .... | 1 | .... | 2 | 4 | 59.15 | 97.90 | 15 00–15 99 |
| 16 00–17 99 | .... | 1 | 2 | .... | 2 | .... | .... | .... | .... | .... | .... | 1 | .... | 4 | .... | 5 | 5 | 66.20 | 99.20 | 16 00–17 99 |
| 18 00–19 99 | .... | .... | 1 | 2 | .... | .... | .... | .... | .... | .... | .... | .... | .... | 2 | .... | 4 | 1 | 71.83 | 99.50 | 18 00–19 99 |
| 20 00–24 99 | .... | 2 | .... | 1 | .... | .... | 1 | .... | .... | 1 | .... | .... | .... | 5 | .... | 8 | 2 | 83.10 | 100.00 | 20 00–24 99 |
| 25 00–29 99 | .... | .... | .... | .... | .... | .... | .... | .... | .... | .... | .... | .... | .... | 8 | .... | 8 | .... | 94.34 | .... | 25 00–29 99 |
| 30 00–34 99 | .... | .... | .... | .... | .... | .... | .... | .... | .... | .... | .... | .... | .... | 1 | .... | 1 | .... | 95.77 | .... | 30 00 34 99 |
| 35 00–39 99 | 1 | .... | .... | .... | .... | .... | .... | .... | .... | .... | .... | .... | .... | 1 | .... | 2 | .... | 98.60 | .... | 35 00–39 99 |
| 40 00 and over | .... | .... | .... | .... | .... | .... | .... | .... | .... | .... | .... | .... | .... | 1 | .... | 1 | .... | 100.00 | .... | 40 00 and over. |
| Not reported | .... | .... | .... | .... | 1 | .... | .... | .... | .... | .... | .... | .... | .... | .... | .... | .... | 1 | .... | .... | Not reported |
| Total | 1 | 8 | 36 | 20 | 86 | 1 | 16 | 1 | 1 | 175 | 9 | 53 | 1 | 39 | 2 | 71 | 378 | .... | .... | Total |

STATE OF NEW YORK

66. TABLE X, A, 2, b

**NEIGHBORHOOD STORES — OFFICE**

Number and Per Cent. of Employees Classified According to Actual Weekly Earnings by Conjugal Condition and Sex

| Actual Weekly Earnings in Dollars | Conjugal Condition | | | | | | | | | | | | Actual Weekly Earnings in Dollars |
|---|---|---|---|---|---|---|---|---|---|---|---|---|---|
| | Single | | Married | | Widowed or Divorced | | Not Reported | | Total | | Cumulative Per Cent. of Total | | |
| | Male | Female | Male | Female | Male | Female | Male | Female | Male | Female | Male | Female | |
| Less than $3 00 | 1 | 5 | ....... | ....... | ....... | ....... | ....... | ....... | 1 | 5 | 1.41 | 1.33 | Less than $3 00 |
| $3 00–$3 49 | ....... | 15 | ....... | ....... | ....... | ....... | ....... | ....... | ....... | 15 | ....... | 5.30 | $3 00– 3 49 |
| 3 50– 3 99 | ....... | 21 | ....... | ....... | ....... | ....... | ....... | ....... | ....... | 21 | ....... | 10.87 | 3 50– 3 99 |
| 4 00– 4 49 | 1 | 44 | ....... | 1 | ....... | ....... | ....... | ....... | 1 | 45 | 2.82 | 22.80 | 4 00– 4 49 |
| 4 50– 4 99 | ....... | 28 | ....... | ....... | ....... | ....... | ....... | 1 | ....... | 29 | ....... | 30.50 | 4 50– 4 99 |
| 5 00– 5 49 | 7 | 50 | ....... | ....... | ....... | ....... | ....... | ....... | 7 | 50 | 12.67 | 43.80 | 5 00– 5 49 |
| 5 50– 5 99 | 1 | 26 | ....... | ....... | ....... | ....... | ....... | ....... | 1 | 26 | 14.08 | 50.30 | 5 50– 5 99 |
| 6 00– 6 49 | 1 | 47 | ....... | ....... | ....... | 1 | 1 | ....... | 2 | 48 | 16.90 | 63.40 | 6 00– 6 49 |
| 6 50– 6 99 | ....... | 4 | ....... | ....... | ....... | 1 | ....... | ....... | ....... | 5 | ....... | 64.70 | 6 50– 6 99 |
| 7 00– 7 49 | 7 | 44 | ....... | 2 | ....... | 1 | ....... | ....... | 7 | 47 | 26.76 | 77.20 | 7 00– 7 49 |
| 7 50– 7 99 | ....... | 8 | ....... | ....... | ....... | ....... | 1 | ....... | 1 | 8 | 28.17 | 79.30 | 7 50– 7 99 |
| 8 00– 8 99 | 4 | 17 | ....... | 1 | ....... | 2 | ....... | 1 | 4 | 21 | 33.80 | 84.80 | 8 00– 8 99 |
| 9 00– 9 99 | 2 | 13 | ....... | ....... | ....... | ....... | ....... | 1 | 2 | 14 | 36.62 | 88.60 | 9 00– 9 99 |
| 10 00–10 99 | 2 | 12 | ....... | ....... | ....... | ....... | 2 | 1 | 4 | 13 | 42.25 | 92.00 | 10 00–10 99 |
| 11 00–11 99 | ....... | 5 | ....... | ....... | ....... | ....... | ....... | ....... | ....... | 5 | ....... | 93.40 | 11 00–11 99 |
| 12 00–12 99 | 1 | 10 | 1 | ....... | ....... | ....... | ....... | ....... | 2 | 10 | 45.07 | 96.00 | 12 00–12 99 |
| 13 00–13 99 | ....... | 1 | 1 | ....... | 1 | ....... | ....... | ....... | 2 | 1 | 47.89 | 96.30 | 13 00–13 99 |
| 14 00–14 99 | 3 | 2 | 3 | ....... | ....... | ....... | ....... | ....... | 6 | 2 | 56.34 | 96.80 | 14 00–14 99 |
| 15 00–15 99 | ....... | 4 | 2 | ....... | ....... | ....... | ....... | ....... | 2 | 4 | 59.15 | 97.90 | 15 00–15 99 |
| 16 00–17 99 | 5 | 4 | ....... | ....... | ....... | ....... | ....... | 1 | 5 | 5 | 66.20 | 99.20 | 16 00–17 99 |
| 18 00–19 99 | 1 | 1 | 2 | ....... | ....... | ....... | 1 | ....... | 4 | 1 | 71.83 | 99.50 | 18 00–19 99 |
| 20 00–24 99 | 1 | 2 | 5 | ....... | ....... | ....... | 2 | ....... | 8 | 2 | 83.10 | 100.00 | 20 00–24 99 |
| 25 00–29 99 | 1 | ....... | 7 | ....... | ....... | ....... | ....... | ....... | 8 | ....... | 93.34 | ....... | 25 00–29 99 |
| 30 00–34 99 | ....... | ....... | 1 | ....... | ....... | ....... | ....... | ....... | 1 | ....... | 95.77 | ....... | 30 00–34 99 |
| 35 00–39 99 | ....... | ....... | 2 | ....... | ....... | ....... | ....... | ....... | 2 | ....... | 98.60 | ....... | 35 00–39 99 |
| 40 00 and over | ....... | ....... | 1 | ....... | ....... | ....... | ....... | ....... | 1 | ....... | 100.00 | ....... | 40 00 and over |
| Not reported | ....... | 1 | ....... | ....... | ....... | ....... | ....... | ....... | ....... | 1 | ....... | ....... | Not reported |
| Total | 38 | 364 | 25 | 4 | 1 | 5 | 7 | 5 | 71 | 378 | ....... | ....... | Total |

67. TABLE XI, A, 2, b

NEW YORK STATE

**NEIGHBORHOOD STORES — OFFICE**

Number and Per Cent. of Employees Classified According to Actual Weekly Earnings by Nativity and Sex

| Actual Weekly Earnings in Dollars | Nativity: Native | | Nativity: Foreign | | Nativity: Not reported | | Nativity: Total | | Cumulative per cent. of total | | Actual Weekly Earnings in Dollars |
|---|---|---|---|---|---|---|---|---|---|---|---|
| | Male | Female | Male | Female | Male | Female | Male | Female | Male | Female | |
| Less than $3 00 | 1 | 4 | | 1 | | | 1 | 5 | 1.41 | 1.33 | Less than $3 00 |
| $3 00–$3 49 | | 14 | | 1 | | | | 15 | | 5.30 | $3 00– 3 49 |
| 3 50– 3 99 | | 19 | | 2 | | | | 21 | | 10.87 | 3 50– 3 99 |
| 4 00– 4 49 | 1 | 43 | | 1 | | 1 | 1 | 45 | 2.82 | 22.80 | 4 00– 4 49 |
| 4 50– 4 99 | | 26 | | 3 | | | | 29 | | 30.50 | 4 50– 4 99 |
| 5 00– 5 49 | 7 | 47 | | 3 | | | 7 | 50 | 12.67 | 43.80 | 5 00– 5 49 |
| 5 50– 5 99 | 1 | 23 | | 1 | | 2 | 1 | 26 | 14.08 | 50.30 | 5 50– 5 99 |
| 6 00– 6 49 | | 44 | 2 | 4 | | | 2 | 48 | 16.90 | 63.40 | 6 00– 6 49 |
| 6 50– 6 99 | | 4 | | 1 | | | | 5 | | 64.70 | 6 50– 6 99 |
| 7 00– 7 49 | 7 | 43 | | 4 | | | 7 | 47 | 26.76 | 77.20 | 7 00– 7 49 |
| 7 50– 7 99 | 1 | 6 | | 2 | | | 1 | 8 | 28.17 | 79.30 | 7 50– 7 99 |
| 8 00– 8 99 | 3 | 19 | | 2 | 1 | | 4 | 21 | 33.80 | 84.80 | 8 00– 8 99 |
| 9 00– 9 99 | 2 | 11 | | 3 | | | 2 | 14 | 36.62 | 88.60 | 9 00– 9 99 |
| 10 00–10 99 | 3 | 13 | 1 | | | | 4 | 13 | 42.25 | 92.00 | 10 00–10 99 |
| 11 00–11 99 | | 5 | | | | | | 5 | | 93.40 | 11 00–11 99 |
| 12 00–12 99 | | 9 | 2 | 1 | | | 2 | 10 | 45.07 | 96.00 | 12 00–12 99 |
| 13 00–13 99 | 1 | 1 | 1 | | | | 2 | 1 | 47.89 | 96.30 | 13 00–13 99 |
| 14 00–14 99 | 3 | 2 | 3 | | | | 6 | 2 | 56.34 | 96.80 | 14 00–14 99 |
| 15 00–15 99 | 1 | 4 | 1 | | | | 2 | 4 | 59.15 | 97.90 | 15 00–15 99 |
| 16 00–17 99 | 3 | 5 | 2 | | | | 5 | 5 | 66.20 | 99.20 | 16 00–17 99 |
| 18 00–19 99 | 3 | 1 | | | 1 | | 4 | 1 | 71.83 | 99.50 | 18 00–19 99 |
| 20 00–24 99 | 5 | 1 | 3 | 1 | | | 8 | 2 | 83.10 | 100.00 | 20 00–24 99 |
| 25 00–29 99 | 6 | | 2 | | | | 8 | | 94.34 | | 25 00–29 99 |
| 30 00–34 99 | 1 | | | | | | 1 | | 95.77 | | 30 00–34 99 |
| 35 00–39 99 | | | 2 | | | | 2 | | 98.60 | | 35 00–39 99 |
| 40 00 and over | | | 1 | | | | 1 | | 100.00 | | 40 00 and over |
| Not reported | | 1 | | | | | | 1 | | | Not reported |
| Total | 49 | 345 | 20 | 30 | 2 | 3 | 71 | 378 | | | Total |

NEW YORK STATE

68. TABLE XII, A, 2, b

**NEIGHBORHOOD STORES — OFFICE**

NUMBER OF EMPLOYEES FOR EACH SEX CLASSIFIED ACCORDING TO ACTUAL WEEKLY EARNINGS BY THE NUMBER OF YEARS IN THE TRADE

| ACTUAL WEEKLY EARNINGS IN DOLLARS | YEARS IN THE TRADE | | | | | | | | | | | | ACTUAL WEEKLY EARNINGS IN DOLLARS |
|---|---|---|---|---|---|---|---|---|---|---|---|---|---|
| | LESS THAN 1 | | 1 | | 2 | | 3 | | 4 | | 5 | | |
| | Male | Female | Male | Female | Male | Female | Male | Female | Male | Female | Male | Female | |
| Less than $3 00 | 1 | 4 | | | | | | | | 1 | | | Less than $3 00 |
| $3 00–$3 49 | | 9 | | 4 | | 1 | | 1 | | | | | $3 00– 3 49 |
| 3 50– 3 99 | | 17 | | 2 | | 1 | | | | 1 | | | 3 50– 3 99 |
| 4 00– 4 49 | 1 | 20 | | 16 | | 5 | | 1 | | 2 | | | 4 00– 4 49 |
| 4 50– 4 99 | | 13 | | 8 | | 6 | | 1 | | 1 | | | 4 50– 4 99 |
| 5 00– 5 49 | 4 | 6 | 2 | 13 | | 17 | | 4 | | 3 | | 1 | 5 00– 5 49 |
| 5 50– 5 99 | 1 | | | 5 | | 8 | | 5 | | 5 | | 3 | 5 50– 5 99 |
| 6 00– 6 49 | | 6 | | 4 | | 13 | 1 | 10 | | 4 | | 4 | 6 00– 6 49 |
| 6 50– 6 99 | | 1 | | | | | | 1 | | | | 1 | 6 50– 6 99 |
| 7 00– 7 49 | 2 | 4 | 1 | 6 | | 7 | 3 | 10 | | 9 | 1 | 1 | 7 00– 7 49 |
| 7 50– 7 99 | | 1 | | 1 | | 1 | | | | 1 | | | 7 50– 7 99 |
| 8 00– 8 99 | | | | | 1 | 3 | 2 | | | 5 | | 3 | 8 00– 8 99 |
| 9 00– 9 99 | | 1 | | | | | 1 | 2 | | | | | 9 00– 9 99 |
| 10 00–10 99 | 1 | | 1 | | 2 | | | 1 | | 2 | | 1 | 10 00–10 99 |
| 11 00–11 99 | | | | | | | | 1 | | | | | 11 00–11 99 |
| 12 00–12 99 | | 1 | | | | 1 | | | | | | | 12 00–12 99 |
| 13 00–13 99 | | | | 1 | | | 1 | | | | | | 13 00–13 99 |
| 14 00–14 99 | | | 1 | | 1 | | | | 1 | | | | 14 00–14 99 |
| 16 00–17 99 | 1 | | | | | | | | 1 | | 1 | 1 | 16 00–17 99 |
| 18 00–19 99 | | | | | | | 1 | | | | 1 | | 18 00–19 99 |
| 20 00–24 99 | | | | | | | | | | | 1 | | 20 00–24 99 |
| Not reported | | 1 | | | | | | | | | | | Not reported |
| Total | 11 | 84 | 5 | 60 | 4 | 63 | 9 | 37 | 2 | 34 | 4 | 15 | Total |

NEW YORK STATE

68. TABLE XII, A, 2, b — (*continued*)

**NEIGHBORHOOD STORES — OFFICE**

NUMBER OF EMPLOYEES FOR EACH SEX CLASSIFIED ACCORDING TO ACTUAL WEEKLY EARNINGS BY THE NUMBER OF YEARS IN THE TRADE

| ACTUAL WEEKLY EARNINGS IN DOLLARS | YEARS IN THE TRADE | | | | | | | | | | | | ACTUAL WEEKLY EARNINGS IN DOLLARS |
|---|---|---|---|---|---|---|---|---|---|---|---|---|---|
| | 6 | | 7 | | 8 | | 9 | | 10–14 | | 15–19 | | |
| | Male | Female | Male | Female | Male | Female | Male | Female | Male | Female | Male | Female | |
| $4 00–$4 49 | ....... | 1 | ....... | ....... | ....... | ....... | ....... | ....... | ....... | ....... | ....... | ....... | $4 00–$4 49 |
| 5 00– 5 49 | ....... | 4 | ....... | 1 | ....... | ....... | ....... | ....... | ....... | ....... | ....... | ....... | 5 00– 5 49 |
| 6 00– 6 49 | ....... | 1 | ....... | 2 | ....... | 2 | 1 | ....... | ....... | ....... | ....... | ....... | 6 00– 6 49 |
| 6 50– 6 99 | ....... | 1 | ....... | 1 | ....... | ....... | ....... | ....... | ....... | ....... | ....... | ....... | 6 50– 6 99 |
| 7 00– 7 49 | ....... | 4 | ....... | 2 | ....... | ....... | ....... | 2 | ....... | 1 | ....... | ....... | 7 00– 7 49 |
| 7 50– 7 99 | ....... | ....... | ....... | 1 | ....... | 1 | ....... | 1 | 1 | 1 | ....... | ....... | 7 50– 7 99 |
| 8 00– 8 99 | 1 | 2 | ....... | 2 | ....... | 1 | ....... | 2 | ....... | 2 | ....... | ....... | 8 00– 8 99 |
| 9 00– 9 99 | ....... | 2 | ....... | 3 | ....... | 1 | ....... | 2 | ....... | 3 | 1 | ....... | 9 00– 9 99 |
| 10 00–10 99 | ....... | 2 | ....... | 1 | ....... | 2 | ....... | ....... | ....... | 3 | ....... | 1 | 10 00–10 99 |
| 11 00–11 99 | ....... | ....... | ....... | ....... | ....... | 1 | ....... | ....... | ....... | 2 | ....... | ....... | 11 00–11 99 |
| 12 00–12 99 | 1 | 2 | ....... | 1 | ....... | 1 | ....... | 1 | 1 | 2 | ....... | ....... | 12 00–12 99 |
| 14 00–14 99 | ....... | ....... | 1 | ....... | ....... | ....... | ....... | ....... | 1 | 1 | ....... | 1 | 14 00–14 99 |
| 15 00–15 99 | ....... | 1 | ....... | ....... | ....... | 1 | ....... | ....... | 1 | 2 | ....... | ....... | 15 00–15 99 |
| 16 00–17 99 | ....... | ....... | ....... | ....... | 1 | 1 | ....... | ....... | ....... | 1 | ....... | 2 | 16 00–17 99 |
| 18 00–19 99 | ....... | ....... | ....... | ....... | ....... | 1 | ....... | ....... | ....... | ....... | ....... | ....... | 18 00–19 99 |
| 20 00–24 99 | ....... | ....... | 1 | ....... | 2 | ....... | ....... | ....... | 1 | 1 | 1 | ....... | 20 00–24 99 |
| 25 00–29 99 | ....... | ....... | ....... | ....... | ....... | ....... | ....... | ....... | 5 | ....... | 2 | ....... | 25 00–29 99 |
| 30 00–34 99 | ....... | ....... | ....... | ....... | ....... | ....... | ....... | ....... | ....... | ....... | 1 | ....... | 30 00–34 99 |
| 35 00–39 99 | ....... | ....... | ....... | ....... | ....... | ....... | ....... | ....... | ....... | ....... | 1 | ....... | 35 00–39 99 |
| 40 00 and over | ....... | ....... | ....... | ....... | ....... | ....... | ....... | ....... | 1 | ....... | ....... | ....... | 40 00 and over |
| Total | 2 | 20 | 2 | 14 | 3 | 12 | 1 | 8 | 11 | 19 | 6 | 4 | Total |

68. TABLE XII, A, 2, b — (*concluded*)

NEW YORK STATE

**NEIGHBORHOOD STORES — OFFICE**

Number of Employees for Each Sex Classified According to Actual Weekly Earnings by the Number of Years in the Trade

| Actual Weekly Earnings in Dollars | Years in the Trade: 20–24 | 25–29 | | 30–34 | | 35–44 | Not reported | | Total | | Cumulative per cent. of total | | Actual Weekly Earnings in Dollars |
|---|---|---|---|---|---|---|---|---|---|---|---|---|---|
| | Male | Male | Female | Male | Female | Male | Male | Female | Male | Female | Male | Female | |
| Less than $3 00. | ...... | ...... | ...... | ...... | ...... | ...... | ...... | ...... | 1 | 5 | 1.41 | 1.33 | Less than $3 00 |
| $3 00–$3 49.... | ...... | ...... | ...... | ...... | ...... | ...... | ...... | ...... | ...... | 15 | ...... | 5.30 | ...$3 00– 3 49 |
| 3 50– 3 99.... | ...... | ...... | ...... | ...... | ...... | ...... | ...... | ...... | ...... | 21 | ...... | 10.87 | ... 3 50– 3 99 |
| 4 0C– 4 49.... | ...... | ...... | ...... | ...... | ...... | ...... | ...... | ...... | 1 | 45 | 2.82 | 22.80 | ... 4 00– 4 49 |
| 4 50– 4 99.... | ...... | ...... | ...... | ...... | ...... | ...... | ...... | ...... | ...... | 29 | ...... | 30.50 | ... 4 50– 4 99 |
| 5 00– 5 49.... | ...... | ...... | ...... | ...... | ...... | ...... | 1 | 1 | 7 | 50 | 12.67 | 43.80 | ... 5 00– 5 49 |
| 5 50– 5 99.... | ...... | ...... | ...... | ...... | ...... | ...... | ...... | ...... | 1 | 26 | 14.08 | 50.30 | ... 5 50– 5 99 |
| 6 00– 6 49.... | ...... | ...... | ...... | ...... | ...... | ...... | ...... | 2 | 2 | 48 | 16.90 | 63.40 | ... 6 00– 6 49 |
| 6 50– 6 99.... | ...... | ...... | ...... | ...... | ...... | ...... | ...... | ...... | ...... | 5 | ...... | 64.70 | ... 6 50– 6 99 |
| 7 00– 7 49.... | ...... | ...... | ...... | ...... | ...... | ...... | ...... | 1 | 7 | 47 | 26.76 | 77.20 | ... 7 00– 7 49 |
| 7 50– 7 99.... | ...... | ...... | ...... | ...... | ...... | ...... | ...... | ...... | 1 | 8 | 28.17 | 79.30 | ... 7 50– 7 99 |
| 8 00– 8 99.... | ...... | ...... | ...... | ...... | ...... | ...... | ...... | 1 | 4 | 21 | 33.80 | 84.80 | ... 8 00– 8 99 |
| 9 00– 9 99.... | ...... | ...... | ...... | ...... | ...... | ...... | ...... | ...... | 2 | 14 | 36.62 | 88.60 | ... 9 00– 9 99 |
| 10 00–10 99.... | ...... | ...... | ...... | ...... | ...... | ...... | ...... | ...... | 4 | 13 | 42.25 | 92.00 | 10 00–10 99 |
| 11 00–11 99.... | ...... | ...... | ...... | ...... | ...... | ...... | ...... | 1 | ...... | 5 | ...... | 93.04 | ...11 00–11 99 |
| 12 00–12 99.... | ...... | ...... | ...... | ...... | ...... | ...... | ...... | 1 | 2 | 10 | 45.07 | 96.00 | ...12 00–12 99 |
| 13 00–13 99.... | ...... | ...... | ...... | ...... | ...... | ...... | 1 | ...... | 2 | 1 | 47.89 | 96.30 | ...13 00–13 99 |
| 14 00–14 99.... | 1 | ...... | ...... | ...... | ...... | ...... | ...... | ...... | 6 | 2 | 56.34 | 96.80 | ...14 00–14 99 |
| 15 00–15 99.... | ...... | ...... | ...... | ...... | ...... | 1 | ...... | ...... | 2 | 4 | 59.15 | 97.90 | ...15 00–15 99 |
| 00–17 99.... | ...... | ...... | ...... | ...... | ...... | ...... | 1 | ...... | 5 | 5 | 66.20 | 99.20 | ...16 00–17 99 |
| 00–19 99.... | 1 | ...... | ...... | ...... | ...... | ...... | 1 | ...... | 4 | 1 | 71.83 | 99.50 | ...18 00–19 99 |
| 00–24 99.... | 1 | 1 | 1 | ...... | ...... | ...... | ...... | ...... | 8 | 2 | 83.10 | 100.00 | ...20 00–24 99 |
| 00–29 99.... | ...... | ...... | ...... | 1 | ...... | ...... | ...... | ...... | 8 | ...... | 94.34 | ...... | ...25 00–29 99 |
| 00–34 99.... | ...... | ...... | ...... | ...... | ...... | ...... | ...... | ...... | 1 | ...... | 95.77 | ...... | ...30 00–34 99 |
| 00–39 99.... | 1 | ...... | ...... | ...... | ...... | ...... | ...... | ...... | 2 | ...... | 98.60 | ...... | ...35 00–39 99 |
| 40 00 and over.. | ...... | ...... | ...... | ...... | ...... | ...... | ...... | ...... | 1 | ...... | 100.00 | ...... | .40 00 and over |
| Not reported.... | ...... | ...... | ...... | ...... | ...... | ...... | ...... | ...... | ...... | 1 | ...... | ...... | ...Not reported |
| Total..... | 4 | 1 | 1 | 1 | ...... | 1 | 4 | 7 | 71 | 378 | ...... | ...... | .....Total |

NEW YORK STATE

69. TABLE XIII, A, 2, b

**NEIGHBORHOOD STORES — OFFICE**

NUMBER OF EMPLOYEES FOR EACH SEX, CLASSIFIED ACCORDING TO ACTUAL WEEKLY EARNINGS BY THE NUMBER OF YEARS WITH THE FIRM

| ACTUAL WEEKLY EARNINGS IN DOLLARS | YEARS WITH FIRM | | | | | | | | | | | | | | | | ACTUAL WEEKLY EARNINGS IN DOLLARS |
|---|---|---|---|---|---|---|---|---|---|---|---|---|---|---|---|---|---|
| | Less than 1 | | 1 | | 2 | | 3 | | 4 | | 5 | | 6 | | 7 | | |
| | Male | Female | Male | Female | Male | Female | Male | Female | Male | Female | Male | Female | Male | Female | Male | Female | |
| Less than $3 00 | 1 | 4 | .... | .... | .... | 1 | .... | .... | .... | .... | .... | .... | .... | .... | .... | .... | Less than $3 00 |
| $3 00–$3 49 | .... | 12 | .... | 3 | .... | .... | .... | .... | .... | .... | .... | .... | .... | .... | .... | .... | $3 00– 3 49 |
| 3 50– 3 99 | .... | 18 | .... | 3 | .... | .... | .... | .... | .... | .... | .... | .... | .... | .... | .... | .... | 3 50– 3 99 |
| 4 00– 4 49 | 1 | 28 | .... | 12 | .... | 4 | .... | 1 | .... | .... | .... | .... | .... | .... | .... | .... | 4 00– 4 49 |
| 4 50– 4 99 | .... | 15 | .... | 8 | .... | 5 | .... | 1 | .... | .... | .... | .... | .... | .... | .... | .... | 4 50– 4 99 |
| 5 00– 5 49 | 4 | 9 | 2 | 17 | 1 | 15 | .... | 4 | .... | 3 | .... | .... | .... | .... | .... | 1 | 5 00– 5 49 |
| 5 50– 5 99 | 1 | 3 | .... | 7 | .... | 5 | .... | 5 | .... | 3 | .... | 3 | .... | .... | .... | .... | 5 50– 5 99 |
| 6 00– 6 49 | .... | 15 | .... | 5 | .... | 10 | 2 | 8 | .... | 5 | .... | 2 | .... | 2 | .... | 1 | 6 00– 6 49 |
| 6 50– 6 99 | .... | 2 | .... | .... | .... | .... | .... | 1 | .... | .... | .... | 1 | .... | 1 | .... | .... | 6 50– 6 99 |
| 7 00– 7 49 | 2 | 13 | 2 | 9 | 1 | 4 | 2 | 8 | .... | 6 | .... | 1 | .... | 2 | .... | 3 | 7 00– 7 49 |
| 7 50– 7 99 | .... | 2 | .... | 1 | .... | .... | .... | .... | .... | 1 | 1 | .... | .... | .... | .... | 1 | 7 50– 7 99 |
| 8 00– 8 99 | 1 | 5 | .... | 4 | 1 | 4 | 1 | 2 | .... | 2 | .... | 1 | 1 | 1 | .... | 1 | 8 00– 8 99 |
| 9 00– 9 99 | .... | 2 | .... | .... | .... | 1 | 1 | 1 | .... | .... | .... | .... | .... | 2 | .... | 3 | 9 00– 9 99 |
| 10 00–10 99 | 2 | .... | 1 | 2 | .... | .... | .... | 2 | 1 | 1 | .... | .... | .... | 2 | .... | 2 | 10 00–10 99 |
| 11 00–11 99 | .... | .... | .... | .... | .... | .... | .... | 1 | .... | .... | .... | .... | .... | .... | .... | .... | 11 00–11 99 |
| 12 00–12 99 | 1 | 2 | 1 | .... | .... | 1 | .... | .... | .... | 1 | .... | 1 | .... | 1 | .... | 1 | 12 00–12 99 |
| 13 00–13 99 | 1 | .... | 1 | 1 | .... | .... | .... | .... | .... | .... | .... | .... | .... | .... | .... | .... | 13 00–13 99 |
| 14 00–14 99 | 1 | .... | .... | .... | 1 | .... | 2 | .... | 1 | .... | .... | 1 | .... | .... | .... | .... | 14 00–14 99 |
| 15 00–15 99 | 1 | .... | .... | .... | .... | .... | .... | .... | .... | .... | .... | .... | .... | 1 | .... | .... | 15 00–15 99 |
| 16 00–17 99 | 3 | .... | 1 | .... | 1 | 2 | .... | 1 | .... | .... | .... | .... | .... | .... | .... | .... | 16 00–17 99 |
| 18 00–19 99 | 1 | .... | .... | .... | .... | .... | 2 | .... | .... | .... | .... | .... | .... | .... | .... | .... | 18 00–19 99 |
| 20 00–24 99 | 2 | .... | 1 | .... | .... | .... | 2 | .... | .... | .... | 1 | .... | .... | .... | .... | .... | 20 00–24 99 |
| 25 00–29 99 | .... | .... | 1 | .... | 1 | .... | 1 | .... | .... | .... | .... | .... | 1 | .... | .... | .... | 25 00–29 99 |
| 30 00–34 99 | .... | .... | .... | .... | .... | .... | .... | .... | .... | .... | .... | .... | 1 | .... | .... | .... | 30 00–34 99 |
| 35 00–39 99 | 1 | .... | .... | .... | .... | .... | .... | .... | .... | .... | .... | .... | .... | .... | .... | .... | 35 00–39 99 |
| 40 00 and over | .... | .... | .... | .... | .... | .... | .... | .... | .... | .... | .... | .... | .... | .... | 1 | .... | 40 00 and over |
| Not reported | .... | 1 | .... | .... | .... | .... | .... | .... | .... | .... | .... | .... | .... | .... | .... | .... | Not reported |
| Total | 23 | 131 | 10 | 72 | 6 | 52 | 13 | 35 | 2 | 22 | 2 | 10 | 3 | 12 | 1 | 13 | Total |

69. TABLE XIII, A, 2, b — (*concluded*)

NEW YORK STATE

**NEIGHBORHOOD STORES — OFFICE**

NUMBER OF EMPLOYEES FOR EACH SEX, CLASSIFIED ACCORDING TO ACTUAL WEEKLY EARNINGS BY THE NUMBER OF YEARS WITH THE FIRM

| ACTUAL WEEKLY EARNINGS IN DOLLARS | YEARS WITH FIRM | | | | | | | | | | | | | | | ACTUAL WEEKLY EARNINGS IN DOLLARS |
|---|---|---|---|---|---|---|---|---|---|---|---|---|---|---|---|---|
| | 8 | | 9 | | 10–14 | | 15–19 | | 20–24 | 25–29 | NOT REPORTED | TOTAL | | CUMULATIVE PER CENT. OF TOTAL | | |
| | Male | Female | Male | Female | Male | Female | Male | Female | Male | Female | Female | Male | Female | Male | Female | |
| Less than $3 00 | ..... | ..... | ..... | ..... | ..... | ..... | ..... | ..... | ..... | ..... | ..... | 1 | 5 | 1.41 | 1.33 | Less than $3 00 |
| $3 00–$3 49 | ..... | ..... | ..... | ..... | ..... | ..... | ..... | ..... | ..... | ..... | ..... | ..... | 15 | ..... | 5.30 | $3 00– 3 49 |
| 3 50– 3 99 | ..... | ..... | ..... | ..... | ..... | ..... | ..... | ..... | ..... | ..... | ..... | ..... | 21 | ..... | 10.87 | 3 50– 3 99 |
| 4 00– 4 49 | ..... | ..... | ..... | ..... | ..... | ..... | ..... | ..... | ..... | ..... | ..... | 1 | 45 | 2.82 | 22.80 | 4 00– 4 49 |
| 4 50– 4 99 | ..... | ..... | ..... | ..... | ..... | ..... | ..... | ..... | ..... | ..... | ..... | ..... | 29 | ..... | 30.50 | 4 50– 4 99 |
| 5 00– 5 49 | ..... | ..... | ..... | ..... | ..... | ..... | ..... | ..... | ..... | ..... | 1 | 7 | 50 | 12.67 | 43.80 | 5 00– 5 49 |
| 5 50– 5 99 | ..... | ..... | ..... | ..... | ..... | ..... | ..... | ..... | ..... | ..... | ..... | 1 | 26 | 14.08 | 50.30 | 5 50– 5 99 |
| 6 00– 6 49 | ..... | ..... | ..... | ..... | ..... | ..... | ..... | ..... | ..... | ..... | ..... | 2 | 48 | 16.90 | 63.40 | 6 00– 6 49 |
| 6 50– 6 99 | ..... | ..... | ..... | ..... | ..... | ..... | ..... | ..... | ..... | ..... | ..... | ..... | 5 | ..... | 64.70 | 6 50– 6 99 |
| 7 00– 7 49 | ..... | ..... | ..... | 1 | ..... | ..... | ..... | ..... | ..... | ..... | ..... | 7 | 47 | 26.76 | 77.20 | 7 00– 7 49 |
| 7 50– 7 99 | ..... | 2 | ..... | ..... | ..... | 1 | ..... | ..... | ..... | ..... | ..... | 1 | 8 | 28.17 | 79.30 | 7 50– 7 99 |
| 8 00– 8 99 | ..... | 1 | ..... | ..... | ..... | ..... | ..... | ..... | ..... | ..... | ..... | 4 | 21 | 33.80 | 84.80 | 8 00– 8 99 |
| 9 00– 9 99 | ..... | 1 | 1 | 2 | ..... | 2 | ..... | ..... | ..... | ..... | ..... | 2 | 14 | 36.62 | 88.60 | 9 00– 9 99 |
| 10 00–10 99 | ..... | 1 | ..... | ..... | ..... | 2 | ..... | 1 | ..... | ..... | ..... | 4 | 13 | 42.25 | 92.00 | 10 00–10 99 |
| 11 00–11 99 | ..... | 1 | ..... | ..... | ..... | 2 | ..... | ..... | ..... | ..... | 1 | ..... | 5 | ..... | 93.40 | 11 00–11 99 |
| 12 00–12 99 | ..... | ..... | ..... | 1 | ..... | 2 | ..... | ..... | ..... | ..... | ..... | 2 | 10 | 45.07 | 96.00 | 12 00–12 99 |
| 13 00–13 99 | ..... | ..... | ..... | ..... | ..... | ..... | ..... | ..... | ..... | ..... | ..... | 2 | 1 | 47.89 | 96.30 | 13 00–13 99 |
| 14 00–14 99 | ..... | ..... | ..... | ..... | ..... | ..... | ..... | 1 | 1 | ..... | ..... | 6 | 2 | 56.34 | 96.80 | 14 00–14 99 |
| 15 00–15 99 | 1 | 1 | ..... | ..... | ..... | 2 | ..... | ..... | ..... | ..... | ..... | 2 | 4 | 59.15 | 97.90 | 15 00–15 99 |
| 16 00–17 99 | ..... | ..... | ..... | ..... | ..... | 1 | ..... | 1 | ..... | ..... | ..... | 5 | 5 | 66.20 | 99.20 | 16 00–17 99 |
| 18 00–19 99 | ..... | 1 | ..... | ..... | 1 | ..... | ..... | ..... | ..... | ..... | ..... | 4 | 1 | 71.83 | 99.50 | 18 00–19 99 |
| 20 00–24 99 | ..... | 1 | ..... | ..... | 1 | ..... | 1 | ..... | ..... | 1 | ..... | 8 | 2 | 83.10 | 100.00 | 20 00–24 99 |
| 25 00–29 99 | 2 | ..... | ..... | ..... | 1 | ..... | 1 | ..... | ..... | ..... | ..... | 8 | ..... | 94.34 | ..... | 25 00–29 99 |
| 30 00–34 99 | ..... | ..... | ..... | ..... | ..... | ..... | ..... | ..... | ..... | ..... | ..... | 1 | ..... | 95.77 | ..... | 30 00–34 99 |
| 35 00–39 99 | ..... | ..... | ..... | ..... | 1 | ..... | ..... | ..... | ..... | ..... | ..... | 2 | ..... | 98.60 | ..... | 35 00–39 99 |
| 40 00 and over | ..... | ..... | ..... | ..... | ..... | ..... | ..... | ..... | ..... | ..... | ..... | 1 | ..... | 100.00 | ..... | 40 00 and over |
| Not reported | ..... | ..... | ..... | ..... | ..... | ..... | ..... | ..... | ..... | ..... | ..... | ..... | 1 | ..... | ..... | Not reported |
| Total | 3 | 9 | 1 | 4 | 4 | 12 | 2 | 3 | 1 | 1 | 2 | 71 | 378 | ..... | ..... | Total |

NEW YORK STATE

70. TABLE XV, A, 2, c, d, e

**NEIGHBORHOOD STORES — SHIPPING AND DELIVERY, MANUFACTURING, PLANT**

NUMBER OF EMPLOYEES EARNING SPECIFIED WEEKLY RATES BY DEPARTMENT AND SEX

| WEEKLY RATES IN DOLLARS | DEPARTMENT | | | | | | | | | WEEKLY RATES IN DOLLARS |
|---|---|---|---|---|---|---|---|---|---|---|
| | SHIPPING AND DELIVERY | MANUFACTURING | | PLANT | | TOTAL | | CUMULATIVE PER CENT. OF TOTAL | | |
| | Male | Male | Female | Male | Female | Male | Female | Male | Female | |
| Less than $3 00 | ........ | ........ | 2 | ........ | ........ | ........ | 2 | ........ | 2.50 | Less than $3 00 |
| $3 00–$3 49 | 1 | ........ | ........ | ........ | 3 | 1 | 3 | .20 | 6.40 | $3 00– 3 49 |
| 3 50– 3 99 | 1 | ........ | ........ | 1 | ........ | 2 | ........ | .70 | ........ | 3 50– 3 99 |
| 4 00– 4 49 | 8 | ........ | 2 | 2 | ........ | 10 | 2 | 3.20 | 9.00 | 4 00– 4 49 |
| 4 50– 4 99 | 4 | ........ | ........ | 9 | ........ | 13 | ........ | 6.30 | ........ | 4 50– 4 99 |
| 5 00– 5 49 | 35 | ........ | 4 | 1 | 6 | 36 | 10 | 15.10 | 21.80 | 5 00– 5 49 |
| 5 50– 5 99 | 2 | ........ | 2 | 6 | ........ | 8 | 2 | 17.10 | 24.40 | 5 50– 5 99 |
| 6 00– 6 49 | 29 | ........ | 6 | ........ | 4 | 29 | 10 | 24.10 | 37.20 | 6 00– 6 49 |
| 6 50– 6 99 | 2 | ........ | 1 | 3 | 2 | 5 | 3 | 25.40 | 41.00 | 6 50– 6 99 |
| 7 00– 7 49 | 5 | ........ | 3 | 3 | 3 | 8 | 6 | 27.30 | 48.60 | 7 00– 7 49 |
| 7 50– 7 99 | 1 | ........ | 3 | 10 | 1 | 11 | 4 | 30.00 | 53.80 | 7 50– 7 99 |
| 8 00– 8 99 | 8 | 1 | 5 | 8 | 1 | 17 | 6 | 34.20 | 61.50 | 8 00– 8 99 |
| 9 00– 9 99 | 4 | ........ | 5 | 16 | ........ | 20 | 5 | 39.00 | 67.80 | 9 00– 9 99 |
| 10 00–10 99 | 22 | ........ | 10 | 13 | ........ | 35 | 10 | 47.50 | 80.70 | 10 00–10 99 |
| 11 00–11 99 | 3 | 2 | 2 | 30 | ........ | 35 | 2 | 56.10 | 83.20 | 11 00–11 99 |
| 12 00–12 99 | 60 | 3 | 2 | 7 | 1 | 70 | 3 | 73.20 | 88.00 | 12 00–12 99 |
| 13 00–13 99 | 19 | 4 | 2 | 7 | ........ | 30 | 2 | 80.50 | 89.70 | 13 00–13 99 |
| 14 00–14 99 | 9 | 4 | 3 | 7 | 1 | 20 | 4 | 85.50 | 94.80 | 14 00–14 99 |
| 15 00–15 99 | 10 | 6 | 1 | 4 | ........ | 20 | 1 | 90.20 | 96.10 | 15 00–15 99 |
| 16 00–17 99 | 9 | 10 | ........ | 4 | ........ | 23 | ........ | 95.70 | ........ | 16 00–17 99 |
| 18 00–19 99 | 2 | 3 | 1 | 2 | ........ | 7 | 1 | 97.60 | 97.40 | 18 00–19 99 |
| 20 00–24 99 | 4 | 2 | 2 | 1 | ........ | 7 | 2 | 99.70 | 100.00 | 20 00–24 99 |
| 25 00–29 99 | 1 | ........ | ........ | ........ | ........ | 1 | ........ | 99.80 | ........ | 25 00–29 99 |
| 30 00–34 99 | 1 | ........ | ........ | ........ | ........ | 1 | ........ | 99.90 | ........ | 30 00–34 99 |
| 40 00 and over | ........ | 1 | ........ | ........ | ........ | 1 | ........ | 100.00 | ........ | 40 00 and over |
| Not reported | ........ | ........ | ........ | ........ | ........ | ........ | ........ | ........ | ........ | not reported |
| Total | 240 | 36 | 56 | 134 | 22 | 410 | 78 | ........ | ........ | Total |

NEW YORK STATE

**NEIGHBORHOOD STORES — SHIPPING AND DELIVERY, MANUFACTURING, PLANT**

71. TABLE XVI, A, 2, c, d, e, NUMBER OF EMPLOYEES CLASSIFIED ACCORDING TO ACTUAL WEEKLY EARNINGS BY DEPARTMENT AND SEX

| ACTUAL WEEKLY EARNINGS IN DOLLARS | DEPARTMENT | | | | | | | | | ACTUAL WEEKLY EARNINGS IN DOLLARS |
|---|---|---|---|---|---|---|---|---|---|---|
| | SHIPPING AND DELIVERY | MANUFACTURING | | PLANT | | TOTAL | | CUMULATIVE PER CENT. OF TOTAL | | |
| | Male | Male | Female | Male | Female | Male | Female | Male | Female | |
| Less than $3 00 | 7 | ........ | 2 | ........ | ........ | 7 | 2 | 1.70 | 2.50 | Less than $3 00 |
| $3 00–$3 49 | 3 | ........ | ........ | 1 | 3 | 4 | 3 | 2.70 | 6.30 | $3 00– 3 49 |
| 3 50– 3 99 | 1 | ........ | ........ | 1 | ........ | 2 | ........ | 3.20 | ........ | 3 50– 3 99 |
| 4 00– 4 49 | 7 | ........ | 1 | 3 | ........ | 10 | 1 | 5.60 | 7.60 | 4 00– 4 49 |
| 4 50– 4 99 | 4 | ........ | 2 | ........ | ........ | 4 | 2 | 6.60 | 10.10 | 4 50– 4 99 |
| 5 00– 5 49 | 34 | ........ | 5 | 10 | 6 | 44 | 11 | 17.30 | 24.00 | 5 00– 5 49 |
| 5 50– 5 99 | 2 | ........ | 1 | 2 | ........ | 4 | 1 | 18.30 | 25.00 | 5 50– 5 99 |
| 6 00– 6 49 | 26 | ........ | 5 | 5 | 6 | 31 | 11 | 25.80 | 39.00 | 6 00– 6 49 |
| 6 50– 6 99 | 2 | ........ | 2 | 2 | 2 | 4 | 4 | 26.80 | 44.00 | 6 50– 6 99 |
| 7 00– 7 49 | 6 | ........ | 3 | 2 | 4 | 8 | 7 | 28.00 | 53.00 | 7 00– 7 49 |
| 7 50– 7 99 | 1 | ........ | 1 | 4 | ........ | 5 | 1 | 29.60 | 54.50 | 7 50– 7 99 |
| 8 00– 8 99 | 9 | 1 | 8 | 8 | 1 | 18 | 9 | 34.40 | 66.00 | 8 00– 8 99 |
| 9 00– 9 99 | 4 | 1 | 5 | 5 | ........ | 10 | 5 | 36.80 | 72.00 | 9 00– 9 99 |
| 10 00–10 99 | 21 | ........ | 8 | 17 | ........ | 38 | 8 | 46.00 | 82.30 | 10 00–10 99 |
| 11 00–11 99 | 3 | 3 | 3 | 15 | ........ | 21 | 3 | 51.20 | 86.10 | 11 00–11 99 |
| 12 00–12 99 | 54 | 3 | 2 | 28 | ........ | 85 | 2 | 72.00 | 88.60 | 12 00–12 99 |
| 13 00–13 99 | 20 | 4 | 1 | 5 | ........ | 29 | 1 | 79.00 | 90.00 | 13 00–13 99 |
| 14 00–14 99 | 10 | 1 | 4 | 6 | ........ | 17 | 4 | 83.20 | 95.00 | 14 00–14 99 |
| 15 00–15 99 | 10 | 7 | 1 | 8 | ........ | 25 | 1 | 89.20 | 96.20 | 15 00–15 99 |
| 16 00–17 99 | 8 | 9 | ........ | 4 | ........ | 21 | ........ | 94.30 | ........ | 16 00–17 99 |
| 18 00–19 99 | 2 | 4 | 1 | 4 | ........ | 10 | 1 | 96.80 | 97.50 | 18 00–19 99 |
| 20 00–24 99 | 4 | 1 | 2 | 3 | ........ | 8 | 2 | 98.70 | 100.00 | 20 00–24 99 |
| 25 00–29 99 | 1 | 1 | ........ | 1 | ........ | 3 | ........ | 99.20 | ........ | 25 00–29 99 |
| 30 00–34 99 | 1 | ........ | ........ | ........ | ........ | 1 | ........ | 99.60 | ........ | 30 00–34 99 |
| 40 00 and over | ........ | 1 | ........ | ........ | ........ | 1 | ........ | 100.00 | ........ | 40 00 and over |
| Total | 240 | 36 | 57 | 134 | 22 | 410 | 79 | ........ | ........ | Total |

72. TABLE XVII, A, 2, c, d, e

NEW YORK STATE

**NEIGHBORHOOD STORES — SHIPPING AND DELIVERY, MANUFACTURING, PLANT**

Number of Employees Classified by Age Groups by Departments and Sex

| Age Groups in Years | Department | | | | | | | | | Age Groups in Years |
|---|---|---|---|---|---|---|---|---|---|---|
| | Shipping and Delivery | Manufacturing | | Plant | | Total | | Per Cent of Total | | |
| | Male | Male | Female | Male | Female | Male | Female | Male | Female | |
| 14–15 | 11 | ........ | ........ | 1 | ........ | 12 | ........ | 2.90 | ........ | 14–15 |
| 16–17 | 44 | ........ | 7 | 10 | ........ | 54 | 7 | 13.30 | 9.00 | 16–17 |
| 18–20 | 43 | ........ | 10 | 14 | ........ | 57 | 10 | 14.00 | 13.00 | 18–20 |
| 21–24 | 51 | 1 | 11 | 12 | 1 | 64 | 12 | 15.80 | 15.60 | 21–24 |
| 25–29 | 25 | 6 | 5 | 13 | 4 | 44 | 9 | 10.50 | 11.70 | 25–29 |
| 30–34 | 22 | 5 | 4 | 10 | 2 | 37 | 6 | 9.10 | 7.80 | 30–34 |
| 35–39 | 12 | 3 | 6 | 11 | 3 | 26 | 9 | 6.40 | 11.70 | 35–39 |
| 40–44 | 9 | 10 | 8 | 15 | 6 | 34 | 14 | 8.40 | 18.40 | 40–44 |
| 45–54 | 16 | 8 | 4 | 27 | 5 | 51 | 9 | 12.60 | 11.70 | 45–54 |
| 55–64 | 5 | 3 | ........ | 11 | 1 | 19 | 1 | 4.80 | 1.30 | 55–64 |
| 65 and over | 1 | ........ | ........ | 8 | ........ | 9 | ........ | 2.20 | ........ | 65 and over |
| Not reported | 1 | ........ | 2 | 2 | ........ | 3 | 2 | ........ | ........ | Not reported |
| Total | 240 | 36 | 57 | 134 | 22 | 410 | 79 | 100.00 | 100.00 | Total |

NEW YORK STATE

**FIVE AND TEN CENT STORES — STOCK AND SALES**

73. **TABLE VII, A, 3, a** NUMBER AND PER CENT OF EMPLOYEES BY SEX ACCORDING TO OCCUPATION AND NATIVITY

| NATIVITY | OCCUPATION | | | | | | | | | | | |
|---|---|---|---|---|---|---|---|---|---|---|---|---|
| | TOTAL | | SUPERINTENDENTS | ASSISTANT BUYERS AND HEADS OF STOCK | RECEIVING AND STOCK CLERKS | STOCK PEOPLE | FLOOR MANAGERS | | SALES PEOPLE | | MESSENGERS, WRAPPERS, ERRAND BOYS | |
| | Male | Female | Male | Male | Male | Male | Male | Female | Male | Female | Male | Female |
| Native | 170 | 1,189 | 11 | 1 | 33 | 67 | 40 | 52 | 8 | 1,136 | 10 | 1 |
| Foreign | 26 | 111 | 1 | 1 | 2 | 13 | 4 | 1 | 3 | 110 | 2 | ........ |
| Not reported | 4 | 3 | ........ | ........ | ........ | 3 | 1 | ........ | ........ | 3 | ........ | ........ |
| Total | 200 | 1,303 | 12 | 2 | 35 | 83 | 45 | 53 | 11 | 1,249 | 12 | 1 |
| Per cent of total | 100.0 | 100.0 | 6.0 | 1.0 | 17.5 | 41.5 | 22.5 | 4.07 | 5.5 | 95.96 | 6.0 | .07 |

NEW YORK STATE

**FIVE AND TEN CENT STORES — STOCK AND SALES**

74. TABLE V, A, 3, a — Number and Per Cent of Employees Earning Specified Weekly Rates by Age Groups and Sex

| Weekly Rates in Dollars | Age Groups in Years | | | | | | | | | | | | | | Weekly Rates in Dollars |
|---|---|---|---|---|---|---|---|---|---|---|---|---|---|---|---|
| | 14–15 | | 16–17 | | 18–20 | | 21–24 | | 25–29 | | 30–34 | | 35–39 | | |
| | Male | Female | Male | Female | Male | Female | Male | Female | Male | Female | Male | Female | Male | Female | |
| Less than $3 00 | .... | ...... | .... | 1 | ...... | ...... | ...... | ...... | ...... | ...... | ...... | ...... | ...... | ...... | Less than $3 00 |
| $3 00–$3 49... | 1 | ...... | 1 | 2 | ...... | ...... | ...... | ...... | ...... | ...... | ...... | ...... | ...... | ...... | ...$3 00– 3 49 |
| 3 50– 3 99... | .... | ...... | .... | 8 | ...... | 1 | ...... | ...... | ...... | ...... | ...... | ...... | ...... | ...... | ... 3 50– 3 99 |
| 4 00– 4 49... | 1 | 1 | .... | 23 | ...... | 22 | ...... | 3 | ...... | 1 | ...... | 1 | ...... | 1 | ... 4 00– 4 49 |
| 4 50– 4 99... | 1 | 1 | .... | 84 | ...... | 58 | ...... | 23 | ...... | 7 | ...... | 1 | ...... | 1 | ... 4 50– 4 99 |
| 5 00– 5 49... | 3 | 6 | 4 | 130 | ...... | 139 | ...... | 49 | ...... | 17 | ...... | 6 | ...... | 1 | ... 5 00– 5 49 |
| 5 50– 5 99... | 2 | 1 | 1 | 28 | ...... | 46 | ...... | 19 | ...... | 5 | ...... | ...... | ...... | ...... | ... 5 50– 5 99 |
| 6 00– 6 49... | 2 | ...... | 6 | 50 | 4 | 183 | ...... | 83 | ...... | 25 | ...... | 9 | ...... | 3 | ... 6 00– 6 49 |
| 6 50– 6 99... | .... | ...... | .... | 2 | ...... | 24 | ...... | 26 | ...... | 7 | ...... | ...... | ...... | 1 | ... 6 50– 6 99 |
| 7 00– 7 49... | .... | ...... | 4 | 3 | 7 | 28 | 3 | 31 | ...... | 7 | ...... | 4 | ...... | ...... | ... 7 00– 7 49 |
| 7 50– 7 99... | .... | ...... | .... | 1 | 1 | 3 | ...... | 8 | ...... | 3 | ...... | ...... | ...... | ...... | ... 7 50– 7 99 |
| 8 00– 8 99... | .... | ...... | 1 | 1 | 8 | 9 | 2 | 13 | 1 | 7 | ...... | 1 | ...... | 1 | ... 8 00– 8 99 |
| 9 00– 9 99... | .... | ...... | 2 | ...... | 8 | 2 | 5 | 9 | 1 | 1 | 2 | 2 | ...... | ...... | ... 9 00– 9 99 |
| 10 00–10 99... | .... | ...... | 1 | 1 | 11 | 3 | 14 | 7 | 1 | 4 | 2 | ...... | 2 | ...... | ...10 00–10 99 |
| 11 00–11 99... | .... | ...... | 1 | 1 | ...... | 1 | 10 | 2 | 1 | ...... | 3 | ...... | ...... | ...... | ...11 00–11 99 |
| 12 00–12 99... | .... | ...... | .... | ...... | 2 | 1 | 10 | 2 | 8 | 2 | 2 | 1 | ...... | ...... | ...12 00–12 99 |
| 13 00–13 99... | .... | ...... | .... | ...... | ...... | ...... | 5 | ...... | 1 | ...... | 1 | ...... | ...... | ...... | ...13 00–13 99 |
| 14 00–14 99... | .... | ...... | .... | ...... | ...... | ...... | 6 | ...... | 5 | ...... | 2 | ...... | ...... | ...... | ...14 00–14 99 |
| 15 00–15 99... | .... | ...... | .... | ...... | ...... | 1 | 7 | 1 | 4 | ...... | 1 | ...... | 1 | ...... | ...15 00–15 99 |
| 16 00–17 99... | .... | ...... | .... | ...... | ...... | ...... | ...... | ...... | 1 | ...... | 3 | 1 | ...... | ...... | ...16 00–17 99 |
| 18 00–19 99... | .... | ...... | .... | ...... | ...... | ...... | 1 | ...... | 1 | ...... | 1 | ...... | ...... | ...... | ...18 00–19 99 |
| 20 00–24 99... | .... | ...... | .... | ...... | ...... | ...... | ...... | ...... | 2 | ...... | ...... | ...... | ...... | ...... | ...20 00–24 99 |
| Not reported... | 1 | ...... | 3 | 8 | ...... | 10 | ...... | 8 | 1 | 1 | ...... | 1 | ...... | 1 | ...Not reported |
| Total..... | 11 | 9 | 24 | 343 | 41 | 531 | 63 | 284 | 27 | 87 | 17 | 27 | 3 | 9 | .....Total |

74. TABLE V, A, 3, a — *(concluded)*

NEW YORK STATE

**FIVE AND TEN CENT STORES — STOCK AND SALES**

NUMBER AND PER CENT OF EMPLOYEES EARNING SPECIFIED WEEKLY RATES BY AGE GROUPS AND SEX

| WEEKLY RATES IN DOLLARS | AGE GROUPS IN YEARS—*(concluded)* 40–44 | | 45–54 | | 55–64 | 65 AND OVER | NOT REPORTED | | TOTAL | | CUMULATIVE PER CENT OF TOTAL | | WEEKLY RATES IN DOLLARS |
|---|---|---|---|---|---|---|---|---|---|---|---|---|---|
| | Male | Female | Male | Female | Male | Male | Male | Female | Male | Female | Male | Female | |
| Less than $3 00 | | | | | | | | | | 1 | | .08 | Less than $3 00 |
| $3 00–$3 49 | | | | | | | | | 2 | 2 | 1.0 | .24 | $3 00– 3 49 |
| 3 50– 3 99 | | | | | | | | | | 9 | | .94 | 3 50– 3 99 |
| 4 00– 4 49 | | | | 1 | | | | | 1 | 53 | 1.5 | 5.10 | 4 00– 4 49 |
| 4 50– 4 99 | | | | | | | | | 1 | 175 | 2.0 | 18.90 | 4 50– 4 99 |
| 5 00– 5 49 | | | | | | | | | 7 | 348 | 5.7 | 46.30 | 5 00– 5 49 |
| 5 50– 5 99 | | | | | | | | | 3 | 99 | 7.2 | 54.10 | 5 50– 5 99 |
| 6 00– 6 49 | | 1 | | 1 | | | | 1 | 12 | 356 | 13.3 | 82.10 | 6 00– 6 49 |
| 6 50– 6 99 | | 1 | | | | | | | | 61 | | 86.90 | 6 50– 6 99 |
| 7 00– 7 49 | | 3 | | 1 | | | 1 | | 15 | 77 | 21.0 | 92.90 | 7 00– 7 49 |
| 7 50– 7 99 | | | | 2 | | | | | 1 | 17 | 21.6 | 94.20 | 7 50– 7 99 |
| 8 00– 8 99 | | | | | | | | | | 12 | 27.7 | 96.70 | 8 00– 8 99 |
| 9 00– 9 99 | | | 1 | | | | | | 19 | 14 | 37.4 | 97.90 | 9 00– 9 99 |
| 10 00–10 99 | | | 2 | | | 1 | | | 34 | 15 | 54.9 | 99.00 | 10 00–10 99 |
| 11 00–11 99 | | | | | 1 | | | | 16 | 4 | 63.1 | 99.40 | 11 00–11 99 |
| 12 00–12 99 | 1 | | 1 | | | | | | 24 | 6 | 75.5 | 99.80 | 12 00–12 99 |
| 13 00–13 99 | | | | | | | | | 7 | | 79.0 | | 13 00–13 99 |
| 14 00–14 99 | 1 | | 1 | | | | | | 15 | | 86.7 | | 14 00–14 99 |
| 15 00–15 99 | 1 | | 1 | | | | | | 15 | 2 | 94.5 | 99.90 | 15 00–15 99 |
| 16 00–17 99 | 1 | | | | | | | | 5 | 1 | 97.0 | 100.00 | 16 00–17 99 |
| 18 00–19 99 | | | 1 | | | | | | 4 | | 99.5 | | 18 00–19 99 |
| 20 00–24 99 | | | | | | | | | 2 | | 100.0 | | 20 00–24 99 |
| 25 00–29 99 | | | | | | | | | | | | | 25 00–29 99 |
| 30 00–34 99 | | | | | | | | | | | | | 30 00–34 99 |
| 35 00–39 99 | | | | | | | | | | | | | 35 00–39 99 |
| Not reported | | | | | | | | 2 | 5 | 31 | | | Not reported |
| Total | 4 | 5 | 7 | 5 | 1 | 1 | 1 | 3 | 200 | 1,303 | | | Total |

NEW YORK STATE

**FIVE AND TEN CENT STORES — STOCK AND SALES**

75. TABLE VIII, A, 3, a — NUMBER AND PER CENT OF EMPLOYEES EARNING SPECIFIED WEEKLY RATES BY OCCUPATION AND SEX

| WEEKLY RATES IN DOLLARS | OCCUPATION: SUPERINTENDENTS | ASSISTANT BUYERS AND HEADS OF STOCK | RECEIVING AND STOCK CLERKS | STOCK PEOPLE | FLOOR MANAGERS | | SALES PEOPLE | | MESSENGERS, WRAPPERS, ERRAND BOYS | | TOTAL | | CUMULATIVE PER CENT OF TOTAL | | WEEKLY RATES IN DOLLARS |
|---|---|---|---|---|---|---|---|---|---|---|---|---|---|---|---|
| | Male | Male | Male | Male | Male | Female | Male | Female | Male | Female | Male | Female | Male | Female | |
| Less than $3 00 | ...... | ...... | ........ | ........ | .... | ...... | .... | 1 | .... | ...... | .... | 1 | ...... | .08 | Less than $3 00 |
| $3 00–$3 49... | ...... | ...... | ........ | ........ | .... | ...... | .... | 2 | 2 | ...... | 2 | 2 | 1.0 | .24 | ...$3 00– 3 49 |
| 3 50– 3 99... | ...... | ...... | ........ | ........ | .... | ...... | .... | 9 | .... | ...... | .... | 9 | ...... | .94 | ... 3 50– 3 99 |
| 4 00– 4 49... | ...... | ...... | ........ | ........ | .... | ...... | .... | 53 | 1 | ...... | 1 | 53 | 1.5 | 5.10 | ... 4 00– 4 49 |
| 4 50– 4 99... | ...... | ...... | ........ | ........ | .... | ...... | 1 | 175 | .... | ...... | 1 | 175 | 2.0 | 18.90 | ... 4 50– 4 99 |
| 5 00– 5 49... | ...... | ...... | ........ | 3 | .... | ...... | 1 | 347 | 3 | 1 | 7 | 348 | 5.7 | 46.30 | ... 5 00– 5 49 |
| 5 50– 5 99... | ...... | ...... | ........ | ........ | .... | ...... | .... | 99 | 3 | ...... | 3 | 99 | 7.2 | 54.10 | ... 5 50– 5 99 |
| 6 00– 6 49... | ...... | ...... | 1 | 10 | .... | 9 | .... | 347 | 1 | ...... | 12 | 356 | 13.3 | 82.10 | ... 6 00– 6 49 |
| 6 50– 6 99... | ...... | ...... | ........ | ........ | .... | 2 | .... | 59 | .... | ...... | .... | 61 | ...... | 86.90 | ... 6 50– 6 99 |
| 7 00– 7 49... | ...... | ...... | 2 | 11 | 1 | 9 | .... | 68 | 1 | ...... | 15 | 77 | 21.0 | 92.90 | ... 7 00– 7 49 |
| 7 50– 7 99... | ...... | ...... | ........ | 1 | .... | 2 | .... | 15 | .... | ...... | 1 | 17 | 21.6 | 94.20 | ... 7 50– 7 99 |
| 8 00– 8 99... | ...... | ...... | 2 | 9 | .... | 9 | 1 | 23 | .... | ...... | 12 | 32 | 27.7 | 96.70 | ... 8 00– 8 99 |
| 9 00– 9 99... | ...... | ...... | 6 | 10 | 3 | 6 | .... | 8 | .... | ...... | 19 | 14 | 37.4 | 97.90 | ... 9 00– 9 99 |
| 10 00–10 99... | 1 | ...... | 8 | 17 | 7 | 9 | 1 | 6 | .... | ...... | 34 | 15 | 54.9 | 99.00 | ...10 00–10 99 |
| 11 00–11 99... | ...... | ...... | 2 | 7 | 6 | 1 | 1 | 3 | .... | ...... | 16 | 4 | 63.1 | 99.40 | ...11 00–11 99 |
| 12 00–12 99... | 4 | ...... | 2 | 9 | 8 | 3 | 1 | 3 | .... | ...... | 24 | 6 | 75.5 | 99.80 | ...12 00–12 99 |
| 13 00–13 99... | 1 | 1 | ........ | ........ | 4 | ...... | 1 | ...... | .... | ...... | 7 | ...... | 79.0 | ...... | ...13 00–13 99 |
| 14 00–14 99... | 2 | ...... | 6 | 2 | 5 | ...... | .... | ...... | .... | ...... | 15 | ...... | 86.7 | ...... | ...14 00–14 99 |
| 15 00–15 99... | 2 | ...... | 3 | 1 | 7 | 1 | 2 | 1 | .... | ...... | 15 | 2 | 94.5 | 99.90 | ...15 00–15 99 |
| 16 00–17 99... | 1 | ...... | 2 | 1 | 1 | 1 | .... | ...... | .... | ...... | 5 | 1 | 97.0 | 100.00 | ...16 00–17 99 |
| 18 00–19 99... | 1 | 1 | 1 | 1 | .... | ...... | .... | ...... | .... | ...... | 4 | ...... | 99.5 | ...... | ...18 00–19 99 |
| 20 00–24 99... | ...... | ...... | ........ | ........ | 2 | ...... | .... | ...... | .... | ...... | 2 | ...... | 100.0 | ...... | ...20 00–24 99 |
| Not reported... | ...... | ...... | ........ | 1 | 1 | 1 | 2 | 30 | 1 | ...... | 5 | 31 | ...... | ...... | ...Not reported |
| Total..... | 12 | 2 | 35 | 83 | 45 | 53 | 11 | 1,249 | 12 | 1 | 200 | 1,303 | ...... | ...... | .....Total |

76. TABLE V, A, 3, a.

NEW YORK STATE

**FIVE AND TEN CENT STORES — STOCK AND SALES**

NUMBER AND PER CENT OF EMPLOYEES CLASSIFIED ACCORDING TO ACTUAL WEEKLY EARNINGS BY AGE GROUPS AND SEX

| ACTUAL WEEKLY EARNINGS IN DOLLARS | AGE GROUPS IN YEARS | | | | | | | | | | | | | | ACTUAL WEEKLY EARNINGS IN DOLLARS |
|---|---|---|---|---|---|---|---|---|---|---|---|---|---|---|---|
| | 14–15 | | 16–17 | | 18–20 | | 21–24 | | 25–29 | | 30–34 | | 35–39 | | |
| | Male | Female | Male | Female | Male | Female | Male | Female | Male | Female | Male | Female | Male | Female | |
| Less than $3 00 | 1 | 2 | .... | 15 | ...... | 16 | ...... | 10 | ...... | 3 | ...... | 1 | ...... | ...... | Less than $3 00 |
| $3 00–$3 49... | .... | 1 | 1 | 7 | ...... | 13 | 1 | 4 | ...... | ...... | ...... | ...... | ...... | ...... | ...$3 00– 3 49 |
| 3 50– 3 99... | 1 | 1 | 2 | 13 | ...... | 13 | ...... | 7 | ...... | 1 | ...... | 1 | ...... | ...... | ... 3 50– 3 99 |
| 4 00– 4 49... | .... | ...... | .... | 34 | ...... | 39 | ...... | 10 | ...... | 5 | ...... | 2 | ...... | 2 | ... 4 00– 4 49 |
| 4 50– 4 99... | 2 | ...... | .... | 77 | ...... | 49 | ...... | 23 | ...... | 8 | ...... | 2 | ...... | 1 | ... 4 50– 4 99 |
| 5 00– 5 49... | 2 | 4 | 4 | 93 | 1 | 110 | ...... | 35 | ...... | 10 | ...... | 4 | ...... | 1 | ... 5 00– 5 49 |
| 5 50– 5 99... | 3 | 1 | 1 | 47 | 1 | 62 | ...... | 27 | ...... | 9 | ...... | ...... | ...... | 1 | ... 5 50– 5 99 |
| 6 00– 6 49... | 2 | ...... | 6 | 44 | 3 | 141 | ...... | 58 | ...... | 19 | ...... | 6 | ...... | 3 | ... 6 00– 6 49 |
| 6 50– 6 99... | .... | ...... | 3 | 6 | ...... | 40 | ...... | 36 | ...... | 8 | ...... | 3 | ...... | ...... | ... 6 50– 6 99 |
| 7 00– 7 49... | .... | ...... | .... | 4 | 3 | 27 | 1 | 28 | ...... | 4 | ...... | ...... | ...... | ...... | ... 7 00– 7 49 |
| 7 50– 7 99... | .... | ...... | 1 | ...... | 4 | 4 | 2 | 13 | ...... | 7 | ...... | 3 | ...... | ...... | ... 7 50– 7 99 |
| 8 00– 8 99... | .... | ...... | 1 | 1 | 8 | 9 | 3 | 12 | 1 | 6 | ...... | 1 | ...... | 1 | ... 8 00– 8 99 |
| 9 00– 9 99... | .... | ...... | 1 | ...... | 8 | 2 | 5 | 10 | 1 | 2 | 1 | 2 | ...... | ...... | ... 9 00– 9 99 |
| 10 00–10 99... | .... | ...... | 1 | 1 | 8 | 3 | 7 | 6 | 1 | 1 | ...... | ...... | ...... | ...... | ...10 00–10 99 |
| 11 00–11 99... | .... | ...... | 2 | 1 | 3 | 1 | 10 | 2 | ...... | 2 | 6 | ...... | 2 | ...... | ...11 00–11 99 |
| 12 00–12 99... | .... | ...... | .... | ...... | 2 | 1 | 11 | 2 | 8 | ...... | ...... | ...... | ...... | ...... | ...12 00–12 99 |
| 13 00–13 99... | .... | ...... | .... | ...... | ...... | ...... | 8 | ...... | 1 | 2 | 1 | 1 | ...... | ...... | ...13 00–13 99 |
| 14 00–14 99... | .... | ...... | .... | ...... | ...... | ...... | 6 | ...... | 4 | ...... | 2 | ...... | ...... | ...... | ...14 00–14 99 |
| 15 00–15 99... | .... | ...... | .... | ...... | ...... | 1 | 8 | ...... | 5 | ...... | 2 | ...... | ...... | ...... | ...15 00–15 99 |
| 16 00–17 99... | .... | ...... | .... | ...... | ...... | ...... | ...... | 1 | 3 | ...... | 4 | 1 | 1 | ...... | ...16 00–17 99 |
| 18 00–19 99... | .... | ...... | .... | ...... | ...... | ...... | 1 | ...... | 1 | ...... | 1 | ...... | ...... | ...... | ...18 00–19 99 |
| 20 00–24 99... | .... | ...... | .... | ...... | ...... | ...... | ...... | ...... | 2 | ...... | ...... | ...... | ...... | ...... | ...20 00–24 99 |
| Not reported... | .... | ...... | 1 | ...... | ...... | ...... | ...... | ...... | ...... | ...... | ...... | ...... | ...... | ...... | ...Not reported |
| Total..... | 11 | 9 | 24 | 343 | 41 | 531 | 63 | 284 | 27 | 87 | 17 | 27 | 3 | 9 | .....Total |

NEW YORK STATE

76. TABLE V, A, 3, a. FIVE AND TEN CENT STORES — STOCK AND SALES

NUMBER AND PER CENT. OF EMPLOYEES CLASSIFIED ACCORDING TO ACTUAL WEEKLY EARNINGS BY AGE GROUPS AND SEX

| ACTUAL WEEKLY EARNINGS IN DOLLARS | AGE GROUPS IN YEARS | | | | | | | | | | | | ACTUAL WEEKLY EARNINGS IN DOLLARS |
|---|---|---|---|---|---|---|---|---|---|---|---|---|---|
| | 40–44 | | 45–54 | | 55–64 | 65 AND OVER | NOT REPORTED | | TOTAL | | CUMULATIVE PER CENT. OF TOTAL | | |
| | Male | Female | Male | Female | Male | Male | Male | Female | Male | Female | Male | Female | |
| Less than $3 00 | ....... | ....... | ....... | ....... | ....... | ....... | ....... | ....... | 1 | 47 | .5 | 3.6 | Less than $3 00 |
| $3 00–$3 49 | ....... | ....... | ....... | ....... | ....... | ....... | ....... | ....... | 2 | 25 | 1.5 | 5.5 | $3 00– 3 49 |
| 3 50– 3 99 | ....... | ....... | ....... | ....... | ....... | ....... | ....... | 1 | 3 | 37 | 3.0 | 8.4 | 3 50– 3 99 |
| 4 00– 4 49 | ....... | ....... | ....... | 1 | ....... | ....... | ....... | ....... | ....... | 93 | ....... | 15.5 | 4 00– 4 49 |
| 4 50– 4 99 | ....... | ....... | ....... | ....... | ....... | ....... | ....... | 1 | 2 | 161 | 4.0 | 27.9 | 4 50– 4 99 |
| 5 00– 5 49 | ....... | ....... | ....... | 1 | ....... | ....... | ....... | ....... | 7 | 258 | 7.5 | 47.6 | 5 00– 5 49 |
| 5 50– 5 99 | ....... | 1 | ....... | 1 | ....... | ....... | ....... | ....... | 5 | 149 | 10.1 | 59.1 | 5 50– 5 99 |
| 6 00– 6 49 | ....... | 1 | ....... | ....... | ....... | ....... | ....... | 1 | 11 | 273 | 15.6 | 80.1 | 6 00– 6 49 |
| 6 50– 6 99 | ....... | 2 | ....... | ....... | ....... | ....... | ....... | ....... | 3 | 95 | 17.1 | 87.5 | 6 50– 6 99 |
| 7 00– 7 49 | ....... | ....... | ....... | ....... | ....... | ....... | ....... | ....... | 4 | 63 | 19.1 | 92.2 | 7 00– 7 49 |
| 7 50– 7 99 | ....... | 1 | ....... | 2 | ....... | ....... | 1 | ....... | 8 | 30 | 23.1 | 94.5 | 7 50– 7 99 |
| 8 00– 8 99 | ....... | ....... | ....... | ....... | ....... | ....... | ....... | ....... | 13 | 30 | 29.6 | 96.7 | 8 00– 8 99 |
| 9 00– 9 99 | ....... | ....... | 1 | ....... | ....... | ....... | ....... | ....... | 17 | 16 | 38.1 | 98.0 | 9 00– 9 99 |
| 10 00–10 99 | ....... | ....... | 1 | ....... | ....... | 1 | ....... | ....... | 19 | 11 | 47.7 | 98.8 | 10 00–10 99 |
| 11 00–11 99 | ....... | ....... | 1 | ....... | ....... | ....... | ....... | ....... | 24 | 6 | 59.8 | 99.4 | 11 00–11 99 |
| 12 00–12 99 | ....... | ....... | ....... | ....... | 1 | ....... | ....... | ....... | 22 | 3 | 70.8 | 99.6 | 12 00–12 99 |
| 13 00–13 99 | 1 | ....... | 1 | ....... | ....... | ....... | ....... | ....... | 12 | 3 | 76.9 | 99.8 | 13 00–13 99 |
| 14 00–14 99 | ....... | ....... | ....... | ....... | ....... | ....... | ....... | ....... | 12 | ....... | 82.9 | ....... | 14 00–14 99 |
| 15 00–15 99 | 1 | ....... | 1 | ....... | ....... | ....... | ....... | ....... | 17 | 1 | 91.5 | 99.9 | 15 00–15 99 |
| 16 00–17 99 | 2 | ....... | 1 | ....... | ....... | ....... | ....... | ....... | 11 | 2 | 97.0 | 100.0 | 16 00–17 99 |
| 18 00–19 99 | ....... | ....... | 1 | ....... | ....... | ....... | ....... | ....... | 4 | ....... | 99.1 | ....... | 18 00–19 99 |
| 20 00–24 99 | ....... | ....... | ....... | ....... | ....... | ....... | ....... | ....... | 2 | ....... | 100.0 | ....... | 20 00–24 99 |
| Not reported | ....... | ....... | ....... | ....... | ....... | ....... | ....... | ....... | 1 | ....... | ....... | ....... | Not reported |
| Total | 4 | 5 | 7 | 5 | 1 | 1 | 1 | 3 | 200 | 1,303 | ....... | ....... | Total |

NEW YORK STATE

77. TABLE IX, A, 3, a. **FIVE AND TEN CENT STORES — STOCK AND SALES**

NUMBER AND PER CENT. OF EMPLOYEES CLASSIFIED ACCORDING TO ACTUAL WEEKLY EARNINGS BY OCCUPATION AND SEX

| ACTUAL WEEKLY EARNINGS IN DOLLARS | OCCUPATION | | | | | | | | | | | | | | ACTUAL WEEKLY EARNINGS IN DOLLARS |
|---|---|---|---|---|---|---|---|---|---|---|---|---|---|---|---|
| | SUPERINTENDENTS | ASSISTANT BUYERS AND HEADS OF STOCK | RECEIVING AND STOCK CLERKS | STOCK PEOPLE | FLOOR MANAGERS | | SALES PEOPLE | | MESSENGERS, WRAPPERS, ERRAND BOYS | | TOTAL | | CUMULATIVE PER CENT. OF TOTAL | | |
| | Male | Female | Male | Female | Male | Female | Male | Female | Male | Female | Male | Female | Male | Female | |
| Less than $3 00 | ........ | ............ | ........ | ...... | .... | ..... | .... | 47 | 1 | ..... | 1 | 47 | .5 | 3.6 | Less than $3 00 |
| $3 00–$3 49... | ........ | ............ | ........ | 1 | .... | ..... | .... | 25 | 1 | ..... | 2 | 25 | 1.5 | 5.5 | ...$3 00– 3 49 |
| 3 50– 3 99... | ........ | ............ | ........ | 1 | .... | ..... | .... | 37 | 2 | ..... | 3 | 37 | 3.0 | 8.4 | ... 3 50– 3 99 |
| 4 00– 4 49... | ........ | ............ | ........ | ...... | .... | ..... | .... | 93 | .... | ..... | .... | 93 | ..... | 15.5 | ... 4 00– 4 49 |
| 4 50– 4 99... | ........ | ............ | ........ | ...... | .... | ..... | 1 | 161 | 1 | ..... | 2 | 161 | 4.0 | 27.9 | ... 4 50– 4 99 |
| 5 00– 5 49... | ........ | ............ | ........ | 4 | .... | ..... | 2 | 257 | 1 | 1 | 7 | 258 | 7.5 | 47.6 | ... 5 00– 5 49 |
| 5 50– 5 99... | ........ | ............ | ........ | 2 | .... | ..... | .... | 149 | 3 | ..... | 5 | 149 | 10.1 | 59.1 | ... 5 50– 5 99 |
| 6 00– 6 49... | ........ | ............ | 1 | 8 | .... | 7 | .... | 266 | 2 | ..... | 11 | 273 | 15.6 | 80.1 | ... 6 00– 6 49 |
| 6 50– 6 99... | ........ | ............ | 1 | 1 | .... | 6 | 1 | 89 | .... | ..... | 3 | 95 | 17.1 | 87.5 | ... 6 50– 6 99 |
| 7 00– 7 49... | ........ | ............ | 1 | 3 | .... | 4 | .... | 59 | .... | ..... | 4 | 63 | 19.1 | 92.2 | ... 7 00– 7 49 |
| 7 50– 7 99... | ........ | ............ | ........ | 6 | 1 | 8 | .... | 22 | 1 | ..... | 8 | 30 | 23.1 | 94.5 | ... 7 50– 7 99 |
| 8 00– 8 99... | ........ | ............ | 2 | 9 | 1 | 8 | 1 | 22 | .... | ..... | 13 | 30 | 29.6 | 96.7 | ... 8 00– 8 99 |
| 9 00– 9 99... | ........ | ............ | 5 | 9 | 3 | 6 | .... | 10 | .... | ..... | 17 | 16 | 38.1 | 98.0 | ... 9 00– 9 99 |
| 10 00–10 99... | 1 | ............ | 3 | 9 | 5 | 6 | 1 | 5 | .... | ..... | 19 | 11 | 47.7 | 98.8 | ...10 00–10 99 |
| 11 00–11 99... | ........ | ............ | 8 | 12 | 4 | 3 | .... | 3 | .... | ..... | 24 | 6 | 59.8 | 99.4 | ...11 00–11 99 |
| 12 00–12 99... | 1 | ............ | 1 | 8 | 10 | ..... | 2 | 3 | .... | ..... | 22 | 3 | 70.8 | 99.6 | ...12 00–12 99 |
| 13 00–13 99... | 2 | ............ | 1 | 4 | 4 | 3 | 1 | ..... | .... | ..... | 12 | 3 | 76.9 | 99.8 | ...13 00–13 99 |
| 14 00–14 99... | 4 | 1 | 3 | 1 | 3 | ..... | .... | ..... | .... | ..... | 12 | ..... | 82.9 | ..... | ...14 00–14 99 |
| 15 00–15 99... | 2 | ............ | 3 | 2 | 8 | 1 | 2 | ..... | .... | ..... | 17 | 1 | 91.5 | 99.9 | ...15 00–15 99 |
| 16 00–17 99... | 1 | ............ | 5 | 1 | 4 | 1 | .... | 1 | .... | ..... | 11 | 2 | 97.0 | 100.0 | ...16 00–17 99 |
| 18 00–19 99... | 1 | 1 | 1 | 1 | .... | ..... | .... | ..... | .... | ..... | 4 | ..... | 99.1 | ..... | ...18 00–19 99 |
| 20 00–24 99... | ........ | ............ | ........ | ...... | 2 | ..... | .... | ..... | .... | ..... | 2 | ..... | 100.0 | ..... | ...20 00–24 99 |
| Not reported... | ........ | ............ | ........ | 1 | .... | ..... | .... | ..... | .... | ..... | 1 | ..... | ..... | ..... | ...Not reported |
| Total..... | 12 | 2 | 35 | 83 | 45 | 53 | 11 | 1,249 | 12 | 1 | 200 | 1,303 | ..... | ..... | .....Total |

NEW YORK STATE

78. TABLE X, A, 3, a.

**FIVE AND TEN CENT STORES — STOCK AND SALES**

NUMBER AND PER CENT. OF EMPLOYEES CLASSIFIED ACCORDING TO ACTUAL WEEKLY EARNINGS BY CONJUGAL CONDITION AND SEX

| ACTUAL WEEKLY EARNINGS IN DOLLARS | CONJUGAL CONDITION | | | | | | | | | | | | ACTUAL WEEKLY EARNINGS IN DOLLARS |
|---|---|---|---|---|---|---|---|---|---|---|---|---|---|
| | SINGLE | | MARRIED | | WIDOWED OR DIVORCED | | NOT REPORTED | | TOTAL | | CUMULATIVE PER CENT. OF TOTAL | | |
| | Male | Female | Male | Female | Male | Female | Male | Female | Male | Female | Male | Female | |
| Less than $3 00 | 1 | 44 | ....... | 1 | ....... | 1 | ....... | 1 | 1 | 47 | .5 | 3.6 | Less than $3 00 |
| $3 00–$3 49.... | 1 | 23 | 1 | 2 | ....... | ....... | ....... | ....... | 2 | 25 | 1.5 | 5.5 | ...$3 00– 3 49 |
| 3 50– 3 99.... | 3 | 35 | ....... | 2 | ....... | ....... | ....... | ....... | 3 | 37 | 3.0 | 8.4 | ... 3 50– 3 99 |
| 4 00– 4 49.... | ....... | 85 | ....... | 7 | ....... | 1 | ....... | ....... | ....... | 93 | ....... | 15.5 | ... 4 00– 4 49 |
| 4 50– 4 99.... | 2 | 154 | ....... | 6 | ....... | 1 | ....... | ....... | 2 | 161 | 4.0 | 27.9 | ... 4 50– 4 99 |
| 5 00– 5 49.... | 7 | 237 | ....... | 14 | ....... | 4 | ....... | 3 | 7 | 258 | 7.5 | 47.6 | ... 5 00– 5 49 |
| 5 50– 5 99.... | 5 | 141 | ....... | 4 | ....... | 4 | ....... | ....... | 5 | 149 | 10.1 | 59.1 | ... 5 50– 5 99 |
| 6 00– 6 49.... | 11 | 240 | ....... | 14 | ....... | 10 | ....... | 9 | 11 | 273 | 15.6 | 80.1 | ... 6 00– 6 49 |
| 6 50– 6 99.... | 3 | 87 | ....... | 4 | ....... | 4 | ....... | ....... | 3 | 95 | 17.1 | 87.5 | ... 6 50– 6 99 |
| 7 00– 7 49.... | 4 | 60 | ....... | 1 | ....... | ....... | ....... | 2 | 4 | 63 | 19.1 | 92.2 | ... 7 00– 7 49 |
| 7 50– 7 99.... | 8 | 25 | ....... | 3 | ....... | 1 | ....... | 1 | 8 | 30 | 23.1 | 94.5 | ... 7 50– 7 99 |
| 8 00– 8 99.... | 12 | 29 | 1 | 1 | ....... | ....... | ....... | ....... | 13 | 30 | 29.6 | 96.7 | ... 8 00– 8 99 |
| 9 00– 9 99.... | 13 | 16 | 2 | ....... | 2 | ....... | ....... | ....... | 17 | 16 | 38.1 | 98.0 | ... 9 00– 9 99 |
| 10 00–10 99.... | 17 | 10 | 1 | ....... | 1 | ....... | ....... | 1 | 19 | 11 | 47.7 | 98.8 | ...10 00–10 99 |
| 11 00–11 99.... | 17 | 6 | 7 | ....... | ....... | ....... | ....... | ....... | 24 | 6 | 59.8 | 99.4 | ...11 00–11 99 |
| 12 00–12 99.... | 14 | 2 | 5 | ....... | ....... | ....... | 3 | 1 | 22 | 3 | 70.8 | 99.6 | ...12 00–12 99 |
| 13 00–13 99.... | 6 | 3 | 5 | ....... | ....... | ....... | 1 | ....... | 12 | 3 | 76.9 | 99.8 | ...13 00–13 99 |
| 14 00–14 99.... | 9 | ....... | 3 | ....... | ....... | ....... | ....... | ....... | 12 | ....... | 82.9 | ....... | ...14 00–14 99 |
| 15 00–15 99.... | 10 | 1 | 6 | ....... | ....... | ....... | 1 | ....... | 17 | 1 | 91.5 | 99.9 | ...15 00–15 99 |
| 16 00–17 99.... | ....... | 2 | 10 | ....... | 1 | ....... | ....... | ....... | 11 | 2 | 97.0 | 100.0 | ...16 00–17 99 |
| 18 00–19 99.... | 2 | ....... | 2 | ....... | ....... | ....... | ....... | ....... | 4 | ....... | 99.1 | ....... | ...18 00–19 99 |
| 20 00–24 99.... | 1 | ....... | ....... | ....... | 1 | ....... | ....... | ....... | 2 | ....... | 100.0 | ....... | ...20 00–24 99 |
| Not reported.... | 1 | ....... | ....... | ....... | ....... | ....... | ....... | ....... | 1 | ....... | ....... | ....... | ...Not reported |
| Total...... | 147 | 1,200 | 43 | 59 | 5 | 26 | 5 | 18 | 200 | 1,303 | ....... | ....... | .....Total |

79. TABLE XI, A, 3, a.

NEW YORK STATE

**FIVE AND TEN CENT STORES — STOCK AND SALES**

NUMBER AND PER CENT. OF EMPLOYEES CLASSIFIED ACCORDING TO ACTUAL WEEKLY EARNINGS BY NATIVITY AND SEX

| ACTUAL WEEKLY EARNINGS IN DOLLARS | NATIVITY: NATIVE | | FOREIGN | | NOT REPORTED | | TOTAL | | CUMULATIVE PER CENT. OF TOTAL | | ACTUAL WEEKLY EARNINGS IN DOLLARS |
|---|---|---|---|---|---|---|---|---|---|---|---|
| | Male | Female | Male | Female | Male | Female | Male | Female | Male | Female | |
| Less than $3 00 | 1 | 45 | ........ | 2 | ........ | ........ | 1 | 47 | .5 | 3.6 | Less than $3 00 |
| $3 00–$3 49 | 1 | 25 | ........ | ........ | 1 | ........ | 2 | 25 | 1.5 | 5.5 | $3 00– 3 49 |
| 3 50– 3 99 | 3 | 32 | ........ | 3 | ........ | 2 | 3 | 37 | 3.0 | 8.4 | 3 50– 3 99 |
| 4 00– 4 49 | ........ | 87 | ........ | 6 | ........ | ........ | ........ | 93 | ........ | 15.5 | 4 00– 4 49 |
| 4 50– 4 99 | 2 | 152 | ........ | 9 | ........ | ........ | 2 | 161 | 4.0 | 27.9 | 4 50– 4 99 |
| 5 00– 5 49 | 7 | 243 | ........ | 14 | ........ | 1 | 7 | 258 | 7.5 | 47.6 | 5 00– 5 49 |
| 5 50– 5 99 | 2 | 137 | 3 | 137 | 3 | 12 | 5 | 149 | 10.1 | 59.1 | 5 50– 5 99 |
| 6 00– 6 49 | 10 | 239 | 1 | 34 | ........ | ........ | 11 | 273 | 15.6 | 80.1 | 6 00– 6 49 |
| 6 50– 6 99 | 3 | 84 | ........ | 11 | ........ | ........ | 3 | 95 | 17.1 | 87.5 | 6 50– 6 99 |
| 7 00– 7 49 | 3 | 51 | 1 | 12 | ........ | ........ | 4 | 63 | 19.1 | 92.2 | 7 00– 7 49 |
| 7 50– 7 99 | 7 | 27 | ........ | 3 | 1 | ........ | 8 | 30 | 23.1 | 94.5 | 7 50– 7 99 |
| 8 00– 8 99 | 13 | 29 | ........ | 1 | ........ | ........ | 13 | 30 | 29.6 | 96.7 | 8 00– 8 99 |
| 9 00– 9 99 | 14 | 13 | 2 | 3 | 1 | ........ | 17 | 16 | 38.1 | 98.0 | 9 00– 9 99 |
| 10 00–10 99 | 16 | 11 | 2 | ........ | 1 | ........ | 19 | 11 | 47.7 | 98.8 | 10 00–10 99 |
| 11 00–11 99 | 22 | 6 | 2 | ........ | ........ | ........ | 24 | 6 | 59.8 | 99.4 | 11 00–11 99 |
| 12 00–12 99 | 17 | 2 | 5 | 1 | ........ | ........ | 22 | 3 | 70.8 | 99.6 | 12 00–12 99 |
| 13 00–13 99 | 10 | 3 | 2 | ........ | ........ | ........ | 12 | 3 | 76.9 | 99.8 | 13 00–13 99 |
| 14 00–14 99 | 11 | ........ | 1 | ........ | ........ | ........ | 12 | ........ | 82.9 | ........ | 14 00–14 99 |
| 15 00–15 99 | 12 | 1 | 5 | ........ | ........ | ........ | 17 | 1 | 91.5 | 99.9 | 15 00–15 99 |
| 16 00–17 99 | 10 | 2 | 1 | ........ | ........ | ........ | 11 | 2 | 97.0 | 100.0 | 16 00–17 99 |
| 18 00–19 99 | 4 | ........ | ........ | ........ | ........ | ........ | 4 | ........ | 99.1 | ........ | 18 00–19 99 |
| 20 00–24 99 | 2 | ........ | ........ | ........ | ........ | ........ | 2 | ........ | 100.0 | ........ | 20 00–24 99 |
| Not reported | ........ | ........ | 1 | ........ | ........ | ........ | 1 | ........ | ........ | ........ | Not reported |
| Total | 170 | 1,189 | 26 | 111 | 4 | 3 | 200 | 1,303 | ........ | ........ | Total |

NEW YORK STATE

80. TABLE XII, A, 3, a

**FIVE AND TEN CENT STORES — STOCK AND SALES**

NUMBER OF EMPLOYEES FOR EACH SEX CLASSIFIED ACCORDING TO ACTUAL WEEKLY EARNINGS BY THE NUMBER OF YEARS IN THE TRADE

| ACTUAL WEEKLY EARNINGS IN DOLLARS | YEARS IN TRADE | | | | | | | | | | | | | | | | ACTUAL WEEKLY EARNINGS IN DOLLARS |
|---|---|---|---|---|---|---|---|---|---|---|---|---|---|---|---|---|---|
| | LESS THAN 1 | | 1 | | 2 | | 3 | | 4 | | 5 | | 6 | | 7 | | |
| | Male | Female | Male | Female | Male | Female | Male | Female | Male | Female | Male | Female | Male | Female | Male | Female | |
| Less than $3 00 | ...... | 31 | 1 | 3 | ...... | 5 | .... | 4 | .... | 1 | .... | 2 | .... | .... | .... | .... | Less than $3 00 |
| $3 00–$3 49... | ...... | 18 | ...... | 2 | 1 | ..... | .... | 2 | .... | .... | .... | 1 | .... | 1 | .... | .... | ...$3 00– 3 49 |
| 3 50– 3 99... | 3 | 29 | ...... | 4 | ...... | 3 | .... | 1 | .... | .... | .... | .... | .... | .... | .... | .... | ... 3 50– 3 99 |
| 4 00– 4 49... | ...... | 54 | ...... | 10 | ...... | 4 | .... | 6 | .... | 4 | .... | 2 | .... | .... | .... | 2 | ... 4 00– 4 49 |
| 4 50– 4 99... | 1 | 89 | 1 | 33 | ...... | 12 | .... | 13 | .... | 8 | .... | 4 | .... | .... | .... | .... | ... 4 50– 4 99 |
| 5 00– 5 49... | 7 | 156 | ...... | 37 | ...... | 31 | .... | 16 | .... | 10 | .... | 5 | .... | 2 | .... | .... | ... 5 00– 5 49 |
| 5 50– 5 99... | 5 | 54 | ...... | 40 | ...... | 24 | .... | 14 | .... | 9 | .... | 2 | .... | 2 | .... | 2 | ... 5 50– 5 99 |
| 6 00– 6 49... | 8 | 79 | 3 | 70 | ...... | 50 | .... | 32 | .... | 16 | .... | 5 | .... | 5 | .... | 2 | ... 6 00– 6 49 |
| 6 50– 6 99... | 1 | 5 | 2 | 14 | ...... | 30 | .... | 9 | .... | 15 | .... | 7 | .... | 9 | .... | 3 | ... 6 50– 6 99 |
| 7 00– 7 49... | 3 | 1 | ...... | 10 | 1 | 15 | .... | 11 | .... | 11 | .... | 5 | .... | 4 | .... | 4 | ... 7 00– 7 49 |
| 7 50– 7 99... | 7 | 2 | 1 | 2 | ...... | 3 | .... | .... | .... | 6 | .... | 7 | .... | 3 | .... | 1 | ... 7 50– 7 99 |
| 8 00– 8 99... | 8 | 2 | 3 | 4 | 2 | 5 | .... | 5 | .... | 1 | .... | 2 | .... | 3 | .... | 1 | ... 8 00– 8 99 |
| 9 00– 9 99... | 11 | ...... | 4 | 2 | ...... | 3 | .... | 1 | 1 | 1 | .... | 2 | 1 | 1 | .... | 3 | ... 9 00– 9 99 |
| 10 00–10 99... | 8 | ...... | 5 | 1 | 2 | 2 | 1 | 1 | 2 | 1 | 1 | 2 | .... | 1 | .... | .... | ...10 00–10 99 |
| 11 00–11 99... | 11 | 1 | 7 | ...... | 2 | ..... | 1 | 1 | 2 | .... | .... | 1 | 1 | .... | .... | .... | ...11 00–11 99 |
| 12 00–12 99... | 5 | ...... | 6 | ...... | 4 | ..... | 2 | .... | 2 | .... | .... | 1 | 1 | 1 | .... | 1 | ...12 00–12 99 |
| 13 00–13 99... | 2 | ...... | 1 | ...... | 3 | ..... | 4 | .... | .... | .... | .... | .... | .... | .... | 1 | .... | ...13 00–13 99 |
| 14 00–14 99... | 1 | ...... | 1 | ...... | 3 | ..... | 4 | .... | 1 | .... | 1 | .... | 1 | .... | .... | .... | ...14 00–14 99 |
| 15 00–15 99... | 3 | ...... | ...... | ...... | 3 | ..... | 4 | .... | 1 | 1 | 1 | .... | 2 | .... | 2 | .... | ...15 00–15 99 |
| 16 00–17 99... | 1 | ...... | 2 | ...... | ...... | ..... | 3 | .... | 1 | .... | .... | 1 | 1 | .... | 1 | .... | ...16 00–17 99 |
| 18 00–19 99... | 2 | ...... | ...... | ...... | ...... | ..... | .... | .... | .... | .... | 1 | .... | .... | .... | .... | .... | ...18 00–19 99 |
| 20 00–24 99... | ...... | ...... | ...... | ...... | 1 | ..... | .... | .... | 1 | .... | .... | .... | .... | .... | .... | .... | ...20 00–24 99 |
| Not reported... | ...... | ...... | 1 | ...... | ...... | ..... | .... | .... | .... | .... | .... | .... | .... | .... | .... | .... | ...Not reported |
| Total..... | 87 | 521 | 38 | 250 | 22 | 187 | 18 | 116 | 11 | 84 | 4 | 49 | 7 | 32 | 4 | 19 | .....Total |

80. TABLE XII, A, 3, a — *concluded*

NEW YORK STATE

**FIVE AND TEN CENT STORES — STOCK AND SALES**

NUMBER OF EMPLOYEES FOR EACH SEX CLASSIFIED ACCORDING TO ACTUAL WEEKLY EARNINGS BY THE NUMBER OF YEARS IN THE TRADE

| ACTUAL WEEKLY EARNINGS IN DOLLARS | YEARS IN TRADE | | | | | | | | | | | | TOTAL | | CUMULATIVE PER CENT OF TOTAL | | ACTUAL WEEKLY EARNINGS IN DOLLARS |
|---|---|---|---|---|---|---|---|---|---|---|---|---|---|---|---|---|---|
| | 8 | | 9 | | 10–14 | | 15–19 | | 25–29 | | NOT REPORTED | | | | | | |
| | Male | Female | Male | Female | Male | Female | Fe-male | Male | Male | Fe-male | Male | Fe-male | Male | Fe-male | Male | Fe-male | |
| Less than $3 00 | | | | | | | | | | | | 1 | 1 | 47 | .5 | 3.6 | Less than $3 00 |
| $3 00–$3 49 | | | | | | | | | | | 1 | 1 | 2 | 25 | 1.5 | 5.5 | $3 00–$3 49 |
| 3 50– 3 99 | | | | | | | | | | | | | 3 | 37 | 3.0 | 8.4 | 3 50– 3 99 |
| 4 00– 4 49 | | 1 | | | | 1 | | | | | | | .... | 93 | .... | 15.5 | 4 00– 4 49 |
| 4 50– 4 99 | | | | 1 | | | | | | | | 1 | 2 | 161 | 4.0 | 27.9 | 4 50– 4 99 |
| 5 00– 5 49 | | | | | | | | | | | | 1 | 7 | 258 | 7.5 | 47.6 | 5 00– 5 49 |
| 5 50– 5 99 | | | | | | | | | | 1 | | 1 | 5 | 149 | 10.1 | 59.1 | 5 50– 5 99 |
| 6 00– 6 49 | | 1 | | 1 | | | 1 | | | | | 2 | 11 | 273 | 15.6 | 80.1 | 6 00– 6 49 |
| 6 50– 6 99 | | 1 | | | | 2 | | | | | | | 3 | 95 | 17.1 | 87.5 | 6 50– 6 99 |
| 7 00– 7 49 | | 2 | | | | | | | | | | | 4 | 63 | 19.1 | 92.2 | 7 00– 7 49 |
| 7 50– 7 99 | | 2 | | 1 | | 2 | 1 | | | | | | 8 | 30 | 23.1 | 94.5 | 7 50– 7 99 |
| 8 00– 8 99 | | | | 3 | | 4 | | | | | | | 13 | 30 | 29.6 | 96.7 | 8 00– 8 99 |
| 9 00– 9 99 | | | | | | 2 | 1 | | | | | | 17 | 16 | 38.1 | 98.0 | 9 00– 9 99 |
| 10 00–10 99 | | 1 | | 1 | | 1 | | | | | | | 19 | 11 | 47.7 | 98.8 | 10 00–10 99 |
| 11 00–11 99 | | | | 1 | | 2 | | | | | | | 24 | 6 | 59.8 | 99.4 | 11 00–11 99 |
| 12 00–12 99 | 1 | | | | 1 | | | | | | | | 22 | 3 | 70.8 | 99.6 | 12 00–12 99 |
| 13 00–13 99 | | | 1 | | | 2 | 1 | | | | | | 12 | 3 | 76.9 | 99.8 | 13 00–13 99 |
| 14 00–14 99 | 1 | | | | | | | | | | | | 12 | .... | 82.9 | .... | 14 00–14 99 |
| 15 00–15 99 | | | 1 | | | | | | | | | | 17 | 1 | 91.5 | 99.9 | 15 00–15 99 |
| 16 00–17 99 | 1 | | | | | | 1 | 1 | | | | | 11 | 2 | 97.0 | 100.0 | 16 00–17 99 |
| 18 00–19 99 | | | | | | | | | 1 | | | | 4 | .... | 99.1 | .... | 18 00–19 99 |
| 20 00–24 99 | | | | | | | | | | | | | 2 | .... | 100.0 | .... | 20 00–24 99 |
| Not reported | | | | | | | | | | | | | 1 | .... | .... | .... | Not reported |
| Total | 3 | 8 | 2 | 8 | 1 | 16 | 5 | 1 | 1 | 1 | 1 | 7 | 200 | 1,303 | .... | .... | Total |

NEW YORK STATE

81. TABLE XIII, A, 3, a

**FIVE AND TEN CENT STORES—STOCK AND SALES**

Number of Employees for Each Sex Classified According to Actual Weekly Earnings by the Number of Years with the Firm

| Actual Weekly Earnings in Dollars | Years with Firm: Less than 1 | | 1 | | 2 | | 3 | | 4 | | 5 | | 6 | | Actual Weekly Earnings in Dollars |
|---|---|---|---|---|---|---|---|---|---|---|---|---|---|---|---|
| | Male | Female | Male | Female | Male | Female | Male | Female | Male | Female | Male | Female | Male | Female | |
| Less than $3 00 | .... | 40 | 1 | 1 | ...... | 2 | ...... | 1 | ...... | 2 | ...... | 1 | ...... | ...... | Less than $3 00 |
| $3 00–$3 49... | 2 | 23 | .... | 1 | ...... | ...... | ...... | ...... | ...... | ...... | ...... | ...... | ...... | 1 | ...$3 00– 3 49 |
| 3 50– 3 99... | 3 | 34 | .... | 2 | ...... | 1 | ...... | ...... | ...... | ...... | ...... | ...... | ...... | ...... | ... 3 50– 3 99 |
| 4 00– 4 49... | .... | 74 | .... | 13 | ...... | ...... | ...... | 5 | ...... | ...... | ...... | 1 | ...... | ...... | ... 4 00– 4 49 |
| 4 50– 4 99... | 1 | 111 | 1 | 27 | ...... | 7 | ...... | 5 | ...... | 7 | ...... | 2 | ...... | ...... | ... 4 50– 4 99 |
| 5 00– 5 49... | 7 | 200 | .... | 40 | ...... | 12 | ...... | 1 | ...... | 2 | ...... | ...... | ...... | 2 | ... 5 00– 5 49 |
| 5 50– 5 99... | 5 | 78 | .... | 33 | ...... | 21 | ...... | 11 | ...... | 5 | ...... | ...... | ...... | ...... | ... 5 50– 5 99 |
| 6 00– 6 49... | 9 | 125 | 2 | 77 | ...... | 40 | ...... | 17 | ...... | 9 | ...... | 1 | ...... | 2 | ... 6 00– 6 49 |
| 6 50– 6 99... | 1 | 11 | 2 | 19 | ...... | 30 | ...... | 9 | ...... | 11 | ...... | 6 | ...... | 6 | ... 6 50– 6 99 |
| 7 00– 7 49... | 3 | 4 | .... | 15 | 1 | 15 | ...... | 7 | ...... | 10 | ...... | 4 | ...... | 1 | ... 7 00– 7 49 |
| 7 50– 7 99... | 7 | 2 | 1 | 3 | ...... | 4 | ...... | ...... | ...... | 6 | ...... | 6 | ...... | 3 | ... 7 50– 7 99 |
| 8 00– 8 99... | 8 | 4 | 3 | 4 | 2 | 5 | ...... | 5 | ...... | 1 | ...... | 1 | ...... | 3 | ... 8 00– 8 99 |
| 9 00– 9 99... | 11 | 4 | 4 | 4 | ...... | 2 | ...... | ...... | 1 | ...... | ...... | 1 | 1 | 1 | ... 9 00– 9 99 |
| 10 00–10 99... | 11 | 1 | 4 | 1 | 2 | 3 | ...... | 1 | ...... | 2 | 1 | ...... | ...... | 1 | ...10 00–10 99 |
| 11 00–11 99... | 13 | 2 | 6 | 1 | 3 | ...... | ...... | 1 | 1 | ...... | ...... | ...... | 1 | ...... | ...11 00–11 99 |
| 12 00–12 99... | 8 | 2 | 9 | ...... | 2 | 1 | 2 | ...... | ...... | ...... | ...... | ...... | ...... | ...... | ...12 00–12 99 |
| 13 00–13 99... | 3 | ...... | 1 | ...... | 3 | ...... | 4 | ...... | ...... | ...... | ...... | ...... | ...... | ...... | ...13 00–13 99 |
| 14 00–14 99... | 2 | ...... | 1 | ...... | 3 | ...... | 2 | ...... | 1 | ...... | 1 | ...... | 1 | ...... | ...14 00–14 99 |
| 15 00–15 99... | 7 | ...... | .... | 1 | 3 | ...... | 3 | ...... | ...... | ...... | ...... | ...... | 1 | ...... | ...15 00–15 99 |
| 16 00–17 99... | 1 | ...... | 2 | 1 | ...... | ...... | 4 | ...... | 2 | ...... | ...... | ...... | 1 | ...... | ...16 00–17 99 |
| 18 00–19 99... | 3 | ...... | .... | ...... | ...... | ...... | ...... | ...... | ...... | ...... | ...... | ...... | ...... | ...... | ...18 00–19 99 |
| 20 00–24 99... | .... | ...... | .... | ...... | 2 | ...... | ...... | ...... | ...... | ...... | ...... | ...... | ...... | ...... | ...20 00–24 99 |
| Not reported... | .... | ...... | 1 | ...... | ...... | ...... | ...... | ...... | ...... | ...... | ...... | ...... | ...... | ...... | ...Not reported |
| Total..... | 105 | 715 | 38 | 243 | 21 | 143 | 15 | 63 | 5 | 55 | 2 | 23 | 5 | 20 | .....Total |

NEW YORK STATE

81. TABLE XIII, A, 3, a

FIVE AND TEN CENT STORES — STOCK AND SALES

NUMBER OF EMPLOYEES FOR EACH SEX CLASSIFIED ACCORDING TO ACTUAL WEEKLY EARNINGS BY THE NUMBER OF YEARS WITH THE FIRM

| ACTUAL WEEKLY EARNINGS IN DOLLARS | YEARS WITH FIRM: 7 | | 8 | | 9 | | 10—14 | | 15-19 | NOT REPORTED | | TOTAL | | CUMULATIVE PER CENT. OF TOTAL | | ACTUAL WEEKLY EARNINGS IN DOLLARS |
|---|---|---|---|---|---|---|---|---|---|---|---|---|---|---|---|---|
| | Male | Female | Male | Female | Male | Female | Male | Female | Female | Male | Female | Male | Female | Male | Female | |
| Less than $3 00 | | | | | | | | | | | | 1 | 47 | .5 | 3.6 | Less than $3 00 |
| $3 00-$3 49 | | | | | | | | | | | | 2 | 25 | 1.5 | 5.5 | $3 00- 3 49 |
| 3 50- 3 99 | | | | | | | | | | | | 3 | 37 | 3.0 | 8.4 | 3 50- 3 99 |
| 4 00- 4 49 | | | | | | | | | | | | | 93 | | 15.5 | 4 00- 4 49 |
| 4 50- 4 99 | | | | | | 1 | | | | | 1 | 2 | 161 | 4.0 | 27.9 | 4 50- 4 99 |
| 5 00- 5 49 | | | | | | | | 1 | | | | 7 | 258 | 7.5 | 47.6 | 5 00- 5 49 |
| 5 50- 5 99 | | 1 | | | | | | | | | | 5 | 149 | 10.1 | 59.1 | 5 50- 5 99 |
| 6 00- 6 49 | | 1 | | 1 | | | | | | | | 11 | 273 | 15.6 | 80.1 | 6 00- 6 49 |
| 6 50- 6 99 | | 2 | | | | | | 1 | | | | 3 | 95 | 17.1 | 87.5 | 6 50- 6 99 |
| 7 00- 7 49 | | 4 | | 2 | | | | | | | 1 | 4 | 63 | 19.1 | 92.2 | 7 00- 7 49 |
| 7 50- 7 99 | | 2 | | 1 | | | | 2 | 1 | | | 8 | 30 | 23.1 | 94.5 | 7 50- 7 99 |
| 8 00- 8 99 | | | | | | 3 | | 4 | | | | 13 | 30 | 29.6 | 96.7 | 8 00- 8 99 |
| 9 00- 9 99 | | 1 | | | | | | 2 | 1 | | | 17 | 16 | 38.1 | 98.0 | 9 00- 9 99 |
| 10 00-10 99 | | | | 1 | | | | 1 | | 1 | | 19 | 11 | 47.7 | 98.8 | 10 00-10 99 |
| 11 00-11 99 | | | | | | | | 2 | | | | 24 | 6 | 59.8 | 99.4 | 11 00-11 99 |
| 12 00-12 99 | | | 1 | | | | | | | | | 22 | 3 | 70.8 | 99.6 | 12 00-12 99 |
| 13 00-13 99 | 1 | | | | | | | 2 | 1 | | | 12 | 3 | 76.9 | 99.8 | 13 00-13 99 |
| 14 00-14 99 | | | 1 | | | | | | | | | 12 | | 82.9 | | 14 00-14 99 |
| 15 00-15 99 | 2 | | | | 1 | | | | | | | 17 | 1 | 91.5 | 99.9 | 15 00-15 99 |
| 16 00-17 99 | 1 | | | | | | | | 1 | | | 11 | 2 | 97.0 | 100.0 | 16 00-17 99 |
| 18 00-19 99 | | | | | | | 1 | | | | | 4 | | 99.1 | | 18 00-19 99 |
| 20 00-24 99 | | | | | | | | | | | | 2 | | 100.0 | | 20 00-24 99 |
| Not reported | | | | | | | | | | | | 1 | | | | Not reported |
| Total | 4 | 11 | 2 | 5 | 1 | 4 | 1 | 15 | 4 | 1 | 2 | 200 | 1,303 | | | Total |

82. TABLE XV, A, 3, b, c, e

NEW YORK STATE

**FIVE AND TEN CENT STORES — OFFICE, SHIPPING AND DELIVERY, PLANT**

Number of Employees Earning Specified Weekly Rates by Department and Sex

| Weekly Rates in Dollars | Department | | | | | | | | | Weekly Rates in Dollars |
|---|---|---|---|---|---|---|---|---|---|---|
| | Office | | Shipping and Delivery | Plant | | Total | | Cumulative per cent. of total | | |
| | Male | Female | Male | Male | Female | Male | Female | Male | Female | |
| Less than $3 00 | | | | | | | | | | Less than $3 00 |
| $3 00–$3 49 | | | | | | | | | | $3 00– 3 49 |
| 3 50– 3 99 | | | 1 | | 1 | 1 | 1 | 2.00 | 1.00 | 3 50– 3 99 |
| 4 00– 4 49 | | | | | 3 | | 3 | | 4.10 | 4 00– 4 49 |
| 4 50– 4 99 | | | | | | | | | | 4 50– 4 99 |
| 5 00– 5 49 | | 2 | | | 3 | | 5 | | 9.20 | 5 00– 5 49 |
| 5 50– 5 99 | | | | | 1 | | 1 | | 10.20 | 5 50– 5 99 |
| 6 00– 6 49 | | 10 | 2 | 2 | 3 | 4 | 13 | 10.20 | 23.50 | 6 00– 6 49 |
| 6 50– 6 99 | | 1 | | | 1 | | 2 | | 25.60 | 6 50– 6 99 |
| 7 00– 7 49 | | 15 | | | 3 | | 18 | | 43.90 | 7 00– 7 49 |
| 7 50– 7 99 | | 3 | | 1 | 2 | 1 | 5 | 12.50 | 49.00 | 7 50– 7 99 |
| 8 00– 8 99 | | 14 | 1 | 6 | 1 | 7 | 15 | 26.50 | 64.60 | 8 00– 8 99 |
| 9 00– 9 99 | | 6 | 3 | 3 | | 6 | 6 | 38.80 | 70.50 | 9 00– 9 99 |
| 10 00–10 99 | 1 | 12 | 2 | 6 | | 9 | 12 | 57.20 | 82.70 | 10 00–10 99 |
| 11 00–11 99 | | 6 | | 3 | | 3 | 6 | 63.20 | 89.00 | 11 00–11 99 |
| 12 00–12 99 | 1 | 4 | 2 | 2 | | 5 | 4 | 73.50 | 93.00 | 12 00–12 99 |
| 13 00–13 99 | 2 | 3 | | 3 | | 5 | 3 | 83.60 | 96.00 | 13 00–13 99 |
| 14 00–14 99 | 1 | 1 | 1 | 1 | | 3 | 1 | 89.80 | 97.00 | 14 00–14 99 |
| 15 00–15 99 | 1 | 2 | | 2 | | 3 | 2 | 96.00 | 99.00 | 15 00–15 99 |
| 16 00–17 99 | 1 | | | | | 1 | | 98.00 | | 16 00–17 99 |
| 18 00–19 99 | 1 | 1 | | | | 1 | 1 | 100.00 | 100.00 | 18 00–19 99 |
| Not reported | | 4 | | | | | 4 | | | Not reported |
| Total | 8 | 84 | 12 | 29 | 18 | 49 | 102 | | | Total |

NEW YORK STATE

83. TABLE XVI, A, 3, b, c, e **FIVE AND TEN CENT STORES — OFFICE, SHIPPING AND DELIVERY, PLANT**

NUMBER AND PER CENT. OF EMPLOYEES CLASSIFIED ACCORDING TO ACTUAL WEEKLY EARNINGS BY DEPARTMENT AND SEX

| Actual Weekly Earnings in Dollars | Department: Office | | Shipping and Delivery | Plant | | Total | | Cumulative Per Cent. of Total | | Actual Weekly Earnings in Dollars |
|---|---|---|---|---|---|---|---|---|---|---|
| | Male | Female | Male | Male | Female | Male | Female | Male | Female | |
| Less than $3 00 | ........ | 1 | ........ | ........ | 1 | ........ | 2 | ........ | 2.00 | Less than $3 00 |
| $3 00–$3 49 | ........ | ........ | ........ | ........ | 1 | ........ | 1 | ........ | 3.00 | $3 00– 3 49 |
| 3 50– 3 99 | ........ | 1 | 1 | ........ | 1 | 1 | 2 | 2.00 | 5.00 | 3 50– 3 99 |
| 4 00– 4 49 | ........ | 1 | ........ | ........ | 1 | ........ | 2 | ........ | 7.00 | 4 00– 4 49 |
| 4 50– 4 99 | ........ | ........ | ........ | ........ | ........ | ........ | ........ | ........ | ........ | 4 50– 4 99 |
| 5 00– 5 49 | ........ | 1 | ........ | ........ | 1 | ........ | 2 | ........ | 8.90 | 5 00– 5 49 |
| 5 50– 5 99 | ........ | 1 | ........ | ........ | 3 | ........ | 4 | ........ | 12.90 | 5 50– 5 99 |
| 6 00– 6 49 | ........ | 4 | 2 | 2 | 2 | 4 | 6 | 10.20 | 18.80 | 6 00– 6 49 |
| 6 50– 6 99 | ........ | 8 | ........ | ........ | 2 | ........ | 10 | ........ | 28.80 | 6 50– 6 99 |
| 7 00– 7 49 | ........ | 9 | ........ | ........ | 2 | ........ | 11 | ........ | 39.60 | 7 00– 7 49 |
| 7 50– 7 99 | ........ | 5 | ........ | 1 | 2 | 1 | 7 | 12.20 | 46.60 | 7 50– 7 99 |
| 8 00– 8 99 | ........ | 16 | 1 | 6 | 2 | 7 | 18 | 26.50 | 64.50 | 8 00– 8 99 |
| 9 00– 9 99 | ........ | 6 | 3 | 3 | ........ | 6 | 6 | 38.80 | 70.40 | 9 00– 9 99 |
| 10 00–10 99 | 1 | 7 | 1 | 3 | ........ | 5 | 7 | 49.00 | 77.20 | 10 00–10 99 |
| 11 00–11 99 | ........ | 11 | 1 | 5 | ........ | 6 | 11 | 61.20 | 88.20 | 11 00–11 99 |
| 12 00–12 99 | 1 | 3 | 1 | 3 | ........ | 5 | 3 | 71.40 | 91.10 | 12 00–12 99 |
| 13 00–13 99 | 1 | 4 | ........ | 1 | ........ | 2 | 4 | 75.50 | 95.10 | 13 00–13 99 |
| 14 00–14 99 | ........ | 1 | ........ | 3 | ........ | 3 | 1 | 81.50 | 96.10 | 14 00–14 99 |
| 15 00–15 99 | 1 | 3 | 1 | 1 | ........ | 3 | 3 | 87.70 | 99.10 | 15 00–15 99 |
| 16 00–17 99 | 1 | ........ | 1 | 1 | ........ | 3 | ........ | 93.70 | ........ | 16 00–17 99 |
| 18 00–19 99 | 3 | 1 | ........ | ........ | ........ | 3 | 1 | 100.00 | 100.00 | 18 00–19 99 |
| Not reported | ........ | 1 | ........ | ........ | ........ | ........ | 1 | ........ | ........ | Not reported |
| Total | 8 | 84 | 12 | 29 | 18 | 49 | 102 | ........ | ........ | Total |

NEW YORK STATE

84. TABLE XVII, A, 3, b, c, e

**FIVE AND TEN CENT STORES — OFFICE, SHIPPING AND DELIVERY, PLANT**

NUMBER OF EMPLOYEES CLASSIFIED BY AGE GROUPS BY DEPARTMENT AND SEX

| AGE GROUPS IN YEARS | DEPARTMENT | | | | | | | | | AGE GROUPS IN YEARS |
|---|---|---|---|---|---|---|---|---|---|---|
| | OFFICE | | SHIPPING AND DELIVERY | PLANT | | TOTAL | | PER CENT. OF TOTAL | | |
| | Male | Female | Male | Male | Female | Male | Female | Male | Female | |
| 14–15 | ........ | ........ | ........ | ........ | ........ | ........ | ........ | ........ | ........ | 14–15 |
| 16–17 | ........ | 6 | 3 | 2 | ........ | 5 | 6 | 10.20 | 5.90 | 16–17 |
| 18–20 | ........ | 27 | 2 | 5 | 2 | 7 | 29 | 14.30 | 28.30 | 18–20 |
| 21–24 | 4 | 32 | 3 | 5 | 1 | 12 | 33 | 24.50 | 32.50 | 21–24 |
| 25–29 | 3 | 13 | 1 | 4 | 1 | 8 | 14 | 16.30 | 13.70 | 25–29 |
| 30–34 | ........ | 2 | ........ | 3 | 1 | 3 | 3 | 6.10 | 2.90 | 30–34 |
| 35–39 | 1 | 4 | 1 | 3 | 2 | 5 | 6 | 10.20 | 5.90 | 35–39 |
| 40–44 | ........ | ........ | 2 | ........ | 3 | 2 | 3 | 4.10 | 2.90 | 40–44 |
| 45–54 | ........ | ........ | ........ | 4 | 6 | 4 | 6 | 8.20 | 5.90 | 45–54 |
| 55–64 | ........ | ........ | ........ | 3 | 1 | 3 | 1 | 6.10 | 1.00 | 55–64 |
| 65 and over | ........ | ........ | ........ | ........ | 1 | ........ | 1 | ........ | 1.00 | 65 and over |
| Not reported | ........ | ........ | ........ | ........ | ........ | ........ | ........ | ........ | ........ | Not reported |
| Total | 8 | 84 | 12 | 29 | 18 | 49 | 102 | 100.00 | 100.00 | Total |

NEW YORK STATE

THE MEN'S SHIRT INDUSTRY

85. TABLE XVIII, B NUMBER OF EMPLOYEES IN EACH DEPARTMENT ACCORDING TO ACTUAL WEEKLY EARNINGS BY SEX

| Actual Weekly Earnings in Dollars | Department | | | | | | | | | | | | Actual Weekly Earnings in Dollars |
|---|---|---|---|---|---|---|---|---|---|---|---|---|---|
| | Factory | | Office | | Shipping | | Plant | | Total | | Cumulative per cent. of total | | |
| | Male | Female | Male | Female | Male | Female | Male | Female | Male | Female | Male | Female | |
| Less than $3 00 | 66 | 538 | 1 | 2 | 1 | ....... | 2 | ....... | 70 | 540 | 1.94 | 5.8 | Less than $3 00 |
| $3 00– 3 49 | 29 | 361 | 2 | ....... | ....... | ....... | ....... | ....... | 31 | 361 | 2.80 | 9.6 | $3 00– 3 49 |
| 3 50– 3 99 | 54 | 382 | 1 | ....... | 1 | ....... | 3 | 2 | 59 | 384 | 4.40 | 13.8 | 3 50– 3 99 |
| 4 00– 4 49 | 63 | 523 | 3 | 4 | ....... | ....... | 3 | 1 | 69 | 528 | 6.30 | 19.4 | 4 00– 4 49 |
| 4 50– 4 99 | 56 | 533 | 2 | 1 | 4 | ....... | 1 | ....... | 63 | 534 | 8.10 | 25.2 | 4 50– 4 99 |
| 5 00– 5 49 | 118 | 710 | 4 | 8 | 5 | 2 | 12 | ....... | 139 | 720 | 11.90 | 32.8 | 5 00– 5 49 |
| 5 50– 5 99 | 67 | 593 | 2 | 5 | 2 | 5 | 3 | 1 | 74 | 604 | 14.00 | 39.3 | 5 50– 5 99 |
| 6 00– 6 49 | 153 | 727 | 10 | 21 | 22 | 4 | 6 | 6 | 191 | 758 | 19.30 | 47.3 | 6 00– 6 49 |
| 6 50– 6 99 | 82 | 511 | 3 | 3 | 7 | 2 | 6 | 2 | 98 | 518 | 22.00 | 53.0 | 6 50– 6 99 |
| 7 00– 7 49 | 105 | 645 | 12 | 24 | 29 | 3 | 10 | 5 | 156 | 677 | 26.30 | 60.3 | 7 00– 7 49 |
| 7 50– 7 99 | 97 | 485 | 2 | 2 | 7 | ....... | 3 | 3 | 109 | 490 | 29.30 | 65.7 | 7 50– 7 99 |
| 8 00– 8 99 | 257 | 905 | 15 | 40 | 28 | 2 | 9 | 4 | 309 | 951 | 37.90 | 75.7 | 8 00– 8 99 |
| 9 00– 9 99 | 181 | 654 | 15 | 20 | 30 | ....... | 25 | 3 | 251 | 677 | 45.00 | 83.0 | 9 00– 9 99 |
| 10 00–10 99 | 170 | 510 | 22 | 38 | 35 | 2 | 25 | ....... | 252 | 550 | 51.80 | 88.8 | 10 00–10 99 |
| 11 00–11 99 | 176 | 283 | 6 | 18 | 24 | ....... | 14 | ....... | 220 | 301 | 58.00 | 92.0 | 11 00–11 99 |
| 12 00–12 99 | 203 | 254 | 21 | 18 | 19 | ....... | 22 | 1 | 265 | 273 | 65.00 | 95.3 | 12 00–12 99 |
| 13 00–13 99 | 174 | 162 | 7 | 8 | 13 | ....... | 18 | ....... | 212 | 170 | 71.20 | 96.8 | 13 00–13 99 |
| 14 00–14 99 | 146 | 110 | 6 | 3 | 13 | ....... | 25 | ....... | 190 | 113 | 76.50 | 98.0 | 14 00–14 99 |
| 15 00–15 99 | 140 | 80 | 5 | 9 | 13 | ....... | 25 | ....... | 183 | 89 | 81.50 | 99.0 | 15 00–15 99 |
| 16 00–17 99 | 182 | 51 | 16 | 8 | 18 | ....... | 23 | ....... | 239 | 59 | 88.00 | 99.5 | 16 00–17 99 |
| 18 00–19 99 | 132 | 21 | 6 | 3 | 11 | ....... | 26 | ....... | 175 | 24 | 92.70 | 99.8 | 18 00–19 99 |
| 20 00–24 99 | 182 | 8 | 16 | 2 | 7 | ....... | 15 | ....... | 170 | 10 | 98.00 | 99.9 | 20 00–24 99 |
| 25 00–29 99 | 30 | 1 | 7 | ....... | 4 | ....... | 14 | 1 | 55 | 2 | 99.00 | 100.0 | 25 00–29 99 |
| 30 00–34 99 | 15 | ....... | 6 | ....... | ....... | ....... | 3 | ....... | 24 | ....... | 99.70 | ....... | 30 00–34 99 |
| 35 00–39 99 | 2 | ....... | 3 | ....... | ....... | ....... | 2 | ....... | 7 | ....... | 99.90 | ....... | 35 00–39 99 |
| 40 00 and over | 4 | ....... | 2 | ....... | ....... | ....... | ....... | ....... | 6 | ....... | 100.00 | ....... | 40 00 and over |
| Not reported | 10 | 91 | ....... | ....... | 2 | ....... | 2 | ....... | 14 | 91 | ....... | ....... | Not reported |
| Total | 2,844 | 9,138 | 195 | 237 | 295 | 20 | 297 | 29 | 3,631 | 9,424 | ....... | ....... | Total |

86. TABLE I, B

NEW YORK STATE
THE MEN'S SHIRT INDUSTRY
Number of Employees According to Age Groups, by Locality and Sex

| | Locality | Sex | Age Groups in Years | | | | | | | | | | | | |
|---|---|---|---|---|---|---|---|---|---|---|---|---|---|---|---|
| | | | Total | 14–15 | 16–17 | 18–20 | 21–24 | 25–29 | 30–34 | 35–39 | 40–44 | 45–54 | 55–64 | 65 and over | Not reported |
| Factory workers | New York city... | Male..... | 1,941 | 23 | 138 | 345 | 343 | 342 | 228 | 209 | 132 | 139 | 31 | 5 | 6 |
| | | Female... | 4,776 | 256 | 1,138 | 1,884 | 840 | 307 | 126 | 105 | 45 | 58 | 8 | ....... | 14 |
| | Troy........... | Male..... | 497 | 2 | 17 | 23 | 73 | 84 | 91 | 85 | 54 | 52 | 10 | 2 | 4 |
| | | Female... | 1,454 | 5 | 85 | 224 | 272 | 240 | 190 | 184 | 116 | 100 | 15 | 4 | 19 |
| | Albany.......... | Male..... | 22 | 2 | 2 | 5 | 5 | 4 | ....... | 1 | 2 | 1 | ....... | ....... | ....... |
| | | Female... | 953 | 8 | 84 | 223 | 253 | 171 | 94 | 60 | 30 | 16 | 8 | ....... | 6 |
| | Buffalo.......... | Male..... | 12 | ....... | 1 | 5 | 1 | 2 | ....... | 1 | ....... | 2 | ....... | ....... | ....... |
| | | Female... | 179 | 1 | 41 | 48 | 30 | 28 | 14 | 14 | 3 | 4 | 1 | ....... | ....... |
| | Other cities and towns......... | Male..... | 372 | 1 | 22 | 36 | 49 | 83 | 52 | 54 | 40 | 26 | 7 | 1 | 1 |
| | | Female... | 1,776 | 22 | 137 | 299 | 339 | 275 | 169 | 184 | 118 | 146 | 50 | 13 | 24 |
| Office, shipping and plant | All localities..... | Male..... | 787 | 14 | 75 | 131 | 146 | 103 | 67 | 71 | 51 | 81 | 31 | 13 | 4 |
| | | Female... | 286 | 6 | 30 | 95 | 74 | 35 | 12 | 6 | 8 | 8 | 7 | 5 | ....... |
| All workers | State........... | Male..... | 3,631 | 42 | 255 | 545 | 617 | 618 | 438 | 421 | 279 | 301 | 79 | 21 | 15 |
| | | Female... | 9,424 | 298 | 1,510 | 2,773 | 1,808 | 1,051 | 605 | 553 | 320 | 332 | 89 | 22 | 63 |
| | Cumulative per cent for state... | Male..... | 100 | 1.16 | 8.21 | 23.28 | 40.34 | 57.43 | 69.54 | 81.18 | 88.90 | 97.23 | 99.42 | 100 | ....... |
| | | Female... | 100 | 3.18 | 19.31 | 48.93 | 68.25 | 79.48 | 85.94 | 91.85 | 95.27 | 98.82 | 99.77 | 100 | ....... |

87. TABLE II, B

NEW YORK STATE

**THE MEN'S SHIRT INDUSTRY**

NUMBER AND PER CENT. OF ALL EMPLOYEES ACCORDING TO NATIVITY, BY LOCALITY

| | Locality | Distribution of foreign and native born | | | | | | | Distribution of foreign born, according to country of birth | | | | | | | | | | | |
|---|---|---|---|---|---|---|---|---|---|---|---|---|---|---|---|---|---|---|---|---|
| | | Total | | Not given | Native | | Foreign | | Russia | | Italy | | Austria | | Ireland | | England | | Germany | |
| | | Number | Per cent | Number | Number | Per cent | Number | Per cent | Number | Per cent | Number | Per cent | Number | Per cent | Number | Per cent | Number | Per cent | Number | Per cent |
| Factory workers | New York city | 6,717 | 100.00 | 26 | 1,582 | 23.64 | 5,109 | 76.36 | 2,524 | 49.4 | 1,844 | 36.1 | 334 | 6.5 | 20 | .4 | 37 | .7 | 50 | 1.0 |
| | Troy | 1,951 | 100.00 | 23 | 1,378 | 71.48 | 550 | 28.52 | 74 | 13.5 | 27 | 4.9 | 104 | 18.9 | 89 | 16.2 | 43 | 7.8 | 36 | 6.6 |
| | Albany | 975 | 100.00 | 6 | 848 | 87.51 | 121 | 12.49 | 51 | 42.1 | 19 | 15.7 | ...... | ...... | 6 | 5.0 | 3 | 2.5 | 9 | 7.4 |
| | Buffalo | 191 | 100.00 | 1 | 159 | 83.69 | 31 | 16.31 | 5 | 16.1 | 10 | 32.2 | 2 | 6.5 | ...... | ...... | 2 | 6.5 | 6 | 19.3 |
| | Other cities and towns | 2,148 | 100.00 | 11 | 1,913 | 89.51 | 224 | 10.49 | 28 | 12.5 | 38 | 17.0 | 7 | 3.1 | 72 | 32.2 | 17 | 7.6 | 9 | 4.0 |
| Office, shipping and plant | All localities | 1,073 | 100.00 | 9 | 766 | 71.99 | 298 | 28.01 | 127 | 42.6 | 33 | 11.1 | 39 | 13.1 | 23 | 7.7 | 22 | 7.4 | 19 | 6.4 |
| All workers | State | 13,055 | 100.00 | 76 | 6,646 | 51.20 | 6,333 | 48.80 | 2,809 | 44.37 | 1,971 | 31.13 | 486 | 7.68 | 210 | 3.32 | 124 | 1.91 | 129 | 2.04 |

87. TABLE II, B — (*concluded*)

NEW YORK STATE

THE MEN'S SHIRT INDUSTRY

NUMBER AND PER CENT OF ALL EMPLOYEES ACCORDING TO NATIVITY, BY LOCALITY

| | Locality | Distribution of Foreign Born According to Country of Birth — (*concluded*) | | | | | | | | | | | | | | | | | |
|---|---|---|---|---|---|---|---|---|---|---|---|---|---|---|---|---|---|---|---|
| | | Hungary | | Poland | | Canada | | Turkey | | Roumania | | Scotland | | Armenia | | Denmark | | All other | |
| | | Number | Per cent. | Number | Per cent. | Number | Per cent. | Number | Per cent. | Number | Per cent. | Number | Per cent. | Number | Per cent. | Number | Per cent. | Number | Per cent. |
| Factory workers | New York City | 102 | 2.0 | 59 | 1.2 | ..... | ..... | ..... | ..... | 43 | .8 | ..... | ..... | ..... | ..... | ..... | ..... | 96 | 1.9 |
| | Troy | ..... | ..... | 18 | 3.3 | 49 | 3.9 | 65 | 11.8 | ..... | ..... | 10 | 1.8 | 9 | 1.6 | 10 | 1.8 | 16 | 2.9 |
| | Albany | ..... | ..... | 15 | 12.4 | 6 | 5.0 | ..... | ..... | ..... | ..... | ..... | ..... | ..... | ..... | ..... | ..... | 12 | 9.9 |
| | Buffalo | ..... | ..... | ..... | ..... | 2 | 5.5 | ..... | ..... | ..... | ..... | ..... | ..... | ..... | ..... | ..... | ..... | 4 | 12.9 |
| | Other cities and towns | ..... | ..... | 3 | 1.3 | 26 | 11.6 | 4 | 1.8 | ..... | ..... | 5 | 2.2 | 6 | 2.7 | ..... | ..... | 9 | 4.0 |
| Office, shipping and plant | All localities | 5 | 1.7 | ..... | ..... | 4 | 1.3 | ..... | ..... | 10 | 3.3 | 5 | 1.7 | ..... | ..... | ..... | ..... | 11 | 3.7 |
| All workers | State | 107 | 1.69 | 95 | 1.50 | 87 | 1.37 | 69 | 1.09 | 53 | .84 | 20 | .32 | 15 | .24 | 10 | .16 | 148 | 2.34 |

88. TABLE III, B

NEW YORK STATE
THE MEN'S SHIRT INDUSTRY
NUMBER OF EMPLOYEES EARNING SPECIFIED WEEKLY RATES BY LOCALITY AND SEX

| Weekly Rates in Dollars | Factory Workers | | | | | | | | | | Offices Plant and Shipping | | All Workers | | | | Weekly Rates in Dollars |
|---|---|---|---|---|---|---|---|---|---|---|---|---|---|---|---|---|---|
| | New York City | | Troy | | Albany | | Buffalo | | Other Cities and Towns | | All Localities | | State | | Cumulative Per Cent. for State | | |
| | Male | Female | Male | Female | Male | Female | Male | Female | Male | Female | Male | Female | Male | Female | Male | Female | |
| Less than $3 00 | 1 | 6 | ...... | ..... | .... | .... | .... | .... | .... | .... | 1 | .... | 2 | 6 | .10 | .10 | Less than $3 00 |
| $3 00–$3 49... | 6 | 108 | ...... | ..... | .... | .... | .... | .... | .... | 4 | 1 | .... | 7 | 107 | .45 | 3.50 | ...$3 00– 3 49 |
| 3 50– 3 99... | 8 | 125 | ...... | ..... | .... | .... | .... | .... | 3 | 7 | 3 | 1 | 14 | 183 | 1.25 | 7.70 | ... 3 50– 3 99 |
| 4 00– 4 49... | 24 | 206 | 1 | 4 | .... | 11 | .... | 17 | 3 | 15 | 4 | 2 | 32 | 255 | 2.75 | 15.60 | ... 4 00– 4 49 |
| 4 50– 4 99... | 18 | 162 | 1 | 1 | 1 | 12 | .... | 2 | 3 | 9 | 7 | 3 | 25 | 189 | 4.00 | 21.50 | ... 4 50– 4 99 |
| 5 00– 5 49... | 46 | 238 | 8 | 13 | .... | 26 | .... | 12 | 9 | 17 | 19 | 9 | 82 | 315 | 8.15 | 31.20 | ... 5 00– 5 49 |
| 5 50– 5 99... | 17 | 151 | 1 | 18 | .... | 2 | 1 | 3 | 5 | 16 | 5 | 6 | 29 | 196 | 9.60 | 37.40 | ... 5 50– 5 99 |
| 6 00– 6 49... | 63 | 259 | 4 | 27 | 1 | 35 | 4 | 3 | 4 | 68 | 35 | 36 | 111 | 428 | 15.20 | 50.60 | ... 6 00– 6 49 |
| 6 50– 6 99... | 10 | 127 | ...... | 2 | .... | 6 | .... | 2 | 2 | 12 | 12 | 4 | 33 | 153 | 16.80 | 55.50 | ... 6 50– 6 99 |
| 7 00– 7 49... | 66 | 182 | 3 | 43 | 1 | 18 | .... | 2 | 9 | 25 | 55 | 34 | 134 | 304 | 23.50 | 65.00 | ... 7 00– 7 49 |
| 7 50– 7 99... | 18 | 110 | 6 | 2 | .... | 2 | 1 | 3 | .... | 14 | 10 | 6 | 35 | 137 | 25.30 | 69.00 | ... 7 50– 7 99 |
| 8 00– 8 99... | 98 | 223 | 6 | 35 | .... | 8 | .... | 1 | 8 | 26 | 45 | 45 | 157 | 338 | 33.20 | 80.00 | ... 8 00– 8 99 |
| 9 00– 9 99... | 66 | 172 | 8 | 37 | 2 | 13 | 1 | 1 | 6 | 36 | 83 | 24 | 166 | 283 | 41.50 | 88.50 | ... 9 00– 9 99 |
| 10 00–10 99... | 48 | 87 | 9 | 13 | 1 | 18 | .... | .... | 10 | 6 | 86 | 41 | 149 | 160 | 49.00 | 93.50 | ...10 00–10 99 |
| 11 00–11 99... | 48 | 26 | 5 | 7 | .... | 3 | .... | 1 | 7 | 2 | 45 | 17 | 100 | 56 | 54.00 | 95.50 | ...11 00–11 99 |
| 12 00–12 99... | 68 | 31 | 12 | 15 | 1 | 1 | .... | .... | 6 | 6 | 74 | 18 | 156 | 71 | 62.00 | 97.50 | ...12 00–12 99 |
| 13 00–13 99... | 58 | 9 | 5 | 4 | 1 | 3 | 1 | .... | 5 | 1 | 29 | 9 | 99 | 26 | 67.00 | 98.00 | ...13 00–13 99 |
| 14 00–14 99... | 43 | 6 | 9 | ..... | .... | 1 | 1 | .... | 4 | 1 | 36 | 4 | 93 | 12 | 71.50 | 98.60 | ...14 00–14 99 |
| 15 00–15 99... | 42 | 2 | 26 | 2 | 2 | 2 | .... | 2 | 18 | 3 | 49 | 8 | 137 | 19 | 78.50 | 99.40 | ...15 00–15 99 |
| 16 00–17 99... | 52 | 3 | 13 | 1 | 1 | .... | 1 | .... | 13 | .... | 49 | 8 | 129 | 12 | 85.00 | 99.60 | ...16 00–17 99 |
| 18 00–19 99... | 50 | ...... | 10 | 1 | .... | 1 | .... | .... | 7 | 2 | 40 | 3 | 107 | 7 | 90.00 | 99.80 | ...18 00–19 99 |
| 20 00–24 99... | 55 | 1 | 7 | ..... | 1 | .... | .... | .... | 10 | 2 | 36 | 2 | 109 | 5 | 95.50 | 99.90 | ...20 00–24 99 |
| 25 00–29 99... | 16 | ...... | 3 | ..... | .... | .... | 2 | .... | 4 | .... | 24 | 1 | 49 | 1 | 98.00 | 100.00 | ...25 00–29 99 |
| 30 00–34 99... | 8 | ...... | 1 | ..... | 1 | .... | .... | .... | 2 | .... | 9 | .... | 21 | .... | 99.00 | ...... | ...30 00–34 99 |
| 35 00–39 99... | 2 | ...... | ...... | ..... | .... | .... | .... | .... | 1 | .... | 5 | .... | 8 | .... | 99.60 | ...... | ..35 00–39 99 |
| 40 00 and over. | 3 | ...... | ...... | ..... | .... | .... | .... | .... | .... | .... | 2 | .... | 5 | .... | 100.00 | ...... | .40 00 and over |
| Not reported... | 5 | 5 | 3 | 268 | .... | 1 | .... | .... | 1 | 28 | 21 | 4 | 30 | 306 | ...... | ...... | ...Not reported |
| Total..... | 928 | 2,234 | 141 | 493 | 13 | 158 | 12 | 49 | 140 | 300 | 785 | 285 | 2,019 | 3,519 | ...... | ...... | .....Total |

NEW YORK STATE
THE MEN'S SHIRT INDUSTRY

89. TABLE IV, B — Number of Employees According to Actual Weekly Earnings by Locality and Sex

| Actual Weekly Earnings in Dollars | Factory Workers | | | | | | | | | | Office, Plant and Shipping | | All Workers | | | | Actual Weekly Earnings in Dollars |
|---|---|---|---|---|---|---|---|---|---|---|---|---|---|---|---|---|---|
| | New York City | | Troy | | Albany | | Buffalo | | Other Cities and Towns | | All Localities | | State | | Cumulative per cent. for State | | |
| | Male | Female | Male | Female | Male | Female | Male | Female | Male | Female | Male | Female | Male | Female | Male | Female | |
| Less than $3 00 | 52 | 263 | 8 | 54 | 1 | 56 | .... | 4 | 5 | 161 | 4 | 2 | 70 | 540 | 1.94 | 5.8 | Less than $3 00 |
| $3 00–$3 49... | 26 | 226 | 2 | 23 | .... | 29 | .... | 2 | 1 | 81 | 2 | ..... | 31 | 361 | 2.80 | 9.6 | ...$3 00– 3 49 |
| 3 50– 3 99... | 29 | 228 | 19 | 19 | 1 | 28 | .... | 19 | 5 | 88 | 5 | 2 | 59 | 584 | 4.40 | 15.8 | ... 3 50– 3 99 |
| 4 00– 4 49... | 43 | 312 | 14 | 39 | .... | 53 | .... | 12 | 6 | 107 | 6 | 5 | 69 | 528 | 6.30 | 19.4 | ... 4 00– 4 49 |
| 4 50– 4 99... | 35 | 306 | 15 | 38 | 1 | 64 | .... | 6 | 5 | 119 | 7 | 1 | 63 | 534 | 8.10 | 25.2 | ... 4 50– 4 99 |
| 5 00– 5 49... | 64 | 400 | 39 | 62 | 2 | 79 | 1 | 23 | 12 | 146 | 21 | 10 | 139 | 720 | 11.90 | 32.8 | ... 5 00– 5 49 |
| 5 50– 5 99... | 46 | 289 | 9 | 94 | .... | 64 | 1 | 15 | 11 | 131 | 7 | 11 | 74 | 604 | 14.00 | 39.3 | ... 5 50– 5 99 |
| 6 00– 6 49... | 103 | 396 | 30 | 87 | 3 | 103 | 8 | 7 | 14 | 134 | 38 | 31 | 191 | 758 | 19.30 | 47.3 | ... 6 00– 6 49 |
| 6 50– 6 99... | 60 | 304 | 16 | 56 | .... | 61 | .... | 19 | 6 | 71 | 16 | 7 | 98 | 518 | 22.00 | 53.0 | ... 6 50– 6 99 |
| 7 00– 7 49... | 82 | 355 | 14 | 87 | 2 | 73 | .... | 9 | 7 | 121 | 51 | 32 | 156 | 677 | 26.30 | 60.3 | ... 7 00– 7 49 |
| 7 50– 7 99... | 65 | 263 | 26 | 72 | .... | 48 | 1 | 13 | 5 | 89 | 12 | 5 | 109 | 490 | 29.30 | 65.7 | ... 7 50– 7 99 |
| 8 00– 8 99... | 166 | 482 | 75 | 163 | .... | 91 | .... | 12 | 16 | 157 | 52 | 46 | 309 | 951 | 37.90 | 75.7 | ... 8 00– 8 99 |
| 9 00– 9 99... | 152 | 316 | 15 | 141 | 1 | 69 | 1 | 15 | 12 | 113 | 70 | 23 | 251 | 677 | 45.00 | 83.0 | ... 9 00– 9 99 |
| 10 00–10 99... | 121 | 234 | 31 | 124 | 1 | 62 | .... | 5 | 17 | 85 | 82 | 40 | 252 | 550 | 51.80 | 88.8 | ...10 00–10 99 |
| 11 00–11 99... | 120 | 92 | 30 | 101 | 2 | 25 | .... | 9 | 24 | 56 | 44 | 18 | 220 | 301 | 58.00 | 92.0 | ...11 00–11 99 |
| 12 00–12 99... | 135 | 98 | 39 | 89 | .... | 21 | .... | 2 | 29 | 44 | 62 | 19 | 265 | 273 | 65.00 | 95.3 | ...12 00–12 99 |
| 13 00–13 99... | 114 | 46 | 24 | 79 | 2 | 11 | 1 | 5 | 33 | 21 | 38 | 8 | 212 | 170 | 71.20 | 96.8 | ...13 00–13 99 |
| 14 00–14 99... | 95 | 27 | 20 | 55 | 1 | 12 | .... | ..... | 30 | 16 | 44 | 3 | 190 | 113 | 76.50 | 98.0 | ...14 00–14 99 |
| 15 00–15 99... | 79 | 22 | 23 | 40 | 2 | 3 | 1 | 2 | 35 | 13 | 43 | 9 | 183 | 89 | 81.50 | 99.0 | ...15 00–15 99 |
| 16 00–17 99... | 131 | 14 | 11 | 26 | 1 | ..... | 1 | ..... | 38 | 11 | 57 | 8 | 239 | 59 | 88.00 | 99.5 | ...16 00–17 99 |
| 18 00–19 99... | 88 | 8 | 13 | 4 | .... | 1 | .... | ..... | 31 | 8 | 43 | 3 | 175 | 24 | 92.70 | 99.8 | ...18 00–19 99 |
| 20 00–24 99... | 92 | 4 | 17 | 1 | 1 | ..... | .... | ..... | 22 | 3 | 38 | 2 | 170 | 10 | 98.00 | 99.9 | ...20 00–24 99 |
| 25 00–29 99... | 18 | 1 | 5 | ..... | .... | ..... | 2 | ..... | 5 | ..... | 25 | 1 | 55 | 2 | 99.00 | 100.0 | ...25 00–29 99 |
| 30 00–34 99... | 11 | ..... | 1 | ..... | 1 | ..... | .... | ..... | 2 | ..... | 9 | ..... | 24 | ..... | 99.70 | ..... | ...30 00–34 99 |
| 35 00–39 99... | 1 | ..... | .... | ..... | .... | ..... | .... | ..... | 1 | ..... | 5 | ..... | 7 | ..... | 99.90 | ..... | ...35 00–39 99 |
| 40 00 and over. | 4 | ..... | .... | ..... | .... | ..... | .... | ..... | .... | ..... | 2 | ..... | 6 | ..... | 100.00 | ..... | .40 00 and over |
| Not reported... | 9 | 90 | 1 | ..... | .... | ..... | .... | ..... | .... | 1 | 4 | ..... | 14 | 91 | ..... | ..... | ...Not reported |
| Total..... | 1,941 | 4,776 | 497 | 1,454 | 22 | 953 | 12 | 179 | 372 | 1,776 | 787 | 286 | 3,631 | 9,424 | ..... | ..... | .....Total |

NEW YORK STATE

**THE MEN'S SHIRT INDUSTRY — FACTORY WORKERS**

90. TABLE VII, B, a — NUMBER AND PER CENT. OF ALL EMPLOYEES BY SEX ACCORDING TO OCCUPATION AND NATIVITY

| NATIVITY | OCCUPATION | | | | | | | | | | | | | | NATIVITY |
|---|---|---|---|---|---|---|---|---|---|---|---|---|---|---|---|
| | TOTAL | | MARKERS | | CUTTERS | | TRIMMERS | | CUTTERS | | FOREMEN AND FOREWOMEN | | OPERATORS | | |
| | Male | Female | Male | Female | Male | Female | Male | Female | Male | Female | Male | Female | Male | Female | |
| Native......... | 855 | 5,025 | 15 | ..... | 210 | 1 | 25 | 4 | 73 | 38 | 73 | 118 | 39 | 3,290 | .........Native |
| Foreign........ | 1,973 | 4,063 | 27 | 1 | 126 | ...... | 22 | ...... | 125 | 2 | 72 | 30 | 750 | 2,956 | ........Foreign |
| Not reported.... | 16 | 50 | .... | ..... | 4 | ...... | 1 | ...... | 1 | ...... | 1 | 1 | 4 | 26 | ....Not reported |
| Total...... | 2,844 | 9,138 | 42 | 1 | 340 | 1 | 48 | 4 | 199 | 40 | 146 | 149 | 793 | 6,272 | ......Total |
| Per cent. of total | 100.0 | 100.0 | 1.5 | .01 | 12.0 | .01 | 1.7 | .04 | 7.0 | .44 | 5.15 | 1.6 | 27.9 | 68.8 | Per cent. of total |

90. TABLE VII, B, a — (*concluded*)

NEW YORK STATE

**THE MEN'S SHIRT INDUSTRY — FACTORY WORKERS**

NUMBER AND PER CENT. OF ALL EMPLOYEES BY SEX ACCORDING TO OCCUPATION AND NATIVITY

| NATIVITY | OCCUPATION | | | | | | | | | | | | | | | | NATIVITY |
|---|---|---|---|---|---|---|---|---|---|---|---|---|---|---|---|---|---|
| | FLOOR WORK | | LAUNDRY HELPERS | | STARCHERS AND DAMPNERS | | IRONERS AND PRESSERS | | EXAMINERS | | FOLDERS | | PACKERS | | NOT REPORTED | | |
| | Male | Female | Male | Female | Male | Female | Male | Female | Male | Female | Male | Female | Male | Female | Male | Female | |
| Native | 26 | 388 | 35 | 35 | 4 | 135 | 290 | 248 | 28 | 543 | 16 | 101 | 21 | 118 | ..... | 6 | Native |
| Foreign | 50 | 382 | 18 | 24 | 4 | 89 | 694 | 284 | 9 | 103 | 30 | 140 | 41 | 36 | 5 | 16 | Foreign |
| Not reported | 1 | 9 | .... | 1 | .... | 2 | 4 | 2 | ... | 4 | .... | 4 | .... | 1 | ..... | ..... | Not reported |
| Total | 77 | 779 | 53 | 60 | 8 | 226 | 988 | 534 | 37 | 650 | 46 | 245 | 62 | 155 | 5 | 22 | Total |
| Per cent. of total | 2.7 | 8.6 | 1.87 | .65 | .28 | 2.5 | 34.8 | 5.85 | 1.3 | 7.1 | 1.6 | 2.7 | 2.2 | 1.7 | ..... | ..... | Per cent. of total |

NEW YORK STATE

**THE MEN'S SHIRT INDUSTRY — FACTORY WORKERS**

91. TABLE V, B, a — NUMBER AND PER CENT OF EMPLOYEES EARNING SPECIFIED WEEKLY RATES BY AGE GROUPS AND SEX

| WEEKLY RATES IN DOLLARS | AGE GROUPS IN YEARS | | | | | | | | | | | | | | WEEKLY RATES IN DOLLARS |
|---|---|---|---|---|---|---|---|---|---|---|---|---|---|---|---|
| | 14–15 | | 16–17 | | 18–20 | | 21–24 | | 25–29 | | 30–34 | | 35–39 | | |
| | Male | Female | Male | Female | Male | Female | Male | Female | Male | Female | Male | Female | Male | Female | |
| Less than $3 00 | 1 | 4 | .... | ...... | ...... | 2 | ...... | ...... | ...... | ...... | ...... | ...... | ...... | ...... | Less than $3 00 |
| $3 00–$3 49... | 4 | 53 | 2 | 35 | ...... | 9 | ...... | 4 | ...... | 2 | ...... | 1 | ...... | 2 | ...$3 00–$3 49 |
| 3 50– 3 99... | 3 | 50 | 6 | 48 | 2 | 21 | ...... | 2 | ...... | 4 | ...... | 2 | ...... | 3 | ... 3 50– 3 99 |
| 4 00– 4 49... | 3 | 39 | 13 | 119 | 7 | 56 | 2 | 20 | 2 | 6 | ...... | 2 | ...... | 3 | ... 4 00– 4 49 |
| 4 50– 4 99... | 3 | 28 | 11 | 86 | 3 | 39 | 1 | 11 | ...... | 9 | ...... | 3 | ...... | 2 | ... 4 50– 4 99 |
| 5 00– 5 49... | 5 | 12 | 37 | 144 | 15 | 98 | 6 | 23 | ...... | 11 | ...... | 6 | ...... | 4 | ... 5 00– 5 49 |
| 5 50– 5 99... | 2 | 10 | 9 | 79 | 9 | 51 | 2 | 20 | ...... | 15 | 1 | 2 | ...... | 6 | ... 5 50– 5 99 |
| 6 00– 6 49... | 2 | 8 | 26 | 105 | 82 | 144 | 7 | 59 | 4 | 27 | 3 | 8 | ...... | 13 | ... 6 00– 6 49 |
| 6 50– 6 99... | .... | 2 | 7 | 28 | 9 | 72 | 2 | 24 | 1 | 13 | ...... | 2 | 1 | 3 | ... 6 50– 6 99 |
| 7 00– 7 49... | .... | 2 | 17 | 45 | 42 | 114 | 10 | 51 | 3 | 24 | 2 | 10 | 1 | 7 | ... 7 00– 7 49 |
| 7 50– 7 99... | .... | ...... | 3 | 26 | 7 | 55 | 7 | 26 | 4 | 6 | 1 | 3 | ...... | 6 | ... 7 50– 7 99 |
| 8 00– 8 99... | .... | 1 | 13 | 85 | 51 | 114 | 19 | 67 | 9 | 30 | 3 | 13 | 5 | 18 | ... 8 00– 8 99 |
| 9 00– 9 99... | .... | ...... | 7 | 11 | 30 | 78 | 14 | 79 | 6 | 36 | 2 | 18 | 6 | 14 | ... 9 00– 9 99 |
| 10 00–10 99... | .... | ...... | 1 | 6 | 18 | 31 | 13 | 43 | 9 | 12 | 5 | 12 | 5 | 7 | ...10 00–10 99 |
| 11 00–11 99... | .... | ...... | .... | 1 | 10 | 12 | 11 | 11 | 13 | 7 | 8 | 4 | 2 | 2 | ...10 00–11 99 |
| 12 00–12 99... | .... | ...... | .... | 1 | 7 | 7 | 24 | 12 | 18 | 11 | 9 | 11 | 10 | 5 | ...12 00–12 99 |
| 13 00–13 99... | .... | ...... | .... | 1 | 8 | 8 | 16 | 4 | 17 | 4 | 8 | 1 | 8 | 3 | ...13 00–13 99 |
| 14 00–14 99... | .... | ...... | .... | 1 | 5 | 1 | 15 | ...... | 24 | 2 | 4 | ...... | 4 | 2 | ...14 00–14 99 |
| 15 00–15 99... | .... | ...... | .... | ...... | 3 | ...... | 17 | ...... | 16 | 2 | 14 | 4 | 20 | 1 | ...15 00–15 99 |
| 16 00–17 99... | .... | ...... | .... | ...... | 1 | ...... | 12 | ...... | 19 | 2 | 20 | ...... | 8 | 2 | ...16 00–17 99 |
| 18 00–19 99... | .... | ...... | .... | ...... | 1 | ...... | 11 | ...... | 16 | 1 | 14 | ...... | 16 | ...... | ...18 00–19 99 |
| 20 00–24 99... | .... | ...... | .... | ...... | ...... | ...... | 4 | ...... | 16 | ...... | 14 | 2 | 19 | 1 | ...20 00–24 99 |
| 25 00–29 99... | .... | ...... | .... | ...... | ...... | ...... | ...... | ...... | 4 | ...... | 4 | ...... | 12 | ...... | ...25 00–29 99 |
| 30 00–34 99... | .... | ...... | .... | ...... | ...... | ...... | ...... | ...... | ...... | ...... | 3 | ...... | 3 | ...... | ...30 00–34 99 |
| 35 00–39 99... | .... | ...... | .... | ...... | ...... | ...... | ...... | ...... | ...... | ...... | ...... | ...... | 1 | ...... | ...35 00–39 99 |
| 40 00 and over. | .... | ...... | .... | ...... | ...... | ...... | ...... | ...... | ...... | ...... | ...... | ...... | 1 | ...... | 40 00 and over |
| Not reported... | .... | 1 | 1 | 17 | 2 | 56 | 3 | 63 | ...... | 45 | 2 | 43 | 1 | 26 | ...Not reported |
| Total..... | 23 | 210 | 153 | 788 | 262 | 963 | 196 | 520 | 181 | 269 | 117 | 147 | 123 | 130 | .....Total |

91. TABLE V, B, a — *(concluded)*

NEW YORK STATE

**THE MEN'S SHIRT INDUSTRY — FACTORY WORKERS**

NUMBER AND PER CENT. OF EMPLOYEES EARNING SPECIFIED WEEKLY RATES BY AGE GROUPS AND SEX

| Weekly Rates in Dollars | Age Groups in Years | | | | | | | | | | | | | | | | Weekly Rates in Dollars |
|---|---|---|---|---|---|---|---|---|---|---|---|---|---|---|---|---|---|
| | 40–44 | | 45–54 | | 55–64 | | 65 and over | | Not reported | | Total | | Cumulative per cent. of total | | | | |
| | Male | Female | Male | Female | Male | Female | Male | Female | Male | Female | Male | Female | Male | Female | | | |
| Less than $3 00 | | | | | | | | | | | 1 | 6 | .08 | .20 | | | Less than $3 00 |
| $3 00–$3 49 | | 1 | | | | | | | | | 6 | 107 | .57 | 3.85 | | | $3 00– 3 49 |
| 3 50– 3 99 | | | | 1 | | | | | | 1 | 11 | 132 | 1.47 | 8.36 | | | 3 50– 3 99 |
| 4 00– 4 49 | | 2 | | 5 | 1 | 1 | | | | | 28 | 253 | 3.76 | 16.95 | | | 4 00– 4 49 |
| 4 50– 4 99 | | 3 | | 3 | | 1 | | | | 1 | 18 | 186 | 5.23 | 23.40 | | | 4 50– 4 99 |
| 5 00– 5 49 | | 4 | | 2 | | 1 | | | | 1 | 63 | 306 | 10.36 | 33.80 | | | 5 00– 5 49 |
| 5 50– 5 99 | | 2 | 1 | 4 | | | | | | 1 | 24 | 190 | 12.34 | 40.30 | | | 5 50– 5 99 |
| 6 00– 6 49 | | 3 | 1 | 15 | 1 | 8 | | | | 2 | 76 | 392 | 18.65 | 53.70 | | | 6 00– 6 49 |
| 6 50– 6 99 | 1 | 1 | | 2 | | 2 | | | | | 21 | 149 | 20.21 | 58.80 | | | 6 50– 6 99 |
| 7 00– 7 49 | | 8 | 3 | 7 | 1 | 2 | | | | | 79 | 270 | 26.65 | 68.00 | | | 7 00– 7 49 |
| 7 50– 7 99 | 1 | 1 | 1 | 6 | 1 | | | | | 2 | 25 | 131 | 28.78 | 72.50 | | | 7 50– 7 99 |
| 8 00– 8 99 | 2 | 4 | 7 | 8 | 2 | 2 | 1 | 1 | | | 112 | 293 | 37.95 | 82.50 | | | 8 00– 8 99 |
| 9 00– 9 99 | 6 | 4 | 9 | 11 | 2 | 1 | 1 | 2 | | 5 | 83 | 259 | 44.60 | 91.20 | | | 9 00– 9 99 |
| 10 00–10 99 | 4 | 3 | 6 | 3 | 1 | 1 | | | 1 | 1 | 63 | 119 | 49.80 | 95.30 | | | 10 00–10 99 |
| 11 00–11 99 | 7 | 1 | 2 | | 2 | 1 | | | | | 55 | 39 | 54.40 | 96.50 | | | 11 00–11 99 |
| 12 00–12 99 | 7 | 5 | 4 | | 2 | | 1 | | | | 82 | 53 | 61.10 | 98.50 | | | 12 00–12 99 |
| 13 00–13 99 | 7 | | 5 | | | | | 1 | 1 | | 70 | 17 | 66.75 | 99.00 | | | 13 00–13 99 |
| 14 00–14 99 | 2 | 1 | 2 | 1 | 1 | | | | | | 57 | 8 | 71.40 | 99.25 | | | 14 00–14 99 |
| 15 00–15 99 | 8 | 1 | 7 | 3 | 2 | | | | 1 | | 88 | 11 | 78.50 | 99.65 | | | 15 00–15 99 |
| 16 00–17 99 | 13 | | 7 | | | | | | | | 80 | 4 | 85.10 | 99.80 | | | 16 00–17 99 |
| 18 00–19 99 | 3 | | 2 | 3 | 2 | | | | 1 | | 67 | 4 | 90.50 | 99.92 | | | 18 00–19 99 |
| 20 00–24 99 | 8 | | 11 | | 1 | | | | | | 73 | 3 | 96.50 | 100.00 | | | 20 00–24 99 |
| 25 00–29 99 | 1 | | 3 | | 1 | | | | | | 25 | | 98.50 | | | | 25 00–29 99 |
| 30 00–34 99 | 3 | | 2 | | 1 | | | | | | 12 | | 99.50 | | | | 30 00–34 99 |
| 35 00–39 99 | | | 2 | | | | | | | | 3 | | 99.75 | | | | 35 00–39 99 |
| 40 00 and over | 1 | | 1 | | | | | | | | 3 | | 100.00 | | | | 40 00 and over |
| Not reported | | 20 | | 20 | | 2 | | 1 | | 8 | 9 | 302 | | | | | Not reported |
| Total | 74 | 64 | 76 | 94 | 28 | 22 | 8 | 5 | 4 | 22 | 1,234 | 3,234 | | | | | Total |

92. TABLE VIII, B, a

NEW YORK STATE

**THE MEN'S SHIRT INDUSTRY — FACTORY WORKERS**

NUMBER AND PER CENT. OF EMPLOYEES EARNING SPECIFIED WEEKLY RATES ACCORDING TO OCCUPATION AND SEX

| WEEKLY RATES IN DOLLARS | OCCUPATION | | | | | | | | | | | | | | | WEEKLY RATES IN DOLLARS |
|---|---|---|---|---|---|---|---|---|---|---|---|---|---|---|---|---|
| | MARKERS | | CUTTERS | TRIMMERS | | CUTTERS' HELPERS | | FOREMEN AND FOREWOMEN | | OPERATORS | | FLOOR WORK | | LAUNDRY HELPERS | | |
| | Male | Female | Male | Male | Female | Male | Female | Male | Female | Male | Female | Male | Female | Male | Female | |
| Less than $3 00 | .... | .... | .... | .... | .... | .... | .... | .... | .... | 1 | 3 | .... | 1 | .... | .... | Less than $3 00 |
| $3 00–$3 49 | .... | .... | .... | .... | .... | .... | 2 | .... | .... | 2 | 35 | 4 | 52 | .... | .... | $3 00– 3 49 |
| 3 50– 3 99 | .... | .... | .... | .... | .... | 4 | .... | .... | .... | 1 | 59 | 5 | 56 | .... | .... | 3 50– 3 99 |
| 4 00– 4 49 | .... | .... | .... | .... | .... | 10 | 3 | .... | .... | 7 | 106 | 7 | 84 | 1 | 1 | 4 00– 4 49 |
| 4 50– 4 99 | .... | .... | .... | .... | .... | 8 | 8 | .... | 1 | 3 | 89 | 3 | 48 | 2 | 2 | 4 50– 4 99 |
| 5 00– 5 49 | .... | .... | 6 | 1 | .... | 29 | .... | .... | .... | 6 | 131 | 5 | 77 | 3 | 7 | 5 00– 5 49 |
| 5 50– 5 99 | .... | .... | 2 | 1 | .... | 9 | 1 | .... | .... | 1 | 96 | 3 | 34 | 1 | 4 | 5 50– 5 99 |
| 6 00– 6 49 | .... | .... | 5 | 2 | .... | 31 | 5 | .... | 5 | 8 | 159 | 6 | 66 | 2 | 6 | 6 00– 6 49 |
| 6 50– 6 99 | .... | .... | 1 | .... | .... | 6 | 3 | .... | 3 | 3 | 82 | 2 | 21 | .... | 3 | 6 50– 6 99 |
| 7 00– 7 49 | .... | .... | 6 | 6 | .... | 30 | 3 | .... | 5 | 9 | 113 | 7 | 31 | 1 | 4 | 7 00– 7 49 |
| 7 50– 7 99 | .... | .... | 3 | .... | .... | 5 | 1 | .... | 4 | 5 | 92 | 1 | 10 | 2 | 2 | 7 50– 7 99 |
| 8 00– 8 99 | .... | .... | 9 | 7 | .... | 42 | 1 | 2 | 18 | 17 | 191 | 2 | 17 | 2 | 3 | 8 00– 8 99 |
| 9 00– 9 99 | 2 | .... | 18 | 3 | .... | 13 | 2 | 3 | 32 | 10 | 154 | 2 | 11 | 8 | 1 | 9 00– 9 99 |
| 10 00–10 99 | 1 | .... | 13 | 5 | .... | 3 | 1 | 1 | 16 | 14 | 70 | .... | 3 | 7 | 4 | 10 00–10 99 |
| 11 00–11 99 | 1 | .... | 14 | 5 | 1 | 1 | .... | 3 | 8 | 19 | 24 | .... | .... | 2 | 2 | 11 00–11 99 |
| 12 00–12 99 | .... | .... | 18 | 4 | .... | 1 | .... | 8 | 20 | 40 | 20 | .... | .... | 4 | .... | 12 00–12 99 |
| 13 00–13 99 | 1 | .... | 21 | 3 | .... | 1 | .... | 7 | 6 | 27 | 6 | .... | 2 | 3 | 2 | 13 00–13 99 |
| 14 00–14 99 | 2 | 1 | 23 | 6 | .... | .... | .... | 5 | 5 | 17 | 1 | 1 | .... | .... | .... | 14 00–14 99 |
| 15 00–15 99 | 1 | .... | 33 | 3 | .... | .... | .... | 12 | 10 | 26 | .... | 2 | .... | 2 | .... | 15 00–15 99 |
| 16 00–17 99 | 3 | .... | 36 | 1 | .... | .... | .... | 21 | 4 | 15 | .... | 1 | .... | .... | .... | 16 00–17 99 |
| 18 00–19 99 | 4 | .... | 34 | 1 | .... | .... | .... | 18 | 4 | 6 | .... | .... | .... | 4 | .... | 18 00–19 99 |
| 20 00–24 99 | 23 | .... | 15 | .... | .... | .... | .... | 31 | 3 | 2 | .... | .... | .... | 1 | .... | 20 00–24 99 |
| 25 00–29 99 | 1 | .... | 3 | .... | .... | .... | .... | 19 | .... | 1 | .... | .... | .... | 1 | .... | 25 00–29 99 |
| 30 00–34 99 | 1 | .... | 2 | .... | .... | .... | .... | 9 | .... | .... | .... | .... | .... | .... | .... | 30 00–34 99 |
| 35 00–39 99 | 1 | .... | .... | .... | .... | .... | .... | 2 | .... | .... | .... | .... | .... | .... | .... | 35 00–39 99 |
| 40 00 and over | .... | .... | .... | .... | .... | .... | .... | 3 | .... | .... | .... | .... | .... | .... | .... | 40 00 and over |
| Not reported | 1 | .... | 1 | .... | .... | 1 | .... | .... | .... | 2 | 245 | .... | 5 | .... | .... | Not reported |
| Total | 42 | 1 | 263 | 48 | 1 | 194 | 30 | 144 | 144 | 242 | 1,676 | 51 | 518 | 46 | 41 | Total |

NEW YORK STATE

92. TABLE VIII, B, a — *(concluded)* **THE MEN'S SHIRT INDUSTRY — FACTORY WORKERS**

NUMBER AND PER CENT. OF EMPLOYEES EARNING SPECIFIED WEEKLY RATES ACCORDING TO OCCUPATION AND SEX

| WEEKLY RATES IN DOLLARS | OCCUPATION | | | | | | | | | | | | | | | | WEEKLY RATES IN DOLLARS |
|---|---|---|---|---|---|---|---|---|---|---|---|---|---|---|---|---|---|
| | STARCHERS AND DAMPNERS | | IRONERS AND PRESSERS | | EXAMINERS | | FOLDERS | | PACKERS | | NOT REPORTED | | TOTAL | | CUMULATIVE PER CENT. OF TOTAL | | |
| | Male | Female | Male | Female | Male | Female | Male | Female | Male | Female | Male | Female | Male | Female | Male | Female | |
| Less than $3 00 | .... | ..... | .... | ..... | .... | ..... | .... | 2 | .... | ..... | .... | ..... | 1 | 6 | .08 | .20 | Less than $3 00 |
| $3 00–$3 49 | .... | ..... | .... | ..... | .... | 4 | .... | 13 | .... | 1 | .... | ..... | 6 | 107 | .57 | 3.85 | $3 00– 3 49 |
| 3 50– 3 99 | .... | ..... | 1 | ..... | .... | 5 | .... | 4 | .... | 6 | .... | 2 | 11 | 132 | 1.47 | 8.36 | 3 50– 3 99 |
| 4 00– 4 49 | 1 | 4 | .... | 3 | .... | 29 | .... | 9 | 1 | 14 | 1 | ..... | 28 | 253 | 3.76 | 16.95 | 4 00– 4 49 |
| 4 50– 4 99 | 1 | ..... | .... | 1 | 1 | 22 | .... | 3 | .... | 10 | .... | 2 | 18 | 186 | 5.23 | 23.40 | 4 50– 4 99 |
| 5 00– 5 49 | .... | 3 | 2 | 5 | 1 | 42 | 2 | 3 | 8 | 36 | .... | 2 | 63 | 306 | 10.36 | 33.80 | 5 00– 5 49 |
| 5 50– 5 99 | .... | 4 | 1 | 5 | 1 | 33 | 1 | 2 | 4 | 10 | .... | 1 | 24 | 190 | 12.34 | 40.30 | 5 50– 5 99 |
| 6 00– 6 49 | 1 | 9 | 6 | 17 | 1 | 105 | 3 | 4 | 11 | 12 | .... | 4 | 76 | 393 | 18.65 | 53.70 | 6 00– 6 49 |
| 6 50– 6 99 | .... | 3 | 3 | 4 | 2 | 20 | 1 | 3 | 3 | 7 | .... | ..... | 21 | 149 | 20.21 | 58.80 | 6 50– 6 99 |
| 7 00– 7 49 | .... | 8 | 12 | 10 | 2 | 80 | 2 | 3 | 3 | 13 | 1 | ..... | 79 | 270 | 26.65 | 68.00 | 7 00– 7 49 |
| 7 50– 7 99 | .... | 3 | 7 | 8 | 2 | 8 | .... | 1 | .... | 2 | .... | ..... | 25 | 131 | 28.78 | 72.50 | 7 50– 7 99 |
| 8 00– 8 99 | 1 | 2 | 19 | 10 | 1 | 45 | 2 | ..... | 8 | 6 | .... | ..... | 112 | 293 | 37.95 | 82.50 | 8 00– 8 99 |
| 9 00– 9 99 | .... | ..... | 14 | 5 | 3 | 40 | 1 | 1 | 6 | 10 | .... | 3 | 83 | 259 | 44.60 | 91.20 | 9 00– 9 99 |
| 10 00–10 99 | 1 | ..... | 7 | 2 | 4 | 19 | 3 | 1 | 4 | 3 | .... | ..... | 63 | 119 | 49.80 | 95.30 | 10 00–10 99 |
| 11 00–11 99 | 1 | ..... | 6 | ..... | 1 | 4 | 2 | ..... | .... | ..... | .... | ..... | 55 | 39 | 54.40 | 96.50 | 11 00–11 99 |
| 12 00–12 99 | .... | 1 | 2 | ..... | 5 | 11 | .... | 1 | .... | ..... | .... | ..... | 82 | 53 | 61.10 | 98.50 | 12 00–12 99 |
| 13 00–13 99 | .... | ..... | 1 | ..... | 2 | 1 | 2 | ..... | 2 | ..... | .... | ..... | 70 | 17 | 66.75 | 99.00 | 13 00–13 99 |
| 14 00–14 99 | .... | ..... | 1 | ..... | 1 | ..... | 1 | ..... | .... | 1 | .... | ..... | 57 | 8 | 71.40 | 99.25 | 14 00–14 99 |
| 15 00–15 99 | .... | ..... | 1 | ..... | 7 | 1 | 1 | ..... | .... | ..... | .... | ..... | 88 | 11 | 78.50 | 99.65 | 15 00–15 99 |
| 16 00–17 99 | .... | ..... | 1 | ..... | 2 | ..... | .... | ..... | .... | ..... | .... | ..... | 80 | 4 | 85.10 | 99.80 | 16 00–17 99 |
| 18 00–19 99 | .... | ..... | .... | ..... | .... | ..... | .... | ..... | .... | ..... | .... | ..... | 67 | 4 | 90.50 | 99.92 | 18 00–19 99 |
| 20 00–24 99 | .... | ..... | .... | ..... | .... | ..... | .... | ..... | .... | ..... | 1 | ..... | 73 | 3 | 96.50 | 100.00 | 20 00–24 99 |
| 25 00–29 99 | .... | ..... | .... | ..... | .... | ..... | .... | ..... | .... | ..... | .... | ..... | 25 | ..... | 98.50 | ..... | 25 00–29 99 |
| 30 00–34 99 | .... | ..... | .... | ..... | .... | ..... | .... | ..... | .... | ..... | .... | ..... | 12 | ..... | 99.50 | ..... | 30 00–34 99 |
| 35 00–39 99 | .... | ..... | .... | ..... | .... | ..... | .... | ..... | .... | ..... | .... | ..... | 3 | ..... | 99.75 | ..... | 35 00–39 99 |
| 40 00 and over | .... | ..... | .... | ..... | .... | ..... | .... | ..... | .... | ..... | .... | ..... | 3 | ..... | 100.00 | ..... | 40 00 and over |
| Not reported | .... | 18 | 2 | 6 | 1 | 24 | .... | ..... | 1 | 4 | .... | ..... | 9 | 302 | ..... | ..... | Not reported |
| Total | 6 | 55 | 86 | 76 | 37 | 493 | 21 | 50 | 51 | 135 | 3 | 14 | 1,234 | 3,234 | ..... | ..... | Total |

93. TABLE VI-B, a

NEW YORK STATE

THE MEN'S SHIRT INDUSTRY — FACTORY WORKERS

NUMBER AND PER CENT. OF EMPLOYEES CLASSIFIED ACCORDING TO ACTUAL WEEKLY EARNINGS BY AGE GROUPS AND SEX

| Actual Weekly Earnings in Dollars | Age Groups in Years | | | | | | | | | | | | | | Actual Weekly Earnings in Dollars |
|---|---|---|---|---|---|---|---|---|---|---|---|---|---|---|---|
| | 14–15 | | 16–17 | | 18–20 | | 21–24 | | 25–29 | | 30–34 | | 35–39 | | |
| | Male | Female | Male | Female | Male | Female | Male | Female | Male | Female | Male | Female | Male | Female | |
| Less than $3 00 | 5 | 58 | 12 | 135 | 12 | 135 | 12 | 71 | 12 | 31 | 3 | 23 | 2 | 20 | Less than $3 00 |
| $3 00– 3 49... | 6 | 60 | 8 | 96 | 4 | 84 | 7 | 39 | 3 | 24 | 1 | 11 | ...... | 19 | ...$3 00– 3 49 |
| 3 50– 3 99... | .... | 48 | 10 | 106 | 7 | 97 | 7 | 44 | 10 | 29 | 6 | 16 | 4 | 13 | ... 3 50– 3 99 |
| 4 00– 4 49... | 2 | 31 | 19 | 161 | 9 | 140 | 4 | 76 | 10 | 43 | 3 | 18 | 6 | 16 | ... 4 00– 4 49 |
| 4 50– 4 99... | 3 | 29 | 17 | 158 | 8 | 154 | 9 | 75 | 5 | 34 | 6 | 19 | 2 | 24 | ... 4 50– 4 99 |
| 5 00– 5 49... | 8 | 25 | 24 | 174 | 24 | 244 | 21 | 100 | 9 | 50 | 10 | 37 | 10 | 23 | ... 5 00– 5 49 |
| 5 50– 5 99... | 2 | 10 | 12 | 135 | 20 | 194 | 8 | 104 | 4 | 52 | 6 | 28 | 9 | 26 | ... 5 50– 5 99 |
| 6 00– 6 49... | 2 | 4 | 28 | 123 | 42 | 246 | 15 | 148 | 16 | 68 | 10 | 36 | 11 | 44 | ... 6 00– 6 49 |
| 6 50– 6 99... | .... | 2 | 11 | 64 | 20 | 205 | 12 | 103 | 17 | 58 | 3 | 21 | 7 | 21 | ... 6 50– 6 99 |
| 7 00– 7 49... | .... | 8 | 14 | 88 | 32 | 225 | 225 | 140 | 140 | 76 | 8 | 34 | 8 | 29 | ... 7 00– 7 49 |
| 7 50– 7 99... | .... | 1 | 7 | 59 | 23 | 164 | 15 | 99 | 9 | 43 | 14 | 33 | 5 | 37 | ... 7 50– 7 99 |
| 8 00– 8 99... | .... | 2 | 11 | 73 | 61 | 282 | 47 | 220 | 44 | 118 | 29 | 81 | 25 | 57 | ... 8 00– 8 99 |
| 9 00– 9 99... | .... | 1 | 8 | 81 | 39 | 184 | 32 | 172 | 34 | 96 | 23 | 59 | 12 | 50 | ... 9 00– 9 99 |
| 10 00–10 99... | .... | ...... | 1 | 20 | 28 | 146 | 40 | 111 | 25 | 97 | 17 | 49 | 22 | 39 | ...10 00–10 99 |
| 11 00–11 99... | .... | ...... | 2 | 7 | 21 | 51 | 32 | 69 | 41 | 53 | 29 | 29 | 19 | 34 | ...11 00–11 99 |
| 12 00–12 99... | .... | ...... | .... | 10 | 19 | 44 | 40 | 54 | 89 | 43 | 34 | 40 | 34 | 36 | ...12 00–12 99 |
| 13 00–13 99... | .... | ...... | .... | 5 | 16 | 21 | 32 | 38 | 86 | 35 | 27 | 20 | 24 | 23 | ...13 00–13 99 |
| 14 00–14 99... | .... | ...... | 1 | ...... | 7 | 17 | 33 | 29 | 82 | 27 | 15 | 12 | 22 | 10 | ...14 00–14 99 |
| 15 00–15 99... | .... | ...... | .... | 2 | 7 | 7 | 21 | 17 | 81 | 16 | 18 | 18 | 33 | 10 | ...15 00–15 99 |
| 16 00–17 99... | .... | ...... | .... | ...... | 6 | 8 | 27 | 13 | 53 | 9 | 43 | 5 | 22 | 12 | ...16 00–17 99 |
| 18 00–19 99... | .... | ...... | .... | ...... | 4 | 4 | 19 | 5 | 36 | 4 | 27 | 2 | 26 | 2 | ...18 00–19 99 |
| 20 00–24 99... | .... | ...... | .... | ...... | 3 | 1 | 16 | 2 | 26 | 1 | 29 | 2 | 29 | 1 | ...20 00–24 99 |
| 25 00–29 99... | .... | ...... | .... | ...... | ...... | 1 | 2 | ...... | 5 | ...... | 7 | ...... | 10 | ...... | ...25 00–29 99 |
| 30 00–34 99... | .... | ...... | .... | ...... | ...... | ...... | ...... | ...... | 1 | ...... | 3 | ...... | 5 | ...... | ...30 00–34 99 |
| 35 00–39 99... | .... | ...... | .... | ...... | ...... | ...... | ...... | ...... | ...... | ...... | ...... | ...... | ...... | ...... | ...35 00–39 99 |
| 40 00 and over. | .... | ...... | .... | ...... | ...... | ...... | ...... | ...... | ...... | ...... | ...... | ...... | 2 | ...... | .40 00 and over |
| Not reported... | .... | 18 | .... | 33 | 2 | 24 | 3 | 5 | 3 | 9 | ...... | ...... | 1 | 1 | ..Not reported |
| Total..... | 28 | 292 | 180 | 1,480 | 414 | 2,678 | 471 | 1,734 | 515 | 1,016 | 371 | 593 | 350 | 547 | .....Total |

NEW YORK STATE

98. TABLE VI-B, a — *(concluded)* **THE MEN'S SHIRT INDUSTRY — FACTORY WORKERS**

NUMBER AND PER CENT. OF EMPLOYEES CLASSIFIED ACCORDING TO ACTUAL WEEKLY EARNINGS BY AGE GROUPS AND SEX

| ACTUAL WEEKLY EARNINGS IN DOLLARS | AGE GROUPS IN YEARS: 40–44 | | 45–54 | | 55–64 | | 65 AND OVER | | NOT REPORTED | | TOTAL | | CUMULATIVE PER CENT. OF TOTAL | | ACTUAL WEEKLY EARNINGS IN DOLLARS |
|---|---|---|---|---|---|---|---|---|---|---|---|---|---|---|---|
| | Male | Female | Male | Female | Male | Female | Male | Female | Male | Female | Male | Female | Male | Female | |
| Less than $3 00 | 1 | 21 | 3 | 30 | 3 | 10 | ...... | 3 | 1 | 1 | 66 | 538 | 2.33 | 5.94 | Less than $3 00 |
| $3 00–$3 49... | .... | 6 | 4 | 8 | ...... | 9 | 1 | 4 | ...... | 1 | 29 | 361 | 3.35 | 9.93 | ...$3 00– 3 49 |
| 3 50– 3 99... | 1 | 9 | 8 | 12 | ...... | 3 | ...... | 1 | 1 | 4 | 54 | 382 | 5.26 | 14.30 | ... 3 50– 3 99 |
| 4 00– 4 49... | 5 | 15 | 3 | 18 | 2 | 3 | ...... | ...... | ...... | 2 | 63 | 523 | 7.48 | 19.90 | ... 4 00– 4 49 |
| 4 50– 4 99... | 2 | 10 | 3 | 20 | ...... | 7 | 1 | 2 | ...... | 1 | 56 | 533 | 9.46 | 25.80 | ... 4 50– 4 99 |
| 5 00– 5 49... | 5 | 24 | 6 | 17 | ...... | 11 | 1 | ...... | ...... | 5 | 118 | 710 | 13.60 | 33.70 | ... 5 00– 5 49 |
| 5 50– 5 99... | 3 | 11 | 2 | 23 | 1 | 4 | ...... | ...... | ...... | 6 | 67 | 593 | 16.00 | 40.20 | ... 5 50– 5 99 |
| 6 00– 6 49... | 9 | 25 | 10 | 19 | 8 | 9 | 1 | 2 | 1 | 3 | 153 | 727 | 21.40 | 48.30 | ... 6 00– 6 49 |
| 6 50– 6 99... | 5 | 12 | 3 | 18 | 1 | 3 | 1 | ...... | 2 | 4 | 82 | 511 | 24.30 | 53.90 | ... 6 50– 6 99 |
| 7 00– 7 49... | 2 | 17 | 9 | 20 | 1 | 3 | ...... | 1 | ...... | 9 | 105 | 645 | 28.00 | 61.30 | ... 7 00– 7 49 |
| 7 50– 7 99... | 5 | 24 | 16 | 19 | 3 | 1 | ...... | ...... | ...... | 5 | 97 | 485 | 31.40 | 66.30 | ... 7 50– 7 99 |
| 8 00– 8 99... | 17 | 37 | 18 | 26 | 4 | 3 | 1 | 2 | ...... | 4 | 257 | 905 | 40.50 | 76.50 | ... 8 00– 8 99 |
| 9 00– 9 99... | 15 | 24 | 16 | 24 | 2 | 5 | ...... | 1 | ...... | 7 | 181 | 654 | 46.80 | 83.70 | ... 9 00– 9 99 |
| 10 00–10 99... | 19 | 21 | 14 | 21 | 1 | 3 | 1 | ...... | 2 | 3 | 170 | 510 | 52.90 | 89.20 | ...10 00–10 99 |
| 11 00–11 99... | 18 | 20 | 8 | 13 | 5 | 2 | 1 | ...... | ...... | 5 | 176 | 283 | 59.10 | 92.40 | ...11 00–11 99 |
| 12 00–12 99... | 18 | 13 | 13 | 11 | 6 | 2 | ...... | ...... | ...... | 1 | 203 | 254 | 66.20 | 95.20 | ...12 00–12 99 |
| 13 00–13 99... | 21 | 9 | 16 | 9 | 1 | ...... | ...... | 1 | 1 | 1 | 174 | 162 | 72.40 | 96.70 | ...13 00–13 99 |
| 14 00–14 99... | 16 | 7 | 19 | 5 | 1 | 2 | ...... | ...... | ...... | 1 | 146 | 110 | 77.50 | 98.20 | ...14 00–14 99 |
| 15 00–15 99... | 16 | 4 | 11 | 5 | 2 | 1 | ...... | ...... | 1 | ...... | 140 | 80 | 82.40 | 99.10 | ...15 00–15 99 |
| 16 00–17 99... | 24 | 3 | 7 | ...... | ...... | 1 | ...... | ...... | ...... | ...... | 182 | 51 | 88.80 | 99.60 | ...16 00–17 99 |
| 18 00–19 99... | 9 | ...... | 6 | 4 | 4 | ...... | ...... | ...... | 1 | ...... | 132 | 21 | 93.50 | 99.90 | ...18 00–19 99 |
| 20 00–24 99... | 11 | ...... | 16 | 1 | 1 | ...... | ...... | ...... | 1 | ...... | 132 | 8 | 98.20 | 99.99 | ...20 00–24 99 |
| 25 00–29 99... | 2 | ...... | 3 | ...... | 1 | ...... | ...... | ...... | ...... | ...... | 30 | 1 | 99.20 | 100.00 | ...25 00–29 99 |
| 30 00–34 99... | 3 | ...... | 2 | ...... | 1 | ...... | ...... | ...... | ...... | ...... | 15 | ...... | 99.80 | ...... | ...30 00–34 99 |
| 35 00–39 99... | .... | ...... | 2 | ...... | ...... | ...... | ...... | ...... | ...... | ...... | 2 | ...... | 99.90 | ...... | ...35 00–39 99 |
| 40 00 and over. | 1 | ...... | 1 | ...... | ...... | ...... | ...... | ...... | ...... | ...... | 4 | ...... | 100.00 | ...... | 40 00 and over |
| Not reported... | .... | ...... | 1 | 1 | ...... | ...... | ...... | ...... | ...... | ...... | 10 | 91 | ...... | ...... | ...Not reported |
| Total..... | 228 | 312 | 220 | 324 | 48 | 82 | 8 | 17 | 11 | 63 | 2,844 | 9,138 | ...... | ...... | .....Total |

NEW YORK STATE

94. TABLE IX, B, a

**THE MEN'S SHIRT INDUSTRY — FACTORY WORKERS**

NUMBER AND PER CENT. OF EMPLOYEES CLASSIFIED ACCORDING TO ACTUAL WEEKLY EARNINGS BY OCCUPATION AND SEX

| ACTUAL WEEKLY EARNINGS IN DOLLARS | OCCUPATION | | | | | | | | | | | | | | | | ACTUAL WEEKLY EARNINGS IN DOLLARS |
|---|---|---|---|---|---|---|---|---|---|---|---|---|---|---|---|---|---|
| | MARKERS | | CUTTERS | | TRIMMERS | | CUTTERS' HELPERS | | FOREMEN AND FOREWOMEN | | OPERATORS | | FLOOR WORK | | LAUNDRY HELPERS | | |
| | Male | Female | Male | Female | Male | Female | Male | Female | Male | Female | Male | Female | Male | Female | Male | Female | |
| Less than $3 00 | .... | ..... | 4 | .... | .... | .... | 6 | 1 | ...... | 1 | 30 | 370 | 4 | 85 | ...... | 3 | Less than $3 00 |
| $3 00–$3 49... | .... | ..... | 2 | 1 | .... | .... | 3 | 3 | ...... | 2 | 11 | 227 | 6 | 79 | ...... | ...... | ...$3 00– 3 49 |
| 3 50– 3 99... | .... | ..... | .... | .... | .... | .... | 6 | .... | ...... | 1 | 12 | 236 | 5 | 78 | ...... | 1 | ... 3 50– 3 99 |
| 4 00– 4 49... | .... | ..... | 3 | .... | .... | 1 | 9 | 4 | 1 | ...... | 15 | 323 | 8 | 102 | 3 | 1 | ... 4 00– 4 49 |
| 4 50– 4 99... | .... | ..... | 2 | .... | .... | .... | 12 | 6 | ...... | 1 | 11 | 352 | 1 | 65 | 5 | 5 | ... 4 50– 4 99 |
| 5 00– 5 49... | .... | ..... | 7 | .... | 1 | .... | 24 | 1 | ...... | 1 | 23 | 443 | 5 | 96 | 2 | 5 | ... 5 00– 5 49 |
| 5 50– 5 99... | .... | ..... | 3 | .... | 1 | .... | 13 | 5 | ...... | 2 | 17 | 389 | 4 | 50 | 1 | 7 | ... 5 50– 5 99 |
| 6 00– 6 49... | .... | ..... | 8 | .... | 3 | 1 | 21 | 4 | ...... | 5 | 35 | 476 | 13 | 61 | 4 | 8 | ... 6 00– 6 49 |
| 6 50– 6 99... | .... | ..... | 2 | .... | 1 | .... | 16 | 2 | ...... | 4 | 22 | 362 | 3 | 31 | 1 | 2 | ... 6 50– 6 99 |
| 7 00– 7 49... | .... | ..... | 4 | .... | 4 | 1 | 16 | 3 | ...... | 6 | 31 | 455 | 10 | 31 | 1 | 4 | ... 7 00– 7 49 |
| 7 50– 7 99... | .... | ..... | 12 | .... | 2 | .... | 13 | 4 | ...... | 8 | 22 | 348 | 1 | 18 | 5 | 5 | ... 7 50– 7 99 |
| 8 00– 8 99... | .... | ..... | 18 | .... | 6 | .... | 33 | 2 | 3 | 17 | 60 | 703 | 5 | 31 | 1 | 1 | ... 8 00– 8 99 |
| 9 00– 9 99... | 1 | ..... | 17 | .... | 3 | 1 | 15 | 3 | 2 | 25 | 61 | 482 | 4 | 21 | 6 | 3 | ... 9 00– 9 99 |
| 10 00–10 99... | 1 | ..... | 22 | .... | 3 | .... | 7 | 1 | 1 | 14 | 60 | 392 | .... | 9 | 4 | 10 | ...10 00–10 99 |
| 11 00–11 99... | .... | ..... | 23 | .... | 7 | .... | 2 | .... | 5 | 10 | 65 | 198 | .... | 3 | 4 | 3 | ...11 00–11 99 |
| 12 00–12 99... | 1 | ..... | 27 | .... | 3 | .... | 2 | .... | 7 | 18 | 75 | 176 | .... | 2 | 2 | ...... | ...12 00–12 99 |
| 13 00–13 99... | 1 | ..... | 29 | .... | 5 | 1 | 1 | .... | 5 | 6 | 49 | 103 | 2 | 1 | 3 | 1 | ...13 00–13 99 |
| 14 00–14 99... | 3 | 1 | 22 | .... | 4 | .... | .... | .... | 5 | 5 | 48 | 76 | 1 | 1 | ...... | 1 | ...14 00–14 99 |
| 15 00–15 99... | . | ..... | 24 | .... | 3 | .... | .... | .... | 14 | 11 | 41 | 34 | 3 | ...... | 2 | ...... | ...15 00–15 99 |
| 16 00–17 99... | 4 | ..... | 30 | .... | 1 | .... | .... | .... | 19 | 4 | 53 | 38 | 1 | ...... | ...... | ...... | ...16 00–17 99 |
| 18 00–19 99... | 5 | ..... | 38 | .... | 1 | .... | .... | .... | 19 | 4 | 24 | 15 | .... | ...... | 7 | ...... | ...18 00–19 99 |
| 20 00–24 99... | 22 | ..... | 33 | .... | .... | .... | .... | .... | 32 | 4 | 18 | 4 | .... | ...... | 1 | ...... | ...20 00–24 99 |
| 25 00–29 99... | 2 | ..... | 6 | .... | .... | .... | .... | .... | 17 | ...... | 3 | 1 | .... | ...... | 1 | ...... | ...25 00–29 99 |
| 30 00–34 99... | 1 | ..... | 3 | .... | .... | .... | .... | .... | 11 | ...... | .... | .... | .... | ...... | ...... | ...... | ...30 00–34 99 |
| 35 00–39 99... | .... | ..... | .... | .... | .... | .... | .... | .... | 2 | ...... | .... | .... | .... | ...... | ...... | ...... | ...35 00–39 99 |
| 40 00 and over. | 1 | ..... | .... | .... | .... | .... | .... | .... | 3 | ...... | .... | .... | .... | ...... | ...... | ...... | .40 00 and over |
| Not reported... | .... | ..... | 1 | .... | .... | .... | .... | .... | ...... | ...... | 7 | 69 | 1 | 15 | ...... | ...... | ...Not reported |
| Total..... | 42 | 1 | 340 | 1 | 48 | 5 | 199 | 39 | 146 | 149 | 793 | 6,272 | 77 | 779 | 53 | 60 | .....Total |

NEW YORK STATE

94. TABLE IX, B, a — (*concluded*) · **THE MEN'S SHIRT INDUSTRY — FACTORY WORKERS**

NUMBER AND PER CENT. OF EMPLOYEES CLASSIFIED ACCORDING TO ACTUAL WEEKLY EARNINGS BY OCCUPATION AND SEX

| ACTUAL WEEKLY EARNINGS IN DOLLARS | OCCUPATION | | | | | | | | | | | | | | | | ACTUAL WEEKLY EARNINGS IN DOLLARS |
|---|---|---|---|---|---|---|---|---|---|---|---|---|---|---|---|---|---|
| | STARCHERS AND DAMPNERS | | IRONERS AND PRESSERS | | EXAMINERS | | FOLDERS | | PACKERS | | NOT REPORTED | | TOTAL | | CUMULATIVE PER CENT. OF TOTAL | | |
| | Male | Female | Male | Female | Male | Female | Male | Female | Male | Female | Male | Female | Male | Female | Male | Female | |
| Less than $3 00 | .... | 21 | 17 | 12 | .... | 24 | .... | 13 | 4 | 7 | 1 | 1 | 66 | 538 | 2.33 | 5.94 | Less than $3 00 |
| $3 00–$3 49... | .... | 6 | 7 | 10 | .... | 7 | .... | 20 | ...... | 5 | .... | 1 | 29 | 361 | 3.35 | 9.93 | ...$3 00– 3 49 |
| 3 50– 3 99... | .... | 8 | 27 | 9 | .... | 26 | 4 | 13 | ...... | 8 | .... | 2 | 54 | 382 | 5.26 | 14.30 | ... 3 50– 3 99 |
| 4 00– 4 49... | .... | 5 | 18 | 16 | .... | 36 | 3 | 16 | 3 | 19 | .... | .... | 63 | 523 | 7.48 | 19.90 | ... 4 00– 4 49 |
| 4 50– 4 99... | 1 | 5 | 19 | 20 | 1 | 45 | 1 | 12 | 3 | 20 | .... | 2 | 56 | 533 | 9.46 | 25.80 | ... 4 50– 4 99 |
| 5 00– 5 49... | .... | 10 | 44 | 27 | 1 | 84 | 6 | 11 | 5 | 27 | .... | 5 | 118 | 710 | 13.60 | 33.70 | ... 5 00– 5 49 |
| 5 50– 5 99... | .... | 19 | 19 | 33 | 1 | 54 | 3 | 24 | 4 | 8 | 1 | 2 | 67 | 593 | 16.00 | 40.20 | ... 5 50– 5 99 |
| 6 00– 6 49... | 1 | 13 | 48 | 40 | 2 | 89 | 7 | 14 | 11 | 14 | .... | 2 | 153 | 727 | 21.40 | 48.30 | ... 6 00– 6 49 |
| 6 50– 6 99... | .... | 8 | 30 | 37 | 2 | 44 | 1 | 13 | 3 | 8 | 1 | .... | 82 | 511 | 24.30 | 53.90 | ... 6 50– 6 99 |
| 7 00– 7 49... | .... | 25 | 32 | 28 | 2 | 62 | 2 | 16 | 3 | 13 | .... | 1 | 105 | 645 | 28.00 | 61.30 | ... 7 00– 7 49 |
| 7 50– 7 99... | .... | 25 | 36 | 35 | 4 | 31 | .... | 9 | 2 | 2 | .... | .... | 97 | 485 | 31.40 | 66.30 | ... 7 50– 7 99 |
| 8 00– 8 99... | 1 | 16 | 114 | 58 | .... | 52 | 4 | 15 | 12 | 9 | .... | 1 | 257 | 905 | 40.50 | 76.50 | ... 8 00– 8 99 |
| 9 00– 9 99... | .... | 13 | 62 | 37 | 2 | 47 | 2 | 13 | 6 | 7 | .... | 2 | 181 | 654 | 46.80 | 83.70 | ... 9 00– 9 99 |
| 10 00–10 99... | 1 | 10 | 63 | 43 | 3 | 18 | 3 | 8 | 2 | 5 | .... | .... | 170 | 510 | 52.90 | 89.20 | ...10 00–10 99 |
| 11 00–11 99... | 2 | 14 | 63 | 39 | 2 | 8 | 2 | 7 | 1 | 1 | .... | .... | 176 | 283 | 59.10 | 92.40 | ...11 00–11 99 |
| 12 00–12 99... | 1 | 2 | 77 | 37 | 5 | 12 | 2 | 7 | 1 | ...... | .... | .... | 203 | 254 | 66.28 | 95.20 | ...12 00–12 99 |
| 13 00–13 99... | .... | 4 | 73 | 38 | 3 | 2 | 1 | 5 | 2 | 1 | .... | .... | 174 | 162 | 72.40 | 96.70 | ...13 00–13 99 |
| 14 00–14 99... | .... | 4 | 61 | 9 | 1 | 2 | 1 | 11 | ...... | ...... | .... | .... | 146 | 110 | 77.50 | 98.20 | ...14 00–14 99 |
| 15 00–15 99... | 1 | 16 | 45 | 4 | 5 | 2 | 2 | 13 | ...... | ...... | .... | .... | 140 | 80 | 82.40 | 99.10 | ...15 00–15 99 |
| 16 00–17 99... | .... | 2 | 71 | 1 | 2 | 2 | 1 | 4 | ...... | ...... | .... | .... | 182 | 51 | 88.80 | 99.60 | ...16 00–17 99 |
| 18 00–19 99... | .... | ..... | 38 | .... | .... | 1 | .... | 1 | ...... | ...... | .... | .... | 132 | 21 | 93.60 | 99.90 | ...18 00–19 99 |
| 20 00–24 99... | .... | ..... | 24 | .... | .... | .... | 1 | .... | ...... | ...... | 1 | .... | 132 | 8 | 98.20 | 99.99 | ...20 00–24 99 |
| 25 00–29 99... | .... | ..... | 1 | .... | .... | .... | .... | .... | ...... | ...... | .... | .... | 30 | 1 | 99.20 | 100.00 | ...25 00–29 99 |
| 30 00–34 99... | .... | ..... | .... | .... | .... | .... | .... | .... | ...... | ...... | .... | .... | 15 | ...... | 99.80 | ...... | ...30 00–34 99 |
| 35 00–39 99... | .... | ..... | .... | .... | .... | .... | .... | .... | ...... | ...... | .... | .... | 2 | ...... | 99.90 | ...... | ...35 00–39 99 |
| 40 00 and over. | .... | ..... | .... | .... | .... | .... | .... | .... | ...... | ...... | .... | .... | 4 | ...... | 100.00 | ...... | .40 00 and over |
| Not reported... | .... | ..... | .... | 1 | 1 | 2 | .... | .... | ...... | 1 | .... | 3 | 10 | 91 | ...... | ...... | ...Not reported |
| Total..... | 8 | 226 | 989 | 534 | 37 | 650 | 46 | 245 | 62 | 155 | 4 | 22 | 2,844 | 9,138 | ...... | ...... | .....Total |

95. TABLE X, B. a

NEW YORK STATE

**THE MEN'S SHIRT INDUSTRY — FACTORY WORKERS**

NUMBER AND PER CENT. OF EMPLOYEES CLASSIFIED ACCORDING TO ACTUAL WEEKLY EARNINGS BY CONJUGAL CONDITION AND SEX

| ACTUAL WEEKLY EARNINGS IN DOLLARS | CONJUGAL CONDITION | | | | | | | | | | | | ACTUAL WEEKLY EARNINGS IN DOLLARS |
|---|---|---|---|---|---|---|---|---|---|---|---|---|---|
| | SINGLE | | MARRIED | | WIDOWED OR DIVORCED | | NOT REPORTED | | TOTAL | | CUMULATIVE PER CENT. OF TOTAL | | |
| | Male | Female | Male | Female | Male | Female | Male | Female | Male | Female | Male | Female | |
| Less than $3 00 | 45 | 424 | 21 | 69 | ....... | 35 | ....... | 10 | 66 | 538 | 2.38 | 5.94 | Less than $3 00 |
| $3 00–$3 49 | 19 | 302 | 9 | 35 | 1 | 18 | ....... | 6 | 29 | 361 | 3.35 | 9.98 | $3 00–$3 49 |
| 3 50– 3 99 | 32 | 334 | 21 | 32 | 1 | 14 | ....... | 2 | 54 | 382 | 5.26 | 14.30 | 3 50– 3 99 |
| 4 00– 4 49 | 42 | 447 | 19 | 45 | 1 | 23 | 1 | 8 | 63 | 523 | 7.48 | 19.90 | 4 00– 4 49 |
| 4 50– 4 99 | 38 | 446 | 17 | 62 | ....... | 21 | 1 | 4 | 56 | 533 | 9.46 | 25.80 | 4 50– 4 99 |
| 5 00– 5 49 | 87 | 595 | 27 | 78 | 3 | 30 | 1 | 7 | 118 | 710 | 13.60 | 33.70 | 5 00– 5 49 |
| 5 50– 5 99 | 42 | 491 | 23 | 58 | ....... | 35 | 2 | 9 | 67 | 593 | 16 00 | 40.20 | 5 50– 5 99 |
| 6 00– 6 49 | 101 | 605 | 49 | 80 | 1 | 34 | 2 | 8 | 153 | 727 | 21.40 | 48.30 | 6 00– 6 49 |
| 6 50– 6 99 | 48 | 441 | 31 | 40 | 1 | 21 | 2 | 9 | 82 | 511 | 24.30 | 53.90 | 6 50– 6 99 |
| 7 00– 7 49 | 64 | 539 | 37 | 68 | 3 | 26 | 1 | 12 | 105 | 645 | 28.00 | 61.30 | 7 00– 7 49 |
| 7 50– 7 99 | 56 | 403 | 39 | 48 | ....... | 29 | 2 | 5 | 97 | 485 | 31.40 | 66.30 | 7 50– 7 99 |
| 8 00– 8 99 | 143 | 732 | 107 | 96 | 2 | 62 | 5 | 15 | 257 | 905 | 40.50 | 76.50 | 8 00– 8 99 |
| 9 00– 9 99 | 101 | 520 | 79 | 73 | 1 | 50 | ....... | 11 | 181 | 654 | 46.80 | 83.70 | 9 00– 9 99 |
| 10 00–10 99 | 78 | 412 | 91 | 50 | ....... | 40 | 1 | 8 | 170 | 510 | 52.90 | 89.20 | 10 00–10 99 |
| 11 00–11 99 | 79 | 210 | 94 | 46 | 1 | 21 | 2 | 6 | 176 | 283 | 59.10 | 92.40 | 11 00–11 99 |
| 12 00–12 99 | 81 | 191 | 120 | 38 | 1 | 20 | 1 | 5 | 203 | 254 | 66.20 | 95.20 | 12 00–12 99 |
| 13 00–13 99 | 60 | 118 | 108 | 28 | 4 | 13 | 2 | 3 | 174 | 162 | 72.40 | 96.70 | 13 00–13 99 |
| 14 00–14 99 | 52 | 78 | 88 | 20 | 5 | 8 | 1 | 4 | 146 | 110 | 77.50 | 98.20 | 14 00–14 99 |
| 15 00–15 99 | 44 | 47 | 91 | 17 | 4 | 11 | 1 | 5 | 140 | 80 | 82.40 | 99.10 | 15 00–15 99 |
| 16 00–17 99 | 52 | 32 | 128 | 12 | 1 | 7 | 1 | ....... | 182 | 51 | 88.80 | 99.60 | 16 00–17 99 |
| 18 00–19 99 | 39 | 19 | 90 | 2 | ....... | ....... | 3 | ....... | 132 | 21 | 93.60 | 99.90 | 18 00–19 99 |
| 20 00–24 99 | 29 | 7 | 100 | 1 | 2 | ....... | 1 | ....... | 132 | 8 | 98.20 | 99.99 | 20 00–24 99 |
| 25 00–29 99 | 2 | 1 | 27 | ....... | 1 | ....... | ....... | ....... | 30 | 1 | 99.20 | 100.00 | 25 00–29 99 |
| 30 00–34 99 | ....... | ....... | 13 | ....... | 1 | ....... | 1 | ....... | 15 | ....... | 99.80 | ....... | 30 00–34 99 |
| 35 00–39 99 | ....... | ....... | 2 | ....... | ....... | ....... | ....... | ....... | 2 | ....... | 99.90 | ....... | 35 00–39 99 |
| 40 00 and over | ....... | ....... | 4 | ....... | ....... | ....... | ....... | ....... | 4 | ....... | 100.00 | ....... | 40 00 and over |
| Not reported | 5 | 74 | 3 | 9 | 1 | 3 | 1 | 5 | 10 | 91 | ....... | ....... | Not reported |
| Total | 1,339 | 7,468 | 1,438 | 1,007 | 35 | 521 | 32 | 142 | 2,844 | 9,138 | ....... | ....... | Total |

96. TABLE XI, B, a

NEW YORK STATE

**THE MEN'S SHIRT INDUSTRY — FACTORY WORKERS**

Number and Per Cent. of Employees Classified According to Actual Weekly Earnings by Nativity and Sex

| Actual Weekly Earnings in Dollars | Nativity | | | | | | | | | | Actual Weekly Earnings in Dollars |
|---|---|---|---|---|---|---|---|---|---|---|---|
| | Native | | Foreign | | Not Reported | | Total | | Cumulative Per Cent. of Total | | |
| | Male | Female | Male | Female | Male | Female | Male | Female | Male | Female | |
| Less than $3 00 | 15 | 299 | 51 | 236 | ........ | 3 | 66 | 538 | 2.33 | 5.94 | Less than $3 00 |
| $3 00-$3 49 | 8 | 200 | 20 | 158 | 1 | 3 | 29 | 361 | 3.35 | 9.93 | $3 00- 3 49 |
| 3 50- 3 99 | 12 | 214 | 42 | 167 | ........ | 1 | 54 | 382 | 5.26 | 14.30 | 3 50- 3 99 |
| 4 00- 4 49 | 16 | 287 | 47 | 232 | ........ | 4 | 63 | 523 | 7.48 | 19.90 | 4 00- 4 49 |
| 4 50- 4 99 | 18 | 279 | 38 | 251 | ........ | 3 | 56 | 533 | 9.46 | 25.80 | 4 50- 4 99 |
| 5 00- 5 49 | 37 | 389 | 80 | 319 | 1 | 2 | 118 | 710 | 13.60 | 33.70 | 5 00- 5 49 |
| 5 50- 5 99 | 21 | 338 | 46 | 250 | ........ | 5 | 67 | 593 | 16.00 | 40.20 | 5 50- 5 99 |
| 6 00- 6 49 | 46 | 369 | 105 | 353 | 2 | 5 | 153 | 727 | 21.40 | 48.30 | 6 00- 6 49 |
| 6 50- 6 99 | 20 | 256 | 62 | 252 | ........ | 3 | 82 | 511 | 24.30 | 53.90 | 6 50- 6 99 |
| 7 00- 7 49 | 26 | 356 | 78 | 286 | 1 | 3 | 105 | 645 | 28.00 | 61.30 | 7 00- 7 49 |
| 7 50- 7 99 | 33 | 261 | 64 | 221 | ........ | 3 | 97 | 485 | 31.40 | 66.30 | 7 50- 7 99 |
| 8 00- 8 99 | 81 | 469 | 175 | 432 | 1 | 4 | 257 | 905 | 40.50 | 76.50 | 8 00- 8 99 |
| 9 00- 9 99 | 28 | 356 | 150 | 295 | 3 | 3 | 181 | 654 | 46.80 | 83.70 | 9 00- 9 99 |
| 10 00-10 99 | 51 | 297 | 117 | 213 | 2 | ........ | 170 | 510 | 52.90 | 89.20 | 10 00-10 99 |
| 11 00-11 99 | 55 | 174 | 120 | 107 | 1 | 2 | 176 | 283 | 59.10 | 92.40 | 11 00-11 99 |
| 12 00-12 99 | 63 | 166 | 138 | 84 | 2 | 4 | 203 | 254 | 66.20 | 95.20 | 12 00-12 99 |
| 13 00-13 99 | 55 | 105 | 119 | 56 | ........ | 1 | 174 | 162 | 72.40 | 96.70 | 13 00-13 99 |
| 14 00-14 99 | 48 | 79 | 98 | 31 | ........ | ........ | 146 | 110 | 77.50 | 98.20 | 14 00-14 99 |
| 15 00-15 99 | 60 | 55 | 79 | 25 | 1 | ........ | 140 | 80 | 82.40 | 99.10 | 15 00-15 99 |
| 16 00-17 99 | 45 | 34 | 137 | 16 | ........ | 1 | 182 | 51 | 88.80 | 99.60 | 16 00-17 99 |
| 18 00-19 99 | 42 | 18 | 88 | 3 | 2 | ........ | 132 | 21 | 93.60 | 99.90 | 18 00-19 99 |
| 20 00-24 99 | 48 | 7 | 84 | 1 | ........ | ........ | 132 | 8 | 98.20 | 99.99 | 20 00-24 99 |
| 25 00-29 99 | 15 | ........ | 15 | 1 | ........ | ........ | 30 | 1 | 99.20 | 100.00 | 25 00-29 99 |
| 30 00-34 99 | 8 | ........ | 7 | ........ | ........ | ........ | 15 | ........ | 99.80 | ........ | 30 00-34 99 |
| 35 00-39 99 | 2 | ........ | ........ | ........ | ........ | ........ | 2 | ........ | 99.90 | ........ | 35 00-39 99 |
| 40 00 and over | ........ | ........ | 4 | ........ | ........ | ........ | 4 | ........ | 100.00 | ........ | 40 00 and over |
| Not reported | 2 | 17 | 8 | 74 | ........ | ........ | 10 | 91 | ........ | ........ | Not reported |
| Total | 855 | 5,025 | 1,972 | 4,063 | 17 | 50 | 2,844 | 9,138 | ........ | ........ | Total |

NEW YORK STATE

97. TABLE XII, B, a

**THE MEN'S SHIRT INDUSTRY — FACTORY WORKERS**

NUMBER OF EMPLOYEES FOR EACH SEX CLASSIFIED ACCORDING TO ACTUAL WEEKLY EARNINGS BY THE NUMBER OF YEARS IN THE TRADE

| Actual Weekly Earnings in Dollars | Years in Trade | | | | | | | | | | | | | | Actual Weekly Earnings in Dollars |
|---|---|---|---|---|---|---|---|---|---|---|---|---|---|---|---|
| | Less than 1 | | 1 | | 2 | | 3 | | 4 | | 5 | | 6 | | |
| | Male | Female | Male | Female | Male | Female | Male | Female | Male | Female | Male | Female | Male | Female | |
| Less than $3 00 | 31 | 232 | 10 | 88 | 4 | 51 | 2 | 29 | ...... | 25 | 2 | 17 | 2 | 12 | Less than $3 00 |
| $3 00-$3 49... | 12 | 191 | 3 | 40 | 4 | 28 | 1 | 19 | 2 | 16 | 2 | 9 | 1 | 3 | ...$3 00- 3 49 |
| 3 50- 3 99... | 20 | 181 | 15 | 74 | 6 | 35 | 3 | 20 | 2 | 13 | 1 | 5 | ...... | 8 | ....3 50- 3 99 |
| 4 00- 4 49... | 29 | 244 | 7 | 79 | 4 | 57 | 4 | 29 | 2 | 23 | 3 | 17 | ...... | 9 | ....4 00- 4 49 |
| 4 50- 4 99... | 21 | 203 | 10 | 120 | 7 | 55 | 3 | 39 | 3 | 24 | 3 | 16 | ...... | 12 | ....4 50- 4 99 |
| 5 00- 5 49... | 49 | 217 | 19 | 162 | 7 | 114 | 2 | 48 | 8 | 37 | 13 | 30 | 2 | 16 | ....5 00- 5 49 |
| 5 50- 5 99... | 25 | 139 | 6 | 134 | 10 | 101 | 5 | 47 | 1 | 40 | 5 | 26 | 1 | 12 | ....5 50- 5 99 |
| 6 00- 6 49... | 56 | 168 | 12 | 160 | 16 | 115 | 9 | 62 | 13 | 49 | 14 | 30 | 2 | 28 | ....6 00- 6 49 |
| 6 50- 6 99... | 20 | 86 | 16 | 90 | 9 | 95 | 5 | 48 | 5 | 57 | 5 | 25 | 2 | 21 | ....6 50- 6 99 |
| 7 00- 7 49... | 27 | 99 | 24 | 92 | 10 | 103 | 7 | 83 | 8 | 74 | 5 | 35 | 3 | 25 | ....7 00- 7 49 |
| 7 50- 7 99... | 16 | 56 | 14 | 75 | 15 | 85 | 4 | 51 | 10 | 56 | 6 | 27 | 1 | 15 | ....7 50- 7 99 |
| 8 00- 8 99... | 29 | 87 | 35 | 105 | 32 | 132 | 21 | 106 | 15 | 100 | 25 | 75 | 13 | 38 | ....8 00- 8 99 |
| 9 00- 9 99... | 20 | 48 | 31 | 51 | 25 | 77 | 21 | 71 | 13 | 75 | 10 | 65 | 9 | 44 | ....9 00- 9 99 |
| 10 00-10 99... | 12 | 35 | 25 | 40 | 15 | 47 | 11 | 60 | 19 | 59 | 19 | 45 | 7 | 25 | ...10 00-10 99 |
| 11 00-11 99... | 6 | 14 | 5 | 21 | 19 | 22 | 17 | 25 | 20 | 23 | 13 | 25 | 10 | 21 | ...11 00-11 99 |
| 12 00-12 99... | 4 | 11 | 8 | 23 | 22 | 19 | 14 | 16 | 18 | 13 | 10 | 19 | 16 | 19 | ...12 00-12 99 |
| 13 00-13 99... | 3 | 5 | 5 | 9 | 14 | 11 | 15 | 16 | 15 | 15 | 21 | 9 | 7 | 11 | ...13 00-13 99 |
| 14 00-14 99... | 1 | 7 | 7 | 2 | 2 | 9 | 11 | 14 | 14 | 12 | 16 | 9 | 8 | 4 | ...14 00-14 99 |
| 15 00-15 99... | 2 | 3 | 2 | 5 | 5 | 5 | 5 | 2 | 11 | 5 | 11 | 5 | 2 | 8 | ...15 00-15 99 |
| 16 00-17 99... | .... | 3 | 4 | ...... | 3 | 4 | 13 | 2 | 15 | 10 | 15 | 3 | 15 | 3 | ...16 00-17 99 |
| 18 00-19 99... | .... | 2 | .... | ...... | 1 | 1 | 7 | ...... | 7 | 2 | 6 | 1 | 8 | 2 | ...18 00-19 99 |
| 20 00-24 99... | .... | 1 | 1 | ...... | 3 | ...... | 4 | ...... | 2 | 2 | 3 | 1 | 7 | ...... | ...20 00-24 99 |
| 30 00-34 99... | .... | ...... | .... | ...... | ...... | ...... | ...... | ...... | ...... | ...... | ...... | ...... | 1 | ...... | ...30 00-34 99 |
| Not reported... | 1 | 46 | 1 | 14 | 4 | 8 | ...... | 4 | ...... | 3 | ...... | ...... | ...... | ...... | ...Not reported |
| Total..... | 384 | 2,078 | 260 | 1,384 | 237 | 1,174 | 184 | 791 | 203 | 733 | 208 | 494 | 117 | 336 | .....Total |

NEW YORK STATE

97. TABLE XII, B, a. — (*continued*) THE MEN'S SHIRT INDUSTRY — FACTORY WORKERS

NUMBER OF EMPLOYEES FOR EACH SEX CLASSIFIED ACCORDING TO ACTUAL WEEKLY EARNINGS BY THE NUMBER OF YEARS IN THE TRADE

| ACTUAL WEEKLY EARNINGS IN DOLLARS | YEARS IN TRADE (*continued*) | | | | | | | | | | | | ACTUAL WEEKLY EARNINGS IN DOLLARS |
|---|---|---|---|---|---|---|---|---|---|---|---|---|---|
| | 7 | | 8 | | 9 | | 10–14 | | 15–19 | | 20–24 | | |
| | Male | Female | Male | Female | Male | Female | Male | Female | Male | Female | Male | Female | |
| Less than $3 00. | 4 | 4 | 3 | 6 | 1 | 2 | 4 | 23 | 3 | 13 | ....... | 13 | Less than $3 00 |
| $3 00–$3 49.... | ....... | 2 | ....... | 9 | 1 | 1 | 2 | 15 | 1 | 7 | ....... | 7 | ...$3 00– 3 49 |
| 3 50– 3 99.... | ....... | 6 | 2 | 6 | ....... | 3 | 2 | 10 | 1 | 11 | 1 | 1 | ....3 50– 3 99 |
| 4 00– 4 49.... | ....... | 6 | 2 | 15 | 2 | 5 | 8 | 19 | 1 | 8 | 1 | 5 | ....4 00– 4 49 |
| 4 50– 4 99.... | 4 | 8 | 1 | 7 | 2 | 1 | 1 | 17 | ....... | 8 | 1 | 4 | ....4 50– 4 99 |
| 5 00– 5 49.... | 3 | 14 | 1 | 10 | 2 | 7 | 7 | 26 | 3 | 7 | 1 | 5 | ....5 00– 5 49 |
| 5 50– 5 99.... | 1 | 20 | 2 | 10 | ....... | 4 | 7 | 24 | 1 | 12 | 3 | 11 | ....5 50– 5 99 |
| 6 00– 6 49.... | 5 | 17 | 2 | 17 | 5 | 6 | 5 | 30 | 5 | 14 | 7 | 15 | ....6 00– 6 49 |
| 6 50– 6 99.... | 3 | 12 | 2 | 14 | 3 | 7 | 5 | 18 | 4 | 16 | 1 | 7 | ....6 50– 6 99 |
| 7 00– 7 49.... | 3 | 32 | 3 | 18 | 1 | 5 | 5 | 39 | 4 | 16 | 2 | 10 | ....7 00– 7 49 |
| 7 50– 7 99.... | 3 | 14 | 3 | 12 | ....... | 11 | 7 | 34 | 7 | 18 | 5 | 13 | ....7 50– 7 99 |
| 8 00– 8 99.... | 11 | 46 | 10 | 22 | 5 | 19 | 27 | 96 | 14 | 36 | 11 | 19 | ....8 00– 8 99 |
| 9 00– 9 99.... | 4 | 29 | 7 | 43 | 3 | 17 | 20 | 58 | 10 | 32 | 6 | 18 | ....9 00– 9 99 |
| 10 00–10 99.... | 11 | 25 | 6 | 24 | 3 | 19 | 20 | 62 | 9 | 29 | 8 | 18 | ...10 00–10 99 |
| 11 00–11 99.... | 11 | 14 | 3 | 23 | 13 | 5 | 30 | 36 | 13 | 19 | 5 | 12 | ...11 00–11 99 |
| 12 00–12 99.... | 14 | 14 | 20 | 10 | 8 | 10 | 32 | 36 | 14 | 36 | 18 | 10 | ...12 00–12 99 |
| 13 00–13 99.... | 10 | 8 | 16 | 10 | 9 | 3 | 25 | 33 | 15 | 14 | 11 | 10 | ...13 00–13 99 |
| 14 00–14 99.... | 16 | 4 | 11 | 7 | 5 | 5 | 32 | 14 | 7 | 8 | 11 | 6 | ...14 00–14 99 |
| 15 00–15 99.... | 11 | 5 | 9 | 7 | 14 | 4 | 23 | 17 | 26 | 6 | 14 | 6 | ...15 00–15 99 |
| 16 00–17 99.... | 13 | 3 | 16 | 2 | 12 | ....... | 33 | 9 | 25 | 6 | 12 | 2 | ...16 00–17 99 |
| 18 00–19 99.... | 14 | 2 | 12 | 1 | 7 | 1 | 33 | 2 | 17 | 2 | 10 | ....... | ...18 00–19 99 |
| 20 00–24 99.... | 4 | ....... | 9 | ....... | 6 | 1 | 34 | 1 | 31 | ....... | 15 | 2 | ...20 00–24 99 |
| 25 00–29 99.... | 1 | 1 | 3 | ....... | 1 | ....... | 7 | ....... | 3 | ....... | 9 | ....... | ...25 00–29 99 |
| 30 00–34 99.... | ....... | ....... | ....... | ....... | ....... | ....... | 1 | ....... | 6 | ....... | 2 | ....... | ...30 00–34 99 |
| 40 00 and over.. | ....... | ....... | ....... | ....... | ....... | ....... | ....... | ....... | 1 | ....... | 2 | ....... | .40 00 and over |
| Not reported.... | ....... | 2 | 1 | 1 | ....... | ....... | 1 | ....... | ....... | ....... | ....... | ....... | ...Not reported |
| Total...... | 146 | 288 | 144 | 274 | 103 | 136 | 371 | 619 | 221 | 318 | 156 | 194 | ....Total |

NEW YORK STATE

97. TABLE XII, B, a — (*concluded*) **THE MEN'S SHIRT INDUSTRY — FACTORY WORKERS**

NUMBER OF EMPLOYEES FOR EACH SEX CLASSIFIED ACCORDING TO ACTUAL WEEKLY EARNINGS BY THE NUMBER OF YEARS IN THE TRADE

| Actual Weekly Earnings in Dollars | Years in Trade (*concluded*) | | | | | | | | | | | | | | Actual Weekly Earnings in Dollars |
|---|---|---|---|---|---|---|---|---|---|---|---|---|---|---|
| | 25–29 | | 30–34 | | 35–44 | | 45 and over | Not reported | | Total | | Cumulative per cent. of total | | |
| | Male | Female | Male | Female | Male | Female | Female | Male | Female | Male | Female | Male | Female | |
| Less than $3 00 | ...... | 8 | ...... | 2 | ...... | ...... | ...... | ...... | 13 | 66 | 538 | 2.33 | 5.94 | Less than $3 00 |
| $3 00–$3 49 | ...... | 4 | ...... | 4 | ...... | 2 | ...... | ...... | 4 | 29 | 361 | 3.35 | 9.93 | $3 00– 3 49 |
| 3 50– 3 99 | ...... | 4 | ...... | ...... | ...... | ...... | ...... | 1 | 5 | 54 | 382 | 5.26 | 14.30 | 3 50– 3 99 |
| 4 00– 4 49 | ...... | 3 | ...... | 2 | ...... | ...... | ...... | ...... | 2 | 63 | 523 | 7.48 | 19.90 | 4 00– 4 49 |
| 4 50– 4 99 | ...... | 6 | ...... | 4 | ...... | ...... | ...... | ...... | 9 | 56 | 533 | 9.46 | 25.80 | 4 50– 4 99 |
| 5 00– 5 49 | ...... | 4 | ...... | 2 | 1 | 1 | ...... | ...... | 10 | 118 | 710 | 13.60 | 33.70 | 5 00– 5 49 |
| 5 50– 5 99 | ...... | 2 | ...... | 1 | ...... | 2 | ...... | ...... | 8 | 67 | 593 | 16.00 | 40.20 | 5 50– 5 99 |
| 6 00– 6 49 | ...... | 3 | ...... | 5 | ...... | ...... | ...... | 2 | 8 | 153 | 727 | 21.40 | 48.30 | 6 00– 6 49 |
| 6 50– 6 99 | 2 | 3 | ...... | 2 | ...... | 2 | ...... | ...... | 8 | 82 | 511 | 24.30 | 53.90 | 6 50– 6 99 |
| 7 00– 7 49 | 2 | 3 | ...... | ...... | ...... | 1 | ...... | 1 | 10 | 105 | 645 | 28.00 | 61.30 | 7 00– 7 49 |
| 7 50– 7 99 | 2 | 4 | ...... | 1 | 1 | 1 | ...... | 3 | 12 | 97 | 485 | 31.40 | 66.30 | 7 50– 7 99 |
| 8 00– 8 99 | 2 | 6 | 1 | 4 | ...... | 2 | ...... | 6 | 12 | 257 | 905 | 40.50 | 76.50 | 8 00– 8 99 |
| 9 00– 9 99 | 2 | 8 | ...... | 3 | ...... | 2 | ...... | ...... | 13 | 181 | 654 | 46.80 | 83.70 | 9 00– 9 99 |
| 10 00–10 99 | 3 | 5 | ...... | 5 | ...... | 4 | ...... | 2 | 8 | 170 | 510 | 52.90 | 89.20 | 10 00–10 99 |
| 11 00–11 99 | 3 | 5 | 2 | ...... | 3 | 1 | ...... | 3 | 17 | 176 | 283 | 59.10 | 92.40 | 11 00–11 99 |
| 12 00–12 99 | 2 | 6 | 2 | 3 | ...... | ...... | ...... | 1 | 9 | 203 | 254 | 66.20 | 95.20 | 12 00–12 99 |
| 13 00–13 99 | 6 | 3 | ...... | 1 | 1 | ...... | 1 | 1 | 3 | 174 | 162 | 72.40 | 96.70 | 13 00–13 99 |
| 14 00–14 99 | 4 | 3 | 1 | 1 | ...... | ...... | ...... | ...... | 5 | 146 | 110 | 77.50 | 98.20 | 14 00–14 99 |
| 15 00–15 99 | 1 | ...... | 3 | 2 | 1 | ...... | ...... | ...... | ...... | 140 | 80 | 82.40 | 99.10 | 15 00–15 99 |
| 16 00–17 99 | 4 | 1 | ...... | ...... | 1 | ...... | ...... | 1 | 3 | 182 | 51 | 88.80 | 99.60 | 16 00–17 99 |
| 18 00–19 99 | 4 | 1 | 1 | 1 | 2 | 2 | ...... | 3 | 1 | 132 | 21 | 93.60 | 99.90 | 18 00–19 99 |
| 20 00–24 99 | 5 | ...... | 4 | ...... | 3 | ...... | ...... | 1 | ...... | 132 | 8 | 98.20 | 99.99 | 20 00–24 99 |
| 25 00–29 99 | 2 | ...... | 1 | ...... | 2 | ...... | ...... | 1 | ...... | 30 | 1 | 99.20 | 100.00 | 25 00–29 00 |
| 30 00–34 99 | 2 | ...... | 1 | ...... | 2 | ...... | ...... | ...... | ...... | 15 | ...... | 99.80 | ...... | 30 00–34 99 |
| 35 00–39 00 | 1 | ...... | 1 | ...... | ...... | ...... | ...... | ...... | ...... | 2 | ...... | 99.90 | ...... | 35 00–39 99 |
| 40 00 and over | 1 | ...... | ...... | ...... | ...... | ...... | ...... | ...... | ...... | 4 | ...... | 100.00 | ...... | 40 00 and over |
| Not reported | ...... | ...... | ...... | ...... | ...... | ...... | ...... | 2 | 13 | 10 | 91 | ...... | ...... | Not reported |
| Total | 48 | 82 | 17 | 43 | 17 | 20 | 1 | 28 | 173 | 2,844 | 9,138 | ...... | ...... | Total |

NEW YORK STATE

98. TABLE XIII, B, a. THE MEN'S SHIRT INDUSTRY — FACTORY WORKERS

Number of Employees for Each Sex Classified According to Actual Weekly Earnings by the Number of Years With the Firm

| Actual Weekly Earnings in Dollars | Years With Firm | | | | | | | | | | | | | | Actual Weekly Earnings in Dollars |
|---|---|---|---|---|---|---|---|---|---|---|---|---|---|---|---|
| | Less than 1 | | 1 | | 2 | | 3 | | 4 | | 5 | | 6 | | |
| | Male | Female | Male | Female | Male | Female | Male | Female | Male | Female | Male | Female | Male | Female | |
| Less than $3 00 | 44 | 298 | 9 | 81 | 5 | 38 | 2 | 27 | ...... | 20 | 1 | 16 | 3 | 8 | Less than $3 00 |
| $3 00–$3 49... | 17 | 231 | 5 | 38 | 2 | 21 | 2 | 15 | 1 | 11 | ...... | 5 | ...... | 3 | ...$3 00– 3 49 |
| 3 50– 3 99... | 29 | 231 | 16 | 67 | 6 | 27 | ...... | 11 | 1 | 14 | ...... | 7 | ...... | 5 | ....3 50– 3 99 |
| 4 00– 4 49... | 39 | 298 | 10 | 78 | 7 | 40 | 2 | 27 | 1 | 18 | 2 | 10 | ...... | 10 | ....4 00– 4 49 |
| 4 50– 4 99... | 34 | 266 | 8 | 120 | 6 | 43 | 2 | 24 | 2 | 21 | ...... | 9 | 1 | 14 | ....4 50– 4 99 |
| 5 00– 5 49... | 60 | 313 | 20 | 155 | 6 | 88 | 12 | 38 | 8 | 29 | 5 | 25 | 2 | 8 | ....5 00– 5 49 |
| 5 50– 5 99... | 40 | 214 | 8 | 145 | 6 | 84 | 3 | 39 | 1 | 25 | 1 | 21 | ...... | 12 | ....5 50– 5 99 |
| 6 00– 6 49... | 81 | 259 | 14 | 158 | 14 | 84 | 7 | 62 | 11 | 39 | 8 | 29 | 5 | 18 | ....6 00– 6 49 |
| 6 50– 6 99... | 33 | 139 | 18 | 119 | 9 | 84 | 2 | 33 | 6 | 40 | 6 | 17 | ...... | 18 | ....6 50– 6 99 |
| 7 00– 7 49... | 48 | 178 | 28 | 122 | 9 | 83 | 2 | 59 | 3 | 65 | 5 | 36 | ...... | 24 | ....7 00– 7 49 |
| 7 50– 7 99... | 37 | 131 | 20 | 87 | 10 | 69 | 4 | 41 | 6 | 40 | 4 | 29 | ...... | 11 | ....7 50– 7 99 |
| 8 00– 8 99... | 80 | 183 | 43 | 153 | 31 | 129 | 13 | 100 | 19 | 79 | 15 | 62 | 5 | 24 | ....8 00– 8 99 |
| 9 00– 9 99... | 62 | 120 | 44 | 88 | 20 | 74 | 17 | 63 | 8 | 69 | 7 | 58 | 3 | 30 | ....9 00– 9 99 |
| 10 00–10 99... | 49 | 104 | 37 | 54 | 17 | 52 | 16 | 57 | 11 | 53 | 16 | 44 | 5 | 11 | ...10 00–10 99 |
| 11 00–11 99... | 36 | 43 | 21 | 31 | 27 | 22 | 20 | 32 | 13 | 31 | 13 | 17 | 7 | 22 | ...11 00–11 99 |
| 12 00–12 99... | 42 | 48 | 28 | 38 | 34 | 19 | 25 | 24 | 21 | 20 | 9 | 15 | 12 | 13 | ...12 00–12 99 |
| 13 00–13 99... | 41 | 20 | 23 | 13 | 23 | 13 | 18 | 19 | 11 | 19 | 17 | 8 | 9 | 11 | ...13 00–13 99 |
| 14 00–14 99... | 19 | 17 | 23 | 8 | 12 | 12 | 27 | 15 | 13 | 12 | 16 | 7 | 11 | 3 | ...14 00–14 99 |
| 15 00–15 99... | 28 | 14 | 17 | 10 | 9 | 3 | 14 | 14 | 13 | 4 | 15 | 7 | 8 | 3 | ...15 00–15 99 |
| 16 00–17 99... | 41 | 11 | 31 | 3 | 12 | 4 | 13 | 4 | 16 | 9 | 14 | 3 | 13 | 3 | ...16 00–17 99 |
| 18 00–19 99... | 32 | 6 | 11 | 1 | 10 | 1 | 10 | ...... | 5 | 2 | 12 | 2 | 6 | 2 | ...18 00–19 99 |
| 20 00–24 99... | 19 | 2 | 16 | 2 | 10 | ...... | 9 | ...... | 11 | ...... | 9 | 2 | 11 | ...... | ...20 00–24 99 |
| 25 00–29 99... | 6 | ...... | 3 | ...... | 6 | ...... | ...... | 1 | 1 | ...... | ...... | ...... | ...... | ...... | ...25 00–29 99 |
| 30 00–34 99... | 3 | ...... | 1 | ...... | 1 | ...... | ...... | ...... | 3 | ...... | 1 | ...... | ...... | ...... | ...30 00–34 99 |
| 35 00–39 99... | .... | ...... | 1 | ...... | ...... | ...... | ...... | ...... | ...... | ...... | ...... | ...... | ...... | ...... | ...35 00–39 99 |
| 40 00 and over. | .... | ...... | .... | ...... | ...... | ...... | ...... | ...... | ...... | ...... | ...... | ...... | 1 | ...... | .40 00 and over |
| Not reported... | 2 | 68 | 2 | 16 | 4 | 4 | ...... | 2 | ...... | 1 | ...... | ...... | ...... | ...... | ...Not reported |
| Total..... | 922 | 3,194 | 457 | 1,587 | 296 | 994 | 220 | 707 | 185 | 621 | 176 | 429 | 102 | 253 | .....Total |

NEW YORK STATE

98. TABLE XIII, B, a — (*continued*) **THE MEN'S SHIRT INDUSTRY — FACTORY WORKERS**

NUMBER OF EMPLOYEES FOR EACH SEX CLASSIFIED ACCORDING TO ACTUAL WEEKLY EARNINGS BY THE NUMBER OF YEARS WITH THE FIRM

| ACTUAL WEEKLY EARNINGS IN DOLLARS | YEARS WITH FIRM (*continued*) | | | | | | | | | | | | ACTUAL WEEKLY EARNINGS IN DOLLARS |
|---|---|---|---|---|---|---|---|---|---|---|---|---|---|
| | 7 | | 8 | | 9 | | 10–14 | | 15–19 | | 20–24 | | |
| | Male | Female | Male | Female | Male | Female | Male | Female | Male | Female | Male | Female | |
| Less than $3 00. | ...... | 2 | ...... | 6 | ...... | 1 | 2 | 13 | ...... | 12 | ...... | 9 | Less than $3 00 |
| $3 00–$3 49.... | 1 | 7 | ...... | 3 | ...... | ...... | 1 | 11 | ...... | 5 | ...... | 5 | ...$3 00– 3 49 |
| 3 50– 3 99.... | ...... | 4 | 2 | ...... | ...... | 1 | ...... | 9 | ...... | 2 | ...... | 2 | ....3 50– 3 99 |
| 4 00– 4 49.... | ...... | 9 | ...... | 9 | ...... | 2 | 2 | 12 | ...... | 5 | ...... | 2 | ....4 00– 4 49 |
| 4 50– 4 99.... | 1 | 11 | 1 | 3 | ...... | 2 | 1 | 8 | ...... | 5 | ...... | 2 | ....4 50– 4 99 |
| 5 00– 5 49.... | 2 | 9 | 1 | 8 | ...... | 6 | 2 | 16 | ...... | 4 | ...... | 2 | ....5 00– 5 49 |
| 5 50– 5 99.... | 1 | 11 | 2 | 3 | ...... | 7 | 4 | 12 | ...... | 7 | 1 | 7 | ....5 50– 5 99 |
| 6 00– 6 49.... | 4 | 17 | 1 | 15 | 2 | 3 | 2 | 15 | 1 | 13 | ...... | 7 | ....6 00– 6 49 |
| 6 50– 6 99.... | 1 | 12 | 1 | 13 | 1 | 5 | 4 | 11 | 1 | 7 | ...... | 4 | ....6 50– 6 99 |
| 7 00– 7 49.... | 3 | 24 | 4 | 11 | ...... | 4 | 2 | 23 | 1 | 4 | ...... | 4 | ....7 00– 7 49 |
| 7 50– 7 99.... | 3 | 13 | 4 | 8 | 1 | 7 | 3 | 31 | 2 | 7 | 1 | 6 | ....7 50– 7 99 |
| 8 00– 8 99.... | 11 | 48 | 7 | 17 | 2 | 17 | 14 | 49 | 10 | 21 | 3 | 12 | ....8 00– 8 99 |
| 9 00– 9 99.... | 6 | 32 | 2 | 26 | 1 | 17 | 6 | 41 | 4 | 18 | 1 | 8 | ....9 00– 9 99 |
| 10 00–10 99.... | 5 | 23 | 3 | 21 | 2 | 11 | 4 | 42 | 2 | 17 | 1 | 12 | ...10 00–10 99 |
| 11 00–11 99.... | 11 | 14 | 1 | 18 | 5 | 3 | 17 | 24 | ...... | 13 | ...... | 6 | ...11 00–11 99 |
| 12 00–12 99.... | 4 | 9 | 6 | 8 | 4 | 5 | 10 | 27 | 4 | 18 | 3 | 5 | ...12 00–12 99 |
| 13 00–13 99.... | 5 | 7 | 7 | 9 | 5 | 1 | 11 | 21 | 2 | 8 | ...... | 8 | ...13 00–13 99 |
| 14 00–14 99.... | 8 | 7 | 5 | 5 | 2 | 2 | 10 | 12 | ...... | 4 | ...... | 1 | ...14 00–14 99 |
| 15 00–15 99.... | 5 | 5 | 4 | 4 | 6 | 4 | 14 | 8 | 3 | 2 | 2 | 1 | ...15 00–15 99 |
| 16 00–17 99.... | 7 | 2 | 11 | 3 | 3 | ...... | 13 | 5 | 6 | 3 | ...... | ...... | ...16 00–17 99 |
| 18 00–19 99.... | 7 | 1 | 9 | 1 | 4 | 1 | 15 | 2 | 5 | ...... | 3 | ...... | ...18 00–19 99 |
| 20 00–24 99.... | 10 | 1 | 4 | 1 | 4 | ...... | 17 | ...... | 9 | ...... | 1 | ...... | ...20 00–24 99 |
| 25 00–29 99.... | 2 | ...... | 1 | ...... | ...... | ...... | 4 | ...... | 4 | ...... | 1 | ...... | ...25 00–29 99 |
| 30 00–34 99.... | 1 | ...... | 1 | ...... | 2 | ...... | ...... | ...... | 1 | ...... | ...... | ...... | ...30 00–34 99 |
| 40 00 and over.. | 1 | ...... | ...... | ...... | ...... | ...... | ...... | ...... | 1 | ...... | 1 | ...... | .40 00 and over |
| Not reported.... | ...... | ...... | ...... | ...... | 1 | ...... | ...... | ...... | ...... | ...... | ...... | ...... | ...Not reported |
| Total...... | 99 | 268 | 77 | 192 | 45 | 99 | 158 | 392 | 56 | 175 | 18 | 103 | ....Total |

NEW YORK STATE

98. TABLE XIII, B, a — (*concluded*) **THE MEN'S SHIRT INDUSTRY — FACTORY WORKERS**

NUMBER OF EMPLOYEES FOR EACH SEX CLASSIFIED ACCORDING TO ACTUAL WEEKLY EARNINGS BY THE NUMBER OF YEARS WITH THE FIRM

| ACTUAL WEEKLY EARNINGS IN DOLLARS | YEARS WITH FIRM (*concluded*) | | | | | | | | | | | | | | ACTUAL WEEKLY EARNINGS IN DOLLARS |
|---|---|---|---|---|---|---|---|---|---|---|---|---|---|---|---|
| | 25–29 | | 30–34 | | 35–44 | | 45 AND OVER | NOT REPORTED | | TOTAL | | CUMULATIVE PER CENT. OF TOTAL | | | |
| | Male | Female | Male | Female | Male | Female | Female | Male | Female | Male | Female | Male | Female | | |
| Less than $3 00 | ...... | 3 | ...... | 1 | ...... | ...... | ...... | ...... | 3 | 66 | 538 | 3.33 | 5.94 | Less than $3 00 |
| $3 00–$3 49 | ...... | 2 | ...... | 1 | ...... | ...... | ...... | ...... | 3 | 29 | 361 | 3.35 | 9.93 | $3 00– 3 49 |
| 3 50– 3 99 | ...... | 2 | ...... | ...... | ...... | ...... | ...... | ...... | ...... | 54 | 382 | 5.26 | 14.30 | 3 50– 3 99 |
| 4 00– 4 49 | ...... | 1 | ...... | ...... | ...... | ...... | ...... | ...... | 2 | 63 | 523 | 7.48 | 19.90 | 4 00– 4 49 |
| 4 50– 4 99 | ...... | 3 | ...... | ...... | ...... | ...... | ...... | ...... | 2 | 56 | 533 | 9.46 | 25.80 | 4 50– 4 99 |
| 5 00– 5 49 | ...... | 4 | ...... | 1 | ...... | ...... | ...... | ...... | 4 | 118 | 710 | 13.60 | 33.70 | 5 00– 5 49 |
| 5 50– 5 99 | ...... | 1 | ...... | ...... | ...... | ...... | ...... | ...... | 5 | 67 | 593 | 16.00 | 40.20 | 5 50– 5 99 |
| 6 00– 6 49 | ...... | 2 | ...... | 2 | ...... | ...... | ...... | 3 | 4 | 153 | 727 | 21.40 | 48.30 | 6 00– 6 49 |
| 6 50– 6 99 | ...... | 3 | ...... | ...... | ...... | 2 | ...... | ...... | 4 | 82 | 511 | 24.30 | 53.90 | 6 50– 6 99 |
| 7 00– 7 49 | ...... | 1 | ...... | ...... | ...... | ...... | ...... | ...... | 7 | 105 | 645 | 28.00 | 61.30 | 7 00– 7 49 |
| 7 50– 7 99 | ...... | 2 | ...... | ...... | ...... | ...... | ...... | 2 | 3 | 97 | 485 | 31.40 | 66.30 | 7 50– 7 99 |
| 8 00– 8 99 | ...... | 5 | ...... | 2 | ...... | 1 | ...... | 4 | 3 | 257 | 905 | 40.50 | 76.50 | 8 00– 8 99 |
| 9 00– 9 99 | ...... | 4 | ...... | 2 | ...... | ...... | ...... | ...... | 4 | 181 | 654 | 46.80 | 83.70 | 9 00– 9 99 |
| 10 00–10 99 | ...... | 3 | ...... | 2 | ...... | 1 | ...... | 2 | 3 | 170 | 510 | 52.90 | 89.20 | 10 00–10 99 |
| 11 00–11 99 | 1 | 3 | ...... | ...... | 1 | ...... | ...... | 3 | 4 | 176 | 283 | 59.10 | 92.40 | 11 00–11 99 |
| 12 00–12 99 | ...... | 3 | 1 | 1 | ...... | ...... | ...... | ...... | 1 | 203 | 254 | 66.20 | 95.20 | 12 00–12 99 |
| 13 00–13 99 | 2 | 2 | ...... | 1 | ...... | ...... | 1 | ...... | 1 | 174 | 162 | 72.40 | 96.70 | 13 00–13 99 |
| 14 00–14 99 | ...... | 1 | ...... | 1 | ...... | ...... | ...... | ...... | 3 | 146 | 110 | 77.50 | 98.20 | 14 00–14 99 |
| 15 00–15 99 | 2 | ...... | ...... | ...... | ...... | ...... | ...... | ...... | 1 | 140 | 80 | 82.40 | 99.10 | 15 00–15 99 |
| 16 00–17 99 | 2 | 1 | ...... | ...... | ...... | ...... | ...... | ...... | ...... | 182 | 51 | 88.80 | 99.60 | 16 00–17 99 |
| 18 00–19 99 | 1 | ...... | ...... | ...... | 1 | 2 | ...... | 1 | ...... | 132 | 21 | 93.60 | 99.90 | 18 00–19 99 |
| 20 00–24 99 | 1 | ...... | ...... | ...... | ...... | ...... | ...... | 1 | ...... | 132 | 8 | 98.20 | 99.90 | 20 00–24 99 |
| 25 00–29 99 | ...... | ...... | 1 | ...... | ...... | ...... | ...... | 1 | ...... | 30 | 1 | 99.20 | 100.00 | 25 00–29 99 |
| 30 00–34 99 | 1 | ...... | ...... | ...... | ...... | ...... | ...... | ...... | ...... | 15 | ...... | 99.80 | ...... | 30 00–34 99 |
| 35 00–39 99 | ...... | ...... | ...... | ...... | ...... | ...... | ...... | 1 | ...... | 2 | ...... | 99.90 | ...... | 35 00–39 99 |
| 40 00 and over | ...... | ...... | ...... | ...... | ...... | ...... | ...... | ...... | ...... | 4 | ...... | 100.00 | ...... | 40 00 and over |
| Not reported | ...... | ...... | ...... | ...... | ...... | ...... | ...... | 1 | ...... | 10 | 91 | ...... | ...... | Not reported |
| Total | 10 | 46 | 2 | 14 | 2 | 6 | 1 | 19 | 57 | 2,844 | 9,138 | ...... | ...... | Total |

NEW YORK STATE
**THE PAPER BOX INDUSTRY**

9. TABLE VXIII, c — NUMBER AND PER CENT. OF ALL EMPLOYEES IN EACH DEPARTMENT, ACCORDING TO ACTUAL WEEKLY EARNINGS

| Actual Weekly Earnings in Dollars | Department: Factory | | Office | | Shipping | | Plant | | Total | | Cumulative Per Cent of Total | | Actual Weekly Earnings in Dollars |
|---|---|---|---|---|---|---|---|---|---|---|---|---|---|
| | Male | Female | Male | Female | Male | Female | Male | Female | Male | Female | Male | Female | |
| Less than $3 00 | 38 | 231 | ....... | ....... | 2 | ....... | 5 | 1 | 45 | 232 | 1.10 | 3.00 | Less than $3 00 |
| $3 00–$3 49 | 27 | 219 | ....... | ....... | 1 | ....... | ....... | 1 | 28 | 220 | 1.80 | 5.90 | $3 00– 3 49 |
| 3 50– 3 99 | 26 | 266 | ....... | ....... | 4 | ....... | 1 | ....... | 31 | 266 | 2.60 | 9.40 | 3 50– 3 99 |
| 4 00– 4 49 | 56 | 428 | ....... | 1 | 11 | ....... | 5 | 1 | 72 | 430 | 4.40 | 15.00 | 4 00– 4 49 |
| 4 50– 4 99 | 49 | 493 | 4 | 2 | 14 | ....... | 7 | 1 | 74 | 496 | 6.30 | 21.50 | 4 50– 4 99 |
| 5 00– 5 49 | 103 | 716 | 3 | 6 | 29 | 1 | 8 | 4 | 143 | 727 | 9.80 | 31.00 | 5 00– 5 49 |
| 5 50– 5 99 | 79 | 569 | ....... | 2 | 10 | 3 | 3 | 2 | 92 | 576 | 12.01 | 38.50 | 5 50– 5 99 |
| 6 00– 6 49 | 130 | 662 | 3 | 10 | 20 | ....... | 14 | ....... | 167 | 672 | 16.30 | 47.20 | 6 00– 6 49 |
| 6 50– 6 99 | 76 | 435 | 1 | 7 | 4 | 5 | 9 | 2 | 90 | 449 | 18.60 | 53.20 | 6 50– 6 99 |
| 7 00– 7 49 | 112 | 508 | ....... | 15 | 13 | 1 | 11 | 4 | 136 | 528 | 21.90 | 60.00 | 7 00– 7 49 |
| 7 50– 7 99 | 81 | 390 | 2 | 2 | 4 | 2 | 9 | 5 | 96 | 399 | 24.30 | 65.20 | 7 50– 7 99 |
| 8 00– 8 99 | 207 | 824 | 8 | 31 | 24 | 4 | 35 | 11 | 274 | 870 | 31.20 | 76.70 | 8 00– 8 99 |
| 9 00– 9 99 | 212 | 672 | 5 | 23 | 33 | 1 | 54 | 7 | 304 | 703 | 39.00 | 86.00 | 9 00– 9 99 |
| 10 00–10 99 | 214 | 449 | 4 | 28 | 48 | 2 | 41 | 2 | 307 | 481 | 46.40 | 92.20 | 10 00–10 99 |
| 11 00–11 99 | 180 | 236 | 3 | 7 | 45 | 3 | 43 | ....... | 271 | 246 | 53.00 | 95.20 | 11 00–11 99 |
| 12 00–12 99 | 211 | 172 | 9 | 18 | 66 | ....... | 53 | ....... | 339 | 190 | 61.60 | 97.60 | 12 00–12 99 |
| 13 00–13 99 | 173 | 56 | 5 | 7 | 47 | ....... | 26 | ....... | 251 | 63 | 68.00 | 98.60 | 13 00–13 99 |
| 14 00–14 99 | 147 | 29 | 5 | 11 | 31 | ....... | 23 | ....... | 206 | 40 | 73.20 | 99.20 | 14 00–14 99 |
| 15 00–15 99 | 173 | 11 | 8 | 7 | 27 | ....... | 25 | ....... | 233 | 18 | 79.00 | 99.40 | 15 00–15 99 |
| 16 00–17 99 | 232 | 17 | 8 | 9 | 30 | ....... | 44 | ....... | 314 | 26 | 86.80 | 99.70 | 16 00–17 99 |
| 18 00–19 99 | 139 | 3 | 3 | 4 | 8 | ....... | 55 | ....... | 205 | 7 | 91.80 | 99.80 | 18 00–19 99 |
| 20 00–24 99 | 157 | 2 | 11 | 3 | 6 | ....... | 45 | ....... | 219 | 5 | 97.80 | 99.90 | 20 00–24 99 |
| 25 00–29 99 | 37 | 1 | 10 | 2 | 1 | ....... | 14 | ....... | 62 | 3 | 99.00 | 100.00 | 25 00–29 99 |
| 30 00–34 99 | 19 | ....... | 6 | ....... | 1 | ....... | 1 | ....... | 27 | ....... | 99.60 | ....... | 30 00–34 99 |
| 35 00–39 99 | 8 | ....... | 3 | ....... | ....... | ....... | 1 | ....... | 12 | ....... | 99.90 | ....... | 35 00–39 99 |
| 40 00 and over | ....... | ....... | 2 | ....... | ....... | ....... | ....... | ....... | 2 | ....... | 100.00 | ....... | 40 00 and over |
| Not reported | 34 | 67 | 16 | 14 | 3 | ....... | 2 | ....... | 55 | 81 | ....... | ....... | Not reported |
| Total | 2,920 | 7,456 | 119 | 209 | 482 | 22 | 534 | 41 | 4,055 | 7,728 | ....... | ....... | Total |

100. TABLE I, C

NEW YORK STATE

THE PAPER BOX INDUSTRY

NUMBER OF EMPLOYEES ACCORDING TO AGE GROUPS, BY LOCALITY AND SEX

| | Locality | Sex | Age groups in years | | | | | | | | | | | |
|---|---|---|---|---|---|---|---|---|---|---|---|---|---|---|
| | | | Total | 14–15 | 16–17 | 18–20 | 21–24 | 25–29 | 30–34 | 35–39 | 40–44 | 45–54 | 55–64 | 65 and over | Not reported |
| Factory workers | New York city | Male | 2,233 | 47 | 218 | 422 | 466 | 380 | 236 | 167 | 108 | 125 | 46 | 5 | 13 |
| | | Female | 5,522 | 362 | 1,269 | 1,713 | 1,024 | 458 | 234 | 185 | 127 | 109 | 30 | ...... | 11 |
| | Buffalo | Male | 129 | 4 | 17 | 24 | 31 | 16 | 18 | 2 | 6 | 5 | 6 | ...... | ....... |
| | | Female | 655 | 49 | 140 | 222 | 169 | 38 | 10 | 9 | 7 | 7 | 1 | ...... | 3 |
| | Rochester | Male | 108 | 1 | 8 | 14 | 22 | 22 | 13 | 10 | 6 | 5 | 4 | 3 | ....... |
| | | Female | 510 | 30 | 105 | 118 | 114 | 63 | 43 | 14 | 8 | 9 | 1 | ...... | 5 |
| | Troy | Male | 196 | 19 | 25 | 21 | 32 | 27 | 21 | 13 | 15 | 15 | 6 | 1 | 1 |
| | | Female | 143 | 1 | 21 | 29 | 26 | 14 | 13 | 12 | 11 | 9 | 5 | ...... | 2 |
| | Other cities and towns | Male | 254 | 14 | 22 | 53 | 40 | 42 | 31 | 20 | 13 | 9 | 7 | 2 | 1 |
| | | Female | 626 | 40 | 120 | 167 | 118 | 63 | 32 | 38 | 11 | 21 | 7 | 1 | 8 |
| Office, shipping and plant | All localities | Male | 1,135 | 33 | 86 | 166 | 199 | 179 | 130 | 98 | 73 | 110 | 38 | 11 | 12 |
| | | Female | 272 | 3 | 37 | 75 | 69 | 43 | 19 | 11 | 3 | 4 | 2 | ...... | 6 |
| All workers | State | Male | 4,055 | 118 | 376 | 700 | 790 | 666 | 449 | 310 | 221 | 269 | 107 | 22 | 27 |
| | | Female | 7,728 | 485 | 1,692 | 2,324 | 1,520 | 679 | 351 | 269 | 167 | 159 | 46 | 1 | 35 |
| | Cumulative per cent. for state | Male | 100 | 2.93 | 12.26 | 29.66 | 49.29 | 65.71 | 76.91 | 84.62 | 90.10 | 96.79 | 99.45 | 100 | ....... |
| | | Female | 100 | 6.29 | 28.17 | 58.37 | 78.37 | 87.15 | 91.70 | 95.17 | 97.33 | 99.39 | 99.99 | 100 | ....... |

101. TABLE II, C.

NEW YORK STATE

THE PAPER BOX INDUSTRY

NUMBER AND PER CENT. OF ALL EMPLOYEES ACCORDING TO NATIVITY, BY LOCALITY

| | Locality | Distribution of native and foreign born | | | | | | | Distribution of foreign born, according to country of birth | | | | | | | | | | | |
|---|---|---|---|---|---|---|---|---|---|---|---|---|---|---|---|---|---|---|---|---|
| | | Total | | Not reported | Native | | Foreign | | Russia | | Italy | | Austria | | Germany | | England | | Ireland | |
| | | Number | Per cent | Number | Number | Per cent | Number | Per cent | Number | Per cent | Number | Per cent | Number | Per cent | Number | Per cent | Number | Per cent | Number | Per cent |
| Factory workers | New York city | 7,755 | 100.00 | 25 | 4,758 | 61.50 | 2,972 | 38.50 | 1,531 | 51.50 | 606 | 20.40 | 307 | 10.35 | 142 | 4.77 | 76 | 2.56 | 83 | 2.80 |
| | Buffalo | 784 | 100.00 | 1 | 688 | 88.00 | 95 | 12.00 | 7 | 7.37 | 10 | 10.52 | ...... | ..... | 21 | 22.14 | 3 | 3.15 | 3 | 3.15 |
| | Rochester | 618 | 100.00 | 3 | 506 | 82.00 | 109 | 18.00 | 16 | 14.68 | 19 | 17.43 | 12 | 11.00 | 13 | 11.92 | 15 | 13.75 | 2 | 1.84 |
| | Troy | 339 | 100.00 | 2 | 311 | 92.50 | 26 | 7.50 | ...... | ..... | 4 | 15.40 | 2 | 7.70 | 2 | 7.70 | 6 | 23.04 | 4 | 15.40 |
| | Other cities and towns | 880 | 100.00 | 5 | 757 | 86.50 | 118 | 13.50 | 12 | 10.16 | 30 | 26.41 | 8 | 6.79 | 12 | 10.16 | 12 | 10.16 | 5 | 4.26 |
| Office, shipping and plant | All localities | 1,407 | 100.00 | 14 | 957 | 68.80 | 436 | 31.20 | 101 | 23.18 | 136 | 31.18 | 22 | 5.06 | 68 | 15.61 | 16 | 3.58 | 15 | 3.45 |
| All workers | State | 11,783 | 100.00 | 50 | 7,977 | 68.00 | 3,756 | 32.00 | 1,667 | 44.43 | 805 | 21.41 | 351 | 9.34 | 258 | 6.86 | 128 | 3.41 | 112 | 2.94 |

101. TABLE II. C—(*concluded*)

NEW YORK STATE
**THE PAPER BOX INDUSTRY**
NUMBER AND PER CENT OF ALL EMPLOYEES, ACCORDING TO NATIVITY, BY LOCALITY

| | LOCALITY | DISTRIBUTION OF FOREIGN BORN, ACCORDING TO COUNTRY OF BIRTH—*Concluded* | | | | | | | | | | | | | | | | | | | |
|---|---|---|---|---|---|---|---|---|---|---|---|---|---|---|---|---|---|---|---|---|---|
| | | Canada | | Poland | | Roumania | | Hungary | | Scotland | | Holland | | Turkey | | Greece | | France | | All other* | |
| | | Number | Per cent | Number | Per cent | Number | Per cent | Number | Per cent | Number | Per cent | Number | Per cent | Number | Per cent | Number | Per cent | Number | Per cent | Number | Per cent |
| Factory workers | New York city | 18 | .60 | 21 | .71 | 46 | 1.55 | 29 | .97 | 27 | .91 | | | 20 | .67 | 18 | .60 | 12 | .40 | 36 | 1.21 |
| | Buffalo | 22 | 23.15 | 22 | 23.15 | | | | | | | | | | | | | | | 7 | 7.37 |
| | Rochester | 16 | 14.68 | 2 | 1.84 | | | 2 | 1.84 | | | 4 | 3.68 | | | | | | | 8 | 7.34 |
| | Troy | 5 | 19.21 | | | | | | | 2 | 7.70 | | | | | | | | | 1 | 3.85 |
| | Other cities and towns | 9 | 7.61 | 2 | 1.70 | | | | | | | 20 | 16.95 | | | | | | | 8 | 6.79 |
| Office, shipping and plant | All localities | 19 | 4.37 | 9 | 2.07 | 8 | 1.84 | 5 | 1.15 | 5 | 1.15 | 5 | 1.15 | 5 | 1.15 | | | | | 22 | 5.06 |
| All workers | State | 89 | 2.45 | 56 | 1.47 | 54 | 1.42 | 36 | .96 | 34 | .90 | 29 | .77 | 25 | .67 | 18 | .48 | 12 | .32 | 82 | 2.17 |

* Includes for each locality (New York City excepted) countries representing less than one per cent of the total foreign born employees in the industry in that locality.

NEW YORK STATE

THE PAPER BOX INDUSTRY

102. TABLE III, C — NUMBER OF EMPLOYEES, BY SEX, EARNING SPECIFIED RATES, ACCORDING TO LOCALITY

| Weekly Rates in Dollars | Locality: New York City | | Buffalo | | Rochester | | Troy | | Other Cities and Towns | | Office, Shipping and Plant. All Localities | | State | | Cumulative Per Cent. for State | | Weekly Rates in Dollars |
|---|---|---|---|---|---|---|---|---|---|---|---|---|---|---|---|---|---|
| | Male | Female | Male | Female | Male | Female | Male | Female | Male | Female | Male | Female | Male | Female | Male | Female | |
| Less than $3 00 | 1 | 4 | | 5 | | | | | | | | | 1 | 9 | .03 | .21 | Less than $3 00 |
| $3 00–$3 49 | 2 | 45 | | 5 | | 2 | 1 | | 1 | 6 | 2 | | 6 | 58 | .21 | 1.55 | $3 00– 3 49 |
| 3 50– 3 99 | 9 | 62 | | 5 | | 3 | 2 | | | 18 | 1 | | 12 | 88 | .58 | 3.06 | 3 50– 3 99 |
| 4 00– 4 49 | 28 | 172 | 2 | 9 | | 4 | 5 | 2 | 2 | 11 | 8 | 1 | 45 | 199 | 1.95 | 8.04 | 4 00– 4 49 |
| 4 50– 4 99 | 17 | 262 | 1 | 8 | 1 | 9 | 6 | 3 | | 7 | 18 | 1 | 43 | 290 | 3.28 | 15.02 | 4 50– 4 99 |
| 5 00– 5 49 | 92 | 461 | 1 | 51 | | 18 | 4 | 6 | 2 | 8 | 43 | 6 | 142 | 550 | 7.65 | 28.02 | 5 00– 5 49 |
| 5 50– 5 99 | 37 | 94 | 1 | 14 | | 10 | 3 | | | | 17 | 3 | 58 | 321 | 9.42 | 35.08 | 5 50– 5 99 |
| 6 00– 6 49 | 122 | 501 | 6 | 65 | | 32 | 1 | 5 | 1 | 14 | 44 | 12 | 174 | 629 | 14.07 | 50.08 | 6 00– 6 49 |
| 6 50– 6 99 | 45 | 143 | | 8 | | 11 | | | 1 | 4 | 3 | 6 | 49 | 172 | 16.03 | 54.05 | 6 50– 6 99 |
| 7 00– 7 49 | 105 | 177 | 7 | 48 | 1 | 15 | 5 | 3 | 1 | 4 | 18 | 27 | 137 | 274 | 20.03 | 61.02 | 7 00– 7 49 |
| 7 50– 7 99 | 34 | 127 | 6 | 6 | 1 | 15 | 3 | 1 | 1 | | 14 | 4 | 59 | 153 | 22.02 | 64.08 | 7 50– 7 99 |
| 8 00– 8 99 | 119 | 404 | 7 | 19 | 7 | 24 | 4 | 5 | 1 | 9 | 48 | 40 | 186 | 501 | 28.00 | 76.08 | 8 00– 8 99 |
| 9 00– 9 99 | 113 | 352 | 12 | 10 | 4 | 16 | 19 | 6 | 5 | 5 | 84 | 34 | 237 | 423 | 35.02 | 86.05 | 9 00– 9 99 |
| 10 00–10 99 | 136 | 264 | 12 | 7 | 7 | 15 | 12 | 6 | 8 | 4 | 91 | 30 | 266 | 326 | 43.03 | 94.03 | 10 00–10 99 |
| 11 00–11 99 | 104 | 68 | 4 | 2 | 4 | 1 | 6 | 1 | 1 | | 68 | 9 | 187 | 81 | 49.02 | 96.02 | 11 00–11 99 |
| 12 00–12 99 | 146 | 57 | 13 | 2 | 10 | 4 | 11 | | 12 | 2 | 137 | 21 | 329 | 86 | 59.02 | 98.02 | 12 00–12 99 |
| 13 00–13 99 | 117 | 13 | 2 | | 3 | 1 | 8 | | 14 | | 81 | 8 | 225 | 22 | 66.01 | 98.06 | 13 00–13 99 |
| 14 00–14 99 | 104 | 5 | 3 | 1 | 3 | | 2 | | 5 | | 43 | 12 | 160 | 18 | 70.08 | 99.00 | 14 00–14 99 |
| 15 00–15 99 | 152 | 6 | 7 | | 7 | | 4 | | 13 | | 59 | 10 | 242 | 16 | 78.08 | 99.04 | 15 00–15 99 |
| 16 00–17 99 | 158 | 4 | 9 | 1 | 12 | 1 | 4 | | 8 | | 57 | 9 | 248 | 15 | 86.01 | 99.07 | 16 00–17 99 |
| 18 00–19 99 | 91 | | 4 | | 6 | 1 | 1 | | 6 | | 67 | 4 | 175 | 5 | 91.05 | 99.08 | 18 00–19 99 |
| 20 00–24 99 | 106 | 1 | 8 | | 6 | | 7 | | 4 | | 54 | 3 | 185 | 4 | 97.00 | 99.09 | 20 00–24 99 |
| 25 00–29 99 | 26 | | 4 | | 1 | 1 | 1 | | 2 | | 22 | 2 | 56 | 3 | 99.00 | 100.00 | 25 00–29 99 |
| 30 00–34 99 | 14 | | 2 | | | | 1 | | 1 | | 9 | | 27 | | 99.08 | | 30 00–34 99 |
| 35 00–39 99 | 6 | | | | | | | | | | 5 | | 11 | | 99.09 | | 35 00–39 99 |
| 40 00 and over | | | | | | | | | | | 2 | | 2 | | 100.00 | | 40 00 and over |
| Not reported | 14 | 30 | 4 | 5 | 29 | 48 | 3 | | 123 | 122 | 108 | 18 | 281 | 233 | | | Not reported |
| Total | 1,898 | 3,452 | 115 | 271 | 102 | 231 | 113 | 38 | 212 | 214 | 1,103 | 260 | 3,543 | 4,466 | 100.00 | 100.00 | Total |

NEW YORK STATE
**THE PAPER BOX INDUSTRY**

103. TABLE IV, C — NUMBER OF EMPLOYEES, BY SEX, CLASSIFIED ACCORDING TO ACTUAL WEEKLY EARNINGS BY LOCALITY

| ACTUAL WEEKLY EARNINGS IN DOLLARS | LOCALITY | | | | | | | | | | | | | | | | ACTUAL WEEKLY EARNINGS IN DOLLARS |
|---|---|---|---|---|---|---|---|---|---|---|---|---|---|---|---|---|---|
| | NEW YORK CITY | | BUFFALO | | ROCHESTER | | TROY | | OTHER CITIES AND TOWNS | | OFFICE, SHIPPING AND PLANT. ALL LOCALITIES | | STATE | | CUMULATIVE PER CENT. FOR STATE | | |
| | Male | Female | Male | Female | Male | Female | Male | Female | Male | Female | Male | Female | Male | Female | Male | Female | |
| Less than $3 00 | 24 | 154 | 3 | 33 | 1 | 13 | 6 | 3 | 4 | 28 | 7 | 1 | 45 | 232 | 1.01 | 3.00 | Less than $3 00 |
| $3 00–$3 49 | 21 | 153 | | 18 | | 12 | 6 | 2 | | 34 | 1 | 1 | 28 | 220 | 1.08 | 5.09 | $3 00– 3 49 |
| 3 50– 3 99 | 17 | 173 | 1 | 30 | | 10 | 4 | 4 | 4 | 49 | 5 | | 31 | 266 | 2.06 | 9.04 | 3 50– 3 99 |
| 4 00– 4 49 | 40 | 304 | 2 | 43 | | 20 | 7 | 7 | 7 | 54 | 16 | 2 | 72 | 430 | 4.04 | 15.00 | 4 00– 4 49 |
| 4 50– 4 99 | 35 | 363 | | 51 | 1 | 29 | 7 | 6 | 6 | 44 | 25 | 3 | 74 | 496 | 6.03 | 21.05 | 4 50– 4 99 |
| 5 00– 5 49 | 85 | 517 | 4 | 82 | 1 | 44 | 5 | 11 | 8 | 62 | 40 | 11 | 143 | 727 | 9.08 | 31.00 | 5 00– 5 49 |
| 5 50– 5 99 | 59 | 416 | 4 | 70 | 1 | 28 | 10 | 12 | 5 | 43 | 13 | 7 | 92 | 576 | 12.01 | 38.05 | 5 50– 5 99 |
| 6 00– 6 49 | 113 | 495 | 5 | 73 | 1 | 40 | 6 | 9 | 5 | 45 | 37 | 10 | 167 | 672 | 16.03 | 47.02 | 6 00– 6 49 |
| 6 50– 6 99 | 61 | 280 | 1 | 61 | 5 | 42 | 3 | 4 | 6 | 48 | 14 | 14 | 90 | 449 | 18.06 | 53.02 | 6 50– 6 99 |
| 7 00– 7 49 | 91 | 353 | 7 | 64 | 1 | 46 | 7 | 10 | 6 | 35 | 24 | 20 | 136 | 528 | 21.09 | 60.00 | 7 00– 7 49 |
| 7 50– 7 99 | 60 | 295 | 3 | 25 | 5 | 28 | 7 | 7 | 6 | 35 | 15 | 9 | 96 | 399 | 24.03 | 65.02 | 7 50– 7 99 |
| 8 00– 8 99 | 139 | 611 | 10 | 58 | 11 | 69 | 21 | 13 | 26 | 73 | 67 | 46 | 274 | 870 | 31.02 | 76.07 | 8 00– 8 99 |
| 9 00– 9 99 | 141 | 545 | 10 | 28 | 12 | 48 | 17 | 21 | 32 | 30 | 92 | 31 | 304 | 703 | 39.00 | 86.00 | 9 00– 9 99 |
| 10 00–10 99 | 146 | 379 | 12 | 9 | 11 | 29 | 14 | 19 | 31 | 13 | 93 | 32 | 307 | 481 | 46.04 | 92.02 | 10 00–10 99 |
| 11 00–11 99 | 137 | 181 | 6 | 5 | 5 | 31 | 16 | 6 | 16 | 13 | 91 | 10 | 271 | 246 | 53.00 | 95.02 | 11 00–11 99 |
| 12 00–12 99 | 155 | 141 | 9 | 2 | 14 | 13 | 10 | 6 | 23 | 10 | 128 | 18 | 339 | 190 | 61.06 | 97.06 | 12 00–12 99 |
| 13 00–13 99 | 128 | 49 | 4 | | 4 | 4 | 11 | 1 | 26 | 2 | 78 | 7 | 251 | 63 | 68.00 | 98.06 | 13 00–13 99 |
| 14 00–14 99 | 122 | 25 | 7 | 1 | 4 | | 4 | | 10 | 3 | 59 | 11 | 206 | 40 | 73.02 | 99.02 | 14 00–14 99 |
| 15 00–15 99 | 131 | 10 | 11 | | 8 | | 14 | | 9 | 1 | 60 | 7 | 233 | 18 | 79.00 | 99.04 | 15 00–15 99 |
| 16 00–17 99 | 192 | 11 | 8 | 2 | 12 | 2 | 8 | 2 | 12 | | 82 | 9 | 314 | 26 | 86.08 | 99.07 | 16 00–17 99 |
| 18 00–19 99 | 124 | 2 | 3 | | 5 | 1 | 2 | | 5 | | 66 | 4 | 205 | 7 | 91.08 | 99.08 | 18 00–19 99 |
| 20 00–24 99 | 133 | 2 | 6 | | 5 | | 9 | | 4 | | 62 | 3 | 219 | 5 | 97.08 | 99.09 | 20 00–24 99 |
| 25 00–29 99 | 32 | | 1 | | 1 | 1 | 1 | | 2 | | 25 | 2 | 62 | 3 | 99.00 | 100.00 | 25 00–29 99 |
| 30 00–34 99 | 16 | | 1 | | | | 1 | | 1 | | 8 | | 27 | | 99.06 | | 30 00–34 99 |
| 35 00–39 99 | 8 | | | | | | | | | | 4 | | 12 | | 99.09 | | 35 00–39 99 |
| 40 00 and over | | | | | | | | | | | 2 | | 2 | | 100.00 | | 40 00 and over |
| Not reported | 23 | 63 | 11 | | | | | | | 4 | 21 | 14 | 55 | 81 | | | Not reported |
| Total | 2,233 | 5,522 | 129 | 655 | 108 | 510 | 196 | 143 | 254 | 626 | 1,135 | 272 | 4,055 | 7,728 | | | Total |

104. TABLE VII, C, a

NEW YORK STATE

THE PAPER BOX INDUSTRY — FACTORY WORKERS

NUMBER AND PER CENT. OF EMPLOYEES BY SEX ACCORDING TO OCCUPATION AND NATIVITY

| NATIVITY | OCCUPATION | | | | | | | | | | | | | | | | | | | | | |
|---|---|---|---|---|---|---|---|---|---|---|---|---|---|---|---|---|---|---|---|---|---|---|
| | FOREMEN AND FOREWOMEN | | CUTTERS | | GLUE MAKERS | SETTERS-UP | | GENERAL MACHINE WORK | | GLUE TABLE WORK | TURNERS-IN, STRIPPERS, TOP LABELERS | | TABLE WORK | | CLOSING AND TYING | | FLOOR WORK | | NOT REPORTED | | TOTAL | |
| | Male | Female | Male | Female | Male | Male | Female | Male | Female | Ma e | Male | Female | Male | Female | Male | Female | Male | Female | Male | Female | Male | Female |
| Native | 154 | 123 | 492 | 48 | 4 | 179 | 272 | 128 | 475 | 31 | 113 | 2,275 | 33 | 1,914 | 116 | 216 | 127 | 258 | 22 | 40 | 1,399 | 5,621 |
| Foreign | 60 | 11 | 365 | 10 | 8 | 211 | 41 | 179 | 104 | 120 | 30 | 772 | 285 | 699 | 72 | 77 | 165 | 94 | 14 | 3 | 1,509 | 1,811 |
| Not reported | ...... | 1 | 2 | ...... | ........ | 1 | 1 | 2 | 2 | ........ | 1 | 6 | ...... | 8 | ...... | ...... | ...... | 4 | 6 | 2 | 12 | 24 |
| Total | 214 | 135 | 859 | 58 | 12 | 391 | 314 | 309 | 581 | 151 | 144 | 3,053 | 318 | 2,621 | 188 | 293 | 292 | 356 | 42 | 45 | 2,920 | 7,456 |
| Per cent. of total | 7.45 | 1.8 | 29.8 | .8 | .4 | 13.6 | 4.2 | 10.7 | 7.8 | 5.25 | 5.0 | 41.2 | 11.1 | 35.4 | 6.54 | 4.0 | 10.16 | 4.8 | ...... | ...... | 100.0 | 100.0 |

NEW YORK STATE
**THE PAPER BOX INDUSTRY — FACTORY WORKERS**

105. TABLE V, C, a — Number and Per Cent. of Employees Earning Specified Weekly Rates by Age Groups and Sex

| Weekly Rates in Dollars | Age Groups in Years | | | | | | | | | | | | | | Weekly Rates in Dollars |
|---|---|---|---|---|---|---|---|---|---|---|---|---|---|---|---|
| | 14–15 | | 16–17 | | 18–20 | | 21–24 | | 25–29 | | 30–34 | | 35–39 | | |
| | Male | Female | Male | Female | Male | Female | Male | Female | Male | Female | Male | Female | Male | Female | |
| Less than $3 00 | 1 | 8 | .... | 1 | ...... | ...... | ...... | ...... | ...... | ...... | ...... | ...... | ...... | ...... | Less than $3 00 |
| $3 00–$3 49 | 1 | 27 | 3 | 22 | ...... | 3 | ...... | ...... | ...... | ...... | ...... | ...... | ...... | ...... | $3 00– 3 49 |
| 3 50– 3 99 | 4 | 50 | 5 | 33 | ...... | 4 | ...... | 1 | 1 | ...... | 1 | ...... | ...... | ...... | 3 50– 3 99 |
| 4 00– 4 49 | 14 | 55 | 13 | 104 | 2 | 30 | 4 | 6 | 1 | 1 | ...... | ...... | 1 | 1 | 4 00– 4 49 |
| 4 50– 4 99 | 10 | 58 | 12 | 161 | 2 | 55 | ...... | 10 | ...... | 2 | ...... | ...... | ...... | 2 | 4 50– 4 99 |
| 5 00– 5 49 | 12 | 46 | 52 | 253 | 24 | 168 | 8 | 41 | 1 | 14 | 1 | 13 | ...... | 4 | 5 00– 5 49 |
| 5 50– 5 99 | 2 | 28 | 20 | 148 | 12 | 92 | 5 | 29 | 1 | 7 | ...... | 6 | 1 | 1 | 5 50– 5 99 |
| 6 00– 6 49 | 6 | 13 | 48 | 200 | 41 | 243 | 11 | 119 | 6 | 22 | 4 | 6 | 5 | 3 | 6 00– 6 49 |
| 6 50– 6 99 | 1 | ...... | 14 | 57 | 19 | 69 | 8 | 22 | 2 | 8 | 1 | 4 | 1 | 3 | 6 50– 6 99 |
| 7 00– 7 49 | .... | 1 | 28 | 32 | 57 | 117 | 17 | 57 | 2 | 14 | 4 | 9 | 3 | 7 | 7 00– 7 49 |
| 7 50– 7 99 | .... | ...... | 8 | 24 | 20 | 60 | 6 | 33 | 1 | 11 | ...... | 8 | ...... | 3 | 7 50– 7 99 |
| 8 00– 8 99 | .... | 1 | 16 | 30 | 54 | 177 | 29 | 103 | 13 | 69 | 6 | 24 | 4 | 25 | 8 00– 8 99 |
| 9 00– 9 99 | .... | ...... | 13 | 17 | 54 | 109 | 37 | 114 | 18 | 51 | 14 | 33 | 5 | 25 | 9 00– 9 99 |
| 10 00–10 99 | .... | ...... | 2 | 8 | 45 | 83 | 44 | 82 | 30 | 50 | 22 | 27 | 7 | 17 | 10 00–10 99 |
| 11 00–11 99 | .... | ...... | 1 | ...... | 18 | 9 | 36 | 26 | 20 | 23 | 16 | 3 | 8 | 7 | 11 00–11 99 |
| 12 00–12 99 | .... | ...... | 1 | 1 | 24 | 3 | 54 | 25 | 30 | 14 | 22 | 8 | 22 | 6 | 12 00–12 99 |
| 13 00–13 99 | .... | ...... | .... | ...... | 12 | 2 | 49 | 2 | 33 | 4 | 18 | 2 | 13 | 3 | 13 00–13 99 |
| 14 00–14 99 | .... | ...... | .... | ...... | 7 | ...... | 37 | 1 | 33 | ...... | 16 | 1 | 11 | 2 | 14 00–14 99 |
| 15 00–15 99 | .... | ...... | .... | ...... | 8 | 1 | 46 | ...... | 46 | 1 | 36 | 2 | 19 | 1 | 15 00–15 99 |
| 16 00–17 99 | .... | ...... | .... | ...... | 2 | ...... | 25 | 1 | 70 | 1 | 33 | 2 | 22 | 1 | 16 00–17 99 |
| 18 00–19 99 | .... | ...... | .... | ...... | 2 | ...... | 17 | ...... | 29 | ...... | 19 | 1 | 22 | ...... | 18 00–19 99 |
| 20 00–24 99 | .... | ...... | .... | ...... | ...... | ...... | 9 | ...... | 21 | 1 | 40 | ...... | 12 | ...... | 20 00–24 99 |
| 25 00–29 99 | .... | ...... | .... | ...... | ...... | ...... | ...... | ...... | 7 | ...... | 4 | ...... | 6 | 1 | 25 00–29 99 |
| 30 00–34 99 | .... | ...... | .... | ...... | ...... | ...... | ...... | ...... | 1 | ...... | 4 | ...... | 6 | ...... | 30 00–34 99 |
| 35 00–39 99 | .... | ...... | .... | ...... | ...... | ...... | ...... | ...... | ...... | ...... | 1 | ...... | 2 | ...... | 35 00–39 99 |
| Not reported | 15 | 20 | 18 | 43 | 35 | 48 | 30 | 28 | 26 | 23 | 13 | 12 | 14 | 9 | Not reported |
| Total | 66 | 307 | 254 | 1,134 | 438 | 1,273 | 472 | 700 | 392 | 316 | 275 | 161 | 184 | 121 | Total |

105. TABLE V, C, a — (*concluded*)

NEW YORK STATE

**THE PAPER BOX INDUSTRY — FACTORY WORKERS**

NUMBER AND PER CENT. OF EMPLOYEES EARNING SPECIFIED WEEKLY RATES BY AGE GROUPS AND SEX

| Weekly Rates in Dollars | Age Groups in Years | | | | | | | | | | | | | | Weekly Rates in Dollars |
|---|---|---|---|---|---|---|---|---|---|---|---|---|---|---|---|
| | 40–44 | | 45–54 | | 55–64 | | 65 and over | | Not reported | | Total | | Cumulative per cent of total | | |
| | Male | Female | Male | Female | Male | Female | Male | Female | Male | Female | Male | Female | Male | Female | |
| Less than $3 00 | .... | ...... | .... | ...... | ...... | ...... | ...... | ...... | ...... | ...... | 1 | 9 | .04 | .23 | Less than $3 00 |
| $3 00–$3 49... | .... | ...... | .... | ...... | ...... | ...... | ...... | ...... | ...... | 6 | 4 | 58 | .22 | 1.68 | ...$3 00– 3 49 |
| 3 50– 3 99... | .... | ...... | .... | ...... | ...... | ...... | ...... | ...... | ...... | ...... | 11 | 88 | .71 | 3.87 | ... 3 50– 3 99 |
| 4 00– 4 49... | .... | ...... | .... | ...... | ...... | ...... | ...... | ...... | 2 | 1 | 37 | 198 | 2.34 | 8.82 | ... 4 00– 4 49 |
| 4 50– 4 99... | .... | ...... | .... | 1 | ...... | ...... | ...... | ...... | 1 | ...... | 25 | 289 | 3.44 | 16.05 | ... 4 50– 4 99 |
| 5 00– 5 49... | .... | 2 | .... | 1 | 1 | 2 | ...... | ...... | ...... | ...... | 99 | 544 | 7.81 | 29.70 | ... 5 00– 5 49 |
| 5 50– 5 99... | .... | ...... | .... | 2 | ...... | ...... | ...... | ...... | ...... | 5 | 41 | 318 | 9.62 | 37.60 | ... 5 50– 5 99 |
| 6 00– 6 49... | 2 | 3 | 2 | 5 | 4 | 1 | 1 | ...... | ...... | 2 | 130 | 617 | 15.30 | 53.00 | ... 6 00– 6 49 |
| 6 50– 6 99... | .... | 2 | .... | ...... | ...... | 1 | ...... | ...... | ...... | ...... | 46 | 166 | 17.40 | 57.10 | ... 6 50– 6 99 |
| 7 00– 7 49... | 1 | 1 | 4 | 5 | 2 | 2 | 1 | 1 | ...... | 1 | 119 | 247 | 22.80 | 63.40 | ... 7 00– 7 49 |
| 7 50– 7 99... | 1 | 6 | 1 | 2 | ...... | ...... | ...... | ...... | 8 | 2 | 45 | 149 | 24.60 | 67.10 | ... 7 50– 7 99 |
| 8 00– 8 99... | 5 | 14 | 5 | 15 | 5 | 2 | ...... | ...... | 1 | 1 | 138 | 461 | 30.70 | 78.60 | ... 8 00– 8 99 |
| 9 00– 9 99... | 3 | 24 | 2 | 9 | 5 | 6 | 1 | ...... | 1 | 1 | 153 | 389 | 37.45 | 88.30 | ... 9 00– 9 99 |
| 10 00–10 99... | 9 | 11 | 12 | 13 | 3 | 2 | 1 | ...... | ...... | 3 | 175 | 296 | 45.30 | 95.60 | ...10 00–10 99 |
| 11 00–11 99... | 6 | 3 | 10 | 1 | 4 | ...... | ...... | ...... | ...... | ...... | 119 | 72 | 50.40 | 97.40 | ...11 00–11 99 |
| 12 00–12 99... | 14 | 5 | 11 | 3 | 9 | ...... | 1 | ...... | 4 | ...... | 192 | 65 | 58.90 | 99.10 | ...12 00–12 99 |
| 13 00–13 99... | 8 | 1 | 7 | ...... | 4 | ...... | ...... | ...... | ...... | ...... | 144 | 14 | 65.20 | 99.50 | ...13 00–13 99 |
| 14 00–14 99... | 2 | ...... | 7 | 1 | 4 | ...... | ...... | ...... | ...... | 1 | 117 | 6 | 70.40 | 99.60 | ...14 00–14 99 |
| 15 00–15 99... | 11 | ...... | 10 | 1 | 6 | ...... | 1 | ...... | ...... | ...... | 183 | 6 | 78.50 | 99.80 | ...15 00–15 99 |
| 16 00–17 99... | 16 | 1 | 18 | ...... | 4 | ...... | 1 | ...... | ...... | ...... | 191 | 6 | 86.90 | 99.93 | ...16 00–17 99 |
| 18 00–19 99... | 6 | ...... | 10 | ...... | 3 | ...... | ...... | ...... | ...... | ...... | 108 | 1 | 91.60 | 99.95 | ...18 00–19 99 |
| 20 00–24 99... | 22 | ...... | 22 | ...... | 5 | ...... | ...... | ...... | ...... | ...... | 131 | 1 | 97.40 | 99.98 | ...20 00–24 99 |
| 25 00–29 99... | 8 | ...... | 8 | ...... | 1 | ...... | ...... | ...... | ...... | ...... | 34 | 1 | 99.00 | 100.00 | ...25 00–29 99 |
| 30 00–34 99... | 3 | ...... | 3 | ...... | 1 | ...... | ...... | ...... | ...... | ...... | 18 | ...... | 99.80 | ...... | ...30 00–34 99 |
| 35 00–39 99... | 1 | ...... | 2 | ...... | ...... | ...... | ...... | ...... | ...... | ...... | 6 | ...... | 100.00 | ...... | ...35 00–39 99 |
| Not reported.. | 8 | 4 | 7 | 11 | 3 | 4 | 3 | 1 | 1 | 2 | 173 | 205 | ...... | ...... | ..Not reported |
| Total..... | 126 | 77 | 141 | 70 | 64 | 20 | 10 | 2 | 18 | 25 | 2,440 | 4,206 | ...... | ...... | .....Total |

NEW YORK STATE

**THE PAPER BOX INDUSTRY — FACTORY WORKERS**

106. TABLE VIII, C, a — NUMBER AND PER CENT. OF EMPLOYEES EARNING SPECIFIED WEEKLY RATES, BY OCCUPATION AND SEX

| WEEKLY RATES IN DOLLARS | OCCUPATION | | | | | | | | | | | | WEEKLY RATES IN DOLLARS |
|---|---|---|---|---|---|---|---|---|---|---|---|---|---|
| | FOREMEN AND FOREWOMEN | | CUTTERS | | GLUE MAKERS | SETTERS-UP | | GENERAL MACHINE WORK | | GLUE TABLE WORK | TURNERS-IN | | |
| | Male | Female | Male | Female | Male | Male | Female | Male | Female | Male | Male | Female | |
| Less than $3 00 | ....... | ....... | ....... | ....... | ....... | ....... | 2 | ....... | ....... | ....... | ....... | 1 | Less than $3 00 |
| $3 00–$3 49 | ....... | ....... | ....... | ....... | ....... | ....... | 3 | ....... | ....... | ....... | 1 | 17 | $3 00– 3 49 |
| 3 50– 3 99 | ....... | ....... | 1 | 1 | ....... | 2 | 7 | ....... | ....... | ....... | 1 | 28 | 3 50– 3 99 |
| 4 00– 4 49 | ....... | ....... | 2 | 1 | ....... | 6 | 7 | ....... | 13 | 4 | ....... | 94 | 4 00– 4 49 |
| 4 50– 4 99 | ....... | ....... | 1 | 1 | ....... | 10 | 12 | 1 | 8 | 1 | ....... | 127 | 4 50– 4 99 |
| 5 00– 5 49 | ....... | ....... | 15 | 4 | ....... | 19 | 18 | 11 | 55 | 4 | ....... | 188 | 5 00– 5 49 |
| 5 50– 5 99 | ....... | ....... | ....... | 1 | ....... | 5 | 8 | 6 | 31 | ....... | ....... | 163 | 5 50– 5 99 |
| 6 00– 6 49 | ....... | 1 | 26 | 7 | ....... | 16 | 20 | 26 | 80 | 2 | 1 | 225 | 6 00– 6 49 |
| 6 50– 6 99 | ....... | 2 | 14 | ....... | ....... | 3 | 8 | 14 | 8 | 1 | ....... | 42 | 6 50– 6 99 |
| 7 00– 7 49 | ....... | 7 | 19 | 3 | 1 | 16 | 9 | 16 | 44 | 3 | ....... | 7 | 7 00– 7 49 |
| 7 50– 7 99 | ....... | 4 | 17 | 3 | ....... | 3 | 1 | 8 | 16 | 1 | ....... | ....... | 7 50– 7 99 |
| 8 00– 8 99 | 2 | 15 | 33 | 1 | ....... | 12 | 22 | 19 | 11 | 5 | ....... | 4 | 8 00– 8 99 |
| 9 00– 9 99 | ....... | 15 | 48 | 2 | 2 | 13 | 12 | 20 | 7 | 6 | ....... | 1 | 9 00– 9 99 |
| 10 00–10 99 | ....... | 27 | 43 | 2 | 2 | 18 | 24 | 31 | 4 | 13 | ....... | 1 | 10 00–10 99 |
| 11 00–11 99 | 1 | 12 | 33 | ....... | 4 | 10 | 8 | 18 | 1 | 10 | ....... | ....... | 11 00–11 99 |
| 12 00–12 99 | 7 | 25 | 72 | ....... | 1 | 22 | 7 | 30 | 3 | 25 | ....... | ....... | 12 00–12 99 |
| 13 00–13 99 | 6 | 5 | 46 | ....... | ....... | 45 | 4 | 4 | ....... | 29 | ....... | ....... | 13 00–13 99 |
| 14 00–14 99 | 6 | 5 | 42 | ....... | 1 | 43 | ....... | 5 | ....... | 16 | ....... | ....... | 14 00–14 99 |
| 15 00–15 99 | 8 | 2 | 73 | ....... | 1 | 57 | 1 | 7 | ....... | 17 | ....... | ....... | 15 00–15 99 |
| 16 00–17 99 | 30 | 3 | 123 | 1 | ....... | 27 | ....... | 1 | ....... | 6 | ....... | ....... | 16 00–17 99 |
| 18 00–19 99 | 25 | 1 | 73 | ....... | ....... | 3 | ....... | 4 | ....... | ....... | ....... | ....... | 18 00–19 99 |
| 20 00–24 99 | 69 | 1 | 56 | ....... | ....... | 2 | ....... | ....... | ....... | ....... | ....... | ....... | 20 00–24 99 |
| 25 00–29 00 | 28 | 1 | 6 | ....... | ....... | ....... | ....... | ....... | ....... | ....... | ....... | ....... | 25 00–29 99 |
| 30 00–34 99 | 17 | ....... | ....... | ....... | ....... | ....... | ....... | ....... | ....... | ....... | ....... | ....... | 30 00–34 99 |
| 35 00–39 99 | 6 | ....... | ....... | ....... | ....... | ....... | ....... | ....... | ....... | ....... | ....... | ....... | 35 00–39 99 |
| Not reported | 9 | 2 | 44 | 11 | ....... | 11 | 13 | 35 | 23 | 1 | 1 | 18 | Not reported |
| Total | 214 | 128 | 787 | 38 | 12 | 343 | 186 | 256 | 304 | 144 | 4 | 916 | Total |

NEW YORK STATE

106. TABLE VIII, C, a—(*concluded*). **THE PAPER BOX INDUSTRY — FACTORY WORKERS**

Number and Per Cent. of Employees Earning Specified Weekly Rates by Occupation and Sex

| Weekly Rates in Dollars | Occupation (*concluded*) | | | | | | | | | | | | | | Weekly Rates in Dollars |
|---|---|---|---|---|---|---|---|---|---|---|---|---|---|---|---|
| | Strippers and Top Labelers | | Table Work | | Closing and Tying | | Floor Work | | Not Reported | | Total | | Cumulative Per Cent. of Total | | |
| | Male | Female | Male | Female | Male | Female | Male | Female | Male | Female | Male | Female | Male | Female | |
| Less than $3 00 | ...... | 2 | ...... | 2 | ...... | 2 | 1 | ...... | .... | ...... | 1 | 9 | .04 | .23 | Less than $3 00 |
| $3 00–$3 49... | ...... | 7 | 1 | 15 | ...... | 10 | 2 | 6 | .... | ...... | 4 | 58 | .22 | 1.68 | ...$3 00– 3 49 |
| 3 50– 3 99... | ...... | 12 | 1 | 14 | ...... | 8 | 4 | 13 | 2 | 5 | 11 | 88 | .71 | 3.87 | ... 3 50– 3 99 |
| 4 00– 4 49... | 1 | 19 | 7 | 34 | 6 | 9 | 11 | 21 | .... | ...... | 37 | 198 | 2.34 | 8.82 | ... 4 00– 4 49 |
| 4 50– 4 99... | ...... | 13 | ...... | 81 | 5 | 13 | 7 | 29 | .... | 5 | 25 | 289 | 3.44 | 16.05 | ... 4 50– 4 99 |
| 5 00– 5 49... | 2 | 60 | 10 | 135 | 12 | 24 | 24 | 56 | 2 | 4 | 99 | 544 | 7.81 | 29.70 | ... 5 00– 5 49 |
| 5 50– 5 99... | 5 | 47 | 5 | 41 | 5 | 16 | 15 | 11 | .... | ...... | 41 | 318 | 9.62 | 37.60 | ... 5 50– 5 99 |
| 6 00– 6 49... | 1 | 119 | 9 | 96 | 22 | 29 | 27 | 35 | .... | 5 | 130 | 617 | 15.30 | 53.00 | ... 6 00– 6 49 |
| 6 50– 6 99... | 1 | 44 | 4 | 44 | 2 | 1 | 6 | 17 | 1 | ...... | 46 | 166 | 17.40 | 57.10 | ... 6 50– 6 99 |
| 7 00– 7 49... | 3 | 68 | 8 | 68 | 17 | 12 | 28 | 28 | 8 | 1 | 119 | 247 | 22.80 | 63.40 | ... 7 00– 7 49 |
| 7 50– 7 99... | ...... | 62 | 4 | 46 | 4 | 3 | 8 | 13 | .... | 1 | 45 | 149 | 24.60 | 67.10 | ... 7 50– 7 99 |
| 8 00– 8 99... | 4 | 167 | 13 | 191 | 27 | 9 | 23 | 36 | .... | 5 | 138 | 461 | 30.70 | 78.60 | ... 8 00– 8 99 |
| 9 00– 9 99... | 8 | 174 | 13 | 165 | 25 | 1 | 18 | 11 | .... | 1 | 153 | 389 | 37.45 | 88.30 | ... 9 00– 9 99 |
| 10 00–10 99... | 5 | 141 | 19 | 93 | 12 | 1 | 28 | 3 | 4 | ...... | 175 | 296 | 45.30 | 95.60 | ...10 00–10 99 |
| 11 00–11 99... | 9 | 28 | 8 | 23 | 8 | ...... | 15 | ...... | 3 | ...... | 119 | 72 | 50.40 | 97.40 | ...11 00–11 99 |
| 12 00–12 99... | 7 | 13 | 15 | 17 | 3 | ...... | 8 | ...... | 2 | ...... | 192 | 65 | 58.90 | 99.10 | ...12 00–12 99 |
| 13 00–13 99... | 2 | 1 | 3 | 2 | 1 | ...... | 6 | ...... | 2 | 2 | 144 | 14 | 65.20 | 99.50 | ...13 00–13 99 |
| 14 00–14 99... | 1 | ...... | 3 | 1 | ...... | ...... | ...... | ...... | .... | ...... | 117 | 6 | 70.40 | 99.60 | ...14 00–14 99 |
| 15 00–15 99... | 2 | 1 | 9 | 2 | 1 | ...... | 3 | ...... | 5 | ...... | 183 | 6 | 78.50 | 99.80 | ...15 00–15 99 |
| 16 00–17 99... | ...... | ...... | 1 | 1 | 1 | ...... | 1 | 1 | 1 | ...... | 191 | 6 | 86.90 | 99.93 | ...16 00–17 99 |
| 18 00–19 99... | 1 | ...... | 1 | ...... | ...... | ...... | ...... | ...... | 1 | ...... | 108 | 1 | 91.60 | 99.95 | ...18 00–19 99 |
| 20 00–24 99... | ...... | ...... | 1 | ...... | ...... | ...... | 1 | ...... | 2 | ...... | 131 | 1 | 97.40 | 99.98 | ...20 00–24 99 |
| 25 00–29 99... | ...... | ...... | ...... | ...... | ...... | ...... | ...... | ...... | .... | ...... | 34 | 1 | 99.00 | 100.00 | ...25 00–29 99 |
| 30 00–34 99... | ...... | ...... | ...... | ...... | ...... | ...... | 1 | ...... | .... | ...... | 18 | ...... | 99.80 | ...... | ...30 00–34 99 |
| 35 00–39 99... | ...... | ...... | ...... | ...... | ...... | ...... | ...... | ...... | .... | ...... | 6 | ...... | 100.00 | ...... | ...35 00–39 99 |
| Not reported... | 3 | 36 | 2 | 67 | 20 | 8 | 42 | 20 | 5 | 7 | 173 | 205 | ...... | ...... | ...Not reported |
| Total .... | 55 | 1,014 | 137 | 1,138 | 171 | 146 | 279 | 300 | 38 | 36 | 2,440 | 4,206 | ...... | ...... | .....Total |

NEW YORK STATE

**THE PAPER BOX INDUSTRY — FACTORY WORKERS**

107. TABLE VI, C, a  NUMBER AND PER CENT. OF EMPLOYEES CLASSIFIED ACCORDING TO ACTUAL WEEKLY EARNINGS, BY AGE GROUPS AND SEX

| Actual Weekly Earnings in Dollars | Age Groups in Years: 14–15 Male | 14–15 Female | 16–17 Male | 16–17 Female | 18–20 Male | 18–20 Female | 21–24 Male | 21–24 Female | 25–29 Male | 25–29 Female | 30–34 Male | 30–34 Female | 35–39 Male | 35–39 Female | Actual Weekly Earnings in Dollars |
|---|---|---|---|---|---|---|---|---|---|---|---|---|---|---|---|
| Less than $3 00 | 7 | 51 | 11 | 78 | 8 | 63 | 4 | 17 | 1 | 5 | .... | 5 | 4 | 4 | Less than $3 00 |
| $3 00–$3 49... | 4 | 66 | 9 | 84 | 5 | 33 | 2 | 19 | 2 | 5 | 2 | 4 | 1 | 3 | ...$3 00– 3 49 |
| 3 50– 3 99... | 11 | 65 | 8 | 106 | 3 | 57 | 4 | 13 | .... | 12 | .... | 2 | ...... | 4 | ... 3 50– 3 99 |
| 4 00– 4 49... | 18 | 84 | 25 | 178 | 2 | 102 | 6 | 35 | 1 | 11 | 1 | 5 | 1 | 6 | ... 4 00– 4 49 |
| 4 50– 4 99... | 13 | 64 | 24 | 175 | 7 | 145 | 2 | 57 | 2 | 16 | .... | 9 | ...... | 8 | ... 4 50– 4 99 |
| 5 00– 5 49... | 13 | 61 | 42 | 256 | 25 | 205 | 14 | 99 | 3 | 37 | 2 | 16 | 2 | 12 | ... 5 00– 5 49 |
| 5 50– 5 99... | 7 | 45 | 27 | 198 | 30 | 191 | 7 | 81 | 2 | 18 | 1 | 14 | 1 | 11 | ... 5 50– 5 99 |
| 6 00– 6 49... | 7 | 22 | 41 | 190 | 41 | 238 | 17 | 113 | 11 | 34 | 2 | 21 | 3 | 11 | ... 6 00– 6 49 |
| 6 50– 6 99... | 2 | 7 | 21 | 102 | 28 | 159 | 14 | 89 | 5 | 30 | 1 | 12 | 3 | 17 | ... 6 50– 6 99 |
| 7 00– 7 49... | ...... | 9 | 20 | 74 | 44 | 174 | 16 | 126 | 10 | 48 | 6 | 25 | 2 | 20 | ... 7 00– 7 49 |
| 7 50– 7 99... | ...... | 3 | 14 | 54 | 39 | 132 | 10 | 98 | 8 | 42 | 1 | 27 | 2 | 10 | ... 7 50– 7 99 |
| 8 00– 8 99... | 1 | 3 | 21 | 79 | 81 | 283 | 40 | 206 | 20 | 109 | 14 | 47 | 9 | 42 | ... 8 00– 8 99 |
| 9 00– 9 99... | ...... | ...... | 14 | 35 | 67 | 203 | 53 | 182 | 30 | 91 | 17 | 59 | 5 | 38 | ... 9 00– 9 99 |
| 10 00–10 99... | ...... | ...... | 4 | 21 | 46 | 112 | 56 | 123 | 40 | 85 | 21 | 36 | 15 | 32 | ...10 00–10 99 |
| 11 00–11 99... | ...... | ...... | 2 | 9 | 27 | 59 | 50 | 89 | 32 | 37 | 22 | 17 | 9 | 15 | ...11 00–11 99 |
| 12 00–12 99... | ...... | ...... | 2 | 5 | 22 | 27 | 36 | 64 | 42 | 34 | 26 | 16 | 21 | 11 | ...12 00–12 99 |
| 13 00–13 99... | ...... | ...... | ...... | ...... | 20 | 18 | 56 | 19 | 33 | 9 | 27 | 4 | 15 | 3 | ...13 00–13 99 |
| 14 00–14 99... | ...... | ...... | ...... | ...... | 11 | 6 | 47 | 8 | 35 | 3 | 18 | 4 | 16 | 3 | ...14 00–14 99 |
| 15 00–15 99... | ...... | ...... | ...... | ...... | 13 | 2 | 38 | 2 | 45 | 3 | 34 | 3 | 19 | 1 | ...15 00–15 99 |
| 16 00–17 99... | ...... | ...... | ...... | ...... | 7 | 2 | 42 | 3 | 71 | 4 | 43 | 3 | 27 | 2 | ...16 00–17 99 |
| 18 00–19 99... | ...... | ...... | ...... | ...... | 4 | ...... | 26 | ...... | 45 | ...... | 22 | 2 | 22 | 1 | ...18 00–19 00 |
| 20 00–24 99... | ...... | ...... | ...... | ...... | ...... | ...... | 12 | 1 | 35 | 1 | 43 | ...... | 17 | ...... | ...20 00–24 99 |
| 25 00–29 99... | ...... | ...... | ...... | ...... | ...... | ...... | ...... | ...... | 11 | ...... | 4 | ...... | 6 | 1 | ...25 00–29 99 |
| 30 00–34 99... | ...... | ...... | ...... | ...... | ...... | ...... | 1 | ...... | 1 | ...... | 4 | ...... | 6 | ...... | ...30 00–34 99 |
| 35 00–39 99... | ...... | ...... | ...... | ...... | ...... | ...... | ...... | ...... | .... | ...... | 2 | ...... | 2 | ...... | ...35 00–39 99 |
| Not reported... | 2 | 2 | 5 | 11 | 4 | 38 | 3 | 7 | 2 | 2 | 6 | 1 | 4 | 3 | ...Not reported |
| Total..... | 85 | 482 | 290 | 1,655 | 534 | 2,249 | 591 | 1,451 | 487 | 636 | 319 | 332 | 212 | 258 | ......Total |

NEW YORK STATE

107. TABLE VI, C, a.—(*concluded*)

**THE PAPER BOX INDUSTRY — FACTORY WORKERS**

NUMBER AND PER CENT. OF EMPLOYEES CLASSIFIED ACCORDING TO ACTUAL WEEKLY EARNINGS BY AGE GROUPS AND SEX

| ACTUAL WEEKLY EARNINGS IN DOLLARS | AGE GROUPS IN YEARS (*concluded*) 40–44 | | 45–54 | | 55–64 | | 65 AND OVER | | NOT REPORTED | | TOTAL | | CUMULATIVE PER CENT. OF TOTAL | | ACTUAL WEEKLY EARNINGS IN DOLLARS |
|---|---|---|---|---|---|---|---|---|---|---|---|---|---|---|---|
| | Male | Female | Male | Female | Male | Female | Male | Female | Male | Female | Male | Female | Male | Female | |
| Less than $3 00 | ...... | 3 | ...... | 4 | 1 | ...... | 1 | ...... | 1 | 1 | 38 | 231 | 1.32 | 3.12 | Less than $3 00 |
| $3 00–$3 49... | ...... | 4 | 1 | 1 | ...... | ...... | ...... | ...... | 1 | ...... | 27 | 219 | 2.25 | 6.10 | ...$3 00– 3 49 |
| 3 50– 3 99... | ...... | ...... | ...... | 5 | ...... | 1 | ...... | ...... | .... | 1 | 26 | 266 | 3.15 | 9.70 | ... 3 50– 3 99 |
| 4 00– 4 49... | 1 | 2 | ...... | 3 | ...... | 1 | ...... | ...... | 1 | 1 | 56 | 428 | 5.09 | 14.15 | ... 4 00– 4 49 |
| 4 50– 4 99... | ...... | 5 | ...... | 6 | 1 | 3 | ...... | ...... | .... | 5 | 49 | 493 | 6.79 | 22.18 | ... 4 50– 4 99 |
| 5 00– 5 49... | 1 | 10 | ...... | 12 | 1 | 6 | ...... | 1 | .... | 1 | 103 | 716 | 10.70 | 31.85 | ... 5 00– 5 49 |
| 5 50– 5 99... | 1 | 2 | 1 | 4 | 2 | 4 | ...... | ...... | .... | 1 | 79 | 569 | 13.10 | 39.60 | ... 5 50– 5 99 |
| 6 00– 6 49... | 3 | 11 | 1 | 17 | 3 | 3 | 1 | ...... | .... | 2 | 130 | 662 | 17.63 | 48.60 | ... 6 00– 6 49 |
| 6 50– 6 99... | ...... | 4 | 1 | 9 | 1 | 4 | ...... | ...... | .... | 2 | 76 | 435 | 20.24 | 55.50 | ... 6 50– 6 99 |
| 7 00– 7 49... | 2 | 11 | 7 | 17 | 1 | 2 | 1 | ...... | 3 | 2 | 112 | 508 | 24.10 | 61.30 | ... 7 00– 7 49 |
| 7 50– 7 99... | 2 | 10 | 3 | 8 | ...... | 4 | 1 | ...... | 1 | 2 | 81 | 390 | 26.90 | 66.70 | ... 7 50– 7 99 |
| 8 00– 8 99... | 7 | 27 | 9 | 21 | 5 | 2 | ...... | ...... | .... | 5 | 207 | 824 | 34.08 | 77.80 | ... 8 00– 8 99 |
| 9 00– 9 99... | 8 | 35 | 4 | 20 | 5 | 7 | 3 | ...... | 1 | 2 | 212 | 672 | 41.40 | 87.00 | ... 9 00– 9 99 |
| 10 00–10 99... | 12 | 20 | 13 | 16 | 6 | 2 | 1 | ...... | .... | 2 | 214 | 449 | 48.80 | 93.00 | ...10 00–10 99 |
| 11 00–11 99... | 14 | 3 | 15 | 3 | 8 | 3 | ...... | ...... | 1 | 1 | 180 | 236 | 55.00 | 96.00 | ...11 00–11 00 |
| 12 00–12 99... | 8 | 8 | 13 | 6 | 10 | ...... | 1 | ...... | .... | 1 | 211 | 172 | 62.40 | 98.50 | ...12 00–12 99 |
| 13 00–13 99... | 11 | 1 | 8 | 1 | 3 | 1 | ...... | ...... | .... | ...... | 173 | 56 | 68.40 | 99.20 | ...13 00–13 99 |
| 14 00–14 99... | 8 | 4 | 6 | 1 | 5 | ...... | ...... | ...... | 1 | ...... | 147 | 29 | 73.50 | 99.60 | ...14 00–14 99 |
| 15 00–15 99... | 9 | ...... | 12 | ...... | 3 | ...... | ...... | ...... | .... | ...... | 173 | 11 | 79.40 | 99.80 | ...15 00–15 99 |
| 16 00–17 99... | 17 | 2 | 19 | 1 | 4 | ...... | 2 | ...... | .... | ...... | 232 | 17 | 87.50 | 99.93 | ...16 00–17 99 |
| 18 00–19 99... | 6 | ...... | 11 | ...... | 3 | ...... | ...... | ...... | .... | ...... | 139 | 3 | 92.40 | 99.96 | ...18 00–19 99 |
| 20 00–24 99... | 24 | ...... | 21 | ...... | 5 | ...... | ...... | ...... | .... | ...... | 157 | 2 | 97.80 | 99.98 | ...20 00–24 99 |
| 25 00–29 99... | 7 | ...... | 8 | ...... | 1 | ...... | ...... | ...... | .... | ...... | 37 | 1 | 99.00 | 100.00 | ...25 00–29 99 |
| 30 00–34 99... | 3 | ...... | 3 | ...... | 1 | ...... | ...... | ...... | .... | ...... | 19 | ...... | 99.70 | ...... | ...30 00–34 99 |
| 35 00–39 99... | 2 | ...... | 2 | ...... | ...... | ...... | ...... | ...... | .... | ...... | 8 | ...... | 100.00 | ...... | ...35 00–39 99 |
| Not reported... | 2 | 2 | 1 | ...... | ...... | 1 | ...... | ...... | 5 | ...... | 34 | 67 | ...... | ...... | ...Not reported |
| Total..... | 148 | 164 | 159 | 155 | 69 | 44 | 11 | 1 | 15 | 29 | 2,920 | 7,456 | ...... | ...... | .....Total |

NEW YORK STATE

108. TABLE IX, C, a.

**THE PAPER BOX INDUSTRY — FACTORY WORKERS**

NUMBER AND PER CENT. OF EMPLOYEES CLASSIFIED ACCORDING TO ACTUAL WEEKLY EARNINGS BY OCCUPATION AND SEX

| ACTUAL WEEKLY EARNINGS IN DOLLARS | OCCUPATION | | | | | | | | | | | | | ACTUAL WEEKLY EARNINGS IN DOLLARS |
|---|---|---|---|---|---|---|---|---|---|---|---|---|---|---|
| | FOREMEN AND FOREWOMEN | | CUTTERS | | GLUE MAKERS | SETTERS-UP | | GENERAL MACHINE WORK | | GLUE TABLE WORK | TURNERS-IN | | | |
| | Male | Female | Male | Female | Male | Male | Female | Male | Female | Male | Male | Female | | |
| Less than $3 00 | ....... | ....... | 6 | 1 | ....... | 5 | 14 | 5 | 19 | ....... | 4 | 56 | | Less than $3 00 |
| 3 00– 3 49 | ....... | ....... | 4 | 1 | ....... | 3 | 11 | 2 | 11 | 1 | 2 | 69 | | 3 00– 3 49 |
| 3 50– 3 99 | ....... | ....... | 3 | 1 | ....... | 3 | 7 | 3 | 13 | ....... | 1 | 77 | | 3 50– 3 99 |
| 4 00– 4 49 | ....... | 2 | 8 | 2 | ....... | 3 | 12 | 3 | 31 | 7 | 2 | 124 | | 4 00– 4 49 |
| 4 50– 4 99 | ....... | ....... | 5 | 4 | ....... | 11 | 15 | 6 | 41 | ....... | 5 | 146 | | 4 50– 4 99 |
| 5 00– 5 49 | ....... | ....... | 12 | 3 | ....... | 13 | 28 | 11 | 85 | 3 | ....... | 205 | | 5 00– 5 49 |
| 5 50– 5 99 | ....... | 2 | 11 | 5 | ....... | 9 | 15 | 16 | 63 | 1 | 6 | 146 | | 5 50– 5 99 |
| 6 00– 6 49 | ....... | 2 | 23 | 6 | ....... | 13 | 30 | 26 | 79 | 2 | 3 | 144 | | 6 00– 6 49 |
| 6 50– 6 99 | ....... | 5 | 21 | 4 | ....... | 3 | 17 | 15 | 55 | 4 | ....... | 39 | | 6 50– 6 99 |
| 7 00– 7 49 | ....... | 8 | 25 | 8 | 1 | 15 | 23 | 13 | 57 | 4 | ....... | 25 | | 7 00– 7 49 |
| 7 50– 7 99 | ....... | 4 | 21 | 5 | ....... | 9 | 17 | 13 | 27 | 1 | ....... | 2 | | 7 50– 7 99 |
| 8 00– 8 99 | 3 | 16 | 41 | 3 | ....... | 19 | 36 | 18 | 51 | 8 | ....... | 9 | | 8 00– 8 99 |
| 9 00– 9 99 | 1 | 14 | 56 | 7 | 2 | 23 | 22 | 35 | 29 | 8 | ....... | 6 | | 9 00– 9 99 |
| 10 00–10 99 | ....... | 23 | 66 | 5 | 1 | 17 | 29 | 30 | 5 | 13 | ....... | 1 | | 10 00–10 99 |
| 11 00–11 99 | 1 | 13 | 55 | 2 | 4 | 22 | 13 | 20 | 9 | 11 | ....... | 3 | | 11 00–11 99 |
| 12 00–12 99 | 9 | 24 | 68 | ....... | 2 | 24 | 12 | 32 | 4 | 22 | ....... | 2 | | 12 00–12 99 |
| 13 00–13 99 | 7 | 6 | 50 | ....... | 1 | 41 | 9 | 17 | ....... | 25 | ....... | ....... | | 13 00–13 99 |
| 14 00–14 99 | 5 | 8 | 43 | ....... | ....... | 39 | ....... | 19 | ....... | 15 | ....... | ....... | | 14 00–14 99 |
| 15 00–15 99 | 9 | 1 | 69 | ....... | ....... | 43 | 1 | 7 | ....... | 15 | ....... | ....... | | 15 00–15 99 |
| 16 00–17 99 | 27 | 4 | 118 | 1 | ....... | 41 | ....... | 11 | 1 | 9 | ....... | ....... | | 16 00–17 99 |
| 18 00–19 99 | 25 | 1 | 80 | ....... | 1 | 11 | ....... | 3 | ....... | 2 | ....... | ....... | | 18 00–19 99 |
| 20 00–24 99 | 65 | 1 | 64 | ....... | ....... | 4 | ....... | 1 | ....... | ....... | ....... | ....... | | 20 00–24 99 |
| 25 00–29 99 | 26 | 1 | 6 | ....... | ....... | ....... | ....... | ....... | ....... | ....... | ....... | ....... | | 25 00–29 99 |
| 30 00–34 99 | 17 | ....... | ....... | ....... | ....... | ....... | ....... | 1 | ....... | ....... | ....... | ....... | | 30 00–34 99 |
| 35 00–39 99 | 6 | ....... | ....... | ....... | ....... | ....... | ....... | ....... | ....... | ....... | ....... | ....... | | 35 00–39 99 |
| Not reported | 13 | ....... | 4 | ....... | ....... | 1 | 3 | 2 | 1 | ....... | ....... | 1 | | Not reported |
| Total | 214 | 135 | 859 | 58 | 12 | 394 | 314 | 309 | 581 | 151 | 23 | 1,055 | | Total |

NEW YORK STATE

108. TABLE IX, C, a—(*concluded*)

**THE PAPER BOX INDUSTRY — FACTORY WORKERS**

NUMBER AND PER CENT. OF EMPLOYEES CLASSIFIED ACCORDING TO ACTUAL WEEKLY EARNINGS BY OCCUPATION AND SEX

| Actual Weekly Earnings in Dollars | Occupation (*concluded*) | | | | | | | | | | | | | | | | Actual Weekly Earnings in Dollars |
|---|---|---|---|---|---|---|---|---|---|---|---|---|---|---|---|---|---|
| | Strippers and top labelers | | Table work | | Closing and tying | | Floor work | | Not reported | | Total | | Cumulative per cent. of total | | | | |
| | Male | Female | Male | Female | Male | Female | Male | Female | Male | Female | Male | Female | Male | Female | | | |
| Less than $3 00 | .... | 29 | 4 | 60 | 6 | 20 | 7 | 32 | 1 | ...... | 38 | 231 | 1.32 | 3.12 | | | Less than $3 00 |
| $3 00–$3 49 | .... | 21 | 5 | 65 | 2 | 23 | 7 | 16 | 1 | 2 | 27 | 219 | 2.25 | 6.10 | | | $3 00– 3 49 |
| 3 50– 3 99 | .... | 44 | 2 | 86 | 5 | 14 | 8 | 21 | 1 | 3 | 26 | 266 | 3.15 | 9.70 | | | 3 50– 3 99 |
| 4 00– 4 49 | 1 | 63 | 6 | 138 | 10 | 21 | 12 | 34 | 1 | 1 | 56 | 428 | 5.09 | 14.15 | | | 4 00– 4 49 |
| 4 50– 4 99 | 1 | 66 | 5 | 154 | 7 | 30 | 8 | 31 | 1 | 6 | 49 | 493 | 6.79 | 22.18 | | | 4 50– 4 99 |
| 5 00– 5 49 | 5 | 114 | 8 | 198 | 17 | 28 | 29 | 46 | 2 | 9 | 103 | 716 | 10.70 | 31.85 | | | 5 00– 5 49 |
| 5 50– 5 99 | 7 | 119 | 9 | 162 | 7 | 38 | 13 | 15 | ...... | 4 | 79 | 569 | 13 10 | 39 60 | | | 5 50– 5 99 |
| 6 00– 6 49 | 2 | 161 | 10 | 184 | 20 | 28 | 23 | 25 | 3 | 3 | 130 | 662 | 17.63 | 48.60 | | | 6 00– 6 49 |
| 6 50– 6 99 | 2 | 122 | 6 | 154 | 7 | 18 | 12 | 19 | 1 | 2 | 76 | 435 | 20.24 | 55.50 | | | 6 50– 6 99 |
| 7 00– 7 49 | 5 | 152 | 17 | 191 | 10 | 14 | 21 | 29 | 1 | 1 | 112 | 508 | 24.10 | 61.30 | | | 7 00– 7 49 |
| 7 50– 7 99 | 5 | 142 | 9 | 164 | 10 | 15 | 10 | 12 | 3 | 2 | 81 | 390 | 26.90 | 66.70 | | | 7 50– 7 99 |
| 8 00– 8 99 | 27 | 291 | 26 | 383 | 32 | 15 | 31 | 16 | 2 | 4 | 207 | 824 | 34.08 | 77.80 | | | 8 00– 8 99 |
| 9 00– 9 99 | 12 | 258 | 25 | 309 | 22 | 14 | 25 | 8 | ...... | 5 | 212 | 672 | 41.40 | 87.00 | | | 9 00– 9 99 |
| 10 00–10 99 | 8 | 194 | 29 | 179 | 12 | 6 | 31 | 6 | 7 | 1 | 214 | 449 | 48.80 | 93.00 | | | 10 00–10 99 |
| 11 00–11 99 | 14 | 100 | 23 | 90 | 9 | 5 | 17 | 1 | 4 | ...... | 180 | 236 | 55.00 | 96.00 | | | 11 00–11 99 |
| 12 00–12 99 | 9 | 70 | 27 | 57 | 6 | 2 | 9 | ...... | 3 | 1 | 211 | 172 | 62.40 | 98.50 | | | 12 00–12 99 |
| 13 00–13 99 | 8 | 27 | 13 | 13 | 2 | ...... | 7 | ...... | 2 | 1 | 173 | 56 | 68.40 | 99.20 | | | 13 00–13 99 |
| 14 00–14 99 | 2 | 11 | 17 | 10 | 1 | ...... | 6 | ...... | ...... | ...... | 147 | 29 | 73.50 | 99.60 | | | 14 00–14 99 |
| 15 00–15 99 | 7 | 7 | 15 | 2 | 2 | ...... | 2 | ...... | 4 | ...... | 173 | 11 | 79.40 | 99.80 | | | 15 00–15 99 |
| 16 00–17 99 | 3 | 6 | 19 | 4 | 1 | ...... | 3 | 1 | ...... | ...... | 232 | 17 | 87.50 | 99.93 | | | 16 00–17 99 |
| 18 00–19 99 | 2 | ...... | 15 | 2 | .... | ...... | .... | ...... | ...... | ...... | 139 | 3 | 92.40 | 99.96 | | | 18 00–19 99 |
| 20 00–24 99 | 1 | ...... | 21 | 1 | .... | ...... | 1 | ...... | ...... | ...... | 157 | 2 | 97.80 | 99.98 | | | 20 00–24 99 |
| 25 00–29 99 | .... | ...... | 5 | ...... | .... | ...... | .... | ...... | ...... | ...... | 37 | 1 | 99.00 | 100.00 | | | 25 00–29 99 |
| 30 00–34 99 | .... | ...... | .... | ...... | .... | ...... | 1 | ...... | ...... | ...... | 19 | ...... | 99.70 | ...... | | | 30.00–34 99 |
| 35 00–39 99 | .... | ...... | 2 | ...... | .... | ...... | .... | ...... | ...... | ...... | 8 | ...... | 100.00 | ...... | | | 35 00–39 99 |
| Not reported | .... | 1 | .... | 15 | .... | 2 | 9 | 44 | 5 | ...... | 34 | 67 | ...... | ...... | | | Not reported |
| Total | 121 | 1,998 | 318 | 2,621 | 188 | 293 | 292 | 356 | 42 | 45 | 2,920 | 7,456 | ...... | ...... | | | Total |

NEW YCRK STATE

109. TABLE X, C, a

**THE PAPER BOX INDUSTRY — FACTORY WORKERS**

NUMBER AND PER CENT. OF EMPLOYEES CLASSIFIED ACCORDING TO ACTUAL WEEKLY EARNINGS, BY CONJUGAL CONDITION AND SEX

| ACTUAL WEEKLY EARNINGS IN DOLLARS | CONJUGAL CONDITION | | | | | | | | | | | | ACTUAL WEEKLY EARNINGS IN DOLLARS |
|---|---|---|---|---|---|---|---|---|---|---|---|---|---|
| | SINGLE | | MARRIED | | WIDOWED OR DIVORCED | | NOT REPORTED | | TOTAL | | CUMULATIVE PER CENT. OF TOTAL | | |
| | Male | Female | Male | Female | Male | Female | Male | Female | Male | Female | Male | Female | |
| Less than $3 00. | 30 | 208 | 6 | 16 | 1 | 3 | 1 | 4 | 38 | 231 | 1.32 | 3.12 | Less than $3 00 |
| $3 00–$3 49.... | 22 | 202 | 4 | 14 | ....... | 2 | 1 | 1 | 27 | 219 | 2.25 | 6.10 | ...$3 00– 3 49 |
| 3 50– 3 99.... | 25 | 247 | 1 | 12 | ....... | 5 | ....... | 2 | 26 | 266 | 3.15 | 9.70 | ....3 50– 3 99 |
| 4 00– 4 49.... | 53 | 389 | 1 | 28 | 1 | 6 | 1 | 5 | 56 | 428 | 5.09 | 14.15 | ....4 00– 4 49 |
| 4 50– 4 99.... | 46 | 448 | 3 | 28 | ....... | 13 | ....... | 4 | 49 | 493 | 6.79 | 22.18 | ....4 50– 4 99 |
| 5 00– 5 49.... | 92 | 633 | 11 | 51 | ....... | 29 | ....... | 3 | 103 | 716 | 10.70 | 31.85 | ....5 00– 5 49 |
| 5 50– 5 99.... | 71 | 521 | 7 | 30 | ....... | 17 | 1 | 1 | 79 | 569 | 13.10 | 39.60 | ....5 50– 5 99 |
| 6 00– 6 49.... | 112 | 589 | 18 | 46 | ....... | 19 | ....... | 8 | 130 | 662 | 17.63 | 48.60 | ....6 00– 6 49 |
| 6 50– 6 99.... | 66 | 385 | 8 | 33 | 1 | 15 | 1 | 2 | 76 | 435 | 20.24 | 55.50 | ....6 50– 6 99 |
| 7 00– 7 49.... | 88 | 436 | 20 | 48 | 1 | 21 | 3 | 3 | 112 | 508 | 24.10 | 61.30 | ....7 00– 7 49 |
| 7 50– 7 99.... | 65 | 337 | 14 | 37 | ....... | 14 | 2 | 2 | 81 | 390 | 26.90 | 66.70 | ....7 50– 7 99 |
| 8 00– 8 99.... | 159 | 720 | 45 | 59 | 2 | 43 | 1 | 2 | 207 | 824 | 34.08 | 77.80 | ....8 00– 8 99 |
| 9 00– 9 99.... | 151 | 569 | 57 | 58 | 2 | 44 | 2 | 1 | 212 | 672 | 41.40 | 87.00 | ....9 00– 9 99 |
| 10 00–10 99.... | 128 | 368 | 77 | 48 | 3 | 32 | 6 | 1 | 214 | 449 | 48.80 | 93.00 | ...10 00–10 99 |
| 11 00–11 99.... | 101 | 205 | 75 | 18 | 1 | 9 | 3 | 4 | 180 | 236 | 55.00 | 96.00 | ...11 00–11 99 |
| 12 00–12 99.... | 113 | 144 | 91 | 21 | 6 | 7 | 1 | ....... | 211 | 172 | 62.40 | 98.50 | ...12 00–12 99 |
| 13 00–13 99.... | 87 | 50 | 83 | 4 | 1 | 2 | 2 | ....... | 173 | 56 | 68.40 | 99.20 | ...13 00–13 99 |
| 14 00–14 99.... | 69 | 24 | 73 | 3 | 3 | 2 | 2 | ....... | 147 | 29 | 73.50 | 99.60 | ...14 00–14 99 |
| 15 00–15 99.... | 68 | 9 | 99 | 2 | 4 | ....... | 2 | ....... | 173 | 11 | 79.40 | 98.80 | ...15 00–15 99 |
| 16 00–17 99.... | 76 | 10 | 150 | 5 | 3 | 2 | 3 | ....... | 232 | 17 | 87.50 | 99.93 | ...16 00–17 99 |
| 18 00–19 99.... | 44 | 1 | 93 | 2 | 1 | ....... | 1 | ....... | 139 | 3 | 92.40 | 99.96 | ...18 00–19 99 |
| 20 00–24 99.... | 17 | 2 | 133 | ....... | 4 | ....... | 3 | ....... | 157 | 2 | 97.80 | 99.98 | ...20 00–24 99 |
| 25 00–29 99.... | 5 | 1 | 32 | ....... | ....... | ....... | ....... | ....... | 37 | 1 | 99.00 | 100.00 | ...25 00–29 99 |
| 30 00–34 99.... | 3 | ....... | 16 | ....... | ....... | ....... | ....... | ....... | 19 | ....... | 99.70 | ....... | ...30 00–34 99 |
| 35 00–39 99.... | 1 | ....... | 7 | ....... | ....... | ....... | ....... | ....... | 8 | ....... | 100.00 | ....... | ...35 00–39 99 |
| Not reported.... | 15 | 60 | 14 | 4 | ....... | 1 | 5 | 2 | 34 | 67 | ....... | ....... | ...Not reported |
| Total...... | 1,707 | 6,558 | 1,138 | 567 | 34 | 286 | 41 | 45 | 2,920 | 7,456 | ....... | ....... | .....Total |

NEW YORK STATE

**THE PAPER BOX INDUSTRY — FACTORY WORKERS**

110. TABLE XI, C, a NUMBER AND PER CENT. OF EMPLOYEES CLASSIFIED ACCORDING TO ACTUAL WEEKLY EARNINGS, BY NATIVITY AND SEX

| ACTUAL WEEKLY EARNINGS IN DOLLARS | NATIVITY — NATIVE | | FOREIGN | | NOT REPORTED | | TOTAL | | CUMULATIVE PER CENT. OF TOTAL | | ACTUAL WEEKLY EARNINGS IN DOLLARS |
|---|---|---|---|---|---|---|---|---|---|---|---|
| | Male | Female | Male | Female | Male | Female | Male | Female | Male | Female | |
| Less than $3 00 | 21 | 172 | 16 | 58 | 1 | 1 | 38 | 231 | 1.32 | 3.12 | Less than $3 00 |
| $3 00–$3 49 | 11 | 167 | 15 | 50 | 1 | 2 | 27 | 219 | 2.25 | 6.10 | $3 00– 3 49 |
| 3 50– 3 99 | 14 | 218 | 12 | 47 | ........ | 1 | 26 | 266 | 3.15 | 9.70 | 3 50– 3 99 |
| 4 00– 4 49 | 30 | 356 | 25 | 71 | 1 | 1 | 56 | 428 | 5.09 | 14.15 | 4 00– 4 49 |
| 4 50– 4 99 | 31 | 387 | 18 | 103 | ........ | 3 | 49 | 403 | 6.79 | 22.18 | 4 50– 4 99 |
| 5 00– 5 49 | 47 | 536 | 56 | 179 | ........ | 1 | 103 | 716 | 10.70 | 31.85 | 5 00– 5 49 |
| 5 50– 5 99 | 39 | 420 | 40 | 140 | ........ | 1 | 79 | 569 | 13.10 | 39.60 | 5 50– 5 99 |
| 6 00– 6 49 | 58 | 480 | 72 | 181 | ........ | 1 | 130 | 662 | 17.63 | 48.60 | 6 00– 6 49 |
| 6 50– 6 99 | 28 | 322 | 48 | 110 | ........ | 3 | 76 | 435 | 20.24 | 55.50 | 6 50– 6 99 |
| 7 00– 7 49 | 45 | 393 | 63 | 114 | 4 | 1 | 112 | 508 | 24.10 | 61.30 | 7 00– 7 49 |
| 7 50– 7 99 | 40 | 281 | 41 | 106 | ........ | 3 | 81 | 390 | 26.90 | 66.70 | 7 50– 7 99 |
| 8 00– 8 99 | 104 | 642 | 102 | 181 | 1 | 1 | 207 | 824 | 34.00 | 77.80 | 8 00– 8 99 |
| 9 00– 9 99 | 100 | 520 | 112 | 150 | ........ | 2 | 212 | 672 | 41.40 | 87.00 | 9 00– 9 99 |
| 10 00–10 99 | 93 | 317 | 121 | 130 | ........ | 2 | 214 | 449 | 48.80 | 93.00 | 10 00–10 99 |
| 11 00–11 99 | 78 | 181 | 102 | 55 | ........ | ........ | 180 | 236 | 55.00 | 96.00 | 11 00–11 99 |
| 12 00–12 99 | 95 | 118 | 116 | 53 | ........ | 1 | 211 | 172 | 62.40 | 98.50 | 12 00–12 99 |
| 13 00–13 99 | 95 | 39 | 77 | 17 | 1 | ........ | 173 | 56 | 68.40 | 99.20 | 13 00–13 99 |
| 14 00–14 99 | 68 | 22 | 77 | 7 | 2 | ........ | 147 | 29 | 73.50 | 99.60 | 14 00–14 99 |
| 15 00–15 99 | 84 | 10 | 88 | 1 | 1 | ........ | 173 | 11 | 79.40 | 99.80 | 15 00–15 99 |
| 16 00–17 99 | 121 | 12 | 111 | 5 | ........ | ........ | 232 | 17 | 87.50 | 99.93 | 16 00–17 99 |
| 18 00–19 99 | 65 | 2 | 74 | 1 | ........ | ........ | 139 | 3 | 92.40 | 99.96 | 18 00–19 99 |
| 20 00–24 99 | 79 | 1 | 78 | 1 | ........ | ........ | 157 | 2 | 97.80 | 99.98 | 20 00–24 99 |
| 25 00–29 99 | 23 | 1 | 14 | ........ | ........ | ........ | 37 | 1 | 99.00 | 100.00 | 25 00–29 99 |
| 30 00–34 99 | 11 | ........ | 8 | ........ | ........ | ........ | 19 | ........ | 99.70 | ........ | 30 00–34 99 |
| 35 00–39 99 | 3 | ........ | 5 | ........ | ........ | ........ | 8 | ........ | 100.00 | ........ | 35 00–39 99 |
| Not reported | 16 | 24 | 18 | 43 | ........ | ........ | 34 | 67 | ........ | ........ | Not reported |
| Total | 1,399 | 5,621 | 1,509 | 1,811 | 12 | 24 | 2,920 | 7,456 | ........ | ........ | Total |

111. TABLE XII, C, a

NEW YORK STATE

THE PAPER BOX INDUSTRY — FACTORY WORKERS

NUMBER OF EMPLOYEES FOR EACH SEX CLASSIFIED ACCORDING TO ACTUAL WEEKLY EARNINGS BY THE NUMBER OF YEARS IN THE TRADE

| ACTUAL WEEKLY EARNINGS IN DOLLARS | YEARS IN TRADE | | | | | | | | | | | | | | ACTUAL WEEKLY EARNINGS IN DOLLARS |
|---|---|---|---|---|---|---|---|---|---|---|---|---|---|---|---|
| | LESS THAN 1 | | 1 | | 2 | | 3 | | 4 | | 5 | | 6 | | |
| | Male | Female | Male | Female | Male | Female | Male | Female | Male | Female | Male | Female | Male | Female | |
| Less than $3 00 | 25 | 137 | 3 | 30 | 3 | 20 | 1 | 15 | ...... | 5 | ...... | 2 | ...... | 2 | Less than $3 00 |
| $3 00–$3 49... | 17 | 145 | 5 | 28 | ...... | 16 | 1 | 7 | ...... | 4 | ...... | 5 | 1 | 3 | ...$3 00– 3 49 |
| 3 50– 3 99... | 16 | 154 | 9 | 44 | ...... | 29 | 1 | 16 | ...... | 5 | ...... | 2 | ...... | ...... | ... 3 50– 3 99 |
| 4 00– 4 49... | 37 | 238 | 11 | 77 | 3 | 47 | 1 | 24 | ...... | 9 | ...... | 5 | 1 | 8 | ... 4 00– 4 49 |
| 4 50– 4 99... | 27 | 252 | 16 | 88 | 3 | 48 | 1 | 32 | ...... | 19 | ...... | 10 | ...... | 9 | ... 4 50– 4 99 |
| 5 00– 5 49... | 64 | 317 | 20 | 122 | 6 | 76 | 2 | 55 | 2 | 35 | ...... | 24 | 1 | 12 | ... 5 00– 5 49 |
| 5 50– 5 99... | 37 | 200 | 20 | 110 | 8 | 88 | 5 | 54 | 1 | 29 | 1 | 18 | ...... | 12 | ... 5 50– 5 99 |
| 6 00– 6 49... | 78 | 137 | 25 | 137 | 9 | 112 | 2 | 83 | 4 | 50 | 3 | 35 | 2 | 24 | ... 6 00– 6 49 |
| 6 50– 6 99... | 44 | 58 | 11 | 60 | 7 | 84 | 2 | 57 | ...... | 42 | 2 | 36 | 1 | 25 | ... 6 50– 6 99 |
| 7 00– 7 49... | 42 | 49 | 23 | 64 | 17 | 67 | 11 | 79 | 1 | 57 | 4 | 37 | 3 | 34 | ... 7 00– 7 49 |
| 7 50– 7 99... | 29 | 28 | 11 | 45 | 21 | 50 | 8 | 45 | 1 | 51 | ...... | 31 | 3 | 16 | ... 7 50– 7 99 |
| 8 00– 8 99... | 58 | 49 | 31 | 53 | 20 | 90 | 18 | 116 | 18 | 86 | 10 | 59 | 10 | 69 | ... 8 00– 8 99 |
| 9 00– 9 99... | 49 | 21 | 34 | 29 | 25 | 44 | 18 | 65 | 13 | 68 | 12 | 74 | 15 | 68 | ... 9 00– 9 99 |
| 10 00–10 99... | 30 | 7 | 17 | 12 | 29 | 22 | 20 | 31 | 14 | 26 | 19 | 47 | 19 | 45 | ...10 00–10 99 |
| 11 00–11 99... | 23 | 4 | 19 | 7 | 17 | 21 | 15 | 18 | 14 | 20 | 10 | 25 | 9 | 15 | ...11 00–11 99 |
| 12 00–12 99... | 9 | 1 | 13 | 4 | 8 | 15 | 17 | 6 | 23 | 6 | 22 | 16 | 24 | 13 | ...12 00–12 99 |
| 13 00–13 99... | 5 | ...... | 9 | 1 | 7 | 2 | 13 | 7 | 17 | 3 | 11 | 3 | 10 | 5 | ...13 00–13 99 |
| 14 00–14 99... | 3 | ...... | 5 | ...... | 5 | 3 | 13 | 1 | 8 | 1 | 10 | 2 | 11 | 2 | ...14 00–14 99 |
| 15 00–15 99... | 2 | ...... | 2 | ...... | 6 | 3 | 10 | ...... | 11 | ...... | 10 | ...... | 18 | ...... | ...15 00–15 99 |
| 16 00–17 99... | 2 | ...... | 6 | ...... | 9 | ...... | 12 | 1 | 5 | ...... | 5 | 3 | 11 | 2 | ...16 00–17 99 |
| 18 00–19 99... | 3 | ...... | 3 | ...... | 2 | ...... | 3 | ...... | 1 | ...... | 6 | ...... | 10 | ...... | ...18 00–19 99 |
| 20 00–24 99... | 2 | ...... | .... | ...... | ...... | ...... | 2 | ...... | 1 | ...... | 5 | ...... | 4 | 1 | ...20 00–24 99 |
| 25 00–29 99... | .... | ...... | 1 | ...... | ...... | ...... | 1 | ...... | ...... | ...... | ...... | ...... | ...... | ...... | ...25 00–29 99 |
| 30 00–34 99... | .... | ...... | 2 | ...... | ...... | ...... | ...... | ...... | ...... | ...... | ...... | ...... | ...... | ...... | ...30 00–34 99 |
| Not reported... | 9 | 17 | 1 | 3 | 2 | 7 | 3 | 16 | ...... | 7 | 1 | 4 | 1 | 3 | ...Not reported |
| Total..... | 611 | 1,814 | 297 | 914 | 207 | 844 | 180 | 729 | 134 | 523 | 131 | 438 | 154 | 368 | .....Total |

111. TABLE XII, C, a — *(continued)*

NEW YORK STATE

**THE PAPER BOX INDUSTRY — FACTORY WORKERS**

NUMBER OF EMPLOYEES FOR EACH SEX CLASSIFIED ACCORDING TO ACTUAL WEEKLY EARNINGS BY THE NUMBER OF YEARS IN THE TRADE

| ACTUAL WEEKLY EARNINGS IN DOLLARS | YEARS IN TRADE *(continued)* | | | | | | | | | | | | | | ACTUAL WEEKLY EARNINGS IN DOLLARS |
|---|---|---|---|---|---|---|---|---|---|---|---|---|---|---|---|
| | 7 | | 8 | | 9 | | 10–14 | | 15–19 | | 20–24 | | 25–29 | | |
| | Male | Female | Male | Female | Male | Female | Male | Female | Male | Female | Male | Female | Male | Female | |
| Less than $3 00 | 1 | 2 | .... | 3 | ...... | 1 | ...... | 1 | 2 | 5 | ...... | ...... | 1 | 3 | Less than $3 00 |
| $3 00–$3 49... | 1 | 1 | .... | 1 | ...... | 2 | ...... | 2 | 1 | 2 | ...... | 2 | ...... | 1 | ...$3 00– 3 49 |
| 3 50– 3 99... | .... | 1 | .... | 4 | ...... | ...... | ...... | 3 | ...... | 1 | ...... | ...... | ...... | 1 | ... 3 50– 3 99 |
| 4 00– 4 49... | 2 | 2 | .... | ...... | ...... | 1 | ...... | 7 | ...... | 3 | ...... | 2 | ...... | 1 | ... 4 00– 4 49 |
| 4 50– 4 99... | 1 | 8 | .... | 7 | ...... | 3 | 1 | 7 | ...... | 3 | ...... | 2 | ...... | 2 | ... 4 50– 4 99 |
| 5 00– 5 49... | .... | 18 | 3 | 7 | ...... | 3 | 1 | 18 | 1 | 8 | ...... | 9 | 1 | 2 | ... 5 00– 5 49 |
| 5 50– 5 99... | .... | 11 | .... | 8 | 1 | 7 | 2 | 15 | ...... | 7 | ...... | 4 | ...... | 1 | ... 5 50– 5 99 |
| 6 00– 6 49... | 1 | 13 | 2 | 8 | 1 | 7 | 1 | 18 | ...... | 13 | 1 | 12 | ...... | 4 | ... 6 00– 6 49 |
| 6 50– 6 99... | 1 | 14 | 1 | 9 | 1 | 9 | ...... | 16 | 3 | 7 | ...... | 5 | ...... | 3 | ... 6 50– 6 99 |
| 7 00– 7 49... | .... | 26 | .... | 16 | 1 | 8 | 4 | 31 | 2 | 14 | ...... | 12 | ...... | 7 | ... 7 00– 7 49 |
| 7 50– 7 99... | 1 | 29 | 1 | 10 | ...... | 8 | 2 | 37 | ...... | 19 | 1 | 10 | ...... | 5 | ... 7 50– 7 99 |
| 8 00– 8 99... | 9 | 52 | 6 | 47 | 3 | 18 | 12 | 96 | 3 | 29 | 5 | 29 | 1 | 14 | ... 8 00– 8 99 |
| 9 00– 9 99... | 10 | 44 | 1 | 32 | 4 | 24 | 15 | 91 | 8 | 50 | 3 | 25 | 1 | 20 | ... 9 00– 9 99 |
| 10 00–10 99... | 6 | 40 | 10 | 34 | 3 | 20 | 25 | 86 | 7 | 32 | 7 | 24 | 1 | 13 | ...10 00–10 99 |
| 11 00–11 99... | 12 | 29 | 6 | 15 | 4 | 15 | 18 | 35 | 14 | 13 | 5 | 8 | 2 | 6 | ...11 00–11 99 |
| 12 00–12 99... | 8 | 14 | 10 | 17 | 9 | 9 | 29 | 33 | 12 | 18 | 10 | 8 | 9 | 4 | ...12 00–12 99 |
| 13 00–13 99... | 14 | 4 | 18 | 3 | 9 | 5 | 24 | 14 | 18 | 4 | 6 | 2 | 8 | 2 | ...13 00–13 99 |
| 14 00–14 99... | 11 | ...... | 16 | 4 | 5 | 1 | 32 | 6 | 9 | 3 | 7 | 3 | 8 | 1 | ...14 00–14 99 |
| 15 00–15 99... | 15 | 1 | 11 | ...... | 9 | 2 | 32 | 2 | 22 | 2 | 11 | 1 | 5 | ...... | ...15 00–15 99 |
| 16 00–17 99... | 12 | ...... | 22 | ...... | 10 | 1 | 54 | 2 | 40 | 3 | 17 | 3 | 7 | 2 | ...16 00–17 99 |
| 18 00–19 99... | 8 | ...... | 10 | ...... | 7 | ...... | 36 | ...... | 16 | 3 | 18 | ...... | 7 | ...... | ...18 00–19 99 |
| 20 00–24 99... | 3 | ...... | 2 | ...... | 3 | ...... | 42 | 1 | 35 | ...... | 22 | ...... | 13 | ...... | ...20 00–24 99 |
| 25 00–29 99... | .... | ...... | 1 | ...... | 1 | ...... | 7 | ...... | 8 | ...... | 5 | 1 | 8 | ...... | ...25 00–29 99 |
| 30 00–34 99... | 1 | ...... | 1 | ...... | ...... | ...... | 2 | ...... | 4 | ...... | 3 | ...... | 3 | ...... | ...30 00–34 99 |
| 35 00–39 99... | .... | ...... | .... | ...... | ...... | ...... | 1 | ...... | 2 | ...... | 2 | ...... | 1 | ...... | ...35 00–39 00 |
| Not reported... | 2 | 1 | .... | 2 | ...... | ...... | 5 | 1 | 3 | 1 | 2 | 1 | ...... | 2 | ...Not reported |
| Total..... | 119 | 310 | 121 | 227 | 71 | 144 | 345 | 522 | 210 | 240 | 125 | 163 | 76 | 94 | .....Total |

111. TABLE XII, C, a — (*concluded*)

NEW YORK STATE

**THE PAPER BOX INDUSTRY — FACTORY WORKERS**

NUMBER OF EMPLOYEES FOR EACH SEX CLASSIFIED ACCORDING TO ACTUAL WEEKLY EARNINGS BY THE NUMBER OF YEARS IN THE TRADE

| ACTUAL WEEKLY EARNINGS IN DOLLARS | YEARS IN TRADE (*concluded*) 30–34 | | 35–44 | | 45 AND OVER | | NOT REPORTED | | TOTAL | | CUMULATIVE PER CENT. OF TOTAL | | ACTUAL WEEKLY EARNINGS IN DOLLARS |
|---|---|---|---|---|---|---|---|---|---|---|---|---|---|
| | Male | Female | Male | Female | Male | Female | Male | Female | Male | Female | Male | Female | |
| Less than $3 00 | | 1 | | | | | 2 | 4 | 38 | 231 | 1.32 | 3.12 | Less than $3 00 |
| $3 00–$3 49 | | | | | | | 1 | | 27 | 219 | 2.25 | 6.10 | $3 00– 3 49 |
| 3 50– 3 99 | | 1 | | 2 | | | | 3 | 26 | 266 | 3.15 | 9.70 | 3 50– 3 99 |
| 4 00– 4 49 | | | | | | | 1 | 4 | 56 | 428 | 5.09 | 14.15 | 4 00– 4 49 |
| 4 50– 4 99 | | | | | | | | 3 | 49 | 493 | 6.79 | 22.18 | 4 50– 4 99 |
| 5 00– 5 49 | | 2 | | 2 | | | 2 | 6 | 103 | 716 | 10.70 | 31.85 | 5 00– 5 49 |
| 5 50– 5 99 | 1 | | | 1 | | | 3 | 4 | 79 | 569 | 13.10 | 39.60 | 5 50– 5 99 |
| 6 00– 6 49 | | 3 | | 1 | | | 1 | 5 | 130 | 662 | 17.63 | 48.60 | 6 00– 6 49 |
| 6 50– 6 99 | 1 | 2 | | 2 | | 1 | 2 | 5 | 76 | 435 | 20.24 | 55.50 | 6 50– 6 99 |
| 7 00– 7 49 | | 3 | | 2 | | | 4 | 2 | 112 | 508 | 24.10 | 61.30 | 7 00– 7 49 |
| 7 50– 7 99 | 1 | 2 | 1 | 2 | | | 1 | 1 | 81 | 390 | 26.90 | 66.70 | 7 50– 7 99 |
| 8 00– 8 99 | | 8 | 1 | 1 | 1 | | 1 | 8 | 207 | 824 | 34.08 | 77.80 | 8 00– 8 99 |
| 9 00– 9 99 | | 7 | 1 | 6 | | | 3 | 4 | 212 | 672 | 41.40 | 87.00 | 9 00– 9 99 |
| 10 00–10 99 | 1 | 4 | 3 | 3 | | | 3 | 3 | 214 | 449 | 48.80 | 93.00 | 10 00–10 99 |
| 11 00–11 99 | 7 | 2 | 3 | | | | 2 | 3 | 180 | 236 | 55.00 | 96.00 | 11 00–11 99 |
| 12 00–12 99 | 4 | 2 | 3 | 2 | | | 1 | 4 | 211 | 172 | 62.40 | 98.50 | 12 00–12 99 |
| 13 00–13 99 | 1 | 1 | 1 | | | | 2 | | 173 | 56 | 68.40 | 99.20 | 13 00–13 99 |
| 14 00–14 99 | 2 | 2 | | | | | 2 | | 147 | 29 | 73.50 | 99.60 | 14 00–14 99 |
| 15 00–15 99 | 6 | | 1 | | | | 2 | | 173 | 11 | 79.40 | 99.80 | 15 00–15 99 |
| 16 00–17 99 | 11 | | 5 | | 2 | | 2 | | 232 | 17 | 87.50 | 99.93 | 16 00–17 99 |
| 18 00–19 99 | 3 | | 5 | | 1 | | | | 139 | 3 | 92.40 | 99.96 | 18 00–19 99 |
| 20 00–24 99 | 17 | | 6 | | | | | | 157 | 2 | 97.80 | 99.98 | 20 00–24 99 |
| 25 00–29 99 | 4 | | 1 | | | | | | 37 | 1 | 99.00 | 100.00 | 25 00–29 99 |
| 30 00–34 99 | 2 | | 1 | | | | | | 19 | | 99.70 | | 30 00–34 99 |
| 35 00–39 99 | 1 | | 1 | | | | | | 8 | | 100.00 | | 35 00–39 99 |
| Not reported | | | | 1 | | | 5 | 1 | 34 | 67 | | | Not reported |
| Total | 62 | 40 | 33 | 25 | 4 | 1 | 40 | 60 | 2,920 | 7,456 | | | Total |

NEW YORK STATE

112. TABLE XIII, C, a

THE PAPER BOX INDUSTRY — FACTORY WORKERS

NUMBER OF EMPLOYEES FOR EACH SEX CLASSIFIED ACCORDING TO ACTUAL WEEKLY EARNINGS BY THE NUMBER OF YEARS WITH THE FIRM

| ACTUAL WEEKLY EARNINGS IN DOLLARS | YEARS IN FIRM | | | | | | | | | | | | | | ACTUAL WEEKLY EARNINGS IN DOLLARS |
|---|---|---|---|---|---|---|---|---|---|---|---|---|---|---|---|
| | LESS THAN 1 | | 1 | | 2 | | 3 | | 4 | | 5 | | 6 | | |
| | Male | Female | Male | Female | Male | Female | Male | Female | Male | Female | Male | Female | Male | Female | |
| Less than $3 00 | 33 | 169 | 2 | 28 | 1 | 11 | 1 | 7 | ...... | 5 | ...... | 3 | ...... | ...... | Less than $3 00 |
| $3 00–$3 49 | 19 | 163 | 5 | 25 | 1 | 11 | ...... | 6 | ...... | 2 | ...... | 5 | 1 | 1 | $3 00– 3 49 |
| 3 50– 3 99 | 19 | 183 | 6 | 42 | ...... | 22 | 1 | 9 | ...... | 3 | ...... | 1 | ...... | 2 | 3 50– 3 99 |
| 4 00– 4 49 | 41 | 269 | 8 | 69 | 3 | 43 | 1 | 18 | ...... | 7 | 1 | 3 | 1 | 6 | 4 00– 4 49 |
| 4 50– 4 99 | 32 | 300 | 16 | 84 | 1 | 36 | ...... | 28 | ...... | 18 | ...... | 5 | ...... | 6 | 4 50– 4 99 |
| 5 00– 5 49 | 75 | 400 | 19 | 118 | 6 | 61 | 1 | 37 | ...... | 28 | ...... | 17 | ...... | 8 | 5 00– 5 49 |
| 5 50– 5 99 | 50 | 278 | 19 | 110 | 5 | 73 | 2 | 42 | 2 | 15 | 1 | 14 | ...... | 6 | 5 50– 5 99 |
| 6 00– 6 49 | 89 | 260 | 21 | 137 | 9 | 79 | 3 | 62 | 4 | 35 | 3 | 25 | ...... | 13 | 6 00– 6 49 |
| 6 50– 6 99 | 48 | 103 | 15 | 83 | 6 | 78 | 2 | 44 | 1 | 28 | ...... | 31 | 1 | 20 | 6 50– 6 99 |
| 7 00– 7 49 | 61 | 118 | 15 | 82 | 13 | 64 | 11 | 66 | 1 | 48 | 2 | 31 | 2 | 22 | 7 00– 7 49 |
| 7 50– 7 99 | 39 | 80 | 14 | 56 | 19 | 75 | 5 | 34 | ...... | 44 | ...... | 20 | 1 | 15 | 7 50– 7 99 |
| 8 00– 8 99 | 97 | 146 | 39 | 101 | 21 | 112 | 17 | 111 | 11 | 74 | 5 | 61 | 3 | 41 | 8 00– 8 99 |
| 9 00– 9 99 | 75 | 145 | 42 | 82 | 31 | 77 | 14 | 70 | 10 | 53 | 11 | 56 | 9 | 34 | 9 00– 9 99 |
| 10 00–10 99 | 75 | 90 | 31 | 48 | 28 | 65 | 15 | 39 | 13 | 31 | 13 | 29 | 14 | 25 | 10 00–10 99 |
| 11 00–11 99 | 47 | 31 | 38 | 33 | 18 | 34 | 17 | 25 | 15 | 20 | 4 | 16 | 4 | 11 | 11 00–11 99 |
| 12 00–12 99 | 52 | 26 | 29 | 20 | 18 | 22 | 18 | 13 | 21 | 14 | 15 | 16 | 7 | 4 | 12 00–12 99 |
| 13 00–13 99 | 40 | 5 | 28 | 10 | 13 | 4 | 21 | 7 | 15 | 3 | 14 | 5 | 8 | 5 | 13 00–13 99 |
| 14 00–14 99 | 23 | 6 | 20 | ...... | 21 | 3 | 22 | 6 | 10 | 3 | 7 | 4 | 4 | 2 | 14 00–14 99 |
| 15 00–15 99 | 37 | ...... | 24 | 1 | 21 | 3 | 17 | ...... | 15 | ...... | 8 | 2 | 8 | ...... | 15 00–15 99 |
| 16 00–17 99 | 43 | 1 | 31 | 1 | 24 | 1 | 19 | 3 | 15 | ...... | 19 | 2 | 12 | ...... | 16 00–17 99 |
| 18 00–19 99 | 21 | 1 | 12 | ...... | 20 | ...... | 14 | ...... | 5 | ...... | 14 | 1 | 4 | ...... | 18 00–19 99 |
| 20 00–24 99 | 22 | ...... | 14 | ...... | 20 | ...... | 9 | 1 | 2 | ...... | 16 | ...... | 8 | ...... | 20 00–24 99 |
| 25 00–29 99 | 4 | ...... | 3 | ...... | ...... | ...... | 4 | ...... | 2 | ...... | 2 | ...... | 3 | ...... | 25 00–29 99 |
| 30 00–34 99 | 3 | ...... | 3 | ...... | ...... | ...... | 1 | ...... | 1 | ...... | ...... | ...... | ...... | ...... | 30 00–34 99 |
| 35 00–39 99 | .... | ...... | 2 | ...... | 1 | ...... | 1 | ...... | ...... | ...... | 1 | ...... | ...... | ...... | 35 00–39 99 |
| Not reported | 13 | 21 | 2 | 7 | 1 | 10 | 1 | 11 | ...... | 7 | 2 | 3 | 1 | 2 | Not reported |
| Total | 1,058 | 2,795 | 453 | 1,137 | 301 | 884 | 217 | 639 | 143 | 438 | 138 | 350 | 91 | 223 | Total |

NEW YORK STATE

112. TABLE XIII, C, a—(*continued*) THE PAPER BOX INDUSTRY — FACTORY WORKERS

NUMBER OF EMPLOYEES FOR EACH SEX CLASSIFIED ACCORDING TO ACTUAL WEEKLY EARNINGS BY THE NUMBER OF YEARS WITH THE FIRM

| Actual Weekly Earnings in Dollars | Years in Firm | | | | | | | | | | | | | | Actual Weekly Earnings in Dollars |
|---|---|---|---|---|---|---|---|---|---|---|---|---|---|---|---|
| | 7 | | 8 | | 9 | | 10–14 | | 15–19 | | 20–24 | | 25–29 | | |
| | Male | Female | Male | Female | Male | Female | Male | Female | Male | Female | Male | Female | Male | Female | |
| Less than $3 00 | .... | 2 | .... | .... | .... | .... | 1 | 2 | .... | 2 | .... | .... | .... | 1 | Less than $3 00 |
| $3 00–$3 49 | 1 | .... | .... | .... | .... | 3 | .... | 3 | .... | .... | .... | .... | .... | .... | $3 00– 3 49 |
| 3 50– 3 99 | .... | 2 | .... | 1 | .... | .... | .... | .... | .... | .... | .... | .... | .... | .... | 3 50– 3 99 |
| 4 00– 4 49 | .... | 2 | .... | 1 | .... | .... | .... | 7 | .... | .... | .... | 1 | .... | .... | 4 00– 4 49 |
| 4 50– 4 99 | .... | 5 | .... | 1 | .... | .... | .... | 6 | .... | .... | .... | 1 | .... | 1 | 4 50– 4 99 |
| 5 00– 5 49 | .... | 13 | 2 | 5 | .... | 2 | .... | 15 | .... | 4 | .... | 4 | .... | .... | 5 00– 5 49 |
| 5 50– 5 99 | .... | 7 | .... | 1 | .... | 6 | .... | 14 | .... | 3 | .... | .... | .... | .... | 5 50– 5 99 |
| 6 00– 6 49 | .... | 15 | 1 | 6 | .... | 7 | .... | 7 | .... | 8 | .... | 6 | .... | .... | 6 00– 6 49 |
| 6 50– 6 99 | .... | 11 | 1 | 6 | .... | 6 | .... | 16 | .... | 3 | .... | 3 | .... | 1 | 6 50– 6 99 |
| 7 00– 7 49 | .... | 14 | .... | 10 | .... | 7 | 2 | 25 | .... | 9 | .... | 4 | .... | 4 | 7 00– 7 49 |
| 7 50– 7 99 | .... | 21 | .... | 4 | .... | 4 | 1 | 26 | .... | 4 | 1 | 3 | .... | 1 | 7 50– 7 99 |
| 8 00– 8 99 | 3 | 29 | 3 | 37 | 1 | 15 | 4 | 64 | .... | 9 | 3 | 15 | .... | 6 | 8 00– 8 99 |
| 9 00– 9 99 | 4 | 25 | 1 | 20 | 2 | 16 | 6 | 48 | 2 | 21 | 2 | 13 | .... | 5 | 9 00– 9 99 |
| 10 00–10 99 | 5 | 21 | 2 | 22 | 2 | 13 | 12 | 41 | 1 | 15 | 2 | 7 | .... | 3 | 10 00–10 99 |
| 11 00–11 99 | 9 | 22 | 5 | 10 | 5 | 4 | 16 | 16 | 3 | 7 | 1 | 2 | 1 | 3 | 11 00–11 99 |
| 12 00–12 99 | 8 | 11 | 5 | 6 | 5 | 6 | 15 | 22 | 6 | 4 | 7 | 2 | 2 | 4 | 12 00–12 99 |
| 13 00–13 99 | 5 | 5 | 3 | .... | 6 | 2 | 13 | 5 | 3 | 1 | 1 | 2 | 3 | 1 | 13 00–13 99 |
| 14 00–14 99 | 8 | .... | 5 | .... | 5 | .... | 8 | 3 | 4 | .... | 3 | 2 | 4 | .... | 14 00–14 99 |
| 15 00–15 99 | 9 | .... | 6 | .... | 2 | 1 | 13 | 3 | 7 | 1 | 4 | .... | 1 | .... | 15 00–15 99 |
| 16 00–17 99 | 11 | .... | 7 | .... | 4 | 2 | 21 | 5 | 13 | 1 | 4 | 1 | 4 | .... | 16 00–17 99 |
| 18 00–19 99 | 5 | 1 | 8 | .... | 2 | .... | 23 | .... | 4 | .... | 3 | .... | 1 | .... | 18 00–19 99 |
| 20 00–24 99 | 12 | .... | 6 | .... | 2 | .... | 13 | 1 | 12 | .... | 7 | .... | 7 | .... | 20 00–24 99 |
| 25 00–29 99 | .... | .... | 2 | .... | .... | .... | 4 | .... | 3 | .... | 3 | 1 | 3 | .... | 25 00–29 99 |
| 30 00–34 99 | .... | .... | 1 | .... | .... | .... | 4 | .... | 1 | .... | 1 | .... | 2 | .... | 30 00–34 99 |
| 35 00–39 99 | .... | .... | .... | .... | .... | .... | 2 | .... | .... | .... | 1 | .... | .... | .... | 35 00–39 99 |
| Not reported | 2 | 1 | .... | .... | 1 | .... | 3 | 2 | 3 | .... | .... | 1 | .... | 2 | Not reported |
| Total | 82 | 207 | 58 | 130 | 37 | 94 | 161 | 331 | 62 | 92 | 43 | 68 | 28 | 32 | Total |

NEW YORK STATE

112. TABLE XIII, C, a—(*concluded*)

**THE PAPER BOX INDUSTRY — FACTORY WORKERS**

NUMBER OF EMPLOYEES FOR EACH SEX CLASSIFIED ACCORDING TO ACTUAL WEEKLY EARNINGS BY THE NUMBER OF YEARS WITH THE FIRM

| ACTUAL WEEKLY EARNINGS IN DOLLARS | YEARS IN FIRM | | | | | | | | | | | ACTUAL WEEKLY EARNINGS IN DOLLARS |
|---|---|---|---|---|---|---|---|---|---|---|---|---|
| | 30–34 | | 35–44 | | 45 AND OVER | NOT REPORTED | | TOTAL | | CUMULATIVE PER CENT. OF TOTAL | | |
| | Male | Female | Male | Female | Female | Male | Female | Male | Female | Male | Female | |
| Less than $3 00 | ....... | ....... | ....... | 1 | ....... | ....... | ....... | 38 | 231 | 1.32 | 3.12 | Less than $3 00 |
| $3 00–$3 49 | ....... | ....... | ....... | ....... | ....... | ....... | ....... | 27 | 219 | 2.25 | 6.10 | $3 00– 3 49 |
| 3 50– 3 99 | ....... | ....... | ....... | 1 | ....... | ....... | ....... | 26 | 266 | 3.15 | 9.70 | 3 50– 3 99 |
| 4 00– 4 49 | ....... | ....... | ....... | ....... | ....... | 1 | 2 | 56 | 428 | 5.09 | 14.15 | 4 00– 4 49 |
| 4 50– 4 99 | ....... | ....... | ....... | ....... | 1 | ....... | 1 | 49 | 493 | 6.79 | 22.18 | 4 50– 4 99 |
| 5 00– 5 49 | ....... | 1 | ....... | 1 | ....... | ....... | 2 | 103 | 716 | 10.70 | 31.85 | 5 00– 5 49 |
| 5 50– 5 99 | ....... | ....... | ....... | ....... | ....... | ....... | ....... | 79 | 569 | 13.10 | 39.60 | 5 50– 5 99 |
| 6 00– 6 49 | ....... | ....... | ....... | ....... | 1 | ....... | 1 | 130 | 662 | 17.63 | 48.60 | 6 00– 6 49 |
| 6 50– 6 99 | 1 | 1 | ....... | ....... | 1 | 1 | ....... | 76 | 435 | 20.24 | 55.50 | 6 50– 6 99 |
| 7 00– 7 49 | ....... | 2 | ....... | ....... | 1 | 5 | 1 | 112 | 508 | 24.10 | 61.30 | 7 00– 7 49 |
| 7 50– 7 99 | 1 | 3 | ....... | ....... | ....... | ....... | ....... | 81 | 390 | 26.90 | 66.70 | 7 50– 7 99 |
| 8 00– 8 99 | ....... | 3 | ....... | ....... | ....... | ....... | ....... | 207 | 824 | 34.08 | 77.80 | 8 00– 8 99 |
| 9 00– 9 99 | ....... | 2 | ....... | 3 | 2 | 3 | ....... | 212 | 672 | 41.40 | 87.00 | 9 00– 9 99 |
| 10 00–10 99 | ....... | ....... | 1 | ....... | ....... | ....... | ....... | 214 | 449 | 48.80 | 93.00 | 10 00–10 99 |
| 11 00–11 99 | ....... | 1 | 1 | ....... | ....... | 1 | 1 | 180 | 236 | 55.00 | 96.00 | 11 00–11 99 |
| 12 00–12 99 | 2 | 1 | 1 | ....... | 1 | ....... | ....... | 211 | 172 | 62.40 | 98.50 | 12 00–12 99 |
| 13 00–13 99 | ....... | 1 | ....... | ....... | ....... | ....... | ....... | 173 | 56 | 68.40 | 99.20 | 13 00–13 99 |
| 14 00–14 99 | 1 | ....... | ....... | ....... | ....... | 2 | ....... | 147 | 29 | 73.50 | 99.60 | 14 00–14 99 |
| 15 00–15 99 | 1 | ....... | ....... | ....... | ....... | ....... | ....... | 173 | 11 | 79.40 | 99.80 | 15 00–15 99 |
| 16 00–17 99 | 4 | ....... | 1 | ....... | ....... | ....... | ....... | 232 | 17 | 87.50 | 99.93 | 16 00–17 99 |
| 18 00–19 99 | ....... | ....... | 3 | ....... | ....... | ....... | ....... | 139 | 3 | 92.40 | 99.96 | 18 00–19 99 |
| 20 00–24 99 | 7 | ....... | ....... | ....... | ....... | ....... | ....... | 157 | 2 | 97.80 | 99.98 | 20 00–24 99 |
| 25 00–29 99 | 3 | ....... | ....... | ....... | ....... | 1 | ....... | 37 | 1 | 99.00 | 100.00 | 25 00–29 99 |
| 30 00–34 99 | 2 | ....... | ....... | ....... | ....... | ....... | ....... | 19 | ....... | 99.70 | ....... | 30 00–34 99 |
| 35 00–39 99 | ....... | ....... | ....... | ....... | ....... | ....... | ....... | 8 | ....... | 100.00 | ....... | 35 00–39 99 |
| Not reported | ....... | ....... | ....... | ....... | ....... | 5 | ....... | 34 | 67 | ....... | ....... | Not reported |
| Total | 22 | 15 | 7 | 6 | 7 | 19 | 8 | 2,920 | 7,456 | ....... | ....... | Total |

113. TABLE XIX, C, a

NEW YORK STATE

**THE PAPER BOX INDUSTRY — FACTORY WORKERS**

NUMBER AND PER CENT. OF EMPLOYEES, ACCORDING TO AVERAGE ACTUAL WEEKLY EARNINGS BY OCCUPATION AND SEX

| AVERAGE ACTUAL WEEKLY EARNINGS IN DOLLARS | OCCUPATION | | | | | | | | | | | AVERAGE ACTUAL WEEKLY EARNINGS IN DOLLARS |
|---|---|---|---|---|---|---|---|---|---|---|---|---|
| | FOREMEN AND FOREWOMEN | | CUTTERS | | SETTERS-UP | | GENERAL MACHINE WORK | | GLUE TABLE WORK | TURNERS-IN | | |
| | Male | Female | Male | Female | Male | Female | Male | Female | Male | Male | Female | |
| Less than $3 00 | .... | .... | .... | .... | .... | 1 | .... | .... | .... | .... | 9 | Less than $3 00 |
| $3 00–$3 49 | .... | .... | .... | .... | 1 | 2 | .... | .... | .... | .... | 17 | $3 00– 3 49 |
| 3 50– 3 99 | .... | .... | 1 | 1 | 1 | 1 | .... | .... | .... | 1 | 22 | 3 50– 3 99 |
| 4 00– 4 49 | .... | .... | 3 | .... | .... | 2 | .... | .... | .... | .... | 15 | 4 00– 4 49 |
| 4 50– 4 99 | .... | .... | .... | .... | 2 | 2 | .... | 1 | .... | 4 | 20 | 4 50– 4 99 |
| 5 00– 5 49 | .... | .... | 2 | .... | .... | 1 | 1 | .... | .... | 3 | 18 | 5 00– 5 49 |
| 5 50– 5 99 | .... | .... | 3 | .... | 1 | 1 | .... | 1 | .... | 1 | 7 | 5 50– 5 99 |
| 6 00– 6 49 | .... | .... | 6 | 1 | 2 | 1 | 1 | .... | .... | .... | 2 | 6 00– 6 49 |
| 6 50– 6 99 | .... | .... | 5 | .... | 2 | .... | .... | .... | .... | .... | .... | 6 50– 6 99 |
| 7 00– 7 49 | .... | .... | 1 | .... | 1 | 3 | .... | 1 | .... | .... | .... | 7 00– 7 49 |
| 7 50– 7 99 | .... | .... | 2 | .... | .... | .... | .... | .... | 1 | .... | 1 | 7 50– 7 99 |
| 8 00– 8 99 | .... | 1 | 12 | .... | 5 | 1 | 2 | .... | 1 | .... | .... | 8 00– 8 99 |
| 9 00– 9 99 | .... | 1 | 6 | 1 | 6 | .... | 1 | .... | 1 | .... | .... | 9 00– 9 99 |
| 10 00–10 99 | .... | 1 | 3 | .... | 2 | 2 | 1 | .... | 4 | .... | .... | 10 00–10 99 |
| 11 00–11 99 | 1 | .... | 8 | .... | 5 | .... | 1 | 1 | 7 | .... | .... | 11 00–11 99 |
| 12 00–12 99 | .... | 1 | 5 | .... | 5 | 2 | 1 | .... | 2 | .... | .... | 12 00–12 99 |
| 13 00–13 99 | 2 | .... | 6 | .... | 3 | .... | .... | .... | .... | .... | .... | 13 00–13 99 |
| 14 00–14 99 | .... | .... | 9 | .... | 3 | .... | .... | .... | 1 | .... | .... | 14 00–14 99 |
| 15 00–15 99 | .... | .... | 9 | .... | 2 | .... | 2 | .... | .... | .... | .... | 15 00–15 99 |
| 16 00–17 99 | 4 | .... | 10 | .... | .... | .... | .... | .... | .... | .... | .... | 16 00–17 99 |
| 18 00–19 99 | 1 | .... | 2 | .... | .... | .... | .... | .... | .... | .... | .... | 18 00–19 99 |
| 20 00–24 99 | 8 | .... | 4 | .... | .... | .... | .... | .... | .... | .... | .... | 20 00–24 99 |
| 30 00–34 99 | 2 | .... | .... | .... | .... | .... | .... | .... | .... | .... | .... | 30 00–34 99 |
| Total | 18 | 4 | 97 | 3 | 41 | 19 | 10 | 4 | 17 | 9 | 111 | Total |

NEW YORK STATE

113. TABLE XIX, C, a — (*concluded*) **THE PAPER BOX INDUSTRY — FACTORY WORKERS**

NUMBER AND PER CENT. OF EMPLOYEES, ACCORDING TO AVERAGE ACTUAL WEEKLY EARNINGS BY OCCUPATION AND SEX

| AVERAGE ACTUAL WEEKLY EARNINGS IN DOLLARS | OCCUPATION | | | | | | | | | | | | AVERAGE ACTUAL WEEKLY EARNINGS IN DOLLARS |
|---|---|---|---|---|---|---|---|---|---|---|---|---|---|
| | STRIPPERS AND TOP LABELERS | | TABLE WORK | | CLOSING AND TYING | | FLOOR WORK | | TOTAL | | CUMULATIVE PER CENT OF TOTAL | | |
| | Male | Female | Male | Female | Male | Female | Male | Female | Male | Female | Male | Female | |
| Less than $3 00 | ....... | ....... | ....... | 1 | 1 | 8 | ....... | 6 | 1 | 25 | .04 | 4.06 | Less than $3 00 |
| $3 00–$3 49 | ....... | ....... | ....... | 3 | ....... | 4 | 1 | 2 | 2 | 28 | 1.15 | 9.08 | $3 00– 3 49 |
| 3 50– 3 99 | ....... | 4 | ....... | 7 | 3 | 1 | ....... | 2 | 6 | 38 | 3.46 | 16.08 | 3 50– 3 99 |
| 4 00– 4 49 | ....... | 10 | ....... | 6 | 2 | 1 | 1 | 1 | 6 | 35 | 5.08 | 23.03 | 4 00– 4 49 |
| 4 50– 4 99 | ....... | 13 | 1 | 13 | 4 | 1 | 1 | 2 | 12 | 52 | 10.04 | 33.00 | 4 50– 4 99 |
| 5 00– 5 49 | 1 | 17 | ....... | 13 | 5 | ....... | ....... | ....... | 12 | 49 | 15.00 | 42.00 | 5 00– 5 49 |
| 5 50– 5 99 | 1 | 18 | ....... | 18 | 1 | ....... | 1 | ....... | 8 | 45 | 18.01 | 50.04 | 5 50– 5 99 |
| 6 00– 6 49 | 1 | 7 | ....... | 19 | ....... | ....... | ....... | ....... | 10 | 30 | 21.09 | 56.00 | 6 00– 6 49 |
| 6 50– 6 99 | 1 | 7 | 1 | 15 | 3 | ....... | 2 | ....... | 14 | 22 | 27.03 | 60.00 | 6 50– 6 99 |
| 7 00– 7 49 | 2 | 14 | ....... | 19 | ....... | ....... | ....... | ....... | 4 | 37 | 28.09 | 67.00 | 7 00– 7 49 |
| 7 50– 7 99 | ....... | 17 | ....... | 28 | 1 | 3 | ....... | ....... | 4 | 49 | 30.04 | 76.00 | 7 50– 7 99 |
| 8 00– 8 99 | 3 | 27 | ....... | 28 | 1 | ....... | 2 | ....... | 26 | 57 | 40.04 | 86.08 | 8 00– 8 99 |
| 9 00– 9 99 | 4 | 10 | 2 | 28 | ....... | ....... | ....... | ....... | 20 | 40 | 48.01 | 94.00 | 9 00– 9 99 |
| 10 00–10 99 | 3 | 7 | ....... | 10 | ....... | ....... | 1 | ....... | 14 | 20 | 53.05 | 97.08 | 10 00–10 99 |
| 11 00–11 99 | 2 | 2 | 1 | 1 | ....... | ....... | ....... | ....... | 25 | 4 | 63.01 | 98.04 | 11 00–11 99 |
| 12 00–12 99 | 2 | 2 | 1 | ....... | 1 | ....... | ....... | ....... | 17 | 5 | 69.07 | 99.03 | 12 00–12 99 |
| 13 00–13 99 | 1 | 2 | ....... | ....... | ....... | ....... | ....... | ....... | 12 | 2 | 74.03 | 99.07 | 13 00–13 99 |
| 14 00–14 99 | 1 | 1 | 2 | ....... | 2 | ....... | ....... | ....... | 18 | 1 | 81.02 | 99.09 | 14 00–14 99 |
| 15 00–15 99 | 4 | 1 | ....... | ....... | ....... | ....... | ....... | ....... | 17 | 1 | 87.07 | 100.00 | 15 00–15 99 |
| 16 00–17 99 | 1 | ....... | ....... | ....... | ....... | ....... | ....... | ....... | 15 | ....... | 93.05 | ....... | 16 00–17 99 |
| 18 00–19 99 | 1 | ....... | ....... | ....... | ....... | ....... | ....... | ....... | 4 | ....... | 95.00 | ....... | 18 00–19 99 |
| 20 00–24 99 | ....... | ....... | ....... | ....... | ....... | ....... | ....... | ....... | 12 | ....... | 99.02 | ....... | 20 00–24 99 |
| 30 00–34 99 | ....... | ....... | ....... | ....... | ....... | ....... | ....... | ....... | 2 | ....... | 100.00 | ....... | 30 00–34 99 |
| Total | 28 | 159 | 8 | 209 | 24 | 18 | 9 | 13 | 261 | 540 | ....... | ....... | Total |

114. TABLE XX, C, a

NEW YORK STATE
THE PAPER BOX INDUSTRY — FACTORY WORKERS

Number and Per Cent. of All Employees, Working 43 Weeks or More According to Actual Annual Earnings by Occupation and Sex

| Actual Annual Earnings in Dollars | Occupation | | | | | | | | | | | Annual Actual Earnings in Dollars |
|---|---|---|---|---|---|---|---|---|---|---|---|---|
| | Foremen and Forewomen | | Cutters | | Setters-up | | General Machine Work | | Glue Table Work | Turners-in | | |
| | Male | Female | Male | Female | Male | Female | Male | Female | Male | Male | Female | |
| Less than $200 | | | | | | | | | | | 5 | Less than $200 |
| $200-$249 | | | | | 1 | 3 | | | | 1 | 11 | 200- 249 |
| 250- 299 | | | 3 | | | 1 | | 1 | | 3 | 11 | 250- 299 |
| 300- 349 | | | 2 | | 2 | | | 1 | | 1 | 2 | 300- 349 |
| 350- 399 | | | 1 | | 2 | 2 | | | 1 | | | 350- 399 |
| 400- 449 | | 1 | 2 | | 2 | | | | | | 1 | 400- 449 |
| 450- 499 | | | 3 | 1 | 3 | | 1 | | | | | 450- 499 |
| 500- 549 | | 2 | 3 | | 2 | 1 | 1 | | | | | 500- 549 |
| 550- 599 | 1 | 1 | 6 | | 1 | 1 | 1 | 1 | | | | 550- 599 |
| 600- 649 | | | 4 | | 4 | 1 | 1 | | 2 | | | 600- 649 |
| 650- 699 | 1 | | 4 | | 1 | 1 | | | | | | 650- 699 |
| 700- 749 | 1 | | 3 | | 2 | | | | | | | 700- 749 |
| 750- 799 | | | 8 | | 2 | | | | | | | 750- 799 |
| 800- 899 | 3 | | 6 | | | | 1 | | | | | 800- 899 |
| 900- 999 | 1 | | 3 | | | | | | | | | 900- 999 |
| 1,000-1,099 | 4 | | 5 | | | | | | | | | 1,000-1,099 |
| 1,100-1,199 | 1 | | | | | | | | | | | 1,100-1,199 |
| 1,200-1,299 | 2 | | | | | | | | | | | 1,200-1,299 |
| 1,500-1,599 | 1 | | | | | | | | | | | 1,500-1,599 |
| 1,600-1,799 | 1 | | | | | | | | | | | 1,600-1,799 |
| Total | 16 | 4 | 58 | 1 | 22 | 10 | 5 | 3 | 3 | 5 | 30 | Total |

NEW YORK STATE

114. TABLE XX, C, a (*concluded*) **THE PAPER BOX INDUSTRY — FACTORY WORKERS**

NUMBER AND PER CENT. OF ALL EMPLOYEES, WORKING 43 WEEKS OR MORE, ACCORDING TO ACTUAL ANNUAL EARNINGS BY OCCUPATION AND SEX

| ACTUAL ANNUAL EARNINGS IN DOLLARS | OCCUPATION (*concluded*) | | | | | | | | | | | | ACTUAL ANNUAL EARNINGS IN DOLLARS |
|---|---|---|---|---|---|---|---|---|---|---|---|---|---|
| | STRIPPERS AND TOP LABELERS | | TABLE WORK | | CLOSING AND TYING | | FLOOR WORK | | TOTAL | | CUMULATIVE PER CENT. OF TOTAL | | |
| | Male | Female | Male | Female | Male | Female | Male | Female | Male | Female | Male | Female | |
| Less than $200.. | ....... | 2 | ....... | 1 | 2 | 2 | ....... | 1 | 2 | 11 | 1.30 | 3.70 | .Less than $200 |
| $200– $249.... | ....... | 6 | ....... | 6 | ....... | ....... | ....... | 2 | 2 | 28 | 2.70 | 13.20 | ... $200– 249 |
| 250– 299.... | 1 | 18 | ....... | 17 | 4 | ....... | ....... | ....... | 11 | 48 | 10.20 | 29.30 | .....250– 299 |
| 300– 349.... | 1 | 12 | ....... | 26 | 1 | ....... | 1 | ....... | 8 | 41 | 15.49 | 43.00 | .....300– 349 |
| 350– 399.... | ....... | 21 | ....... | 34 | 1 | 3 | 1 | ....... | 6 | 60 | 19.50 | 63.20 | .....350– 399 |
| 400– 449.... | 1 | 22 | ....... | 20 | 1 | ....... | 1 | ....... | 7 | 44 | 24.10 | 78.09 | .....400– 449 |
| 450– 499.... | 6 | 12 | 1 | 21 | ....... | ....... | 1 | ....... | 15 | 34 | 34.20 | 89.30 | .....450– 499 |
| 500– 549.... | 1 | 5 | 1 | 10 | ....... | ....... | 1 | ....... | 9 | 18 | 40.20 | 95.70 | .....500– 549 |
| 550– 599.... | 1 | 3 | ....... | ....... | ....... | ....... | ....... | ....... | 10 | 6 | 52.20 | 97.50 | .....550– 599 |
| 600– 649.... | 4 | 2 | 2 | ....... | 1 | ....... | ....... | ....... | 18 | 3 | 59.00 | 98.50 | .....600– 649 |
| 650– 699.... | 1 | 1 | ....... | ....... | ....... | ....... | ....... | ....... | 7 | 2 | 64.00 | 99.20 | .....650– 699 |
| 700– 749.... | 1 | 2 | 1 | ....... | 1 | ....... | ....... | ....... | 9 | 2 | 70.00 | 100.00 | .....700– 749 |
| 750– 799.... | 2 | ....... | ....... | ....... | 1 | ....... | ....... | ....... | 13 | ....... | 78.00 | ....... | .....750– 799 |
| 800– 899.... | 1 | ....... | ....... | ....... | ....... | ....... | ....... | ....... | 11 | ....... | 86.00 | ....... | .....800– 899 |
| 900– 999.... | 3 | ....... | ....... | ....... | ....... | ....... | ....... | ....... | 7 | ....... | 90.00 | ....... | .....900– 999 |
| 1,000–1,099.... | ....... | ....... | ....... | ....... | ....... | ....... | ....... | ....... | 9 | ....... | 96.80 | ....... | ...1,000–1,099 |
| 1,100–1,199.... | ....... | ....... | ....... | ....... | ....... | ....... | ....... | ....... | 1 | ....... | 97.50 | ....... | ...1,100–1,199 |
| 1,200–1,299.... | ....... | ....... | ....... | ....... | ....... | ....... | ....... | ....... | 2 | ....... | 98.70 | ....... | ...1,200–1,299 |
| 1,500–1,599.... | ....... | ....... | ....... | ....... | ....... | ....... | ....... | ....... | 1 | ....... | 99.40 | ....... | ...1,500–1,599 |
| 1,600–1,799.... | ....... | ....... | ....... | ....... | ....... | ....... | ....... | ....... | 1 | ....... | 100.00 | ....... | ...1,600–1,799 |
| Total...... | 23 | 106 | 5 | 135 | 12 | 5 | 5 | 3 | 149 | 297 | ....... | ....... | .....Total |

NEW YORK STATE
**THE CONFECTIONERY INDUSTRY**

115. TABLE XVIII, D — NUMBER AND PER CENT. OF ALL EMPLOYEES IN EACH DEPARTMENT ACCORDING TO ACTUAL WEEKLY EARNINGS

| ACTUAL WEEKLY EARNINGS IN DOLLARS | DEPARTMENT | | | | | | | | | | | | ACTUAL WEEKLY EARNINGS IN DOLLARS |
|---|---|---|---|---|---|---|---|---|---|---|---|---|---|
| | FACTORY | | OFFICE | | SHIPPING | | PLANT | | TOTAL | | CUMULATIVE PER CENT. OF TOTAL | | |
| | Male | Female | Male | Female | Male | Female | Male | Female | Male | Female | Male | Female | |
| Less than $3 00 | 57 | 315 | ....... | ....... | 2 | ....... | 3 | 1 | 62 | 316 | 1.50 | 5.60 | Less than $3 00 |
| $3 00–$3 49.... | 21 | 186 | ....... | ....... | 3 | ....... | ....... | 2 | 24 | 188 | 2.10 | 8.90 | ...$3 00– 3 49 |
| 3 50– 3 99.... | 20 | 236 | ....... | ....... | ....... | ....... | 2 | ....... | 22 | 236 | 2.60 | 13.30 | ....3 50– 3 99 |
| 4 00– 4 49.... | 26 | 413 | ....... | 1 | 5 | 1 | 2 | 4 | 33 | 419 | 3.50 | 20.30 | ....4 00– 4 49 |
| 4 50– 4 99.... | 50 | 537 | ....... | ....... | 5 | 1 | 3 | 2 | 58 | 540 | 4.70 | 30.20 | ....4 50– 4 99 |
| 5 00– 5 49.... | 77 | 753 | 6 | 2 | 4 | 1 | 12 | 5 | 99 | 761 | 7.40 | 43.80 | ....5 00– 5 49 |
| 5 50– 5 99.... | 62 | 522 | ....... | ....... | 6 | 3 | 4 | 2 | 72 | 527 | 9.10 | 53.30 | ....5 50– 5 99 |
| 6 00– 6 49.... | 95 | 514 | 11 | 13 | 18 | 2 | 9 | 5 | 133 | 534 | 12.50 | 62.60 | ....6 00– 6 49 |
| 6 50– 6 99.... | 110 | 326 | ....... | 3 | 6 | 5 | 10 | 3 | 126 | 337 | 15.50 | 68.60 | ....6 50– 6 99 |
| 7 00– 7 49.... | 166 | 309 | 8 | 9 | 23 | 2 | 5 | 4 | 202 | 324 | 20.50 | 74.50 | ....7 00– 7 49 |
| 7 50– 7 99.... | 155 | 249 | ....... | 2 | 9 | 4 | 8 | 6 | 172 | 261 | 24.80 | 79.00 | ....7 50– 7 99 |
| 8 00– 8 99.... | 319 | 388 | 10 | 17 | 32 | 2 | 18 | 8 | 379 | 415 | 34.10 | 86.50 | ....8 00– 8 99 |
| 9 00– 9 99.... | 290 | 265 | 12 | 15 | 23 | 1 | 36 | 2 | 361 | 283 | 43.00 | 91.50 | ....9 00– 9 99 |
| 10 00–10 99.... | 239 | 191 | 14 | 19 | 49 | ....... | 31 | ....... | 333 | 210 | 51.20 | 95.20 | ...10 00–10 99 |
| 11 00–11 99.... | 190 | 82 | 6 | 7 | 32 | 1 | 25 | ....... | 253 | 90 | 57.40 | 96.70 | ...11 00–11 99 |
| 12 00–12 99.... | 231 | 50 | 8 | 23 | 47 | ....... | 45 | 1 | 331 | 74 | 65.50 | 98.30 | ...12 00–12 99 |
| 13 00–13 99.... | 150 | 14 | 6 | 3 | 33 | ....... | 30 | ....... | 219 | 17 | 71.00 | 98.50 | ...13 00–13 99 |
| 14 00–14 99.... | 135 | 13 | 13 | 7 | 25 | ....... | 40 | ....... | 213 | 20 | 76.00 | 98.80 | ...14 00–14 99 |
| 15 00–15 99.... | 112 | 8 | 18 | 12 | 38 | ....... | 38 | ....... | 206 | 20 | 81.20 | 99.20 | ...15 00–15 99 |
| 16 00–17 99.... | 129 | 11 | 18 | 6 | 45 | ....... | 51 | ....... | 243 | 17 | 87.10 | 99.50 | ...16 00–17 99 |
| 18 00–19 99.... | 84 | 9 | 12 | 4 | 14 | ....... | 46 | ....... | 156 | 13 | 91.00 | 99.60 | ...18 00–19 99 |
| 20 00–24 99.... | 93 | 4 | 27 | 6 | 29 | ....... | 64 | ....... | 213 | 10 | 96.20 | 99.70 | ...20 00–24 99 |
| 25 00–29 99.... | 33 | 1 | 23 | 1 | 5 | ....... | 26 | ....... | 87 | 2 | 98.50 | 99.80 | ...25 00–29 99 |
| 30 00–34 99.... | 14 | ....... | 8 | ....... | 1 | ....... | 8 | ....... | 31 | ....... | 99.10 | ....... | ...30 00–34 99 |
| 35 00–39 99.... | 12 | ....... | 7 | 1 | ....... | ....... | 2 | ....... | 21 | 1 | 99.70 | 99.90 | ...35 00–39 99 |
| 40 00 and over.. | 6 | ....... | 1 | 2 | ....... | ....... | 4 | ....... | 11 | 2 | 100.00 | 100.00 | .40 00 and over |
| Not reported.... | 18 | 47 | 17 | 12 | 12 | ....... | 5 | ....... | 52 | 59 | ....... | ....... | ...Not reported |
| Total...... | 2,894 | 5,443 | 225 | 165 | 466 | 23 | 527 | 45 | 4,112 | 5,676 | ....... | ....... | .....Total |

116. TABLE I, D

NEW YORK STATE
THE CONFECTIONERY INDUSTRY
NUMBER OF EMPLOYEES ACCORDING TO AGE GROUPS, BY LOCALITY AND SEX

| | Locality | Sex | Age Groups in Years | | | | | | | | | | | |
|---|---|---|---|---|---|---|---|---|---|---|---|---|---|---|
| | | | Total | 14–15 | 16–17 | 18–20 | 21–24 | 25–29 | 30–34 | 35–39 | 40–44 | 45–54 | 55–64 | 65 and over | Not reported |
| Factory workers | New York city | Male | 2,533 | 13 | 94 | 359 | 412 | 425 | 306 | 272 | 200 | 292 | 110 | 28 | 22 |
| | | Female | 4,797 | 256 | 1,215 | 1,414 | 755 | 454 | 211 | 180 | 122 | 180 | 35 | 4 | 21 |
| | Rochester | Male | 99 | ...... | 2 | 16 | 16 | 16 | 16 | 11 | 9 | 9 | 4 | ...... | ...... |
| | | Female | 170 | 2 | 16 | 48 | 36 | 24 | 12 | 16 | 5 | 8 | 2 | ...... | 1 |
| | Buffalo | Male | 80 | ...... | 3 | 15 | 21 | 10 | 5 | 8 | 5 | 9 | 3 | 1 | ...... |
| | | Female | 167 | 3 | 56 | 53 | 29 | 18 | 5 | 2 | 1 | ...... | ...... | ...... | ...... |
| | Other cities and towns | Male | 182 | ...... | 10 | 35 | 31 | 17 | 16 | 20 | 16 | 22 | 13 | 1 | 1 |
| | | Female | 309 | 8 | 61 | 82 | 77 | 28 | 17 | 15 | 9 | 8 | 3 | ...... | 1 |
| Office, and shipping plant | All localities | Male | 1,218 | 10 | 49 | 169 | 187 | 198 | 153 | 120 | 110 | 152 | 48 | 21 | ...... |
| | | Female | 233 | 1 | 21 | 69 | 54 | 33 | 14 | 20 | 7 | 6 | 3 | 1 | 4 |
| All workers | State | Male | 4,112 | 23 | 158 | 594 | 667 | 666 | 496 | 431 | 340 | 484 | 178 | 52 | 23 |
| | | Female | 5,676 | 270 | 1,360 | 1,666 | 951 | 557 | 259 | 233 | 144 | 152 | 43 | 5 | 27 |
| | Cumulative per cent. for state | Male | 100.00 | .6 | 4.4 | 19.0 | 35.3 | 53.6 | 64.7 | 74.2 | 82.5 | 94.2 | 98.5 | 100.00 | ...... |
| | | Female | 100 | 4.8 | 29.1 | 59.3 | 75.2 | 85.2 | 90.0 | 94.2 | 96.5 | 99.0 | 99.9 | 100.00 | ...... |

117. TABLE II, D.

## NEW YORK STATE
## THE CONFECTIONERY INDUSTRY

Number and Per Cent. of Employees According to Nativity, by Locality

| | Locality | Distribution of native and foreign born | | | | | | | | Distribution of foreign born, according to country of birth | | | | | | | | | | | |
|---|---|---|---|---|---|---|---|---|---|---|---|---|---|---|---|---|---|---|---|---|---|
| | | Total | | Not reported | | Native | | Foreign | | Italy | | Russia | | Germany | | Austria | | Hungary | | England | |
| | | Number | Per cent | Number | Per cent | Number | Per cent | Number | Per cent | Number | Per cent | Number | Per cent | Number | Per cent | Number | Per cent | Number | Per cent | Number | Per cent |
| Factory workers | New York city | 7,330 | 100.00 | 168 | .... | 3,202 | 45.0 | 3,942 | 55.0 | 3,019 | 76.5 | 270 | 6.9 | 157 | 3.98 | 136 | 3.47 | 78 | 1.98 | 58 | 1.48 |
| | Rochester | 269 | 100.00 | 2 | .... | 168 | 63.0 | 99 | 37.0 | 66 | 66.7 | 3 | 3.0 | 6 | 6.1 | 3 | 3.0 | ...... | ..... | 6 | 6.1 |
| | Buffalo | 247 | 100.00 | 1 | .... | 188 | 76.5 | 58 | 23.5 | 36 | 62.0 | 5 | 8.6 | 6 | 10.5 | 2 | 3.4 | ...... | ..... | 2 | 3.4 |
| | Other cities and towns | 491 | 100.00 | 9 | .... | 399 | 83.0 | 83 | 17.0 | 39 | 47.0 | 2 | 2.4 | 4 | 4.8 | ...... | ..... | ...... | ..... | 10 | 12.1 |
| Office, shipping and plant | All localities | 1,451 | 100.00 | 27 | .... | 864 | 60.5 | 560 | 39.5 | 204 | 36.2 | 40 | 7.1 | 100 | 18.0 | 39 | 7.0 | 33 | 5.9 | 23 | 4.1 |
| All workers | State | 9,788 | 100.00 | 207 | ..... | 4,839 | 50.5 | 4,742 | 49.5 | 3,364 | 71.1 | 320 | 6.7 | 273 | 5.8 | 180 | 3.8 | 111 | 2.3 | 99 | 2.1 |

NEW YORK STATE

THE CONFECTIONERY INDUSTRY

117. TABLE II. D.— (*concluded*) NUMBER AND PER CENT OF EMPLOYEES, ACCORDING TO NATIVITY, BY LOCATION

| | LOCALITY | DISTRIBUTION OF FOREIGN BORN, ACCORDING TO COUNTRY OF BIRTH—*Concluded* | | | | | | | | | | | | | | | | | | | | | |
|---|---|---|---|---|---|---|---|---|---|---|---|---|---|---|---|---|---|---|---|---|---|---|---|
| | | Ireland | | Canada | | France | | Scotland | | Poland | | West Indies | | Roumania | | Switzerland | | Turkey | | Sweden | | All Other* | |
| | | Number | Per cent | Number | Per cent | Number | Per cent | Number | Per cent | Number | Per cent | Number | Per cent | Number | Per cent | Number | Per cent | Number | Per cent | Number | Per cent | Number | Per cent |
| Factory workers | New York city | 51 | 1.29 | 11 | .28 | 37 | .94 | 24 | .61 | 31 | .79 | ... | ... | 15 | .38 | ... | ... | 11 | .28 | ... | ... | 44 | 1.12 |
| | Rochester | ... | ... | 9 | 9.1 | ... | ... | ... | ... | 2 | 2.0 | ... | ... | ... | ... | ... | ... | ... | ... | ... | ... | 4 | .4 |
| | Buffalo | ... | ... | 4 | 6.9 | ... | ... | ... | ... | ... | ... | ... | ... | ... | ... | ... | ... | ... | ... | ... | ... | 3 | 5.2 |
| | Other cities and towns | 3 | 3.6 | 15 | 18.1 | ... | ... | 3 | 3.6 | ... | ... | ... | ... | ... | ... | 7 | 8.4 | ... | ... | ... | ... | ... | ... |
| Office, shipping and plant | All localities | 36 | 6.4 | 12 | 2.2 | ... | ... | 10 | 1.8 | ... | ... | 16 | 2.9 | ... | ... | 8 | 1.4 | ... | ... | 9 | 1.6 | 30 | 5.4 |
| All workers | State | 90 | 1.9 | 51 | 1.1 | 37 | .8 | 37 | .8 | 33 | .7 | 16 | .3 | 15 | .3 | 15 | .3 | 11 | .2 | 9 | .1 | 81 | 1.7 |

* Includes for each locality (New York City excepted) all countries representing less than one per cent of the total foreign born employees in the industry in that locality.

NEW YORK STATE
**THE CONFECTIONERY INDUSTRY**

118. TABLE III, D. Number of Employees, by Sex, Earning Specified Weekly Rate According to Locality

| Weekly Rates in Dollars | Locality: New York City | | Rochester | | Buffalo | | Other Cities and Towns | | Office, Shipping Plant, All Localities | | State | | Cumulative Per Cent. for State | | Weekly Rates in Dollars |
|---|---|---|---|---|---|---|---|---|---|---|---|---|---|---|---|
| | Male | Female | Male | Female | Male | Female | Male | Female | Male | Female | Male | Female | Male | Female | |
| Less than $3 00 | .... | ...... | .... | ...... | ...... | ...... | ...... | 5 | ...... | ...... | ...... | 5 | ...... | .10 | Less than $3 00 |
| $3 00–$3 49... | .... | ...... | .... | ...... | ...... | ...... | ...... | 3 | 1 | 1 | 1 | 4 | .03 | .19 | ...$3 00–$3 49 |
| 3 50– 3 99... | 3 | 129 | .... | ...... | ...... | 3 | ...... | 13 | ...... | ...... | 3 | 145 | .10 | 3.20 | ....3 50– 3 99 |
| 4 00– 4 49... | 6 | 213 | .... | ...... | ...... | 47 | ...... | 17 | 4 | 3 | 10 | 280 | .35 | 9.10 | ....4 00– 4 49 |
| 4 50– 4 99... | 10 | 477 | .... | ...... | ...... | 28 | 2 | 17 | 1 | 2 | 13 | 524 | .68 | 20.00 | ....4 50– 4 99 |
| 5 00– 5 49... | 37 | 887 | .... | ...... | ...... | 19 | ...... | 28 | 24 | 11 | 61 | 945 | 2.20 | 39.10 | ....5 00– 5 49 |
| 5 50– 5 99... | 36 | 458 | .... | 1 | ...... | 4 | ...... | 7 | 4 | 5 | 40 | 475 | 3.20 | 49.80 | ....5 50– 5 99 |
| 6 00– 6 49... | 121 | 565 | .... | 1 | 3 | 16 | 8 | 49 | 46 | 25 | 178 | 656 | 7.70 | 63.50 | ....6 00– 6 49 |
| 6 50– 6 99... | 25 | 223 | .... | 11 | ...... | 6 | 1 | 14 | 4 | 6 | 30 | 260 | 8.40 | 68.70 | ....6 50– 6 99 |
| 7 00– 7 49... | 232 | 319 | 3 | 5 | 5 | 8 | 3 | 19 | 44 | 20 | 287 | 371 | 15.60 | 76.50 | ....7 00– 7 49 |
| 7 50– 7 99... | 110 | 172 | 11 | 6 | 4 | 2 | 3 | 1 | 10 | 10 | 138 | 191 | 19.10 | 80.50 | ....7 50– 7 99 |
| 8 00– 8 99... | 322 | 266 | 16 | 3 | 13 | 5 | 8 | 4 | 69 | 26 | 428 | 304 | 29.80 | 87.10 | ....8 00– 8 99 |
| 9 00– 9 99... | 331 | 171 | 10 | 19 | 10 | 2 | 16 | 6 | 84 | 21 | 451 | 219 | 41.20 | 91.50 | ....9 00– 9 99 |
| 10 00–10 99... | 232 | 117 | 6 | 24 | 6 | 2 | 14 | 5 | 107 | 25 | 365 | 173 | 50.20 | 95.00 | ...10 00–10 99 |
| 11 00–11 99... | 144 | 46 | 7 | 17 | 2 | ...... | 9 | ...... | 59 | 8 | 221 | 71 | 55.70 | 96.70 | ...11 00–11 99 |
| 12 00–12 99... | 229 | 30 | 9 | 2 | 9 | ...... | 24 | 1 | 126 | 25 | 397 | 58 | 65.70 | 97.70 | ...12 00–12 99 |
| 13 00–13 99... | 114 | 4 | 8 | 1 | 1 | 1 | 10 | ...... | 67 | 3 | 200 | 9 | 70.80 | 98.00 | ...13 00–13 99 |
| 14 00–14 99... | 132 | 6 | 4 | ...... | 3 | ...... | 4 | ...... | 73 | 8 | 216 | 14 | 76.30 | 98.30 | ...14 00–14 99 |
| 15 00–15 99... | 105 | 6 | 7 | 1 | 7 | ...... | 12 | 2 | 104 | 13 | 235 | 22 | 82.20 | 98.90 | ...15 00–15 99 |
| 16 00–17 99... | 100 | 8 | 6 | ...... | ...... | ...... | 6 | ...... | 111 | 6 | 223 | 14 | 87.70 | 99.10 | ...16 00–17 99 |
| 18 00–19 99... | 73 | 8 | 3 | ...... | 8 | ...... | 6 | ...... | 72 | 4 | 162 | 12 | 91.70 | 99.50 | ...18 00–19 99 |
| 20 00–24 99... | 65 | 5 | 6 | ...... | 9 | ...... | 4 | ...... | 107 | 6 | 191 | 11 | 96.70 | 99.60 | ...20 00–24 99 |
| 25 00–29 99... | 22 | ...... | 1 | ...... | ...... | ...... | 5 | ...... | 42 | 1 | 70 | 1 | 98.40 | 99.70 | ...25 00–29 99 |
| 30 00–34 99... | 13 | 1 | .... | ...... | ...... | ...... | 1 | ...... | 21 | ...... | 35 | 1 | 99.20 | 99.80 | ...30 00–34 99 |
| 35 00–39 99... | 12 | ...... | .... | ...... | ...... | ...... | ...... | ...... | 9 | 1 | 21 | 1 | 99.70 | 99.90 | ...35 00–39 99 |
| 40 00 and over. | 5 | ...... | .... | ...... | ...... | ...... | ...... | ...... | 5 | 2 | 10 | 2 | 100.00 | 100.00 | .40 00 and over |
| Not reported... | 9 | 21 | 1 | 8 | ...... | ...... | 29 | 5 | 20 | 1 | 59 | 35 | ...... | ...... | ...Not reported |
| Total..... | 2,488 | 4,132 | 98 | 99 | 80 | 143 | 165 | 196 | 1,214 | 233 | 4,045 | 4,803 | ...... | ...... | .....Total |

NEW YORK STATE

**THE CONFECTIONERY INDUSTRY**

119. TABLE IV, D. NUMBER OF EMPLOYEES CLASSIFIED ACCORDING TO ACTUAL WEEKLY EARNINGS, BY LOCALITY

| ACTUAL WEEKLY EARNINGS IN DOLLARS | LOCALITY | | | | | | | | | | | | | | ACTUAL WEEKLY EARNINGS IN DOLLARS |
|---|---|---|---|---|---|---|---|---|---|---|---|---|---|---|---|
| | NEW YORK CITY | | ROCHESTER | | BUFFALO | | OTHER CITIES AND TOWNS | | OFFICE, SHIPPING PLANT, ALL LOCALITIES | | STATE | | CUMULATIVE PER CENT. FOR STATE | | |
| | Male | Female | Male | Female | Male | Female | Male | Female | Male | Female | Male | Female | Male | Female | |
| Less than $3 00 | 49 | 253 | 4 | 4 | 4 | 22 | ...... | 36 | 5 | 1 | 62 | 316 | 1.50 | 5.60 | Less than $3 00 |
| $3 00—$3 49.. | 19 | 134 | .... | 4 | 2 | 26 | ...... | 22 | 3 | 2 | 24 | 188 | 2.10 | 8.90 | ...$3 00–$3 49 |
| 3 50– 3 99... | 14 | 199 | 2 | 3 | 3 | 18 | 1 | 16 | 2 | ...... | 22 | 236 | 2.60 | 13.30 | ....3 50– 3 99 |
| 4 00– 4 49... | 23 | 371 | 1 | 8 | 1 | 17 | 1 | 17 | 7 | 6 | 33 | 419 | 3.50 | 20.30 | ....4 00– 4 49 |
| 4 0– 4 99... | 41 | 474 | 1 | 14 | 4 | 19 | 4 | 30 | 8 | 3 | 58 | 540 | 4.70 | 30.20 | ....4 50– 4 99 |
| 5 00– 5 49... | 65 | 693 | 2 | 8 | 7 | 17 | 3 | 35 | 22 | 8 | 99 | 761 | 7.40 | 43.80 | ....5 00– 5 49 |
| 5 50– 5 99... | 50 | 468 | 3 | 13 | 2 | 15 | 7 | 26 | 10 | 5 | 72 | 527 | 9.10 | 53.30 | ....5 50– 5 99 |
| 6 00– 6 49... | 86 | 463 | 6 | 7 | 3 | 13 | ...... | 31 | 38 | 20 | 133 | 534 | 12.50 | 62.60 | ....6 00– 6 49 |
| 6 50– 6 99... | 95 | 281 | 7 | 13 | 4 | 3 | 4 | 29 | 16 | 11 | 126 | 337 | 15.50 | 68.60 | ....6 50– 6 99 |
| 7 00– 7 49... | 152 | 274 | 5 | 13 | 2 | 6 | 7 | 16 | 36 | 15 | 202 | 324 | 20.50 | 74.50 | ....7 00– 7 49 |
| 7 50– 7 99... | 138 | 221 | 5 | 11 | 2 | 2 | 10 | 15 | 17 | 12 | 172 | 261 | 24.80 | 79.00 | ....7 50– 7 99 |
| 8 00– 8 99... | 287 | 342 | 15 | 25 | 5 | 5 | 12 | 16 | 60 | 27 | 379 | 415 | 34.10 | 86.50 | ....8 00– 8 99 |
| 9 00– 9 99... | 260 | 232 | 8 | 24 | 5 | 1 | 17 | 8 | 71 | 18 | 361 | 283 | 43.00 | 91.50 | ....9 00– 9 99 |
| 10 00–10 99... | 202 | 166 | 5 | 16 | 7 | 3 | 25 | 6 | 94 | 19 | 333 | 210 | 51.20 | 95.20 | ...10 00–10 99 |
| 11 00–11 99... | 144 | 77 | 10 | 4 | 4 | ...... | 32 | 1 | 63 | 8 | 253 | 90 | 57.40 | 96.70 | ...11 00–11 99 |
| 12 00–12 99... | 209 | 43 | 2 | 2 | 4 | ...... | 16 | 5 | 100 | 24 | 331 | 74 | 65.50 | 98.30 | ...12 00–12 99 |
| 13 00–13 99... | 128 | 14 | 6 | ...... | 1 | ...... | 15 | ...... | 69 | 3 | 219 | 17 | 71.00 | 98.50 | ...13 00–13 99 |
| 14 00–14 99... | 128 | 12 | 3 | 1 | 1 | ...... | 3 | ...... | 78 | 7 | 213 | 20 | 76.00 | 98.80 | ...14 00–14 99 |
| 15 00–15 99... | 95 | 8 | 5 | ...... | 7 | ...... | 5 | ...... | 94 | 12 | 206 | 20 | 81.20 | 99.20 | ...15 00–15 99 |
| 16 00–17 99... | 115 | 11 | 2 | ...... | 3 | ...... | 9 | ...... | 114 | 6 | 243 | 17 | 87.10 | 99.50 | ...16 00–17 99 |
| 18 00–19 99... | 75 | 9 | 2 | ...... | 4 | ...... | 3 | ...... | 72 | 4 | 156 | 13 | 91.00 | 99.60 | ...18 00–19 99 |
| 20 00–24 99... | 81 | 4 | 4 | ...... | 5 | ...... | 3 | ...... | 120 | 6 | 213 | 10 | 96.20 | 99.70 | ...20 00–24 99 |
| 25 00–29 99... | 29 | 1 | 1 | ...... | ...... | ...... | 3 | ...... | 54 | 1 | 87 | 2 | 98.50 | 99.80 | ...25 00–29 99 |
| 30 00–34 99... | 13 | ...... | .... | ...... | ...... | ...... | 1 | ...... | 17 | ...... | 31 | ...... | 99.10 | ...... | ...30 00–34 99 |
| 35 00–39 99... | 12 | ...... | .... | ...... | ...... | ...... | ...... | ...... | 9 | 1 | 21 | 1 | 99.70 | 99.90 | ...35 00–39.99 |
| 40 00 and over. | 6 | ...... | .... | ...... | ...... | ...... | ...... | ...... | 5 | 2 | 11 | 2 | 100.00 | 100.00 | 40 00 and over |
| Not reported... | 17 | 47 | .... | ...... | ...... | ...... | 1 | ...... | 34 | 12 | 52 | 59 | ...... | ...... | ...Not reported |
| Total..... | 2,533 | 4,797 | 99 | 170 | 80 | 167 | 182 | 309 | 1,218 | 233 | 4,112 | 5,676 | ...... | ...... | .....Total |

120. TABLE VII, D, a

NEW YORK STATE

**THE CONFECTIONERY INDUSTRY — FACTORY WORKERS**

NUMBER AND PER CENT. OF EMPLOYEES BY SEX ACCORDING TO OCCUPATION AND NATIVITY

| NATIVITY | TOTAL | | FOREMEN AND FOREWOMEN | | CANDY MAKERS | | MACHINE OPERATORS | | DIPPERS | | PACKERS AND WRAPPERS | | HELPERS | | LABORERS | | NOT REPORTED | |
|---|---|---|---|---|---|---|---|---|---|---|---|---|---|---|---|---|---|---|
| | Male | Female | Male | Female | Male | Female | Male | Female | Male | Female | Male | Female | Male | Female | Male | Female | Male | Female |
| Native | 527 | 3,448 | 61 | 174 | 114 | 3 | 29 | 16 | 18 | 646 | 23 | 2,008 | 245 | 554 | 37 | 41 | ..... | 6 |
| Foreign | 2,296 | 1,886 | 129 | 33 | 255 | ..... | 134 | 1 | 2 | 369 | 30 | 859 | 1,502 | 588 | 212 | 28 | 32 | 8 |
| Not reported | 71 | 109 | 5 | 3 | 8 | ..... | 2 | 1 | 2 | 9 | 1 | 51 | 45 | 36 | 8 | ..... | ..... | 9 |
| Total | 2,894 | 5,443 | 195 | 210 | 377 | 3 | 165 | 18 | 22 | 1,024 | 54 | 2,918 | 1,792 | 1,178 | 257 | 69 | 32 | 23 |
| Per cent. of total | 100 | 100 | 6.8 | 3.87 | 13.2 | .06 | 5.76 | .3 | .77 | 18.9 | 1.89 | 53.8 | 62.6 | 21.8 | 8.98 | 1.27 | ..... | ..... |

NEW YORK STATE

**THE CONFECTIONERY INDUSTRY — FACTORY WORKERS**

121. TABLE V-D, a — NUMBER AND PER CENT. OF EMPLOYEES EARNING SPECIFIED WEEKLY RATES, BY AGE GROUPS AND SEX

| Weekly Rates in Dollars | Age Groups in Years | | | | | | | | | | | | | | Weekly Rates in Dollars |
|---|---|---|---|---|---|---|---|---|---|---|---|---|---|---|---|
| | 14–15 | | 16–17 | | 18–20 | | 21–24 | | 25–29 | | 30–34 | | 35–39 | | |
| | Male | Female | Male | Female | Male | Female | Male | Female | Male | Female | Male | Female | Male | Female | |
| Less than $3 00 | .... | 2 | .... | 1 | ...... | 2 | ...... | ...... | ...... | ...... | ...... | ...... | ...... | ...... | Less than $3 00 |
| $3 00–$3 49... | .... | ...... | .... | 3 | ...... | ...... | ...... | ...... | ...... | ...... | ...... | ...... | ...... | ...... | ...$3 00– 3 49 |
| 3 50– 3 99... | 3 | 71 | .... | 39 | ...... | 15 | ...... | 7 | ...... | 3 | ...... | 1 | ...... | 4 | ....3 50– 3 99 |
| 4 00– 4 49... | 5 | 71 | 1 | 115 | ...... | 36 | ...... | 15 | ...... | 5 | ...... | 5 | ...... | 10 | ....4 00– 4 49 |
| 4 50– 4 99... | 2 | 68 | 7 | 211 | 1 | 120 | ...... | 34 | ...... | 20 | ...... | 15 | 1 | 11 | ....4 50– 4 99 |
| 5 00– 5 49... | 2 | 13 | 21 | 384 | 9 | 269 | 2 | 83 | 1 | 59 | ...... | 27 | ...... | 34 | ....5 00– 5 49 |
| 5 50– 5 99... | 2 | 7 | 10 | 157 | 18 | 153 | 5 | 50 | ...... | 31 | ...... | 13 | ...... | 18 | ....5 50– 5 99 |
| 6 00– 6 49... | .... | 3 | 31 | 153 | 59 | 238 | 19 | 112 | 13 | 46 | 3 | 27 | 2 | 21 | ....6 00– 6 49 |
| 6 50– 6 99... | .... | ...... | 6 | 24 | 10 | 110 | 4 | 57 | 2 | 29 | ...... | 6 | 2 | 7 | ....6 50– 6 99 |
| 7 00– 7 49... | .... | ...... | 15 | 42 | 76 | 153 | 52 | 81 | 37 | 41 | 20 | 17 | 15 | 9 | ....7 00– 7 49 |
| 7 50– 7 99... | .... | ...... | 3 | 18 | 37 | 44 | 28 | 58 | 17 | 39 | 11 | 11 | 11 | 5 | ....7 50– 7 99 |
| 8 00– 8 99... | .... | ...... | 6 | 17 | 96 | 65 | 67 | 102 | 57 | 53 | 28 | 22 | 25 | 16 | ....8 00– 8 99 |
| 9 00– 9 99... | .... | ...... | 3 | 7 | 58 | 45 | 95 | 53 | 68 | 38 | 43 | 24 | 27 | 17 | ....9 00– 9 99 |
| 10 00–10 99... | .... | ...... | 1 | ...... | 21 | 12 | 51 | 36 | 48 | 35 | 36 | 27 | 23 | 15 | ...10 00–10 99 |
| 11 00–11 99... | .... | ...... | .... | ...... | 7 | 2 | 32 | 12 | 43 | 15 | 25 | 6 | 22 | 9 | ...11 00–11 99 |
| 12 00–12 99... | .... | ...... | 1 | ...... | 10 | 2 | 41 | 5 | 58 | 11 | 32 | 5 | 38 | 4 | ...12 00–12 99 |
| 13 00–13 99... | .... | ...... | .... | ...... | 1 | ...... | 20 | 1 | 22 | ...... | 26 | 1 | 24 | 1 | ...13 00–13 99 |
| 14 00–14 99... | .... | ...... | .... | ...... | 1 | ...... | 20 | 1 | 38 | 2 | 30 | 1 | 18 | 1 | ...14 00–14 99 |
| 15 00–15 99... | .... | ...... | 1 | ...... | 4 | 1 | 9 | ...... | 15 | 1 | 22 | 1 | 31 | 3 | ...15 00–15 99 |
| 16 00–17 99... | .... | ...... | .... | ...... | ...... | ...... | 6 | ...... | 20 | 1 | 20 | 2 | 21 | 3 | ...16 00–17 99 |
| 18 00–19 99... | .... | ...... | .... | ...... | ...... | ...... | 7 | ...... | 10 | 3 | 14 | 2 | 14 | 2 | ...18 00–19 99 |
| 20 00–24 99... | .... | ...... | .... | ...... | ...... | ...... | 1 | ...... | 8 | 1 | 14 | 1 | 15 | 1 | ...20 00–24 99 |
| 25 00–29 99... | .... | ...... | .... | ...... | ...... | ...... | 1 | ...... | 2 | ...... | 4 | ...... | 5 | ...... | ...25 00–29 99 |
| 30 00–34 99... | .... | ...... | .... | ...... | ...... | ...... | ...... | ...... | 1 | ...... | 3 | 1 | 1 | ...... | ...30 00–34 99 |
| 35 00–39 99... | .... | ...... | .... | ...... | ...... | ...... | ...... | ...... | 1 | ...... | 2 | ...... | 2 | ...... | ...35 00–39 99 |
| 40 00 and over. | .... | ...... | .... | ...... | ...... | ...... | ...... | ...... | ...... | ...... | 1 | ...... | 1 | ...... | 40 00 and over |
| Not reported... | .... | 1 | .... | 5 | 8 | 10 | 2 | 8 | 2 | 2 | 5 | 1 | 5 | 2 | ...Not reported |
| Total..... | 14 | 236 | 106 | 1,176 | 416 | 1,277 | 462 | 715 | 463 | 435 | 339 | 216 | 303 | 193 | .....Total |

121. TABLE V-D, a, *(concluded)*

NEW YORK STATE

**THE CONFECTIONERY INDUSTRY — FACTORY WORKERS**

NUMBER AND PER CENT. OF EMPLOYEES EARNING SPECIFIED WEEKLY RATES, BY AGE GROUPS AND SEX

| WEEKLY RATES IN DOLLARS | AGE GROUPS IN YEARS *(concluded)* | | | | | | | | | | | | | | WEEKLY RATES IN DOLLARS |
|---|---|---|---|---|---|---|---|---|---|---|---|---|---|---|---|
| | 40–44 | | 45–54 | | 55–64 | | 65 AND OVER | | NOT REPORTED | | TOTAL | | CUMULATIVE PER CENT. OF TOTAL | | |
| | Male | Female | Male | Female | Male | Femz le | Male | Female | Male | Female | Male | Female | Male | Female | |
| Less than $3 00 | .... | .... | .... | .... | .... | .... | .... | .... | .... | .... | .... | 5 | .... | .10 | Less than $3 00 |
| $3 00–$3 49 | .... | .... | .... | .... | .... | .... | .... | .... | .... | .... | .... | 3 | .... | .18 | $3 00–$3 49 |
| 3 50– 3 99 | .... | 2 | .... | 3 | .... | .... | .... | .... | .... | .... | 3 | 145 | .15 | 3.40 | 3 50– 3 99 |
| 4 00– 4 49 | .... | 3 | .... | 13 | .... | 3 | .... | 1 | .... | .... | 6 | 277 | .32 | 9.50 | 4 00– 4 49 |
| 4 50– 4 99 | .... | 16 | .... | 22 | .... | 2 | .... | 1 | 1 | 2 | 12 | 522 | .75 | 21.00 | 4 50– 4 99 |
| 5 00– 5 49 | .... | 23 | .... | 24 | 1 | 13 | .... | 1 | 1 | 5 | 37 | 935 | 2.80 | 41.80 | 5 00– 5 49 |
| 5 50– 5 99 | .... | 15 | 1 | 12 | .... | 3 | .... | .... | .... | 11 | 36 | 470 | 3.40 | 52.00 | 5 50– 5 99 |
| 6 00– 6 49 | 1 | 14 | 2 | 16 | 1 | 8 | .... | .... | 1 | 3 | 132 | 641 | 8.10 | 66.00 | 6 00– 6 49 |
| 6 50– 6 99 | .... | 6 | .... | 8 | .... | 1 | .... | .... | 2 | .... | 26. | 248 | 9.10 | 71.80 | 6 50– 6 99 |
| 7 00– 7 49 | 6 | 3 | 15 | 4 | 5 | 1 | .... | .... | 2 | 1 | 243 | 352 | 17.80 | 79.50 | 7 00– 7 49 |
| 7 50– 7 99 | 7 | 2 | 12 | .... | .... | .... | 2 | .... | .... | 1 | 128 | 178 | 22.30 | 83 20 | 7 50– 7 99 |
| 8 00– 8 99 | 26 | 12 | 33 | 6 | 16 | 1 | 3 | .... | 2 | .... | 359 | 294 | 35.20 | 89.70 | 8 00– 8 99 |
| 9 00– 9 99 | 21 | 10 | 31 | 5 | 17 | 1 | 3 | .... | 1 | 3 | 367 | 203 | 48.50 | 94.20 | 9 00– 9 99 |
| 10 00–10 99 | 24 | 8 | 41 | 5 | 10 | 2 | 3 | .... | .... | 1 | 258 | 141 | 57.70 | 97.20 | 10 00–10 99 |
| 11 00–11 99 | 10 | 1 | 16 | 2 | 7 | .... | .... | .... | .... | 1 | 162 | 48 | 63.50 | 98.40 | 11 00–11 99 |
| 12 00–12 99 | 22 | 3 | 50 | 2 | 14 | .... | 5 | .... | .... | .... | 271 | 32 | 73.20 | 99.00 | 12 00–12 99 |
| 13 00–13 99 | 15 | 1 | 14 | 1 | 7 | .... | 4 | .... | .... | .... | 133 | 5 | 77.80 | 99.10 | 13 00–13 99 |
| 14 00–14 99 | 15 | .... | 14 | .... | 3 | 1 | 2 | .... | 2 | 1 | 143 | 7 | 83.00 | 99.20 | 14 00–14 99 |
| 15 00–15 99 | 21 | .... | 22 | 1 | 6 | .... | .... | .... | .... | 1 | 131 | 8 | 88.00 | 99.40 | 15 00–15 99 |
| 16 00–17 99 | 17 | .... | 15 | 2 | 8 | .... | 4 | .... | 1 | .... | 112 | 8 | 91.80 | 99.60 | 16 00–17 99 |
| 18 00–19 99 | 11 | .... | 24 | 1 | 9 | .... | .... | .... | 1 | .... | 90 | 8 | 95.00 | 99.80 | 18 00–19 99 |
| 20 00–24 99 | 15 | 1 | 25 | 1 | 6 | .... | .... | .... | .... | .... | 84 | 5 | 98.00 | 99.90 | 20 00–24 99 |
| 25 00–29 99 | 8 | .... | 5 | .... | 2 | .... | .... | .... | 1 | .... | 28 | .... | 99.00 | .... | 25 00–29 99 |
| 30 00–34 99 | 2 | .... | 3 | .... | 3 | .... | 1 | .... | .... | .... | 14 | 1 | 99.50 | 100.00 | 30 00–34 99 |
| 35 00–39 99 | 4 | .... | 1 | .... | 1 | .... | .... | .... | 1 | .... | 12 | .... | 99.90 | .... | 35 00–39 99 |
| 40 00 and over | 1 | .... | 1 | .... | 1 | .... | .... | .... | .... | .... | 5 | .... | 100.00 | .... | 40 00 and over |
| Not reported | 3 | 2 | 4 | 2 | 5 | 1 | .... | .... | 5 | .... | 39 | 34 | .... | .... | Not reported |
| Total | 229 | 122 | 329 | 130 | 122 | 37 | 27 | 3 | 21 | 30 | 2,831 | 4,570 | .... | .... | Total |

NEW YORK STATE

**THE CONFECTIONERY INDUSTRY — FACTORY WORKERS**

122. TABLE VIII, D, a — NUMBER AND PER CENT. OF EMPLOYEES EARNING SPECIFIED WEEKLY RATES, BY OCCUPATION AND SEX

| WEEKLY RATES IN DOLLARS | OCCUPATION | | | | | | | | | | | | | | | | | | | | WEEKLY RATES IN DOLLARS |
|---|---|---|---|---|---|---|---|---|---|---|---|---|---|---|---|---|---|---|---|---|---|
| | FOREMEN AND FOREWOMEN | | CANDY MAKERS | | MACHINE OPERATORS | | DIPPERS | | PACKERS AND WRAPPERS | | HELPERS | | LABORERS | | NOT REPORTED | | TOTAL | | CUMULATIVE PER CENT. OF TOTAL | | |
| | Male | Female | Male | Female | Male | Female | Male | Female | Male | Female | Male | Female | Male | Female | Male | Female | Male | Female | Male | Female | |
| Less than $3 00 | | | | | | | | | | 5 | | | | | | | | 5 | | .01 | Less than $3 00 |
| $3 00-$3 49 | | | | | | | | | | 3 | | | | | | | | 3 | | .18 | $3 00-$3 49 |
| 3 50- 3 99 | | | | | | | | 17 | | 91 | 2 | 36 | 1 | | | 1 | 3 | 145 | .15 | 3.04 | 3 50- 3 99 |
| 4 00- 4 49 | | | | 1 | | | | 28 | | 170 | 6 | 73 | | 5 | | | 6 | 277 | .32 | 9.05 | 4 00- 4 49 |
| 4 50- 4 99 | | | | | | | | 54 | 1 | 239 | 8 | 201 | 3 | 21 | | 7 | 12 | 522 | .75 | 21.00 | 4 50- 4 99 |
| 5 00- 5 49 | | 2 | | | | | | 59 | 2 | 559 | 25 | 296 | 10 | 13 | | 6 | 37 | 935 | 2.08 | 41.08 | 5 00- 5 49 |
| 5 50- 5 99 | | 1 | | | | | | 52 | 1 | 278 | 34 | 131 | | 8 | 1 | | 36 | 470 | 3.40 | 52.00 | 5 50- 5 99 |
| 6 00- 6 49 | | 8 | | | | | | 67 | 4 | 406 | 104 | 151 | 24 | 8 | | 1 | 132 | 641 | 8.10 | 66.00 | 6 00- 6 49 |
| 6 50- 6 99 | | 2 | | 1 | | | | 40 | | 159 | 22 | 39 | 4 | 2 | | 5 | 26 | 248 | 9.10 | 71.80 | 6 50- 6 99 |
| 7 00- 7 49 | | 9 | 1 | 1 | | 1 | | 49 | 12 | 217 | 198 | 69 | 32 | 2 | | 4 | 243 | 352 | 17.80 | 79.50 | 7 00- 7 49 |
| 7 50- 7 99 | | 4 | 2 | | | 2 | 1 | 45 | 4 | 104 | 110 | 21 | 10 | | 1 | 2 | 128 | 178 | 22.30 | 83.20 | 7 50- 7 99 |
| 8 00- 8 99 | | 24 | 5 | | 3 | 2 | 1 | 119 | 11 | 100 | 291 | 45 | 48 | 1 | | 3 | 359 | 294 | 35.20 | 89.70 | 8 00- 8 99 |
| 9 00- 9 99 | 2 | 35 | 15 | | 4 | 1 | | 98 | 2 | 38 | 308 | 30 | 34 | 1 | 2 | | 367 | 203 | 48.50 | 94.20 | 9 00- 9 99 |
| 10 00-10 99 | | 39 | 20 | | 10 | 9 | 1 | 76 | 5 | 10 | 193 | 5 | 21 | 1 | 5 | 1 | 258 | 141 | 57.70 | 97.20 | 10 00-10 99 |
| 11 00-11 99 | 1 | 19 | 17 | | 19 | 1 | | 23 | 1 | 5 | 101 | | 19 | | 4 | | 162 | 48 | 63.50 | 98.40 | 11 00-11 99 |
| 12 00-12 99 | 7 | 24 | 55 | | 25 | 1 | | 3 | 2 | | 156 | 2 | 26 | | | 2 | 271 | 32 | 73.20 | 99.00 | 12 00-12 99 |
| 13 00-13 99 | 8 | 4 | 30 | | 23 | | | 1 | 1 | | 60 | | 7 | | 4 | | 133 | 5 | 77.80 | 99.10 | 13 00-13 99 |
| 14 00-14 99 | 11 | 6 | 35 | | 24 | | | 1 | 1 | | 70 | | 2 | | | | 143 | 7 | 83.00 | 99.20 | 14 00-14 99 |
| 15 00-15 99 | 16 | 8 | 54 | | 15 | | | | 3 | | 29 | | 5 | | 9 | | 131 | 8 | 88.00 | 99.40 | 15 00-15 99 |
| 16 00-17 99 | 24 | 7 | 50 | | 10 | | | | 1 | 1 | 24 | | 3 | | | | 112 | 8 | 91.80 | 99.60 | 16 00-17 99 |
| 18 00-19 99 | 26 | 7 | 47 | | 10 | | | | | 1 | 5 | | 2 | | | | 90 | 8 | 95.00 | 99.80 | 18 00-19 99 |
| 20 00-24 99 | 52 | 5 | 24 | | 5 | | | | | | 1 | | | | 2 | | 84 | 5 | 98.00 | 99.90 | 20 00-24 99 |
| 25 00-29 99 | 19 | | 8 | | 1 | | | | | | | | | | | | 28 | | 99.00 | | 25 00-29 99 |
| 30 00-34 99 | 12 | 1 | 1 | | | | | | | | | | | | 1 | | 14 | 1 | 99.50 | 100.00 | 30 00-34 99 |
| 35 00-39 99 | 11 | | 1 | | | | | | | | | | | | | | 12 | | 99.90 | | 35 00-39 99 |
| 40 00 and over | 3 | | 1 | | | | | | | | | | | | 1 | | 5 | | 100.00 | | 40 00 and over |
| Not reported | 2 | 2 | 6 | | 13 | 1 | | 4 | 3 | 15 | 13 | 10 | 2 | | | 2 | 39 | 34 | | | Not reported |
| Total | 194 | 207 | 372 | 3 | 162 | 18 | 3 | 736 | 54 | 2,401 | 1,760 | 1,109 | 256 | 62 | 30 | 34 | 2,831 | 4,570 | | | Total |

NEW YORK STATE

123. TABLE VI, D, a

THE CONFECTIONERY INDUSTRY — FACTORY WORKERS

NUMBER AND PER CENT. OF EMPLOYEES CLASSIFIED ACCORDING TO ACTUAL WEEKLY EARNINGS, BY AGE GROUPS AND SEX

| ACTUAL WEEKLY EARNINGS IN DOLLARS | AGE GROUPS IN YEARS | | | | | | | | | | | | | | ACTUAL WEEKLY EARNINGS IN DOLLARS |
|---|---|---|---|---|---|---|---|---|---|---|---|---|---|---|---|
| | 14–15 | | 16–17 | | 18–20 | | 21–24 | | 25–29 | | 30–34 | | 35–39 | | |
| | Male | Female | Male | Female | Male | Female | Male | Female | Male | Female | Male | Female | Male | Female | |
| Less than $3 00 | 1 | 45 | 6 | 102 | 18 | 76 | 15 | 36 | 7 | 13 | 2 | 14 | 4 | 10 | Less than $3 00 |
| $3 00–$3 49... | 1 | 21 | 2 | 72 | 8 | 55 | 4 | 22 | 1 | 5 | 2 | 3 | ...... | 5 | ...$3 00–$3 49 |
| 3 50– 3 99... | .... | 56 | 8 | 85 | 4 | 47 | 4 | 15 | 2 | 8 | 2 | 8 | ...... | 7 | ....3 50– 3 99 |
| 4 00– 4 49... | 6 | 69 | 6 | 157 | 5 | 88 | 3 | 36 | 2 | 23 | 2 | 9 | ...... | 11 | ....4 00– 4 49 |
| 4 50– 4 99... | 3 | 43 | 9 | 206 | 19 | 147 | 10 | 47 | 2 | 25 | 3 | 17 | 1 | 14 | ....4 50– 4 99 |
| 5 00– 5 49... | 1 | 10 | 19 | 277 | 20 | 221 | 16 | 83 | 8 | 59 | 2 | 20 | 2 | 24 | ....5 00– 5 49 |
| 5 50– 5 99... | 1 | 11 | 8 | 154 | 22 | 174 | 8 | 74 | 8 | 35 | 4 | 13 | 7 | 19 | ....5 50– 5 99 |
| 6 00– 6 49... | .... | 8 | 13 | 112 | 35 | 192 | 18 | 95 | 9 | 43 | 9 | 18 | 3 | 14 | ....6 00– 6 49 |
| 6 50– 6 99... | .... | ...... | 10 | 50 | 34 | 140 | 12 | 62 | 17 | 29 | 2 | 16 | 13 | 12 | ....6 50– 6 99 |
| 7 00– 7 49... | .... | 2 | 13 | 40 | 45 | 119 | 37 | 72 | 17 | 39 | 16 | 15 | 10 | 12 | ....7 00– 7 49 |
| 7 50– 7 99... | .... | 1 | 5 | 28 | 43 | 72 | 26 | 71 | 30 | 47 | 12 | 13 | 10 | 9 | ....7 50– 7 99 |
| 8 00– 8 99... | .... | 1 | 4 | 33 | 76 | 109 | 67 | 110 | 56 | 65 | 22 | 34 | 20 | 14 | ....8 00– 8 99 |
| 9 00– 9 99... | .... | ...... | 2 | 16 | 43 | 78 | 68 | 66 | 44 | 44 | 38 | 22 | 30 | 19 | ....9 00– 9 99 |
| 10 00–10 99... | .... | ...... | 1 | 5 | 19 | 36 | 43 | 56 | 47 | 44 | 36 | 20 | 28 | 13 | ...10 00–10 99 |
| 11 00–11 99... | .... | ...... | 1 | ...... | 11 | 20 | 40 | 25 | 45 | 19 | 24 | 4 | 20 | 9 | ...11 00–11 99 |
| 12 00–12 99... | .... | ...... | 1 | 1 | 13 | 7 | 37 | 11 | 44 | 10 | 39 | 6 | 31 | 6 | ...12 00–12 99 |
| 13 00–13 99... | .... | ...... | .... | 1 | 2 | 1 | 25 | 7 | 31 | 1 | 20 | 2 | 18 | 1 | ...13 00–13 99 |
| 14 00–14 99... | .... | ...... | .... | ...... | 1 | ...... | 14 | 3 | 33 | 3 | 27 | 2 | 22 | 2 | ...14 00–14 99 |
| 15 00–15 99... | .... | ...... | 1 | ...... | 4 | 2 | 10 | ...... | 16 | 2 | 19 | 1 | 22 | 2 | ...15 00–15 99 |
| 16 00–17 99... | .... | ...... | .... | ...... | ...... | 1 | 10 | ...... | 23 | 1 | 19 | 4 | 24 | 3 | ...16 00–17 99 |
| 18 00–19 99... | .... | ...... | .... | ...... | ...... | ...... | 4 | 1 | 11 | 3 | 4 | 2 | 17 | 2 | ...18 00–19 99 |
| 20 00–24 99... | .... | ...... | .... | ...... | 1 | ...... | 4 | ...... | 8 | 1 | 17 | 1 | 15 | ...... | ...20 00–24 99 |
| 25 00–29 99... | .... | ...... | .... | ...... | ...... | ...... | 1 | ...... | 2 | ...... | 5 | ...... | 6 | 1 | ...25 00–29 99 |
| 30 00–34 99... | .... | ...... | .... | ...... | ...... | ...... | ...... | ...... | ...... | ...... | 2 | ...... | 3 | ...... | ...30 00–34 99 |
| 35 00–39 99... | .... | ...... | .... | ...... | ...... | ...... | ...... | ...... | 1 | ...... | 2 | ...... | 2 | ...... | ...35 00–39 99 |
| 40 00 and over. | .... | ...... | .... | ...... | ...... | ...... | ...... | ...... | ...... | ...... | 1 | ...... | 1 | ...... | .40 00 and over |
| Not reported... | .... | 2 | .... | 9 | 2 | 12 | 4 | 5 | 4 | 5 | 2 | 1 | 2 | 4 | ...Not reported |
| Total..... | 13 | 269 | 109 | 1,348 | 425 | 1,597 | 480 | 897 | 468 | 524 | 343 | 245 | 311 | 213 | .....Total |

NEW YORK STATE

123. TABLE VI, D, a — (*concluded*) **THE CONFECTIONERY INDUSTRY — FACTORY WORKERS**

NUMBER AND PER CENT. OF EMPLOYEES CLASSIFIED ACCORDING TO ACTUAL WEEKLY EARNINGS BY AGE

| ACTUAL WEEKLY EARNINGS IN DOLLARS | AGE GROUPS IN YEARS (*concluded*) | | | | | | | | | | | | | | ACTUAL WEEKLY EARNINGS IN DOLLARS |
|---|---|---|---|---|---|---|---|---|---|---|---|---|---|---|---|
| | 40–44 | | 45–54 | | 55–64 | | 65 AND OVER | | NOT REPORTED | | TOTAL | | CUMULATIVE PER CENT OF TOTAL | | |
| | Male | Female | Male | Female | Male | Female | Male | Female | Male | Female | Male | Female | Male | Female | |
| Less than $3 00 | 1 | 6 | .... | 10 | 2 | 2 | ...... | ...... | 1 | 1 | 57 | 315 | 2.00 | 5.80 | Less than $3 00 |
| $3 00–$3 49... | 1 | ...... | 1 | 2 | 1 | 1 | ...... | ...... | ...... | ...... | 21 | 186 | 2.70 | 9.30 | ...$3 00– 3 49 |
| 3 50– 3 99... | .... | 2 | .... | 7 | ...... | 1 | ...... | ...... | ...... | ...... | 20 | 236 | 3.40 | 13.70 | ... 3 50– 3 99 |
| 4 00– 4 49... | .... | 10 | .... | 5 | 2 | 4 | ...... | 1 | ...... | ...... | 26 | 413 | 4.30 | 21.30 | ... 4 00– 4 49 |
| 4 50– 4 99... | 1 | 14 | 1 | 16 | 1 | 3 | ...... | 1 | ...... | 4 | 50 | 537 | 6.10 | 31.30 | ... 4 50– 4 99 |
| 5 00– 5 49... | 5 | 21 | 2 | 24 | ...... | 11 | ...... | 1 | 2 | 2 | 77 | 753 | 8.70 | 45.20 | ... 5 00– 5 49 |
| 5 50– 5 99... | .... | 19 | 4 | 17 | ...... | 4 | ...... | 1 | ...... | 1 | 62 | 522 | 10.90 | 54.80 | ... 5 50– 5 99 |
| 6 00– 6 49... | .... | 10 | 4 | 15 | 1 | 5 | ...... | ...... | 3 | 2 | 95 | 514 | 14.50 | 64.40 | ... 6 00– 6 49 |
| 6 50– 6 99... | 8 | 5 | 8 | 11 | 4 | ...... | ...... | ...... | 2 | 1 | 110 | 326 | 18.00 | 70.50 | ... 6 50– 6 99 |
| 7 00– 7 49... | 7 | 2 | 14 | 6 | 4 | 1 | 1 | ...... | 2 | 1 | 166 | 309 | 23.70 | 76.10 | ... 7 00– 7 49 |
| 7 50– 7 99... | 7 | 6 | 18 | 1 | 3 | 1 | 1 | ...... | ...... | ...... | 155 | 249 | 29.20 | 80.80 | ... 7 50– 7 99 |
| 8 00– 8 99... | 25 | 15 | 29 | 3 | 15 | 1 | 5 | ...... | ...... | 3 | 319 | 388 | 39.20 | 88.00 | ... 8 00– 8 99 |
| 9 00– 9 99... | 17 | 9 | 31 | 6 | 15 | 2 | 2 | ...... | ...... | 3 | 290 | 265 | 50.30 | 92.70 | ... 9 00– 9 99 |
| 10 00–10 99... | 17 | 8 | 34 | 6 | 10 | 2 | 4 | ...... | ...... | 1 | 239 | 191 | 58.50 | 96.50 | ...10 00–10 99 |
| 11 00–11 99... | 14 | 3 | 25 | 2 | 6 | ...... | 1 | ...... | 3 | ...... | 190 | 82 | 65.30 | 97.70 | ...11 00–11 99 |
| 12 00–12 99... | 16 | 3 | 31 | 6 | 13 | ...... | 4 | ...... | 2 | ...... | 231 | 50 | 73.50 | 98.80 | ...12 00–12 99 |
| 13 00–13 99... | 19 | ...... | 21 | 1 | 7 | ...... | 5 | ...... | 2 | ...... | 150 | 14 | 78.50 | 99.10 | ...13 00–13 99 |
| 14 00–14 99... | 14 | ...... | 19 | ...... | 4 | 2 | 1 | ...... | ...... | 1 | 135 | 13 | 83.20 | 99.40 | ...14 00–14 99 |
| 15 00–15 99... | 16 | ...... | 13 | ...... | 9 | ...... | 2 | ...... | ...... | 1 | 112 | 8 | 87.20 | 99.50 | ...15 00–15 99 |
| 16 00–17 99... | 19 | ...... | 25 | 2 | 7 | ...... | 2 | ...... | ...... | ...... | 129 | 11 | 91.50 | 99.70 | ...16 00–17 99 |
| 18 00–19 99... | 9 | ...... | 20 | 1 | 9 | ...... | ...... | ...... | ...... | ...... | 84 | 9 | 94.50 | 99.80 | ...18 00–19 99 |
| 20 00–24 99... | 19 | 1 | 21 | 1 | 8 | ...... | ...... | ...... | ...... | ...... | 93 | 4 | 97.70 | 99.90 | ...20 00–24 99 |
| 25 00–29 99... | 7 | ...... | 5 | ...... | 4 | ...... | ...... | ...... | 3 | ...... | 33 | 1 | 98.70 | 100.00 | ...25 00–29 99 |
| 30 00–34 99... | 3 | ...... | 4 | ...... | 1 | ...... | 1 | ...... | ...... | ...... | 14 | ...... | 99.40 | ...... | ...30 00–34 99 |
| 35 00–39 99... | 3 | ...... | 1 | ...... | 2 | ...... | ...... | ...... | 1 | ...... | 12 | ...... | 99.80 | ...... | ...35 00–39 99 |
| 40 00 and over. | 2 | ...... | .... | ...... | 1 | ...... | ...... | ...... | 1 | ...... | 6 | ...... | 100.00 | ...... | .40 00 and over |
| Not reported... | .... | 3 | 1 | 4 | 1 | ...... | 1 | ...... | 1 | 2 | 18 | 47 | ...... | ...... | ...Not reported |
| Total..... | 230 | 137 | 332 | 146 | 130 | 40 | 30 | 4 | 23 | 23 | 2,894 | 5,443 | ...... | ...... | .....Total |

NEW YORK STATE

124. TABLE IX, D, a

THE CONFECTIONERY INDUSTRY — FACTORY WORKERS

NUMBER AND PER CENT. OF EMPLOYEES CLASSIFIED ACCORDING TO ACTUAL WEEKLY EARNINGS, BY OCCUPATION AND SEX

| ACTUAL WEEKLY EARNINGS IN DOLLARS | OCCUPATION: FOREMEN AND FOREWOMEN | | CANDY MAKERS | | MACHINE OPERATORS | | DIPPERS | | PACKERS AND WRAPPERS | | HELPERS | | LABORERS | | NOT REPORTED | | TOTAL OF TOTAL | | CUMULATIVE PER CENT. OF TOTAL | | ACTUAL WEEKLY EARNINGS IN DOLLARS |
|---|---|---|---|---|---|---|---|---|---|---|---|---|---|---|---|---|---|---|---|---|---|
| | Male | Female | Male | Female | Male | Female | Male | Female | Male | Female | Male | Female | Male | Female | Male | Female | Male | Female | Male | Female | |
| Less than $3 00 | 1 | 2 | | | 1 | | | 35 | 2 | 202 | 49 | 73 | 4 | 1 | | 2 | 57 | 315 | 2.00 | 5.80 | Less than $3 00 |
| 3 00– 3 49 | 1 | | 1 | 1 | | | 1 | 8 | | 127 | 15 | 49 | 1 | 1 | 2 | | 21 | 186 | 2.70 | 9.30 | $3 00–$3 49 |
| 3 50– 3 99 | | 1 | 1 | | | 1 | | 31 | 1 | 150 | 18 | 51 | | 2 | | | 20 | 236 | 3.40 | 13.70 | 3 50– 3 99 |
| 4 00– 4 49 | | | | | | | | 45 | 1 | 256 | 22 | 97 | 3 | 12 | | 3 | 26 | 413 | 4.30 | 21.30 | 4 00– 4 49 |
| 4 50– 4 99 | | 1 | 1 | | 1 | | | 60 | 2 | 288 | 43 | 176 | 3 | 12 | | | 50 | 537 | 6.10 | 31.30 | 4 50– 4 99 |
| 5 00– 5 49 | 1 | 7 | | | 1 | | | 58 | 4 | 437 | 60 | 233 | 11 | 17 | | 1 | 77 | 753 | 8.70 | 45.20 | 5 00– 5 49 |
| 5 50– 5 99 | | 5 | 1 | | | | | 62 | 2 | 325 | 57 | 122 | 1 | 6 | 1 | 2 | 62 | 522 | 10.90 | 54.80 | 5 50– 5 99 |
| 6 00– 6 49 | | 7 | 1 | | | | 1 | 87 | 2 | 294 | 73 | 114 | 18 | 9 | | 3 | 95 | 514 | 14.50 | 64.40 | 6 00– 6 49 |
| 6 50– 6 99 | 1 | 4 | | 1 | 2 | | | 65 | | 204 | 95 | 49 | 12 | 2 | | 1 | 110 | 326 | 18.00 | 70.50 | 6 50– 6 99 |
| 7 00– 7 49 | | 6 | 1 | 1 | | 1 | | 71 | 11 | 184 | 124 | 43 | 30 | 2 | | 1 | 166 | 309 | 23.70 | 76.10 | 7 00– 7 49 |
| 7 50– 7 99 | 1 | 9 | 8 | | 1 | | 2 | 70 | 2 | 137 | 122 | 32 | 18 | | 1 | 1 | 155 | 249 | 29.20 | 80.80 | 7 50– 7 99 |
| 8 00– 8 99 | | 29 | 10 | | 4 | 4 | 4 | 130 | 9 | 159 | 257 | 63 | 35 | 2 | | 1 | 319 | 388 | 39.20 | 88.00 | 8 00– 8 99 |
| 9 00– 9 99 | 1 | 29 | 16 | | 6 | 4 | 3 | 112 | 3 | 76 | 226 | 43 | 35 | 1 | | | 290 | 265 | 50.30 | 92.70 | 9 00– 9 99 |
| 10 00–10 99 | 1 | 34 | 31 | | 15 | 6 | 2 | 103 | 4 | 33 | 162 | 13 | 20 | 2 | 4 | | 239 | 191 | 58.50 | 96.50 | 10 00–10 99 |
| 11 00–11 99 | 6 | 15 | 28 | | 28 | | 4 | 49 | 2 | 12 | 103 | 6 | 19 | | | | 190 | 82 | 65.30 | 97.70 | 11 00–11 99 |
| 12 00–12 99 | 4 | 23 | 38 | | 17 | 2 | 4 | 13 | 4 | 5 | 139 | 5 | 25 | | | 2 | 231 | 50 | 73.50 | 98.80 | 12 00–12 99 |
| 13 00–13 99 | 11 | 4 | 30 | | 23 | | | 8 | 2 | 2 | 71 | | 7 | | 6 | | 150 | 14 | 78.50 | 99.10 | 13 00–13 99 |
| 14 00–14 99 | 11 | 7 | 28 | | 17 | | 1 | 5 | | | 76 | 1 | 1 | | 1 | | 135 | 13 | 83.20 | 99.40 | 14 00–14 99 |
| 15 00–15 99 | 13 | 5 | 44 | | 15 | | | 3 | 1 | | 25 | | 4 | | 10 | | 112 | 8 | 87.20 | 99.50 | 15 00–15 99 |
| 16 00–17 99 | 17 | 8 | 54 | | 14 | | | 2 | 1 | 1 | 37 | | 6 | | | | 129 | 11 | 91.50 | 99.70 | 16 00–17 99 |
| 18 00–19 99 | 29 | 7 | 35 | | 9 | | | 1 | | 1 | 6 | | 3 | | 2 | | 84 | 9 | 94.50 | 99.80 | 18 00–19 99 |
| 20 00–24 99 | 48 | 4 | 31 | | 8 | | | | | | 4 | | | | 2 | | 93 | 4 | 97.70 | 99.90 | 20 00–24 99 |
| 25 00–29 99 | 21 | 1 | 11 | | 1 | | | | | | | | | | | | 33 | 1 | 98.70 | 100.00 | 25 00–29 99 |
| 30 00–34 99 | 12 | | 1 | | | | | | | | | | | | 1 | | 14 | | 99.40 | | 30 00–34 99 |
| 35 00–39 99 | 10 | | 1 | | | | | | | | | | | | 1 | | 12 | | 99.80 | | 35 00–39 99 |
| 40 00 and over | 5 | | 1 | | | | | | | | | | | | | | 6 | | 100.00 | | 40 00 and over |
| Not reported | 1 | 2 | 4 | | 2 | | | 6 | 1 | 25 | 8 | 8 | 1 | | 1 | 6 | 18 | 47 | | | Not reported |
| Total | 195 | 210 | 377 | 3 | 165 | 18 | 22 | 1,024 | 54 | 2,918 | 1,792 | 1,178 | 257 | 69 | 32 | 23 | 2,894 | 5,443 | | | Total |

125. TABLE X, D, a.

NEW YORK STATE

THE CONFECTIONERY INDUSTRY — FACTORY WORKERS

NUMBER AND PER CENT. OF EMPLOYEES CLASSIFIED ACCORDING TO ACTUAL WEEKLY EARNINGS BY CONJUGAL CONDITION ANND SEX

| Actual Weekly Earnings in Dollars | Conjugal Condition | | | | | | | | | | | | Actual Weekly Earnings in Dollars |
|---|---|---|---|---|---|---|---|---|---|---|---|---|---|
| | Single | | Married | | Widowed or Divorced | | Not Reported | | Total | | Cumulative Per Cent. of Total | | |
| | Male | Female | Male | Female | Male | Female | Male | Female | Male | Female | Male | Female | |
| Less than $3 00. | 37 | 227 | 15 | 44 | ....... | 18 | 5 | 26 | 57 | 315 | 2.00 | 5.80 | Less than $3 00 |
| $3 00–$3 49.... | 14 | 149 | 6 | 20 | 1 | 5 | ....... | 12 | 21 | 186 | 2.70 | 9.30 | ...$3 00– 3 49 |
| 3 50– 3 99.... | 15 | 193 | 5 | 16 | ....... | 13 | ....... | 14 | 20 | 236 | 3.40 | 13.70 | ... 3 50– 3 99 |
| 4 00– 4 49.... | 21 | 316 | 3 | 53 | ....... | 11 | 2 | 33 | 26 | 413 | 4.30 | 21.30 | ... 4 00– 4 49 |
| 4 50– 4 99.... | 39 | 408 | 9 | 58 | ....... | 25 | 2 | 46 | 50 | 537 | 6.10 | 31.30 | ... 4 50– 4 99 |
| 5 00– 5 49.... | 55 | 555 | 13 | 119 | 2 | 38 | 7 | 41 | 77 | 753 | 8.70 | 45.20 | ... 5 00– 5 49 |
| 5 50– 5 99.... | 44 | 378 | 15 | 85 | ....... | 21 | 3 | 38 | 62 | 522 | 10.90 | 54.80 | ... 5 50– 5 99 |
| 6 00– 6 49.... | 69 | 388 | 22 | 65 | ....... | 27 | 4 | 34 | 95 | 514 | 14.50 | 64.40 | ... 6 00– 6 49 |
| 6 50– 6 99.... | 63 | 263 | 43 | 35 | 1 | 14 | 3 | 14 | 110 | 326 | 18.00 | 70.50 | ... 6 50– 6 99 |
| 7 00– 7 49.... | 96 | 254 | 58 | 34 | 1 | 13 | 11 | 8 | 166 | 309 | 23.70 | 76.10 | ... 7 00– 7 49 |
| 7 50– 7 99.... | 80 | 189 | 65 | 39 | 2 | 11 | 8 | 10 | 155 | 249 | 29.20 | 80.80 | ... 7 50– 7 99 |
| 8 00– 8 99.... | 166 | 306 | 131 | 53 | 4 | 20 | 18 | 9 | 319 | 388 | 39.20 | 88.00 | ... 8 00– 8 99 |
| 9 00– 9 99.... | 150 | 210 | 132 | 36 | 3 | 13 | 5 | 6 | 290 | 265 | 50.30 | 92.70 | ... 9 00– 9 99 |
| 10 00–10 99.... | 89 | 149 | 135 | 23 | 9 | 17 | 6 | 2 | 239 | 191 | 58.50 | 96.50 | ...10 00–10 99 |
| 11 00–11 99.... | 70 | 65 | 104 | 7 | 7 | 5 | 9 | 5 | 190 | 82 | 65.30 | 97.70 | ...11 00–11 99 |
| 12 00–12 99.... | 82 | 34 | 143 | 12 | 2 | 4 | 4 | ....... | 231 | 50 | 73.50 | 98.80 | ...12 00–12 99 |
| 13 00–13 99.... | 39 | 11 | 104 | 2 | 3 | 1 | 4 | ....... | 150 | 14 | 78.50 | 99.10 | ...13 00–13 99 |
| 14 00–14 99.... | 33 | 7 | 95 | 2 | 4 | 3 | 3 | 1 | 135 | 13 | 83.20 | 99.40 | ...14 00–14 99 |
| 15 00–1 99.... | 33 | 5 | 72 | 2 | 3 | ....... | 4 | 1 | 112 | 8 | 87.20 | 99.50 | ...15 00–15 99 |
| 16 00–17 99.... | 37 | 6 | 87 | 4 | 5 | 1 | ....... | ....... | 129 | 11 | 91.50 | 99.70 | ...16 00–17 99 |
| 18 00–19 99.... | 11 | 6 | 69 | 3 | 2 | ....... | 2 | ....... | 84 | 9 | 94.50 | 99.80 | ...18 00–19 99 |
| 20 00–24 99.... | 10 | 1 | 80 | 3 | 1 | ....... | 2 | ....... | 93 | 4 | 97.70 | 99.90 | ...20 00–24 99 |
| 25 00–29 99.... | 5 | 1 | 23 | ....... | 1 | ....... | 4 | ....... | 33 | 1 | 98.70 | 100.00 | ...25 00–29 99 |
| 30 00–34 99.... | ....... | ....... | 12 | ....... | 2 | ....... | ....... | ....... | 14 | ....... | 99.40 | ....... | ...30 00–34 99 |
| 35 00–39 00.... | 1 | ....... | 11 | ....... | ....... | ....... | ....... | ....... | 12 | ....... | 99.80 | ....... | ..335 00–39 99 |
| 40 00 and over.. | 1 | ....... | 4 | ....... | ....... | ....... | 1 | ....... | 6 | ....... | 100.00 | ....... | .40 00 and over |
| Not reported.... | 5 | 28 | 11 | 15 | ....... | 2 | 2 | 2 | 18 | 47 | ....... | ....... | ...Not reported |
| Total...... | 1,265 | 4,149 | 1,467 | 730 | 53 | 262 | 109 | 302 | 2,894 | 5,443 | ....... | ....... | .....Total |

NEW YORK STATE

126. TABLE XI D, a. **THE CONFECTIONERY INDUSTRY — FACTORY WORKERS**

Number and Per Cent. of Employees Classified According to Actual Weekly Earnings by Nativity and Sex

| Actual Weekly Earnings in Dollars | Nativity: Native | | Foreign | | Not Reported | | Total | | Cumulative Per Cent. of Total | | Actual Weekly Earnings in Dollars |
|---|---|---|---|---|---|---|---|---|---|---|---|
| | Male | Female | Male | Female | Male | Female | Male | Female | Male | Female | |
| Less than $3 00 | 10 | 204 | 46 | 96 | 1 | 15 | 57 | 315 | 2.00 | 5.80 | Less than $3 00 |
| $3 00–$3 49 | 5 | 129 | 16 | 48 | ........ | 9 | 21 | 186 | 2.70 | 9.30 | $3 00– 3 49 |
| 3 50– 3 99 | 5 | 156 | 15 | 74 | ........ | 6 | 20 | 236 | 3.40 | 13.70 | 3 50– 3 99 |
| 4 00– 4 49 | 10 | 250 | 14 | 147 | 2 | 16 | 26 | 413 | 4.30 | 21.30 | 4 00– 4 49 |
| 4 50– 4 99 | 17 | 325 | 32 | 197 | 1 | 15 | 50 | 537 | 6.10 | 31.30 | 4 50– 4 99 |
| 5 00– 5 49 | 10 | 423 | 63 | 313 | 4 | 17 | 77 | 753 | 8.70 | 45.20 | 5 00– 5 49 |
| 5 50– 5 99 | 12 | 322 | 48 | 194 | 2 | 6 | 62 | 522 | 10.90 | 54.80 | 5 50– 5 99 |
| 6 00– 6 49 | 10 | 328 | 81 | 178 | 4 | 8 | 95 | 514 | 14.50 | 64.40 | 6 00– 6 49 |
| 6 50– 6 99 | 16 | 222 | 91 | 98 | 3 | 6 | 110 | 326 | 18.00 | 70.50 | 6 50– 6 99 |
| 7 00– 7 49 | 20 | 205 | 140 | 104 | 6 | ........ | 166 | 309 | 23.70 | 76.10 | 7 00– 7 49 |
| 7 50– 7 99 | 21 | 156 | 128 | 91 | 6 | 2 | 155 | 249 | 29.20 | 80.80 | 7 50– 7 99 |
| 8 00– 8 99 | 36 | 257 | 275 | 129 | 8 | 2 | 319 | 388 | 39.20 | 88.00 | 8 00– 8 99 |
| 9 00– 9 99 | 46 | 187 | 239 | 75 | 5 | 3 | 290 | 265 | 50.30 | 92.70 | 9 00– 9 99 |
| 10 00–10 99 | 49 | 120 | 185 | 70 | 5 | 1 | 239 | 191 | 58.50 | 96.50 | 10 00–10 99 |
| 11 00–11 99 | 36 | 55 | 150 | 27 | 4 | ........ | 190 | 82 | 65.30 | 97.70 | 11 00–11 99 |
| 12 00–12 99 | 36 | 40 | 190 | 9 | 5 | 1 | 231 | 50 | 73.50 | 98.80 | 12 00–12 99 |
| 13 00–13 99 | 28 | 11 | 121 | 3 | 1 | ........ | 150 | 14 | 78.50 | 99.10 | 13 00–13 99 |
| 14 00–14 99 | 18 | 11 | 115 | 1 | 2 | 1 | 135 | 13 | 83.20 | 99.40 | 14 00–14 99 |
| 15 00–15 99 | 28 | 5 | 82 | 2 | 2 | 1 | 112 | 8 | 87.20 | 99.50 | 15 00–15 99 |
| 16 00–17 99 | 25 | 8 | 102 | 3 | 2 | ........ | 129 | 11 | 91.50 | 99.70 | 16 00–17 99 |
| 18 00–19 99 | 30 | 7 | 54 | 2 | ........ | ........ | 84 | 9 | 94.50 | 99.80 | 18 00–19 99 |
| 20 00–24 99 | 30 | 4 | 63 | ........ | ........ | ........ | 93 | 4 | 97.70 | 99.90 | 20 00–24 99 |
| 25 00–29 99 | 9 | 1 | 20 | ........ | 4 | ........ | 33 | 1 | 98.70 | 100.00 | 25 00–29 99 |
| 30 00–34 99 | 7 | ........ | 7 | ........ | ........ | ........ | 14 | ........ | 99.40 | ........ | 30 00–34 99 |
| 35 00–39 99 | 5 | ........ | 6 | ........ | 1 | ........ | 12 | ........ | 99.80 | ........ | 35 00–39 99 |
| 40 00 and over | 3 | ........ | 2 | ........ | 1 | ........ | 6 | ........ | 100.00 | ........ | 40 00 and over |
| Not reported | 5 | 22 | 11 | 25 | 2 | ........ | 18 | 47 | ........ | ........ | Not reported |
| Total | 527 | 3,448 | 2,296 | 1,886 | 71 | 109 | 2,894 | 5,443 | ........ | ........ | Total |

127. TABLE XII, D, a.

NEW YORK STATE

**THE CONFECTIONERY INDUSTRY — FACTORY WORKERS**

NUMBER OF EMPLOYEES FOR EACH SEX CLASSIFIED ACCORDING TO ACTUAL WEEKLY EARNINGS BY THE NUMBER OF YEARS IN THE TRADE

| ACTUAL WEEKLY EARNINGS IN DOLLARS | YEARS IN TRADE | | | | | | | | | | | | | | ACTUAL WEEKLY EARNINGS IN DOLLARS |
|---|---|---|---|---|---|---|---|---|---|---|---|---|---|---|---|
| | LESS THAN 1 | | 1 | | 2 | | 3 | | 4 | | 5 | | 6 | | |
| | Male | Female | Male | Female | Male | Female | Male | Female | Male | Female | Male | Female | Male | Female | |
| Less than $3 00 | 34 | 212 | 5 | 23 | 6 | 17 | 1 | 14 | 4 | 5 | 1 | 4 | ...... | 3 | Less than $3 00 |
| $3 00–$3 49... | 13 | 113 | 1 | 30 | ...... | 16 | ...... | 5 | ...... | 3 | 1 | 3 | ...... | 3 | ...$3 00– 3 49 |
| 3 50– 3 99... | 17 | 160 | 2 | 31 | ...... | 19 | ...... | 4 | 1 | 5 | ...... | 3 | ...... | 1 | ... 3 50– 3 99 |
| 4 00– 4 49... | 14 | 261 | 8 | 69 | 1 | 29 | ...... | 19 | ...... | 7 | 1 | 3 | ...... | 1 | ... 4 00– 4 49 |
| 4 50– 4 99... | 35 | 321 | 9 | 86 | 1 | 41 | 1 | 29 | 2 | 15 | ...... | 7 | ...... | 5 | ... 4 50– 4 99 |
| 5 00– 5 49... | 46 | 405 | 16 | 131 | 4 | 86 | 1 | 50 | 2 | 17 | ...... | 14 | ...... | 11 | ... 5 00– 5 49 |
| 5 50– 5 99... | 35 | 178 | 13 | 118 | 6 | 81 | 2 | 50 | 1 | 25 | 1 | 16 | 1 | 12 | ... 5 50– 5 99 |
| 6 00– 6 49... | 51 | 120 | 14 | 125 | 8 | 92 | 8 | 64 | 2 | 29 | 2 | 20 | 1 | 17 | ... 6 00– 6 49 |
| 6 50– 6 99... | 53 | 44 | 16 | 54 | 13 | 55 | 4 | 56 | 4 | 36 | 3 | 15 | 6 | 11 | ... 6 50– 6 99 |
| 7 00– 7 49... | 83 | 45 | 30 | 52 | 11 | 57 | 12 | 36 | 6 | 35 | 3 | 18 | 4 | 17 | ... 7 00– 7 49 |
| 7 50– 7 99... | 64 | 23 | 24 | 25 | 23 | 28 | 8 | 34 | 7 | 24 | 3 | 21 | 5 | 13 | ... 7 50– 7 99 |
| 8 00– 8 99... | 119 | 30 | 40 | 35 | 33 | 46 | 23 | 34 | 27 | 46 | 19 | 27 | 13 | 28 | ... 8 00– 8 99 |
| 9 00– 9 99... | 61 | 13 | 59 | 12 | 26 | 24 | 19 | 32 | 17 | 25 | 18 | 18 | 8 | 22 | ... 9 00– 9 99 |
| 10 00–10 99... | 40 | 4 | 29 | 8 | 20 | 10 | 27 | 11 | 11 | 13 | 18 | 10 | 17 | 13 | ...10 00–10 99 |
| 11 00–11 99... | 16 | 6 | 22 | 3 | 14 | 1 | 21 | 10 | 20 | 3 | 14 | 3 | 6 | 8 | ...11 00–11 99 |
| 12 00–12 99... | 22 | 3 | 22 | 3 | 16 | 1 | 19 | 4 | 23 | 2 | 13 | 3 | 13 | 3 | ...12 00–12 99 |
| 13 00–13 99... | 12 | ...... | 9 | 1 | 8 | ...... | 9 | 1 | 14 | 1 | 9 | 2 | 9 | 1 | ...13 00–13 99 |
| 14 00–14 99... | 4 | ...... | 8 | ...... | 3 | ...... | 9 | 1 | 12 | 1 | 10 | 2 | 8 | 1 | ...14 00–14 99 |
| 15 00–15 99... | .... | ...... | 3 | ...... | 1 | ...... | 6 | 1 | 8 | ...... | 8 | ...... | 8 | 1 | ...15 00–15 99 |
| 16 00–17 99... | 1 | ...... | .... | ...... | 2 | ...... | 2 | 1 | 1 | ...... | 3 | 2 | 7 | ...... | ...16 00–17 99 |
| 18 00–19 99... | .... | ...... | .... | ...... | 1 | ...... | ...... | ...... | 1 | ...... | 1 | ...... | 3 | 1 | ...18 00–19 99 |
| 20 00–24 99... | 1 | ...... | 1 | ...... | 1 | ...... | ...... | ...... | ...... | ...... | ...... | ...... | 2 | ...... | ...20 00–24 99 |
| 25 00–29 99... | .... | ...... | .... | ...... | ...... | ...... | 1 | ...... | 1 | ...... | ...... | ...... | ...... | ...... | ...30 00–34 99 |
| 30 00–34 99... | .... | ...... | .... | ...... | ...... | ...... | ...... | ...... | ...... | ...... | ...... | ...... | ...... | ...... | ...25 00–29 99 |
| 35 00–39 99... | .... | ...... | .... | ...... | ...... | ...... | 1 | ...... | ...... | ...... | ...... | ...... | ...... | ...... | ...35 00–39 99 |
| 40 00 and over. | .... | ...... | .... | ...... | ...... | ...... | ...... | ...... | ...... | ...... | ...... | ...... | ...... | ...... | .40 00 and over |
| Not reported... | 2 | 23 | 5 | 5 | ...... | 7 | ...... | 1 | 1 | 1 | 1 | 4 | ...... | 1 | ...Not reported |
| Total..... | 723 | 1,961 | 336 | 811 | 198 | 610 | 174 | 457 | 165 | 293 | 129 | 195 | 111 | 173 | .....Total |

NEW YORK STATE

127. TABLE XII, D, a (*continued*) **THE CONFECTIONERY INDUSTRY — FACTORY WORKERS**

NUMBER OF EMPLOYEES FOR EACH SEX CLASSIFIED ACCORDING TO ACTUAL WEEKLY EARNINGS BY THE NUMBER OF YEARS IN THE TRADE

| ACTUAL WEEKLY EARNINGS IN DOLLARS | YEARS IN TRADE (*continued*) | | | | | | | | | | | | | | ACTUAL WEEKLY EARNINGS IN DOLLARS |
|---|---|---|---|---|---|---|---|---|---|---|---|---|---|---|---|
| | 7 | | 8 | | 9 | | 10–14 | | 15–19 | | 20–24 | | 25–29 | | |
| | Male | Female | Male | Female | Male | Female | Male | Female | Male | Female | Male | Female | Male | Female | |
| Less than $3 00 | .... | 1 | 1 | 5 | ...... | 1 | 1 | 2 | ...... | 1 | ...... | ...... | ...... | ...... | Less than $3 00 |
| $3 00–$3 49... | .... | 1 | 1 | 1 | ...... | ...... | 2 | 3 | ...... | ...... | ...... | ...... | ...... | ...... | ...$3 00– 3 49 |
| 3 50– 3 99... | .... | 2 | .... | ...... | ...... | 2 | ...... | 3 | ...... | 1 | ...... | ...... | ...... | ...... | ... 3 50– 3 99 |
| 4 00– 4 49... | .... | 4 | .... | 1 | ...... | 1 | ...... | 2 | ...... | ...... | ...... | ...... | 1 | ...... | ... 4 00– 4 49 |
| 4 50– 4 99... | .... | 2 | .... | 3 | ...... | 4 | 1 | 2 | ...... | 2 | ...... | ...... | ...... | ...... | ... 4 50– 4 99 |
| 5 00– 5 49... | 1 | 1 | 1 | 5 | ...... | 1 | ...... | 10 | 2 | 2 | ...... | 1 | ...... | ...... | ... 5 00– 5 49 |
| 5 50– 5 99... | 1 | 11 | .... | 6 | ...... | ...... | 1 | 10 | 1 | 2 | ...... | 1 | ...... | 2 | ... 5 50– 5 99 |
| 6 00– 6 49... | 1 | 10 | 1 | 9 | 1 | 7 | ...... | 10 | 1 | 3 | ...... | 1 | ...... | 2 | ... 6 00– 6 49 |
| 6 50– 6 99... | 1 | 10 | .... | 10 | ...... | 3 | 3 | 17 | 1 | 3 | 2 | 1 | ...... | 2 | ... 6 50– 6 99 |
| 7 00– 7 49... | 1 | 6 | .... | 13 | ...... | 3 | 3 | 12 | ...... | 5 | 4 | 5 | ...... | 1 | ... 7 00– 7 49 |
| 7 50– 7 99... | 7 | 17 | 2 | 11 | ...... | 10 | 4 | 29 | 2 | 8 | 2 | 1 | ...... | ...... | ... 7 50– 7 99 |
| 8 00– 8 99... | 10 | 30 | 7 | 28 | 1 | 12 | 11 | 45 | 1 | 16 | 6 | 4 | 1 | 2 | ... 8 00– 8 99 |
| 9 00– 9 99... | 8 | 14 | 10 | 22 | 5 | 9 | 20 | 44 | 11 | 20 | 3 | 4 | 3 | 2 | ... 9 00– 9 99 |
| 10 00–10 99... | 8 | 17 | 17 | 17 | 4 | 8 | 22 | 39 | 8 | 27 | 6 | 9 | 5 | 4 | ...10 00–10 99 |
| 11 00–11 99... | 16 | 7 | 10 | 8 | 5 | 6 | 24 | 12 | 5 | 8 | 7 | 7 | 3 | ...... | ...11 00–11 99 |
| 12 00–12 99... | 9 | 5 | 15 | 4 | 11 | 3 | 18 | 10 | 12 | 5 | 10 | 3 | 7 | 1 | ...12 00–12 99 |
| 13 00–13 99... | 15 | 2 | 11 | ...... | 1 | ...... | 19 | 2 | 7 | 3 | 15 | ...... | 5 | 1 | ...13 00–13 99 |
| 14 00–14 99... | 12 | ...... | 8 | ...... | 9 | ...... | 25 | 7 | 5 | ...... | 11 | ...... | 6 | ...... | ...14 00–14 99 |
| 15 00–15 99... | 8 | ...... | 2 | ...... | 9 | ...... | 22 | 1 | 6 | 3 | 16 | 1 | 3 | ...... | ...15 00–15 99 |
| 16 00–17 99... | 10 | ...... | 6 | ...... | 8 | ...... | 38 | 1 | 11 | 3 | 21 | 3 | 9 | ...... | ...16 00–17 99 |
| 18 00–19 99... | 2 | ...... | 2 | 1 | 5 | ...... | 17 | 1 | 14 | ...... | 15 | 5 | 9 | ...... | ...18 00–19 99 |
| 20 00–24 99... | 2 | ...... | 2 | ...... | 2 | ...... | 20 | 2 | 12 | ...... | 15 | 2 | 14 | ...... | ...20 00–24 99 |
| 25 00–29 99... | .... | ...... | 1 | ...... | 1 | ...... | 3 | ...... | 4 | ...... | 9 | 1 | 3 | ...... | ...25 00–29 99 |
| 30 00–34 99... | 1 | ...... | .... | ...... | ...... | ...... | ...... | ...... | 1 | ...... | 5 | ...... | 3 | ...... | ...30 00–34 99 |
| 35 00–39 99... | .... | ...... | .... | ...... | ...... | ...... | 2 | ...... | 3 | ...... | 3 | ...... | ...... | ...... | ...35 00–39 99 |
| 40 00 and over. | .... | ...... | .... | ...... | ...... | ...... | 2 | ...... | ...... | ...... | 1 | ...... | ...... | ...... | 40 00 and over |
| Not reported... | .... | 1 | .... | 1 | 1 | ...... | 4 | 1 | ...... | 1 | 1 | 1 | 2 | ...... | ...Not reported |
| Total..... | 113 | 141 | 97 | 145 | 63 | 70 | 262 | 265 | 107 | 113 | 152 | 50 | 74 | 17 | .....Total |

NEW YORK STATE

127. TABLE XII, D, a — (*concluded*) **THE CONFECTIONERY INDUSTRY — FACTORY WORKERS**

NUMBER OF EMPLOYEES FOR EACH SEX CLASSIFIED ACCORDING TO ACTUAL WEEKLY EARNINGS BY THE NUMBER OF YEARS IN THE TRADE

| ACTUAL WEEKLY EARNINGS IN DOLLARS | YEARS IN TRADE (*concluded*) | | | | | | | | | | | ACTUAL WEEKLY EARNINGS IN DOLLARS |
|---|---|---|---|---|---|---|---|---|---|---|---|---|
| | 30–34 | | 35–44 | | 45 AND OVER | NOT REPORTED | | TOTAL | | CUMULATIVE PER CENT. OF TOTAL | | |
| | Male | Female | Male | Female | Male | Male | Female | Male | Female | Male | Female | |
| Less than $3 00 | ... | ... | ... | ... | ... | 4 | 27 | 57 | 315 | 2.00 | 5.80 | Less than $3 00 |
| $3 00–$3 49 | ... | ... | 1 | ... | ... | 2 | 8 | 21 | 186 | 2.70 | 9.30 | $3 00– 3 49 |
| 3 50– 3 99 | ... | ... | ... | ... | ... | ... | 5 | 20 | 236 | 3.40 | 13.70 | 3 50– 3 99 |
| 4 00– 4 49 | ... | ... | ... | ... | ... | 1 | 16 | 26 | 413 | 4.30 | 21.30 | 4 00– 4 49 |
| 4 50– 4 99 | ... | ... | ... | 1 | ... | 1 | 19 | 50 | 537 | 6.10 | 31.30 | 4 50– 4 99 |
| 5 00– 5 49 | 1 | ... | ... | ... | ... | 3 | 19 | 77 | 753 | 8.70 | 45.20 | 5 00– 5 49 |
| 5 50– 5 99 | ... | 1 | ... | ... | ... | ... | 9 | 62 | 522 | 10.90 | 54.80 | 5 50– 5 99 |
| 6 00– 6 49 | ... | 1 | ... | ... | ... | 5 | 4 | 95 | 514 | 14.50 | 64.40 | 6 00– 6 49 |
| 6 50– 6 99 | ... | ... | 1 | 1 | ... | 3 | 8 | 110 | 326 | 18.00 | 75.50 | 6 50– 6 99 |
| 7 00– 7 49 | 1 | 1 | ... | 1 | ... | 8 | 2 | 166 | 309 | 23.70 | 76.10 | 7 00– 7 49 |
| 7 50– 7 99 | ... | ... | ... | 1 | ... | 4 | 4 | 155 | 249 | 29.20 | 80.80 | 7 50– 7 99 |
| 8 00– 8 99 | ... | ... | 1 | ... | 2 | 5 | 5 | 319 | 388 | 39.20 | 88.00 | 8 00– 8 99 |
| 9 00– 9 99 | 5 | ... | 1 | 1 | 1 | 15 | 3 | 290 | 265 | 50.30 | 92.70 | 9 00– 9 99 |
| 10 00–10 99 | 2 | ... | 3 | 1 | ... | 2 | ... | 239 | 191 | 58.50 | 96.50 | 10 00–10 99 |
| 11 00–11 99 | 2 | ... | ... | ... | 1 | 4 | ... | 190 | 82 | 65.30 | 97.70 | 11 00–11 99 |
| 12 00–12 99 | 2 | ... | 6 | ... | ... | 13 | ... | 231 | 50 | 73.50 | 98.80 | 12 00–12 99 |
| 13 00–13 99 | 2 | ... | 2 | ... | 3 | ... | ... | 150 | 14 | 78.50 | 99.10 | 13 00–13 99 |
| 14 00–14 99 | 1 | ... | 2 | ... | ... | 2 | 1 | 135 | 13 | 83.20 | 99.40 | 14 00–14 99 |
| 15 00–15 99 | 3 | ... | 4 | ... | 4 | 1 | 1 | 112 | 8 | 87.20 | 99.50 | 15 00–15 99 |
| 16 00–17 99 | 2 | 1 | 6 | ... | 1 | 1 | ... | 129 | 11 | 91.50 | 99.70 | 16 00–17 99 |
| 18 00–19 99 | 9 | ... | 4 | ... | 1 | ... | 1 | 84 | 9 | 94.50 | 99.80 | 18 00–19 99 |
| 20 00–24 00 | 14 | ... | 5 | ... | ... | 2 | ... | 93 | 4 | 97.70 | 99.90 | 20 00–24 99 |
| 25 00–29 99 | 5 | ... | 3 | ... | ... | 2 | ... | 33 | 1 | 98.70 | 100.00 | 25 00–29 99 |
| 30 00–34 99 | 2 | ... | ... | ... | 1 | 1 | ... | 14 | ... | 99.40 | ... | 30 00–34 99 |
| 35 00–39 99 | ... | ... | 2 | ... | ... | 1 | ... | 12 | ... | 99.80 | ... | 35 00–39 99 |
| 40 00 and over | 1 | ... | ... | ... | 1 | 1 | ... | 6 | ... | 100.00 | ... | 40 00 and over |
| Not reported | 1 | ... | ... | ... | ... | ... | ... | 18 | 47 | ... | ... | Not reported |
| Total | 53 | 4 | 41 | 6 | 15 | 81 | 132 | 2,894 | 5,443 | ... | ... | Total |

NEW YORK STATE

128 TABLE XIII, D, a THE CONFECTIONERY INDUSTRY — FACTORY WORKERS

NUMBER OF EMPLOYEES FOR EACH SEX, CLASSIFIED ACCORDING TO ACTUAL WEEKLY EARNINGS, BY THE NUMBER OF YEARS IN THE FIRM

| ACTUAL WEEKLY EARNINGS IN DOLLARS | YEARS WITH FIRM | | | | | | | | | | | | | | ACTUAL WEEKLY EARNINGS IN DOLLARS |
|---|---|---|---|---|---|---|---|---|---|---|---|---|---|---|---|
| | LESS THAN 1 | | 1 | | 2 | | 3 | | 4 | | 5 | | 6 | | |
| | Male | Female | Male | Female | Male | Female | Male | Female | Male | Female | Male | Female | Male | Female | |
| Less than $3 00 | 46 | 245 | 2 | 23 | 2 | 16 | 2 | 8 | 3 | 4 | ...... | 2 | ...... | 2 | Less than $3 00 |
| $3 00–$3 49... | 20 | 136 | .... | 25 | ...... | 13 | ...... | 3 | ...... | 3 | 1 | 1 | ...... | ...... | ...$3 00–$3 49 |
| 3 50– 3 99... | 19 | 183 | 1 | 23 | ...... | 18 | ...... | 1 | ...... | 2 | ...... | 3 | ...... | ...... | ....3 50– 3 99 |
| 4 00– 4 49... | 16 | 310 | 7 | 67 | ...... | 14 | ...... | 8 | ...... | 3 | 1 | 1 | ...... | 2 | ....4 00– 4 49 |
| 4 50– 4 99... | 40 | 371 | 6 | 85 | 2 | 33 | ...... | 20 | 2 | 10 | ...... | 5 | ...... | 2 | ....4 50– 4 99 |
| 5 00– 5 49... | 55 | 474 | 13 | 135 | 1 | 61 | 1 | 45 | 2 | 8 | ...... | 4 | ...... | 5 | ....5 00– 5 49 |
| 5 50– 5 99... | 41 | 232 | 12 | 122 | 4 | 71 | 2 | 39 | ...... | 16 | ...... | 10 | 1 | 8 | ....5 50– 5 99 |
| 6 00– 6 49... | 65 | 168 | 15 | 131 | 5 | 83 | 4 | 52 | ...... | 25 | 3 | 16 | ...... | 14 | ....6 00– 6 49 |
| 6 50– 6 99... | 71 | 65 | 14 | 62 | 12 | 56 | 2 | 49 | 2 | 33 | 2 | 10 | 4 | 10 | ....6 50– 6 99 |
| 7 00– 7 49... | 107 | 78 | 28 | 59 | 10 | 47 | 7 | 33 | 3 | 30 | 2 | 13 | 2 | 14 | ....7 00– 7 49 |
| 7 50– 7 99... | 87 | 38 | 26 | 43 | 17 | 34 | 8 | 26 | 5 | 29 | 3 | 18 | 4 | 9 | ....7 50– 7 99 |
| 8 00– 8 99... | 150 | 59 | 47 | 46 | 33 | 55 | 18 | 44 | 18 | 41 | 18 | 25 | 7 | 22 | ....8 00– 8 99 |
| 9 00– 9 99... | 94 | 32 | 64 | 25 | 32 | 36 | 24 | 40 | 13 | 20 | 15 | 17 | 6 | 17 | ....9 00– 9 99 |
| 10 00–10 99... | 61 | 8 | 32 | 17 | 25 | 18 | 31 | 22 | 10 | 12 | 15 | 14 | 16 | 8 | ...10 00–10 99 |
| 11 00–11 99... | 27 | 12 | 35 | 6 | 15 | 3 | 23 | 11 | 17 | 10 | 12 | 5 | 5 | 9 | ...11 00–11 99 |
| 12 00–12 99... | 33 | 8 | 29 | 3 | 22 | 2 | 23 | 5 | 27 | 2 | 16 | 3 | 13 | 4 | ...12 00–12 99 |
| 13 00–13 99... | 21 | 3 | 9 | 1 | 11 | 1 | 12 | ...... | 15 | 1 | 8 | 2 | 10 | 2 | ...13 00–13 99 |
| 14 00–14 99... | 13 | ...... | 9 | 1 | 8 | ...... | 16 | 1 | 14 | 1 | 12 | 2 | 8 | 2 | ...14 00–14 99 |
| 15 00–15 99... | 7 | 1 | 9 | 2 | 4 | ...... | 9 | 1 | 9 | ...... | 11 | ...... | 10 | ...... | ...15 00–15 99 |
| 16 00–17 99... | 17 | ...... | 6 | 1 | 12 | 2 | 6 | 1 | 3 | 1 | 4 | 1 | 4 | 1 | ...16 00–17 99 |
| 18 00–19 99... | 2 | ...... | 5 | ...... | 5 | ...... | 4 | 1 | 3 | 2 | 4 | 1 | 3 | ...... | ...18 00–19 99 |
| 20 00–24 99... | 8 | 1 | 12 | ...... | 4 | ...... | 4 | ...... | 3 | ...... | 2 | ...... | 2 | ...... | ...20 00–24 99 |
| 25 00–29 99... | 1 | ...... | 1 | ...... | 1 | ...... | 2 | ...... | 3 | ...... | 1 | ...... | 2 | ...... | ...25 00–29 99 |
| 30 00–34 99... | .... | ...... | .... | ...... | ...... | ...... | ...... | ...... | ...... | ...... | ...... | ...... | 1 | ...... | ...30 00–34 99 |
| 35 00–39 99... | 1 | ...... | 1 | ...... | ...... | ...... | 1 | ...... | ...... | ...... | 1 | ...... | ...... | ...... | ...35 00–39 99 |
| 40 00 and over. | 3 | ...... | .... | ...... | ...... | ...... | ...... | ...... | ...... | ...... | ...... | ...... | ...... | ...... | .40 00 and over |
| Not reported... | 4 | 25 | 3 | 5 | ...... | 6 | ...... | 3 | 1 | 1 | 3 | 3 | ...... | 1 | ...Not reported |
| Total..... | 1,009 | 2,449 | 386 | 882 | 225 | 569 | 199 | 413 | 153 | 254 | 134 | 158 | 98 | 135 | .....Total |

NEW YORK STATE

128. TABLE XIII, D, a (*continued*) **THE CONFECTIONERY INDUSTRY — FACTORY WORKERS**

NUMBER OF EMPLOYEES FOR EACH SEX, CLASSIFIED ACCORDING TO ACTUAL WEEKLY EARNINGS, BY THE NUMBER OF YEARS IN THE FIRM

| ACTUAL WEEKLY EARNINGS IN DOLLARS | YEARS WITH FIRM (*continued*) | | | | | | | | | | | | ACTUAL WEEKLY EARNINGS IN DOLLARS |
|---|---|---|---|---|---|---|---|---|---|---|---|---|---|
| | 7 | | 8 | | 9 | | 10–14 | | 15–19 | | 20–24 | | |
| | Male | Female | Male | Female | Male | Female | Male | Female | Male | Female | Male | Female | |
| Less than $3 00. | ....... | ....... | ....... | 2 | ....... | ....... | ....... | 2 | ....... | ....... | ....... | ....... | Less than $3 00 |
| $3 00–$3 49.... | ....... | 1 | ....... | ....... | ....... | ....... | ....... | 2 | ....... | ....... | ....... | ....... | ...$3 00–$3 49 |
| 3 50– 3 99.... | ....... | 1 | ....... | ....... | ....... | 2 | ....... | 2 | ....... | ....... | ....... | ....... | ....3 50– 3 99 |
| 4 00– 4 49.... | ....... | 1 | ....... | 1 | ....... | ....... | 1 | 2 | ....... | ....... | ....... | ....... | ....4 00– 4 49 |
| 4 50– 4 99.... | ....... | 1 | ....... | 1 | ....... | 1 | ....... | 1 | ....... | ....... | ....... | ....... | ....4 50– 4 99 |
| 5 00– 5 49.... | 1 | ....... | ....... | 2 | ....... | ....... | ....... | 7 | 1 | ....... | ....... | 1 | ....5 00– 5 49 |
| 5 50– 5 99.... | ....... | 8 | ....... | 2 | ....... | ....... | 1 | 6 | 1 | 1 | ....... | ....... | ....5 50– 5 99 |
| 6 00– 6 49.... | ....... | 7 | ....... | 5 | ....... | 3 | 1 | 5 | ....... | 1 | ....... | 1 | ....6 00– 6 49 |
| 6 50– 6 99.... | ....... | 7 | ....... | 9 | ....... | 3 | 1 | 14 | ....... | 3 | 1 | 1 | ....6 50– 6 99 |
| 7 00– 7 49.... | ....... | 7 | ....... | 9 | ....... | 4 | 2 | 8 | ....... | 3 | 2 | 2 | ....7 00– 7 49 |
| 7 50– 7 99.... | 3 | 13 | ....... | 5 | ....... | 7 | 1 | 25 | 1 | 1 | ....... | ....... | ....7 50– 7 99 |
| 8 00– 8 99.... | 4 | 26 | 6 | 20 | 1 | 11 | 6 | 25 | 1 | 10 | 5 | 2 | ....8 00– 8 99 |
| 9 00– 9 99.... | 6 | 13 | 9 | 15 | 4 | 8 | 14 | 26 | 8 | 11 | ....... | 4 | ....9 00– 9 99 |
| 10 00–10 99.... | 8 | 17 | 11 | 17 | 3 | 7 | 17 | 31 | 1 | 13 | 5 | 4 | ...10 00–10 99 |
| 11 00–11 99.... | 13 | 10 | 7 | 2 | 5 | 5 | 17 | 4 | 3 | 2 | 4 | 3 | ...11 00–11 99 |
| 12 00–12 99.... | 5 | 4 | 13 | 2 | 10 | 4 | 16 | 8 | 8 | 2 | 6 | 2 | ...12 00–12 99 |
| 13 00–13 99.... | 17 | 1 | 7 | ....... | 1 | ....... | 19 | 2 | 5 | ....... | 9 | 1 | ...13 00–13 99 |
| 14 00–14 99.... | 7 | ....... | 10 | ....... | 5 | ....... | 16 | 5 | 6 | ....... | 8 | ....... | ...14 00–14 99 |
| 15 00–15 99.... | 7 | ....... | 5 | ....... | 8 | ....... | 18 | ....... | 6 | 2 | 8 | 1 | ...15 00–15 99 |
| 16 00–17 99.... | 10 | ....... | 7 | ....... | 9 | ....... | 24 | 2 | 13 | 2 | 6 | ....... | ...16 00–17 99 |
| 18 00–19 99.... | 5 | ....... | 2 | ....... | 5 | ....... | 18 | 2 | 8 | 1 | 10 | 2 | ...18 00–19 99 |
| 20 00–24 99.... | 6 | ....... | 2 | ....... | 4 | ....... | 19 | 2 | 9 | ....... | 8 | 1 | ...20 00–24 99 |
| 25 00–29 99.... | ....... | ....... | 2 | ....... | 1 | ....... | 2 | ....... | 6 | ....... | 5 | 1 | ...25 00–29 99 |
| 30 00–34 99.... | 1 | ....... | ....... | ....... | ....... | ....... | 2 | ....... | 4 | ....... | 2 | ....... | ...30 00–34 99 |
| 35 00–39 99.... | ....... | ....... | ....... | ....... | ....... | ....... | 3 | ....... | 2 | ....... | 1 | ....... | ...35 00–39 99 |
| 40 00 and over.. | ....... | ....... | ....... | ....... | ....... | ....... | 1 | ....... | ....... | ....... | ....... | ....... | .40 00 and over |
| Not reported.... | ....... | ....... | 1 | 1 | ....... | ....... | 3 | 1 | ....... | 1 | 2 | ....... | ...Not reported |
| Total...... | 93 | 117 | 82 | 93 | 56 | 55 | 202 | 182 | 83 | 53 | 82 | 26 | .....Total |

NEW YORK STATE

128. TABLE XIII, D, a *(concluded)* **THE CONFECTIONERY INDUSTRY — FACTORY WORKERS**

Number of Employees for Each Sex, Classified According to Actual Weekly Earnings, by the Number of Years in the Firm

| Actual Weekly Earnings in Dollars | Years With Firm *(concluded)* | | | | | | | | Total | | Cumulative per cent of total | | Actual Weekly Earnings in Dollars |
|---|---|---|---|---|---|---|---|---|---|---|---|---|---|
| | 25–29 | | 30–34 | | 35–44 | | Not reported | | | | | | |
| | Male | Female | Male | Female | Male | Female | Male | Female | Male | Female | Male | Female | |
| Less than $3 49. | ...... | ...... | ...... | ...... | ...... | ...... | 2 | 11 | 57 | 315 | 2.00 | 5.80 | Less than $3 00 |
| $3 00–$3 00.... | ...... | ...... | ...... | ...... | ...... | ...... | ...... | 2 | 21 | 186 | 2.70 | 9.30 | ...$3 00–$3 49 |
| 3 50– 3 99.... | ...... | ...... | ...... | ...... | ...... | ...... | ...... | 1 | 20 | 236 | 3.40 | 13.70 | ....3 50– 3 99 |
| 4 00– 4 49.... | ...... | ...... | ...... | ...... | ...... | ...... | 1 | 4 | 26 | 413 | 4.30 | 21.30 | ....4 00– 4 49 |
| 4 50– 4 99.... | ...... | ...... | ...... | ...... | ...... | ...... | ...... | 7 | 50 | 537 | 6.10 | 31.30 | ....4 50– 4 99 |
| 5 00– 5 49.... | ...... | ...... | ...... | ...... | ...... | ...... | 3 | 6 | 77 | 753 | 8.70 | 45.20 | ....5 00– 5 49 |
| 5 50– 5 99.... | ...... | 1 | ...... | 1 | ...... | ...... | ...... | 5 | 62 | 522 | 10.90 | 54.80 | ....5 50– 5 99 |
| 6 00– 6 49.... | ...... | 1 | ...... | ...... | ...... | ...... | 2 | 2 | 95 | 514 | 14.50 | 64.40 | ....6 00– 6 49 |
| 6 50– 6 99.... | ...... | 1 | ...... | ...... | ...... | ...... | 1 | 3 | 110 | 326 | 18.00 | 70.50 | ....6 50– 6 99 |
| 7 00– 7 49.... | ...... | ...... | 1 | 1 | ...... | ...... | 2 | 1 | 166 | 309 | 23.70 | 76.10 | ....7 00– 7 49 |
| 7 50– 7 99.... | ...... | ...... | ...... | ...... | ...... | ...... | ...... | 1 | 155 | 249 | 29.20 | 80.80 | ....7 50– 7 99 |
| 8 00– 8 99.... | 1 | 1 | ...... | ...... | ...... | ...... | 4 | 1 | 319 | 388 | 39.20 | 88.00 | ....8 00– 8 99 |
| 9 00– 9 99.... | ...... | ...... | ...... | ...... | ...... | 1 | 1 | ...... | 290 | 265 | 50.30 | 92.70 | ....9 00– 9 99 |
| 10 00–10 99.... | 1 | 2 | 1 | ...... | 1 | 1 | 1 | ...... | 239 | 191 | 58.50 | 96.50 | ...10 00–10 99 |
| 11 00–11 99.... | 1 | ...... | 1 | ...... | ...... | ...... | 5 | ...... | 190 | 82 | 65.30 | 97.70 | ...11 00–11 99 |
| 12 00–12 99.... | 4 | 1 | 1 | ...... | ...... | ...... | 5 | ...... | 231 | 50 | 73.50 | 98.80 | ...12 00–12 99 |
| 13 00–13 99.... | 3 | ...... | 1 | ...... | 1 | ...... | 1 | ...... | 150 | 14 | 78.50 | 99.10 | ...13 00–13 99 |
| 14 00–14 99.... | 3 | ...... | ...... | ...... | ...... | ...... | ...... | 1 | 135 | 13 | 83.20 | 99.40 | ...14 00–14 99 |
| 15 00–15 99.... | ...... | ...... | 1 | ...... | ...... | ...... | ...... | 1 | 112 | 8 | 87.20 | 99.50 | ...15 00–15 99 |
| 16 00–17 99.... | 5 | ...... | 1 | ...... | 2 | ...... | ...... | ...... | 129 | 11 | 91.50 | 99.70 | ...16 00–17 99 |
| 18 00–19 99.... | 4 | ...... | 6 | ...... | ...... | ...... | ...... | ...... | 84 | 9 | 94.50 | 99.80 | ...18 00–19 99 |
| 20 00–24 99.... | 7 | ...... | 2 | ...... | 1 | ...... | ...... | ...... | 93 | 4 | 97.70 | 99.90 | ...20 00–24 99 |
| 25 00–29 99.... | 2 | ...... | ...... | ...... | 1 | ...... | 3 | ...... | 33 | 1 | 98.70 | 100.00 | ...25 00–29 99 |
| 30 00–34 99.... | 2 | ...... | 1 | ...... | 1 | ...... | ...... | ...... | 14 | ...... | 99.40 | ...... | ...30 00–34 99 |
| 35 00–35 99.... | ...... | ...... | ...... | ...... | 1 | ...... | 1 | ...... | 12 | ...... | 99.80 | ...... | ...35 00–39 99 |
| 40 00 and over.. | ...... | ...... | 1 | ...... | ...... | ...... | 1 | ...... | 6 | ...... | 100.00 | ...... | .40 00 and over |
| Not reported.... | ...... | ...... | ...... | ...... | ...... | ...... | 1 | ...... | 18 | 47 | ...... | ...... | Not reported... |
| Total...... | 33 | 7 | 17 | 2 | 8 | 2 | 34 | 46 | 2,894 | 5,443 | ...... | ...... | .....Total |

NEW YORK STATE

**MEN'S SHIRTS, CONFECTIONERY AND PAPER BOX INDUSTRIES — OFFICE FORCE**

129. **TABLE VII, B, C, D, 6** NUMBER AND PER CENT. OF EMPLOYEES BY SEX ACCORDING TO OCCUPATION AND NATIVITY

| NATIVITY | OCCUPATION | | | | | | | | | | | | | | | | | |
|---|---|---|---|---|---|---|---|---|---|---|---|---|---|---|---|---|---|---|
| | TOTAL | | SUPERIN-TENDENTS | | BOOKKEEPERS | | CLERKS | | SECRETARIES | | STENOG-RAPHERS | | OFFICE BOYS AND GIRLS | | CASHIERS | | TELEPHONE OPERATORS | |
| | Male | Female | Male | Female | Male | Female | Male | Female | Male | Female | Male | Female | Male | Female | Male | Female | Male | Female |
| Native | 439 | 555 | 49 | 4 | 80 | 174 | 266 | 239 | 2 | 1 | 10 | 103 | 24 | 5 | 8 | 4 | ..... | 25 |
| Foreign | 95 | 53 | 9 | ..... | 16 | 27 | 68 | 17 | ..... | ..... | ..... | 8 | 1 | ..... | 1 | ..... | ..... | 1 |
| Not reported | 5 | 3 | 1 | ..... | ..... | ..... | 3 | 3 | ..... | ..... | ..... | ..... | 1 | ..... | ..... | ..... | ..... | ..... |
| Total | 539 | 611 | 59 | 4 | 96 | 201 | 337 | 259 | 2 | 1 | 10 | 111 | 26 | 5 | 9 | 4 | ..... | 26 |
| Per cent. of total | 100 | 100 | 11.0 | .65 | 17.8 | 32.9 | 62.5 | 42.4 | .37 | .16 | 1.86 | 18.2 | 4.8 | .8 | 1.67 | .65 | ..... | 4.24 |

130. TABLE V,B, c, D, e,

NEW YORK STATE

**MEN'S SHIRTS, CONFECTIONERY AND PAPER BOX INDUSTRIES — OFFICE FORCE**

NUMBER AND PER CENT. OF EMPLOYEES EARNING SPECIFIED WEEKLY RATES, BY AGE GROUPS AND SEX

| WEEKLY RATES IN DOLLARS | AGE GROUPS IN YEARS | | | | | | | | | | | | | | WEEKLY RATES IN DOLLARS |
|---|---|---|---|---|---|---|---|---|---|---|---|---|---|---|---|
| | 14–15 | | 16–17 | | 18–20 | | 21–24 | | 25–29 | | 30–34 | | 35–39 | | |
| | Male | Female | Male | Female | Male | Female | Male | Female | Male | Female | Male | Female | Male | Female | |
| Less than $3 00 | 1 | ...... | .... | ...... | ...... | ...... | ...... | ...... | ...... | ...... | ...... | ...... | ...... | ...... | Less than $3 00 |
| $3 00–$3 49... | .... | ...... | 1 | ...... | ...... | ...... | ...... | ...... | ...... | ...... | ...... | ...... | ...... | ...... | ...$3 00– 3 49 |
| 3 50– 3 99... | 1 | ...... | .... | ...... | ...... | ...... | ...... | ...... | ...... | ...... | ...... | ...... | ...... | ...... | ...3 50– 3 99 |
| 4 00– 4 49... | 1 | 2 | 3 | 1 | ...... | 1 | ...... | ...... | ...... | ...... | ...... | ...... | ...... | ...... | ...4 00– 4 49 |
| 4 50– 4 99... | 3 | ...... | 2 | 3 | ...... | 1 | ...... | ...... | ...... | ...... | ...... | ...... | ...... | ...... | ...4 50– 4 99 |
| 5 00– 5 49... | 7 | 2 | 8 | 8 | 2 | 2 | ...... | 1 | ...... | 1 | ...... | ...... | ...... | ...... | ...5 00– 5 49 |
| 5 50– 5 99... | .... | 1 | 1 | 2 | ...... | 1 | ...... | ...... | ...... | ...... | ...... | ...... | ...... | ...... | ...5 50– 5 99 |
| 6 00– 6 49... | 3 | 1 | 17 | 18 | 7 | 17 | ...... | 8 | ...... | 2 | ...... | ...... | ...... | ...... | ...6 00– 6 49 |
| 6 50– 6 99... | 1 | ...... | .... | 6 | 1 | 1 | ...... | ...... | ...... | ...... | ...... | ...... | ...... | ...... | ...6 50– 6 99 |
| 7 00– 7 49... | 1 | 1 | 6 | 8 | 11 | 31 | ...... | 10 | ...... | 5 | ...... | ...... | ...... | ...... | ...7 00– 7 49 |
| 7 50– 7 99... | .... | ...... | 2 | ...... | 1 | 1 | ...... | 2 | ...... | 1 | ...... | ...... | ...... | ...... | ...7 50– 7 99 |
| 8 00– 8 99... | 1 | 1 | 6 | 13 | 18 | 43 | 9 | 24 | 1 | 2 | ...... | 2 | ...... | 1 | ...8 00– 8 99 |
| 9 00– 9 99... | .... | ...... | 2 | 7 | 17 | 24 | 11 | 23 | 2 | 10 | ...... | ...... | 1 | 1 | ...9 00– 9 99 |
| 10 00–10 99... | .... | ...... | 1 | 3 | 27 | 37 | 12 | 26 | 1 | 18 | 1 | 4 | 1 | 1 | ...10 00–10 99 |
| 11 00–11 99... | .... | ...... | .... | 1 | 9 | 11 | 6 | 12 | ...... | 2 | ...... | 2 | ...... | 1 | ...11 00–11 99 |
| 12 00–12 99... | .... | ...... | 1 | ...... | 8 | 15 | 19 | 20 | 2 | 14 | 3 | 8 | ...... | 1 | ...12 00–12 99 |
| 13 00–13 99... | .... | ...... | .... | ...... | 7 | 5 | 5 | 5 | 2 | 7 | 1 | 1 | 1 | 1 | ...13 00–13 99 |
| 14 00–14 99... | .... | ...... | .... | ...... | 1 | 5 | 14 | 10 | 5 | 4 | 4 | 3 | ...... | 1 | ...14 00–14 99 |
| 15 00–15 99... | .... | ...... | .... | ...... | 3 | 2 | 11 | 13 | 10 | 11 | 2 | 4 | 2 | ...... | ...15 00–15 99 |
| 16 00–17 99... | .... | ...... | .... | ...... | 3 | 1 | 13 | 10 | 12 | 6 | 6 | 2 | 6 | 2 | ...16 00–17 99 |
| 18 00–19 99... | .... | ...... | .... | ...... | ...... | ...... | 5 | 4 | 7 | 4 | 3 | 2 | 2 | 1 | ...18 00–19 99 |
| 20 00–24 99... | .... | ...... | .... | ...... | ...... | ...... | 6 | 2 | 17 | 5 | 6 | ...... | 12 | 2 | ...20 00–24 99 |
| 25 00–29 99... | .... | ...... | .... | ...... | 1 | ...... | ...... | 2 | 8 | ...... | 12 | 1 | 6 | ...... | ...25 00–29 99 |
| 30 00–34 99... | .... | ...... | .... | ...... | ...... | ...... | 1 | ...... | 5 | ...... | 5 | ...... | 4 | ...... | ...30 00–34 99 |
| 35 00–39 99... | .... | ...... | .... | ...... | ...... | ...... | ...... | ...... | 2 | ...... | ...... | ...... | 5 | 1 | ...35 00–39 99 |
| 40 00 and over. | .... | ...... | .... | ...... | ...... | ...... | ...... | ...... | 1 | ...... | ...... | ...... | 1 | 1 | .40 00 and over |
| Not reported... | .... | ...... | 1 | 2 | 1 | 4 | ...... | 1 | 1 | 1 | ...... | ...... | ...... | ...... | ...Not reported |
| Total..... | 19 | 8 | 51 | 72 | 117 | 202 | 112 | 173 | 76 | 93 | 43 | 29 | 41 | 14 | .....Total |

130. TABLE V, B, c, D, e — (*concluded*)

NEW YORK STATE

**MEN'S SHIRTS, CONFECTIONERY AND PAPER BOX INDUSTRIES — OFFICE FORCE**

NUMBER AND PER CENT. OF EMPLOYEES EARNING SPECIFIED WEEKLY RATES, BY AGE GROUPS AND SEX

| WEEKLY RATES IN DOLLARS | AGE GROUPS IN YEARS (*concluded*) 40–44 | | 45–54 | | 55–64 | | 65 AND OVER | NOT REPORTED | | TOTAL | | CUMULATIVE PER CENT. OF TOTAL | | WEEKLY RATES IN DOLLARS |
|---|---|---|---|---|---|---|---|---|---|---|---|---|---|---|
| | Male | Female | Male | Female | Male | Female | Male | Male | Female | Male | Female | Male | Female | |
| Less than $3 00 | ...... | ...... | ...... | ...... | ...... | ...... | ...... | ...... | ...... | 1 | ...... | .19 | ...... | Less than $3 00 |
| $3 00–$3 49 | ...... | ...... | ...... | ...... | ...... | ...... | ...... | ...... | ...... | 1 | ...... | .37 | ...... | $3 00– 3 49 |
| 3 50– 3 99 | ...... | ...... | ...... | ...... | ...... | ...... | ...... | ...... | ...... | 1 | ...... | .56 | ...... | 3 50– 3 99 |
| 4 00– 4 49 | ...... | ...... | ...... | ...... | ...... | ...... | ...... | ...... | ...... | 4 | 4 | 1.31 | .67 | 4 00– 4 49 |
| 4 50– 4 99 | ...... | ...... | ...... | ...... | ...... | ...... | ...... | ...... | ...... | 5 | 4 | 2.24 | 1.33 | 4 50– 4 99 |
| 5 00– 5 49 | ...... | ...... | ...... | ...... | ...... | ...... | ...... | ...... | ...... | 17 | 14 | 5.42 | 3.66 | 5 00– 5 49 |
| 5 50– 5 99 | ...... | ...... | ...... | ...... | ...... | ...... | ...... | ...... | ...... | 1 | 4 | 5.61 | 4.35 | 5 50– 5 99 |
| 6 00– 6 49 | ...... | ...... | ...... | ...... | ...... | ...... | ...... | ...... | ...... | 27 | 46 | 10.70 | 12.00 | 6 00– 6 49 |
| 6 50– 6 99 | ...... | ...... | ...... | ...... | ...... | ...... | ...... | ...... | ...... | 2 | 7 | 11.00 | 13.10 | 6 50– 6 99 |
| 7 00– 7 49 | ...... | ...... | ...... | ...... | ...... | ...... | ...... | ...... | ...... | 18 | 55 | 14.40 | 22.30 | 7 00– 7 49 |
| 7 50– 7 99 | ...... | ...... | ...... | ...... | ...... | ...... | ...... | ...... | ...... | 3 | 4 | 15.00 | 23.00 | 7 50– 7 99 |
| 8 00– 8 99 | ...... | 1 | ...... | 1 | ...... | 1 | ...... | ...... | 1 | 35 | 90 | 21.50 | 37.90 | 8 00– 8 99 |
| 9 00– 9 99 | ...... | ...... | 2 | ...... | 1 | ...... | ...... | ...... | 1 | 36 | 66 | 28.20 | 48.90 | 9 00– 9 99 |
| 10 00–10 99 | 1 | ...... | 1 | ...... | ...... | ...... | ...... | 1 | 1 | 46 | 90 | 36.80 | 63.90 | 10 00–10 99 |
| 11 00–11 99 | ...... | 1 | ...... | ...... | ...... | ...... | ...... | ...... | ...... | 15 | 30 | 39.60 | 68.90 | 11 00–11 99 |
| 12 00–12 99 | 3 | 2 | 4 | 1 | ...... | ...... | ...... | ...... | ...... | 40 | 61 | 47.10 | 79.00 | 12 00–12 99 |
| 13 00–13 99 | ...... | ...... | 2 | 1 | ...... | ...... | ...... | ...... | ...... | 18 | 20 | 50.50 | 82.30 | 13 00–13 99 |
| 14 00–14 99 | 1 | 1 | ...... | ...... | 1 | ...... | ...... | ...... | ...... | 26 | 24 | 53.30 | 86.30 | 14 00–14 99 |
| 15 00–15 99 | 2 | 1 | 2 | ...... | ...... | ...... | 2 | ...... | ...... | 34 | 31 | 61.70 | 91.60 | 15 00–15 99 |
| 16 00–17 99 | 3 | 2 | 5 | ...... | ...... | ...... | ...... | ...... | ...... | 48 | 23 | 70.70 | 95.40 | 16 00–17 99 |
| 18 00–19 99 | 1 | ...... | 1 | ...... | ...... | ...... | 1 | ...... | ...... | 20 | 11 | 74.60 | 92.20 | 18 00–19 99 |
| 20 00–24 99 | 6 | ...... | 5 | ...... | 1 | ...... | ...... | ...... | 2 | 53 | 11 | 84.30 | 99.00 | 20 00–24 99 |
| 25 00–29 99 | 6 | ...... | 5 | ...... | 1 | ...... | ...... | 1 | ...... | 40 | 3 | 91.80 | 99.50 | 25 00–29 99 |
| 30 00–34 99 | 3 | ...... | 4 | ...... | ...... | ...... | 2 | ...... | ...... | 24 | ...... | 96.20 | ...... | 30 00–34 99 |
| 35 00–39 99 | 5 | ...... | 3 | ...... | ...... | ...... | ...... | ...... | ...... | 15 | 1 | 99.10 | 99.70 | 35 00–39 99 |
| 40 00 and over | 1 | 1 | 2 | ...... | ...... | ...... | ...... | ...... | ...... | 5 | 2 | 100.00 | 100.00 | 40 00 and over |
| Not reported | ...... | ...... | ...... | ...... | ...... | ...... | ...... | ...... | ...... | 3 | 8 | ...... | ...... | Not reported |
| Total | 32 | 9 | 36 | 3 | 4 | 1 | 5 | 2 | 5 | 538 | 609 | ...... | ...... | Total |

NEW YORK STATE

131. TABLE VIII, B, C, D, 6 **MEN'S SHIRTS, CONFECTIONERY AND PAPER BOX INDUSTRIES — OFFICE FORCE**

Number and Per Cent. of Employees Earning Specified Weekly Rates According to Occupation and Sex

| Weekly Earnings in Dollars | Occupation | | | | | | | | | | | | | | | | | | | | Weekly Earnings in Dollars |
|---|---|---|---|---|---|---|---|---|---|---|---|---|---|---|---|---|---|---|---|---|---|
| | Superintendents | | Bookkeepers | | Clerks | | Secretaries | | Stenographers | | Office Boys and Girls | | Cashiers | | Telephone Operators | Total | | Cumulative Per Cent. of Total | | |
| | Male | Female | Male | Female | Male | Female | Male | Female | Male | Female | Male | Female | Male | Female | Female | Male | Female | Male | Female | |
| Less than $3 00 | .... | ..... | .... | ..... | .... | ..... | .... | ..... | .... | ..... | 1 | ..... | .... | ..... | ....... | 1 | ..... | .19 | ..... | Less than $3 00 |
| $3 00–$3 49... | .... | ..... | .... | ..... | 1 | ..... | .... | ..... | .... | ..... | .... | ..... | .... | ..... | ....... | 1 | ..... | .37 | ..... | ...$3 00– 3 49 |
| 3 50– 3 99... | .... | ..... | .... | ..... | .... | ..... | .... | ..... | .... | ..... | 1 | ..... | .... | ..... | ....... | 1 | ..... | .56 | ..... | ... 3 50– 3 99 |
| 4 00– 4 49... | .... | ..... | .... | ..... | 2 | 3 | .... | ..... | .... | ..... | 2 | 1 | .... | ..... | ....... | 4 | 4 | 1.31 | .67 | ... 4 00– 4 49 |
| 4 50– 4 99... | .... | ..... | .... | ..... | 1 | 4 | .... | ..... | .... | ..... | 4 | ..... | .... | ..... | ....... | 5 | 4 | 2.24 | 1.33 | ... 4 50– 4 99 |
| 5 00– 5 49... | .... | ..... | .... | ..... | 8 | 8 | .... | ..... | .... | 2 | 9 | 2 | .... | ..... | 2 | 17 | 14 | 5.42 | 3.66 | ... 5 00– 5 49 |
| 5 50– 5 99... | .... | ..... | .... | ..... | 1 | 4 | .... | ..... | .... | ..... | .... | ..... | .... | ..... | ....... | 1 | 4 | 5.61 | 4.35 | ... 5 50– 5 99 |
| 6 00– 6 49... | .... | ..... | 1 | 15 | 19 | 20 | .... | ..... | 1 | 6 | 6 | 1 | .... | ..... | 4 | 27 | 46 | 10.70 | 12.00 | ... 6 00– 6 49 |
| 6 50– 6 99... | .... | ..... | .... | 2 | 2 | 4 | .... | ..... | .... | ..... | .... | ..... | .... | ..... | 1 | 2 | 7 | 11.00 | 13.10 | ... 6 50– 6 99 |
| 7 00– 7 49... | .... | ..... | .... | 6 | 17 | 39 | .... | ..... | .... | 9 | 1 | ..... | .... | ..... | 1 | 18 | 55 | 14.40 | 22.30 | ... 7 00– 7 49 |
| 7 50– 7 99... | .... | ..... | .... | 2 | 3 | 2 | .... | ..... | .... | ..... | .... | ..... | .... | ..... | ....... | 3 | 4 | 15.00 | 23.00 | ... 7 50– 7 99 |
| 8 00– 8 99... | .... | ..... | 6 | 23 | 28 | 40 | .... | ..... | 1 | 20 | .... | ..... | .... | ..... | 7 | 35 | 90 | 21.50 | 37.90 | ... 8 00– 8 99 |
| 9 00– 9 99... | 1 | ..... | 3 | 15 | 31 | 34 | .... | ..... | .... | 11 | 1 | ..... | .... | 1 | 5 | 36 | 66 | 28.20 | 48.90 | ... 9 00– 9 99 |
| 10 00–10 99... | .... | ..... | 7 | 22 | 37 | 37 | .... | ..... | 2 | 26 | .... | 1 | .... | 1 | 3 | 46 | 90 | 36.80 | 63.90 | ...10 00–10 99 |
| 11 00–11 99... | .... | ..... | .... | 13 | 15 | 6 | .... | ..... | .... | 11 | .... | ..... | .... | ..... | ....... | 15 | 30 | 39.60 | 68.90 | ...11 00–11 99 |
| 12 00–12 99... | 2 | 2 | 9 | 29 | 27 | 20 | .... | ..... | 2 | 8 | .... | ..... | .... | ..... | 2 | 40 | 61 | 47.10 | 79.00 | ...12 00–12 99 |
| 13 00–13 99... | .... | ..... | 4 | 10 | 13 | 8 | .... | ..... | 1 | 2 | .... | ..... | .... | ..... | ....... | 18 | 20 | 50.50 | 82.30 | ...13 00–13 99 |
| 14 00–14 99... | .... | ..... | 5 | 13 | 19 | 9 | .... | ..... | 1 | 2 | .... | ..... | 1 | ..... | ....... | 26 | 24 | 55.30 | 86.30 | ...14 00–14 99 |
| 15 00–15 99... | 2 | 1 | 8 | 16 | 23 | 6 | .... | ..... | .... | 6 | .... | ..... | 1 | 1 | 1 | 34 | 31 | 61.70 | 91.60 | ...15 00–15 99 |
| 16 00–17 99... | 1 | ..... | 13 | 14 | 32 | 5 | .... | ..... | 1 | 3 | .... | ..... | 1 | 1 | ....... | 48 | 23 | 70.70 | 95.40 | ...16 00–17 99 |
| 18 00–19 99... | .... | ..... | 4 | 8 | 15 | 1 | .... | ..... | .... | 2 | .... | ..... | 1 | ..... | ....... | 20 | 11 | 74.60 | 97.20 | ...18 00–19 99 |
| 20 00–24 99... | 13 | 1 | 16 | 7 | 20 | 2 | 1 | ..... | .... | 1 | .... | ..... | 3 | ..... | ....... | 53 | 11 | 84.30 | 99.00 | ...20 00–24 99 |
| 25 00–29 99... | 14 | ..... | 10 | 1 | 15 | 1 | .... | 1 | 1 | ..... | .... | ..... | .... | ..... | ....... | 40 | 3 | 91.80 | 99.50 | ...25 00–29 99 |
| 30 00–34 99... | 15 | ..... | 4 | ..... | 3 | ..... | 1 | ..... | .... | ..... | .... | ..... | 1 | ..... | ....... | 24 | ..... | 96.20 | ..... | ...30 00–34 99 |
| 35 00–39 99... | 6 | ..... | 5 | 1 | 3 | ..... | .... | ..... | .... | ..... | .... | ..... | 1 | ..... | ....... | 15 | 1 | 99.10 | 99.70 | ...35 00–39 99 |
| 40 00 and over. | 4 | ..... | 1 | ..... | .... | 2 | .... | ..... | .... | ..... | .... | ..... | .... | ..... | ....... | 5 | 2 | 100.00 | 100.00 | .40 00 and over |
| Not reported... | .... | ..... | .... | 3 | 2 | 3 | .... | ..... | .... | 2 | 1 | ..... | .... | ..... | ....... | 3 | 8 | ..... | ..... | ...Not reported |
| Total...... | 58 | 4 | 96 | 200 | 337 | 258 | 2 | 1 | 10 | 111 | 26 | 5 | 9 | 4 | 26 | 538 | 609 | ..... | ..... | .....Total |

NEW YORK STATE

132. TABLE VI, B, C, D, b. **MEN'S SHIRTS, CONFECTIONERY AND PAPER BOX INDUSTRIES — OFFICE FORCE**

NUMBER AND PER CENT. OF EMPLOYEES CLASSIFIED ACCORDING TO ACTUAL WEEKLY EARNINGS BY AGE GROUPS AND SEX

| ACTUAL WEEKLY EARNINGS IN DOLLARS | AGE GROUPS IN YEARS | | | | | | | | | | | | | | ACTUAL WEEKLY EARNINGS IN DOLLARS |
|---|---|---|---|---|---|---|---|---|---|---|---|---|---|---|---|
| | 14–15 | | 16–17 | | 18–20 | | 21–24 | | 25–29 | | 30–34 | | 35–39 | | |
| | Male | Female | Male | Female | Male | Female | Male | Female | Male | Female | Male | Female | Male | Female | |
| Less than $3 00 | .... | ...... | .... | ...... | 1 | 1 | ...... | 1 | ...... | ...... | ...... | ...... | ...... | ...... | Less than $3 00 |
| $3 00–$3 49... | 1 | ...... | .... | ...... | 1 | ...... | ...... | ...... | ...... | ...... | ...... | ...... | ...... | ...... | ...$3 00– 3 49 |
| 3 50– 3 99... | 1 | ...... | .... | ...... | ...... | ...... | ...... | ...... | ...... | ...... | ...... | ...... | ...... | ...... | ... 3 50– 3 99 |
| 4 00– 4 49... | 1 | 2 | 2 | 3 | ...... | 1 | ...... | ...... | ...... | ...... | ...... | ...... | ...... | ...... | ... 4 00– 4 49 |
| 4 50– 4 99... | 3 | ...... | 2 | 1 | 1 | 1 | ...... | 1 | ...... | ...... | ...... | ...... | ...... | ...... | ... 4 50– 4 99 |
| 5 00– 5 49... | 5 | 2 | 6 | 8 | 2 | 3 | ...... | 1 | ...... | 2 | ...... | ...... | ...... | ...... | ... 5 00– 5 49 |
| 5 50– 5 99... | .... | 1 | 1 | 3 | 1 | 2 | ...... | 1 | ...... | ...... | ...... | ...... | ...... | ...... | ... 5 50– 5 99 |
| 6 00– 6 49... | 2 | 1 | 16 | 17 | 5 | 16 | ...... | 7 | 1 | 3 | ...... | ...... | ...... | ...... | ... 6 00– 6 49 |
| 6 50– 6 99... | .... | ...... | 2 | 7 | 2 | 3 | ...... | 2 | ...... | 1 | ...... | ...... | ...... | ...... | ... 6 50– 6 99 |
| 7 00– 7 49... | 3 | 1 | 5 | 9 | 9 | 27 | 3 | 7 | ...... | 4 | ...... | ...... | ...... | ...... | ... 7 00– 7 49 |
| 7 50– 7 99... | .... | ...... | 2 | ...... | 2 | 3 | ...... | 2 | ...... | 1 | ...... | ...... | ...... | ...... | ... 7 50– 7 99 |
| 8 00– 8 99... | .... | 1 | 5 | 13 | 17 | 41 | 8 | 22 | 1 | 4 | ...... | 2 | 1 | 1 | ... 8 00– 8 99 |
| 9 00– 9 99... | .... | ...... | 2 | 6 | 15 | 24 | 10 | 19 | 1 | 7 | ...... | ...... | 1 | 1 | ... 9 00– 9 99 |
| 10 00–10 99... | .... | ...... | 1 | 3 | 23 | 36 | 12 | 22 | ...... | 17 | 1 | 4 | 1 | 1 | ...10 00–10 99 |
| 11 00–11 99... | .... | ...... | .... | 1 | 11 | 10 | 3 | 13 | 1 | 2 | ...... | 3 | ...... | 1 | ...11 00–11 99 |
| 12 00–12 99... | .... | ...... | 1 | ...... | 5 | 16 | 20 | 19 | 3 | 13 | 3 | 8 | ...... | 1 | ...12 00–12 99 |
| 13 00–13 99... | .... | ...... | .... | ...... | 6 | 5 | 4 | 5 | 3 | 5 | 1 | 2 | 1 | 1 | ...13 00–13 99 |
| 14 00–14 99... | .... | ...... | .... | ...... | 1 | 4 | 12 | 10 | 6 | 3 | 3 | 2 | ...... | 1 | ...14 00–14 99 |
| 15 00–15 99... | .... | ...... | .... | ...... | 2 | 3 | 11 | 11 | 8 | 10 | 3 | 3 | 1 | ...... | ...15 00–15 99 |
| 16 00–17 99... | .... | ...... | .... | ...... | 2 | 1 | 12 | 10 | 11 | 6 | 5 | 2 | 7 | 2 | ...16 00–17 99 |
| 18 00–19 99... | .... | ...... | .... | ...... | 2 | ...... | 6 | 4 | 4 | 4 | 2 | 2 | 2 | 1 | ...18 00–19 99 |
| 20 00–24 99... | .... | ...... | .... | ...... | ...... | ...... | 5 | 2 | 18 | 5 | 7 | ...... | 12 | 2 | ...20 00–24 99 |
| 25 00–29 99... | .... | ...... | .... | ...... | 1 | ...... | ...... | 2 | 8 | ...... | 12 | 1 | 6 | ...... | ...25 00–29 99 |
| 30 00–34 99... | .... | ...... | .... | ...... | ...... | ...... | ...... | ...... | 5 | ...... | 4 | ...... | 3 | ...... | ...30 00–34 99 |
| 35 00–39 99... | .... | ...... | .... | ...... | ...... | ...... | ...... | ...... | 1 | ...... | ...... | ...... | 5 | 1 | ...35 00–39 99 |
| 40 00 and over. | .... | ...... | .... | ...... | ...... | ...... | ...... | ...... | 1 | ...... | ...... | ...... | 1 | 1 | .40 00 and over |
| Not reported... | 3 | ...... | 6 | 1 | 8 | 6 | 6 | 12 | 4 | 6 | 2 | 1 | 1 | ...... | ...Not reported |
| Total..... | 19 | 8 | 51 | 72 | 117 | 203 | 112 | 173 | 76 | 93 | 43 | 30 | 42 | 14 | .....Total |

132. TABLE VI, B, C, D, b — (*concluded*) NEW YORK STATE

**MEN'S SHIRTS, CONFECTIONERY AND PAPER BOX INDUSTRIES — OFFICE FORCE**

Number and Per Cent. of Employees Classified According to Actual Weekly Earnings by Age Groups and Sex

| Actual Weekly Earnings in Dollars | Age Groups in Years (*concluded*) | | | | | | | | | | | | | Actual Weekly Earnings in Dollars |
|---|---|---|---|---|---|---|---|---|---|---|---|---|---|---|
| | 40–44 | | 45–54 | | 55–64 | | 65 and over | Not reported | | Total | | Cumulative per cent. of total | | |
| | Male | Female | Male | Female | Male | Female | Male | Male | Female | Male | Female | Male | Female | |
| Less than $3 00 | ...... | ...... | ...... | ...... | ...... | ...... | ...... | ...... | ...... | 1 | 2 | .20 | .34 | Less than $3 00 |
| $3 00–$3 49 | ...... | ...... | ...... | ...... | ...... | ...... | ...... | ...... | ...... | 2 | ...... | .59 | .34 | $3 00– 3 49 |
| 3 50– 3 99 | ...... | ...... | ...... | ...... | ...... | ...... | ...... | ...... | ...... | 1 | ...... | .79 | .34 | 3 50– 3 99 |
| 4 00– 4 49 | ...... | ...... | ...... | ...... | ...... | ...... | ...... | ...... | ...... | 3 | 6 | 1.36 | 1.37 | 4 00– 4 49 |
| 4 50– 4 99 | ...... | ...... | ...... | ...... | ...... | ...... | ...... | ...... | ...... | 6 | 3 | 2.56 | 1.88 | 4 50– 4 99 |
| 5 00– 5 49 | ...... | ...... | ...... | ...... | ...... | ...... | ...... | ...... | ...... | 13 | 16 | 5.19 | 4.62 | 5 00– 5 49 |
| 5 50– 5 99 | ...... | ...... | ...... | ...... | ...... | ...... | ...... | ...... | ...... | 2 | 7 | 5.51 | 5.82 | 5 50– 5 99 |
| 6 00– 6 49 | ...... | ...... | ...... | ...... | ...... | ...... | ...... | ...... | ...... | 24 | 44 | 10.35 | 13.34 | 6 00– 6 49 |
| 6 50– 6 99 | ...... | ...... | ...... | ...... | ...... | ...... | ...... | ...... | ...... | 4 | 13 | 11.15 | 15.56 | 6 50– 6 99 |
| 7 00– 7 49 | ...... | ...... | ...... | ...... | ...... | ...... | ...... | ...... | ...... | 20 | 48 | 15.12 | 23.78 | 7 00– 7 49 |
| 7 50– 7 99 | ...... | ...... | ...... | ...... | ...... | ...... | ...... | ...... | ...... | 4 | 6 | 15.62 | 24.80 | 7 50– 7 99 |
| 8 00– 8 99 | ...... | 1 | 1 | 1 | ...... | 1 | ...... | ...... | 1 | 33 | 88 | 21.80 | 39.98 | 8 00– 8 99 |
| 9 00– 9 99 | ...... | ...... | 2 | ...... | 1 | ...... | ...... | ...... | 1 | 32 | 58 | 28.62 | 49.75 | 9 00– 9 99 |
| 10 00–10 99 | 1 | 1 | ...... | ...... | ...... | ...... | ...... | 1 | 1 | 40 | 85 | 36.60 | 64.30 | 10 00–10 99 |
| 11 00–11 99 | ...... | 1 | ...... | 1 | ...... | ...... | ...... | ...... | ...... | 15 | 32 | 39.50 | 69.90 | 11 00–11 99 |
| 12 00–12 99 | 3 | 1 | 3 | 1 | ...... | ...... | ...... | ...... | ...... | 38 | 59 | 47.10 | 79.90 | 12 00–12 99 |
| 13 00–13 99 | 1 | ...... | 2 | ...... | ...... | ...... | ...... | ...... | ...... | 18 | 18 | 50.60 | 83.00 | 13 00–13 99 |
| 14 00–14 99 | ...... | 1 | 1 | ...... | 1 | ...... | ...... | ...... | ...... | 24 | 21 | 55.40 | 86.60 | 14 00–14 99 |
| 15 00–15 99 | 2 | 1 | 2 | ...... | ...... | ...... | 2 | ...... | ...... | 31 | 28 | 61.50 | 91.30 | 15 00–15 99 |
| 16 00–17 99 | 2 | 2 | 3 | ...... | ...... | ...... | ...... | ...... | ...... | 42 | 23 | 69.75 | 95.25 | 16 00–17 99 |
| 18 00–19 99 | 2 | ...... | 2 | ...... | ...... | ...... | 1 | ...... | ...... | 21 | 11 | 73.95 | 97.30 | 18 00–19 99 |
| 20 00–24 99 | 6 | ...... | 5 | ...... | 1 | ...... | ...... | ...... | 2 | 54 | 11 | 84.90 | 99.00 | 20 00–24 99 |
| 25 00–29 99 | 6 | ...... | 5 | ...... | 1 | ...... | ...... | 1 | ...... | 40 | 3 | 92.75 | 99.50 | 25 00–29 99 |
| 30 00–34 99 | 3 | ...... | 3 | ...... | ...... | ...... | 2 | ...... | ...... | 20 | ...... | 96.70 | 99.50 | 30 00–34 99 |
| 35 00–39 99 | 4 | ...... | 3 | ...... | ...... | ...... | ...... | ...... | ...... | 13 | 1 | 99.00 | 99.65 | 35 00–39 99 |
| 40 00 and over | 1 | 1 | 2 | ...... | ...... | ...... | ...... | ...... | ...... | 5 | 2 | 100.00 | 100.00 | 40 00 and over |
| Not reported | 1 | ...... | 2 | ...... | ...... | ...... | ...... | ...... | ...... | 33 | 26 | ...... | ...... | Not reported |
| Total | 32 | 9 | 36 | 3 | 4 | 1 | 5 | 2 | 5 | 539 | 611 | ...... | ...... | Total |

NEW YORK STATE

133. TABLE IX, B, C, D, b **MEN'S SHIRTS, CONFECTIONERY AND PAPER BOX INDUSTRIES — OFFICE FORCE**

NUMBER AND PER CENT. OF EMPLOYEES CLASSIFIED ACCORDING TO ACTUAL WEEKLY EARNINGS, BY OCCUPATION AND SEX

| ACTUAL WEEKLY EARNINGS IN DOLLARS | OCCUPATION | | | | | | | | | | | | | | | | | | | | ACTUAL WEEKLY EARNINGS IN DOLLARS |
|---|---|---|---|---|---|---|---|---|---|---|---|---|---|---|---|---|---|---|---|---|---|
| | SUPERINTENDENTS | | BOOKKEEPERS | | CLERKS | | SECRETARIES | | STENOGRAPHERS | | OFFICE BOYS AND GIRLS | | CASHIERS | | TELEPHONE OPERATORS | TOTAL | | CUMULATIVE PER CENT. OF TOTAL | | |
| | Male | Female | Male | Female | Male | Female | Male | Female | Male | Female | Male | Female | Male | Female | Female | Male | Female | Male | Female | |
| Less than $3 00 | .... | .... | .... | .... | 1 | 2 | .... | .... | .... | .... | .... | .... | .... | .... | .... | 1 | 2 | .20 | .34 | Less than $3 00 |
| $3 00–$3 49 | .... | .... | .... | .... | 1 | .... | .... | .... | .... | .... | 1 | .... | .... | .... | .... | 2 | .... | .59 | .34 | $3 00– 3 49 |
| 3 50– 3 99 | .... | .... | .... | .... | .... | .... | .... | .... | .... | .... | 1 | .... | .... | .... | .... | 1 | .... | .79 | .34 | 3 50– 3 99 |
| 4 00– 4 49 | .... | .... | .... | .... | 1 | 5 | .... | .... | .... | .... | 2 | 1 | .... | .... | .... | 3 | 6 | 1.36 | 1.37 | 4 00– 4 49 |
| 4 50– 4 99 | .... | .... | .... | .... | 2 | 3 | .... | .... | .... | .... | 4 | .... | .... | .... | .... | 6 | 3 | 2.56 | 1.88 | 4 50– 4 99 |
| 5 00– 5 49 | .... | .... | .... | .... | 7 | 10 | .... | .... | .... | 2 | 6 | 2 | .... | .... | 2 | 13 | 16 | 5.14 | 4.62 | 5 00– 5 49 |
| 5 50– 5 99 | .... | .... | .... | 1 | 2 | 4 | .... | .... | .... | .... | .... | 1 | .... | .... | 1 | 2 | 7 | 5.51 | 5.82 | 5 50– 5 99 |
| 6 00– 6 49 | .... | .... | 1 | 15 | 18 | 20 | .... | .... | 1 | 6 | 4 | .... | .... | .... | 3 | 24 | 44 | 10.35 | 13.34 | 6 00– 6 49 |
| 6 50– 6 99 | .... | .... | .... | 2 | 3 | 9 | .... | .... | .... | 1 | 1 | .... | .... | .... | 1 | 4 | 13 | 11.15 | 15.56 | 6 50– 6 99 |
| 7 00– 7 49 | .... | .... | 1 | 6 | 17 | 32 | .... | .... | 1 | 9 | 1 | .... | .... | .... | 1 | 20 | 48 | 15.12 | 23.78 | 7 00– 7 49 |
| 7 50– 7 99 | .... | .... | .... | 2 | 4 | 3 | .... | .... | .... | 1 | .... | .... | .... | .... | .... | 4 | 6 | 15.62 | 24.80 | 7 50– 7 99 |
| 8 00– 8 99 | .... | .... | 5 | 26 | 28 | 39 | .... | .... | .... | 19 | .... | .... | .... | .... | 4 | 33 | 88 | 21.80 | 39.98 | 8 00– 8 99 |
| 9 00– 9 99 | 1 | .... | 3 | 15 | 26 | 28 | .... | .... | 1 | 10 | 1 | .... | .... | 1 | 4 | 32 | 58 | 28.62 | 49.75 | 9 00– 9 99 |
| 10 00–10 99 | 1 | .... | 6 | 20 | 32 | 34 | .... | .... | 1 | 26 | .... | 1 | .... | 1 | 3 | 40 | 85 | 36.60 | 64.30 | 10 00–10 99 |
| 11 00–11 99 | .... | .... | 1 | 15 | 14 | 6 | .... | .... | .... | 11 | .... | .... | .... | .... | .... | 15 | 32 | 39.50 | 69.90 | 11 00–11 99 |
| 12 00–12 99 | 2 | 2 | 9 | 28 | 25 | 18 | .... | .... | 2 | 9 | .... | .... | .... | .... | 2 | 38 | 59 | 47.10 | 79.90 | 12 00–12 99 |
| 13 00–13 99 | .... | .... | 4 | 9 | 13 | 8 | .... | .... | 1 | 1 | .... | .... | .... | .... | .... | 18 | 18 | 50.60 | 83.00 | 13 00–13 99 |
| 14 00–14 99 | .... | .... | 5 | 12 | 17 | 7 | .... | .... | 1 | 2 | .... | .... | 1 | .... | .... | 24 | 21 | 55.40 | 86.60 | 14 00–14 99 |
| 15 00–15 99 | 2 | 1 | 8 | 15 | 20 | 7 | .... | .... | .... | 3 | .... | .... | 1 | 1 | 1 | 31 | 28 | 61.50 | 91.20 | 15 00–15 99 |
| 16 00–17 99 | 1 | .... | 13 | 14 | 26 | 5 | .... | .... | 1 | 3 | .... | .... | 1 | 1 | .... | 42 | 23 | 69.75 | 95.25 | 16 00–17 99 |
| 18 00–19 99 | .... | .... | 4 | 8 | 17 | 1 | .... | .... | .... | 2 | .... | .... | .... | .... | .... | 21 | 11 | 73.95 | 97.30 | 18 00–19 99 |
| 20 00–24 99 | 12 | 1 | 16 | 7 | 21 | 2 | 1 | .... | .... | 1 | .... | .... | 4 | .... | .... | 54 | 11 | 84.90 | 99.00 | 20 00–24 99 |
| 25 00–29 99 | 14 | .... | 9 | 1 | 16 | 1 | 1 | 1 | .... | .... | .... | .... | .... | .... | .... | 40 | 3 | 92.75 | 99.50 | 25 00–29 99 |
| 30 00–34 99 | 13 | .... | 4 | .... | 2 | .... | .... | .... | .... | .... | .... | .... | 1 | .... | .... | 20 | .... | 96.70 | 99.50 | 30 00–34 99 |
| 35 00–39 99 | 6 | .... | 4 | 1 | 2 | .... | .... | .... | .... | .... | .... | .... | 1 | .... | .... | 13 | 1 | 99.00 | 99.65 | 35 00–39 99 |
| 40 00 and over | 4 | .... | 1 | .... | .... | 2 | .... | .... | .... | .... | .... | .... | .... | .... | .... | 5 | 2 | 100.00 | 100.00 | 40 00 and over |
| Not reported | 3 | .... | 2 | 4 | 22 | 13 | .... | .... | 1 | 5 | 5 | .... | .... | .... | 4 | 33 | 26 | .... | .... | Not reported |
| Total | 59 | 4 | 96 | 201 | 337 | 259 | 2 | 1 | 10 | 111 | 26 | 5 | 9 | 4 | 26 | 539 | 611 | .... | .... | Total |

NEW YORK STATE

134. TABLE X, B, C, D, b. **MEN'S SHIRTS, CONFECTIONERY AND PAPER BOX INDUSTRIES — OFFICE FORCE**

NUMBER AND PER CENT. OF EMPLOYEES CLASSIFIED ACCORDING TO ACTUAL WEEKLY EARNINGS BY CONJUGAL CONDITION AND SEX

| ACTUAL WEEKLY EARNINGS IN DOLLARS | CONJUGAL CONDITION | | | | | | | | | | | | ACTUAL WEEKLY EARNINGS IN DOLLARS |
|---|---|---|---|---|---|---|---|---|---|---|---|---|---|
| | SINGLE | | MARRIED | | WIDOWED OR DIVORCED | | NOT REPORTED | | TOTAL | | CUMULATIVE PER CENT. OF TOTAL | | |
| | Male | Female | Male | Female | Male | Female | Male | Female | Male | Female | Male | Female | |
| Less than $3 00. | 1 | 2 | ....... | ....... | ....... | ....... | ....... | ....... | 1 | 2 | .20 | .34 | Less than $3 00 |
| $3 00–$3 49.... | 2 | ....... | ....... | ....... | ....... | ....... | ....... | ....... | 2 | ....... | .59 | .34 | ...$3 00– 3 49 |
| 3 50– 3 99.... | 1 | ....... | ....... | ....... | ....... | ....... | ....... | ....... | 1 | ....... | .79 | .34 | ... 3 50– 3 99 |
| 4 00– 4 49.... | 3 | 6 | ....... | ....... | ....... | ....... | ....... | ....... | 3 | 6 | 1.36 | 1.37 | ... 4 00– 4 49 |
| 4 50– 4 99.... | 6 | 2 | ....... | ....... | ....... | ....... | ....... | 1 | 6 | 3 | 2.56 | 1.88 | ... 4 50– 4 99 |
| 5 00– 5 49.... | 13 | 14 | ....... | ....... | ....... | ....... | ....... | 2 | 13 | 16 | 5.14 | 4.62 | ... 5 00– 5 49 |
| 5 50– 5 99.... | 2 | 7 | ....... | ....... | ....... | ....... | ....... | ....... | 2 | 7 | 5.51 | 5.82 | ... 5 50– 5 99 |
| 6 00– 6 49.... | 23 | 44 | 1 | ....... | ....... | ....... | ....... | ....... | 24 | 44 | 10.35 | 13.34 | ... 6 00– 6 49 |
| 6 50– 6 99.... | 4 | 13 | ....... | ....... | ....... | ....... | ....... | ....... | 4 | 13 | 11.15 | 15.56 | ... 6 50– 6 99 |
| 7 00– 7 49.... | 18 | 46 | 1 | 1 | ....... | ....... | 1 | 1 | 20 | 48 | 15.12 | 23.78 | ... 7 00– 7 49 |
| 7 50– 7 99.... | 4 | 6 | ....... | ....... | ....... | ....... | ....... | ....... | 4 | 6 | 15.62 | 24.80 | ... 7 50– 7 99 |
| 8 00– 8 99.... | 30 | 84 | 3 | 2 | ....... | 1 | ....... | 1 | 33 | 88 | 21.80 | 39.98 | ... 8 00– 8 99 |
| 9 00– 9 99.... | 23 | 56 | 6 | ....... | ....... | 1 | 3 | 1 | 32 | 58 | 28.62 | 49.75 | ... 9 00– 9 99 |
| 10 00–10 99.... | 33 | 82 | 5 | 2 | ....... | 1 | 2 | ....... | 40 | 85 | 36.60 | 64.30 | ...10 00–10 99 |
| 11 00–11 99.... | 15 | 28 | ....... | 2 | ....... | 1 | ....... | 1 | 15 | 32 | 39.50 | 69.90 | ...11 00–11 99 |
| 12 00–12 99.... | 31 | 55 | 5 | 2 | 2 | 2 | ....... | ....... | 38 | 59 | 47.10 | 79.90 | ...12 00–12 99 |
| 13 00–13 99.... | 14 | 17 | 4 | ....... | ....... | 1 | ....... | ....... | 18 | 18 | 50.60 | 83.00 | ...13 00–13 99 |
| 14 00–14 99.... | 17 | 19 | 7 | 1 | ....... | ....... | ....... | 1 | 24 | 21 | 55.40 | 86.60 | ...14 00–14 99 |
| 15 00–15 99.... | 22 | 27 | 8 | ....... | 1 | ....... | ....... | 1 | 31 | 28 | 61.50 | 91.30 | ...15 00–15 99 |
| 16 00–17 99.... | 19 | 22 | 21 | ....... | ....... | ....... | 2 | 1 | 42 | 23 | 69.75 | 95.25 | ...16 00–17 99 |
| 18 00–19 99.... | 14 | 11 | 6 | ....... | 1 | ....... | ....... | ....... | 21 | 11 | 73.95 | 97.30 | ...18 00–19 99 |
| 20 00–24 99.... | 18 | 10 | 34 | ....... | 1 | ....... | 1 | 1 | 54 | 11 | 84.90 | 99.00 | ...20 00–24 99 |
| 25 00–29 99.... | 8 | 2 | 30 | 1 | 1 | ....... | 1 | ....... | 40 | 3 | 92.75 | 99.50 | ...25 00–29 99 |
| 30 00–34 99.... | 4 | ....... | 14 | ....... | 1 | ....... | 1 | ....... | 20 | ....... | 96.70 | 99.50 | ...30 00–34 99 |
| 35 00–39 99.... | 2 | 1 | 9 | ....... | 2 | ....... | ....... | ....... | 13 | 1 | 99.00 | 99.65 | ...35 00–39 99 |
| 40 00 and over.. | ....... | 2 | 5 | ....... | ....... | ....... | ....... | ....... | 5 | 2 | 100.00 | 100.00 | .40 00 and over |
| Not reported.... | 26 | 25 | 6 | 1 | ....... | ....... | 1 | ....... | 33 | 26 | ....... | ....... | ...Not reported |
| Total...... | 353 | 581 | 165 | 12 | 9 | 7 | 12 | 11 | 539 | 611 | ....... | ....... | .....Total |

NEW YORK STATE

135. TABLE XI, B, C, D, b. **MEN'S SHIRTS, CONFECTIONERY AND PAPER BOX INDUSTRIES — OFFICE FORCE**

NUMBER AND PER CENT. OF EMPLOYEES CLASSIFIED ACCORDING TO ACTUAL WEEKLY EARNINGS BY NATIVITY AND SEX

| ACTUAL WEEKLY EARNINGS IN DOLLARS | NATIVITY | | | | | | | | | | ACTUAL WEEKLY EARNINGS IN DOLLARS |
|---|---|---|---|---|---|---|---|---|---|---|---|
| | NATIVE | | FOREIGN | | NOT REPORTED | | TOTAL | | CUMULATIVE PER CENT. OF TOTAL | | |
| | Male | Female | Male | Female | Male | Female | Male | Female | Male | Female | |
| Less than $3 00 | 1 | 2 | ........ | ........ | ........ | ........ | 1 | 2 | .20 | .34 | Less than $3 00 |
| $3 00–$3 49 | 2 | ........ | ........ | ........ | ........ | ........ | 2 | ........ | .59 | .34 | $3 00– 3 49 |
| 3 50– 3 99 | ........ | ........ | 1 | ........ | ........ | ........ | 1 | ........ | .79 | .34 | 3 50– 3 99 |
| 4 00– 4 49 | 3 | 5 | ........ | ........ | ........ | 1 | 3 | 6 | 1.36 | 1.37 | 4 00– 4 49 |
| 4 50– 4 99 | 6 | 2 | ........ | 1 | ........ | ........ | 6 | 3 | 2.56 | 1.88 | 4 50– 4 99 |
| 5 00– 5 49 | 12 | 12 | 1 | 4 | ........ | ........ | 13 | 16 | 5.14 | 4.62 | 5 00– 5 49 |
| 5 50– 5 99 | 1 | 7 | 1 | ........ | ........ | ........ | 2 | 7 | 5.51 | 5.82 | 5 50– 5 99 |
| 6 00– 6 49 | 18 | 38 | 6 | 6 | ........ | ........ | 24 | 44 | 10.35 | 13.34 | 6 00– 6 49 |
| 6 50– 6 99 | 1 | 11 | 3 | 2 | ........ | ........ | 4 | 13 | 11.15 | 15.56 | 6 50– 6 99 |
| 7 00– 7 49 | 15 | 44 | 5 | 4 | ........ | ........ | 20 | 48 | 15.12 | 23.78 | 7 00– 7 49 |
| 7 50– 7 99 | 4 | 6 | ........ | ........ | ........ | ........ | 4 | 6 | 15.62 | 24.80 | 7 50– 7 99 |
| 8 00– 8 99 | 28 | 83 | 5 | 5 | ........ | ........ | 33 | 88 | 21.80 | 39.98 | 8 00– 8 99 |
| 9 00– 9 99 | 27 | 53 | 5 | 4 | ........ | 1 | 32 | 58 | 28.62 | 49.75 | 9 00– 9 99 |
| 10 00–10 99 | 33 | 80 | 6 | 5 | 1 | ........ | 40 | 85 | 36.60 | 64.30 | 10 00–10 99 |
| 11 00–11 99 | 13 | 27 | 2 | 5 | ........ | ........ | 15 | 32 | 39.50 | 69.90 | 11 00–11 99 |
| 12 00–12 99 | 28 | 53 | 10 | 6 | ........ | ........ | 38 | 59 | 47.10 | 79.90 | 12 00–12 99 |
| 13 00–13 99 | 15 | 17 | 3 | 1 | ........ | ........ | 18 | 18 | 50.60 | 83.00 | 13 00–13 99 |
| 14 00–14 99 | 21 | 20 | 3 | 1 | ........ | ........ | 24 | 21 | 55.40 | 86.60 | 14 00–14 99 |
| 15 00–15 99 | 26 | 25 | 5 | 3 | ........ | ........ | 31 | 28 | 61.50 | 91.30 | 15 00–15 99 |
| 16 00–17 99 | 33 | 20 | 9 | 3 | ........ | ........ | 42 | 23 | 69.75 | 95.25 | 16 00–17 99 |
| 18 00–19 99 | 19 | 10 | 2 | 1 | ........ | ........ | 21 | 11 | 73.95 | 97.30 | 18 00–19 99 |
| 20 00–24 99 | 40 | 9 | 14 | 2 | ........ | ........ | 54 | 11 | 84.90 | 99.00 | 20 00–24 99 |
| 25 00–29 99 | 32 | 3 | 7 | ........ | 1 | ........ | 40 | 3 | 92.75 | 99.50 | 25 00–29 99 |
| 30 00–34 99 | 17 | ........ | 3 | ........ | ........ | ........ | 20 | ........ | 96.70 | 99.50 | 30 00–34 99 |
| 35 00–39 00 | 9 | 1 | 3 | ........ | 1 | ........ | 13 | 1 | 99.00 | 99.65 | 35 00–39 99 |
| 40 00 and over | 4 | 2 | 1 | ........ | ........ | ........ | 5 | 2 | 100.00 | 100.00 | 40 00 and over |
| Not reported | 31 | 25 | ........ | ........ | 2 | 1 | 33 | 26 | ........ | ........ | Not reported |
| Total | 439 | 555 | 95 | 53 | 5 | 3 | 539 | 611 | ........ | ........ | Total |

NEW YORK STATE

136. TABLE XII, B, C, D, b. **MEN'S SHIRTS, CONFECTIONERY AND PAPER BOX INDUSTRIES — OFFICE FORCE**

Number of Employees for Each Sex, Classified According to Actual Weekly Earnings, by the Number of Years in the Trade

| Actual Weekly Earnings in Dollars | Years in Trade | | | | | | | | | | | | | | Actual Weekly Earnings in Dollars |
|---|---|---|---|---|---|---|---|---|---|---|---|---|---|---|---|
| | Less than 1 | | 1 | | 2 | | 3 | | 4 | | 5 | | 6 | | |
| | Male | Female | Male | Female | Male | Female | Male | Female | Male | Female | Male | Female | Male | Female | |
| Less than $3 00 | .... | ...... | .... | 1 | 1 | ...... | ...... | ...... | ...... | ...... | ...... | ...... | ...... | ...... | Less than $3 00 |
| $3 00–$3 49... | .... | ...... | 1 | ...... | ...... | ...... | ...... | ...... | ...... | ...... | ...... | ...... | 1 | ...... | ...$3 00– 3 49 |
| 3 50– 3 99... | 1 | ...... | .... | ...... | ...... | ...... | ...... | ...... | ...... | ...... | ...... | ...... | ...... | ...... | ....3 50– 3 99 |
| 4 00– 4 49... | 2 | 3 | 1 | 2 | ...... | ...... | ...... | ...... | ...... | ...... | ...... | ...... | ...... | ...... | ....4 00– 4 49 |
| 4 50– 4 99... | 4 | 2 | 2 | ...... | ...... | ...... | ...... | ...... | ...... | ...... | ...... | 1 | ...... | ...... | ....4 50– 4 99 |
| 5 00– 5 49... | 9 | 8 | 2 | 3 | 1 | 3 | ...... | ...... | ...... | 2 | ...... | ...... | ...... | ...... | ....5 00– 5 49 |
| 5 50– 5 99... | 2 | 3 | .... | 2 | ...... | ...... | ...... | 1 | ...... | 1 | ...... | ...... | ...... | ...... | ....5 50– 5 99 |
| 6 00– 6 49... | 15 | 22 | 7 | 5 | 2 | 5 | ...... | 4 | ...... | 4 | ...... | 2 | ...... | 1 | ....6 00– 6 49 |
| 6 50– 6 99... | 1 | 4 | 3 | 3 | ...... | ...... | ...... | 2 | ...... | 1 | ...... | ...... | ...... | 1 | ....6 50– 6 99 |
| 7 00– 7 49... | 10 | 13 | 7 | 9 | 1 | 9 | ...... | 10 | 1 | 2 | 1 | 2 | ...... | 1 | ....7 00– 7 49 |
| 7 50– 7 99... | .... | ...... | .... | 4 | 3 | ...... | 1 | 1 | ...... | ...... | ...... | 1 | ...... | ...... | ....7 50– 7 99 |
| 8 00– 8 99... | 9 | 13 | 6 | 22 | 8 | 17 | 3 | 10 | 4 | 10 | ...... | 2 | ...... | 5 | ....8 00– 8 99 |
| 9 00– 9 99... | 5 | 5 | 8 | 10 | 9 | 10 | 2 | 5 | 2 | 7 | 1 | 5 | 2 | 4 | ....9 00– 9 99 |
| 10 00–10 99... | 10 | 10 | 7 | 5 | 3 | 15 | 4 | 18 | 4 | 11 | 3 | 4 | 2 | 6 | ...10 00–10 99 |
| 11 00–11 99... | .... | 1 | 2 | 1 | 4 | 5 | 5 | 6 | 3 | 4 | ...... | 4 | 1 | 2 | ...11 00–11 99 |
| 12 00–12 99... | 4 | 1 | 2 | 4 | 5 | 5 | 5 | 7 | 4 | 9 | 3 | 7 | 2 | 5 | ...12 00–12 99 |
| 13 00–13 99... | .... | ...... | 2 | 2 | 3 | ...... | 1 | 3 | 1 | 3 | 3 | 1 | 1 | ...... | ...13 00–13 99 |
| 14 00–14 99... | 3 | 1 | 1 | 1 | 4 | 1 | 2 | 1 | 3 | 4 | 2 | 2 | 3 | 3 | ...14 00–14 99 |
| 15 00–15 99... | 1 | 1 | 4 | ...... | 5 | 1 | 6 | 2 | 1 | 3 | 2 | 2 | 1 | 1 | ...15 00–15 99 |
| 16 00–17 99... | .... | 1 | 1 | 2 | 1 | 1 | 2 | ...... | 3 | 2 | 5 | 1 | 2 | 1 | ...16 00–17 99 |
| 18 00–19 99... | .... | 1 | 1 | ...... | ...... | 1 | 2 | ...... | ...... | ...... | 3 | ...... | 1 | 2 | ...18 00–19 99 |
| 20 00–24 99... | 3 | ...... | 1 | ...... | 6 | ...... | 2 | ...... | 1 | ...... | 4 | ...... | 3 | ...... | ...20 00–24 99 |
| 25 00–29 99... | .... | ...... | 3 | ...... | 2 | ...... | 2 | ...... | ...... | ...... | 1 | ...... | ...... | 1 | ...25 00–29 99 |
| 30 00–34 99... | 1 | ...... | .... | ...... | 2 | ...... | ...... | ...... | 3 | ...... | ...... | ...... | ...... | ...... | ...30 00–34 99 |
| Not reported... | 9 | 1 | 6 | 3 | 3 | 2 | 3 | 4 | 2 | 2 | 1 | 4 | 3 | 1 | ...Not reported |
| Total..... | 89 | 90 | 67 | 79 | 63 | 75 | 40 | 74 | 32 | 65 | 29 | 38 | 22 | 34 | .....Total |

136. TABLE XII, B, C, D, b — (*continued*)

NEW YORK STATE

**MEN'S SHIRTS, CONFECTIONERY AND PAPER BOX INDUSTRIES — OFFICE FORCE**

NUMBER OF EMPLOYEES FOR EACH SEX, CLASSIFIED ACCORDING TO ACTUAL WEEKLY EARNINGS, BY THE NUMBER OF YEARS IN THE TRADE

| ACTUAL WEEKLY EARNINGS IN DOLLARS | YEARS IN TRADE (*continued*) | | | | | | | | | | | | ACTUAL WEEKLY EARNINGS IN DOLLARS |
|---|---|---|---|---|---|---|---|---|---|---|---|---|---|
| | 7 | | 8 | | 9 | | 10–14 | | 15–19 | | 20–24 | | |
| | Male | Female | Male | Female | Male | Female | Male | Female | Male | Female | Male | Female | |
| $6 50–$6 99 | ....... | ....... | ....... | ....... | ....... | ....... | ....... | 1 | ....... | ....... | ....... | ....... | $6 50–$6 99 |
| 7 00– 7 49 | ....... | ....... | ....... | 2 | ....... | ....... | ....... | ....... | ....... | ....... | ....... | ....... | 7 00– 7 49 |
| 8 00– 8 99 | ....... | 2 | 1 | 2 | ....... | 1 | ....... | ....... | ....... | ....... | 1 | 1 | 8 00– 8 99 |
| 9 00– 9 99 | ....... | 4 | 1 | 2 | ....... | ....... | 1 | 2 | ....... | ....... | ....... | ....... | 9 00– 9 99 |
| 10 00–10 99 | ....... | 4 | 1 | ....... | 1 | 1 | 1 | 7 | ....... | 2 | ....... | ....... | 10 00–10 99 |
| 11 00–11 99 | ....... | 3 | ....... | ....... | ....... | 3 | ....... | 1 | ....... | 1 | ....... | 1 | 11 00–11 99 |
| 12 00–12 99 | 4 | 5 | 1 | 5 | ....... | ....... | 4 | 9 | 1 | ....... | ....... | 1 | 12 00–12 99 |
| 13 00–13 99 | 1 | 2 | 1 | 2 | 1 | ....... | 2 | 3 | ....... | 2 | 2 | ....... | 13 00–13 99 |
| 14 00–14 99 | 4 | 1 | 1 | 3 | ....... | ....... | 1 | 1 | ....... | 2 | ....... | 1 | 14 00–14 99 |
| 15 00–15 99 | 2 | 2 | 1 | 7 | 1 | ....... | 2 | 7 | 1 | 2 | ....... | ....... | 15 00–15 99 |
| 16 00–17 99 | 2 | 2 | 4 | 5 | 3 | 2 | 8 | 3 | 4 | 3 | 5 | ....... | 16 00–17 99 |
| 18 00–19 99 | 2 | 1 | 1 | ....... | ....... | 1 | 4 | 2 | 3 | 3 | 1 | ....... | 18 00–19 99 |
| 20 00–24 99 | 3 | 1 | ....... | ....... | 2 | ....... | 10 | 7 | 7 | 3 | 6 | ....... | 20 00–24 99 |
| 25 00–29 99 | ....... | ....... | 2 | 1 | 1 | 1 | 9 | ....... | 6 | ....... | 4 | ....... | 25 00–29 99 |
| 30 00–34 99 | 1 | ....... | 1 | ....... | ....... | ....... | 5 | ....... | 2 | ....... | 1 | ....... | 30 00–34 99 |
| 35 00–39 99 | ....... | ....... | ....... | ....... | 1 | ....... | 2 | ....... | 1 | ....... | 1 | 1 | 35 00–39 99 |
| 40 00 and over | ....... | ....... | ....... | ....... | 1 | ....... | ....... | ....... | ....... | 1 | 2 | 1 | 40 00 and over |
| Not reported | ....... | 3 | 2 | 3 | ....... | 1 | 1 | 2 | ....... | ....... | ....... | ....... | Not reported |
| Total | 19 | 30 | 17 | 32 | 11 | 10 | 50 | 45 | 25 | 19 | 23 | 6 | Total |

136. TABLE XII, B, C, D, b — (*concluded*)

NEW YORK STATE

**MEN'S SHIRTS, CONFECTIONERY AND PAPER BOX INDUSTRIES — OFFICE FORCE**

NUMBER OF EMPLOYEES FOR EACH SEX, CLASSIFIED ACCORDING TO ACTUAL WEEKLY EARNINGS, BY THE NUMBER OF YEARS IN THE TRADE

| ACTUAL WEEKLY EARNINGS IN DOLLARS | YEARS IN TRADE (*concluded*) | | | | | | | | | | | | ACTUAL WEEKLY EARNINGS IN DOLLARS |
|---|---|---|---|---|---|---|---|---|---|---|---|---|---|
| | 25–29 | | 30–34 | | 35–44 | | NOT REPORTED | | TOTAL | | CUMULATIVE PER CENT. OF TOTAL | | |
| | Male | Female | Male | Female | Male | Female | Male | Female | Male | Female | Male | Female | |
| Less than $3 00 | ...... | ...... | ...... | ...... | ...... | ...... | ...... | 1 | 1 | 2 | .20 | .34 | Less than $3 00 |
| $3 00–$3 49 | ...... | ...... | ...... | ...... | ...... | ...... | ...... | ...... | 2 | ...... | .59 | .34 | $3 00– 3 49 |
| 3 50– 3 99 | ...... | ...... | ...... | ...... | ...... | ...... | ...... | ...... | 1 | ...... | .79 | .34 | 3 50– 3 99 |
| 4 00– 4 49 | ...... | ...... | ...... | ...... | ...... | ...... | ...... | 1 | 3 | 6 | 1.36 | 1.37 | 4 00– 4 99 |
| 4 50– 4 99 | ...... | ...... | ...... | ...... | ...... | ...... | ...... | ...... | 6 | 3 | 2.56 | 1.88 | 4 50– 4 99 |
| 5 00– 5 49 | ...... | ...... | ...... | ...... | ...... | ...... | 1 | ...... | 13 | 16 | 5.14 | 4.62 | 5 00– 5 49 |
| 5 50– 5 99 | ...... | ...... | ...... | ...... | ...... | ...... | ...... | ...... | 2 | 7 | 5.51 | 5.82 | 5 50– 5 99 |
| 6 00– 6 49 | ...... | ...... | ...... | ...... | ...... | ...... | ...... | 1 | 24 | 44 | 10.35 | 13.34 | 6 00– 6 49 |
| 6 50– 6 99 | ...... | ...... | ...... | ...... | ...... | ...... | ...... | 1 | 4 | 13 | 11.15 | 15.56 | 6 50– 6 99 |
| 7 00– 7 49 | ...... | ...... | ...... | ...... | ...... | ...... | ...... | ...... | 20 | 48 | 15.12 | 23.78 | 7 00– 7 49 |
| 7 50– 7 99 | ...... | ...... | ...... | ...... | ...... | ...... | ...... | ...... | 4 | 6 | 15.62 | 24.80 | 7 50– 7 99 |
| 8 00– 8 99 | 1 | 1 | ...... | ...... | ...... | 1 | ...... | 1 | 33 | 88 | 21.80 | 39.98 | 8 00– 8 49 |
| 9 00– 9 99 | ...... | ...... | ...... | ...... | ...... | ...... | 1 | 4 | 32 | 58 | 28.62 | 49.75 | 9 00– 9 99 |
| 10 00–10 99 | ...... | ...... | ...... | ...... | ...... | ...... | 4 | 2 | 40 | 85 | 36.60 | 64.30 | 10 00–10 99 |
| 11 00–11 99 | ...... | ...... | ...... | ...... | ...... | ...... | ...... | ...... | 15 | 32 | 39.50 | 69.90 | 11 00–11 99 |
| 12 00–12 99 | 1 | ...... | 1 | ...... | ...... | ...... | 1 | 1 | 38 | 59 | 47.10 | 79.90 | 12.00–12 99 |
| 13 00–13 99 | ...... | ...... | ...... | ...... | ...... | ...... | ...... | ...... | 18 | 18 | 50.60 | 83.00 | 13 00–13 99 |
| 14 00–14 99 | ...... | ...... | ...... | ...... | ...... | ...... | ...... | ...... | 24 | 21 | 55.40 | 86.60 | 14 00–14 99 |
| 15 00–15 99 | 3 | ...... | 1 | ...... | ...... | ...... | ...... | ...... | 31 | 28 | 61.50 | 91.30 | 15 00–15 99 |
| 16 00–17 99 | 1 | ...... | 1 | ...... | ...... | ...... | ...... | ...... | 42 | 23 | 69.75 | 95.25 | 16 00–17 99 |
| 18 00–19 99 | ...... | ...... | 1 | ...... | ...... | ...... | 2 | ...... | 21 | 11 | 73.95 | 97.30 | 18 00–19 99 |
| 20 00–24 99 | 2 | ...... | ...... | ...... | 1 | ...... | 3 | ...... | 54 | 11 | 84.90 | 99.00 | 20 00–24 99 |
| 25 00–29 99 | 5 | ...... | 2 | ...... | 1 | ...... | 2 | ...... | 40 | 3 | 92.75 | 99.50 | 25 00–29 99 |
| 30 00–34 99 | 3 | ...... | ...... | ...... | 1 | ...... | ...... | ...... | 20 | ...... | 96.70 | 99.50 | 30 00–34 99 |
| 35 00–39 99 | 6 | ...... | 1 | ...... | 1 | ...... | ...... | ...... | 13 | 1 | 99.00 | 99.65 | 35 00–39 99 |
| 40 00 and over | ...... | ...... | 1 | ...... | 1 | ...... | ...... | ...... | 5 | 2 | 100.00 | 100.00 | 40 00 and over |
| Not reported | ...... | ...... | ...... | ...... | ...... | ...... | 3 | ...... | 33 | 26 | ...... | ...... | Not reported |
| Total | 22 | 1 | 8 | ...... | 5 | 1 | 17 | 12 | 539 | 611 | ...... | ...... | Total |

137. TABLE XIII, B, C, D, b.

NEW YORK STATE

**MEN'S SHIRTS, CONFECTIONERY AND PAPER BOX INDUSTRIES — OFFICE FORCE**

NUMBER OF EMPLOYEES FOR EACH SEX, CLASSIFIED ACCORDING TO ACTUAL WEEKLY EARNINGS, BY THE NUMBER OF YEARS WITH THE FIRM

| ACTUAL WEEKLY EARNINGS IN DOLLARS | YEARS WITH FIRM | | | | | | | | | | | | | | ACTUAL WEEKLY EARNINGS IN DOLLARS |
|---|---|---|---|---|---|---|---|---|---|---|---|---|---|---|---|
| | LESS THAN 1 | | 1 | | 2 | | 3 | | 4 | | 5 | | 6 | | |
| | Male | Female | Male | Female | Male | Female | Male | Female | Male | Female | Male | Female | Male | Female | |
| Less than $3 00 | .... | ...... | .... | 1 | 1 | 1 | ...... | ...... | ...... | ...... | ...... | ...... | ...... | ...... | Less than $3 00 |
| $3 00–$3 49... | .... | ...... | 1 | ...... | ...... | ...... | ...... | ...... | ...... | ...... | ...... | ...... | 1 | ...... | ...$3 00– 3 49 |
| 3 50– 3 99... | 1 | ...... | .... | ...... | ...... | ...... | ...... | ...... | ...... | ...... | ...... | ...... | ...... | ...... | ....3 50– 3 99 |
| 4 00– 4 49... | 2 | 3 | 1 | 2 | ...... | ...... | ...... | ...... | ...... | ...... | ...... | ...... | ...... | ...... | ....4 00– 4 49 |
| 4 50– 4 99... | 4 | 2 | 2 | ...... | ...... | ...... | ...... | ...... | ...... | ...... | ...... | 1 | ...... | ...... | ....4 50– 4 99 |
| 5 00– 5 49... | 11 | 8 | 2 | 3 | ...... | 3 | ...... | ...... | ...... | 2 | ...... | ...... | ...... | ...... | ....5 00– 5 49 |
| 5 50– 5 99... | 2 | 3 | .... | 3 | ...... | ...... | ...... | 1 | ...... | ...... | ...... | ...... | ...... | ...... | ....5 50– 5 99 |
| 6 00– 6 49... | 18 | 30 | 6 | 3 | ...... | 4 | ...... | 3 | ...... | 1 | ...... | 2 | ...... | 1 | ....6 00– 6 49 |
| 6 50– 6 99... | 1 | 5 | 3 | 4 | ...... | ...... | ...... | 2 | ...... | 1 | ...... | ...... | ...... | ...... | ....6 50– 6 99 |
| 7 00– 7 49... | 12 | 21 | 6 | 12 | 1 | 3 | 1 | 8 | ...... | 1 | ...... | ...... | ...... | 1 | ....7 00– 7 49 |
| 7 50– 7 99... | .... | 2 | .... | 2 | 2 | ...... | 2 | 1 | ...... | ...... | ...... | 1 | ...... | ...... | ....7 50– 7 99 |
| 8 00– 8 99... | 18 | 26 | 5 | 21 | 3 | 16 | 3 | 5 | 2 | 6 | ...... | 1 | 1 | 5 | ....8 00– 8 99 |
| 9 00– 9 99... | 10 | 17 | 7 | 14 | 6 | 10 | 1 | 6 | 4 | 2 | 1 | 4 | 1 | 2 | ....9 00– 9 99 |
| 10 00–10 99... | 19 | 24 | 7 | 10 | 3 | 11 | 4 | 12 | 1 | 11 | 2 | 3 | 1 | 4 | ...10 00–10 99 |
| 11 00–11 99... | 1 | 4 | 3 | 4 | 4 | 3 | 4 | 4 | 2 | 4 | ...... | 4 | 1 | 2 | ...11 00–11 99 |
| 12 00–12 99... | 7 | 8 | 5 | 5 | 4 | 10 | 6 | 4 | 2 | 8 | 4 | 3 | 2 | 6 | ...12 00–12 99 |
| 13 00–13 99... | .... | 2 | 2 | 3 | 4 | 2 | 2 | 2 | ...... | 2 | 2 | 1 | 1 | ...... | ...13 00–13 99 |
| 14 00–14 99... | 3 | 1 | 3 | 2 | 4 | 4 | 5 | 1 | 3 | 3 | 3 | 1 | 2 | 2 | ...14 00–14 99 |
| 15 00–15 99... | 3 | 2 | 4 | 1 | 10 | 5 | 5 | 3 | 1 | 2 | ...... | 1 | 2 | ...... | ...15 00–15 99 |
| 16 00–17 99... | 4 | 2 | 2 | 2 | 2 | 3 | 2 | 4 | 3 | 2 | 5 | 1 | 5 | 1 | ...16 00–17 99 |
| 18 00–19 99... | .... | 2 | 2 | ...... | 1 | 2 | 4 | 1 | 2 | 1 | 4 | ...... | ...... | ...... | ...18 00–19 99 |
| 20 00–24 99... | 4 | ...... | 3 | 1 | 6 | 1 | 3 | ...... | 2 | ...... | 5 | ...... | 5 | ...... | ...20 00–24 99 |
| 25 00–29 99... | 5 | ...... | 3 | ...... | 5 | ...... | 1 | ...... | 1 | ...... | 2 | ...... | 1 | 1 | ...25 00–29 99 |
| 30 00–34 99... | 3 | ...... | .... | ...... | 2 | ...... | 1 | ...... | 3 | ...... | 1 | ...... | ...... | ...... | ...30 00–34 99 |
| 35 00–39 99... | .... | ...... | 1 | ...... | ...... | ...... | 1 | ...... | ...... | ...... | 1 | ...... | 1 | ...... | ...35 00–39 99 |
| 40 00 and over. | .... | ...... | 1 | ...... | ...... | ...... | ...... | ...... | ...... | ...... | ...... | ...... | ...... | ...... | 40 00 and over |
| Not reported... | 11 | 5 | 6 | 2 | 2 | 3 | 4 | 2 | 3 | 2 | ...... | 4 | 3 | ...... | ...Not reported |
| Total..... | 139 | 167 | 75 | 95 | 60 | 81 | 49 | 59 | 29 | 48 | 30 | 27 | 27 | 25 | .....Total |

137. TABLE XIII, B, C, D, b — (*continued*)

NEW YORK STATE

**MEN'S SHIRTS, CONFECTIONERY AND PAPER BOX INDUSTRIES — OFFICE FORCE**

NUMBER OF EMPLOYEES FOR EACH SEX, CLASSIFIED ACCORDING TO ACTUAL WEEKLY EARNINGS, BY THE NUMBER OF YEARS WITH THE FIRM

| ACTUAL WEEKLY EARNINGS IN DOLLARS | YEARS WITH FIRM | | | | | | | | | | | | ACTUAL WEEKLY EARNINGS IN DOLLARS |
|---|---|---|---|---|---|---|---|---|---|---|---|---|---|
| | 7 | | 8 | | 9 | | 10–14 | | 15–19 | | 20–24 | | |
| | Male | Female | Male | Female | Male | Female | Male | Female | Male | Female | Male | Female | |
| $6 50–$6 99.... | ....... | ....... | ....... | ....... | ....... | ....... | ....... | 1 | ....... | ....... | ....... | ....... | ...$6 50–$6 99 |
| 7 00– 7 49.... | ....... | 1 | ....... | 1 | ....... | ....... | ....... | ....... | ....... | ....... | ....... | ....... | ....7 00– 7 49 |
| 8 00– 8 99.... | ....... | 3 | ....... | 1 | ....... | 1 | 1 | 1 | ....... | ....... | ....... | 1 | ....8 00– 8 99 |
| 9 00– 9 99.... | ....... | ....... | 1 | 2 | ....... | ....... | 1 | ....... | ....... | ....... | ....... | ....... | ....9 00– 9 99 |
| 10 00–10 99.... | 1 | 1 | 1 | 1 | 1 | 1 | ....... | 4 | ....... | 1 | ....... | ....... | ...10 00–10 99 |
| 11 00–11 99.... | ....... | 2 | ....... | ....... | ....... | 3 | ....... | 1 | ....... | 1 | ....... | ....... | ...11 00–11 99 |
| 12 00–12 99.... | 4 | 6 | ....... | 3 | ....... | 1 | 4 | 4 | ....... | 1 | ....... | ....... | ...12 00–12 99 |
| 13 00–13 99.... | 1 | 2 | 2 | ....... | 1 | 1 | 1 | 1 | ....... | 2 | 2 | ....... | ...13 00–13 99 |
| 14 00–14 99.... | 1 | ....... | ....... | 3 | ....... | ....... | ....... | 1 | ....... | 1 | ....... | 1 | ...14 00–14 99 |
| 15 00–15 99.... | 1 | 4 | ....... | 5 | 1 | 1 | 1 | 4 | ....... | ....... | ....... | ....... | ...15 00–15 99 |
| 16 00–17 99.... | 1 | 2 | 4 | 3 | 4 | ....... | 5 | 1 | 2 | 2 | 2 | ....... | ...16 00–17 99 |
| 18 00–19 99.... | 1 | ....... | 1 | 1 | ....... | 1 | 3 | 1 | 2 | 2 | 1 | ....... | ...18 00–19 99 |
| 20 00–24 99.... | 4 | 1 | 1 | ....... | 2 | ....... | 8 | 6 | 4 | 2 | 6 | ....... | ...20 00–24 99 |
| 25 00–29 99.... | ....... | ....... | ....... | 1 | 1 | 1 | 11 | ....... | 4 | ....... | 3 | ....... | ...25 00–29 99 |
| 30·00–34 99.... | ....... | ....... | ....... | ....... | ....... | ....... | 1 | ....... | 4 | ....... | 2 | ....... | ...30 00–34 99 |
| 35 00–39 99.... | ....... | ....... | ....... | ....... | 1 | ....... | 2 | 1 | 4 | ....... | ....... | ....... | ...35 00–39 99 |
| 40 00 and over.. | ....... | ....... | ....... | ....... | 1 | ....... | 1 | 1 | ....... | ....... | 2 | 1 | .40 00 and over |
| Not reported.... | ....... | 3 | 3 | 3 | ....... | ....... | 1 | 2 | ....... | ....... | ....... | ....... | .Not reported.. |
| Total...... | 14 | 25 | 13 | 24 | 12 | 10 | 40 | 29 | 20 | 12 | 18 | 3 | .....Total |

137. TABLE XIII, B, C, D, b — (*concluded*) NEW YORK STATE

**MEN'S SHIRTS, CONFECTIONERY AND PAPER BOX INDUSTRIES — OFFICE FORCE**

NUMBER OF EMPLOYEES FOR EACH SEX, CLASSIFIED ACCORDING TO ACTUAL WEEKLY EARNINGS, BY THE NUMBER OF YEARS WITH THE FIRM

| ACTUAL WEEKLY EARNINGS IN DOLLARS | YEARS WITH FIRM (*concluded*) | | | | | | | | | | ACTUAL WEEKLY EARNINGS IN DOLLARS |
|---|---|---|---|---|---|---|---|---|---|---|---|
| | 25–29 | 30–34 | 35–44 | | NOT REPORTED | | TOTAL | | CUMULATIVE PER CENT. OF TOTAL | | |
| | Male | Male | Male | Female | Male | Female | Male | Female | Male | Female | |
| Less than $3 00 | ........ | ........ | ........ | ........ | ........ | ........ | 1 | 2 | .20 | .34 | Less than $3 00 |
| $3 00–$3 49 | ........ | ........ | ........ | ........ | ........ | ........ | 2 | ........ | .59 | .34 | $3 00– 3 49 |
| 3 50– 3 99 | ........ | ........ | ........ | ........ | ........ | ........ | 1 | ........ | .79 | .34 | 3 50– 3 99 |
| 4 00– 4 49 | ........ | ........ | ........ | ........ | ........ | 1 | 3 | 6 | 1.36 | 1.37 | 4 00– 4 49 |
| 4 50– 4 99 | ........ | ........ | ........ | ........ | ........ | ........ | 6 | 3 | 2.56 | 1.88 | 4 50– 4 99 |
| 5 00– 5 49 | ........ | ........ | ........ | ........ | ........ | ........ | 13 | 16 | 5.14 | 4.62 | 5 00– 5 49 |
| 5 50– 5 99 | ........ | ........ | ........ | ........ | ........ | ........ | 2 | 7 | 5.51 | 5.82 | 5 50– 5 99 |
| 6 00– 6 49 | ........ | ........ | ........ | ........ | ........ | ........ | 24 | 44 | 10.35 | 13.34 | 6 00– 6 49 |
| 6 50– 6 99 | ........ | ........ | ........ | ........ | ........ | ........ | 4 | 13 | 11.15 | 15.56 | 6 50– 6 99 |
| 7 00– 7 49 | ........ | ........ | ........ | ........ | ........ | ........ | 20 | 48 | 15.12 | 23.78 | 7 00– 7 49 |
| 7 50– 7 99 | ........ | ........ | ........ | ........ | ........ | ........ | 4 | 6 | 15.62 | 24.80 | 7 50– 7 99 |
| 8 00– 8 99 | ........ | ........ | ........ | 1 | ........ | ........ | 33 | 88 | 21.80 | 39.98 | 8 00– 8 99 |
| 9 00– 9 99 | ........ | ........ | ........ | ........ | ........ | 1 | 32 | 58 | 28.62 | 49.75 | 9 00– 9 99 |
| 10 00–10 99 | ........ | ........ | ........ | ........ | ........ | 2 | 40 | 85 | 36.60 | 64.30 | 10 00–10 99 |
| 11 00–11 99 | ........ | ........ | ........ | ........ | ........ | ........ | 15 | 32 | 39.50 | 69.90 | 11 00–11 99 |
| 12 00–12 99 | ........ | ........ | ........ | ........ | ........ | ........ | 38 | 59 | 47.10 | 79.90 | 12 00–12 99 |
| 13 00–13 99 | ........ | ........ | ........ | ........ | ........ | ........ | 18 | 18 | 50.60 | 83.00 | 13 00–13 99 |
| 14 00–14 99 | ........ | ........ | ........ | ........ | ........ | 1 | 24 | 21 | 55.40 | 86.60 | 14 00–14 99 |
| 15 00–15 99 | 2 | 1 | ........ | ........ | ........ | ........ | 31 | 28 | 61.50 | 91.30 | 15 00–15 99 |
| 16 00–17 99 | ........ | 1 | ........ | ........ | ........ | ........ | 42 | 23 | 69.75 | 95.25 | 16 00–17 99 |
| 18 00–19 99 | ........ | ........ | ........ | ........ | ........ | ........ | 21 | 11 | 73.95 | 97.30 | 18 00–19 99 |
| 20 00–24 99 | 1 | ........ | ........ | ........ | ........ | ........ | 54 | 11 | 84.90 | 99.00 | 20 00–24 99 |
| 25 00–29 99 | 1 | ........ | 1 | ........ | 1 | ........ | 40 | 3 | 92.75 | 99.50 | 25 00–29 99 |
| 30 00–34 99 | 2 | ........ | 1 | ........ | ........ | ........ | 20 | ........ | 96.70 | 99.50 | 30 00–34 99 |
| 35 00–39 99 | ........ | 1 | ........ | ........ | 1 | ........ | 13 | 1 | 99.00 | 99.65 | 35 00–39 99 |
| 40 00 and over | ........ | ........ | ........ | ........ | ........ | ........ | 5 | 2 | 100.00 | 100.00 | 40 00 and over |
| Not reported | ........ | ........ | ........ | ........ | ........ | ........ | 33 | 26 | ........ | ........ | Not reported |
| Total | 6 | 3 | 2 | 1 | 2 | 5 | 539 | 611 | ........ | ........ | Total |

NEW YORK STATE

**MEN'S SHIRTS, CONFECTIONERY AND PAPER BOX INDUSTRIES — SHIPPING AND DELIVERY**

138. TABLE VII, B, C, D, c. NUMBER AND PER CENT. OF EMPLOYEES BY SEX ACCORDING TO OCCUPATION AND NATIVITY

| NATIVITY | OCCUPATION | | | | | | | | | | | | | NATIVITY |
|---|---|---|---|---|---|---|---|---|---|---|---|---|---|---|
| | TOTAL | | FOREMEN | CLERKS AND ROUTERS | | DRIVERS | WAGON BOYS AND HELPERS | CHAUFFEURS | GENERAL LABOR | | PACKING | | STABLEMEN | |
| | Male | Female | Male | Male | Female | Male | Male | Male | Male | Female | Male | Female | Male | |
| Native.......... | 779 | 54 | 19 | 335 | 49 | 153 | 79 | 28 | 30 | 3 | 134 | 2 | 1 | ..........Native |
| Foreign.......... | 450 | 10 | 11 | 172 | 10 | 79 | 40 | 6 | 44 | ...... | 98 | ...... | ...... | ..........Foreign |
| Not reported...... | 14 | 1 | ...... | 3 | ...... | 2 | ...... | ...... | 4 | ...... | 5 | 1 | ...... | .....Not reported |
| Total........ | 1,243 | 65 | 30 | 510 | 59 | 234 | 119 | 34 | 78 | 3 | 237 | 3 | 1 | .......Total |
| Per Cent of Total.. | 100.00 | 100.00 | 2.42 | 41.00 | 90.80 | 18.80 | 9.60 | 2.70 | 6.30 | 4.60 | 19.10 | 4.60 | 0.08 | .Per Cent of Total |

NEW YORK STATE

MEN'S SHIRTS, CONFECTIONERY AND PAPER BOX INDUSTRIES — SHIPPING AND DELIVERY

139. TABLE V, B, C, D, c. NUMBER AND PER CENT. OF EMPLOYEES EARNING SPECIFIED WEEKLY RATES BY AGE GROUPS AND SEX

| WEEKLY RATES IN DOLLARS | AGE GROUPS IN YEARS | | | | | | | | | | | | | | WEEKLY RATES IN DOLLARS |
|---|---|---|---|---|---|---|---|---|---|---|---|---|---|---|---|
| | 14–15 | | 16–17 | | 18–20 | | 21–24 | | 25–29 | | 30–34 | | 35–39 | | |
| | Male | Female | Male | Female | Male | Female | Male | Female | Male | Female | Male | Female | Male | Female | |
| $3 00–$3 49... | 1 | ...... | 2 | ...... | ...... | ...... | ...... | ...... | ...... | ...... | ...... | ...... | ...... | ...... | ...$3 00–$3 49 |
| 3 50– 3 99... | 1 | ...... | .... | ...... | ...... | ...... | ...... | ...... | ...... | ...... | ...... | ...... | ...... | ...... | ... 3 50– 3 99 |
| 4 00– 4 49... | 3 | ...... | 2 | 1 | ...... | ...... | 1 | ...... | ...... | ...... | 1 | ...... | ...... | ...... | ... 4 00– 4 49 |
| 4 50– 4 99... | 9 | ...... | 3 | ...... | 1 | ...... | 1 | ...... | ...... | ...... | ...... | ...... | ...... | ...... | ... 4 50– 4 99 |
| 5 00– 5 49... | 5 | ...... | 26 | 1 | 7 | 1 | 1 | ...... | 2 | ...... | ...... | ...... | 1 | ...... | ... 5 00– 5 49 |
| 5 50– 5 99... | 4 | ...... | 14 | 3 | ...... | 3 | ...... | 1 | ...... | ...... | ...... | ...... | ...... | ...... | ... 5 50– 5 99 |
| 6 00– 6 49... | 2 | ...... | 36 | 2 | 28 | 6 | 4 | 1 | 1 | 2 | ...... | 1 | ...... | 1 | ... 6 00– 6 49 |
| 6 50– 6 99... | .... | ...... | 3 | ...... | 6 | 3 | 1 | 1 | ...... | ...... | ...... | ...... | ...... | ...... | ... 6 50– 6 99 |
| 7 00– 7 49... | 2 | ...... | 11 | 2 | 40 | 6 | 11 | 1 | 4 | ...... | 2 | ...... | ...... | 1 | ... 7 00– 7 49 |
| 7 50– 7 99... | .... | ...... | 3 | ...... | 9 | ...... | 2 | 2 | 1 | 1 | ...... | ...... | 1 | ...... | ... 7 50– 7 99 |
| 8 00– 8 99... | .... | 1 | 6 | ...... | 45 | 4 | 19 | 2 | 2 | ...... | 4 | 1 | 1 | ...... | ... 8 00– 8 99 |
| 9 00– 9 99... | .... | ...... | 1 | ...... | 42 | ...... | 26 | ...... | 8 | 1 | 5 | ...... | 4 | 1 | ... 9 00– 9 99 |
| 10 00–10 99... | .... | ...... | .... | ...... | 23 | ...... | 52 | 2 | 16 | ...... | 7 | 2 | 5 | ...... | ...10 00–10 99 |
| 11 00–11 99... | .... | ...... | 2 | ...... | 11 | ...... | 28 | 1 | 24 | 1 | 11 | 1 | 4 | ...... | ...11 00–11 99 |
| 12 00–12 99... | .... | ...... | .... | ...... | 12 | ...... | 43 | ...... | 38 | ...... | 13 | ...... | 13 | 1 | ...12 00–12 99 |
| 13 00–13 99... | .... | ...... | .... | ...... | 5 | ...... | 20 | ...... | 28 | ...... | 13 | ...... | 13 | ...... | ...13 00–13 99 |
| 14 00–14 99... | .... | ...... | .... | ...... | 1 | ...... | 4 | ...... | 11 | ...... | 14 | ...... | 14 | ...... | ...14 00–14 99 |
| 15 00–15 99... | .... | ...... | .... | ...... | 1 | ...... | 10 | ...... | 24 | ...... | 14 | ...... | 11 | ...... | ...15 00–15 99 |
| 16 00–17 99... | .... | ...... | .... | ...... | 3 | ...... | 11 | ...... | 10 | ...... | 21 | ...... | 13 | ...... | ...16 00–17 99 |
| 18 00–19 99... | .... | ...... | .... | ...... | ...... | ...... | ...... | ...... | 4 | ...... | 8 | ...... | 4 | ...... | ...18 00–19 99 |
| 20 00–24 99... | .... | ...... | .... | ...... | ...... | ...... | 5 | ...... | 7 | ...... | 6 | ...... | 10 | ...... | ...20 00–24 99 |
| 25 00–29 99... | .... | ...... | .... | ...... | ...... | ...... | 1 | ...... | 2 | ...... | 2 | ...... | ...... | ...... | ...25 00–29 99 |
| 30 00–34 99... | .... | ...... | .... | ...... | ...... | ...... | ...... | ...... | 1 | ...... | ...... | ...... | 1 | ...... | ...30 00–34 99 |
| Not reported... | .... | ...... | 2 | 1 | 5 | ...... | 9 | 1 | 11 | ...... | 3 | ...... | 3 | ...... | ...Not reported |
| Total..... | 27 | 1 | 111 | 10 | 239 | 23 | 249 | 12 | 194 | 5 | 124 | 5 | 98 | 4 | .....Total |

139. V, B, C, D, c—(*concluded*)

NEW YORK STATE

**MEN'S SHIRTS, CONFECTIONERY AND PAPER BOX INDUSTRIES — SHIPPING AND DELIVERY**

NUMBER AND PER CENT OF EMPLOYEES EARNING SPECIFIED WEEKLY RATES BY AGE GROUPS AND SEX

| WEEKLY RATES IN DOLLARS | AGE GROUPS IN YEARS | | | | | | | | | | | WEEKLY RATES IN DOLLARS |
|---|---|---|---|---|---|---|---|---|---|---|---|---|
| | 40–44 | | 45–54 | | 55–64 | 65 AND OVER | NOT REPORTED | TOTAL | | CUMULATIVE PER CENT OF TOTAL | | |
| | Male | Female | Male | Female | Male | Male | Male | Male | Female | Male | Female | |
| $3 00–$3 49 | ....... | ....... | ....... | ....... | ....... | ....... | ....... | 3 | ....... | 0.25 | ....... | $3 00–$3 49 |
| 3 50– 3 99 | ....... | ....... | ....... | ....... | ....... | ....... | ....... | 1 | ....... | 0.34 | ....... | 3 50– 3 99 |
| 4 00– 4 49 | ....... | ....... | ....... | ....... | ....... | ....... | ....... | 7 | 1 | 0.93 | 1.64 | 4 00– 4 49 |
| 4 50– 4 99 | ....... | ....... | ....... | ....... | ....... | ....... | ....... | 14 | ....... | 2.12 | ....... | 4 50– 4 99 |
| 5 00– 5 49 | ....... | ....... | 2 | ....... | ....... | ....... | 1 | 45 | 2 | 5.92 | 4.92 | 5 00– 5 49 |
| 5 50– 5 99 | ....... | ....... | ....... | ....... | ....... | ....... | ....... | 18 | 7 | 7.45 | 16.40 | 5 50– 5 99 |
| 6 00– 6 49 | ....... | 1 | ....... | ....... | ....... | ....... | ....... | 71 | 14 | 13.50 | 39.40 | 6 00– 6 49 |
| 6 50– 6 99 | ....... | ....... | ....... | 1 | ....... | ....... | ....... | 10 | 5 | 14.30 | 47.60 | 6 50– 6 99 |
| 7 00– 7 49 | 2 | ....... | ....... | ....... | ....... | ....... | ....... | 72 | 10 | 20.40 | 64.00 | 7 00– 7 49 |
| 7 50– 7 99 | ....... | ....... | ....... | ....... | ....... | ....... | ....... | 16 | 3 | 21.80 | 69.00 | 7 50– 7 99 |
| 8 00– 8 99 | ....... | ....... | 2 | ....... | ....... | ....... | ....... | 79 | 8 | 28.40 | 82.00 | 8 00– 8 99 |
| 9 00– 9 99 | 2 | ....... | 2 | ....... | 1 | ....... | ....... | 91 | 2 | 36.20 | 85.30 | 9 00– 9 99 |
| 10 00–10 99 | 5 | ....... | 14 | ....... | 5 | 1 | ....... | 128 | 4 | 47.00 | 91.90 | 10 00–10 99 |
| 11 00–11 99 | 9 | 1 | 3 | ....... | 1 | ....... | ....... | 93 | 4 | 54.90 | 98.40 | 11 00–11 99 |
| 12 00–12 99 | 9 | ....... | 13 | ....... | 4 | 3 | ....... | 148 | 1 | 67.40 | 100.00 | 12 00–12 99 |
| 13 00–13 99 | 7 | ....... | 9 | ....... | 1 | ....... | ....... | 96 | ....... | 75.50 | ....... | 13 00–13 99 |
| 14 00–14 99 | 3 | ....... | 10 | ....... | ....... | ....... | ....... | 57 | ....... | 80.40 | ....... | 14 00–14 99 |
| 15 00–15 99 | 11 | ....... | 7 | ....... | 2 | ....... | ....... | 80 | ....... | 87.10 | ....... | 15 00–15 99 |
| 16 00–17 99 | 7 | ....... | 11 | ....... | 1 | ....... | ....... | 77 | ....... | 93.70 | ....... | 16 00–17 99 |
| 18 00–19 99 | 5 | ....... | 6 | ....... | 2 | 1 | ....... | 30 | ....... | 96.20 | ....... | 18 00–19 99 |
| 20 00–24 99 | 3 | ....... | 3 | ....... | 1 | ....... | ....... | 35 | ....... | 99.10 | ....... | 20 00–24 99 |
| 25 00–29 99 | ....... | ....... | 3 | ....... | ....... | ....... | ....... | 8 | ....... | 99.80 | ....... | 25 00–29 99 |
| 30 00–34 99 | ....... | ....... | ....... | ....... | ....... | ....... | ....... | 2 | ....... | 100.00 | ....... | 30 00–34 99 |
| Not reported | 3 | ....... | 3 | ....... | 2 | ....... | ....... | 41 | 2 | ....... | ....... | Not reported |
| Total | 66 | 2 | 88 | 1 | 20 | 5 | 1 | 1,222 | 63 | ....... | ....... | Total |

140. TABLE VIII, B, C, D, c.

NEW YORK STATE

~~MEN'S SHIRTS,~~ CONFECTIONERY AND PAPER BOX INDUSTRIES — SHIPPING AND DELIVERY

NUMBER AND PER CENT. OF EMPLOYEES EARNING SPECIFIED WEEKLY RATES BY OCCUPATION AND SEX

| WEEKLY RATES IN DOLLARS | OCCUPATION | | | | | | | | | | | | | | | WEEKLY RATES IN DOLLARS |
|---|---|---|---|---|---|---|---|---|---|---|---|---|---|---|---|---|
| | FOREMEN | CLERKS AND ROUTERS | | DRIVERS | WAGON BOYS AND HELPERS | CHAUFFEURS | GENERAL LABOR | | PACKING | | STABLEMEN | TOTAL | | CUMULATIVE PER CENT. OF TOTAL | | |
| | Male | Male | Female | Male | Male | Male | Male | Female | Male | Female | Male | Male | Female | Male | Female | |
| $3 00–$3 49 | ...... | .... | ...... | .... | 1 | ...... | 1 | ...... | 1 | ...... | ...... | 3 | ...... | .25 | ...... | $3 00–$3 49 |
| 3 50– 3 99 | ...... | .... | ...... | .... | 1 | ...... | .... | ...... | .... | ...... | ...... | 1 | ...... | .34 | ...... | 3 50– 3 99 |
| 4 00– 4 49 | ...... | .... | 1 | .... | 5 | ...... | .... | ...... | 2 | ...... | ...... | 7 | 1 | .93 | 1.64 | 4 00– 4 49 |
| 4 50– 4 99 | ...... | 3 | ...... | .... | 8 | ...... | 2 | ...... | 1 | ...... | ...... | 14 | ...... | 2.12 | ...... | 4 50– 4 99 |
| 5 00– 5 49 | ...... | 7 | 2 | 1 | 30 | 2 | 1 | ...... | 4 | ...... | ...... | 45 | 2 | 5.92 | 4.92 | 5 00– 5 49 |
| 5 50– 5 99 | ...... | 5 | 7 | .... | 12 | ...... | .... | ...... | 1 | ...... | ...... | 18 | 7 | 7.45 | 16.40 | 5 50– 5 99 |
| 6 00– 6 49 | ...... | 29 | 12 | 1 | 24 | 1 | 3 | 2 | 13 | ...... | ...... | 71 | 14 | 13.50 | 39.40 | 6 00– 6 49 |
| 6 50– 6 99 | 1 | 5 | 4 | 1 | 1 | ...... | .... | 1 | 2 | ...... | ...... | 10 | 5 | 14.30 | 47.60 | 6 50– 6 99 |
| 7 00– 7 49 | ...... | 37 | 10 | 2 | 12 | ...... | 14 | ...... | 7 | ...... | ...... | 72 | 10 | 20.40 | 64.00 | 7 00– 7 49 |
| 7 50– 7 99 | ...... | 6 | 2 | 2 | 1 | ...... | .... | ...... | 7 | 1 | ...... | 16 | 3 | 21.80 | 69.00 | 7 50– 7 99 |
| 8 00– 8 99 | ...... | 38 | 8 | 6 | 7 | ...... | 7 | ...... | 21 | ...... | ...... | 79 | 8 | 28.40 | 82.00 | 8 00– 8 99 |
| 9 00– 9 99 | 1 | 39 | 1 | 15 | 9 | ...... | 7 | ...... | 20 | 1 | ...... | 91 | 2 | 36.20 | 85.30 | 9 00– 9 99 |
| 10 00–10 99 | 1 | 48 | 4 | 30 | 4 | 1 | 9 | ...... | 34 | ...... | 1 | 128 | 4 | 47.00 | 91.90 | 10 00–10 99 |
| 11 00–11 99 | 1 | 37 | 4 | 20 | 2 | ...... | 10 | ...... | 23 | ...... | ...... | 93 | 4 | 54.90 | 98.40 | 11 00–11 99 |
| 12 00–12 99 | 6 | 55 | 1 | 47 | 1 | 2 | 5 | ...... | 32 | ...... | ...... | 148 | 1 | 67.40 | 100.00 | 12 00–12 99 |
| 13 00–13 99 | 1 | 29 | ...... | 44 | ...... | 1 | 5 | ...... | 16 | ...... | ...... | 96 | ...... | 75.50 | ...... | 13 00–13 99 |
| 14 00–14 99 | 2 | 15 | ...... | 23 | ...... | 5 | 2 | ...... | 10 | ...... | ...... | 57 | ...... | 80.40 | ...... | 14 00–14 99 |
| 15 00–15 99 | 1 | 39 | ...... | 15 | ...... | 9 | 4 | ...... | 12 | ...... | ...... | 80 | ...... | 87.10 | ...... | 15 00–15 99 |
| 16 00–17 99 | 5 | 42 | ...... | 16 | ...... | 6 | 3 | ...... | 5 | ...... | ...... | 77 | ...... | 93.70 | ...... | 16 00–17 99 |
| 18 00–19 99 | 3 | 22 | ...... | 1 | ...... | 1 | 1 | ...... | 2 | ...... | ...... | 30 | ...... | 96.20 | ...... | 18 00–19 99 |
| 20 00–24 99 | 6 | 20 | ...... | 1 | ...... | 6 | .... | ...... | 2 | ...... | ...... | 35 | ...... | 99.10 | ...... | 20 00–24 99 |
| 25 00–29 99 | 1 | 7 | ...... | .... | ...... | ...... | .... | ...... | .... | ...... | ...... | 8 | ...... | 99.80 | ...... | 25 00–29 99 |
| 30 00–34 99 | 1 | 1 | ...... | .... | ...... | ...... | .... | ...... | .... | ...... | ...... | 2 | ...... | 100.00 | ...... | 30 00–34 99 |
| Not reported | ...... | 25 | 2 | 5 | 1 | ...... | 4 | ...... | 6 | ...... | ...... | 41 | 2 | .... | ...... | Not reported |
| Total | 30 | 509 | 58 | 230 | 119 | 34 | 78 | 3 | 221 | 2 | 1 | 1,222 | 63 | .... | ...... | Total |

141. TABLE VI, B, C, D, c.

NEW YORK STATE

**MEN'S SHIRTS, CONFECTIONERY AND PAPER BOX INDUSTRIES — SHIPPING AND DELIVERY**

Number and Per Cent. of Employees Classified According to Actual Weekly Earnings by Age Groups and Sex

| Actual Weekly Earnings in Dollars | Age Groups in Years | | | | | | | | | | | | | | Actual Weekly Earnings in Dollars |
|---|---|---|---|---|---|---|---|---|---|---|---|---|---|---|---|
| | 14–15 | | 16–17 | | 18–20 | | 21–24 | | 25–29 | | 30–34 | | 35–39 | | |
| | Male | Female | Male | Female | Male | Female | Male | Female | Male | Female | Male | Female | Male | Female | |
| Less than $3 00 | | | 3 | | 1 | | | | | | | | 1 | | Less than $3 00 |
| $3 00–$3 49 | | | 2 | | 2 | | | | | | | | | | $3 00– 3 49 |
| 3 50– 3 99 | 4 | | 1 | | | | | | | | | | | | 3 50– 3 99 |
| 4 00– 4 49 | 4 | | 5 | 1 | 1 | | 2 | | 3 | | 1 | | | | 4 00– 4 49 |
| 4 50– 4 99 | 8 | | 8 | | 5 | | 1 | | | | | | | 1 | 4 50– 4 99 |
| 5 00– 5 49 | 4 | | 23 | 2 | 7 | 1 | | | 1 | | | | 1 | | 5 00– 5 49 |
| 5 50– 5 99 | 3 | | 9 | 3 | 4 | 5 | 2 | 1 | | 1 | | | | | 5 50– 5 99 |
| 6 00– 6 49 | 2 | | 31 | 1 | 22 | 3 | 3 | 1 | 2 | | | 1 | | | 6 00– 6 49 |
| 6 50– 6 99 | | | 5 | 1 | 9 | 6 | 3 | 3 | | 1 | | | | | 6 50– 6 99 |
| 7 00– 7 49 | 2 | | 11 | 2 | 35 | 2 | 10 | | 3 | 1 | 2 | | | 1 | 7 00– 7 49 |
| 7 50– 7 99 | | | 2 | | 9 | 4 | 6 | 1 | 2 | | | | 1 | 1 | 7 50– 7 99 |
| 8 00– 8 99 | | 1 | 4 | | 47 | 2 | 20 | 3 | 5 | | 4 | 1 | 2 | | 8 00– 8 99 |
| 9 00– 9 99 | | | 2 | | 37 | | 21 | | 10 | 2 | 4 | | 5 | | 9 00– 9 99 |
| 10 00–10 99 | | | 1 | | 26 | | 51 | 2 | 16 | | 7 | 2 | 4 | | 10 00–10 99 |
| 11 00–11 99 | | | 2 | | 8 | | 30 | 1 | 24 | | 15 | 1 | 4 | 1 | 11 00–11 99 |
| 12 00–12 99 | | | | | 10 | | 38 | | 37 | | 11 | | 11 | | 12 00–12 99 |
| 13 00–13 99 | | | | | 4 | | 22 | | 28 | | 9 | | 10 | | 13 00–13 99 |
| 14 00–14 99 | | | | | 5 | | 7 | | 16 | | 17 | | 15 | | 14 00–14 99 |
| 15 00–15 99 | | | | | 1 | | 11 | | 19 | | 15 | | 12 | | 15 00–15 99 |
| 16 00–17 99 | | | | | 2 | | 15 | | 17 | | 19 | | 17 | | 16 00–17 99 |
| 18 00–19 99 | | | | | 1 | | 2 | | 2 | | 10 | | 5 | | 18 00–19 99 |
| 20 00–24 99 | | | | | 1 | | 5 | | 8 | | 10 | | 9 | | 20 00–24 99 |
| 25 00–29 99 | | | | | | | 1 | | 4 | | 2 | | | | 25 00–29 99 |
| 30 00–34 99 | | | | | | | | | | | | | 1 | | 30 00–34 99 |
| Not reported | | | 4 | | 3 | | 4 | | 2 | | | | 1 | | Not reported |
| Total | 27 | 1 | 113 | 10 | 240 | 23 | 254 | 12 | 199 | 5 | 126 | 5 | 99 | 4 | Total |

141. TABLE VI, B, C, D, c — *concluded*)

NEW YORK STATE

**MENS SHIRTS, CONFECTIONERY AND PAPER BOX INDUSTRIES — SHIPPING AND DELIVERY**

NUMBER AND PER CENT. OF EMPLOYEES CLASSIFIED ACCORDING TO ACTUAL WEEKLY EARNINGS BY AGE GROUPS AND SEX

| ACTUAL WEEKLY EARNINGS IN DOLLARS | AGE GROUPS IN YEARS (*concluded*) | | | | | | | | | | | | ACTUAL WEEKLY EARNINGS IN DOLLARS |
|---|---|---|---|---|---|---|---|---|---|---|---|---|---|
| | 40–44 | | 45–54 | | 55–64 | 65 AND OVER | NOT REPORTED | | TOTAL | | CUMULATIVE PER CENT. OF TOTAL | | |
| | Male | Female | Male | Female | Male | Male | Male | Female | Male | Female | Male | Female | |
| Less than $3 00 | | | | | | | | | 5 | | .41 | | Less than $3 00 |
| $3 00–$3 49 | | | | | | | | | 4 | | .73 | | $3 00– 3 49 |
| 3 50– 3 99 | | | | | | | | | 5 | | 1.14 | | 3 50– 3 99 |
| 4 00– 4 49 | | | | | | | | | 16 | 1 | 2.45 | 1.54 | 4 00– 4 49 |
| 4 50– 4 99 | | | | | | | 1 | | 23 | 1 | 4.33 | 3.08 | 4 50– 4 99 |
| 5 00– 5 49 | | | 2 | | | | | 1 | 38 | 4 | 7.42 | 9.25 | 5 00– 5 49 |
| 5 50– 5 99 | | 1 | | | | | | | 18 | 11 | 8.90 | 26.15 | 5 50– 5 99 |
| 6 00– 6 49 | | | | | | | | | 60 | 6 | 13.80 | 35.40 | 6 00– 6 49 |
| 6 50– 6 99 | | | | 1 | | | | | 17 | 12 | 15.35 | 53.80 | 6 50– 6 99 |
| 7 00– 7 49 | 2 | | | | | | | | 65 | 6 | 20.45 | 63.10 | 7 00– 7 49 |
| 7 50– 7 99 | | | | | | | | | 20 | 6 | 22.10 | 72.40 | 7 50– 7 99 |
| 8 00– 8 99 | | | 2 | | | | | 1 | 84 | 8 | 28.95 | 84.60 | 8 00– 8 99 |
| 9 00– 9 99 | 2 | | 3 | | 2 | | | | 86 | 2 | 36.00 | 87.75 | 9 00– 9 99 |
| 10 00–10 99 | 8 | | 11 | | 6 | 2 | | | 132 | 4 | 46.75 | 93.90 | 10 00–10 99 |
| 11 00–11 99 | 10 | 1 | 6 | | 2 | | | | 101 | 4 | 55.00 | 100.00 | 11 00–11 99 |
| 12 00–12 99 | 6 | | 14 | | 3 | 2 | | | 132 | | 65.75 | | 12 00–12 99 |
| 13 00–13 99 | 9 | | 10 | | 1 | | | | 93 | | 73.30 | | 13 00–13 99 |
| 14 00–14 99 | 2 | | 7 | | | | | | 69 | | 79.00 | | 14 00–14 99 |
| 15 00–15 99 | 9 | | 9 | | 2 | | | | 78 | | 85.30 | | 15 00–15 99 |
| 16 00–17 99 | 10 | | 11 | | 2 | | | | 93 | | 92.90 | | 16 00–17 99 |
| 18 00–19 99 | 5 | | 6 | | 1 | 1 | | | 33 | | 95.60 | | 18 00–19 99 |
| 20 00–24 99 | 5 | | 3 | | 1 | | | | 42 | | 99.00 | | 20 00–24 99 |
| 25 00–29 99 | | | 3 | | | | | | 10 | | 99.80 | | 25 00–29 99 |
| 30 00–34 99 | | | 1 | | | | | | 2 | | 100.00 | | 30 00–34 99 |
| Not reported | 1 | | 1 | | 1 | | | | 17 | | | | Not reported |
| Total | 69 | 2 | 89 | 1 | 21 | 5 | 1 | 2 | 1,243 | 65 | | | Total |

142. TABLE IX, B, C, D, c.

NEW YORK STATE

**MEN'S SHIRTS, CONFECTIONERY AND PAPER BOX INDUSTRIES — SHIPPING AND DELIVERY**

Number and Per Cent. of Employees Classified According to Actual Weekly Earnings by Occupation and Sex

| Actual Weekly Earnings in Dollars | Occupation | | | | | | | | | | | | | | | Actual Weekly Earnings in Dollars |
|---|---|---|---|---|---|---|---|---|---|---|---|---|---|---|---|---|
| | Foremen | Clerks and Routers | | Drivers | Wagon Boys and | Chauffeurs | General Labor | | Packing | | Stablemen | Total | | Cumulative Per Cent. of Total | | |
| | Male | Male | Female | Male | Male | Male | Male | Female | Male | Female | Male | Male | Female | Male | Female | |
| Less than $3 00 | .... | 2 | ...... | 1 | 2 | ...... | .... | ...... | .... | ...... | ...... | 5 | ...... | .41 | ...... | Less than $3 00 |
| $3 00–$3 49 | .... | .... | ...... | 1 | 2 | ...... | 1 | ...... | .... | ...... | ...... | 4 | ...... | .73 | ...... | $3 00– 3 49 |
| 3 50– 3 99 | .... | 1 | ...... | .... | 2 | ...... | .... | ...... | 2 | ...... | ...... | 5 | ...... | 1.14 | ...... | 3 50– 3 99 |
| 4 00– 4 49 | .... | 4 | 1 | .... | 7 | 2 | .... | ...... | 3 | ...... | ...... | 16 | 1 | 2.45 | 1.54 | 4 00– 4 49 |
| 4 50– 4 99 | .... | 6 | ...... | .... | 11 | ...... | 2 | 1 | 4 | ...... | ...... | 23 | 1 | 4.33 | 3.08 | 4 50– 4 99 |
| 5 00– 5 49 | .... | 4 | 4 | 2 | 26 | ...... | 2 | ...... | 4 | ...... | ...... | 38 | 4 | 7.42 | 9.25 | 5 00– 5 49 |
| 5 50– 5 99 | .... | 2 | 10 | .... | 12 | ...... | 1 | 1 | 3 | ...... | ...... | 18 | 11 | 8.90 | 26.15 | 5 50– 5 99 |
| 6 00– 6 49 | 1 | 29 | 6 | 1 | 17 | 1 | 2 | ...... | 9 | ...... | ...... | 60 | 6 | 13.80 | 35.40 | 6 00– 6 49 |
| 6 50– 6 99 | .... | 8 | 11 | 1 | 3 | ...... | .... | 1 | 5 | ...... | ...... | 17 | 12 | 15.35 | 53.80 | 6 50– 6 99 |
| 7 00– 7 49 | .... | 33 | 5 | 2 | 11 | ...... | 11 | ...... | 8 | 1 | ...... | 65 | 6 | 20.45 | 63.10 | 7 00– 7 49 |
| 7 50– 7 99 | .... | 6 | 5 | 1 | 1 | ...... | 2 | ...... | 10 | 1 | ...... | 20 | 6 | 22.10 | 72.40 | 7 50– 7 99 |
| 8 00– 8 99 | .... | 43 | 7 | 11 | 8 | ...... | 6 | ...... | 16 | 1 | ...... | 84 | 8 | 28.95 | 84.60 | 8 00– 8 99 |
| 9 00– 9 99 | 1 | 39 | 2 | 16 | 7 | ...... | 5 | ...... | 18 | ...... | ...... | 86 | 2 | 36.00 | 87.75 | 9 00– 9 99 |
| 10 00–10 99 | 4 | 50 | 4 | 33 | 6 | 1 | 10 | ...... | 28 | ...... | ...... | 132 | 4 | 46.75 | 93.90 | 10 00–10 99 |
| 11 00–11 99 | 2 | 36 | 4 | 22 | 1 | ...... | 9 | ...... | 30 | ...... | 1 | 101 | 4 | 55.00 | 100.00 | 11 00–11 99 |
| 12 00–12 99 | 3 | 50 | ...... | 43 | 2 | 2 | 7 | ...... | 25 | ...... | ...... | 132 | ...... | 65.75 | ...... | 12 00–12 99 |
| 13 00–13 99 | .... | 31 | ...... | 40 | ...... | 1 | 3 | ...... | 18 | ...... | ...... | 93 | ...... | 73.30 | ...... | 13 00–13 99 |
| 14 00–14 99 | 2 | 22 | ...... | 23 | ...... | 5 | 1 | ...... | 16 | ...... | ...... | 69 | ...... | 79.00 | ...... | 14 00–14 99 |
| 15 00–15 99 | .... | 33 | ...... | 19 | ...... | 9 | 2 | ...... | 15 | ...... | ...... | 78 | ...... | 85.30 | ...... | 15 00–15 99 |
| 16 00–17 99 | 6 | 49 | ...... | 13 | ...... | 5 | 7 | ...... | 13 | ...... | ...... | 93 | ...... | 92.90 | ...... | 16 00–17 99 |
| 18 00–19 99 | 2 | 21 | ...... | 2 | ...... | 1 | 4 | ...... | 3 | ...... | ...... | 33 | ...... | 95.60 | ...... | 18 00–19 99 |
| 20 00–24 99 | 6 | 21 | ...... | 3 | ...... | 7 | 1 | ...... | 4 | ...... | ...... | 42 | ...... | 99.00 | ...... | 20 00–24 99 |
| 25 00–29 99 | 2 | 8 | ...... | .... | ...... | ...... | .... | ...... | .... | ...... | ...... | 10 | ...... | 99.80 | ...... | 25 00–29 99 |
| 30 00–34 99 | 1 | 1 | ...... | .... | ...... | ...... | .... | ...... | .... | ...... | ...... | 2 | ...... | 100.00 | ...... | 30 00–34 99 |
| Not reported | .... | 11 | ...... | .... | 1 | ...... | 2 | ...... | 3 | ...... | ...... | 17 | ...... | ...... | ...... | Not reported |
| Total | 30 | 510 | 59 | 234 | 119 | 34 | 78 | 3 | 237 | 3 | 1 | 1,243 | 65 | ...... | ...... | Total |

143. TABLE X, B, C, D, c. NEW YORK STATE

**MEN'S SHIRTS, CONFECTIONERY AND PAPER BOX INDUSTRIES — SHIPPING AND DELIVERY**

NUMBER AND PER CENT. OF EMPLOYEES CLASSIFIED ACCORDING TO ACTUAL WEEKLY EARNINGS BY CONJUGAL CONDITION AND SEX

| ACTUAL WEEKLY EARNINGS IN DOLLARS | CONJUGAL CONDITION | | | | | | | | | | | ACTUAL WEEKLY EARNINGS IN DOLLARS |
|---|---|---|---|---|---|---|---|---|---|---|---|---|
| | SINGLE | | MARRIED | WIDOWED OR DIVORCED | | NOT REPORTED | | TOTAL | | CUMULATIVE PER CENT OF TOTAL | | |
| | Male | Female | Male | Male | Female | Male | Female | Male | Female | Male | Female | |
| Less than $3.00 | 3 | ....... | 1 | ....... | ....... | 1 | ....... | 5 | ....... | .41 | ....... | Less than $3 00 |
| $3 00–$3 49 | 3 | ....... | ....... | ....... | ....... | 1 | ....... | 4 | ....... | .73 | ....... | $3 00– 3 49 |
| 3 50– 3 99 | 5 | ....... | ....... | ....... | ....... | ....... | ....... | 5 | ....... | 1.14 | ....... | 3 50– 3 99 |
| 4 00– 4 49 | 14 | 1 | 1 | ....... | ....... | 1 | ....... | 16 | 1 | 2.45 | 1.54 | 4 00– 4 49 |
| 4 50– 4 99 | 23 | ....... | ....... | ....... | 1 | ....... | ....... | 23 | 1 | 4.33 | 3.08 | 4 50– 4 99 |
| 5 00– 5 49 | 34 | 4 | 4 | ....... | ....... | ....... | ....... | 38 | 4 | 7.42 | 9.25 | 5 00– 5 49 |
| 5 50– 5 99 | 18 | 10 | ....... | ....... | 1 | ....... | ....... | 18 | 11 | 8.90 | 26.15 | 5 50– 5 99 |
| 6 00– 6 49 | 55 | 6 | 4 | ....... | ....... | 1 | ....... | 60 | 6 | 13.80 | 35.40 | 6 00– 6 49 |
| 6 50– 6 99 | 15 | 12 | ....... | ....... | ....... | 2 | ....... | 17 | 12 | 15.35 | 53.80 | 6 50– 6 99 |
| 7 00– 7 49 | 58 | 5 | 4 | ....... | ....... | 3 | 1 | 65 | 6 | 20.45 | 63.10 | 7 00– 7 49 |
| 7 50– 7 99 | 16 | 6 | 4 | ....... | ....... | ....... | ....... | 20 | 6 | 22.10 | 72.40 | 7 50– 7 99 |
| 8 00– 8 99 | 69 | 7 | 10 | ....... | ....... | 5 | 1 | 84 | 8 | 28.95 | 84.60 | 8 00– 8 99 |
| 9 00– 9 99 | 62 | 2 | 20 | 1 | ....... | 3 | ....... | 86 | 2 | 36.00 | 87.75 | 9 00– 9 99 |
| 10 00–10 99 | 89 | 4 | 34 | 3 | ....... | 6 | ....... | 132 | 4 | 46.75 | 93.90 | 10 00–10 99 |
| 11 00–11 99 | 55 | 3 | 40 | 1 | 1 | 5 | ....... | 101 | 4 | 55.00 | 100.00 | 11 00–11 99 |
| 12 00–12 99 | 66 | ....... | 58 | 5 | ....... | 3 | ....... | 132 | ....... | 65.75 | ....... | 12 00–12 99 |
| 13 00–13 99 | 35 | ....... | 53 | 1 | ....... | 4 | ....... | 93 | ....... | 73.30 | ....... | 13 00–13 99 |
| 14 00–14 99 | 24 | ....... | 41 | ....... | ....... | 4 | ....... | 69 | ....... | 79.00 | ....... | 14 00–14 99 |
| 15 00–15 99 | 22 | ....... | 50 | 1 | ....... | 5 | ....... | 78 | ....... | 85.30 | ....... | 15 00–15 99 |
| 16 00–17 99 | 30 | ....... | 57 | 3 | ....... | 3 | ....... | 93 | ....... | 92.90 | ....... | 16 00–17 99 |
| 18 00–19 99 | 7 | ....... | 23 | 1 | ....... | 2 | ....... | 33 | ....... | 95.60 | ....... | 18 00–19 99 |
| 20 00–24 99 | 11 | ....... | 31 | ....... | ....... | ....... | ....... | 42 | ....... | 99.00 | ....... | 20 00–24 99 |
| 25 00–29 99 | 4 | ....... | 6 | ....... | ....... | ....... | ....... | 10 | ....... | 99.80 | ....... | 25 00–29 99 |
| 30 00–34 99 | ....... | ....... | 1 | 1 | ....... | ....... | ....... | 2 | ....... | 100.00 | ....... | 30 00–34 99 |
| Not reported | 10 | ....... | 6 | ....... | ....... | 1 | ....... | 17 | ....... | ....... | ....... | Not reported |
| Total | 728 | 60 | 448 | 17 | 3 | 50 | 2 | 1,243 | 65 | ....... | ....... | Total |

144. TABLE XI, B, C, D, c. NEW YORK STATE

**MEN'S SHIRTS, CONFECTIONERY AND PAPER BOX INDUSTRIES — SHIPPING AND DELIVERY**

Number and Per Cent. of Employees Classified According to Actual Weekly Earnings by Nativity and Sex

| Actual Weekly Earnings in Dollars | Nativity — Native | | Foreign | | Not Reported | | Total | | Actual Weekly Earnings in Dollars |
|---|---|---|---|---|---|---|---|---|---|
| | Male | Female | Male | Female | Male | Female | Male | Female | |
| Less than $3 00 | 3 | ........ | 2 | ........ | ........ | ........ | 5 | ........ | Less than $3 00 |
| $3 00–$3 49 | 4 | ........ | ........ | ........ | ........ | ........ | 4 | ........ | $3 00– 3 49 |
| 3 50– 3 99 | 5 | ........ | ........ | ........ | ........ | ........ | 5 | ........ | 3 50– 3 99 |
| 4 00– 4 49 | 13 | 1 | 3 | ........ | ........ | ........ | 16 | 1 | 4 00– 4 49 |
| 4 50– 4 99 | 16 | 1 | 6 | ........ | 1 | ........ | 23 | 1 | 4 50– 4 99 |
| 5 00– 5 49 | 27 | 4 | 11 | ........ | ........ | ........ | 38 | 4 | 5 00– 5 49 |
| 5 50– 5 99 | 9 | 9 | 9 | 2 | ........ | ........ | 18 | 11 | 5 50– 5 99 |
| 6 00– 6 49 | 41 | 4 | 19 | 2 | ........ | ........ | 60 | 6 | 6 00– 6 49 |
| 6 50– 6 99 | 11 | 9 | 6 | 3 | ........ | ........ | 17 | 12 | 6 50– 6 99 |
| 7 00– 7 49 | 39 | 5 | 24 | 1 | 2 | ........ | 65 | 6 | 7 00– 7 49 |
| 7 50– 7 99 | 12 | 5 | 8 | 1 | ........ | ........ | 20 | 6 | 7 50– 7 99 |
| 8 00– 8 99 | 49 | 7 | 32 | ........ | 3 | 1 | 84 | 8 | 8 00– 8 99 |
| 9 00– 9 99 | 46 | 2 | 39 | ........ | 1 | ........ | 86 | 2 | 9 00– 9 99 |
| 10 00–10 99 | 90 | 3 | 42 | 1 | ........ | ........ | 132 | 4 | 10 00–10 99 |
| 11 00–11 99 | 57 | 4 | 44 | ........ | ........ | ........ | 101 | 4 | 11 00–11 99 |
| 12 00–12 99 | 80 | ........ | 51 | ........ | 1 | ........ | 132 | ........ | 12 00–12 99 |
| 13 00–13 99 | 52 | ........ | 40 | ........ | 1 | ........ | 93 | ........ | 13 00–13 99 |
| 14 00–14 99 | 45 | ........ | 24 | ........ | ........ | ........ | 69 | ........ | 14 00–14 99 |
| 15 00–15 99 | 55 | ........ | 23 | ........ | ........ | ........ | 78 | ........ | 15 00–15 99 |
| 16 00–17 99 | 59 | ........ | 33 | ........ | 1 | ........ | 93 | ........ | 16 00–17 99 |
| 18 00–19 99 | 23 | ........ | 10 | ........ | ........ | ........ | 33 | ........ | 18 00–19 99 |
| 20 00–24 99 | 26 | ........ | 14 | ........ | 2 | ........ | 42 | ........ | 20 00–24 99 |
| 25 00–29 99 | 5 | ........ | 5 | ........ | ........ | ........ | 10 | ........ | 25 00–29 99 |
| 30 00–34 99 | 1 | ........ | 1 | ........ | ........ | ........ | 2 | ........ | 30 00–34 99 |
| Not reported | 11 | ........ | 4 | ........ | 2 | ........ | 17 | ........ | Not reported |
| Total | 779 | 54 | 450 | 10 | 14 | 1 | 1,243 | 65 | Total |

145. TABLE XII, B, C, D, c.

NEW YORK STATE

**MEN'S SHIRTS, CONFECTIONERY AND PAPER BOX INDUSTRIES — SHIPPING AND DELIVERY**

NUMBER AND PER CENT. OF EMPLOYEES FOR EACH SEX, CLASSIFIED ACCORDING TO ACTUAL WEEKLY EARNINGS BY THE NUMBER OF YEARS IN THE TRADE

| Actual Weekly Earnings in Dollars | Years in Trade | | | | | | | | | | | | | | | | | Actual Weekly Earnings in Dollars |
|---|---|---|---|---|---|---|---|---|---|---|---|---|---|---|---|---|---|---|
| | Less than 1 | | 1 | | 2 | | 3 | | 4 | | 5 | | 5 | 7 | | 8 | | |
| | Male | Female | Male | Female | Male | Female | Male | Female | Male | Female | Male | Female | Male | Male | Female | Male | Female | |
| Less than $3 00... | 4 | .... | .... | .... | .... | .... | .... | .... | .... | .... | .... | .... | .... | .... | .... | .... | .... | .. Less than $3 00 |
| $3 00–$3 49...... | 2 | .... | .... | .... | 1 | .... | .... | .... | .... | .... | .... | .... | .... | .... | .... | .... | .... | ......$3 00– 3 49 |
| 3 50– 3 99...... | 4 | .... | 1 | .... | .... | .... | .... | .... | .... | .... | .... | .... | .... | .... | .... | .... | .... | ......3 50– 3 99 |
| 4 00– 4 49...... | 12 | 1 | 1 | .... | .... | .... | 1 | .... | 1 | .... | .... | .... | .... | 1 | .... | .... | .... | ......4 00– 4 49 |
| 4 50– 4 99...... | 15 | .... | 6 | .... | 1 | .... | 1 | .... | .... | 1 | .... | .... | .... | .... | .... | .... | .... | ......4 50– 4 99 |
| 5 00– 5 49...... | 19 | 1 | 11 | 1 | 2 | 1 | 4 | 1 | 1 | .... | .... | .... | .... | .... | .... | .... | .... | ......5 00– 5 49 |
| 5 50– 5 99...... | 8 | 3 | 9 | 3 | .... | 1 | .... | 3 | .... | .... | .... | 1 | 1 | .... | .... | .... | .... | ......5 50– 5 99 |
| 6 00– 6 49...... | 40 | .... | 6 | 3 | 5 | .... | 3 | 1 | .... | 2 | .... | .... | 1 | 1 | .... | .... | .... | ......6 00– 6 49 |
| 6 50– 6 99...... | 5 | 1 | 5 | 2 | 3 | 2 | 2 | 2 | 2 | 2 | .... | .... | .... | .... | .... | .... | 1 | ......6 50– 6 99 |
| 7 00– 7 49...... | 28 | .... | 11 | 1 | 7 | 2 | 7 | 2 | 5 | .... | 3 | .... | 1 | .... | 1 | 1 | .... | ......7 00– 7 49 |
| 7 50– 7 99...... | 6 | .... | 5 | .... | 2 | 1 | 4 | 2 | 1 | 1 | .... | .... | .... | 2 | 1 | .... | .... | ......7 50– 7 99 |
| 8 00– 8 99...... | 34 | 1 | 13 | .... | 18 | 2 | 5 | 1 | 1 | .... | 1 | .... | 2 | 1 | .... | 2 | 2 | ......8 00– 8 99 |
| 9 00– 9 99...... | 28 | .... | 14 | .... | 9 | .... | 8 | .... | 10 | .... | 3 | .... | 4 | 1 | .... | 3 | 1 | ......9 00– 9 99 |
| 10 00–10 99...... | 25 | .... | 19 | .... | 13 | 1 | 12 | .... | 12 | .... | 10 | 1 | 7 | 5 | 1 | 6 | .... | .....10 00–10 99 |
| 11 00–11 99...... | 23 | .... | 10 | .... | 11 | .... | 12 | .... | 7 | .... | 6 | .... | 2 | 4 | 2 | 4 | .... | .....11 00–11 99 |
| 12 00–12 99...... | 20 | .... | 6 | .... | 19 | .... | 5 | .... | 10 | .... | 16 | .... | 6 | 6 | .... | 4 | .... | .....12 00–12 99 |
| 13 00–13 99...... | 8 | .... | 7 | .... | 7 | .... | 4 | .... | 5 | .... | 5 | .... | 7 | 5 | .... | 5 | .... | .....13 00–13 99 |
| 14 00–14 99...... | 8 | .... | 5 | .... | 6 | .... | 4 | .... | 2 | .... | 4 | .... | 3 | 3 | .... | 6 | .... | .....14 00–14 99 |
| 15 00–15 99...... | 2 | .... | 4 | .... | 9 | .... | 3 | .... | 2 | .... | 5 | .... | 5 | 2 | .... | 3 | .... | .....15 00–15 99 |
| 16 00–17 99...... | 5 | .... | 6 | .... | 4 | .... | 5 | .... | 10 | .... | 7 | .... | 5 | 4 | .... | 6 | .... | .....16 00–17 99 |
| 18 00–19 99...... | .... | .... | .... | .... | 2 | .... | .... | .... | 2 | .... | 1 | .... | 2 | 1 | .... | 2 | .... | .....18 00–19 99 |
| 20 00–24 99...... | 1 | .... | .... | .... | 2 | .... | 4 | .... | 2 | .... | 3 | .... | 1 | 2 | .... | 4 | .... | .....20 00–24 99 |
| 25 00–29 99...... | .... | .... | .... | .... | .... | .... | .... | .... | .... | .... | .... | .... | 1 | .... | .... | 1 | .... | .....25 00–29 99 |
| 30 00–34 99...... | .... | .... | .... | .... | .... | .... | .... | .... | .... | .... | 1 | .... | .... | .... | .... | .... | .... | .....30 00–34 99 |
| Not reported..... | 1 | .... | 6 | .... | 3 | .... | 1 | .... | .... | .... | .... | .... | 2 | 1 | .... | 1 | .... | ....Not reported |
| Total........ | 298 | 7 | 145 | 10 | 124 | 10 | 85 | 12 | 73 | 6 | 65 | 2 | 50 | 39 | 5 | 50 | 4 | .......Total |

145. TABLE XII, B, C, D, c — (*concluded*) NEW YORK STATE

**MEN'S SHIRTS, CONFECTIONERY AND PAPER BOX INDUSTRIES — SHIPPING AND DELIVERY**

NUMBER AND PER CENT. OF EMPLOYEES FOR EACH SEX, CLASSIFIED ACCORDING TO ACTUAL WEEKLY EARNINGS, BY THE NUMBER OF YEARS IN THE TRADE

| ACTUAL WEEKLY EARNINGS IN DOLLARS | YEARS IN TRADE (*concluded*) | | | | | | | | | | | | TOTAL | | CUMULATIVE PER CENT. OF TOTAL | | ACTUAL WEEKLY EARNINGS IN DOLLARS |
|---|---|---|---|---|---|---|---|---|---|---|---|---|---|---|---|---|---|
| | 9 | | 10–14 | | 15–19 | | 20–24 | 25–29 | 30–34 | 35–44 | NOT REPORTED | | | | | | |
| | Male | Female | Male | Female | Male | Female | Male | Male | Male | Male | Male | Female | Male | Female | Male | Female | |
| Less than $3 00 | .... | .... | .... | .... | 1 | ...... | .... | .... | .... | .... | .... | ...... | 5 | ...... | .41 | ...... | Less than $3 00 |
| $3 00–$3 49.... | .... | .... | .... | .... | .... | ...... | .... | .... | .... | .... | 1 | ...... | 4 | ...... | .73 | ...... | ...$3 00– 3 49 |
| 3 50– 3 99.... | .... | .... | .... | .... | .... | ...... | .... | .... | .... | .... | .... | ...... | 5 | ...... | 1.14 | ...... | ....3 50– 3 99 |
| 4 00– 4 49.... | .... | .... | .... | .... | .... | ...... | .... | .... | .... | .... | .... | ...... | 16 | 1 | 2.45 | 1.54 | ....4 00– 4 49 |
| 4 50– 4 99.... | .... | .... | .... | .... | .... | ...... | .... | .... | .... | .... | .... | ...... | 23 | 1 | 4.33 | 3.08 | ....4 50– 4 99 |
| 5 00– 5 49.... | .... | .... | 1 | .... | .... | ...... | .... | .... | .... | .... | .... | ...... | 38 | 4 | 7.42 | 9.25 | ....5 00– 5 49 |
| 5 50– 5 99.... | .... | .... | .... | .... | .... | ...... | .... | .... | .... | .... | .... | ...... | 18 | 11 | 8.90 | 26.15 | ....5 50– 5 99 |
| 6 00– 6 49.... | .... | .... | .... | .... | .... | ...... | .... | .... | .... | .... | 4 | ...... | 60 | 6 | 13.80 | 35.40 | ....6 00– 6 49 |
| 6 50– 6 99.... | .... | 1 | .... | 1 | .... | ...... | .... | .... | .... | .... | .... | ...... | 17 | 12 | 15.35 | 53.80 | ....6 50– 6 99 |
| 7 00– 7 49.... | .... | .... | 1 | .... | .... | ...... | .... | .... | .... | .... | 1 | ...... | 65 | 6 | 20.45 | 63.10 | ....7 00– 7 49 |
| 7 50– 7 99.... | .... | .... | .... | 1 | .... | ...... | .... | .... | .... | .... | .... | ...... | 20 | 6 | 22.10 | 72.40 | ....7 50– 7 99 |
| 8 00– 8 99.... | .... | .... | 1 | .... | 1 | 1 | .... | .... | 1 | .... | 4 | 1 | 84 | 8 | 28.95 | 84.60 | ....8 00– 8 99 |
| 9 00– 9 99.... | .... | .... | 1 | .... | 1 | 1 | 2 | .... | .... | .... | 2 | ...... | 86 | 2 | 36.00 | 87.75 | ....9 00– 9 99 |
| 10 00–10 99.... | 3 | .... | 6 | .... | 5 | 1 | 2 | 1 | 1 | 1 | 4 | ...... | 132 | 4 | 46.75 | 93.90 | ...10 00–10 99 |
| 11 00–11 99.... | 3 | .... | 11 | .... | .... | 1 | 5 | 1 | 1 | .... | 1 | 1 | 101 | 4 | 55.00 | 100.00 | ...11 00–11 99 |
| 12 00–12 99.... | 4 | .... | 16 | .... | 8 | ...... | 3 | 2 | 1 | 2 | 4 | ...... | 132 | ...... | 65.75 | ...... | ...12 00–12 99 |
| 13 00–13 99.... | 4 | .... | 22 | .... | 7 | ...... | 3 | 1 | 2 | .... | 1 | ...... | 93 | ...... | 73.30 | ...... | ...13 00–13 99 |
| 14 00–14 99.... | 4 | .... | 11 | .... | 7 | ...... | 3 | 1 | 1 | .... | 1 | ...... | 69 | ...... | 79.00 | ...... | ...14 00–14 99 |
| 15 00–15 99.... | 3 | .... | 16 | .... | 11 | ...... | 3 | 5 | 1 | 1 | 1 | ...... | 78 | ...... | 85.30 | ...... | ...15 00–15 99 |
| 16 00–17 99.... | 1 | .... | 17 | .... | 6 | ...... | 8 | 3 | 4 | 2 | .... | ...... | 93 | ...... | 92.90 | ...... | ...16 00–17 99 |
| 18 00–19 99.... | 1 | .... | 8 | .... | 4 | ...... | 6 | 1 | .... | 2 | 1 | ...... | 33 | ...... | 95.60 | ...... | ...18 00–19 99 |
| 20 00–24 99.... | 6 | .... | 6 | .... | 5 | ...... | 6 | .... | .... | .... | .... | ...... | 42 | ...... | 99.00 | ...... | ...20 00–24 99 |
| 25 00–29 99.... | 2 | .... | 5 | .... | 1 | ...... | .... | .... | .... | .... | .... | ...... | 10 | ...... | 99.80 | ...... | ...25 00–29 99 |
| 30 00–34 99.... | .... | .... | .... | .... | .... | ...... | .... | 1 | .... | .... | .... | ...... | 2 | ...... | 100.00 | ...... | ...30 00–34 99 |
| Not reported.... | .... | .... | .... | .... | .... | ...... | .... | .... | .... | .... | 2 | ...... | 17 | ...... | ...... | ...... | ...Not reported |
| Total...... | 31 | 1 | 122 | 2 | 57 | 4 | 41 | 16 | 12 | 8 | 27 | 2 | 1,243 | 65 | ...... | ...... | .....Total |

146. TABLE XIII, B, C, D, c.

NEW YORK STATE

**MEN'S SHIRTS, CONFECTIONERY AND PAPER BOX INDUSTRIES — SHIPPING AND DELIVERY**

NUMBER AND PER CENT. OF EMPLOYEES FOR EACH SEX, CLASSIFIED ACCORDING TO ACTUAL WEEKLY EARNINGS, BY THE NUMBER OF YEARS WITH THE FIRM

| ACTUAL WEEKLY EARNINGS IN DOLLARS | YEARS WITH FIRM | | | | | | | | | | | | | | | | | | ACTUAL WEEKLY EARNINGS IN DOLLARS |
|---|---|---|---|---|---|---|---|---|---|---|---|---|---|---|---|---|---|---|---|
| | LESS THAN 0 | | 0 | | | | 3 | | 4 | | 5 | | 6 | | 7 | | 8 | | |
| | Male | Female | Male | Female | Male | Female | Male | Female | Male | Female | Male | Female | Male | Female | Male | Female | Male | Female | |
| Less than $3 00 | 4 | .... | .... | .... | .... | .... | .... | .... | .... | .... | .... | .... | .... | .... | .... | .... | 1 | ... | Less than $3 00 |
| $3 00-$3 49... | 3 | .... | 1 | .... | .... | .... | .... | .... | .... | .... | .... | .... | .... | .... | .... | .... | .... | ... | ...$3 00- 3 49 |
| 3 50- 3 99... | 4 | .... | 1 | .... | .... | .... | .... | .... | .... | .... | .... | .... | .... | .... | .... | .... | .... | ... | ....3 50- 3 99 |
| 4 00- 4 49... | 14 | 1 | 1 | .... | .... | .... | 1 | .... | .... | .... | .... | .... | .... | .... | .... | .... | .... | ... | ....4 00- 4 49 |
| 4 50- 4 99... | 19 | 1 | 4 | .... | .... | .... | .... | .... | .... | .... | .... | .... | .... | .... | .... | .... | ... | ... | ....4 50- 4 99 |
| 5 00- 5 49... | 30 | 1 | 5 | 1 | 2 | 1 | 1 | 1 | .... | .... | .... | .... | .... | .... | .... | .... | ... | ... | ....5 00- 5 49 |
| 5 50- 5 99... | 11 | 3 | 6 | 3 | .... | 1 | .... | 3 | .... | .... | .... | 1 | 1 | .... | .... | .... | ... | ... | ....5 50- 5 99 |
| 6 00- 6 49... | 48 | .... | 8 | 4 | 2 | .... | 2 | 1 | .... | 1 | .... | .... | .... | .... | .... | .... | ... | ... | ....6 00- 6 49 |
| 6 50- 6 99... | 7 | 2 | 6 | 2 | 4 | 2 | ... | 2 | .... | 2 | .... | .... | .... | .... | .... | .... | ... | ... | ....6 50- 6 99 |
| 7 00- 7 49... | 38 | .... | 11 | 1 | 8 | 1 | 6 | 2 | 2 | .... | .... | 1 | .... | .... | .... | 1 | ... | ... | ....7 00- 7 49 |
| 7 50- 7 99... | 9 | .... | 4 | .... | 3 | 1 | 3 | 2 | 1 | 1 | .... | .... | .... | 1 | .... | 1 | ... | ... | ....7 50- 7 99 |
| 8 00- 8 99... | 42 | 1 | 15 | .... | 21 | 2 | 2 | 1 | 1 | .... | 1 | .... | 1 | .... | 1 | .... | ... | 2 | ....8 00- 8 99 |
| 9 00- 9 99... | 34 | .... | 17 | .... | 9 | .... | 6 | .... | 8 | .... | 4 | .... | 4 | .... | .... | .... | 2 | 1 | ....9 00- 9 99 |
| 10 00-10 99... | 50 | .... | 25 | .... | 10 | 1 | 13 | .... | 11 | .... | 4 | 1 | 3 | 1 | 3 | .... | 4 | ... | ...10 00-10 99 |
| 11 00-11 99... | 36 | .... | 12 | .... | 11 | .... | 6 | .... | 7 | 1 | 7 | .... | 5 | .... | 2 | 1 | 1 | ... | ...11 00-11 99 |
| 12 00-12 99... | 30 | .... | 18 | .... | 20 | .... | 8 | .... | 15 | .... | 9 | .... | 3 | .... | 7 | .... | 3 | ... | ...12 00-12 99 |
| 13 00-13 99... | 16 | .... | 12 | .... | 13 | .... | 7 | .... | 6 | .... | 8 | .... | 5 | .... | 6 | .... | 5 | ... | ...13 00-13 99 |
| 14 00-14 99... | 14 | .... | 7 | .... | 9 | .... | 5 | .... | 3 | .... | 3 | .... | 3 | .... | 3 | .... | 6 | ... | ...14 00-14 99 |
| 15 00-15 99... | 9 | .... | 9 | .... | 8 | .... | 4 | .... | 4 | .... | 7 | .... | 4 | .... | 3 | .... | 3 | ... | ...15 00-15 99 |
| 16 00-17 99... | 11 | .... | 4 | .... | 7 | .... | 6 | .... | 10 | .... | 7 | .... | 4 | .... | 4 | .... | 6 | ... | ...16 00-17 99 |
| 18 00-19 99... | 2 | .... | 1 | .... | 4 | .... | 3 | .... | 2 | .... | .... | .... | 2 | .... | 2 | .... | 3 | ... | ...18 00-19 99 |
| 20 00-24 99... | 2 | .... | 2 | .... | 3 | .... | 5 | .... | 4 | .... | 5 | .... | 1 | .... | 1 | .... | 6 | ... | ...20 00-24 99 |
| 25 00-29 99... | .... | .... | .... | .... | .... | .... | .... | .... | 1 | .... | 4 | .... | 1 | .... | .... | .... | ... | ... | ...25 00-29 99 |
| 30 00-34 99... | .... | .... | .... | .... | .... | .... | 1 | .... | .... | .... | .... | .... | .... | .... | .... | .... | ... | ... | ...30 00-34 99 |
| Not reported... | 3 | .... | 7 | .... | 3 | .... | 1 | .... | .... | .... | .... | .... | 1 | .... | 1 | .... | 1 | ... | ...Not reported |
| Total..... | 436 | 9 | 176 | 11 | 137 | 9 | 80 | 12 | 75 | 5 | 59 | 3 | 38 | 2 | 33 | 3 | 41 | 3 | .....Total |

146. TABLE XIII, B, C, D, c — *(concluded)*

NEW YORK STATE

**MEN'S SHIRTS, CONFECTIONERY AND PAPER BOX INDUSTRIES — SHIPPING AND DELIVERY**

NUMBER AND PER CENT. OF EMPLOYEES FOR EACH SEX, CLASSIFIED ACCORDING TO ACTUAL WEEKLY EARNINGS, BY THE NUMBER OF YEARS WITH THE FIRM

| ACTUAL WEEKLY EARNINGS IN DOLLARS | YEARS WITH FIRM *(concluded)* | | | | | | | | | | | | | | | | ACTUAL WEEKLY EARNINGS IN DOLLARS |
|---|---|---|---|---|---|---|---|---|---|---|---|---|---|---|---|---|---|
| | 9 | | 10–14 | | 15–19 | | 20–24 | 25–29 | 30–34 | 35–44 | NOT REPORTED | | TOTAL | | CUMULATIVE PER CENT. OF TOTAL | | |
| | Male | Female | Male | Female | Male | Female | Male | Male | Male | Male | Male | Female | Male | Female | Male | Female | |
| Less than $3 00 | .... | .... | .... | .... | .... | .... | .... | .... | .... | .... | .... | ...... | 5 | ...... | .41 | ...... | Less than $3 00 |
| $3 00–$3 49 | .... | .... | .... | .... | .... | .... | .... | .... | .... | .... | .... | ...... | 4 | ...... | .73 | ...... | $3 00– 3 49 |
| 3 50– 3 99 | .... | .... | .... | .... | .... | .... | .... | .... | .... | .... | .... | ...... | 5 | ...... | 1.14 | ...... | 3 50– 3 99 |
| 4 00– 4 49 | .... | .... | .... | .... | .... | .... | .... | .... | .... | .... | .... | ...... | 16 | 1 | 2.45 | 1.54 | 4 00– 4 49 |
| 4 50– 4 99 | .... | .... | .... | .... | .... | .... | .... | .... | .... | .... | .... | ...... | 23 | 1 | 4.33 | 3.08 | 4 50– 4 99 |
| 5 00– 5 49 | .... | .... | .... | .... | .... | .... | .... | .... | .... | .... | .... | ...... | 38 | 4 | 7.42 | 9.25 | 5 00– 5 49 |
| 5 50– 5 99 | .... | .... | .... | .... | .... | .... | .... | .... | .... | .... | .... | ...... | 18 | 11 | 8.90 | 26.15 | 5 50– 5 99 |
| 6 00– 6 49 | .... | .... | .... | .... | .... | .... | .... | .... | .... | .... | .... | ...... | 60 | 6 | 13.80 | 35.40 | 6 00– 6 49 |
| 6 50– 6 99 | .... | 1 | .... | 1 | .... | .... | .... | .... | .... | .... | .... | ...... | 17 | 12 | 15.35 | 53.80 | 6 50– 6 99 |
| 7 00– 7 49 | .... | .... | .... | .... | .... | .... | .... | .... | .... | .... | .... | ...... | 65 | 6 | 20.45 | 63.10 | 7 00– 7 49 |
| 7 50– 7 99 | .... | .... | .... | .... | .... | .... | .... | .... | .... | .... | .... | ...... | 20 | 6 | 22.10 | 72.40 | 7 50– 7 99 |
| 8 00– 8 99 | .... | .... | .... | .... | .... | 1 | .... | .... | .... | .... | .... | 1 | 84 | 8 | 28.95 | 84.60 | 8 00– 8 99 |
| 9 00– 9 99 | .... | .... | .... | 1 | 1 | .... | .... | .... | .... | .... | 1 | ...... | 86 | 2 | 36.00 | 87.75 | 9 00– 9 99 |
| 10 00–10 99 | 1 | .... | 5 | .... | 2 | 1 | 1 | .... | .... | .... | .... | ...... | 132 | 4 | 46.75 | 93.90 | 10 00–10 99 |
| 11 00–11 99 | 3 | .... | 8 | 1 | .... | 1 | 2 | .... | 1 | .... | .... | ...... | 101 | 4 | 55.00 | 100.00 | 11 00–11 99 |
| 12 00–12 99 | 1 | .... | 10 | .... | 3 | .... | 1 | 3 | 1 | .... | .... | ...... | 132 | ...... | 65.75 | ...... | 12 00–12 99 |
| 13 00–13 99 | 2 | .... | 8 | .... | 4 | .... | 1 | .... | .... | .... | .... | ...... | 93 | ...... | 73.30 | ...... | 13 00–13 99 |
| 14 00–14 99 | 3 | .... | 11 | .... | 1 | .... | .... | 1 | .... | .... | .... | ...... | 69 | ...... | 79.00 | ...... | 14 00–14 99 |
| 15 00–15 99 | 4 | .... | 10 | .... | 8 | .... | 1 | 2 | 1 | .... | 1 | ...... | 78 | ...... | 85.30 | ...... | 15 00–15 99 |
| 16 00–17 99 | 2 | .... | 16 | .... | 6 | .... | 4 | 3 | 2 | 1 | .... | ...... | 93 | ...... | 92.90 | ...... | 16 00–17 99 |
| 18 00–19 99 | 1 | .... | 7 | .... | .... | .... | 3 | 1 | 1 | 1 | .... | ...... | 33 | ...... | 95.60 | ...... | 18 00–19 99 |
| 20 00–24 99 | 1 | .... | 4 | .... | 3 | .... | 4 | 1 | .... | .... | .... | ...... | 42 | ...... | 99.00 | ...... | 20 00–24 99 |
| 25 00–29 99 | 1 | .... | 3 | .... | .... | .... | .... | .... | .... | .... | .... | ...... | 10 | ...... | 99.80 | ...... | 25 00–29 99 |
| 30 00–34 99 | .... | .... | .... | .... | .... | .... | 1 | .... | .... | .... | .... | ...... | 2 | ...... | 100.00 | ...... | 30 00–34 99 |
| Not reported | .... | .... | .... | .... | .... | .... | .... | .... | .... | .... | .... | ...... | 17 | ...... | ...... | ...... | Not reported |
| Total | 19 | 1 | 82 | 3 | 28 | 3 | 18 | 11 | 6 | 2 | 2 | 1 | 1,243 | 65 | ...... | ...... | Total |

NEW YORK STATE

MEN'S SHIRT, CONFECTIONERY AND PAPER BOX INDUSTRIES — PLANT

147. TABLE VII, B, C, D, c. NUMBER AND PER CENT. OF EMPLOYEES BY SEX ACCORDING TO OCCUPATION AND NATIVITY

| NATIVITY | OCCUPATION | | | | | | | | | | | | | NATIVITY |
|---|---|---|---|---|---|---|---|---|---|---|---|---|---|---|
| | TOTAL | | FOREMEN | MECHANICS | JANITORIAL FORCE | | ERRAND BOYS AND GIRLS | | GENERAL LABOR | | PERSONAL SERVICE | | NOT REPORTED | |
| | Male | Female | Male | Male | Male | Female | Male | Female | Male | Female | Male | Female | Male | |
| Native........... | 695 | 65 | 9 | 344 | 271 | 55 | 22 | 4 | 46 | 1 | 2 | 5 | 1 | ...........Native |
| Foreign.......... | 641 | 45 | 6 | 290 | 305 | 43 | 9 | ...... | 31 | ...... | ...... | 2 | ...... | ..........Foreign |
| Not reported...... | 22 | 5 | ...... | 15 | 6 | 5 | ...... | ...... | 1 | ...... | ...... | ...... | ...... | .....Not reported |
| Total........ | 1,358 | 115 | 15 | 649 | 582 | 103 | 31 | 4 | 78 | 1 | 2 | 7 | 1 | .......Total |
| Per cent. of total.. | 100.0 | 100.0 | 1.1 | 57.0 | 33.8 | 89.6 | 2.3 | 3.5 | 5.7 | .8 | .1 | 6.1 | ...... | .Per cent. of total |

NEW YORK STATE

MEN'S SHIRT, CONFECTIONERY AND PAPER BOX INDUSTRIES — PLANT

148. TABLE V, B, C, D, e, NUMBER AND PER CENT. OF EMPLOYEES EARNING SPECIFIED WEEKLY RATES, BY AGE GROUPS AND SEX

| WEEKLY RATES IN DOLLARS | AGE GROUPS IN YEARS | | | | | | | | | | | | | | WEEKLY RATES IN DOLLARS |
|---|---|---|---|---|---|---|---|---|---|---|---|---|---|---|---|
| | 14–15 | | 16–17 | | 18–20 | | 21–24 | | 25–29 | | 30–34 | | 35–39 | | |
| | Male | Female | Male | Female | Male | Female | Male | Female | Male | Female | Male | Female | Male | Female | |
| $3 50–$3 99... | 1 | 1 | 1 | ...... | ...... | ...... | ...... | ...... | ...... | ...... | ...... | ...... | ...... | ...... | ...$3 50–$3 99 |
| 4 00– 4 49... | 1 | ...... | 3 | ...... | ...... | 1 | ...... | ...... | ...... | ...... | ...... | ...... | ...... | ...... | ... 4 00– 4 49 |
| 4 50– 4 99... | 2 | ...... | 5 | 1 | ...... | 1 | ...... | ...... | ...... | ...... | ...... | ...... | ...... | ...... | ... 4 50– 4 99 |
| 5 00– 5 49... | 2 | ...... | 9 | 1 | 8 | 2 | ...... | ...... | 1 | 1 | ...... | ...... | ...... | 1 | ... 5 00– 5 49 |
| 5 50– 5 99... | .... | ...... | 2 | 1 | 1 | 1 | 1 | ...... | ...... | ...... | 1 | ...... | ...... | ...... | ... 5 50– 5 99 |
| 6 00– 6 49... | 2 | ...... | 11 | 1 | 7 | ...... | 3 | 1 | 2 | 2 | ...... | 2 | ...... | 2 | ... 6 00– 6 49 |
| 6 50– 6 99... | .... | ...... | 1 | 1 | 4 | 1 | 2 | 1 | ...... | ...... | ...... | ...... | ...... | 1 | ... 6 50– 6 99 |
| 7 00– 7 49... | .... | ...... | 4 | ...... | 9 | 1 | 5 | 1 | 4 | 3 | 2 | 1 | ...... | 1 | ... 7 00– 7 49 |
| 7 50– 7 99... | .... | ...... | 1 | ...... | 3 | 1 | 2 | 1 | 2 | 1 | 2 | 2 | ...... | 3 | ... 7 50– 7 99 |
| 8 00– 8 99... | .... | ...... | 2 | ...... | 16 | ...... | 13 | 4 | 4 | ...... | 4 | 2 | 4 | 1 | ... 8 00– 8 99 |
| 9 00– 9 99... | .... | ...... | 2 | ...... | 17 | ...... | 22 | 1 | 17 | 1 | 17 | 2 | 10 | 5 | ... 9 00– 9 99 |
| 10 00–10 99... | .... | ...... | 3 | ...... | 9 | ...... | 23 | ...... | 18 | ...... | 10 | ...... | 11 | ...... | ...10 00–10 99 |
| 11 00–11 99... | .... | ...... | .... | ...... | 5 | ...... | 13 | ...... | 7 | ...... | 9 | ...... | 9 | ...... | ...11 00–11 99 |
| 12 00–12 99... | .... | ...... | .... | ...... | 7 | ...... | 18 | ...... | 29 | 1 | 20 | ...... | 12 | 1 | ...12 00–12 99 |
| 13 00–13 99... | .... | ...... | .... | ...... | 1 | ...... | 7 | ...... | 6 | ...... | 7 | ...... | 9 | ...... | ...13 00–13 99 |
| 14 00–14 99... | .... | ...... | .... | ...... | 1 | ...... | 9 | ...... | 7 | ...... | 12 | ...... | 10 | ...... | ...14 00–14 99 |
| 15 00–15 99... | .... | ...... | .... | ...... | 2 | ...... | 12 | ...... | 12 | ...... | 17 | ...... | 11 | ...... | ...15 00–15 99 |
| 16 00–17 99... | .... | ...... | .... | ...... | ...... | ...... | 12 | ...... | 23 | ...... | 13 | ...... | 13 | ...... | ...16 00–17 99 |
| 18 00–19 99... | .... | ...... | .... | ...... | ...... | ...... | 6 | ...... | 31 | ...... | 29 | ...... | 14 | ...... | ...18 00–19 99 |
| 20 00–24 99... | .... | ...... | .... | ...... | ...... | ...... | 1 | ...... | 15 | ...... | 19 | ...... | 27 | ...... | ...20 00–24 99 |
| 25 00–29 99... | .... | ...... | .... | ...... | ...... | ...... | 1 | ...... | 4 | ...... | 3 | ...... | 6 | 1 | ...25 00–29 99 |
| 30 00–34 99... | .... | ...... | .... | ...... | ...... | ...... | ...... | ...... | ...... | ...... | 1 | ...... | 3 | ...... | ...30 00–34 99 |
| 35 00–39 99... | .... | ...... | .... | ...... | ...... | ...... | ...... | ...... | ...... | ...... | ...... | ...... | 1 | ...... | ...35 00–39 99 |
| 40 00 and over. | .... | ...... | .... | ...... | ...... | ...... | ...... | ...... | ...... | ...... | ...... | ...... | 1 | ...... | .40 00 and over |
| Not reported... | 3 | ...... | 1 | 1 | 19 | 1 | 12 | 2 | 16 | 2 | 14 | ...... | 5 | 3 | ...Not reported |
| Total..... | 11 | 1 | 45 | 6 | 109 | 9 | 162 | 11 | 198 | 11 | 180 | 9 | 146 | 19 | .....Total |

148. TABLE V, B, C, D, e — (*concluded*)

NEW YORK STATE

**MEN'S SHIRT, CONFECTIONERY AND PAPER BOX INDUSTRIES — PLANT**

NUMBER AND PER CENT. OF EMPLOYEES EARNING SPECIFIED WEEKLY RATES, BY AGE GROUPS AND SEX

| WEEKLY RATES IN DOLLARS | Age Groups in Years — (*concluded*) 40–44 | | 45–54 | | 55–64 | | 65 AND OVER | | NOT REPORTED | | TOTAL | | CUMULATIVE PER CENT. OF TOTAL | | WEEKLY RATES IN DOLLARS |
|---|---|---|---|---|---|---|---|---|---|---|---|---|---|---|---|
| | Male | Female | Male | Female | Male | Female | Male | Female | Male | Female | Male | Female | Male | Female | |
| $3 00–$3 49 | .... | ...... | .... | ...... | ...... | ...... | ...... | 1 | ...... | ...... | ...... | 1 | ...... | 1.08 | $3 00–$3 49 |
| 3 50– 3 99 | .... | ...... | .... | ...... | ...... | ...... | ...... | ...... | ...... | ...... | 2 | 1 | .16 | 2.15 | 3 50– 3 99 |
| 4 00– 4 49 | .... | ...... | .... | ...... | ...... | ...... | ...... | ...... | 1 | ...... | 5 | 1 | .57 | 3.23 | 4 00– 4 49 |
| 4 50– 4 99 | .... | ...... | .... | ...... | ...... | ...... | ...... | ...... | ...... | ...... | 7 | 2 | 1.13 | 5.38 | 4 50– 4 99 |
| 5 00– 5 49 | 1 | ...... | 2 | 3 | 1 | 2 | ...... | ...... | ...... | ...... | 24 | 10 | 3.07 | 16.25 | 5 00– 5 49 |
| 5 50– 5 99 | .... | 1 | .... | ...... | 2 | ...... | ...... | ...... | ...... | ...... | 7 | 3 | 3.64 | 19.37 | 5 50– 5 99 |
| 6 00– 6 49 | 1 | 1 | 1 | 1 | ...... | 1 | ...... | 2 | ...... | ...... | 27 | 13 | 5.82 | 33.20 | 6 00– 6 49 |
| 6 50– 6 99 | .... | ...... | .... | ...... | ...... | ...... | ...... | ...... | ...... | ...... | 7 | 4 | 6.39 | 37.60 | 6 50– 6 99 |
| 7 00– 7 49 | .... | 3 | 1 | 2 | 2 | 3 | ...... | ...... | ...... | 1 | 27 | 16 | 8.58 | 54.90 | 7 00– 7 49 |
| 7 50– 7 99 | 1 | ...... | 2 | 3 | 2 | ...... | ...... | 2 | ...... | ...... | 15 | 13 | 9.78 | 63.90 | 7 50– 7 99 |
| 8 00– 8 99 | 1 | ...... | 1 | 2 | 2 | 2 | 1 | 1 | ...... | 1 | 48 | 13 | 13.70 | 82.80 | 8 00– 8 99 |
| 9 00– 9 99 | 9 | ...... | 12 | 1 | 9 | 1 | 9 | ...... | ...... | ...... | 124 | 11 | 23.70 | 94.60 | 9 00– 9 99 |
| 10 00–10 99 | 10 | 1 | 15 | 1 | 4 | ...... | 7 | ...... | ...... | ...... | 110 | 2 | 32.60 | 96.80 | 10 00–10 99 |
| 11 00–11 99 | 6 | ...... | 9 | ...... | 5 | ...... | ...... | ...... | 1 | ...... | 64 | ...... | 37.80 | ...... | 11 00–11 99 |
| 12 00–12 99 | 8 | ...... | 28 | ...... | 19 | ...... | 6 | ...... | 2 | ...... | 149 | 2 | 49.80 | 98.08 | 12 00–12 99 |
| 13 00–13 99 | 10 | ...... | 15 | ...... | 5 | ...... | 2 | ...... | 1 | ...... | 63 | ...... | 54.90 | ...... | 13 00–13 99 |
| 14 00–14 99 | 9 | ...... | 15 | ...... | 4 | ...... | 2 | ...... | ...... | ...... | 69 | ...... | 60.47 | ...... | 14 00–14 99 |
| 15 00–15 99 | 11 | ...... | 17 | ...... | 13 | ...... | 2 | ...... | 1 | ...... | 98 | ...... | 67.60 | ...... | 15 00–15 99 |
| 16 00–17 99 | 12 | ...... | 18 | ...... | 1 | ...... | ...... | ...... | ...... | ...... | 92 | ...... | 75.80 | ...... | 16 00–17 99 |
| 18 00–19 99 | 15 | ...... | 23 | ...... | 8 | ...... | 2 | ...... | 1 | ...... | 129 | ...... | 86.25 | ...... | 18 00–19 99 |
| 20 00–24 99 | 8 | ...... | 24 | ...... | 10 | ...... | 2 | ...... | 3 | ...... | 109 | ...... | 95.00 | ...... | 20 00–24 99 |
| 25 00–29 99 | 14 | ...... | 11 | ...... | 1 | ...... | ...... | ...... | ...... | ...... | 40 | 1 | 98.40 | 100.00 | 25 00–29 99 |
| 30 00–34 99 | 2 | ...... | 6 | ...... | ...... | ...... | ...... | ...... | 1 | ...... | 13 | ...... | 99.30 | ...... | 30 00–34 99 |
| 35 00–39 99 | 2 | ...... | .... | ...... | ...... | ...... | ...... | ...... | 1 | ...... | 4 | ...... | 99.70 | ...... | 35 00–39 99 |
| 40 00 and over | .... | ...... | 2 | ...... | 1 | ...... | ...... | ...... | ...... | ...... | 4 | ...... | 100.00 | ...... | 40 00 and over |
| Not reported | 13 | 1 | 14 | 1 | 4 | 2 | 3 | ...... | 1 | ...... | 105 | 13 | ...... | ...... | Not reported |
| Total | 133 | 7 | 216 | 14 | 93 | 11 | 36 | 6 | 13 | 2 | 1,342 | 106 | ...... | ...... | Total |

149. TABLE VIII, B, C, D, e

NEW YORK STATE

**MEN'S SHIRT, CONFECTIONERY AND PAPER BOX INDUSTRIES — PLANT**

NUMBER AND PER CENT. OF EMPLOYEES EARNING SPECIFIED WEEKLY RATES, BY OCCUPATION AND SEX

| WEEKLY RATES IN DOLLARS | OCCUPATION | | | | | | | | | | | | | | | |
|---|---|---|---|---|---|---|---|---|---|---|---|---|---|---|---|---|
| | FOREMEN | MECHANICS | JANITORIAL FORCE | | ERRAND BOYS AND GIRLS | | GENERAL LABOR | | PERSONAL SERVICE | | NOT REPORTED | TOTAL | | CUMULATIVE PER CENT. OF TOTAL | | WEEKLY RATES IN DOLLARS |
| | Male | Male | Male | Female | Male | Female | Male | Female | Male | Female | Male | Male | Female | Male | Female | |
| $3 00–$3 49... | .... | ...... | .... | 1 | .... | ...... | .... | ...... | .... | ...... | .... | ..... | 1 | ...... | 1.08 | ...$3 00–$3 49 |
| 3 50– 3 99... | .... | ...... | 1 | 1 | 1 | ...... | .... | ...... | .... | ...... | .... | 2 | 1 | .16 | 2.15 | ... 3 50– 3 99 |
| 4 00– 4 49... | .... | ...... | 3 | ...... | 2 | 1 | .... | ...... | .... | ...... | .... | 5 | 1 | .57 | 3.23 | ... 4 00– 4 49 |
| 4 50– 4 99... | .... | ...... | 2 | 2 | 5 | ...... | .... | ...... | .... | ...... | .... | 7 | 2 | 1.13 | 5.38 | ... 4 50– 4 99 |
| 5 00– 5 49... | .... | 3 | 13 | 9 | 7 | ...... | 1 | ...... | .... | 1 | .... | 24 | 10 | 3.07 | 16.25 | ... 5 00– 5 49 |
| 5 50– 5 99... | .... | 1 | 5 | 2 | 1 | 1 | .... | ...... | .... | ...... | .... | 7 | 3 | 3.64 | 19.37 | ... 5 50– 5 99 |
| 6 00– 6 49... | .... | 2 | 14 | 13 | 10 | ...... | 1 | ...... | .... | ...... | .... | 27 | 13 | 5.82 | 33.20 | ... 6 00– 6 49 |
| 6 50– 6 99... | .... | 2 | 4 | 4 | .... | ...... | 1 | ...... | .... | ...... | .... | 7 | 4 | 6.39 | 37.60 | ... 6 50– 6 99 |
| 7 00– 7 49... | .... | 3 | 21 | 16 | 2 | ...... | 1 | ...... | .... | ...... | .... | 27 | 16 | 8.58 | 54.90 | ... 7 00– 7 49 |
| 7 50– 7 99... | .... | 2 | 13 | 11 | .... | 1 | .... | ...... | .... | 1 | .... | 15 | 13 | 9.78 | 63.90 | ... 7 50– 7 99 |
| 8 00– 8 99... | .... | 6 | 36 | 11 | 1 | ...... | 5 | ...... | .... | 2 | .... | 48 | 13 | 13.70 | 82.80 | ... 8 00– 8 99 |
| 9 00– 9 99... | .... | 18 | 92 | 11 | 1 | ...... | 12 | ...... | 1 | ...... | .... | 124 | 11 | 23.70 | 94.60 | ... 9 00– 9 99 |
| 10 00–10 99... | .... | 18 | 77 | 1 | .... | ...... | 14 | ...... | 1 | 1 | .... | 110 | 2 | 32.60 | 96.80 | ...10 00–10 99 |
| 11 00–11 99... | .... | 22 | 38 | ...... | .... | ...... | 4 | ...... | .... | ...... | .... | 64 | ...... | 37.80 | ...... | ...11 00–11 99 |
| 12 00–12 99... | 1 | 50 | 81 | 1 | .... | ...... | 16 | 1 | .... | ...... | 1 | 149 | 2 | 49.80 | 98.08 | ...12 00–12 99 |
| 13 00–13 99... | .... | 28 | 34 | ...... | .... | ...... | 1 | ...... | .... | ...... | .... | 63 | ...... | 54.90 | ...... | ...13 00–13 99 |
| 14 00–14 99... | .... | 40 | 25 | ...... | .... | ...... | 4 | ...... | .... | ...... | .... | 69 | ...... | 60.47 | ...... | ...14 00–14 99 |
| 15 00–15 99... | 1 | 71 | 21 | ...... | .... | ...... | 5 | ...... | .... | ...... | .... | 98 | ...... | 67.60 | ...... | ...15 00–15 99 |
| 16 00–17 99... | 2 | 75 | 13 | ...... | .... | ...... | 2 | ...... | .... | ...... | .... | 92 | ...... | 75.80 | ...... | ...16 00–17 99 |
| 18 00–19 99... | 3 | 112 | 14 | ...... | .... | ...... | .... | ...... | .... | ...... | .... | 129 | ...... | 86.25 | ...... | ...18 00–19 99 |
| 20 00–24 99... | 3 | 100 | 6 | ...... | .... | ...... | .... | ...... | .... | ...... | .... | 109 | ...... | 95.00 | ...... | ...20 00–24 99 |
| 25 00–29 99... | 1 | 38 | 1 | ...... | .... | ...... | .... | ...... | .... | 1 | .... | 40 | 1 | 98.40 | 100.00 | ...25 00–29 99 |
| 30 00–34 99... | 3 | 10 | .... | ...... | .... | ...... | .... | ...... | .... | ...... | .... | 13 | ...... | 99.30 | ...... | ...30 00–34 99 |
| 35 00–39 99... | .... | 4 | .... | ...... | .... | ...... | .... | ...... | .... | ...... | .... | 4 | ...... | 99.70 | ...... | ...35 00–39 99 |
| 40 00 and over. | 1 | 3 | .... | ...... | .... | ...... | .... | ...... | .... | ...... | .... | 4 | ...... | 100.00 | ...... | .40 00 and over |
| Not reported... | .... | 34 | 61 | 11 | 1 | 1 | 9 | ...... | .... | 1 | .... | 105 | 13 | ...... | ...... | ...Not reported |
| Total..... | 15 | 642 | 575 | 94 | 31 | 4 | 76 | 1 | 2 | 7 | 1 | 1,342 | 106 | ...... | ...... | .....Total |

NEW YORK STATE

150. TABLE VI, B, C, D, e — MEN'S SHIRT, CONFECTIONERY AND PAPER BOX INDUSTRIES — PLANT

NUMBER AND PER CENT. OF EMPLOYEES CLASSIFIED ACCORDING TO ACTUAL WEEKLY EARNINGS, BY AGE GROUPS AND SEX

| Actual Weekly Earnings in Dollars | Age Groups in Years | | | | | | | | | | | | | | Actual Weekly Earnings Dollars |
|---|---|---|---|---|---|---|---|---|---|---|---|---|---|---|---|
| | 14–15 | | 16–17 | | 18–20 | | 21–24 | | 25–29 | | 30–34 | | 35–39 | | |
| | Male | Female | Male | Female | Male | Female | Male | Female | Male | Female | Male | Female | Male | Female | |
| Less than $3.00 | .... | ...... | .... | 1 | 2 | 1 | 2 | ...... | ...... | ...... | ...... | ...... | ...... | ...... | Less than $3 00 |
| $3 00–$3 49 | .... | ...... | .... | ...... | ...... | 2 | ...... | ...... | ...... | ...... | ...... | ...... | ...... | ...... | $3 00–$3 49 |
| 3 50– 3 99 | 2 | ...... | 1 | ...... | ...... | ...... | 1 | ...... | 2 | ...... | ...... | 1 | ...... | ...... | 3 50– 3 99 |
| 4 00– 4 49 | 2 | 1 | 5 | 1 | ...... | 2 | ...... | ...... | 2 | 1 | ...... | ...... | ...... | 1 | 4 00– 4 49 |
| 4 50– 4 99 | 2 | ...... | 4 | ...... | 2 | ...... | 2 | 2 | 1 | ...... | ...... | ...... | ...... | ...... | 4 50– 4 99 |
| 5 00– 5 49 | 3 | ...... | 10 | 1 | 8 | 3 | 3 | ...... | ...... | ...... | 1 | 1 | 1 | ...... | 5 00– 5 49 |
| 5 50– 5 99 | .... | ...... | 3 | 2 | 1 | ...... | ...... | ...... | 2 | 1 | 2 | ...... | ...... | 1 | 5 50– 5 99 |
| 6 00– 6 49 | 2 | ...... | 10 | ...... | 9 | ...... | 2 | 1 | 2 | 2 | 2 | ...... | ...... | 2 | 6 00– 6 49 |
| 6 50– 6 99 | .... | ...... | 2 | 1 | 9 | 3 | 4 | ...... | 3 | ...... | 4 | 1 | ...... | 1 | 6 50– 6 99 |
| 7 00– 7 49 | .... | ...... | 4 | ...... | 9 | 1 | 3 | ...... | 2 | 4 | 1 | 2 | 1 | 1 | 7 00– 7 49 |
| 7 50– 7 99 | .... | ...... | 1 | ...... | 6 | ...... | 3 | 2 | 2 | 1 | 1 | 2 | 1 | 1 | 7 50– 7 99 |
| 8 00– 8 99 | .... | ...... | 2 | ...... | 21 | 1 | 15 | 5 | 6 | 1 | 7 | 2 | 4 | 4 | 8 00– 8 99 |
| 9 00– 9 99 | .... | ...... | 2 | ...... | 15 | ...... | 23 | 2 | 16 | 2 | 17 | 1 | 8 | 5 | 9 00– 9 99 |
| 10 00–10 99 | .... | ...... | 2 | ...... | 12 | ...... | 17 | ...... | 15 | ...... | 8 | ...... | 9 | 1 | 10 00–10 99 |
| 11 00–11 99 | .... | ...... | .... | ...... | 4 | ...... | 20 | ...... | 11 | ...... | 14 | ...... | 7 | ...... | 11 00–11 99 |
| 12 00–12 99 | .... | ...... | .... | ...... | 6 | ...... | 10 | ...... | 25 | 1 | 12 | ...... | 14 | 1 | 12 00–12 99 |
| 13 00–13 99 | .... | ...... | .... | ...... | 2 | ...... | 15 | ...... | 13 | ...... | 9 | ...... | 8 | ...... | 13 00–13 99 |
| 14 00–14 99 | .... | ...... | .... | ...... | ...... | ...... | 10 | ...... | 12 | ...... | 12 | ...... | 10 | ...... | 14 00–14 99 |
| 15 00–15 99 | .... | ...... | .... | ...... | 2 | ...... | 9 | ...... | 11 | ...... | 14 | ...... | 10 | ...... | 15 00–15 99 |
| 16 00–17 99 | .... | ...... | .... | ...... | 1 | ...... | 17 | ...... | 26 | ...... | 20 | ...... | 15 | ...... | 16 00–17 99 |
| 18 00–19 99 | .... | ...... | .... | ...... | ...... | ...... | 6 | ...... | 29 | ...... | 25 | ...... | 18 | ...... | 18 00–19 99 |
| 20 00–24 99 | .... | ...... | .... | ...... | ...... | ...... | 2 | ...... | 21 | ...... | 23 | ...... | 26 | ...... | 20 00–24 99 |
| 25 00–29 99 | .... | ...... | .... | ...... | ...... | ...... | 1 | ...... | 4 | ...... | 8 | ...... | 9 | 1 | 25 00–29 99 |
| 30 00–34 99 | .... | ...... | .... | ...... | ...... | ...... | ...... | ...... | ...... | ...... | 1 | ...... | 3 | ...... | 30 00–34 99 |
| 35 00–39 99 | .... | ...... | .... | ...... | ...... | ...... | ...... | ...... | ...... | ...... | ...... | ...... | 1 | ...... | 35 00–39 99 |
| 40 00 and over | .... | ...... | .... | ...... | ...... | ...... | ...... | ...... | ...... | ...... | ...... | ...... | 1 | ...... | 40 00 and over |
| Not reported | .... | ...... | .... | ...... | ...... | ...... | 1 | ...... | ...... | ...... | ...... | ...... | 2 | ...... | Not reported |
| Total | 11 | 1 | 46 | 6 | 109 | 13 | 166 | 12 | 205 | 13 | 181 | 10 | 148 | 19 | Total |

NEW YORK STATE

150. TABLE VI, B, C, D, e **MEN'S SHIRT, CONFECTIONERY AND PAPER BOX INDUSTRIES — PLANT**

NUMBER AND PER CENT. OF EMPLOYEES CLASSIFIED ACCORDING TO ACTUAL WEEKLY EARNINGS, BY AGE GROUPS AND SEX

| ACTUAL WEEKLY EARNINGS IN DOLLARS | AGE GROUPS IN YEARS — (*concluded*) 40–44 | | 45–54 | | 55–64 | | 65 AND OVER | | NOT REPORTED | | TOTAL | | CUMULATIVE PER CENT. OF TOTAL | | ACTUAL WEEKLY EARNINGS IN DOLLARS |
|---|---|---|---|---|---|---|---|---|---|---|---|---|---|---|---|
| | Male | Female | Male | Female | Male | Female | Male | Female | Male | Female | Male | Female | Male | Female | |
| Less than $3 00. | 2 | ...... | 3 | ...... | 1 | ...... | ...... | ...... | ...... | ...... | 10 | 2 | .74 | 1.74 | .Less than $ 300 |
| $3 00–$3 49... | .... | ...... | .... | ...... | ...... | ...... | ...... | 1 | ...... | ...... | ...... | 3 | .74 | 4.35 | ...$3 00– 3 49 |
| 3 50– 3 99... | .... | 1 | .... | ...... | ...... | ...... | ...... | ...... | ...... | ...... | 6 | 2 | 1.19 | 6.09 | ... 3 50– 3 99 |
| 4 00– 4 49... | .... | ...... | 1 | ...... | ...... | ...... | ...... | ...... | ...... | ...... | 10 | 6 | 1.93 | 11.30 | ... 4 00– 4 49 |
| 4 50– 4 99... | .... | ...... | .... | ...... | ...... | 1 | ...... | ...... | ...... | ...... | 11 | 3 | 2.72 | 13.90 | ... 4 50– 4 99 |
| 5 00– 5 49... | 1 | ...... | 3 | 3 | 2 | 1 | ...... | ...... | ...... | ...... | 32 | 9 | 5.12 | 21.70 | ... 5 00– 5 49 |
| 5 50– 5 99... | .... | 1 | .... | ...... | 1 | ...... | 1 | ...... | ...... | ...... | 10 | 5 | 5.86 | 26.10 | ... 5 50– 5 99 |
| 6 00– 6 49... | 1 | 2 | 1 | 1 | ...... | 1 | ...... | 2 | ...... | ...... | 29 | 11 | 8.01 | 35.60 | ... 6 00– 6 49 |
| 6 50– 6 99... | .... | ...... | 2 | ...... | 1 | ...... | ...... | ...... | ...... | 1 | 25 | 7 | 9.86 | 41.80 | ... 6 50– 6 99 |
| 7 00– 7 49... | .... | ...... | 2 | 2 | 3 | 2 | 1 | ...... | ...... | 1 | 26 | 13 | 11.80 | 53.10 | ... 7 00– 7 49 |
| 7 50– 7 99... | 1 | 2 | 2 | 3 | 2 | 1 | ...... | 2 | 1 | ...... | 20 | 14 | 13.30 | 65.30 | ... 7 50– 7 99 |
| 8 00– 8 99... | 2 | 1 | 2 | 3 | 1 | 4 | 2 | 1 | ...... | 1 | 62 | 23 | 17.90 | 85.20 | ... 8 00– 8 99 |
| 9 00– 9 99... | 10 | ...... | 12 | 1 | 7 | 1 | 5 | ...... | ...... | ...... | 115 | 12 | 26.20 | 95.70 | ... 9 00– 9 99 |
| 10 00–10 99... | 8 | ...... | 13 | 1 | 4 | ...... | 9 | ...... | ...... | ...... | 97 | 2 | 33.60 | 97.50 | ...10 00–10 99 |
| 11 00–11 99... | 6 | ...... | 9 | ...... | 7 | ...... | 2 | ...... | 2 | ...... | 82 | ...... | 39.70 | 97.50 | ...11 00–11 99 |
| 12 00–12 99... | 9 | ...... | 23 | ...... | 16 | ...... | 5 | ...... | ...... | ...... | 120 | 2 | 48.60 | 99.20 | ...12 00–12 99 |
| 13 00–13 99... | 8 | ...... | 15 | ...... | 2 | ...... | 2 | ...... | ...... | ...... | 74 | ...... | 54.10 | ...... | ...13 00–13 99 |
| 14 00–14 99... | 12 | ...... | 22 | ...... | 6 | ...... | 2 | ...... | 2 | ...... | 88 | ...... | 60.60 | ...... | ...14 00–14 99 |
| 15 00–15 99... | 13 | ...... | 16 | ...... | 12 | ...... | 1 | ...... | ...... | ...... | 88 | ...... | 67.10 | ...... | ...15 00–15 99 |
| 16 00–17 99... | 12 | ...... | 20 | ...... | 5 | ...... | 1 | ...... | 1 | ...... | 118 | ...... | 75.90 | ...... | ...16 00–17 99 |
| 18 00–19 99... | 15 | ...... | 21 | ...... | 9 | ...... | 2 | ...... | 2 | ...... | 127 | ...... | 85.30 | ...... | ...18 00–19 99 |
| 20 00–24 99... | 13 | ...... | 24 | ...... | 10 | ...... | 2 | ...... | 3 | ...... | 124 | ...... | 94.50 | ...... | ...20 00–24 99 |
| 25 00–29 99... | 15 | ...... | 15 | ...... | 2 | ...... | ...... | ...... | ...... | ...... | 54 | 1 | 98.50 | 100.00 | ...25 00–29 99 |
| 30 00–34 99... | 2 | ...... | 5 | ...... | ...... | ...... | ...... | ...... | 1 | ...... | 12 | ...... | 994 | ...... | ...30 00–34 99 |
| 35 00–39 99... | 2 | ...... | 1 | ...... | ...... | ...... | ...... | ...... | 1 | ...... | 5 | ...... | 99.70 | ...... | ...35 00–39 99 |
| 40 00 and over. | .... | ...... | 2 | ...... | 1 | ...... | ...... | ...... | ...... | ...... | 4 | ...... | 100.00 | ...... | .40 00 and over |
| Not reported... | 1 | ...... | 3 | ...... | 1 | ...... | 1 | ...... | ...... | ...... | 9 | ...... | ...... | ...... | ...Not reported |
| Total..... | 133 | 7 | 217 | 14 | 93 | 11 | 36 | 6 | 13 | 3 | 1,358 | 115 | ...... | ...... | .....Total |

NEW YORK STATE

151. TABLE IX, B, C, D, e **MEN'S SHIRT, CONFECTIONERY AND PAPER BOX INDUSTRIES — PLANT**

NUMBER AND PER CENT OF EMPLOYEES CLASSIFIED ACCORDING TO ACTUAL WEEKLY EARNINGS, BY OCCUPATION AND SEX

| ACTUAL WEEKLY EARNINGS IN DOLLARS | OCCUPATION | | | | | | | | | | | | | | | ACTUAL WEEKLY EARNINGS IN DOLLARS |
|---|---|---|---|---|---|---|---|---|---|---|---|---|---|---|---|---|
| | FOREMEN | MECHANICS | JANITORIAL FORCE | | ERRAND BOYS AND GIRLS | | GENERAL LABOR | | PERSONAL SERVICE | | NOT REPORTED | TOTAL | | CUMULATIVE PER CENT. OF TOTAL | | |
| | Male | Male | Male | Female | Male | Female | Male | Female | Male | Female | Male | Male | Female | Male | Female | |
| Less than $3.00 | | 3 | 6 | 2 | | | 1 | | | | | 10 | 2 | .74 | 1.74 | Less than $3 00 |
| $3 00–$3 49 | | | | 2 | | 1 | | | | | | | 3 | | 4.35 | 3 00– 3 49 |
| 3 50– 3 99 | | 1 | 3 | 2 | 2 | | | | | | | 6 | 2 | 1.19 | 6.09 | 3 50– 3 99 |
| 4 00– 4 49 | | 2 | 6 | 5 | 2 | 1 | | | | | | 10 | 6 | 1.93 | 11.30 | 4 00– 4 49 |
| 4 50– 4 99 | | 1 | 5 | 2 | 5 | | | | | 1 | | 11 | 3 | 2.72 | 13.90 | 4 50– 4 99 |
| 5 00– 5 49 | | 4 | 20 | 8 | 7 | 1 | 1 | | | | | 32 | 9 | 5.12 | 21.70 | 5 00– 5 49 |
| 5 50– 5 99 | | 1 | 5 | 5 | 2 | | 2 | | | | | 10 | 5 | 5.86 | 26.10 | 5 50– 5 99 |
| 6 00– 6 49 | | 6 | 11 | 11 | 10 | | 2 | | | | | 29 | 11 | 8.01 | 35.60 | 6 00– 6 49 |
| 6 50– 6 99 | | 5 | 16 | 6 | | 1 | 4 | | | | | 25 | 7 | 9.86 | 41.80 | 5 60– 6 99 |
| 7 00– 7 49 | | 3 | 21 | 13 | 1 | | 1 | | | | | 26 | 13 | 11.80 | 53.10 | 7 00– 7 49 |
| 7 50– 7 99 | | 3 | 14 | 14 | 1 | | 2 | | | | | 20 | 14 | 13.30 | 65.30 | 7 50– 7 99 |
| 8 00– 8 99 | | 6 | 50 | 20 | | | 6 | | | 3 | | 62 | 23 | 17.90 | 85.20 | 8 00– 8 99 |
| 9 00– 9 99 | | 19 | 84 | 12 | | | 12 | | | | | 115 | 12 | 26.20 | 95.70 | 9 00– 9 99 |
| 10 00–10 99 | | 16 | 66 | | 1 | | 12 | | 2 | 2 | | 97 | 2 | 33.60 | 97.50 | 10 00–10 99 |
| 11 00–11 99 | | 18 | 58 | | | | 6 | | | | | 82 | | 39.70 | | 11 00–11 99 |
| 12 00–12 99 | 1 | 43 | 66 | 1 | | | 10 | 1 | | | | 120 | 2 | 48.60 | 99.20 | 12 00–12 99 |
| 13 00–13 99 | | 32 | 41 | | | | 1 | | | | | 74 | | 54.10 | | 13 00–13 99 |
| 14 00–14 99 | | 46 | 35 | | | | 6 | | | | 1 | 88 | | 60.60 | | 14 00–14 99 |
| 15 00–15 99 | | 61 | 24 | | | | 3 | | | | | 88 | | 67.10 | | 15 00–15 99 |
| 16 00–17 99 | | 90 | 20 | | | | 8 | | | | | 118 | | 75.90 | | 16 00–17 99 |
| 18 00–19 99 | 2 | 110 | 15 | | | | | | | | | 127 | | 85.30 | | 18 00–19 99 |
| 20 00–24 99 | 7 | 106 | 11 | | | | | | | | | 124 | | 94.50 | | 20 00–24 99 |
| 25 00–29 99 | 1 | 52 | 1 | | | | | | | 1 | | 54 | 1 | 98.50 | 100.00 | 25 00–29 99 |
| 30 00–34 99 | 2 | 10 | | | | | | | | | | 12 | | 99.40 | | 30 00–34 99 |
| 35 00–39 99 | | 5 | | | | | | | | | | 5 | | 99.70 | | 35 00–39 99 |
| 40 00 and over | 1 | 3 | | | | | | | | | | 4 | | 100.00 | | 40 00 and over |
| Not reported | 1 | 3 | 4 | | | | 1 | | | | | 9 | | | | Not reported |
| Total | 15 | 649 | 582 | 103 | 31 | 4 | 78 | 1 | 2 | 7 | 1 | 1,358 | 115 | | | Total |

NEW YORK STATE

152. TABLE X, B, C, D, e — **MEN'S SHIRT, CONFECTIONERY AND PAPER BOX INDUSTRY — PLANT**

NUMBER AND PER CENT. OF EMPLOYEES CLASSIFIED ACCORDING TO ACTUAL WEEKLY EARNINGS, BY CONJUGAL CONDITION AND SEX

| ACTUAL WEEKLY EARNINGS IN DOLLARS | CONJUGAL CONDITION | | | | | | | | | | | | ACTUAL WEEKLY EARNINGS IN DOLLARS |
|---|---|---|---|---|---|---|---|---|---|---|---|---|---|
| | SINGLE | | MARRIED | | WIDOWED OR DIVORCED | | NOT REPORTED | TOTAL | | CUMULATIVE PER CENT. OF TOTAL | | | |
| | Male | Female | Male | Female | Male | Female | Male | Male | Female | Male | Female | | |
| Less than $3 00 | 4 | 2 | 6 | ........ | ........ | ........ | ........ | 10 | 2 | .74 | 1.74 | Less than $3 00 |
| $3 00–$3 49 | ........ | 2 | ........ | ........ | ........ | 1 | ........ | ........ | 3 | ........ | 4.35 | $3 00– 3 49 |
| 3 50– 3 99 | 4 | ........ | 2 | 2 | ........ | ........ | ........ | 6 | 2 | 1.19 | 6.09 | 3 50– 3 99 |
| 4 00– 4 49 | 9 | 4 | 1 | 2 | ........ | ........ | ........ | 10 | 6 | 1.93 | 11.30 | 4 00– 4 49 |
| 4 50– 4 99 | 10 | 1 | 1 | 1 | ........ | 1 | ........ | 11 | 3 | 2.72 | 13.90 | 4 50– 4 99 |
| 5 00– 5 49 | 25 | 4 | 7 | 1 | ........ | 4 | ........ | 32 | 9 | 5.12 | 21.70 | 5 00– 5 49 |
| 5 50– 5 99 | 5 | 2 | 4 | 1 | 1 | 2 | ........ | 10 | 5 | 5.86 | 26.10 | 5 50– 5 99 |
| 6 00– 6 49 | 24 | 1 | 3 | 4 | ........ | 6 | 2 | 29 | 11 | 8.01 | 35.60 | 6 00– 6 49 |
| 6 50– 6 99 | 18 | 4 | 7 | 3 | ........ | ........ | ........ | 25 | 7 | 9.86 | 41.80 | 6 50– 6 99 |
| 7 00– 7 49 | 19 | 4 | 7 | 5 | ........ | 4 | ........ | 26 | 13 | 11.80 | 53.10 | 7 00– 7 49 |
| 7 50– 7 99 | 10 | 3 | 9 | 6 | ........ | 5 | 1 | 20 | 14 | 13.30 | 65.30 | 7 50– 7 99 |
| 8 00– 8 99 | 38 | 9 | 20 | 8 | 2 | 6 | 2 | 62 | 23 | 17.90 | 85.20 | 8 00– 8 99 |
| 9 00– 9 99 | 56 | 4 | 54 | 5 | 4 | 3 | 1 | 115 | 12 | 26.20 | 95.70 | 9 00– 9 99 |
| 10 00–10 99 | 37 | ........ | 53 | 1 | 5 | 1 | 2 | 97 | 2 | 33.60 | 97.50 | 10 00–10 99 |
| 11 00–11 99 | 34 | ........ | 41 | ........ | 4 | ........ | 3 | 82 | ........ | 39.70 | ........ | 11 00–11 99 |
| 12 00–12 99 | 32 | 1 | 76 | 1 | 6 | ........ | 6 | 120 | 2 | 48.60 | 99.20 | 12 00–12 99 |
| 13 00–13 99 | 28 | ........ | 43 | ........ | 2 | ........ | 1 | 74 | ........ | 54.10 | ........ | 13 00–13 99 |
| 14 00–14 99 | 17 | ........ | 61 | ........ | 3 | ........ | 7 | 88 | ........ | 60.60 | ........ | 14 00–14 99 |
| 15 00–15 99 | 17 | ........ | 64 | ........ | 3 | ........ | 4 | 88 | ........ | 67.10 | ........ | 15 00–15 99 |
| 16 00–17 99 | 22 | ........ | 86 | ........ | 6 | ........ | 4 | 118 | ........ | 75.90 | ........ | 16 00–17 99 |
| 18 00–19 99 | 27 | ........ | 88 | ........ | 5 | ........ | 7 | 127 | ........ | 85.30 | ........ | 18 00–19 99 |
| 20 00–24 99 | 15 | ........ | 99 | ........ | 4 | ........ | 6 | 124 | ........ | 94.50 | ........ | 20 00–24 99 |
| 25 00–29 99 | 4 | 1 | 48 | ........ | ........ | ........ | 2 | 54 | 1 | 98.50 | 100.00 | 25 00–29 99 |
| 30 00–34 99 | ........ | ........ | 12 | ........ | ........ | ........ | ........ | 12 | ........ | 99.40 | ........ | 30 00–34 99 |
| 35 00–39 99 | ........ | ........ | 4 | ........ | ........ | ........ | 1 | 5 | ........ | 99.70 | ........ | 35 00–39 99 |
| 40 00 and over | ........ | ........ | 4 | ........ | ........ | ........ | ........ | 4 | ........ | 100.00 | ........ | 40 00 and over |
| Not reported | 1 | ........ | 7 | ........ | ........ | ........ | 1 | 9 | ........ | ........ | ........ | Not reported |
| Total | 456 | 42 | 807 | 40 | 45 | 33 | 50 | 1,358 | 115 | ........ | ........ | Total |

NEW YORK STATE

153. TABLE XI, B, C, D, c. MEN'S SHIRT, CONFECTIONERY AND PAPER BOX INDUSTRIES — PLANT

NUMBER AND PER CENT. OF EMPLOYEES CLASSIFIED ACCORDING TO ACTUAL WEEKLY EARNINGS BY NATIVITY AND SEX

| ACTUAL WEEKLY EARNINGS IN DOLLARS | NATIVITY | | | | | | | | | | ACTUAL WEEKLY EARNINGS IN DOLLARS |
|---|---|---|---|---|---|---|---|---|---|---|---|
| | NATIVE | | FOREIGN | | NOT REPORTED | | TOTAL | | CUMULATIVE PER CENT. OF TOTAL | | |
| | Male | Female | Male | Female | Male | Female | Male | Female | Male | Female | |
| Less than $3 00 | 4 | 1 | 6 | 1 | ........ | ........ | 10 | 2 | .7 | 1.7 | Less than $3 00 |
| $3 00–$3 40 | ........ | 2 | ........ | 1 | ........ | ........ | ........ | 3 | ........ | 4.4 | $3 00– 3 49 |
| 3 50– 3 99 | 5 | ........ | 1 | 1 | ........ | 1 | 6 | 2 | 1.2 | 6.1 | 3 50– 3 99 |
| 4 00– 4 49 | 4 | 3 | 6 | 3 | ........ | ........ | 10 | 6 | 1.9 | 11.3 | 4 00– 4 49 |
| 4 50– 4 99 | 6 | 2 | 5 | 1 | ........ | ........ | 11 | 3 | 2.7 | 13.9 | 4 50– 4 99 |
| 5 00– 5 49 | 18 | 4 | 14 | 5 | ........ | ........ | 32 | 9 | 5.1 | 21.7 | 5 00– 5 49 |
| 5 50– 5 99 | 5 | 2 | 5 | 3 | ........ | ........ | 10 | 5 | 5.9 | 26.1 | 5 50– 5 99 |
| 6 00– 6 49 | 17 | 7 | 12 | 3 | ........ | 1 | 29 | 11 | 8.0 | 35.6 | 6 00– 6 49 |
| 6 50– 6 99 | 13 | 6 | 12 | 1 | ........ | ........ | 25 | 7 | 9.9 | 41.8 | 6 50– 6 99 |
| 7 00– 7 49 | 10 | 7 | 15 | 5 | 1 | 1 | 26 | 13 | 11.8 | 53.1 | 7 00– 7 49 |
| 7 50– 7 99 | 9 | 6 | 10 | 7 | 1 | 1 | 20 | 14 | 13.3 | 65.3 | 7 50– 7 99 |
| 8 00– 8 99 | 32 | 15 | 30 | 7 | ........ | 1 | 62 | 23 | 17.9 | 85.2 | 8 00– 8 99 |
| 9 00– 9 99 | 41 | 7 | 72 | 5 | 2 | ........ | 115 | 12 | 26.2 | 95.7 | 9 00– 9 99 |
| 10 00–10 99 | 48 | 1 | 48 | 1 | 1 | ........ | 97 | 2 | 33.6 | 97.5 | 10 00–10 99 |
| 11 00–11 99 | 44 | ........ | 35 | ........ | 3 | ........ | 82 | ........ | 39.7 | ........ | 11 00–11 99 |
| 12 00–12 99 | 62 | 1 | 57 | 1 | 1 | ........ | 120 | 2 | 48.6 | 99.2 | 12 00–12 99 |
| 13 00–13 99 | 39 | ........ | 35 | ........ | ........ | ........ | 74 | ........ | 54.1 | ........ | 13 00–13 99 |
| 14 00–14 99 | 43 | ........ | 43 | ........ | 2 | ........ | 88 | ........ | 60.6 | ........ | 14 00–14 99 |
| 15 00–15 99 | 51 | ........ | 34 | ........ | 3 | ........ | 88 | ........ | 67.1 | ........ | 15 00–15 99 |
| 16 00–17 99 | 69 | ........ | 47 | ........ | 2 | ........ | 118 | ........ | 75.9 | ........ | 16 00–17 99 |
| 18 00–19 99 | 70 | ........ | 56 | ........ | 1 | ........ | 127 | ........ | 85.3 | ........ | 18 00–19 99 |
| 20 00–24 99 | 63 | ........ | 58 | ........ | 3 | ........ | 124 | ........ | 94.5 | ........ | 20 00–24 99 |
| 25 00–29 00 | 31 | 1 | 22 | ........ | 1 | ........ | 54 | 1 | 98.5 | 100.0 | 25 00–29 99 |
| 30 00–34 99 | 5 | ........ | 7 | ........ | ........ | ........ | 12 | ........ | 99.4 | ........ | 30 00–34 99 |
| 35 00–39 99 | 2 | ........ | 2 | ........ | 1 | ........ | 5 | ........ | 99.7 | ........ | 35 00–39 99 |
| 40 00 and over | 2 | ........ | 2 | ........ | ........ | ........ | 4 | ........ | 100.0 | ........ | 40 00 and over |
| Not reported | 2 | ........ | 7 | ........ | ........ | ........ | 9 | ........ | ........ | ........ | Not reported |
| Total | 695 | 65 | 641 | 45 | 22 | 5 | 1,358 | 115 | ........ | ........ | Total |

NEW YORK STATE

154. TABLE XII, B,C, D, c. MEN'S SHIRT, CONFECTIONERY AND PAPER BOX INDUSTRIES — PLANT

Number of Employees for Each Sex Classified According to Actual Weekly Earnings by the Number of Years in the Trade

| Actual Weekly Earnings in Dollars | Years in Trade | | | | | | | | | | | | | | Actual Weekly Earnings in Dollars |
|---|---|---|---|---|---|---|---|---|---|---|---|---|---|---|---|
| | Less than 1 | | 1 | | 2 | | 3 | | 4 | | | | 6 | | |
| | Male | Female | Male | Female | Male | Female | Male | Female | Male | Female | Male | Female | Male | Female | |
| Less than $3 00 | 3 | 2 | .... | ...... | 1 | ...... | 1 | ...... | 1 | ...... | ...... | ...... | ...... | ...... | Less than $3 00 |
| $3 00–$3 49... | .... | 1 | .... | 1 | ...... | ...... | ...... | ...... | ...... | ...... | ...... | ...... | ...... | ...... | ...$3 00– 3 49 |
| 3 50– 3 99... | 2 | 1 | 2 | 1 | ...... | ...... | 1 | ...... | 1 | ...... | ...... | ...... | ...... | ...... | ... 3 50– 3 99 |
| 4 00– 4 49... | 5 | 4 | 2 | 1 | 1 | ...... | 2 | ...... | ...... | ...... | ...... | ...... | ...... | ...... | ... 4 00– 4 49 |
| 4 50– 4 99... | 10 | ...... | .... | 1 | ...... | 1 | ...... | ...... | ...... | ...... | ...... | ...... | ...... | ...... | ... 4 50– 4 99 |
| 5 00– 5 49... | 21 | 4 | 3 | 1 | 1 | 1 | 1 | 1 | ...... | 2 | 1 | ...... | 1 | ...... | ... 5 00– 5 49 |
| 5 50– 5 99... | 5 | ...... | 2 | 3 | 1 | ...... | ...... | 1 | 1 | ...... | ...... | ...... | ...... | 1 | ... 5 50– 5 99 |
| 6 00– 6 49... | 13 | 3 | 5 | 1 | 7 | ...... | 1 | 1 | ...... | 2 | ...... | ...... | 1 | 1 | ... 6 00– 6 49 |
| 6 50– 6 99... | 11 | 4 | 4 | ...... | 1 | ...... | 1 | 2 | 1 | 1 | 1 | ...... | ...... | ...... | ... 6 50– 6 99 |
| 7 00– 7 49... | 16 | 5 | 2 | 2 | 1 | ...... | 1 | ...... | 3 | 1 | ...... | ...... | ...... | ...... | ... 7 00– 7 49 |
| 7 50– 7 99... | 6 | 3 | 6 | ...... | 1 | ...... | 3 | ...... | ...... | 1 | 1 | 1 | ...... | 1 | ... 7 50– 7 99 |
| 8 00– 8 99... | 22 | 3 | 8 | 2 | 9 | 3 | 7 | 2 | 7 | 2 | 1 | 1 | 1 | ...... | ... 8 00– 8 99 |
| 9 00– 9 99... | 33 | 1 | 19 | 1 | 17 | 2 | 10 | 2 | 9 | ...... | 4 | 2 | 3 | ...... | ... 9 00– 9 99 |
| 10 00–10 99... | 12 | ...... | 9 | ...... | 14 | ...... | 17 | 1 | 5 | ...... | 6 | ...... | 2 | ...... | ...10 00–10 99 |
| 11 00–11 99... | 13 | ...... | 4 | ...... | 12 | ...... | 5 | ...... | 6 | ...... | 5 | ...... | 4 | ...... | ...11 00–11 99 |
| 12 00–12 99... | 19 | ...... | 6 | ...... | 10 | ...... | 12 | ...... | 11 | 1 | 6 | ...... | 5 | ...... | ...12 00–12 99 |
| 13 00–13 99... | 6 | ...... | 7 | ...... | 8 | ...... | 9 | ...... | 2 | ...... | 4 | ...... | 3 | ...... | ...13 00–13 99 |
| 14 00–14 99... | 5 | ...... | 4 | ...... | 8 | ...... | 4 | ...... | 5 | ...... | 2 | ...... | 4 | ...... | ...14 00–14 99 |
| 15 00–15 99... | 3 | ...... | 5 | ...... | 5 | ...... | 3 | ...... | 4 | ...... | 4 | ...... | 3 | ...... | ...15 00–15 99 |
| 16 00–17 99... | 5 | ...... | 4 | ...... | 4 | ...... | 10 | ...... | 4 | ...... | 2 | ...... | 5 | ...... | ...16 00–17 99 |
| 18 00–19 99... | 2 | ...... | 1 | ...... | ...... | ...... | 5 | ...... | 2 | ...... | 5 | ...... | 5 | ...... | ...18 00–19 99 |
| 20 00–24 99... | 2 | ...... | 3 | ...... | 1 | ...... | 2 | ...... | 1 | ...... | ...... | ...... | 6 | ...... | ...20 00–24 99 |
| 25 00–29 99... | 1 | ...... | 3 | ...... | ...... | ...... | 3 | ...... | ...... | ...... | 1 | ...... | 1 | ...... | ...25 00–29 99 |
| Not reported... | 1 | ...... | 1 | ...... | 1 | ...... | ...... | ...... | ...... | ...... | ...... | ...... | ...... | ...... | ...Not reported |
| Total..... | 216 | 31 | 100 | 14 | 103 | 7 | 98 | 10 | 63 | 10 | 43 | 4 | 44 | 3 | .....Total |

154. TABLE XII, B, C, D, c.— (*continued*)

NEW YORK STATE

MEN'S SHIRT, CONFECTIONERY AND PAPER BOX INDUSTRIES — PLANT

NUMBER OF EMPLOYEES FOR EACH SEX CLASSIFIED ACCORDING TO ACTUAL WEEKLY EARNINGS BY THE NUMBER OF YEARS IN THE TRADE

| ACTUAL WEEKLY EARNINGS IN DOLLARS | YEARS IN TRADE (*continued*) | | | | | | | | | | | | ACTUAL WEEKLY EARNINGS IN DOLLARS |
|---|---|---|---|---|---|---|---|---|---|---|---|---|---|
| | 7 | | 8 | | 9 | | 10–14 | | 15–19 | | 20–14 | | |
| | Male | Female | Male | Female | Male | Female | Male | Female | Male | Female | Male | Female | |
| Less than $3 00. | ....... | ....... | ....... | ....... | ....... | ....... | 2 | ....... | ....... | ....... | ....... | ....... | Less than $3 00 |
| $3 00–$3 49.... | ....... | ....... | ....... | ....... | ....... | ....... | ....... | 1 | ....... | ....... | ....... | ....... | ...$3 00– 3 49 |
| 4 50– 4 99.... | ....... | ....... | ....... | 1 | ....... | ....... | ....... | ....... | ....... | ....... | ....... | ....... | ... 4 50– 4 99 |
| 5 00– 5 49.... | 1 | ....... | ....... | ....... | ....... | ....... | ....... | ....... | ....... | ....... | 1 | ....... | ... 5 50– 5 99 |
| 5 50– 5 99.... | ....... | ....... | ....... | ....... | ....... | ....... | ....... | ....... | ....... | ....... | 1 | ....... | ... 5 00– 5 49 |
| 6 00– 6 49.... | ....... | ....... | ....... | 1 | ....... | ....... | 2 | ....... | ....... | 1 | ....... | ....... | ... 6 00– 6 49 |
| 6 50– 6 99.... | 1 | ....... | ....... | ....... | 1 | ....... | 2 | ....... | 1 | ....... | ....... | ....... | ... 6 50– 6 99 |
| 7 00– 7 49.... | ....... | 1 | ....... | ....... | ....... | 1 | 1 | ....... | ....... | ....... | ....... | 1 | ... 7 00– 7 49 |
| 7 50– 7 99.... | 1 | 1 | ....... | 1 | 1 | ....... | ....... | 3 | ....... | 2 | ....... | 1 | ... 7 50– 7 99 |
| 8 00– 8 99.... | 2 | 2 | ....... | 1 | ....... | ....... | 1 | 4 | 1 | ....... | ....... | 1 | ... 8 00– 8 99 |
| 9 00– 9 99.... | 3 | 1 | 2 | 1 | 1 | 1 | 6 | 1 | 2 | ....... | 1 | ....... | ... 9 00– 9 99 |
| 10 00–10 99.... | 3 | ....... | 5 | ....... | 3 | ....... | 8 | 1 | 3 | ....... | 1 | ....... | ...10 00–10 99 |
| 11 00–11 99.... | 2 | ....... | 1 | ....... | 1 | ....... | 9 | ....... | 2 | ....... | 3 | ....... | ...11 00–11 99 |
| 12 00–12 99.... | 3 | ....... | 4 | ....... | 3 | ....... | 17 | 1 | 10 | ....... | 2 | ....... | ...12 00–12 99 |
| 13 00–13 99.... | 6 | ....... | 1 | ....... | 2 | ....... | 13 | ....... | 6 | ....... | 3 | ....... | ...13 00–13 99 |
| 14 00–14 99.... | 5 | ....... | 2 | ....... | 4 | ....... | 11 | ....... | 14 | ....... | 4 | ....... | ...14 00–14 99 |
| 15 00–15 99.... | 3 | ....... | 8 | ....... | 1 | ....... | 13 | ....... | 7 | ....... | 8 | ....... | ...15 00–15 99 |
| 16 00–17 99.... | 4 | ....... | 11 | ....... | 6 | ....... | 23 | ....... | 17 | ....... | 9 | ....... | ...16 00–17 99 |
| 18 00–19 99.... | 9 | ....... | 4 | ....... | 4 | ....... | 29 | ....... | 28 | ....... | 16 | ....... | ...18 00–19 99 |
| 20 00–24 99.... | 1 | ....... | 2 | ....... | 3 | ....... | 28 | ....... | 23 | ....... | 25 | ....... | ...20 00–24 99 |
| 25 00–29 99.... | 1 | ....... | 1 | 1 | 3 | ....... | 7 | ....... | 7 | ....... | 7 | ....... | ...25 00–29 99 |
| 30 00–34 99.... | 1 | ....... | ....... | ....... | ....... | ....... | ....... | ....... | 1 | ....... | 3 | ....... | ...30 00–34 99 |
| 35 00–39 99.... | ....... | ....... | ....... | ....... | ....... | ....... | ....... | ....... | 1 | ....... | 1 | ....... | ...35 00–39 99 |
| 40 00 and over.. | ....... | ....... | ....... | ....... | ....... | ....... | ....... | ....... | ....... | ....... | 1 | ....... | .40 00 and over |
| Not reported.... | ....... | ....... | ....... | ....... | ....... | ....... | 1 | ....... | 2 | ....... | 1 | ....... | ...Not reported |
| Total...... | 46 | 5 | 41 | 6 | 33 | 2 | 173 | 11 | 125 | 3 | 87 | 3 | .....Total |

154. TABLE XII, B, C, D, c – (*concluded*) NEW YORK STATE

**MEN'S SHIRT, CONFECTIONERY AND PAPER BOX INDUSTRIES — PLANT**

Number of Employees for Each Sex Classified According to Actual Weekly Earnings by the Number of Years in the Trade

| Actual Weekly Earnings in Dollars | Years in Trade (*concluded*) 25–29 | | 30–34 | 35–44 | 45 and over | Not reported | | Total | | Cumulative per cent. of total | | Actual Weekly Earnings in Dollars |
|---|---|---|---|---|---|---|---|---|---|---|---|---|
| | Male | Female | Male | Male | Male | Male | Female | Male | Female | Male | Female | |
| Less than $3 00 | ........ | ........ | 1 | 1 | ....... | ....... | ....... | 10 | 2 | .7 | 1.7 | Less than $3 00 |
| $3 00–$3 49 | ........ | ........ | ........ | ....... | ....... | ....... | ....... | ....... | 3 | ....... | 4.4 | $3 00– 3 49 |
| 3 50– 3 99 | ........ | ........ | ........ | ....... | ....... | ....... | ....... | 6 | 2 | 1.2 | 6.1 | 3 50– 3 99 |
| 4 00– 4 49 | ........ | ........ | ........ | ....... | ....... | ....... | 1 | 10 | 6 | 1.9 | 11.3 | 4 00– 4 49 |
| 4 50– 4 99 | ........ | ........ | ........ | ....... | ....... | 1 | ....... | 11 | 3 | 2.7 | 13.9 | 4 50– 4 99 |
| 5 00– 5 49 | ........ | ........ | ........ | ....... | ....... | 2 | ....... | 32 | 9 | 5.1 | 21.7 | 5 00– 5 49 |
| 5 50– 5 99 | ........ | ........ | ........ | ....... | ....... | ....... | ....... | 10 | 5 | 5.9 | 26.1 | 5 50– 5 99 |
| 6 00– 6 49 | ........ | 1 | ........ | ....... | ....... | ....... | ....... | 29 | 11 | 8.0 | 35.6 | 6 00– 6 49 |
| 6 50– 6 99 | ........ | ........ | ........ | ....... | ....... | 1 | ....... | 25 | 7 | 9.9 | 41.8 | 6 50– 6 99 |
| 7 00– 7 49 | ........ | ........ | ........ | 1 | ....... | 1 | 2 | 26 | 13 | 11.8 | 53.1 | 7 00– 7 49 |
| 7 50– 7 99 | ........ | ........ | ........ | ....... | ....... | 1 | ....... | 20 | 14 | 13.3 | 65.3 | 7 50– 7 99 |
| 8 00– 8 99 | ........ | 1 | ........ | ....... | ....... | 3 | 1 | 62 | 23 | 17.9 | 85.2 | 8 00– 8 99 |
| 9 00– 9 99 | ........ | ........ | 1 | ....... | ....... | 4 | ....... | 115 | 12 | 26.2 | 95.7 | 9 00– 9 99 |
| 10 00–10 99 | 3 | ........ | ........ | 2 | ....... | 4 | ....... | 97 | 2 | 33.6 | 97.5 | 10 00–10 99 |
| 11 00–11 99 | 3 | ........ | 2 | 2 | 1 | 7 | ....... | 82 | ....... | 39.7 | ....... | 11 00–11 99 |
| 12 00–12 99 | 1 | ........ | 3 | 1 | 3 | 4 | ....... | 120 | 2 | 48.6 | 99.2 | 12 00–12 99 |
| 13 00–13 99 | 1 | ........ | 2 | ....... | ....... | 1 | ....... | 74 | ....... | 54.1 | ....... | 13 00–13 99 |
| 14 00–14 99 | 5 | ........ | 4 | 1 | 2 | 4 | ....... | 88 | ....... | 60.6 | ....... | 14 00–14 99 |
| 15 00–15 99 | 3 | ........ | 4 | 7 | 3 | 4 | ....... | 88 | ....... | 67.1 | ....... | 15 00–15 99 |
| 16 00–17 99 | 3 | ........ | 3 | 2 | 1 | 5 | ....... | 118 | ....... | 75.9 | ....... | 16 00–17 99 |
| 18 00–19 99 | 6 | ........ | 3 | 4 | 2 | 2 | ....... | 127 | ....... | 85.3 | ....... | 18 00–19 99 |
| 20 00–24 99 | 11 | ........ | 5 | 2 | 5 | 4 | ....... | 124 | ....... | 94.5 | ....... | 20 00–24 99 |
| 25 00–29 99 | 9 | ........ | 6 | 2 | ....... | 2 | ....... | 54 | 1 | 98.5 | 100.0 | 25 00–29 99 |
| 30 00–34 99 | 3 | ........ | 3 | 1 | ....... | ....... | ....... | 12 | ....... | 99.4 | ....... | 30 00–34 99 |
| 35 00–39 99 | 1 | ........ | 1 | ....... | ....... | 1 | ....... | 5 | ....... | 99.7 | ....... | 35 00–39 99 |
| 40 00 and over | 1 | ........ | 2 | ....... | ....... | ....... | ....... | 4 | ....... | 100.0 | ....... | 40 00 and over |
| Not reported | ........ | ........ | 1 | ....... | ....... | 1 | ....... | 9 | ....... | ....... | ....... | Not reported |
| Total | 50 | 2 | 41 | 26 | 17 | 52 | 4 | 1,358 | 115 | ....... | ....... | Total |

NEW YORK STATE

155. TABLE XII, B, C, D, c. **MEN'S SHIRT, CONFECTIONERY AND PAPER BOX INDUSTRIES — PLANT**

Number and Per Cent of Employees for Each Sex Classified According to Actual Weekly Earnings by the Number of Years With the Firm

| Actual Weekly Earnings in Dollars | Years With Firm | | | | | | | | | | | | | | Actual Weekly Earnings in Dollars |
|---|---|---|---|---|---|---|---|---|---|---|---|---|---|---|---|
| | Less than 1 | | 1 | | 2 | | 3 | | 4 | | 5 | | 6 | | |
| | Male | Female | Male | Female | Male | Female | Male | Female | Male | Female | Male | Female | Male | Female | |
| Less than $3 00 | 6 | 2 | 1 | ...... | 1 | ...... | 1 | ...... | ...... | ...... | ...... | ...... | ...... | ...... | Less than $3 00 |
| $3 00–$3 49... | .... | 2 | .... | ...... | ...... | ...... | ...... | ...... | ...... | 1 | ...... | ...... | ...... | ...... | ...$3 00–$3 49 |
| 3 50– 3 99... | 2 | 1 | 2 | 1 | 1 | ...... | ...... | ...... | 1 | ...... | ...... | ...... | ...... | ...... | ... 3 50– 3 99 |
| 4 00– 4 49... | 7 | 4 | 1 | 1 | ...... | ...... | 2 | ...... | ...... | ...... | ...... | ...... | ...... | ...... | ... 4 00– 4 49 |
| 4 50– 4 99... | 10 | ...... | 1 | 1 | ...... | 1 | ...... | ...... | ...... | ...... | ...... | ...... | ...... | ...... | ... 4 50– 4 99 |
| 5 00– 5 49... | 23 | 4 | 4 | 1 | 1 | 2 | ...... | 1 | ...... | 1 | 1 | ...... | 1 | ...... | ... 5 00– 5 49 |
| 5 50– 5 99... | 6 | 1 | 2 | 3 | 1 | ...... | ...... | 1 | ...... | ...... | ...... | ...... | ...... | ...... | ... 5 50– 5 99 |
| 6 00– 6 49... | 20 | 3 | 4 | 1 | 4 | ...... | ...... | 1 | ...... | 2 | ...... | ...... | 1 | 1 | ... 6 00– 6 49 |
| 6 50– 6 99... | 13 | 4 | 4 | ...... | 1 | ...... | 2 | 2 | 2 | 1 | 2 | ...... | ...... | ...... | ... 6 50– 6 99 |
| 7 00– 7 49... | 19 | 6 | 4 | 2 | 1 | 1 | ...... | ...... | 1 | 1 | ...... | ...... | ...... | ...... | ... 7 00– 7 49 |
| 7 50– 7 99... | 7 | 3 | 5 | 4 | 1 | 1 | 3 | ...... | ...... | 1 | 1 | ...... | ...... | ...... | ... 7 50– 7 99 |
| 8 00– 8 99... | 29 | 3 | 9 | 2 | 6 | 5 | 8 | 3 | 5 | 1 | 1 | 1 | 1 | ...... | ... 8 00– 8 99 |
| 9 00– 9 99... | 47 | 3 | 25 | 2 | 13 | 2 | 10 | 1 | 6 | ...... | 4 | 1 | 4 | ...... | ... 9 00– 9 99 |
| 10 00–10 99... | 20 | 1 | 17 | ...... | 15 | 1 | 18 | ...... | 7 | ...... | 4 | ...... | 2 | ...... | ...10 00–10 99 |
| 11 00–11 99... | 24 | ...... | 7 | ...... | 15 | ...... | 11 | ...... | 2 | ...... | 1 | ...... | 6 | ...... | ...11 00–11 99 |
| 12 00–12 99... | 35 | ...... | 13 | ...... | 12 | ...... | 11 | 1 | 8 | ...... | 8 | ...... | 6 | ...... | ...12 00–12 99 |
| 13 00–13 99... | 18 | ...... | 10 | ...... | 9 | ...... | 11 | ...... | 2 | ...... | 4 | ...... | 3 | ...... | ...13 00–13 99 |
| 14 00–14 99... | 19 | ...... | 12 | ...... | 11 | ...... | 3 | ...... | 1 | ...... | 2 | ...... | 4 | ...... | ...14 00–14 99 |
| 15 00–15 99... | 18 | ...... | 17 | ...... | 7 | ...... | 9 | ...... | 8 | ...... | 4 | ...... | 1 | ...... | ...15 00–15 99 |
| 16 00–17 99... | 27 | ...... | 16 | ...... | 9 | ...... | 12 | ...... | 10 | ...... | 3 | ...... | 6 | ...... | ...16 00–17 99 |
| 18 00–19 99... | 27 | ...... | 20 | ...... | 15 | ...... | 13 | ...... | 5 | ...... | 8 | ...... | 3 | ...... | ...18 00–19 99 |
| 20 00–24 99... | 25 | ...... | 16 | ...... | 12 | ...... | 10 | ...... | 8 | ...... | 6 | ...... | 1 | ...... | ...20 00–24 99 |
| 25 00–29 99... | 11 | ...... | 4 | 1 | 7 | ...... | 6 | ...... | 3 | ...... | 3 | ...... | 4 | ...... | ...25 00–29 99 |
| 30 00–34 99... | 2 | ...... | 2 | ...... | ...... | ...... | 1 | ...... | ...... | ...... | ...... | ...... | ...... | ...... | ...30 00–34 99 |
| 35 00–39 99... | 1 | ...... | 1 | ...... | 1 | ...... | 1 | ...... | ...... | ...... | ...... | ...... | ...... | ...... | ...35 00–39 99 |
| 40 00 and over. | 1 | ...... | .... | ...... | ...... | ...... | 1 | ...... | 1 | ...... | ...... | ...... | ...... | ...... | .40 00 and over |
| Not reported... | 1 | ...... | 1 | ...... | 1 | ...... | ...... | ...... | ...... | ...... | ...... | ...... | ...... | ...... | ...Not reported |
| Total..... | 418 | 37 | 198 | 19 | 144 | 13 | 133 | 10 | 70 | 8 | 52 | 2 | 43 | 1 | .....Total |

155. TABLE XIII, B, C, D, c—(*continued.*)

NEW YORK STATE

**MEN'S SHIRT, CONFECTIONERY AND PAPER BOX INDUSTRIES — PLANT**

NUMBER AND PER CENT OF EMPLOYEES FOR EACH SEX CLASSIFIED ACCORDING TO ACTUAL WEEKLY EARNINGS BY THE NUMBER OF YEARS WITH THE FIRM

| ACTUAL WEEKLY EARNINGS IN DOLLARS | YEARS WITH FIRM | | | | | | | | | | | | ACTUAL WEEKLY EARNINGS IN DOLLARS |
|---|---|---|---|---|---|---|---|---|---|---|---|---|---|
| | 7 | | 8 | | 9 | | 10–14 | | 15–19 | | 20–24 | | |
| | Male | Female | Male | Female | Male | Female | Male | Female | Male | Female | Male | Female | |
| Less than $3 00 | | | | | | | 1 | | | | | | Less than $3 00 |
| $4 00–$4 49 | | 1 | | | | | | | | | | | $4 00– 4 49 |
| 4 50– 4 99 | | | | 1 | | | | | | | | | 4 50– 4 99 |
| 5 00– 5 49 | 1 | | | | | | | | | | 1 | | 5 00– 5 49 |
| 5 50– 5 99 | | | | | | | | | | | 1 | | 5 50– 5 99 |
| 6 00– 6 49 | | | | 1 | | | | | | 1 | | | 6 00– 6 49 |
| 6 50– 6 99 | | | | | 1 | | | | | | | | 6 50– 6 99 |
| 7 00– 7 49 | | 1 | | | | 1 | | | | | | 1 | 7 00– 7 49 |
| 7 50– 7 99 | 1 | 1 | | | 1 | | | 3 | | | | 1 | 7 50– 7 99 |
| 8 00– 8 99 | 1 | 2 | | | | | 2 | 4 | | | | | 8 00– 8 99 |
| 9 00– 9 99 | 1 | | 1 | 1 | | 1 | 2 | 1 | | | 1 | | 9 00– 9 99 |
| 10 00–10 99 | 4 | | 4 | | 1 | | 3 | | 1 | | | | 10 00–10 99 |
| 11 00–11 99 | 1 | | 1 | | 1 | | 5 | | 5 | | 2 | | 11 00–11 99 |
| 12 00–12 99 | 5 | | 4 | | 4 | | 8 | 1 | 2 | | 2 | | 12 00–12 99 |
| 13 00–13 99 | 3 | | 2 | | 2 | | 6 | | 4 | | | | 13 00–13 99 |
| 14 00–14 99 | 4 | | 5 | | 3 | | 11 | | 10 | | | | 14 00 14 99 |
| 15 00–15 99 | 3 | | 2 | | 1 | | 11 | | 5 | | | | 15 00–15 99 |
| 16 00–17 99 | 5 | | 6 | | 3 | | 14 | | 4 | | 1 | | 16 00–17 99 |
| 18 00–19 99 | 3 | | 4 | | 1 | | 16 | | 3 | | 5 | | 18 00–19 99 |
| 20 00–24 99 | 7 | | 3 | | 3 | | 18 | | 6 | | 3 | | 20 00–24 99 |
| 25 00–29 99 | 3 | | 4 | | 2 | | 3 | | | | 2 | | 25 00–29 99 |
| 30 00–34 99 | 2 | | | | | | 1 | | 1 | | 1 | | 30 00–34 99 |
| 35 00–39 99 | | | | | | | | | 1 | | | | 35 00–39 99 |
| 40 00 and over | | | | | 1 | | | | | | | | 40 00 and over |
| Not reported | | | 1 | | | | 2 | | 2 | | 1 | | Not reported |
| Total | 44 | 5 | 37 | 3 | 24 | 2 | 103 | 9 | 44 | 1 | 20 | 2 | Total |

155. TABLE XIII, B, C, D, c—(*concluded.*)

NEW YORK STATE

**MEN'S SHIRT, CONFECTIONERY AND PAPER BOX INDUSTRIES — PLANT**

NUMBER AND PER CENT OF EMPLOYEES FOR EACH SEX CLASSIFIED ACCORDING TO ACTUAL WEEKLY EARNINGS BY THE NUMBER OF YEARS WITH THE FIRM

| ACTUAL WEEKLY EARNINGS IN DOLLARS | YEARS WITH FIRM — (*concluded*) | | | | | | | | | | ACTUAL WEEKLY EARNINGS IN DOLLARS |
|---|---|---|---|---|---|---|---|---|---|---|---|
| | 25–29 | | 30–34 | 35–44 | 45 AND OVER | NOT REPORTED | TOTAL | | CUMULATIVE PER CENT OF TOTAL | | |
| | Male | Female | Male | Female | Male | Male | Male | Female | Male | Female | |
| Less than $3 00 | | | | | | | 10 | 2 | 0.74 | 1.74 | Less than $3 00 |
| $3 00–$3 49 | | | | | | | | 3 | .74 | 4.35 | $3 00–$3 49 |
| 3 50– 3 99 | | | | | | | 6 | 2 | 1.19 | 6.09 | 3 50– 3 99 |
| 4 00– 4 49 | | | | | | | 10 | 6 | 1.93 | 11.30 | 4 00– 4 49 |
| 4 50– 4 99 | | | | | | | 11 | 3 | 2.72 | 13.09 | 4 50– 4 99 |
| 5 00– 5 49 | | | | | | | 32 | 9 | 5.12 | 21.70 | 5 00– 5 49 |
| 5 50– 5 99 | | | | | | | 10 | 5 | 5.86 | 26.10 | 5 50– 5 99 |
| 6 00– 6 49 | | 1 | | | | | 29 | 11 | 8.01 | 35.60 | 6 00– 6 49 |
| 6 50– 6 99 | | | | | | | 25 | 7 | 9.86 | 41.80 | 6 50– 6 99 |
| 7 00– 7 49 | | | | 1 | | | 26 | 13 | 11.80 | 53.10 | 7 00– 7 49 |
| 7 50– 7 99 | | | | | | 1 | 20 | 14 | 13.90 | 65.30 | 7 50– 7 99 |
| 8 00– 8 99 | | 2 | | | | | 62 | 23 | 17.90 | 85.20 | 8 00– 8 99 |
| 9 00– 9 99 | | | | | | 1 | 115 | 12 | 26.20 | 95.70 | 9 00– 9 99 |
| 10 00–10 99 | 1 | | | | | | 97 | 2 | 33.60 | 97.50 | 10 00–10 99 |
| 11 00–11 99 | | | | | | 1 | 82 | | 39.70 | 97.50 | 11 00–11 99 |
| 12 00–12 99 | 1 | | | | | 1 | 120 | 2 | 48.60 | 99.20 | 12 00–12 99 |
| 13 00–13 99 | | | | | | | 74 | | 54.10 | | 13 00–13 99 |
| 14 00–14 99 | 1 | | 1 | | | 1 | 88 | | 60.60 | | 14 00–14 99 |
| 15 00–15 99 | 1 | | | 1 | | | 88 | | 67.10 | | 15 00–15 99 |
| 16 00–17 99 | | | 1 | | | 1 | 118 | | 75.90 | | 16 00–17 99 |
| 18 00–19 99 | | | 1 | 1 | | 2 | 127 | | 85.30 | | 18 00–19 99 |
| 20 00–24 99 | 2 | | 2 | | 1 | 1 | 124 | | 94.50 | | 20 00–24 99 |
| 25 00–29 99 | 1 | | 1 | | | | 54 | 1 | 98.50 | 100.00 | 25 00–29.99 |
| 30 00–34 99 | 1 | | 1 | | | | 12 | | 99.40 | | 30 00–34 99 |
| 35 00–39 99 | | | | | | | 5 | | 99.70 | | 35 00–39 99 |
| 40 00 and over | | | | | | | 4 | | 100.00 | | 40 00 and over |
| Not reported | | | | | | | 9 | | | | Not reported |
| Total | 8 | 3 | 7 | 3 | 1 | 9 | 1,358 | 115 | | | Total |

NEW YORK STATE
DEPARTMENT STORES — STOCK AND SALES

156. TABLE V, A, I, a. NUMBER AND PER CENT OF EMPLOYEES EARNING SPECIFIED WEEKLY RATES BY AGE GROUPS AND SEX

| Weekly Rates in Dollars | Age Groups in Years | | | | | | | | | | | | | | Weekly Rates in Dollars |
|---|---|---|---|---|---|---|---|---|---|---|---|---|---|---|---|
| | 14–15 | | 16–17 | | 18–20 | | 21–24 | | 25–29 | | 30–34 | | 35–39 | | |
| | Male | Female | Male | Female | Male | Female | Male | Female | Male | Female | Male | Female | Male | Female | |
| Less than $3.00 | 5 | 38 | .... | 1 | ...... | 1 | ...... | ...... | ...... | 1 | ...... | ...... | ...... | ...... | Less than $3.00 |
| $3.00–$3.49 | 26 | 73 | 6 | 83 | ...... | 6 | ...... | 1 | ...... | 1 | ...... | ...... | ...... | ...... | $3.00–$3.49 |
| 3.50–3.99 | 39 | 115 | 8 | 109 | ...... | 15 | ...... | ...... | ...... | ...... | ...... | ...... | ...... | ...... | 3.50–3.99 |
| 4.00–4.49 | 63 | 44 | 32 | 141 | 4 | 52 | 1 | 4 | ...... | ...... | ...... | 1 | ...... | ...... | 4.00–4.49 |
| 4.50–4.99 | 12 | 12 | 12 | 50 | ...... | 38 | 1 | 6 | ...... | ...... | ...... | 2 | ...... | ...... | 4.50–4.99 |
| 5.00–5.49 | 22 | 7 | 43 | 117 | 11 | 177 | ...... | 67 | ...... | 27 | ...... | 15 | ...... | 4 | 5.00–5.49 |
| 5.50–5.99 | 1 | 2 | 6 | 6 | ...... | 12 | ...... | 2 | ...... | 7 | ...... | 3 | ...... | ...... | 5.50–5.99 |
| 6.00–6.49 | 2 | 1 | 34 | 58 | 14 | 351 | 2 | 269 | 1 | 112 | ...... | 43 | ...... | 27 | 6.00–6.49 |
| 6.50–6.99 | .... | ...... | 1 | 1 | 1 | 8 | ...... | 9 | ...... | 6 | ...... | 5 | ...... | 2 | 6.50–6.99 |
| 7.00–7.49 | .... | ...... | 11 | 6 | 35 | 145 | 4 | 280 | 3 | 194 | 1 | 75 | ...... | 44 | 7.00–7.49 |
| 7.50–7.99 | .... | 1 | 2 | 1 | 3 | 7 | ...... | 28 | ...... | 24 | ...... | 7 | ...... | 5 | 7.50–7.99 |
| 8.00–8.99 | .... | ...... | 10 | 4 | 40 | 43 | 12 | 204 | 3 | 190 | 3 | 81 | ...... | 66 | 8.00–8.99 |
| 9.00–9.99 | .... | ...... | 1 | ...... | 35 | 10 | 12 | 57 | 5 | 107 | 3 | 70 | 1 | 42 | 9.00–9.99 |
| 10.00–10.99 | .... | ...... | 1 | ...... | 25 | 8 | 62 | 50 | 16 | 103 | 8 | 74 | 5 | 56 | 10.00–10.99 |
| 11.00–11.99 | .... | ...... | 1 | ...... | 4 | ...... | 21 | 7 | 6 | 26 | 1 | 25 | 1 | 11 | 11.00–11.99 |
| 12.00–12.99 | .... | ...... | 2 | ...... | 14 | 1 | 74 | 18 | 52 | 43 | 28 | 68 | 13 | 60 | 12.00–12.99 |
| 13.00–13.99 | .... | ...... | .... | ...... | ...... | ...... | 12 | 2 | 17 | 8 | 11 | 13 | 3 | 11 | 13.00–13.99 |
| 14.00–14.99 | .... | ...... | .... | ...... | 1 | ...... | 27 | 1 | 41 | 9 | 22 | 14 | 20 | 17 | 14.00–14.99 |
| 15.00–15.99 | .... | ...... | .... | ...... | 1 | 1 | ...... | 22 | 2 | 50 | 17 | 39 | 25 | 32 | 15.00–15.99 |
| 16.00–17.99 | .... | ...... | .... | ...... | ...... | 1 | 5 | 2 | 34 | 8 | 42 | 11 | 28 | 9 | 16.00–17.00 |
| 18.00–19.99 | .... | ...... | .... | ...... | ...... | ...... | 3 | ...... | 26 | 8 | 38 | 8 | 27 | 8 | 18.00–19.99 |
| 20.00–24.99 | .... | ...... | .... | ...... | ...... | ...... | 4 | 1 | 28 | 3 | 40 | 10 | 38 | 7 | 20.00–24.99 |
| 25.00–29.99 | .... | ...... | .... | ...... | ...... | ...... | ...... | ...... | 6 | ...... | 16 | 3 | 17 | 7 | 25.00–29.99 |
| 30.00–34.99 | .... | ...... | .... | ...... | ...... | ...... | ...... | ...... | 1 | ...... | 5 | ...... | 11 | 2 | 30.00–34.99 |
| 35.00–39.99 | .... | ...... | .... | ...... | ...... | ...... | ...... | ...... | ...... | ...... | 2 | ...... | 2 | 2 | 35.00–39.99 |
| 40.00 and over | .... | ...... | .... | ...... | ...... | ...... | ...... | ...... | 1 | ...... | 5 | ...... | 9 | ...... | 40.00 and over |
| Not reported | .... | ...... | 1 | ...... | 1 | 1 | 1 | 1 | ...... | ...... | ...... | 1 | 2 | 1 | Not reported |
| Total | 170 | 293 | 171 | 573 | 189 | 876 | 263 | 1,011 | 291 | 894 | 264 | 554 | 209 | 407 | Total |

156. TABLE V, A, I, a—(*concluded*)

NEW YORK STATE, EXCLUSIVE OF NEW YORK CITY
DEPARTMENT STORES — STOCK AND SALES
NUMBER AND PER CENT. OF EMPLOYEES EARNING SPECIFIED WEEKLY RATES, BY AGE GROUPS AND SEX

| Weekly Rates in Dollars | Age Groups in Years — (*concluded*) 40–44 | | 45–54 | | 55–64 | | 65 and over | | Not reported | | Total | | Cumulative per cent. of total | | Weekly Rates in Dollars |
|---|---|---|---|---|---|---|---|---|---|---|---|---|---|---|---|
| | Male | Female | Male | Female | Male | Female | Male | Female | Male | Female | Male | Female | Male | Female | |
| Less than $3 00 | .... | ...... | .... | ...... | ...... | ...... | ...... | ...... | 1 | ...... | 6 | 41 | .27 | .81 | Less than $3 00 |
| $3 00–$3 49 | .... | ...... | .... | ...... | ...... | ...... | ...... | ...... | 1 | ...... | 33 | 164 | 1.78 | 4.05 | $3 00– 3 49 |
| 3 50– 3 99 | 1 | ...... | .... | ...... | ...... | ...... | ...... | ...... | ...... | 1 | 48 | 240 | 3.97 | 8.78 | 3 50– 3 99 |
| 4 00– 4 49 | .... | ...... | .... | ...... | ...... | ...... | ...... | ...... | ...... | ...... | 100 | 242 | 8.54 | 13.55 | 4 00– 4 49 |
| 4 50– 4 99 | .... | ...... | .... | ...... | ...... | ...... | ...... | ...... | ...... | 1 | 25 | 109 | 9.66 | 15.45 | 4 50– 4 99 |
| 5 00– 5 49 | .... | 2 | .... | 2 | ...... | ...... | ...... | ...... | 2 | 2 | 78 | 420 | 13.22 | 24.00 | 5 00– 5 49 |
| 5 50– 5 99 | .... | 1 | .... | ...... | ...... | ...... | ...... | ...... | ...... | 1 | 7 | 29 | 13.55 | 24.58 | 5 50– 5 99 |
| 6 00– 6 49 | .... | 10 | .... | 9 | 1 | ...... | ...... | ...... | ...... | 9 | 54 | 889 | 16.00 | 42.10 | 6 00– 6 49 |
| 6 50– 6 99 | .... | 1 | .... | ...... | ...... | ...... | ...... | ...... | ...... | ...... | 2 | 32 | 16.10 | 42.75 | 6 50– 6 99 |
| 7 00– 7 49 | .... | 22 | .... | 13 | 1 | ...... | ...... | ...... | 1 | 10 | 56 | 789 | 18.68 | 53.25 | 7 00– 7 49 |
| 7 50– 7 99 | .... | 3 | .... | 3 | ...... | ...... | ...... | ...... | ...... | ...... | 5 | 79 | 18.90 | 59.80 | 7 50– 7 99 |
| 8 00– 8 99 | 1 | 27 | .... | 33 | 1 | 1 | ...... | 1 | 1 | 16 | 71 | 666 | 22.10 | 73.00 | 8 00– 8 99 |
| 9 00– 9 99 | 2 | 13 | 2 | 12 | ...... | ...... | ...... | ...... | ...... | 12 | 61 | 323 | 24.90 | 79.30 | 9 00– 9 99 |
| 10 00–10 99 | 2 | 25 | 6 | 20 | 5 | 4 | 2 | ...... | 1 | 19 | 133 | 359 | 31.00 | 86.50 | 10 00–10 99 |
| 11 00–11 99 | .... | 7 | 2 | 2 | 2 | ...... | 1 | ...... | 1 | 9 | 40 | 87 | 32.80 | 88.20 | 11 00–11 99 |
| 12 00–12 99 | 8 | 34 | 19 | 20 | 13 | 2 | 1 | ...... | 2 | 8 | 226 | 254 | 43.10 | 93.20 | 12 00–12 99 |
| 13 00–13 99 | 6 | 4 | 7 | 5 | 2 | ...... | 3 | ...... | ...... | 2 | 61 | 45 | 45.80 | 94.10 | 13 00–13 99 |
| 14 00–14 99 | 13 | 8 | 25 | 3 | 9 | 1 | 4 | ...... | 2 | 6 | 164 | 59 | 53.40 | 95.15 | 14 00–14 99 |
| 15 00–15 99 | 17 | 15 | 42 | 11 | 13 | ...... | 6 | ...... | 4 | 7 | 226 | 104 | 63.60 | 97.20 | 15 00–15 99 |
| 16 00–17 99 | 26 | 6 | 39 | 7 | 14 | ...... | 4 | ...... | ...... | 5 | 192 | 49 | 72.40 | 98.25 | 16 00–17 99 |
| 18 00–19 99 | 29 | 4 | 30 | 4 | 9 | ...... | 4 | ...... | 1 | 1 | 167 | 33 | 80.00 | 98.90 | 18 00–19 99 |
| 20 00–24 99 | 46 | 1 | 53 | 3 | 13 | 1 | 3 | 1 | 1 | 1 | 227 | 28 | 90.50 | 99.40 | 20 00–24 99 |
| 25 00–29 99 | 24 | ...... | 34 | 3 | 10 | ...... | ...... | ...... | ...... | 2 | 107 | 15 | 95.25 | 99.70 | 25 00–29 99 |
| 30 00–34 99 | 9 | 3 | 14 | 1 | 7 | ...... | ...... | ...... | ...... | 2 | 47 | 8 | 97.25 | 99.90 | 30 00–34 99 |
| 35 00–39 99 | 4 | ...... | 7 | 1 | 3 | ...... | 1 | ...... | ...... | 1 | 19 | 4 | 98.10 | 99.97 | 35 00–39 99 |
| 40 00 and over | 7 | ...... | 13 | 1 | 3 | 1 | 2 | ...... | ...... | ...... | 40 | 2 | 100.00 | 100.00 | 40 00 and over |
| Not reported | .... | ...... | .... | ...... | ...... | ...... | ...... | ...... | ...... | ...... | 5 | 4 | ...... | ...... | Not reported |
| Total | 195 | 186 | 293 | 153 | 106 | 10 | 31 | 2 | 18 | 115 | 2,200 | 5,074 | ...... | ...... | Total |

## NEW YORK STATE, EXCLUSIVE OF NEW YORK CITY
## DEPARTMENT STORES — STOCK AND SALES

157. TABLE VIII, R, 1, a   NUMBER AND PER CENT. OF EMPLOYEES EARNING SPECIFIED WEEKLY RATES, BY OCCUPATION AND SEX

| Weekly Rates in Dollars | Occupation: Superintendents | Buyers | | Assistant Buyers and Heads of Stock | | Receiving and Stock Clerks | | Stock People | | Floor Managers | | Sales People | | Messengers, Wrappers and Errand Boys | | Total | | Cumulative Per Cent. of Total | | Weekly Rates in Dollars |
|---|---|---|---|---|---|---|---|---|---|---|---|---|---|---|---|---|---|---|---|---|
| | Male | Male | Female | Male | Female | Male | Female | Male | Female | Male | Female | Male | Female | Male | Female | Male | Female | Male | Female | |
| Less than $3 00 | | | | | | 1 | | 1 | 3 | | | | 3 | 4 | 35 | 6 | 41 | .27 | .81 | Less than $3 00 |
| $3 00–$3 49 | | | | | | | | 2 | 13 | | | 1 | 14 | 30 | 137 | 33 | 164 | 1.78 | 4.05 | $3 00– 3 49 |
| 3 50– 3 99 | | | | | | 1 | | 8 | 34 | | | 1 | 13 | 38 | 193 | 48 | 240 | 3.97 | 8.78 | 3 50– 3 99 |
| 4 00– 4 49 | | | | | | 1 | 1 | 33 | 35 | | | 2 | 76 | 64 | 130 | 100 | 242 | 8.54 | 13.55 | 4 00 4 49 |
| 4 50– 4 99 | | | | | | | 2 | 9 | 13 | | | | 45 | 16 | 49 | 25 | 109 | 9.66 | 15.45 | 4 50– 4 99 |
| 5 00– 5 49 | | | | | | | 2 | 35 | 35 | | | 8 | 331 | 35 | 52 | 78 | 420 | 13.22 | 24.00 | 5 00– 5 49 |
| 5 50– 5 99 | | | | | | | | 1 | 1 | | | | 26 | 6 | 2 | 7 | 29 | 13.55 | 24.58 | 5 50– 5 99 |
| 6 00– 6 49 | | | | | | 1 | 4 | 15 | 21 | | | 23 | 849 | 15 | 15 | 54 | 889 | 16.00 | 42.10 | 6 00– 6 49 |
| 6 50– 6 99 | | | | | | | | | | | | 1 | 32 | 1 | | 2 | 32 | 16.10 | 42.75 | 6 50– 6 99 |
| 7 00– 7 49 | | | | | 1 | 1 | 4 | 12 | 10 | | | 28 | 771 | 15 | 3 | 56 | 789 | 18.68 | 53.25 | 7 00– 7 49 |
| 7 50– 7 99 | | | | | | | | 2 | 1 | | | 1 | 78 | 2 | | 5 | 79 | 18.90 | 59.80 | 7 50– 7 99 |
| 8 00– 8 99 | | | 1 | 2 | 1 | 3 | 1 | 10 | 2 | | 1 | 50 | 654 | 6 | 6 | 71 | 666 | 22.10 | 73.00 | 8 00– 8 99 |
| 9 00– 9 99 | | | | | 2 | 4 | 6 | 10 | 1 | | | 38 | 314 | | | 61 | 323 | 24.90 | 79.30 | 9 00– 9 99 |
| 10 00–10 99 | | 1 | 3 | 3 | 12 | 10 | 1 | 18 | 1 | 1 | 1 | 91 | 341 | 9 | | 133 | 359 | 31.00 | 86.50 | 10 00–10 99 |
| 11 00–11 99 | | | 2 | | 4 | 2 | 2 | 7 | | | | 31 | 79 | | | 40 | 87 | 32.80 | 88.20 | 11 00–11 99 |
| 12 00–12 99 | | 2 | 2 | 4 | 17 | 20 | | 24 | | | 3 | 172 | 231 | 4 | 1 | 226 | 254 | 43.10 | 93.20 | 12 00–12 99 |
| 13 00–13 99 | | | | 2 | 3 | 5 | 1 | 3 | | | | 50 | 41 | 1 | | 61 | 45 | 45.80 | 94.10 | 13 00–13 99 |
| 14 00–14 99 | | | 1 | 4 | 5 | 9 | 1 | 4 | | 5 | | 140 | 52 | 2 | | 164 | 59 | 53.40 | 95.15 | 14 00–14 99 |
| 15 00–15 99 | | 1 | 4 | 2 | 15 | 8 | 1 | 8 | | 17 | | 187 | 84 | 3 | | 226 | 104 | 63.60 | 97.20 | 15 00 15 99 |
| 16 00–17 99 | | 8 | 3 | 5 | 9 | 4 | | 7 | | 16 | 1 | 152 | 36 | | | 192 | 49 | 72.40 | 98.25 | 16 00–17 99 |
| 18 00–19 99 | | 2 | | 13 | 5 | 2 | | | | 24 | 3 | 126 | 25 | | | 167 | 33 | 80.00 | 98.90 | 18 00–19 99 |
| 20 00–24 99 | 2 | 10 | 3 | 28 | 7 | 1 | | 1 | | 39 | 3 | 146 | 15 | | | 227 | 28 | 90.50 | 99.40 | 20 00–24 99 |
| 25 00–29 99 | 3 | 19 | 6 | 18 | 6 | 1 | | | | 20 | 1 | 46 | 2 | | | 107 | 15 | 95.25 | 99.70 | 25 00–29 99 |
| 30 00–34 99 | 2 | 22 | 4 | 4 | 3 | 1 | | | | 6 | | 12 | 1 | | | 47 | 8 | 97.25 | 99.90 | 30 00–34 99 |
| 35 00–39 99 | 1 | 10 | 4 | 1 | | | | | | 6 | | 1 | | | | 19 | 4 | 98.10 | 99.97 | 35 00–39 99 |
| 40 00 and over | 3 | 31 | 2 | 2 | | | | | | 4 | | | | | | 40 | 2 | 100.00 | 100.00 | 40 00 and over |
| Not reported | | | | 2 | | | | | | | | 1 | 4 | 2 | | 5 | 4 | | | Not reported |
| Total | 11 | 106 | 35 | 90 | 90 | 75 | 26 | 210 | 170 | 138 | 13 | 1,308 | 4,117 | 262 | 623 | 2,200 | 5,074 | | | Total |

158. TABLE VI, A, 1, a

NEW YORK STATE, EXCLUSIVE OF NEW YORK CITY
DEPARTMENT STORES — STOCK AND SALES

NUMBER AND PER CENT. OF EMPLOYEES CLASSIFIED ACCORDING TO ACTUAL WEEKLY EARNINGS, BY AGE GROUPS AND SEX

| Actual Weekly Earnings in Dollars | Age Groups in Years | | | | | | | | | | | | | | Actual Weekly Earnings in Dollars |
|---|---|---|---|---|---|---|---|---|---|---|---|---|---|---|---|
| | 14–15 | | 16–17 | | 18–20 | | 21–24 | | 25–29 | | 30–34 | | 35–39 | | |
| | Male | Female | Male | Female | Male | Female | Male | Female | Male | Female | Male | Female | Male | Female | |
| Less than $3 00 | 14 | 60 | 5 | 29 | ...... | 21 | 1 | 12 | ...... | 13 | ...... | 5 | ...... | 1 | Less than $3 00 |
| $3 00–$3 49... | 25 | 68 | 8 | 82 | 1 | 13 | 2 | 6 | ...... | 1 | ...... | 1 | ...... | 1 | ...$3 00– 3 49 |
| 3 50– 3 99... | 41 | 102 | 11 | 108 | ...... | 31 | ...... | 7 | ...... | 3 | ...... | 4 | ...... | ...... | ... 3 50– 3 99 |
| 4 00– 4 49... | 54 | 40 | 27 | 141 | 6 | 67 | 1 | 15 | ...... | 8 | ...... | 5 | ...... | 2 | ... 4 00– 4 49 |
| 4 50– 4 99... | 12 | 12 | 14 | 52 | 3 | 47 | 1 | 13 | ...... | 8 | ...... | 3 | ...... | 2 | ... 4 50– 4 99 |
| 5 00– 5 49... | 21 | 7 | 38 | 96 | 9 | 165 | ...... | 84 | ...... | 36 | ...... | 16 | ...... | 8 | ... 5 00– 5 49 |
| 5 50– 5 99... | 1 | 2 | 7 | 5 | 1 | 34 | 1 | 26 | 1 | 30 | ...... | 7 | ...... | 3 | ... 5 50– 5 99 |
| 6 00– 6 49... | 1 | 1 | 32 | 43 | 15 | 261 | 3 | 224 | 2 | 95 | 1 | 44 | ...... | 23 | ... 6 00– 6 49 |
| 6 50– 6 99... | .... | ...... | 2 | 4 | 4 | 28 | ...... | 31 | ...... | 21 | ...... | 9 | ...... | 10 | ... 6 50– 6 99 |
| 7 00– 7 49... | .... | ...... | 8 | 6 | 35 | 126 | 5 | 239 | 3 | 158 | 1 | 58 | ...... | 35 | ... 7 00– 7 49 |
| 7 50– 7 99... | .... | ...... | 2 | 1 | 3 | 13 | 1 | 28 | ...... | 35 | ...... | 13 | ...... | 13 | ... 7 50– 7 99 |
| 8 00– 8 99... | .... | 1 | 9 | 4 | 37 | 48 | 14 | 177 | 4 | 158 | 3 | 78 | ...... | 58 | ... 8 00– 8 99 |
| 9 00– 9 99... | .... | ...... | 1 | ...... | 31 | 9 | 12 | 61 | 5 | 99 | 4 | 70 | 1 | 40 | ... 9 00– 9 99 |
| 10 00–10 99... | .... | ...... | 1 | ...... | 22 | 4 | 65 | 42 | 16 | 100 | 7 | 62 | 5 | 55 | ...10 00–10 99 |
| 11 00–11 99... | .... | ...... | 1 | ...... | 5 | ...... | 18 | 12 | 14 | 26 | 8 | 29 | 2 | 16 | ...11 00–11 99 |
| 12 00–12 99... | .... | ...... | 2 | ...... | 13 | 1 | 61 | 16 | 44 | 37 | 23 | 59 | 12 | 39 | ...12 00–12 99 |
| 13 00–13 99... | .... | ...... | .... | ...... | ...... | ...... | 17 | 5 | 15 | 9 | 8 | 16 | 3 | 16 | ...13 00–13 99 |
| 14 00–14 99... | .... | ...... | .... | ...... | 1 | ...... | 25 | 1 | 36 | 9 | 20 | 18 | 17 | 20 | ...14 00–14 99 |
| 15 00–15 99... | .... | ...... | .... | ...... | 1 | ...... | 21 | 2 | 50 | 14 | 38 | 20 | 29 | 24 | ...15 00–15 99 |
| 16 00–17 99... | .... | ...... | .... | ...... | ...... | 1 | 5 | 2 | 33 | 13 | 35 | 11 | 32 | 13 | ...16 00–17 99 |
| 18 00–19 99... | .... | ...... | .... | ...... | ...... | ...... | 3 | ...... | 27 | 7 | 40 | 10 | 27 | 7 | ...18 00–19 99 |
| 20 00–24 99... | .... | ...... | .... | ...... | ...... | ...... | 4 | 1 | 30 | 2 | 42 | 9 | 37 | 5 | ...20 00–24 99 |
| 25 00–29 99... | .... | ...... | .... | ...... | ...... | ...... | ...... | ...... | 6 | ...... | 18 | 3 | 18 | 5 | ...25 00–29 99 |
| 30 00–34 99... | .... | ...... | .... | ...... | ...... | ...... | ...... | ...... | 1 | ...... | 5 | ...... | 12 | 2 | ...30 00–34 99 |
| 35 00–39 99... | .... | ...... | .... | ...... | ...... | ...... | ...... | ...... | ...... | ...... | 2 | ...... | 3 | 2 | ...35 00–39 99 |
| 40 00 and over. | .... | ...... | .... | ...... | ...... | ...... | ...... | ...... | 1 | ...... | 5 | ...... | 10 | ...... | .40 00 and over |
| Not reported... | 1 | ...... | 3 | 2 | 3 | 7 | 3 | 7 | 3 | 12 | 4 | 4 | 1 | 7 | ...Not reported |
| Total..... | 170 | 293 | 171 | 573 | 190 | 876 | 263 | 1,011 | 291 | 894 | 264 | 554 | 209 | 407 | .....Total |

158. TABLE VI, A, 1, a — (*concluded*)

NEW YORK STATE, EXCLUSIVE OF NEW YORK CITY

**DEPARTMENT STORES — STOCK AND SALES**

NUMBER AND PER CENT. OF EMPLOYEES CLASSIFIED ACCORDING TO ACTUAL WEEKLY EARNINGS, BY AGE GROUPS AND SEX

| ACTUAL WEEKLY EARNINGS IN DOLLARS | AGE GROUPS IN YEARS (*Concluded*) | | | | | | | | | | | | | | ACTUAL WEEKLY EARNINGS IN DOLLARS |
|---|---|---|---|---|---|---|---|---|---|---|---|---|---|---|---|
| | 40–44 | | 45–54 | | 55–64 | | 65 AND OVER | | NOT REPORTED | | TOTAL | | CUMULATIVE PER CENT. OF TOTAL | | |
| | Male | Female | Male | Female | Male | Female | Male | Female | Male | Female | Male | Female | Male | Female | |
| Less than $3 00 | .... | ...... | .... | ...... | ...... | ...... | ...... | ...... | 1 | 1 | 21 | 142 | .90 | 2.80 | Less than $3 00 |
| $3 00–$3 49 | .... | ...... | .... | ...... | ...... | ...... | ...... | ...... | 2 | ...... | 38 | 172 | 2.70 | 6.30 | $3 00– 3 49 |
| 3 50– 3 99 | 1 | ...... | .... | ...... | ...... | ...... | ...... | ...... | ...... | 1 | 53 | 256 | 5.20 | 11.40 | 3 50– 3 99 |
| 4 00– 4 49 | .... | 2 | .... | ...... | ...... | ...... | ...... | ...... | ...... | ...... | 88 | 280 | 9.20 | 16.90 | 4 00– 4 49 |
| 4 50– 4 99 | .... | ...... | .... | ...... | ...... | ...... | ...... | ...... | ...... | 1 | 30 | 138 | 10.60 | 19.70 | 4 50– 4 99 |
| 5 00– 5 49 | .... | 4 | .... | 6 | ...... | ...... | ...... | ...... | 2 | 3 | 70 | 425 | 13.80 | 28.20 | 5 00– 5 49 |
| 5 50– 5 99 | .... | 2 | .... | 2 | ...... | ...... | ...... | ...... | ...... | ...... | 11 | 111 | 14.70 | 30.40 | 5 50– 5 99 |
| 6 00– 6 49 | .... | 11 | .... | 9 | 1 | ...... | ...... | ...... | ...... | 10 | 55 | 721 | 16.90 | 44.70 | 6 00– 6 49 |
| 6 50– 6 99 | .... | ...... | .... | ...... | ...... | ...... | ...... | ...... | ...... | 4 | 6 | 107 | 17.30 | 46.80 | 6 50– 6 99 |
| 7 00– 7 49 | .... | 20 | 1 | 11 | 1 | ...... | ...... | ...... | 1 | 9 | 55 | 662 | 19.70 | 60.00 | 7 00– 7 49 |
| 7 50– 7 99 | .... | 6 | .... | 4 | 1 | ...... | ...... | ...... | ...... | 1 | 7 | 114 | 20.00 | 62.40 | 7 50– 7 99 |
| 8 00– 8 99 | 1 | 23 | .... | 29 | 1 | ...... | ...... | 1 | 1 | 17 | 70 | 594 | 23.20 | 74.10 | 8 00– 8 99 |
| 9 00– 9 99 | 2 | 12 | 5 | 10 | ...... | ...... | ...... | ...... | ...... | 11 | 61 | 312 | 26.10 | 80.30 | 9 00– 9 99 |
| 10 00–10 99 | 3 | 24 | 5 | 17 | 5 | 3 | 2 | ...... | 1 | 15 | 132 | 322 | 32.20 | 86.80 | 10 00–10 99 |
| 11 00–11 99 | .... | 8 | 1 | 5 | 1 | ...... | 2 | ...... | ...... | 8 | 52 | 104 | 34.60 | 88.90 | 11 00–11 99 |
| 12 00–12 99 | 7 | 29 | 20 | 14 | 14 | 2 | 1 | ...... | 2 | 8 | 199 | 205 | 43.70 | 93.00 | 12 00–12 99 |
| 13 00–13 99 | 5 | 4 | 9 | 7 | 1 | ...... | 2 | ...... | ...... | 1 | 60 | 58 | 46.50 | 94.10 | 13 00–13 99 |
| 14 00–14 99 | 13 | 12 | 21 | 2 | 10 | 1 | 3 | ...... | 2 | 7 | 148 | 70 | 53.20 | 95.40 | 14 00–14 99 |
| 15 00–15 99 | 17 | 12 | 39 | 9 | 10 | ...... | 4 | ...... | 4 | 7 | 213 | 88 | 60.30 | 97.20 | 15 00–15 99 |
| 16 00–17 99 | 23 | 5 | 37 | 8 | 15 | ...... | 5 | ...... | ...... | 3 | 185 | 56 | 71.60 | 98.20 | 16 00–17 99 |
| 18 00–19 99 | 27 | 4 | 31 | 2 | 8 | ...... | 5 | ...... | 1 | 1 | 169 | 31 | 79.40 | 99.00 | 18 00–19 99 |
| 20 00–24 99 | 47 | 2 | 50 | 3 | 13 | 1 | 3 | 1 | 1 | 1 | 227 | 25 | 89.90 | 99.50 | 20–00 24 99 |
| 25 00–29 99 | 25 | ...... | 36 | 3 | 10 | ...... | ...... | ...... | ...... | 2 | 113 | 13 | 95.30 | 99.70 | 25 00–29 99 |
| 30 00–34 99 | 9 | 3 | 14 | 1 | 8 | ...... | ...... | ...... | ...... | 2 | 49 | 8 | 97.30 | 99.90 | 30 00–34 99 |
| 35 00–39 99 | 4 | ...... | 7 | 1 | 2 | ...... | 1 | ...... | ...... | 1 | 19 | 4 | 98.20 | 99.90 | 35 00–39 99 |
| 40 00 and over | 7 | ...... | 13 | 1 | 3 | 1 | 2 | ...... | ...... | ...... | 41 | 2 | 100.00 | 100.00 | 40 00 and over |
| Not reported | 4 | 3 | 4 | 9 | 2 | 2 | 1 | ...... | ...... | 1 | 29 | 54 | ...... | ...... | Not reported |
| Total | 195 | 186 | 293 | 153 | 106 | 10 | 31 | 2 | 18 | 115 | 2,201 | 5,074 | ...... | ...... | Total |

NEW YORK STATE, EXCLUSIVE OF NEW YORK CITY
**DEPARTMENT STORES — STOCK AND SALES**

159. TABLE IX, A, 1, a  NUMBER AND PER CENT. OF EMPLOYEES CLASSIFIED ACCORDING TO ACTUAL WEEKLY EARNINGS, BY OCCUPATION AND SEX

| Actual Weekly Earnings in Dollars | Occupation: Superintendents | Buyers | | Assistant Buyers and Heads of Stock | | Receiving and Stock Clerks | | Stock People | | Floor Managers | | Sales People | | Messengers, Wrappers and Errand Boys | | Total | | Cumulative Per Cent. of Total | | Actual Weekly Earnings in Dollars |
|---|---|---|---|---|---|---|---|---|---|---|---|---|---|---|---|---|---|---|---|---|
| | Male | Male | Female | Male | Female | Male | Female | Male | Female | Male | Female | Male | Female | Male | Female | Male | Female | Male | Female | |
| Less than $3 00 | | | 1 | | 1 | 1 | | 6 | 8 | | | 1 | 56 | 13 | 76 | 21 | 142 | .90 | 2.80 | Less than $3 00 |
| 3 00–$3 49 | | | | | | | | 5 | 14 | | | 4 | 28 | 29 | 130 | 38 | 172 | 2.70 | 6.30 | $3 00– 3 49 |
| 3 50– 3 99 | | | | | | 2 | | 8 | 35 | | | 2 | 43 | 41 | 178 | 53 | 256 | 5.20 | 11.40 | 3 50– 3 99 |
| 4 00– 4 49 | | | | | | | 2 | 31 | 31 | | | 2 | 127 | 55 | 120 | 88 | 280 | 9.20 | 16.90 | 4 00– 4 49 |
| 4 50– 4 99 | | | | | | | 2 | 11 | 14 | | | 2 | 80 | 17 | 42 | 30 | 138 | 10.60 | 19.70 | 4 50– 4 99 |
| 5 00– 5 49 | | | 1 | | 1 | | 2 | 31 | 34 | | | 6 | 333 | 33 | 54 | 70 | 425 | 13.80 | 28.20 | 5 00– 5 49 |
| 5 50– 5 99 | | | | | | | | 2 | 1 | | | 3 | 107 | 6 | 3 | 11 | 111 | 14.70 | 30.40 | 5 50– 5 99 |
| 6 00– 6 49 | | | | | | 1 | 3 | 14 | 20 | | | 26 | 689 | 14 | 9 | 55 | 721 | 16.90 | 44.70 | 6 00– 6 49 |
| 6 50– 6 99 | | | | | 1 | | 1 | | | | | 4 | 105 | 2 | | 6 | 107 | 17.30 | 46.80 | 6 50– 6 99 |
| 7 00– 7 49 | | | | 1 | 1 | 1 | 3 | 10 | 9 | | | 28 | 646 | 15 | 3 | 55 | 662 | 19.70 | 60.00 | 7 00– 7 49 |
| 7 50– 7 99 | | | | | | | | 2 | 1 | | | 3 | 113 | 2 | | 7 | 114 | 20.00 | 62.40 | 7 50– 7 99 |
| 8 00– 8 99 | | | 1 | 1 | 2 | 3 | 2 | 10 | 2 | | | 50 | 581 | 6 | 6 | 70 | 594 | 23.20 | 74.10 | 8 00– 8 99 |
| 9 00– 9 99 | | | | 1 | 3 | 4 | 6 | 11 | 1 | 2 | | 36 | 302 | 7 | | 61 | 312 | 26.10 | 80.30 | 9 00– 9 99 |
| 10 00–10 99 | | 1 | 2 | 3 | 13 | 10 | 1 | 17 | | 1 | 2 | 92 | 304 | 8 | | 132 | 322 | 32.10 | 86.80 | 10 00–10 99 |
| 11 00–11 99 | | | 2 | | 3 | 4 | 1 | 8 | | | | 40 | 98 | | | 52 | 104 | 34.60 | 88.90 | 11 00–11 99 |
| 12 00–12 99 | | 2 | 2 | 3 | 15 | 20 | | 21 | | | 2 | 149 | 185 | 4 | 1 | 199 | 205 | 43.70 | 93.00 | 12 00–12 99 |
| 13 00–13 99 | | | | 2 | 3 | 4 | 1 | 4 | | | | 49 | 54 | 1 | | 60 | 58 | 46.50 | 94.10 | 13 00–13 99 |
| 14 00–14 99 | | | 1 | 4 | 3 | 8 | 1 | 4 | | 4 | | 126 | 65 | 2 | | 148 | 70 | 53.20 | 95.40 | 14 00 14 99 |
| 15 00–15 99 | | 1 | 3 | 2 | 13 | 8 | 1 | 7 | | 17 | | 175 | 71 | 3 | | 213 | 88 | 63.00 | 97.20 | 15 00–15 99 |
| 16 00–17 99 | | 9 | 4 | 3 | 12 | 4 | | 7 | | 17 | 1 | 145 | 39 | | | 185 | 56 | 71.60 | 98.20 | 16 00–17 99 |
| 18 00–19 99 | | 2 | | 12 | 5 | 2 | | | | 22 | 2 | 131 | 24 | | | 169 | 31 | 79.40 | 99.00 | 18 00–19 99 |
| 20 00–24 99 | 2 | 10 | 2 | 28 | 6 | 1 | | 1 | | 38 | 3 | 147 | 14 | | | 227 | 25 | 89.90 | 99.50 | 20 00–24 99 |
| 25 00–29 99 | 3 | 18 | 6 | 18 | 4 | 1 | | | | 20 | 1 | 53 | 2 | | | 113 | 13 | 95.30 | 99.70 | 25 00–29 99 |
| 30 00–34 99 | 2 | 23 | 4 | 5 | 3 | 1 | | | | 6 | | 12 | 1 | | | 49 | 8 | 97.30 | 99.90 | 30 00–34 99 |
| 35 00–39 99 | 1 | 9 | 4 | 2 | | | | | | 6 | | 1 | | | | 19 | 4 | 98.20 | 99.90 | 35 00–39 99 |
| 40 00 and over | 3 | 31 | 2 | 3 | | | | | | 4 | | | | | | 41 | 2 | 100.00 | 100.00 | 40 00 and over |
| Not reported | | | | 2 | 1 | | | | | 1 | 2 | 22 | 50 | 4 | 1 | 29 | 54 | | | Not reported |
| Total | 11 | 106 | 35 | 90 | 90 | 75 | 26 | 210 | 170 | 138 | 13 | 1,309 | 4,117 | 262 | 623 | 2,201 | 5,074 | | | Total |

160. TABLE XIX, A, 1, a

NEW YORK STATE, EXCLUSIVE OF NEW YORK CITY — FIRST AND SECOND CLASS CITIES
MERCANTILE ESTABLISHMENTS — DEPARTMENT STORES — STOCK AND SALES
NUMBER AND PER CENT. OF EMPLOYEES CLASSIFIED ACCORDING TO AVERAGE ACTUAL WEEKLY EARNINGS, BY OCCUPATION AND SEX

| Average Actual Weekly Earnings in Dollars | Occupation: Superintendents | Buyers | | Assistant Buyers and Heads of Stock | | Receiving and Stock Clerks | Stock People | | Floor Managers | | Sales People | | Messengers, Wrappers and Errand Boys | | Total | | Cumulative Per Cent. of Total | | Average Actual Weekly Earnings in Dollars |
|---|---|---|---|---|---|---|---|---|---|---|---|---|---|---|---|---|---|---|---|
| | Male | Male | Female | Male | Female | Male | Male | Female | Male | Female | Male | Female | Male | Female | Male | Female | Male | Female | |
| Less than $3 00 | ........ | .... | .... | .... | .... | ........ | .... | 4 | .... | .... | .... | 2 | 3 | 18 | 3 | 24 | 1.00 | 3.60 | Less than $3 00 |
| $3 00–$3 49 | ........ | .... | .... | .... | .... | ........ | 1 | 1 | .... | .... | .... | 1 | 1 | 5 | 2 | 7 | 1.80 | 4.70 | $3 00–$3 49 |
| 3 50– 3 99 | ........ | .... | .... | .... | .... | ........ | 2 | .... | .... | .... | .... | 6 | .... | 11 | 2 | 17 | 2.50 | 7.30 | 3 50– 3 99 |
| 4 00– 4 49 | ........ | .... | .... | .... | .... | ........ | 1 | 1 | .... | .... | 1 | 14 | .... | 6 | 2 | 21 | 3.20 | 10.50 | 4 00– 4 49 |
| 4 50– 4 99 | ........ | .... | .... | .... | .... | ........ | 2 | 2 | .... | .... | .... | 53 | 2 | 4 | 4 | 59 | 4.60 | 19.50 | 4 50– 4 99 |
| 5 00– 5 49 | ........ | .... | .... | .... | .... | ........ | .... | 1 | .... | .... | 2 | 31 | 2 | .... | 4 | 32 | 6.10 | 24.40 | 5 00– 5 49 |
| 5 50– 5 99 | ........ | .... | .... | .... | .... | ........ | 2 | 1 | 1 | .... | .... | 82 | .... | 1 | 3 | 84 | 7.30 | 37.20 | 5 50– 5 99 |
| 6 00– 6 49 | ........ | .... | .... | .... | .... | ........ | 1 | .... | .... | 1 | .... | 45 | 2 | .... | 3 | 46 | 8.20 | 44.30 | 6 00– 6 49 |
| 6 50– 6 99 | ........ | .... | .... | .... | .... | ........ | .... | .... | .... | .... | 1 | 57 | .... | .... | 1 | 57 | 8.60 | 53.00 | 6 50– 6 99 |
| 7 00– 7 49 | ........ | .... | .... | .... | .... | ........ | 1 | .... | .... | .... | 6 | 39 | .... | .... | 7 | 39 | 11.10 | 59.00 | 7 00– 7 49 |
| 7 50– 7 99 | ........ | .... | .... | .... | .... | ........ | .... | .... | .... | .... | 6 | 55 | 1 | .... | 7 | 55 | 13.60 | 68.30 | 7 50– 7 99 |
| 8 00– 8 99 | ........ | .... | .... | .... | 2 | ........ | 1 | .... | .... | .... | 5 | 50 | .... | .... | 6 | 52 | 15.70 | 75.40 | 8 00– 8 99 |
| 9 00– 9 99 | ........ | .... | .... | .... | 5 | ........ | .... | .... | .... | .... | 10 | 41 | .... | .... | 10 | 46 | 19.40 | 82.30 | 9 00– 9 99 |
| 10 00–10 99 | ........ | .... | .... | 1 | 1 | ........ | 1 | .... | .... | .... | 6 | 22 | 1 | .... | 9 | 23 | 22.50 | 85.70 | 10 00–10 99 |
| 11 00–11 99 | ........ | .... | .... | 2 | 1 | ........ | 3 | .... | .... | 1 | 11 | 24 | .... | .... | 16 | 26 | 28.20 | 89.80 | 11 00–11 99 |
| 12 00–12 99 | ........ | .... | .... | 1 | 5 | ........ | .... | .... | 1 | .... | 14 | 19 | .... | .... | 16 | 24 | 34.00 | 93.50 | 12 00–12 99 |
| 13 00–13 99 | ........ | .... | .... | 1 | 3 | ........ | 1 | .... | 1 | .... | 15 | 8 | .... | .... | 18 | 11 | 40.50 | 95.20 | 13 00–13 99 |
| 14 00–14 99 | ........ | .... | .... | 1 | 2 | ........ | .... | .... | 3 | .... | 24 | 6 | .... | .... | 28 | 8 | 50.50 | 96.40 | 14 00–14 99 |
| 15 00–15 99 | ........ | .... | .... | 2 | 1 | ........ | .... | .... | 2 | .... | 13 | 4 | .... | .... | 17 | 5 | 56.50 | 97.20 | 15 00–15 99 |
| 16 00–17 99 | ........ | .... | .... | 3 | 1 | 1 | .... | .... | 2 | .... | 17 | 3 | .... | .... | 23 | 4 | 65.00 | 97.80 | 16 00–17 99 |
| 18 00–19 99 | ........ | .... | .... | 5 | 3 | ........ | .... | .... | 2 | .... | 28 | 3 | .... | .... | 30 | 6 | 75.50 | 98.60 | 18 00–19 99 |
| 20 00–24 99 | ........ | 4 | 1 | 4 | .... | ........ | .... | .... | 7 | 1 | 24 | 3 | .... | .... | 39 | 5 | 89.50 | 99.40 | 20 00–24 99 |
| 25 00–29 99 | ........ | 5 | 1 | 5 | 1 | ........ | .... | .... | 6 | .... | 3 | .... | .... | .... | 19 | 2 | 96.80 | 99.70 | 25 00–29 99 |
| 30 00–34 99 | ........ | 5 | .... | .... | .... | ........ | .... | .... | 1 | .... | .... | 2 | .... | .... | 6 | 2 | 98.60 | 100.00 | 30 00–34 99 |
| 35 00–39 99 | 1 | 3 | .... | .... | .... | ........ | .... | .... | .... | .... | .... | .... | .... | .... | 4 | .... | 100.00 | ..... | 35 00–39 99 |
| Total | 1 | 17 | 8 | 25 | 25 | 1 | 16 | 10 | 26 | 3 | 181 | 570 | 12 | 45 | 279 | 655 | ..... | ..... | Total |

NEW YORK STATE, EXCLUSIVE OF NEW YORK CITY — FIRST AND SECOND CLASS CITIES

161. TABLE XX, A, 1, a — MERCANTILE ESTABLISHMENTS — DEPARTMENT STORES — STOCK AND SALES

NUMBER AND PER CENT. OF EMPLOYEES, WORKING 43 WEEKS OR MORE, CLASSIFIED ACCORDING TO ACTUAL ANNUAL EARNINGS BY OCCUPATION AND SEX

| ACTUAL ANNUAL EARNINGS IN DOLLARS | OCCUPATION | | | | | | | | | | | | | | | | | | ACTUAL ANNUAL EARNINGS IN DOLLARS |
|---|---|---|---|---|---|---|---|---|---|---|---|---|---|---|---|---|---|---|---|
| | SUPERINTENDENTS | BUYERS | | ASSISTANT BUYERS AND HEADS OF STOCK | | RECEIVING AND STOCK CLERKS | STOCK PEOPLE | | FLOOR MANAGERS | | SALES PEOPLE | | WRAPPERS AND MESSENGERS ERRAND BOYS | | TOTAL | | CUMULATIVE PER CENT. OF TOTAL | | |
| | Male | Male | Female | Male | Female | Male | Male | Female | Male | Female | Male | Female | Male | Female | Male | Female | Male | Female | |
| Less than $200 | ........ | .... | .... | ..... | ..... | ........ | 2 | 2 | .... | .... | .... | 3 | ..... | 6 | 2 | 11 | 1.00 | 2.70 | Less than $200 |
| $200– $249 | ........ | .... | .... | ..... | ..... | ........ | 1 | .... | .... | .... | .... | 31 | ..... | 3 | 1 | 34 | 1.40 | 11.30 | $200– 249 |
| 250– 299 | ........ | .... | .... | ..... | ..... | ........ | 1 | 1 | 1 | .... | 1 | 56 | ..... | 1 | 3 | 58 | 2.90 | 25.70 | 250– 299 |
| 300– 349 | ........ | .... | .... | ..... | ..... | ........ | 1 | 1 | .... | 1 | 1 | 72 | 1 | ..... | 3 | 74 | 4.40 | 44.20 | 300– 349 |
| 350– 399 | ........ | .... | .... | ..... | ..... | ........ | 1 | .... | .... | .... | 3 | 64 | 1 | ..... | 5 | 64 | 6.80 | 60.20 | 350– 399 |
| 400– 449 | ........ | .... | .... | ..... | 1 | ........ | .... | .... | .... | .... | 5 | 34 | ..... | ..... | 5 | 35 | 9.20 | 69.00 | 400– 449 |
| 450– 499 | ........ | .... | .... | ..... | 5 | ........ | .... | .... | .... | .... | 7 | 29 | ..... | ..... | 7 | 34 | 12.60 | 77.50 | 450– 499 |
| 500– 549 | ........ | .... | .... | ..... | 2 | ........ | 1 | .... | .... | .... | 4 | 23 | ..... | ..... | 5 | 25 | 15.00 | 83.80 | 500– 549 |
| 550– 599 | ........ | .... | .... | 2 | 2 | ........ | 2 | .... | .... | .... | 7 | 14 | 1 | ..... | 12 | 16 | 20.70 | 88.00 | 550– 599 |
| 600– 649 | ........ | .... | .... | 1 | 4 | ........ | 1 | .... | 1 | .... | 12 | 12 | ..... | ..... | 15 | 16 | 28.00 | 92.00 | 600– 649 |
| 650– 699 | ........ | .... | .... | 1 | 3 | ........ | .... | .... | .... | .... | 8 | 4 | ..... | ..... | 9 | 7 | 32.30 | 93.20 | 650– 699 |
| 700– 749 | ........ | .... | .... | 1 | 1 | ........ | 1 | .... | 4 | .... | 12 | 6 | ..... | ..... | 18 | 7 | 41.00 | 95.20 | 700– 749 |
| 750– 799 | ........ | .... | .... | 2 | 2 | ........ | .... | .... | 2 | .... | 15 | 4 | ..... | ..... | 19 | 6 | 50.00 | 97.00 | 750– 799 |
| 800– 899 | ........ | .... | .... | 3 | 1 | 1 | .... | .... | 1 | .... | 17 | 2 | ..... | ..... | 22 | 3 | 61.00 | 97.70 | 800– 899 |
| 900– 999 | ........ | .... | .... | 4 | 3 | ........ | .... | .... | 1 | .... | 18 | 2 | ..... | ..... | 23 | 5 | 72.00 | 98.80 | 900– 999 |
| 1,000–1,099 | ........ | 3 | 1 | 1 | ..... | ........ | .... | .... | 4 | .... | 13 | 1 | ..... | ..... | 21 | 2 | 82.00 | 99.30 | 1,000–1,099 |
| 1,100–1,199 | ........ | 1 | .... | 3 | ..... | ........ | .... | .... | 3 | .... | 4 | .... | ..... | ..... | 11 | .... | 87.50 | ..... | 1,100–1,199 |
| 1,200–1,299 | ........ | .... | 1 | 2 | ..... | ........ | .... | .... | 3 | .... | 3 | 1 | ..... | ..... | 8 | 2 | 91.50 | 99.80 | 1,200–1,299 |
| 1,300–1,399 | ........ | 3 | .... | ..... | ..... | ........ | .... | .... | 1 | .... | 1 | .... | ..... | ..... | 5 | .... | 94.00 | ..... | 1,300–1,399 |
| 1,400–1,499 | ........ | 1 | .... | 1 | ..... | ........ | .... | .... | .... | .... | 1 | .... | ..... | ..... | 3 | .... | 95.00 | ..... | 1,400–1,499 |
| 1,500–1,599 | ........ | 4 | .... | ..... | ..... | ........ | .... | .... | .... | .... | .... | 1 | ..... | ..... | 4 | 1 | 97.00 | 100.00 | 1,500–1,599 |
| 1,600–1,799 | ........ | 4 | .... | ..... | ..... | ........ | .... | .... | 1 | .... | .... | .... | ..... | ..... | 5 | .... | 99.40 | ..... | 1,600–1,799 |
| 2,500–2,999 | 1 | .... | .... | ..... | ..... | ........ | .... | .... | .... | .... | .... | .... | ..... | ..... | 1 | .... | 100.00 | ..... | 2,500–2,999 |
| Total | 1 | 16 | 2 | 21 | 24 | 1 | 11 | 4 | 22 | 1 | 132 | 359 | 3 | 10 | 207 | 400 | ..... | ..... | Total |

## NEW YORK STATE, EXCLUSIVE OF NEW YORK CITY
## DEPARTMENT STORES — OFFICE

162. TABLE V, A, 1, b NUMBER AND PER CENT. OF EMPLOYEES EARNING SPECIFIED WEEKLY RATES, BY AGE GROUPS AND SEX

| WEEKLY RATES IN DOLLARS | AGE GROUPS IN YEARS | | | | | | | | | | | | | | WEEKLY RATES IN DOLLARS |
|---|---|---|---|---|---|---|---|---|---|---|---|---|---|---|---|
| | 14–15 | | 16–17 | | 18–20 | | 21–24 | | 25–29 | | 30–34 | | 35–39 | | |
| | Male | Female | Male | Female | Male | Female | Male | Female | Male | Female | Male | Female | Male | Female | |
| Less than $3 00 | 1 | 1 | .... | ...... | ...... | ...... | ...... | ...... | ...... | ...... | ...... | ...... | ...... | ...... | Less than $3 00 |
| $3 00–$3 49 | 1 | 2 | 1 | 5 | ...... | 1 | ...... | ...... | ...... | ...... | ...... | ...... | ...... | ...... | $3 50– 3 49 |
| 3 50– 3 99 | 2 | 9 | 1 | 10 | 1 | 2 | 1 | 1 | ...... | ...... | ...... | ...... | ...... | ...... | 5 30– 3 99 |
| 4 00– 4 49 | 12 | 16 | 7 | 34 | ...... | 15 | ...... | ...... | ...... | 1 | ...... | ...... | ...... | ...... | 4 00– 4 49 |
| 4 50– 4 99 | 2 | 3 | 2 | 13 | ...... | 13 | ...... | 1 | ...... | 1 | ...... | 1 | ...... | ...... | 4 50– 4 99 |
| 5 00– 5 49 | 4 | 3 | 11 | 63 | 1 | 85 | ...... | 19 | ...... | 1 | ...... | 1 | ...... | 1 | 5 00– 5 49 |
| 5 50– 5 99 | .... | ...... | 3 | 7 | ...... | 9 | ...... | 2 | ...... | ...... | ...... | ...... | ...... | ...... | 5 50– 5 99 |
| 6 00– 6 49 | 1 | 2 | 13 | 36 | 10 | 158 | 1 | 71 | 3 | 16 | ...... | 5 | ...... | 2 | 6 00– 6 49 |
| 6 50– 6 99 | .... | ...... | 1 | 1 | 3 | 12 | ...... | 6 | ...... | ...... | ...... | ...... | ...... | ...... | 6 50– 6 99 |
| 7 00– 7 49 | .... | ...... | 2 | 11 | 12 | 78 | ...... | 78 | ...... | 24 | ...... | 12 | ...... | 1 | 7 00– 7 49 |
| 7 50– 7 99 | .... | ...... | 1 | ...... | ...... | 3 | 2 | 5 | ...... | 1 | ...... | ...... | ...... | ...... | 7 50– 7 99 |
| 8 00– 8 99 | .... | ...... | 2 | 4 | 13 | 30 | 1 | 73 | ...... | 34 | ...... | 5 | ...... | 4 | 8 00– 8 99 |
| 9 00– 9 99 | .... | ...... | 1 | 1 | 16 | 12 | 7 | 30 | ...... | 17 | ...... | 11 | ...... | 2 | 9 00– 9 99 |
| 10 00–10 99 | .... | ...... | 1 | ...... | 6 | 13 | 5 | 47 | 3 | 27 | 2 | 6 | 1 | 5 | 10 00–10 99 |
| 11 00–11 99 | .... | ...... | .... | ...... | 2 | 1 | 2 | 6 | 1 | 12 | ...... | 2 | ...... | 4 | 11 00–11 99 |
| 12 00–12 99 | .... | ...... | .... | ...... | 5 | 3 | 25 | 10 | 12 | 25 | 4 | 6 | 7 | 6 | 12 00–12 99 |
| 13 00–13 99 | .... | ...... | .... | ...... | 3 | ...... | 9 | 1 | 4 | 6 | 2 | 3 | 3 | 2 | 13 00–13 99 |
| 14 00–14 99 | .... | ...... | .... | ...... | ...... | 1 | 4 | 2 | 4 | 4 | 1 | 2 | 3 | 4 | 14.00–14 99 |
| 15 00–15 99 | .... | ...... | .... | ...... | ...... | ...... | 12 | 4 | 8 | 7 | 5 | 4 | 5 | 2 | 15 00–15 99 |
| 16 00–17 99 | .... | ...... | .... | ...... | ...... | ...... | 3 | 1 | 7 | ...... | 11 | 3 | 5 | 2 | 16 00–17 99 |
| 18 00–19 99 | .... | ...... | .... | ...... | ...... | ...... | 1 | 1 | 5 | 2 | 4 | 1 | 4 | 3 | 18 00–19 99 |
| 20 00–24 99 | .... | ...... | .... | ...... | ...... | ...... | 1 | ...... | 11 | 1 | 6 | 1 | 6 | 2 | 20 00–24 99 |
| 25 00–29 99 | .... | ...... | .... | ...... | ...... | ...... | ...... | ...... | 5 | ...... | 7 | ...... | 2 | ...... | 25 00–29 99 |
| 30 00–34 99 | .... | ...... | .... | ...... | ...... | ...... | ...... | ...... | ...... | ...... | 7 | ...... | 3 | ...... | 30 00–34 99 |
| 35 00–39 99 | .... | ...... | .... | ...... | ...... | ...... | ...... | ...... | ...... | ...... | 2 | ...... | 1 | ...... | 35 00–39 99 |
| 40 00 and over | .... | ...... | .... | ...... | ...... | ...... | 1 | ...... | ...... | ...... | 3 | ...... | 1 | ...... | 40 00 and over |
| Not reported | .... | 1 | .... | ...... | ...... | ...... | ...... | ...... | ...... | ...... | ...... | ...... | ...... | ...... | Not reported |
| Total | 23 | 37 | 46 | 185 | 72 | 436 | 75 | 358 | 63 | 179 | 54 | 63 | 41 | 40 | Total |

162. TABLE V, A, 1, b — (*concluded*)

NEW YORK STATE, EXCLUSIVE OF NEW YORK CITY
DEPARTMENT STORES — OFFICE
NUMBER AND PER CENT. OF EMPLOYEES EARNING SPECIFIED WEEKLY RATES, BY AGE GROUPS AND SEX

| WEEKLY RATES IN DOLLARS | AGE GROUPS IN YEARS — (*concluded*) 40–44 | | 45–54 | | 55–64 | 65 AND OVER | NOT REPORTED | | TOTAL | | CUMULATIVE PER CENT OF TOTAL | | WEEKLY RATES IN DOLLARS |
|---|---|---|---|---|---|---|---|---|---|---|---|---|---|
| | Male | Female | Male | Female | Male | Male | Male | Female | Male | Female | Male | Female | |
| Less than $3 00.. | ....... | ....... | ....... | ....... | ....... | ....... | ....... | ....... | 1 | 1 | .21 | .07 | .Less than $3 00 |
| $3 00–$3 49.... | ....... | ....... | ....... | ....... | ....... | ....... | ....... | ....... | 2 | 8 | .63 | .67 | ...$3 00– 3 49 |
| 3 50– 3 99.... | ....... | ....... | ....... | ....... | ....... | ....... | ....... | ....... | 5 | 22 | 1.60 | 2.30 | ... 3 50– 3 99 |
| 4 00– 4 49.... | ....... | ....... | ....... | ....... | ....... | ....... | ....... | ....... | 19 | 66 | 5.63 | 7.20 | ... 4 00– 4 49 |
| 4 50– 4 99.... | ....... | ....... | ....... | ....... | ....... | ....... | ....... | ....... | 4 | 32 | 6.47 | 9.58 | ... 4 50– 4 99 |
| 5 00– 5.49.... | ....... | ....... | ....... | ....... | ....... | ....... | ....... | 2 | 16 | 175 | 9.80 | 22.58 | ... 5 00– 5 49 |
| 5 50– 5 99.... | ....... | ....... | ....... | ....... | ....... | ....... | ....... | ....... | 3 | 18 | 10.42 | 23.90 | ... 5 50– 5 99 |
| 6 00– 6 49.... | ....... | ....... | ....... | 2 | ....... | ....... | 1 | 1 | 29 | 293 | 16.48 | 45.65 | ... 6 00– 6 49 |
| 6 50– 6 99.... | ....... | ....... | ....... | ....... | ....... | ....... | ....... | ....... | 4 | 19 | 17.30 | 47.00 | ... 6 50– 6 99 |
| 7 00– 7 49.... | ....... | 1 | ....... | ....... | ....... | ....... | ....... | ....... | 14 | 205 | 20.20 | 62.25 | ... 7 00– 7 49 |
| 7 50– 7 99.... | ....... | ....... | ....... | ....... | ....... | ....... | ....... | ....... | 3 | 9 | 20.85 | 63.00 | ... 7 50– 7 99 |
| 8 00– 8 99.... | ....... | 3 | ....... | ....... | ....... | ....... | ....... | 1 | 16 | 154 | 24.20 | 74.25 | ... 8 00– 8 99 |
| 9 00– 9 99.... | ....... | 1 | ....... | ....... | ....... | 1 | ....... | 2 | 25 | 76 | 29.40 | 80.00 | ... 9 00– 9 99 |
| 10 00–10 99.... | ....... | 4 | 1 | 1 | 3 | 1 | ....... | 2 | 23 | 105 | 34.20 | 87.75 | ...10 00–10 99 |
| 11 00–11 99.... | 1 | 2 | 2 | ....... | ....... | ....... | ....... | 2 | 8 | 29 | 35.90 | 89.90 | ...11 00–11 99 |
| 12 00–12 99.... | 5 | 4 | 5 | 1 | 2 | 1 | ....... | 3 | 66 | 58 | 49.60 | 94.10 | ...12 00–12 99 |
| 13 00–13 99.... | ....... | ....... | 1 | 2 | 2 | 2 | ....... | 1 | 26 | 15 | 55.00 | 95.30 | ...13 00–13 99 |
| 14 00–14 99.... | ....... | ....... | 3 | ....... | 2 | ....... | ....... | 3 | 17 | 16 | 58.60 | 96.50 | ...14 00–14 99 |
| 15 00–15 99.... | 4 | 1 | 8 | 1 | 3 | ....... | 2 | 2 | 47 | 21 | 68.40 | 98.00 | ...15 00–15 99 |
| 16 00–17 99.... | ....... | 1 | 1 | 1 | 1 | ....... | 2 | ....... | 30 | 8 | 74.70 | 98.60 | ...16 00–17 99 |
| 18 00–19 99.... | 2 | ....... | 8 | ....... | 1 | 1 | ....... | 1 | 26 | 8 | 80.00 | 99.25 | ...18 00–19 99 |
| 20 00–24 99.... | 4 | 1 | 5 | 1 | 2 | ....... | ....... | ....... | 35 | 6 | 86.50 | 99.65 | ...20 00–24 99 |
| 25 00–29 99.... | 6 | ....... | 2 | 1 | 3 | ....... | 1 | 1 | 26 | 2 | 92.80 | 99.80 | ...25 00–29 99 |
| 30 00–34 99.... | 1 | 2 | 4 | ....... | 1 | ....... | ....... | ....... | 16 | 2 | 96.00 | 99.90 | ...30 00–34 99 |
| 35 00–39 99.... | 2 | ....... | 4 | ....... | ....... | 1 | 1 | ....... | 11 | ....... | 98.25 | 99.90 | ...35 00–39 99 |
| 40 00 and over.. | ....... | ....... | ....... | ....... | 2 | 1 | ....... | 1 | 8 | 1 | 100.00 | 100.00 | .40 00 and over |
| Not reported.... | ....... | ....... | ....... | ....... | 1 | ....... | ....... | ....... | 1 | 1 | ....... | ....... | ...Not reported |
| Total...... | 25 | 20 | 44 | 10 | 23 | 8 | 7 | 22 | 481 | 1,350 | ....... | ....... | .....Total |

NEW YORK STATE, EXCLUSIVE OF NEW YORK CITY

**DEPARTMENT STORES — OFFICE**

163. TABLE VIII, A, 1, b Number and Per Cent. of Employees Earning Specified Weekly Rates, by Occupation and Sex

| Actual Weekly Earnings in Dollars | Occupation | | | | | | | | | | | | | Actual Weekly Earnings in Dollars |
|---|---|---|---|---|---|---|---|---|---|---|---|---|---|---|
| | Superintendents | | Bookkeepers | | Clerks | | Secretaries | Stenographers | | Office Boys and Girls | | Cashiers | | |
| | Male | Female | Male | Female | Male | Female | Female | Male | Female | Male | Female | Male | Female | |
| Less than $3.00 | ...... | ...... | ...... | ...... | 1 | 1 | ...... | ...... | ...... | ...... | ...... | ...... | ...... | Less than $3 00 |
| $3 00–$3 49 | ...... | ...... | ...... | ...... | ...... | 2 | ...... | ...... | ...... | 1 | 1 | 1 | 2 | 3 00– 3 49 |
| 3 50– 3 99 | ...... | ...... | ...... | ...... | 3 | 6 | ...... | ...... | ...... | 1 | 1 | ...... | 13 | 3 50– 3 99 |
| 4 00– 4 49 | ...... | ...... | ...... | ...... | 12 | 18 | ...... | ...... | 1 | 7 | 5 | ...... | 26 | 4 00– 4 49 |
| 4 50– 4 99 | ...... | ...... | ...... | ...... | ...... | 11 | ...... | ...... | ...... | 4 | 1 | ...... | 15 | 4 50– 4 99 |
| 5 00– 5 49 | ...... | ...... | ...... | 9 | 8 | 75 | ...... | ...... | 1 | 5 | 12 | ...... | 49 | 5 00– 5 49 |
| 5 50– 5 99 | ...... | ...... | ...... | 1 | 3 | 7 | ...... | ...... | ...... | ...... | ...... | ...... | 7 | 5 50– 5 99 |
| 6 00– 6 49 | ...... | ...... | ...... | 15 | 21 | 106 | ...... | ...... | 9 | 1 | 7 | 2 | 117 | 6 00– 6 49 |
| 6 50– 6 99 | ...... | ...... | ...... | 2 | 4 | 12 | ...... | ...... | ...... | ...... | ...... | ...... | 3 | 6 50– 6 99 |
| 7 00– 7 49 | ...... | ...... | ...... | 25 | 11 | 59 | ...... | ...... | 15 | ...... | 2 | ...... | 71 | 7 00– 7 49 |
| 7 50– 7 99 | ...... | ...... | ...... | 1 | 1 | 1 | ...... | ...... | 1 | ...... | ...... | 1 | 5 | 7 50– 7 99 |
| 8 00– 8 99 | ...... | ...... | 1 | 35 | 8 | 59 | ...... | ...... | 9 | ...... | 1 | 1 | 33 | 8 00– 8 99 |
| 9 00– 9 99 | ...... | ...... | 3 | 23 | 15 | 27 | ...... | 1 | 6 | ...... | ...... | 1 | 15 | 9 00– 9 99 |
| 10 00–10 99 | ...... | ...... | 1 | 34 | 14 | 23 | ...... | 1 | 22 | 1 | ...... | 1 | 16 | 10 00–10 99 |
| 11 00–11 99 | ...... | ...... | ...... | 12 | 7 | 8 | ...... | ...... | 5 | ...... | ...... | ...... | 3 | 11 00–11 99 |
| 12 00–12 99 | ...... | ...... | 14 | 20 | 42 | 16 | ...... | ...... | 7 | ...... | ...... | 2 | 9 | 12 00–12 99 |
| 13 00–13 99 | ...... | ...... | 10 | 4 | 12 | 2 | ...... | 1 | 4 | ...... | ...... | 2 | 5 | 13 00–13 99 |
| 14 00–14 99 | ...... | 1 | 2 | 9 | 13 | 2 | ...... | ...... | 1 | ...... | ...... | 1 | 2 | 14 00–14 99 |
| 15 00–15 99 | ...... | ...... | 12 | 8 | 24 | 6 | ...... | ...... | 4 | ...... | ...... | 1 | 3 | 15 00–15 99 |
| 16 00–17 99 | ...... | ...... | 14 | 2 | 12 | 1 | 1 | ...... | 1 | ...... | ...... | 1 | 2 | 16 00–17 99 |
| 18 00–19 99 | ...... | ...... | 7 | 2 | 11 | 1 | ...... | ...... | 3 | ...... | ...... | ...... | ...... | 18 00–19 99 |
| 20 00–24 99 | 1 | ...... | 6 | ...... | 15 | 3 | ...... | ...... | 2 | ...... | ...... | 2 | ...... | 20 00–24 99 |
| 25 00–29.99 | 2 | ...... | 4 | ...... | 8 | 2 | ...... | ...... | ...... | ...... | ...... | 1 | ...... | 25 00–29 99 |
| 30 00–34 99 | 1 | ...... | ...... | 1 | 3 | ...... | ...... | ...... | ...... | ...... | ...... | ...... | ...... | 30 00–34 99 |
| 35 00–39 99 | 1 | ...... | 2 | ...... | 6 | ...... | ...... | ...... | ...... | ...... | ...... | 2 | ...... | 35 00–39 99 |
| 40 00 and over | ...... | ...... | 1 | ...... | ...... | 1 | ...... | ...... | ...... | ...... | ...... | 1 | ...... | 40 00 and over |
| Not reported | ...... | ...... | ...... | ...... | 1 | ...... | ...... | ...... | ...... | ...... | ...... | ...... | 1 | Not reported |
| Total | 5 | 1 | 77 | 208 | 255 | 449 | 1 | 3 | 91 | 20 | 30 | 20 | 397 | Total |

163. TABLE VIII, A, 1, b — (*concluded*)

NEW YORK STATE, EXCLUSIVE OF NEW YORK CITY

**DEPARTMENT STORES — OFFICE**

NUMBER AND PER CENT. OF EMPLOYEES EARNING SPECIFIED WEEKLY RATES, BY OCCUPATION AND SEX

| ACTUAL WEEKLY EARNINGS IN DOLLARS | OCCUPATION — (*concluded*) | | | | | | | | | | | ACTUAL WEEKLY EARNINGS IN DOLLARS |
|---|---|---|---|---|---|---|---|---|---|---|---|---|
| | TELEPHONE OPERATORS | AUDITORS | | DETECTIVES | | ADVERTISERS AND WINDOW DRESSERS | | TOTAL | | CUMULATIVE PER CENT. OF TOTAL | | |
| | Female | Male | Female | Male | Female | Male | Female | Male | Female | Male | Female | |
| Less than $3 00. | ........ | ........ | ........ | ........ | ........ | ........ | ........ | 1 | 1 | .21 | .07 | Less than $3.00 |
| $3 00–$3 49... | 1 | ........ | 2 | ........ | ........ | ........ | ........ | 2 | 8 | .63 | .67 | ...$3 00– 3 49 |
| 3 50– 3 99... | 1 | ........ | 1 | ........ | ........ | 1 | ........ | 5 | 22 | 1.60 | 2.30 | ... 3 50– 3 99 |
| 4 00– 4 49... | 5 | ........ | 11 | ........ | ........ | ........ | ........ | 19 | 66 | 5.63 | 7.20 | ... 4 00– 4 49 |
| 4 50– 4 99... | 2 | ........ | 3 | ........ | ........ | ........ | ........ | 4 | 32 | 6.47 | 9.58 | ... 4 50– 4 99 |
| 5 00– 5 49... | 6 | ........ | 23 | ........ | ........ | 3 | ........ | 16 | 175 | 9.80 | 22.58 | ... 5 00– 5 49 |
| 5 50– 5 99... | 1 | ........ | 2 | ........ | ........ | ........ | ........ | 3 | 18 | 10.42 | 23.90 | ... 5 50– 5 99 |
| 6 00– 6 49... | 11 | ........ | 27 | ........ | ........ | 5 | 1 | 29 | 293 | 16.48 | 45.65 | ... 6 00– 6 49 |
| 6 50– 6 99... | ........ | ........ | 2 | ........ | ........ | ........ | ........ | 4 | 19 | 17.30 | 47.00 | ... 6 50– 6 99 |
| 7 00– 7 49... | 11 | ........ | 21 | ........ | ........ | 3 | 1 | 14 | 205 | 20.20 | 62.25 | ... 7 00– 7 49 |
| 7 50– 7 99... | 1 | 1 | ........ | ........ | ........ | ........ | ........ | 3 | 9 | 20.85 | 63.00 | ... 7 50– 7 99 |
| 8 00– 8 99... | 10 | ........ | 7 | ........ | ........ | 6 | ........ | 16 | 154 | 24.20 | 74.25 | ... 8 00– 8 99 |
| 9 00– 9 99... | 4 | ........ | 1 | ........ | ........ | 5 | ........ | 25 | 76 | 29.40 | 80.00 | ... 9 00– 9 99 |
| 10 00–10 99... | 3 | 2 | 6 | ........ | ........ | 3 | 1 | 23 | 105 | 34.20 | 87.75 | ...10 00–10 99 |
| 11 00–11 99... | ........ | ........ | 1 | ........ | ........ | 1 | ........ | 8 | 29 | 35.90 | 89.90 | ...11 00–11 99 |
| 12 00–12 99... | 2 | 2 | ........ | ........ | 1 | 6 | 3 | 66 | 58 | 49.60 | 94.10 | ...12 00–12 99 |
| 13 00–13 99... | ........ | ........ | ........ | ........ | ........ | 1 | ........ | 26 | 15 | 55.00 | 95.30 | ...13 00–13 99 |
| 14 00–14 99... | ........ | ........ | ........ | ........ | ........ | 1 | 1 | 17 | 16 | 58.60 | 96.50 | ...14 00–14 99 |
| 15 00–15 99... | ........ | 1 | ........ | ........ | ........ | 9 | ........ | 47 | 21 | 68.40 | 98.00 | ...15 00–15 99 |
| 16 00–17 99... | ........ | ........ | 1 | ........ | ........ | 3 | ........ | 30 | 8 | 74.70 | 98.60 | ...16 00–17 99 |
| 18 00–19 99... | ........ | 1 | ........ | ........ | ........ | 7 | 2 | 26 | 8 | 80.00 | 99.25 | ...18 00–19 99 |
| 20 00–24 99... | ........ | ........ | ........ | 1 | ........ | 10 | 1 | 35 | 6 | 86.50 | 99.65 | ...20 00–24 99 |
| 25 00–29 99... | ........ | 1 | ........ | ........ | ........ | 10 | ........ | 26 | 2 | 92.80 | 99.80 | ...25 00–29 99 |
| 30 00–34 99... | ........ | 2 | ........ | ........ | ........ | 10 | 1 | 16 | 2 | 96.00 | 99.90 | ...30 00–34 99 |
| 35 00–39 99... | ........ | ........ | ........ | ........ | ........ | ........ | ........ | 11 | ........ | 98.25 | 99.90 | ...35 00–39 99 |
| 40 00 and over. | ........ | 1 | ........ | ........ | ........ | 5 | ........ | 8 | 1 | 100.00 | 100.00 | .40 00 and over |
| Not reported... | ........ | ........ | ........ | ........ | ........ | ........ | ........ | 1 | 1 | ........ | ........ | ...Not reported |
| Total..... | 58 | 11 | 108 | 1 | 1 | 89 | 11 | 481 | 1,350 | ........ | ........ | .....Total |

164. TABLE VI, A, 1, b

NEW YORK STATE, EXCLUSIVE OF NEW YORK CITY
**DEPARTMENT STORES — OFFICE**
NUMBER AND PER CENT. OF EMPLOYEES CLASSIFIED ACCORDING TO ACTUAL WEEKLY EARNINGS, BY AGE GROUPS AND SEX

| Actual Weekly Earnings in Dollars | Age Groups in Years | | | | | | | | | | | | | | Actual Weekly Earnings in Dollars |
|---|---|---|---|---|---|---|---|---|---|---|---|---|---|---|---|
| | 14–15 | | 16–17 | | 18–20 | | 21–24 | | 25–29 | | 30–34 | | 35–39 | | |
| | Male | Female | Male | Female | Male | Female | Male | Female | Male | Female | Male | Female | Male | Female | |
| Less than $3 00. | 1 | 2 | 1 | 4 | 1 | ...... | ...... | 2 | ...... | ...... | ...... | ...... | ...... | ...... | .Less than $3 00 |
| $3 00–$3 49... | 2 | 2 | 2 | 6 | ...... | 4 | ...... | ...... | ...... | ...... | ...... | 1 | ...... | 1 | ...$3 00– 3 49 |
| 3 50– 3 99... | 2 | 10 | 1 | 14 | ...... | 7 | 1 | 1 | ...... | ...... | ...... | ...... | ...... | ...... | ... 3 50– 3 99 |
| 4 00– 4 49... | 11 | 14 | 6 | 35 | ...... | 18 | 1 | 2 | ...... | 1 | ...... | ...... | ...... | ...... | ... 4 00– 4 49 |
| 4 50– 4 99... | 2 | 3 | 3 | 12 | ...... | 17 | ...... | 7 | ...... | 1 | ...... | 1 | ...... | 1 | ... 4 50– 4 99 |
| 5 00– 5 49... | 4 | 3 | 11 | 58 | 1 | 82 | ...... | 18 | ...... | 1 | ...... | 1 | ...... | ...... | ... 5 00– 5 49 |
| 5 50– 5 99... | .... | ...... | 2 | 10 | 1 | 18 | ...... | 12 | ...... | 3 | ...... | 1 | ...... | ...... | ... 5 50– 5 99 |
| 6 00– 6 49... | 1 | 2 | 13 | 30 | 11 | 147 | 2 | 68 | 3 | 16 | ...... | 5 | ...... | 2 | ... 6 00– 6 49 |
| 6 50– 6 99... | .... | ...... | 1 | 1 | 3 | 9 | 1 | 11 | ...... | 1 | ...... | ...... | ...... | ...... | ... 6 50– 6 99 |
| 7 00– 7 49... | .... | ...... | 1 | 10 | 12 | 73 | ...... | 64 | ...... | 22 | ...... | 12 | ...... | 1 | ... 7 00– 7 49 |
| 7 50– 7 99... | .... | ...... | 1 | ...... | ...... | 3 | 2 | 3 | ...... | 1 | ...... | 1 | ...... | ...... | ... 7 50– 7 99 |
| 8 00– 8 99... | .... | ...... | 2 | 4 | 13 | 28 | 2 | 69 | ...... | 34 | ...... | 5 | ...... | 4 | ... 8 00– 8 99 |
| 9 00– 9 99... | .... | ...... | 1 | ...... | 15 | 14 | 6 | 38 | ...... | 16 | ...... | 7 | ...... | 2 | ... 9 00– 9 99 |
| 10 00–10 99... | .... | ...... | 1 | ...... | 7 | 10 | 4 | 36 | 3 | 26 | 2 | 7 | 2 | 5 | ...10 00–10 99 |
| 11 00–11 99... | .... | ...... | .... | ...... | 2 | 1 | 2 | 6 | 4 | 13 | ...... | 2 | ...... | 4 | ...11 00–11 99 |
| 12 00–12 99... | .... | ...... | .... | ...... | 4 | 2 | 23 | 9 | 10 | 23 | 4 | 6 | 7 | 5 | ...12 00–12 99 |
| 13 00 13 99... | .... | ...... | .... | ...... | 2 | ...... | 9 | 1 | 3 | 6 | 2 | 2 | 2 | 2 | ...13 00–13 99 |
| 14 00–14 99... | .... | ...... | .... | ...... | ...... | 1 | 4 | 2 | 4 | 4 | 1 | 2 | 3 | 4 | ...14 00–14 99 |
| 15 00–15 99... | .... | ...... | .... | ...... | ...... | ...... | 11 | 4 | 7 | 7 | 5 | 4 | 5 | 2 | ...15 00–15 99 |
| 16 00–17 99... | .... | ...... | .... | ...... | ...... | ...... | 3 | 1 | 8 | ...... | 11 | 3 | 5 | 2 | ...16 00–17 99 |
| 18 00–19 99... | .... | ...... | .... | ...... | ...... | ...... | 1 | 1 | 5 | 1 | 4 | 1 | 4 | 3 | ...18 00–19 99 |
| 20 00–24 99... | .... | ...... | .... | ...... | ...... | ...... | 2 | ...... | 11 | 1 | 6 | 1 | 6 | 2 | ...20 00–24 99 |
| 25 00–29 99... | .... | ...... | .... | ...... | ...... | ...... | ...... | ...... | 5 | ...... | 7 | ...... | 2 | ...... | ...25 00–29 99 |
| 30 00–34 99... | .... | ...... | .... | ...... | ...... | ...... | ...... | ...... | ...... | ...... | 7 | ...... | 3 | ...... | ...30 00–34 99 |
| 35 00–39 99... | .... | ...... | .... | ...... | ...... | ...... | ...... | ...... | ...... | ...... | 2 | ...... | 1 | ...... | ...35 00–39 99 |
| 40 00 and over | .... | ...... | .... | ...... | ...... | ...... | ...... | ...... | ...... | ...... | 3 | ...... | 1 | ...... | .40 00 and over |
| Not reported... | .... | 1 | .... | 1 | ...... | 2 | 1 | 3 | ...... | 2 | ...... | 1 | ...... | ...... | ...Not reported |
| Total..... | 23 | 37 | 46 | 185 | 72 | 436 | 75 | 358 | 63 | 179 | 54 | 63 | 41 | 40 | .....Total |

164. TABLE VI, A, 1, b — (*concluded*)

## NEW YORK STATE, EXCLUSIVE OF NEW YORK CITY
## DEPARTMENT STORES — OFFICE

NUMBER AND PER CENT. OF EMPLOYEES CLASSIFIED ACCORDING TO ACTUAL WEEKLY EARNINGS, BY AGE GROUP AND SEX

| Actual Weekly Earnings in Dollars | Age Groups in Years — (Continued) 40–44 | | 45–54 | | 55–64 | 65 and over | Not reported | | Total | | Cumulative per cent of total | | Actual Weekly Earnings in Dollars |
|---|---|---|---|---|---|---|---|---|---|---|---|---|---|
| | Male | Female | Male | Female | Male | Male | Male | Female | Male | Female | Male | Female | |
| Less than $3 00 | | | | | | | | 1 | 3 | 9 | .60 | .70 | Less than $3 00 |
| $3 00–$3 49 | | | | | | | | | 4 | 14 | 1.50 | 1.70 | $3 00– 3 49 |
| 3 50– 3 99 | | | | | | | | | 4 | 32 | 2.30 | 4.10 | 3 50– 3 99 |
| 4 00– 4 49 | | | | | | | | | 18 | 70 | 6.10 | 9.30 | 4 00– 4 49 |
| 4 50– 4 99 | | | | | | | | | 5 | 42 | 7.10 | 12.50 | 4 50– 4 99 |
| 5 00– 5 49 | | | | | | | | 3 | 16 | 166 | 10.50 | 24.90 | 5 00– 5 49 |
| 5 50– 5 99 | | | | | | | | | 3 | 44 | 11.10 | 28.20 | 5 50– 5 99 |
| 6 00– 6 49 | | | | 2 | | | 1 | | 31 | 272 | 17.60 | 48.50 | 6 00– 6 49 |
| 6 50– 6 99 | | | | | | | | | 5 | 22 | 18.60 | 50.10 | 6 50– 6 99 |
| 7 00– 7 49 | 1 | 1 | | | | | | | 14 | 183 | 21.60 | 63.80 | 7 00– 7 49 |
| 7 50– 7 99 | | | | | | | | | 3 | 8 | 22.20 | 64.50 | 7 50– 7 99 |
| 8 00– 8 99 | | 4 | | | | | | | 17 | 148 | 25.80 | 75.50 | 8 00– 8 99 |
| 9 00– 9 99 | | 1 | | | | 1 | | 3 | 23 | 81 | 30.60 | 81.50 | 9 00– 9 99 |
| 10 00–10 99 | | 4 | 1 | 1 | 3 | 1 | 1 | 2 | 25 | 91 | 35.80 | 88.50 | 10 00–10 99 |
| 11 00–11 99 | 1 | 2 | 2 | | | | | 2 | 11 | 30 | 38.10 | 90.50 | 11 00–11 99 |
| 12 00–12 99 | 4 | 3 | 5 | 1 | 2 | 1 | | 3 | 60 | 52 | 50.70 | 94.50 | 12 00–12 99 |
| 13 00–13 99 | | | 1 | 2 | 2 | 2 | | 1 | 23 | 14 | 55.50 | 95.50 | 13 00–13 99 |
| 14 00–14 99 | | | 3 | | 2 | | | 2 | 17 | 15 | 59.10 | 96.60 | 14 00–14 99 |
| 15 00–15 99 | 4 | 1 | 8 | 1 | 3 | | 2 | 2 | 45 | 21 | 68.50 | 98.20 | 15 00–15 99 |
| 16 00–17 99 | | 1 | 1 | 1 | 1 | | 1 | | 30 | 8 | 74.80 | 98.80 | 16 00–17 99 |
| 18 00–19 99 | 2 | | 7 | | 1 | 1 | | | 25 | 6 | 80.00 | 99.30 | 18 00–19 99 |
| 20 00–24 99 | 5 | 1 | 5 | 2 | 2 | | 1 | | 38 | 7 | 88.10 | 99.70 | 20 00–24 99 |
| 25 00–29 99 | 5 | | 2 | | 3 | | | 1 | 24 | 1 | 93.10 | 99.80 | 25 00–29 99 |
| 30 00–34 99 | 1 | 2 | 3 | | 1 | | | | 15 | 2 | 96.30 | 99.90 | 30 00–34 99 |
| 35 00–39 99 | 2 | | 4 | | | 1 | 1 | | 11 | | 98.50 | | 35 00–39 99 |
| 40 00 and over | | | | | 2 | 1 | | 1 | 7 | 1 | 100.00 | 100.00 | 40 00 and over |
| Not reported | | | 2 | | 1 | | | 1 | 4 | 11 | | | Not reported |
| Total | 25 | 20 | 44 | 10 | 23 | 8 | 7 | 22 | 481 | 1,350 | | | Total |

165. TABLE IX, A, 1, b

NEW YORK STATE, EXCLUSIVE OF NEW YORK CITY

**DEPARTMENT STORES — OFFICE**

NUMBER AND PER CENT. OF EMPLOYEES CLASSIFIED ACCORDING TO ACTUAL WEEKLY EARNINGS, BY OCCUPATION AND SEX

| ACTUAL WEEKLY EARNINGS IN DOLLARS | OCCUPATION | | | | | | | | | | | | | ACTUAL WEEKLY EARNINGS IN DOLLARS |
|---|---|---|---|---|---|---|---|---|---|---|---|---|---|---|
| | SUPERINTENDENTS | | BOOKKEEPERS | | CLERKS | | SECRETARIES | STENOGRAPHERS | | OFFICE BOYS AND GIRLS | | CASHIERS | | |
| | Male | Female | Male | Female | Male | Female | Female | Male | Female | Male | Female | Male | Female | |
| Less than $3 00 | ...... | ...... | ...... | ...... | 3 | 2 | ...... | ...... | ...... | ...... | 1 | ...... | 8 | Less than $3 00 |
| $3 00–$3 49 | ...... | ...... | ...... | ...... | 1 | 6 | ...... | ...... | ...... | 2 | 1 | 1 | 3 | $3 00– 3 49 |
| 3 50– 3 99 | ...... | ...... | ...... | ...... | 2 | 11 | ...... | ...... | ...... | 1 | ...... | ...... | 15 | 3 50– 3 99 |
| 4 00– 4 49 | ...... | ...... | ...... | 1 | 12 | 18 | ...... | ...... | 1 | 6 | 5 | ...... | 29 | 4 00– 4 49 |
| 4 50– 4 99 | ...... | ...... | ...... | 1 | 1 | 14 | ...... | ...... | ...... | 4 | 1 | ...... | 20 | 4 50– 4 99 |
| 5 00– 5 49 | ...... | ...... | ...... | 8 | 8 | 68 | ...... | ...... | 1 | 5 | 12 | ...... | 54 | 5 00– 5 49 |
| 5 50– 5 99 | ...... | ...... | ...... | 1 | 3 | 15 | ...... | ...... | 1 | ...... | 1 | ...... | 18 | 5 50– 5.99 |
| 6 00– 6 49 | ...... | ...... | ...... | 20 | 22 | 99 | ...... | ...... | 9 | 1 | 7 | 2 | 100 | 6 00– 6 49 |
| 6 50– 6 99 | ...... | ...... | ...... | 2 | 4 | 11 | ...... | ...... | ...... | ...... | ...... | ...... | 6 | 6 50– 6 99 |
| 7 00– 7 49 | ...... | ...... | ...... | 22 | 10 | 56 | ...... | ...... | 16 | ...... | 1 | ...... | 60 | 7 00– 7 49 |
| 7 50– 7 99 | ...... | ...... | ...... | 2 | 1 | 1 | ...... | ...... | 1 | ...... | ...... | 1 | 3 | 7 50– 7 99 |
| 8 00– 8 99 | ...... | ...... | 1 | 31 | 9 | 58 | ...... | ...... | 10 | ...... | 1 | 1 | 30 | 8 00– 8 99 |
| 9 00– 9 99 | ...... | ...... | 3 | 25 | 14 | 30 | ...... | 1 | 7 | ...... | ...... | 1 | 14 | 9 00– 9 99 |
| 10 00–10 99 | ...... | ...... | 2 | 30 | 15 | 19 | ...... | 1 | 18 | 1 | ...... | 1 | 15 | 10 00–10 99 |
| 11 00–11 99 | ...... | ...... | 2 | 11 | 8 | 9 | ...... | ...... | 6 | ...... | ...... | ...... | 3 | 11 00–11 99 |
| 12 00–12 99 | ...... | ...... | 14 | 19 | 37 | 15 | ...... | ...... | 6 | ...... | ...... | 2 | 9 | 12 00–12 99 |
| 13 00–13 99 | ...... | ...... | 8 | 4 | 11 | 1 | ...... | 1 | 4 | ...... | ...... | 2 | 5 | 13 00–13 99 |
| 14 00–14 99 | ...... | 1 | 2 | 9 | 13 | 1 | ...... | ...... | 1 | ...... | ...... | 1 | 2 | 14 00–14 99 |
| 15 00–15 99 | ...... | ...... | 11 | 8 | 23 | 6 | ...... | ...... | 4 | ...... | ...... | 1 | 3 | 15 00–15 99 |
| 16 00–17 99 | ...... | ...... | 14 | 2 | 13 | 1 | 1 | ...... | 1 | ...... | ...... | 1 | 2 | 16 00–17 99 |
| 18 00–19 99 | ...... | ...... | 7 | 2 | 10 | 1 | ...... | ...... | 2 | ...... | ...... | ...... | ...... | 18 00–19 99 |
| 20 00–24 99 | 1 | ...... | 7 | ...... | 16 | 4 | ...... | ...... | 2 | ...... | ...... | 2 | ...... | 20 00–24 99 |
| 25 00–29 99 | 2 | ...... | 3 | ...... | 7 | 1 | ...... | ...... | ...... | ...... | ...... | 1 | ...... | 25 00–29 99 |
| 30 00–34 99 | 1 | ...... | ...... | 1 | 2 | ...... | ...... | ...... | ...... | ...... | ...... | ...... | ...... | 30 00–34 99 |
| 35 00–39 99 | 1 | ...... | 2 | ...... | 6 | ...... | ...... | ...... | ...... | ...... | ...... | 2 | ...... | 35 00–39 99 |
| 40 00 and over | ...... | ...... | 1 | ...... | ...... | 1 | ...... | ...... | ...... | ...... | ...... | 1 | ...... | 40 00 and over |
| Not reported | ...... | ...... | ...... | 4 | 4 | 1 | ...... | ...... | 1 | ...... | ...... | ...... | 3 | Not reported |
| Total | 5 | 1 | 77 | 203 | 256 | 449 | 1 | 3 | 91 | 20 | 30 | 20 | 397 | Total |

165. TABLE IX, A, 1, b — (*concluded*)

NEW YORK STATE EXCLUSIVE OF NEW YORK CITY
**DEPARTMENT STORES — OFFICE**
NUMBER AND PER CENT. OF EMPLOYEES CLASSIFIED ACCORDING TO ACTUAL WEEKLY EARNINGS, BY OCCUPATION AND SEX

| ACTUAL WEEKLY EARNINGS IN DOLLARS | OCCUPATION—(*Continued*) | | | | | | | | | | | ACTUAL WEEKLY EARNINGS IN DOLLARS |
|---|---|---|---|---|---|---|---|---|---|---|---|---|
| | TELEPHONE OPERATORS | AUDITORS | | DETECTIVES | | ADVERTISERS AND WINDOW DRESSERS | | TOTAL | | CUMULATIVE PER CENT. OF TOTAL | | |
| | Female | Male | Female | Male | Female | Male | Female | Male | Female | Male | Female | |
| Less than $3.00 | 1 | ........ | 2 | ........ | ........ | ........ | ........ | 3 | 9 | .60 | .70 | Less than $3 00 |
| $3 00–$3 49 | 1 | ........ | 2 | ........ | 1 | ........ | ........ | 4 | 14 | 1.50 | 1.70 | $3 00– 3 49 |
| 3 50– 3 99 | 2 | ........ | 4 | ........ | ........ | 1 | ........ | 4 | 32 | 2.30 | 4.10 | 3 50– 3 99 |
| 4 00– 4 49 | 6 | ........ | 10 | ........ | ........ | ........ | ........ | 18 | 70 | 6.10 | 9.30 | 4 00– 4 49 |
| 4 50– 4 99 | 1 | ........ | 5 | ........ | ........ | ........ | ........ | 5 | 42 | 7.10 | 12.50 | 4 50– 4 99 |
| 5 00– 5 49 | 4 | ........ | 19 | ........ | ........ | 3 | ........ | 16 | 166 | 10.50 | 24.90 | 5 00– 5 49 |
| 5 50– 5 99 | 3 | ........ | 5 | ........ | ........ | ........ | ........ | 3 | 44 | 11.10 | 28.20 | 5 50– 5 99 |
| 6 00– 6 49 | 10 | ........ | 26 | ........ | ........ | 6 | 1 | 31 | 272 | 17.60 | 48.50 | 6 00– 6 49 |
| 6 50– 6 99 | ........ | 1 | 3 | ........ | ........ | ........ | ........ | 5 | 22 | 18.60 | 50.10 | 6 50– 6 99 |
| 7 00– 7 49 | 9 | ........ | 18 | ........ | ........ | 4 | 1 | 14 | 183 | 21.60 | 63.80 | 7 00– 7 49 |
| 7 50– 7 99 | 1 | 1 | ........ | ........ | ........ | ........ | ........ | 3 | 8 | 22.22 | 64.50 | 7 50– 7 99 |
| 8 00– 8 99 | 12 | ........ | 6 | ........ | ........ | 6 | ........ | 17 | 148 | 25.80 | 75.50 | 8 00– 8 99 |
| 9 00– 9 99 | 4 | ........ | 1 | ........ | ........ | 4 | ........ | 23 | 81 | 30.60 | 81.50 | 9 00– 9 99 |
| 10 00–10 99 | 3 | 1 | 5 | ........ | ........ | 4 | 1 | 25 | 91 | 35.80 | 88.50 | 10 00–10 99 |
| 11 00–11 99 | ........ | ........ | 1 | ........ | ........ | 1 | ........ | 11 | 30 | 38.10 | 90.50 | 11 00–11 99 |
| 12 00–12 99 | ........ | 2 | ........ | ........ | ........ | 5 | 3 | 60 | 52 | 50.70 | 94.50 | 12 00–12 99 |
| 13 00–13 99 | ........ | ........ | ........ | ........ | ........ | 1 | ........ | 23 | 14 | 55.50 | 95.50 | 13 00–13 99 |
| 14 00–14 99 | ........ | ........ | ........ | ........ | ........ | 1 | 1 | 17 | 15 | 59.10 | 96.60 | 14 00–14 99 |
| 15 00–15 99 | ........ | 1 | ........ | ........ | ........ | 9 | ........ | 45 | 21 | 68.50 | 98.20 | 15 00–15 99 |
| 16 00–17 99 | ........ | ........ | 1 | ........ | ........ | 2 | ........ | 30 | 8 | 74.80 | 98.80 | 16 00–17 99 |
| 18 00–19 99 | ........ | 1 | ........ | ........ | ........ | 7 | 1 | 25 | 6 | 80.00 | 99.30 | 18 00–19 99 |
| 20 00–24 99 | ........ | ........ | ........ | 1 | ........ | 11 | 1 | 38 | 7 | 88.10 | 99.70 | 20 00–24 99 |
| 25 00–29 99 | ........ | 1 | ........ | ........ | ........ | 10 | ........ | 24 | 1 | 93.10 | 99.80 | 25 00–29 99 |
| 30 00–34 99 | ........ | 2 | ........ | ........ | ........ | 10 | 1 | 15 | 2 | 96.30 | 99.90 | 30 00–34 99 |
| 35 00–39 99 | ........ | ........ | ........ | ........ | ........ | ........ | ........ | 11 | ........ | 98.50 | ........ | 35 00–39 99 |
| 40 00 an over | ........ | 1 | ........ | ........ | ........ | 4 | ........ | 7 | 1 | 100.00 | 100.00 | 40 00 and over |
| Not reported | 1 | ........ | ........ | ........ | ........ | ........ | 1 | 4 | 11 | ........ | ........ | Not reported |
| Total | 58 | 11 | 108 | 1 | 1 | 89 | 11 | 481 | 1,350 | ........ | ........ | Total |

166. TABLE XIX, A, 1, b

NEW YORK STATE EXCLUSIVE OF NEW YORK CITY—FIRST AND SECOND CLASS CITIES

**MERCANTILE ESTABLISHMENTS — DEPARTMENT STORES — OFFICE**

NUMBER AND PER CENT. OF EMPLOYEES CLASSIFIED ACCORDING TO AVERAGE ACTUAL WEEKLY EARNINGS, BY OCCUPATION AND SEX

| AVERAGE ACTUAL WEEKLY EARNINGS IN DOLLARS | OCCUPATION: BOOK-KEEPERS | | CLERKS | | STENOG-RAPHERS | OFFICE BOYS AND GIRLS | | CASHIERS | TELEPHONE OPERATORS | AUDITORS | | ADVERTISERS AND WINDOW DRESSERS | | TOTAL | | CUMULATIVE PER CENT. OF TOTAL | | AVERAGE ACTUAL WEEKLY EARNINGS IN DOLLARS |
|---|---|---|---|---|---|---|---|---|---|---|---|---|---|---|---|---|---|---|
| | Male | Female | Male | Female | Female | Male | Female | Female | Female | Male | Female | Male | Female | Male | Female | Male | Female | |
| Less than $3 00 | .... | .... | 1 | 1 | .... | .... | .... | .... | .... | 1 | 1 | .... | .... | 2 | 2 | 3.90 | 1.50 | Less than $3 00 |
| $3 00–$3 49 | .... | .... | 1 | .... | .... | 1 | 1 | .... | .... | .... | .... | 1 | .... | 3 | 1 | 9.60 | 2.20 | $3 00– 3 49 |
| 3 50– 3 99 | .... | .... | .... | 1 | .... | 1 | 2 | 3 | 1 | .... | .... | .... | .... | 1 | 7 | 11.50 | 7.40 | 3 50– 3 99 |
| 4 00– 4 49 | .... | .... | 1 | 3 | .... | .... | .... | .... | .... | .... | .... | .... | 1 | 1 | 4 | 13.50 | 10.40 | 4 00– 4 49 |
| 4 50– 4 99 | .... | 2 | 1 | 4 | .... | .... | .... | .... | 1 | .... | .... | .... | .... | 1 | 7 | 15.40 | 15.60 | 4 50– 4 99 |
| 5 00– 5 49 | .... | 2 | .... | 2 | 1 | .... | .... | 4 | .... | .... | 1 | .... | .... | .... | 10 | ..... | 23.00 | 5 00– 5 49 |
| 5 50– 5 99 | .... | 3 | 1 | 1 | 3 | .... | .... | 7 | .... | .... | 2 | .... | .... | 1 | 16 | 17.30 | 35.00 | 5 50– 5 99 |
| 6 00– 6 49 | .... | 1 | .... | 2 | 2 | .... | .... | 6 | 1 | .... | .... | .... | .... | .... | 12 | ..... | 43.70 | 6 00– 6 49 |
| 6 50– 6 99 | .... | 4 | .... | 5 | 2 | .... | .... | 2 | .... | .... | 1 | .... | .... | .... | 14 | ..... | 54.00 | 6 50– 6 99 |
| 7 00– 7 49 | .... | 1 | 1 | 2 | .... | .... | 1 | 2 | .... | .... | 2 | .... | .... | 1 | 8 | 19.30 | 60.00 | 7 00– 7 49 |
| 7 50– 7 99 | .... | 4 | .... | 2 | 1 | .... | .... | 4 | .... | .... | .... | .... | .... | .... | 11 | ..... | 68.00 | 7 50– 7 99 |
| 8 00– 8 99 | .... | 2 | 2 | 1 | .... | .... | .... | 4 | 1 | .... | .... | .... | .... | 2 | 8 | 23.00 | 74.00 | 8 00– 8 99 |
| 9 00– 9 99 | .... | 5 | 5 | .... | 1 | .... | .... | 1 | .... | .... | .... | .... | .... | 5 | 7 | 32.70 | 79.00 | 9 00– 9 99 |
| 10 00–10 99 | .... | 2 | 2 | 5 | 1 | 1 | .... | .... | .... | .... | 1 | .... | .... | 3 | 9 | 38.50 | 86.00 | 10 00–10 99 |
| 11 00–11 99 | 1 | .... | 4 | 2 | .... | .... | 1 | .... | .... | .... | .... | .... | .... | 5 | 3 | 48.00 | 88.00 | 11 00–11 99 |
| 12 00–12 99 | 1 | 1 | 3 | .... | 1 | .... | .... | 1 | .... | .... | .... | .... | 1 | 4 | 4 | 56.00 | 91.00 | 12 00–12 99 |
| 13 00–13 99 | .... | .... | 1 | .... | .... | .... | .... | .... | .... | .... | .... | .... | .... | 1 | .... | 58.00 | ..... | 13 00–13 99 |
| 14 00–14 99 | .... | 1 | 1 | 2 | .... | .... | .... | .... | .... | .... | .... | 1 | .... | 2 | 3 | 61.50 | 93.00 | 14 00–14 99 |
| 15 00–15 99 | .... | 1 | 1 | 1 | .... | .... | .... | 2 | .... | .... | .... | 1 | .... | 2 | 4 | 65.50 | 96.00 | 15 00–15 99 |
| 16 00–17 99 | 1 | .... | 1 | 3 | .... | .... | .... | .... | .... | .... | .... | 1 | .... | 3 | 8 | 71.00 | 98.00 | 16 00–17 99 |
| 18 00–19 99 | .... | .... | 2 | .... | .... | .... | .... | .... | .... | .... | .... | 2 | .... | 4 | .... | 79.00 | ..... | 18 00–19 99 |
| 20 00–24 99 | 2 | .... | 2 | 1 | .... | .... | .... | .... | .... | .... | .... | 1 | .... | 5 | 1 | 88.50 | 99.00 | 20 00–24 99 |
| 25 00–29 99 | .... | 1 | 1 | .... | .... | .... | .... | .... | .... | .... | .... | 4 | .... | 5 | 1 | 98.00 | 100.00 | 25 00–29 99 |
| 35 00–39 99 | 1 | .... | .... | .... | .... | .... | .... | .... | .... | .... | .... | .... | .... | 1 | .... | 100.00 | ..... | 35 00–39 99 |
| Total | 6 | 30 | 31 | 38 | 12 | 3 | 5 | 56 | 4 | 1 | 8 | 11 | 2 | 52 | 135 | ..... | ..... | Total |

NEW YORK STATE, EXCLUSIVE OF NEW YORK CITY—FIRST AND SECOND CLASS CITIES

167. TABLE XX, A, 1, b

**MERCANTILE ESTABLISHMENTS — DEPARTMENT STORES — OFFICE**

NUMBER AND PER CENT. OF EMPLOYEES WORKING 48 WEEKS OR MORE, CLASSIFIED ACCORDING TO ACTUAL ANNUAL EARNINGS, BY OCCUPATION AND SEX

| ACTUAL ANNUAL EARNINGS IN DOLLARS | OCCUPATION | | | | | | | | | | | | | | | | | ACTUAL ANNUAL EARNINGS IN DOLLARS |
|---|---|---|---|---|---|---|---|---|---|---|---|---|---|---|---|---|---|---|
| | BOOK-KEEPERS | | CLERKS | | STENOG-RAPHERS | OFFICE BOYS AND GIRLS | | CASHIERS | TELEPHONE OPERATORS | AUDITORS | | ADVERTISERS | | TOTAL | | CUMULATIVE PER CENT. OF TOTAL | | |
| | Male | Female | Male | Female | Female | Male | Female | Female | Female | Male | Female | Male | Female | Male | Female | Male | Female | |
| Less than $200 | .... | .... | 2 | 2 | ........ | 2 | 3 | 2 | .......... | 1 | 1 | .... | .... | 5 | 8 | 12.20 | 7.00 | Less than $200 |
| $200- $249 | .... | .... | .... | 5 | ........ | .... | .... | 1 | 1 | .... | 1 | .... | 1 | .... | 9 | ..... | 14.80 | $200- 249 |
| 250- 299 | .... | 1 | .... | 2 | 1 | .... | .... | 7 | .......... | .... | 1 | .... | .... | .... | 12 | ..... | 25.20 | 250- 299 |
| 300- 349 | .... | 3 | .... | 5 | 5 | .... | .... | 9 | .......... | .... | 2 | .... | .... | .... | 24 | ..... | 46.00 | 300- 349 |
| 350- 399 | .... | 6 | 1 | 5 | 1 | .... | 1 | 3 | .......... | .... | 2 | .... | .... | 1 | 18 | 14.60 | 62.00 | 350- 399 |
| 400- 449 | .... | 1 | 1 | 2 | ........ | .... | .... | 5 | 1 | .... | .... | .... | .... | 1 | 9 | 17.00 | 69.80 | 400- 449 |
| 450- 499 | .... | 5 | 1 | .... | ........ | .... | .... | 1 | .......... | .... | .... | .... | .... | 1 | 6 | 19.50 | 75.00 | 450- 499 |
| 500- 549 | .... | 3 | 5 | 5 | 2 | 1 | 1 | ........ | .......... | .... | .... | .... | .... | 6 | 11 | 34.00 | 84.50 | 500- 549 |
| 550- 599 | 1 | .... | .... | 1 | ........ | .... | .... | ........ | .......... | .... | .... | .... | .... | 1 | 1 | 36.50 | 85.40 | 550- 599 |
| 600- 649 | 1 | 1 | 4 | 1 | 1 | .... | .... | 1 | .......... | .... | .... | .... | 1 | 5 | 5 | 48.70 | 89.80 | 600- 649 |
| 650- 699 | .... | 1 | 1 | .... | ........ | .... | .... | ........ | .......... | .... | .... | .... | .... | 1 | 1 | 51.10 | 90.70 | 650- 699 |
| 700- 749 | .... | .... | 1 | 2 | ........ | .... | .... | ........ | .......... | .... | .... | .... | .... | 1 | 2 | 53.50 | 92.40 | 700- 749 |
| 750- 799 | .... | 1 | .... | 1 | ........ | .... | .... | 2 | .......... | .... | .... | 2 | .... | 2 | 4 | 58.50 | 95.90 | 750- 799 |
| 800- 899 | 1 | .... | 2 | 2 | ........ | .... | .... | ........ | .......... | .... | .... | 1 | .... | 4 | 2 | 68.00 | 97.50 | 800- 899 |
| 900- 999 | .... | .... | 1 | 1 | ........ | .... | .... | ........ | .......... | .... | .... | 1 | .... | 2 | 1 | 73.00 | 98.40 | 900- 999 |
| 1,000-1,099 | 1 | .... | .... | 1 | ........ | .... | .... | ........ | .......... | .... | .... | 1 | .... | 2 | 1 | 78.00 | 99.20 | 1,000-1,099 |
| 1,100-1,199 | 1 | .... | 2 | .... | ........ | .... | .... | ........ | .......... | .... | .... | .... | .... | 3 | .... | 85.50 | ..... | 1,100-1,199 |
| 1,300-1,399 | .... | 1 | 1 | .... | ........ | .... | .... | ........ | .......... | .... | .... | 2 | .... | 3 | 1 | 92.50 | 100.00 | 1,300-1,399 |
| 1,400-1,499 | .... | .... | .... | .... | ........ | .... | .... | ........ | .......... | .... | .... | 1 | .... | 1 | .... | 95.00 | ..... | 1,400-1,499 |
| 1,500-1,599 | .... | .... | .... | .... | ........ | .... | .... | ........ | .......... | .... | .... | 1 | .... | 1 | .... | 97.50 | ..... | 1,500-1,599 |
| 1,800-1,999 | 1 | .... | .... | .... | ........ | .... | .... | ........ | .......... | .... | .... | .... | .... | 1 | .... | 100.00 | ..... | 1,800-1,999 |
| Total | 6 | 23 | 22 | 35 | 10 | 3 | 5 | 31 | 2 | 1 | 7 | 9 | 2 | 41 | 115 | ..... | ..... | Total |

NEW YORK STATE, EXCLUSIVE OF NEW YORK CITY
DEPARTMENT STORES — SHIPPING AND DELIVERY

168. TABLE V, A, 1, c NUMBER AND PER CENT. OF EMPLOYEES EARNING SPECIFIED WEEKLY RATES, BY AGE GROUPS AND SEX

| WEEKLY RATES IN DOLLARS | AGE GROUPS IN YEARS | | | | | | | | | | | | | | | | | | WEEKLY RATES DOLLARS |
|---|---|---|---|---|---|---|---|---|---|---|---|---|---|---|---|---|---|---|---|
| | 14–15 | 16–17 | | 18–20 | | 21–24 | 25–29 | 30–34 | 35–39 | 40–44 | 45–54 | 55–64 | 65 AND OVER | NOT REPORTED | TOTAL | | CUMULATIVE PER CENT. OF TOTAL | | |
| | Male | Male | Female | Male | Female | Male | Male | Male | Male | Male | Male | Male | Male | Male | Male | Female | Male | Female | |
| Less than $3 00 | 3 | ..... | ..... | ..... | ..... | ..... | ..... | ..... | ..... | ..... | ..... | ..... | ..... | ..... | 3 | ..... | .39 | ..... | Less than $3 00 |
| $3 00–$3 49 | ..... | 1 | ..... | ..... | ..... | ..... | ..... | ..... | ..... | ..... | ..... | ..... | ..... | ..... | 1 | ..... | .52 | ..... | $3 00– 3 49 |
| 3 50– 3 99 | 8 | ..... | ..... | ..... | ..... | ..... | ..... | ..... | ..... | ..... | ..... | ..... | ..... | ..... | 8 | ..... | 1.57 | ..... | 3 50– 3 99 |
| 4 00– 4 49 | 20 | 7 | ..... | ..... | ..... | ..... | ..... | ..... | ..... | ..... | ..... | ..... | ..... | ..... | 27 | ..... | 5.11 | ..... | 4 00– 4 49 |
| 4 50– 4 99 | 9 | 7 | ..... | ..... | ..... | ..... | ..... | ..... | ..... | ..... | ..... | ..... | ..... | ..... | 16 | ..... | 7.20 | ..... | 4 50– 4 99 |
| 5 00– 5 49 | 15 | 78 | 1 | 11 | ..... | ..... | ..... | ..... | ..... | ..... | ..... | ..... | ..... | 1 | 105 | 1 | 20.99 | 33.33 | 5 00– 5 49 |
| 6 00– 6 49 | ..... | 13 | 1 | 2 | ..... | 2 | ..... | ..... | ..... | ..... | ..... | ..... | ..... | ..... | 17 | 1 | 23.20 | 66.67 | 6 00– 6 49 |
| 7 00– 7 49 | ..... | 1 | ..... | 8 | 1 | 3 | ..... | 1 | 1 | ..... | ..... | ..... | ..... | ..... | 14 | 1 | 25.00 | 100.00 | 7 00– 7 49 |
| 7 50– 7 99 | ..... | 1 | ..... | ..... | ..... | ..... | ..... | ..... | ..... | ..... | ..... | ..... | ..... | ..... | 1 | ..... | 25.19 | ..... | 7 50– 7 99 |
| 8 00– 8 99 | 1 | 1 | ..... | 8 | ..... | ..... | ..... | 1 | ..... | ..... | ..... | ..... | ..... | ..... | 11 | ..... | 26.55 | ..... | 8 00– 8 99 |
| 9 00– 9 99 | ..... | ..... | ..... | 5 | ..... | 4 | 4 | 1 | 2 | ..... | 1 | 1 | ..... | ..... | 18 | ..... | 28.90 | ..... | 9 00– 9 99 |
| 10 00–10 99 | ..... | 1 | ..... | 6 | ..... | 8 | 8 | 2 | 1 | 1 | 6 | 3 | 2 | ..... | 38 | ..... | 35.00 | ..... | 10 00–10 99 |
| 11 00–11 99 | ..... | ..... | ..... | 2 | ..... | 4 | 2 | 3 | ..... | 2 | 5 | 2 | 1 | ..... | 21 | ..... | 36.60 | ..... | 11 00–11 99 |
| 12 00–12 99 | ..... | ..... | ..... | 11 | ..... | 24 | 25 | 14 | 15 | 17 | 25 | 12 | 3 | 1 | 147 | ..... | 55.90 | ..... | 12 00–12 99 |
| 13 00–13 99 | ..... | ..... | ..... | 5 | ..... | 28 | 12 | 5 | 8 | 5 | 7 | 2 | ..... | ..... | 72 | ..... | 64.25 | ..... | 13 00–13 99 |
| 14 00–14 99 | ..... | ..... | ..... | ..... | ..... | 7 | 12 | 6 | 3 | 2 | 4 | 1 | 1 | ..... | 36 | ..... | 70.10 | ..... | 14 00–14 99 |
| 15 00–15 99 | ..... | 1 | ..... | 2 | ..... | 35 | 38 | 24 | 17 | 10 | 19 | 2 | ..... | ..... | 148 | ..... | 89.50 | ..... | 15 00–15 99 |
| 16 00–17 99 | ..... | ..... | ..... | ..... | ..... | 4 | 9 | 12 | 10 | 8 | 4 | 3 | ..... | ..... | 50 | ..... | 96.00 | ..... | 16 00–17 99 |
| 18 00–19 99 | ..... | ..... | ..... | ..... | ..... | 2 | 2 | 3 | 5 | 3 | 4 | 3 | ..... | ..... | 22 | ..... | 98.90 | ..... | 18 00–19 99 |
| 20 00–24 99 | ..... | ..... | ..... | ..... | ..... | ..... | 1 | 1 | 1 | 1 | 2 | ..... | ..... | ..... | 6 | ..... | 99.70 | ..... | 20 00–24 99 |
| 25 00–29 99 | ..... | ..... | ..... | ..... | ..... | ..... | ..... | 1 | ..... | 1 | ..... | ..... | ..... | ..... | 2 | ..... | 100.00 | ..... | 25 00–29 99 |
| Not reported | 1 | ..... | ..... | ..... | ..... | ..... | ..... | ..... | 1 | ..... | ..... | ..... | ..... | ..... | 2 | ..... | ..... | ..... | Not reported |
| Total | 57 | 110 | 2 | 61 | 1 | 121 | 113 | 74 | 64 | 50 | 77 | 29 | 7 | 2 | 765 | 3 | ..... | ..... | Total |

NEW YORK STATE, EXCLUSIVE OF NEW YORK CITY

**DEPARTMENT STORES — SHIPPING AND DELIVERY**

169. TABLE VIII, A, 1, c    NUMBER AND PER CENT. OF EMPLOYEES EARNING SPECIFIED WEEKLY RATES, BY OCCUPATION AND SEX

| WEEKLY RATES IN DOLLARS | OCCUPATION | | | | | | | | | | | | | WEEKLY RATES IN DOLLARS |
|---|---|---|---|---|---|---|---|---|---|---|---|---|---|---|
| | FOREMEN | CLERKS AND ROUTERS | | DRIVERS | WAGON BOYS AND HELPERS | CHAUFFEURS | GENERAL LABOR | PACKING | STABLE MEN | TOTAL | | CUMULATIVE PER CENT. OF TOTAL | | |
| | Male | Male | Female | Male | Male | Male | Male | Male | Male | Male | Female | Male | Female | |
| Less than $3.00 | ...... | ...... | ...... | ...... | 3 | ...... | ...... | ...... | ...... | 3 | ...... | .39 | ...... | Less than $3 00 |
| $3 00–$3.49 | ...... | ...... | ...... | ...... | 1 | ...... | ...... | ...... | ...... | 1 | ...... | .52 | ...... | $3 00– 3 49 |
| 3 50– 3 99 | ...... | ...... | ...... | ...... | 8 | ...... | ...... | ...... | ...... | 8 | ...... | 1.57 | ...... | 3 50– 3 99 |
| 4 00– 4 49 | ...... | ...... | ...... | ...... | 27 | ...... | ...... | ...... | ...... | 27 | ...... | 5.11 | ...... | 4 00– 4 49 |
| 4 50– 4 99 | ...... | ...... | ...... | ...... | 14 | ...... | 1 | 1 | ...... | 16 | ...... | 7.20 | ...... | 4 50– 4 99 |
| 5 00– 5 49 | ...... | 3 | 1 | ...... | 99 | ...... | 2 | 1 | ...... | 105 | 1 | 20.99 | 33.33 | 5 00– 5 49 |
| 6 00– 6 49 | ...... | 7 | 1 | ...... | 9 | ...... | 1 | ...... | ...... | 17 | 1 | 23.20 | 66.67 | 6 00– 6 49 |
| 7 00– 7 49 | ...... | 2 | 1 | 1 | 2 | 1 | 1 | 6 | 1 | 14 | 1 | 25.00 | 100.00 | 7 00– 7 49 |
| 7 50– 7 99 | ...... | 1 | ...... | ...... | ...... | ...... | ...... | ...... | ...... | 1 | ...... | 25.19 | ...... | 7 50– 7 99 |
| 8 00– 8 99 | ...... | 1 | ...... | ...... | 1 | 1 | 1 | 7 | ...... | 11 | ...... | 26.55 | ...... | 8 00– 8 99 |
| 9 00– 9 99 | ...... | 7 | ...... | 1 | ...... | 1 | 3 | 5 | 1 | 18 | ...... | 28.90 | ...... | 9 00– 9 99 |
| 10 00–10 99 | ...... | 12 | ...... | 4 | 1 | 6 | 1 | 13 | 1 | 38 | ...... | 35.00 | ...... | 10 00–10 99 |
| 11 00–11 99 | ...... | 3 | ...... | 5 | ...... | ...... | 1 | 9 | 3 | 21 | ...... | 36.60 | ...... | 11 00–11 99 |
| 12 00–12 99 | ...... | 19 | ...... | 40 | 4 | 7 | 9 | 43 | 25 | 147 | ...... | 55.90 | ...... | 12 00–12 99 |
| 13 00–13 99 | 2 | 9 | ...... | 41 | 1 | 6 | 4 | 6 | 3 | 72 | ...... | 64.25 | ...... | 13 00–13 99 |
| 14 00–14 99 | ...... | 7 | ...... | 8 | ...... | 10 | 1 | 9 | 1 | 36 | ...... | 70.10 | ...... | 14 00–14 99 |
| 15 00–15 99 | 1 | 16 | ...... | 87 | 1 | 36 | 3 | 3 | 1 | 148 | ...... | 89.50 | ...... | 15 00–15 99 |
| 16 00–17 99 | ...... | 12 | ...... | 26 | ...... | 8 | ...... | 2 | 2 | 50 | ...... | 96.00 | ...... | 16 00–17 99 |
| 18 00–19 99 | 3 | 11 | ...... | 4 | ...... | 2 | ...... | 1 | 1 | 22 | ...... | 98.90 | ...... | 18 00–19 99 |
| 20 00–24 99 | 2 | 3 | ...... | ...... | ...... | ...... | ...... | ...... | 1 | 6 | ...... | 99.70 | ...... | 20 00–24 99 |
| 25 00–29 99 | 1 | 1 | ...... | ...... | ...... | ...... | ...... | ...... | ...... | 2 | ...... | 100.00 | ...... | 25 00–29 99 |
| Not reported | ...... | ...... | ...... | ...... | 1 | ...... | ...... | 1 | ...... | 2 | ...... | ...... | ...... | Not reported |
| Total | 9 | 114 | 3 | 217 | 172 | 78 | 28 | 107 | 40 | 765 | 3 | ...... | ...... | Total |

170. TABLE VI, A, 1, c

NEW YORK STATE, EXCLUSIVE OF NEW YORK CITY
**DEPARTMENT STORES — SHIPPING AND DELIVERY**
Number and Per Cent. of Employees Classified According to Actual Weekly Earnings, by Age Groups and Sex

| Actual Weekly Earnings in Dollars | Age Groups in Years | | | | | | | | | | | | | | | | | | Actual Weekly Earnings in Dollars |
|---|---|---|---|---|---|---|---|---|---|---|---|---|---|---|---|---|---|---|---|
| | 14-15 | 16-17 | | 18-20 | | 21-24 | 25-29 | 30-34 | 35-39 | 40-44 | 45-54 | 55-64 | 65 and over | Not reported | Total | | Cumulative per cent. of total | | |
| | Male | Male | Female | Male | Female | Male | Male | Male | Male | Male | Male | Male | Male | Male | Male | Female | Male | Female | |
| Less than $3 00 | 4 | ..... | ..... | 1 | ..... | ..... | ..... | ..... | ..... | ..... | ..... | 1 | ..... | 1 | 7 | ..... | .92 | ..... | Less than $3 00 |
| $3 00-$3 49 | 3 | 1 | ..... | ..... | ..... | ..... | 1 | ..... | ..... | ..... | ..... | ..... | ..... | ..... | 5 | ..... | 1.58 | ..... | $3 00- 3 49 |
| 3 50- 3 99 | 7 | 1 | ..... | ..... | ..... | ..... | ..... | ..... | ..... | ..... | ..... | ..... | ..... | ..... | 8 | ..... | 2.66 | ..... | 3 50- 3 99 |
| 4 00- 4 49 | 20 | 9 | ..... | 1 | ..... | ..... | ..... | ..... | ..... | ..... | ..... | 1 | ..... | ..... | 31 | ..... | 6.72 | ..... | 4 00- 4 49 |
| 4 50- 4 99 | 9 | 7 | ..... | ..... | ..... | ..... | ..... | ..... | ..... | ..... | ..... | ..... | ..... | ..... | 16 | ..... | 8.84 | ..... | 4 50- 4 99 |
| 5 00- 5 49 | 13 | 74 | 1 | 9 | ..... | ..... | ..... | ..... | ..... | ..... | ..... | ..... | ..... | ..... | 96 | 1 | 21.48 | 33.33 | 5 00- 5 49 |
| 6 00- 6 49 | ..... | 13 | 1 | 2 | ..... | 2 | ..... | 1 | ..... | ..... | ..... | ..... | ..... | ..... | 18 | 1 | 23.85 | 66.67 | 6 00- 6 49 |
| 6 50- 6 99 | ..... | ..... | ..... | ..... | ..... | 1 | 1 | ..... | ..... | ..... | ..... | ..... | ..... | ..... | 2 | ..... | 24.10 | ..... | 6 50- 6 99 |
| 7 00- 7 49 | ..... | 1 | ..... | 8 | 1 | 3 | ..... | 1 | 1 | ..... | ..... | ..... | ..... | ..... | 14 | 1 | 26.00 | 100.00 | 7 00- 7 49 |
| 7 50- 7 99 | ..... | 1 | ..... | ..... | ..... | ..... | 1 | ..... | ..... | ..... | 1 | ..... | ..... | ..... | 3 | ..... | 26.35 | ..... | 7 50- 7 99 |
| 8 00- 8 99 | 1 | 1 | ..... | 9 | ..... | ..... | 1 | 1 | ..... | ..... | ..... | ..... | ..... | 1 | 14 | ..... | 28 20 | ..... | 8 00- 8 99 |
| 9 00- 9 99 | ..... | ..... | ..... | 5 | ..... | 4 | 5 | 1 | 2 | ..... | 1 | 1 | ..... | ..... | 19 | ..... | 30.75 | ..... | 9 00- 9 99 |
| 10 00-10 99 | ..... | 1 | ..... | 6 | ..... | 8 | 9 | 2 | 1 | 2 | 6 | 3 | 3 | ..... | 41 | ..... | 36.15 | ..... | 10 00-10 99 |
| 11 00-11 99 | ..... | ..... | ..... | 2 | ..... | 8 | 2 | 3 | 1 | 2 | 5 | 2 | 1 | ..... | 26 | ..... | 39.60 | ..... | 11 00-11 99 |
| 12 00-12 99 | ..... | ..... | ..... | 10 | ..... | 24 | 22 | 13 | 14 | 16 | 25 | 10 | 2 | ..... | 136 | ..... | 57.50 | ..... | 12 00-12 99 |
| 13 00-13 99 | ..... | ..... | ..... | 5 | ..... | 27 | 10 | 5 | 8 | 5 | 6 | 2 | ..... | ..... | 68 | ..... | 66.50 | ..... | 13 00-13 99 |
| 14 00-14 99 | ..... | ..... | ..... | ..... | ..... | 7 | 11 | 6 | 3 | 1 | 3 | ..... | 1 | ..... | 32 | ..... | 70.60 | ..... | 14 00-14 99 |
| 15 00-15 99 | ..... | 1 | ..... | 2 | ..... | 32 | 38 | 24 | 18 | 10 | 19 | 2 | ..... | ..... | 146 | ..... | 89.90 | ..... | 15 00-15 99 |
| 16 00-17 99 | ..... | ..... | ..... | ..... | ..... | 4 | 8 | 12 | 9 | 8 | 4 | 3 | ..... | ..... | 48 | ..... | 96.20 | ..... | 16 00-17 99 |
| 18 00-19 99 | ..... | ..... | ..... | ..... | ..... | 1 | 1 | 3 | 5 | 3 | 4 | 3 | ..... | ..... | 20 | ..... | 98.90 | ..... | 18 00-19 99 |
| 20 00-24 99 | ..... | ..... | ..... | ..... | ..... | ..... | 2 | 1 | 1 | 1 | 2 | ..... | ..... | ..... | 7 | ..... | 99.75 | ..... | 20 00-24 99 |
| 25 00-29 99 | ..... | ..... | ..... | ..... | ..... | ..... | ..... | 1 | ..... | 1 | ..... | ..... | ..... | ..... | 2 | ..... | 100.00 | ..... | 25 00-29 99 |
| Not reported | ..... | ..... | ..... | 1 | ..... | ..... | 1 | ..... | 1 | 1 | 1 | 1 | ..... | ..... | 6 | ..... | ..... | ..... | Not reported |
| Total | 57 | 110 | 2 | 61 | 1 | 121 | 113 | 74 | 64 | 50 | 77 | 29 | 7 | 2 | 765 | 3 | ..... | ..... | Total |

171. TABLE, IX A, 1, c

NEW YORK STATE, EXCLUSIVE OF NEW YORK CITY

**DEPARTMENT STORES — SHIPPING AND DELIVERY**

NUMBER AND PER CENT. OF EMPLOYEES CLASSIFIED ACCORDING TO ACTUAL WEEKLY EARNINGS, BY OCCUPATION AND SEX

| ACTUAL WEEKLY EARNINGS IN DOLLARS | OCCUPATION | | | | | | | | | | | | | ACTUAL WEEKLY EARNINGS IN DOLLARS |
|---|---|---|---|---|---|---|---|---|---|---|---|---|---|---|
| | FOREMEN | CLERKS AND ROUTERS | | DRIVERS | WAGON BOYS AND HELPERS | CHAUFFEURS | GENERAL LABOR | PACKING | STABLE MEN | TOTAL | | CUMULATIVE PER CENT. OF TOTAL | | |
| | Male | Male | Female | Male | Male | Male | Male | Male | Male | Male | Female | Male | Female | |
| Less than $3 00 | ...... | 1 | ...... | ...... | 5 | ...... | 1 | ...... | ...... | 7 | ...... | .92 | ...... | Less than $3.00 |
| $3 00–$3 49 | ...... | ...... | ...... | ...... | 4 | 1 | ...... | ...... | ...... | 5 | ...... | 1.58 | ...... | $3 00– 3 49 |
| 3 50– 3 99 | ...... | ...... | ...... | ...... | 8 | ...... | ...... | ...... | ...... | 8 | ...... | 2.66 | ...... | 3 50– 3 99 |
| 4 00– 4 49 | ...... | ...... | ...... | ...... | 30 | ...... | ...... | ...... | 1 | 31 | ...... | 6.72 | ...... | 4 00– 4 49 |
| 4 50– 4 99 | ...... | ...... | ...... | ...... | 14 | ...... | 1 | 1 | ...... | 16 | ...... | 8.84 | ...... | 4 50– 4 99 |
| 5 00– 5 49 | ...... | 2 | 1 | ...... | 91 | ...... | 2 | 1 | ...... | 96 | 1 | 21.48 | 33.33 | 5 00– 5 49 |
| 6 00– 6 49 | ...... | 7 | 1 | ...... | 10 | ...... | 1 | ...... | ...... | 18 | 1 | 23.85 | 66.67 | 6 00– 6 49 |
| 6 50– 6 99 | ...... | ...... | ...... | 1 | 1 | ...... | ...... | ...... | ...... | 2 | ...... | 24.10 | ...... | 6 50– 6 99 |
| 7 00– 7 49 | ...... | 2 | 1 | 1 | 2 | 1 | 1 | 6 | 1 | 14 | 1 | 26.00 | 100.00 | 7 00– 7 49 |
| 7 50– 7 99 | ...... | 1 | ...... | ...... | ...... | ...... | 2 | ...... | ...... | 3 | ...... | 26.35 | ...... | 7 50– 7 99 |
| 8 00– 8 99 | ...... | 2 | ...... | 1 | 1 | 1 | 1 | 8 | ...... | 14 | ...... | 28.20 | ...... | 8 00– 8 99 |
| 9 00– 9 99 | ...... | 7 | ...... | 2 | ...... | 1 | 3 | 5 | 1 | 19 | ...... | 30.75 | ...... | 9 00– 9 99 |
| 10 00–10 99 | ...... | 12 | ...... | 6 | 1 | 6 | 1 | 14 | 1 | 41 | ...... | 36.15 | ...... | 10 00–10 99 |
| 11 00–11 99 | ...... | 4 | ...... | 7 | ...... | 1 | 2 | 9 | 3 | 26 | ...... | 39.60 | ...... | 11 00–11 99 |
| 12 00–12 99 | ...... | 17 | ...... | 37 | 3 | 6 | 8 | 41 | 24 | 136 | ...... | 57.50 | ...... | 12 00–12 99 |
| 13 00–13 99 | 2 | 10 | ...... | 38 | ...... | 7 | 3 | 6 | 2 | 68 | ...... | 66.50 | ...... | 13 00–13 99 |
| 14 00–14 99 | ...... | 7 | ...... | 8 | ...... | 7 | ...... | 9 | 1 | 32 | ...... | 70.60 | ...... | 14 00–14 99 |
| 15 00–15 99 | 1 | 16 | ...... | 85 | 1 | 36 | 2 | 3 | 2 | 146 | ...... | 89.90 | ...... | 15 00–15 99 |
| 16 00–17 99 | ...... | 12 | ...... | 26 | ...... | 6 | ...... | 2 | 2 | 48 | ...... | 96.20 | ...... | 16 00–17 99 |
| 18 00–19 99 | 2 | 10 | ...... | 4 | ...... | 2 | ...... | 1 | 1 | 20 | ...... | 98.90 | ...... | 18 00–19 99 |
| 20 00–24 99 | 3 | 3 | ...... | ...... | ...... | ...... | ...... | ...... | 1 | 7 | ...... | 99.75 | ...... | 20 00–24 99 |
| 25 00–29 99 | 1 | 1 | ...... | ...... | ...... | ...... | ...... | ...... | ...... | 2 | ...... | 100.00 | ...... | 25 00–29 99 |
| Not reported | ...... | ...... | ...... | 1 | 1 | 3 | ...... | 1 | ...... | 6 | ...... | ...... | ...... | Not reported |
| Total | 9 | 114 | 3 | 217 | 172 | 78 | 28 | 107 | 40 | 765 | 3 | ...... | ...... | Total |

NEW YORK STATE, EXCLUSIVE OF NEW YORK CITY
DEPARTMENT STORES — MANUFACTURING

172. TABLE V, A, 1, d — NUMBER AND PER CENT. OF EMPLOYEES EARNING SPECIFIED WEEKLY RATES, BY AGE GROUPS AND SEX

| WEEKLY RATES IN DOLLARS | AGE GROUPS IN YEARS | | | | | | | | | | | | | WEEKLY RATES IN DOLLARS |
|---|---|---|---|---|---|---|---|---|---|---|---|---|---|---|
| | 14–15 | 16–17 | | 18–20 | | 21–24 | | 25–29 | | 30–34 | | 35–39 | | |
| | Female | Male | Female | Male | Female | Male | Female | Male | Female | Male | Female | Male | Female | |
| Less than $3 00 | 2 | ...... | 15 | ...... | 2 | ...... | ...... | ...... | ...... | ...... | ...... | ...... | 1 | Less than $3.00 |
| $3 00–$3 49 | 3 | 1 | 11 | ...... | 5 | ...... | ...... | ...... | ...... | ...... | ...... | ...... | ...... | $3 00– 3 49 |
| 3 50– 3 99 | ...... | ...... | 1 | ...... | 1 | ...... | ...... | ...... | ...... | ...... | ...... | ...... | ...... | 3 50– 3 99 |
| 4 00– 4 49 | 1 | ...... | 5 | ...... | 9 | ...... | 1 | ...... | ...... | ...... | ...... | ...... | ...... | 4 00– 4 49 |
| 4 50– 4 99 | ...... | 1 | 1 | ...... | 1 | ...... | 1 | ...... | ...... | ...... | ...... | ...... | ...... | 4 50– 4 99 |
| 5 00– 5 49 | 1 | 1 | 5 | ...... | 25 | ...... | 6 | ...... | 1 | ...... | ...... | ...... | ...... | 5 00– 5 49 |
| 5 50– 5 99 | ...... | ...... | 1 | ...... | 3 | ...... | ...... | ...... | 1 | ...... | ...... | ...... | ...... | 5 50– 5 99 |
| 6 00– 6 49 | ...... | 1 | 3 | ...... | 33 | ...... | 17 | ...... | 7 | ...... | 4 | ...... | 8 | 6 00– 6 49 |
| 6 50– 6 99 | ...... | ...... | ...... | ...... | 2 | ...... | 3 | ...... | ...... | ...... | ...... | ...... | ...... | 6 50– 6 99 |
| 7 00– 7 49 | ...... | 1 | ...... | 1 | 26 | ...... | 34 | 1 | 16 | 1 | 13 | ...... | 16 | 7 00– 7 49 |
| 7 50– 7 99 | ...... | ...... | ...... | ...... | 4 | ...... | 6 | 1 | 7 | 1 | 4 | ...... | 10 | 7 50– 7 99 |
| 8 00– 8 99 | ...... | ...... | ...... | 2 | 9 | 2 | 36 | ...... | 26 | ...... | 15 | ...... | 27 | 8 00– 8 99 |
| 9 00– 9 99 | ...... | ...... | ...... | 1 | 4 | 1 | 21 | 1 | 37 | ...... | 19 | ...... | 25 | 9 00– 9 99 |
| 10 00–10 99 | ...... | ...... | ...... | 2 | 1 | ...... | 13 | ...... | 16 | ...... | 10 | ...... | 11 | 10 00–10 99 |
| 11 00–11 99 | ...... | ...... | ...... | 2 | ...... | ...... | 1 | 1 | 15 | ...... | 2 | 1 | 2 | 11 00–11 99 |
| 12 00–12 99 | ...... | ...... | ...... | ...... | ...... | 8 | 11 | 4 | 16 | 2 | 20 | ...... | 17 | 12 00–12 99 |
| 13 00–13 99 | ...... | ...... | ...... | 1 | ...... | 2 | 1 | 4 | 2 | 4 | 4 | 1 | 3 | 13 00–13 99 |
| 14 00–14 99 | ...... | ...... | ...... | ...... | ...... | 3 | 2 | 1 | 3 | 3 | 5 | 2 | 7 | 14 00–14 99 |
| 15 00–15 99 | ...... | ...... | ...... | ...... | ...... | 6 | 1 | 9 | 8 | 7 | 3 | 3 | 5 | 15 00–15 99 |
| 16 00–17 99 | ...... | ...... | ...... | ...... | 1 | ...... | ...... | 6 | 4 | 11 | 2 | 9 | 2 | 16 00–17 99 |
| 18 00–19 99 | ...... | ...... | ...... | ...... | ...... | 5 | 3 | 5 | 1 | 8 | 1 | 8 | 4 | 18 00–19 99 |
| 20 00–24 99 | ...... | ...... | ...... | ...... | ...... | 1 | ...... | 5 | 5 | 4 | 3 | 5 | 5 | 20 00–24 99 |
| 25 00–29 99 | ...... | ...... | ...... | ...... | ...... | ...... | ...... | ...... | ...... | 1 | 5 | 2 | 4 | 25 00–29 99 |
| 30 00–34 99 | ...... | ...... | ...... | ...... | ...... | ...... | ...... | 1 | 1 | ...... | 2 | ...... | ...... | 30 00–34 99 |
| 35 00–39 99 | ...... | ...... | ...... | ...... | ...... | ...... | ...... | 1 | 1 | 2 | 1 | ...... | 2 | 35 00–39 99 |
| 40 00 and over | ...... | ...... | ...... | ...... | ...... | ...... | ...... | 1 | 2 | ...... | 1 | 2 | ...... | 40 00 and over |
| Not reported | ...... | ...... | ...... | 1 | ...... | ...... | 3 | ...... | ...... | 2 | ...... | ...... | ...... | Not reported |
| Total | 7 | 5 | 42 | 10 | 126 | 28 | 130 | 41 | 169 | 46 | 114 | 33 | 149 | Total |

172. TABLE V, A, 1, d — (*concluded*)

NEW YORK STATE, EXCLUSIVE OF NEW YORK CITY
**DEPARTMENT STORES — MANUFACTURING**
NUMBER AND PER CENT. OF EMPLOYEES EARNING SPECIFIED WEEKLY RATES, BY AGE GROUPS AND SEX

| WEEKLY RATES IN DOLLARS | AGE GROUPS IN YEARS — (*concluded*) | | | | | | | | | | | | | | WEEKLY RATES IN DOLLARS |
|---|---|---|---|---|---|---|---|---|---|---|---|---|---|---|---|
| | 40–44 | | 45–54 | | 55–64 | | 65 AND OVER | | NOT REPORTED | | TOTAL | | CUMULATIVE PER CENT. OF TOTAL | | |
| | Male | Female | Male | Female | Male | Female | Male | Female | Male | Female | Male | Female | Male | Female | |
| Less than $3 00 | .... | ...... | .... | ...... | ...... | ...... | ...... | ...... | ...... | ...... | ...... | 20 | ...... | 1.80 | Less than $3 00 |
| $3 00–$3 49 | .... | ...... | .... | ...... | ...... | ...... | ...... | ...... | ...... | ...... | 1 | 19 | .35 | 3.50 | $3 00– 3 49 |
| 3 50– 3 99 | .... | ...... | .... | ...... | ...... | ...... | ...... | ...... | ...... | ...... | ...... | 2 | ...... | 3.70 | 3 50– 3 99 |
| 4 00– 4 49 | .... | ...... | .... | ...... | ...... | ...... | ...... | ...... | ...... | ...... | ...... | 16 | ...... | 5.10 | 4 00– 4 49 |
| 4 50– 4 99 | .... | ...... | .... | ...... | ...... | ...... | ...... | ...... | ...... | ...... | 1 | 3 | .70 | 5.40 | 4 50– 4 99 |
| 5 00– 5 49 | .... | ...... | .... | 1 | ...... | ...... | ...... | ...... | ...... | ...... | 1 | 39 | 1.10 | 8.90 | 5 00– 5 49 |
| 5 50– 5 99 | .... | ...... | .... | ...... | ...... | ...... | ...... | ...... | ...... | ...... | ...... | 5 | ...... | 9.30 | 5 01– 5 99 |
| 6 00– 6 49 | .... | 3 | .... | 3 | ...... | 5 | ...... | 1 | ...... | 4 | 1 | 88 | 1.40 | 17.20 | 6 00– 6 49 |
| 6 50– 6 99 | .... | ...... | .... | ...... | ...... | ...... | ...... | ...... | ...... | ...... | ...... | 5 | ...... | 17.70 | 6 50– 6 99 |
| 7 00– 7 49 | 1 | 9 | 1 | 14 | ...... | 3 | ...... | ...... | ...... | 4 | 6 | 135 | 3.60 | 29.80 | 7 00– 7 49 |
| 7 50– 7 99 | .... | 7 | .... | 12 | ...... | 4 | ...... | 1 | ...... | 4 | 2 | 59 | 4.30 | 35.10 | 7 50– 7 99 |
| 8 00– 8 99 | 1 | 18 | .... | 28 | ...... | 15 | ...... | 1 | ...... | 13 | 5 | 188 | 6.80 | 52.00 | 8 00– 8 99 |
| 9 00– 9 99 | .... | 17 | .... | 28 | ...... | 6 | ...... | 2 | ...... | 16 | 3 | 175 | 7.10 | 67.60 | 9 00– 9 99 |
| 10 00–10 99 | .... | 8 | .... | 22 | ...... | 7 | 1 | ...... | 1 | 11 | 4 | 99 | 8.60 | 76.50 | 10 00–10 99 |
| 11 00–11 99 | 1 | ...... | .... | 2 | 1 | ...... | ...... | ...... | ...... | ...... | 6 | 22 | 10.70 | 78.50 | 11 00–11 99 |
| 12 00–12 99 | 2 | 8 | 2 | 10 | 2 | 2 | 2 | ...... | ...... | 6 | 22 | 90 | 18.60 | 86.50 | 12 00–12 99 |
| 13 00–13 99 | 1 | 1 | 2 | 3 | ...... | 1 | ...... | ...... | ...... | 1 | 15 | 16 | 24.90 | 88.00 | 13 00–13 99 |
| 14 00–14 99 | 2 | 3 | 3 | 3 | 2 | 1 | ...... | ...... | 1 | 3 | 17 | 27 | 30.00 | 90.50 | 14 00–14 99 |
| 15 00–15 99 | 3 | 8 | 7 | 6 | 3 | ...... | 2 | ...... | 1 | 6 | 41 | 37 | 44.70 | 93.70 | 15 00–15 99 |
| 16 00–17 99 | 9 | ...... | 10 | ...... | 4 | 1 | 2 | ...... | ...... | 2 | 51 | 12 | 62.90 | 94.80 | 16 00–17 99 |
| 18 00–19 99 | 6 | ...... | 11 | ...... | 8 | ...... | ...... | ...... | 1 | 2 | 52 | 11 | 81.50 | 95.80 | 18 00–19 99 |
| 20 00–24 99 | 7 | 2 | 12 | 2 | 1 | ...... | ...... | ...... | ...... | ...... | 35 | 17 | 94.00 | 97.40 | 20 00–24 99 |
| 25 00–29 99 | 1 | 2 | 1 | ...... | 1 | 1 | ...... | ...... | ...... | 1 | 6 | 13 | 96.10 | 98.50 | 25 00–29 99 |
| 30 00–34 99 | 1 | 1 | .... | ...... | 1 | ...... | ...... | ...... | ...... | ...... | 3 | 4 | 97.20 | 98.80 | 30 00–34 99 |
| 35 00–39 99 | 2 | 1 | .... | ...... | ...... | ...... | ...... | ...... | ...... | ...... | 5 | 5 | 99.00 | 99.30 | 35 00–39 99 |
| 40 00 and over | .... | 2 | .... | 1 | ...... | ...... | ...... | ...... | ...... | 1 | 3 | 7 | 100.00 | 100.00 | 40 00 and over |
| Not reported | .... | ...... | .... | ...... | ...... | ...... | ...... | ...... | ...... | ...... | 3 | 3 | ...... | ...... | Not reported |
| Total | 37 | 90 | 49 | 135 | 23 | 46 | 7 | 5 | 4 | 74 | 283 | 1,117 | ...... | ...... | Total |

NEW YORK STATE, EXCLUSIVE OF NEW YORK CITY
DEPARTMENT STORES — MANUFACTURING

173. TABLE VIII, A, 1, d NUMBER AND PER CENT. OF EMPLOYEES EARNING SPECIFIED WEEKLY RATES, BY OCCUPATION AND SEX

| WEEKLY RATES IN DOLLARS | OCCUPATION: SEWING | | HOUSE FURNISHINGS | | CABINET WORK, FRAMING | PHOTOGRAVURES | METAL WORK, JEWELRY, GLASS WORK | SHOE REPAIRING, BUCKLES, ETC. | BOX MAKING | TOTAL | | CUMULATIVE PER CENT. OF TOTAL | | WEEKLY RATES IN DOLLARS |
|---|---|---|---|---|---|---|---|---|---|---|---|---|---|---|
| | Male | Female | Male | Female | Male | Female | Male | Male | Female | Male | Female | Male | Female | |
| Less than $3 00 | ...... | 20 | ...... | ...... | ...... | ...... | ...... | ...... | ...... | ...... | 20 | ...... | 1.80 | Less than $3 00 |
| $3 00–$3 49 | ...... | 19 | ...... | ...... | ...... | ...... | ...... | 1 | ...... | 1 | 19 | .35 | 3.50 | $3 00– 3 49 |
| 3 50– 3 99 | ...... | 2 | ...... | ...... | ...... | ...... | ...... | ...... | ...... | ...... | 2 | ...... | 3.70 | 3 50– 3 99 |
| 4 00– 4 49 | ...... | 16 | ...... | ...... | ...... | ...... | ...... | ...... | ...... | ...... | 16 | ...... | 5.10 | 4 00– 4 49 |
| 4 50– 4 99 | ...... | 3 | ...... | ...... | 1 | ...... | ...... | ...... | ...... | 1 | 3 | .70 | 5.40 | 4 50– 4 99 |
| 5 00– 5 49 | ...... | 38 | 1 | ...... | ...... | 1 | ...... | ...... | ...... | 1 | 39 | 1.10 | 8.90 | 5 00– 5 49 |
| 5 50– 5 99 | ...... | 5 | ...... | ...... | ...... | ...... | ...... | ...... | ...... | ...... | 5 | ...... | 9.30 | 5 50– 5 99 |
| 6 00– 6 49 | ...... | 84 | 1 | 3 | ...... | 1 | ...... | ...... | ...... | 1 | 88 | 1.40 | 17.20 | 6 00– 6 49 |
| 6 50– 6 99 | ...... | 5 | ...... | ...... | ...... | ...... | ...... | ...... | ...... | ...... | 5 | ...... | 17.70 | 6 50– 6 99 |
| 7 00– 7 49 | 1 | 129 | 4 | 5 | 1 | ...... | ...... | ...... | 1 | 6 | 135 | 3.60 | 29.80 | 7 00– 7 49 |
| 7 50– 7 99 | ...... | 53 | 2 | 6 | ...... | ...... | ...... | ...... | ...... | 2 | 59 | 4.30 | 35.10 | 7 50– 7 99 |
| 8 00– 8 99 | 2 | 185 | 2 | 3 | 1 | ...... | ...... | ...... | ...... | 5 | 188 | 6.80 | 52.00 | 8 00– 8 99 |
| 9 00– 9 99 | ...... | 168 | 2 | 7 | 1 | ...... | ...... | ...... | ...... | 3 | 175 | 7.10 | 67.60 | 9 00– 9 99 |
| 10 00–10 99 | ...... | 89 | ...... | 9 | 3 | 1 | ...... | 1 | ...... | 4 | 99 | 8.60 | 76.50 | 10 00–10 99 |
| 11 00–11 99 | 1 | 21 | 3 | ...... | ...... | 1 | 1 | 1 | ...... | 6 | 22 | 10.70 | 78.50 | 11 00–11 99 |
| 12 00–12 99 | 2 | 84 | 9 | 6 | 8 | ...... | 1 | 2 | ...... | 22 | 90 | 18.60 | 86.50 | 12 00–12 99 |
| 13 00–13 99 | 4 | 16 | 7 | ...... | 4 | ...... | ...... | ...... | ...... | 15 | 16 | 24 90 | 88 00 | 13 00–13 99 |
| 14 00–14 99 | 5 | 26 | 8 | 1 | 3 | ...... | ...... | 1 | ...... | 17 | 27 | 30.00 | 90.50 | 14 00–14 99 |
| 15 00–15 99 | 9 | 37 | 21 | ...... | 10 | ...... | ...... | 1 | ...... | 41 | 37 | 44.70 | 93.70 | 15 00–15 99 |
| 16 00–17 99 | 6 | 12 | 29 | ...... | 16 | ...... | ...... | ...... | ...... | 51 | 12 | 62.90 | 94.80 | 16 00–17 99 |
| 18 00–19 99 | 9 | 11 | 41 | ...... | 2 | ...... | ...... | ...... | ...... | 52 | 11 | 81.50 | 95.80 | 18 00–19 99 |
| 20 00–24 99 | 7 | 17 | 23 | ...... | 5 | ...... | ...... | ...... | ...... | 35 | 17 | 94.00 | 97.40 | 20 00–24 99 |
| 25 00–29 99 | 3 | 13 | 3 | ...... | ...... | ...... | ...... | ...... | ...... | 6 | 13 | 96 10 | 98.50 | 25 00–29 99 |
| 30 00–34 99 | 3 | 4 | ...... | ...... | ...... | ...... | ...... | ...... | ...... | 3 | 4 | 97 20 | 98 80 | 30 00–34 99 |
| 35 00–39 99 | 4 | 5 | 1 | ...... | ...... | ...... | ...... | ...... | ...... | 5 | 5 | 99 00 | 99.30 | 35 00–39 99 |
| 40 00 and over | 3 | 7 | ...... | ...... | ...... | ...... | ...... | ...... | ...... | 3 | 7 | 100.00 | 100.00 | 40 00 and over |
| Not reported | 3 | 3 | ...... | ...... | ...... | ...... | ...... | ...... | ...... | 3 | ...... | ...... | ...... | Not reported |
| Total | 62 | 1,072 | 157 | 40 | 55 | 4 | 2 | 7 | 1 | 283 | 1,117 | ...... | ...... | Total |

174. TABLE VI, A, 1, d

NEW YORK STATE, EXCLUSIVE OF NEW YORK CITY

**DEPARTMENT STORES — MANUFACTURING**

NUMBER AND PER CENT. OF EMPLOYEES CLASSIFIED ACCORDING TO ACTUAL WEEKLY EARNINGS, BY AGE GROUPS AND SEX

| Actual Weekly Earnings in Dollars | Age Groups in Years | | | | | | | | | | | | | Actual Weekly Earnings in Dollars |
|---|---|---|---|---|---|---|---|---|---|---|---|---|---|---|
| | 14–15 | 16–17 | | 18–20 | | 21–24 | | 25–29 | | 30–34 | | 35–39 | | |
| | Female | Male | Female | Male | Female | Male | Female | Male | Female | Male | Female | Male | Female | |
| Less than $3 00... | 2 | ...... | 15 | ...... | 6 | ...... | ...... | ...... | 1 | ...... | 1 | ...... | 3 | ..Less than $3 00 |
| $3 00–$3 49...... | 4 | 1 | 12 | ...... | 6 | ...... | 1 | ...... | ...... | ...... | ...... | ...... | 1 | .....$3 00– 3 49 |
| 3 50– 3 99...... | ...... | ...... | 1 | ...... | 2 | ...... | ...... | ...... | ...... | ...... | ...... | ...... | 1 | ..... 3 50– 3 99 |
| 4 00– 4 49...... | ...... | ...... | 4 | ...... | 7 | ...... | 3 | ...... | 3 | ...... | ...... | ...... | 1 | ..... 4 00– 4 49 |
| 4 50– 4 99...... | ...... | 1 | 1 | ...... | 2 | ...... | 2 | ...... | 3 | ...... | ...... | ...... | 1 | ..... 4 50– 4 99 |
| 5 00– 5 49...... | 1 | 1 | 5 | ...... | 26 | ...... | 7 | ...... | ...... | ...... | 1 | ...... | 2 | ..... 5 00– 5 49 |
| 5 50– 5 99...... | ...... | ...... | 1 | 1 | 8 | ...... | 7 | ...... | 3 | ...... | 2 | ...... | 3 | ..... 5 50– 5 99 |
| 6 00– 6 49...... | ...... | 1 | 3 | ...... | 24 | 1 | 15 | ...... | 8 | ...... | 4 | ...... | 7 | ..... 6 00– 6 49 |
| 6 50– 6 99...... | ...... | ...... | ...... | ...... | 2 | ...... | 4 | ...... | 5 | ...... | ...... | ...... | 2 | ..... 6 50– 6 99 |
| 7 00– 7 49...... | ...... | 1 | ...... | 1 | 24 | 1 | 31 | 1 | 15 | 1 | 11 | ...... | 13 | ..... 7 00– 7 49 |
| 7 50– 7 99...... | ...... | ...... | ...... | ...... | 3 | ...... | 9 | 1 | 6 | 1 | 5 | ...... | 10 | ..... 7 50– 7 99 |
| 8 00– 8 99...... | ...... | ...... | ...... | 2 | 9 | 2 | 31 | ...... | 26 | 1 | 17 | ...... | 25 | ..... 8 00– 8 99 |
| 9 00– 9 99...... | ...... | ...... | ...... | 1 | 3 | 1 | 18 | 1 | 31 | ...... | 15 | ...... | 21 | ..... 9 00– 9 99 |
| 10 00–10 99...... | ...... | ...... | ...... | 2 | 1 | ...... | 14 | ...... | 14 | ...... | 12 | ...... | 10 | .....10 00–10 99 |
| 11 00–11 99...... | ...... | ...... | ...... | 2 | ...... | ...... | ...... | 2 | 17 | 1 | 1 | 1 | 3 | .....11 00–11 99 |
| 12 00–12 99...... | ...... | ...... | ...... | ...... | ...... | 7 | 11 | 5 | 11 | 2 | 18 | ...... | 14 | .....12 00–12 99 |
| 13 00–13 99...... | ...... | ...... | ...... | 1 | ...... | 3 | ...... | 4 | 2 | 5 | 6 | 2 | 3 | .....13 00–13 99 |
| 14 00–14 99...... | ...... | ...... | ...... | ...... | ...... | 2 | 2 | 1 | 3 | 4 | 3 | 3 | 7 | .....14 00–14 99 |
| 15 00–15 99...... | ...... | ...... | ...... | ...... | ...... | 6 | 1 | 8 | 8 | 6 | 3 | 4 | 4 | .....15 00–15 99 |
| 16 00–17 99...... | ...... | ...... | ...... | ...... | 1 | ...... | ...... | 5 | 4 | 11 | 2 | 9 | 2 | .....16 00–17 99 |
| 18 00–19 99...... | ...... | ...... | ...... | ...... | ...... | 4 | 3 | 5 | 2 | 7 | 1 | 7 | 3 | .....18 00–19 99 |
| 20 00–24 99...... | ...... | ...... | ...... | ...... | ...... | 1 | ...... | 5 | 4 | 4 | 3 | 6 | 5 | .....20 00–24 99 |
| 25 00–29 99...... | ...... | ...... | ...... | ...... | ...... | ...... | ...... | ...... | ...... | 1 | 4 | 1 | 3 | .....25 00–29 99 |
| 30 00–34 99...... | ...... | ...... | ...... | ...... | ...... | ...... | ...... | 1 | 1 | ...... | 2 | ...... | ...... | .....30 00–34 99 |
| 35 00–39 99...... | ...... | ...... | ...... | ...... | ...... | ...... | ...... | 1 | 1 | 2 | 1 | ...... | 2 | .....35 00–39 99 |
| 40 00 and over.... | ...... | ...... | ...... | ...... | ...... | ...... | ...... | 1 | 2 | ...... | 1 | 1 | ...... | ...40 00 and over |
| Not reported...... | ...... | ...... | ...... | ...... | 4 | ...... | 1 | ...... | 1 | ...... | 1 | ...... | 3 | .....Not reported |
| Total........ | 7 | 5 | 42 | 10 | 128 | 28 | 160 | 41 | 171 | 46 | 114 | 34 | 149 | .......Total |

174. TABLE VI, A, 1, d — (*concluded*)

NEW YORK STATE, EXCLUSIVE OF NEW YORK CITY
**DEPARTMENT STORES — MANUFACTURING**
NUMBER AND PER CENT. OF EMPLOYEES CLASSIFIED ACCORDING TO ACTUAL WEEKLY EARNINGS, BY AGE GROUPS AND SEX

| ACTUAL WEEKLY EARNINGS IN DOLLARS | AGE GROUPS IN YEARS—(*Concluded*) 40–44 | | 45–54 | | 55–64 | | 65 AND OVER | | NOT REPORTED | | TOTAL | | CUMULATIVE PER CENT. OF TOTAL | | ACTUAL WEEKLY EARNINGS IN DOLLARS |
|---|---|---|---|---|---|---|---|---|---|---|---|---|---|---|---|
| | Male | Female | Male | Female | Male | Female | Male | Female | Male | Female | Male | Female | Male | Female | |
| Less than $3 00 | .... | ...... | .... | ...... | ...... | ...... | ...... | ...... | ...... | ...... | ...... | 28 | ...... | 2.54 | Less than $3 00 |
| $3 00–$3 49... | .... | 1 | .... | ...... | ...... | 1 | ...... | ...... | ...... | ...... | 1 | 26 | .35 | 4.92 | ...$3 00– 3 49 |
| 3 50– 3 99... | .... | 1 | 1 | ...... | ...... | ...... | ...... | ...... | ...... | ...... | 1 | 5 | .71 | 5.36 | ... 3 50– 3 99 |
| 4 00– 4 49... | .... | ...... | .... | 1 | ...... | 1 | ...... | ...... | ...... | ...... | ...... | 20 | ...... | 7.10 | ... 4 00– 4 49 |
| 4 50– 4 99... | .... | ...... | .... | 1 | ...... | 1 | ...... | ...... | ...... | ...... | 1 | 11 | 1.06 | 8.20 | ... 4 50– 4 99 |
| 5 00– 5 49... | .... | ...... | .... | 2 | ...... | 1 | ...... | ...... | ...... | ...... | 1 | 45 | 1.42 | 12.28 | ... 5 00– 5 49 |
| 5 50– 5 99... | .... | 2 | .... | 2 | ...... | 1 | ...... | ...... | ...... | 1 | 1 | 30 | 1.77 | 15.00 | ... 5 50– 5 99 |
| 6 00– 6 49... | .... | 5 | .... | 6 | ...... | 3 | ...... | 1 | ...... | 4 | 2 | 80 | 2.48 | 22.28 | ... 6 00– 6 49 |
| 6 50– 6 99... | 1 | 2 | .... | 2 | ...... | 1 | ...... | ...... | ...... | 2 | 1 | 20 | 2.84 | 24.10 | ... 6 50– 6 99 |
| 7 00– 7 49... | 1 | 8 | .... | 11 | ...... | 2 | ...... | ...... | ...... | 6 | 6 | 121 | 4.96 | 35.10 | ... 7 00– 7 49 |
| 7 50– 7 99... | .... | 8 | .... | 10 | ...... | 4 | ...... | 1 | ...... | 2 | 2 | 58 | 5.68 | 40.40 | ... 7 50– 7 99 |
| 8 00– 8 99... | 1 | 18 | .... | 27 | ...... | 12 | ...... | 1 | ...... | 14 | 6 | 180 | 7.80 | 56.75 | ... 8 00– 8 99 |
| 9 00– 9 99... | .... | 10 | .... | 26 | ...... | 5 | ...... | 2 | ...... | 12 | 3 | 143 | 8.87 | 69.75 | ... 9 00– 9 99 |
| 10 00–10 99... | .... | 5 | .... | 19 | ...... | 6 | 1 | ...... | 1 | 10 | 4 | 91 | 10.30 | 78.00 | ...10 00–10 99 |
| 11 00–11 99... | 2 | ...... | .... | 2 | 1 | ...... | ...... | ...... | 1 | ...... | 10 | 23 | 13.84 | 80.00 | ...11 00–11 99 |
| 12 00–12 99... | 2 | 7 | 2 | 8 | 2 | 2 | 2 | ...... | 1 | 6 | 23 | 77 | 22.00 | 87.20 | ...12 00–12 99 |
| 13 00–13 99... | .... | 1 | 1 | 3 | ...... | 1 | ...... | ...... | ...... | 2 | 16 | 18 | 27.68 | 88.75 | ...13 00–13 99 |
| 14 00–14 99... | 2 | 3 | 3 | 2 | 2 | 1 | ...... | ...... | ...... | 3 | 17 | 24 | 33.70 | 91.00 | ...14 00–14 99 |
| 15 00–15 99... | 3 | 8 | 8 | 4 | 3 | ...... | 2 | ...... | ...... | 5 | 40 | 33 | 47.90 | 94.00 | ...15 00–15 99 |
| 16 00–17 99... | 9 | ...... | 9 | 1 | 5 | 1 | 1 | ...... | ...... | 2 | 49 | 13 | 65.30 | 65.00 | ...16 00–17 99 |
| 18 00–19 99... | 6 | ...... | 11 | ...... | 7 | ...... | ...... | ...... | 1 | 2 | 48 | 11 | 82.30 | 97.20 | ...18 00–19 99 |
| 20 00–24 99... | 6 | 2 | 12 | 2 | 1 | ...... | ...... | ...... | ...... | ...... | 35 | 16 | 94.75 | 97.50 | ...20 00–24 99 |
| 25 00–29 99... | 1 | 2 | 1 | ...... | 1 | ...... | ...... | ...... | ...... | 1 | 5 | 11 | 96.50 | 98.50 | ...25 00–29 99 |
| 30 00–34 99... | 1 | 1 | .... | ...... | 1 | ...... | ...... | ...... | ...... | ...... | 3 | 4 | 97.50 | 98.80 | ...30 00–34 99 |
| 35 00–39 99... | 2 | 1 | .... | ...... | ...... | ...... | ...... | ...... | ...... | ...... | 5 | 5 | 99.30 | 99.40 | ...35 00–39 99 |
| 40 00 and over. | .... | 2 | .... | 1 | ...... | ...... | ...... | ...... | ...... | 1 | 2 | 7 | 100.00 | 100.00 | .40 00 and over |
| Not reported... | .... | 3 | 1 | 5 | ...... | 2 | 1 | ...... | ...... | 1 | 2 | 21 | ...... | ...... | ...Not reported |
| Total.... | 37 | 90 | 49 | 135 | 23 | 46 | 7 | 5 | 4 | 74 | 284 | 1,121 | ...... | ...... | .....Total |

175. TABLE IX, A, 1, d

NEW YORK STATE, EXCLUSIVE OF NEW YORK CITY

**DEPARTMENT STORES — MANUFACTURING**

NUMBER AND PER CENT. OF EMPLOYEES CLASSIFIED ACCORDING TO ACTUAL WEEKLY EARNINGS, BY OCCUPATION AND SEX

| ACTUAL WEEKLY EARNINGS IN DOLLARS | OCCUPATION | | | | | | | | | | | | | ACTUAL WEEKLY EARNINGS IN DOLLARS |
|---|---|---|---|---|---|---|---|---|---|---|---|---|---|---|
| | SEWING | | HOUSE-FURNISHING | | CABINET WORK, FRAMING | PHOTOGRAVURES, PRINTING | METAL WORK, JEWELRY, GLASS WORK | SHOE REPAIRING, BUCKLES, ETC. | BOX MAKING | TOTAL | | CUMULATIVE PER CENT. OF TOTAL | | |
| | Male | Female | Male | Female | Male | Female | Male | Male | Female | Male | Female | Male | Female | |
| Less than $3 00 | | 28 | | | | | | | | | 28 | | 2.54 | Less than $3 00 |
| $3 00–$3 49 | | 26 | | | | | | 1 | | 1 | 26 | .35 | 4.92 | $3 00– 3 49 |
| 3 50– 3 99 | | 4 | 1 | 1 | | | | | | 1 | 5 | .71 | 5.36 | 3 50– 3 99 |
| 4 00– 4 49 | | 19 | | 1 | | | | | | | 20 | | 7.10 | 4 00– 4 49 |
| 4 50– 4 99 | | 10 | | 1 | 1 | | | | | 1 | 11 | 1.06 | 8.20 | 4 50– 4 99 |
| 5 00– 5 49 | | 42 | 1 | 2 | | 1 | | | | 1 | 45 | 1.42 | 12.28 | 5 00– 5 49 |
| 5 50– 5 99 | 1 | 29 | | | | 1 | | | | 1 | 30 | 1.77 | 15.00 | 5 50– 5 99 |
| 6 00– 6 49 | | 78 | 2 | 2 | | | | | | 2 | 80 | 2.48 | 22.28 | 6 00– 6 49 |
| 6 50– 6 99 | 1 | 20 | | | | | | | | 1 | 20 | 2.84 | 24.10 | 6 50– 6 99 |
| 7 00– 7 49 | 2 | 115 | 3 | 5 | 1 | | | | 1 | 6 | 121 | 4.96 | 35.10 | 7 00– 7 49 |
| 7 50– 7 99 | | 52 | 2 | 6 | | | | | | 2 | 58 | 5.68 | 40.40 | 7 50– 7 99 |
| 8 00– 8 99 | 3 | 177 | 2 | 3 | 1 | | | | | 6 | 180 | 7.80 | 56.75 | 8 00– 8 99 |
| 9 00– 9 99 | | 139 | 2 | 4 | 1 | | | | | 3 | 143 | 8.87 | 69.75 | 9 00– 9 99 |
| 10 00–10 99 | | 82 | | 8 | 3 | 1 | | 1 | | 4 | 91 | 10.30 | 78.00 | 10 00–10 99 |
| 11 00–11 99 | 2 | 22 | 5 | | 1 | 1 | 1 | 1 | | 10 | 23 | 13.84 | 80.00 | 11 00–11 99 |
| 12 00–12 99 | 3 | 70 | 8 | 7 | 8 | | 1 | 3 | | 23 | 77 | 22.00 | 87.20 | 12 00–12 99 |
| 13 00–13 99 | 4 | 18 | 9 | | 3 | | | | | 16 | 18 | 27.68 | 88.75 | 13 00–13 99 |
| 14 00–14 99 | 6 | 24 | 7 | | 3 | | | 1 | | 17 | 24 | 33.70 | 91.00 | 14 00–14 99 |
| 15 00–15 99 | 7 | 33 | 23 | | 10 | | | | | 40 | 33 | 47.90 | 94.00 | 15 00–15 99 |
| 16 00–17 99 | 6 | 13 | 27 | | 16 | | | | | 49 | 13 | 65.30 | 95.00 | 16 00–17 99 |
| 18 00–19 99 | 9 | 11 | 37 | | 2 | | | | | 48 | 11 | 82.30 | 97.20 | 18 00–19 99 |
| 20 00–24 99 | 7 | 16 | 23 | | 5 | | | | | 35 | 16 | 94.75 | 97.50 | 20 00–24 99 |
| 25 00–29 99 | 2 | 11 | 3 | | | | | | | 5 | 11 | 96.50 | 98.50 | 25 00–29 99 |
| 30 00–34 99 | 3 | 4 | | | | | | | | 3 | 4 | 97.50 | 98.80 | 30 00–34 99 |
| 35 00–39 99 | 4 | 5 | 1 | | | | | | | 5 | 5 | 99.30 | 99.40 | 35 00–39 99 |
| 40 00 and over | 2 | 7 | | | | | | | | 2 | 7 | 100.00 | 100.00 | 40 00 and over |
| Not reported | | 21 | 2 | | | | | | | 2 | 21 | | | Not reported |
| Total | 62 | 1,076 | 158 | 40 | 55 | 4 | 2 | 7 | 1 | 284 | 1,121 | | | Total |

NEW YORK STATE, EXCLUSIVE OF NEW YORK CITY
**DEPARTMENT STORES — PLANT**

176. TABLE V, A, 1, e NUMBER AND PER CENT. OF EMPLOYEES EARNING SPECIFIED WEEKLY RATES, BY AGE GROUPS AND SEX

| WEEKLY RATES IN DOLLARS | AGE GROUPS IN YEARS | | | | | | | | | | | | | | | | WEEKLY RATES IN DOLLARS |
|---|---|---|---|---|---|---|---|---|---|---|---|---|---|---|---|---|---|
| | 14–15 | | 16–17 | | 18–20 | | 21–24 | | 25–29 | | 30–34 | | 35–39 | | | |
| | Male | Female | Male | Female | Male | Female | Male | Female | Male | Female | Male | Female | Male | Fema e | |
| Less than $3 00 | .... | ...... | .... | ...... | ...... | 1 | ...... | 1 | ...... | ...... | ...... | ...... | ...... | ...... | Less than $3 00 |
| $3 00–$3 49... | .... | ...... | .... | 2 | ...... | 4 | ...... | 17 | ...... | 14 | ...... | 10 | ...... | 9 | ...$3 00– 3 49 |
| 3 50– 3 99... | .... | 1 | .... | ...... | ...... | 3 | ...... | 4 | ...... | 4 | ...... | 2 | ...... | 6 | ... 3 50– 3 99 |
| 4 00– 4 49... | .... | ...... | 1 | 4 | ...... | 3 | ...... | 3 | 1 | 6 | ...... | 7 | ...... | 2 | ... 4 00– 4 49 |
| 4 50– 4 99... | .... | ...... | 2 | 1 | ...... | 1 | ...... | ...... | ...... | 2 | ...... | ...... | ...... | 1 | ... 4 50– 4 99 |
| 5 00– 5 49... | .... | ...... | 4 | 2 | ...... | 15 | ...... | 23 | ...... | 20 | ...... | 13 | ...... | 10 | ... 5 00– 5 49 |
| 5 50– 5 99... | .... | ...... | .... | ...... | ...... | 1 | ...... | 2 | ...... | ...... | ...... | 4 | ...... | ...... | ... 5 50– 5 99 |
| 6 00– 6 49... | 1 | ...... | 3 | 1 | 1 | 14 | 1 | 19 | ...... | 9 | ...... | 15 | ...... | 7 | ... 6 00– 6 49 |
| 7 00– 7 49... | .... | ...... | 2 | 1 | 5 | ...... | ...... | 5 | ...... | 5 | ...... | 7 | ...... | 6 | ... 7 00– 7 49 |
| 7 50– 7 99... | .... | ...... | 1 | ...... | ...... | ...... | ...... | ...... | ...... | 1 | ...... | 1 | ...... | ...... | ... 7 50– 7 99 |
| 8 00– 8 99... | .... | ...... | 2 | ...... | 9 | 2 | 5 | 2 | 4 | 2 | ...... | 3 | ...... | 3 | ... 8 00– 8 99 |
| 9 00– 9 99... | .... | ...... | 2 | ...... | 5 | ...... | 3 | 2 | 5 | 2 | 1 | 2 | ...... | 3 | ... 9 00– 9 99 |
| 10 00–10 99... | .... | ...... | .... | ...... | 9 | ...... | 14 | ...... | 8 | 2 | 4 | 1 | 5 | 4 | ...10 00–10 99 |
| 11 00–11 99... | .... | ...... | .... | ...... | 1 | ...... | 6 | ...... | 2 | ...... | 3 | 1 | 2 | 1 | ...10 10–11 99 |
| 12 00–12 99... | .... | ...... | .... | ...... | 5 | ...... | 21 | ...... | 31 | 1 | 25 | 3 | 14 | ...... | ...12 00–12 99 |
| 13 00–13 99... | .... | ...... | .... | ...... | ...... | ...... | 1 | ...... | 2 | ...... | 3 | ...... | 1 | ...... | ...13 00–13 99 |
| 14 00–14 99... | .... | ...... | .... | ...... | ...... | ...... | 2 | ...... | 1 | ...... | 7 | ...... | 6 | ...... | ...14 00–14 99 |
| 15 00–15 99... | .... | ...... | .... | ...... | ...... | ...... | 2 | ...... | 10 | ...... | 8 | ...... | 5 | 1 | ...15 00–15 99 |
| 16 00–17 99... | .... | ...... | .... | ...... | 1 | ...... | ...... | ...... | 8 | 1 | 4 | ...... | 6 | ...... | ...16 00–17 99 |
| 18 00–19 99... | .... | ...... | .... | ...... | ...... | ...... | ...... | ...... | 4 | ...... | 7 | ...... | 4 | ...... | ...18 00–19 99 |
| 20 00–24 99... | .... | ...... | .... | ...... | ...... | ...... | 1 | ...... | 8 | ...... | 6 | ...... | 10 | ...... | ...20 00–24 99 |
| 25 00–29 99... | .... | ...... | .... | ...... | ...... | ...... | ...... | ...... | ...... | ...... | 2 | ...... | ...... | ...... | ...25 00–29 99 |
| Not reported... | .... | ...... | .... | ...... | ...... | ...... | ...... | ...... | 2 | ...... | 2 | ...... | ...... | ...... | ...Not reported |
| Total..... | 1 | 1 | 17 | 11 | 36 | 44 | 56 | 78 | 86 | 69 | 72 | 69 | 53 | 53 | .....Total |

NEW YORK STATE, EXCLUSIVE OF NEW YORK CITY

176. TABLE V, A, 1, e — (*concluded*)

DEPARTMENT STORES — PLANT

NUMBER AND PER CENT. OF EMPLOYEES EARNING SPECIFIED WEEKLY RATES, BY AGE GROUPS AND SEX

| WEEKLY RATES IN DOLLARS | AGE GROUPS IN YEARS — (*concluded*) | | | | | | | | | | | | | | WEEKLY RATES IN DOLLARS |
|---|---|---|---|---|---|---|---|---|---|---|---|---|---|---|---|
| | 40–44 | | 45–54 | | 55–64 | | 65 AND OVER | | NOT REPORTED | | TOTAL | | CUMULATIVE PER CENT. OF TOTAL | | |
| | Male | Female | Male | Female | Male | Female | Male | Female | Male | Female | Male | Female | Male | Female | |
| Less than $3 00 | .... | ...... | .... | ...... | ...... | ...... | ...... | ...... | ...... | ...... | ...... | 2 | ...... | .50 | Less than $3 00 |
| $3 00–$3 49... | .... | 2 | .... | 1 | ...... | ...... | ...... | ...... | ...... | ...... | ...... | 59 | ...... | 13 80 | ...$3 00– 3 49 |
| 3 50– 3 99... | .... | ...... | .... | ...... | ...... | ...... | ...... | ...... | ...... | ...... | ...... | 20 | ...... | 18.40 | ... 3 50– 3 99 |
| 4 00– 4 49... | .... | 1 | .... | 1 | ...... | 1 | ...... | ...... | ...... | ...... | 2 | 28 | .30 | 24.70 | ... 4 00– 4 49 |
| 4 50– 4 99... | .... | 1 | .... | 6 | ...... | 2 | ...... | ...... | ...... | ...... | 2 | 14 | .60 | 27.60 | ... 4 50– 4 99 |
| 5 00– 5 49... | .... | 7 | .... | 8 | ...... | 1 | ...... | ...... | ...... | ...... | 4 | 99 | 1.30 | 50.40 | ... 5 00– 5 49 |
| 5 50– 5 99... | .... | ...... | .... | ...... | ...... | 1 | ...... | ...... | ...... | ...... | ...... | 8 | ...... | 52.20 | ... 5 50– 5 99 |
| 6 00– 6 49... | .... | 6 | .... | 19 | ...... | 2 | ...... | 1 | ...... | ...... | 6 | 93 | 2.30 | 73.30 | ... 6 00– 6 49 |
| 7 00– 7 49... | 2 | 11 | .... | 10 | ...... | 6 | 1 | ...... | 1 | 1 | 11 | 52 | 4.10 | 85.10 | ... 7 00– 7 49 |
| 7 50– 7 99... | .... | 1 | .... | 2 | ...... | ...... | ...... | ...... | ...... | 1 | 1 | 6 | 4.20 | 86.40 | ... 7 50– 7 99 |
| 8 00– 8 99... | .... | 4 | .... | 1 | 3 | 1 | 1 | ...... | ...... | ...... | 24 | 18 | 8.10 | 90.50 | ... 8 00– 8 99 |
| 9 00– 9 99... | .... | 3 | .... | 1 | 4 | 2 | 1 | 1 | ...... | ...... | 21 | 16 | 11.50 | 94.20 | ... 9 00– 9 99 |
| 10 00–10 99... | 6 | 1 | 11 | 4 | 17 | ...... | 6 | ...... | ...... | ...... | 80 | 12 | 24 50 | 96.80 | ...10 00–10 99 |
| 11 00–11 99... | 4 | ...... | 6 | ...... | 7 | ...... | 1 | ...... | ...... | ...... | 32 | 2 | 29.70 | 98.40 | ...11 00–11 99 |
| 12 00–12 99... | 22 | 3 | 38 | ...... | 41 | 1 | 4 | ...... | ...... | ...... | 201 | 8 | 62.30 | 99.20 | ...12 00–12 99 |
| 13 00–13 99... | 2 | ...... | 8 | ...... | 1 | ...... | ...... | ...... | ...... | ...... | 18 | ...... | 65.20 | ...... | ...13 00–13 99 |
| 14 00–14 99... | 3 | ...... | 8 | 1 | 14 | ...... | 2 | ...... | ...... | ...... | 43 | 1 | 72.20 | 99.50 | ...14 00–14 99 |
| 15 00–15 99... | 4 | ...... | 13 | 1 | 7 | ...... | 1 | ...... | 1 | ...... | 51 | 2 | 80.50 | 99.80 | ...15 00–15 99 |
| 16 00–17 99... | 7 | ...... | 8 | ...... | 3 | ...... | 1 | ...... | ...... | ...... | 38 | 1 | 86.70 | 100.00 | ...16 00–17 99 |
| 18 00–19 99... | 2 | ...... | 6 | ...... | 8 | ...... | ...... | ...... | 1 | ...... | 32 | ...... | 92.00 | ...... | ...18 00–19 99 |
| 20 00–24 99... | 3 | ...... | 9 | ...... | 1 | ...... | 1 | ...... | 1 | ...... | 40 | ...... | 98.40 | ...... | ...20 00–24 99 |
| 25 00–29 99... | 2 | ...... | 4 | ...... | ...... | ...... | ...... | ...... | ...... | ...... | 8 | ...... | 99.70 | ...... | ...25 00–29 99 |
| 30 00–34 99... | .... | ...... | 1 | ...... | ...... | ...... | ...... | ...... | ...... | ...... | 1 | ...... | 99.80 | ...... | ...30 00–34 99 |
| 35 00–39 99... | 1 | ...... | .... | ...... | ...... | ...... | ...... | ...... | ...... | ...... | ...... | 1 | 100.00 | ...... | ...35 00–39 99 |
| Not reported... | 2 | ...... | 2 | ...... | ...... | ...... | ...... | ...... | ...... | ...... | 8 | ...... | ...... | ...... | ...Not reported |
| Total..... | 60 | 40 | 114 | 55 | 108 | 17 | 19 | 2 | 4 | 2 | 624 | 441 | ...... | ...... | .....Total |

NEW YORK STATE, EXCLUSIVE OF NEW YORK CITY

**DEPARTMENT STORES — PLANT**

177. TABLE VIII, A, 1, e NUMBER AND PER CENT. OF EMPLOYEES EARNING SPECIFIED WEEKLY RATES, BY OCCUPATION AND SEX

| SPECIFIED WEEKLY RATES | OCCUPATION: FOREMEN | MECHANICS | JANITORIAL FORCE | | ERRAND BOYS | GENERAL LABOR | PERSONAL SERVICE | | NOT REPORTED | TOTAL | | CUMULATIVE PER CENT. OF TOTAL | | SPECIFIED WEEKLY RATES |
|---|---|---|---|---|---|---|---|---|---|---|---|---|---|---|
| | Male | Male | Male | Female | Male | Male | Male | Female | Male | Male | Female | Male | Female | |
| Less than $3 00 | ...... | ...... | ...... | ...... | ...... | ...... | ...... | 2 | ...... | ...... | 2 | ...... | .50 | Less than $3 00 |
| $3 00–$3 49 | ...... | ...... | ...... | ...... | ...... | ...... | ...... | 59 | ...... | ...... | 59 | ...... | 13.80 | $3 00– 3 49 |
| 3 50– 3 99 | ...... | ...... | ...... | ...... | ...... | ...... | ...... | 20 | ...... | ...... | 20 | ...... | 18.40 | 3 50– 3 99 |
| 4 00– 4 49 | ...... | 1 | 1 | ...... | ...... | ...... | ...... | 28 | ...... | 2 | 28 | .30 | 24.70 | 4 00– 4 49 |
| 4 50– 4 99 | ...... | ...... | 2 | ...... | ...... | ...... | ...... | 14 | ...... | 2 | 14 | .60 | 27.60 | 4 50– 4 99 |
| 5 00– 5 49 | ...... | 1 | 3 | ...... | ...... | ...... | ...... | 99 | ...... | 4 | 99 | 1.30 | 50.40 | 5 00– 5 49 |
| 5 50– 5 99 | ...... | ...... | ...... | ...... | ...... | ...... | ...... | 8 | ...... | ...... | 8 | ...... | 52.20 | 5 50– 5 99 |
| 6 00– 6 49 | ...... | 2 | 3 | 18 | 1 | ...... | ...... | 75 | ...... | 6 | 93 | 2.30 | 73.30 | 6 00– 6 49 |
| 7 00– 7 49 | ...... | 1 | 5 | 18 | 1 | ...... | 4 | 34 | ...... | 11 | 52 | 4.10 | 85.10 | 7 00– 7 49 |
| 7 50– 7 99 | ...... | ...... | 1 | 4 | ...... | ...... | ...... | 2 | ...... | 1 | 6 | 4.20 | 86.40 | 7 50– 7 99 |
| 8 00– 8 99 | ...... | ...... | 19 | 2 | ...... | 1 | 4 | 16 | ...... | 24 | 18 | 8.10 | 90.50 | 8 00– 8 99 |
| 9 00– 9 99 | ...... | 1 | 17 | 8 | ...... | 1 | 2 | 8 | ...... | 21 | 16 | 11.50 | 94.20 | 9 00– 9 99 |
| 10 00–10 99 | ...... | 4 | 72 | 3 | ...... | ...... | 4 | 9 | ...... | 80 | 12 | 24.50 | 96.80 | 10 00–10 99 |
| 11 00–11 99 | ...... | 1 | 31 | ...... | ...... | ...... | ...... | 2 | ...... | 32 | 2 | 29.70 | 98.40 | 11 00–11 99 |
| 12 00–12 99 | ...... | 13 | 179 | ...... | ...... | 1 | 8 | 8 | ...... | 201 | 8 | 62.30 | 99.20 | 12 00–12 99 |
| 13 00–13 99 | ...... | 6 | 12 | ...... | ...... | ...... | ...... | ...... | ...... | 18 | ...... | 65.20 | ...... | 13 00–13 99 |
| 14 00–14 99 | ...... | 5 | 31 | ...... | ...... | 2 | 5 | 1 | ...... | 43 | 1 | 72.29 | 99.50 | 14 00–14 99 |
| 15 00–15 99 | ...... | 27 | 19 | ...... | ...... | ...... | 5 | 2 | ...... | 51 | 2 | 80.50 | 99.80 | 15 00–15 99 |
| 16 00–17 99 | 1 | 17 | 13 | ...... | ...... | ...... | 6 | 1 | 1 | 38 | 1 | 86.70 | 100.00 | 16 00–17 99 |
| 18 00–19 99 | 2 | 24 | 3 | ...... | ...... | ...... | 3 | ...... | ...... | 32 | ...... | 92.00 | ...... | 18 00–19 99 |
| 20 00–24 99 | 1 | 31 | ...... | ...... | ...... | ...... | 8 | ...... | ...... | 40 | ...... | 98.40 | ...... | 20 00–24 99 |
| 25 00–29 99 | ...... | 7 | 1 | ...... | ...... | ...... | ...... | ...... | ...... | 8 | ...... | 99.70 | ...... | 25 00–29 99 |
| 30 00–34 99 | 1 | ...... | ...... | ...... | ...... | ...... | ...... | ...... | ...... | 1 | ...... | 99.80 | ...... | 30 00–34 99 |
| 35 00–39 99 | ...... | 1 | ...... | ...... | ...... | ...... | ...... | ...... | ...... | 1 | ...... | 100.00 | ...... | 35 00–39 99 |
| Not reported | ...... | 7 | 1 | ...... | ...... | ...... | ...... | ...... | ...... | 8 | ...... | ...... | ...... | Not reported |
| Total | 5 | 149 | 413 | 53 | 2 | 5 | 49 | 388 | 1 | 624 | 441 | ...... | ...... | Total |

NEW YORK STATE, EXCLUSIVE OF NEW YORK CITY
DEPARTMENT STORES — PLANT

178. TABLE VI, A, 1, e — NUMBER AND PER CENT. OF EMPLOYEES CLASSIFIED ACCORDING TO ACTUAL WEEKLY EARNINGS, BY AGE GROUPS AND SEX

| ACTUAL WEEKLY EARNINGS IN DOLLARS | AGE GROUPS IN YEARS | | | | | | | | | | | | | | ACTUAL WEEKLY EARNING IN DOLLARS |
|---|---|---|---|---|---|---|---|---|---|---|---|---|---|---|---|
| | 14–15 | | 16–17 | | 18–20 | | 21–24 | | 25–29 | | 30–34 | | 35–39 | | |
| | Male | Female | Male | Female | Male | Female | Male | Female | Male | Female | Male | Female | Male | Female | |
| Less than $3 00 | .... | ...... | .... | 1 | ...... | 3 | 1 | 4 | ...... | 5 | ...... | 1 | ...... | 4 | Less than $3 00 |
| $3 00–$3 49... | .... | ...... | .... | 2 | ...... | 4 | ...... | 12 | 1 | 8 | ...... | 9 | ...... | 6 | ...$3 00– 3 49 |
| 3 50– 3 99... | .... | 1 | .... | 1 | ...... | 1 | ...... | 5 | ...... | 6 | ...... | 3 | ...... | 5 | ... 3 50– 3 99 |
| 4 00– 4 49... | .... | ...... | 1 | 3 | ...... | 3 | ...... | 6 | 2 | 7 | ...... | 8 | ...... | 3 | ... 4 00– 4 49 |
| 4 50– 4 99... | .... | ...... | 3 | ...... | ...... | 1 | ...... | ...... | ...... | 2 | ...... | ...... | 1 | 1 | ... 4 50– 4 99 |
| 5 00– 5 49... | 1 | ...... | 3 | 2 | ...... | 17 | ...... | 24 | ...... | 18 | ...... | 12 | ...... | 10 | ... 5 00– 5 49 |
| 5 50– 5 99... | .... | ...... | .... | ...... | ...... | 1 | ...... | 3 | ...... | 2 | ...... | 4 | ...... | 1 | ... 5 50– 5 99 |
| 6 00– 6 49... | .... | ...... | 3 | 2 | 1 | 12 | ...... | 17 | ...... | 8 | ...... | 14 | ...... | 7 | ... 6 00– 6 49 |
| 6 50– 6 99... | .... | ...... | .... | ...... | ...... | 1 | 1 | ...... | ...... | ...... | ...... | ...... | ...... | 1 | ... 6 50– 6 99 |
| 7 00– 7 49... | .... | ...... | 2 | ...... | 5 | 1 | ...... | 4 | ...... | 4 | ...... | 7 | ...... | 5 | ... 7 00– 7 49 |
| 7 50– 7 99... | .... | ...... | 1 | ...... | 1 | ...... | ...... | ...... | ...... | 1 | ...... | 1 | ...... | ...... | ... 7 50– 7 99 |
| 8 00– 8 99... | .... | ...... | 2 | ...... | 9 | ...... | 5 | 1 | 5 | 2 | ...... | 3 | ...... | 2 | ... 8 00– 8 99 |
| 9 00– 9 99... | .... | ...... | 1 | ...... | 4 | ...... | 3 | 2 | 4 | 2 | 1 | 2 | ...... | 3 | ... 9 00– 9 99 |
| 10 00–10 99... | .... | ...... | 1 | ...... | 9 | ...... | 15 | ...... | 8 | 2 | 3 | 1 | 5 | 3 | ...10 00–10 99 |
| 11 00–11 99... | .... | ...... | .... | ...... | 1 | ...... | 7 | ...... | 3 | ...... | 4 | 1 | 2 | 1 | ...11 00–11 99 |
| 12 00–12 99... | .... | ...... | .... | ...... | 4 | ...... | 18 | ...... | 28 | 1 | 25 | 3 | 13 | ...... | ...12 00–12 99 |
| 13 00–13 99... | .... | ...... | .... | ...... | 1 | ...... | 1 | ...... | 2 | ...... | 3 | ...... | 1 | ...... | ...13 00–13 99 |
| 14 00–14 99... | .... | ...... | .... | ...... | ...... | ...... | 2 | ...... | ...... | ...... | 6 | ...... | 6 | ...... | ...14 00–14 99 |
| 15 00–15 99... | .... | ...... | .... | ...... | ...... | ...... | 2 | ...... | 10 | ...... | 8 | ...... | 4 | 1 | ...15 00–15 99 |
| 16 00–17 99... | .... | ...... | .... | ...... | 1 | ...... | ...... | ...... | 9 | 1 | 4 | ...... | 6 | ...... | ...16 00–17 99 |
| 18 00–19 99... | .... | ...... | .... | ...... | ...... | ...... | ...... | ...... | 5 | ...... | 8 | ...... | 4 | ...... | ...18 00–19 99 |
| 20 00–24 99... | .... | ...... | .... | ...... | ...... | ...... | 1 | ...... | 9 | ...... | 7 | ...... | 10 | ...... | ...20 00–24 99 |
| 25 00–29 99... | .... | ...... | .... | ...... | ...... | ...... | ...... | ...... | ...... | ...... | 3 | ...... | ...... | ...... | ...25 00–29 99 |
| 30 00–34 99... | .... | ...... | .... | ...... | ...... | ...... | ...... | ...... | ...... | ...... | ...... | ...... | ...... | ...... | ...30 00–34 99 |
| Not reported... | .... | ...... | .... | ...... | ...... | ...... | ...... | ...... | ...... | ...... | ...... | ...... | 1 | ...... | ...Not reported |
| Total.... | 1 | 1 | 17 | 11 | 36 | 44 | 56 | 78 | 86 | 69 | 72 | 69 | 53 | 53 | .....Total |

178. TABLE VI, A, 1, e — (*concluded*)

NEW YORK STATE, EXCLUSIVE OF NEW YORK CITY

DEPARTMENT STORES — PLANT

NUMBER AND PER CENT. OF EMPLOYEES CLASSIFIED ACCORDING TO ACTUAL WEEKLY EARNINGS, BY AGE GROUPS AND SEX

| ACTUAL WEEKLY EARNINGS IN DOLLARS | AGE GROUPS IN YEARS — (*concluded*) | | | | | | | | | | | | | | ACTUAL WEEKLY EARNINGS IN DOLLARS |
|---|---|---|---|---|---|---|---|---|---|---|---|---|---|---|---|
| | 40–44 | | 45–54 | | 55–64 | | 65 AND OVER | | NOT REPORTED | | TOTAL | | CUMULATIVE PER CENT. OF TOTAL | | |
| | Male | Female | Male | Female | Male | Female | Male | Female | Male | Female | Male | Female | Male | Female | |
| Less than $3 00 | .... | ...... | .... | ...... | ...... | ...... | ...... | ...... | ...... | ...... | 1 | 18 | .16 | 4.08 | Less than $3 50 |
| $3 00–$3 49... | .... | 2 | .... | 2 | 1 | ...... | ...... | ...... | ...... | ...... | 2 | 43 | .48 | 14.30 | ...$3 00– 3 49 |
| 3 50– 3 99... | .... | 1 | 1 | 1 | ...... | ...... | ...... | ...... | ...... | ...... | 1 | 24 | .64 | 19.70 | ... 3 50– 3 99 |
| 4 00– 4 49... | .... | 1 | .... | 1 | 1 | 1 | ...... | ...... | ...... | ...... | 4 | 33 | 1.29 | 27.20 | ... 4 00– 4 49 |
| 4 50– 4 99... | .... | 1 | .... | 6 | ...... | 2 | ...... | ...... | ...... | ...... | 4 | 13 | 1.93 | 32.00 | ... 4 50– 4 99 |
| 5 00– 5 49... | .... | 6 | .... | 8 | ...... | 1 | ...... | ...... | ...... | ...... | 4 | 98 | 2.57 | 52.40 | ... 5 00– 5 49 |
| 5 50– 5 99... | .... | ...... | .... | 1 | ...... | 1 | ...... | ...... | ...... | ...... | ...... | 13 | ...... | 55.40 | ... 5 50– 5 99 |
| 6 00– 6 49... | .... | 7 | 1 | 16 | ...... | 2 | ...... | 1 | ...... | ...... | 5 | 86 | 3.38 | 74.80 | ... 6 00– 6 49 |
| 6 50– 6 99... | .... | ...... | .... | ...... | ...... | ...... | ...... | ...... | ...... | ...... | 1 | 2 | 3.54 | 75.30 | ... 6 50– 6 99 |
| 7 00– 7 49... | 2 | 10 | .... | 9 | ...... | 6 | ...... | ...... | 1 | 1 | 10 | 47 | 5.31 | 85.60 | ... 7 00– 7 49 |
| 7 50– 7 99... | .... | 1 | .... | 2 | ...... | ...... | ...... | ...... | ...... | 1 | 2 | 6 | 5.47 | 87.30 | ... 7 50– 7 99 |
| 8 00– 8 99... | .... | 4 | .... | 1 | 3 | 2 | 1 | 1 | ...... | ...... | 25 | 16 | 9.50 | 90.90 | ... 8 00– 8 99 |
| 9 00– 9 99... | .... | 3 | 1 | 2 | 5 | 1 | 1 | ...... | ...... | ...... | 20 | 15 | 12.55 | 94.25 | ... 9 00– 9 99 |
| 10 00–10 99... | 6 | 1 | 10 | 5 | 16 | ...... | 6 | ...... | ...... | ...... | 79 | 12 | 25.40 | 97.20 | ...10 00–10 99 |
| 11 00–11 99... | 3 | ...... | 8 | ...... | 6 | ...... | 1 | ...... | ...... | ...... | 35 | 2 | 31.05 | 97.50 | ...11 00–11 99 |
| 12 00–12 99... | 20 | 3 | 35 | ...... | 40 | 1 | 4 | ...... | ...... | ...... | 187 | 8 | 61.10 | 99.50 | ...12 00–12 99 |
| 13 00–13 99... | 4 | ...... | 8 | ...... | 1 | ...... | ...... | ...... | ...... | ...... | 21 | ...... | 66.00 | ...... | ...13 00–13 99 |
| 14 00–14 99... | 4 | ...... | 8 | ...... | 15 | ...... | 2 | ...... | ...... | ...... | 43 | ...... | 71.50 | ...... | ...14 00–14 99 |
| 15 00–15 99... | 4 | ...... | 13 | 1 | 6 | ...... | 1 | ...... | 1 | ...... | 49 | 2 | 79.40 | 99.85 | ...15 00–15 99 |
| 16 00–17 99... | 7 | ...... | 8 | ...... | 3 | ...... | 1 | ...... | ...... | ...... | 39 | 1 | 85.60 | 100.00 | ...16 00–17 99 |
| 18 00–19 99... | 3 | ...... | 6 | ...... | 7 | ...... | ...... | ...... | 1 | ...... | 34 | ...... | 91.00 | ...... | ...18 00–19 99 |
| 20 00–24 99... | 4 | ...... | 9 | ...... | 2 | ...... | 1 | ...... | 1 | ...... | 44 | ...... | 98.00 | ...... | ...20 00–24 99 |
| 25 00–29 99... | 2 | ...... | 5 | ...... | ...... | ...... | ...... | ...... | ...... | ...... | 10 | ...... | 99.70 | ...... | ...25 00–29 99 |
| 30 00–34 99... | .... | ...... | 1 | ...... | ...... | ...... | ...... | ...... | ...... | ...... | 1 | ...... | 99.85 | ...... | ...30 00–34 99 |
| 35 00–39 99... | 1 | ...... | .... | ...... | ...... | ...... | ...... | ...... | ...... | ...... | 1 | ...... | 100.00 | ...... | ...35 00–39 99 |
| Not reported... | .... | ...... | .... | ...... | ...... | ...... | 1 | ...... | ...... | ...... | 2 | ...... | ...... | ...... | ...Not reported |
| Total..... | 60 | 40 | 114 | 55 | 106 | 17 | 19 | 2 | 4 | 2 | 624 | 441 | ...... | ...... | .....Total |

179. TABLE IX, A,I, e.

NEW YORK STATE EXCLUSIVE OF NEW YORK CITY
DEPARTMENT STORES — PLANT

NUMBER AND PER CENT OF EMPLOYEES CLASSIFIED ACCORDING TO ACTUAL WEEKLY EARNINGS BY OCCUPATION AND SEX

| ACTUAL WEEKLY EARNINGS IN DOLLARS | OCCUPATION: FOREMEN | MECHANICS | JANITORIAL FORCE | | ERRAND BOYS | GENERAL LABOR | PERSONAL SERVICE | | NOT REPORTED | TOTAL | | CUMULATIVE PER CENT OF TOTAL | | ACTUAL WEEKLY EARNINGS IN DOLLARS |
|---|---|---|---|---|---|---|---|---|---|---|---|---|---|---|
| | Male | Male | Male | Female | Male | Male | Male | Female | Male | Male | Female | Male | Female | |
| Less than $3 00 | ...... | ...... | 1 | ...... | ...... | ...... | ...... | 18 | ...... | 1 | 18 | .16 | 4.08 | Less than $3 00 |
| $3 00–$3 49 | ...... | 1 | 1 | 1 | ...... | ...... | ...... | 44 | ...... | 2 | 45 | .48 | 14.30 | $3 00–$3 49 |
| 3 50– 3 99 | ...... | 1 | ...... | 1 | ...... | ...... | ...... | 23 | ...... | 1 | 24 | .64 | 19.70 | 3 50– 3 99 |
| 4 00– 4 49 | ...... | 1 | 3 | ...... | ...... | ...... | ...... | 33 | ...... | 4 | 33 | 1.29 | 27.20 | 4 00– 4 49 |
| 4 50– 4 99 | ...... | 1 | 2 | ...... | ...... | ...... | 1 | 13 | ...... | 4 | 13 | 1.93 | 32.00 | 4 50– 4 99 |
| 5 00– 5 49 | ...... | ...... | 3 | ...... | 1 | ...... | ...... | 98 | ...... | 4 | 98 | 2.57 | 52.40 | 5 00– 5 49 |
| 5 50– 5 99 | ...... | ...... | ...... | 1 | ...... | ...... | ...... | 12 | ...... | ...... | 13 | ...... | 55.40 | 5 50– 5 99 |
| 6 00– 6 49 | ...... | 2 | 3 | 17 | ...... | ...... | ...... | 69 | ...... | 5 | 86 | 3.38 | 74.80 | 6 00– 6 49 |
| 6 50– 6 99 | ...... | ...... | 1 | ...... | ...... | ...... | ...... | 2 | ...... | 1 | 2 | 3.54 | 75.30 | 6 50– 6 99 |
| 7 00– 7 49 | ...... | 1 | 4 | 16 | 1 | ...... | 4 | 31 | ...... | 10 | 47 | 5.31 | 85.60 | 7 00– 7 49 |
| 7 50– 7 99 | ...... | ...... | 2 | 4 | ...... | ...... | ...... | 2 | ...... | 2 | 6 | 5.47 | 87.30 | 7 50– 7 99 |
| 8 00– 8 99 | ...... | ...... | 19 | 4 | ...... | 1 | 5 | 12 | ...... | 25 | 16 | 9.50 | 90.90 | 8 00– 8 99 |
| 9 00– 9 99 | ...... | 1 | 18 | 6 | ...... | 1 | ...... | 9 | ...... | 20 | 15 | 12.55 | 94.25 | 9 00– 9 99 |
| 10 00–10 99 | ...... | 3 | 71 | 3 | ...... | ...... | 5 | 9 | ...... | 79 | 12 | 25.40 | 97.20 | 10 00–10 99 |
| 11 00–11 99 | ...... | 1 | 34 | ...... | ...... | ...... | ...... | 2 | ...... | 35 | 2 | 31.05 | 97.50 | 11 00–11 99 |
| 12 00–12 99 | ...... | 13 | 166 | ...... | ...... | 1 | 7 | 8 | ...... | 187 | 8 | 61.10 | 99.50 | 12 00–12 99 |
| 13 00–13 99 | ...... | 5 | 15 | ...... | ...... | ...... | 1 | ...... | ...... | 21 | ...... | 66.00 | ...... | 13 00–13.99 |
| 14 00–14 99 | ...... | 5 | 32 | ...... | ...... | 2 | 4 | ...... | ...... | 43 | ...... | 71.50 | ...... | 14 00–14 99 |
| 15 00–15 99 | ...... | 27 | 18 | ...... | ...... | ...... | 4 | 2 | ...... | 49 | 2 | 79.40 | 99.85 | 15 00–15 99 |
| 16 00–17 99 | 1 | 17 | 14 | ...... | ...... | ...... | 6 | 1 | 1 | 39 | 1 | 85.60 | 100.00 | 16 00–17 99 |
| 18 00–19 99 | 2 | 26 | 3 | ...... | ...... | ...... | 3 | ...... | ...... | 34 | ...... | 91.00 | ...... | 18 00–19 99 |
| 20 00–24 99 | 1 | 34 | ...... | ...... | ...... | ...... | 9 | ...... | ...... | 44 | ...... | 98.00 | ...... | 20 00–24 99 |
| 25 00–29 99 | ...... | 9 | 1 | ...... | ...... | ...... | ...... | ...... | ...... | 10 | ...... | 99.70 | ...... | 25 00–29 99 |
| 30 00–34 99 | 1 | ...... | ...... | ...... | ...... | ...... | ...... | ...... | ...... | 1 | ...... | 99.85 | ...... | 30 00–34 99 |
| 35 00–39 99 | ...... | 1 | ...... | ...... | ...... | ...... | ...... | ...... | ...... | 1 | ...... | 100.00 | ...... | 35 00–39 99 |
| Not reported | ...... | ...... | 2 | ...... | ...... | ...... | ...... | ...... | ...... | 2 | ...... | ...... | ...... | Not reported |
| Total | 5 | 149 | 413 | 53 | 2 | 5 | 49 | 388 | 1 | 624 | 441 | ...... | ...... | Total |

NEW YORK STATE EXCLUSIVE OF NEW YORK CITY
FIVE AND TEN CENT STORES — STOCK AND SALES

180. TABLE V, A, 3, a. NUMBER AND PER CENT OF EMPLOYEES EARNING SPECIFIED WEEKLY RATES BY AGE GROUPS AND SEX

| WEEKLY RATES IN DOLLARS | Age Groups in Years | | | | | | | | | | | | | | WEEKLY RATE IN DOLLARS |
|---|---|---|---|---|---|---|---|---|---|---|---|---|---|---|---|
| | 14–15 | | 16–17 | | 18–20 | | 21–24 | | 25–29 | | 30–34 | | 35–39 | | |
| | Male | Female | Male | Female | Male | Female | Male | Female | Male | Female | Male | Female | Male | Female | |
| Less than $3 00 | | | | 1 | | | | | | | | | | | Less than $3 00 |
| $3 00–$3 49... | | | | 1 | | | | | | | | | | | ...$3 00–$3 49 |
| 3 50– 3 99... | | | | 8 | | 1 | | | | | | | | | ... 3 50– 3 99 |
| 4 00– 4 49... | | 1 | | 22 | | 21 | | 3 | | 1 | | 1 | | | ... 4 00– 4 49 |
| 4 50– 4 99... | | 1 | | 49 | | 37 | | 21 | | 7 | | 1 | | 1 | ... 4 50– 4 99 |
| 5 00– 5 49... | 1 | 4 | 2 | 66 | | 66 | | 20 | | 6 | | 3 | | 1 | ... 5 00– 5 49 |
| 5 50– 5 99... | 2 | 1 | 1 | 16 | | 11 | | 10 | | | | | | | ... 5 50– 5 99 |
| 6 00– 6 49... | 2 | | 5 | 28 | 3 | 128 | | 55 | | 15 | | 8 | | 3 | ... 6 00– 6 49 |
| 6 50– 6 99... | | | | 2 | | 14 | | 12 | | 3 | | | | 1 | ... 6 50– 6 99 |
| 7 00– 7 49... | | | 3 | 2 | 6 | 11 | 1 | 12 | | 2 | | | | | ... 7 00– 7 49 |
| 7 50– 7 99... | | | | 1 | 1 | 1 | | 3 | | 1 | | | | | ... 7 50– 7 99 |
| 8 00– 8 99... | | | 1 | | 4 | 6 | 2 | 6 | | 1 | | | | 1 | ... 8 00– 8 99 |
| 9 00– 9 99... | | | 1 | | 7 | 1 | 3 | 4 | | 1 | 1 | | | | ... 9 00– 9 99 |
| 10 00–10 99... | | | 1 | | 6 | 1 | 9 | 5 | | | 1 | | 1 | | ...10 00–10 99 |
| 11 00–11 99... | | | 1 | | | 1 | 6 | | 1 | | 1 | | | | ...11 00–11 99 |
| 12 00–12 99... | | | | | 1 | | 5 | 2 | 5 | 1 | | | | | ...12 00–12 99 |
| 13 00–13 99... | | | | | | | 4 | | | | | | | | ...13 00–13 99 |
| 14 00–14 99... | | | | | | | 5 | | 3 | | 2 | | | | ...14 00–14 99 |
| 15 00–15 99... | | | | | | | 5 | | 1 | | 1 | | | | ...15 00–15 99 |
| 16 00–17 99... | | | | | | | | | | | 3 | 1 | | | ...16 00–17 99 |
| 18 00–19 99... | | | | | | | 1 | | 1 | | 1 | | | | ...18 00–19 99 |
| 20 00–24 99... | | | | | | | | | 2 | | | | | | ...20 00–24 99 |
| Not reported... | 1 | | 3 | 8 | | 8 | | 8 | | 1 | | 1 | | | ...Not reported |
| Total..... | 6 | 7 | 18 | 204 | 28 | 307 | 41 | 161 | 13 | 39 | 10 | 15 | 1 | 7 | .....Total |

180. TABLE V, A, 3, a. — (*concluded*)

NEW YORK STATE EXCLUSIVE OF NEW YORK CITY

**FIVE AND TEN CENT STORES — STOCK AND SALES**

NUMBER AND PER CENT EMPLOYEES OF EARNING SPECIFIED WEEKLY RATES BY AGE GROUPS AND SEX

| WEEKLY RATES IN DOLLARS | AGE GROUPS IN YEARS — (*Concluded*) | | | | | | | | | | | WEEKLY RATES IN DOLLARS |
|---|---|---|---|---|---|---|---|---|---|---|---|---|
| | 40–44 | | 45–54 | | 65 AND OVER | NOT REPORTED | | TOTAL | | CUMULATIVE PER CENT OF TOTAL | | |
| | Male | Female | Male | Female | Male | Male | Female | Male | Female | Male | Female | |
| Less than $3 00 | ........ | ........ | ........ | ........ | ........ | ........ | ........ | ........ | 1 | ........ | .14 | Less than $3 00 |
| $3 00–$3 49... | ........ | ........ | ........ | ........ | ........ | ........ | ........ | ........ | 1 | ........ | .28 | ...$3 00–$3 49 |
| 3 50– 3 99... | ........ | ........ | ........ | ........ | ........ | ........ | ........ | ........ | 9 | ........ | 1.55 | ... 3 50– 3 99 |
| 4 00– 4 49... | ........ | ........ | ........ | 1 | ........ | ........ | ........ | ........ | 50 | ........ | 8.46 | ... 4 00– 4 49 |
| 4 50– 4 99... | ........ | ........ | ........ | ........ | ........ | ........ | ........ | ........ | 117 | ........ | 24.70 | ... 4 50– 4 99 |
| 5 00– 5 49... | ........ | ........ | ........ | ........ | ........ | ........ | ........ | 3 | 166 | 2.50 | 47.75 | ... 5 00– 5 49 |
| 5 50– 5 99... | ........ | ........ | ........ | ........ | ........ | ........ | ........ | 3 | 38 | 5.00 | 53.00 | ... 5 50– 5 99 |
| 6 00– 6 49... | ........ | 1 | ........ | ........ | ........ | ........ | 1 | 10 | 239 | 13.65 | 86.10 | ... 6 00– 6 49 |
| 6 50– 6 99... | ........ | 1 | ........ | ........ | ........ | ........ | ........ | ........ | 33 | ........ | 90.75 | ... 6 50– 6 99 |
| 7 00– 7 49... | ........ | 1 | ........ | ........ | ........ | 1 | ........ | 11 | 28 | 22.50 | 94.60 | ... 7 00– 7 49 |
| 7 50– 7 99... | ........ | ........ | ........ | 2 | ........ | ........ | ........ | 1 | 8 | 23.38 | 95.70 | ... 7 50– 7 99 |
| 8 00– 8 99... | ........ | ........ | ........ | ........ | ........ | ........ | ........ | 7 | 14 | 29.20 | 97.60 | ... 8 00– 8 99 |
| 9 00– 9 99... | ........ | ........ | ........ | ........ | ........ | ........ | ........ | 12 | 6 | 39.20 | 98.50 | ... 9 00– 9 99 |
| 10 00–10 99... | ........ | ........ | 2 | ........ | 1 | ........ | ........ | 21 | 6 | 56.75 | 99.30 | ...10 00–10 99 |
| 11 00–11 99... | ........ | ........ | ........ | ........ | ........ | ........ | ........ | 9 | 1 | 64.25 | 99.45 | ...11 00–11 99 |
| 12 00–12 99... | 1 | ........ | ........ | ........ | ........ | ........ | ........ | 12 | 3 | 74.25 | 99.85 | ...12 00–12 99 |
| 13 00–13 99... | ........ | ........ | ........ | ........ | ........ | ........ | ........ | 4 | ........ | 77.50 | ........ | ...13 00–13 99 |
| 14 00–14 99... | ........ | ........ | ........ | ........ | ........ | ........ | ........ | 10 | ........ | 86.00 | ........ | ...14 00–14 99 |
| 15 00–15 99... | ........ | ........ | 1 | ........ | ........ | ........ | ........ | 8 | ........ | 92.50 | ........ | ...15 00–15 99 |
| 16 00–17 99... | ........ | ........ | ........ | ........ | ........ | ........ | ........ | 3 | 1 | 95.00 | 100.00 | ...16 00–17 99 |
| 18 00–19 99... | ........ | ........ | 1 | ........ | ........ | ........ | ........ | 4 | ........ | 98.50 | ........ | ...18 00–19 99 |
| 20 00–24 99... | ........ | ........ | ........ | ........ | ........ | ........ | ........ | 2 | ........ | 100.00 | ........ | ...20 00–24 99 |
| Not reported... | ........ | ........ | ........ | ........ | ........ | ........ | 2 | 4 | 28 | ........ | ........ | ...Not reported |
| Total..... | 1 | 3 | 4 | 3 | 1 | 1 | 3 | 124 | 749 | ........ | ........ | .....Total |

NEW YORK STATE EXCLUSIVE OF NEW YORK CITY
**FIVE AND TEN CENT STORES — STOCK AND SALES**

181. TABLE, VIII, A, 3, a. NUMBER AND PER CENT OF EMPLOYEES EARNING SPECIFIED WEEKLY RATES BY OCCUPATION AND SEX

| WEEKLY RATES IN DOLLARS | OCCUPATION | | | | | | | | | | | | | | WEEKLY RATES IN DOLLARS |
|---|---|---|---|---|---|---|---|---|---|---|---|---|---|---|---|
| | SUPERINTENDENTS | ASSISTANT BUYERS AND HEADS OF STOCK | RECEIVING AND STOCK CLERKS | STOCK PEOPLE | FLOOR MANAGERS | | SALES PEOPLE | | MESSENGERS, WRAPPERS, ERRAND BOYS | | TOTAL | | CUMULATIVE PER CENT OF TOTAL | | |
| | Male | Male | Male | Male | Male | Female | Male | Female | Male | Female | Male | Female | Male | Female | |
| Less than $3 00 | | | | | | | | 1 | | | | 1 | | .14 | Less than $3 00 |
| $3 00–$3 49 | | | | | | | | 1 | | | | 1 | | .28 | $3 00–$3 49 |
| 3 50– 3 99 | | | | | | | | 9 | | | | 9 | | 1.55 | 3 50– 3 99 |
| 4 00– 4 49 | | | | | | | | 50 | | | | 50 | | 8.46 | 4 00– 4 49 |
| 4 50– 4 99 | | | | | | | | 117 | | | | 117 | | 24.70 | 4 50– 4 99 |
| 5 00– 5 49 | | | | 1 | | | | 165 | 2 | 1 | 3 | 166 | 2.50 | 47.75 | 5 00– 5 49 |
| 5 50– 5 99 | | | | | | | | 38 | 3 | | 3 | 38 | 5.00 | 53.00 | 5 50– 5 99 |
| 6 00– 6 49 | | | 1 | 8 | | 8 | | 231 | 1 | | 10 | 239 | 13.65 | 86.10 | 6 00– 6 49 |
| 6 50– 6 99 | | | | | | 2 | | 31 | | | | 33 | | 90.75 | 6 50– 6 99 |
| 7 00– 7 49 | | | 1 | 9 | | 4 | | 24 | 1 | | 11 | 28 | 22.50 | 94.60 | 7 00– 7 49 |
| 7 50– 7 99 | | | | 1 | | | | 8 | | | 1 | 8 | 23.38 | 95.70 | 7 50– 7 99 |
| 8 00– 8 99 | | | | 7 | | 8 | | 6 | | | 7 | 14 | 29.20 | 97.60 | 8 00– 8 99 |
| 9 00– 9 99 | | | 3 | 8 | 1 | 4 | | 2 | | | 12 | 6 | 39.20 | 98.50 | 9 00– 9 99 |
| 10 00–10 99 | 1 | | 4 | 14 | 2 | 2 | | 4 | | | 21 | 6 | 56.75 | 99.30 | 10 00–10 99 |
| 11 00–11 99 | | | 2 | 3 | 4 | | | 1 | | | 9 | 1 | 64.25 | 99.45 | 11 00–11 99 |
| 12 00–12 99 | 2 | | 1 | 4 | 5 | 1 | | 2 | | | 12 | 3 | 74.25 | 99.85 | 12 00–12 99 |
| 13 00–13 99 | | | | | 3 | | 1 | | | | 4 | | 77.50 | | 13 00–13 99 |
| 14 00–14 99 | 2 | | 2 | 1 | 5 | | | | | | 10 | | 86.00 | | 14 00–14 99 |
| 15 00–15 99 | 2 | | 1 | | 5 | | | | | | 8 | | 92.50 | | 15 00–15 99 |
| 16 00–17 99 | 1 | | 1 | | 1 | 1 | | | | | 3 | 1 | 95.00 | 100.00 | 16 00–17 99 |
| 18 00–19 99 | 1 | 1 | 1 | 1 | | | | | | | 4 | | 98.50 | | 18 00–19 99 |
| 20 00–24 99 | | | | | 2 | | | | | | 2 | | 100.00 | | 20 00–24 99 |
| Not reported | | | | 1 | | 1 | 2 | 27 | 1 | | 4 | 28 | | | Not reported |
| Total | 9 | 1 | 17 | 58 | 28 | 31 | 3 | 717 | 8 | 1 | 124 | 749 | | | Total |

182. TABLE VI, A, 3, a.

NEW YORK STATE EXCLUSIVE OF NEW YORK CITY
FIVE AND TEN CENT STORES — STOCK AND SALES
NUMBER AND PER CENT OF EMPLOYEES CLASSIFIED ACCORDING TO ACTUAL WEEKLY EARNINGS BY AGE GROUPS AND SEX

| ACTUAL WEEKLY EARNINGS IN DOLLARS | AGE GROUPS IN YEARS | | | | | | | | | | | | | | ACTUAL WEEKLY EARNINGS IN DOLLARS |
|---|---|---|---|---|---|---|---|---|---|---|---|---|---|---|---|
| | 14–15 | | 16–17 | | 18–20 | | 21–24 | | 25–29 | | 30–34 | | 35–39 | | |
| | Male | Female | Male | Female | Male | Female | Male | Female | Male | Female | Male | Female | Male | Female | |
| Less than $3 00 | 1 | 1 | .... | 7 | ...... | 11 | ...... | 7 | ...... | 2 | ...... | 1 | ...... | ...... | Less than $3 00 |
| $3 00–$3 49... | .... | 1 | 1 | 5 | ...... | 10 | 1 | 3 | ...... | ...... | ...... | ...... | ...... | ...... | ...$3 00–$3 49 |
| 3 50– 3 99... | .... | 1 | 1 | 13 | ...... | 9 | ...... | 6 | ...... | 1 | ...... | ...... | ...... | ...... | ... 3 50– 3 99 |
| 4 00– 4 49... | .... | ...... | .... | 26 | ...... | 30 | ...... | 7 | ...... | 3 | ...... | 2 | ...... | ...... | ... 4 00– 4 49 |
| 4 50– 4 99... | .... | ...... | .... | 51 | ...... | 30 | ...... | 16 | ...... | 6 | ...... | 2 | ...... | 1 | ... 4 50– 4 99 |
| 5 00– 5 49... | 1 | 3 | 3 | 46 | ...... | 59 | ...... | 20 | ...... | 2 | ...... | 2 | ...... | 1 | ... 5 00– 5 49 |
| 5 50– 5 99... | 2 | 1 | 1 | 27 | 1 | 25 | ...... | 15 | ...... | 5 | ...... | ...... | ...... | 1 | ... 5 50– 5 99 |
| 6 00– 6 49... | 2 | ...... | 4 | 24 | 2 | 93 | ...... | 40 | ...... | 12 | ...... | 5 | ...... | 3 | ... 6 00– 6 49 |
| 6 50– 6 99... | .... | ...... | 2 | 2 | ...... | 21 | ...... | 17 | ...... | 2 | ...... | 2 | ...... | ...... | ... 6 50– 6 99 |
| 7 00– 7 49... | .... | ...... | .... | 3 | 2 | 10 | 1 | 10 | ...... | 2 | ...... | ...... | ...... | ...... | ... 7 00– 7 49 |
| 7 50– 7 99... | .... | ...... | 1 | ...... | 4 | 2 | ...... | 5 | ...... | 1 | ...... | ...... | ...... | ...... | ... 7 50– 7 99 |
| 8 00– 8 99... | .... | ...... | 1 | ...... | 5 | 4 | 3 | 5 | ...... | 1 | ...... | ...... | ...... | 1 | ... 8 00– 8 99 |
| 9 00– 9 99... | .... | ...... | .... | ...... | 7 | 1 | 3 | 4 | ...... | 1 | 1 | ...... | ...... | ...... | ... 9 00– 9 99 |
| 10 00–10 99... | .... | ...... | 1 | ...... | 5 | 1 | 5 | 4 | ...... | ...... | ...... | ...... | ...... | ...... | ...10 00–10 99 |
| 11 00–11 99... | .... | ...... | 2 | ...... | 1 | 1 | 6 | ...... | ...... | ...... | 2 | ...... | 1 | ...... | ...11 00–11 99 |
| 12 00–12 99... | .... | ...... | .... | ...... | 1 | ...... | 5 | 2 | 4 | ...... | ...... | ...... | ...... | ...... | ...12 00–12 99 |
| 13 00–13 99... | .... | ...... | .... | ...... | ...... | ...... | 6 | ...... | 1 | 1 | ...... | ...... | ...... | ...... | ...13 00–13 99 |
| 14 00–14 99... | .... | ...... | .... | ...... | ...... | ...... | 4 | ...... | 2 | ...... | ...... | ...... | ...... | ...... | ...14 00–14 99 |
| 15 00–15 99... | .... | ...... | .... | ...... | ...... | ...... | 6 | ...... | 2 | ...... | 2 | ...... | ...... | ...... | ...15 00–15 99 |
| 16 00–17 99... | .... | ...... | .... | ...... | ...... | ...... | ...... | ...... | 1 | ...... | 4 | 1 | ...... | ...... | ...16 00–17 99 |
| 18 00–19 99... | .... | ...... | .... | ...... | ...... | ...... | 1 | ...... | 1 | ...... | 1 | ...... | ...... | ...... | ...18 00–19 99 |
| 20 00–24 99... | .... | ...... | .... | ...... | ...... | ...... | ...... | ...... | 2 | ...... | ...... | ...... | ...... | ...... | ...20 00–24 99 |
| Not reported... | .... | ...... | 1 | ...... | ...... | ...... | ...... | ...... | ...... | ...... | ...... | ...... | ...... | ...... | ...Not reported |
| Total..... | 6 | 7 | 18 | 204 | 28 | 307 | 41 | 161 | 13 | 39 | 10 | 15 | 1 | 7 | .....Total |

182. TABLE VI, A, 3, a — (*Concluded*)

NEW YORK STATE EXCLUSIVE OF NEW YORK CITY

**FIVE AND TEN CENT STORES — STOCK AND SALES**

NUMBER AND PER CENT OF EMPLOYEES CLASSIFIED ACCORDING TO ACTUAL WEEKLY EARNINGS BY AGE GROUPS AND SEX

| ACTUAL WEEKLY EARNINGS IN DOLLARS | AGE GROUPS IN YEARS — (*Concluded*) | | | | | | | | | | | | ACTUAL WEEKLY EARNINGS IN DOLLARS |
|---|---|---|---|---|---|---|---|---|---|---|---|---|---|
| | 40–44 | | 45–54 | | 65 AND OVER | NOT REPORTED | | TOTAL | | CUMULATIVE PER CENT OF TOTAL | | | |
| | Male | Female | Male | Female | Male | Male | Female | Male | Female | Male | Female | | |
| Less than $3 00 | ........ | ........ | ........ | ........ | ........ | ........ | ........ | 1 | 29 | .80 | 3.90 | Less than $3 00 |
| $3 00–$3 49... | ........ | ........ | ........ | ........ | ........ | ........ | ........ | 2 | 19 | 2.40 | 6.40 | .. $3 00– 3 49 |
| 3 50– 3 99... | ........ | ........ | ........ | ........ | ........ | ........ | 1 | 1 | 31 | 3.30 | 10.50 | ... 3 50– 3 99 |
| 4 00– 4 49... | ........ | ........ | ........ | 1 | ........ | ........ | ........ | ........ | 69 | ........ | 19.70 | ... 4 00– 4 49 |
| 4 50– 4 99... | ........ | ........ | ........ | ........ | ........ | ........ | 1 | ........ | 107 | ........ | 34.00 | ... 4 50– 4 99 |
| 5 00– 5 49... | ........ | ........ | ........ | 1 | ........ | ........ | ........ | 4 | 134 | 6.50 | 51.90 | ... 5 00– 5 49 |
| 5 50– 5 99... | ........ | 1 | ........ | ........ | ........ | ........ | ........ | 4 | 75 | 9.80 | 62.00 | ... 5 50– 5 99 |
| 6 00– 6 49... | ........ | ........ | ........ | ........ | ........ | ........ | 1 | 8 | 178 | 16.50 | 85.70 | ... 6 00– 6 49 |
| 6 50– 6 99... | ........ | 2 | ........ | ........ | ........ | ........ | ........ | 2 | 46 | 17.90 | 91.90 | ... 6 50– 6 99 |
| 7 00– 7 49... | ........ | ........ | ........ | ........ | ........ | ........ | ........ | 3 | 25 | 20.40 | 95.20 | ... 7 00– 7 49 |
| 7 50– 7 99... | ........ | ........ | ........ | 1 | ........ | 1 | ........ | 6 | 9 | 25.20 | 96.50 | ... 7 50– 7 99 |
| 8 00– 8 99... | ........ | ........ | ........ | ........ | ........ | ........ | ........ | 9 | 11 | 32.60 | 97.90 | ... 8 00– 8 99 |
| 9 00– 9 99... | ........ | ........ | ........ | ........ | ........ | ........ | ........ | 11 | 6 | 41.50 | 98.70 | ... 9 00– 9 99 |
| 10 00–10 99... | ........ | ........ | 1 | ........ | 1 | ........ | ........ | 13 | 5 | 52.00 | 99.40 | ...10 00–10 99 |
| 11 00–11 99... | ........ | ........ | 1 | ........ | ........ | ........ | ........ | 13 | 1 | 62.60 | 99.50 | ...11 00–11 99 |
| 12 00–12 99... | ........ | ........ | ........ | ........ | ........ | ........ | ........ | 10 | 2 | 70.80 | 99.80 | ...12 00–12 99 |
| 13 00–13 99... | 1 | ........ | ........ | ........ | ........ | ........ | ........ | 8 | 1 | 77.30 | 99.90 | ...13 00–13 99 |
| 14 00–14 99... | ........ | ........ | ........ | ........ | ........ | ........ | ........ | 6 | ........ | 82.20 | ........ | ...14 00–14 99 |
| 15 00–15 99... | ........ | ........ | ........ | ........ | ........ | ........ | ........ | 10 | ........ | 90.30 | ........ | ...15 00–15 99 |
| 16 00–17 99... | ........ | ........ | 1 | ........ | ........ | ........ | ........ | 6 | 1 | 95.20 | 100.00 | ...16 00–17 99 |
| 18 00–19 99... | ........ | ........ | 1 | ........ | ........ | ........ | ........ | 4 | ........ | 98.50 | ........ | ...18 00–19 99 |
| 20 00–24 99... | ........ | ........ | ........ | ........ | ........ | ........ | ........ | 2 | ........ | 100.00 | ........ | ...20 00–24 99 |
| Not reported... | ........ | ........ | ........ | ........ | ........ | ........ | ........ | 1 | ........ | ........ | ........ | ...Not reported |
| Total..... | 1 | 3 | 4 | 3 | 1 | 1 | 3 | 124 | 749 | ........ | ........ | .....Total |

183. TABLE IX, A, 3, a.

NEW YORK STATE EXCLUSIVE OF NEW YORK CITY
**FIVE AND TEN CENT STORES — STOCK AND SALES**
NUMBER AND PER CENT OF EMPLOYEES CLASSIFIED ACCORDING TO ACTUAL WEEKLY EARNINGS BY OCCUPATION AND SEX

| ACTUAL WEEKLY EARNINGS IN DOLLARS | OCCUPATION | | | | | | | | | | | | | | ACTUAL WEEKLY EARNINGS IN DOLLARS |
|---|---|---|---|---|---|---|---|---|---|---|---|---|---|---|---|
| | SUPERINTENDENTS | ASSISTANT BUYERS AND HEADS OF STOCK | RECEIVING AND STOCK CLERKS | STOCK PEOPLE | FLOOR MANAGERS | | SALES PEOPLE | | MESSENGERS, WRAPPAERS, ERRAND BOYS | | TOTAL | | CUMULATIVE PER CENT OF TOTAL | | |
| | Male | Male | Male | Male | Male | Female | Male | Female | Male | Female | Male | Female | Male | Female | |
| Less than $3 00 | ......... | ............ | ......... | ......... | ...... | ...... | ...... | 29 | 1 | ...... | 1 | 29 | .80 | 3.90 | Less than $3 00 |
| $3 00–$3 49... | ......... | ............ | ......... | 1 | ...... | ...... | ...... | 19 | 1 | ...... | 2 | 19 | 2.40 | 6.40 | ...$3 00–$3 49 |
| 3 50– 3 99... | ......... | ............ | ......... | 1 | ...... | ...... | ...... | 31 | ...... | ...... | 1 | 31 | 3.30 | 10.50 | ... 3 50– 3 99 |
| 4 00– 4 49... | ......... | ............ | ......... | ......... | ...... | ...... | ...... | 69 | ...... | ...... | ...... | 69 | ...... | 19.70 | ... 4 00– 4 49 |
| 4 50– 4 99... | ......... | ............ | ......... | ......... | ...... | ...... | ...... | 107 | ...... | ...... | ...... | 107 | ...... | 34.00 | ... 4 50– 4 99 |
| 5 00– 5 49... | ......... | ............ | ......... | 1 | ...... | ...... | 2 | 133 | 1 | 1 | 4 | 134 | 6.50 | 51.90 | ... 5 00– 5 49 |
| 5 50– 5 99... | ......... | ............ | ......... | 2 | ...... | ...... | ...... | 75 | 2 | ...... | 4 | 75 | 9.80 | 62.00 | ... 5 50– 5 99 |
| 6 00– 6 49... | ......... | ............ | ......... | 6 | ...... | 7 | ...... | 171 | 2 | ...... | 8 | 178 | 16.50 | 85.70 | ... 6 00– 6 49 |
| 6 50– 6 99... | ......... | ............ | 1 | 1 | ...... | 5 | ...... | 41 | ...... | ...... | 2 | 46 | 17.90 | 91.90 | ... 6 50– 6 99 |
| 7 00– 7 49... | ......... | ............ | 1 | 2 | ...... | 2 | ...... | 23 | ...... | ...... | 3 | 25 | 20.40 | 95.20 | ... 7 00– 7 49 |
| 7 50– 7 99... | ......... | ............ | ......... | 5 | ...... | 3 | ...... | 6 | 1 | ...... | 6 | 9 | 25.20 | 96.50 | ... 7 50– 7 99 |
| 8 00– 8 99... | ......... | ............ | ......... | 8 | 1 | 6 | ...... | 5 | ...... | ...... | 9 | 11 | 32.60 | 97.90 | ... 8 00– 8 99 |
| 9 00– 9 99... | ......... | ............ | 3 | 7 | 1 | 4 | ...... | 2 | ...... | ...... | 11 | 6 | 41.50 | 98.70 | ... 9 00– 9 99 |
| 10 00–10 99... | 1 | ............ | 2 | 8 | 2 | 2 | ...... | 3 | ...... | ...... | 13 | 5 | 52.00 | 99.40 | ...10 00–10 99 |
| 11 00–11 99... | ......... | ............ | 4 | 8 | 1 | ...... | ...... | 1 | ...... | ...... | 13 | 1 | 62.60 | 99.50 | ...11 00–11 99 |
| 12 00–12 99... | 1 | ............ | 1 | 2 | 6 | ...... | ...... | 2 | ...... | ...... | 10 | 2 | 70.80 | 99.80 | ...12 00–12 99 |
| 13 00–13 99... | 1 | ............ | ......... | 3 | 3 | 1 | 1 | ...... | ...... | ...... | 8 | 1 | 77.30 | 99.90 | ...13 00–13 99 |
| 14 00–14 99... | 2 | ............ | 1 | 1 | 2 | ...... | ...... | ...... | ...... | ...... | 6 | ...... | 82.20 | ...... | ...14 00–14 99 |
| 15 00–15 99... | 2 | ............ | 1 | ......... | 7 | ...... | ...... | ...... | ...... | ...... | 10 | ...... | 90.30 | ...... | ...15 00–15 99 |
| 16 00–17 99... | 1 | ............ | 2 | ......... | 3 | 1 | ...... | ...... | ...... | ...... | 6 | 1 | 95.20 | 100.00 | ...16 00–17 99 |
| 18 00–19 99... | 1 | 1 | 1 | 1 | ...... | ...... | ...... | ...... | ...... | ...... | 4 | ...... | 98.50 | ...... | ...18 00–19 99 |
| 20 00–24 99... | ......... | ............ | ......... | ......... | 2 | ...... | ...... | ...... | ...... | ...... | 2 | ...... | 100.00 | ...... | ...20 00–24 99 |
| Not reported... | ......... | ............ | ......... | 1 | ...... | ...... | ...... | ...... | ...... | ...... | 1 | ...... | ...... | ...... | ...Not reported |
| Total..... | 9 | 1 | 17 | 58 | 28 | 31 | 3 | 717 | 8 | 1 | 124 | 749 | ...... | ...... | .....Total |

NEW YORK STATE EXCLUSIVE OF NEW YORK CITY

184. TABLE XV, A, 3, b,c,e. **FIVE AND TEN CENT STORES — OFFICE, SHIPPING AND DELIVERY, PLANT**

NUMBER AND PER CENT OF EMPLOYEES EARNING SPECIFIED WEEKLY RATES ACCORDING TO DEPARTMENT AND SEX

| WEEKLY RATES IN DOLLARS | DEPARTMENT | | | | | | | | | WEEKLY RATES IN DOLLARS |
|---|---|---|---|---|---|---|---|---|---|---|
| | OFFICE | | PLANT | | SHIPPING AND DELIVERY | TOTAL | | CUMULATIVE PER CENT OF TOTAL | | |
| | Male | Female | Male | Female | Male | Male | Female | Male | Female | |
| $3 50–$3 99 | ........ | ........ | ........ | ........ | 1 | 1 | ........ | 5.00 | ........ | $3 50–$3 99 |
| 5 00– 5 49 | ........ | 1 | ........ | 1 | ........ | ........ | 2 | ........ | 4.16 | 5 00– 5 49 |
| 6 00– 6 49 | ........ | 4 | 1 | ........ | 1 | 2 | 4 | 15.00 | 12.50 | 6 00– 6 49 |
| 6 50– 6 99 | ........ | 1 | ........ | 1 | ........ | ........ | 2 | ........ | 16.65 | 6 50– 6 99 |
| 7 00– 7 49 | ........ | 11 | ........ | ........ | ........ | ........ | 11 | ........ | 39.50 | 7 00– 7 49 |
| 7 50– 7 99 | ........ | 1 | 1 | ........ | ........ | 1 | 1 | 20.00 | 41.60 | 7 50– 7 99 |
| 8 00– 8 99 | ........ | 8 | 2 | ........ | ........ | 2 | 8 | 30.00 | 58.25 | 8 00– 8 99 |
| 9 00– 9 99 | ........ | 4 | ........ | ........ | ........ | ........ | 4 | ........ | 66.80 | 9 00– 9 99 |
| 10 00–10 99 | ........ | 5 | 4 | ........ | 1 | 5 | 5 | 55.00 | 77.00 | 10 00–10 99 |
| 11 00–11 99 | ........ | 4 | 2 | ........ | ........ | 2 | 4 | 65.00 | 85.50 | 11 00–11 99 |
| 12 00–12 99 | 1 | 2 | ........ | ........ | 1 | 2 | 2 | 75.00 | 89.50 | 12 00–12 99 |
| 13 00–13 99 | 2 | 3 | 3 | ........ | ........ | 5 | 3 | 100.00 | 95.80 | 13 00–13 99 |
| 15 00–15 99 | ........ | 2 | ........ | ........ | ........ | ........ | 2 | ........ | 100.00 | 15 00–15 99 |
| Not reported | ........ | 3 | ........ | ........ | ........ | ........ | 3 | ........ | ........ | Not reported |
| Total | 3 | 49 | 13 | 2 | 4 | 20 | 51 | ........ | ........ | Total |

NEW YORK STATE EXCLUSIVE OF NEW YORK CITY

185. TABLE XVI, A, 3, b, c, e **FIVE AND TEN CENT STORES — OFFICE, SHIPPING AND DELIVERY, PLANT**

NUMBER AND PER CENT OF EMPLOYEES CLASSIFIED ACCORDING TO ACTUAL WEEKLY EARNINGS BY DEPARTMENT AND SEX

| ACTUAL WEEKLY EARNINGS IN DOLLARS | DEPARTMENT | | | | | | | | | ACTUAL WEEKLY EARNINGS IN DOLLARS |
|---|---|---|---|---|---|---|---|---|---|---|
| | OFFICE | | PLANT | | SHIPPING AND DELIVERY | TOTAL | | CUMULATIVE PER CENT OF TOTAL | | |
| | Male | Female | Male | Female | Male | Male | Female | Male | Female | |
| Less than $3 00 | ........ | 1 | ........ | ........ | ........ | ........ | 1 | ........ | 1.96 | Less than $3 00 |
| $3 50–$3 99 | ........ | ........ | ........ | ........ | 1 | 1 | ........ | 5.00 | ........ | $3 50– 3 99 |
| 5 00– 5 49 | ........ | 1 | ........ | 1 | ........ | ........ | 2 | ........ | 5.88 | 5 00– 5 49 |
| 5 50– 5 99 | ........ | 1 | ........ | ........ | ........ | ........ | 1 | ........ | 7.85 | 5 50– 5 99 |
| 6 00– 6 49 | ........ | 2 | 1 | ........ | 1 | 2 | 2 | 15.00 | 11.55 | 6 00– 6 49 |
| 6 50– 6 99 | ........ | 3 | ........ | 1 | ........ | ........ | 4 | ........ | 19.60 | 6 50– 6 99 |
| 7 00– 7 49 | ........ | 8 | ........ | ........ | ........ | ........ | 8 | ........ | 35.35 | 7 00– 7 49 |
| 7 50– 7 99 | ........ | 3 | 1 | ........ | ........ | 1 | 3 | 20.00 | 41.20 | 7 50– 7 99 |
| 8 00– 8 99 | ........ | 9 | 2 | ........ | ........ | 2 | 9 | 30.00 | 58.80 | 8 00– 8 99 |
| 9 00– 9 99 | ........ | 4 | ........ | ........ | ........ | ........ | 4 | ........ | 66.70 | 9 00– 9 99 |
| 10 00–10 99 | ........ | 5 | 3 | ........ | 1 | 4 | 5 | 50.00 | 76.50 | 10 00–10 99 |
| 11 00–11 99 | ........ | 4 | 3 | ........ | ........ | 3 | 4 | 65.00 | 84.40 | 11 00–11 99 |
| 12 00–12 99 | 1 | 2 | ........ | ........ | ........ | 1 | 2 | 70.00 | 88.25 | 12 00–12 99 |
| 13 00–13 99 | 1 | 3 | 1 | ........ | ........ | 2 | 3 | 80.00 | 93.20 | 13 00–13 99 |
| 14 00–14 99 | ........ | 1 | 2 | ........ | ........ | 2 | 1 | 90.00 | 96.10 | 14 00–14 99 |
| 15 00–15 99 | ........ | 2 | ........ | ........ | ........ | ........ | 2 | ........ | 100.00 | 15 00–15 99 |
| 16 00–17 99 | ........ | ........ | ........ | ........ | 1 | 1 | ........ | 95.00 | ........ | 16 00–17 99 |
| 18 00–19 99 | 1 | ........ | ........ | ........ | ........ | 1 | ........ | 100.00 | ........ | 18 00–19 99 |
| Total | 3 | 49 | 13 | 2 | 4 | 20 | 51 | ........ | ........ | Total |

186. TABLE XVII, A, 3, b,c,e.

NEW YORK STATE EXCLUSIVE OF NEW YORK CITY

**FIVE AND TEN CENT STORES — OFFICE, SHIPPING AND DELIVERY, PLANT**

NUMBER OF EMPLOYEES CLASSIFIED BY AGE GROUPS ACCORDING TO DEPARTMENT AND SEX

| AGE GROUPS IN YEARS | DEPARTMENT | | | | | | | | | AGE GROUPS IN YEARS |
|---|---|---|---|---|---|---|---|---|---|---|
| | OFFICE | | SHIPPING AND DELIVERY | PLANT | | TOTAL | | PER CENT OF TOTAL | | |
| | Male | Female | Male | Male | Female | Male | Female | Male | Female | |
| 16–17 | ........ | 4 | 2 | 2 | ........ | 4 | 4 | 20.00 | 7.84 | 16–17 |
| 18–20 | ........ | 16 | ........ | 1 | ........ | 1 | 16 | 5.00 | 31.38 | 18–20 |
| 21–24 | 1 | 19 | 2 | 3 | ........ | 6 | 19 | 30.00 | 37.25 | 21–24 |
| 25–29 | 1 | 8 | ........ | 2 | ........ | 3 | 8 | 15.00 | 15.69 | 25–29 |
| 30–34 | ........ | ........ | ........ | 1 | 1 | 1 | 1 | 5.00 | 1.96 | 30–34 |
| 35–39 | 1 | 2 | ........ | 1 | ........ | 2 | 2 | 10.00 | 3.92 | 35–39 |
| 45–54 | ........ | ........ | ........ | 2 | 1 | 2 | 1 | 10.00 | 1.96 | 45–54 |
| 55–64 | ........ | ........ | ........ | 1 | ........ | 1 | ........ | 5.00 | ........ | 55–64 |
| Total | 3 | 49 | 4 | 13 | 2 | 20 | 51 | 100.00 | 100.00 | Total |

187. TABLE V, B, a.

NEW YORK STATE EXCLUSIVE OF NEW YORK CITY
THE MEN'S SHIRT INDUSTRY — FACTORY WORKERS

NUMBER AND PER CENT OF EMPLOYEES EARNING SPECIFIED WEEKLY RATES BY AGE GROUPS AND SEX

| WEEKLY RATES IN DOLLARS | AGE GROUPS IN YEARS | | | | | | | | | | | | | | WEEKLY RATES IN DOLLARS |
|---|---|---|---|---|---|---|---|---|---|---|---|---|---|---|---|
| | 14–15 | | 16–17 | | 18–20 | | 21–24 | | 25–29 | | 30–34 | | 35–39 | | |
| | Male | Female | Male | Female | Male | Female | Male | Female | Male | Female | Male | Female | Male | Female | |
| $3 00–$3 49... | .... | 1 | .... | 3 | ...... | ...... | ...... | ...... | ...... | ...... | ...... | ...... | ...... | ...... | ...$3 00–$3 49 |
| 3 50– 3 99... | .... | 4 | 2 | 1 | 1 | 1 | ...... | ...... | ...... | ...... | ...... | ...... | ...... | ...... | ... 3 50– 3 99 |
| 4 00– 4 49... | .... | 7 | 3 | 27 | 1 | 9 | ...... | 3 | ...... | ...... | ...... | ...... | ...... | ...... | ... 4 00– 4 49 |
| 4 50– 4 99... | .... | ...... | 5 | 10 | ...... | 10 | ...... | 2 | ...... | 1 | ...... | ...... | ...... | ...... | ... 4 50– 4 99 |
| 5 00– 5 49... | 1 | 2 | 14 | 29 | 2 | 21 | ...... | 9 | ...... | 2 | ...... | ...... | ...... | 3 | ... 5 00– 5 49 |
| 5 50– 5 99... | .... | ...... | 3 | 15 | 3 | 11 | 1 | 2 | ...... | 3 | ...... | ...... | ...... | 5 | ... 5 50– 5 99 |
| 6 00– 6 49... | 1 | ...... | 4 | 21 | 7 | 44 | 1 | 23 | ...... | 12 | ...... | 4 | ...... | 11 | ... 6 00– 6 49 |
| 6 50– 6 99... | .... | ...... | 1 | ...... | 1 | 8 | ...... | 3 | ...... | 6 | ...... | 1 | ...... | ...... | ... 6 50– 6 99 |
| 7 00– 7 49... | .... | ...... | 4 | 6 | 8 | 27 | 1 | 19 | ...... | 10 | ...... | 8 | ...... | 4 | ... 7 00– 7 49 |
| 7 50– 7 99... | .... | ...... | .... | ...... | 4 | 1 | 1 | 7 | 1 | 3 | 1 | ...... | ...... | 3 | ... 7 50– 7 99 |
| 8 00– 8 99... | .... | ...... | 1 | ...... | 8 | 5 | 1 | 18 | 1 | 15 | 1 | 7 | 1 | 13 | ... 8 00– 8 99 |
| 9 00– 9 99... | .... | ...... | 1 | ...... | 7 | 1 | 3 | 20 | ...... | 21 | ...... | 13 | ...... | 12 | ... 9 00– 9 99 |
| 10 00–10 99... | .... | ...... | 1 | ...... | 4 | 1 | 2 | 12 | 4 | 5 | 2 | 5 | 3 | 3 | ...10 00–10 99 |
| 11 00–11 99... | .... | ...... | .... | ...... | 1 | ...... | 4 | 3 | 3 | 4 | 1 | 3 | 1 | 1 | ...11 00–11 99 |
| 12 00–12 99... | .... | ...... | .... | ...... | 1 | ...... | 10 | 2 | 2 | 5 | 1 | 10 | 3 | 3 | ...12 00–12 99 |
| 13 00–13 99... | .... | ...... | .... | ...... | 1 | ...... | 4 | 1 | 2 | 2 | 2 | 1 | ...... | 3 | ...13 00–13 99 |
| 14 00–14 99... | .... | ...... | .... | ...... | ...... | ...... | 4 | ...... | 6 | ...... | 1 | ...... | 1 | 1 | ...14 00–14 99 |
| 15 00–15 99... | .... | ...... | .... | ...... | ...... | ...... | 8 | ...... | 10 | 2 | 8 | 2 | 12 | 1 | ...15 00–15 99 |
| 16 00–17 99... | .... | ...... | .... | ...... | ...... | ...... | 2 | ...... | 5 | ...... | 7 | ...... | 3 | 1 | ...16 00–17 99 |
| 18 00–19 99... | .... | ...... | .... | ...... | ...... | ...... | ...... | ...... | 1 | 1 | 7 | ...... | 3 | ...... | ...18 00–19 99 |
| 20 00–24 99... | .... | ...... | .... | ...... | ...... | ...... | ...... | ...... | 2 | ...... | 4 | 1 | 7 | 1 | ...20 00–24 99 |
| 25 00–29 99... | .... | ...... | .... | ...... | ...... | ...... | ...... | ...... | ...... | ...... | 2 | ...... | 5 | ...... | ...25 00–29 99 |
| 30 00–34 99... | .... | ...... | .... | ...... | ...... | ...... | ...... | ...... | ...... | ...... | ...... | ...... | 1 | ...... | ...30 00–34 99 |
| Not reported... | .... | 1 | .... | 16 | 2 | 55 | 1 | 63 | ...... | 42 | 1 | 43 | ...... | 26 | ...Not reported |
| Total..... | 2 | 15 | 39 | 128 | 51 | 194 | 43 | 187 | 37 | 134 | 38 | 98 | 40 | 91 | .....Total |

187. TABLE V, B, a — (*concluded*)

NEW YORK STATE EXCLUSIVE OF NEW YORK CITY
**THE MEN'S SHIRT INDUSTRY — FACTORY WORKERS**
Number and Per Cent of Employees Earning Specified Weekly Rates by Age Groups and Sex

| Weekly Rates in Dollars | Age Groups in Years | | | | | | | | | | | | | Weekly Rates in Dollars |
|---|---|---|---|---|---|---|---|---|---|---|---|---|---|---|
| | 40–44 | | 45–54 | | 55–64 | | 65 and over | | Not reported | Total | | Cumulative per cent of total | | |
| | Male | Female | Male | Female | Male | Female | Male | Female | Female | Male | Female | Male | Female | |
| $3 00–$3 49 | ...... | ...... | ...... | ...... | ...... | ...... | ...... | ...... | ...... | ...... | 4 | ...... | .57 | $3 00–$3 49 |
| 3 50– 3 99 | ...... | ...... | ...... | ...... | ...... | ...... | ...... | ...... | 1 | 3 | 7 | .99 | 1.56 | 3 50– 3 99 |
| 4 00– 4 49 | ...... | ...... | ...... | 1 | ...... | ...... | ...... | ...... | ...... | 4 | 47 | 2.34 | 8.25 | 4 00– 4 49 |
| 4 50– 4 99 | ...... | 1 | ...... | ...... | ...... | ...... | ...... | ...... | ...... | 5 | 24 | 3 97 | 11.65 | 4 50– 4 99 |
| 5 00– 5 49 | ...... | ...... | ...... | 1 | ...... | ...... | ...... | ...... | 1 | 17 | 68 | 9.60 | 21.35 | 5 00– 5 49 |
| 5 50– 5 99 | ...... | 1 | ...... | 1 | ...... | ...... | ...... | ...... | 1 | 7 | 39 | 11.92 | 26 95 | 5 50– 5 99 |
| 6 00– 9 49 | ...... | 3 | ...... | 9 | ...... | 5 | ...... | ...... | 1 | 13 | 133 | 16.25 | 45.80 | 6 00– 6 49 |
| 6 50– 6 99 | ...... | 1 | ...... | 1 | ...... | 2 | ...... | ...... | ...... | 2 | 22 | 16.90 | 48.90 | 6 50– 6 99 |
| 7 00– 7 49 | ...... | 5 | ...... | 7 | ...... | 2 | ...... | ...... | ...... | 13 | 88 | 21.20 | 61.40 | 7 00– 7 49 |
| 7 50– 7 99 | ...... | ...... | ...... | 5 | ...... | ...... | ...... | ...... | 2 | 7 | 21 | 23.50 | 64.50 | 7 50– 7 99 |
| 8 00– 8 99 | 1 | 3 | ...... | 6 | ...... | 2 | ...... | 1 | ...... | 14 | 70 | 27.18 | 74.50 | 8 00– 8 99 |
| 9 00– 9 99 | 2 | 4 | 2 | 10 | 1 | 1 | 1 | 2 | 3 | 17 | 87 | 33.80 | 86.75 | 9 00– 9 99 |
| 10 00–10 99 | 2 | 3 | 2 | 1 | ...... | 1 | ...... | ...... | 1 | 20 | 32 | 40.40 | 91.25 | 10 00–10 99 |
| 11 00–11 99 | 1 | 1 | 1 | ...... | ...... | 1 | ...... | ...... | ...... | 12 | 13 | 44.40 | 93.10 | 11 00–11 99 |
| 12 00–12 99 | ...... | 2 | 1 | ...... | ...... | ...... | 1 | ...... | ...... | 19 | 22 | 50.70 | 96.25 | 12 00–12 99 |
| 13 00–13 99 | 1 | ...... | 2 | ...... | ...... | ...... | ...... | 1 | ...... | 12 | 8 | 54.60 | 97.50 | 13 00–13 99 |
| 14 00–14 99 | ...... | 1 | 1 | ...... | 1 | ...... | ...... | ...... | ...... | 14 | 2 | 59.30 | 97.70 | 14 00–14 99 |
| 15 00–15 99 | 4 | 1 | 3 | 3 | 1 | ...... | ...... | ...... | ...... | 46 | 9 | 62.90 | 99.00 | 15 00–15 99 |
| 16 00–17 99 | 4 | ...... | 7 | ...... | ...... | ...... | ...... | ...... | ...... | 28 | 1 | 83.75 | 99.15 | 16 00–17 99 |
| 18 00–19 99 | 2 | ...... | 1 | 3 | 3 | ...... | ...... | ...... | ...... | 17 | 4 | 89.50 | 99.70 | 18 00–19 99 |
| 20 00–24 99 | 2 | ...... | 3 | ...... | ...... | ...... | ...... | ...... | ...... | 18 | 2 | 95.40 | 100.00 | 20 00–24 99 |
| 25 00–29 99 | ...... | ...... | 1 | ...... | 1 | ...... | ...... | ...... | ...... | 9 | ...... | 98.40 | ...... | 25 00–29 99 |
| 30 00–34 99 | 3 | ...... | ...... | ...... | ...... | ...... | ...... | ...... | ...... | 4 | ...... | 99.40 | ...... | 30 00–34 99 |
| 35 00–39 99 | ...... | ...... | 1 | ...... | ...... | ...... | ...... | ...... | ...... | 1 | ...... | 100.00 | ...... | 35 00–39 99 |
| Not reported | ...... | 20 | ...... | 20 | ...... | 2 | ...... | 1 | 8 | 4 | 297 | ...... | ...... | Not reported |
| Total | 22 | 46 | 25 | 68 | 7 | 16 | 2 | 5 | 18 | 306 | 1,000 | ...... | ...... | Total |

NEW YORK STATE EXCLUSIVE OF NEW YORK CITY

**THE MEN'S SHIRT INDUSTRY — FACTORY WORKERS**

188. TABLE VII, B, a. NUMBER AND PER CENT OF EMPLOYEES EARNING SPECIFIED WEEKLY RATES BY OCCUPATION AND SEX

| WEEKLY RATES IN DOLLARS | OCCUPATION | | | | | | | | | | | | | WEEKLY RATES IN DOLLARS |
|---|---|---|---|---|---|---|---|---|---|---|---|---|---|---|
| | MARKERS | CUTTERS | TRIMMERS | | CUTTERS' HELPERS | | FOREMEN AND FOREWOMEN | | OPERATORS | FLOOR WORK | | LAUNDRY HELPERS | | |
| | Male | Male | Male | Female | Male | Female | Male | Female | Female | Male | Female | Male | Female | |
| $3 00–$3 49...... | ...... | ...... | ...... | ...... | ...... | 1 | ...... | ...... | ...... | ...... | 1 | ...... | ...... | ......$3 00–$3 49 |
| 3 50– 3 99...... | ...... | ...... | ...... | ...... | 1 | ...... | ...... | ...... | ...... | 2 | 2 | ...... | ...... | ......3 50– 3 99 |
| 4 00– 4 49...... | ...... | ...... | ...... | 1 | 2 | 1 | ...... | ...... | 9 | ...... | 12 | 1 | 1 | ......4 00– 4 49 |
| 4 50– 4 99...... | ...... | ...... | ...... | ...... | 2 | ...... | ...... | ...... | 4 | 1 | 4 | 1 | 2 | ......4 50– 4 99 |
| 5 00– 5 49...... | ...... | 2 | ...... | ...... | 8 | ...... | ...... | ...... | 7 | 1 | 18 | 2 | 5 | ......5 00– 5 49 |
| 5 50– 5 99...... | ...... | 2 | 1 | ...... | 1 | 1 | ...... | ...... | 1 | ...... | 4 | 1 | 3 | ......5 50– 5 99 |
| 6 00– 6 49...... | ...... | 4 | 1 | ...... | 6 | 4 | ...... | 4 | 13 | ...... | 10 | ...... | 4 | ......6 00– 6 49 |
| 6 50– 6 99...... | ...... | ...... | ...... | ...... | 1 | 1 | ...... | 2 | 4 | ...... | 1 | ...... | 3 | ......6 50– 6 99 |
| 7 00– 7 49...... | ...... | 4 | 1 | ...... | 3 | 1 | ...... | 3 | 9 | ...... | 1 | ...... | 3 | ......7 00– 7 49 |
| 7 50– 7 99...... | ...... | 2 | ...... | ...... | ...... | 1 | ...... | 2 | 11 | ...... | 2 | 2 | 2 | ......7 50– 7 99 |
| 8 00– 8 99...... | ...... | 3 | 3 | ...... | 1 | 1 | ...... | 9 | 20 | ...... | 1 | 2 | 3 | ......8 00– 8 99 |
| 9 00– 9 99...... | ...... | 7 | ...... | ...... | 1 | 1 | ...... | 22 | 25 | ...... | 4 | 6 | 1 | ......9 00– 9 99 |
| 10 00–10 99...... | ...... | 4 | 4 | ...... | ...... | ...... | 1 | 10 | 4 | ...... | 1 | 7 | 4 | .....10 00–10 99 |
| 11 00–11 99...... | ...... | 7 | 1 | 1 | ...... | ...... | 2 | 4 | 2 | ...... | ...... | 1 | 2 | .....11 00–11 99 |
| 12 00–12 99...... | ...... | 10 | ...... | ...... | ...... | ...... | 4 | 14 | 1 | ...... | ...... | 2 | ...... | .....12 00–12 99 |
| 13 00–13 99...... | ...... | 6 | ...... | ...... | ...... | ...... | 2 | 5 | ...... | ...... | ...... | 3 | 2 | .....13 00–13 99 |
| 14 00–14 99...... | ...... | 11 | 1 | ...... | ...... | ...... | 1 | 2 | ...... | ...... | ...... | ...... | ...... | .....14 00–14 99 |
| 15 00–15 99...... | ...... | 29 | ...... | ...... | ...... | ...... | 7 | 9 | ...... | 2 | ...... | 2 | ...... | .....15 00–15 99 |
| 16 00–17 99...... | ...... | 22 | ...... | ...... | ...... | ...... | 4 | 1 | ...... | 1 | ...... | ...... | ...... | .....16 00–17 99 |
| 18 00–19 99...... | ...... | 5 | ...... | ...... | ...... | ...... | 10 | 4 | ...... | ...... | ...... | 2 | ...... | .....18 00–19 99 |
| 20 00–24 99...... | ...... | 1 | ...... | ...... | ...... | ...... | 16 | 2 | ...... | ...... | ...... | 1 | ...... | .....20 00–24 99 |
| 25 00–29 99...... | ...... | 1 | ...... | ...... | ...... | ...... | 7 | ...... | ...... | ...... | ...... | 1 | ...... | .....25 00–29 99 |
| 30 00–34 99...... | ...... | ...... | ...... | ...... | ...... | ...... | 4 | ...... | ...... | ...... | ...... | ...... | ...... | .....30 00–34 99 |
| 35 00–39 99...... | ...... | ...... | ...... | ...... | ...... | ...... | 1 | ...... | ...... | ...... | ...... | ...... | ...... | .....35 00–39 99 |
| Not reported...... | 1 | 1 | ...... | ...... | ...... | ...... | ...... | ...... | 241 | ...... | 4 | ...... | ...... | .....Not reported |
| Total........ | 1 | 121 | 12 | 2 | 26 | 12 | 59 | 93 | 351 | 7 | 65 | 34 | 35 | .......Total |

188. TABLE VIII, B, a — (*concluded*)

NEW YORK STATE EXCLUSIVE OF NEW YORK CITY

**THE MEN'S SHIRT INDUSTRY — FACTORY WORKERS**

NUMBER AND PER CENT OF EMPLOYEES EARNING SPECIFIED WEEKLY RATES BY OCCUPATION AND SEX

| WEEKLY RATES IN DOLLARS | OCCUPATION (*concluded*) STARCHERS AND DAMPENERS | | IRONERS AND PRESSERS | | EXAMINERS | | FOLDERS | PACKERS | | TOTAL | | CUMULATIVE PER CENT OF TOTAL | | WEEKLY RATES IN DOLLARS |
|---|---|---|---|---|---|---|---|---|---|---|---|---|---|---|
| | Male | Female | Male | Female | Male | Female | Female | Male | Female | Male | Female | Male | Female | |
| $3 00–$3 49 | ...... | ...... | ...... | ...... | ...... | 2 | ...... | ...... | ...... | ...... | 4 | ...... | .57 | $3 00–$3 49 |
| 3 50– 3 99 | ...... | ...... | ...... | ...... | ...... | 4 | ...... | ...... | 1 | 3 | 7 | .99 | 1.56 | 3 50– 3 99 |
| 4 00– 4 99 | ...... | 3 | ...... | ...... | ...... | 19 | 1 | 1 | ...... | 4 | 47 | 2.34 | 8.25 | 4 00– 4 49 |
| 4 50– 4 99 | ...... | ...... | ...... | ...... | 1 | 13 | ...... | ...... | 1 | 5 | 24 | 3.97 | 11.65 | 4 50– 4 99 |
| 5 00– 5 49 | ...... | ...... | 1 | 2 | 1 | 29 | ...... | 2 | 7 | 17 | 68 | 9.60 | 21.35 | 5 00– 5 49 |
| 5 50– 5 99 | ...... | 1 | ...... | 2 | ...... | 26 | ...... | 2 | 1 | 7 | 39 | 11.92 | 26.95 | 5 50– 5 99 |
| 6 00– 6 49 | ...... | 1 | ...... | 4 | 1 | 87 | ...... | 1 | 6 | 13 | 133 | 16.25 | 45.80 | 6 00– 6 49 |
| 6 50– 6 99 | ...... | ...... | 1 | ...... | ...... | 10 | ...... | ...... | 1 | 2 | 22 | 16.90 | 48.90 | 6 50– 6 99 |
| 7 00– 7 49 | ...... | ...... | 2 | 1 | 2 | 64 | ...... | 1 | 6 | 13 | 88 | 21.20 | 61.40 | 7 00– 7 49 |
| 7 50– 7 99 | ...... | ...... | 1 | ...... | 2 | 3 | ...... | ...... | ...... | 7 | 21 | 23.50 | 64.50 | 7 50– 7 99 |
| 8 00– 8 99 | ...... | ...... | 1 | 2 | 1 | 30 | ...... | 3 | 4 | 14 | 70 | 27.18 | 74.50 | 8 00– 8 99 |
| 9 00– 9 99 | ...... | ...... | ...... | ...... | 3 | 26 | ...... | ...... | 8 | 17 | 87 | 33.80 | 86.75 | 9 00– 9 99 |
| 10 00–10 99 | 1 | ...... | ...... | 1 | 2 | 11 | 1 | 1 | ...... | 20 | 32 | 40.40 | 91.25 | 10 00–10 99 |
| 11 00–11 99 | 1 | ...... | ...... | ...... | ...... | 4 | ...... | ...... | ...... | 12 | 13 | 44.40 | 93.10 | 11 00–11 99 |
| 12 00–12 99 | ...... | 1 | ...... | ...... | 3 | 5 | 1 | ...... | ...... | 19 | 22 | 50.70 | 96.25 | 12 00–12 99 |
| 13 00–13 99 | ...... | ...... | ...... | ...... | 1 | 1 | ...... | ...... | ...... | 12 | 8 | 54.60 | 97.50 | 13 00–13 99 |
| 14 00–14 99 | ...... | ...... | ...... | ...... | 1 | ...... | ...... | ...... | ...... | 14 | 2 | 59.30 | 97.70 | 14 00–14 99 |
| 15 00–15 99 | ...... | ...... | ...... | ...... | 6 | ...... | ...... | ...... | ...... | 46 | 9 | 62.90 | 99.00 | 15 00–15 99 |
| 16 00–17 99 | ...... | ...... | ...... | ...... | 1 | ...... | ...... | ...... | ...... | 28 | 1 | 83.75 | 99.15 | 16 00–17 99 |
| 18 00–19 99 | ...... | ...... | ...... | ...... | ...... | ...... | ...... | ...... | ...... | 17 | 4 | 89.50 | 99.70 | 18 00–19 99 |
| 20 00–24 99 | ...... | ...... | ...... | ...... | ...... | ...... | ...... | ...... | ...... | 18 | 2 | 95.40 | 100.00 | 20 00–24 99 |
| 25 00–29 99 | ...... | ...... | ...... | ...... | ...... | ...... | ...... | ...... | ...... | 9 | ...... | 98.40 | ...... | 25 00–29 99 |
| 30 00–34 99 | ...... | ...... | ...... | ...... | ...... | ...... | ...... | ...... | ...... | 4 | ...... | 99.40 | ...... | 30 00–34 99 |
| 35 00–39 99 | ...... | ...... | ...... | ...... | ...... | ...... | ...... | ...... | ...... | 1 | ...... | 100.00 | ...... | 35 00–39 99 |
| Not reported | ...... | 18 | ...... | 6 | 1 | 24 | ...... | 1 | 4 | 4 | 297 | ...... | ...... | Not reported |
| Total | 2 | 24 | 6 | 18 | 26 | 358 | 3 | 12 | 39 | 306 | 1,000 | ...... | ...... | Total |

NEW YORK STATE EXCLUSIVE OF NEW YORK CITY
**THE MEN'S SHIRT INDUSTRY — FACTORY WORKERS**

189. TABLE VI, B, a NUMBER AND PER CENT. OF EMPLOYEES CLASSIFIED ACCORDING TO ACTUAL WEEKLY EARNINGS BY AGE GROUPS AND SEX

| ACTUAL WEEKLY EARNINGS IN DOLLARS | AGE GROUPS IN YEARS | | | | | | | | | | | | | | ACTUAL WEEKLY EARNINGS IN DOLLARS |
|---|---|---|---|---|---|---|---|---|---|---|---|---|---|---|---|
| | 14–15 | | 16–17 | | 18–20 | | 21–24 | | 25–29 | | 30–34 | | 35–39 | | |
| | Male | Female | Male | Female | Male | Female | Male | Female | Male | Female | Male | Female | Male | Female | |
| Less than $3 00 | 2 | 13 | 2 | 47 | ...... | 57 | 1 | 41 | 4 | 21 | 1 | 20 | 1 | 17 | Less than $3 00 |
| $3 00–$3 49... | .... | 2 | .... | 21 | ...... | 30 | 2 | 17 | ...... | 18 | ...... | 9 | ...... | 13 | ...$3 00– 3 49 |
| 3 50– 3 99... | .... | 5 | 4 | 32 | 2 | 35 | 5 | 24 | 6 | 19 | 4 | 8 | 1 | 8 | ... 3 50– 3 99 |
| 4 00– 4 49... | .... | 6 | 6 | 35 | 1 | 47 | 3 | 44 | 5 | 28 | ...... | 14 | 5 | 12 | ... 4 00– 4 49 |
| 4 50– 4 99... | .... | 2 | 8 | 43 | 1 | 59 | 3 | 39 | 2 | 23 | 4 | 13 | 1 | 18 | ... 4 50– 4 99 |
| 5 00– 5 49... | 2 | 3 | 6 | 43 | 10 | 98 | 10 | 52 | 9 | 27 | 7 | 27 | 5 | 17 | ... 5 00– 5 49 |
| 5 50– 5 99... | .... | 1 | 3 | 38 | 7 | 79 | 2 | 67 | 2 | 38 | 1 | 23 | 5 | 23 | ... 5 50– 5 99 |
| 6 00– 6 49... | 1 | ...... | 7 | 30 | 9 | 76 | 4 | 77 | 8 | 40 | 8 | 25 | 6 | 38 | ... 6 00– 6 49 |
| 6 50– 6 99... | .... | ...... | 2 | 10 | 2 | 50 | 5 | 41 | 7 | 41 | 1 | 20 | 1 | 15 | ... 6 50– 6 99 |
| 7 00– 7 49... | .... | 1 | 1 | 17 | 4 | 59 | 4 | 74 | 6 | 50 | 3 | 26 | 4 | 23 | ... 7 00– 7 49 |
| 7 50– 7 99... | .... | ...... | .... | 9 | 7 | 28 | 2 | 55 | 1 | 35 | 6 | 24 | 3 | 26 | ... 7 50– 7 99 |
| 8 00– 8 99... | .... | 1 | 2 | 8 | 7 | 48 | 11 | 101 | 16 | 86 | 15 | 60 | 18 | 53 | ... 8 00– 8 99 |
| 9 00– 9 99... | .... | 1 | .... | 4 | 5 | 42 | 6 | 75 | 6 | 68 | 5 | 52 | 1 | 41 | ... 9 00– 9 99 |
| 10 00–10 99... | .... | ...... | .... | 4 | 5 | 34 | 14 | 54 | 7 | 68 | 8 | 40 | 5 | 34 | ...10 00–10 99 |
| 11 00–11 99... | .... | ...... | 1 | 1 | 1 | 15 | 12 | 37 | 13 | 45 | 7 | 28 | 8 | 27 | ...11 00–11 99 |
| 12 00–12 99... | .... | ...... | .... | 3 | 3 | 14 | 15 | 27 | 12 | 30 | 13 | 32 | 13 | 30 | ...12 00–12 99 |
| 13 00–13 99... | .... | ...... | .... | 1 | 2 | 5 | 4 | 24 | 15 | 31 | 9 | 17 | 8 | 18 | ...13 00–13 99 |
| 14 00–14 99... | .... | ...... | .... | ...... | ...... | 10 | 9 | 22 | 8 | 20 | 4 | 10 | 9 | 7 | ...14 00–14 99 |
| 15 00–15 99... | .... | ...... | .... | 1 | 1 | 3 | 6 | 13 | 15 | 11 | 7 | 12 | 17 | 9 | ...15 00–15 99 |
| 16 00–17 99... | .... | ...... | .... | ...... | ...... | 4 | 3 | 9 | 13 | 6 | 14 | 4 | 7 | 10 | ...16 00–17 99 |
| 18 00–19 99... | .... | ...... | .... | ...... | ...... | 1 | 3 | 1 | 9 | 3 | 12 | 2 | 7 | 2 | ...18 00–19 99 |
| 20 00–24 99... | .... | ...... | .... | ...... | 1 | ...... | 3 | ...... | 9 | 1 | 10 | 1 | 10 | 1 | ...20 00–24 99 |
| 25 00–29 99... | .... | ...... | .... | ...... | ...... | ...... | 1 | ...... | ...... | ...... | 4 | ...... | 5 | ...... | ...25 00–29 99 |
| 30 00–34 99... | .... | ...... | .... | ...... | ...... | ...... | ...... | ...... | ...... | ...... | ...... | ...... | 1 | ...... | ...30 00–34 99 |
| Not reported... | .... | 1 | .... | ...... | 1 | ...... | ...... | ...... | ...... | ...... | ...... | ...... | ...... | ...... | ...Not reported |
| Total..... | 5 | 36 | 42 | 347 | 69 | 794 | 128 | 894 | 173 | 709 | 143 | 467 | 141 | 442 | ......Total |

189. TABLE VI, B, a — (*concluded*)

NEW YORK STATE EXCLUSIVE OF NEW YORK CITY

**THE MEN'S SHIRT INDUSTRY — FACTORY WORKERS**

Number and Per Cent. of Employees Classified According to Actual Weekly Earnings by Age Groups and Sex

| Actual Weekly Earnings in Dollars | Age Groups in Years (*concluded*) | | | | | | | | | | | | | | Actual Weekly Earnings in Dollars |
|---|---|---|---|---|---|---|---|---|---|---|---|---|---|---|---|
| | 40–44 | | 45–54 | | 55–64 | | 65 and over | | Not reported | | Total | | Cumulative per cent. of total | | |
| | Male | Female | Male | Female | Male | Female | Male | Female | Male | Female | Male | Female | Male | Female | |
| Less than $3 00 | 1 | 20 | 1 | 25 | ...... | 10 | ...... | 3 | 1 | 1 | 14 | 275 | 1.3 | 6.3 | Less than $3 00 |
| $3 00–$3 49... | .... | 6 | 1 | 6 | ...... | 8 | ...... | 4 | ...... | 1 | 3 | 135 | 1.9 | 9.4 | ...$3 00– 3 49 |
| 3 50– 3 99... | .... | 7 | 2 | 10 | ...... | 3 | ...... | 1 | 1 | 2 | 25 | 154 | 4.7 | 12.9 | ... 3 50 3 99 |
| 4 00– 4 49... | .... | 11 | .... | 10 | ...... | 3 | ...... | ...... | ...... | 1 | 20 | 211 | 6.9 | 17.8 | ... 4 00– 4 49 |
| 4 50– 4 99... | .... | 8 | 1 | 14 | ...... | 5 | 1 | 2 | ...... | 1 | 21 | 227 | 9.2 | 23.4 | ... 4 50– 4 99 |
| 5 00– 5 49... | 3 | 18 | 1 | 13 | ...... | 9 | 1 | ...... | ...... | 3 | 54 | 310 | 16.2 | 30.1 | ... 5 00– 5 49 |
| 5 50– 5 99... | .... | 9 | .... | 18 | 1 | 4 | ...... | ...... | ...... | 4 | 21 | 304 | 17.5 | 37.0 | ... 5 50– 5 99 |
| 6 00– 6 49... | 4 | 21 | 2 | 13 | ...... | 6 | ...... | 2 | 1 | 3 | 50 | 331 | 23.1 | 44.6 | ... 6 00– 6 49 |
| 6 50– 6 99... | .... | 8 | 2 | 16 | ...... | 3 | ...... | ...... | 2 | 3 | 22 | 207 | 25.5 | 44.2 | ... 6 50– 6 99 |
| 7 00– 7 49... | .... | 14 | 1 | 15 | ...... | 3 | ...... | 1 | ...... | 7 | 23 | 290 | 28.0 | 56.0 | ... 7 00– 7 49 |
| 7 50– 7 99... | 4 | 22 | 7 | 18 | 2 | 1 | ...... | ...... | ...... | 4 | 32 | 222 | 31.6 | 61.1 | ... 7 50– 7 99 |
| 8 00– 8 99... | 12 | 35 | 9 | 22 | 1 | 3 | ...... | 2 | ...... | 4 | 91 | 423 | 41.7 | 70.8 | ... 8 00– 8 99 |
| 9 00– 9 99... | 4 | 21 | 2 | 23 | ...... | 5 | ...... | 1 | ...... | 5 | 29 | 338 | 44.9 | 78.5 | ... 9 00– 9 99 |
| 10 00–10 99... | 7 | 18 | 3 | 18 | ...... | 3 | ...... | ...... | ...... | 3 | 49 | 276 | 50.4 | 84.8 | ...10 00–10 99 |
| 11 00–11 99... | 8 | 18 | 3 | 13 | 2 | 2 | 1 | ...... | ...... | 5 | 56 | 191 | 57.6 | 89.2 | ...11 00–11 99 |
| 12 00–12 99... | 2 | 9 | 7 | 9 | 3 | 2 | ...... | ...... | ...... | ...... | 68 | 156 | 64.2 | 92.7 | ...12 00–12 99 |
| 13 00–13 99... | 13 | 9 | 8 | 9 | 1 | ...... | ...... | 1 | ...... | 1 | 60 | 116 | 70.8 | 95.5 | ...13 00–13 99 |
| 14 00–14 99... | 7 | 7 | 13 | 4 | 1 | 2 | ...... | ...... | ...... | 1 | 51 | 83 | 76.5 | 97.4 | ...14 00–14 99 |
| 15 00–15 99... | 10 | 3 | 4 | 5 | 1 | 1 | ...... | ...... | ...... | ...... | 61 | 58 | 83.2 | 98.6 | ...15 00–15 99 |
| 16 00–17 99... | 9 | 3 | 5 | ...... | ...... | 1 | ...... | ...... | ...... | ...... | 51 | 37 | 88.8 | 99.5 | ...16 00–17 99 |
| 18 00–19 99... | 6 | ...... | 3 | 4 | 4 | ...... | ...... | ...... | ...... | ...... | 44 | 13 | 93.8 | 99.9 | ...18 00–19 99 |
| 20 00–24 99... | 3 | ...... | 4 | 1 | ...... | ...... | ...... | ...... | ...... | ...... | 40 | 4 | 98.2 | 100.0 | ...20 00–24 99 |
| 25 00–29 99... | .... | ...... | 1 | ...... | 1 | ...... | ...... | ...... | ...... | ...... | 12 | ...... | 99.5 | ...... | ...25 00–29 99 |
| 30 00–34 99... | 3 | ...... | .... | ...... | ...... | ...... | ...... | ...... | ...... | ...... | 4 | ...... | 99.9 | ...... | ...30 00–34 99 |
| 35 00–39 99... | .... | ...... | 1 | ...... | ...... | ...... | ...... | ...... | ...... | ...... | 1 | ...... | 100.0 | ...... | ...35 00–39 99 |
| Not reported... | .... | ...... | .... | ...... | ...... | ...... | ...... | ...... | ...... | ...... | 1 | 1 | ...... | ...... | ...Not reported |
| Total..... | 96 | 267 | 81 | 266 | 17 | 74 | 3 | 17 | 5 | 49 | 903 | 4,362 | ...... | ...... | .....Total |

190. TABLE B, a

NEW YORK STATE EXCLUSIVE OF NEW YORK CITY
THE MEN'S SHIRT INDUSTRY — FACTORY WORKERS
NUMBER AND PER CENT. OF EMPLOYEES CLASSIFIED ACCORDING TO ACTUAL WEEKLY EARNINGS BY OCCUPATION AND SEX

| ACTUAL WEEKLY EARNINGS IN DOLLARS | OCCUPATION | | | | | | | | | | | | | ACTUAL WEEKLY EARNINGS IN DOLLARS |
|---|---|---|---|---|---|---|---|---|---|---|---|---|---|---|
| | MARKERS | CUTTERS | | TRIMMERS | | CUTTERS' HELPERS | | FOREMEN AND FOREWOMEN | | OPERATORS | | FLOOR WORK | | |
| | Male | Male | Female | Male | Female | Male | Female | Male | Female | Male | Female | Male | Female | |
| Less than $3 00 | ...... | 3 | ...... | ...... | ...... | ...... | 1 | ...... | 1 | 1 | 191 | ...... | 26 | Less than $3 00 |
| $3 00-$3 49 | ...... | 1 | 1 | ...... | ...... | ...... | 2 | ...... | 1 | ...... | 99 | ...... | 13 | $3 00- 3 49 |
| 3 50- 3 99 | ...... | ...... | ...... | ...... | ...... | 3 | ...... | ...... | 1 | ...... | 103 | 2 | 9 | 3 50- 3 99 |
| 4 00- 4 49 | ...... | 2 | ...... | ...... | 1 | 3 | 2 | ...... | ...... | ...... | 143 | 1 | 19 | 4 00- 4 49 |
| 4 50- 4 99 | ...... | 2 | ...... | ...... | ...... | 3 | 2 | ...... | ...... | ...... | 141 | ...... | 16 | 4 50- 4 99 |
| 5 00- 5 49 | ...... | 4 | ...... | ...... | ...... | 8 | ...... | ...... | 1 | ...... | 179 | 2 | 28 | 5 00- 5 49 |
| 5 50- 5 99 | ...... | 3 | ...... | 1 | ...... | 4 | 4 | ...... | 2 | 3 | 184 | ...... | 9 | 5 50- 5 99 |
| 6 00- 6 49 | ...... | 7 | ...... | 2 | 1 | 3 | 2 | ...... | 5 | ...... | 194 | ...... | 13 | 6 00- 6 49 |
| 6 50- 6 99 | ...... | ...... | ...... | ...... | ...... | 2 | 1 | ...... | 1 | 2 | 133 | ...... | 6 | 6 50- 6 99 |
| 7 00- 7 49 | ...... | 3 | ...... | 1 | 1 | 1 | ...... | ...... | 5 | ...... | 182 | 1 | 4 | 7 00- 7 49 |
| 7 50- 7 99 | ...... | 6 | ...... | 1 | ...... | ...... | 2 | ...... | 4 | ...... | 134 | ...... | 6 | 7 50- 7 99 |
| 8 00- 8 99 | ...... | 12 | ...... | 3 | ...... | 1 | 1 | ...... | 11 | ...... | 304 | 1 | 11 | 8 00- 8 99 |
| 9 00- 9 99 | ...... | 4 | ...... | ...... | 1 | ...... | 1 | ...... | 15 | 2 | 236 | ...... | 9 | 9 00- 9 99 |
| 10 00-10 99 | ...... | 15 | ...... | 2 | ...... | 2 | ...... | 1 | 8 | 3 | 204 | ...... | 7 | 10 00-10 99 |
| 11 00-11 99 | ...... | 18 | ...... | ...... | ...... | ...... | ...... | 2 | 6 | 3 | 125 | ...... | 3 | 11 00-11 99 |
| 12 00-12 99 | ...... | 17 | ...... | 1 | ...... | ...... | ...... | 4 | 12 | 2 | 100 | ...... | 1 | 12 00-12 99 |
| 13 00-13 99 | ...... | 14 | ...... | 1 | 1 | ...... | ...... | 2 | 5 | 1 | 61 | 1 | ...... | 13 00-13 99 |
| 14 00-14 99 | ...... | 13 | ...... | ...... | ...... | ...... | ...... | 1 | 2 | ...... | 59 | ...... | 1 | 14 00-14 99 |
| 15 00-15 99 | ...... | 16 | ...... | ...... | ...... | ...... | ...... | 7 | 10 | ...... | 20 | 3 | ...... | 15 00-15 99 |
| 16 00-17 99 | ...... | 16 | ...... | ...... | ...... | ...... | ...... | 4 | 1 | ...... | 29 | 1 | ...... | 16 00-17 99 |
| 18 00-19 99 | ...... | 11 | ...... | ...... | ...... | ...... | ...... | 11 | 4 | ...... | 7 | ...... | ...... | 18 00-19 99 |
| 20 00-24 99 | 1 | 17 | ...... | ...... | ...... | ...... | ...... | 15 | 3 | 1 | 1 | ...... | ...... | 20 00-24 99 |
| 25 00-29 99 | ...... | 4 | ...... | ...... | ...... | ...... | ...... | 7 | ...... | ...... | ...... | ...... | ...... | 25 00-29 99 |
| 30 00-34 99 | ...... | ...... | ...... | ...... | ...... | ...... | ...... | 4 | ...... | ...... | ...... | ...... | ...... | 30 00-34 99 |
| 35 00-39 99 | ...... | ...... | ...... | ...... | ...... | ...... | ...... | 1 | ...... | ...... | ...... | ...... | ...... | 35 00-39 99 |
| Total | 1 | 188 | 1 | 12 | 5 | 30 | 18 | 59 | 98 | 18 | 2,829 | 12 | 181 | Total |

190. TABLE B, a — (*concluded*)

NEW YORK STATE EXCLUSIVE OF NEW YORK CITY

**THE MEN'S SHIRT INDUSTRY — FACTORY WORKERS**

NUMBER AND PER CENT OF EMPLOYEES CLASSIFIED ACCORDING TO ACTUAL WEEKLY EARNINGS BY OCCUPATION AND SEX

| ACTUAL WEEKLY EARNINGS IN DOLLARS | OCCUPATION: LAUNDRY HELPERS | | STARCHERS AND DAMPENERS | | IRONERS AND PRESSERS | | EXAMINERS | | FOLDERS | | PACKERS | | TOTAL | | CUMULATIVE PER CENT OF TOTAL | | ACTUAL WEEKLY EARNINGS IN DOLLARS |
|---|---|---|---|---|---|---|---|---|---|---|---|---|---|---|---|---|---|
| | Male | Female | Male | Female | Male | Female | Male | Female | Male | Female | Male | Female | Male | Female | Male | Female | |
| Less than $3 00 | .... | 3 | .... | 21 | 8 | 7 | .... | 17 | .... | 7 | 2 | 1 | 14 | 275 | 1.30 | 6.30 | Less than $3 00 |
| $3 00–$3 49... | .... | ...... | .... | 6 | 2 | 3 | .... | 4 | .... | 6 | .... | ..... | 3 | 135 | 1.90 | 9.40 | ...$3 00– 3 49 |
| 3 50– 3 99... | .... | 1 | .... | 8 | 16 | 4 | .... | 23 | 4 | 3 | .... | 2 | 25 | 154 | 4.70 | 12.90 | ... 3 50– 3 99 |
| 4 00– 4 49... | 2 | 1 | .... | 4 | 9 | 7 | .... | 21 | 2 | 11 | 1 | 2 | 20 | 211 | 6.90 | 17.80 | ... 4 00– 4 49 |
| 4 50– 4 99... | 3 | 5 | .... | 5 | 11 | 8 | 1 | 35 | .... | 10 | 1 | 5 | 21 | 227 | 9.20 | 23.40 | ... 4 50– 4 99 |
| 5 00– 5 49... | 1 | 3 | .... | 3 | 33 | 16 | 1 | 70 | 4 | 6 | 1 | 4 | 54 | 310 | 15.20 | 30.10 | ... 5 00– 5 49 |
| 5 50– 5 99... | 1 | 6 | .... | 14 | 6 | 18 | .... | 49 | 3 | 14 | .... | 4 | 21 | 304 | 17.50 | 37.00 | ... 5 50– 5 99 |
| 6 00– 6 49... | 1 | 6 | .... | 8 | 28 | 15 | 2 | 70 | 4 | 12 | 3 | 5 | 50 | 331 | 23.10 | 44.60 | ... 6 00– 6 49 |
| 6 50– 6 99... | 1 | 2 | .... | 5 | 17 | 19 | .... | 30 | .... | 8 | .... | 2 | 22 | 207 | 25.50 | 44.20 | ... 6 50– 6 99 |
| 7 00– 7 49... | .... | 3 | .... | 11 | 15 | 13 | 2 | 53 | .... | 13 | .... | 5 | 23 | 290 | 28.00 | 56.00 | ... 7 00– 7 49 |
| 7 50– 7 99... | 4 | 5 | .... | 23 | 18 | 20 | 3 | 21 | .... | 7 | .... | ..... | 32 | 222 | 31.60 | 61.10 | ... 7 50– 7 99 |
| 8 00– 8 99... | 1 | 1 | .... | 12 | 68 | 24 | .... | 38 | 1 | 13 | 4 | 8 | 91 | 423 | 41.70 | 70.80 | ... 8 00– 8 99 |
| 9 00– 9 99... | 5 | 3 | .... | 8 | 14 | 20 | 2 | 30 | 1 | 11 | 1 | 4 | 29 | 338 | 44.90 | 78.50 | ... 9 00– 9 99 |
| 10 00–10 99... | 3 | 10 | 1 | 8 | 20 | 25 | 2 | 8 | .... | 6 | .... | ..... | 49 | 276 | 50.40 | 84.80 | ...10 00–10 99 |
| 11 00–11 99... | 4 | 3 | .... | 11 | 27 | 28 | 1 | 8 | 1 | 6 | .... | 1 | 56 | 191 | 57.60 | 89.20 | ...11 00–11 99 |
| 12 00–12 99... | .... | ...... | 1 | 2 | 40 | 27 | 3 | 7 | .... | 7 | .... | ..... | 68 | 156 | 64.20 | 92.70 | ...12 00–12 99 |
| 13 00–13 99... | 3 | 1 | .... | 3 | 36 | 37 | 2 | 2 | .... | 5 | .... | 1 | 60 | 116 | 70.80 | 95.50 | ...13 00–13 99 |
| 14 00–14 99... | .... | ...... | .... | 2 | 36 | 6 | 1 | 2 | .... | 11 | .... | ..... | 51 | 83 | 76.50 | 97.40 | ...14 00–14 99 |
| 15 00–15 99... | 2 | ...... | 1 | 12 | 28 | 3 | 4 | ..... | .... | 13 | .... | ..... | 61 | 58 | 83.20 | 98.60 | ...15 00–15 99 |
| 16 00–17 99... | .... | ...... | .... | 1 | 29 | ..... | 1 | 2 | .... | 4 | .... | ..... | 51 | 37 | 88.80 | 99.50 | ...16 00–17 99 |
| 18 00–19 99... | 5 | ...... | .... | ..... | 17 | ..... | .... | 1 | .... | 1 | .... | ..... | 44 | 13 | 93.80 | 99.90 | ...18 00–19 99 |
| 20 00–24 99... | 1 | ...... | .... | ..... | 5 | ..... | .... | ..... | .... | ..... | .... | ..... | 40 | 4 | 98.20 | 100.00 | ...20 00–24 99 |
| 25 00–29 99... | 1 | ...... | .... | ..... | .... | ..... | .... | ..... | .... | ..... | .... | ..... | 12 | ..... | 99.50 | ..... | ...25 00–29 99 |
| 30 00–34 99... | .... | ...... | .... | ..... | .... | ..... | .... | ..... | .... | ..... | .... | ..... | 4 | ..... | 99.90 | ..... | ...30 00–34 99 |
| 35 00–39 99... | .... | ...... | .... | ..... | .... | ..... | .... | ..... | .... | ..... | .... | ..... | 1 | ..... | 100.00 | ..... | ...35 00–39 99 |
| Not reported.. | .... | ...... | .... | ..... | .... | ..... | 1 | 1 | .... | ..... | .... | ..... | 1 | 1 | ..... | ..... | ..Not reported |
| Total..... | 38 | 53 | 3 | 167 | 483 | 300 | 26 | 492 | 20 | 174 | 13 | 44 | 903 | 4,362 | ..... | ..... | .....Total |

191. TABLE XIX, B, a

## NEW YORK STATE EXCLUSIVE OF NEW YORK CITY — EASTERN DIVISION
## THE MEN'S SHIRT INDUSTRY — FACTORY WORKERS

NUMBER AND PER CENT OF EMPLOYEES CLASSIFIED ACCORDING TO AVERAGE ACTUAL WEEKLY EARNINGS BY OCCUPATION AND SEX

| AVERAGE ACTUAL WEEKLY EARNINGS IN DOLLARS | OCCUPATION | | | | | | | | | | | | | | | AVERAGE ACTUAL WEEKLY EARNINGS IN DOLLARS |
|---|---|---|---|---|---|---|---|---|---|---|---|---|---|---|---|---|
| | MARKERS | | CUTTERS | | TRIMMERS | CUTTERS' HELPERS | | FOREMEN AND FOREWOMEN | | OPERATORS | | FLOOR WORK | | LAUNDRY HELPERS | | |
| | Male | Female | Male | Female | Male | Male | Female | Male | Female | Male | Female | Male | Female | Male | Female | |
| Less than $3 00 | .... | ...... | .... | ...... | .... | ...... | ..... | ..... | 1 | ..... | 15 | 1 | 3 | ...... | ...... | Less than $3 00 |
| $3 00–$3 49... | .... | ...... | .... | ...... | .... | 2 | ..... | ..... | ..... | ..... | 16 | ..... | 1 | ...... | ...... | ...$3 00– 3 49 |
| 3 50– 3 99... | .... | ...... | .... | ...... | .... | 1 | ..... | ..... | ..... | ..... | 21 | ..... | 2 | ...... | ...... | ... 3 50– 3 99 |
| 4 00– 4 49... | .... | ...... | 1 | ...... | .... | 3 | 2 | ..... | ..... | ..... | 26 | 1 | 2 | 1 | ...... | ... 4 00– 4 49 |
| 4 50– 4 99... | .... | ...... | 2 | ...... | .... | 2 | 3 | ..... | ..... | 1 | 45 | ..... | 4 | ...... | ...... | ... 4 50– 4 99 |
| 5 00– 5 49... | .... | ...... | 3 | ...... | .... | ...... | 1 | ..... | 1 | ..... | 45 | 1 | 2 | ...... | ...... | ... 5 00– 5 49 |
| 5 50– 5 99... | .... | 1 | .... | ...... | .... | 1 | ..... | ..... | ..... | ..... | 59 | 1 | 3 | ...... | 1 | ... 5 50– 5 99 |
| 6 00– 6 49... | .... | ...... | .... | ...... | 2 | 3 | 1 | ..... | 1 | ..... | 75 | ..... | 2 | ...... | ...... | ... 6 00– 6 49 |
| 6 50– 6 99... | .... | ...... | 1 | ...... | .... | 2 | 1 | ..... | ..... | ..... | 85 | ..... | 2 | ...... | ...... | ... 6 50– 6 99 |
| 7 00– 7 49... | .... | ...... | .... | ...... | .... | ...... | ..... | ..... | 3 | ..... | 75 | ..... | 1 | ...... | ...... | ... 7 00– 7 49 |
| 7 50– 7 99... | .... | ...... | 3 | ...... | .... | 1 | ..... | ..... | 3 | ..... | 72 | ..... | 1 | ...... | ...... | ... 7 50– 7 99 |
| 8 00– 8 99... | .... | ...... | 3 | ...... | 1 | 2 | 1 | ..... | 10 | ..... | 141 | ..... | ...... | 1 | ...... | ... 8 00– 8 99 |
| 9 00– 9 99... | .... | ...... | 4 | ...... | 1 | ...... | ..... | ..... | 5 | ..... | 94 | ..... | 1 | 2 | ...... | ... 9 00– 9 99 |
| 10 00–10 99... | .... | ...... | 4 | ...... | .... | ...... | ..... | 1 | 4 | 2 | 83 | ..... | ...... | ...... | ...... | ...10 00–10 99 |
| 11 00–11 99... | .... | ...... | 7 | ...... | 1 | ...... | ..... | 1 | 1 | 1 | 51 | ..... | ...... | ...... | ...... | ...11 00–11 99 |
| 12 00–12 99... | .... | ...... | 11 | ...... | .... | ...... | ..... | 1 | 1 | ..... | 36 | ..... | 1 | ...... | ...... | ...12 00–12 99 |
| 13 00–13 99... | .... | ...... | 11 | ...... | 1 | ...... | ..... | 1 | 1 | ..... | 25 | ..... | ...... | ...... | ...... | ...13 00–13 99 |
| 14 00–14 99... | .... | ...... | 15 | ...... | .... | ...... | ..... | ..... | 2 | ..... | 15 | ..... | ...... | ...... | ...... | ...14 00–14 99 |
| 15 00–15 99... | .... | ...... | 8 | ...... | 1 | ...... | ..... | ..... | 1 | ..... | 8 | ..... | ...... | ...... | ...... | ...15 00–15 99 |
| 16 00–17 99... | .... | ...... | 12 | ...... | .... | ...... | 1 | 2 | 2 | ..... | 13 | ..... | ...... | ...... | ...... | ...16 00–17 99 |
| 18 00–19 99... | .... | ...... | 10 | 1 | .... | ...... | ..... | ..... | ..... | ..... | 2 | ..... | ...... | 1 | ...... | ...18 00–19 99 |
| 20 00–24 99... | 1 | ...... | 4 | ...... | .... | ...... | ..... | 3 | 3 | 1 | 4 | ..... | ...... | 1 | ...... | ...20 00–24 99 |
| 25 00–29 99... | .... | ...... | 1 | ...... | .... | ...... | ..... | 2 | ..... | ..... | ..... | ..... | ...... | ...... | ...... | ...25 00–29 99 |
| 30 00–34 99... | 1 | ...... | .... | ...... | .... | ...... | ..... | ..... | ..... | 1 | ..... | ..... | ...... | ...... | ...... | ...30 00–34 99 |
| 35 00–39 99... | .... | ...... | .... | ...... | .... | ...... | ..... | 1 | ..... | ..... | ..... | ..... | ...... | ...... | ...... | ...35 00–39 99 |
| Not reported.. | .... | ...... | .... | ...... | .... | ...... | ..... | ..... | ..... | ..... | ..... | ..... | ...... | ...... | ...... | ..Not reported |
| Total..... | 2 | 1 | 100 | 1 | 7 | 17 | 10 | 12 | 39 | 6 | 1,006 | 4 | 25 | 6 | 1 | .....Total |

NEW YORK STATE EXCLUSIVE OF NEW YORK CITY — EASTERN DIVISION

191. TABLE XIX, B, a — (*concluded*) **THE MEN'S SHIRT INDUSTRY — FACTORY WORKERS**

Number and Per Cent of Employees Classified According to Average Actual Weekly Earnings by Occupation and Sex

| Average Actual Weekly Earnings in Dollars | Occupation — (*Concluded*) | | | | | | | | | | | | Average Actual Weekly Earnings in Dollars |
|---|---|---|---|---|---|---|---|---|---|---|---|---|---|
| | Starchers and Dampeners | Ironers and Pressers | | Examiners | | Folders | Packers | | Total | | Cumulative per cent of total | | |
| | Female | Male | Female | Male | Female | Female | Male | Female | Male | Female | Male | Female | |
| Less than $3 00 | ........ | ....... | ....... | ....... | 4 | ....... | ....... | ....... | 1 | 23 | .35 | 1.75 | Less than $3 00 |
| $3 00–$3 49... | 1 | ....... | ....... | ....... | 5 | ....... | ....... | 1 | 2 | 24 | 11.06 | 3.60 | ...$3 00– 3 49 |
| 3 50– 3 99... | 1 | 1 | ....... | 1 | 7 | ....... | 1 | 2 | 4 | 33 | 2.50 | 6.10 | ... 3 50– 3 99 |
| 4 00– 4 49... | ........ | ....... | ....... | ....... | 7 | ....... | 1 | 2 | 7 | 39 | 4.90 | 9.00 | ... 4 00– 4 49 |
| 4 50– 4 99... | 1 | ....... | ....... | 1 | 29 | 1 | 1 | 3 | 7 | 86 | 7.40 | 15.50 | ... 4 50– 4 99 |
| 5 00– 5 49... | 1 | ....... | ....... | ....... | 23 | ....... | ....... | 4 | 4 | 77 | 8.80 | 21.40 | ... 5 00– 5 49 |
| 5 50– 5 99... | ........ | ....... | ....... | 1 | 15 | ....... | ....... | 1 | 3 | 80 | 9.90 | 27.40 | ... 5 50– 5 99 |
| 6 00– 6 49... | 1 | 1 | 2 | ....... | 7 | ....... | 1 | 3 | 7 | 92 | 12.40 | 34.40 | ... 6 00– 6 49 |
| 6 50– 6 99... | 4 | 1 | ....... | ....... | 13 | ....... | ....... | 2 | 4 | 107 | 13.80 | 42.50 | ... 6 50– 6 99 |
| 7 00– 7 49... | 6 | 2 | 1 | 1 | 9 | ....... | ....... | ....... | 3 | 95 | 18.80 | 49.70 | ... 7 00– 7 49 |
| 7 50– 7 99... | 1 | 3 | 1 | ....... | 9 | ....... | ....... | 2 | 7 | 89 | 17.30 | 57.20 | ... 7 50– 7 99 |
| 8 00– 8 99... | 7 | 3 | 2 | ....... | 10 | ....... | 1 | 3 | 11 | 174 | 21.20 | 69.60 | ... 8 00– 8 99 |
| 9 00– 9 99... | 3 | 10 | 1 | ....... | 9 | ....... | ....... | ....... | 17 | 113 | 27.20 | 78.00 | ... 9 00– 9 99 |
| 10 00–10 99... | 4 | 11 | 3 | 1 | 7 | ....... | ....... | 1 | 19 | 102 | 34.00 | 85.80 | ...10 00–10 99 |
| 11 00–11 99... | 2 | 16 | 1 | ....... | 5 | ....... | ....... | 1 | 26 | 61 | 43.20 | 90.60 | ...11 00–11 99 |
| 12 00–12 99... | 1 | 13 | 1 | ....... | ....... | ....... | ....... | 1 | 25 | 41 | 52.00 | 93.80 | ...12 00–12 99 |
| 13 00–13 99... | ........ | 11 | 2 | 1 | 1 | ....... | ....... | ....... | 25 | 29 | 60.90 | 95.80 | ...13 00–13 99 |
| 14 00–14 99... | ........ | 16 | 4 | 1 | 1 | ....... | ....... | ....... | 32 | 22 | 73.50 | 97.60 | ...14 00–14 99 |
| 15 00–15 99... | ........ | 4 | ....... | 1 | ....... | ....... | ....... | ....... | 14 | 9 | 77.00 | 98.00 | ...15 00–15 99 |
| 16 00–17 99... | ........ | 16 | ....... | 1 | ....... | ....... | ....... | ....... | 31 | 16 | 88.00 | 99.30 | ...16 00–17 99 |
| 18 00–19 99.. | ........ | 6 | ....... | ....... | ....... | ....... | ....... | ....... | 17 | 3 | 94.00 | 99.50 | ...18 00–19 99 |
| 20 00–24 99... | ........ | 1 | ....... | ....... | ....... | ....... | ....... | ....... | 11 | 7 | 98.00 | 100.00 | ...20 00–24 99 |
| 25 00–29 99... | ........ | ....... | ....... | ....... | ....... | ....... | ....... | ....... | 3 | ....... | 99.00 | ....... | ...25 00–29 99 |
| 30 00–34 99... | ........ | ....... | ....... | ....... | ....... | ....... | ....... | ....... | 2 | ....... | 99.60 | ....... | ...30 00–34 99 |
| 35 00–39 99... | ........ | ....... | ....... | ....... | ....... | ....... | ....... | ....... | 1 | ....... | 100.00 | ....... | ...35 00–39 99 |
| Total..... | 33 | 115 | 18 | 9 | 161 | 1 | 5 | 26 | 283 | 1,322 | ....... | ....... | .....Total |

192. TABLE XX, B, a

## NEW YORK STATE EXCLUSIVE OF NEW YORK CITY — EASTERN DIVISION

### THE MEN'S SHIRT INDUSTRY — FACTORY WORKERS

NUMBER AND PER CENT OF ALL EMPLOYEES, WORKING 43 WEEKS OR MORE, CLASSIFIED ACCORDING TO ACTUAL ANNUAL EARNINGS BY OCCUPATION AND SEX

| ACTUAL ANNUAL EARNINGS IN DOLLARS | OCCUPATION | | | | | | | | | | | | | | ACTUAL ANNUAL EARNINGS IN DOLLARS |
|---|---|---|---|---|---|---|---|---|---|---|---|---|---|---|---|
| | MARKERS | CUTTERS | | TRIMMERS | CUTTERS' HELPERS | | FOREMEN AND FOREWOMEN | | OPERATORS | | FLOOR WORK | | LAUNDRY HELPERS | | |
| | Male | Male | Female | Male | Male | Female | Male | Female | Male | Female | Male | Female | Male | Female | |
| Less than $2 00 | .... | .... | ...... | ...... | 1 | ...... | ...... | ...... | ...... | 23 | 1 | 5 | 1 | ...... | Less than $2 00 |
| $2 00–$2 49... | .... | 2 | ...... | ...... | 1 | 2 | ...... | ...... | 1 | 23 | 1 | 1 | ...... | ...... | ...$2 00– 2 49 |
| 2 50– 2 99... | .... | 1 | ...... | 1 | ...... | 1 | ...... | ...... | ...... | 60 | ...... | 6 | ...... | 1 | ....2 50– 2 99 |
| 3 00– 3 49... | .... | 1 | ...... | ...... | 3 | ...... | ...... | 1 | ...... | 101 | ...... | 3 | ...... | ...... | ....3 00– 3 49 |
| 3 50– 3 99... | .... | .... | ...... | ...... | ...... | ...... | ...... | 5 | ...... | 112 | ...... | 2 | 1 | ...... | ....3 50– 3 99 |
| 4 00– 4 49... | .... | 6 | ...... | ...... | 1 | 1 | ...... | 10 | ...... | 100 | ...... | 1 | 1 | ...... | ....4 00– 4 49 |
| 4 50– 4 99... | .... | .... | ...... | ...... | ...... | ...... | ...... | 5 | ...... | 69 | ...... | ...... | ...... | ...... | ....4 50– 4 99 |
| 5 00– 5 49... | .... | 4 | ...... | 1 | ...... | ...... | 1 | 3 | ...... | 46 | ...... | ...... | ...... | ...... | ....5 00– 5 49 |
| 5 50– 5 99... | .... | 3 | ...... | ...... | ...... | ...... | ...... | 2 | 1 | 47 | ...... | 1 | ...... | ...... | ....5 50– 5 99 |
| 6 00– 6 49... | .... | 6 | ...... | 1 | ...... | ...... | 2 | 2 | ...... | 22 | ...... | 1 | ...... | ...... | ....6 00– 6 49 |
| 6 50– 6 99... | .... | 13 | ...... | ...... | ...... | ...... | 1 | 1 | ...... | 9 | ...... | ...... | ...... | ...... | ....6 50– 6 99 |
| 7 00– 7 49... | .... | 14 | ...... | ...... | ...... | ...... | ...... | 1 | ...... | 6 | ...... | ...... | ...... | ...... | ....7 00– 7 49 |
| 7 50– 7 99... | .... | 6 | ...... | 1 | ...... | ...... | ...... | ...... | ...... | 3 | ...... | ...... | ...... | ...... | ....7 50– 7 99 |
| 8 00– 8 99... | .... | 12 | 1 | ...... | ...... | ...... | 2 | ...... | ...... | 1 | ...... | ...... | ...... | ...... | ....8 00– 8 99 |
| 9 00– 9 99... | .... | 7 | ...... | ...... | ...... | ...... | ...... | 2 | ...... | ...... | ...... | ...... | 1 | ...... | ....9 00– 9 99 |
| 10 00–10 99... | .... | 1 | ...... | ...... | ...... | ...... | 2 | 1 | 1 | ...... | ...... | ...... | ...... | ...... | ...10 00–10 99 |
| 11 00–11 99... | 1 | 2 | ...... | ...... | ...... | ...... | ...... | ...... | ...... | ...... | ...... | ...... | 1 | ...... | ...11 00–11 99 |
| 12 00–12 99... | .... | .... | ...... | ...... | ...... | ...... | 1 | ...... | ...... | ...... | ...... | ...... | ...... | ...... | ...12 00–12 99 |
| 15 00–15 99... | 1 | .... | ...... | ...... | ...... | ...... | ...... | ...... | ...... | ...... | ...... | ...... | ...... | ...... | ...15 00–15 99 |
| Total..... | 2 | 78 | 1 | 4 | 6 | 4 | 9 | 33 | 3 | 622 | 2 | 20 | 5 | 1 | .....Total |

NEW YORK STATE EXCLUSIVE OF NEW YORK CITY — EASTERN DIVISION

192. TABLE XX, B, a — (*concluded*) **THE MEN'S SHIRT INDUSTRY — FACTORY WORKERS**

NUMBER AND PER CENT OF ALL EMPLOYEES, WORKING 43 WEEKS OR MORE, CLASSIFIED ACCORDING TO ACTUAL ANNUAL EARNINGS BY OCCUPATION AND SEX

| ACTUAL ANNUAL EARNINGS IN DOLLARS | OCCUPATION (*concluded*) | | | | | | | | | | | | ACTUAL ANNUAL EARNINGS IN DOLLARS |
|---|---|---|---|---|---|---|---|---|---|---|---|---|---|
| | STARCHERS AND DAMPENERS | IRONERS AND PRESSERS | | EXAMINERS | | FOLDERS | PACKERS | | TOTAL | | CUMULATIVE PER CENT OF TOTAL | | |
| | Female | Male | Female | Male | Female | Female | Male | Female | Male | Female | Male | Female | |
| Less than $2 00. | 1 | ....... | ....... | ....... | 7 | ....... | ....... | 1 | 3 | 37 | 1.50 | 4.40 | Less than $2 00 |
| $2 00–$2 49.... | ....... | ....... | ....... | ....... | 17 | 1 | ....... | 4 | 5 | 48 | 4.20 | 10.20 | ...$2 00– 2 49 |
| 2 50– 2 99.... | 1 | ....... | ....... | ....... | 26 | ....... | ....... | 2 | 2 | 97 | 5.20 | 21.70 | ....2 50– 2 99 |
| 3 00– 3 49.... | 2 | ....... | 1 | ....... | 18 | ....... | 1 | 3 | 5 | 129 | 7.80 | 37.20 | ....3 00– 3 49 |
| 3 50– 3 99.... | 6 | ....... | 2 | 1 | 14 | ....... | ....... | 1 | 2 | 142 | 8.80 | 54.00 | ....3 50– 3 99 |
| 4 00– 4 49.... | 6 | 3 | ....... | ....... | 8 | ....... | 1 | 4 | 12 | 130 | 15.00 | 69.50 | ....4 00– 4 49 |
| 4 50– 4 99.... | ....... | 4 | 2 | ....... | 5 | ....... | ....... | ....... | 4 | 81 | 17.00 | 79.20 | ....4 50– 4 99 |
| 5 00– 5 49.... | 3 | 6 | 1 | 1 | 8 | ....... | ....... | 1 | 13 | 62 | 24.00 | 86.60 | ....5 00– 5 49 |
| 5 50– 5 99.... | ....... | 7 | 1 | ....... | 2 | ....... | ....... | ....... | 11 | 53 | 29.50 | 92.80 | ....5 50– 5 99 |
| 6 00– 6 49.... | 1 | 10 | 1 | ....... | ....... | ....... | ....... | 1 | 19 | 28 | 39.50 | 96.50 | ....6 00– 6 49 |
| 6 50– 6 99.... | ....... | 10 | 1 | 1 | 1 | ....... | ....... | ....... | 25 | 12 | 52.40 | 97.60 | ....6 50– 6 99 |
| 7 00– 7 49.... | ....... | 9 | 4 | 1 | ....... | ....... | ....... | ....... | 24 | 11 | 64.80 | 99.00 | ....7 00– 7 49 |
| 7 50– 7 99.... | ....... | 7 | ....... | 1 | ....... | ....... | ....... | ....... | 15 | 3 | 72.50 | 99.40 | ....7 50– 7 99 |
| 8 00– 8 99.... | ....... | 11 | ....... | 1 | ....... | ....... | ....... | ....... | 26 | 2 | 86.00 | 99.70 | ....8 00– 8 99 |
| 9 00– 9 99.... | ....... | 5 | ....... | ....... | ....... | ....... | ....... | ....... | 13 | 2 | 92.70 | 99.90 | ....9 00– 9 99 |
| 10 00–10 99.... | ....... | 3 | ....... | ....... | ....... | ....... | ....... | ....... | 7 | 1 | 96.40 | 100.00 | ...10 00–10 99 |
| 11 00–11 99.... | ....... | 1 | ....... | ....... | ....... | ....... | ....... | ....... | 5 | ....... | 99.00 | ....... | ...11 00–11 99 |
| 12 00–12 99.... | ....... | ....... | ....... | ....... | ....... | ....... | ....... | ....... | 1 | ....... | 99.50 | ....... | ...12 00–12 99 |
| 15 00–15 99.... | ....... | ....... | ....... | ....... | ....... | ....... | ....... | ....... | 1 | ....... | 100.00 | ....... | ...15 00–15 99 |
| Total...... | 20 | 76 | 13 | 6 | 106 | 1 | 2 | 17 | 193 | 838 | ....... | ....... | .....Total |

193. TABLE V, C, a

NEW YORK STATE EXCLUSIVE OF NEW YORK CITY
**THE PAPER BOX INDUSTRY — FACTORY WORKERS**
NUMBER AND PER CENT OF EMPLOYEES EARNING SPECIFIED WEEKLY RATES BY AGE GROUPS AND SEX

| WEEKLY RATES IN DOLLARS | AGE GROUPS IN YEARS | | | | | | | | | | | | | | WEEKLY RATES IN DOLLARS |
|---|---|---|---|---|---|---|---|---|---|---|---|---|---|---|---|
| | 14–15 | | 16–17 | | 18–20 | | 21–24 | | 25–29 | | 30–34 | | 35–39 | | |
| | Male | Female | Male | Female | Male | Female | Male | Female | Male | Female | Male | Female | Male | Female | |
| Less than $3 00 | .... | 5 | .... | ...... | ...... | ...... | ...... | ...... | ...... | ...... | ...... | ...... | ...... | ...... | Less than $3 00 |
| $3 00–$3 49... | 1 | 8 | 1 | 5 | ...... | ...... | ...... | ...... | ...... | ...... | ...... | ...... | ...... | ...... | ...$3 00– 3 49 |
| 3 50– 3 99... | 1 | 19 | 1 | 6 | ...... | 1 | ...... | ...... | ...... | ...... | ...... | ...... | ...... | ...... | ...3 50– 3 99 |
| 4 00– 4 49... | 6 | 3 | 3 | 15 | ...... | 6 | ...... | 1 | ...... | ...... | ...... | ...... | ...... | 1 | ...4 00– 4 49 |
| 4 50– 4 99... | 4 | 9 | 3 | 10 | 1 | 5 | ...... | 2 | ...... | ...... | ...... | ...... | ...... | ...... | ...4 50– 4 99 |
| 5 00– 5 49... | 2 | 3 | 5 | 31 | ...... | 27 | ...... | 10 | ...... | 5 | ...... | 3 | ...... | ...... | ...5 00– 5 49 |
| 5 50– 5 99... | .... | 1 | 4 | 4 | ...... | 10 | ...... | 5 | ...... | 2 | ...... | 1 | ...... | ...... | ...5 50– 5 99 |
| 6 00– 6 49... | .... | ...... | 6 | 25 | 2 | 40 | ...... | 34 | ...... | 5 | ...... | 1 | ...... | 3 | ...6 00– 6 49 |
| 6 50– 6 99... | .... | ...... | .... | 8 | 1 | 7 | ...... | 2 | ...... | 2 | ...... | 2 | ...... | 1 | ...6 50– 6 99 |
| 7 00– 7 49... | .... | ...... | 5 | 4 | 7 | 21 | ...... | 23 | ...... | 10 | 1 | 5 | ...... | 2 | ...7 00– 7 49 |
| 7 50– 7 99... | .... | ...... | 1 | 2 | 6 | 6 | 3 | 7 | 1 | 4 | ...... | 2 | ...... | ...... | ...7 50– 7 99 |
| 8 00– 8 99... | .... | 1 | 6 | 2 | 4 | 7 | 4 | 20 | 2 | 11 | ...... | 6 | ...... | 5 | ...8 00– 8 99 |
| 9 00– 9 99... | .... | ...... | 1 | ...... | 12 | 3 | 10 | 16 | 4 | 6 | 6 | 4 | 3 | 1 | ...9 00– 9 99 |
| 10 00–10 99... | .... | ...... | 1 | 1 | 8 | 1 | 13 | 7 | 4 | 9 | 3 | 5 | 2 | 1 | ...10 00–10 99 |
| 11 00–11 99... | .... | ...... | .... | ...... | 2 | ...... | 5 | 1 | 3 | 2 | 2 | 1 | ...... | ...... | ...11 00–11 99 |
| 12 00–12 99... | .... | ...... | .... | ...... | 6 | ...... | 17 | 2 | 6 | 2 | 4 | 2 | 4 | 1 | ...12 00–12 99 |
| 13 00–13 99... | .... | ...... | .... | ...... | ...... | ...... | 7 | ...... | 9 | ...... | 3 | ...... | ...... | 1 | ...13 00–13 99 |
| 14 00–14 99... | .... | ...... | .... | ...... | ...... | ...... | 3 | ...... | 3 | ...... | 3 | 1 | 1 | ...... | ...14 00–14 99 |
| 15 00–15 99... | .... | ...... | .... | ...... | 1 | ...... | 6 | ...... | 8 | ...... | 7 | ...... | 4 | ...... | ...15 00–15 99 |
| 16 00–17 99... | .... | ...... | .... | ...... | ...... | ...... | 5 | ...... | 10 | ...... | 3 | 1 | 4 | ...... | ...16 00–17 99 |
| 18 00–19 99... | .... | ...... | .... | ...... | ...... | ...... | ...... | ...... | 5 | ...... | 6 | 1 | 3 | ...... | ...18 00–19 99 |
| 20 00–24 99... | .... | ...... | .... | ...... | ...... | ...... | ...... | ...... | 1 | ...... | 10 | ...... | 2 | ...... | ...20 00–24 99 |
| 25 00–29 99... | .... | ...... | .... | ...... | ...... | ...... | ...... | ...... | 2 | ...... | 1 | ...... | ...... | 1 | ...25 00–29 99 |
| 30 00–34 99... | .... | ...... | .... | ...... | ...... | ...... | ...... | ...... | ...... | ...... | 2 | ...... | 1 | ...... | ...30 00–34 99 |
| Not reported... | 12 | 16 | 16 | 37 | 34 | 41 | 28 | 27 | 24 | 19 | 12 | 9 | 13 | 8 | ...Not reported |
| Total..... | 26 | 65 | 53 | 150 | 84 | 175 | 101 | 157 | 82 | 77 | 63 | 44 | 37 | 25 | .....Total |

193. TABLE V, C, a — (*concluded*)

NEW YORK STATE EXCLUSIVE OF NEW YORK CITY

**THE PAPER BOX INDUSTRY — FACTORY WORKERS**

NUMBER AND PER CENT OF EMPLOYEES EARNING SPECIFIED WEEKLY RATES BY AGE GROUPS AND SEX

| WEEKLY RATES IN DOLLARS | AGE GROUPS IN YEARS (*concluded*) | | | | | | | | | | | | | | WEEKLY RATES IN DOLLARS |
|---|---|---|---|---|---|---|---|---|---|---|---|---|---|---|---|
| | 40–44 | | 45–54 | | 55–64 | | 65 AND OVER | | NOT REPORTED | | TOTAL | | CUMULATIVE PER CENT OF TOTAL | | |
| | Male | Female | Male | Female | Male | Female | Male | Female | Male | Female | Male | Female | Male | Female | |
| Less than $3 00 | ... | ... | ... | ... | ... | ... | ... | ... | ... | ... | ... | 5 | ... | .90 | Less than $3 00 |
| $3 00–$3 49... | ... | ... | ... | ... | ... | ... | ... | ... | ... | ... | 2 | 13 | .50 | 3.10 | ...$3 00– 3 49 |
| 3 50– 3 99... | ... | ... | ... | ... | ... | ... | ... | ... | ... | ... | 2 | 26 | 1.50 | 7.60 | ....3 50– 3 99 |
| 4 00– 4 49... | ... | ... | ... | ... | ... | ... | ... | ... | ... | ... | 9 | 26 | 3.40 | 12.10 | ....4 00– 4 49 |
| 4 50– 4 99... | ... | ... | ... | 1 | ... | ... | ... | ... | ... | ... | 8 | 27 | 5.50 | 16.70 | ....4 50– 4 99 |
| 5 00– 5 49... | ... | 1 | ... | 1 | ... | 2 | ... | ... | ... | ... | 7 | 83 | 7.30 | 31.10 | ....5 00– 5 49 |
| 5 50– 5 99... | ... | ... | ... | 1 | ... | ... | ... | ... | ... | ... | 4 | 24 | 8.40 | 41.40 | ....5 50– 5 99 |
| 6 00– 6 49... | ... | 3 | ... | 3 | ... | ... | ... | ... | ... | 2 | 8 | 116 | 10.50 | 55.20 | ....6 00– 6 49 |
| 6 50– 6 99... | ... | 1 | ... | ... | ... | ... | ... | ... | ... | ... | 1 | 23 | 10.70 | 59.20 | ....6 50– 6 99 |
| 7 00– 7 49... | ... | ... | ... | 3 | ... | 1 | 1 | ... | ... | 1 | 14 | 70 | 14.40 | 71.30 | ....7 00– 7 49 |
| 7 50– 7 99... | ... | 1 | ... | ... | ... | ... | ... | ... | ... | ... | 11 | 22 | 17.20 | 75.00 | ....7 50– 7 99 |
| 8 00– 8 99... | 2 | 2 | ... | 1 | 1 | 1 | ... | ... | ... | 1 | 19 | 57 | 22.20 | 84.80 | ....8 00– 8 99 |
| 9 00– 9 99... | ... | 6 | 1 | 1 | 2 | ... | 1 | ... | ... | ... | 40 | 37 | 32.60 | 91.40 | ....9 00– 9 99 |
| 10 00–10 99... | 5 | 3 | ... | 4 | 3 | 1 | ... | ... | ... | ... | 39 | 32 | 42.80 | 96.80 | ...10 00–10 99 |
| 11 00–11 99... | 2 | ... | 1 | ... | ... | ... | ... | ... | ... | ... | 15 | 4 | 46.80 | 97.50 | ...11 00–11 99 |
| 12 00–12 99... | 1 | 1 | 1 | ... | 5 | ... | 1 | ... | 1 | ... | 46 | 8 | 58.20 | 99.00 | ...12 00–12 99 |
| 13 00–13 99... | 3 | ... | 4 | ... | 1 | ... | ... | ... | ... | ... | 27 | 1 | 65.80 | 91.10 | ...13 00–13 99 |
| 14 00–14 99... | ... | ... | 1 | ... | 2 | ... | ... | ... | ... | ... | 13 | 1 | 69.30 | 99.30 | ...14 00–14 99 |
| 15 00–15 99... | 3 | ... | 1 | ... | 1 | ... | ... | ... | ... | ... | 31 | ... | 77.40 | ... | ...15 00–15 99 |
| 16 00–17 99... | 5 | 1 | 4 | ... | 2 | ... | ... | ... | ... | ... | 33 | 2 | 86.00 | 99.50 | ...16 00–17 99 |
| 18 00–19 99... | 1 | ... | 2 | ... | ... | ... | ... | ... | ... | ... | 17 | 1 | 90.40 | 99.80 | ...18 00–19 99 |
| 20 00–24 99... | 4 | ... | 6 | ... | 2 | ... | ... | ... | ... | ... | 25 | ... | 96.90 | ... | ...20 00–24 99 |
| 25 00–29 99... | 3 | ... | 1 | ... | 1 | ... | ... | ... | ... | ... | 8 | 1 | 98.00 | 100.00 | ...25 00–29 99 |
| 30 00–34 99... | 1 | ... | ... | ... | ... | ... | ... | ... | ... | ... | 4 | ... | 100.00 | ... | ...30 00–34 99 |
| Not reported... | 6 | 1 | 7 | 11 | 3 | 3 | 3 | 1 | 1 | 2 | 159 | 175 | ... | ... | ...Not reported |
| Total..... | 36 | 20 | 29 | 26 | 23 | 8 | 6 | 1 | 2 | 6 | 542 | 754 | ... | ... | .....Total |

NEW YORK STATE EXCLUSIVE OF NEW YORK CITY
THE PAPER BOX INDUSTRY — FACTORY WORKERS

194. TABLE VIII, C, a — NUMBER AND PER CENT OF EMPLOYEES EARNING SPECIFIED WEEKLY RATES BY OCCUPATION AND SEX

| WEEKLY RATES IN DOLLARS | OCCUPATION | | | | | | | | | | | | WEEKLY RATES IN DOLLARS |
|---|---|---|---|---|---|---|---|---|---|---|---|---|---|
| | FOREMEN AND FOREWOMEN | | CUTTERS | | GLUE MAKERS | SETTERS UP | | GENERAL MACHINE WORK | | GLUE TABLE WORK | TURNERS IN | | |
| | Male | Female | Male | Female | Male | Male | Female | Male | Female | Male | Male | Female | |
| Less than $3 00 | ...... | ...... | ...... | ...... | ...... | ...... | 2 | ...... | ...... | ...... | ...... | ...... | Less than $3 00 |
| $3 00–$3 49 | ...... | ...... | ...... | ...... | ...... | ...... | ...... | ...... | ...... | ...... | 1 | 1 | $3 00– 3 49 |
| 3 50– 3 99 | ...... | ...... | ...... | ...... | ...... | 1 | ...... | ...... | ...... | ...... | 1 | 4 | 3 50– 3 99 |
| 4 00– 4 49 | ...... | ...... | ...... | 1 | ...... | 4 | ...... | ...... | 4 | ...... | ...... | 10 | 4 00– 4 49 |
| 4 50– 4 99 | ...... | ...... | ...... | ...... | ...... | 3 | ...... | ...... | 1 | ...... | ...... | 13 | 4 50– 4 99 |
| 5 00– 5 49 | ...... | ...... | 3 | 1 | ...... | 2 | 4 | ...... | 13 | ...... | ...... | 11 | 5 00– 5 49 |
| 5 50– 5 99 | ...... | ...... | ...... | ...... | ...... | 2 | 1 | ...... | 6 | ...... | ...... | 3 | 5 50– 5 99 |
| 6 00– 6 49 | ...... | ...... | ...... | 3 | ...... | ...... | 5 | 2 | 31 | ...... | ...... | 3 | 6 00– 6 49 |
| 6 50– 6 99 | ...... | ...... | 1 | ...... | ...... | ...... | 3 | ...... | 5 | ...... | ...... | 1 | 6 50– 6 99 |
| 7 00– 7 49 | ...... | 5 | 5 | 2 | ...... | 1 | 4 | 1 | 28 | ...... | ...... | 1 | 7 00– 7 49 |
| 7 50– 7 99 | ...... | 1 | 4 | 2 | ...... | 1 | 1 | 2 | 7 | ...... | ...... | ...... | 7 50– 7 99 |
| 8 00– 8 99 | 1 | 12 | 4 | ...... | ...... | 1 | 6 | 2 | 3 | ...... | ...... | ...... | 8 00– 8 99 |
| 9 00– 9 99 | ...... | 11 | 18 | 1 | ...... | 3 | 3 | 8 | 2 | ...... | ...... | ...... | 9 00– 9 99 |
| 10 00–10 99 | ...... | 10 | 13 | 2 | ...... | 5 | 4 | 4 | 1 | 3 | ...... | ...... | 10 00–10 99 |
| 11 00–11 99 | ...... | 3 | 8 | ...... | ...... | 1 | ...... | 2 | 1 | 1 | ...... | ...... | 11 00–11 99 |
| 12 00–12 99 | 4 | 7 | 26 | ...... | ...... | 2 | ...... | 7 | ...... | ...... | ...... | ...... | 12 00–12 99 |
| 13 00–13 99 | 3 | ...... | 17 | ...... | ...... | 3 | ...... | 1 | ...... | ...... | ...... | ...... | 13 00–13 99 |
| 14 00–14 99 | 3 | 1 | 6 | ...... | 1 | 1 | ...... | 2 | ...... | ...... | ...... | ...... | 14 00–14 99 |
| 15 00–15 99 | 5 | ...... | 15 | ...... | ...... | 1 | ...... | 3 | ...... | ...... | ...... | ...... | 15 00–15 99 |
| 16 00–17 99 | 13 | ...... | 20 | 1 | ...... | ...... | ...... | ...... | ...... | ...... | ...... | ...... | 16 00–17 99 |
| 18 00–19 99 | 12 | 1 | 5 | ...... | ...... | ...... | ...... | ...... | ...... | ...... | ...... | ...... | 18 00–19 99 |
| 20 00–24 99 | 21 | ...... | 4 | ...... | ...... | ...... | ...... | ...... | ...... | ...... | ...... | ...... | 20 00–24 99 |
| 25 00–29 99 | 8 | 1 | ...... | ...... | ...... | ...... | ...... | ...... | ...... | ...... | ...... | ...... | 25 00–29 99 |
| 30 00–34 99 | 4 | ...... | ...... | ...... | ...... | ...... | ...... | ...... | ...... | ...... | ...... | ...... | 30 00–34 99 |
| Not reported | 7 | 1 | 42 | 11 | ...... | 9 | 12 | 35 | 22 | ...... | 1 | 17 | Not reported |
| Total | 81 | 53 | 191 | 24 | 1 | 40 | 45 | 69 | 124 | 4 | 3 | 64 | Total |

194. TABLE VIII, C, a — (*concluded*)

NEW YORK STATE EXCLUSIVE OF NEW YORK CITY

**THE PAPER BOX INDUSTRY — FACTORY WORKERS**

NUMBER AND PER CENT OF EMPLOYEES EARNING SPECIFIED WEEKLY RATES BY OCCUPATION AND SEX

| WEEKLY RATES IN DOLLARS | OCCUPATION (*concluded*) | | | | | | | | | | | | | | WEEKLY RATES IN DOLLARS |
|---|---|---|---|---|---|---|---|---|---|---|---|---|---|---|---|
| | STRIPPERS AND TOP LABELERS | | TABLE WORK | | CLOSING AND TYING | | FLOOR WORK | | NOT REPORTED | | TOTAL | | CUMULATIVE PER CENT OF TOTAL | | |
| | Male | Female | Male | Female | Male | Female | Male | Female | Male | Female | Male | Female | Male | Female | |
| Less than $3 00 | .... | 2 | .... | 1 | ...... | ...... | ...... | ..... | ...... | ...... | ...... | 5 | ...... | .90 | Less than $3 00 |
| $3 00–$3 49... | .... | 6 | .... | 2 | ...... | ...... | 1 | 4 | ...... | ...... | 2 | 13 | .50 | 3.10 | ...$3 00– 3 49 |
| 3 50– 3 99... | .... | 9 | .... | 4 | ...... | 2 | ...... | 7 | ...... | ...... | 2 | 26 | 1.50 | 7.60 | ....3 50– 3 99 |
| 4 00– 4 49... | .... | 3 | .... | 4 | 2 | 1 | 3 | 3 | ...... | ...... | 9 | 26 | 3.40 | 12.10 | ....4 00– 4 49 |
| 4 50– 4 99... | .... | 2 | .... | 4 | 3 | 4 | 2 | 3 | ...... | ...... | 8 | 27 | 5.50 | 16.70 | ....4 50– 4 99 |
| 5 00– 5 49... | .... | 12 | .... | 12 | 1 | 8 | 1 | 22 | ...... | ...... | 7 | 83 | 7.30 | 31.10 | ....5 00– 5 49 |
| 5 50– 5 99... | .... | 4 | .... | 5 | 1 | 5 | 1 | ..... | ...... | ...... | 4 | 24 | 8.40 | 41.40 | ....5 50– 5 99 |
| 6 00– 6 49... | .... | 20 | .... | 22 | 2 | 15 | 4 | 17 | ...... | ...... | 8 | 116 | 10.50 | 55.20 | ....6 00– 6 49 |
| 6 50 –6 99... | .... | 4 | .... | 2 | ...... | 1 | ...... | 7 | ...... | ...... | 1 | 23 | 10.70 | 59.20 | ....6 50– 6 99 |
| 7 00– 7 49... | .... | 2 | .... | 10 | 3 | 7 | 4 | 11 | ...... | ...... | 14 | 70 | 14.40 | 71.30 | ....7 00– 7 49 |
| 7 50– 7 99... | .... | 1 | 1 | 4 | 2 | 2 | 1 | 4 | ...... | ...... | 11 | 22 | 17.20 | 75.00 | ....7 50– 7 99 |
| 8 00– 8 99... | .... | 8 | 1 | 16 | 4 | 1 | 6 | 9 | ...... | 2 | 19 | 57 | 22.20 | 84.80 | ....8 00– 8 99 |
| 9 00– 9 99... | 5 | 7 | 2 | 9 | 4 | ...... | ...... | 4 | ...... | ...... | 40 | 37 | 32.60 | 91.40 | ....9 00– 9 99 |
| 10 00–10 99... | 4 | 3 | 2 | 10 | ...... | 1 | 6 | 1 | 2 | ...... | 39 | 32 | 42.80 | 96.80 | ...10 00–10 99 |
| 11 00–11 99... | 1 | ...... | .... | ...... | ...... | ...... | 2 | ..... | ...... | ...... | 15 | 4 | 46.80 | 97.50 | ...11 00–11 99 |
| 12 00–12 99... | 2 | ...... | 1 | 1 | ...... | ...... | 2 | ..... | 2 | ...... | 46 | 8 | 58.20 | 99.00 | ...12 00–12 99 |
| 13 00–13 99... | 1 | ...... | .... | 1 | ...... | ...... | 1 | ..... | 1 | ...... | 27 | 1 | 65.80 | 99.10 | ...13 00–13 99 |
| 14 00–14 99... | .... | ...... | .... | ...... | ...... | ...... | ...... | ..... | ...... | ...... | 13 | 1 | 69.30 | 99.30 | ...14 00–14 99 |
| 15 00–15 99... | 1 | ...... | 2 | ...... | ...... | ...... | ...... | ..... | 4 | ...... | 31 | ...... | 77.40 | ...... | ...15 00–15 99 |
| 16 00–17 99... | .... | ...... | .... | 1 | ...... | ...... | ...... | ..... | ...... | ...... | 33 | 2 | 86.00 | 99.50 | ...16 00–17 99 |
| 18 00–19 99... | .... | ...... | .... | ...... | ...... | ...... | ...... | ..... | ...... | ...... | 17 | 1 | 90.40 | 99.80 | ...18 00–19 99 |
| 20 00–24 99... | .... | ...... | .... | ...... | ...... | ...... | ...... | ..... | ...... | ...... | 25 | ...... | 96.90 | ...... | ...20 00–24 99 |
| 25 00–29 99... | .... | ...... | .... | ...... | ...... | ...... | ...... | ..... | ...... | ...... | 8 | 1 | 98.00 | 100.00 | ...25 00–29 99 |
| 30 00–34 99... | .... | ...... | .... | ...... | ...... | ...... | ...... | ..... | ...... | ...... | 4 | ...... | 100.00 | ...... | ...30 00–34 99 |
| Not reported... | 3 | 29 | .... | 54 | 19 | 6 | 39 | 19 | 4 | 4 | 159 | 175 | ...... | ...... | ...Not reported |
| Total..... | 17 | 112 | 9 | 162 | 41 | 53 | 73 | 111 | 13 | 6 | 542 | 754 | ...... | ...... | .....Total |

195. TABLE VI, C, a

NEW YORK STATE EXCLUSIVE OF NEW YORK CITY

THE PAPER BOX INDUSTRY — FACTORY WORKERS

NUMBER AND PER CENT OF EMPLOYEES CLASSIFIED ACCORDING TO ACTUAL WEEKLY EARNINGS BY AGE GROUPS AND SEX

| ACTUAL WEEKLY EARNINGS IN DOLLARS | AGE GROUPS IN YEARS | | | | | | | | | | | | | | ACTUAL WEEKLY EARNINGS IN DOLLARS |
|---|---|---|---|---|---|---|---|---|---|---|---|---|---|---|---|
| | 14–15 | | 16–17 | | 18–20 | | 21–24 | | 25–29 | | 30–34 | | 35–39 | | |
| | Male | Female | Male | Female | Male | Female | Male | Female | Male | Female | Male | Female | Male | Female | |
| Less than $3 00 | 5 | 21 | 5 | 24 | 3 | 17 | 1 | 5 | ... | 3 | ... | 1 | ... | 2 | Less than $3 00 |
| $3 00–$3 49... | 3 | 23 | 3 | 19 | ... | 12 | ... | 9 | ... | 3 | ... | ... | ... | ... | ...$3 00– 3 49 |
| 3 50– 3 99... | 7 | 28 | 2 | 28 | ... | 21 | ... | 5 | ... | 7 | ... | ... | ... | 1 | ... 3 50– 3 99 |
| 4 00– 4 49... | 9 | 17 | 6 | 46 | ... | 33 | 1 | 16 | ... | 5 | ... | 3 | ... | 1 | ... 4 00– 4 49 |
| 4 50– 4 99... | 6 | 12 | 7 | 22 | 1 | 47 | ... | 26 | ... | 8 | ... | 3 | ... | 3 | ... 4 50– 4 99 |
| 5 00– 5 49... | 5 | 7 | 7 | 65 | 5 | 49 | ... | 41 | 1 | 14 | ... | 5 | ... | 3 | ... 5 00– 5 49 |
| 5 50– 5 99... | 3 | 3 | 9 | 45 | 7 | 52 | 1 | 32 | ... | 9 | ... | 1 | ... | 7 | ... 5 50– 5 99 |
| 6 00– 6 49... | ... | 5 | 8 | 36 | 4 | 50 | 3 | 38 | ... | 15 | ... | 6 | ... | 6 | ... 6 00– 6 49 |
| 6 50– 6 99... | ... | ... | 7 | 26 | 5 | 56 | 2 | 42 | 1 | 13 | ... | 4 | ... | 9 | ... 6 50– 6 99 |
| 7 00– 7 49... | ... | 2 | 4 | 21 | 7 | 37 | 4 | 46 | 3 | 20 | 2 | 11 | ... | 5 | ... 7 00– 7 49 |
| 7 50– 7 99... | ... | ... | 3 | 12 | 9 | 30 | 3 | 28 | 3 | 8 | ... | 7 | 1 | 3 | ... 7 50– 7 99 |
| 8 00– 8 99... | ... | 2 | 9 | 24 | 23 | 61 | 9 | 60 | 9 | 22 | 6 | 17 | 5 | 14 | ... 8 00– 8 99 |
| 9 00– 9 99... | ... | ... | 2 | 8 | 15 | 36 | 23 | 35 | 9 | 15 | 9 | 16 | 2 | 6 | ... 9 00– 9 99 |
| 10 00–10 99... | ... | ... | ... | 3 | 12 | 11 | 19 | 18 | 17 | 16 | 5 | 8 | 5 | 5 | ...10 00–10 99 |
| 11 00–11 99... | ... | ... | ... | 5 | 6 | 13 | 12 | 18 | 5 | 11 | 7 | 5 | 2 | 2 | ...11 00–11 99 |
| 12 00–12 99... | ... | ... | ... | 2 | 7 | 4 | 12 | 4 | 15 | 7 | 6 | 6 | 5 | 3 | ...12 00–12 99 |
| 13 00–13 99... | ... | ... | ... | ... | 3 | 3 | 12 | 2 | 9 | ... | 10 | 1 | 4 | 1 | ...13 00–13 99 |
| 14 00–14 99... | ... | ... | ... | ... | 3 | 3 | 8 | ... | 2 | ... | 5 | 1 | 3 | ... | ...14 00–14 99 |
| 15 00–15 99... | ... | ... | ... | ... | ... | ... | 6 | ... | 16 | 1 | 8 | ... | 6 | ... | ...15 00–15 99 |
| 16 00–17 99... | ... | ... | ... | ... | 2 | ... | 8 | 1 | 8 | 1 | 5 | 2 | 6 | ... | ...16 00–17 99 |
| 18 00–19 99... | ... | ... | ... | ... | ... | ... | ... | ... | 4 | ... | 5 | 1 | 3 | ... | ...18 00–19 99 |
| 20 00–24 99... | ... | ... | ... | ... | ... | ... | ... | ... | 1 | ... | 8 | ... | 2 | ... | ...20 00–24 99 |
| 25 00–29 99... | ... | ... | ... | ... | ... | ... | ... | ... | 2 | ... | ... | ... | ... | 1 | ...25 00–29 99 |
| 30 00–34 99... | ... | ... | ... | ... | ... | ... | ... | ... | ... | ... | 2 | ... | ... | ... | ...30 00–34 99 |
| Not reported... | ... | ... | ... | ... | ... | 1 | 1 | 1 | 2 | ... | 5 | ... | 1 | 1 | ...Not reported |
| Total..... | 38 | 120 | 72 | 386 | 112 | 536 | 125 | 427 | 107 | 178 | 83 | 98 | 45 | 73 | .....Total |

195. TABLE VI, C, a — (*concluded*)

NEW YORK STATE EXCLUSIVE OF NEW YORK CITY
**THE PAPER BOX INDUSTRY — FACTORY WORKERS**
NUMBER AND PER CENT OF EMPLOYEES CLASSIFIED ACCORDING TO ACTUAL WEEKLY EARNINGS BY AGE GROUPS AND SEX

| ACTUAL WEEKLY EARNINGS IN DOLLARS | AGE GROUPS IN YEARS (*concluded*) | | | | | | | | | | | | | | ACTUAL WEEKLY EARNINGS IN DOLLARS |
|---|---|---|---|---|---|---|---|---|---|---|---|---|---|---|---|
| | 40–44 | | 45–54 | | 55–64 | | 65 AND OVER | | NOT REPORTED | | TOTAL | | CUMULATIVE PER CENT OF TOTAL | | |
| | Male | Female | Male | Female | Male | Female | Male | Female | Male | Female | Male | Female | Male | Female | |
| Less than $3 00 | .... | 2 | .... | 1 | .... | .... | .... | .... | .... | 1 | 14 | 77 | 2.07 | 4.00 | Less than $3 00 |
| $3 00–$3 49... | .... | .... | .... | .... | .... | .... | .... | .... | .... | .... | 6 | 66 | 2.96 | 7.40 | ...$3 00– 3 49 |
| 3 50– 3 99... | .... | .... | .... | 1 | .... | 1 | .... | .... | .... | 1 | 9 | 93 | 4.29 | 12.22 | ... 3 50– 3 99 |
| 4 00– 4 49... | .... | .... | .... | 1 | .... | 1 | .... | .... | .... | 1 | 16 | 124 | 6.66 | 18.65 | ... 4 00– 4 49 |
| 4 50– 4 99... | .... | 1 | .... | 3 | .... | 1 | .... | .... | .... | 4 | 14 | 130 | 8.73 | 25.40 | ... 4 50– 4 99 |
| 5 00– 5 49... | .... | 4 | .... | 4 | .... | 5 | .... | 1 | .... | 1 | 18 | 199 | 11.40 | 35.35 | ... 5 00– 5 49 |
| 5 50– 5 99... | .... | 1 | .... | 2 | .... | .... | .... | .... | .... | 1 | 20 | 153 | 14.35 | 43.60 | ... 5 50– 5 99. |
| 6 00– 6 49... | .... | 3 | 1 | 4 | 1 | 2 | .... | .... | .... | 2 | 17 | 167 | 16.89 | 56.50 | ... 6 00– 6 49 |
| 6 50– 6 99... | .... | 1 | .... | 3 | .... | 1 | .... | .... | .... | .... | 15 | 155 | 19.10 | 60.25 | ... 6 50– 6 99 |
| 7 00– 7 49... | .... | 2 | .... | 8 | .... | 1 | 1 | .... | .... | 2 | 21 | 155 | 22.20 | 68.25 | ... 7 00– 7 49 |
| 7 50– 7 99... | .... | 1 | 1 | 5 | .... | .... | 1 | .... | .... | 1 | 21 | 95 | 25.15 | 73.30 | ... 7 50– 7 99 |
| 8 00– 8 99... | 3 | 5 | 2 | 5 | 2 | .... | .... | .... | .... | 3 | 68 | 213 | 35.45 | 84.30 | ... 8 00– 8 99 |
| 9 00– 9 99... | 3 | 6 | 2 | 4 | 2 | 1 | 3 | .... | 1 | .... | 71 | 127 | 45.80 | 91.00 | ... 9 00– 9 99 |
| 10 00–10 99... | 5 | 5 | 1 | 3 | 4 | .... | .... | .... | .... | 1 | 68 | 70 | 56.00 | 94.50 | ...10 00–10 99 |
| 11 00–11 99... | 6 | .... | 2 | .... | 2 | 1 | .... | .... | 1 | .... | 43 | 55 | 62.25 | 97.20 | ...11 00–11 99 |
| 12 00–12 99... | 1 | 3 | 5 | 2 | 4 | .... | 1 | .... | .... | .... | 56 | 31 | 70.05 | 99.00 | ...12 00–12 99 |
| 13 00–13 99... | 3 | .... | 3 | .... | 1 | .... | .... | .... | .... | .... | 45 | 7 | 77.10 | 99.30 | ...13 00–13 99 |
| 14 00–14 99... | 1 | .... | 1 | .... | 2 | .... | .... | .... | .... | .... | 25 | 4 | 81.00 | 99.50 | 14 00–14 99 |
| 15 00–15 99... | 3 | .... | 3 | .... | .... | .... | .... | .... | .... | .... | 42 | 1 | 87.10 | 99.60 | ...15 00–15 99 |
| 16 00–17 99... | 5 | 2 | 4 | .... | 2 | .... | .... | .... | .... | .... | 40 | 6 | 93.00 | 99.90 | ...16 00–17 99 |
| 18 00–19 99... | 1 | .... | 1 | .... | 1 | .... | .... | .... | .... | .... | 15 | 1 | 95.30 | 99.95 | .18 00–19 99 |
| 20 00–24 99... | 5 | .... | 7 | .... | 1 | .... | .... | .... | .... | .... | 24 | .... | 98.80 | .... | ...20 00–24 99 |
| 25 00–29 99... | 2 | .... | .... | .... | 1 | .... | .... | .... | .... | .... | 5 | 1 | 99.50 | 100.00 | ...25 00–29 00 |
| 30 00–34 99... | 1 | .... | .... | .... | .... | .... | .... | .... | .... | .... | 3 | .... | 100.00 | .... | ...30 00–34 99 |
| Not reported... | 1 | 1 | 1 | .... | .... | .... | .... | .... | .... | .... | 11 | 4 | .... | .... | ...Not reported |
| Total..... | 40 | 37 | 34 | 46 | 23 | 14 | 6 | 1 | 2 | 18 | 687 | 1,934 | .... | .... | .....Total |

196. TABLE IX, C, a

NEW YORK STATE EXCLUSIVE OF NEW YORK CITY
THE PAPER BOX INDUSTRY — FACTORY WORKERS
NUMBER AND PER CENT OF EMPLOYEES CLASSIFIED ACCORDING TO ACTUAL WEEKLY EARNINGS BY OCCUPATION AND SEX

| ACTUAL WEEKLY EARNINGS IN DOLLARS | OCCUPATION | | | | | | | | | | | | | ACTUAL WEEKLY EARNINGS IN DOLLARS |
|---|---|---|---|---|---|---|---|---|---|---|---|---|---|---|
| | FOREMEN AND FOREWOMEN | | CUTTERS | | SETTERS UP | | GENERAL MACHINE WORK | | GLUE TABLE WORK | TURNERS IN | | STRIPPERS AND TOP-LABELERS | | |
| | Male | Female | Male | Female | Male | Female | Male | Female | Male | Male | Female | Male | Female | |
| Less than $3 00 | ...... | ...... | 3 | ...... | 2 | 5 | ...... | 14 | ...... | 4 | 13 | ...... | 16 | Less than $3 00 |
| $3 00–$3 49 | ...... | ...... | ...... | ...... | 3 | 3 | ...... | 6 | ...... | 2 | 17 | ...... | 13 | $3 00– 3 49 |
| 3 50– 3 99 | ...... | ...... | ...... | 1 | 1 | 3 | 1 | 7 | ...... | 1 | 23 | ...... | 20 | 3 50– 3 99 |
| 4 00– 4 49 | ...... | 1 | 2 | 2 | 3 | 2 | ...... | 9 | ...... | 2 | 27 | ...... | 26 | 4 00– 4 49 |
| 4 50– 4 99 | ...... | ...... | 1 | 1 | 1 | 3 | ...... | 15 | ...... | 5 | 23 | ...... | 22 | 4 50– 4 99 |
| 5 00– 5 49 | ...... | ...... | 2 | ...... | 3 | 12 | 2 | 41 | ...... | ...... | 26 | 3 | 35 | 5 00– 5 49 |
| 5 50– 5 99 | ...... | 2 | 2 | 1 | 3 | 6 | 1 | 27 | ...... | 6 | 14 | 1 | 39 | 5 50– 5 99 |
| 6 00– 6 49 | ...... | 2 | 2 | 3 | 2 | 13 | 2 | 34 | ...... | 2 | 10 | ...... | 34 | 6 00– 6 49 |
| 6 50– 6 99 | ...... | 2 | 2 | 4 | ...... | 12 | 5 | 35 | ...... | ...... | 6 | 1 | 31 | 6 50– 6 99 |
| 7 00– 7 49 | ...... | 5 | 5 | 4 | 3 | 9 | 3 | 35 | ...... | ...... | 5 | 2 | 25 | 7 00– 7 49 |
| 7 50– 7 99 | ...... | 3 | 4 | 4 | 4 | 8 | 4 | 15 | ...... | ...... | 1 | 2 | 25 | 7 50– 7 99 |
| 8 00– 8 99 | 1 | 12 | 17 | 1 | 7 | 11 | 5 | 33 | 1 | ...... | 5 | 11 | 58 | 8 00– 8 99 |
| 9 00– 9 99 | ...... | 9 | 22 | 2 | 13 | 6 | 13 | 19 | ...... | ...... | 4 | 6 | 31 | 9 00– 9 99 |
| 10 00–10 99 | ...... | 7 | 31 | 2 | 3 | 5 | 8 | 4 | 2 | ...... | ...... | 6 | 23 | 10 00–10 99 |
| 11 00–11 99 | ...... | 4 | 17 | ...... | 4 | 4 | 3 | 5 | 1 | ...... | 3 | 5 | 22 | 11 00–11 99 |
| 12 00–12 99 | 8 | 7 | 25 | ...... | 4 | 2 | 7 | ...... | 1 | ...... | 2 | 4 | 13 | 12 00–12 99 |
| 13 00–13 99 | 3 | ...... | 20 | ...... | 5 | 1 | 8 | ...... | ...... | ...... | ...... | 6 | 4 | 13 00–13 99 |
| 14 00–14 99 | 3 | 1 | 8 | ...... | 1 | ...... | 9 | ...... | ...... | ...... | ...... | 2 | 3 | 14 00–14 99 |
| 15 00–15 99 | 6 | ...... | 17 | ...... | 4 | ...... | 4 | ...... | ...... | ...... | ...... | 6 | 1 | 15 00–15 99 |
| 16 00–17 99 | 13 | ...... | 16 | 1 | 3 | ...... | 6 | 1 | ...... | ...... | ...... | 2 | 2 | 16 00–17 99 |
| 18 00–19 99 | 11 | 1 | 3 | ...... | ...... | ...... | ...... | ...... | ...... | ...... | ...... | 1 | ...... | 18 00–19 99 |
| 20 00–24 99 | 18 | ...... | 5 | ...... | ...... | ...... | 1 | ...... | ...... | ...... | ...... | ...... | ...... | 20 00–24 99 |
| 25 00–29 99 | 5 | 1 | ...... | ...... | ...... | ...... | ...... | ...... | ...... | ...... | ...... | ...... | ...... | 25 00–29 99 |
| 30 00–34 99 | 3 | ...... | ...... | ...... | ...... | ...... | ...... | ...... | ...... | ...... | ...... | ...... | ...... | 30 00–34 99 |
| Not reported | 10 | ...... | 1 | ...... | ...... | 1 | ...... | ...... | ...... | ...... | ...... | ...... | ...... | Not reported |
| Total | 81 | 57 | 205 | 26 | 69 | 106 | 82 | 300 | 5 | 22 | 179 | 58 | 443 | Total |

196. TABLE IX, C, a — (*concluded*)

NEW YORK STATE EXCLUSIVE OF NEW YORK CITY
THE PAPER BOX INDUSTRY — FACTORY WORKERS

Number and Per Cent of Employees Classified According to Actual Weekly Earnings by Occupation and Sex

| Actual Weekly Earnings in Dollars | Occupation — (*Concluded*) | | | | | | | | | | | | | Actual Week Earnings in Dollars |
|---|---|---|---|---|---|---|---|---|---|---|---|---|---|---|
| | Table Work | | Closing and Tying | | Floor Work | | Glue Makers | Not Reported | | Total | | Cumulative Per Cent of Total | | |
| | Male | Female | Male | Female | Male | Female | Male | Male | Female | Male | Female | Male | Female | |
| Less than $3 00... | ...... | 13 | 3 | 4 | 1 | 12 | ...... | 1 | ..... | 14 | 77 | 2.07 | 4.00 | ..Less than $3 00 |
| $3 00–$3 49...... | ...... | 19 | ...... | 2 | 1 | 5 | ...... | ...... | 1 | 6 | 66 | 2.96 | 7.40 | .....$3 00– 3 49 |
| 3 50– 3 99...... | ...... | 23 | 4 | 5 | 2 | 9 | ...... | ...... | 2 | 9 | 93 | 4.29 | 12.22 | ..... 3 50– 3 99 |
| 4 00– 4 49...... | ...... | 37 | 3 | 8 | 5 | 12 | ...... | 1 | ...... | 16 | 124 | 6.66 | 18.65 | ..... 4 00– 4 49 |
| 4 50– 4 99...... | ...... | 36 | 4 | 16 | 2 | 9 | ...... | 1 | 5 | 14 | 130 | 8.73 | 25.40 | ..... 4 50– 4 99 |
| 5 00– 5 49...... | ...... | 43 | 3 | 7 | 4 | 27 | ...... | 1 | 8 | 18 | 199 | 11.40 | 35.35 | ..... 5 00– 5 49 |
| 5 50– 5 99...... | 1 | 38 | 2 | 13 | 4 | 10 | ...... | ...... | 3 | 20 | 153 | 14.35 | 43.60 | ..... 5 50– 5 99 |
| 6 00– 6 49...... | ...... | 45 | 2 | 13 | 5 | 11 | ...... | 2 | 2 | 17 | 167 | 16.89 | 56.50 | ..... 6.00– 6.49 |
| 6 50– 6 99...... | ...... | 42 | 3 | 11 | 4 | 10 | ...... | ...... | 2 | 15 | 155 | 19.10 | 60.25 | ..... 6 50– 6 99 |
| 7 00– 7 49...... | ...... | 47 | 3 | 8 | 4 | 17 | ...... | 1 | ...... | 21 | 155 | 22.20 | 68.25 | ..... 7 00– 7 49 |
| 7 50– 7 99...... | ...... | 29 | 3 | 4 | 3 | 4 | ...... | 1 | 2 | 21 | 95 | 25.15 | 73.30 | ..... 7 50– 7 99 |
| 8 00– 8 99...... | 3 | 72 | 8 | 7 | 14 | 12 | ...... | 1 | 2 | 68 | 213 | 35.45 | 84.30 | ..... 8 00– 8 99 |
| 9 00– 9 99...... | 3 | 41 | 4 | 7 | 10 | 5 | ...... | ...... | 3 | 71 | 127 | 45.80 | 91.00 | ..... 9 00– 9 99 |
| 10 00–10 99...... | ...... | 21 | 1 | 6 | 12 | 2 | ...... | 5 | ...... | 68 | 70 | 56.00 | 94.50 | .....10 00–10 99 |
| 11 00–11 99...... | 2 | 13 | 4 | 3 | 5 | 1 | ...... | 2 | ...... | 43 | 55 | 62.25 | 97.20 | .....11 00–11 99 |
| 12 00–12 99...... | ...... | 7 | ...... | ...... | 3 | ...... | 1 | 3 | ...... | 56 | 31 | 70.05 | 99.00 | .....12 00–12 99 |
| 13 00–13 99...... | ...... | 2 | ...... | ...... | 2 | ...... | ...... | 1 | ...... | 45 | 7 | 77.10 | 99.30 | .....13 00–13 99 |
| 14 00–14 99...... | ...... | ...... | 1 | ...... | 1 | ...... | ...... | ...... | ...... | 25 | 4 | 81.00 | 99.50 | .....14 00–14 99 |
| 15 00–15 99...... | 3 | ...... | 1 | ...... | ...... | ...... | ...... | 1 | ...... | 42 | 6 | 87.10 | 99.60 | .....15 00–15 99 |
| 16 00–17 99...... | ...... | 2 | ...... | ...... | ...... | ...... | ...... | ...... | ...... | 40 | 6 | 93.00 | 99.90 | .....16 00–17 99 |
| 18 00–19 99...... | ...... | ...... | ...... | ...... | ...... | ...... | ...... | ...... | ...... | 15 | 1 | 95.30 | 99.95 | .....18 00–19 99 |
| 20 00–24 99...... | ...... | ...... | ...... | ...... | ...... | ...... | ...... | ...... | ...... | 24 | ...... | 98.80 | ...... | .....20 00–24 99 |
| 25 00–29 99...... | ...... | ...... | ...... | ...... | ...... | ...... | ...... | ...... | ...... | 5 | 1 | 99.50 | 100.00 | .....25 00–29 99 |
| 30 00–34 99...... | ...... | ...... | ...... | ...... | ...... | ...... | ...... | ...... | ...... | 3 | ...... | 100.00 | ...... | .....30 00–34 99 |
| Not reported...... | ...... | 2 | ...... | 1 | ...... | ...... | ...... | ...... | ...... | 11 | 4 | ...... | ...... | .....Not reported |
| Total........ | 12 | 532 | 49 | 115 | 82 | 146 | 1 | 21 | 30 | 687 | 1,934 | ...... | ...... | .......Total |

197. TABLE V, D, a

NEW YORK STATE EXCLUSIVE OF NEW YORK CITY
THE CONFECTIONERY INDUSTRY — FACTORY WORKERS
NUMBER AND PER CENT OF EMPLOYEES EARNING SPECIFIED WEEKLY RATES BY AGE GROUPS AND SEX

| WEEKLY RATES DOLLARS IN | AGE GROUPS IN YEARS | | | | | | | | | | | | | WEEKLY RATES IN DOLLARS |
|---|---|---|---|---|---|---|---|---|---|---|---|---|---|---|
| | 14–15 | 16–17 | | 18–20 | | 21–24 | | 25–29 | | 30–34 | | 35–39 | | |
| | Female | Male | Female | Male | Female | Male | Female | Male | Female | Male | Female | Male | Female | |
| Less than $3 00 | 2 | ...... | 1 | ...... | 2 | ...... | ...... | ...... | ...... | ...... | ...... | ...... | ...... | Less than $3 00 |
| $3 00–$3 49 | ...... | ...... | 3 | ...... | ...... | ...... | ...... | ...... | ...... | ...... | ...... | ...... | ...... | $3 00– 3 49 |
| 3 50– 3 99 | 2 | ...... | 6 | ...... | 1 | ...... | 1 | ...... | 1 | ...... | 1 | ...... | 2 | 3 50– 3 99 |
| 4 00– 4 49 | 3 | ...... | 37 | ...... | 14 | ...... | 5 | ...... | ...... | ...... | 3 | ...... | 2 | 4 00– 4 49 |
| 4 50– 4 99 | 1 | 1 | 14 | ...... | 23 | ...... | 5 | ...... | 1 | ...... | ...... | 1 | 1 | 4 50– 4 99 |
| 5 00– 5 49 | 1 | ...... | 13 | ...... | 18 | ...... | 11 | ...... | 3 | ...... | 1 | ...... | ...... | 5 00– 5 49 |
| 5 50– 5 99 | ...... | ...... | 4 | ...... | 5 | ...... | 3 | ...... | ...... | ...... | ...... | ...... | ...... | 5 50– 5 99 |
| 6 00– 6 49 | ...... | 9 | 10 | 1 | 25 | 1 | 22 | ...... | 7 | ...... | 4 | ...... | 3 | 6 00– 6 49 |
| 6 50– 6 99 | ...... | ...... | 5 | 1 | 7 | ...... | 9 | ...... | 3 | ...... | 1 | ...... | ...... | 6 50– 6 99 |
| 7 00– 7 49 | ...... | ...... | 4 | 6 | 9 | 4 | 10 | ...... | 4 | ...... | 3 | 1 | 1 | 7 00– 7 49 |
| 7 50– 7 99 | ...... | 1 | 1 | 11 | ...... | 2 | 1 | 2 | 2 | ...... | 1 | 1 | ...... | 7 50– 7 99 |
| 8 00– 8 99 | ...... | 3 | 1 | 14 | 8 | 6 | 6 | 5 | 9 | 5 | 1 | ...... | 1 | 8 00– 8 99 |
| 9 00– 9 99 | ...... | 1 | ...... | 12 | 2 | 7 | 10 | 4 | 4 | 1 | 3 | 3 | 5 | 9 00– 9 99 |
| 10 00–10 99 | ...... | ...... | ...... | 6 | ...... | 8 | 4 | 2 | 8 | 1 | 5 | 1 | 4 | 10 00–10 99 |
| 11 00–11 99 | ...... | ...... | ...... | 1 | ...... | 6 | ...... | 1 | ...... | 3 | 1 | 3 | 1 | 11 00–11 99 |
| 12 00–12 99 | ...... | ...... | ...... | 3 | ...... | 14 | ...... | 8 | ...... | 1 | ...... | 1 | 1 | 12 00–12 99 |
| 13 00–13 99 | ...... | ...... | ...... | ...... | ...... | 4 | ...... | 3 | ...... | 5 | ...... | 2 | ...... | 13 00–13 99 |
| 14 00–14 99 | ...... | ...... | ...... | ...... | ...... | 3 | 1 | 1 | ...... | 2 | ...... | ...... | ...... | 14 00–14 99 |
| 15 00–15 99 | ...... | ...... | ...... | ...... | ...... | 2 | ...... | 4 | ...... | 6 | ...... | 7 | 1 | 15 00–15 99 |
| 16 00–17 99 | ...... | ...... | ...... | ...... | ...... | 2 | ...... | 2 | ...... | 1 | ...... | 4 | ...... | 16 00–17 99 |
| 18 00–19 99 | ...... | ...... | ...... | ...... | ...... | 3 | ...... | 3 | ...... | 2 | ...... | 3 | ...... | 18 00–19 99 |
| 20 00–24 99 | ...... | ...... | ...... | ...... | ...... | ...... | ...... | 3 | ...... | 3 | ...... | 4 | ...... | 20 00–24 99 |
| 25 00–29 99 | ...... | ...... | ...... | ...... | ...... | 1 | ...... | 1 | ...... | 1 | ...... | ...... | ...... | 25 00–29 99 |
| 30 00–34 99 | ...... | ...... | ...... | ...... | ...... | ...... | ...... | ...... | ...... | ...... | ...... | ...... | ...... | 30 00–34 99 |
| Not reported | 1 | ...... | 1 | 8 | 5 | 1 | 3 | 2 | 1 | 3 | 1 | 5 | ...... | Not reported |
| Total | 10 | 15 | 100 | 63 | 119 | 64 | 91 | 41 | 43 | 34 | 25 | 36 | 22 | Total |

197. TABLE V, D, a — (*concluded*)

NEW YORK STATE EXCLUSIVE OF NEW YORK CITY
THE CONFECTIONERY INDUSTRY — FACTORY WORKERS
NUMBER AND PER CENT OF EMPLOYEES EARNING SPECIFIED WEEKLY RATES BY AGE GROUPS AND SEX

| WEEKLY RATES IN DOLLARS | AGE GROUPS IN YEARS (*concluded*) 40–44 | | 45–54 | | 55–64 | | 65 AND OVER | NOT REPORTED | TOTAL | | CUMULATIVE PER CENT OF TOTAL | | WEEKLY RATES IN DOLLARS |
|---|---|---|---|---|---|---|---|---|---|---|---|---|---|
| | Male | Female | Male | Female | Male | Female | Male | Female | Male | Female | Male | Female | |
| Less than $3 00 | ....... | ....... | ....... | ....... | ....... | ....... | ....... | ....... | ....... | 5 | ....... | 1.18 | Less than $3 00 |
| $3 00–$3 49 | ....... | ....... | ....... | ....... | ....... | ....... | ....... | ....... | ....... | 3 | ....... | 1.84 | ...$3 00– 3 49 |
| 3 50– 3 99 | ....... | 2 | ....... | ....... | ....... | ....... | ....... | ....... | ....... | 16 | ....... | 5.65 | ... 3 50– 3 99 |
| 4 00– 4 49 | ....... | ....... | ....... | ....... | ....... | ....... | ....... | ....... | ....... | 64 | ....... | 20.65 | ... 4 00– 4 49 |
| 4 50– 4 99 | ....... | ....... | ....... | ....... | ....... | ....... | ....... | ....... | 2 | 45 | .64 | 31.30 | ... 4 50– 4 99 |
| 5 00– 5 49 | ....... | 1 | ....... | ....... | ....... | ....... | ....... | ....... | ....... | 48 | ....... | 42.60 | ... 5 00– 5 49 |
| 5 50– 5 99 | ....... | ....... | ....... | ....... | ....... | ....... | ....... | ....... | ....... | 12 | ....... | 45.40 | ... 5 50– 5 99 |
| 6 00– 6 49 | ....... | 3 | ....... | 1 | ....... | 1 | ....... | ....... | 11 | 76 | 4.15 | 63.30 | ... 6 00– 6 49 |
| 6 50– 6 99 | ....... | ....... | ....... | ....... | ....... | ....... | ....... | ....... | 1 | 25 | 4.48 | 69.20 | ... 6 50– 6 99 |
| 7 00– 7 49 | ....... | ....... | ....... | 1 | ....... | ....... | ....... | 1 | 11 | 33 | 8.00 | 77.00 | ... 7 00– 7 49 |
| 7 50– 7 99 | 1 | 1 | ....... | ....... | ....... | ....... | ....... | ....... | 18 | 6 | 13.80 | 79.00 | ... 7 50– 7 99 |
| 8 00– 8 99 | ....... | 1 | 1 | ....... | 3 | 1 | ....... | ....... | 37 | 28 | 25.05 | 85.00 | ... 8 00– 8 99 |
| 9 00– 9 99 | 4 | 3 | 2 | 4 | 2 | ....... | ....... | 1 | 36 | 32 | 37.05 | 92.50 | ... 9 00– 9 99 |
| 10 00–10 99 | ....... | 2 | 4 | 1 | 3 | ....... | 1 | ....... | 26 | 24 | 45.40 | 98.20 | ...10 00–10 99 |
| 11 00–11 99 | 1 | ....... | 3 | ....... | ....... | ....... | ....... | ....... | 18 | 2 | 51.10 | 98.60 | ...11 00–11 99 |
| 12 00–12 99 | 4 | ....... | 8 | 1 | 3 | ....... | ....... | ....... | 42 | 2 | 64.50 | 99.00 | ...12 00–12 99 |
| 13 00–13 99 | 2 | 1 | 1 | ....... | 1 | ....... | 1 | ....... | 19 | 1 | 70.70 | 99.25 | ...13 00–13 99 |
| 14 00–14 99 | 2 | ....... | 3 | ....... | ....... | ....... | ....... | ....... | 11 | 1 | 74.20 | 99.50 | ...14 00–14 99 |
| 15 00–15 99 | 4 | ....... | 2 | 1 | 1 | ....... | ....... | ....... | 26 | 2 | 82.50 | 100.00 | ...15 00–15 99 |
| 16 00–17 99 | 2 | ....... | 1 | ....... | ....... | ....... | ....... | ....... | 12 | ....... | 86.30 | ....... | ...16 00–17 99 |
| 18 00–19 99 | 2 | ....... | 3 | ....... | 1 | ....... | ....... | ....... | 17 | ....... | 91.60 | ....... | ...18 00–19 99 |
| 20 00–24 99 | 3 | ....... | 5 | ....... | 1 | ....... | ....... | ....... | 19 | ....... | 92.90 | ....... | ...20 00–24 99 |
| 25 00–29 99 | 2 | ....... | 1 | ....... | ....... | ....... | ....... | ....... | 6 | ....... | 99.70 | ....... | ...25 00–29 99 |
| 30 00–34 99 | 1 | ....... | ....... | ....... | ....... | ....... | ....... | ....... | 1 | ....... | 100.00 | ....... | ...30 00–34 99 |
| Not reported | 2 | ....... | 4 | ....... | 5 | 1 | ....... | ....... | 30 | 13 | ....... | ....... | ..Not reported |
| Total | 30 | 14 | 38 | 9 | 20 | 3 | 2 | 2 | 343 | 438 | ....... | ....... | .....Total |

### NEW YORK STATE EXCLUSIV OF NEW YORK CITY
### THE CONFECTIONERY INDUSTRY — FACTORY WORKERS

198. TABLE VIII, D, a  NUMBER AND PER CENT OF EMPLOYEES EARNING SPECIFIED WEEKLY RATES, BY OCCUPATION AND SEX

| WEEKLY RATES IN DOLLARS | OCCUPATION | | | | | | | | | | | | | | | | | | | WEEKLY RATES IN DOLLARS |
|---|---|---|---|---|---|---|---|---|---|---|---|---|---|---|---|---|---|---|---|---|
| | FOREMEN AND FOREWOMEN | | CANDY MAKERS | | DIPPERS | | PACKERS | | WRAPPERS | | MACHINE OPERATORS | | HELPERS | | GENERAL LABORERS | TOTAL | | CUMULATIVE PER CENT. OF TOTAL | | |
| | Male | Female | Male | Female | Male | Female | Male | Female | Male | Female | Male | Female | Male | Female | Male | Male | Female | Male | Female | |
| Less than $3 00 | | | | | | | | 3 | | 2 | | | | | | | 5 | | 1.18 | Less than $3 00 |
| $3 00–$3 49 | | | | | | | | 1 | | 2 | | | | | | | 3 | | 1.84 | $3 00– 3 49 |
| 3 50– 3 99 | | | | | | 1 | | 10 | | 4 | | | | 1 | | | 16 | | 5.65 | 3 50– 3 99 |
| 4 00– 4 49 | | | | 1 | | 6 | | 43 | | 1 | | | | 13 | | | 64 | | 20.65 | 4 00– 4 49 |
| 4 50– 4 99 | | | | | | 4 | 1 | 26 | | 5 | | | 1 | 10 | | 2 | 45 | .64 | 31.30 | 4 50– 4 99 |
| 5 00– 5 49 | | | | | | 3 | | 23 | | 7 | | | | 15 | | | 48 | | 42.60 | 5 00– 5 49 |
| 5 50– 5 99 | | | | | | 2 | | 4 | | 3 | | | | 3 | | | 12 | | 45.40 | 5 50– 5 99 |
| 6 00– 6 49 | | 4 | | | | 4 | 1 | 38 | | 7 | | | 10 | 23 | | 11 | 76 | 4.15 | 63.30 | 6 00– 6 49 |
| 6 50– 6 99 | | 1 | | | | 3 | | 14 | | 3 | | | 1 | 4 | | 1 | 25 | 4.48 | 69.20 | 6 50– 6 99 |
| 7 00– 7 49 | | 3 | | | | 4 | | 17 | | 8 | | | 11 | 1 | | 11 | 33 | 8.00 | 77.00 | 7 00– 7 49 |
| 7 50– 7 99 | | | | | | 1 | | 4 | | | | | 18 | 1 | | 18 | 6 | 13.80 | 79.00 | 7 50– 7 99 |
| 8 00– 8 99 | | 2 | 1 | | | 1 | 1 | 12 | 2 | | 1 | | 30 | 13 | 1 | 37 | 28 | 25.05 | 85.00 | 8 00– 8 99 |
| 9 00– 9 99 | | 11 | 5 | | | | 1 | 10 | | 1 | | | 30 | 10 | | 36 | 32 | 37.05 | 92.50 | 9 00– 9 99 |
| 10 00–10 99 | | 10 | 2 | | 1 | 1 | 1 | 3 | | 1 | 2 | 9 | 19 | | 1 | 26 | 24 | 45.40 | 98.20 | 10 00–10 99 |
| 11 00–11 99 | | 2 | 4 | | | | 1 | | | | 2 | | 10 | | 1 | 18 | 2 | 51.10 | 98.60 | 11.00 11 99 |
| 12 00–12 99 | 2 | 2 | 19 | | | | 1 | | | | 4 | | 14 | | 2 | 42 | 2 | 64.50 | 99.00 | 12 00–12 99 |
| 13 00–13 99 | 5 | | 9 | | | 1 | | | | | 3 | | 2 | | | 19 | 1 | 70.70 | 99.25 | 13 00–13 99 |
| 11 00–14 99 | 3 | 1 | 3 | | | | | | | | 1 | | 4 | | | 11 | 1 | 74.20 | 99.50 | 14 00–14 99 |
| 15 00–15 99 | 4 | 2 | 15 | | | | 3 | | | | | | 2 | | 2 | 26 | 2 | 82.50 | 100.00 | 15 00–15 99 |
| 16 00–17 99 | 2 | | 8 | | | | | | | | | | 2 | | | 12 | | 86.30 | | 16 00–17 99 |
| 18 00–19 99 | 2 | | 13 | | | | | | | | | | 1 | | 1 | 17 | | 91.60 | | 18 00–19 99 |
| 20 00–24 99 | 8 | | 11 | | | | | | | | | | | | | 19 | | 92.90 | | 20 00–24 99 |
| 25 00–29 99 | 4 | | 2 | | | | | | | | | | | | | 6 | | 99.70 | | 25 00–29 99 |
| 30 00–34 99 | 1 | | | | | | | | | | | | | | | 1 | | 100.00 | | 30 00–34 99 |
| Not reported | 2 | 1 | 5 | | | 1 | 1 | 6 | 1 | | 12 | 1 | 9 | 4 | | 30 | 13 | | | Not reported. |
| Total | 33 | 39 | 98 | 1 | 1 | 32 | 11 | 214 | 3 | 44 | 25 | 10 | 164 | 98 | 8 | 343 | 438 | | | Total |

199. TABLE VI, D, a

NEW YORK STATE EXCLUSIVE OF NEW YORK CITY
THE CONFECTIONERY INDUSTRY — FACTORY WORKERS
NUMBER AND PER CENT OF EMPLOYEES CLASSIFIED ACCORDING TO ACTUAL WEEKLY EARNINGS BY AGE GROUPS AND SEX

| ACTUAL WEEKLY EARNINGS IN DOLLARS | AGE GROUPS IN YEARS | | | | | | | | | | | | | ACTUAL WEEKLY EARNINGS IN DOLLARS |
|---|---|---|---|---|---|---|---|---|---|---|---|---|---|---|
| | 14–15 | 16–17 | | 18–20 | | 21–24 | | 25–29 | | 30–34 | | 35–39 | | |
| | Female | Male | Female | Male | Female | Male | Female | Male | Female | Male | Female | Male | Female | |
| Less than $3 00 | 4 | ...... | 24 | 3 | 13 | 2 | 9 | 2 | 2 | ...... | 3 | ...... | 4 | Less than $3 00 |
| $3 00–$3 49 | 2 | ...... | 19 | 2 | 21 | ...... | 7 | ...... | 1 | ...... | 2 | ...... | ...... | $3 00– 3 49 |
| 3 50– 3 99 | 3 | 1 | 16 | 2 | 11 | 3 | 5 | ...... | 1 | ...... | ...... | ...... | 1 | 3 50– 3 99 |
| 4 00– 4 49 | 3 | 1 | 18 | ...... | 10 | ...... | 5 | 1 | 3 | 1 | 1 | ...... | 2 | 4 00– 4 49 |
| 4 50– 4 99 | ...... | 1 | 14 | 3 | 33 | 1 | 9 | ...... | 3 | ...... | ...... | 1 | 1 | 4 50– 4 99 |
| 5 00– 5 49 | ...... | 2 | 13 | 1 | 20 | 4 | 19 | 2 | 2 | 1 | 4 | 1 | 1 | 5 00– 5 49 |
| 5 50– 5 99 | ...... | 4 | 7 | 3 | 18 | 2 | 18 | 1 | 5 | ...... | 1 | 2 | 1 | 5 50– 5 99 |
| 6 00– 6 49 | ...... | 1 | 5 | 4 | 14 | 1 | 15 | 2 | 8 | 1 | 3 | ...... | 1 | 6 00– 6 49 |
| 6 50– 6 99 | ...... | 1 | 5 | 8 | 15 | 2 | 9 | ...... | 9 | ...... | 3 | 2 | 3 | 6 50– 6 99 |
| 7 00– 7 49 | ...... | 2 | 3 | 4 | 9 | 5 | 10 | 1 | 4 | ...... | 5 | ...... | 1 | 7 00– 7 49 |
| 7 50– 7 99 | ...... | 1 | 7 | 9 | 5 | 1 | 12 | 3 | 4 | 1 | ...... | ...... | ...... | 7 50– 7 99 |
| 8 00– 8 99 | 1 | 1 | 2 | 12 | 8 | 8 | 12 | ...... | 11 | 2 | 4 | ...... | 6 | 8 00– 8 99 |
| 9 00– 9 99 | ...... | ...... | ...... | 4 | 4 | 6 | 7 | 5 | 5 | 3 | 5 | 4 | 4 | 9 00– 9 99 |
| 10 00–10 99 | ...... | ...... | ...... | 6 | 1 | 9 | 3 | 6 | 10 | 3 | 3 | 3 | 4 | 10 00–10 99 |
| 11 00–11 99 | ...... | ...... | ...... | 4 | 1 | 10 | 1 | 4 | 2 | 7 | ...... | 7 | 1 | 11 00–11 99 |
| 12 00–12 99 | ...... | ...... | ...... | 1 | ...... | 4 | ...... | ...... | ...... | 5 | ...... | 2 | 3 | 12 00–12 99 |
| 13 00–13 99 | ...... | ...... | ...... | ...... | ...... | 4 | ...... | 2 | ...... | 2 | ...... | 5 | ...... | 13 00–13 99 |
| 14 00–14 99 | ...... | ...... | ...... | ...... | ...... | ...... | 1 | 2 | ...... | 2 | ...... | ...... | ...... | 14 00–14 99 |
| 15 00–15 99 | ...... | ...... | ...... | ...... | ...... | 1 | ...... | 4 | ...... | 3 | ...... | 4 | ...... | 15 00–15 99 |
| 16 00–17 99 | ...... | ...... | ...... | ...... | ...... | 2 | ...... | 3 | ...... | ...... | ...... | 5 | ...... | 16 00–17 99 |
| 18 00–19 99 | ...... | ...... | ...... | ...... | ...... | 2 | ...... | 2 | ...... | 1 | ...... | 1 | ...... | 18 00–19 99 |
| 20 00–24 99 | ...... | ...... | ...... | ...... | ...... | ...... | ...... | 2 | ...... | 4 | ...... | 2 | ...... | 20 00–24 99 |
| 25 00–29 99 | ...... | ...... | ...... | ...... | ...... | 1 | ...... | ...... | ...... | 1 | ...... | ...... | ...... | 25 00–29 99 |
| Not reported | ...... | ...... | ...... | ...... | ...... | ...... | ...... | 1 | ...... | ...... | ...... | ...... | ...... | Not reported |
| Total | 13 | 15 | 133 | 66 | 133 | 68 | 142 | 43 | 70 | 37 | 34 | 39 | 33 | Total |

199. TABLE VI, D, a — (*concluded*)

NEW YORK STATE EXCLUSIVE OF NEW YORK CITY
THE CONFECTIONERY INDUSTRY — FACTORY WORKERS
NUMBER AND PER CENT OF EMPLOYEES CLASSIFIED ACCORDING TO ACTUAL WEEKLY EARNINGS BY AGE GROUPS AND SEX

| ACTUAL WEEKLY EARNINGS IN DOLLARS | AGE GROUPS IN YEARS (*concluded*) | | | | | | | | | | | | | ACTUAL WEEKLY EARNINGS IN DOLLARS |
|---|---|---|---|---|---|---|---|---|---|---|---|---|---|---|
| | 40–44 | | 45–54 | | 55–64 | | 65 AND OVER | NOT REPORTED | | TOTAL | | CUMULATIVE PER CENT OF TOTAL | | |
| | Male | Female | Male | Female | Male | Female | Male | Male | Female | Male | Female | Male | Female | |
| Less than $3 00... | ...... | 2 | ...... | 1 | 1 | ...... | ...... | ...... | ...... | 8 | 62 | 2.20 | 9.60 | ..Less than $3 00 |
| $3 00–$3 49...... | ...... | ...... | ...... | ...... | ...... | ...... | ...... | ...... | ...... | 2 | 52 | 2.80 | 17.60 | .....$3 00– 3 49 |
| 3 50– 3 99...... | ...... | ...... | ...... | ...... | ...... | ...... | ...... | ...... | ...... | 6 | 37 | 4.40 | 23.40 | ..... 3 50– 3 99 |
| 4 00– 4 49...... | ...... | ...... | ...... | ...... | ...... | ...... | ...... | ...... | ...... | 3 | 42 | 5.30 | 29.60 | ..... 4 00– 4 49 |
| 4 50– 4 99...... | 1 | 2 | 1 | ...... | 1 | 1 | ...... | ...... | ...... | 9 | 63 | 7.80 | 39.60 | ..... 4 50– 4 99 |
| 5 00– 5 49...... | 1 | 1 | ...... | ...... | ...... | ...... | ...... | ...... | ...... | 12 | 60 | 11.10 | 48.90 | ..... 5 00– 5 49 |
| 5 50– 5 99...... | ...... | 2 | ...... | 1 | ...... | 1 | ...... | ...... | ...... | 12 | 54 | 14.50 | 57.30 | ..... 5 50– 5 99 |
| 6 00– 6 49...... | ...... | 2 | ...... | 3 | ...... | ...... | ...... | ...... | ...... | 9 | 51 | 17.00 | 65.10 | ..... 6 00– 6 49 |
| 6 50– 6 99...... | 1 | ...... | ...... | 1 | 1 | ...... | ...... | ...... | ...... | 15 | 45 | 21.10 | 72.10 | ..... 6 50– 6 99 |
| 7 00– 7 49...... | ...... | ...... | 1 | 1 | 1 | 1 | ...... | ...... | 1 | 14 | 35 | 25.00 | 77.50 | ..... 7 00– 7 49 |
| 7 50– 7 99...... | 1 | ...... | ...... | ...... | 1 | ...... | ...... | ...... | ...... | 17 | 28 | 29.80 | 81.90 | ..... 7 50– 7 99 |
| 8 00– 8 99...... | 3 | 1 | 4 | ...... | 2 | 1 | ...... | ...... | ...... | 32 | 46 | 38.60 | 89.00 | ..... 8 00– 8 99 |
| 9 00– 9 99...... | ...... | 2 | 5 | 4 | 3 | 1 | ...... | ...... | 1 | 30 | 33 | 47.00 | 94.20 | ..... 9 00– 9 99 |
| 10 00–10 99...... | 1 | 3 | 5 | 1 | 3 | ...... | 1 | ...... | ...... | 37 | 25 | 57.30 | 98.00 | .....10 00–10 99 |
| 11 00–11 99...... | 6 | ...... | 7 | ...... | 1 | ...... | ...... | ...... | ...... | 46 | 5 | 70.00 | 9.80 | .....11.00–11 99 |
| 12 00–12 99...... | 2 | ...... | 4 | 4 | 4 | ...... | ...... | ...... | ...... | 22 | 7 | 76.20 | 99.80 | .....12 00–12 99 |
| 13 00–13 99...... | 4 | ...... | 3 | ...... | ...... | ...... | 1 | 1 | ...... | 22 | ...... | 82.40 | ...... | .....13 00–13 99 |
| 14 00–14 99...... | 1 | ...... | 2 | ...... | ...... | ...... | ...... | ...... | ...... | 7 | 1 | 84.20 | 100.00 | .....14 00–14 99 |
| 15 00–15 99...... | 1 | ...... | 3 | ...... | 1 | ...... | ...... | ...... | ...... | 17 | ...... | 89.00 | ...... | .....15 00–15 99 |
| 16 00–17 99...... | 1 | ...... | 2 | ...... | 1 | ...... | ...... | ...... | ...... | 14 | ...... | 92.80 | ...... | .....16 00–17 99 |
| 18 00–19 99...... | 2 | ...... | 1 | ...... | ...... | ...... | ...... | ...... | ...... | 9 | ...... | 95.40 | ...... | .....18 00–19 99 |
| 20 00–24 99...... | 3 | ...... | 1 | ...... | ...... | ...... | ...... | ...... | ...... | 12 | ...... | 93.70 | ...... | .....20 00–24 99 |
| 25 00–29 99...... | 1 | ...... | 1 | ...... | ...... | ...... | ...... | ...... | ...... | 4 | ...... | 99.80 | ...... | .....25 00–29 99 |
| 30 00–34 99...... | 1 | ...... | ...... | ...... | ...... | ...... | ...... | ...... | ...... | 1 | ...... | 100.00 | ...... | .....30 00–34 99 |
| Not reported...... | ...... | ...... | ...... | ...... | ...... | ...... | ...... | ...... | ...... | 1 | ...... | ...... | ...... | .....Not reported |
| Total........ | 30 | 15 | 40 | 16 | 20 | 5 | 2 | 1 | 2 | 361 | 646 | ...... | ...... | .......Total |

200. TABLE IX, D, a

NEW YORK STATE EXCLUSIVE OF NEW YORK CITY
THE PAPER BOX INDUSTRY — FACTORY WORKERS
NUMBER AND PER CENT OF EMPLOYEES CLASSIFIED ACCORDING TO ACTUAL WEEKLY EARNINGS BY OCCUPATION AND SEX

| ACTUAL WEEKLY EARNINGS IN DOLLARS | OCCUPATION: FOREMEN AND FOREWOMEN | | CANDY MAKERS | | DIPPERS | | PACKERS | | WRAPPERS | | MACHINE OPERATORS | | HELPERS | | GENERAL LABORERS | TOTAL | | CUMULATIVE PER CENT OF TOTAL | | ACTUAL WEEKLY EARNINGS IN DOLLARS |
|---|---|---|---|---|---|---|---|---|---|---|---|---|---|---|---|---|---|---|---|---|
| | Male | Female | Male | Female | Male | Female | Male | Female | Male | Female | Male | Female | Male | Female | Male | Male | Female | Male | Female | |
| Less than $3 00 | | 2 | | | | 12 | | 30 | | 10 | | | 8 | 8 | | 8 | 62 | 2.20 | 9.60 | Less than $3 00 |
| $3 00-$3 49 | | | | 1 | | 2 | | 28 | | 9 | | | 2 | 12 | | 2 | 52 | 2.80 | 17.60 | $3 00- 3 49 |
| 3 50- 3 99 | | | 1 | | | 3 | | 23 | | 2 | | 1 | 5 | 8 | | 6 | 37 | 4.40 | 23.40 | 3 50- 3 99 |
| 4 00- 4 49 | | | | | | 3 | | 27 | | 1 | | | 3 | 11 | | 3 | 42 | 5.30 | 29.60 | 4 00- 4 49 |
| 4 50- 4 99 | | | 1 | | | 8 | 1 | 31 | | 9 | | | 7 | 15 | | 9 | 63 | 7.80 | 39.60 | 4 50- 4 99 |
| 5 00- 5 49 | 1 | 2 | | | | 8 | | 27 | | 8 | | | 11 | 15 | | 12 | 60 | 11.10 | 48.90 | 5 00- 5 49 |
| 5 50- 5 99 | | 2 | | | | 12 | 1 | 19 | | 10 | | | 11 | 11 | | 12 | 54 | 14.50 | 57.30 | 5 50- 5 99 |
| 6 00- 6 49 | | 3 | | | | 12 | | 17 | 1 | 15 | | | 8 | 4 | | 9 | 51 | 17.00 | 65.10 | 6 00- 6 49 |
| 6 50- 6 99 | | | | | | 13 | | 18 | | 11 | 2 | | 12 | 3 | 1 | 15 | 45 | 21.10 | 72.10 | 6 50- 6 99 |
| 7 00- 7 49 | | 3 | 1 | | | 6 | 1 | 16 | 1 | 7 | | | 11 | 3 | | 14 | 35 | 25.00 | 77.50 | 7 00- 7 49 |
| 7 50- 7 99 | | 3 | 5 | | | 7 | | 10 | | 7 | 1 | | 11 | 1 | | 17 | 28 | 29.80 | 81.90 | 7 50- 7 49 |
| 8 00- 8 99 | | 6 | 2 | | | 9 | | 13 | 1 | 8 | | 1 | 29 | 9 | | 32 | 46 | 38.60 | 89.00 | 8 00- 8 99 |
| 9 00- 9 99 | | 8 | 7 | | 1 | 2 | 2 | 11 | | 1 | 2 | 2 | 18 | 9 | | 30 | 33 | 47.00 | 94.20 | 9 00- 9 99 |
| 10 00-10 99 | 1 | 7 | 14 | | 1 | 5 | 1 | 5 | | 2 | 7 | 6 | 12 | | 1 | 37 | 25 | 57.30 | 98.00 | 10 00-10 99 |
| 11 00-11 99 | 5 | | 13 | | | 1 | 2 | 2 | | 2 | 10 | | 13 | | 3 | 46 | 5 | 70.00 | 98.80 | 11 00-11 99 |
| 12 00-12 99 | 2 | 4 | 7 | | | | 2 | 2 | | 1 | | | 9 | | 2 | 22 | 7 | 76.20 | 99.80 | 12 00-12 99 |
| 13 00-13 99 | 5 | | 10 | | | | | | | | 3 | | 4 | | | 22 | | 82.40 | | 13 00-13 99 |
| 14 00-14 99 | 2 | 1 | 2 | | | | | | | | | | 3 | | | 7 | 1 | 84.20 | 100.00 | 14 00-14 99 |
| 15 00-15 99 | 4 | | 11 | | | | 1 | | | | | | | | 1 | 17 | | 89.00 | | 15 00-15 99 |
| 16 00-17 99 | | | 11 | | | | | | | | | | 3 | | | 14 | | 92.80 | | 16 00-17 99 |
| 18 00-19 99 | 2 | | 6 | | | | | | | | | | 1 | | | 9 | | 95.40 | | 18 00-19 99 |
| 20 00-24 99 | 6 | | 6 | | | | | | | | | | | | | 12 | | 93.70 | | 20 00-24 99 |
| 25 00-29 99 | 3 | | 1 | | | | | | | | | | | | | 4 | | 99.80 | | 25 00-29 99 |
| 30 00-34 99 | 1 | | | | | | | | | | | | | | | 1 | | 100.00 | | 30 00-34 99 |
| Not reported | 1 | | | | | | | | | | | | | | | 1 | | | | Not reported |
| Total | 33 | 41 | 98 | 1 | 2 | 103 | 11 | 279 | 3 | 103 | 25 | 10 | 181 | 109 | 8 | 361 | 646 | | | Total |

## NEW YORK CITY
## DEPARTMENT STORES — STOCK AND SALES

201. TABLE V, A, 1, a — Number and Per Cent of Employees Earning Specified Weekly Rates by Age Groups and Sex

| Weekly Rates in Dollars | Age Groups in Years | | | | | | | | | | | | | | Weekly Rates in Dollars |
|---|---|---|---|---|---|---|---|---|---|---|---|---|---|---|---|
| | 14–15 | | 16–17 | | 18–20 | | 21–24 | | 25–29 | | 30–34 | | 35–39 | | |
| | Male | Female | Male | Female | Male | Female | Male | Female | Male | Female | Male | Female | Male | Female | |
| Less than $3 00 | .... | 2 | .... | ...... | ...... | ...... | ...... | ...... | ...... | ...... | ...... | ...... | ...... | ...... | Less than $3 00 |
| $3 00–$3 49... | 12 | 147 | 3 | 30 | ...... | 3 | ...... | ...... | ...... | ...... | ...... | 1 | ...... | ...... | ...$3 00– 3 00 |
| 3 50– 3 99... | 20 | 309 | 3 | 129 | 2 | 10 | ...... | 3 | ...... | ...... | ...... | ...... | ...... | ...... | ... 3 50– 3 99 |
| 4 00– 4 49... | 163 | 322 | 44 | 529 | 7 | 107 | 4 | 10 | 5 | 2 | 4 | ...... | 2 | ...... | ... 4 00– 4 49 |
| 4 50– 4 99... | 26 | 60 | 26 | 218 | 1 | 117 | 1 | 21 | 1 | 22 | ...... | 13 | 1 | 18 | ... 4 50– 4 99 |
| 5 00– 5 49... | 45 | 44 | 86 | 295 | 14 | 300 | 2 | 40 | 1 | 11 | 4 | 2 | 1 | 2 | ... 5 00– 5 49 |
| 5 50– 5 99... | 3 | 6 | 7 | 40 | 2 | 73 | 1 | 28 | ...... | 11 | ...... | 2 | ...... | ...... | ... 5 50– 5 99 |
| 6 00– 6 49... | 9 | 6 | 118 | 182 | 76 | 633 | 8 | 278 | 1 | 72 | 2 | 28 | ...... | 14 | ... 6 00– 6 49 |
| 6 50– 6 99... | .... | 5 | 7 | 10 | 6 | 63 | 4 | 36 | 2 | 10 | ...... | 3 | ...... | ...... | ... 6 50– 6 99 |
| 7 00– 7 49... | 2 | 1 | 49 | 53 | 112 | 545 | 17 | 570 | 1 | 224 | 4 | 120 | ...... | 77 | ... 7 00– 7 49 |
| 7 50– 7 99... | 1 | ...... | 1 | 3 | 8 | 28 | 2 | 36 | ...... | 10 | ...... | 2 | ...... | 4 | ... 7 50– 7 99 |
| 8 00– 8 99... | .... | 2 | 23 | 13 | 134 | 305 | 35 | 670 | 7 | 309 | 6 | 135 | 4 | 98 | ... 8 00– 8 99 |
| 9 00– 9 99... | 1 | ...... | 3 | 3 | 62 | 97 | 54 | 393 | 7 | 277 | 3 | 99 | 1 | 86 | ... 9 00– 9 99 |
| 10 00–10 99... | .... | ...... | 3 | 1 | 73 | 49 | 102 | 322 | 47 | 309 | 18 | 131 | 14 | 95 | ...10 00–10 99 |
| 11 00–11 99... | .... | ...... | .... | ...... | 17 | 18 | 41 | 114 | 26 | 144 | 10 | 62 | 10 | 38 | ...11 00–11 99 |
| 12 00–12 99... | .... | ...... | .... | 1 | 38 | 24 | 177 | 150 | 101 | 266 | 69 | 158 | 54 | 87 | ...12 00–12 99 |
| 13 00–13 99... | .... | ...... | .... | 1 | 4 | ...... | 30 | 25 | 30 | 52 | 14 | 39 | 10 | 26 | ...13 00–13 99 |
| 14 00–14 99... | .... | ...... | .... | ...... | 4 | 5 | 68 | 40 | 73 | 90 | 53 | 65 | 32 | 58 | ...14 00–14 99 |
| 15 00–15 99... | .... | ...... | 1 | 1 | 1 | ...... | 76 | 31 | 131 | 90 | 84 | 68 | 81 | 58 | ...15 00–15 99 |
| 16 00–17 99... | .... | ...... | .... | 2 | 2 | 1 | 38 | 11 | 83 | 54 | 68 | 58 | 43 | 52 | ...16 00–17 99 |
| 18 00–19 99... | .... | ...... | .... | ...... | 5 | 2 | 25 | 8 | 74 | 51 | 93 | 43 | 66 | 55 | ...18 00–19 99 |
| 20 00–24 99... | .... | ...... | .... | ...... | ...... | ...... | 19 | 7 | 99 | 40 | 122 | 49 | 130 | 52 | ...20 00–24 99 |
| 25 00–29 99... | .... | ...... | .... | ...... | ...... | ...... | 1 | ...... | 36 | 17 | 57 | 18 | 82 | 24 | ...25 00–29 99 |
| 30 00–34 99... | .... | ...... | .... | ...... | ...... | 1 | ...... | ...... | 9 | 9 | 25 | 7 | 31 | 9 | ...30 00–34 99 |
| 35 00–39 99... | .... | ...... | .... | ...... | ...... | 1 | ...... | ...... | 2 | 1 | 6 | 6 | 8 | 7 | ...35 00–39 99 |
| 40 00 and over. | .... | ...... | .... | ...... | ...... | ...... | ...... | ...... | 2 | 3 | 11 | 6 | 32 | 8 | .40 00 and over |
| Not reported... | .... | 1 | 1 | 1 | 3 | 2 | 5 | ...... | 8 | 1 | 4 | ...... | 13 | ...... | ...Not reported |
| Total..... | 282 | 905 | 375 | 1,512 | 571 | 2,384 | 710 | 2,793 | 746 | 2,075 | 657 | 1,115 | 615 | 868 | .....Total |

201. TABLE V, A, 1, a — (*concluded*)

NEW YORK CITY
DEPARTMENT STORES — STOCK AND SALES
NUMBER AND PER CENT OF EMPLOYEES EARNINGS SPECIFIED WEEKLY RATES BY AGE GROUPS AND SEX

| WEEKLY RATES IN DOLLARS | AGE GROUPS IN YEARS (*concluded*) | | | | | | | | | | | | | | WEEKLY RATES IN DOLLARS |
|---|---|---|---|---|---|---|---|---|---|---|---|---|---|---|---|
| | 40–44 | | 45–54 | | 55–64 | | 65 AND OVER | | NOT REPORTED | | TOTAL | | CUMULATIVE PER CENT OF TOTAL | | |
| | Male | Female | Male | Female | Male | Female | Male | Female | Male | Female | Male | Female | Male | Female | |
| Less than $3 00 | .... | ...... | .... | ...... | ...... | ...... | ...... | ...... | ...... | ...... | ...... | 2 | ...... | .01 | Less than $3 00 |
| 3 00–$3 49... | .... | ...... | .... | ...... | ...... | ...... | ...... | ...... | 1 | ...... | 16 | 181 | .3 | 1.4 | ...$3 00– 3 49 |
| 3 50– 3 99... | .... | ...... | .... | ...... | ...... | ...... | ...... | ...... | ...... | 17 | 25 | 468 | .7 | 5.1 | ... 3 50– 3 99 |
| 4 00– 4 49... | 6 | 1 | 5 | ...... | 1 | ...... | ...... | ...... | 3 | 17 | 244 | 988 | 5.1 | 12.7 | ... 4 00– 4 49 |
| 4 50– 4 99... | .... | 8 | .... | 6 | ...... | ...... | ...... | ...... | 2 | 12 | 58 | 495 | 6.2 | 16.6 | ... 4 50– 4 99 |
| 5 00– 5 49... | .... | 2 | .... | 1 | 1 | ...... | ...... | ...... | ...... | 25 | 154 | 722 | 8.9 | 22.2 | ... 5 00– 5 49 |
| 5 50– 5 99... | .... | 1 | .... | ...... | ...... | ...... | ...... | ...... | ...... | 85 | 13 | 246 | 9.2 | 24.1 | ... 5 50– 5 99 |
| 6 00– 6 49... | .... | 12 | 1 | 10 | ...... | 1 | 1 | ...... | ...... | 58 | 216 | 1,294 | 13.0 | 34.1 | ... 6 00– 6 49 |
| 6 50– 6 99... | .... | 3 | .... | ...... | ...... | ...... | ...... | ...... | ...... | 79 | 19 | 209 | 13.4 | 35.8 | ... 6 50– 6 99 |
| 7 00– 7 49... | 1 | 41 | 3 | 27 | 4 | 2 | 2 | 2 | 1 | 39 | 196 | 1,701 | 16.9 | 48.9 | ... 7 00– 7 49 |
| 7 50– 7 99... | .... | ...... | .... | ...... | ...... | ...... | ...... | ...... | ...... | 24 | 12 | 107 | 17.1 | 49.8 | ... 7 50– 7 99 |
| 8 00– 8 99... | 4 | 37 | 8 | 22 | 10 | 6 | 4 | ...... | 5 | 56 | 240 | 1,653 | 21.4 | 62.7 | ... 8 00– 8 99 |
| 9 00– 9 99... | 3 | 33 | 8 | 18 | ...... | 1 | ...... | ...... | 4 | 67 | 146 | 1,074 | 24.0 | 71.0 | ... 9 00– 9 00 |
| 10 00–10 99... | 9 | 32 | 14 | 20 | 11 | 4 | 2 | 1 | 4 | 39 | 297 | 1,003 | 29.4 | 78.8 | ...10 00–10 99 |
| 11 00–11 99... | 6 | 18 | 5 | 1 | 4 | 1 | ...... | ...... | 6 | 12 | 125 | 408 | 31.6 | 81.9 | ...11 00–11 99 |
| 12 00–12 99... | 39 | 39 | 55 | 22 | 19 | ...... | 9 | ...... | 6 | 24 | 567 | 771 | 41.8 | 88.0 | ...12 00–12 99 |
| 13 00–13 99... | 10 | 10 | 17 | 3 | 4 | ...... | 2 | ...... | 1 | 14 | 122 | 170 | 44.0 | 89.3 | ...13 00–13 99 |
| 14 00–14 99... | 20 | 18 | 37 | 5 | 18 | ...... | 4 | ...... | 2 | 10 | 311 | 291 | 49.6 | 91.5 | ...14 00–14 99 |
| 15 00–15 99... | 62 | 28 | 83 | 13 | 33 | ...... | 5 | ...... | 3 | 13 | 560 | 302 | 59.7 | 93.8 | ...15 00–15 99 |
| 16 00–17 99... | 41 | 27 | 76 | 13 | 23 | 1 | 7 | ...... | 6 | 19 | 387 | 238 | 66.7 | 95.7 | ...16 00–17 99 |
| 18 00–19 99... | 55 | 14 | 98 | 8 | 19 | 1 | 4 | ...... | 4 | 13 | 443 | 195 | 74 6 | 97.2 | ...18 00–19 99 |
| 20 00–24 99... | 112 | 24 | 158 | 7 | 59 | ...... | 4 | ...... | 5 | 19 | 708 | 198 | 87.3 | 98.7 | ...20 00–24 99 |
| 25 00–29 99... | 73 | 11 | 96 | 9 | 27 | ...... | 7 | ...... | ...... | 8 | 379 | 87 | 94.1 | 99.4 | ...25 00–29 00 |
| 30 00–34 99... | 35 | 2 | 39 | 3 | 10 | ...... | 3 | ...... | 1 | 4 | 153 | 35 | 96.9 | 99.6 | ...30 00–34 99 |
| 35 00–39 99... | 12 | 5 | 21 | 1 | 6 | ...... | 2 | ...... | 1 | 1 | 58 | 22 | 97.9 | 99.9 | ...35 00–39 99 |
| 40 00 and over. | 25 | 4 | 33 | 3 | 7 | ...... | 2 | ...... | 1 | 8 | 113 | 32 | 100.0 | 100.0 | .40 00 and over |
| Not reported... | 3 | ...... | 11 | ...... | 7 | ...... | 2 | ...... | ...... | 1 | 57 | 6 | ...... | ...... | ...Not reported |
| Total..... | 516 | 370 | 768 | 192 | 263 | 17 | 60 | 8 | 56 | 664 | 5,619 | 12,898 | ...... | ...... | .....Total |

NEW YORK CITY

DEPARTMENT STORES — STOCK AND SALES

202. TABLE IX, D. a — NUMBER AND PER CENT OF EMPLOYEES EARNING SPECIFIED WEEKLY RATES BY OCCUPATION AND SEX

| WEEKLY RATES IN DOLLARS | OCCUPATION: SUPERINTENDENTS | BUYERS | | ASSISTANT BUYERS AND HEADS OF STOCK | | RECEIVING AND STOCK CLERKS | | STOCK PEOPLE | | FLOOR MANAGERS | | SALES PEOPLE | | MESSENGER, WRAPPERS, ERRAND BOYS | | TOTAL | | CUMULATIVE PER CENT OF TOTAL | | WEEKLY RATES IN DOLLARS |
|---|---|---|---|---|---|---|---|---|---|---|---|---|---|---|---|---|---|---|---|---|
| | Male | Male | Female | Male | Female | Male | Female | Male | Female | Male | Female | Male | Female | Male | Female | Male | Female | Male | Female | |
| Less than $3 00 | | | | | | | | | | | | | | | 2 | | 2 | | .01 | Less than $3 00 |
| $3 00–$3 49 | | | | | | 1 | 16 | | 8 | | | | 3 | 15 | 154 | 16 | 181 | .30 | 1.40 | $3 00– 3 49 |
| 3 50– 3 99 | | | | | | 1 | 42 | | 72 | | | | 27 | 24 | 327 | 25 | 468 | .70 | 5.10 | 3 50– 3 99 |
| 4 00– 4 49 | | | | | | 6 | 69 | 14 | 118 | | | 8 | 97 | 216 | 704 | 244 | 988 | 5.10 | 12.70 | 4 00– 4 49 |
| 4 50– 4 99 | | | | | | 6 | 59 | 13 | 90 | | | 1 | 159 | 38 | 187 | 58 | 495 | 6.20 | 16.60 | 4 50– 4 99 |
| 5 00– 5 49 | | | | | 1 | 17 | 119 | 66 | 198 | | 1 | 5 | 162 | 66 | 241 | 154 | 722 | 8.90 | 22.20 | 5 00– 5 49 |
| 5 50– 5 99 | | | | | 1 | 3 | 13 | 3 | 31 | | | 1 | 164 | 6 | 37 | 13 | 246 | 9.20 | 24.10 | 5 50– 5 99 |
| 6 00– 6 49 | | | | | 3 | 52 | 111 | 99 | 101 | | | 17 | 951 | 48 | 128 | 216 | 1,294 | 13.00 | 34.10 | 6 00– 6 49 |
| 6 50– 6 99 | | | | | | 2 | 5 | 6 | 15 | | | 4 | 136 | 7 | 53 | 19 | 209 | 13.40 | 35.80 | 6 50– 6 99 |
| 7 00– 7 49 | | | | | 8 | 43 | 77 | 67 | 51 | 1 | | 28 | 1,511 | 57 | 54 | 196 | 1,701 | 16.90 | 48.90 | 7 00– 7 49 |
| 7 50– 7 99 | | | | 1 | 2 | 2 | 8 | 4 | 7 | | 2 | 3 | 72 | 2 | 16 | 12 | 107 | 17.10 | 49.80 | 7 50– 7 99 |
| 8 00– 8 99 | | | | 1 | 18 | 65 | 51 | 47 | 36 | | 2 | 44 | 1,507 | 83 | 39 | 240 | 1,653 | 21.40 | 62.70 | 8 00– 8 99 |
| 9 00– 9 99 | | | | 1 | 35 | 38 | 36 | 23 | 25 | | 16 | 58 | 958 | 26 | 4 | 146 | 1,074 | 24.00 | 71.00 | 9 00– 9 99 |
| 10 00–10 99 | | | | 2 | 26 | 63 | 28 | 61 | 13 | | 7 | 146 | 925 | 25 | 4 | 297 | 1,003 | 29.40 | 78.80 | 10 00–10 99 |
| 11 00–11 99 | | | | 1 | 26 | 47 | 13 | 21 | 14 | | 5 | 52 | 348 | 4 | 2 | 125 | 408 | 31.60 | 81.90 | 11 00–11 99 |
| 12 00–12 99 | | 1 | | 5 | 37 | 108 | 14 | 81 | 14 | 5 | 2 | 353 | 703 | 14 | 1 | 567 | 771 | 41.80 | 88.00 | 12 00–12 99 |
| 13 00–13 99 | | | | 2 | 11 | 36 | 5 | 14 | 3 | | 3 | 68 | 147 | 2 | 1 | 122 | 170 | 44.00 | 89.30 | 13 00–13 99 |
| 14 00–14 99 | | | | 8 | 32 | 46 | 10 | 23 | | | | 233 | 247 | 1 | 2 | 311 | 291 | 49.60 | 91.50 | 14 00–14 99 |
| 15 00–15 99 | 1 | 2 | 1 | 19 | 35 | 29 | 4 | 16 | | 8 | 1 | 484 | 261 | 1 | | 560 | 302 | 59.70 | 93.80 | 15 00–15 99 |
| 16 00–17 99 | 1 | | | 24 | 27 | 27 | 7 | 15 | | 17 | 3 | 302 | 201 | 1 | | 387 | 238 | 66.70 | 95.70 | 16 00–17 99 |
| 18 00–19 99 | | 3 | | 27 | 38 | 18 | 3 | 9 | | 44 | | 341 | 154 | 1 | | 443 | 195 | 74.60 | 97.20 | 18 00–19 99 |
| 20 00–24 99 | 3 | 4 | 4 | 39 | 42 | 16 | 2 | 6 | 1 | 161 | | 479 | 149 | | | 708 | 198 | 87.30 | 98.70 | 20 00–24 99 |
| 25 00–29 99 | 6 | 5 | 4 | 39 | 31 | 5 | | 3 | | 152 | | 169 | 52 | | | 379 | 87 | 94.10 | 99.40 | 25 00–29 99 |
| 30 00–34 99 | 2 | 4 | 5 | 28 | 12 | 1 | | 2 | | 62 | | 54 | 18 | | | 153 | 35 | 96.90 | 99.60 | 30 00–34 99 |
| 35 00–39 99 | 1 | | 1 | 9 | 11 | 3 | | 1 | | 25 | | 19 | 10 | | | 58 | 22 | 97.90 | 99.90 | 35 00–39 99 |
| 40 00 and over | 6 | 29 | 12 | 19 | 6 | 1 | | 1 | | 16 | | 41 | 14 | | | 113 | 32 | 100.00 | 100.00 | 40 00 and over |
| Not reported | | | | | | | | 1 | | 2 | | 54 | 5 | | 1 | 57 | 6 | | | Not reported |
| Total | 20 | 48 | 27 | 225 | 402 | 636 | 692 | 596 | 797 | 493 | 42 | 2,964 | 8,981 | 637 | 1,957 | 5,619 | 12,898 | | | Total |

NEW YORK CITY

DEPARTMENT STORES — STOCK AND SALES

203. TABLE VI, A, 1, a NUMBER AND PER CENT OF EMPLOYEES CLASSIFIED ACCORDING TO ACTUAL WEEKLY EARNINGS BY AGE GROUPS AND SEX

| ACTUAL WEEKLY EARNINGS IN DOLLARS | AGE GROUPS IN YEARS | | | | | | | | | | | | | | ACTUAL WEEKLY EARNINGS IN DOLLARS |
|---|---|---|---|---|---|---|---|---|---|---|---|---|---|---|---|
| | 14–15 | | 16–17 | | 18–20 | | 21–24 | | 25–29 | | 30–34 | | 35–39 | | |
| | Male | Female | Male | Female | Male | Female | Male | Female | Male | Female | Male | Female | Male | Female | |
| Less than $3 00 | 11 | 54 | 10 | 36 | 6 | 29 | 4 | 26 | 4 | 15 | 1 | 5 | ...... | 7 | Less than $3 00 |
| 3 00–$3 49... | 19 | 152 | 11 | 72 | 1 | 24 | ...... | 6 | 1 | 5 | ...... | 2 | 1 | ...... | ...$3 00– 3 49 |
| 3 50– 3 99... | 20 | 205 | 5 | 160 | 4 | 21 | 2 | 12 | ...... | 7 | 1 | 2 | ...... | 4 | ... 3 50– 3 99 |
| 4 00– 4 49... | 150 | 377 | 40 | 467 | 9 | 120 | ...... | 17 | ...... | 7 | 1 | 4 | 2 | 1 | ... 4 00– 4 49 |
| 4 50– 4 99... | 25 | 54 | 30 | 188 | 6 | 89 | 2 | 17 | 1 | 17 | ...... | 10 | 1 | 9 | ... 4 50– 4 99 |
| 5 00– 5 49... | 42 | 39 | 78 | 253 | 14 | 243 | 6 | 51 | 1 | 19 | 3 | 15 | ...... | 7 | ... 5 00– 5 49 |
| 5 50– 5 99... | 3 | 5 | 14 | 56 | 17 | 147 | 3 | 74 | 1 | 24 | 2 | 10 | ...... | 8 | ... 5 50– 5 99 |
| 6 00– 6 49... | 8 | 7 | 102 | 156 | 59 | 459 | 8 | 222 | 6 | 54 | 2 | 25 | 1 | 16 | ... 6 00– 6 49 |
| 6 50– 6 99... | .... | 5 | 14 | 20 | 22 | 174 | 4 | 129 | 1 | 50 | ...... | 22 | ...... | 8 | ... 6 50– 6 99 |
| 7 00– 7 49... | 2 | 1 | 39 | 66 | 90 | 424 | 17 | 389 | 1 | 170 | 3 | 83 | ...... | 59 | ... 7 00– 7 49 |
| 7 50– 7 99... | 1 | 1 | 3 | 9 | 18 | 108 | 5 | 159 | 3 | 48 | 1 | 23 | ...... | 15 | ... 7 50– 7 99 |
| 8 00– 8 99... | .... | 2 | 20 | 16 | 122 | 301 | 40 | 585 | 8 | 300 | 7 | 124 | 6 | 90 | ....8 00– 8 99 |
| 9 00– 9 99... | 1 | ...... | 5 | 4 | 51 | 118 | 66 | 385 | 10 | 268 | 4 | 109 | 2 | 84 | ....9 00– 9 99 |
| 10 00–10 99... | .... | ...... | 2 | 1 | 67 | 65 | 81 | 317 | 47 | 268 | 17 | 113 | 10 | 78 | ...10 00–10 99 |
| 11 00–11 99... | .... | ...... | .... | ...... | 27 | 19 | 60 | 124 | 36 | 169 | 16 | 72 | 11 | 44 | ...11 00–11 99 |
| 12 00–12 99... | .... | 1 | 1 | 1 | 32 | 24 | 130 | 133 | 76 | 210 | 56 | 120 | 47 | 73 | ...12 00–12 99 |
| 13 00–13 99... | .... | ...... | .... | ...... | 8 | 5 | 49 | 46 | 44 | 77 | 18 | 46 | 13 | 31 | ...13 00–13 99 |
| 14 00–14 99... | .... | ...... | .... | 1 | 6 | 4 | 64 | 41 | 63 | 100 | 45 | 62 | 30 | 62 | ...14 00–14 99 |
| 15 00–15 99... | .... | ...... | 1 | 1 | 3 | 1 | 65 | 26 | 92 | 83 | 71 | 72 | 59 | 57 | ...15 00–15 99 |
| 16 00–17 99... | .... | ...... | .... | 1 | 3 | 2 | 45 | 10 | 90 | 70 | 70 | 63 | 46 | 64 | ...16 00–17 99 |
| 18 00–19 99... | .... | ...... | .... | ...... | 3 | 1 | 31 | 10 | 78 | 51 | 84 | 41 | 77 | 49 | ...18 00–19 99 |
| 20 00–24 99... | .... | ...... | .... | 1 | 1 | 1 | 25 | 11 | 108 | 35 | 142 | 52 | 142 | 54 | ...20 00–24 99 |
| 25 00–29 99... | .... | ...... | .... | ...... | ...... | ...... | 1 | 1 | 50 | 16 | 63 | 17 | 85 | 24 | ...25 00–29 99 |
| 30 00–34 99... | .... | ...... | .... | ...... | ...... | 1 | ...... | ...... | 18 | 7 | 29 | 6 | 34 | 9 | ...30 00–34 99 |
| 35 00–39 99... | .... | ...... | .... | ...... | ...... | 1 | ...... | ...... | 4 | 1 | 8 | 6 | 15 | 6 | ...35 00–39 99 |
| 40 00 and over. | .... | ...... | .... | ...... | ...... | ...... | ...... | ...... | 3 | 3 | 12 | 6 | 33 | 8 | .40 00 and over |
| Not reported... | .... | 2 | .... | 3 | 2 | 5 | 2 | 2 | ...... | 2 | 1 | 5 | ...... | 1 | ...Not reported |
| Total..... | 282 | 905 | 375 | 1,512 | 571 | 2,386 | 710 | 2,793 | 746 | 2,076 | 657 | 1,115 | 615 | 868 | .....Total |

203. TABLE VI, A, 1, a — (*concluded*)

NEW YORK CITY

**DEPARTMENT STORES — STOCK AND SALES**

NUMBER AND PER CENT OF EMPLOYEES CLASSIFIED ACCORDING TO ACTUAL WEEKLY EARNINGS BY AGE GROUPS AND SEX

| ACTUAL WEEKLY EARNINGS IN DOLLARS | AGE GROUPS IN YEARS (*concluded*) 40–44 | | 45–54 | | 55-64 | | 65 AND OVER | | NOT REPORTED | | TOTAL | | CUMULATIVE PER CENT OF TOTAL | | ACTUAL WEEKLY EARNINGS IN DOLLARS |
|---|---|---|---|---|---|---|---|---|---|---|---|---|---|---|---|
| | Male | Female | Male | Female | Male | Female | Male | Female | Male | Female | Male | Female | Male | Female | |
| Less than $3 00 | 2 | 2 | 1 | ...... | 1 | 1 | ...... | ...... | ...... | 1 | 40 | 176 | .71 | 1.37 | Less than $3 00 |
| $3 00–$3 49... | .... | 3 | .... | ...... | ...... | ...... | ...... | ...... | 1 | 2 | 84 | 266 | 1.32 | 3.43 | ...$3 00– 3 49 |
| 3 50– 3 99... | .... | 3 | .... | 1 | ...... | ...... | ...... | ...... | 1 | 13 | 33 | 428 | 1.91 | 6.76 | ....3 50– 3 99 |
| 4 00– 4 49... | .... | ...... | 2 | 1 | 1 | ...... | ...... | ...... | 2 | 16 | 207 | 1,010 | 5.60 | 14.60 | ....4 00– 4 49 |
| 4 50– 4 99... | .... | 3 | 1 | 4 | ...... | ...... | ...... | ...... | 2 | 5 | 68 | 396 | 6.80 | 17.68 | ....4 50– 4 99 |
| 5 00– 5 49... | 1 | 4 | 1 | 6 | ...... | 1 | ...... | ...... | ...... | 2 | 146 | 640 | 9.42 | 22.65 | ....5 00– 5 49 |
| 5 50– 5 99... | .... | 4 | .... | 5 | ...... | ...... | ...... | ...... | ...... | 7 | 40 | 340 | 9.95 | 25.30 | ....5 50– 5 99 |
| 6 00– 6 49... | 1 | 12 | 3 | 8 | ...... | 1 | 1 | 1 | ...... | 17 | 191 | 978 | 13.52 | 32.85 | ....6 00– 6 49 |
| 6 50– 6 99... | .... | 3 | 2 | 1 | 1 | ...... | 2 | ...... | ...... | 27 | 46 | 430 | 14.35 | 36.30 | ....6 50– 6 99 |
| 7 00– 7 49... | 1 | 36 | 3 | 17 | 5 | 2 | 1 | 1 | 1 | 20 | 163 | 1,268 | 17.50 | 46.10 | ....7 00– 7 49 |
| 7 50– 7 99... | 1 | 2 | .... | 3 | 1 | ...... | 1 | ...... | 2 | 28 | 36 | 396 | 18.50 | 49.20 | ....7 50– 7 99 |
| 8 00– 8 99... | 4 | 35 | 9 | 24 | 10 | 4 | 3 | ...... | 2 | 88 | 231 | 1,569 | 22.00 | 61.50 | ....8 00– 8 99 |
| 9 00– 9 99... | 4 | 32 | 9 | 18 | 2 | 1 | 1 | ...... | 2 | 103 | 157 | 1,122 | 24.80 | 70.10 | ....9 00– 9 99 |
| 10 00–10 99... | 11 | 29 | 13 | 17 | 8 | 2 | 2 | ...... | 2 | 64 | 260 | 954 | 29.45 | 77.50 | ...10 00–10 99 |
| 11 00–11 99... | 7 | 18 | 9 | 2 | 3 | 2 | 1 | 1 | 2 | 43 | 172 | 494 | 32.50 | 81.30 | ...11 00–11 99 |
| 12 00–12 99... | 33 | 34 | 39 | 15 | 14 | 1 | 9 | ...... | 4 | 55 | 441 | 667 | 40.40 | 86.50 | ...12 00–12 99 |
| 13 00–13 99... | 8 | 12 | 21 | 6 | 6 | ...... | 2 | ...... | 3 | 28 | 172 | 251 | 43.35 | 88.50 | ...13 00–13 99 |
| 14 00–14 99... | 15 | 13 | 41 | 6 | 21 | ...... | 3 | ...... | 5 | 27 | 293 | 316 | 48.60 | 91.00 | ...14 00–14 99 |
| 15 00–15 99... | 43 | 26 | 69 | 13 | 25 | ...... | 3 | ...... | 2 | 31 | 433 | 310 | 56.40 | 93.50 | ...15 00–15 99 |
| 16 00–17 99... | 52 | 31 | 68 | 12 | 27 | 1 | 8 | ...... | 7 | 27 | 416 | 281 | 63.70 | 95.60 | ...16 00–17 99 |
| 18 00–19 99... | 58 | 15 | 103 | 11 | 22 | 1 | 4 | ...... | 6 | 20 | 466 | 199 | 72.00 | 97.00 | ...18 00–19 99 |
| 20 00–24 99... | 120 | 27 | 172 | 6 | 61 | ...... | 4 | ...... | 8 | 16 | 783 | 203 | 86.00 | 98.60 | ...20 00–24 99 |
| 25 00–29 99... | 79 | 14 | 100 | 9 | 31 | ...... | 8 | ...... | 1 | 7 | 418 | 88 | 93.40 | 99.25 | ...25 00–29 99 |
| 30 00–34 99... | 35 | 1 | 46 | 3 | 11 | ...... | 3 | ...... | 1 | 4 | 177 | 31 | 96.60 | 99.60 | ...30 00–34 99 |
| 35 00–39 99... | 12 | 5 | 22 | 1 | 6 | ...... | 2 | ...... | 1 | 1 | 70 | 21 | 97.90 | 99.75 | ...35 00–39 99 |
| 40 00 and over. | 27 | 4 | 33 | 3 | 7 | ...... | 2 | ...... | 1 | 8 | 118 | 32 | 100.00 | 100.00 | .40 00 and over |
| Not reported... | 2 | 2 | 1 | ...... | ...... | ...... | ...... | ...... | ...... | 4 | 8 | 26 | ...... | ...... | ...Not reported |
| Total..... | 516 | 370 | 768 | 192 | 263 | 17 | 60 | 3 | 56 | 664 | 5,619 | 12,901 | ...... | ...... | .....Total |

NEW YORK CITY

DEPARTMENT STORES — STOCK AND SALES

204. TABLE IX, A, 1, a    Number and Per Cent of Employees Classified According to Actual Weekly Earnings by Occupation and Sex

| Actual Weekly Earnings in Dollars | Occupation | | | | | | | | | | | | | | | | | | | | Actual Weekly Earnings in Dollars |
|---|---|---|---|---|---|---|---|---|---|---|---|---|---|---|---|---|---|---|---|---|---|
| | Superintendents | Buyers | | Assistant Buyers and Heads of Stock | | Receiving and Stock Clerks | | Stock People | | Floor Managers | | Sales People | | Messenger, Wrappers, Errand Boys | | Total | | Cumulative Per Cent of Total | | |
| | Male | Male | Female | Male | Female | Male | Female | Male | Female | Male | Female | Male | Female | Male | Female | Male | Female | Male | Female | |
| Less than $3 00 | | | | | 2 | 5 | 6 | 6 | 17 | | | 11 | 77 | 18 | 74 | 40 | 176 | .71 | 1.37 | Less than $3 00 |
| $3 00-$3 49 | | | | | | 1 | 22 | 2 | 19 | | | 3 | 25 | 28 | 200 | 34 | 266 | 1.32 | 3.43 | $3 00- 3 49 |
| 3 50- 3 99 | | | | 1 | | 3 | 44 | 2 | 83 | | | 1 | 50 | 26 | 251 | 33 | 428 | 1.91 | 6.76 | 3 50- 3 99 |
| 4 00- 4 49 | | | | | 1 | 4 | 72 | 13 | 141 | 2 | | 5 | 74 | 183 | 722 | 207 | 1,010 | 5.60 | 14.60 | 4 00- 4 49 |
| 4 50- 4 99 | | | | | 1 | 8 | 61 | 20 | 79 | 1 | | 1 | 76 | 38 | 179 | 68 | 396 | 6.80 | 17.68 | 4 50- 4 99 |
| 5 00- 5 49 | | | | | | 17 | 108 | 62 | 162 | | 1 | 10 | 160 | 57 | 209 | 146 | 640 | 9.42 | 22.65 | 5 00- 5 49 |
| 5 50- 5 99 | | | | | | 12 | 27 | 15 | 40 | | | 3 | 228 | 10 | 45 | 40 | 340 | 9.95 | 25.30 | 5 50- 5 99 |
| 6 00- 6 49 | | | | | 3 | 43 | 90 | 84 | 86 | 1 | | 16 | 688 | 47 | 111 | 191 | 978 | 13.52 | 32.85 | 6 00- 6 49 |
| 6 50- 6 99 | | | | | 4 | 7 | 16 | 10 | 18 | | 1 | 17 | 344 | 12 | 56 | 46 | 439 | 14.35 | 36.30 | 6 50- 6 99 |
| 7 00- 7 49 | | | | | 8 | 38 | 68 | 57 | 44 | | | 25 | 1,101 | 43 | 47 | 163 | 1,268 | 17.50 | 46.10 | 7 00- 7 49 |
| 7 50- 7 99 | | | | 1 | 4 | 5 | 9 | 12 | 11 | | 3 | 9 | 357 | 9 | 12 | 36 | 396 | 18.50 | 49.20 | 7 50- 7 99 |
| 8 00- 8 99 | | | | | 16 | 62 | 51 | 38 | 34 | | 2 | 53 | 1,436 | 78 | 30 | 231 | 1,560 | 22.00 | 61.50 | 8 00- 8 99 |
| 9 00- 9 99 | | | | 1 | 27 | 44 | 31 | 36 | 24 | 1 | 15 | 52 | 1,020 | 23 | 5 | 157 | 1,122 | 24.80 | 70.10 | 9 00- 9 99 |
| 10 00-10 99 | | | | 2 | 29 | 61 | 27 | 46 | 15 | 1 | 7 | 125 | 872 | 25 | 4 | 260 | 954 | 29.45 | 77.50 | 10 00-10 99 |
| 11 00-11 99 | | | | 1 | 19 | 51 | 15 | 25 | 10 | | 4 | 84 | 443 | 11 | 3 | 172 | 494 | 32.50 | 81.30 | 11 00-11 99 |
| 12 00-12 99 | | 1 | | 5 | 41 | 91 | 13 | 74 | 12 | 4 | 2 | 252 | 599 | 14 | | 441 | 667 | 40.40 | 86.50 | 12 00-12 99 |
| 13 00-13 99 | | | | 4 | 12 | 34 | 5 | 11 | 2 | | 3 | 118 | 228 | 5 | 1 | 172 | 251 | 43.35 | 88.50 | 13 00-13 99 |
| 14 00-14 99 | 1 | | | 8 | 35 | 50 | 10 | 23 | | 1 | | 205 | 269 | 5 | 2 | 293 | 316 | 48.60 | 91.00 | 14 00-14 99 |
| 15 00-15 99 | | 2 | 1 | 16 | 32 | 27 | 4 | 18 | | 7 | 1 | 361 | 272 | 2 | | 433 | 310 | 56.40 | 93.50 | 15 00-15 99 |
| 16 00-17 99 | 1 | | | 22 | 29 | 27 | 7 | 18 | | 19 | 2 | 328 | 242 | 1 | | 416 | 281 | 63.70 | 95.60 | 16 00-17 99 |
| 18 00-19 99 | | 3 | 1 | 23 | 38 | 21 | 3 | 7 | | 48 | | 363 | 157 | 1 | | 466 | 199 | 72.00 | 97.00 | 18 00-19 99 |
| 20 00-24 99 | 8 | 4 | 3 | 43 | 43 | 16 | 1 | 8 | 1 | 157 | | 552 | 155 | | | 783 | 203 | 86.00 | 98.60 | 20 00-24 99 |
| 25 00-29 99 | 6 | 5 | 5 | 38 | 30 | 4 | 1 | 4 | | 149 | | 212 | 52 | | | 418 | 88 | 93.40 | 99.25 | 25 00-29 99 |
| 30 00-34 99 | 2 | 4 | 4 | 30 | 11 | 1 | | 1 | | 60 | | 79 | 16 | | | 177 | 31 | 96.60 | 99.60 | 30 00-34 99 |
| 35 00-39 99 | 1 | | 1 | 11 | 11 | 3 | | 1 | | 25 | | 29 | 9 | | | 70 | 21 | 97.90 | 99.75 | 35 00-39 99 |
| 40 00 and over | 6 | 99 | 12 | 19 | 6 | 1 | | 1 | | 16 | | 46 | 14 | | | 118 | 32 | 100.00 | 100.00 | 40 00 and over |
| Not reported | | | | | | | 2 | 2 | | 1 | | 4 | 18 | 1 | 6 | 8 | 26 | | | Not reported |
| Total | 20 | 48 | 27 | 225 | 402 | 636 | 693 | 596 | 798 | 493 | 42 | 2,964 | 8,982 | 637 | 1,957 | 5,619 | 12,901 | | | Total |

205. TABLE V, A, 1, b

NEW YORK CITY
DEPARTMENT STORES — OFFICE
NUMBER AND PER CENT OF EMPLOYEES EARNING SPECIFIED WEEKLY RATES BY AGE GROUPS AND SEX

| Weekly Rates in Dollars | Age Groups in Years | | | | | | | | | | | | | | Weekly Rates in Dollars |
|---|---|---|---|---|---|---|---|---|---|---|---|---|---|---|---|
| | 14–15 | | 16–17 | | 18–20 | | 21–24 | | 25–29 | | 30–34 | | 35–39 | | |
| | Male | Female | Male | Female | Male | Female | Male | Female | Male | Female | Male | Female | Male | Female | |
| $3 00–$3 49 | .... | 22 | 1 | 23 | ...... | 1 | ...... | ...... | ...... | ...... | ...... | ...... | ...... | ...... | $3 00–$3 49 |
| 3 50– 3 99 | 2 | 67 | 2 | 49 | ...... | 11 | ...... | 1 | ...... | 1 | ...... | ...... | ...... | ...... | 3 50– 3 99 |
| 4 00– 4 49 | 37 | 74 | 16 | 112 | 2 | 29 | 9 | 2 | 1 | ...... | 1 | 1 | 1 | ...... | 4 00– 4 49 |
| 4 50– 4 99 | 10 | 17 | 14 | 89 | ...... | 37 | ...... | 2 | ...... | ...... | ...... | ...... | ...... | ...... | 4 50– 4 99 |
| 5 00– 5 49 | 33 | 21 | 51 | 201 | 7 | 167 | 3 | 17 | 1 | 2 | 1 | ...... | ...... | ...... | 5 00– 5 49 |
| 5 50– 5 99 | 4 | 3 | 11 | 42 | 2 | 59 | ...... | 14 | ...... | 1 | ...... | ...... | ...... | ...... | 5 50– 5 99 |
| 6 00– 6 49 | 5 | 7 | 42 | 156 | 23 | 394 | 2 | 102 | ...... | 13 | ...... | 1 | ...... | 3 | 6 00– 6 49 |
| 6 50– 6 99 | .... | 2 | 3 | 17 | 6 | 73 | ...... | 16 | ...... | 2 | ...... | ...... | ...... | 1 | 6 50– 6 99 |
| 7 00– 7 49 | 1 | 3 | 23 | 58 | 28 | 328 | 2 | 212 | 1 | 47 | 1 | 14 | 1 | 9 | 7 00– 7 49 |
| 7 50– 7 99 | .... | ...... | .... | 2 | 4 | 19 | 1 | 25 | ...... | 1 | 1 | ...... | ...... | ...... | 7 50– 7 99 |
| 8 00– 8 99 | .... | 4 | 16 | 24 | 60 | 198 | 12 | 273 | 1 | 59 | 2 | 21 | 1 | 7 | 8 00– 8 99 |
| 9 00– 9 99 | .... | ...... | 2 | 11 | 42 | 105 | 18 | 169 | 2 | 63 | 1 | 23 | 1 | 8 | 9 00– 9 99 |
| 10 00–10 99 | .... | ...... | 2 | 4 | 52 | 64 | 51 | 133 | 18 | 86 | 13 | 21 | 6 | 11 | 10 00–10 99 |
| 11 00–11 99 | .... | ...... | .... | 2 | 13 | 12 | 27 | 69 | 7 | 49 | 2 | 14 | 1 | 6 | 11 00–11 99 |
| 12 00–12 99 | .... | ...... | .... | ...... | 21 | 23 | 76 | 57 | 40 | 55 | 22 | 18 | 18 | 11 | 12 00–12 99 |
| 13 00–13 99 | .... | ...... | .... | ...... | 7 | ...... | 20 | 26 | 12 | 27 | 6 | 10 | 3 | 7 | 13 00–13 99 |
| 14 00–14 99 | .... | ...... | .... | ...... | 4 | 8 | 21 | 18 | 27 | 34 | 18 | 8 | 13 | 11 | 14 00–14 99 |
| 15 00–15 99 | .... | ...... | .... | 1 | 6 | 3 | 34 | 21 | 43 | 20 | 24 | 12 | 24 | 8 | 15 00–15 99 |
| 16 00–17 99 | .... | ...... | .... | ...... | 1 | 1 | 23 | 4 | 39 | 11 | 23 | 7 | 16 | 9 | 16 00–17 99 |
| 18 00–19 99 | .... | ...... | .... | 1 | ...... | 1 | 20 | 4 | 46 | 13 | 34 | 10 | 21 | 6 | 18 00–19 99 |
| 20 00–24 99 | .... | ...... | .... | ...... | ...... | 1 | 13 | 1 | 46 | 12 | 43 | 9 | 40 | 6 | 20 00–24 99 |
| 25 00–29 99 | .... | ...... | .... | ...... | ...... | 1 | 2 | 1 | 17 | 3 | 16 | 4 | 17 | 2 | 25 00–29 99 |
| 30 00–34 99 | .... | ...... | .... | ...... | ...... | 1 | 1 | ...... | 7 | 1 | 16 | ...... | 18 | 2 | 30 00–34 99 |
| 35 00–39 99 | .... | ...... | .... | ...... | ...... | ...... | 1 | ...... | 1 | ...... | 5 | ...... | ...... | ...... | 35 00–39 99 |
| 40 00 and over | .... | ...... | .... | ...... | 1 | ...... | 1 | ...... | 3 | ...... | 9 | 3 | 18 | ...... | 40 00 and over |
| Not reported | .... | ...... | .... | 1 | ...... | ...... | ...... | 1 | 1 | ...... | ...... | ...... | 1 | ...... | Not reported |
| Total | 92 | 220 | 183 | 793 | 279 | 1,536 | 337 | 1,168 | 313 | 500 | 238 | 176 | 200 | 107 | Total |

205. TABLE V, A, 1, b — (*concluded*)

NEW YORK CITY

DEPARTMENT STORES — OFFICE

NUMBER AND PER CENT OF EMPLOYEES EARNING SPECIFIED WEEKLY RATES BY AGE GROUPS AND SEX

| WEEKLY RATES IN DOLLARS | AGE GROUPS IN YEARS (*concluded*) | | | | | | | | | | | | | WEEKLY RATES IN DOLLARS |
|---|---|---|---|---|---|---|---|---|---|---|---|---|---|---|
| | 40–44 | | 45–54 | | 55–64 | | 65 AND OVER | NOT REPORTED | | TOTAL | | CUMULATIVE PER CENT OF TOTAL | | |
| | Male | Female | Male | Female | Male | Female | Male | Male | Female | Male | Female | Male | Female | |
| $3 00–$3 49 | ...... | ...... | ...... | ...... | ...... | ...... | ...... | ...... | ...... | 1 | 46 | .05 | .98 | $3 00–$3 49 |
| 3 50– 3 99 | ...... | ...... | ...... | ...... | ...... | ...... | ...... | ...... | 6 | 4 | 135 | .25 | 3.86 | 3 50– 3 99 |
| 4 00– 4 49 | ...... | ...... | ...... | ...... | ...... | ...... | ...... | ...... | 5 | 67 | 223 | 3.58 | 8.63 | 4 00– 4 49 |
| 4 50– 4 99 | ...... | ...... | ...... | ...... | ...... | ...... | ...... | ...... | 1 | 24 | 146 | 4.77 | 11.75 | 4 50– 4 99 |
| 5 00– 5 49 | ...... | ...... | ...... | 1 | ...... | ...... | ...... | 1 | 2 | 97 | 411 | 9.70 | 20.50 | 5 00– 5 49 |
| 5 50– 5 99 | ...... | ...... | ...... | ...... | 1 | ...... | ...... | ...... | 4 | 18 | 123 | 10.55 | 23.10 | 5 50– 5 99 |
| 6 00– 6 49 | ...... | 1 | ...... | ...... | ...... | ...... | ...... | 1 | 3 | 73 | 680 | 14.25 | 37.60 | 6 00– 6 49 |
| 6 50– 6 99 | ...... | ...... | ...... | ...... | ...... | ...... | ...... | ...... | 9 | 9 | 120 | 14.58 | 40.20 | 6 50– 6 99 |
| 7 00– 7 49 | ...... | 1 | ...... | 3 | ...... | ...... | ...... | ...... | 14 | 57 | 689 | 17.40 | 54.90 | 7 00– 7 49 |
| 7 50– 7 99 | ...... | ...... | ...... | 1 | ...... | ...... | ...... | ...... | 3 | 6 | 51 | 17.70 | 56.00 | 7 50– 7 99 |
| 8 00– 8 99 | ...... | ...... | ...... | 2 | ...... | ...... | ...... | 1 | 13 | 93 | 601 | 22.35 | 68.90 | 8 00– 8 99 |
| 9 00– 9 99 | ...... | 2 | 2 | 1 | ...... | ...... | ...... | ...... | 10 | 68 | 392 | 25.80 | 77.10 | 9 00– 9 99 |
| 10 00–10 99 | 4 | 5 | 7 | ...... | 7 | ...... | 1 | 2 | 19 | 163 | 343 | 33.80 | 84.50 | 10 00–10 99 |
| 11 00–11 99 | 1 | 1 | 5 | ...... | 1 | ...... | ...... | ...... | 14 | 57 | 167 | 36.60 | 88.00 | 11 00–11 99 |
| 12 00–12 99 | 10 | 4 | 23 | 6 | 8 | 2 | 2 | 3 | 10 | 223 | 186 | 47.70 | 92.00 | 12 00–12 99 |
| 13 00–13 99 | 3 | ...... | 2 | 1 | ...... | ...... | ...... | ...... | 4 | 53 | 75 | 50.30 | 93.50 | 13 00–13 99 |
| 14 00–14 99 | 9 | 3 | 11 | 1 | 1 | ...... | 2 | 2 | 4 | 108 | 87 | 55.75 | 95.50 | 14 00–14 99 |
| 15 00–15 99 | 8 | 1 | 11 | 3 | 5 | 1 | 1 | ...... | 5 | 156 | 75 | 63.50 | 97.00 | 15 00–15 99 |
| 16 00–17 99 | 12 | 6 | 12 | 2 | 3 | ...... | ...... | ...... | 1 | 129 | 41 | 70.00 | 98.00 | 16 00–17 99 |
| 18 00–19 99 | 13 | 3 | 20 | ...... | 2 | ...... | ...... | 1 | 4 | 157 | 42 | 77.80 | 98.75 | 18 00–19 99 |
| 20 00–24 99 | 26 | 2 | 27 | 2 | 9 | ...... | ...... | 3 | 3 | 207 | 36 | 88.00 | 99.50 | 20 00–24 99 |
| 25 00–29 99 | 12 | 2 | 10 | ...... | 2 | 2 | 1 | 4 | ...... | 81 | 15 | 92.00 | 99.80 | 25 00–29 99 |
| 30 00–34 99 | 9 | 3 | 12 | ...... | 5 | ...... | ...... | 1 | ...... | 69 | 7 | 95.50 | 99.95 | 30 00–34 99 |
| 35 00–39 99 | 5 | ...... | 3 | ...... | 3 | ...... | ...... | ...... | ...... | 18 | ...... | 96.30 | ...... | 35 00–39 99 |
| 40 00 and over | 14 | ...... | 18 | 1 | 3 | ...... | ...... | ...... | ...... | 67 | 4 | 100.00 | 100.00 | 40 00 and over |
| Not reported | ...... | ...... | ...... | ...... | 1 | ...... | ...... | ...... | ...... | 3 | 2 | ...... | ...... | Not reported |
| Total | 126 | 34 | 163 | 24 | 51 | 5 | 7 | 19 | 134 | 2,008 | 4,697 | ...... | ...... | Total |

266. TABLE VIII, A, 1, b

## NEW YORK CITY
## DEPARTMENT STORES — OFFICE

Number and Per Cent of Employees Earning Specified Weekly Rates by Occupation and Sex

| Weekly Rates in Dollars | Superintendents | | Bookkeepers | | Clerks | | Secretaries | | Stenographers | | Office Boys and Girls | | Cashiers | | Weekly Rates in Dollars |
|---|---|---|---|---|---|---|---|---|---|---|---|---|---|---|---|
| | Male | Female | Male | Female | Male | Female | Male | Female | Male | Female | Male | Female | Male | Female | |
| $3 00–$3 49 | | | | 1 | 1 | 23 | | | | | | 4 | | 2 | $3 00–$3 49 |
| 3 50– 3 99 | | | | 1 | | 60 | | | | | 4 | 14 | | 14 | 3 50– 3 99 |
| 4 00– 4 49 | | | | | 27 | 120 | | | | 1 | 39 | 13 | 1 | 31 | 4 00– 4 49 |
| 4 50– 4 99 | | | | | 7 | 65 | | | | 4 | 17 | 8 | | 19 | 4 50– 4 99 |
| 5 00– 5 49 | | | | 3 | 42 | 223 | | | | 16 | 48 | 12 | 1 | 67 | 5 00– 5 49 |
| 5 50– 5 99 | | | 1 | 2 | 5 | 73 | | | | 9 | 11 | 3 | | 15 | 5 50– 5 99 |
| 6 00– 6 49 | | | 1 | 17 | 38 | 356 | | | | 70 | 22 | 3 | 1 | 143 | 6 00– 6 49 |
| 6 50– 6 99 | | | | 4 | 5 | 64 | | 1 | | 8 | 3 | | | 31 | 6 50– 6 99 |
| 7 00– 7 49 | | | 2 | 23 | 35 | 322 | | | 4 | 77 | 3 | 1 | 3 | 184 | 7 00– 7 49 |
| 7 50– 7 99 | | | 1 | 2 | 4 | 34 | | | 1 | 2 | | | | 5 | 7 50– 7 99 |
| 8 00– 8 99 | | | 5 | 34 | 68 | 302 | | | 3 | 76 | 4 | 1 | | 116 | 8 00– 8 99 |
| 9 00– 9 99 | | | 5 | 50 | 44 | 211 | | | 4 | 56 | 2 | | 2 | 39 | 9 00– 9 99 |
| 10 00–10 99 | | | 6 | 58 | 135 | 153 | | 1 | 4 | 54 | | | 4 | 45 | 10 00–10 99 |
| 11 00–11 99 | | | 4 | 32 | 47 | 88 | | | | 16 | | | 2 | 19 | 11 00–11 99 |
| 12 00–12 99 | | | 11 | 50 | 193 | 71 | | 3 | 2 | 35 | 1 | | 2 | 10 | 12 00–12 99 |
| 13 00–13 99 | | | 1 | 24 | 43 | 32 | | 1 | 1 | 8 | | | 2 | 5 | 13 00–13 99 |
| 14 00–14 99 | | | 8 | 21 | 90 | 40 | | | | 14 | | | 4 | 7 | 14 00–14 99 |
| 15 00–15 99 | | | 15 | 17 | 112 | 34 | | | 4 | 15 | | | 7 | 1 | 15 00–15 99 |
| 16 00–17 99 | | | 30 | 8 | 78 | 19 | | | | 1 | | | 8 | 4 | 16 00–17 99 |
| 18 00–19 99 | | 2 | 35 | 4 | 77 | 14 | | 2 | 3 | 7 | | | 16 | 2 | 18 00–19 99 |
| 20 00–24 99 | 1 | 1 | 37 | 4 | 126 | 14 | 1 | | 1 | 5 | | | 16 | 1 | 20 00–24 99 |
| 25 00–29 99 | 4 | | 8 | 2 | 53 | 6 | 1 | | | | | | 2 | 4 | 25 00–29 99 |
| 30 00–34 99 | 12 | | 3 | | 36 | 4 | | | | 1 | | | 2 | | 30 00–34 99 |
| 35 00–39 99 | | | 1 | | 8 | | 2 | | | | | | 1 | | 35 00–39 99 |
| 40 00 and over | 14 | 1 | 5 | | 22 | 1 | | | | | | | 3 | | 40 00 and over |
| Not reported | | | | | 2 | 1 | | | | | | | | | Not reported |
| Total | 31 | 4 | 179 | 362 | 1,298 | 2,330 | 4 | 8 | 27 | 475 | 154 | 59 | 77 | 764 | Total |

206. TABLE VIII, A, 1, b — (*concluded*)

NEW YORK CITY
DEPARTMENT STORES — OFFICE

Number and Per Cent of Employees Earning Specified Weekly Rates by Occupation and Sex

| Weekly Rates in Dollars | Occupation (concluded) | | | | | | | | | | | | Weekly Rates in Dollars |
|---|---|---|---|---|---|---|---|---|---|---|---|---|---|
| | Telephone Operators | | Auditors | | Detectives | | Advertisers and Window Dressers | | Total | | Cumulative Per Cent of Total | | |
| | Male | Female | Male | Female | Male | Female | Male | Female | Male | Female | Male | Female | |
| $3 00-$3 49 | ....... | ....... | ....... | 16 | ....... | ....... | ....... | ....... | 1 | 46 | .05 | .98 | $3 00-$3 49 |
| 3 50- 3 99 | ....... | ....... | ....... | 46 | ....... | ....... | ....... | ....... | 4 | 135 | .23 | 3.86 | 3 50- 3 99 |
| 4 00- 4 49 | ....... | ....... | ....... | 58 | ....... | ....... | ....... | ....... | 67 | 223 | 3.58 | 8.68 | 4 00- 4 49 |
| 4 50- 4 99 | ....... | 2 | ....... | 48 | ....... | ....... | ....... | ....... | 24 | 146 | 4.77 | 11.75 | 4 50- 4 99 |
| 5 00- 5 49 | ....... | 6 | 1 | 84 | ....... | ....... | 5 | ....... | 97 | 411 | 9.70 | 20.50 | 5 00- 5 49 |
| 5 50- 5 99 | ....... | 3 | ....... | 18 | ....... | ....... | 1 | ....... | 18 | 123 | 10.55 | 23.10 | 5 50- 5 99 |
| 6 00- 6 49 | ....... | 24 | 4 | 66 | ....... | ....... | 7 | 1 | 73 | 680 | 14.25 | 37.60 | 6 00- 6 49 |
| 6 50- 6 99 | ....... | 1 | ....... | 11 | ....... | ....... | 1 | ....... | 9 | 120 | 14.58 | 40.20 | 6 50- 6 99 |
| 7 00- 7 49 | ....... | 15 | 2 | 61 | 1 | 1 | 7 | ....... | 57 | 689 | 17.40 | 54.90 | 7 00- 7 49 |
| 7 50- 7 99 | ....... | ....... | ....... | 8 | ....... | ....... | ....... | ....... | 6 | 51 | 17.70 | 56.00 | 7 50- 7 99 |
| 8 00- 8 99 | 1 | 29 | 5 | 42 | ....... | ....... | 7 | 1 | 93 | 601 | 22.35 | 68.90 | 8 00- 8 99 |
| 9 00- 9 99 | ....... | 17 | 7 | 18 | ....... | ....... | 4 | 1 | 68 | 392 | 25.80 | 77.10 | 9 00- 9 99 |
| 10 00-10 99 | 1 | 19 | 7 | 7 | 2 | 3 | 4 | 3 | 163 | 343 | 33.80 | 84.50 | 10 00-10 99 |
| 11 00-11 99 | ....... | 9 | 3 | 1 | 1 | 1 | ....... | 1 | 57 | 167 | 36.60 | 88.00 | 11 00-11 99 |
| 12 00-12 99 | ....... | 7 | 7 | 7 | 3 | 3 | 4 | ....... | 223 | 186 | 47.70 | 92.00 | 12 00-12 99 |
| 13 00-13 99 | ....... | 1 | 3 | 3 | ....... | ....... | 3 | 1 | 53 | 75 | 50.30 | 93.50 | 13 00-13 99 |
| 14 00-14 99 | ....... | 2 | 2 | 2 | 1 | 1 | 3 | ....... | 108 | 87 | 55.75 | 95.50 | 14 00-14 99 |
| 15 00-15 99 | ....... | 3 | 1 | 3 | 4 | 1 | 13 | 1 | 156 | 75 | 63.50 | 97.00 | 15 00-15 99 |
| 16 00-17 99 | ....... | ....... | 3 | 3 | ....... | 5 | 10 | 1 | 129 | 41 | 70.00 | 98.00 | 16 00-17 99 |
| 18 00-19 99 | ....... | 2 | 5 | 1 | 6 | 8 | 15 | ....... | 157 | 42 | 77.80 | 98.75 | 18 00-19 99 |
| 20 00-24 99 | ....... | 2 | 1 | ....... | 6 | 9 | 18 | ....... | 207 | 36 | 88.00 | 99.50 | 20 00-24 99 |
| 25 00-29 99 | ....... | ....... | 1 | ....... | 1 | 1 | 11 | 2 | 81 | 15 | 92.00 | 99.80 | 25 00-29 99 |
| 30 00-34 99 | ....... | ....... | 1 | ....... | 3 | 1 | 12 | 1 | 69 | 7 | 95.50 | 99.95 | 30 00-34 99 |
| 35 00-39 99 | ....... | ....... | 1 | ....... | 1 | ....... | 4 | ....... | 18 | ....... | 96.30 | ....... | 35 00-39 99 |
| 40 00 and over | ....... | ....... | 1 | ....... | 1 | ....... | 21 | 2 | 67 | 4 | 100.00 | 100.00 | 40 00 and over |
| Not reported | ....... | 1 | ....... | ....... | ....... | ....... | 1 | ....... | 3 | 2 | ....... | ....... | Not reported |
| Total | 2 | 143 | 55 | 503 | 30 | 34 | 151 | 15 | 2,008 | 4,697 | ....... | ....... | ot |

207. TABLE VI, A, 1, b.

NEW YORK CITY

DEPARTMENT STORES — OFFICE

NUMBER AND PER CENT OF EMPLOYEES CLASSIFIED ACCORDING TO ACTUAL WEEKLY EARNINGS BY AGE GROUPS AND SEX

| ACTUAL WEEKLY EARNINGS IN DOLLARS | AGE GROUPS IN YEARS | | | | | | | | | | | | | | ACTUAL WEEKLY EARNINGS IN DOLLARS |
|---|---|---|---|---|---|---|---|---|---|---|---|---|---|---|---|
| | 14–15 | | 16–17 | | 18–20 | | 21–24 | | 25–29 | | 30–34 | | 35–39 | | |
| | Male | Female | Male | Female | Male | Female | Male | Female | Male | Female | Male | Female | Male | Female | |
| Less than $3 00 | 2 | 12 | 1 | 10 | ...... | 18 | 3 | 4 | 1 | 1 | 1 | ...... | ...... | ...... | Less than $3 00 |
| $3 00–$3 49... | 1 | 20 | 3 | 27 | ...... | 9 | ...... | ...... | 1 | ...... | ...... | 1 | ...... | ...... | ...$3 00– 3 49 |
| 3 50– 3 99... | 5 | 64 | 3 | 64 | ...... | 17 | ...... | 2 | ...... | 1 | ...... | ...... | ...... | ...... | ....3 50– 3 99 |
| 4 00– 4 49... | 35 | 72 | 19 | 115 | ...... | 41 | ...... | 7 | ...... | 4 | 2 | ...... | ...... | ...... | ....4 00– 4 49 |
| 4 50– 4 99... | 9 | 12 | 17 | 101 | 1 | 77 | ...... | 7 | 1 | 3 | ...... | ...... | ...... | ...... | ....4 50– 4 99 |
| 5 00– 5 49... | 30 | 19 | 46 | 167 | 8 | 146 | 2 | 26 | ...... | 3 | 4 | ...... | ...... | ...... | ....5 00– 5 49 |
| 5 50– 5 99... | 4 | 5 | 12 | 47 | 3 | 117 | 1 | 28 | ...... | 3 | 2 | ...... | ...... | ...... | ....5 50– 5 99 |
| 6 00– 6 49... | 4 | 6 | 35 | 141 | 20 | 321 | 3 | 87 | ...... | 11 | ...... | 2 | 1 | 5 | ....6 00– 6 49 |
| 6 50– 6 99... | 1 | 3 | 6 | 21 | 12 | 92 | 1 | 45 | ...... | 10 | ...... | 2 | ...... | 2 | ....6 50– 6 99 |
| 7 00– 7 49... | 1 | 2 | 20 | 51 | 23 | 272 | 2 | 185 | 2 | 40 | 2 | 12 | 1 | 7 | ....7 00– 7 49 |
| 7 50– 7 99... | .... | 1 | .... | 3 | 8 | 32 | 1 | 57 | ...... | 8 | 1 | 3 | ...... | ...... | ....7 50– 7 99 |
| 8 00– 8 99... | .... | 3 | 17 | 24 | 58 | 182 | 14 | 252 | 3 | 57 | 2 | 19 | 1 | 7 | ....8 00– 8 99 |
| 9 00– 9 99... | .... | 1 | 2 | 11 | 42 | 99 | 24 | 154 | 3 | 72 | 2 | 26 | 2 | 8 | ....9 00– 9 99 |
| 10 00–10 99... | .... | ...... | 2 | 4 | 45 | 57 | 45 | 116 | 11 | 78 | 8 | 18 | 7 | 11 | ...10 00–10 99 |
| 11 00–11 99... | .... | ...... | .... | 2 | 15 | 15 | 33 | 76 | 9 | 45 | 2 | 16 | 3 | 5 | ...11 00–11 99 |
| 12 00–12 99... | .... | ...... | .... | 2 | 20 | 21 | 67 | 53 | 35 | 51 | 17 | 14 | 13 | 11 | ...12 00–12 99 |
| 13 00–13 99... | .... | ...... | .... | ...... | 8 | ...... | 20 | 22 | 18 | 27 | 7 | 11 | 5 | 9 | ...13 00–13 99 |
| 14 00–14 99... | .... | ...... | .... | ...... | 6 | 10 | 24 | 18 | 25 | 32 | 17 | 7 | 9 | 11 | ...14 00–14 99 |
| 15 00–15 99... | .... | ...... | .... | 1 | 7 | 1 | 36 | 16 | 46 | 16 | 24 | 14 | 24 | 6 | ...15 00–15 99 |
| 16 00–17 99... | .... | ...... | .... | ...... | ...... | 2 | 24 | 5 | 33 | 10 | 24 | 8 | 17 | 8 | ...16 00–17 99 |
| 18 00–19 99... | .... | ...... | .... | 1 | ...... | 1 | 18 | 4 | 49 | 12 | 31 | 7 | 16 | 7 | ...18 00–19 99 |
| 20 00–24 99... | .... | ...... | .... | ...... | 1 | 1 | 13 | 1 | 45 | 12 | 47 | 9 | 42 | 5 | ...20 00–24 99 |
| 25 00–29 99... | .... | ...... | .... | ...... | ...... | 1 | 2 | 1 | 18 | 3 | 16 | 4 | 20 | 2 | ...25 00–29 99 |
| 30 00–34 99... | .... | ...... | .... | ...... | ...... | 1 | 2 | ...... | 7 | 1 | 14 | ...... | 19 | 2 | ...30 00–34 99 |
| 35 00–39 99... | .... | ...... | .... | ...... | ...... | ...... | ...... | ...... | 1 | ...... | 6 | ...... | ...... | ...... | ...35 00–39 99 |
| 40 00 and over. | .... | ...... | .... | ...... | 1 | ...... | 1 | ...... | 4 | ...... | 9 | 3 | 19 | ...... | .40 00 and over |
| Not reported... | .... | ...... | .... | 1 | 1 | 3 | 1 | 2 | 1 | ...... | ...... | ...... | 1 | 1 | ...Not reported |
| Total..... | 92 | 220 | 183 | 793 | 279 | 1,536 | 337 | 1,168 | 313 | 500 | 238 | 176 | 200 | 107 | .....Total |

207. TABLE VI, A, 1, b — (*concluded*)

## NEW YORK CITY
## DEPARTMENT STORES — OFFICE

Number and Per Cent of Employees Classified According to Actual Weekly Earnings by Age Groups and Sex

| Actual Weekly Earnings in Dollars | Age Groups in Years (*concluded*) 40–44 | | 45–54 | | 55–64 | | 65 and over | Not reported | | Total | | Cumulative per cent. of total | | Actual Weekly Earnings in Dollars |
|---|---|---|---|---|---|---|---|---|---|---|---|---|---|---|
| | Male | Female | Male | Female | Male | Female | Male | Male | Female | Male | Female | Male | Female | |
| Less than $3 00 | ...... | ...... | ...... | ...... | ...... | ...... | ...... | ...... | 1 | 8 | 46 | .40 | 1.00 | Less than $3 00 |
| $3 00–$3 49 | ...... | ...... | ...... | ...... | ...... | ...... | ...... | ...... | ...... | 5 | 57 | .60 | 2.20 | $3 00– 3 49 |
| 3 50– 3 99 | ...... | ...... | ...... | ...... | ...... | ...... | ...... | ...... | 8 | 8 | 156 | 1.00 | 5.50 | 3 50– 3 99 |
| 4 00– 4 49 | ...... | ...... | ...... | ...... | ...... | ...... | ...... | ...... | 3 | 56 | 242 | 3.80 | 10.70 | 4 00– 4 49 |
| 4 50– 4 99 | ...... | ...... | ...... | ...... | ...... | ...... | ...... | ...... | 1 | 28 | 201 | 5.20 | 15.00 | 4 50– 4 99 |
| 5 00– 5 49 | ...... | ...... | ...... | 1 | ...... | ...... | ...... | 1 | 2 | 91 | 364 | 10.00 | 22.70 | 5 00– 5 49 |
| 5 50– 5 99 | ...... | ...... | ...... | ...... | 1 | ...... | ...... | ...... | 3 | 23 | 203 | 10.90 | 27.00 | 5 50– 5 99 |
| 6 00– 6 49 | ...... | 1 | ...... | ...... | ...... | ...... | ...... | 1 | 6 | 64 | 580 | 14.30 | 39.60 | 6 00– 6 49 |
| 6 50– 6 99 | ...... | ...... | ...... | ...... | ...... | ...... | ...... | ...... | 7 | 20 | 182 | 15.10 | 43.70 | 6 50– 6 99 |
| 7 00– 7 49 | ...... | 1 | ...... | 3 | ...... | ...... | ...... | ...... | 17 | 51 | 590 | 17.70 | 55.80 | 7 00– 7 49 |
| 7 50– 7 99 | ...... | ...... | ...... | 1 | ...... | ...... | ...... | ...... | 4 | 10 | 109 | 18.20 | 58.20 | 7 50– 7 99 |
| 8 00– 8 99 | ...... | ...... | 1 | 2 | ...... | ...... | ...... | 2 | 11 | 98 | 557 | 23.00 | 70.10 | 8 00– 8 99 |
| 9 00– 9 99 | ...... | 3 | 1 | 1 | ...... | ...... | ...... | 1 | 13 | 77 | 388 | 26.90 | 78.30 | 9 00– 9 99 |
| 10 00–10 99 | 1 | 4 | 4 | ...... | 4 | ...... | 1 | 1 | 13 | 129 | 301 | 33.40 | 84.70 | 10 00–10 99 |
| 11 00–11 99 | 2 | 1 | 5 | 1 | ...... | ...... | ...... | ...... | 15 | 69 | 176 | 36.80 | 88.50 | 11 00–11 99 |
| 12 00–12 99 | 10 | 4 | 23 | 5 | 8 | 2 | 2 | 2 | 10 | 197 | 173 | 46.60 | 92.20 | 12 00–12 99 |
| 13 00–13 99 | 5 | 2 | 1 | 1 | 3 | ...... | ...... | ...... | 5 | 67 | 77 | 49.90 | 93.80 | 13 00–13 99 |
| 14 00–14 99 | 7 | 2 | 11 | 1 | ...... | ...... | 2 | 2 | 3 | 103 | 84 | 55.00 | 95.50 | 14 00–14 99 |
| 15 00–15 99 | 10 | 1 | 14 | 3 | 6 | 1 | 1 | ...... | 4 | 168 | 63 | 63.50 | 97.00 | 15 00–15 99 |
| 16 00–17 99 | 12 | 5 | 12 | 2 | 3 | ...... | ...... | ...... | 1 | 125 | 41 | 69.70 | 97.80 | 16 00–17 99 |
| 18 00–19 99 | 10 | 3 | 24 | ...... | 4 | ...... | ...... | 1 | 4 | 153 | 39 | 77.40 | 98.60 | 18 00–19 99 |
| 20 00–24 99 | 29 | 2 | 24 | 2 | 9 | ...... | ...... | 3 | 3 | 213 | 35 | 88.00 | 99.50 | 20 00–24 99 |
| 25 00–29 99 | 13 | 2 | 8 | ...... | 2 | 2 | 1 | 4 | ...... | 84 | 15 | 92.20 | 99.60 | 25 00–29 99 |
| 30 00–34 99 | 7 | 3 | 12 | ...... | 5 | ...... | ...... | 1 | ...... | 67 | 7 | 95.60 | 99.90 | 30 00–34 99 |
| 35 00–39 99 | 6 | ...... | 6 | ...... | 2 | ...... | ...... | ...... | ...... | 21 | ...... | 96.60 | ...... | 35 00–39 99 |
| 40 00 and over | 14 | ...... | 17 | 1 | 4 | ...... | ...... | ...... | ...... | 69 | 4 | 100.00 | 100.00 | 40 00 and over |
| Not reported | ...... | ...... | ...... | ...... | ...... | ...... | ...... | ...... | ...... | 4 | 7 | ...... | ...... | Not reported |
| Total | 126 | 34 | 163 | 24 | 51 | 5 | 7 | 19 | 134 | 2,008 | 4,697 | ...... | ...... | Total |

908. TABLE IX, A, 1, b.

NEW YORK CITY

**DEPARTMENT STORES — OFFICE**

Number and Per Cent of Employees Classified According to Actual Weekly Earnings by Occupation and Sex

| Actual Weekly Earnings in Dollars | Occupation | | | | | | | | | | | | | | Actual Weekly Earnings in Dollars |
|---|---|---|---|---|---|---|---|---|---|---|---|---|---|---|---|
| | Superintendents | | Bookkeepers | | Clerks | | Secretaries | | Stenographers | | Office Boys and Girls | | Cashiers | | |
| | Male | Female | Male | Female | Male | Female | Male | Female | Male | Female | Male | Female | Male | Female | |
| Less than $3 00 | .... | ...... | .... | 1 | 2 | 15 | ...... | ...... | ...... | 2 | 3 | 2 | ...... | 13 | Less than $3 00 |
| $3 00–$3 49... | .... | ...... | .... | ...... | 1 | 30 | ...... | ...... | ...... | ...... | 3 | 3 | ...... | 3 | ...$3 00– 3 49 |
| 3 50– 3 99... | .... | ...... | .... | 1 | ...... | 66 | ...... | ...... | ...... | 1 | 8 | 13 | ...... | 20 | ....3 50– 3 99 |
| 4 00– 4 49... | .... | ...... | .... | ...... | 19 | 124 | ...... | ...... | ...... | 1 | 36 | 15 | 1 | 41 | ....4 00– 4 49 |
| 4 50– 4 99... | .... | ...... | .... | 1 | 11 | 95 | ...... | ...... | ...... | 6 | 17 | 9 | ...... | 30 | ....4 50– 4 99 |
| 5 00– 5 49... | .... | ...... | .... | 3 | 41 | 199 | ...... | ...... | ...... | 21 | 44 | 9 | 2 | 65 | ....5 00– 5 49 |
| 5 50– 5 99... | .... | ...... | 1 | 9 | 9 | 111 | ...... | ...... | ...... | 15 | 12 | 3 | ...... | 36 | ....5 50– 5 99 |
| 6 00– 6 49... | .... | ...... | 1 | 14 | 33 | 321 | ...... | ...... | ...... | 65 | 18 | 3 | 1 | 102 | ....6 00– 6 49 |
| 6 50– 6 99... | .... | ...... | .... | 9 | 15 | 92 | ...... | 1 | ...... | 15 | 3 | ...... | ...... | 43 | ....6 50– 6 99 |
| 7 00– 7 49... | .... | ...... | 2 | 22 | 31 | 275 | ...... | ...... | 3 | 67 | 3 | 1 | 3 | 160 | ....7 00– 7 49 |
| 7 50– 7 99... | .... | ...... | 1 | 9 | 6 | 56 | ...... | ...... | ...... | 15 | ...... | ...... | ...... | 15 | ....7 50– 7 99 |
| 8 00– 8 99... | .... | ...... | 4 | 32 | 75 | 282 | ...... | ...... | 5 | 73 | 4 | 1 | ...... | 107 | ....8 00– 8 99 |
| 9 00– 9 99... | .... | ...... | 7 | 55 | 45 | 204 | ...... | ...... | 6 | 56 | 2 | ...... | 3 | 33 | ....9 00– 9 99 |
| 10 00–10 99... | .... | ...... | 6 | 53 | 104 | 134 | ...... | 1 | 2 | 42 | ...... | ...... | 5 | 42 | ...10 00–10 99 |
| 11 00–11 99... | .... | ...... | 3 | 34 | 61 | 92 | ...... | ...... | ...... | 20 | ...... | ...... | 1 | 18 | ...11 00–11 99 |
| 12 00–12 99... | .... | ...... | 11 | 46 | 169 | 67 | ...... | 3 | 2 | 30 | 1 | ...... | 2 | 10 | ...12 00–12 99 |
| 13 00–13 99... | .... | 1 | 4 | 24 | 53 | 35 | ...... | 1 | 1 | 7 | ...... | ...... | 2 | 4 | ...13 00–13 99 |
| 14 00–14 99... | .... | ...... | 7 | 20 | 90 | 38 | ...... | ...... | ...... | 14 | ...... | ...... | 2 | 7 | ...14 00–14 99 |
| 15 00–15 99... | .... | ...... | 15 | 12 | 127 | 31 | ...... | ...... | 5 | 12 | ...... | ...... | 4 | 1 | ...15 00–15 99 |
| 16 00–17 99... | .... | ...... | 22 | 7 | 78 | 18 | ...... | ...... | ...... | 2 | ...... | ...... | 9 | 4 | ...16 00–17 99 |
| 18 00–19 99... | .... | 2 | 36 | 4 | 76 | 15 | ...... | 2 | 2 | 5 | ...... | ...... | 16 | 3 | ...18 00–19 99 |
| 20 00–24 99... | 1 | ...... | 41 | 4 | 126 | 14 | 1 | ...... | 1 | 5 | ...... | ...... | 16 | 1 | ...20 00–24 99 |
| 25 00–29 99... | 4 | ...... | 9 | 2 | 55 | 6 | 1 | ...... | ...... | ...... | ...... | ...... | 2 | 4 | ...25 00–29 99 |
| 30 00–34 99... | 12 | ...... | 3 | ...... | 35 | 4 | ...... | ...... | ...... | 1 | ...... | ...... | 2 | ...... | ...30 00–34 99 |
| 35 00–39 99... | .... | ...... | 1 | ...... | 12 | ...... | 2 | ...... | ...... | ...... | ...... | ...... | 1 | ...... | ...35 00–39 99 |
| 40 00 and over. | 14 | 1 | 5 | ...... | 21 | 1 | ...... | ...... | ...... | ...... | ...... | ...... | 4 | ...... | .40 00 and over |
| Not reported... | .... | ...... | .... | ...... | 3 | 5 | ...... | ...... | ...... | ...... | ...... | ...... | 1 | 2 | ...Not reported |
| Total..... | 31 | 4 | 179 | 362 | 1,298 | 2,330 | 4 | 8 | 27 | 475 | 154 | 59 | 77 | 764 | .....Total |

NEW YORK CITY

208. TABLE IX, A, 1, b — *(concluded)*

**DEPARTMENT STORES — OFFICE**

Number and Per Cent of Employees Classified According to Actual Weekly Earnings by Occupation and Sex

| Actual Weekly Earnings in Dollars | Occupation — *(concluded)*: Telephone Operators | | Auditors | | Detectives | | Advertisers and Window Dressers | | Total | | Cumulative Per Cent of Total | | Actual Weekly Earnings in Dollars |
|---|---|---|---|---|---|---|---|---|---|---|---|---|---|
| | Male | Female | Male | Female | Male | Female | Male | Female | Male | Female | Male | Female | |
| Less than $3 00 | ...... | 2 | ...... | 11 | 1 | ...... | 2 | ...... | 8 | 46 | .40 | 1.00 | Less than $3 00 |
| $3 00-$3 49 | ...... | ...... | ...... | 21 | 1 | ...... | ...... | ...... | 5 | 57 | .60 | 2.20 | $3 00- 3 49 |
| 3 50- 3 99 | ...... | 1 | ...... | 54 | ...... | ...... | ...... | ...... | 8 | 156 | 1.00 | 5.50 | 3 50- 3 99 |
| 4 00- 4 49 | ...... | ...... | ...... | 60 | ...... | 1 | ...... | ...... | 56 | 242 | 3.80 | 10.70 | 4 00- 4 49 |
| 4 50- 4 99 | ...... | 1 | ...... | 59 | ...... | ...... | ...... | ...... | 28 | 201 | 5.20 | 15.00 | 4 50- 4 99 |
| 5 00- 5 49 | ...... | 8 | 1 | 59 | ...... | ...... | 3 | ...... | 91 | 364 | 10.00 | 22.70 | 5 00- 5 49 |
| 5 50- 5 99 | ...... | 10 | ...... | 19 | ...... | ...... | 1 | ...... | 23 | 203 | 10.90 | 27.00 | 5 50- 5 99 |
| 6 00- 6 49 | ...... | 20 | 4 | 54 | ...... | ...... | 7 | 1 | 64 | 580 | 14.80 | 39.60 | 6 00- 6 49 |
| 6 50- 6 99 | ...... | 1 | 1 | 21 | ...... | ...... | 1 | ...... | 20 | 182 | 15.10 | 43.70 | 6 50- 6 99 |
| 7 00- 7 49 | ...... | 12 | 2 | 51 | 1 | 1 | 6 | 1 | 51 | 590 | 17.70 | 55.80 | 7 00- 7 49 |
| 7 50- 7 99 | ...... | 2 | 2 | 11 | ...... | ...... | 1 | 1 | 10 | 109 | 18.20 | 58.20 | 7 50- 7 99 |
| 8 00- 8 99 | 1 | 23 | 2 | 39 | ...... | ...... | 7 | ...... | 98 | 557 | 23.00 | 70.10 | 8 00- 8 99 |
| 9 00- 9 99 | 1 | 22 | 8 | 16 | 1 | ...... | 4 | 2 | 77 | 388 | 26.90 | 78.30 | 9 00- 9 99 |
| 10 00-10 99 | ...... | 15 | 7 | 7 | 2 | 4 | 3 | 3 | 129 | 301 | 33.40 | 84.70 | 10 00-10 99 |
| 11 00-11 99 | ...... | 9 | 3 | 2 | ...... | 1 | 1 | ...... | 69 | 176 | 36.80 | 88.50 | 11 00-11 99 |
| 12 00-12 99 | ...... | 6 | 5 | 8 | 3 | 3 | 4 | ...... | 197 | 173 | 46.60 | 92.20 | 12 00-12 99 |
| 13 00-13 99 | ...... | 1 | 3 | 2 | ...... | 1 | 4 | 1 | 67 | 77 | 49.90 | 93.80 | 13 00-13 99 |
| 14 00-14 99 | ...... | 2 | 2 | 2 | ...... | 1 | 2 | ...... | 103 | 84 | 55.00 | 95.50 | 14 00-14 99 |
| 15 00-15 99 | ...... | 3 | 2 | 3 | 2 | 1 | 13 | ...... | 168 | 63 | 63.50 | 97.00 | 15 00-15 99 |
| 16 00-17 99 | ...... | 1 | 2 | 3 | 3 | 5 | 11 | 1 | 125 | 41 | 69.70 | 97.80 | 16 00-17 99 |
| 18 00-19 99 | ...... | 2 | 4 | 1 | 5 | 5 | 14 | ...... | 153 | 39 | 77.40 | 98.60 | 18 00-19 99 |
| 20 00-24 99 | ...... | 2 | 3 | ...... | 5 | 9 | 19 | ...... | 213 | 35 | 88.00 | 99.50 | 20 00-24 99 |
| 25 00-29 99 | ...... | ...... | 1 | ...... | ...... | 1 | 12 | 2 | 84 | 15 | 92.20 | 99.60 | 25 00-29 99 |
| 30 00-34 99 | ...... | ...... | 1 | ...... | 3 | 1 | 11 | 1 | 67 | 7 | 95.60 | 99.90 | 30 00-34 99 |
| 35 00-39 99 | ...... | ...... | 1 | ...... | 1 | ...... | 3 | ...... | 21 | ...... | 96.60 | ...... | 35 00-39 99 |
| 40 00 and over | ...... | ...... | 1 | ...... | 2 | ...... | 22 | 2 | 69 | 4 | 100.00 | 100.00 | 40 00 and over |
| Not reported | ...... | ...... | ...... | ...... | ...... | ...... | ...... | ...... | 4 | 7 | ...... | ...... | Not reported |
| Total | 2 | 143 | 55 | 503 | 30 | 34 | 151 | 15 | 2,008 | 4,697 | ...... | ...... | Total |

209. TABLE V, A, 1, c

NEW YORK CITY

DEPARTMENT STORES — SHIPPING AND DELIVERY

NUMBER AND PER CENT OF EMPLOYEES EARNING SPECIFIED WEEKLY RATES BY AGE GROUPS AND SEX

| WEEKLY RATES IN DOLLARS | AGE GROUPS IN YEARS | | | | | | | | | | | | | WEEKLY RATES IN DOLLARS |
|---|---|---|---|---|---|---|---|---|---|---|---|---|---|---|
| | 14–15 | 16–17 | | 18–20 | | 21–24 | | 25–29 | | 30–34 | | 35–39 | | |
| | Male | Male | Female | Male | Female | Male | Female | Male | Female | Male | Female | Male | Female | |
| $3 50–$3 99 | 5 | 2 | ...... | ...... | ...... | ...... | ...... | ...... | ...... | ...... | ...... | ...... | ...... | $3 50–$3 99 |
| 4 00– 4 49 | ...... | ...... | 1 | ...... | 1 | ...... | ...... | ...... | ...... | ...... | ...... | ...... | ...... | 4 00– 4 49 |
| 4 50– 4 99 | ...... | 5 | 1 | ...... | ...... | ...... | ...... | ...... | ...... | ...... | ...... | ...... | ...... | 4 50– 4 99 |
| 5 00– 5 49 | 3 | 3 | 4 | ...... | 2 | 1 | 1 | ...... | ...... | 1 | ...... | ...... | ...... | 5 00– 5 49 |
| 5 50– 5 99 | ...... | 3 | ...... | 8 | ...... | 1 | ...... | ...... | ...... | ...... | ...... | ...... | ...... | 5 50– 5 99 |
| 6 00– 6 49 | 2 | 46 | ...... | 25 | 5 | ...... | 2 | 1 | 1 | ...... | ...... | ...... | ...... | 6 00– 6 49 |
| 6 50– 6 99 | ...... | 2 | ...... | 5 | ...... | ...... | ...... | ...... | ...... | 1 | ...... | ...... | 1 | 6 50– 6 99 |
| 7 00– 7 49 | ...... | 32 | ...... | 72 | 2 | 8 | 1 | 2 | ...... | ...... | ...... | 1 | ...... | 7 00– 7 49 |
| 7 50– 7 99 | 1 | 32 | ...... | 150 | ...... | 28 | ...... | 1 | ...... | ...... | ...... | ...... | ...... | 7 50– 7 99 |
| 8 00– 8 99 | ...... | 42 | 1 | 227 | ...... | 65 | 7 | 11 | 1 | 5 | ...... | 2 | ...... | 8 00– 8 99 |
| 9 00– 9 99 | ...... | 3 | 1 | 99 | ...... | 55 | 4 | 8 | 1 | 4 | 2 | 1 | 1 | 9 00– 9 99 |
| 10 00–10 99 | ...... | 1 | 2 | 74 | ...... | 93 | 1 | 30 | ...... | 22 | 1 | 16 | ...... | 10 00–10 99 |
| 11 00–11 99 | ...... | 4 | ...... | 24 | 1 | 46 | ...... | 19 | ...... | 8 | ...... | 11 | ...... | 11 00–11 99 |
| 12 00–12 99 | ...... | 1 | ...... | 35 | ...... | 126 | ...... | 96 | ...... | 54 | ...... | 69 | ...... | 12 00–12 99 |
| 13 00–13 99 | ...... | 2 | ...... | 8 | ...... | 59 | ...... | 38 | ...... | 38 | ...... | 24 | ...... | 13 00–13 99 |
| 14 00–14 99 | ...... | ...... | 1 | 3 | ...... | 50 | ...... | 53 | ...... | 54 | ...... | 45 | ...... | 14 00–14 99 |
| 15 00–15 99 | ...... | ...... | 1 | 34 | ...... | 192 | 1 | 140 | ...... | 87 | ...... | 64 | ...... | 15 00–15 99 |
| 16 00–17 99 | ...... | ...... | ...... | 4 | ...... | 34 | ...... | 73 | ...... | 66 | ...... | 69 | ...... | 16 00–17 99 |
| 18 00–19 99 | ...... | ...... | ...... | ...... | ...... | 10 | ...... | 9 | ...... | 19 | ...... | 25 | ...... | 18 00–19 99 |
| 20 00–24 99 | ...... | ...... | ...... | ...... | ...... | 3 | ...... | 4 | ...... | 14 | ...... | 16 | ...... | 20 00–24 99 |
| 25 00–29 99 | ...... | ...... | ...... | ...... | ...... | 2 | ...... | 1 | ...... | 2 | ...... | 10 | ...... | 25 00–29 99 |
| 30 00–34 99 | ...... | ...... | ...... | ...... | ...... | 1 | ...... | ...... | ...... | 1 | ...... | 1 | ...... | 30 00–34 99 |
| 35 00–39 99 | ...... | ...... | ...... | ...... | ...... | ...... | ...... | 1 | ...... | 1 | ...... | 2 | ...... | 35 00–39 99 |
| 40 00 and over | ...... | ...... | ...... | ...... | ...... | ...... | ...... | ...... | ...... | ...... | 1 | 1 | ...... | 40 00 and over |
| Not reported | 1 | ...... | ...... | ...... | ...... | 1 | ...... | 1 | ...... | ...... | ...... | ...... | ...... | Not reported |
| Total | 12 | 178 | 12 | 768 | 11 | 775 | 17 | 488 | 3 | 377 | 4 | 357 | 2 | Total |

NEW YORK CITY

209. TABLE V, A, 1, c — (*concluded*) DEPARTMENT STORES — SHIPPING AND DELIVERY

NUMBER AND PER CENT OF EMPLOYEES EARNING SPECIFIED WEEKLY RATES BY AGE GROUPS AND SEX

| WEEKLY RATES IN DOLLARS | AGE GROUPS IN YEARS (*concluded*) 40-44 | | 45-54 | | 55-64 | 65 AND OVER | NOT REPORTED | | TOTAL | | CUMULATIVE PER CENT OF TOTAL | | WEEKLY RATES IN DOLLARS |
|---|---|---|---|---|---|---|---|---|---|---|---|---|---|
| | Male | Female | Male | Female | Male | Male | Male | Female | Male | Female | Male | Female | |
| $3 50-$3 99 | ....... | ....... | ....... | ....... | ....... | ....... | ....... | ....... | 7 | ....... | .19 | ....... | $3 50-$3 99 |
| 4 00- 4 49 | ....... | ....... | ....... | ....... | ....... | ....... | ....... | ....... | ....... | 2 | ....... | 3.64 | 4 00- 4 49 |
| 4 50- 4 99 | ....... | ....... | ....... | ....... | ....... | ....... | ....... | ....... | 5 | 1 | .32 | 5.45 | 4 50- 4 99 |
| 5 00- 5 49 | ....... | ....... | ....... | ....... | ....... | ....... | ....... | ....... | 8 | 7 | .54 | 18.18 | 5 00- 5 49 |
| 5 50- 5 99 | ....... | ....... | ....... | ....... | ....... | ....... | 1 | ....... | 13 | ....... | .89 | ....... | 5 50- 5 99 |
| 6 00- 6 49 | ....... | ....... | ....... | ....... | ....... | ....... | ....... | ....... | 74 | 8 | 2.90 | 32.80 | 6 00- 6 49 |
| 6 50- 6 99 | ....... | ....... | ....... | ....... | ....... | ....... | ....... | 1 | 8 | 2 | 3.20 | 36.40 | 6 50- 6 99 |
| 7 00- 7 49 | ....... | ....... | ....... | ....... | 1 | 1 | ....... | ....... | 117 | 3 | 6.29 | 41.80 | 7 00- 7 49 |
| 7 50- 7 99 | 1 | 1 | ....... | 1 | ....... | ....... | 3 | 2 | 216 | 4 | 12.35 | 49.10 | 7 50- 7 99 |
| 8 00- 8 99 | 1 | ....... | 3 | ....... | ....... | ....... | 5 | ....... | 361 | 9 | 21.90 | 65.50 | 8 00- 8 99 |
| 9 00- 9 99 | 1 | ....... | 3 | ....... | 1 | ....... | 4 | ....... | 179 | 9 | 26.75 | 81.90 | 9 00- 9 99 |
| 10 00-10 99 | 13 | ....... | 23 | ....... | 5 | 3 | 2 | ....... | 282 | 4 | 34.40 | 89.00 | 10 00-10 99 |
| 11 00-11 99 | 14 | ....... | 20 | ....... | 9 | 1 | 2 | 1 | 158 | 2 | 38.30 | 92.75 | 11 00-11 99 |
| 12 00-12 99 | 42 | ....... | 79 | ....... | 27 | 3 | 2 | ....... | 534 | ....... | 53.20 | ....... | 12 00-12 99 |
| 13 00-13 99 | 23 | ....... | 29 | ....... | 11 | ....... | ....... | ....... | 232 | ....... | 59.40 | ....... | 13 00-13 99 |
| 14 00-14 99 | 40 | ....... | 47 | ....... | 13 | 2 | 2 | ....... | 309 | 1 | 68.00 | 94.50 | 14 00-14 99 |
| 15 00-15 99 | 34 | ....... | 39 | ....... | 9 | 1 | 3 | ....... | 603 | 2 | 84.30 | 98.20 | 15 00-15 99 |
| 16 00-17 99 | 48 | ....... | 63 | ....... | 12 | 1 | ....... | ....... | 370 | ....... | 94.00 | ....... | 16 00-17 99 |
| 18 00-19 99 | 12 | ....... | 18 | ....... | ....... | 1 | 1 | ....... | 95 | ....... | 96.80 | ....... | 18 00-19 99 |
| 20 00-24 99 | 15 | ....... | 13 | ....... | 5 | ....... | 2 | ....... | 72 | ....... | 98.80 | ....... | 20 00-24 99 |
| 25 00-29 99 | 8 | ....... | 2 | ....... | 1 | ....... | ....... | ....... | 26 | ....... | 99.40 | ....... | 25 00-29 99 |
| 30 00-34 99 | 3 | ....... | 5 | ....... | ....... | ....... | ....... | ....... | 11 | ....... | 99.60 | ....... | 30 00-34 99 |
| 35 00-39 99 | 1 | ....... | 2 | ....... | 1 | ....... | ....... | ....... | 8 | ....... | 99.85 | ....... | 35 00-39 99 |
| 40 00 and over | 2 | ....... | 4 | ....... | ....... | ....... | ....... | ....... | 7 | 1 | 100.00 | 100.00 | 40 00 and over |
| Not reported | ....... | ....... | ....... | ....... | ....... | ....... | 2 | ....... | 5 | ....... | ....... | ....... | Not reported |
| Total | 258 | 1 | 350 | 1 | 95 | 13 | 29 | 4 | 3,700 | 55 | ....... | ....... | Total |

210. TABLE VIII, A, 1, e

NEW YORK CITY

DEPARTMENT STORES — SHIPPING AND DELIVERY

NUMBER AND PER CENT OF EMPLOYEES EARNING SPECIFIED WEEKLY RATES BY OCCUPATION AND SEX

| Weekly Rates in Dollars | Occupation: Foremen and Forewomen | | Clerks and Routers | | Drivers | Wagon Boys and Helpers | Chauffeurs | General Labor | Packing | | Stablemen | Not Reported | Total | | Cumulative Per Cent. of Total | | Weekly Rates in Dollars |
|---|---|---|---|---|---|---|---|---|---|---|---|---|---|---|---|---|---|
| | Male | Female | Male | Female | Male | Male | Male | Male | Male | Female | Male | Male | Male | Female | Male | Female | |
| $3 50-$3 99 | ...... | ...... | ...... | ...... | ...... | 7 | ...... | ...... | ...... | ...... | ...... | ...... | 7 | ...... | .19 | ...... | $3 50-$3 99 |
| 4 00- 4 49 | ...... | ...... | ...... | ...... | ...... | ...... | ...... | ...... | ...... | 2 | ...... | ...... | ...... | 2 | ...... | 3.64 | 4 00- 4 49 |
| 4 50- 4 99 | ...... | ...... | ...... | 1 | ...... | 5 | ...... | ...... | ...... | ...... | ...... | ...... | 5 | 1 | .32 | 5.45 | 4 50- 4 99 |
| 5 00- 5 49 | ...... | ...... | 1 | 1 | ...... | 3 | ...... | 2 | 2 | 6 | ...... | ...... | 8 | 7 | .54 | 18.18 | 5 00- 5 49 |
| 5 50- 5 99 | ...... | ...... | ...... | ...... | ...... | 1 | ...... | 1 | 11 | ...... | ...... | ...... | 13 | ...... | .89 | ...... | 5 50- 5 99 |
| 6 00- 6 49 | ...... | ...... | 4 | 4 | ...... | 67 | ...... | ...... | 3 | 4 | ...... | ...... | 74 | 8 | 2.90 | 32.80 | 6 00- 6 49 |
| 6 50- 6 99 | ...... | ...... | ...... | ...... | 1 | 3 | ...... | 1 | 3 | 2 | ...... | ...... | 8 | 2 | 3.20 | 36.40 | 6 50- 6 99 |
| 7 00- 7 49 | ...... | ...... | 10 | 2 | 3 | 86 | ...... | ...... | 18 | 1 | ...... | ...... | 117 | 3 | 6.29 | 41.80 | 7 00- 7 49 |
| 7 50- 7 99 | ...... | ...... | 2 | ...... | 9 | 199 | 1 | 1 | 1 | 4 | 3 | ...... | 216 | 4 | 12.35 | 49.10 | 7 50- 7 99 |
| 8 00- 8 99 | ...... | ...... | 16 | 8 | 7 | 313 | ...... | 5 | 20 | 1 | ...... | ...... | 361 | 9 | 21.90 | 65.50 | 8 00- 8 99 |
| 9 00- 9 99 | ...... | ...... | 11 | 8 | 3 | 142 | ...... | 2 | 20 | 1 | ...... | 1 | 179 | 9 | 26.75 | 81.90 | 9 00- 9 99 |
| 10 00-10 99 | ...... | ...... | 54 | 2 | 25 | 120 | 6 | ...... | 74 | 2 | 3 | ...... | 282 | 4 | 34.40 | 89.00 | 10 00-10 99 |
| 11 00-11 99 | ...... | ...... | 25 | 1 | 14 | 48 | 2 | 4 | 51 | 1 | 14 | ...... | 158 | 2 | 38.30 | 92.75 | 11 00-11 99 |
| 12 00-12 99 | 2 | ...... | 96 | ...... | 48 | 86 | 10 | 12 | 232 | ...... | 48 | ...... | 534 | ...... | 53.20 | ...... | 12 00-12 99 |
| 13 00-13 99 | 1 | ...... | 34 | ...... | 49 | 4 | 4 | ...... | 96 | ...... | 44 | ...... | 232 | ...... | 59.40 | ...... | 13 00-13 99 |
| 14 00-14 99 | 6 | ...... | 33 | ...... | 51 | 4 | 17 | ...... | 96 | 1 | 102 | ...... | 309 | 1 | 68.00 | 94.50 | 14 00-14 99 |
| 15 00-15 99 | 3 | ...... | 38 | 1 | 428 | 6 | 79 | 2 | 33 | 1 | 14 | ...... | 603 | 2 | 84.30 | 98.20 | 15 00-15 99 |
| 16 00-17 99 | 14 | ...... | 49 | ...... | 176 | 3 | 75 | ...... | 34 | ...... | 19 | ...... | 370 | ...... | 94.00 | ...... | 16 00-17 99 |
| 18 00-19 99 | 9 | ...... | 29 | ...... | 15 | 2 | 25 | 1 | 10 | ...... | 4 | ...... | 95 | ...... | 96.80 | ...... | 18 00-19 99 |
| 20 00-24 99 | 23 | ...... | 19 | ...... | 7 | ...... | 10 | ...... | 6 | ...... | 7 | ...... | 72 | ...... | 98.80 | ...... | 20 00-24 99 |
| 25 00-29 99 | 13 | ...... | 6 | ...... | 1 | ...... | 5 | ...... | ...... | ...... | 1 | ...... | 26 | ...... | 99.40 | ...... | 25 00-29 99 |
| 30 00-34 99 | 4 | ...... | 3 | ...... | ...... | ...... | 1 | ...... | ...... | ...... | 3 | ...... | 11 | ...... | 99.60 | ...... | 30 00-34 99 |
| 35 00-39 99 | 6 | ...... | ...... | ...... | ...... | ...... | ...... | ...... | ...... | ...... | 2 | ...... | 8 | ...... | 99.85 | ...... | 35 00-39 99 |
| 40 00 and over | 6 | 1 | ...... | ...... | ...... | ...... | ...... | ...... | ...... | ...... | 1 | ...... | 7 | 1 | 100.00 | 100.00 | 40 00 and over |
| Not reported | ...... | ...... | ...... | ...... | 1 | 3 | 1 | ...... | ...... | ...... | ...... | ...... | 5 | ...... | ...... | ...... | Not reported |
| Total | 87 | 1 | 430 | 28 | 838 | 1,102 | 236 | 31 | 710 | 26 | 265 | 1 | 3,700 | 55 | ...... | ...... | Total |

211. TABLE VI, A, 1, c

NEW YORK CITY

DEPARTMENT STORES — SHIPPING AND DELIVERY

Number and Per Cent of Employees Classified According to Actual Weekly Earnings by Age Groups and Sex

| Weekly Rates in Dollars | Age Groups in Years | | | | | | | | | | | | | Weekly Rates in Dollars |
|---|---|---|---|---|---|---|---|---|---|---|---|---|---|---|
| | 14–15 | 16–17 | | 18–20 | | 21–24 | | 25–29 | | 30–34 | | 35–39 | | |
| | Male | Male | Female | Male | Female | Male | Female | Male | Female | Male | Female | Male | Female | |
| Less than $3 00... | 2 | 2 | 1 | 11 | ...... | 1 | 1 | 2 | ...... | 2 | ...... | ...... | ...... | ..Less than $3 00 |
| $3 00–$3 49...... | ...... | ...... | 1 | 5 | ...... | 2 | ...... | 1 | ...... | ...... | ...... | ...... | ...... | .....$3 00– 3 49 |
| 3 50– 3 99...... | 4 | 2 | ...... | 3 | ...... | ...... | ...... | 1 | ...... | 1 | ...... | ...... | ...... | ..... 3 50– 3 99 |
| 4 00– 4 49...... | ...... | 2 | 1 | 5 | 1 | ...... | ...... | 1 | ...... | 2 | ...... | 1 | ...... | ..... 4 00– 4 49 |
| 4 50– 4 99...... | ...... | 5 | 1 | 4 | ...... | 1 | ...... | ...... | ...... | ...... | ...... | ...... | ...... | ..... 4 50– 4 99 |
| 5 00– 5 49...... | 3 | 8 | 2 | 5 | 2 | 2 | 1 | 4 | ...... | 1 | ...... | 1 | ...... | ..... 5 00– 5 49 |
| 5 50– 5 99...... | ...... | 7 | ...... | 17 | 2 | 2 | ...... | 2 | ...... | ...... | ...... | ...... | ...... | ..... 5 50– 5 99 |
| 6 00– 6 49...... | 2 | 44 | ...... | 31 | 3 | 6 | 3 | 4 | 1 | 2 | ...... | 1 | ...... | ..... 6 00– 6 49 |
| 6 50– 6 99...... | ...... | 4 | ...... | 17 | ...... | 5 | ...... | 3 | ...... | 1 | ...... | ...... | 1 | ..... 6 50– 6 99 |
| 7 00– 7 49...... | ...... | 34 | ...... | 81 | 2 | 6 | ...... | 2 | ...... | ...... | ...... | ...... | ...... | ..... 7 00– 7 49 |
| 7 50– 7 99...... | 1 | 33 | 1 | 163 | ...... | 34 | ...... | 2 | ...... | 2 | 1 | 1 | ...... | ..... 7 50– 7 99 |
| 8 00– 8 99...... | ...... | 26 | ...... | 154 | ...... | 69 | 6 | 8 | 1 | 7 | ...... | 4 | ...... | ..... 8 00– 8 99 |
| 9 00– 9 99...... | ...... | 4 | 1 | 84 | ...... | 46 | 4 | 8 | 1 | 2 | 1 | 4 | 1 | ..... 9 00– 9 99 |
| 10 00–10 99...... | ...... | 1 | 2 | 71 | ...... | 98 | 1 | 31 | ...... | 24 | 1 | 19 | ...... | .....10 00–10 99 |
| 11 00–11 99...... | ...... | 3 | ...... | 32 | 1 | 58 | ...... | 22 | ...... | 13 | ...... | 19 | ...... | .....11 00–11 99 |
| 12 00–12 99...... | ...... | 1 | ...... | 35 | ...... | 106 | ...... | 89 | ...... | 49 | ...... | 58 | ...... | .....12 00–12 99 |
| 13 00–13 99...... | ...... | 2 | ...... | 12 | ...... | 72 | ...... | 43 | ...... | 37 | ...... | 20 | ...... | .....13 00–13 99 |
| 14 00–14 99...... | ...... | ...... | 1 | 9 | ...... | 71 | ...... | 64 | ...... | 56 | ...... | 45 | ...... | .....14 00–14 99 |
| 15 00–15 99...... | ...... | ...... | 1 | 23 | ...... | 134 | 1 | 101 | ...... | 68 | ...... | 56 | ...... | .....15 00–15 99 |
| 16 00–17 99...... | ...... | ...... | ...... | 4 | ...... | 45 | ...... | 83 | ...... | 71 | ...... | 72 | ...... | .....16 00–17 99 |
| 18 00–19 99...... | ...... | ...... | ...... | 1 | ...... | 9 | ...... | 10 | ...... | 20 | ...... | 26 | ...... | .....18 00–19 99 |
| 20 00–24 99...... | ...... | ...... | ...... | ...... | ...... | 2 | ...... | 4 | ...... | 15 | ...... | 15 | ...... | .....20 00–24 99 |
| 25 00–29 99...... | ...... | ...... | ...... | ...... | ...... | 4 | ...... | 1 | ...... | 2 | ...... | 11 | ...... | .....25 00–29 99 |
| 30 00–34 99...... | ...... | ...... | ...... | ...... | ...... | 1 | ...... | ...... | ...... | 1 | ...... | 1 | ...... | .....30 00–34 99 |
| 35 00–39 99...... | ...... | ...... | ...... | ...... | ...... | ...... | ...... | 1 | ...... | 1 | ...... | 2 | ...... | .....35 00–39 99 |
| 40 00 and over.... | ...... | ...... | ...... | ...... | ...... | ...... | ...... | ...... | ...... | ...... | 1 | 1 | ...... | ...40 00 and over |
| Not reported...... | ...... | ...... | ...... | 1 | ...... | 1 | ...... | 1 | ...... | ...... | ...... | ...... | ...... | .....Not reported |
| Total........ | 12 | 178 | 12 | 768 | 11 | 775 | 17 | 488 | 3 | 377 | 4 | 357 | 2 | .......Total |

211. TABLE VI, A, 1, c — (*concluded*)

NEW YORK CITY

DEPARTMENT STORES — SHIPPING AND DELIVERY

Number and Per Cent of Employees Classified According to Actual Weekly Earnings by Age Groups and Sex

| Weekly Rates in Dollars | Age Groups in Years (*concluded*) | | | | | | | | | | | | Weekly Rates in Dollars |
|---|---|---|---|---|---|---|---|---|---|---|---|---|---|
| | 40–44 | | 45–54 | | 55–64 | 65 and over | Not reported | | Total | | Cumulative per cent. of total | | |
| | Male | Female | Male | Female | Male | Male | Male | Female | Male | Female | Male | Female | |
| Less than $3 00. | 2 | ....... | 1 | ....... | ....... | ....... | 2 | ....... | 25 | 2 | .70 | 3.60 | Less than $3 00 |
| $3 00–$3 49.... | ....... | ....... | ....... | ....... | ....... | ....... | ....... | ....... | 8 | 1 | .90 | 5.50 | ...$3 00– 3 49 |
| 3 50– 3 99.... | ....... | ....... | ....... | ....... | ....... | ....... | ....... | ....... | 11 | ....... | 1.10 | ....... | ... 3 50– 3 99 |
| 4 00– 4 49.... | ....... | ....... | ....... | ....... | ....... | ....... | 1 | ....... | 12 | 2 | 1.50 | 9.10 | ... 4 00– 4 49 |
| 4 50– 4 99.... | ....... | ....... | ....... | ....... | ....... | 1 | ....... | ....... | 11 | 1 | 1.80 | 10.90 | ... 4 50– 4 99 |
| 5 00– 5 49.... | ....... | ....... | 3 | ....... | ....... | ....... | ....... | ....... | 27 | 5 | 2.50 | 20.00 | ... 5 00– 5 49 |
| 5 50– 5 99.... | ....... | ....... | ....... | ....... | ....... | ....... | 1 | ....... | 29 | 2 | 3.30 | 23.60 | ... 5 50– 5 99 |
| 6 00– 6 49.... | 1 | ....... | ....... | ....... | ....... | ....... | ....... | ....... | 91 | 7 | 5.80 | 36.40 | ... 6 00– 6 49 |
| 6 50– 6 99.... | 1 | ....... | 2 | ....... | 1 | ....... | 1 | 1 | 35 | 2 | 6.80 | 40.00 | ... 6 50– 6 99 |
| 7 00– 7 49.... | ....... | ....... | 1 | ....... | 1 | 1 | ....... | ....... | 126 | 2 | 10.20 | 43.60 | ... 7 00– 7 49 |
| 7 50– 7 99.... | ....... | 1 | 2 | 1 | 1 | ....... | 4 | 2 | 243 | 6 | 16.70 | 54.50 | ... 7 50– 7 99 |
| 8 00– 8 99.... | 3 | ....... | 5 | ....... | ....... | 1 | 5 | ....... | 282 | 7 | 24.40 | 67.30 | ... 8 00– 8 99 |
| 9 00– 9 99.... | 2 | ....... | 2 | ....... | 1 | ....... | 2 | ....... | 155 | 8 | 28.60 | 81.80 | ... 9 00– 9 99 |
| 10 00–10 99.... | 16 | ....... | 19 | ....... | 5 | 2 | 1 | ....... | 287 | 4 | 36.30 | 89.10 | ...10 00–10 99 |
| 11 00–11 99.... | 17 | ....... | 21 | ....... | 6 | 1 | 2 | 1 | 194 | 2 | 41.50 | 92.70 | ...11 00–11 99 |
| 12 00–12 99.... | 34 | ....... | 67 | ....... | 25 | 2 | 2 | ....... | 468 | ....... | 54.20 | ....... | ...12 00–12 99 |
| 13 00–13 99.... | 23 | ....... | 29 | ....... | 11 | ....... | ....... | ....... | 249 | ....... | 60.90 | ....... | ...13 00–13 99 |
| 14 00–14 99.... | 39 | ....... | 45 | ....... | 13 | 2 | 2 | ....... | 346 | 1 | 70.50 | 94.50 | ...14 00–14 99 |
| 15 00–15 99.... | 32 | ....... | 43 | ....... | 9 | 1 | 3 | ....... | 470 | 2 | 83.10 | 98.20 | ...15 00–15 99 |
| 16 00–17 99.... | 46 | ....... | 62 | ....... | 16 | 1 | ....... | ....... | 400 | ....... | 93.90 | ....... | ...16 00–17 99 |
| 18 00–19 99.... | 11 | ....... | 19 | ....... | ....... | 1 | 1 | ....... | 98 | ....... | 96.60 | ....... | ...18 00–19 99 |
| 20 00–24 99.... | 17 | ....... | 16 | ....... | 5 | ....... | 2 | ....... | 76 | ....... | 98.60 | ....... | ...20 00–24 99 |
| 25 00–29 99.... | 7 | ....... | 2 | ....... | ....... | ....... | ....... | ....... | 27 | ....... | 99.30 | ....... | ...25 00–29 99 |
| 30 00–34 99.... | 4 | ....... | 5 | ....... | ....... | ....... | ....... | ....... | 12 | ....... | 99.60 | ....... | ...30 00–34 99 |
| 35 00–39 99.... | 1 | ....... | 2 | ....... | 1 | ....... | ....... | ....... | 8 | ....... | 99.90 | ....... | ...35 00–39 99 |
| 40 00 and over.. | 2 | ....... | 4 | ....... | ....... | ....... | ....... | ....... | 7 | 1 | 100.00 | 100.00 | .40 00 and over |
| Not reported... | ....... | ....... | ....... | ....... | ....... | ....... | ....... | ....... | 3 | ....... | ....... | ....... | ..Not reported |
| Total...... | 258 | 1 | 350 | 1 | 95 | 13 | 29 | 4 | 3,700 | 55 | ....... | ....... | .....Total |

212. TABLE IX, A, 1, c

NEW YORK CITY

DEPARTMENT STORES — SHIPPING AND DELIVERY

Number and Per Cent. of Employees Classified According to Actual Weekly Earnings, by Occupation and Sex

| Actual Weekly Earnings in Dollars | Occupation | | | | | | | | | | | | Total | | Cumulative Per Cent. of Total | | Actual Weekly Earnings in Dollars |
|---|---|---|---|---|---|---|---|---|---|---|---|---|---|---|---|---|---|
| | Foremen and Forewomen | | Clerks and Routers | | Drivers | Wagon Boys and Helpers | Chauffeurs | General Labor | Packing | | Stablemen | Not Reported | | | | | |
| | Male | Female | Male | Female | Male | Male | Male | Male | Male | Female | Male | Male | Male | Female | Male | Female | |
| Less than $3 00 | | | 1 | 1 | 1 | 18 | | | 5 | 1 | | | 25 | 2 | .70 | 3.60 | Less than $3 00 |
| $3 00–$3 49 | | | | | 1 | 6 | 1 | | | 1 | | | 8 | 1 | .90 | 5.50 | $3 00– 3 49 |
| 3 50– 3 99 | | | 1 | | | 8 | 1 | | | | 1 | | 11 | | 1.10 | | 3 50– 3 99 |
| 4 00– 4 49 | | | | | | 9 | | | 3 | 2 | | | 12 | 2 | 1.50 | 9.10 | 4 00– 4 49 |
| 4 50– 4 99 | | | | 1 | | 10 | | | 1 | | | | 11 | 1 | 1.80 | 10.90 | 4 50– 4 99 |
| 5 00– 5 49 | | | 3 | 1 | 3 | 13 | 1 | 2 | 4 | 4 | 1 | | 27 | 5 | 2.50 | 20.00 | 5 00– 5 49 |
| 5 50– 5 99 | | | 2 | 2 | | 15 | | 1 | 11 | | | | 29 | 2 | 3.30 | 23.60 | 5 50– 5 99 |
| 6 00– 6 49 | | | 5 | 3 | 1 | 79 | | | 6 | 4 | | | 91 | 7 | 5.80 | 36.40 | 6 00– 6 49 |
| 6 50– 6 99 | | | 4 | | 2 | 19 | | 1 | 9 | 2 | | | 35 | 2 | 6.80 | 40.00 | 6 50– 6 99 |
| 7 00– 7 49 | | | 7 | 1 | 5 | 102 | | | 12 | 1 | | | 126 | 2 | 10.20 | 43.60 | 7 00– 7 49 |
| 7 50– 7 99 | | | 3 | 1 | 8 | 220 | 1 | 1 | 6 | 5 | 3 | 1 | 243 | 6 | 16.70 | 54.50 | 7 50– 7 99 |
| 8 00– 8 99 | | | 18 | 7 | 11 | 219 | 2 | 7 | 22 | | 3 | | 282 | 7 | 24.40 | 67.30 | 8 00– 8 99 |
| 9 00– 9 99 | | | 13 | 7 | 4 | 114 | 2 | 2 | 19 | 1 | 1 | | 155 | 8 | 28.60 | 81.80 | 9 00– 9 99 |
| 10 00–10 99 | | | 49 | 2 | 33 | 116 | 13 | 2 | 72 | 2 | 2 | | 287 | 4 | 36.30 | 89.10 | 10 00–10 99 |
| 11 00–11 99 | | | 29 | 1 | 23 | 43 | 7 | 4 | 72 | 1 | 16 | | 194 | 2 | 41.50 | 92.70 | 11 00–11 99 |
| 12 00–12 99 | 2 | | 77 | | 59 | 73 | 18 | 8 | 186 | | 45 | | 468 | | 54.20 | | 12 00–12 99 |
| 13 00–13 99 | 1 | | 37 | | 57 | 17 | 8 | | 88 | | 41 | | 249 | | 60.90 | | 13 00–13 99 |
| 14 00–14 99 | 6 | | 36 | | 87 | 10 | 20 | | 86 | 1 | 101 | | 346 | 1 | 70.50 | 94.50 | 14 00–14 99 |
| 15 00–15 99 | 2 | | 39 | 1 | 307 | 4 | 56 | 2 | 46 | 1 | 14 | | 470 | 2 | 83.10 | 98.20 | 15 00–15 99 |
| 16 00–17 99 | 14 | | 48 | | 209 | 3 | 63 | 1 | 43 | | 19 | | 400 | | 93.90 | | 16 00–17 99 |
| 18 00–19 99 | 9 | | 27 | | 19 | 3 | 24 | | 12 | | 4 | | 98 | | 96.60 | | 18 00–19 99 |
| 20 00–24 99 | 25 | | 22 | | 6 | | 10 | | 6 | | 7 | | 76 | | 98.60 | | 20 00–24 99 |
| 25 00–29 99 | 11 | | 6 | | 1 | | 7 | | 1 | | 1 | | 27 | | 99.30 | | 25 00–29 99 |
| 30 00–34 99 | 5 | | 3 | | 1 | | | | | | 3 | | 12 | | 99.60 | | 30 00–34 99 |
| 35 00–39 99 | 6 | | | | | | | | | | 2 | | 8 | | 99.90 | | 35 00–39 99 |
| 40 00 and over | 6 | 1 | | | | | | | | | 1 | | 7 | 1 | 100.00 | 100.00 | 40 00 and over |
| Not reported | | | | | | 1 | 2 | | | | | | 3 | | | | Not reported |
| Total | 87 | 1 | 430 | 28 | 838 | 1,102 | 236 | 31 | 710 | 26 | 265 | 1 | 3,700 | 55 | | | Total |

NEW YORK CITY

DEPARTMENT STORES — MANUFACTURING

213. TABLE V, a, 1, d NUMBER AND PER CENT OF EMPLOYEES EARNING SPECIFIED WEEKLY RATES BY AGE GROUPS AND SEX

| WEEKLY RATES IN DOLLARS | AGE GROUPS IN YEARS | | | | | | | | | | | | | | WEEKLY RATES IN DOLLARS |
|---|---|---|---|---|---|---|---|---|---|---|---|---|---|---|---|
| | 14–15 | | 16–17 | | 18–20 | | 21–24 | | 25–29 | | 30–34 | | 35–39 | | |
| | Male | Female | Male | Female | Male | Female | Male | Female | Male | Female | Male | Female | Male | Female | |
| Less than $3 00 | .... | ...... | .... | 2 | ...... | 1 | ...... | ...... | ...... | ...... | ...... | ...... | ...... | ...... | Less than $3 00 |
| $3 00–$3 49... | .... | 1 | .... | 1 | ...... | 1 | ...... | ...... | ...... | ...... | ...... | ...... | ...... | ...... | ...$3 00– 3 49 |
| 3 50– 3 99... | 1 | ...... | .... | ...... | ...... | 1 | ...... | ...... | ...... | ...... | ...... | ...... | ...... | ...... | ...3 50– 3 99 |
| 4 00– 4 49... | .... | ...... | 2 | 10 | ...... | 3 | ...... | ...... | ...... | ...... | ...... | ...... | ...... | ...... | ... 4 00– 4 49 |
| 4 50– 4 99... | .... | ...... | .... | 6 | ...... | ...... | ...... | ...... | ...... | ...... | ...... | ...... | ...... | ...... | ... 4 50– 4 99 |
| 5 00– 5 49... | 1 | ...... | .... | 10 | ...... | 13 | ...... | 2 | ...... | 1 | 1 | ...... | ...... | 1 | ... 5 00– 5 49 |
| 5 50– 5 99... | .... | ...... | .... | 2 | ...... | 4 | ...... | ...... | ...... | ...... | ...... | ...... | ...... | ...... | ... 5 50– 5 99 |
| 6 00– 6 49... | 1 | ...... | 1 | 20 | 1 | 16 | ...... | 9 | 1 | 2 | ...... | ...... | 1 | ...... | ... 6 00– 6 49 |
| 6 50– 6 99... | .... | ...... | .... | 1 | 1 | 2 | ...... | ...... | ...... | ...... | ...... | 1 | ...... | ...... | ... 6 50– 6 99 |
| 7 00– 7 49... | 1 | ...... | 2 | 2 | 2 | 14 | 2 | 11 | 1 | 2 | ...... | ...... | ...... | 4 | ... 7 00– 7 49 |
| 7 50– 7 99... | .... | ...... | .... | ...... | ...... | ...... | ...... | ...... | ...... | ...... | 1 | ...... | ...... | ...... | ... 7 50– 7 99 |
| 8 00– 8 99... | .... | ...... | 1 | 4 | 7 | 25 | 3 | 21 | ...... | 15 | ...... | 3 | ...... | 3 | ... 8 00– 8 99 |
| 9 00– 9 99... | .... | ...... | 1 | 1 | 8 | 24 | 1 | 35 | 1 | 15 | ...... | 11 | ...... | 11 | ... 9 00– 9 99 |
| 10 00–10 99... | .... | ...... | .... | 1 | 3 | 7 | 2 | 51 | 3 | 35 | 1 | 24 | 2 | 24 | ...10 00–10 99 |
| 11 00–11 99... | .... | ...... | .... | 1 | ...... | 1 | 2 | 20 | 1 | 25 | ...... | 7 | 1 | 15 | ...11 00–11 99 |
| 12 00–12 99... | .... | ...... | .... | ...... | 2 | 4 | 16 | 26 | 13 | 37 | 9 | 23 | 9 | 25 | ...12 00–12 99 |
| 13 00–13 99... | .... | ...... | .... | ...... | 2 | ...... | 2 | 7 | 6 | 15 | 2 | 7 | 8 | 12 | ...13 00–13 99 |
| 14 00–14 99... | .... | ...... | .... | ...... | 6 | 2 | 13 | 6 | 20 | 23 | 9 | 17 | 19 | 13 | ...14 00–14 99 |
| 15 00–15 99... | .... | ...... | .... | ...... | 5 | ...... | 11 | 7 | 21 | 23 | 29 | 15 | 15 | 13 | ...15 00–15 99 |
| 16 00–17 99... | .... | ...... | .... | ...... | 2 | ...... | 5 | 3 | 23 | 17 | 21 | 24 | 22 | 14 | ...16 00–17 99 |
| 18 00–19 99... | .... | ...... | .... | ...... | ...... | ...... | 5 | 8 | 18 | 13 | 27 | 17 | 19 | 8 | ...18 00–19 99 |
| 20 00–24 99... | .... | ...... | .... | ...... | 1 | ...... | 5 | 4 | 15 | 11 | 23 | 11 | 23 | 19 | ...20 00–24 99 |
| 25 00–29 99... | .... | ...... | .... | ...... | 1 | ...... | 2 | 1 | 6 | 5 | 18 | 11 | 22 | 9 | ...25 00–29 99 |
| 30 00–34 99... | .... | ...... | .... | ...... | ...... | ...... | ...... | ...... | 2 | ...... | 4 | 2 | 6 | 1 | ...30 00–34 99 |
| 35 00–39 99... | .... | ...... | .... | ...... | ...... | ...... | ...... | ...... | 1 | 1 | 2 | 1 | 3 | 3 | ...35 00–39 99 |
| 40 00 and over. | .... | ...... | .... | ...... | ...... | 1 | ...... | 1 | 1 | 2 | 7 | 3 | 4 | 6 | .40 00 and over |
| Not reported... | .... | ...... | .... | ...... | ...... | ...... | 1 | 1 | ...... | 3 | 7 | 5 | 7 | 2 | ...Not reported |
| Total..... | 4 | 1 | 7 | 61 | 41 | 119 | 70 | 213 | 133 | 245 | 161 | 182 | 161 | 183 | .....Total |

213. TABLE V, a, 1, d — (*concluded*)

NEW YORK CITY

DEPARTMENT STORES — MANUFACTURING

Number and Per Cent of Employees Earning Specified Weekly Rates by Age Groups and Sex

| Weekly Rates in Dollars | Age Groups in Years (*concluded*) | | | | | | | | | | | | | | Weekly Rates in Dollars |
|---|---|---|---|---|---|---|---|---|---|---|---|---|---|---|---|
| | 40–44 | | 45–54 | | 55–64 | | 65 and over | | Not reported | | Total | | Cumulative per cent of total | | |
| | Male | Female | Male | Female | Male | Female | Male | Female | Male | Female | Male | Female | Male | Female | |
| Less than $3 00 | .... | ...... | .... | ...... | ...... | ...... | ...... | ...... | ...... | ...... | ...... | 3 | ...... | .20 | Less than $3 00 |
| $3 00–$3 49... | .... | ...... | .... | ...... | ...... | ...... | ...... | ...... | ...... | ...... | ...... | 3 | ...... | .40 | ...$3 00– 3 49 |
| 3 50– 3 99... | .... | ...... | .... | ...... | ...... | ...... | ...... | ...... | ...... | ...... | 1 | 1 | .10 | .50 | ... 3 50– 3 99 |
| 4 00– 4 49... | .... | ...... | .... | 1 | ...... | ...... | ...... | ...... | ...... | ...... | 2 | 14 | .30 | 1.60 | ... 4 00– 4 49 |
| 4 50– 4 99... | .... | ...... | .... | ...... | ...... | ...... | ...... | ...... | ...... | ...... | ...... | 6 | ...... | 2.00 | ... 4 50– 4 99 |
| 5 00– 5 49... | .... | ...... | .... | ...... | ...... | ...... | ...... | ...... | ...... | ...... | 2 | 27 | .50 | 4.10 | ... 5 00– 5 49 |
| 5 50– 5 99... | .... | ...... | .... | ...... | ...... | ...... | ...... | ...... | ...... | ...... | ...... | 6 | ...... | 4.50 | ... 5 50– 5 99 |
| 6 00– 6 49... | 1 | 1 | .... | ...... | ...... | ...... | ...... | ...... | 1 | 2 | 7 | 50 | 1.30 | 8.30 | ... 6 00– 6 49 |
| 6 50– 6 99... | .... | ...... | .... | ...... | ...... | ...... | ...... | ...... | ...... | ...... | 1 | 4 | 1.49 | 8.60 | ... 6 50– 6 99 |
| 7 00– 7 49... | .... | ...... | .... | ...... | ...... | 1 | ...... | ...... | 1 | 3 | 9 | 37 | 2.30 | 11.40 | ... 7 00– 7 49 |
| 7 50– 7 99... | .... | ...... | .... | 1 | ...... | ...... | ...... | ...... | ...... | ...... | 1 | 1 | 2.40 | 11.50 | ... 7 50– 7 99 |
| 8 00– 8 99... | .... | 3 | .... | 3 | ...... | ...... | ...... | 1 | ...... | 4 | 11 | 82 | 3.60 | 17.70 | ... 8 00– 8 99 |
| 9 00– 9 99... | .... | 10 | .... | 7 | ...... | 1 | ...... | 1 | ...... | 3 | 11 | 119 | 4.70 | 26.70 | ... 9 00– 9 99 |
| 10 00–10 99... | 1 | 21 | 1 | 26 | 3 | 4 | ...... | 1 | ...... | 11 | 16 | 205 | 6.40 | 42.30 | ...10 00–10 99 |
| 11 00–11 99... | .... | 6 | 1 | 10 | ...... | 2 | ...... | ...... | 1 | 5 | 6 | 92 | 7.10 | 49.20 | ...11 00–11 99 |
| 12 00–12 99... | 4 | 13 | 9 | 14 | 3 | 5 | 3 | 3 | ...... | 7 | 68 | 157 | 14.20 | 61.10 | ...12 00–12 99 |
| 13 00–13 99... | 5 | 4 | 4 | 4 | 6 | ...... | 1 | 1 | ...... | 3 | 36 | 53 | 18.00 | 65.00 | ...13 00–13 99 |
| 14 00–14 99... | 4 | 7 | 10 | 15 | 7 | 3 | 3 | ...... | 1 | 10 | 92 | 96 | 27.70 | 72.40 | ...14 00–14 99 |
| 15 00–15 99... | 8 | 8 | 22 | 7 | 6 | 1 | 2 | ...... | 3 | 8 | 122 | 82 | 40.50 | 78.60 | ...15 00–15 99 |
| 16 00–17 99... | 10 | 7 | 20 | 6 | 11 | 1 | ...... | ...... | ...... | 5 | 114 | 77 | 57.60 | 84.40 | ...16 00–17 99 |
| 18 00–19 99... | 17 | 5 | 35 | 1 | 15 | 1 | 2 | ...... | 1 | 3 | 139 | 56 | 67.20 | 88.60 | ...18 00–19 99 |
| 20 00–24 99... | 28 | 15 | 36 | 8 | 6 | 1 | 2 | ...... | ...... | 7 | 189 | 76 | 81.80 | 94.40 | ...20 00–24 99 |
| 25 00–29 99... | 20 | 8 | 26 | 4 | 6 | 1 | 1 | ...... | ...... | 2 | 102 | 41 | 92.60 | 97.50 | ...25 00–29 99 |
| 30 00–34 99... | 7 | 4 | 7 | ...... | 3 | ...... | ...... | ...... | 1 | 1 | 30 | 8 | 95.70 | 98.10 | ...30 00–34 99 |
| 35 00–39 99... | 1 | 2 | 5 | ...... | 3 | ...... | ...... | ...... | ...... | 1 | 15 | 8 | 97.30 | 98.89 | ...35 00–39 99 |
| 40 00 and over. | 5 | 1 | 9 | 2 | ...... | ...... | ...... | ...... | ...... | 2 | 26 | 18 | 100.0 | 100.00 | .40 00 and over |
| Not reported... | 5 | 6 | 6 | 4 | 1 | ...... | ...... | ...... | ...... | ...... | 27 | 21 | ...... | ...... | ...Not reported |
| Total..... | 116 | 121 | 191 | 113 | 70 | 21 | 14 | 7 | 9 | 77 | 977 | 1,343 | ...... | ...... | .....Total |

214. TABLE VIII, A, 1, d

NEW YORK CITY
**DEPARTMENT STORES — MANUFACTURING**
NUMBER AND PER CENT OF EMPLOYEES EARNING SPECIFIED WEEKLY RATES BY OCCUPATION AND SEX

| SPECIFIED WEEKLY RATES IN DOLLARS | OCCUPATION | | | | | | | | | | | | | | | | | | | SPECIFIED WEEKLY RATES IN DOLLARS |
|---|---|---|---|---|---|---|---|---|---|---|---|---|---|---|---|---|---|---|---|---|
| | SEWING | | HOUSE FURNISHING | | CABINET WORK, FRAMING | | PHOTO-GRAVURES, PRINTING | | METALWORK JEWELRY, GLASSWORK | | SHOE REPAIRING, BUCKLES, ETC. | | BOX-MAKING | CANDY-MAKING | | TOTAL | | CUMULATIVE PER CENT OF TOTAL | | |
| | Male | Female | Male | Female | Male | Female | Male | Female | Male | Female | Male | Female | Male | Male | Female | Male | Female | Male | Female | |
| Less than $3 00 | .... | 3 | .... | .... | .... | .... | .... | .... | .... | .... | .... | .... | .... | .... | .... | .... | 3 | .... | .20 | Less than $3 00 |
| $3 00–$3 49 | .... | 3 | .... | .... | .... | .... | .... | .... | .... | .... | .... | .... | .... | .... | .... | .... | 3 | .... | .40 | $3 00– 3 49 |
| 3 50– 3 99 | .... | 1 | .... | .... | .... | .... | .... | .... | .... | .... | .... | .... | .... | 1 | .... | 1 | 1 | .10 | .50 | 3 50– 3 99 |
| 4 00– 4 49 | .... | 14 | .... | .... | .... | .... | .... | .... | .... | .... | .... | .... | 1 | 1 | .... | 2 | 14 | .30 | 1.60 | 4 00– 4 49 |
| 4 50– 4 99 | .... | 6 | .... | .... | .... | .... | .... | .... | .... | .... | .... | .... | .... | .... | .... | .... | 6 | .... | 2.00 | 4 50– 4 99 |
| 5 00– 5 49 | 1 | 22 | 1 | 2 | .... | .... | .... | .... | .... | .... | .... | 2 | .... | .... | 1 | 2 | 27 | .50 | 4.10 | 5 00– 5 49 |
| 5 50– 5 99 | .... | 6 | .... | .... | .... | .... | .... | .... | .... | .... | .... | .... | .... | .... | .... | .... | 6 | .... | 4.50 | 5 50– 5 99 |
| 6 00– 6 49 | 2 | 43 | 3 | 4 | .... | .... | .... | .... | 2 | 3 | .... | .... | .... | .... | .... | 7 | 50 | 1.30 | 8.30 | 6 00– 6 49 |
| 6 50– 6 99 | .... | 3 | .... | .... | 1 | .... | .... | 1 | .... | .... | .... | .... | .... | .... | .... | 1 | 4 | 1.40 | 8.60 | 6 50– 6 99 |
| 7 00– 7 49 | .... | 29 | 1 | 6 | 1 | .... | 1 | .... | 4 | 1 | .... | 1 | 1 | 1 | .... | 9 | 37 | 2.30 | 11.40 | 7 00– 7 49 |
| 7 50– 7 99 | .... | 1 | .... | .... | 1 | .... | .... | .... | .... | .... | .... | .... | .... | .... | .... | 1 | 1 | 2.40 | 11.50 | 7 50– 7 99 |
| 8 00– 8 99 | 3 | 65 | 3 | 5 | 3 | .... | 1 | 1 | 1 | 5 | .... | 5 | .... | .... | 1 | 11 | 82 | 3.60 | 17.70 | 8 00– 8 99 |
| 9 00– 9 99 | 3 | 91 | 3 | 21 | 2 | .... | .... | .... | 2 | 1 | .... | 4 | .... | 1 | 2 | 11 | 119 | 4.70 | 26.70 | 9 00– 9 99 |
| 10 00–10 99 | 5 | 151 | 4 | 49 | 3 | .... | .... | .... | 2 | 1 | 2 | 3 | .... | .... | 1 | 16 | 205 | 6.40 | 42.30 | 10 00–10 99 |
| 11 00–11 99 | .... | 76 | 3 | 14 | 1 | .... | .... | .... | 1 | .... | 1 | 2 | .... | .... | .... | 6 | 92 | 7.10 | 49.20 | 11 00–11 99 |
| 12 00–12 99 | 29 | 127 | 17 | 26 | 15 | 1 | .... | .... | 3 | 1 | 3 | 2 | .... | 1 | .... | 68 | 157 | 14.20 | 61.10 | 12 00–12 99 |
| 13 00–13 99 | 19 | 45 | 6 | 6 | 5 | .... | .... | 2 | 1 | .... | 5 | .... | .... | .... | .... | 36 | 53 | 18.00 | 65.00 | 13 00–13 99 |
| 14 00–14 99 | 35 | 89 | 18 | 3 | 27 | .... | 1 | 2 | 8 | 1 | 3 | 1 | .... | .... | .... | 92 | 96 | 27.70 | 72.40 | 14 00–14 99 |
| 15 00–15 99 | 22 | 77 | 28 | 4 | 56 | .... | 1 | .... | 10 | 1 | 3 | .... | .... | 2 | .... | 122 | 82 | 40.50 | 78.60 | 15 00–15 99 |
| 16 00–17 99 | 22 | 75 | 24 | 1 | 42 | .... | .... | 1 | 25 | .... | 1 | .... | .... | .... | .... | 114 | 77 | 51.60 | 84.40 | 16 00–17 99 |
| 18 00–19 99 | 20 | 52 | 39 | 3 | 49 | .... | .... | .... | 26 | .... | 5 | 1 | .... | .... | .... | 139 | 56 | 67.20 | 88.60 | 18 00–19 99 |
| 20 00–24 99 | 29 | 75 | 56 | 1 | 27 | .... | .... | .... | 23 | .... | 4 | .... | .... | .... | .... | 139 | 76 | 81.80 | 94.40 | 20 00–24 99 |
| 25 00–29 99 | 19 | 41 | 70 | .... | 3 | .... | .... | .... | 8 | .... | 1 | .... | .... | 1 | .... | 102 | 41 | 92.60 | 97.50 | 25 00–29 99 |
| 30 00–34 99 | 7 | 7 | 19 | 1 | 2 | .... | 1 | .... | .... | .... | 1 | .... | .... | .... | .... | 30 | 8 | 95.70 | 98.10 | 30 00–34 99 |
| 35 00–39 99 | 10 | 7 | 5 | 1 | .... | .... | .... | .... | .... | .... | .... | .... | .... | .... | .... | 15 | 8 | 97.30 | 98.80 | 35 00–39 99 |
| 40 00 and over | 16 | 18 | 8 | .... | .... | .... | 1 | .... | 1 | .... | .... | .... | .... | .... | .... | 26 | 18 | 100.00 | 100.00 | 40 00 and over |
| Not reported | 7 | 16 | 20 | 4 | .... | .... | .... | 1 | .... | .... | .... | .... | .... | .... | .... | 27 | 21 | .... | .... | Not reported |
| Total | 249 | 1,143 | 328 | 151 | 238 | 1 | 6 | 8 | 117 | 14 | 29 | 21 | 2 | 8 | 5 | 977 | 1,343 | .... | .... | Total |

215. TABLE VI, A, l, d

NEW YORK CITY

**DEPARTMENT STORES — MANUFACTURING**

NUMBER AND PER CENT. OF EMPLOYEES CLASSIFIED ACCCRDING TO ACTUAL WEEKLY EARNINGS BY AGE GROUPS AND SEX

| Actual Weekly Earnings in Dollars | Age Groups in Years | | | | | | | | | | | | | | Actual Weekly Earnings in Dollars |
|---|---|---|---|---|---|---|---|---|---|---|---|---|---|---|---|
| | 14–15 | | 16–17 | | 18–20 | | 21–24 | | 25–29 | | 30–34 | | 35–39 | | |
| | Male | Female | Male | Female | Male | Female | Male | Female | Male | Female | Male | Female | Male | Female | |
| Less than $3 00 | 1 | ...... | .... | 3 | ...... | 3 | ...... | 2 | ...... | 1 | ...... | ...... | ...... | ...... | Less than $3 00 |
| $3 00–$3 49... | .... | 1 | .... | 3 | ...... | 1 | ...... | ...... | 1 | 1 | ...... | ...... | ...... | ...... | ...$3 00– 3 49 |
| 3 50– 3 99... | 1 | ...... | .... | 4 | ...... | 2 | 1 | 1 | ...... | ...... | ...... | 2 | ...... | ...... | ... 3 50– 3 99 |
| 4 00– 4 49... | .... | ...... | 2 | 6 | ...... | 2 | ...... | 1 | ...... | ...... | ...... | ...... | 1 | ...... | ... 4 00– 4 49 |
| 4 50– 4 99... | .... | ...... | .... | 6 | ...... | 3 | ...... | ...... | ...... | ...... | ...... | ...... | ...... | ...... | ... 4 50– 4 99 |
| 5 00– 5 49... | 1 | ...... | .... | 8 | ...... | 11 | ...... | 4 | ...... | 4 | 1 | ...... | ...... | 1 | ... 5 00– 5 49 |
| 5 50– 5 99... | .... | ...... | .... | 2 | ...... | 4 | ...... | 5 | ...... | 3 | ...... | ...... | ...... | 1 | ... 5 50– 5 99 |
| 6 00– 6 49... | .... | ...... | 1 | 19 | 1 | 16 | ...... | 6 | 2 | 2 | 2 | 1 | 2 | 1 | ... 6 00– 6 94 |
| 6 50– 6 99... | .... | ...... | .... | 1 | 1 | 3 | 1 | 4 | 1 | 3 | ...... | ...... | 2 | 3 | ... 6 50– 6 99 |
| 7 00– 7 49... | 1 | ...... | 1 | 2 | 1 | 12 | 2 | 10 | 1 | 2 | ...... | 1 | ...... | 4 | ... 7 00– 7 49 |
| 7 50– 7 99... | .... | ...... | .... | 1 | ...... | 4 | 1 | 6 | ...... | 5 | 2 | 1 | 1 | 3 | ... 7 50– 7 99 |
| 8 00– 8 99... | .... | ...... | 2 | 3 | 9 | 26 | 3 | 23 | 3 | 20 | 2 | 5 | 4 | 3 | ... 8 00– 8 99 |
| 9 00– 9 99... | .... | ...... | .... | 1 | 7 | 22 | 2 | 37 | 2 | 18 | ...... | 11 | ...... | 11 | ... 9 00– 9 99 |
| 10 00–10 99... | .... | ...... | .... | 1 | 3 | 5 | 4 | 44 | 1 | 35 | 1 | 24 | 2 | 27 | ...10 00–10 99 |
| 11 00–11 99... | .... | ...... | 1 | 1 | ...... | 1 | 3 | 17 | 2 | 26 | 4 | 15 | 7 | 23 | ...11 00–11 99 |
| 12 00–12 99... | .... | ...... | .... | ...... | 2 | 4 | 16 | 21 | 15 | 33 | 8 | 16 | 9 | 24 | ...12 00–12 99 |
| 13 00–13 99... | .... | ...... | .... | ...... | 2 | ...... | 5 | 7 | 6 | 16 | 3 | 11 | 9 | 13 | ...13 00–13 99 |
| 14 00–14 99... | .... | ...... | .... | ...... | 4 | 2 | 10 | 7 | 21 | 22 | 9 | 16 | 20 | 10 | ...14 00–14 99 |
| 15 00–15 99... | .... | ...... | .... | ...... | 6 | ...... | 7 | 5 | 21 | 23 | 26 | 16 | 15 | 14 | ...15 00–15 99 |
| 16 00–17 99... | .... | ...... | .... | ...... | 3 | ...... | 10 | 5 | 23 | 18 | 30 | 23 | 22 | 16 | ...16 00–17 99 |
| 18 00–19 99... | .... | ...... | .... | ...... | ...... | ...... | 6 | 8 | 17 | 8 | 23 | 19 | 21 | 8 | ...18 00–19 99 |
| 20 00–24 99... | .... | ...... | .... | ...... | 1 | ...... | 5 | 4 | 19 | 12 | 29 | 14 | 29 | 19 | ...20 00–24 99 |
| 25 00–29 99... | .... | ...... | .... | ...... | 1 | ...... | 2 | 1 | 6 | 4 | 21 | 10 | 20 | 9 | ...25 00–29 99 |
| 30 00–34 99... | .... | ...... | .... | ...... | ...... | ...... | 1 | ...... | 4 | ...... | 6 | 3 | 7 | ...... | ...30 00–34 99 |
| 35 00–39 99... | .... | ...... | .... | ...... | ...... | ...... | ...... | ...... | 2 | 1 | 2 | 1 | 3 | 3 | ...35 00–39 99 |
| 40 00 and over. | .... | ...... | .... | ...... | ...... | 1 | ...... | 1 | 4 | 2 | 7 | 2 | 6 | 6 | .40 00 and over |
| Not reported... | .... | ...... | .... | ...... | ...... | ...... | ...... | ...... | 1 | ...... | 1 | ...... | ...... | ...... | ...Not reported |
| Total..... | 4 | 1 | 7 | 61 | 41 | 122 | 79 | 219 | 152 | 259 | 177 | 191 | 180 | 199 | .....Total |

NEW YORK CITY

215. TABLE VI, A, 1, d — (*concluded*)

**DEPARTMENT STORES — MANUFACTURING**

NUMBER AND PER CENT. OF EMPLOYEES CLASSIFIED ACCORDING TO ACTUAL WEEKLY EARNINGS BY AGE GROUPS AND SEX

| ACTUAL WEEKLY EARNINGS IN DOLLARS | AGE GROUPS IN YEARS (*concluded*) | | | | | | | | | | | | | | ACTUAL WEEKLY EARNINGS IN DOLLARS |
|---|---|---|---|---|---|---|---|---|---|---|---|---|---|---|---|
| | 40–44 | | 45–54 | | 55–64 | | 65 AND OVER | | NOT REPORTED | | TOTAL | | CUMULATIVE PER CENT. OF TOTAL | | |
| | Male | Female | Male | Female | Male | Female | Male | Female | Male | Female | Male | Female | Male | Female | |
| Less than $3 00 | 1 | 2 | 1 | 1 | ...... | ...... | ...... | ...... | ...... | ...... | 3 | 12 | .28 | .85 | Less than $3 00 |
| $3 00–$3 49... | .... | ...... | 1 | 1 | ...... | ...... | ...... | ...... | ...... | ...... | 2 | 7 | .47 | 1.34 | ...$3 00– 3 49 |
| 3 50– 3 99... | .... | ...... | .... | ...... | ...... | ...... | ...... | ...... | ...... | ...... | 2 | 9 | .65 | 1.98 | ... 3 50– 3 99 |
| 4 00– 4 49... | .... | ...... | .... | 1 | ...... | ...... | ...... | ...... | ...... | ...... | 3 | 10 | .93 | 2.68 | ... 4 00– 4 49 |
| 4 50– 4 99... | .... | ...... | .... | ...... | ...... | ...... | ...... | ...... | ...... | ...... | ...... | 9 | ...... | 3.32 | ... 4 50– 4 99 |
| 5 00– 5 49... | .... | ...... | .... | ...... | ...... | ...... | ...... | ...... | ...... | 1 | 2 | 29 | 1.12 | 5.37 | ... 5 00– 5 49 |
| 5 50– 5 99... | .... | ...... | .... | 1 | ...... | ...... | ...... | ...... | ...... | ...... | ...... | 16 | ...... | 6.50 | ... 5 50– 5 99 |
| 6 00– 6 49... | .... | 4 | .... | ...... | ...... | ...... | ...... | ...... | 2 | 2 | 10 | 51 | 2.05 | 10.10 | ... 6 00– 6 49 |
| 6 50– 6 99... | 1 | ...... | 1 | 2 | 1 | 1 | ...... | ...... | ...... | ...... | 8 | 17 | 2.70 | 11.30 | ... 6 50– 6 99 |
| 7 00– 7 49... | .... | ...... | 1 | 2 | ...... | 2 | ...... | ...... | 1 | 4 | 8 | 39 | 3.45 | 14.05 | ... 7 00– 7 49 |
| 7 50– 7 99... | .... | 2 | .... | 2 | ...... | 1 | ...... | ...... | ...... | ...... | 4 | 25 | 3.82 | 16.10 | ... 7 50– 7 99 |
| 8 00– 8 99... | .... | 7 | 1 | 6 | ...... | 1 | ...... | 2 | ...... | 5 | 24 | 101 | 6.05 | 22.95 | ... 8 00– 8 99 |
| 9 00– 9 99... | .... | 15 | .... | 8 | ...... | 1 | ...... | 1 | ...... | 4 | 11 | 129 | 7.09 | 32.05 | ... 9 00– 9 99 |
| 10 00–10 99... | 1 | 16 | 4 | 30 | 4 | 5 | ...... | 1 | ...... | 11 | 20 | 199 | 8.76 | 46.10 | ...10 00–10 99 |
| 11 00–11 99... | 3 | 10 | 3 | 8 | ...... | 2 | ...... | ...... | 1 | 5 | 24 | 108 | 11.17 | 53.75 | ...11 00–11 99 |
| 12 00–12 99... | 7 | 11 | 8 | 12 | 1 | 5 | 3 | 2 | 1 | 7 | 70 | 135 | 17.71 | 63.30 | ...12 00–12 99 |
| 13 00–13 99... | 7 | 4 | 7 | 7 | 6 | ...... | 1 | 1 | ...... | 5 | 46 | 64 | 22.10 | 67.80 | ...13 00–13 99 |
| 14 00–14 99... | 3 | 8 | 12 | 11 | 8 | 3 | 3 | ...... | ...... | 7 | 90 | 86 | 30.45 | 73.80 | ...14 00–14 99 |
| 15 00–15 99... | 10 | 8 | 22 | 8 | 6 | 1 | 2 | ...... | 3 | 6 | 118 | 81 | 41.50 | 79.50 | ...15 00–15 99 |
| 16 00–17 99... | 13 | 7 | 20 | 7 | 10 | 1 | ...... | ...... | ...... | 5 | 131 | 82 | 53.50 | 85.30 | ...16 00–17 99 |
| 18 00–19 99... | 21 | 4 | 35 | 1 | 15 | 1 | 2 | ...... | 1 | 2 | 141 | 51 | 67.00 | 89.00 | ...18 00–19 99 |
| 20 00–24 99... | 30 | 16 | 40 | 9 | 6 | 1 | 2 | ...... | ...... | 7 | 161 | 82 | 81.80 | 94.80 | ...20 00–24 99 |
| 25 00–29 99... | 20 | 8 | 29 | 3 | 6 | 1 | ...... | ...... | ...... | 2 | 105 | 38 | 91.50 | 97.50 | ...25 00–29 99 |
| 30 00–34 99... | 6 | 3 | 7 | ...... | 3 | ...... | ...... | ...... | 1 | 1 | 35 | 7 | 94.75 | 98.00 | ...30 00–34 99 |
| 35 00–39 99... | 2 | 2 | 5 | ...... | 3 | ...... | 1 | ...... | ...... | 1 | 18 | 8 | 96.40 | 98.50 | ...35 00–39 99 |
| 40 00 and over. | 7 | 2 | 10 | 2 | 3 | ...... | ...... | ...... | ...... | 2 | 37 | 18 | 100.00 | 100.00 | .40 00 and over |
| Not reported... | 1 | 2 | .... | 1 | 1 | ...... | ...... | ...... | ...... | 1 | 4 | 4 | ...... | ...... | ...Not reported |
| Total..... | 133 | 131 | 207 | 123 | 73 | 26 | 14 | 7 | 10 | 78 | 1,077 | 1,417 | ...... | ...... | .....Total |

216. TABLE IX, A, 1, d

NEW YORK CITY

**DEPARTMENT STORES — MANUFACTURING**

Number and Per Cent. of Employees Classified According to Actual Weekly Earnings, by Occupation and Sex

| Actual Weekly Earnings in Dollars | Sewing | | House Furnishing | | Cabinet Work, Framing | | Photo Gravures, Printing | | Metalwork Jewelry, Glasswork | | Shoe Repairing, Buckles, etc. | | Box-Making | Candy-Making | | Total | | Cumulative Per Cent. of Total | | Actual Weekly Earnings in Dollars |
|---|---|---|---|---|---|---|---|---|---|---|---|---|---|---|---|---|---|---|---|---|
| | Male | Female | Male | Female | Male | Female | Male | Female | Male | Female | Male | Female | Male | Male | Female | Male | Female | Male | Female | |
| Less than $3 00 | 1 | 11 | 1 | 1 | .... | .... | .... | .... | 1 | .... | .... | .... | .... | .... | .... | 3 | 12 | .28 | .85 | Less than $3 00 |
| $3 00–$3 49 | 1 | 7 | 1 | .... | .... | .... | .... | .... | .... | .... | .... | .... | .... | .... | .... | 2 | 7 | .47 | 1.34 | $3 00– 3 49 |
| 3 50– 3 99 | .... | 9 | .... | .... | .... | .... | 1 | .... | .... | .... | .... | .... | .... | .... | .... | 2 | 9 | .65 | 1.98 | 3 50– 3 99 |
| 4 00– 4 49 | .... | 10 | .... | .... | .... | .... | .... | .... | 1 | .... | .... | .... | .... | 1 | .... | 3 | 10 | .93 | 2.68 | 4 00– 4 49 |
| 4 50– 4 99 | .... | 8 | .... | 1 | .... | .... | .... | .... | .... | .... | .... | .... | 1 | 1 | .... | .... | 9 | .... | 3.32 | 4 50– 4 99 |
| 5 00– 5 49 | 1 | 23 | 1 | 2 | .... | .... | .... | .... | .... | 1 | .... | 2 | .... | .... | 1 | 2 | 29 | 1.12 | 5.37 | 5 00– 5 49 |
| 5 50– 5 99 | .... | 9 | .... | 4 | .... | .... | .... | 1 | .... | .... | .... | 2 | .... | .... | .... | .... | 16 | .... | 6.50 | 5 50– 5 99 |
| 6 00– 6 49 | 5 | 44 | 3 | 4 | .... | .... | .... | .... | 1 | [illegible] | 1 | .... | .... | .... | .... | 10 | 51 | 2.05 | 10.10 | 6 00– 6 49 |
| 6 50– 6 99 | 5 | 16 | .... | .... | 2 | .... | .... | 1 | .... | .... | .... | .... | .... | .... | .... | 7 | 17 | 2.70 | 11.30 | 6 50– 6 99 |
| 7 00– 7 49 | 1 | 32 | .... | 4 | 1 | .... | 1 | 1 | 3 | 1 | .... | 1 | 1 | 1 | .... | 8 | 39 | 3.45 | 14.05 | 7 00– 7 49 |
| 7 50– 7 99 | .... | 20 | .... | 3 | 3 | .... | .... | .... | 1 | [illegible] | .... | .... | .... | .... | .... | 4 | 25 | 3.82 | 16.10 | 7 50– 7 99 |
| 8 00– 8 99 | 9 | 85 | 6 | 8 | 4 | .... | 1 | 1 | 1 | [illegible] | 3 | 4 | .... | .... | 1 | 24 | 101 | 6.06 | 22.95 | 8 00– 8 99 |
| 9 00– 9 99 | 3 | 105 | 3 | 15 | 2 | .... | .... | .... | 2 | [illegible] | .... | 5 | .... | 1 | 2 | 11 | 129 | 7.09 | 32.05 | 9 00– 9 99 |
| 10 00–10 99 | 10 | 149 | 8 | 48 | 2 | .... | .... | .... | 2 | .... | 2 | 1 | .... | 1 | 1 | 20 | 199 | 8.76 | 46.10 | 10 00–10 99 |
| 11 00–11 99 | 7 | 80 | 11 | 25 | 3 | 1 | .... | .... | 2 | .... | 1 | 2 | .... | .... | .... | 24 | 108 | 11.17 | 53.75 | 11 00–11 99 |
| 12 00–12 99 | 36 | 110 | 15 | 21 | 14 | .... | .... | 1 | 2 | 1 | 3 | 2 | .... | .... | .... | 70 | 135 | 17.71 | 63.30 | 12 00–12 99 |
| 13 00–13 99 | 24 | 57 | 13 | 5 | 4 | .... | .... | 2 | 1 | .... | 5 | .... | .... | .... | .... | 47 | 64 | 22.10 | 67.80 | 13 00–13 99 |
| 14 00–14 99 | 32 | 79 | 14 | 4 | 31 | .... | 1 | 1 | 8 | 1 | 4 | 1 | .... | .... | .... | 90 | 86 | 30.45 | 73.80 | 14 00–14 99 |
| 15 00–15 99 | 21 | 73 | 30 | 5 | 51 | .... | 1 | 1 | 10 | 1 | 3 | 1 | .... | 2 | .... | 118 | 81 | 41.50 | 79.50 | 15 00–15 99 |
| 16 00–17 99 | 36 | 81 | 36 | 1 | 38 | .... | 2 | .... | 17 | .... | 2 | .... | .... | .... | .... | 131 | 82 | 53.50 | 85.30 | 16 00–17 99 |
| 18 00–19 99 | 24 | 48 | 33 | 3 | 51 | .... | .... | .... | 28 | .... | 5 | .... | .... | .... | .... | 141 | 51 | 67.00 | 89.00 | 18 00–19 99 |
| 20 00–24 99 | 34 | 81 | 73 | 1 | 27 | .... | 1 | .... | 22 | .... | 4 | .... | .... | .... | .... | 161 | 82 | 81.80 | 94.80 | 20 00–24 99 |
| 25 00–29 99 | 21 | 38 | 68 | .... | 3 | .... | 1 | .... | 9 | .... | 2 | .... | .... | 1 | .... | 105 | 38 | 91.50 | 97.50 | 25 00–29 99 |
| 30 00–34 99 | 6 | 6 | 18 | 1 | 2 | .... | 3 | .... | 6 | .... | .... | .... | .... | .... | .... | 35 | 7 | 94.75 | 98.00 | 30 00–34 99 |
| 35 00–39 99 | 10 | 7 | 5 | 1 | .... | .... | 2 | .... | 1 | .... | .... | .... | .... | .... | .... | 18 | 8 | 96.40 | 98.50 | 35 00–39 99 |
| 40 00 and over | 17 | 18 | 10 | .... | .... | .... | 4 | .... | 6 | .... | .... | .... | .... | .... | .... | 87 | 18 | 100.00 | 100.00 | 40 00 and over |
| Not reported | 4 | 3 | .... | .... | .... | .... | .... | 1 | .... | .... | .... | .... | .... | .... | .... | 4 | 4 | .... | .... | Not reported |
| Total | 308 | 1,209 | 344 | 157 | 238 | 1 | 18 | 10 | 124 | 14 | 35 | 21 | 2 | 8 | 5 | 1,077 | 1,417 | .... | .... | Total |

217. TABLE V, A, I, e

NEW YORR CITY
DEPARTMENT STORES — PLANT
NUMBER AND PER CENT. OF EMPLOYEES EARNING SPECIFIED WEEKLY RATES BY AGE GROUPS AND SEX

| WEEKLY RATES IN DOLLARS | AGE GROUPS IN YEARS 14–15 | | 16–17 | | 18–20 | | 21–24 | | 25–29 | | 30–34 | | 35–39 | | WEEKLY RATES IN DOLLARS |
|---|---|---|---|---|---|---|---|---|---|---|---|---|---|---|---|
| | Male | Female | Male | Female | Male | Female | Male | Female | Male | Female | Male | Female | Male | Female | |
| $3 00–$3 49... | .... | ...... | .... | ...... | ...... | ...... | ...... | ...... | ...... | 2 | ...... | 3 | ...... | 3 | ...$3 00–$3 49 |
| 3 50– 3 99... | .... | 3 | .... | 3 | ...... | 1 | ...... | ...... | ...... | ...... | 1 | ...... | ...... | ...... | ... 3 50– 3 99 |
| 4 00– 4 49... | .... | 1 | 1 | 9 | ...... | 14 | ...... | 52 | 3 | 77 | 6 | 32 | 4 | 22 | ... 4 00– 4 49 |
| 4 50– 4 99... | .... | ...... | 1 | ...... | 2 | 3 | ...... | 6 | ...... | 19 | ...... | 22 | 1 | 11 | ... 4 50– 4 99 |
| 5 00– 5 49... | 1 | ...... | 5 | 3 | 21 | 11 | 12 | 15 | 12 | 25 | 4 | 14 | 3 | 15 | ... 5 00– 5 49 |
| 5 50– 5 99... | .... | ...... | .... | ...... | ...... | ...... | ...... | ...... | ...... | 1 | ...... | ...... | ...... | ...... | ... 5 50– 5 99 |
| 6 00– 6 49... | .... | 1 | 9 | 4 | 17 | 29 | 11 | 51 | 8 | 60 | 4 | 23 | 2 | 25 | ... 6 00– 6 49 |
| 6 50– 6 99... | .... | ...... | .... | ...... | ...... | ...... | ...... | 1 | ...... | 3 | ...... | 1 | ...... | ...... | ... 6 50– 6 99 |
| 7 00– 7 49... | .... | 1 | 2 | 2 | 15 | 20 | 20 | 21 | 4 | 30 | 5 | 22 | 7 | 26 | ... 7 00– 7 49 |
| 7 50– 7 99... | .... | ...... | .... | ...... | 1 | 1 | 3 | 1 | 1 | 1 | ...... | 6 | ...... | 5 | ... 7 50– 7 99 |
| 8 00– 8 99... | .... | ...... | .... | 1 | 9 | 7 | 17 | 7 | 17 | 5 | 11 | 7 | 5 | 13 | ... 8 00– 8 99 |
| 9 00– 9 99... | .... | ...... | 1 | ...... | 10 | 1 | 23 | 3 | 28 | 4 | 13 | 1 | 15 | 8 | ... 9 00– 9 99 |
| 10 00–10 99... | .... | ...... | 3 | ...... | 15 | 1 | 75 | 4 | 83 | 2 | 54 | 8 | 44 | 5 | ...10 00–10 99 |
| 11 00–11 99... | .... | ...... | .... | ...... | 10 | ...... | 49 | 2 | 62 | 1 | 28 | 1 | 32 | ...... | ...11 00–11 99 |
| 12 00–12 99... | .... | ...... | .... | ...... | 15 | ...... | 63 | 3 | 76 | 5 | 83 | 4 | 78 | 2 | ...12 00–12 99 |
| 13 00–13 99... | .... | ...... | .... | ...... | 4 | ...... | 28 | ...... | 35 | ...... | 19 | ...... | 17 | ...... | ...13 00–13 99 |
| 14 00–14 99... | .... | ...... | .... | ...... | 4 | ...... | 12 | 1 | 14 | ...... | 21 | 2 | 24 | 2 | ...14 00–14 99 |
| 15 00–15 99... | .... | ...... | .... | ...... | 4 | ...... | 12 | ...... | 36 | 1 | 26 | ...... | 40 | 5 | ...15 00–15 99 |
| 16 00–17 99... | .... | ...... | .... | ...... | 1 | ...... | 8 | ...... | 26 | ...... | 13 | 2 | 25 | 1 | ...16 00–17 99 |
| 18 00–19 99... | .... | ...... | .... | ...... | 1 | ...... | 9 | ...... | 30 | ...... | 21 | ...... | 23 | 1 | ...18 00–19 99 |
| 20 00–24 99... | .... | ...... | .... | ...... | 1 | ...... | 13 | ...... | 23 | ...... | 42 | 1 | 29 | 1 | ...20 00–24 99 |
| 25 00–29 99... | .... | ...... | .... | ...... | ...... | ...... | 1 | ...... | 5 | ...... | 9 | 1 | 11 | 1 | ...25 00–29 99 |
| 30 00–34 99... | .... | ...... | .... | ...... | ...... | ...... | ...... | ...... | ...... | ...... | 4 | ...... | 9 | ...... | ...30 00–34 99 |
| 35 00–39 99... | .... | ...... | .... | ...... | ...... | ...... | 1 | ...... | 1 | ...... | 2 | ...... | 1 | ...... | ...35 00–39 99 |
| 40 00 and over. | .... | ...... | .... | ...... | ...... | ...... | ...... | ...... | ...... | ...... | 2 | ...... | 4 | ...... | .40 00 and over. |
| Not reported... | .... | ...... | .... | ...... | 8 | ...... | 12 | ...... | 9 | ...... | 18 | ...... | 10 | ...... | ...Not reported. |
| Total..... | 1 | 6 | 22 | 22 | 138 | 88 | 369 | 167 | 473 | 236 | 386 | 150 | 384 | 147 | .....Total |

217. TABLE V, A, I, e — (*concluded*)

NEW YORK CITY
DEPARTMENT STORES — PLANT

NUMBER AND PER CENT. OF EMPLOYEES EARNING SPECIFIED WEEKLY RATES BY AGE GROUPS AND SEX

| WEEKLY RATES IN DOLLARS | AGE GROUPS IN YEARS—(*concluded*) 40–44 | | 45–54 | | 55–64 | | 65 AND OVER | | NOT REPORTED | | TOTAL | | CUMULATIVE PER CENT OF TOTAL | | WEEKLY RATES IN DOLLARS |
|---|---|---|---|---|---|---|---|---|---|---|---|---|---|---|---|
| | Male | Female | Male | Female | Male | Female | Male | Female | Male | Female | Male | Female | Male | Female | |
| $3 00–$3 49... | .... | 3 | .... | 1 | ...... | ...... | ...... | ...... | 1 | ...... | 1 | 12 | .04 | 1.09 | ...$3 00–$3 49 |
| 3 50– 3 99... | .... | ...... | .... | ...... | ...... | ...... | ...... | ...... | ...... | ...... | 1 | 7 | .07 | 1.74 | ... 3 50– 3 99 |
| 4 00– 4 49... | 5 | 7 | 6 | 4 | 2 | ...... | ...... | ...... | ...... | ...... | 27 | 218 | 1.08 | 21.65 | ... 4 00– 4 49 |
| 4 50– 4 99... | .... | 6 | .... | 1 | ...... | ...... | ...... | ...... | ...... | ...... | 4 | 68 | 1.23 | 27 90 | ... 4 50– 4 99 |
| 5 00– 5 49... | 2 | 7 | 5 | 6 | ...... | 1 | ...... | ...... | ...... | 1 | 65 | 98 | 3.64 | 36.80 | ... 5 00– 5 49 |
| 5 50– 5 99... | .... | 1 | .... | 4 | ...... | 1 | ...... | ...... | ...... | ...... | ...... | 7 | ...... | 37.90 | ... 5 50– 5 99 |
| 6 00– 6 49... | 2 | 27 | 5 | 32 | ...... | 6 | ...... | 1 | ...... | 2 | 58 | 261 | 5.80 | 61.30 | ... 6 00– 6 49 |
| 6 50– 6 99... | .... | ...... | .... | 1 | ...... | ...... | ...... | ...... | ...... | ...... | ...... | 6 | ...... | 61.90 | ... 6 50– 6 99 |
| 7 00– 7 49... | .... | 30 | 3 | 29 | 2 | 7 | 1 | 4 | 1 | 5 | 60 | 197 | 8.05 | 79.90 | ... 7 00– 7 49 |
| 7 50– 7 99... | .... | 6 | .... | 9 | ...... | 1 | ...... | ...... | ...... | ...... | 5 | 30 | 8.23 | 82.50 | ... 7 50– 7 99 |
| 8 00– 8 99... | 3 | 17 | 1 | 15 | 1 | 4 | 1 | ...... | 5 | ...... | 70 | 76 | 10.82 | 89.50 | ... 8 00– 8 99 |
| 9 00– 9 99... | 4 | 8 | 11 | 5 | 5 | 1 | 5 | ...... | 3 | 1 | 118 | 32 | 15.22 | 92.50 | ... 9 00– 9 99 |
| 10 00–10 99... | 34 | 3 | 48 | 5 | 23 | 1 | 6 | ...... | 3 | 1 | 388 | 30 | 29.65 | 95.25 | ...10 00–10 99 |
| 11 00–11 99... | 20 | 1 | 41 | ...... | 13 | ...... | 3 | ...... | ...... | ...... | 258 | 5 | 39.20 | 95.55 | ...11 00–11 99 |
| 12 00–12 99... | 66 | 2 | 108 | 2 | 47 | 1 | 11 | ...... | 7 | ...... | 554 | 19 | 59.80 | 97.40 | ...12 00–12 99 |
| 13 00–13 99... | 9 | ...... | 20 | ...... | 13 | ...... | ...... | ...... | 1 | 1 | 146 | 2 | 65.30 | 97.65 | ...13 00–13 99 |
| 14 00–14 99... | 18 | ...... | 50 | 2 | 12 | ...... | 5 | ...... | 1 | ...... | 161 | 6 | 71.25 | 98.10 | ...14 00–14 99 |
| 15 00–15 99... | 21 | 1 | 31 | ...... | 13 | ...... | 2 | ...... | 3 | ...... | 188 | 8 | 78.50 | 99.00 | ...15 00–15 99 |
| 16 00–17 99... | 16 | ...... | 27 | 1 | 11 | ...... | ...... | ...... | ...... | ...... | 127 | 4 | 83.00 | 99.35 | ...16 00–17 99 |
| 18 00–19 99... | 18 | ...... | 21 | ...... | 4 | ...... | 2 | ...... | ...... | ...... | 129 | 1 | 88.00 | 99.45 | ...18 00–19 99 |
| 20 00–24 99... | 28 | ...... | 43 | ...... | 9 | ...... | ...... | ...... | 2 | 1 | 190 | 3 | 95.00 | 99.70 | ...20 00–24 99 |
| 25 00–29 99... | 14 | 1 | 13 | ...... | 6 | ...... | 1 | ...... | ...... | ...... | 60 | 3 | 97.10 | 99.90 | ...25 00–29 99 |
| 30 00–34 99... | 7 | ...... | 18 | ...... | 5 | ...... | ...... | ...... | 1 | ...... | 44 | ...... | 98.60 | ...... | ...30 00–34 99 |
| 35 00–39 99... | 3 | ...... | 5 | ...... | 1 | ...... | ...... | ...... | ...... | ...... | 14 | ...... | 99.50 | ...... | ...35 00–39 99 |
| 40 00 and over. | 3 | 1 | 6 | ...... | 1 | ...... | ...... | ...... | ...... | ...... | 16 | 1 | 100.00 | 100.00 | .40 00 and over |
| Not eported... | 3 | 1 | 11 | ...... | 2 | ...... | 1 | ...... | ...... | ...... | 74 | 1 | ...... | ...... | ...Not reported |
| Total..... | 276 | 122 | 473 | 117 | 170 | 23 | 38 | 5 | 28 | 12 | 27.58 | 1,095 | ...... | ...... | .....Total |

218. TABLE VIII, A, I, e

## NEW YORK CITY
## DEPARTMENT STORES — PLANT

Number and Per Cent. of Employees Earning Specified Weekly Rates by Occupation and Sex

| Weekly Rates in Dollars | Occupation: Foremen | | Mechanics | Janitorial Force | | Errand Boys | | General Labor | Personal Service | | Total | | Cumulative Per Cent of Total | | Weekly Rates in Dollars |
|---|---|---|---|---|---|---|---|---|---|---|---|---|---|---|---|
| | Male | Female | Male | Male | Female | Male | Female | Male | Male | Female | Male | Female | Male | Female | |
| $3 00–$3 49 | ... | ... | ... | ... | ... | ... | ... | ... | 1 | 12 | 1 | 12 | .04 | 1.09 | $3 00–$3 49 |
| 3 50– 3 99 | ... | ... | ... | ... | 1 | ... | 4 | ... | 1 | 2 | 1 | 7 | .07 | 1.74 | 3 50– 3 99 |
| 4 00– 4 49 | ... | ... | ... | ... | 16 | ... | 2 | ... | 27 | 200 | 27 | 218 | 1.08 | 21.65 | 4 00– 4 49 |
| 4 50– 4 99 | ... | ... | ... | ... | 1 | 1 | ... | ... | 3 | 67 | 4 | 68 | 1.23 | 27.90 | 4 50– 4 99 |
| 5 00– 5 49 | ... | ... | 2 | 11 | 3 | 1 | 1 | ... | 51 | 94 | 65 | 98 | 3.64 | 36.80 | 5 00– 5 49 |
| 5 50– 5 90 | ... | ... | ... | ... | ... | ... | ... | ... | ... | 7 | ... | 7 | ... | 37.40 | 5 50– 5 99 |
| 6 00– 6 49 | ... | ... | 2 | 10 | 49 | 4 | ... | 1 | 41 | 212 | 58 | 261 | 5 80 | 61.30 | 6 00– 6 49 |
| 6 50– 6 99 | ... | ... | ... | ... | ... | ... | ... | ... | ... | 6 | ... | 6 | ... | 61.90 | 6 50– 6 99 |
| 7 00– 7 49 | ... | ... | 5 | 10 | 87 | ... | ... | 1 | 44 | 110 | 60 | 197 | 8.05 | 79.90 | 7 00– 7 49 |
| 7 50– 7 99 | ... | ... | ... | 4 | 25 | 1 | ... | ... | ... | 5 | 5 | 30 | 8.23 | 82.50 | 7 50– 7 99 |
| 8 00– 8 99 | ... | ... | 3 | 38 | 32 | ... | ... | 1 | 28 | 44 | 70 | 76 | 10.82 | 89.50 | 8 00– 8 99 |
| 9 00– 9 99 | ... | ... | 4 | 95 | 15 | 1 | ... | 4 | 14 | 17 | 118 | 32 | 15.22 | 92.50 | 9 00– 9 99 |
| 10 00–10 99 | 1 | 1 | 7 | 356 | 12 | 1 | ... | 5 | 18 | 17 | 388 | 30 | 29.65 | 95.25 | 10 00–10 99 |
| 11 00–11.99 | 1 | ... | 6 | 241 | 1 | ... | ... | ... | 10 | 4 | 258 | 5 | 39.20 | 95.55 | 11 00–11 99 |
| 12 00–12 99 | ... | ... | 35 | 473 | 2 | ... | ... | 14 | 32 | 17 | 554 | 19 | 59.80 | 97.40 | 12 00–12 99 |
| 13 00–13 99 | ... | ... | 24 | 106 | ... | ... | ... | 4 | 12 | 2 | 146 | 2 | 65.30 | 97.65 | 13 00–13 99 |
| 14 00–14 99 | 1 | ... | 34 | 108 | ... | ... | ... | ... | 18 | 6 | 161 | 6 | 71.25 | 98.10 | 14 00–14 99 |
| 15 00–15 99 | 4 | ... | 87 | 73 | 2 | ... | ... | 2 | 22 | 6 | 188 | 8 | 78.50 | 99.00 | 15 00–15 99 |
| 16 00–17 99 | 1 | ... | 66 | 37 | 1 | ... | ... | 4 | 19 | 3 | 127 | 4 | 83.00 | 99.35 | 16 00–17 99 |
| 18 00–19 99 | 2 | ... | 98 | 15 | ... | ... | ... | ... | 14 | 1 | 129 | 1 | 88.00 | 99.45 | 18 00–19 99 |
| 20 00–24 99 | 4 | ... | 132 | 17 | 1 | ... | ... | 2 | 35 | 2 | 190 | 3 | 95.00 | 99.70 | 20 00–24 99 |
| 25 00–29 99 | 6 | 1 | 44 | 3 | ... | ... | ... | ... | 7 | 2 | 60 | 3 | 97.10 | 99.90 | 25 00–29 99 |
| 30 00–34 99 | 5 | ... | 34 | 3 | ... | ... | ... | ... | 2 | ... | 44 | ... | 98.60 | ... | 30 00–34 99 |
| 35 00–39 99 | 4 | ... | 4 | 2 | ... | ... | ... | ... | 4 | ... | 14 | ... | 99.50 | ... | 35 00–39 99 |
| 40 00 and over | 3 | ... | 8 | 2 | ... | ... | ... | ... | 3 | 1 | 16 | 1 | 100.00 | 100.00 | 40 00 and over |
| Not reported | ... | ... | 64 | 6 | ... | ... | ... | ... | 4 | 1 | 74 | 1 | ... | ... | Not reported |
| Total | 32 | 2 | 659 | 1,610 | 248 | 9 | 7 | 38 | 410 | 838 | 2,758 | 1,095 | ... | ... | Total |

219. TABLE VI, A, 1, e

NEW YORK CITY

DEPARTMENT STORES — PLANT

NUMBER AND PER CENT OF EMPLOYEES CLASSIFIED ACCORDING TO ACTUAL WEEKLY EARNINGS BY AGE GROUPS AND SEX

| ACTUAL WEEKLY EARNINGS IN DOLLARS | AGE GROUPS IN YEARS | | | | | | | | | | | | | | ACTUAL WEEKLY EARNINGS IN DOLLARS |
|---|---|---|---|---|---|---|---|---|---|---|---|---|---|---|---|
| | 14–15 | | 16–17 | | 18–20 | | 21–24 | | 25–29 | | 30–34 | | 35–39 | | |
| | Male | Female | Male | Female | Male | Female | Male | Female | Male | Female | Male | Female | Male | Female | |
| Less than $3 00 | .... | ...... | .... | ...... | 5 | 3 | 2 | 3 | 3 | 6 | 1 | 4 | 2 | 4 | Less than $3 00 |
| $3 00–$3 49... | .... | ...... | .... | 2 | ...... | 1 | 2 | 14 | 1 | 16 | 1 | 7 | 2 | 7 | ...$3 00– 3 49 |
| 3 50– 3 99... | .... | 3 | 1 | 3 | ...... | 5 | ...... | 6 | ...... | 5 | 1 | 5 | 1 | 2 | ... 3 50– 3 99 |
| 4 00– 4 49... | .... | 1 | 1 | 7 | 2 | 11 | ...... | 44 | 4 | 70 | 7 | 26 | 3 | 16 | ... 4 00– 4 49 |
| 4 50– 4 99... | .... | ...... | 1 | ...... | 2 | 6 | ...... | 10 | 1 | 28 | ...... | 17 | 1 | 17 | ... 4 50– 4 99 |
| 5 00– 5 49... | 1 | ...... | 5 | 3 | 16 | 9 | 10 | 14 | 11 | 24 | 5 | 15 | 3 | 14 | ... 5 00– 5 49 |
| 5 50– 5 99... | .... | ...... | .... | 2 | 2 | 11 | 4 | 14 | 2 | 13 | 1 | 8 | 2 | 7 | ... 5 50– 5 99 |
| 6 00– 6 49... | .... | 1 | 7 | 4 | 17 | 16 | 8 | 23 | 8 | 26 | 4 | 19 | 2 | 12 | ... 6 00– 6 49 |
| 6 50– 6 99... | .... | ...... | .... | ...... | 2 | 7 | 3 | 4 | 3 | 3 | 1 | 7 | 2 | 4 | ... 6 50– 6 99 |
| 7 00– 7 49... | .... | 1 | 2 | ...... | 11 | 11 | 20 | 11 | 1 | 19 | 5 | 12 | 9 | 19 | ... 7 00– 7 49 |
| 7 50– 7 99... | .... | ...... | .... | ...... | 1 | ...... | 2 | 2 | 3 | 1 | ...... | 5 | 1 | 6 | ... 7 50– 7 99 |
| 8 00– 8 99... | .... | ...... | 1 | 1 | 11 | 6 | 18 | 8 | 20 | 7 | 11 | 3 | 5 | 9 | ... 8 00– 8 99 |
| 9 00– 9 99... | .... | ...... | 1 | ...... | 9 | ...... | 24 | 5 | 30 | 6 | 18 | 2 | 12 | 10 | ... 9 00– 9 99 |
| 10 00–10 99... | .... | ...... | 3 | ...... | 14 | 2 | 70 | 3 | 73 | 3 | 48 | 10 | 35 | 6 | ...10 00–10 99 |
| 11 00–11 99... | .... | ...... | .... | ...... | 14 | ...... | 45 | 3 | 50 | 2 | 27 | 1 | 31 | ...... | ...11 00–11 99 |
| 12 00–12 99... | .... | ...... | .... | ...... | 10 | ...... | 60 | 1 | 71 | 6 | 70 | 3 | 68 | 2 | ...12 00–12 99 |
| 13 00–13 99... | .... | ...... | .... | ...... | 7 | ...... | 32 | 1 | 35 | ...... | 15 | ...... | 15 | 1 | ...13 00–13 99 |
| 14 00–14 99... | .... | ...... | .... | ...... | 5 | ...... | 16 | ...... | 20 | ...... | 29 | 3 | 35 | 8 | ...14 00–14 99 |
| 15 00–15 99... | .... | ...... | .... | ...... | 5 | ...... | 15 | 1 | 33 | 1 | 21 | ...... | 34 | 4 | ...15 00–15 99 |
| 16 00–17 99... | .... | ...... | .... | ...... | 2 | ...... | 11 | ...... | 32 | ...... | 21 | 1 | 36 | 1 | ...16 00–17 99 |
| 18 00–19 99... | .... | ...... | .... | ...... | 2 | ...... | 9 | ...... | 31 | ...... | 23 | ...... | 24 | 1 | ...18 00–19 99 |
| 20 00–24 99... | .... | ...... | .... | ...... | 1 | ...... | 15 | ...... | 28 | ...... | 49 | 1 | 33 | 1 | ...20 00–24 99 |
| 25 00–29 99... | .... | ...... | .... | ...... | ...... | ...... | 3 | ...... | 11 | ...... | 13 | 1 | 14 | 1 | ...25 00–29 99 |
| 30 00–34 99... | .... | ...... | .... | ...... | ...... | ...... | ...... | ...... | ...... | ...... | 7 | ...... | 7 | ...... | ...30 00–34 99 |
| 35 00–39 99... | .... | ...... | .... | ...... | ...... | ...... | ...... | ...... | 2 | ...... | 4 | ...... | 2 | ...... | ...35 00–39 99 |
| 40 00 and over. | .... | ...... | .... | ...... | ...... | ...... | ...... | ...... | ...... | ...... | 3 | ...... | 5 | ...... | .40 00 and over |
| Not reported... | .... | ...... | .... | ...... | ...... | ...... | ...... | ...... | ...... | ...... | 1 | ...... | ...... | ...... | ...Not reported |
| Total..... | 1 | 6 | 22 | 22 | 138 | 88 | 369 | 167 | 473 | 236 | 386 | 150 | 384 | 147 | .....Total |

219. TABLE VI, A, I, e — (*concluded*)

NEW YORK CITY
DEPARTMENT STORES — PLANT
NUMBER AND PER CENT OF EMPLOYEES CLASSIFIED ACCORDING TO ACTUAL WEEKLY EARNINGS BY AGE GROUPS AND SEX

| Actual Weekly Earnings in Dollars | Age Groups in Years—(*concluded*) 40–44 | | 45–54 | | 55–64 | | 65 and over | | Not reported | | Total | | Cumulative per cent of total | | Actual Weekly Earnings in Dollars |
|---|---|---|---|---|---|---|---|---|---|---|---|---|---|---|---|
| | Male | Female | Male | Female | Male | Female | Male | Female | Male | Female | Male | Female | Male | Female | |
| Less than $3 00 | 1 | ...... | 1 | 1 | ...... | 1 | ...... | ...... | 1 | ...... | 16 | 22 | .60 | 2.00 | Less than $3 00 |
| $3 00–$3 49... | 1 | 5 | .... | 2 | ...... | ...... | ...... | ...... | ...... | ...... | 7 | 54 | .80 | 6.90 | ...$3 00– 3 49 |
| 3 50– 3 99... | .... | 1 | .... | 2 | 1 | ...... | ...... | ...... | ...... | ...... | 4 | 32 | 1.00 | 9.90 | ... 3 50– 3 99 |
| 4 00– 4 49... | 6 | 7 | 6 | 4 | 2 | ...... | ...... | ...... | ...... | ...... | 31 | 186 | 2.10 | 26.90 | ... 4 00– 4 49 |
| 4 50– 4 99... | 1 | 5 | .... | 3 | ...... | ...... | ...... | ...... | 1 | ...... | 7 | 86 | 2.40 | 34.80 | ... 4 50– 4 99 |
| 5 00– 5 49... | 1 | 9 | 5 | 6 | ...... | 2 | ...... | ...... | ...... | 2 | 57 | 98 | 4.40 | 43.70 | ... 5 00– 5 49 |
| 5 50– 5 99... | .... | 2 | 1 | 9 | ...... | 1 | ...... | 1 | ...... | 1 | 12 | 69 | 4.80 | 50.00 | ... 5 50– 5 99 |
| 6 00– 6 49... | 3 | 25 | 6 | 28 | 1 | 7 | ...... | 1 | ...... | ...... | 56 | 162 | 6.90 | 64.90 | ... 6 00– 6 49 |
| 6 50– 6 99... | .... | 4 | .... | 5 | ...... | ...... | ...... | 1 | ...... | 1 | 11 | 36 | 7.30 | 68.20 | ... 6 50– 6 99 |
| 7 00– 7 49... | 1 | 26 | 4 | 21 | 1 | 4 | 1 | 2 | 1 | 4 | 56 | 130 | 9.40 | 80.00 | ... 7 00– 7 49 |
| 7 50– 7 99... | .... | 7 | .... | 7 | ...... | 2 | ...... | ...... | ...... | ...... | 7 | 30 | 9.60 | 82.80 | ... 7 50– 7 99 |
| 8 00– 8 99... | 4 | 14 | 2 | 14 | 2 | 3 | ...... | ...... | 4 | ...... | 78 | 65 | 12.40 | 88.80 | ... 8 00– 8 99 |
| 9 00– 9 99... | 4 | 7 | 13 | 5 | 6 | 1 | 5 | ...... | 3 | 1 | 125 | 37 | 17.00 | 92.10 | ... 9 00– 9 99 |
| 10 00–10 99... | 22 | 3 | 43 | 5 | 18 | 1 | 5 | ...... | 2 | 1 | 333 | 34 | 29.10 | 95.20 | ...10 00–10.99 |
| 11 00–11 99... | 22 | 1 | 40 | ...... | 15 | ...... | 3 | ...... | ...... | ...... | 247 | 7 | 38.20 | 96.00 | ...11 00–11 99 |
| 12 00–12 99... | 61 | 1 | 97 | 2 | 42 | 1 | 11 | ...... | 8 | ...... | 498 | 16 | 56.20 | 97.40 | ...12 00–12 99 |
| 13 00–13 99... | 12 | ...... | 19 | ...... | 12 | ...... | 1 | ...... | 1 | ...... | 149 | 2 | 61.60 | 97.50 | ...13 00–13 99 |
| 14 00–14 99... | 20 | ...... | 55 | 2 | 17 | ...... | 4 | ...... | 1 | ...... | 202 | 8 | 69.00 | 98.40 | ...14 00–14 99 |
| 15 00–15 99... | 19 | 1 | 39 | ...... | 11 | ...... | 2 | ...... | 3 | ...... | 182 | 7 | 75.60 | 98.90 | ...15 00–15 96 |
| 16 00–17 99... | 21 | ...... | 28 | 1 | 14 | ...... | 1 | ...... | ...... | 1 | 166 | 4 | 80.90 | 99.20 | ...16 00–17 99 |
| 18 00–19 99... | 17 | ...... | 25 | ...... | 6 | ...... | 2 | ...... | ...... | ...... | 139 | 1 | 86.70 | 99.30 | ...18 00–19 99 |
| 20 00–24 99... | 30 | ...... | 44 | ...... | 9 | ...... | 1 | ...... | 2 | 1 | 212 | 3 | 94.40 | 99.60 | ...20 00–24 99 |
| 25 00–29 99... | 14 | 1 | 19 | ...... | 7 | ...... | 1 | ...... | ...... | ...... | 82 | 3 | 97.40 | 99.90 | ...25 00–29 99 |
| 30 00–34 99... | 6 | ...... | 5 | ...... | 2 | ...... | ...... | ...... | 1 | ...... | 28 | ...... | 98.40 | ...... | ...30 00–34 99 |
| 35 00–39 99... | 4 | ...... | 9 | ...... | 2 | ...... | ...... | ...... | ...... | ...... | 23 | ...... | 99.30 | ...... | ...35 00–39 99 |
| 40 00 and over. | 4 | 1 | 11 | ...... | 1 | ...... | ...... | ...... | ...... | ...... | 24 | 1 | 100.00 | 100.00 | .40 00 and over |
| Not reported... | 2 | 2 | 1 | ...... | 1 | ...... | 1 | ...... | ...... | ...... | 6 | 2 | ...... | ...... | ...Not reported |
| Total..... | 276 | 122 | 473 | 117 | 170 | 23 | 38 | 5 | 28 | 12 | 2,758 | 1,095 | ...... | ...... | .....Total |

NEW YORK CITY
DEPARTMENT STORES — PLANT

220. TABLE IX, A, 1, e  NUMBER AND PER CENT OF EMPLOYEES CLASSIFIED ACCORDING TO ACTUAL WEEKLY EARNINGS BY OCCUPATION AND SEX

| ACTUAL WEEKLY EARNINGS IN DOLLARS | OCCUPATION | | | | | | | | | | | | | | ACTUAL WEEKLY EARNINGS IN DOLLARS |
|---|---|---|---|---|---|---|---|---|---|---|---|---|---|---|---|
| | FOREMEN AND FOREWOMEN | | MECHANICS | JANITORIAL FORCE | | ERRAND BOYS AND GIRLS | | GENERAL LABOR | PERSONAL SERVICE | | TOTAL | | CUMULATIVE PER CENT OF TOTAL | | |
| | Male | Female | Male | Male | Female | Male | Female | Male | Male | Female | Male | Female | Male | Female | |
| Less than $3 00 | .... | ...... | 2 | 7 | 3 | ...... | ...... | 1 | 6 | 19 | 16 | 22 | .60 | 2.00 | Less than $3 00 |
| $3 00–$3 49... | .... | ...... | ...... | 3 | 2 | ...... | 1 | ...... | 4 | 51 | 7 | 54 | .80 | 6.90 | ...$3 00– 3 49 |
| 3 50– 3 99... | .... | ...... | ...... | 2 | 2 | ...... | 4 | ...... | 2 | 26 | 4 | 32 | 1.00 | 9.90 | ... 3 50– 3 99 |
| 4 00– 4 49... | .... | ...... | ...... | 2 | 15 | ...... | 1 | ...... | 29 | 170 | 31 | 186 | 2.10 | 26.90 | ... 4 00– 4 49 |
| 4 50– 4 99... | .... | ...... | ...... | 2 | 4 | 1 | ...... | ...... | 4 | 82 | 7 | 86 | 2.40 | 34.80 | ... 4 50– 4 99 |
| 5 00– 5 49... | .... | ...... | 3 | 5 | 5 | 1 | 1 | ...... | 48 | 92 | 57 | 98 | 4.40 | 43.70 | ... 5 00– 5 49 |
| 5 50– 5 99... | .... | ...... | 1 | 7 | 16 | ...... | ...... | ...... | 4 | 53 | 12 | 69 | 4.80 | 50.00 | ... 5 50– 5 99 |
| 6 00– 6 49... | .... | ...... | 1 | 18 | 45 | 4 | ...... | 1 | 32 | 117 | 56 | 162 | 6.90 | 64.90 | ... 6 00– 6 49 |
| 6 50– 6 99... | .... | ...... | 2 | 6 | 13 | ...... | ...... | ...... | 3 | 23 | 11 | 36 | 7.30 | 68.20 | ... 6 50– 6 99 |
| 7 00– 7 49... | .... | ...... | 5 | 12 | 66 | ...... | ...... | 1 | 38 | 64 | 56 | 130 | 9.40 | 80.00 | ... 7 00– 7 49 |
| 7 50– 7 99... | .... | ...... | ...... | 6 | 21 | 1 | ...... | ...... | ...... | 9 | 7 | 30 | 9.60 | 82.80 | ... 7 50– 7 99 |
| 8 00– 8 99... | .... | ...... | 5 | 45 | 24 | ...... | ...... | 1 | 27 | 41 | 78 | 65 | 12.40 | 88.80 | ... 8 00– 8 99 |
| 9 00– 9 99... | .... | ...... | 5 | 101 | 12 | 1 | ...... | 4 | 14 | 25 | 125 | 37 | 17.00 | 92.10 | ... 9 00– 9 99 |
| 10 00–10 99... | 1 | 1 | 8 | 298 | 12 | 1 | ...... | 5 | 20 | 21 | 333 | 34 | 29.10 | 95.20 | ...10 00–10 99 |
| 11 00–11 99... | 1 | ...... | 12 | 227 | ...... | ...... | ...... | ...... | 7 | 7 | 247 | 7 | 38.20 | 96.00 | ...11 00–11 99 |
| 12 00–12 99... | .... | ...... | 28 | 432 | 2 | ...... | ...... | 11 | 27 | 14 | 498 | 16 | 56.20 | 97.40 | ...12 00–12 99 |
| 13 00–13 99... | .... | ...... | 25 | 106 | 1 | ...... | ...... | 2 | 16 | 1 | 149 | 2 | 61.60 | 97.50 | ...13 00–13 99 |
| 14 00–14 99... | 1 | ...... | 39 | 138 | 1 | ...... | ...... | 2 | 22 | 7 | 202 | 8 | 69.00 | 98.40 | ...14 00–14 99 |
| 15 00–15 99... | 3 | ...... | 67 | 89 | 2 | ...... | ...... | 3 | 20 | 5 | 182 | 7 | 75.60 | 98.90 | ...15 00–15 99 |
| 16 00–17 99... | 2 | ...... | 89 | 53 | ...... | ...... | ...... | 4 | 18 | 4 | 166 | 4 | 80.90 | 99.20 | ...16 00–17 99 |
| 18 00–19 99... | 3 | ...... | 100 | 18 | ...... | ...... | ...... | 1 | 17 | 1 | 139 | 1 | 86.70 | 99.30 | ...18 00–19 99 |
| 20 00–24 99... | 3 | ...... | 154 | 19 | 1 | ...... | ...... | 2 | 34 | 2 | 212 | 3 | 94.40 | 99.60 | ...20 00–24 99 |
| 25 00–29 99... | 5 | 1 | 66 | 4 | ...... | ...... | ...... | ...... | 7 | 2 | 82 | 3 | 97.40 | 99.90 | ...25 00–29 99 |
| 30 00–34 99... | 3 | ...... | 19 | 3 | ...... | ...... | ...... | ...... | 3 | ...... | 28 | ...... | 98.40 | ...... | ...30 00–34 99 |
| 35 00–39 99... | 5 | ...... | 14 | 2 | ...... | ...... | ...... | ...... | 2 | ...... | 23 | ...... | 99.30 | ...... | ...35 00–39 99 |
| 40 00 and over. | 5 | ...... | 14 | 2 | ...... | ...... | ...... | ...... | 3 | 1 | 24 | 1 | 100.00 | 100.00 | .40 00 and over |
| Not reported... | .... | ...... | ...... | 3 | 1 | ...... | ...... | ...... | 3 | 1 | 6 | 2 | ...... | ...... | ...Not reported |
| Total.... | 32 | 2 | 659 | 1,610 | 248 | 9 | 7 | 38 | 410 | 838 | 2,758 | 1,095 | ...... | ...... | .....Total |

221. TABLE V, A, 2, a

NEW YORK CITY

**NEIGHBORHOOD STORES — STOCK AND SALES**

NUMBER AND PER CENT OF EMPLOYEES EARNING SPECIFIED WEEKLY RATES BY AGE GROUPS AND SEX

| WEEKLY RATES IN DOLLARS | AGE GROUPS IN YEARS | | | | | | | | | | | | | | WEEKLY RATES IN DOLLARS |
|---|---|---|---|---|---|---|---|---|---|---|---|---|---|---|---|
| | 14–15 | | 16–17 | | 18–20 | | 21–24 | | 25–29 | | 30–34 | | 35–39 | | |
| | Male | Female | Male | Female | Male | Female | Male | Female | Male | Female | Male | Female | Male | Female | |
| $3 00–$3 49... | .... | 6 | 1 | 12 | ...... | 2 | ...... | 1 | ...... | ...... | ...... | ...... | ...... | ...... | ...$3 00–$3 49 |
| 3 50– 3 99... | .... | 4 | 1 | 40 | ...... | 3 | ...... | ...... | ...... | ...... | ...... | 1 | ...... | ...... | ... 3 50– 3 99 |
| 4 00– 4 49... | .... | 3 | 3 | 82 | ...... | 22 | ...... | 2 | ...... | ...... | ...... | 2 | ...... | ...... | ... 4 00– 4 49 |
| 4 50– 4 99... | .... | 1 | 3 | 20 | ...... | 21 | ...... | 4 | ...... | ...... | ...... | ...... | ...... | ...... | ... 4 50– 4 99 |
| 5 00– 5 49... | 2 | ...... | 11 | 27 | 2 | 61 | ...... | 16 | 1 | 2 | ...... | 1 | ...... | 2 | ... 5 00– 5 49 |
| 5 50– 5 99... | .... | ...... | .... | 4 | 1 | 16 | 1 | 7 | ...... | 1 | ...... | ...... | ...... | ...... | ... 5 50– 5 99 |
| 6 00– 6 49... | .... | ...... | 8 | 14 | 12 | 113 | 2 | 70 | 1 | 30 | ...... | 9 | ...... | 12 | ... 6 00– 6 49 |
| 6 50– 6 99... | .... | ...... | 1 | ...... | ...... | 8 | ...... | 7 | ...... | 3 | ...... | ...... | ...... | 2 | ... 6 50– 6 99 |
| 7 00– 7 49... | .... | ...... | .... | 3 | 7 | 58 | ...... | 71 | 2 | 29 | ...... | 10 | ...... | 5 | ... 7 00– 7 49 |
| 7 50– 7 99... | .... | ...... | .... | ...... | ...... | 2 | ...... | 6 | ...... | 1 | ...... | ...... | ...... | 1 | ... 7 50– 7 99 |
| 8 00– 8 99... | .... | ...... | 1 | 1 | 6 | 27 | 6 | 80 | ...... | 37 | 1 | 8 | ...... | 11 | ... 8 00– 8 99 |
| 9 00– 9 99... | .... | ...... | .... | 2 | 4 | 6 | 2 | 42 | ...... | 31 | ...... | 14 | ...... | 6 | ... 9 00– 9 99 |
| 10 00–10 99... | .... | ...... | .... | ...... | 3 | 2 | 16 | 28 | 5 | 25 | 2 | 11 | 2 | 16 | ...10 00–10 99 |
| 11 00–11 99... | .... | ...... | .... | ...... | 1 | ...... | 5 | 5 | 1 | 4 | ...... | 3 | ...... | ...... | ...11 00–11 99 |
| 12 00–12 99... | .... | ...... | .... | ...... | 5 | 1 | 14 | 12 | 7 | 13 | 4 | 6 | 5 | 3 | ...12 00–12 99 |
| 13 00–13 99... | .... | ...... | .... | ...... | ...... | ...... | 3 | 2 | 2 | 4 | 4 | 3 | 4 | 1 | ...13 00–13 99 |
| 14 00–14 99... | .... | ...... | .... | ...... | 1 | ...... | 5 | 2 | 8 | 6 | 8 | 2 | 8 | 4 | ...14 00–14 99 |
| 15 00–15 99... | .... | ...... | .... | ...... | ...... | ...... | 10 | 1 | 7 | 5 | 9 | 4 | 10 | ...... | ...15 00–15 99 |
| 16 00–17 99... | .... | ...... | .... | ...... | ...... | ...... | ...... | ...... | 6 | 1 | 7 | 1 | 6 | ...... | ...16 00–17 99 |
| 18 00–19 99... | .... | ...... | .... | ...... | ...... | ...... | 1 | ...... | 2 | ...... | 1 | 2 | 5 | 2 | ...18 00–19 99 |
| 20 00–24 99... | .... | ...... | .... | ...... | ...... | ...... | ...... | ...... | 3 | 1 | 5 | ...... | 5 | ...... | ...20 00–24 99 |
| 25 00–29 99... | .... | ...... | .... | ...... | ...... | ...... | ...... | 1 | 3 | ...... | 3 | ...... | 7 | 1 | ...25 00–29 99 |
| 30 00–34 99... | .... | ...... | .... | ...... | ...... | ...... | 1 | ...... | 1 | ...... | ...... | 1 | 3 | ...... | ...30 00–34 99 |
| 35 00–39 99... | .... | ...... | .... | ...... | ...... | ...... | 1 | ...... | 2 | ...... | 1 | ...... | ...... | ...... | ...35 00–39 99 |
| 40 00 and over. | .... | ...... | .... | ...... | ...... | ...... | 1 | ...... | ...... | ...... | 1 | ...... | ...... | ...... | .40 00 and over |
| Not reported... | .... | ...... | .... | 1 | 1 | ...... | ...... | ...... | ...... | ...... | ...... | ...... | ...... | ...... | ...Not reported |
| Total..... | 2 | 14 | 29 | 206 | 43 | 342 | 68 | 357 | 51 | 193 | 46 | 78 | 55 | 66 | .....Total |

221. TABLE V, A, 2, e — (*concluded*)

NEW YORK CITY
NEIGHBORHOOD STORES — STOCK AND SALES
Number and Per Cent. of Employees Earning Specified Weekly Rates by Age Groups and Sex

| Weekly Rates in Dollars | Age Groups in Years (*concluded*) 40–44 | | 45–54 | | 55–64 | | 65 and over | Not reported | | Total | | Cumulative per cent of total | | Weekly Rates in Dollars |
|---|---|---|---|---|---|---|---|---|---|---|---|---|---|---|
| | Male | Female | Male | Female | Male | Female | Male | Male | Female | Male | Female | Male | Female | |
| $3 00–$3 49 | ...... | ...... | ...... | ...... | ...... | ...... | ...... | ...... | 1 | 1 | 22 | .20 | 1.70 | $3 00–$3 49 |
| 3 50– 3 99 | ...... | ...... | ...... | ...... | ...... | ...... | ...... | 1 | ...... | 2 | 48 | .70 | 5.30 | 3 50– 3 99 |
| 4 00– 4 49 | ...... | ...... | ...... | ...... | ...... | ...... | ...... | ...... | ...... | 3 | 111 | 1.40 | 13.80 | 4 00– 4 49 |
| 4 50– 4 99 | ...... | ...... | ...... | ...... | ...... | ...... | ...... | ...... | ...... | 3 | 46 | 2.10 | 17.20 | 4 50– 4 99 |
| 5 00– 5 49 | ...... | ...... | ...... | 1 | ...... | ...... | ...... | ...... | ...... | 16 | 110 | 5.80 | 25.60 | 5 00– 5 49 |
| 5 50– 5 99 | ...... | 1 | ...... | ...... | ...... | ...... | ...... | ...... | ...... | 2 | 29 | 6.20 | 27.80 | 5 50– 5 99 |
| 6 00– 6 49 | ...... | 1 | ...... | 2 | ...... | ...... | ...... | ...... | ...... | 23 | 251 | 11.50 | 46.80 | 6 00– 6 49 |
| 6 50– 6 99 | ...... | 1 | ...... | ...... | ...... | ...... | ...... | ...... | ...... | 1 | 21 | 11.70 | 48.50 | 6 50– 6 99 |
| 7 00– 7 49 | ...... | 2 | ...... | 2 | ...... | ...... | ...... | 1 | 5 | 10 | 185 | 14.10 | 62.50 | 7 00– 7 49 |
| 7 50– 7 99 | ...... | 1 | ...... | ...... | ...... | ...... | ...... | ...... | ...... | ...... | 11 | ...... | 63.30 | 7 50– 7 99 |
| 8 00– 8 99 | ...... | 8 | ...... | 5 | ...... | ...... | ...... | ...... | 1 | 14 | 178 | 17.30 | 71.80 | 8 00– 8 99 |
| 9 00– 9 99 | ...... | 3 | 1 | 3 | ...... | ...... | ...... | ...... | ...... | 7 | 107 | 18.90 | 85.00 | 9 00– 9 99 |
| 10 00–10 99 | ...... | 4 | 1 | 1 | 3 | ...... | ...... | 1 | 2 | 33 | 89 | 26.50 | 91.80 | 10 00–10 99 |
| 11 00–11 99 | ...... | ...... | ...... | ...... | ...... | ...... | ...... | 1 | ...... | 8 | 12 | 28.30 | 92.60 | 11 00–11 99 |
| 12 00–12 99 | 6 | 1 | 8 | 1 | 7 | ...... | ...... | 1 | ...... | 57 | 37 | 41.50 | 95.50 | 12 00–12 99 |
| 13 00–13 99 | 1 | 3 | 1 | 2 | 1 | ...... | 1 | ...... | 1 | 17 | 16 | 45.40 | 96.70 | 13 00–13 99 |
| 14 00–14 99 | 3 | 2 | 7 | ...... | ...... | ...... | 2 | 1 | 2 | 43 | 18 | 55.30 | 98.00 | 14 00–14 99 |
| 15 00–15 99 | 9 | 1 | 19 | ...... | 2 | ...... | ...... | ...... | 2 | 66 | 13 | 70.50 | 99.00 | 15 00–15 99 |
| 16 00–17 99 | 5 | ...... | 8 | ...... | 2 | ...... | ...... | 1 | 1 | 35 | 3 | 78.50 | 99.20 | 16 00–17 99 |
| 18 00–19 99 | 6 | ...... | 5 | ...... | 3 | ...... | 3 | ...... | 1 | 26 | 5 | 84.50 | 99.60 | 18 00–19 99 |
| 20 00–24 99 | 5 | ...... | 7 | ...... | 2 | 1 | ...... | ...... | ...... | 27 | 2 | 90.80 | 99.80 | 20 00–24 99 |
| 25 00–29 99 | 1 | ...... | 1 | ...... | ...... | ...... | ...... | ...... | ...... | 15 | 2 | 94.20 | 99.90 | 25 00–29 99 |
| 30 00–34 99 | 3 | ...... | 4 | ...... | ...... | ...... | ...... | 1 | ...... | 13 | 1 | 97.20 | 100.00 | 30 00–34 99 |
| 35 00–39 99 | 2 | ...... | 1 | ...... | ...... | ...... | ...... | ...... | ...... | 7 | ...... | 98.90 | ...... | 35 00–39 99 |
| 40 00 and over | 3 | ...... | ...... | ...... | ...... | ...... | ...... | ...... | ...... | 5 | ...... | 100.00 | ...... | 40 00 and over |
| Not reported | ...... | ...... | ...... | ...... | ...... | ...... | ...... | ...... | ...... | 1 | 1 | ...... | ...... | Not reported |
| Total | 44 | 28 | 63 | 17 | 20 | 1 | 6 | 8 | 16 | 435 | 1,318 | ...... | ...... | Total |

222. TABLE VIII, A, 2, a

NEW YORK CITY

NEIGHBORHOOD STORES — STOCK AND SALES

NUMBER AND PER CENT OF EMPLOYEES EARNING SPECIFIED WEEKLY RATES BY OCCUPATION AND SEX

| Weekly Rates in Dollars | Occupation: Superintendents | Buyers | | Assistant Buyers and Heads of Stock | | Receiving and Stock Clerks | | Stock People | | Floor Managers | Sales People | | Messengers, Wrappers and Errand Boys | | Total | | Cumulative Per Cent of Total | | Weekly Rates in Dollars |
|---|---|---|---|---|---|---|---|---|---|---|---|---|---|---|---|---|---|---|---|
| | Male | Male | Female | Male | Female | Male | Female | Male | Female | Male | Male | Female | Male | Female | Male | Female | Male | Female | |
| $3 00–$3 49 | ........ | .... | .... | .... | .... | .... | .... | .... | 2 | ........ | .... | 2 | 1 | 18 | 1 | 22 | .20 | 1.70 | $3 00–$3 49 |
| 3 50– 3 99 | ........ | .... | .... | .... | .... | .... | 3 | .... | .... | ........ | .... | 9 | 2 | 36 | 2 | 48 | .70 | 5.30 | 3 50– 3 99 |
| 4 00– 4 49 | ........ | .... | .... | .... | .... | .... | .... | .... | 4 | ........ | 1 | 38 | 2 | 69 | 3 | 111 | 1.40 | 13.80 | 4 00– 4 49 |
| 4 50– 4 99 | ........ | .... | .... | .... | .... | 1 | .... | 2 | 1 | ........ | .... | 39 | .... | 6 | 3 | 46 | 2.10 | 17.20 | 4 50– 4 99 |
| 5 00– 5 49 | ........ | .... | .... | .... | .... | .... | 1 | 2 | 3 | ........ | 2 | 104 | 12 | 2 | 16 | 110 | 5.80 | 25.60 | 5 00– 5 49 |
| 5 50– 5 99 | ........ | .... | .... | .... | .... | 1 | .... | .... | 1 | ........ | 1 | 28 | .... | .... | 2 | 29 | 6.20 | 27.80 | 5 50– 5 99 |
| 6 00– 6 49 | ........ | .... | .... | .... | 1 | 4 | 1 | 3 | 4 | ........ | 11 | 245 | 5 | .... | 23 | 251 | 11.50 | 46.80 | 6 00– 6 49 |
| 6 50– 6 99 | ........ | .... | .... | .... | .... | .... | .... | .... | 1 | ........ | 1 | 20 | .... | .... | 1 | 21 | 11.70 | 48.50 | 6 50– 6 99 |
| 7 00– 7 49 | ........ | .... | .... | .... | 2 | 5 | .... | 1 | .... | ........ | 3 | 183 | 1 | .... | 10 | 185 | 14.10 | 62.50 | 7 00– 7 49 |
| 7 50– 7 99 | ........ | .... | .... | .... | 1 | .... | .... | .... | .... | ........ | .... | 10 | .... | .... | .... | 11 | ..... | 63.30 | 7 50– 7 99 |
| 8 00– 8 99 | ........ | .... | 1 | .... | .... | 1 | 1 | .... | 1 | ........ | 12 | 175 | 1 | .... | 14 | 178 | 17.30 | 71.80 | 8 00– 8 99 |
| 9 00– 9 99 | ........ | .... | .... | .... | 4 | .... | .... | .... | 1 | ........ | 7 | 101 | .... | 1 | 7 | 107 | 18.90 | 85.00 | 9 00– 9 99 |
| 10 00–10 99 | ........ | .... | 3 | 1 | 5 | 3 | .... | .... | .... | 1 | 28 | 81 | .... | .... | 33 | 89 | 26.50 | 91.80 | 10 00–10 99 |
| 11 00–11 99 | ........ | .... | .... | 1 | 2 | 1 | .... | .... | .... | ........ | 6 | 10 | .... | .... | 8 | 12 | 28.30 | 92.60 | 11 00–11 99 |
| 12 00–12 99 | 2 | .... | 3 | .... | 4 | 4 | .... | .... | .... | ........ | 51 | 30 | .... | .... | 57 | 37 | 41.50 | 95.50 | 12 00–12 99 |
| 13 00–13 99 | ........ | .... | 3 | 1 | 3 | 2 | .... | .... | 1 | ........ | 14 | 9 | .... | .... | 17 | 16 | 45.40 | 96.70 | 13 00–13 99 |
| 14 00–14 99 | ........ | .... | 5 | 1 | 2 | 3 | .... | .... | .... | ........ | 39 | 11 | .... | .... | 43 | 18 | 55.30 | 98.00 | 14 00–14 99 |
| 15 00–15 99 | ........ | 2 | 4 | 2 | 2 | 2 | .... | 1 | .... | 5 | 54 | 7 | .... | .... | 66 | 13 | 70.50 | 99.00 | 15 00–15 99 |
| 16 00–17 99 | ........ | 3 | .... | 1 | .... | 1 | .... | .... | .... | 2 | 28 | 3 | .... | .... | 35 | 3 | 78.50 | 99.20 | 16 00–17 99 |
| 18 00–19 99 | ........ | 1 | 2 | .... | .... | 1 | .... | .... | .... | 8 | 16 | 3 | .... | .... | 26 | 5 | 84.50 | 99.60 | 18 00–19 99 |
| 20 00–24 99 | 2 | 6 | 2 | 4 | .... | 1 | .... | .... | .... | 6 | 8 | .... | .... | .... | 27 | 2 | 90.80 | 99.80 | 20 00–24 99 |
| 25 00–29 99 | 2 | 8 | 2 | .... | .... | 1 | .... | .... | .... | 1 | 3 | .... | .... | .... | 15 | 2 | 94.20 | 99.90 | 25 00–29 99 |
| 30 00–34 99 | 1 | 8 | 1 | .... | .... | 1 | .... | .... | .... | 2 | 1 | .... | .... | .... | 13 | 1 | 97.20 | 100.00 | 30 00–34 99 |
| 35 00–39 99 | 1 | 6 | .... | .... | .... | .... | .... | .... | .... | ........ | .... | .... | .... | .... | 7 | .... | 98.90 | ..... | 35 00–39 99 |
| 40 00 and over | ........ | 5 | .... | .... | .... | .... | .... | .... | .... | ........ | .... | .... | .... | .... | 5 | .... | 100.00 | ..... | 40 00 and over |
| Not reported | ........ | .... | .... | .... | .... | .... | .... | .... | .... | ........ | 1 | 1 | .... | .... | 1 | 1 | ..... | ..... | Not reported |
| Total | 8 | 39 | 26 | 11 | 26 | 32 | 6 | 9 | 19 | 25 | 287 | 1,109 | 24 | 132 | 435 | 1,318 | ..... | ..... | Total |

223. TABLE VI, A, 2, a

NEW YORK CITY
NEIGHBORHOOD STORES — STOCK AND SALES
NUMBER AND PER CENT OF EMPLOYEES CLASSIFIED ACCORDING TO ACTUAL WEEKLY EARNINGS BY AGE GROUPS AND SEX

| ACTUAL WEEKLY EARNINGS IN DOLLARS | AGE GROUPS IN YEARS | | | | | | | | | | | | | | ACTUAL WEEKLY EARNINGS IN DOLLARS |
|---|---|---|---|---|---|---|---|---|---|---|---|---|---|---|---|
| | 14–15 | | 16–17 | | 18–20 | | 21–24 | | 25–29 | | 30–34 | | 35–39 | | |
| | Male | Female | Male | Female | Male | Female | Male | Female | Male | Female | Male | Female | Male | Female | |
| Less than $3 00 | .... | ...... | 1 | 18 | 2 | 9 | 1 | 7 | ...... | 3 | ...... | 1 | ...... | 1 | Less than $3 00 |
| $3 00–$3 49... | .... | 6 | 1 | 18 | 2 | 8 | 1 | 1 | ...... | 1 | ...... | ...... | ...... | ...... | ...$3 00– 3 49 |
| 3 50– 3 99... | .... | 4 | 1 | 40 | 1 | 7 | ...... | 2 | ...... | 1 | ...... | 2 | ...... | ...... | ... 3 50– 3 99 |
| 4 00– 4 49... | .... | 3 | 3 | 67 | ...... | 24 | ...... | 8 | ...... | ...... | ...... | 2 | 1 | 2 | ... 4 00– 4 49 |
| 4 50– 4 99... | .... | 1 | 3 | 21 | ...... | 20 | ...... | 4 | ...... | 3 | ...... | ...... | ...... | ...... | ... 4 50– 4 99 |
| 5 00– 5 49... | 2 | ...... | 11 | 23 | 2 | 57 | ...... | 15 | 1 | 3 | ...... | 2 | ...... | 1 | ... 5 00– 5 49 |
| 5 50– 5 99... | .... | ...... | .... | 4 | 1 | 27 | ...... | 12 | ...... | 5 | ...... | ...... | ...... | 2 | ... 5 50– 5 99 |
| 6 00– 6 49... | .... | ...... | 7 | 12 | 10 | 90 | 1 | 61 | 1 | 27 | ...... | 8 | ...... | 10 | ... 6 00– 6 49 |
| 6 50– 6 99... | .... | ...... | 1 | ...... | ...... | 14 | 1 | 10 | ...... | 7 | ...... | 1 | 1 | 2 | ... 6 50– 6 99 |
| 7 00– 7 49... | .... | ...... | .... | 1 | 6 | 46 | ...... | 57 | 2 | 17 | ...... | 9 | ...... | 3 | ... 7 00– 7 49 |
| 7 50– 7 99... | .... | ...... | .... | ...... | 1 | 3 | ...... | 12 | ...... | 7 | ...... | 1 | ...... | 1 | ... 7 50– 7 99 |
| 8 00– 8 99... | .... | ...... | 1 | 1 | 4 | 26 | 5 | 68 | ...... | 31 | 1 | 7 | ...... | 11 | ... 8 00– 8 99 |
| 9 00– 9 99... | .... | ...... | .... | 1 | 3 | 5 | 3 | 47 | ...... | 26 | ...... | 13 | ...... | 5 | ... 9 00– 9 99 |
| 10 00–10 99... | .... | ...... | .... | ...... | 4 | 4 | 12 | 23 | 6 | 24 | 2 | 7 | 2 | 15 | ...10 00–10 99 |
| 11 00–11 99... | .... | ...... | .... | ...... | 1 | ...... | 6 | 8 | 1 | 7 | 1 | 2 | ...... | 2 | ...11 00–11 99 |
| 12 00–12 99... | .... | ...... | .... | ...... | 5 | 1 | 14 | 11 | 2 | 10 | 3 | 5 | 4 | 3 | ...12 00–12 99 |
| 13 00–13 99... | .... | ...... | .... | ...... | ...... | ...... | 2 | 4 | 4 | 6 | 6 | 5 | 2 | 1 | ...13 00–13 99 |
| 14 00–14 99... | .... | ...... | .... | ...... | 1 | ...... | 4 | 3 | 6 | 6 | 4 | 3 | 5 | 4 | ...14 00–14 99 |
| 15 00–15 99... | .... | ...... | .... | ...... | ...... | ...... | 7 | 2 | 7 | 5 | 8 | 5 | 6 | ...... | ...15 00–15 99 |
| 16 00–17 99... | .... | ...... | .... | ...... | ...... | ...... | 3 | 1 | 7 | 2 | 6 | 1 | 10 | ...... | ...16 00–17 99 |
| 18 00–19 99... | .... | ...... | .... | ...... | ...... | ...... | 3 | ...... | 3 | 1 | 3 | 2 | 8 | 2 | ...18 00–19 99 |
| 20 00–24 99... | .... | ...... | .... | ...... | ...... | ...... | 2 | ...... | 4 | 1 | 5 | ...... | 5 | ...... | ...20 00–24 99 |
| 25 00–29 99... | .... | ...... | .... | ...... | ...... | ...... | ...... | 1 | 4 | ...... | 5 | ...... | 8 | 1 | ...25 00–29 99 |
| 30 00–34 99... | .... | ...... | .... | ...... | ...... | ...... | 1 | ...... | 1 | ...... | ...... | 1 | 3 | ...... | ...30 00–34 99 |
| 35 00–39 99... | .... | ...... | .... | ...... | ...... | ...... | 1 | ...... | 2 | ...... | 1 | ...... | ...... | ...... | ...35 00–39 99 |
| 40 00 and over. | .... | ...... | .... | ...... | ...... | ...... | 1 | ...... | ...... | ...... | 1 | ...... | ...... | ...... | .40 00 and over |
| Not reported.. | .... | ...... | .... | ...... | ...... | 1 | ...... | ...... | ...... | ...... | ...... | 1 | ...... | ...... | ..Not reported |
| Total..... | 2 | 14 | 29 | 206 | 43 | 342 | 68 | 357 | 51 | 193 | 46 | 78 | 55 | 66 | .....Total |

NEW YORK CITY

228. TABLE VI, A, 2, a — (*concluded*) NEIGHBORHOOD STORES — STOCK AND SALES

NUMBER AND PER CENT OF EMPLOYEES CLASSIFIED ACCORDING TO ACTUAL WEEKLY EARNINGS BY AGE GROUPS AND SEX

| ACTUAL WEEKLY EARNINGS IN DOLLARS | AGE GROUPS IN YEARS (*concluded*) 40–44 | | 45–54 | | 55–64 | | 65 AND OVER | NOT REPORTED | | TOTAL | | CUMULATIVE PER CENT. OF TOTAL | | ACTUAL WEEKLY EARNINGS IN DOLLARS |
|---|---|---|---|---|---|---|---|---|---|---|---|---|---|---|
| | Male | Female | Male | Female | Male | Female | Male | Male | Female | Male | Female | Male | Female | |
| Less than $3 00 | ...... | 1 | ...... | ...... | ...... | ...... | ...... | ...... | 1 | 4 | 41 | .90 | 3.10 | Less than $3 00 |
| $3 00–$3 49 | ...... | ...... | ...... | ...... | ...... | ...... | ...... | ...... | ...... | 4 | 34 | 1.80 | 5.70 | $3 00– 3 49 |
| 3 50– 3 99 | ...... | ...... | ...... | ...... | ...... | ...... | ...... | 1 | ...... | 3 | 56 | 2.50 | 9.90 | 3 50– 3 99 |
| 4 00– 4 49 | ...... | ...... | ...... | ...... | ...... | ...... | ...... | ...... | ...... | 4 | 106 | 3.40 | 18.10 | 4 00– 4 49 |
| 4 50– 4 99 | ...... | ...... | ...... | ...... | ...... | ...... | ...... | ...... | ...... | 3 | 49 | 4.10 | 21.80 | 4 50– 4 99 |
| 5 00– 5 49 | 1 | ...... | ...... | 1 | ...... | ...... | ...... | ...... | ...... | 17 | 102 | 8.00 | 29.50 | 5 00– 5 49 |
| 5 50– 5 99 | ...... | 2 | ...... | ...... | ...... | ...... | ...... | ...... | ...... | 1 | 52 | 8.30 | 33.50 | 5 50– 5 99 |
| 6 00– 6 49 | ...... | 1 | ...... | 2 | ...... | ...... | ...... | ...... | ...... | 19 | 211 | 12.60 | 49.50 | 6 00– 6 49 |
| 6 50– 6 99 | 1 | 1 | ...... | ...... | ...... | ...... | ...... | ...... | ...... | 4 | 35 | 13.60 | 52.20 | 6 50– 6 99 |
| 7 00– 7 49 | ...... | 2 | ...... | 2 | ...... | ...... | ...... | 1 | 3 | 9 | 140 | 15.60 | 62.90 | 7 00– 7 49 |
| 7 50– 7 99 | ...... | 1 | ...... | ...... | ...... | ...... | ...... | ...... | 2 | 1 | 27 | 15.90 | 64.90 | 7 50– 7 99 |
| 8 00– 8 99 | ...... | 6 | ...... | 4 | 1 | ...... | ...... | ...... | 1 | 12 | 155 | 18.60 | 76.60 | 8 00– 8 99 |
| 9 00– 9 99 | ...... | 3 | 1 | 4 | ...... | ...... | ...... | 1 | 2 | 8 | 106 | 20.00 | 84.80 | 9 00– 9 99 |
| 10 00–10 99 | ...... | ...... | 1 | 1 | 2 | ...... | ...... | ...... | 1 | 29 | 75 | 27.10 | 90.50 | 10 00–10 99 |
| 11 00–11 99 | ...... | 1 | ...... | ...... | ...... | ...... | ...... | 1 | ...... | 10 | 20 | 29.40 | 92.00 | 11 00–11 99 |
| 12 00–12 99 | 3 | 3 | 4 | ...... | 4 | ...... | ...... | 1 | ...... | 40 | 33 | 38.60 | 94.50 | 12 00–12 99 |
| 13 00–13 99 | 2 | 4 | 3 | 3 | 2 | ...... | 1 | ...... | 1 | 22 | 24 | 43.70 | 97.30 | 13 00–13 99 |
| 14 00–14 99 | 1 | 2 | 8 | ...... | ...... | ...... | 1 | 1 | 1 | 31 | 19 | 50.80 | 97.80 | 14 00–14 99 |
| 15 00–15 99 | 6 | 1 | 12 | ...... | 2 | ...... | ...... | ...... | 2 | 48 | 15 | 61.80 | 99.00 | 15 00–15 99 |
| 16 00–17 99 | 8 | ...... | 11 | ...... | 4 | ...... | ...... | 1 | 1 | 50 | 5 | 73.30 | 99.30 | 16 00–17 99 |
| 18 00–19 99 | 5 | ...... | 7 | ...... | 3 | ...... | 4 | ...... | 1 | 36 | 6 | 81.50 | 99.70 | 18 00–19 99 |
| 20 00–24 99 | 7 | ...... | 8 | ...... | 2 | 1 | ...... | ...... | ...... | 33 | 2 | 89.20 | 99.80 | 20 00–24 99 |
| 25 00–29 99 | 2 | ...... | 3 | ...... | ...... | ...... | ...... | ...... | ...... | 22 | 2 | 94.30 | 99.90 | 25 00–29 99 |
| 30 00–34 99 | 3 | ...... | 4 | ...... | ...... | ...... | ...... | 1 | ...... | 13 | 1 | 97.20 | 100.00 | 30 00–34 99 |
| 35 00–39 99 | 2 | ...... | 1 | ...... | ...... | ...... | ...... | ...... | ...... | 7 | ...... | 98.80 | ...... | 35 00–39 99 |
| 40 00 and over | 3 | ...... | ...... | ...... | ...... | ...... | ...... | ...... | ...... | 5 | ...... | 100.00 | ...... | 40 00 and over |
| Not reported | ...... | ...... | ...... | ...... | ...... | ...... | ...... | ...... | ...... | ...... | 2 | ...... | ...... | Not reported |
| Total | 44 | 28 | 63 | 17 | 20 | 1 | 6 | 8 | 16 | 435 | 1,318 | ...... | ...... | Total |

224. TABLE IX, A, 2, a

NEW YORK CITY

NEIGHBORHOOD STORES — STOCK AND SALES

NUMBER AND PER CENT OF EMPLOYEES CLASSIFIED ACCORDING TO ACTUAL WEEKLY EARNINGS, BY OCCUPATION AND SEX

| ACTUAL WEEKLY EARNINGS IN DOLLARS | OCCUPATION: SUPERINTENDENTS | BUYERS | | ASSISTANT BUYERS AND HEADS OF STOCK | | RECEIVING AND STOCK CLERKS | | STOCK PEOPLE | | FLOOR MANAGERS | SALES PEOPLE | | MESSENGERS, WRAPPERS AND ERRAND BOYS | | TOTAL | | CUMULATIVE PER CENT OF TOTAL | | ACTUAL WEEKLY EARNINGS IN DOLLARS |
|---|---|---|---|---|---|---|---|---|---|---|---|---|---|---|---|---|---|---|---|
| | Male | Male | Female | Male | Female | Male | Female | Male | Female | Male | Male | Female | Male | Female | Male | Female | Male | Female | |
| Less than $3 00 | | | | | | | | 1 | | | 3 | 30 | | 11 | 4 | 41 | .90 | 3.10 | Less than $3 00 |
| $3 00–$3 49 | | | | | | | | | 2 | | 3 | 10 | 1 | 22 | 4 | 34 | 1.80 | 5.70 | $3 00– 3 49 |
| 3 50– 3 99 | | | | | | | 3 | | 1 | | | 16 | 3 | 36 | 3 | 56 | 2.50 | 9.90 | 3 50– 3 99 |
| 4 00– 4 49 | | | | | | | | | 5 | | 2 | 45 | 2 | 56 | 4 | 106 | 3.40 | 18.10 | 4 00– 4 49 |
| 4 50– 4 99 | | | | | 1 | 1 | | 1 | 1 | | | 43 | 1 | 4 | 3 | 49 | 4.10 | 21.80 | 4 50– 4 99 |
| 5 00– 5 49 | | | | | | | 1 | 3 | 2 | | 3 | 97 | 11 | 2 | 17 | 102 | 8.00 | 29.50 | 5 00– 5 49 |
| 5 50– 5 99 | | | | | | 1 | | | 1 | | | 51 | | | 1 | 52 | 8.30 | 33.50 | 5 50– 5 99 |
| 6 00– 6 49 | | | | | 1 | 4 | 1 | 2 | 3 | | 9 | 206 | 4 | | 19 | 211 | 12.60 | 49.50 | 6 00– 6 49 |
| 6 50– 6 99 | | | | | 1 | 2 | | | 1 | | 2 | 33 | | | 4 | 35 | 13.60 | 52.20 | 6 50– 6 99 |
| 7 00– 7 49 | | | | | | 5 | | 1 | | | 2 | 140 | 1 | | 9 | 140 | 15.60 | 62.90 | 7 00– 7 49 |
| 7 50– 7 99 | | | | | 1 | | | | | | 1 | 26 | | | 1 | 27 | 15.90 | 64.90 | 7 50– 7 99 |
| 8 00– 8 99 | | | 2 | | | | 1 | | 1 | | 11 | 151 | 1 | | 12 | 155 | 18.60 | 76.60 | 8 00– 8 99 |
| 9 00– 9 99 | | | | | 6 | 1 | | | 1 | | 7 | 98 | | 1 | 8 | 106 | 20.00 | 84.80 | 9 00– 9 99 |
| 10 00–10 99 | | | 3 | 1 | 4 | 3 | | | | 1 | 24 | 68 | | | 29 | 75 | 27.10 | 90.50 | 10 00–10 99 |
| 11 00–11 99 | | | | 1 | 1 | 1 | | | | | 8 | 19 | | | 10 | 20 | 29.40 | 92.00 | 11 00–11 99 |
| 12 00–12 99 | 2 | | 4 | | 3 | 4 | | | | | 34 | 26 | | | 40 | 33 | 38.60 | 94.50 | 12 00–12 99 |
| 13 00–13 99 | | | 3 | 1 | 4 | | | | 1 | | 21 | 16 | | | 22 | 24 | 43.70 | 97.30 | 13 00–13 99 |
| 14 00–14 99 | | | 4 | 1 | 2 | 3 | | | | | 27 | 13 | | | 31 | 19 | 50.80 | 97.80 | 14 00–14 99 |
| 15 00–15 99 | | 1 | 3 | 1 | 2 | 2 | | 1 | | 5 | 38 | 10 | | | 48 | 15 | 61.80 | 99.00 | 15 00–15 99 |
| 16 00–17 99 | | 3 | | 1 | | 1 | | | | 2 | 43 | 5 | | | 50 | 5 | 73.30 | 99.30 | 16 00–17 99 |
| 18 00–19 99 | | 1 | 2 | | | 1 | | | | 8 | 26 | 4 | | | 36 | 6 | 81.50 | 99.70 | 18 00–19 99 |
| 20 00–24 99 | 2 | 6 | 2 | 4 | | 1 | | | | 6 | 14 | | | | 33 | 2 | 89.20 | 99.80 | 20 00–24 99 |
| 25 00–29 99 | 2 | 9 | 2 | 1 | | 1 | | | | 1 | 8 | | | | 22 | 2 | 94.30 | 99.90 | 25 00–29 99 |
| 30 00–34 99 | 1 | 8 | 1 | | | 1 | | | | 2 | 1 | | | | 13 | 1 | 97.20 | 100.00 | 30 00–34 99 |
| 35 00–39 99 | 1 | 6 | | | | | | | | | | | | | 7 | | 98.80 | | 35 00–39 99 |
| 40 00 and over | | 5 | | | | | | | | | | | | | 5 | | 100.00 | | 40 00 and over |
| Not reported | | | | | | | | | | | | 2 | | | | 2 | | | Not reported |
| Total | 8 | 39 | 26 | 11 | 26 | 32 | 6 | 9 | 19 | 25 | 287 | 1,109 | 24 | 132 | 435 | 1,318 | | | Total |

225. TABLE V, A, 2, a

NEW YORK CITY
NEIGHBORHOOD STORES — OFFICE
NUMBER AND PER CENT OF EMPLOYEES EARNING SPECIFIED WEEKLY RATES BY AGE GROUPS AND SEX

| WEEKLY RATES IN DOLLARS | AGE GROUPS IN YEARS | | | | | | | | | | | | | WEEKLY RATES IN DOLLARS |
|---|---|---|---|---|---|---|---|---|---|---|---|---|---|---|
| | 14–15 | 16–17 | | 18–20 | | 21–24 | | 25–29 | | 30–34 | | 35–39 | | |
| | Female | Male | Female | Male | Female | Male | Female | Male | Female | Male | Female | Male | Female | |
| Less than $3 00 | ...... | ...... | 1 | ...... | ...... | ...... | ...... | ...... | ...... | ...... | ...... | ...... | ...... | Less than $3 00 |
| $3 00–$3 49 | ...... | ...... | 5 | ...... | ...... | ...... | ...... | ...... | ...... | ...... | ...... | ...... | ...... | $3 00– 3 49 |
| 3 50– 3 99 | 2 | ...... | 16 | ...... | 2 | ...... | ...... | ...... | ...... | ...... | ...... | ...... | ...... | 3 50– 3 99 |
| 4 00– 4 49 | 1 | 1 | 31 | ...... | 7 | ...... | 1 | ...... | ...... | ...... | ...... | ...... | ...... | 4 00– 4 49 |
| 4 50– 4 99 | ...... | ...... | 19 | ...... | 10 | ...... | 1 | ...... | ...... | ...... | ...... | ...... | ...... | 4 50– 4 99 |
| 5 00– 5 49 | ...... | 5 | 21 | 3 | 28 | ...... | 4 | ...... | 1 | ...... | ...... | ...... | ...... | 5 00– 5 49 |
| 5 50– 5 99 | ...... | ...... | 5 | ...... | 14 | ...... | ...... | ...... | ...... | ...... | ...... | ...... | ...... | 5 50– 5 99 |
| 6 00– 6 49 | ...... | 1 | 4 | 1 | 25 | ...... | 13 | ...... | 2 | ...... | ...... | ...... | ...... | 6 00– 6 49 |
| 6 50– 6 99 | ...... | ...... | ...... | ...... | ...... | ...... | 3 | ...... | ...... | ...... | ...... | ...... | ...... | 6 50– 6 99 |
| 7 00– 7 49 | ...... | 1 | 2 | 4 | 29 | 2 | 16 | ...... | 1 | ...... | ...... | ...... | 1 | 7 00– 7 49 |
| 7 50– 7 99 | ...... | ...... | ...... | ...... | 2 | ...... | 4 | ...... | ...... | ...... | ...... | ...... | ...... | 7 50– 7 99 |
| 8 00– 8 99 | ...... | ...... | ...... | 3 | 7 | 1 | 7 | ...... | 3 | ...... | 1 | ...... | 1 | 8 00– 8 99 |
| 9 00– 9 99 | ...... | ...... | ...... | 1 | 3 | ...... | 6 | ...... | 3 | ...... | ...... | 1 | ...... | 9 00– 9 99 |
| 10 00–10 99 | ...... | ...... | ...... | 2 | 2 | 2 | 5 | ...... | 2 | ...... | ...... | ...... | 1 | 10 00–10 99 |
| 11 00–11 99 | ...... | ...... | ...... | ...... | ...... | ...... | ...... | ...... | 2 | ...... | 1 | ...... | ...... | 11 00–11 99 |
| 12 00–12 99 | ...... | ...... | ...... | ...... | 1 | 1 | 6 | ...... | 1 | ...... | ...... | ...... | ...... | 12 00–12 99 |
| 13 00–13 99 | ...... | ...... | ...... | ...... | ...... | ...... | ...... | ...... | ...... | 1 | ...... | 1 | ...... | 13 00–13 99 |
| 14 00–14 99 | ...... | ...... | ...... | 1 | ...... | 2 | ...... | 1 | 2 | 1 | ...... | ...... | ...... | 14 00–14 99 |
| 15 00–15 99 | ...... | ...... | ...... | ...... | ...... | ...... | 1 | ...... | 3 | ...... | ...... | ...... | ...... | 15 00–15 99 |
| 16 00–17 99 | ...... | 1 | ...... | ...... | ...... | 2 | 1 | ...... | 1 | ...... | 1 | ...... | ...... | 16 00–17 99 |
| 18 00–19 99 | ...... | ...... | ...... | ...... | ...... | 1 | 1 | ...... | ...... | ...... | ...... | ...... | ...... | 18 00–19 99 |
| 20 00–24 99 | ...... | ...... | ...... | ...... | ...... | 2 | 1 | 3 | ...... | 2 | ...... | ...... | ...... | 20 00–24 99 |
| 25 00–29 99 | ...... | ...... | ...... | ...... | ...... | 1 | ...... | 2 | ...... | 2 | ...... | ...... | ...... | 25 00–29 99 |
| 30 00–34 99 | ...... | ...... | ...... | ...... | ...... | ...... | ...... | ...... | ...... | ...... | ...... | ...... | ...... | 30 00–34 99 |
| 35 00–39 99 | ...... | ...... | ...... | ...... | ...... | ...... | ...... | ...... | ...... | 1 | ...... | ...... | ...... | 35 00–39 99 |
| 40 00 and over | ...... | ...... | ...... | ...... | ...... | ...... | ...... | ...... | ...... | 1 | ...... | ...... | ...... | 40 00 and over |
| Total | 3 | 9 | 104 | 15 | 130 | 14 | 70 | 6 | 21 | 8 | 3 | 2 | 3 | Total |

225. TABLE V, A, 2, a — (*concluded*)

NEW YORK CITY
NEIGHBORHOOD STORES — OFFICE

NUMBER AND PER CENT OF EMPLOYEES EARNING SPECIFIED WEEKLY RATES BY AGE GROUPS AND SEX

| WEEKLY RATES IN DOLLARS | AGE GROUPS IN YEARS (*concluded*) | | | | | | | | | | | | WEEKLY RATES IN DOLLARS |
|---|---|---|---|---|---|---|---|---|---|---|---|---|---|
| | 40–44 | | 45–54 | | 55–64 | | NOT REPORTED | | TOTAL | | CUMULATIVE PER CENT OF TOTAL | | |
| | Male | Female | Male | Female | Male | Female | Male | Female | Male | Female | Male | Female | |
| Less than $3 00. | | | | | | | | | | 1 | | .30 | Less than $3 00 |
| $3 00–$3 49 | | | | | | | | | | 5 | | 1.70 | $3 00– 3 49 |
| 3 50– 3 99 | | | | | | | | | | 20 | | 7.60 | 3 50– 3 99 |
| 4 00– 4 49 | | | | | | | | | 1 | 40 | 1.50 | 19.20 | 4 00– 4 49 |
| 4 50– 4 99 | | | | | | | | | | 30 | | 28.00 | 4 50– 4 99 |
| 5 00– 5 49 | | | | | | | | 1 | 8 | 55 | 13.40 | 44.00 | 5 00– 5 49 |
| 5 50– 5 99 | | | | | | | | | | 19 | | 48.50 | 5 50– 5 99 |
| 6 00– 6 49 | | | | | | | | | 2 | 44 | 16.40 | 62.40 | 6 00– 6 49 |
| 6 50– 6 99 | | | | | | | | | | 3 | | 63.30 | 6 50– 6 99 |
| 7 00– 7 49 | | 1 | | | | | | | 7 | 50 | 26.80 | 77.80 | 7 00– 7 49 |
| 7 50– 7 99 | | | 1 | 1 | | | | | 1 | 7 | 28.40 | 79.90 | 7 50– 7 99 |
| 8 00– 8 99 | | | | | | 1 | | | 4 | 20 | 34.30 | 85.70 | 8 00– 8 99 |
| 9 00– 9 99 | | | | | | | | 1 | 2 | 13 | 37.30 | 89.50 | 9 00– 9 99 |
| 10 00–10 99 | | | | | | | | | 4 | 10 | 43.30 | 92.50 | 10 00–10 99 |
| 11 00–11 99 | | | | | | | | 1 | | 4 | | 93.50 | 11 00–11 99 |
| 12 00–12 99 | | | 1 | | | | | 1 | 2 | 9 | 46.30 | 96.20 | 12 00–12 99 |
| 13 00–13 99 | | | | | | | | | 2 | | 49.30 | | 13 00–13 99 |
| 14 00–14 99 | | | | | 1 | | | | 6 | 2 | 50.70 | 96.80 | 14 00–14 99 |
| 15 00–15 99 | | | 1 | | 1 | | | | 2 | 4 | 61.20 | 98.00 | 15 00–15 99 |
| 16 00–17 99 | 1 | 1 | | | | | | | 4 | 4 | 67.20 | 99.20 | 16 00–17 99 |
| 18 00–19 99 | 1 | | | | | | 1 | | 3 | 1 | 71.60 | 99.50 | 18 00–19 99 |
| 20 00–24 99 | | 1 | | | 1 | | | | 8 | 2 | 83.50 | 100.00 | 20 00–24 99 |
| 25 00–29 99 | 1 | | 1 | | | | | | 7 | | 94.00 | | 25 00–29 99 |
| 30 00–34 99 | | | | | | | 1 | | 1 | | 95.50 | | 30 00–34 99 |
| 35 00–39 99 | 1 | | | | | | | | 2 | | 98.50 | | 35 00–39 99 |
| 40 00 and over | | | | | | | | | 1 | | 100.00 | | 40 00 and over |
| Total | 4 | 3 | 4 | 1 | 3 | 1 | 2 | 4 | 67 | 343 | | | Total |

226. TABLE VIII, A, 2, a

NEW YORK CITY
NEIGHBORHOOD STORES — OFFICE
NUMBER AND PER CENT OF EMPLOYEES EARNING SPECIFIED WEEKLY RATES BY OCCUPATION AND SEX

| WEEKLY RATES IN DOLLARS | OCCUPATION | | | | | | | | | | | | | | | | | | | WEEKLY RATES IN DOLLARS |
|---|---|---|---|---|---|---|---|---|---|---|---|---|---|---|---|---|---|---|---|---|
| | SUPERINTENDENTS | BOOKKEEPERS | | CLERKS | | STENOGRAPHERS | | OFFICE BOYS | CASHIERS | | TELEPHONE OPERATORS | AUDITORS | DETECTIVES | ADVERTISERS AND WINDOW DRESSERS | | TOTAL | | CUMULATIVE PER CENT OF TOTAL | | |
| | Male | Male | Female | Male | Female | Male | Female | Male | Male | Female | Female | Female | Female | Male | Female | Male | Female | Male | Female | |
| Less than $3 00 | | | | | | | | | | | | 1 | | | | | 1 | | .30 | Less than $3 00 |
| $3 00–$3 49 | | | | | | | | | | 2 | | 3 | | | | | 5 | | 1.70 | $3 00– 3 49 |
| 3 50– 3 99 | | | 1 | | 7 | | | | | 7 | | 5 | | | | | 20 | | 7.60 | 3 50– 3 99 |
| 4 00– 4 49 | | | 5 | | 9 | | | 1 | | 16 | 1 | 9 | | | | 1 | 40 | 1.50 | 19.20 | 4 00– 4 49 |
| 4 50– 4 99 | | | 1 | | 9 | | | | | 17 | | 3 | | | | | 30 | | 28.00 | 4 50– 4 99 |
| 5 00– 5 49 | | | 2 | 2 | 12 | 1 | | | | 26 | 2 | 13 | | 5 | | 8 | 55 | 13.40 | 44.00 | 5 00– 5 49 |
| 5 50– 5 99 | | | | | 1 | | | | | 15 | | 3 | | | | | 19 | | 48.50 | 5 50– 5 99 |
| 6 00– 6 49 | | | 2 | 1 | 8 | | 3 | | | 25 | 2 | 4 | | 1 | | 2 | 44 | 16.40 | 62.40 | 6 00– 6 49 |
| 6 50– 6 99 | | | | | | | | | | 2 | 1 | | | | | | 3 | | 63.30 | 6 50– 6 99 |
| 7 00– 7 49 | | 1 | 4 | 1 | 6 | | 3 | | 1 | 32 | 1 | 4 | | 4 | | 7 | 50 | 26.80 | 77.80 | 7 00– 7 49 |
| 7 50– 7 99 | | | 1 | 1 | 1 | | 1 | | | 4 | | | | | | 1 | 7 | 28.40 | 79.90 | 7 50– 7 99 |
| 8 00– 8 99 | | 2 | 1 | | 6 | | 1 | | | 9 | | 1 | | 2 | 2 | 4 | 20 | 34.30 | 85.70 | 8 00– 8 99 |
| 9 00– 9 99 | | | 4 | 2 | 5 | | | | | 1 | | 3 | | | | 2 | 13 | 37.30 | 89.50 | 9 00– 9 99 |
| 10 00–10 99 | | | 4 | 1 | 3 | | 1 | | | 1 | 1 | | | 3 | | 4 | 10 | 43.30 | 92.50 | 10 00–10 99 |
| 11 00–11 99 | | | | | 2 | | | | | 1 | | 1 | | | | | 4 | | 93.50 | 11 00–11 99 |
| 12 00–12 99 | | | 2 | 2 | 1 | | 3 | | | 1 | | 1 | 1 | | | 2 | 9 | 46.30 | 96.20 | 12 00–12 99 |
| 13 00–13 99 | | | | 2 | | | | | | | | | | | | 2 | | 49.30 | | 13 00–13 99 |
| 14 00–14 99 | | 2 | 1 | 4 | | | | | | 1 | | | | | | 6 | 2 | 50.70 | 96.80 | 14 00–14 99 |
| 15 00–15 99 | | | 1 | 1 | 1 | | | | | 1 | | 1 | | 1 | | 2 | 4 | 61.20 | 98.00 | 15 00–15 99 |
| 16 00–17 99 | | 1 | 1 | | 2 | | | | | | | 1 | | 3 | | 4 | 4 | 67.20 | 99.20 | 16 00–17 99 |
| 18 00–19 99 | | | 1 | 1 | | | | | | | | | | 2 | | 3 | 1 | 71.60 | 99.50 | 18 00–19 99 |
| 20 00–24 99 | | 2 | | 1 | | | 1 | | | 1 | | | | 5 | | 8 | 2 | 83.50 | 100.00 | 20 00–24 99 |
| 25 00–29 99 | | | | | | | | | | | | | | 7 | | 7 | | 94.00 | | 25 00–29 99 |
| 30 00–34 99 | | | | | | | | | | | | | | 1 | | 1 | | 95.50 | | 30 00–34 99 |
| 35 00–39 99 | 1 | | | | | | | | | | | | | 1 | | 2 | | 98.50 | | 35 00–39 99 |
| 40 00 and over | | | | | | | | | | | | | | 1 | | 1 | | 100.00 | | 40 00 and over |
| Total | 1 | 8 | 31 | 19 | 73 | 1 | 13 | 1 | 1 | 162 | 8 | 53 | 1 | 36 | 2 | 67 | 343 | | | Total |

227. TABLE VI, A, 2, a

NEW YORK CITY
NEIGHBORHOOD STORES — OFFICE
Number and Per Cent of Employees Classified According to Actual Weekly Earnings by Age Groups and Sex

| Actual Weekly Earnings in Dollars | Age Groups in Years | | | | | | | | | | | | | Actual Weekly Earnings in Dollars |
|---|---|---|---|---|---|---|---|---|---|---|---|---|---|---|
| | 14–15 | 16–17 | | 18–20 | | 21–24 | | 25–29 | | 30–34 | | 35–39 | | |
| | Female | Male | Female | Male | Female | Male | Female | Male | Female | Male | Female | Male | Female | |
| Less than $3 00 | ...... | 1 | 4 | ...... | 1 | ...... | ...... | ...... | ...... | ...... | ...... | ...... | ...... | Less than $3 00 |
| $3 00–$3 49 | ...... | ...... | 10 | ...... | 4 | ...... | ...... | ...... | ...... | ...... | ...... | ...... | ...... | $3 00– 3 49 |
| 3 50– 3 99 | 2 | ...... | 16 | ...... | 3 | ...... | ...... | ...... | ...... | ...... | ...... | ...... | ...... | 3 50– 3 99 |
| 4 00– 4 49 | 1 | 1 | 31 | ...... | 9 | ...... | 2 | ...... | ...... | ...... | ...... | ...... | ...... | 4 00– 4 49 |
| 4 50– 4 99 | ...... | ...... | 17 | ...... | 10 | ...... | 1 | ...... | ...... | ...... | ...... | ...... | ...... | 4 50– 4 99 |
| 5 00– 5 49 | ...... | 4 | 14 | 3 | 25 | ...... | 4 | ...... | 1 | ...... | ...... | ...... | ...... | 5 00– 5 49 |
| 5 50– 5 99 | ...... | ...... | 5 | ...... | 16 | 1 | 3 | ...... | ...... | ...... | ...... | ...... | ...... | 5 50– 5 99 |
| 6 00– 6 49 | ...... | ...... | 4 | 1 | 22 | ...... | 12 | 1 | 2 | ...... | ...... | ...... | ...... | 6 00– 6 49 |
| 6 50– 6 99 | ...... | ...... | ...... | ...... | ...... | ...... | 3 | ...... | ...... | ...... | ...... | ...... | ...... | 6 50– 6 99 |
| 7 00– 7 49 | ...... | 2 | 2 | 4 | 26 | 1 | 14 | ...... | 1 | ...... | ...... | ...... | 1 | 7 00– 7 49 |
| 7 50– 7 99 | ...... | ...... | ...... | ...... | 2 | ...... | 5 | ...... | ...... | ...... | ...... | ...... | ...... | 7 50– 7 99 |
| 8 00– 8 99 | ...... | ...... | ...... | 3 | 6 | 1 | 6 | ...... | 3 | ...... | 1 | ...... | 1 | 8 00– 8 99 |
| 9 00– 9 99 | ...... | ...... | ...... | 1 | 2 | ...... | 5 | ...... | 3 | ...... | ...... | 1 | ...... | 9 00– 9 99 |
| 10 00–10 99 | ...... | ...... | ...... | 2 | 3 | 2 | 5 | ...... | 2 | ...... | ...... | ...... | 1 | 10 00–10 99 |
| 11 00–11 99 | ...... | ...... | ...... | ...... | ...... | ...... | ...... | ...... | 2 | ...... | 1 | ...... | ...... | 11 00–11 99 |
| 12 00–12 99 | ...... | ...... | ...... | ...... | 1 | 1 | 6 | ...... | 1 | ...... | ...... | ...... | ...... | 12 00–12 99 |
| 13 00–13 99 | ...... | ...... | ...... | ...... | ...... | ...... | ...... | ...... | ...... | 1 | ...... | 1 | ...... | 13 00–13 99 |
| 14 00–14 99 | ...... | ...... | ...... | 1 | ...... | 2 | ...... | ...... | 2 | 1 | ...... | ...... | ...... | 14 00–14 99 |
| 15 00–15 99 | ...... | ...... | ...... | ...... | ...... | ...... | 1 | ...... | 3 | ...... | ...... | ...... | ...... | 15 00–15 99 |
| 16 00–16 99 | ...... | 1 | ...... | ...... | ...... | 2 | 1 | ...... | 1 | ...... | 1 | ...... | ...... | 16 00–17 99 |
| 18 00–19 99 | ...... | ...... | ...... | ...... | ...... | 1 | 1 | 1 | ...... | ...... | ...... | ...... | ...... | 18 00–19 99 |
| 20 00–24 99 | ...... | ...... | ...... | ...... | ...... | 2 | 1 | 2 | ...... | 2 | ...... | ...... | ...... | 20 00–24 99 |
| 25 00–29 99 | ...... | ...... | ...... | ...... | ...... | 1 | ...... | 2 | ...... | 2 | ...... | ...... | ...... | 25 00–29 99 |
| 35 00–39 99 | ...... | ...... | ...... | ...... | ...... | ...... | ...... | ...... | ...... | 1 | ...... | ...... | ...... | 35 00–39 99 |
| 40 00 and over | ...... | ...... | ...... | ...... | ...... | ...... | ...... | ...... | ...... | 1 | ...... | ...... | ...... | 40 00 and over |
| Not reported | ...... | ...... | 1 | ...... | ...... | ...... | ...... | ...... | ...... | ...... | ...... | ...... | ...... | Not reported |
| Total | 3 | 9 | 104 | 15 | 130 | 14 | 70 | 6 | 21 | 8 | 3 | 2 | 3 | Total |

227 TABLE VI, A, 2, a — (*concluded*)

NEW YORK CITY
NEIGHBORHOOD STORES — OFFICE
NUMBER AND PER CENT OF EMPLOYEES CLASSIFIED ACCORDING TO ACTUAL WEEKLY EARNINGS BY AGE GROUPS AND SEX

| ACTUAL WEEKLY EARNINGS IN DOLLARS | AGE GROUPS IN YEARS (*concluded*) | | | | | | | | | | | | ACTUAL WEEKLY EARNINGS IN DOLLARS |
|---|---|---|---|---|---|---|---|---|---|---|---|---|---|
| | 40–44 | | 45–54 | | 55–64 | | NOT REPORTED | | TOTAL | | CUMULATIVE PER CENT. OF TOTAL | | |
| | Male | Female | Male | Female | Male | Female | Male | Female | Male | Female | Male | Female | |
| Less than $3 00 | ....... | ....... | ....... | ....... | ....... | ....... | ....... | ....... | 1 | 5 | 1.50 | 1.50 | Less than $3 00 |
| $3 00–$3 49 | ....... | ....... | ....... | ....... | ....... | ....... | ....... | ....... | ....... | 14 | ....... | 5.60 | $3 00– 3 49 |
| 3 50– 3 99 | ....... | ....... | ....... | ....... | ....... | ....... | ....... | ....... | ....... | 21 | ....... | 11.70 | 3 50– 3 99 |
| 4 00– 4 49 | ....... | ....... | ....... | ....... | ....... | ....... | ....... | ....... | 1 | 43 | 3.00 | 24.20 | 4 00– 4 49 |
| 4 50– 4 99 | ....... | ....... | ....... | ....... | ....... | ....... | ....... | ....... | ....... | 28 | ....... | 32.40 | 4 50– 4 99 |
| 5 00– 5 49 | ....... | ....... | ....... | ....... | ....... | ....... | ....... | 1 | 7 | 45 | 13.40 | 45.60 | 5 00– 5 49 |
| 5 50– 5 99 | ....... | ....... | ....... | ....... | ....... | ....... | ....... | ....... | 1 | 24 | 14.90 | 52.60 | 5 50– 5 99 |
| 6 00– 6 49 | ....... | ....... | ....... | ....... | ....... | ....... | ....... | ....... | 2 | 40 | 17.90 | 64.40 | 6 00– 6 49 |
| 6 50– 6 99 | ....... | ....... | ....... | 1 | ....... | ....... | ....... | ....... | ....... | 4 | ....... | 65.50 | 6 50– 6 99 |
| 7 00– 7 49 | ....... | 1 | ....... | ....... | ....... | ....... | ....... | ....... | 7 | 45 | 28.40 | 78.60 | 7 00– 7 49 |
| 7 50– 7 99 | ....... | ....... | 1 | ....... | ....... | ....... | ....... | ....... | 1 | 7 | 29.80 | 80.70 | 7 50– 7 99 |
| 8 00– 8 99 | ....... | ....... | ....... | ....... | ....... | 1 | ....... | ....... | 4 | 18 | 35.80 | 86.00 | 8 00– 8 99 |
| 9 00– 9 99 | ....... | ....... | ....... | ....... | ....... | ....... | ....... | 1 | 2 | 11 | 38.80 | 89.20 | 9 00– 9 99 |
| 10 00–10 99 | ....... | ....... | ....... | ....... | ....... | ....... | ....... | ....... | 4 | 11 | 44.70 | 92.40 | 10 00–10 99 |
| 11 00–11 99 | ....... | ....... | ....... | ....... | ....... | ....... | ....... | 1 | ....... | 4 | ....... | 93.50 | 11 00–11 99 |
| 12 00–12 99 | ....... | ....... | 1 | ....... | ....... | ....... | ....... | 1 | 2 | 9 | 47.70 | 96.20 | 12 00–12 99 |
| 13 00–13 99 | ....... | ....... | ....... | ....... | ....... | ....... | ....... | ....... | 2 | ....... | 50.70 | ....... | 13 00–13 99 |
| 14 00–14 99 | ....... | ....... | ....... | ....... | 1 | ....... | ....... | ....... | 5 | 2 | 58.20 | 96.80 | 14 00–14 99 |
| 15 00–15 99 | ....... | ....... | 1 | ....... | 1 | ....... | ....... | ....... | 2 | 4 | 61.20 | 98.00 | 15 00–15 99 |
| 16 00–17 99 | 1 | 1 | ....... | ....... | ....... | ....... | ....... | ....... | 4 | 4 | 67.10 | 99.50 | 16 00–17 99 |
| 18 00–19 99 | 1 | ....... | ....... | ....... | ....... | ....... | 1 | ....... | 4 | 1 | 73.00 | 99.40 | 18 00–19 99 |
| 20 00–24 99 | ....... | 1 | ....... | ....... | 1 | ....... | ....... | ....... | 7 | 2 | 83.50 | 100.00 | 20 00–24 99 |
| 25 00–29 99 | 1 | ....... | 1 | ....... | ....... | ....... | ....... | ....... | 7 | ....... | 94.00 | ....... | 25 00–29 99 |
| 30 00–34 99 | ....... | ....... | ....... | ....... | ....... | ....... | 1 | ....... | 1 | ....... | 95.05 | ....... | 30 00–34 99 |
| 35 00–39 99 | 1 | ....... | ....... | ....... | ....... | ....... | ....... | ....... | 2 | ....... | 98.50 | ....... | 35 00–39 99 |
| 40 00 and over | ....... | ....... | ....... | ....... | ....... | ....... | ....... | ....... | 1 | ....... | 100.00 | ....... | 40 00 and over |
| Not reported | ....... | ....... | ....... | ....... | ....... | ....... | ....... | ....... | ....... | 1 | ....... | ....... | Not reported |
| Total | 4 | 3 | 4 | 1 | 3 | 1 | 2 | 4 | 67 | 343 | ....... | ....... | Total |

228. TABLE IX, A, 2, a

NEW YORK CITY
NEIGHBORHOOD STORES — OFFICE

NUMBER AND PER CENT. OF EMPLOYEES CLASSIFIED ACCORDING TO ACTUAL WEEKLY EARNINGS, BY OCCUPATION AND SEX

| ACTUAL WEEKLY RATES IN DOLLARS | OCCUPATION: SUPERINTENDENTS | BOOKKEEPERS | | CLERKS | | STENOGRAPHERS | | OFFICE BOYS | CASHIERS | | TELEPHONE OPERATORS | AUDITORS | DETECTIVES | ADVERTISERS AND WINDOW DRESSERS | | TOTAL | | CUMULATIVE PER CENT. OF TOTAL | | WEEKLY RATES IN DOLLARS |
|---|---|---|---|---|---|---|---|---|---|---|---|---|---|---|---|---|---|---|---|---|
| | Male | Male | Female | Male | Female | Male | Female | Male | Male | Female | Female | Female | Female | Male | Female | Male | Female | Male | Female | |
| Less than $3 00 | | | | 1 | | | | | | 4 | | 1 | | | | 1 | 5 | 1.50 | 1.50 | Less than $3 00 |
| $3 00–$3 49 | | | 1 | | 3 | | | | | 5 | | 5 | | | | | 14 | | 5.60 | $3 00– 3 49 |
| 3 50– 3 99 | | | 1 | | 5 | | | | | 10 | | 5 | | | | | 21 | | 11.70 | 3 50– 3 99 |
| 4 00– 4 49 | | | 4 | | 11 | | | 1 | | 18 | 1 | 9 | | | | 1 | 43 | 3.00 | 24.20 | 4 00– 4 49 |
| 4 50– 4 99 | | | 1 | | 9 | | | | | 15 | | 3 | | | | | 28 | | 32.40 | 4 50– 4 99 |
| 5 00– 5 49 | | | 2 | 1 | 8 | 1 | | | | 22 | 2 | 11 | | 5 | | 7 | 45 | 13.40 | 45.60 | 5 00– 5 49 |
| 5 50– 5 99 | | | | 1 | 2 | | | | | 17 | 2 | 3 | | | | 1 | 24 | 14.90 | 52.60 | 5 50– 5 99 |
| 6 00– 6 49 | | | 3 | 1 | 9 | | 3 | | | 20 | 1 | 4 | | 1 | | 2 | 40 | 17.90 | 64.40 | 6 00– 6 49 |
| 6 50– 6 99 | | | | | 1 | | | | | 3 | | | | | | | 4 | | 65.50 | 6 50– 6 99 |
| 7 00– 7 49 | | 1 | 4 | | 4 | | 3 | | 1 | 29 | 1 | 4 | | 5 | | 7 | 45 | 28.40 | 78.60 | 7 00– 7 49 |
| 7 50– 7 99 | | | 1 | 1 | 1 | | 1 | | | 4 | | | | | | 1 | 7 | 29.80 | 80.70 | 7 50– 7 99 |
| 8 00– 8 99 | | 2 | | | 6 | | 1 | | | 8 | | 1 | | 2 | 2 | 4 | 18 | 35.80 | 86.00 | 8 00– 8 99 |
| 9 00– 9 99 | | | 3 | 2 | 4 | | | | | 1 | | 3 | | | | 2 | 11 | 38.80 | 89.20 | 9 00– 9 99 |
| 10 00–10 99 | | | 5 | 1 | 3 | | 1 | | | 1 | 1 | | | 3 | | 4 | 11 | 44.70 | 92.40 | 10 00–10 99 |
| 11 00–11 99 | | | | | 2 | | | | | 1 | | 1 | | | | | 4 | | 93.50 | 11 00–11 99 |
| 12 00–12 99 | | | 2 | 2 | 1 | | 3 | | | 1 | | 1 | 1 | | | 2 | 9 | 47.70 | 96.20 | 12 00–12 99 |
| 13 00–13 99 | | | | 2 | | | | | | | | | | | | 2 | | 50.70 | | 13 00–13 99 |
| 14 00–14 99 | | 2 | 1 | 3 | | | | | | 1 | | | | | | 5 | 2 | 58.20 | 96.80 | 14 00–14 99 |
| 15 00–15 99 | | | 1 | 1 | 1 | | | | | 1 | | 1 | | 1 | | 2 | 4 | 61.20 | 98.00 | 15 00–15 99 |
| 16 00–17 99 | | 1 | 1 | | 2 | | | | | | | 1 | | 3 | | 4 | 4 | 67.10 | 99.10 | 16 00–17 99 |
| 18 00–19 99 | | | 1 | 2 | | | | | | | | | | 2 | | 4 | 1 | 73.00 | 99.40 | 18 00–19 99 |
| 20 00–24 99 | | 2 | | 1 | | | 1 | | | 1 | | | | 4 | | 7 | 2 | 83.50 | 100.00 | 20 00–24 99 |
| 25 00–29 99 | | | | | | | | | | | | | | 7 | | 7 | | 94.00 | | 25 00–29 99 |
| 30 00–34 99 | | | | | | | | | | | | | | 1 | | 1 | | 95.50 | | 30 00–34 99 |
| 35 00–39 99 | 1 | | | | | | | | | | | | | 1 | | 2 | | 98.50 | | 35 00–39 99 |
| 40 00 and over | | | | | | | | | | | | | | 1 | | 1 | | 100.00 | | 40 00 and over |
| Not reported | | | | | 1 | | | | | | | | | | | | 1 | | | Not reported |
| Total | 1 | 8 | 31 | 19 | 73 | 1 | 13 | 1 | 1 | 162 | 8 | 53 | 1 | 36 | 2 | 67 | 343 | | | Total |

NEW YORK CITY

229. TABLE XV, A,2, c, d, e NEIGHBORHOOD STORES — SHIPPING AND DELIVERY, MANUFACTURING, PLANT

NUMBER OF EMPLOYEES EARNING SPECIFIED WEEKLY RATES, ACCORDING TO DEPARTMENT AND SEX

| WEEKLY RATES IN DOLLARS | DEPARTMENT | | | | | | | | | WEEKLY RATES IN DOLLARS |
|---|---|---|---|---|---|---|---|---|---|---|
| | SHIPPING AND DELIVERY | MANUFACTURING | | PLANT | | TOTAL | | CUMULATIVE PER CENT OF TOTAL | | |
| | Male | Male | Female | Male | Female | Male | Female | Male | Female | |
| $3 00–$3 49 | ........ | ........ | ........ | ........ | 3 | ........ | 3 | ........ | 6.40 | $3 00–$3 49 |
| 3 50– 3 99 | ........ | ........ | ........ | 1 | ........ | 1 | ........ | .30 | ........ | 3 50– 3 99 |
| 4 00– 4 49 | 5 | ........ | 1 | 2 | ........ | 7 | 1 | 2.20 | 8.50 | 4 00– 4 49 |
| 4 50– 4 99 | 4 | ........ | ........ | ........ | ........ | 4 | ........ | 3.30 | ........ | 4 50– 4 99 |
| 5 00– 5 49 | 34 | ........ | 1 | 7 | 6 | 41 | 7 | 14.50 | 23.40 | 5 00– 5 49 |
| 5 50– 5 99 | 2 | ........ | ........ | 1 | ........ | 3 | ........ | 15.30 | ........ | 5 50– 5 99 |
| 6 00– 6 49 | 29 | ........ | 1 | 5 | 4 | 34 | 5 | 24.50 | 34.00 | 6 00– 6 49 |
| 6 50– 6 99 | 2 | ........ | ........ | ........ | 2 | 2 | 2 | 25.10 | 38.30 | 6 50– 6 99 |
| 7 00– 7 49 | 5 | ........ | 3 | 3 | 3 | 8 | 6 | 27.30 | 51.00 | 7 00– 7 49 |
| 7 50– 7 99 | 1 | ........ | ........ | 3 | 1 | 4 | 1 | 28.40 | 53.20 | 7 50– 7 99 |
| 8 00– 8 99 | 7 | 1 | 3 | 10 | 1 | 18 | 4 | 33.20 | 61.60 | 8 00– 8 99 |
| 9 00– 9 99 | 4 | ........ | 2 | 8 | ........ | 12 | 2 | 36.50 | 66.00 | 9 00– 9 99 |
| 10 00–10 99 | 19 | ........ | 7 | 15 | ........ | 34 | 7 | 45.80 | 80.70 | 10 00–10 99 |
| 11 00–11 99 | 3 | 2 | 1 | 10 | ........ | 15 | 1 | 49.90 | 83.00 | 11 00–11 99 |
| 12 00–12 99 | 59 | 3 | 2 | 26 | ........ | 88 | 2 | 73.90 | 87.20 | 12 00–12 99 |
| 13 00–13 99 | 19 | 1 | ........ | 6 | ........ | 26 | ........ | 81.10 | ........ | 13 00–13 99 |
| 14 00–14 99 | 8 | 4 | 2 | 6 | ........ | 18 | 2 | 85.90 | 91.50 | 14 00–14 99 |
| 15 00–15 99 | 5 | 5 | 1 | 7 | ........ | 17 | 1 | 87.80 | 93.60 | 15 00–15 99 |
| 16 00–17 99 | 7 | 6 | ........ | 3 | ........ | 16 | ........ | 94.90 | ........ | 16 00–17 99 |
| 18 00–19 99 | 2 | 3 | 1 | 3 | ........ | 8 | 1 | 97.00 | 95.70 | 18 00–19 99 |
| 20 00–24 99 | 4 | 1 | 2 | 2 | ........ | 7 | 2 | 99.00 | 100.00 | 20 00–24 99 |
| 25 00–29 99 | 1 | ........ | ........ | 1 | ........ | 2 | ........ | 99.50 | ........ | 25 00–29 99 |
| 30 00–34 99 | 1 | ........ | ........ | ........ | ........ | 1 | ........ | 99.80 | ........ | 30 00–34 99 |
| 40 00 and over | ........ | 1 | ........ | ........ | ........ | 1 | ........ | 100.00 | ........ | 40 00 and over |
| Total | 221 | 27 | 27 | 119 | 20 | 367 | 47 | ........ | ........ | Total |

NEW YORK CITY

230. TABLE XVI, A, 2, c, d, e NEIGHBORHOOD STORES — SHIPPING AND DELIVERY, MANUFACTURING, PLANT

NUMBER OF EMPLOYEES CLASSIFIED ACCORDING TO ACTUAL WEEKLY EARNINGS, BY DEPARTMENT AND SEX

| ACTUAL WEEKLY EARNINGS IN DOLLARS | DEPARTMENT | | | | | | | | | ACTUAL WEEKLY EARNINGS IN DOLLARS |
|---|---|---|---|---|---|---|---|---|---|---|
| | SHIPPING AND DELIVERY | MANUFACTURING | | PLANT | | TOTAL | | CUMULATIVE PER CENT OF TOTAL | | |
| | Male | Male | Female | Male | Female | Male | Female | Male | Female | |
| Less than $3 00 | 7 | ........ | ........ | ........ | ........ | 7 | ........ | 1.90 | ........ | Less than $3 00 |
| $3 00–$3 49 | 1 | ........ | ........ | 1 | 3 | 2 | 3 | 2.50 | 6.20 | $3 00– 3 49 |
| 3 50– 3 99 | ........ | ........ | ........ | 1 | ........ | 1 | ........ | 2.70 | ........ | 3 50– 3 99 |
| 4 00– 4 49 | 5 | ........ | 1 | 3 | ........ | 8 | 1 | 4.90 | 8.30 | 4 00– 4 49 |
| 4 50– 4 99 | 4 | ........ | ........ | ........ | ........ | 4 | ........ | 6.00 | ........ | 4 50– 4 99 |
| 5 00– 5 49 | 33 | ........ | 1 | 8 | 6 | 41 | 7 | 17.20 | 22.90 | 5 00– 5 49 |
| 5 50– 5 99 | 2 | ........ | ........ | 2 | ........ | 4 | ........ | 18.30 | ........ | 5 50– 5 99 |
| 6 00– 6 49 | 26 | ........ | 1 | 4 | 5 | 30 | 6 | 26.40 | 35.40 | 6 00– 6 49 |
| 6 50– 6 99 | 2 | ........ | ........ | 2 | 2 | 4 | 2 | 27.50 | 39.60 | 6 50– 6 99 |
| 7 00– 7 49 | 6 | ........ | 3 | 2 | 3 | 8 | 6 | 29.90 | 52.10 | 7 00– 7 49 |
| 7 50– 7 99 | 1 | ........ | ........ | 4 | ........ | 5 | ........ | 31.10 | ........ | 7 50– 7 99 |
| 8 00– 8 99 | 8 | 1 | 3 | 8 | 1 | 17 | 4 | 35.70 | 60.40 | 8 00– 8 99 |
| 9 00– 9 99 | 4 | 1 | 3 | 5 | ........ | 10 | 3 | 38.40 | 66.70 | 9 00– 9 99 |
| 10 00–10 99 | 18 | ........ | 6 | 16 | ........ | 34 | 6 | 47.70 | 79.20 | 10 00–10 99 |
| 11 00–11 99 | 3 | 3 | 2 | 12 | ........ | 18 | 2 | 52.60 | 83.40 | 11 00–11 99 |
| 12 00–12 99 | 53 | 3 | 2 | 24 | ........ | 80 | 2 | 74.40 | 87.50 | 12 00–12 99 |
| 13 00–13 99 | 20 | 1 | ........ | 4 | ........ | 25 | ........ | 81.30 | ........ | 13 00–13 99 |
| 14 00–14 99 | 9 | 1 | 2 | 5 | ........ | 15 | 2 | 85.40 | 91.60 | 14 00–14 99 |
| 15 00–15 99 | 5 | 6 | 1 | 8 | ........ | 19 | 1 | 90.50 | 93.80 | 15 00–15 99 |
| 16 00–17 99 | 6 | 5 | ........ | 3 | ........ | 14 | ........ | 94.30 | ........ | 16 00–17 99 |
| 18 00–19 99 | 2 | 4 | 1 | 4 | ........ | 10 | 1 | 97.10 | 95.90 | 18 00–19 99 |
| 20 00–24 99 | 4 | ........ | 2 | 2 | ........ | 6 | 2 | 98.60 | 100.00 | 20 00–24 99 |
| 25 00–29 99 | 1 | 1 | ........ | 1 | ........ | 3 | ........ | 99.50 | ........ | 25 00–29 99 |
| 30 00–34 99 | 1 | ........ | ........ | ........ | ........ | 1 | ........ | 99.80 | ........ | 30 00–34 99 |
| 40 00 and over | ........ | 1 | ........ | ........ | ........ | 1 | ........ | 100.00 | ........ | 40 00 and over |
| Total | 221 | 27 | 28 | 119 | 20 | 367 | 48 | ........ | ...... | Total |

NEW YORK CITY

231. TABLE A, 2, c. d. e — NEIGHBORHOOD STORES — SHIPPING AND DELIVERY, MANUFACTURING, PLANT

NUMBER OF EMPLOYEES CLASSIFIED ACCORDING TO AGE GROUPS ACCORDING TO DEPARTMENT AND SEX

| AGE GROUPS IN YEARS | DEPARTMENT | | | | | | | | | AGE GROUPS IN YEARS |
|---|---|---|---|---|---|---|---|---|---|---|
| | SHIPPING AND DELIVERY | MANUFACTURING | | PLANT | | TOTAL | | PER CENT OF TOTAL | | |
| | Male | Male | Female | Male | Female | Male | Female | Male | Female | |
| 14–15 | 7 | .......... | .......... | 1 | .......... | 8 | .......... | 2.20 | .......... | 14–15 |
| 16–17 | 41 | .......... | 2 | 9 | .......... | 50 | 2 | 13.60 | 4.20 | 16–17 |
| 18–20 | 41 | .......... | 4 | 12 | .......... | 53 | 4 | 14.40 | 8.30 | 18–20 |
| 21–24 | 47 | 1 | 1 | 11 | 1 | 59 | 2 | 16.10 | 4.20 | 21–24 |
| 25–29 | 24 | 5 | 2 | 12 | 4 | 41 | 6 | 11.20 | 12.50 | 25–29 |
| 30–34 | 19 | 5 | 3 | 10 | 2 | 34 | 5 | 9.30 | 10.40 | 30–34 |
| 35–39 | 12 | 2 | 5 | 8 | 2 | 22 | 7 | 6.00 | 14.60 | 35–39 |
| 40–44 | 8 | 6 | 6 | 14 | 6 | 28 | 12 | 7.60 | 25.00 | 40–44 |
| 45–54 | 15 | 5 | 4 | 23 | 4 | 43 | 8 | 11.70 | 16.60 | 45–54 |
| 55–64 | 5 | 3 | .......... | 10 | 1 | 18 | 1 | 4.90 | 2.10 | 55–64 |
| 65 and over | 1 | .......... | .......... | 7 | .......... | 8 | .......... | 2.20 | .......... | 65 and over |
| Not reported | 1 | .......... | 1 | 2 | .......... | 3 | 1 | .80 | 2.10 | Not reported |
| Total | 221 | 27 | 28 | 119 | 20 | 367 | 48 | .......... | .......... | Total |

232. TABLE V, A, 3, a

NEW YORK CITY

**FIVE AND TEN CENT STORES — STOCK AND SALES**

NUMBER AND PER CENT OF EMPLOYEES EARNING SPECIFIED WEEKLY RATES, BY AGE GROUPS AND SEX

| WEEKLY RATES IN YEARS | AGE GROUPS IN YEARS | | | | | | | | | | | | WEEKLY RATES IN YEARS |
|---|---|---|---|---|---|---|---|---|---|---|---|---|---|
| | 14–15 | | 16–17 | | 18–20 | | 21–24 | | 25–29 | | 30–34 | | |
| | Male | Female | Male | Female | Male | Female | Male | Female | Male | Female | Male | Female | |
| Less than $3 00. | ....... | ....... | ....... | ....... | ....... | ....... | ....... | ....... | ....... | ....... | ....... | ....... | Less than $3 00 |
| $3 00– $3 49... | 1 | ....... | 1 | 1 | ....... | ....... | ....... | ....... | ....... | ....... | ....... | ....... | ...$3 00– 3 49 |
| 3 50– 3 99.... | ....... | ....... | ....... | ....... | ....... | ....... | ....... | ....... | ....... | ....... | ....... | ....... | ... 3 50– 3 99 |
| 4 00– 4 49.... | 1 | ....... | ....... | 1 | ....... | 1 | ....... | ....... | ....... | ....... | ....... | ....... | ... 4 00– 4 49 |
| 4 50– 4 99.... | 1 | ....... | ....... | 35 | ....... | 21 | ....... | 2 | ....... | ....... | ....... | ....... | ... 4 50– 4 89 |
| 5 00– 5 49.... | 2 | 2 | 2 | 64 | ....... | 73 | ....... | 29 | ....... | 11 | ....... | 3 | ... 5 00– 5 49 |
| 5 50– 5 99.... | ....... | ....... | ....... | 12 | ....... | 35 | ....... | 9 | ....... | 5 | ....... | ....... | ... 5 50– 5 99 |
| 6 00– 6 49.... | ....... | ....... | 1 | 22 | 1 | 55 | ....... | 28 | ....... | 10 | ....... | 1 | ... 6 00– 6 49 |
| 6 50– 6 99.... | ....... | ....... | ....... | ....... | ....... | 10 | ....... | 14 | ....... | 4 | ....... | ....... | ... 6 50– 6 99 |
| 7 00– 7 49.... | ....... | ....... | 1 | 1 | 1 | 17 | 2 | 19 | ....... | 5 | ....... | 4 | ... 7 00– 7 49 |
| 7 50– 7 99.... | ....... | ....... | ....... | ....... | ....... | 2 | ....... | 5 | ....... | 2 | ....... | ....... | ... 7 50– 7 99 |
| 8 00– 8 99.... | ....... | ....... | ....... | 1 | 4 | 3 | ....... | 7 | 1 | 6 | ....... | 1 | ... 8 00– 8 99 |
| 9 00– 9 99.... | ....... | ....... | 1 | ....... | 1 | 1 | 2 | 5 | 1 | ....... | 1 | 2 | ... 9 00– 9 99 |
| 10 00–10 99.... | ....... | ....... | ....... | 1 | 5 | 2 | 5 | 2 | 1 | 4 | 1 | ....... | ...10 00–10 99 |
| 11 00–11 99.... | ....... | ....... | ....... | 1 | ....... | ....... | 4 | 2 | ....... | ....... | 2 | ....... | ...11 00–11 99 |
| 12 00–12 99.... | ....... | ....... | ....... | ....... | 1 | 1 | 5 | ....... | 3 | 1 | 2 | 1 | ...12 00–12 99 |
| 13 00–13 99.... | ....... | ....... | ....... | ....... | ....... | ....... | 1 | ....... | 1 | ....... | 1 | ....... | ...13 00–13 99 |
| 14 00–14 99.... | ....... | ....... | ....... | ....... | ....... | ....... | 1 | ....... | 2 | ....... | ....... | ....... | ...14 00–14 99 |
| 15 00–15 99.... | ....... | ....... | ....... | ....... | ....... | 1 | 2 | 1 | 3 | ....... | ....... | ....... | ...15 00–15 99 |
| 16 00–17 99.... | ....... | ....... | ....... | ....... | ....... | ....... | ....... | ....... | 1 | ....... | ....... | ....... | ...16 00–17 99 |
| Not reported.... | ....... | ....... | ....... | ....... | ....... | 2 | ....... | ....... | 1 | ....... | ....... | ....... | ...Not reported |
| Total..... | 5 | 2 | 6 | 139 | 13 | 224 | 22 | 123 | 14 | 48 | 7 | 12 | .....Total |

232. TABLE V. A, 3, a —(*concluded*)

NEW YORK CITY

FIVE AND TEN CENT STORES — STOCK AND SALES

NUMBER AND PER CENT OF EMPLOYEES EARNING SPECIFIED WEEKLY RATES, BY AGE GROUPS AND SEX

| WEEKLY RATES IN YEARS | AGE GROUPS IN YEARS (*concluded*) | | | | | | | | | | | WEEKLY RATES IN YEARS |
|---|---|---|---|---|---|---|---|---|---|---|---|---|
| | 35–39 | | 40–44 | | 45–54 | | 55–64 | Total | | CUMULATIVE PER CENT OF TOTAL | | |
| | Male | Female | Male | Female | Male | Female | Male | Male | Female | Male | Female | |
| $3 00– $3 49 | | | | | | | | 2 | 1 | 2.70 | .20 | $3 00– $3 49 |
| 4 00– 4 49 | | 1 | | | | | | 1 | 3 | 4.00 | .70 | 4 00– 4 49 |
| 4 50– 4 99 | | | | | | | | 1 | 58 | 5.30 | 11.20 | 4 50– 4 99 |
| 5 00– 5 49 | | | | | | | | 4 | 182 | 10.70 | 44.20 | 5 00– 5 49 |
| 5 50– 5 99 | | | | | | | | | 61 | | 55.30 | 5 50– 5 99 |
| 6 00– 6 49 | | | | | | 1 | | 2 | 117 | 13.30 | 76.50 | 6 00– 6 49 |
| 6 50– 6 99 | | | | | | | | | 28 | | 81.50 | 6 50– 6 99 |
| 7 00– 7 49 | | | | 2 | | 1 | | 4 | 49 | 18.60 | 90.50 | 7 00– 7 49 |
| 7 50– 7 99 | | | | | | | | | 9 | | 92.10 | 7 50– 7 99 |
| 8 00– 8 99 | | | | | | | | 5 | 18 | 26.40 | 95.50 | 8 00– 8 99 |
| 9 00– 9 99 | | | | | 1 | | | 7 | 8 | 34.60 | 96.80 | 9 00– 9 99 |
| 10 00–10 99 | 1 | | | | | | | 13 | 9 | 52.00 | 98.50 | 10 00–10 99 |
| 11 00–11 99 | | | | | | | 1 | 7 | 3 | 61.30 | 99.00 | 11 00–11 99 |
| 12 00–12 99 | | | | | 1 | | | 12 | 3 | 77.40 | 99.50 | 12 00–12 99 |
| 13 00–13 99 | | | | | | | | 3 | | 81.30 | | 13 00–13 99 |
| 14 00–14 99 | | | 1 | | 1 | | | 5 | | 88.00 | | 14 00–14 99 |
| 15 00–15 99 | 1 | | 1 | | | | | 7 | 2 | 97.30 | 100.00 | 15 00–15 99 |
| 16 00–17 99 | | | 1 | | | | | 2 | | 100.00 | | 16 00–17 99 |
| Not reported | | 1 | | | | | | 1 | 3 | | | Not reported |
| Total | 2 | 2 | 3 | 2 | 3 | 2 | 1 | 76 | 554 | | | Total |

233. TABLE VIII, A, 3, a

NEW YORK CITY

**FIVE AND TEN CENT STORES — STOCK AND SALES**

Number and Per Cent of Employees Earning Specified Weekly Rates by Occupation and Sex

| Weekly Rates in Dollars | Occupation | | | | | | | | | | | | | Weekly Rates in Dollars |
|---|---|---|---|---|---|---|---|---|---|---|---|---|---|---|
| | Superintendents | Assistant Buyers and Heads of Stock | Receiving and Stock Clerks | Stock People | Floor Managers | | Sales People | | Messengers, Wrappers, Errand Boys | Total | | Cumulative Per Cent of Total | | |
| | Male | Male | Male | Male | Male | Female | Male | Female | Male | Male | Female | Male | Female | |
| $3 00– $3 49 | ...... | ...... | ...... | ...... | ...... | ...... | ...... | 1 | 2 | 2 | 1 | 2.70 | .20 | $3 00– $3 49 |
| 4 00– 4 49 | ...... | ...... | ...... | ...... | ...... | ...... | ...... | 3 | 1 | 1 | 3 | 4.00 | .70 | 4 00– 4 49 |
| 4 50– 4 99 | ...... | ...... | ...... | ...... | ...... | ...... | 1 | 58 | ...... | 1 | 58 | 5.30 | 11.20 | 4 50– 4 99 |
| 5 00– 5 49 | ...... | ...... | ...... | 2 | ...... | ...... | 1 | 182 | 1 | 4 | 182 | 10.70 | 44.20 | 5 00– 5 49 |
| 5 50– 5 99 | ...... | ...... | ...... | ...... | ...... | ...... | ...... | 61 | ...... | ...... | 61 | ...... | 55.30 | 5 50– 5 99 |
| 6 00– 6 49 | ...... | ...... | ...... | 2 | ...... | 1 | ...... | 116 | ...... | 2 | 117 | 13.30 | 76.50 | 6 00– 6 49 |
| 6 50– 6 99 | ...... | ...... | ...... | ...... | ...... | ...... | ...... | 28 | ...... | ...... | 28 | ...... | 81.50 | 6 50– 6 99 |
| 7 00– 7 49 | ...... | ...... | 1 | 2 | 1 | 5 | ...... | 44 | ...... | 4 | 49 | 18.60 | 90.50 | 7 00– 7 49 |
| 7 50– 7 99 | ...... | ...... | ...... | ...... | ...... | 2 | ...... | 7 | ...... | ...... | 9 | ...... | 92.10 | 7 50– 7 99 |
| 8 00– 8 99 | ...... | ...... | 2 | 2 | ...... | 1 | 1 | 17 | ...... | 5 | 18 | 26.40 | 95.50 | 8 00– 8 99 |
| 9 00– 9 99 | ...... | ...... | 3 | 2 | 2 | 2 | ...... | 6 | ...... | 7 | 8 | 34.60 | 96.80 | 9 00– 9 99 |
| 10 00–10 99 | ...... | ...... | 4 | 3 | 5 | 7 | 1 | 2 | ...... | 13 | 9 | 52.00 | 98.50 | 10 00–10 99 |
| 11 00–11 99 | ...... | ...... | ...... | 4 | 2 | 1 | 1 | 2 | ...... | 7 | 3 | 61.30 | 99.00 | 11 00–11 99 |
| 12 00–12 99 | 2 | ...... | 1 | 5 | 3 | 2 | 1 | 1 | ...... | 12 | 3 | 77.40 | 99.50 | 12 00–12 99 |
| 13 00–13 99 | 1 | 1 | ...... | ...... | 1 | ...... | ...... | ...... | ...... | 3 | ...... | 81.30 | ...... | 13 00–13 99 |
| 14 00–14 99 | ...... | ...... | 4 | 1 | ...... | ...... | ...... | ...... | ...... | 5 | ...... | 88.00 | ...... | 14 00–14 99 |
| 15 00–15 99 | ...... | ...... | 2 | 1 | 2 | 1 | 2 | 1 | ...... | 7 | 2 | 97.30 | 100.00 | 15 00–15 99 |
| 16 00–17 99 | ...... | ...... | 1 | 1 | ...... | ...... | ...... | ...... | ...... | 2 | ...... | 100.00 | ...... | 16 00–17 99 |
| Not reported | ...... | ...... | ...... | ...... | 1 | ...... | ...... | 3 | ...... | 1 | 3 | ...... | ...... | Not reported |
| Total | 3 | 1 | 18 | 25 | 17 | 22 | 8 | 532 | 4 | 76 | 554 | ...... | ...... | Total |

234. TABLE VI, A, 3, a

NEW YORK CITY

FIVE AND TEN CENT STORES — STOCK AND SALES

NUMBER AND PER CENT OF EMPLOYEES CLASSIFIED ACCORDING TO ACTUAL WEEKLY EARNINGS BY AGE GROUPS AND SEX

| Actual Weekly Earnings in Dollars | Age Groups in Years | | | | | | | | | | | | Actual Weekly Earnings in Dollars |
|---|---|---|---|---|---|---|---|---|---|---|---|---|---|
| | 14–15 | | 16–17 | | 18–20 | | 21–24 | | 25–29 | | 30–34 | | |
| | Male | Female | Male | Female | Male | Female | Male | Female | Male | Female | Male | Female | |
| Less than $3 00 | ....... | 1 | ....... | 8 | ....... | 5 | ....... | 3 | ....... | 1 | ....... | ....... | Less than $3 00 |
| $3 00–$3 49 | ....... | ....... | ....... | 2 | ....... | 3 | ....... | 1 | ....... | ....... | ....... | ....... | $3 00– 3 49 |
| 3 50– 3 99 | 1 | ....... | 1 | ....... | ....... | 4 | ....... | 1 | ....... | ....... | ....... | 1 | 3 50– 3 99 |
| 4 00– 4 49 | ....... | ....... | ....... | 8 | ....... | 9 | ....... | 3 | ....... | 2 | ....... | ....... | 4 00– 4 49 |
| 4 50– 4 99 | 2 | ....... | ....... | 26 | ....... | 19 | ....... | 7 | ....... | 2 | ....... | ....... | 4 50– 4 99 |
| 5 00– 5 49 | 1 | 1 | 1 | 47 | 1 | 51 | ....... | 15 | ....... | 8 | ....... | 2 | 5 00– 5 49 |
| 5 50– 5 99 | 1 | ....... | ....... | 20 | ....... | 37 | ....... | 12 | ....... | 4 | ....... | ....... | 5 50– 5 99 |
| 6 00– 6 49 | ....... | ....... | 2 | 20 | 1 | 48 | ....... | 18 | ....... | 7 | ....... | 1 | 6 00– 6 49 |
| 6 50– 6 99 | ....... | ....... | 1 | 4 | ....... | 19 | ....... | 19 | ....... | 6 | ....... | 1 | 6 50– 6 99 |
| 7 00– 7 49 | ....... | ....... | ....... | 1 | 1 | 17 | ....... | 18 | ....... | 2 | ....... | ....... | 7 00– 7 49 |
| 7 50– 7 99 | ....... | ....... | ....... | ....... | ....... | 2 | 2 | 8 | ....... | 6 | ....... | 3 | 7 50– 7 99 |
| 8 00– 8 99 | ....... | ....... | ....... | 1 | 3 | 5 | ....... | 7 | 1 | 5 | ....... | 1 | 8 00– 8 99 |
| 9 00– 9 99 | ....... | ....... | 1 | ....... | 1 | 1 | 2 | 6 | 1 | 1 | ....... | 2 | 9 00– 9 99 |
| 10 00–10 99 | ....... | ....... | ....... | 1 | 3 | 2 | 2 | 2 | 1 | 1 | ....... | ....... | 10 00–10 99 |
| 11 00–11 99 | ....... | ....... | ....... | 1 | 2 | ....... | 4 | 2 | ....... | 2 | 4 | ....... | 11 00–11 99 |
| 12 00–12 99 | ....... | ....... | ....... | ....... | 1 | 1 | 6 | ....... | 4 | ....... | ....... | ....... | 12 00–12 99 |
| 13 00–13 99 | ....... | ....... | ....... | ....... | ....... | ....... | 2 | ....... | ....... | 1 | 1 | 1 | 13 00–13 99 |
| 14 00–14 99 | ....... | ....... | ....... | ....... | ....... | ....... | 2 | ....... | 2 | ....... | 2 | ....... | 14 00–14 99 |
| 15 00–15 99 | ....... | ....... | ....... | ....... | ....... | 1 | 2 | ....... | 3 | ....... | ....... | ....... | 15 00–15 99 |
| 16 00–17 99 | ....... | ....... | ....... | ....... | ....... | ....... | ....... | 1 | 2 | ....... | ....... | ....... | 16 00–17 99 |
| Total | 5 | 2 | 6 | 139 | 13 | 224 | 22 | 123 | 14 | 48 | 7 | 12 | Total |

234. TABLE VI, A, 3, a — (*concluded*)

## NEW YORK CITY
## FIVE AND TEN CENT STORES — STOCK AND SALES

Number and Per Cent of Employees Classified According to Actual Weekly Earnings by Age Groups and Sex

| Actual Weekly Earnings in Dollars | Age Groups in Years (*concluded*) | | | | | | | | | | | Actual Weekly Earnings in Dollars |
|---|---|---|---|---|---|---|---|---|---|---|---|---|
| | 35–39 | | 40–44 | | 45–54 | | 55–64 | Total | | Cumulative Per Cent of Total | | |
| | Male | Female | Male | Female | Male | Female | Male | Male | Female | Male | Female | |
| Less than $3 00 | ........ | ........ | ........ | ........ | ........ | ........ | ........ | ........ | 18 | ........ | 3.20 | Less than $3 00 |
| $3 00–$3 49... | ........ | ........ | ........ | ........ | ........ | ........ | ........ | ........ | 6 | ........ | 4.30 | ...$3 00– 3 49 |
| 3 50– 3 99... | ........ | ........ | ........ | ........ | ........ | ........ | ........ | 2 | 6 | 2.60 | 5.40 | ... 3 50– 3 99 |
| 4 00– 4 49... | ........ | 2 | ........ | ........ | ........ | ........ | ........ | ........ | 24 | ........ | 9.70 | ... 4 00– 4 49 |
| 4 50– 4 99... | ........ | ........ | ........ | ........ | ........ | ........ | ........ | 2 | 54 | 5.30 | 19.50 | ... 4 50– 4 99 |
| 5 00– 5 49... | ........ | ........ | ........ | ........ | ........ | ........ | ........ | 3 | 124 | 9.20 | 41.90 | ... 5 00– 5 49 |
| 5 50– 5 99... | ........ | ........ | ........ | ........ | ........ | 1 | ........ | 1 | 74 | 10.50 | 45.20 | ... 5 50– 5 99 |
| 6 00– 6 49... | ........ | ........ | ........ | 1 | ........ | ........ | ........ | 3 | 95 | 14.50 | 72.30 | ... 6 00– 6 49 |
| 6 50– 6 99... | ........ | ........ | ........ | ........ | ........ | ........ | ........ | 1 | 49 | 15.80 | 81.20 | ... 6 50– 6 99 |
| 7 00– 7 49... | ........ | ........ | ........ | ........ | ........ | ........ | ........ | 1 | 38 | 17.10 | 88.00 | ... 7 00– 7 49 |
| 7 50– 7 99... | ........ | ........ | ........ | 1 | ........ | 1 | ........ | 2 | 21 | 19.70 | 91.80 | ... 7 50– 7 99 |
| 8 00– 8 99... | ........ | ........ | ........ | ........ | ........ | ........ | ........ | 4 | 19 | 25.00 | 95.40 | ... 8 00– 8 99 |
| 9 00– 9 99... | ........ | ........ | ........ | ........ | 1 | ........ | ........ | 6 | 10 | 32.90 | 97.00 | ... 9 00– 9 99 |
| 10 00–10 99... | ........ | ........ | ........ | ........ | ........ | ........ | ........ | 6 | 6 | 40.80 | 98.10 | ...10 00–10 99 |
| 11 00–11 99... | 1 | ........ | ........ | ........ | ........ | ........ | ........ | 11 | 5 | 55.30 | 99.10 | ...11 00–11 99 |
| 12 00–12 99... | ........ | ........ | ........ | ........ | ........ | ........ | 1 | 12 | 1 | 71.00 | 99.20 | ...12 00–12 99 |
| 13 00–13 99... | ........ | ........ | ........ | ........ | 1 | ........ | ........ | 4 | 2 | 76.30 | 99.60 | ...13 00–13 99 |
| 14 00–14 99... | ........ | ........ | ........ | ........ | ........ | ........ | ........ | 6 | ........ | 84.20 | ........ | ...14 00–14 99 |
| 15 00–15 99... | ........ | ........ | 1 | ........ | 1 | ........ | ........ | 7 | 1 | 93.50 | 99.80 | ...15 00–15 99 |
| 16 00–17 99... | 1 | ........ | 2 | ........ | ........ | ........ | ........ | 5 | 1 | 100.00 | 100.00 | ...16 00–16 99 |
| Total..... | 2 | 2 | 3 | 2 | 3 | 2 | 1 | 76 | 554 | ........ | ........ | .....Total |

235. TABLE IX, A, 3, a

# NEW YORK CITY

## FIVE AND TEN CENT STORES — STOCK AND SALES

NUMBER AND PER CENT OF EMPLOYEES CLASSIFIED ACCORDING TO ACTUAL WEEKLY EARNINGS BY OCCUPATION AND SEX

| Actual Weekly Earnings in Dollars | Occupation: Superintendents | Occupation: Assistant Buyers and Heads of Stock | Occupation: Receiving and Stock Clerks | Occupation: Stock People | Occupation: Floor Managers | | Occupation: Sales People | | Occupation: Messengers, Wrappers, Errand Boys | Total | | Cumulative Per Cent of Total | | Actual Weekly Earnings in Dollars |
|---|---|---|---|---|---|---|---|---|---|---|---|---|---|---|
| | Male | Male | Male | Male | Male | Female | Male | Female | Male | Male | Female | Male | Female | |
| Less than $3 00. | .......... | ............ | .......... | ........ | .... | .... | .... | 18 | .......... | ... | 18 | ..... | 3.20 | Less than $3 00 |
| $3 00–$3 49.... | .......... | ............ | .......... | ........ | .... | .... | .... | 6 | .......... | ... | 6 | ..... | 4.30 | ...$3 00– 3 49 |
| 3 50– 3 99.... | .......... | ............ | .......... | ........ | .... | .... | .... | 6 | 2 | 2 | 6 | 2.60 | 5.40 | ... 3 50– 3 99 |
| 4 00– 4 49.... | .......... | ............ | .......... | ........ | .... | .... | .... | 24 | .......... | ... | 24 | ..... | 9.70 | ... 4 00– 4 49 |
| 4 50– 4 99.... | .......... | ............ | .......... | ........ | .... | .... | 1 | 54 | 1 | 2 | 54 | 5.30 | 19.50 | ... 4 50– 4 99 |
| 5 00– 5 49.... | .......... | ............ | .......... | 3 | .... | .... | .... | 124 | .......... | 3 | 124 | 9.20 | 41.90 | ... 5 00– 5 49 |
| 5 50– 5 99.... | .......... | ............ | .......... | ........ | .... | .... | .... | 74 | 1 | 1 | 74 | 10.50 | 45.20 | ... 5 50– 5 99 |
| 6 00– 6 49.... | .......... | ............ | 1 | 2 | .... | .... | .... | 95 | .......... | 3 | 95 | 14.50 | 72.30 | ... 6 00– 6 49 |
| 6 50– 6 99.... | .......... | ............ | .......... | ........ | .... | 1 | 1 | 48 | .......... | 1 | 49 | 15.80 | 81.20 | ... 6 50– 6 99 |
| 7 00– 7 49.... | .......... | ............ | .......... | 1 | .... | 2 | .... | 36 | .......... | 1 | 38 | 17.10 | 88.00 | ... 7 00– 7 49 |
| 7 50– 7 99.... | .......... | ............ | .......... | 1 | 1 | 5 | .... | 16 | .......... | 2 | 21 | 19.70 | 91.80 | ... 7 50– 7 99 |
| 8 00– 8 99.... | .......... | ............ | 2 | 1 | .... | 2 | 1 | 17 | .......... | 4 | 19 | 25.00 | 95.40 | ... 8 00– 8 99 |
| 9 00– 9 99.... | .......... | ............ | 2 | 2 | 2 | 2 | .... | 8 | .......... | 6 | 10 | 32.90 | 97.00 | ... 9 00– 9 99 |
| 10 00–10 99.... | .......... | ............ | 1 | 1 | 3 | 4 | 1 | 2 | .......... | 6 | 6 | 40.80 | 98.10 | ...10 00–10 99 |
| 11 00–11 99.... | .......... | ............ | 4 | 4 | 3 | 3 | .... | 2 | .......... | 11 | 5 | 55.30 | 99.10 | ...11 00–11 99 |
| 12 00–12 99.... | .......... | ............ | .......... | 6 | 4 | .... | 2 | 1 | .......... | 12 | 1 | 71.00 | 99.20 | ...12 00–12 99 |
| 13 00–13 99.... | 1 | ............ | 1 | 1 | 1 | 2 | .... | .... | .......... | 4 | 2 | 76.30 | 99.60 | ...13 00–13 99 |
| 14 00–14 99.... | 2 | 1 | 2 | ........ | 1 | .... | .... | .... | .......... | 6 | ... | 84.20 | ..... | ...14 00–14 99 |
| 15 00–15 99.... | .......... | ............ | 2 | 2 | 1 | 1 | 2 | .... | .......... | 7 | 1 | 93.50 | 99.80 | ...15 00–15 99 |
| 16 00–17 99.... | .......... | ............ | 3 | 1 | 1 | .... | .... | 1 | .......... | 5 | 1 | 100.00 | 100.00 | ...16 00–17 99 |
| Total...... | 3 | 1 | 18 | 25 | 17 | 22 | 8 | 532 | 4 | 76 | 554 | ..... | ..... | .....Total |

NEW YORK CITY

236. TABLE XV, A, 3, b, c, e — FIVE AND TEN CENT STORES — OFFICE, SHIPPING AND DELIVERY, PLANT

Number of Employees Earning Specified Weekly Rates According to Department and Sex

| Weekly Rates in Dollars | Departments: Office | | Shipping and Delivery | Plant | | Total | | Cumulative Per Cent. of Total | | Weekly Rates in Dollars |
|---|---|---|---|---|---|---|---|---|---|---|
| | Male | Female | Male | Male | Female | Male | Female | Male | Female | |
| $3 50–$3 99 | ........ | ........ | ........ | ........ | 1 | ........ | 1 | ........ | 2.00 | $3 50–$3 99 |
| 4 00– 4 49 | ........ | ........ | ........ | ........ | 3 | ........ | 3 | ........ | 8.00 | 4 00– 4 49 |
| 5 00– 5 49 | ........ | 1 | ........ | ........ | 2 | ........ | 3 | ........ | 14.00 | 5 00– 5 49 |
| 5 50– 5 99 | ........ | ........ | ........ | ........ | 1 | ........ | 1 | ........ | 16.00 | 5 50– 5 99 |
| 6 00– 6 49 | ........ | 6 | 1 | 1 | 3 | 2 | 9 | 6.90 | 34.00 | 6 00– 6 49 |
| 7 00– 7 49 | ........ | 4 | ........ | ........ | 3 | ........ | 7 | ........ | 48.00 | 7 00– 7 49 |
| 7 50– 7 99 | ........ | 2 | ........ | ........ | 2 | ........ | 4 | ........ | 56.00 | 7 50– 7 99 |
| 8 00– 8 99 | ........ | 6 | 1 | 4 | 1 | 5 | 7 | 24.20 | 70.00 | 8 00– 8 99 |
| 9 00– 9 99 | ........ | 2 | 3 | 3 | ........ | 6 | 2 | 43.80 | 74.00 | 98 00– 9 99 |
| 10 00–10 99 | 1 | 7 | 1 | 2 | ........ | 4 | 7 | 58.60 | 88.00 | 10 00–10 99 |
| 11 00–11 99 | ........ | 2 | ........ | 1 | ........ | 1 | 2 | 62.10 | 92.00 | 11 00–11 99 |
| 12 00–12 99 | ........ | 2 | 1 | 2 | ........ | 3 | 2 | 72.50 | 96.00 | 12 00–12 99 |
| 14 00–14 99 | 1 | 1 | 1 | 1 | ........ | 3 | 1 | 82.80 | 98.00 | 14 00–14 99 |
| 15 00–15 99 | 1 | ........ | ........ | 2 | ........ | 3 | ........ | 93.20 | ........ | 15 00–15 99 |
| 16 00–17 99 | 1 | ........ | ........ | ........ | ........ | 1 | ........ | 96.50 | ........ | 16 00–17 99 |
| 18 00–19 99 | 1 | 1 | ........ | ........ | ........ | 1 | 1 | 100.00 | 100.00 | 18 00–19 99 |
| Not reported | ........ | 1 | ........ | ........ | ........ | ........ | 1 | ........ | ........ | Not reported |
| Total | 5 | 35 | 8 | 16 | 16 | 29 | 51 | ........ | ........ | Total |

NEW YORK CITY

237. TABLE XVI, A, 3, b, c, e **FIVE AND TEN CENT STORES — OFFICE, SHIPPING AND DELIVERY, PLANT**

NUMBER OF EMPLOYEES CLASSIFIED ACCORDING TO ACTUAL WEEKLY EARNINGS, BY DEPARTMENT AND SEX

| ACTUAL WEEKLY EARNINGS IN DOLLARS | DEPARTMENTS | | | | | | | | | ACTUAL WEEKLY EARNINGS IN DOLLARS |
|---|---|---|---|---|---|---|---|---|---|---|
| | OFFICE | | SHIPPING AND DELIVERY | PLANT | | TOTAL | | CUMULATIVE PER CENT. OF TOTAL | | |
| | Male | Female | Male | Male | Female | Male | Female | Male | Female | |
| Less than $3 00 | ........ | ........ | ........ | ........ | 1 | ........ | 1 | ........ | 2.00 | Less than $3 00 |
| $3 00–$3 49 | ........ | ........ | ........ | ........ | 1 | ........ | 1 | ........ | 4.00 | $3 00– 3 49 |
| 3 50– 3 99 | ........ | 1 | ........ | ........ | 1 | ........ | 2 | ........ | 8.00 | 3 50– 3 99 |
| 4 00– 4 49 | ........ | 1 | ........ | ........ | 1 | ........ | 2 | ........ | 12.00 | 4 00– 4 49 |
| 5 50– 5 99 | ........ | ........ | ........ | ........ | 3 | ........ | 3 | ........ | 18.00 | 5 50– 5 99 |
| 6 00– 6 49 | ........ | 2 | 1 | 1 | 2 | 2 | 4 | 6.90 | 26.00 | 6 00– 6 49 |
| 6 50– 6 99 | ........ | 5 | ........ | ........ | 1 | ........ | 6 | ........ | 38.00 | 6 50– 6 99 |
| 7 00– 7 49 | ........ | 1 | ........ | ........ | 2 | ........ | 3 | ........ | 44.00 | 7 00– 7 49 |
| 7 50– 7 99 | ........ | 2 | ........ | ........ | 2 | ........ | 4 | ........ | 52.00 | 7 50– 7 99 |
| 8 00– 8 99 | ........ | 7 | 1 | 4 | 2 | 5 | 9 | 24.20 | 70.00 | 8 00– 8 99 |
| 9 00– 9 99 | ........ | 2 | 3 | 3 | ........ | 6 | 2 | 44.80 | 74.00 | 9 00– 9 99 |
| 10 00–10 99 | 1 | 2 | ........ | ........ | ........ | 1 | 2 | 48.30 | 78.00 | 10 00–10 99 |
| 11 00–11 99 | ........ | 7 | 1 | 2 | ........ | 3 | 7 | 58.60 | 92.00 | 11 00–11 99 |
| 12 00–12 99 | ........ | 1 | 1 | 3 | ........ | 4 | 1 | 72.50 | 94.00 | 12 00–12 99 |
| 13 00–13 99 | ........ | 1 | ........ | ........ | ........ | ........ | 1 | ........ | 96.00 | 13 00–13 99 |
| 14 00–14 99 | ........ | ........ | ........ | 1 | ........ | 1 | ........ | 75.90 | ........ | 14 00–14 99 |
| 15 00–15 99 | 1 | 1 | 1 | 1 | ........ | 3 | 1 | 86.20 | 98.00 | 15 00–15 99 |
| 16 00–17 99 | 1 | ........ | ........ | 1 | ........ | 2 | ........ | 93.20 | ........ | 16 00–17 99 |
| 18 00–19 99 | 2 | 1 | ........ | ........ | ........ | 2 | 1 | 100.00 | 100.00 | 18 00–19 99 |
| Not reported | ........ | 1 | ........ | ........ | ........ | ........ | 1 | ........ | ........ | Not reported |
| Total | 5 | 35 | 8 | 16 | 16 | 29 | 51 | ........ | ........ | Total |

NEW YORK CITY

238. TABLE XVII, A, 3, b, c, e FIVE AND TEN CENT STORES — OFFICE, SHIPPING AND DELIVERY, PLANT

Number of Employees Classified According to Age Groups, by Department and Sex

| Age Groups in Years | Departments | | | | | | | | | Age Groups in Years |
|---|---|---|---|---|---|---|---|---|---|---|
| | Office | | Shipping and Delivery | Plant | | Total | | Per cent. of total | | |
| | Male | Female | Male | Male | Female | Male | Female | Male | Female | |
| 16–17 | ........ | 2 | 1 | ........ | ........ | 1 | 2 | 3.40 | 3.90 | 16–17 |
| 18–20 | ........ | 11 | 2 | 4 | 2 | 6 | 13 | 20.70 | 25.50 | 18–20 |
| 21–24 | 3 | 13 | 1 | 2 | 1 | 6 | 14 | 20.70 | 27.40 | 21–24 |
| 25–29 | 2 | 5 | 1 | 2 | 1 | 5 | 6 | 17.20 | 11.80 | 25–29 |
| 30–34 | ........ | 2 | ........ | 2 | ........ | 2 | 2 | 6.90 | 3.90 | 30–34 |
| 35–39 | ........ | 2 | 1 | 2 | 2 | 3 | 4 | 10.40 | 7.80 | 35–39 |
| 40–44 | ........ | ........ | 2 | ........ | 3 | 2 | 3 | 6.90 | 5.90 | 40–44 |
| 45–54 | ........ | ........ | ........ | 2 | 5 | 2 | 5 | 6.90 | 9.80 | 45–54 |
| 55–64 | ........ | ........ | ........ | 2 | 1 | 2 | 1 | 6.90 | 2.00 | 55–64 |
| 65 and over | ........ | ........ | ........ | ........ | 1 | ........ | 1 | ........ | 2.00 | 65 and over |
| Total | 5 | 35 | 8 | 16 | 16 | 29 | 51 | 100.00 | 100.00 | Total |

NEW YORK CITY
THE MEN'S SHIRT INDUSTRY — FACTORY WORKERS

239. TABLE V, B, a NUMBER AND PER CENT. OF EMPLOYEES EARNING SPECIFIED WEEKLY RATES, BY AGE GROUPS AND SEX

| Weekly Rates in Dollars | Age Groups in Years | | | | | | | | | | | | | | Weekly Rates in Dollars |
|---|---|---|---|---|---|---|---|---|---|---|---|---|---|---|---|
| | 14–15 | | 16–17 | | 18–20 | | 21–24 | | 25–29 | | 30–34 | | 35–39 | | |
| | Male | Female | Male | Female | Male | Female | Male | Female | Male | Female | Male | Female | Male | Female | |
| Less than $3 00 | 1 | 4 | .... | ...... | ...... | 2 | ...... | ...... | ...... | ...... | ...... | ...... | ...... | ...... | Less than $3 00 |
| $3 00–$3 49... | 4 | 52 | 2 | 32 | ...... | 9 | ...... | 4 | ...... | 2 | ...... | 1 | ...... | 2 | ...$3 00– 3 49 |
| 3 50– 3 99... | 3 | 46 | 4 | 47 | 1 | 20 | ...... | 2 | ...... | 4 | ...... | 2 | ...... | 3 | ....3 50– 3 99 |
| 4 00– 4 49... | 3 | 32 | 10 | 92 | 6 | 47 | 2 | 17 | 2 | 6 | ...... | 2 | ...... | 3 | ....4 00– 4 49 |
| 4 50– 4 99... | 3 | 28 | 6 | 76 | 3 | 29 | 1 | 9 | ...... | 8 | ...... | 3 | ...... | 2 | ....4 50– 4 99 |
| 5 00– 5 49... | 4 | 10 | 23 | 115 | 13 | 77 | 6 | 14 | ...... | 9 | ...... | 6 | ...... | 1 | ....5 00– 5 49 |
| 5 50– 5 99... | 2 | 10 | 6 | 64 | 6 | 40 | 1 | 18 | ...... | 12 | 1 | 2 | ...... | 1 | ....5 50– 5 99 |
| 6 00– 6 49... | 1 | 8 | 22 | 84 | 25 | 100 | 6 | 36 | 4 | 15 | 3 | 4 | ...... | 2 | ....6 00– 6 49 |
| 6 50– 6 99... | .... | 2 | 6 | 28 | 8 | 64 | 2 | 21 | 1 | 7 | ...... | 1 | 1 | 3 | ....6 50– 6 99 |
| 7 00– 7 49... | .... | 2 | 13 | 39 | 34 | 87 | 9 | 32 | 3 | 14 | 2 | 2 | 1 | 3 | ....7 00– 7 49 |
| 7 50– 7 99... | .... | ...... | 3 | 26 | 3 | 54 | 6 | 19 | 3 | 3 | ...... | 3 | ...... | 3 | ....7 50– 7 99 |
| 8 00– 8 99... | .... | 1 | 12 | 35 | 43 | 109 | 18 | 49 | 8 | 15 | 2 | 6 | 4 | 5 | ....8 00– 8 99 |
| 9 00– 9 99... | .... | ...... | 6 | 11 | 23 | 77 | 11 | 59 | 6 | 15 | 2 | 5 | 6 | 2 | ....9 00– 9 99 |
| 10 00–10 99... | .... | ...... | .... | 6 | 14 | 30 | 11 | 31 | 5 | 7 | 3 | 7 | 2 | 4 | ...10 00–10 99 |
| 11 00–11 99... | .... | ...... | .... | 1 | 9 | 12 | 7 | 8 | 10 | 3 | 7 | 1 | 1 | 1 | ...11 00–11 99 |
| 12 00–12 99... | .... | ...... | .... | 1 | 6 | 7 | 14 | 11 | 16 | 6 | 8 | 1 | 7 | 2 | ...12 00–12 99 |
| 13 00–13 99... | .... | ...... | .... | 1 | 7 | 3 | 12 | 3 | 15 | 2 | 6 | ...... | 8 | ...... | ...13 00–13 99 |
| 14 00–14 99... | .... | ...... | .... | 1 | 5 | 1 | 11 | ...... | 18 | 2 | 3 | ...... | 3 | 1 | ...14 00–14 99 |
| 15 00–15 99... | .... | ...... | .... | ...... | 3 | ...... | 9 | ...... | 6 | ...... | 6 | 2 | 8 | ...... | ...15 00–15 99 |
| 16 00–17 99... | .... | ...... | .... | ...... | 1 | ...... | 10 | ...... | 14 | 2 | 13 | ...... | 5 | 1 | ...16 00–19 99 |
| 18 00–19 00... | .... | ...... | .... | ...... | 1 | ...... | 11 | ...... | 15 | ...... | 7 | ...... | 13 | ...... | ...18 00–19 99 |
| 20 00–24 99... | .... | ...... | .... | ...... | ...... | ...... | 4 | ...... | 14 | ...... | 10 | 1 | 12 | ...... | ...20 00–24 99 |
| 25 00–29 99... | .... | ...... | .... | ...... | ...... | ...... | ...... | ...... | 4 | ...... | 2 | ...... | 7 | ...... | ...25 00–29 99 |
| 30 00–34 99... | .... | ...... | .... | ...... | ...... | ...... | ...... | ...... | ...... | ...... | 3 | ...... | 2 | ...... | ...30 00–34 99 |
| 35 00–39 99... | .... | ...... | .... | ...... | ...... | ...... | ...... | ...... | ...... | ...... | ...... | ...... | 1 | ...... | ...35 00–39 99 |
| 40 00 and over. | .... | ...... | .... | ...... | ...... | ...... | ...... | ...... | ...... | ...... | ...... | ...... | 1 | ...... | .40 00 and over |
| Not reported... | .... | ...... | 1 | 1 | ...... | 1 | 2 | ...... | ...... | 3 | 1 | ...... | 1 | ...... | ...Not reported |
| Total..... | 21 | 195 | 114 | 660 | 211 | 769 | 153 | 333 | 144 | 135 | 79 | 49 | 83 | 39 | .....Tota |

239. TABLE V, B, a — (*concluded*)

NEW YORK CITY

THE MEN'S SHIRT INDUSTRY — FACTORY WORKERS

NUMBER AND PER CENT. OF EMPLOYEES EARNING SPECIFIED WEEKLY RATES, BY AGE GROUPS AND SEX

| WEEKLY RATES IN DOLLARS | AGE GROUPS IN YEARS (*concluded*) 40–44 | | 45–54 | | 55–64 | | 65 AND OVER | NOT REPORTED | | TOTAL | | CUMULATIVE PER CENT. OF TOTAL | | WEEKLY RATES IN DOLLARS |
|---|---|---|---|---|---|---|---|---|---|---|---|---|---|---|
| | Male | Female | Male | Female | Male | Female | Male | Male | Female | Male | Female | Male | Female | |
| Less than $3 00 | | | | | | | | | | 1 | 6 | .1 | .3 | Less than $3 00 |
| $3 00– 3 49 | | 1 | | | | | | | | 6 | 103 | .7 | 4.9 | $3 00– 3 49 |
| 3 50– 3 99 | | | | 1 | | | | | | 8 | 125 | 1.6 | 10.5 | 3 50– 3 99 |
| 4 00– 4 49 | | 2 | | 4 | 1 | 1 | | | | 24 | 206 | 4.2 | 19.7 | 4 00– 4 49 |
| 4 50– 4 99 | | 2 | | 3 | | 1 | | | 1 | 13 | 162 | 5.6 | 27.0 | 4 50– 4 99 |
| 5 00– 5 49 | | 4 | | 1 | | 1 | | | | 46 | 238 | 10.6 | 37.7 | 5 00– 5 49 |
| 5 50– 5 99 | | 1 | 1 | 3 | | | | | | 17 | 151 | 12.5 | 44.5 | 5 50– 5 99 |
| 6 00– 6 49 | | | 1 | 6 | 1 | 3 | | | 1 | 63 | 259 | 19.3 | 56.1 | 6 00– 6 49 |
| 6 50– 6 99 | 1 | | | 1 | | | | | | 19 | 127 | 21.4 | 61.8 | 6 50– 6 99 |
| 7 00– 7 49 | | 3 | 3 | | 1 | | | | | 66 | 182 | 28.5 | 70.0 | 7 00– 7 49 |
| 7 50– 7 99 | 1 | 1 | 1 | 1 | 1 | | | | | 18 | 110 | 30.4 | 74.9 | 7 50– 7 99 |
| 8 00– 8 99 | 1 | 1 | 7 | 2 | 2 | | 1 | | | 98 | 223 | 41.1 | 84.9 | 8 00– 8 99 |
| 9 00– 9 99 | 4 | | 7 | 1 | 1 | | | | 2 | 66 | 172 | 48.2 | 92.6 | 9 00– 9 99 |
| 10 00–10 99 | 2 | | 4 | 2 | 1 | | | 1 | | 43 | 87 | 52.9 | 96.5 | 10 00–10 99 |
| 11 00–11 99 | 6 | | 1 | | 2 | | | | | 43 | 26 | 57.5 | 97.7 | 11 00–11 99 |
| 12 00–12 99 | 7 | 3 | 3 | | 2 | | | | | 63 | 31 | 64.4 | 99.1 | 12 00–12 99 |
| 13 00–13 99 | 6 | | 3 | | | | | 1 | | 58 | 9 | 70.6 | 99.4 | 13 00–13 99 |
| 14 00–14 99 | 2 | | 1 | 1 | | | | | | 43 | 6 | 75.4 | 99.6 | 14 00–14 99 |
| 15 00–15 99 | 4 | | 4 | | 1 | | | 1 | | 42 | 2 | 79.9 | 99.8 | 15 00–15 99 |
| 16 00–17 99 | 9 | | | | | | | | | 52 | 3 | 85.5 | 99.9 | 16 00–17 99 |
| 18 00–19 00 | 1 | | 1 | | | | | 1 | | 50 | | 91.0 | | 18 00–19 99 |
| 20 00–24 99 | 6 | | 8 | | 1 | | | | | 55 | 1 | 96.9 | 100.0 | 20 00–24 99 |
| 25 00–29 99 | 1 | | 2 | | | | | | | 16 | | 98.5 | | 25 00–29 99 |
| 30 00–34 99 | | | 2 | | 1 | | | | | 8 | | 99.5 | | 30 00–34 99 |
| 35 00–39 99 | | | 1 | | | | | | | 2 | | 99.7 | | 35 00–39 99 |
| 40 00 and over | 1 | | 1 | | | | | | | 3 | | 100.0 | | 40 00 and over |
| Not reported | | | | | | | | | | 5 | 5 | | | Not reported |
| Total | 52 | 18 | 51 | 26 | 15 | 6 | 1 | 4 | 4 | 928 | 2,234 | | | Total |

NEW YORY CITY

**THE MEN'S SHIRT INDUSTRY — FACTORY WORKERS**

240. TABLE VIII, B, a NUMBER AND PER CENT. OF EMPLOYEES EARNING SPECIFIED WEEKLY RATES, BY OCCUPATION AND SEX

| Weekly Rates in Dollars | Occupation | | | | | | | | | | | | | | Weekly Rates in Dollars |
|---|---|---|---|---|---|---|---|---|---|---|---|---|---|---|---|
| | Markers | | Cutters | Trimmers | Cutters' Helpers | | Foremen and Forewomen | | Operators | | Floor Work | | Laundry Helpers | | |
| | Male | Female | Male | Male | Male | Female | Male | Female | Male | Female | Male | Female | Male | Female | |
| Less than $3 00 | .... | ...... | .... | ...... | ...... | ...... | ...... | ...... | 1 | 3 | ...... | 1 | ...... | ...... | Less than $3 00 |
| $3 00-$3 49 | .... | ...... | .... | ...... | ...... | 1 | ...... | ...... | 2 | 35 | 4 | 51 | ...... | ...... | $3 00- 3 49 |
| 3 50- 3 99 | .... | ...... | .... | ...... | 3 | ...... | ...... | ...... | 1 | 59 | 3 | 54 | ...... | ...... | 3 50- 3 99 |
| 4 00- 4 49 | .... | ...... | .... | ...... | 8 | 1 | ...... | ...... | 7 | 97 | 7 | 72 | ...... | ...... | 4 00- 4 49 |
| 4 50- 4 99 | .... | ...... | .... | ...... | 6 | 8 | ...... | 1 | 3 | 85 | 2 | 44 | 1 | ...... | 4 50- 4 99 |
| 5 00- 5 49 | .... | ...... | 4 | 1 | 21 | ...... | ...... | ...... | 6 | 124 | 4 | 59 | 1 | 2 | 5 00- 5 49 |
| 5 50- 5 99 | .... | ...... | .... | ...... | 8 | ...... | ...... | ...... | 1 | 95 | 3 | 30 | ...... | 1 | 5 50- 5 99 |
| 6 00- 6 49 | .... | ...... | 1 | 1 | 25 | 1 | ...... | 1 | 8 | 146 | 6 | 56 | 2 | 2 | 6 00- 6 49 |
| 6 50- 6 99 | .... | ...... | 1 | ...... | 5 | 2 | ...... | 1 | 3 | 78 | 2 | 20 | ...... | ...... | 6 50- 6 99 |
| 7 00- 7 49 | .... | ...... | 2 | 5 | 27 | 2 | ...... | 2 | 9 | 104 | 7 | 30 | 1 | 1 | 7 00- 7 49 |
| 7 50- 7 99 | .... | ...... | 1 | ...... | 5 | ...... | ...... | 2 | 5 | 81 | 1 | 8 | ...... | ...... | 7 50- 7 99 |
| 8 00- 8 99 | .... | ...... | 6 | 4 | 41 | ...... | 2 | 9 | 17 | 171 | 2 | 16 | ...... | ...... | 8 00- 8 99 |
| 9 00- 9 99 | 2 | ...... | 11 | 3 | 12 | 1 | 3 | 10 | 10 | 129 | 2 | 7 | 2 | ...... | 9 00- 9 99 |
| 10 00-10 99 | 1 | ...... | 9 | 1 | 3 | 1 | ...... | 6 | 14 | 66 | ...... | 2 | ...... | ...... | 10 00-10 99 |
| 11 00-11 99 | 1 | ...... | 7 | 4 | 1 | ...... | 1 | 4 | 19 | 22 | ...... | ...... | 1 | ...... | 11 00-11 99 |
| 12 00-12 99 | .... | ...... | 8 | 4 | 1 | ...... | 4 | 6 | 40 | 19 | ...... | ...... | 2 | ...... | 12 00-12 99 |
| 13 00-13 99 | 1 | ...... | 15 | 3 | 1 | ...... | 5 | 1 | 27 | 6 | ...... | 2 | ...... | ...... | 13 00-13 99 |
| 14 00-14 99 | 2 | 1 | 12 | 5 | ...... | ...... | 4 | 3 | 17 | 1 | 1 | ...... | ...... | ...... | 14 00-14 99 |
| 15 00-15 99 | 1 | ...... | 4 | 3 | ...... | ...... | 5 | 1 | 26 | ...... | ...... | ...... | ...... | ...... | 15 00-15 99 |
| 16 00-17 99 | 3 | ...... | 14 | 1 | ...... | ...... | 17 | 3 | 15 | ...... | ...... | ...... | ...... | ...... | 16 00-17 99 |
| 18 00-19 99 | 4 | ...... | 29 | 1 | ...... | ...... | 8 | ...... | 6 | ...... | ...... | ...... | 2 | ...... | 18 00-19 99 |
| 20 00-24 99 | 23 | ...... | 14 | ...... | ...... | ...... | 15 | 1 | 2 | ...... | ...... | ...... | ...... | ...... | 20 00-24 99 |
| 25 00-29 99 | 1 | ...... | 2 | ...... | ...... | ...... | 12 | ...... | 1 | ...... | ...... | ...... | ...... | ...... | 25 00-29 99 |
| 30 00-34 99 | 1 | ...... | 2 | ...... | ...... | ...... | 5 | ...... | ...... | ...... | ...... | ...... | ...... | ...... | 30 00-34 99 |
| 35 00-39 99 | 1 | ...... | .... | ...... | ...... | ...... | 1 | ...... | ...... | ...... | ...... | ...... | ...... | ...... | 35 00-39 99 |
| 40 00 and over | .... | ...... | .... | ...... | ...... | ...... | 3 | ...... | ...... | ...... | ...... | ...... | ...... | ...... | 40 00 and over |
| Not reported | .... | ...... | .... | ...... | 1 | ...... | ...... | ...... | 2 | 4 | ...... | 1 | ...... | ...... | Not reported |
| Total | 41 | 1 | 142 | 36 | 168 | 17 | 85 | 51 | 242 | 1,325 | 44 | 453 | 12 | 6 | Total |

240. TABLE VIII, B, a — (*concluded*)

NEW YORK CITY

**THE MEN'S SHIRT INDUSTRY — FACTORY WORKERS**

NUMBER AND PER CENT. OF EMPLOYEES EARNING SPECIFIED WEEKLY RATES, BY OCCUPATION AND SEX

| WEEKLY RATES IN DOLLARS | OCCUPATION (*concluded*) | | | | | | | | | | | | | | | | WEEKLY RATES IN DOLLARS |
|---|---|---|---|---|---|---|---|---|---|---|---|---|---|---|---|---|---|
| | STARCHERS AND DAMPENERS | | IRONERS AND PRESSERS | | EXAMINERS | | FOLDERS | | PACKERS | | NOT REPORTED | | TOTAL | | CUMULATIVE PER CENT. OF TOTAL | | |
| | Male | Female | Male | Female | Male | Female | Male | Female | Male | Female | Male | Female | Male | Female | Male | Female | |
| Less than $3 00 | .... | ...... | .... | ...... | .... | ..... | .... | 2 | .... | ..... | .... | ..... | 1 | 6 | .1 | .3 | Less than $3 00 |
| $3 00–$3 49... | .... | ...... | .... | ...... | .... | 2 | .... | 13 | .... | 1 | .... | ..... | 6 | 103 | .7 | 4.9 | ...$3 00– 3 49 |
| 3 50– 3 99... | .... | ...... | 1 | ...... | .... | 1 | .... | 4 | .... | 5 | .... | 2 | 8 | 125 | 1.6 | 10.5 | ... 3 50– 3 99 |
| 4 00– 4 49... | 1 | 1 | .... | 3 | .... | 10 | .... | 3 | .... | 14 | 1 | ..... | 24 | 206 | 4.2 | 19.7 | ... 4 00– 4 49 |
| 4 50– 4 99... | 1 | ...... | .... | 1 | .... | 9 | .... | 3 | .... | 9 | .... | 2 | 13 | 162 | 5.6 | 27.0 | ... 4 50– 4 99 |
| 5 00– 5 49... | .... | 3 | 1 | 3 | .... | 13 | 2 | 3 | 6 | 29 | .... | 2 | 46 | 238 | 10.6 | 37.7 | ... 5 00– 5 49 |
| 5 50– 5 99... | .... | 3 | 1 | 3 | 1 | 7 | 1 | 2 | 2 | 9 | .... | 1 | 17 | 151 | 12.5 | 44.5 | ... 5 50– 5 99 |
| 6 00– 6 49... | 1 | 8 | 6 | 13 | .... | 18 | 3 | 4 | 10 | 6 | .... | 4 | 63 | 259 | 19.3 | 56.1 | ... 6 00– 6 49 |
| 6 50– 6 99... | .... | 3 | 2 | 4 | 2 | 10 | 1 | 3 | 3 | 6 | .... | ..... | 19 | 127 | 21.4 | 61.8 | ... 6 50– 6 99 |
| 7 00– 7 49... | .... | 8 | 10 | 9 | .... | 16 | 2 | 3 | 2 | 7 | 1 | ..... | 66 | 182 | 28.5 | 70.0 | ... 7 00– 7 49 |
| 7 50– 7 99... | .... | 3 | 6 | 8 | .... | 5 | .... | 1 | .... | 2 | .... | ..... | 18 | 110 | 30.4 | 74.9 | ... 7 50– 7 99 |
| 8 00– 8 99... | 1 | 2 | 18 | 8 | .... | 15 | 2 | ..... | 5 | 2 | .... | ..... | 98 | 223 | 41.1 | 84.9 | ... 8 00– 8 99 |
| 9 00– 9 99... | .... | ...... | 14 | 5 | .... | 14 | 1 | 1 | 6 | 2 | .... | 3 | 66 | 172 | 48.2 | 92.6 | ... 9 00– 9 99 |
| 10 00–10 99... | .... | ...... | 7 | 1 | 2 | 8 | 3 | ..... | 3 | 3 | .... | ..... | 43 | 87 | 52.9 | 96.5 | ...10 00–10 99 |
| 11 00–11 99... | .... | ...... | 6 | ...... | 1 | ..... | 2 | ..... | .... | ..... | .... | ..... | 43 | 26 | 57.5 | 97.7 | ...11 00–11 99 |
| 12 00–12 99... | .... | ...... | 2 | ...... | 2 | 6 | .... | ..... | .... | ..... | .... | ..... | 63 | 31 | 64.4 | 99.1 | ...12 00–12 99 |
| 13 00–13 99... | .... | ...... | 1 | ...... | 1 | ..... | 2 | ..... | 2 | ..... | .... | ..... | 58 | 9 | 70.6 | 99.4 | ...13 00–13 99 |
| 14 00–14 99... | .... | ...... | 1 | ...... | .... | ..... | 1 | ..... | .... | 1 | .... | ..... | 43 | 6 | 75.4 | 99.6 | ...14 00–14 99 |
| 15 00–15 99... | .... | ...... | 1 | ...... | 1 | 1 | 1 | ..... | .... | ..... | .... | ..... | 42 | 2 | 79.9 | 99.8 | ...15 00–15 99 |
| 16 00–17 99... | .... | ...... | 1 | ...... | 1 | ..... | .... | ..... | .... | ..... | .... | ..... | 52 | 3 | 85.5 | 99.9 | ...16 00–17 99 |
| 18 00–19 99... | .... | ...... | .... | ...... | .... | ..... | .... | ..... | .... | ..... | .... | ..... | 50 | ..... | 91.0 | ..... | ...18 00–19 99 |
| 20 00–24 99... | .... | ...... | .... | ...... | .... | ..... | .... | ..... | .... | ..... | 1 | ..... | 55 | 1 | 96.9 | 100.0 | ...20 00–24 99 |
| 25 00–29 99... | .... | ...... | .... | ...... | .... | ..... | .... | ..... | .... | ..... | .... | ..... | 16 | ..... | 98.5 | ..... | ...25 00–29 99 |
| 30 00–34 99... | .... | ...... | .... | ...... | .... | ..... | .... | ..... | .... | ..... | .... | ..... | 8 | ..... | 99.5 | ..... | ...30 00–34 99 |
| 35 00–39 99... | .... | ...... | .... | ...... | .... | ..... | .... | ..... | .... | ..... | .... | ..... | 2 | ..... | 99.7 | ..... | ...35 00–39 99 |
| 40 00 and over. | .... | ...... | .... | ...... | .... | ..... | .... | ..... | .... | ..... | .... | ..... | 3 | ..... | 100.0 | ..... | .40 00 and over |
| Not reported... | .... | ...... | 2 | ...... | .... | ..... | .... | ..... | .... | ..... | .... | ..... | 5 | 5 | .... | ..... | ...Not reported |
| Total..... | 4 | 31 | 80 | 58 | 11 | 135 | 21 | 47 | 39 | 96 | 3 | 14 | 928 | 2,234 | .... | ..... | .....Total |

241. TABLE VI, B, a

NEW YORK CITY

THE MEN'S SHIRT INDUSTRY — FACTORY WORKERS

NUMBER AND PER CENT. OF EMPLOYEES CLASSIFIED ACCORDING TO ACTUAL WEEKLY EARNINGS, BY AGE GROUPS AND SEX

| Actual Weekly Earnings in Dollars | Age Groups in Years | | | | | | | | | | | | | | Actual Weekly Earnings in Dollars |
|---|---|---|---|---|---|---|---|---|---|---|---|---|---|---|---|
| | 14–15 | | 16–17 | | 18–20 | | 21–24 | | 25–29 | | 30–34 | | 35–39 | | |
| | Male | Female | Male | Female | Male | Female | Male | Female | Male | Female | Male | Female | Male | Female | |
| Less than $3 00 | 3 | 45 | 10 | 88 | 12 | 78 | 11 | 30 | 8 | 10 | 2 | 3 | 1 | 3 | Less than $3 00 |
| $3 00–$3 49... | 6 | 58 | 3 | 75 | 4 | 54 | 5 | 22 | 3 | 6 | 1 | 2 | ...... | 6 | ...$3 00– 3 49 |
| 3 50– 3 99... | .... | 43 | 6 | 74 | 5 | 62 | 2 | 20 | 4 | 10 | 2 | 8 | 3 | 5 | ... 3 50– 3 99 |
| 4 00– 4 49... | 2 | 25 | 13 | 126 | 8 | 93 | 1 | 32 | 5 | 15 | 3 | 4 | 1 | 4 | ... 4 00– 4 49 |
| 4 50– 4 99... | 3 | 27 | 9 | 115 | 7 | 95 | 6 | 36 | 3 | 11 | 2 | 6 | 1 | 6 | ... 4 50– 4 99 |
| 5 00– 5 49... | 6 | 22 | 18 | 131 | 14 | 146 | 11 | 48 | ...... | 23 | 3 | 10 | 5 | 6 | ... 5 00– 5 49 |
| 5 50– 5 99... | 2 | 9 | 9 | 97 | 13 | 115 | 6 | 37 | 2 | 14 | 5 | 5 | 4 | 3 | ... 5 50– 5 99 |
| 6 00– 6 49... | 1 | 4 | 21 | 93 | 33 | 170 | 11 | 71 | 8 | 28 | 2 | 11 | 5 | 6 | ... 6 00– 6 49 |
| 6 50– 6 99... | .... | 2 | 9 | 54 | 18 | 155 | 7 | 62 | 10 | 17 | 2 | 1 | 6 | 6 | ... 6 50– 6 99 |
| 7 00– 7 49... | .... | 2 | 13 | 71 | 28 | 166 | 13 | 66 | 8 | 26 | 5 | 8 | 4 | 6 | ... 7 00– 7 49 |
| 7 50– 7 99... | .... | 1 | 7 | 50 | 16 | 136 | 13 | 44 | 8 | 8 | 8 | 9 | 2 | 11 | ... 7 50– 7 99 |
| 8 00– 8 99... | .... | 1 | 9 | 65 | 54 | 234 | 36 | 119 | 28 | 32 | 14 | 21 | 7 | 4 | ... 8 00– 8 99 |
| 9 00– 9 99... | .... | ...... | 8 | 27 | 34 | 142 | 26 | 97 | 28 | 28 | 18 | 7 | 11 | 9 | ... 9 00– 9 99 |
| 10 00–10 99... | .... | ...... | 1 | 16 | 23 | 112 | 26 | 57 | 18 | 29 | 9 | 9 | 17 | 5 | ...10 00–10 99 |
| 11 00–11 99... | .... | ...... | 1 | 6 | 20 | 36 | 20 | 32 | 28 | 8 | 22 | 1 | 11 | 7 | ...11 00–11 99 |
| 12 00–12 99... | .... | ...... | .... | 7 | 16 | 30 | 25 | 27 | 27 | 13 | 21 | 8 | 21 | 6 | ...12 00–12 99 |
| 13 00–13 99... | .... | ...... | .... | 4 | 14 | 16 | 28 | 14 | 21 | 4 | 18 | 3 | 16 | 5 | ...13 00–13 99 |
| 14 00–14 99... | .... | ...... | 1 | ...... | 7 | 7 | 24 | 7 | 24 | 7 | 11 | 2 | 13 | 3 | ...14 00–14 99 |
| 15 00–15 99... | .... | ...... | .... | 1 | 6 | 4 | 15 | 4 | 16 | 5 | 11 | 6 | 16 | 1 | ...15 00–15 99 |
| 16 00–17 99... | .... | ...... | .... | ...... | 6 | 4 | 24 | 4 | 40 | 3 | 29 | 1 | 15 | 2 | ...16 00–17 99 |
| 18 00–19 99... | .... | ...... | .... | ...... | 4 | 3 | 16 | 4 | 27 | 1 | 15 | ...... | 19 | ...... | ...18 00–19 99 |
| 20 00–24 99... | .... | ...... | .... | ...... | 2 | 1 | 13 | 2 | 17 | ...... | 19 | 1 | 19 | ...... | ...20 00–24 99 |
| 25 00–29 99... | .... | ...... | .... | ...... | ...... | 1 | 1 | ...... | 5 | ...... | 3 | ...... | 5 | ...... | ...25 00–29 99 |
| 30 00–34 99... | .... | ...... | .... | ...... | ...... | ...... | ...... | ...... | 1 | ...... | 3 | ...... | 4 | ...... | ...30 00–34 99 |
| 40 00 and over. | .... | ...... | .... | ...... | ...... | ...... | ...... | ...... | ...... | ...... | ...... | ...... | 2 | ...... | .40 00 and over |
| Not reported... | .... | ...... | .... | ...... | ...... | 4 | 1 | ...... | 1 | 1 | ...... | ...... | ...... | ...... | ...Not reported |
| Total..... | 23 | 239 | 138 | 1,100 | 344 | 1,864 | 341 | 835 | 340 | 299 | 228 | 126 | 208 | 104 | .....Total |

NEW YORK CITY

241. TABLE VI, B, a — (*concluded*) **THE MEN'S SHIRT INDUSTRY — FACTORY WORKERS**

NUMBER AND PER CENT. OF EMPLOYEES CLASSIFIED ACCORDING TO ACTUAL WEEKLY EARNINGS, BY AGE GROUPS AND SEX

| ACTUAL WEEKLY EARNINGS IN DOLLARS | AGE GROUPS IN YEARS | | | | | | | | | | | | | | ACTUAL WEEKLY EARNINGS IN DOLLARS |
|---|---|---|---|---|---|---|---|---|---|---|---|---|---|---|---|
| | 40–44 | | 45–54 | | 55–64 | | 65 AND OVER | NOT REPORTED | | TOTAL | | CUMULATIVE PER CENT. OF TOTAL | | |
| | Male | Female | Male | Female | Male | Female | Male | Male | Female | Male | Female | Male | Female | |
| Less than $3 00 | ...... | 1 | 2 | 5 | 3 | ...... | ...... | ...... | ...... | 52 | 263 | 2.70 | 5.60 | Less than $3 00 |
| $3 00–$3 49 | ...... | ...... | 3 | 2 | ...... | 1 | 1 | ...... | ...... | 26 | 226 | 4.00 | 10.40 | $3 00– 3 49 |
| 3 50– 3 99 | 1 | 2 | 6 | 2 | ...... | ...... | ...... | ...... | 2 | 29 | 228 | 5.50 | 15.30 | 3 50– 3 99 |
| 4 00– 4 49 | 5 | 4 | 3 | 8 | 2 | ...... | ...... | ...... | 1 | 43 | 312 | 7.80 | 21.90 | 4 00– 4 49 |
| 4 50– 4 99 | 2 | 2 | 2 | 6 | ...... | 2 | ...... | ...... | ...... | 35 | 306 | 9.60 | 28.50 | 4 50– 4 99 |
| 5 00– 5 49 | 2 | 6 | 5 | 4 | ...... | 2 | ...... | ...... | 2 | 64 | 400 | 12.90 | 37.00 | 5 00– 5 49 |
| 5 50– 5 99 | 3 | 2 | 2 | 5 | ...... | ...... | ...... | ...... | 2 | 46 | 289 | 15.30 | 43.20 | 5 50– 5 99 |
| 6 00– 6 49 | 5 | 4 | 8 | 6 | 8 | 3 | 1 | ...... | ...... | 103 | 396 | 20.60 | 51.60 | 6 00– 6 49 |
| 6 50– 6 99 | 5 | 4 | 1 | 2 | 1 | ...... | 1 | ...... | 1 | 60 | 304 | 23.70 | 58.10 | 6 50– 6 99 |
| 7 00– 7 49 | 2 | 3 | 8 | 5 | 1 | ...... | ...... | ...... | 2 | 82 | 355 | 28.00 | 65.70 | 7 00– 7 49 |
| 7 50– 7 99 | 1 | 2 | 9 | 1 | 1 | ...... | ...... | ...... | 1 | 65 | 263 | 31.30 | 71.30 | 7 50– 7 99 |
| 8 00– 8 99 | 5 | 2 | 9 | 4 | 3 | ...... | 1 | ...... | ...... | 166 | 482 | 39.90 | 81.50 | 8 00– 8 99 |
| 9 00 9 99 | 11 | 3 | 14 | 1 | 2 | ...... | ...... | ...... | 2 | 152 | 316 | 47.80 | 88.30 | 9 00– 9 99 |
| 10 00–10 99 | 12 | 3 | 11 | 3 | 1 | ...... | 1 | 2 | ...... | 121 | 234 | 54.10 | 93.30 | 10 00–10.99 |
| 11 00–11 99 | 10 | 2 | 5 | ...... | 3 | ...... | ...... | ...... | ...... | 120 | 92 | 60.30 | 95.30 | 11 00–11 99 |
| 12 00–12 99 | 16 | 4 | 6 | 2 | 3 | ...... | ...... | ...... | 1 | 135 | 98 | 67 00 | 97.40 | 12 00–12 99 |
| 13 00–13 99 | 8 | ...... | 8 | ...... | ...... | ...... | ...... | 1 | ...... | 114 | 46 | 73.20 | 98.30 | 13 00–13 99 |
| 14 00–14 99 | 9 | ...... | 6 | 1 | ...... | ...... | ...... | ...... | ...... | 95 | 27 | 78.10 | 98.80 | 14 00–14 99 |
| 15 00–15 99 | 6 | 1 | 7 | ...... | 1 | ...... | ...... | 1 | ...... | 79 | 22 | 82.20 | 99.40 | 15 00–15 99 |
| 16 00–17 99 | 15 | ...... | 2 | ...... | ...... | ...... | ...... | ...... | ...... | 131 | 14 | 89.00 | 99.70 | 16 00–17 99 |
| 18 00–19 99 | 3 | ...... | 3 | ...... | ...... | ...... | ...... | 1 | ...... | 88 | 8 | 93.50 | 99.80 | 18 00–19 99 |
| 20 00–24 99 | 8 | ...... | 12 | ...... | 1 | ...... | ...... | 1 | ...... | 92 | 4 | 98.30 | 99.90 | 20 00–24 99 |
| 25 00–29 99 | 2 | ...... | 2 | ...... | ...... | ...... | ...... | ...... | ...... | 18 | 1 | 99.20 | 100.00 | 25 00–29 99 |
| 30 00–34 99 | ...... | ...... | 2 | ...... | 1 | ...... | ...... | ...... | ...... | 11 | ...... | 99.70 | ...... | 30 00–34 99 |
| 35 00–39 99 | ...... | ...... | 1 | ...... | ...... | ...... | ...... | ...... | ...... | 1 | ...... | 99.80 | ...... | 35 00–39 99 |
| 40 00 and over | 1 | ...... | 1 | ...... | ...... | ...... | ...... | ...... | ...... | 4 | ...... | 100.00 | ...... | 40 00 and over |
| Not reported | ...... | ...... | ...... | ...... | ...... | ...... | ...... | ...... | ...... | 2 | 5 | ...... | ...... | Not reported |
| Total | 132 | 45 | 138 | 57 | 31 | 8 | 5 | 6 | 14 | 1,934 | 4,691 | ...... | ...... | Total |

242. TABLE IX, B, a

NEW YORK CITY

THE MEN'S SHIRT INDUSTRY — FACTORY WORKERS

NUMBER AND PER CENT. OF EMPLOYEES CLASSIFIED ACCORDING TO ACTUAL WEEKLY EARNINGS, BY OCCUPATION AND SEX

| ACTUAL WEEKLY EARNINGS IN DOLLARS | OCCUPATION | | | | | | | | | | | | | | | ACTUAL WEEKLY EARNINGS IN DOLLARS |
|---|---|---|---|---|---|---|---|---|---|---|---|---|---|---|---|---|
| | MARKERS | | CUTTERS | TRIMMERS | CUTTERS' HELPERS | | FOREMEN AND FOREWOMEN | | OPERATORS | | FLOOR WORK | | LAUNDRY HELPERS | | | |
| | Male | Female | Male | Male | Male | Female | Male | Female | Male | Female | Male | Female | Male | Female | | |
| Less than $3 00 | .... | ...... | 1 | ...... | 6 | ...... | ...... | ...... | 29 | 179 | 4 | 59 | ...... | ...... | Less than $3 00 |
| $3 00–$3 49... | .... | ...... | 1 | ...... | 3 | 1 | ...... | 1 | 11 | 128 | 6 | 66 | ...... | ...... | ...$3 00– 3 49 |
| 3 50– 3 99... | .... | ...... | .... | ...... | 3 | ...... | ...... | ...... | 12 | 133 | 3 | 69 | ...... | ...... | ... 3 50– 3 99 |
| 4 00– 4 49... | .... | ...... | 1 | ...... | 6 | 2 | 1 | ...... | 15 | 180 | 7 | 83 | 1 | ...... | ... 4 00– 4 49 |
| 4 50– 4 99... | .... | ...... | .... | ...... | 9 | 4 | ...... | 1 | 11 | 211 | 1 | 49 | 2 | ...... | ... 4 50– 4 99 |
| 5 00– 5 49... | .... | ...... | 3 | 1 | 16 | 1 | ...... | ...... | 23 | 264 | 3 | 68 | 1 | 2 | ... 5 00– 5 49 |
| 5 50– 5 99... | .... | ...... | .... | ...... | 9 | 1 | ...... | ...... | 14 | 205 | 4 | 41 | ...... | 1 | ... 5 50– 5 99 |
| 6 00– 6 49... | .... | ...... | 1 | 1 | 18 | 2 | ...... | ...... | 35 | 282 | 13 | 48 | 3 | 2 | ... 6 00– 6 49 |
| 6 50– 6 99... | .... | ...... | 2 | 1 | 14 | 1 | ...... | 3 | 20 | 229 | 3 | 25 | ...... | ...... | ... 6 50– 6 99 |
| 7 00– 7 49... | .... | ...... | 1 | 3 | 15 | 3 | ...... | 1 | 31 | 273 | 9 | 27 | 1 | 1 | ... 7 00– 7 49 |
| 7 50– 7 99... | .... | ...... | 6 | 1 | 13 | 2 | ...... | 4 | 22 | 214 | 1 | 12 | 1 | ...... | ... 7 50– 7 99 |
| 8 00– 8 99... | .... | ...... | 6 | 3 | 32 | 1 | 3 | 6 | 60 | 399 | 4 | 20 | ...... | ...... | ... 8 00– 8 99 |
| 9 00– 9 99... | 1 | ...... | 13 | 3 | 15 | 2 | 2 | 10 | 59 | 246 | 4 | 12 | 1 | ...... | ... 9 00– 9 99 |
| 10 00–10 99... | 1 | ...... | 7 | 1 | 5 | 1 | ...... | 6 | 57 | 188 | ...... | 2 | 1 | ...... | ...10 00–10 99 |
| 11 00–11 99... | .... | ...... | 5 | 7 | 2 | ...... | 3 | 4 | 62 | 73 | ...... | ...... | ...... | ...... | ...11 00–11 99 |
| 12 00–12 99... | 1 | ...... | 10 | 2 | 2 | ...... | 3 | 6 | 73 | 76 | ...... | 1 | 2 | ...... | ...12 00–12 99 |
| 13 00–13 99... | 1 | ...... | 15 | 4 | 1 | ...... | 3 | 1 | 48 | 42 | 1 | 1 | ...... | ...... | ...13 00–13 99 |
| 14 00–14 99... | 3 | 1 | 9 | 4 | ...... | ...... | 4 | 3 | 48 | 17 | 1 | ...... | ...... | 1 | ...14 00–14 99 |
| 15 00–15 99... | .... | ...... | 8 | 3 | ...... | ...... | 7 | 1 | 41 | 14 | ...... | ...... | ...... | ...... | ...15 00–15 99 |
| 16 00–17 99... | 4 | ...... | 14 | 1 | ...... | ...... | 15 | 3 | 53 | 9 | ...... | ...... | ...... | ...... | ...16 00–17 99 |
| 18 00–19 99... | 5 | ...... | 27 | 1 | ...... | ...... | 8 | ...... | 24 | 8 | ...... | ...... | 2 | ...... | ...18 00–19 99 |
| 20 00–24 99... | 21 | ...... | 16 | ...... | ...... | ...... | 17 | 1 | 17 | 3 | ...... | ...... | ...... | ...... | ...20 00–24 99 |
| 25 00–29 99... | 2 | ...... | 2 | ...... | ...... | ...... | 0 | ...... | 3 | 1 | ...... | ...... | ...... | ...... | ...25 00–29 99 |
| 30 00–34 99... | 1 | ...... | 3 | ...... | ...... | ...... | 7 | ...... | ...... | ...... | ...... | ...... | ...... | ...... | ...30 00–34 99 |
| 35 00–39 99... | .... | ...... | .... | ...... | ...... | ...... | 1 | ...... | ...... | ...... | ...... | ...... | ...... | ...... | ...35 00–39 99 |
| 40 00 and over. | 1 | ...... | .... | ...... | ...... | ...... | 3 | ...... | ...... | ...... | ...... | ...... | ...... | ...... | .40 00 and over |
| Not reported.. | .... | ...... | 1 | ...... | ...... | ...... | ...... | ...... | 7 | 69 | 1 | 15 | ...... | ...... | ..Not reported |
| Total..... | 41 | 1 | 152 | 36 | 169 | 21 | 87 | 51 | 775 | 3,443 | 65 | 598 | 15 | 7 | .....Total |

242. TABLE IX, B, a — (*concluded*)

NEW YORK CITY

THE MEN'S SHIRT INDUSTRY — FACTORY WORKERS

NUMBER AND PER CENT. OF EMPLOYEES CLASSIFIED ACCORDING TO ACTUAL WEEKLY EARNINGS, BY OCCUPATION AND SEX

| ACTUAL WEEKLY EARNINGS IN DOLLARS | OCCUPATION (*concluded*) | | | | | | | | | | | | TOTAL | | CUMULATIVE PER CENT. OF TOTAL | | ACTUAL WEEKLY EARNINGS IN DOLLARS |
|---|---|---|---|---|---|---|---|---|---|---|---|---|---|---|---|---|---|
| | STARCHERS AND DAMPNERS | | IRONERS AND PRESSERS | | EXAMINERS | | FOLDERS | | PACKERS | | NOT REPORTED | | | | | | |
| | Male | Female | Male | Female | Male | Female | Male | Female | Male | Female | Male | Female | Male | Female | Male | Female | |
| Less than $3 00 | .... | .... | 9 | 5 | .... | 7 | .... | 6 | 2 | 6 | 1 | 1 | 52 | 263 | 2.70 | 5.60 | Less than $3 00 |
| $3 00–$3 49... | .... | .... | 5 | 7 | .... | 3 | .... | 14 | .... | 5 | .... | 1 | 26 | 226 | 4.00 | 10.40 | ...$3 00– 3 49 |
| 3 50– 3 99... | .... | .... | 11 | 5 | .... | 3 | .... | 10 | .... | 6 | .... | 2 | 29 | 228 | 5.50 | 15.30 | ... 3 50– 3 99 |
| 4 00– 4 49... | .... | 1 | 9 | 9 | .... | 15 | 1 | 5 | 2 | 17 | .... | .... | 43 | 312 | 7.80 | 21.90 | ... 4 00– 4 49 |
| 4 50– 4 99... | 1 | .... | 8 | 12 | .... | 10 | 1 | 2 | 2 | 15 | .... | 2 | 35 | 306 | 9.60 | 28.50 | ... 4 50– 4 99 |
| 5 00– 5 49... | .... | 7 | 11 | 11 | .... | 14 | 2 | 5 | 4 | 23 | .... | 5 | 64 | 400 | 12.90 | 37.00 | ... 5 00– 5 49 |
| 5 50– 5 99... | .... | 5 | 13 | 15 | 1 | 5 | .... | 10 | 4 | 4 | 1 | 2 | 46 | 289 | 15.30 | 43.20 | ... 5 50– 5 99 |
| 6 00– 6 49... | 1 | 5 | 20 | 25 | .... | 19 | 3 | 2 | 8 | 9 | .... | 2 | 103 | 396 | 20.60 | 51.60 | ... 6 00– 6 49 |
| 6 50– 6 99... | .... | 3 | 13 | 18 | 2 | 14 | 1 | 5 | 3 | 6 | 1 | .... | 60 | 304 | 23.70 | 58.10 | ... 6 50– 6 99 |
| 7 00– 7 49... | .... | 14 | 17 | 15 | .... | 9 | 2 | 3 | 3 | 8 | .... | 1 | 82 | 355 | 28.00 | 65.70 | ... 7 00– 7 49 |
| 7 50– 7 99... | .... | 2 | 18 | 15 | 1 | 10 | .... | 2 | 2 | 2 | .... | .... | 65 | 263 | 31.30 | 71.30 | ... 7 50– 7 99 |
| 8 00– 8 99... | 1 | 4 | 46 | 34 | .... | 14 | 3 | 2 | 8 | 1 | .... | 1 | 166 | 482 | 39.90 | 81.50 | ... 8 00– 8 99 |
| 9 00– 9 99... | .... | 5 | 48 | 17 | .... | 17 | 1 | 2 | 5 | 3 | .... | 2 | 152 | 316 | 47.80 | 88.30 | ... 9 00– 9 99 |
| 10 00–10 99... | .... | 2 | 43 | 18 | 1 | 10 | 3 | 2 | 2 | 5 | .... | .... | 121 | 234 | 54.10 | 93.30 | ...10 00–10 99 |
| 11 00–11 99... | 2 | 3 | 36 | 11 | 1 | .... | 1 | 1 | 1 | .... | .... | .... | 120 | 92 | 60.30 | 95.30 | ...11 00–11 99 |
| 12 00–12 99... | .... | .... | 37 | 10 | 2 | 5 | 2 | .... | 1 | .... | .... | .... | 135 | 98 | 67.00 | 97.40 | ...12 00–12 99 |
| 13 00–13 99... | .... | 1 | 37 | 1 | 1 | .... | 1 | .... | 2 | .... | .... | .... | 114 | 46 | 73.20 | 98.30 | ...13 00–13 99 |
| 14 00–14 99... | .... | 2 | 25 | 3 | .... | .... | 1 | .... | .... | .... | .... | .... | 95 | 27 | 78.10 | 98.80 | ...14 00–14 99 |
| 15 00–15 99... | .... | 4 | 17 | 1 | 1 | 2 | 2 | .... | .... | .... | .... | .... | 79 | 22 | 82.20 | 99.40 | ...15 00–15 99 |
| 16 00–17 99... | .... | 1 | 42 | 1 | 1 | .... | 1 | .... | .... | .... | .... | .... | 131 | 14 | 89.00 | 99.70 | ...16 00–17 99 |
| 18 00–19 99... | .... | .... | 21 | .... | .... | .... | .... | .... | .... | .... | .... | .... | 88 | 8 | 93.50 | 99.80 | ...18 00–19 99 |
| 20 00–24 99... | .... | .... | 19 | .... | .... | .... | 1 | .... | .... | .... | 1 | .... | 92 | 4 | 98.30 | 99.90 | ...20 00–24 99 |
| 25 00–29 99... | .... | .... | 1 | .... | .... | .... | .... | .... | .... | .... | .... | .... | 18 | 1 | 99.20 | 100.00 | ...25 00–29 99 |
| 30 00–34 99... | .... | .... | .... | .... | .... | .... | .... | .... | .... | .... | .... | .... | 11 | .... | 99.70 | .... | ...30 00–34 99 |
| 35 00–39 99... | .... | .... | .... | .... | .... | .... | .... | .... | .... | .... | .... | .... | 1 | .... | 99.80 | .... | ...35 00–39 99 |
| 40 00 and over. | .... | .... | .... | .... | .... | .... | .... | .... | .... | .... | .... | .... | 4 | .... | 100.00 | .... | .40 00 and over |
| Not reported.. | .... | .... | .... | 1 | .... | 1 | .... | .... | .... | 1 | .... | 3 | 9 | 90 | .... | .... | ..Not reported |
| Total..... | 5 | 59 | 506 | 234 | 11 | 158 | 26 | 71 | 49 | 111 | 4 | 22 | 1,941 | 4,776 | .... | .... | .....Total |

NEW YORK CITY

243. TABLE V, B, 1, a — THE MEN'S SHIRT INDUSTRY — NEGLIGEE SHIRTS — FACTORY WORKERS

Number and Per Cent. of Employees Earning Specified Weekly Rates, by Age Groups and Sex

| Weekly Rates in Dollars | Age Groups in Years: 14–15 | | 16–17 | | 18–20 | | 21–24 | | 25–29 | | 30–34 | | 35–39 | | Weekly Rates in Dollars |
|---|---|---|---|---|---|---|---|---|---|---|---|---|---|---|---|
| | Male | Female | Male | Female | Male | Female | Male | Female | Male | Female | Male | Female | Male | Female | |
| Less than $3 00 | 1 | 1 | .... | ...... | ...... | 2 | ...... | ...... | ...... | ...... | ...... | ...... | ...... | ...... | Less than $3 00 |
| $3 00–$3 49... | 3 | 36 | 1 | 30 | ...... | 9 | ...... | 4 | ...... | 2 | ...... | 1 | ...... | 1 | ...$3 00– 3 49 |
| 3 50– 3 99... | 3 | 41 | 4 | 40 | 1 | 16 | ...... | 2 | ...... | 4 | ...... | 2 | ...... | 3 | ... 3 50– 3 99 |
| 4 00– 4 49... | 3 | 31 | 10 | 85 | 3 | 40 | 1 | 15 | 1 | 6 | ...... | 2 | ...... | 2 | ... 4 00– 4 49 |
| 4 50– 4 99... | 1 | 27 | 6 | 73 | 3 | 26 | 1 | 7 | ...... | 7 | ...... | 2 | ...... | 1 | ... 4 50– 4 99 |
| 5 00– 5 49... | 4 | 9 | 15 | 112 | 8 | 73 | 4 | 14 | ...... | 9 | ...... | 5 | ...... | 1 | ... 5 00– 5 49 |
| 5 50– 5 99... | 1 | 9 | 3 | 61 | 4 | 37 | ...... | 16 | ...... | 10 | 1 | 2 | ...... | 1 | ... 5 50– 5 99 |
| 6 00– 6 49... | 1 | 7 | 17 | 79 | 19 | 87 | 5 | 31 | 2 | 14 | 3 | 4 | ...... | 1 | ... 6 00– 6 49 |
| 6 50– 6 99... | .... | 2 | 5 | 25 | 4 | 62 | 2 | 19 | 1 | 7 | ...... | 1 | 1 | 3 | ... 6 50– 6 99 |
| 7 00– 7 49... | .... | 2 | 13 | 33 | 30 | 80 | 9 | 29 | 3 | 14 | 2 | 2 | 1 | 3 | ... 7 00– 7 49 |
| 7 50– 7 99... | .... | ...... | 2 | 25 | 3 | 47 | 6 | 19 | 3 | 3 | ...... | 3 | ...... | 3 | ... 7 50– 7 99 |
| 8 00– 8 99... | .... | 1 | 6 | 35 | 33 | 101 | 14 | 44 | 7 | 15 | 2 | 4 | 2 | 4 | ... 8 00– 8 99 |
| 9 00– 9 99... | .... | ...... | 5 | 11 | 18 | 72 | 9 | 54 | 5 | 13 | 1 | 5 | 5 | 2 | ... 9 00– 9 99 |
| 10 00–10 99... | .... | ...... | .... | 6 | 9 | 26 | 8 | 28 | 4 | 6 | 3 | 7 | 2 | 4 | ...10 00–10 99 |
| 11 00–11 99... | .... | ...... | .... | 1 | 8 | 10 | 6 | 8 | 7 | 2 | 6 | 1 | 1 | 1 | ...11 00–11 99 |
| 12 00–12 99... | .... | ...... | .... | 1 | 4 | 7 | 11 | 10 | 13 | 6 | 8 | 1 | 6 | 1 | ...12 00–12 99 |
| 13 00–13 99... | .... | ...... | .... | 1 | 5 | 3 | 11 | 3 | 11 | 2 | 6 | ...... | 6 | ...... | ...13 00–13 99 |
| 14 00–14 99... | .... | ...... | .... | ...... | 4 | 1 | 6 | ...... | 13 | 2 | 3 | ...... | 3 | 1 | ...14 00–14 99 |
| 15 00–15 99... | .... | ...... | .... | ...... | 3 | ...... | 7 | ...... | 6 | ...... | 6 | 2 | 7 | ...... | ...15 00–15 99 |
| 16 00–17 99... | .... | ...... | .... | ...... | 1 | ...... | 9 | ...... | 12 | 2 | 10 | ...... | 4 | 1 | ...16 00–17 99 |
| 18 00–19 99... | .... | ...... | .... | ...... | ...... | ...... | 9 | ...... | 12 | ...... | 6 | ...... | 8 | ...... | ...18 00–19 99 |
| 20 00–24 99... | .... | ...... | .... | ...... | ...... | ...... | 3 | ...... | 10 | ...... | 9 | ...... | 11 | ...... | ...20 00–24 99 |
| 25 00–29 99... | .... | ...... | .... | ...... | ...... | ...... | ...... | ...... | 4 | ...... | ...... | ...... | 6 | ...... | ...25 00–29 99 |
| 30 00–34 99... | .... | ...... | .... | ...... | ...... | ...... | ...... | ...... | ...... | ...... | 2 | ...... | 2 | ...... | ...30 00–34 99 |
| 35 00–39 99... | .... | ...... | .... | ...... | ...... | ...... | ...... | ...... | ...... | ...... | ...... | ...... | 1 | ...... | ...35 00–39 99 |
| 40 00 and over. | .... | ...... | .... | ...... | ...... | ...... | ...... | ...... | ...... | ...... | ...... | ...... | 1 | ...... | .40 00 and over |
| Not reported.. | .... | ...... | 1 | 1 | ...... | 1 | 2 | ...... | ...... | 2 | ...... | ...... | 1 | ...... | ..Not reported |
| Total..... | 17 | 166 | 88 | 619 | 160 | 700 | 123 | 303 | 114 | 126 | 68 | 44 | 68 | 33 | .....Total |

243. TABLE V, B, 1, a — (*concluded*)

## NEW YORK CITY
### THE MEN'S SHIRT INDUSTRY — NEGLIGEE SHIRTS — FACTORY WORKERS
Number and Per Cent. of Employees Earning Specified Weekly Rates, by Age Groups and Sex

| Weekly Rates in Dollars | Age Groups in Years (*concluded*) 40–44 | | 45–54 | | 55–64 | | 65 and over | Not reported | | Total | | Cumulative per cent. of total | | Weekly Rates in Dollars |
|---|---|---|---|---|---|---|---|---|---|---|---|---|---|---|
| | Male | Female | Male | Female | Male | Female | Male | Male | Female | Male | Female | Male | Female | |
| Less than $3 00 | ...... | ...... | ...... | ...... | ...... | ...... | ...... | ...... | ...... | 1 | 3 | .10 | .10 | Less than $3 00 |
| $3 00–$3 49 | ...... | 1 | ...... | ...... | ...... | ...... | ...... | ...... | ...... | 4 | 84 | .70 | 4.30 | $3 00– 3 49 |
| 3 50– 3 99 | ...... | ...... | ...... | 1 | ...... | ...... | ...... | ...... | ...... | 8 | 109 | 1.80 | 9.60 | 3 50– 3 99 |
| 4 00– 4 49 | ...... | 2 | ...... | 2 | 1 | 1 | ...... | ...... | ...... | 19 | 186 | 4.30 | 18.80 | 4 00– 4 49 |
| 4 50– 4 99 | ...... | 1 | ...... | 2 | ...... | 1 | ...... | ...... | ...... | 11 | 147 | 5.80 | 26.00 | 4 50– 4 99 |
| 5 00– 5 49 | ...... | 4 | ...... | 1 | ...... | 1 | ...... | ...... | ...... | 31 | 229 | 10.00 | 27.40 | 5 00– 5 49 |
| 5 50– 5 99 | ...... | 1 | 1 | 3 | ...... | ...... | ...... | ...... | ...... | 10 | 140 | 11.40 | 44.10 | 5 50– 5 99 |
| 6 00– 6 49 | ...... | ...... | 1 | 5 | ...... | 3 | ...... | ...... | 1 | 48 | 232 | 17.90 | 55.50 | 6 00– 6 49 |
| 6 50– 6 99 | 1 | ...... | ...... | 1 | ...... | ...... | ...... | ...... | ...... | 14 | 120 | 19.80 | 61.50 | 6 50– 6 99 |
| 7 00– 7 49 | ...... | 2 | 3 | ...... | 1 | ...... | ...... | ...... | ...... | 62 | 165 | 28.10 | 69.50 | 7 00– 7 49 |
| 7 50– 7 99 | 1 | 1 | ...... | 1 | 1 | ...... | ...... | ...... | ...... | 16 | 102 | 30.40 | 74.50 | 7 50– 7 99 |
| 8 00– 8 99 | 1 | 1 | 3 | 2 | 2 | ...... | 1 | ...... | ...... | 71 | 207 | 40.00 | 84.80 | 8 00– 8 99 |
| 9 00– 9 99 | 3 | ...... | 7 | 1 | 1 | ...... | ...... | ...... | 2 | 54 | 160 | 47.40 | 92.60 | 9 00– 9 99 |
| 10 00–10 99 | 2 | ...... | 3 | 2 | ...... | ...... | ...... | 1 | ...... | 32 | 79 | 51.70 | 96.50 | 10 00–10 99 |
| 11 00–11 99 | 4 | ...... | 1 | ...... | 2 | ...... | ...... | ...... | ...... | 35 | 23 | 56.50 | 97.50 | 11 00–11 99 |
| 12 00–12 99 | 5 | 3 | 2 | ...... | 2 | ...... | ...... | ...... | ...... | 51 | 29 | 63.40 | 99.10 | 12 00–12 99 |
| 13 00–13 99 | 3 | ...... | 3 | ...... | ...... | ...... | ...... | 1 | ...... | 46 | 9 | 69.60 | 99.50 | 13 00–13 99 |
| 14 00–14 99 | 2 | ...... | 1 | 1 | ...... | ...... | ...... | ...... | ...... | 32 | 5 | 74.00 | 99.80 | 14 00–14 99 |
| 15 00–15 99 | 4 | ...... | 4 | ...... | 1 | ...... | ...... | 1 | ...... | 39 | 2 | 79.30 | 99.90 | 15 00–15 99 |
| 16 00–17 99 | 8 | ...... | ...... | ...... | ...... | ...... | ...... | ...... | ...... | 44 | 3 | 85.20 | 100.00 | 16 00–17 99 |
| 18 00–19 99 | 1 | ...... | 1 | ...... | ...... | ...... | ...... | 1 | ...... | 38 | ...... | 90.40 | ...... | 18 00–19 99 |
| 20 00–24 99 | 4 | ...... | 8 | ...... | 1 | ...... | ...... | ...... | ...... | 46 | ...... | 96.60 | ...... | 20 00–24 99 |
| 25 00–29 99 | 1 | ...... | 2 | ...... | ...... | ...... | ...... | ...... | ...... | 13 | ...... | 98.50 | ...... | 25 00–29 99 |
| 30 00–34 99 | ...... | ...... | 2 | ...... | 1 | ...... | ...... | ...... | ...... | 7 | ...... | 99.40 | ...... | 30 00–34 99 |
| 35 00–39 99 | ...... | ...... | 1 | ...... | ...... | ...... | ...... | ...... | ...... | 2 | ...... | 99.60 | ...... | 35 00–39 99 |
| 40 00 and over | 1 | ...... | 1 | ...... | ...... | ...... | ...... | ...... | ...... | 3 | ...... | 100.00 | ...... | 40 00 and over |
| Not reported | ...... | ...... | ...... | ...... | ...... | ...... | ...... | ...... | ...... | 4 | 4 | ...... | ...... | Not reported |
| Total | 41 | 16 | 44 | 22 | 13 | 6 | 1 | 4 | 3 | 741 | 2,038 | ...... | ...... | Total |

**244. TABLE VIII, B, 1, a**

## NEW YORK CITY
## THE MEN'S SHIRT INDUSTRY — NEGLIGEE SHIRTS — FACTORY WORKERS
### NUMBER AND PER CENT. OF EMPLOYEES EARNING SPECIFIED WEEKLY RATES, BY OCCUPATION AND SEX

| WEEKLY RATES IN DOLLARS | OCCUPATION | | | | | | | | | | | | | | WEEKLY RATES IN DOLLARS |
|---|---|---|---|---|---|---|---|---|---|---|---|---|---|---|---|
| | MARKERS | | CUTTERS | TRIMMERS | CUTTERS' HELPERS | | FOREMEN AND FOREWOMEN | | FOREMEN OPERATORS | | FLOOR WORK | | LAUNDRY HELPERS | | |
| | Male | Female | Male | Male | Male | Female | Male | Female | Male | Female | Male | Female | Male | Female | |
| Less than $3 00 | | | | | | | | | 1 | 3 | | | | | Less than $3 00 |
| $3 00–$3 49 | | | | | | | | | | 32 | 4 | 50 | | | $3 00– 3 49 |
| 3 50– 3 99 | | | | | 3 | | | | 1 | 58 | 3 | 49 | | | 3 50– 3 99 |
| 4 00– 4 49 | | | | | 7 | 1 | | | 4 | 95 | 6 | 71 | | | 4 00– 4 49 |
| 4 50– 4 99 | | | | | 4 | 8 | | 1 | 3 | 82 | 2 | 41 | 1 | | 4 50– 4 99 |
| 5 00– 5 49 | | | 2 | 1 | 13 | | | | 5 | 121 | 3 | 56 | 1 | 2 | 5 00– 5 49 |
| 5 50– 5 99 | | | | | 4 | | | | 1 | 92 | 2 | 27 | | 1 | 5 50– 5 99 |
| 6 00– 6 49 | | | 1 | | 20 | 1 | | 1 | 7 | 138 | 3 | 51 | 2 | 2 | 6 00– 6 49 |
| 6 50– 6 99 | | | 1 | | 5 | 2 | | 1 | 2 | 78 | 2 | 18 | | | 6 50– 6 99 |
| 7 00– 7 49 | | | 1 | 4 | 27 | 2 | | 2 | 9 | 99 | 6 | 27 | 1 | | 7 00– 7 49 |
| 7 50– 7 99 | | | | | 5 | | | 2 | 5 | 80 | 1 | 5 | | | 7 50– 7 99 |
| 8 00– 8 99 | | | 6 | 3 | 27 | | 2 | 7 | 14 | 162 | 1 | 14 | | | 8 00– 8 99 |
| 9 00– 9 99 | 1 | | 7 | 3 | 10 | 1 | 2 | 6 | 9 | 125 | 1 | 7 | 2 | | 9 00– 9 99 |
| 10 00–10 99 | | | 5 | 1 | 3 | 1 | | 6 | 11 | 59 | | 2 | | | 10 00–10 99 |
| 11 00–11 99 | 1 | | 4 | 3 | 1 | | | 3 | 20 | 20 | | | | | 11 00–11 99 |
| 12 00–12 99 | | | 4 | 3 | 1 | | 2 | 5 | 36 | 19 | | | 2 | | 12 00–12 99 |
| 13 00–13 99 | | | 9 | 2 | 1 | | 4 | 1 | 25 | 6 | | 2 | | | 13 00–13 99 |
| 14 00–14 99 | | 1 | 7 | 5 | | | 2 | 3 | 17 | 1 | | | | | 14 00–14 99 |
| 15 00–15 99 | 1 | | 4 | 3 | | | 3 | 1 | 26 | | | | | | 15 00–15 99 |
| 16 00–17 99 | 2 | | 10 | 1 | | | 14 | 3 | 15 | | | | | | 16 00–17 99 |
| 18 00–19 99 | 2 | | 23 | 1 | | | 5 | | 6 | | | | 1 | | 18 00–19 99 |
| 20 00–24 99 | 20 | | 11 | | | | 12 | | 2 | | | | | | 20 00–24 99 |
| 25 00–29 99 | | | 2 | | | | 10 | | 1 | | | | | | 25 00–29 99 |
| 30 00–34 99 | 1 | | 2 | | | | 4 | | | | | | | | 30 00–34 99 |
| 35 00–39 99 | 1 | | | | | | 1 | | | | | | | | 35 00–39 99 |
| 40 00 and over | | | | | | | 3 | | | | | | | | 40 00 and over |
| Not reported | | | | | 1 | | | | 2 | 3 | | 1 | | | Not reported |
| Total | 29 | 1 | 99 | 30 | 132 | 16 | 64 | 42 | 222 | 1,273 | 34 | 421 | 10 | 5 | Total |

244. TABLE VIII, B, 1, a — (*concluded*) NEW YORK CITY

THE MEN'S SHIRT INDUSTRY — NEGLIGEE SHIRTS — FACTORY WORKERS

NUMBER AND PER CENT. OF EMPLOYEES EARNING SPECIFIED WEEKLY RATES, BY OCCUPATION AND SEX

| WEEKLY RATES IN DOLLARS | OCCUPATION (*concluded*) | | | | | | | | | | | | | | | | WEEKLY RATES IN DOLLARS |
|---|---|---|---|---|---|---|---|---|---|---|---|---|---|---|---|---|---|
| | STARCHERS AND DAMPNERS | | IRONERS AND PRESSERS | | EXAMINERS | | FOLDERS | | PACKERS | | NOT REPORTED | | TOTAL | | CUMULATIVE PER CENT. OF TOTAL | | |
| | Male | Female | Male | Female | Male | Female | Male | Female | Male | Female | Male | Female | Male | Female | Male | Female | |
| Less than $3 00 | .... | ..... | .... | ..... | .... | ..... | .... | ..... | .... | ..... | ..... | ..... | 1 | 3 | .10 | .10 | Less than $3 00 |
| $3 00–$3 49... | .... | ..... | .... | ..... | .... | 1 | .... | ..... | .... | 1 | ..... | ..... | 4 | 84 | .70 | 4.30 | ...$3 00– 3 49 |
| 3 50– 3 99... | .... | ..... | 1 | ..... | .... | ..... | .... | ..... | .... | ..... | ..... | 2 | 8 | 109 | 1.80 | 9.60 | ... 3 50– 3 99 |
| 4 00– 4 49... | 1 | 1 | .... | 1 | .... | 8 | .... | 4 | .... | 5 | 1 | ..... | 19 | 186 | 4.30 | 18.80 | ... 4 00– 4 49 |
| 4 50– 4 99... | 1 | ..... | .... | ..... | .... | 6 | .... | 3 | .... | 4 | ..... | 2 | 11 | 147 | 5.80 | 26.00 | ... 4 50– 4 99 |
| 5 00– 5 49... | .... | 3 | 1 | 2 | .... | 13 | 1 | 3 | 4 | 27 | ..... | 2 | 31 | 229 | 10.00 | 27.40 | ... 5 00– 5 49 |
| 5 50– 5 99... | .... | 3 | 1 | ..... | .... | 7 | 1 | 2 | 1 | 7 | ..... | 1 | 10 | 140 | 11.40 | 44.10 | ... 5 50– 5 99 |
| 6 00– 6 99... | .... | 8 | 5 | 4 | .... | 14 | 1 | 3 | 9 | 6 | ..... | 4 | 48 | 232 | 17.90 | 55.50 | ... 6 00– 6 49 |
| 6 50– 6 99... | .... | 3 | 2 | 2 | 1 | 9 | 1 | 2 | .... | 5 | ..... | ..... | 14 | 120 | 19.80 | 61.50 | ... 6 50– 6 99 |
| 7 00– 7 49... | .... | 8 | 10 | 7 | .... | 14 | 2 | 3 | 1 | 3 | 1 | ..... | 62 | 165 | 28.10 | 69.50 | ... 7 00– 7 49 |
| 7 50– 7 99... | .... | 3 | 5 | 5 | .... | 5 | .... | 1 | .... | 1 | ..... | ..... | 16 | 102 | 30.40 | 74.50 | ... 7 50– 7 99 |
| 8 00– 8 99... | 1 | 2 | 12 | 7 | .... | 13 | 1 | ..... | 4 | 2 | ..... | ..... | 71 | 207 | 40.00 | 84.80 | ... 8 00– 8 99 |
| 9 00– 9 99... | .... | ..... | 14 | 4 | .... | 13 | 1 | ..... | 4 | 2 | ..... | 2 | 54 | 160 | 47.40 | 92.60 | ... 9 00– 9 99 |
| 10 00–10 99... | .... | ..... | 6 | 1 | 1 | 7 | 3 | ..... | 2 | 3 | ..... | ..... | 32 | 79 | 51.70 | 96.50 | ...10 00–10 99 |
| 11 00–11 99... | .... | ..... | 6 | ..... | .... | ..... | .... | ..... | .... | ..... | ..... | ..... | 35 | 23 | 56.50 | 97.50 | ...11 00–11 99 |
| 12 00–12 99... | .... | ..... | 2 | ..... | 1 | 5 | .... | ..... | .... | ..... | ..... | ..... | 51 | 29 | 63.40 | 99.10 | ...12 00–12 99 |
| 13 00–13 99... | .... | ..... | 1 | ..... | 1 | ..... | 1 | ..... | 2 | ..... | ..... | ..... | 46 | 9 | 69.60 | 99.50 | ...13 00–13 99 |
| 14 00–14 99... | .... | ..... | 1 | ..... | .... | ..... | .... | ..... | .... | ..... | ..... | ..... | 32 | 5 | 74.00 | 99.80 | ...14 00–14 99 |
| 15 00–15 99... | .... | ..... | 1 | ..... | 1 | 1 | .... | ..... | .... | ..... | ..... | ..... | 39 | 2 | 79.30 | 99.90 | ...15 00–15 99 |
| 16 00–17 99... | .... | ..... | 1 | ..... | 1 | ..... | .... | ..... | .... | ..... | ..... | ..... | 44 | 3 | 85.20 | 100.00 | ...16 00–17 99 |
| 18 00–19 99... | .... | ..... | .... | ..... | .... | ..... | .... | ..... | .... | ..... | ..... | ..... | 38 | ..... | 90.40 | ..... | ...18 00–19 99 |
| 20 00–24 99... | .... | ..... | .... | ..... | .... | ..... | .... | ..... | .... | ..... | 1 | ..... | 46 | ..... | 96.60 | ..... | ...20 00–24 99 |
| 25 00–29 99... | .... | ..... | .... | ..... | .... | ..... | .... | ..... | .... | ..... | ..... | ..... | 13 | ..... | 98.50 | ..... | ...25 00–29 99 |
| 30 00–34 99... | .... | ..... | .... | ..... | .... | ..... | .... | ..... | .... | ..... | ..... | ..... | 7 | ..... | 99.40 | ..... | ...30 00–34 99 |
| 35 00–39 99... | .... | ..... | .... | ..... | .... | ..... | .... | ..... | .... | ..... | ..... | ..... | 2 | ..... | 99.60 | ..... | ...35 00–39 99 |
| 40 00 and over. | .... | ..... | .... | ..... | .... | ..... | .... | ..... | .... | ..... | ..... | ..... | 3 | ..... | 100.00 | ..... | .40 00 and over |
| Not reported.. | .... | ..... | 1 | ..... | .... | ..... | .... | ..... | .... | ..... | ..... | ..... | 4 | 4 | ..... | ..... | ..Not reported |
| Total.... | 3 | 31 | 70 | 33 | 6 | 116 | 12 | 21 | 27 | 66 | 3 | 13 | 741 | 2,038 | ..... | ..... | ....Total |

245. TABLE VI, B. 1. a.

NEW YORK CITY — NEGLIGEE SHIRTS
THE MEN'S SHIRT INDUSTRY — FACTORY WORKERS
NUMBER AND PER CENT. OF EMPLOYEES CLASSIFIED ACCORDING TO ACTUAL WEEKLY EARNINGS, BY AGE GROUPS AND SEX

| WEEKLY RATES IN DOLLARS | AGE GROUPS IN YEARS | | | | | | | | | | | | | | WEEKLY RATES IN DOLLARS |
|---|---|---|---|---|---|---|---|---|---|---|---|---|---|---|---|
| | 14–15 | | 16–17 | | 18–20 | | 21–24 | | 25–29 | | 30–34 | | 35–39 | | |
| | Male | Female | Male | Female | Male | Female | Male | Female | Male | Female | Male | Female | Male | Female | |
| Less than $3 00 | 3 | 34 | 10 | 64 | 8 | 53 | 9 | 20 | 8 | 7 | 2 | 1 | 1 | 2 | Less than $3 00 |
| $3 00–$3 49... | 5 | 37 | 2 | 55 | 3 | 36 | 5 | 16 | 3 | 5 | 1 | 2 | ...... | 3 | ...$3 00– 3 49 |
| 3 50– 3 99... | .... | 33 | 5 | 55 | 4 | 45 | 1 | 12 | 4 | 8 | 2 | 8 | 2 | 4 | ... 3 50– 3 99 |
| 4 00– 4 49... | 2 | 22 | 11 | 103 | 7 | 63 | 1 | 25 | 3 | 9 | 3 | 2 | 1 | 3 | ... 4 00– 4 49 |
| 4 50– 4 99... | 1 | 21 | 8 | 95 | 7 | 69 | 5 | 25 | 2 | 10 | 1 | 3 | 1 | 4 | ... 4 50– 4 99 |
| 5 00– 5 49... | 6 | 15 | 9 | 104 | 11 | 118 | 9 | 38 | ...... | 18 | 3 | 8 | 5 | 5 | ... 5 00– 5 49 |
| 5 50– 5 99... | 1 | 4 | 7 | 76 | 11 | 82 | 3 | 31 | 2 | 10 | 5 | 3 | 4 | 1 | ... 5 50– 5 99 |
| 6 00– 6 49... | 1 | 2 | 17 | 78 | 26 | 116 | 11 | 55 | 7 | 21 | 2 | 8 | 4 | 4 | ... 6 00– 6 49 |
| 6 50– 6 99... | .... | 2 | 8 | 39 | 13 | 116 | 7 | 45 | 9 | 15 | 2 | 1 | 6 | 5 | ... 6 50– 6 99 |
| 7 00– 7 49... | .... | 2 | 13 | 51 | 23 | 119 | 11 | 45 | 7 | 21 | 3 | 5 | 4 | 4 | ... 7 00– 7 49 |
| 7 50– 7 99... | .... | 1 | 4 | 39 | 14 | 96 | 13 | 36 | 8 | 4 | 7 | 7 | 1 | 9 | ... 7 50– 7 99 |
| 8 00– 8 99... | .... | 1 | 5 | 43 | 43 | 171 | 30 | 81 | 25 | 26 | 12 | 18 | 5 | 3 | ... 8 00– 8 99 |
| 9 00– 9 99... | .... | ...... | 7 | 21 | 25 | 104 | 25 | 74 | 26 | 23 | 16 | 6 | 10 | 6 | ... 9 00– 9 99 |
| 10 00–10 99... | .... | ...... | 1 | 12 | 19 | 75 | 20 | 41 | 17 | 22 | 8 | 7 | 16 | 5 | ...10 00–10 99 |
| 11 00–11 99... | .... | ...... | 1 | 5 | 18 | 28 | 18 | 29 | 25 | 3 | 20 | 1 | 9 | 6 | ...11 00–11 99 |
| 12 00–12 99... | .... | ...... | .... | 5 | 14 | 23 | 22 | 26 | 21 | 12 | 21 | 8 | 19 | 5 | ...12 00–12 99 |
| 13 00–13 99... | .... | ...... | .... | 3 | 13 | 14 | 24 | 13 | 18 | 3 | 16 | 3 | 14 | 5 | ...13 00–13 99 |
| 14 00–14 99... | .... | ...... | 1 | ...... | 4 | 5 | 19 | 6 | 20 | 7 | 11 | 2 | 11 | 3 | ...14 00–14 99 |
| 15 00–15 99... | .... | ...... | .... | 1 | 6 | 4 | 14 | 4 | 14 | 5 | 11 | 4 | 15 | 1 | ...15 00–15 99 |
| 16 00–17 99... | .... | ...... | .... | ...... | 6 | 3 | 21 | 4 | 38 | 3 | 22 | 1 | 14 | 2 | ...16 00–17 99 |
| 18 00–19 99... | .... | ...... | .... | ...... | 2 | 3 | 14 | 3 | 21 | 1 | 14 | ...... | 12 | ...... | ...18 00–19 99 |
| 20 00–24 99... | .... | ...... | .... | ...... | 2 | 1 | 9 | 2 | 11 | ...... | 16 | ...... | 17 | ...... | ...20 00–24 99 |
| 25 00–29 99... | .... | ...... | .... | ...... | ...... | 1 | ...... | ...... | 3 | ...... | 1 | ...... | 4 | ...... | ...25 00–29 99 |
| 30 00–34 99... | .... | ...... | .... | ...... | ...... | ...... | ...... | ...... | 1 | ...... | 2 | ...... | 4 | ...... | ...30 00–34 99 |
| 35 00–39 99... | .... | ...... | .... | ...... | ...... | ...... | ...... | ...... | ...... | ...... | ...... | ...... | ...... | ...... | ...35 00–39 99 |
| 40 00 and over. | .... | ...... | .... | ...... | ...... | ...... | ...... | ...... | ...... | ...... | ...... | ...... | 2 | ...... | .40 00 and over |
| Not reported.. | .... | ...... | .... | ...... | ...... | 3 | 1 | ...... | 1 | ...... | ...... | ...... | ...... | ...... | ..Not reported |
| Total..... | 19 | 174 | 109 | 849 | 279 | 1,348 | 292 | 631 | 294 | 233 | 201 | 98 | 181 | 80 | .....Total |

245. TABLE VI, B. 1. a. — (*concluded*)

NEW YORK CITY — NEGLIGEE SHIRTS

**THE MEN'S SHIRT INDUSTRY — FACTORY WORKERS**

NUMBER AND PER CENT. OF EMPLOYEES CLASSIFIED ACCORDING TO ACTUAL WEEKLY EARNINGS, BY AGE GROUPS AND SEX

| WEEKLY RATES IN DOLLARS | AGE GROUPS IN YEARS (*concluded*) 40–44 | | 45–54 | | 55–64 | | 65 AND OVER | NOT REPORTED | | TOTAL | | CUMULATIVE PER CENT. OF TOTAL | | WEEKLY RATES IN DOLLARS |
|---|---|---|---|---|---|---|---|---|---|---|---|---|---|---|
| | Male | Female | Male | Female | Male | Female | Male | Male | Female | Male | Female | Male | Female | |
| Less than $3 00 | ...... | 1 | 2 | 5 | 1 | ...... | ...... | ...... | ...... | 44 | 187 | 2.70 | 5.30 | Less than $3 00 |
| $3 00–$3 49 | ...... | ...... | 1 | 2 | ...... | ...... | 1 | ...... | ...... | 21 | 156 | 3.90 | 9.80 | $3 00– 3 49 |
| 3 50– 3 99 | 1 | 2 | 1 | 2 | ...... | ...... | ...... | ...... | ...... | 20 | 169 | 5.20 | 14.60 | 3 50– 3 99 |
| 4 00– 4 49 | 5 | 3 | 2 | 6 | 2 | ...... | ...... | ...... | ...... | 37 | 236 | 7.40 | 21.40 | 4 00– 4 49 |
| 4 50– 4 99 | 2 | 1 | 2 | 4 | ...... | 2 | ...... | ...... | ...... | 29 | 234 | 9.20 | 28.00 | 4 50– 4 99 |
| 5 00– 5 49 | 2 | 5 | 5 | 3 | ...... | 1 | ...... | ...... | 1 | 50 | 316 | 12.30 | 37.10 | 5 00– 5 49 |
| 5 50– 5 99 | 3 | 2 | 2 | 5 | ...... | ...... | ...... | ...... | 1 | 38 | 215 | 14.60 | 43.20 | 5 50– 5 99 |
| 6 00– 6 49 | 5 | 4 | 8 | 4 | 6 | 3 | ...... | ...... | ...... | 87 | 295 | 19.90 | 51.60 | 6 00– 6 49 |
| 6 50– 6 99 | 5 | 1 | 1 | 1 | 1 | ...... | 1 | ...... | ...... | 53 | 225 | 23.10 | 58.00 | 6 50– 6 99 |
| 7 00– 7 49 | 1 | 1 | 6 | 4 | ...... | ...... | ...... | ...... | 1 | 68 | 253 | 27.20 | 65.40 | 7 00– 7 49 |
| 7 50– 7 99 | 1 | 2 | 8 | 1 | ...... | ...... | ...... | ...... | 1 | 56 | 196 | 30.70 | 71.10 | 7 50– 7 99 |
| 8 00– 8 99 | 5 | 2 | 8 | 4 | 3 | ...... | 1 | ...... | ...... | 137 | 349 | 39.00 | 80.80 | 8 00– 8 99 |
| 9 00– 9 99 | 10 | 3 | 12 | ...... | 2 | ...... | ...... | ...... | 1 | 133 | 238 | 47.20 | 87.60 | 9 00– 9 99 |
| 10 00–10 99 | 11 | 3 | 10 | 3 | 1 | ...... | 1 | 2 | ...... | 106 | 168 | 53.60 | 92.40 | 10 00–10 99 |
| 11 00–11 99 | 8 | 1 | 5 | ...... | 2 | ...... | ...... | ...... | ...... | 106 | 73 | 60.00 | 94.50 | 11 00–11 99 |
| 12 00–12 99 | 13 | 4 | 4 | 1 | 3 | ...... | ...... | ...... | ...... | 117 | 84 | 62.20 | 96.80 | 12 00–12 99 |
| 13 00–13 99 | 6 | ...... | 8 | ...... | ...... | ...... | ...... | 1 | ...... | 100 | 41 | 73.30 | 98.00 | 13 00–13 99 |
| 14 00–14 99 | 9 | ...... | 5 | 1 | ...... | ...... | ...... | ...... | ...... | 80 | 24 | 78.20 | 98.90 | 14 00–14 99 |
| 15 00–15 99 | 6 | 1 | 7 | ...... | 1 | ...... | ...... | 1 | ...... | 75 | 20 | 82.70 | 99.40 | 15 00–15 99 |
| 16 00–17 99 | 13 | ...... | 2 | ...... | ...... | ...... | ...... | ...... | ...... | 116 | 13 | 89.90 | 99.70 | 16 00–17 99 |
| 18 00–19 99 | 3 | ...... | 1 | ...... | ...... | ...... | ...... | 1 | ...... | 68 | 7 | 94.00 | 99.90 | 18 00–19 99 |
| 20 00–24 99 | 6 | ...... | 10 | ...... | 1 | ...... | ...... | ...... | ...... | 72 | 3 | 98.50 | 99.90 | 20 00–24 99 |
| 25 00–29 99 | 2 | ...... | 2 | ...... | ...... | ...... | ...... | ...... | ...... | 12 | 1 | 99.10 | 100.00 | 25 00–29 99 |
| 30 00–34 99 | ...... | ...... | 2 | ...... | 1 | ...... | ...... | ...... | ...... | 10 | ...... | 99.70 | ...... | 30 00–34 99 |
| 35 00–39 99 | ...... | ...... | 1 | ...... | ...... | ...... | ...... | ...... | ...... | 1 | ...... | 99.80 | ...... | 35 00–39 99 |
| 40 00 and over | 1 | ...... | 1 | ...... | ...... | ...... | ...... | ...... | ...... | 4 | ...... | 100.00 | ...... | 40 00 and over |
| Not reported | ...... | ...... | ...... | ...... | ...... | ...... | ...... | ...... | ...... | 2 | 3 | ...... | ...... | Not reported |
| Total | 118 | 36 | 116 | 46 | 24 | 6 | 4 | 5 | 5 | 1,642 | 3,506 | ...... | ...... | Total |

246. TABLE IX, B, 1, a.

NEW YORK CITY—NEGLIGEE SHIRTS

THE MEN'S SHIRT INDUSTRY — FACTORY WORKERS

NUMBER AND PER CENT. OF EMPLOYEES CLASSIFIED ACCORDING TO ACTUAL WEEKLY EARNINGS BY OCCUPATION AND SEX

| ACTUAL WEEKLY EARNINGS IN DOLLARS | OCCUPATION | | | | | | | | | | | | | | ACTUAL WEEKLY EARNINGS IN DOLLARS |
|---|---|---|---|---|---|---|---|---|---|---|---|---|---|---|---|
| | MARKERS | | CUTTERS | TRIMMERS | CUTTERS' HELPERS | | FOREMEN AND FOREWOMEN | | OPERATORS | | FLOOR WORK | | LAUNDRY HELPERS | | |
| | Male | Female | Male | Male | Male | Female | Male | Female | Male | Female | Male | Female | Male | Female | |
| Less than $3 00 | .... | ...... | .... | ...... | 6 | ...... | ...... | ...... | 25 | 125 | 4 | 48 | ...... | ...... | Less than $3 00 |
| $3 00–$3 49... | .... | ...... | 1 | ...... | 3 | ...... | ...... | 1 | 9 | 89 | 5 | 54 | ...... | ...... | ...$3 00– 3 49 |
| 3 50– 3 99... | .... | ...... | .... | ...... | 1 | ...... | ...... | ...... | 11 | 100 | 1 | 57 | ...... | ...... | ... 3 50– 3 99 |
| 4 00– 4 49... | .... | ...... | 1 | ...... | 5 | 2 | 1 | ...... | 13 | 139 | 6 | 72 | 1 | ...... | ... 4 00– 4 49 |
| 4 50– 4 99... | .... | ...... | .... | ...... | 5 | 4 | ...... | 1 | 10 | 165 | 1 | 39 | 2 | ...... | ... 4 50– 4 99 |
| 5 00– 5 49... | .... | ...... | 1 | 1 | 9 | 1 | ...... | ...... | 21 | 201 | 2 | 58 | 1 | 2 | ... 5 00– 5 49 |
| 5 50– 5 99... | .... | ...... | .... | ...... | 6 | 1 | ...... | ...... | 13 | 149 | 2 | 33 | ...... | 1 | ... 5 0– 5 99 |
| 6 00– 6 49... | .... | ...... | 1 | ...... | 15 | 2 | ...... | ...... | 33 | 205 | 10 | 41 | 3 | 2 | ... 6 00– 6 49 |
| 6 50– 6 99... | .... | ...... | 2 | 1 | 14 | 1 | ...... | 3 | 17 | 170 | 3 | 19 | ...... | ...... | ... 6 50– 6 99 |
| 7 00– 7 49... | .... | ...... | .... | 2 | 13 | 2 | ...... | 1 | 27 | 193 | 7 | 21 | 1 | ...... | ... 7 00– 7 49 |
| 7 50– 7 99... | .... | ...... | 5 | 1 | 11 | 2 | ...... | 3 | 19 | 167 | 1 | 6 | 1 | ...... | ... 7 50– 7 99 |
| 8 00– 8 99... | .... | ...... | 6 | 2 | 22 | 1 | 3 | 5 | 50 | 288 | 3 | 14 | ...... | ...... | ... 8 00– 8 99 |
| 9 00– 9 99... | .... | ...... | 6 | 3 | 13 | 2 | 1 | 6 | 55 | 187 | 3 | 10 | 1 | ...... | ... 9 00– 9 99 |
| 10 00–10 99... | .... | ...... | 4 | 1 | 5 | 1 | ...... | 6 | 48 | 133 | ...... | 2 | 1 | ...... | ...10 00–10 99 |
| 11 00–11 99... | .... | ...... | 2 | 6 | 2 | ...... | 1 | 3 | 56 | 57 | ...... | ...... | ...... | ...... | ...11 00–11 99 |
| 12 00–12 99... | 1 | ...... | 6 | ...... | 2 | ...... | 2 | 5 | 66 | 65 | ...... | 1 | 2 | ...... | ...12 00–12 99 |
| 13 00–13 99... | .... | ...... | 8 | 4 | 1 | ...... | 2 | 1 | 44 | 37 | 1 | 1 | ...... | ...... | ...13 00–13 99 |
| 14 00–14 99... | 1 | 1 | 5 | 4 | ...... | ...... | 2 | 3 | 44 | 14 | ...... | ...... | ...... | 1 | ...14 00–14 99 |
| 15 00–15 99... | .... | ...... | 8 | 3 | ...... | ...... | 5 | 1 | 40 | 13 | ...... | ...... | ...... | ...... | ...15 00–15 99 |
| 16 00–17 99... | 3 | ...... | 10 | 1 | ...... | ...... | 12 | 3 | 51 | 8 | ...... | ...... | ...... | ...... | ...16 00–17 99 |
| 18 00–19 99... | 3 | ...... | 21 | 1 | ...... | ...... | 5 | ...... | 22 | 7 | ...... | ...... | 1 | ...... | ...18 00–19 99 |
| 20 00–24 99... | 18 | ...... | 13 | ...... | ...... | ...... | 14 | ...... | 15 | 3 | ...... | ...... | ...... | ...... | ...20 00–24 99 |
| 25 00–29 99... | 1 | ...... | 1 | ...... | ...... | ...... | 8 | ...... | 2 | 1 | ...... | ...... | ...... | ...... | ...25 00–29 99 |
| 30 00–34 99... | 1 | ...... | 3 | ...... | ...... | ...... | 6 | ...... | ...... | ...... | ...... | ...... | ...... | ...... | ...30 00–34 99 |
| 35 00–39 99... | .... | ...... | .... | ...... | ...... | ...... | 1 | ...... | ...... | ...... | ...... | ...... | ...... | ...... | ...35 00–39 99 |
| 40 00 and over. | 1 | ...... | .... | ...... | ...... | ...... | 3 | ...... | ...... | ...... | ...... | ...... | ...... | ...... | .40 00 and over |
| Not reported... | .... | ...... | 1 | ...... | ...... | ...... | ...... | ...... | 1 | 2 | ...... | 1 | ...... | ...... | ...Not reported |
| Total..... | 29 | 1 | 105 | 30 | 133 | 19 | 66 | 42 | 692 | 2,518 | 49 | 477 | 14 | 6 | .....Total |

246. TABLE X, B, 1, a —(*concluded*)

NEW YORK CITY—NEGLIGEE SHIRTS
THE MEN'S SHIRT INDUSTRY — FACTORY WORKERS

Number and Per Cent. of Employees Classified According to Actual Weekly Earnings, by Occupation and Sex

| Actual Weekly Earnings in Dollars | Occupation (*concluded*): Starchers and Dampners |  | Ironers and Pressers |  | Examiners |  | Folders |  | Packers |  | Not Reported |  | Total |  | Cumulative Per Cent. of Total |  | Actual Weekly Earnings Dollars |
|---|---|---|---|---|---|---|---|---|---|---|---|---|---|---|---|---|---|
|  | Male | Female | Male | Female | Male | Female | Male | Female | Male | Female | Male | Female | Male | Female | Male | Female |  |
| Less than $3 00 | .... | ...... | 8 | 4 | .... | 4 | .... | 1 | .... | 5 | 1 | ..... | 44 | 187 | 2.70 | 5.30 | Less than $3 00 |
| $3 00–$3 49... | .... | ...... | 3 | 4 | .... | 2 | .... | 3 | .... | 2 | .... | 1 | 21 | 156 | 3.90 | 9.80 | ...$3 00– 3 49 |
| 3 50– 3 99... | .... | ...... | 7 | 4 | .... | 3 | .... | 3 | .... | 1 | .... | 1 | 20 | 169 | 5.20 | 14.60 | ... 3 50– 3 99 |
| 4 00– 4 49... | .... | 1 | 8 | 3 | .... | 11 | 1 | 2 | 1 | 6 | .... | ..... | 37 | 236 | 7.40 | 21.40 | ... 4 00– 4 49 |
| 4 50– 4 99... | 1 | ...... | 7 | 6 | .... | 6 | 1 | 1 | 2 | 10 | .... | 2 | 29 | 234 | 9.20 | 28.00 | ... 4 50– 4 99 |
| 5 00– 5 49... | .... | 7 | 11 | 8 | .... | 14 | 1 | 4 | 3 | 17 | .... | 4 | 50 | 316 | 12.30 | 37.10 | ... 5 00– 5 49 |
| 5 50– 5 99... | .... | 5 | 13 | 8 | .... | 5 | .... | 8 | 3 | 3 | 1 | 2 | 38 | 215 | 14.60 | 43.20 | ... 5 50– 5 99 |
| 6 00– 6 49... | .... | 5 | 18 | 13 | .... | 16 | 1 | 1 | 6 | 8 | .... | 2 | 87 | 295 | 19.90 | 51.60 | ... 6 00– 6 49 |
| 6 50– 6 99... | .... | 3 | 13 | 6 | 1 | 14 | 1 | 4 | .... | 5 | 1 | ..... | 53 | 225 | 23.10 | 58.00 | ... 6 50– 6 99 |
| 7 00– 7 49... | .... | 14 | 15 | 9 | .... | 6 | 2 | 3 | 1 | 4 | .... | ..... | 68 | 253 | 27.20 | 65.40 | ... 7 00– 7 49 |
| 7 50– 7 99... | .... | 2 | 17 | 6 | .... | 7 | .... | 2 | 1 | 1 | .... | ..... | 56 | 196 | 30 70 | 71.00 | ... 7 50– 7 99 |
| 8 00– 8 99... | 1 | 4 | 43 | 22 | .... | 12 | 2 | 1 | 5 | 1 | .... | 1 | 137 | 349 | 39.00 | 80.80 | ... 8 00– 8 99 |
| 9 00– 9 99... | .... | 5 | 46 | 11 | .... | 12 | 1 | 2 | 4 | 2 | .... | 1 | 133 | 238 | 47.20 | 87.60 | ... 9 00– 9 99 |
| 10 00–10 99... | .... | 2 | 41 | 10 | 1 | 7 | 3 | 2 | 2 | 5 | .... | ..... | 106 | 168 | 53.60 | 92.40 | ...10 00–10 99 |
| 11 00–11 99... | 2 | 3 | 35 | 9 | .... | ..... | 1 | 1 | 1 | ..... | .... | ..... | 106 | 73 | 60.00 | 94.50 | ...11 00–11 99 |
| 12 00–12 99... | .... | ...... | 36 | 9 | 1 | 4 | .... | ..... | 1 | ..... | .... | ..... | 117 | 84 | 62.20 | 96.80 | ...12 00–12 99 |
| 13 00–13 99... | .... | 1 | 36 | 1 | 1 | ..... | 1 | ..... | 2 | ..... | .... | ..... | 100 | 41 | 73.30 | 98.00 | ...13 00–13 99 |
| 14 00–14 99... | .... | 2 | 24 | 3 | .... | ..... | .... | ..... | .... | ..... | .... | ..... | 80 | 24 | 78.20 | 98.90 | ...14 00–14 99 |
| 15 00–15 99... | .... | 4 | 17 | ...... | 1 | 2 | 1 | ..... | .... | ..... | .... | ..... | 75 | 20 | 82.70 | 99.40 | ...15 00–15 99 |
| 16 00–17 99... | .... | 1 | 38 | 1 | 1 | ..... | .... | ..... | .... | ..... | .... | ..... | 116 | 13 | 89.90 | 99.70 | ...16 00–17 99 |
| 18 00–19 99... | .... | ...... | 15 | ...... | .... | ..... | .... | ..... | .... | ..... | .... | ..... | 68 | 7 | 94.00 | 99.90 | ...18 00–19 99 |
| 20 00–24 99... | .... | ...... | 10 | ...... | .... | ..... | 1 | ..... | .... | ..... | 1 | ..... | 72 | 3 | 98.50 | 99.90 | ...20 00–24 99 |
| 25 00–29 99... | .... | ...... | .... | ...... | .... | ..... | .... | ..... | .... | ..... | .... | ..... | 12 | 1 | 99.10 | 100.00 | ...25 00–29 99 |
| 30 00–34 99... | .... | ...... | .... | ...... | .... | ..... | .... | ..... | .... | ..... | .... | ..... | 10 | ..... | 99.70 | ..... | ...30 00–34 99 |
| 35 00–39 99... | .... | ...... | .... | ...... | .... | ..... | .... | ..... | .... | ..... | .... | ..... | 1 | ..... | 99.80 | ..... | ...35 00–39 99 |
| 40 00 and over. | .... | ...... | .... | ...... | .... | ..... | .... | ..... | .... | ..... | .... | ..... | 4 | ..... | 100.00 | ..... | .40 00 and over |
| Not reported... | .... | ...... | .... | ...... | .... | ..... | .... | ..... | .... | ..... | .... | ..... | 2 | 3 | .... | ..... | ...Not reported |
| Total..... | 4 | 59 | 461 | 137 | 6 | 125 | 17 | 38 | 32 | 70 | 4 | 14 | 1,642 | 3,506 | .... | ..... | ...Total |

247. TABLE V, B, 2, a

NEW YORK CITY

THE MEN'S SHIRT INDUSTRY — WORKING SHIRTS — FACTORY WORKERS

NUMBER AND PER CENT. OF EMPLOYEES EARNING SPECIFIED WEEKLY RATES, BY AGE GROUPS AND SEX

| WEEKLY RATES IN DOLLARS | AGE GROUPS IN YEARS | | | | | | | | | | | | | | WEEKLY RATES IN DOLLARS |
|---|---|---|---|---|---|---|---|---|---|---|---|---|---|---|---|
| | 14–15 | | 16–17 | | 18–20 | | 21–24 | | 25–29 | | 30–34 | | 35–39 | | |
| | Male | Female | Male | Female | Male | Female | Male | Female | Male | Female | Male | Female | Male | Female | |
| Less than $3 00 | .... | 3 | .... | ...... | ...... | ...... | ...... | ...... | ...... | ...... | ...... | ...... | ...... | ...... | Less than $3 00 |
| $3 00–$3 49... | 1 | 16 | 1 | 2 | ...... | ...... | ...... | ...... | ...... | ...... | ...... | ...... | ...... | 1 | ...$3 00– 3 49 |
| 3 50– 3 99... | .... | 5 | .... | 7 | ...... | 4 | ...... | ...... | ...... | ...... | ...... | ...... | ...... | ...... | ... 3 50– 3 99 |
| 4 00– 4 49... | .... | 1 | .... | 7 | 3 | 7 | 1 | 2 | 1 | ...... | ...... | ...... | ...... | 1 | ... 4 00– 4 49 |
| 4 50– 4 99... | 2 | 1 | .... | 3 | ...... | 3 | ...... | 2 | ...... | 1 | ...... | 1 | ...... | 1 | ... 4 50– 4 99 |
| 5 00– 5 49... | .... | 1 | 8 | 2 | 5 | 4 | 2 | ...... | ...... | ...... | ...... | 1 | ...... | ...... | ... 5 00– 5 49 |
| 5 50– 5 99... | .... | 1 | 3 | 3 | 2 | 3 | 1 | 2 | ...... | 2 | ...... | ...... | ...... | ...... | ... 5 50– 5 99 |
| 6 00– 6 49... | .... | 1 | 5 | 5 | 6 | 13 | 1 | 5 | ...... | 1 | ...... | ...... | ...... | 1 | ... 6 00– 6 49 |
| 6 50– 6 99... | .... | ...... | 1 | 3 | 4 | 2 | ...... | 2 | ...... | ...... | ...... | ...... | ...... | ...... | ... 6 50– 6 99 |
| 7 00– 7 49... | .... | ...... | .... | 3 | 4 | 6 | ...... | 3 | ...... | ...... | ...... | ...... | ...... | ...... | ... 7 00– 7 49 |
| 7 50– 7 99... | .... | ...... | 1 | 1 | ...... | 7 | ...... | ...... | ...... | ...... | ...... | ...... | ...... | ...... | ... 7 50– 7 99 |
| 8 00– 8 99... | .... | ...... | 6 | ...... | 10 | 8 | 4 | 5 | 1 | ...... | ...... | 1 | 2 | 1 | ... 8 00– 8 99 |
| 9 00– 9 99... | .... | ...... | 1 | ...... | 5 | 5 | 1 | 4 | ...... | 2 | 1 | ...... | 1 | ...... | ... 9 00– 9 99 |
| 10 00–10 99... | .... | ...... | .... | ...... | 5 | 4 | 2 | 2 | 1 | 1 | ...... | ...... | ...... | ...... | ...10 00–10 99 |
| 11 00–11 99... | .... | ...... | .... | ...... | 1 | 2 | 1 | ...... | 3 | 1 | 1 | ...... | ...... | ...... | ...11 00–11 99 |
| 12 00–12 99... | .... | ...... | .... | ...... | 2 | ...... | 2 | 1 | 3 | ...... | ...... | ...... | 1 | ...... | ...12 00–12 99 |
| 13 00–13 99... | .... | ...... | .... | ...... | 2 | ...... | 1 | ...... | 4 | ...... | ...... | ...... | 2 | ...... | ...13 00–13 99 |
| 14 00–14 99... | .... | ...... | .... | ...... | 1 | ...... | 5 | ...... | 5 | ...... | ...... | ...... | ...... | ...... | ...14 00–14 99 |
| 15 00–15 99... | .... | ...... | .... | ...... | ...... | ...... | 2 | ...... | ...... | ...... | ...... | ...... | 1 | ...... | ...15 00–15 99 |
| 16 00–17 99... | .... | ...... | .... | ...... | ...... | ...... | 1 | ...... | 2 | ...... | 3 | ...... | 1 | ...... | ...16 00–17 99 |
| 18 00–19 99... | .... | ...... | .... | ...... | 1 | ...... | 2 | ...... | 3 | ...... | 1 | ...... | 3 | ...... | ...18 00–19 99 |
| 20 00–24 99... | .... | ...... | .... | ...... | ...... | ...... | 1 | ...... | 4 | ...... | ...... | ...... | 1 | ...... | ...20 00–24 99 |
| 25 00–29 99... | .... | ...... | .... | ...... | ...... | ...... | ...... | ...... | ...... | ...... | 2 | ...... | 1 | ...... | ...25 00–29 99 |
| 30 00–34 99... | .... | ...... | .... | ...... | ...... | ...... | ...... | ...... | ...... | ...... | 1 | ...... | ...... | ...... | ...30 00–34 99 |
| Not reported... | .... | ...... | .... | ...... | ...... | ...... | ...... | ...... | ...... | 1 | ...... | ...... | ...... | ...... | ...Not reported |
| Total..... | 3 | 29 | 26 | 36 | 51 | 68 | 27 | 28 | 27 | 9 | 9 | 3 | 13 | 5 | .....Total |

247. TABLE V, B, 2, a (*concluded*)

NEW YORK CITY

THE MEN'S SHIRT INDUSTRY — WORKING SHIRTS — FACTORY WORKERS

NUMBER AND PER CENT. OF EMPLOYEES EARNING SPECIFIED WEEKLY RATES, BY AGE GROUPS AND SEX

| WEEKLY RATES IN DOLLARS | AGE GROUPS IN YEARS (*concluded*) | | | | | | | | | | WEEKLY RATES IN DOLLARS |
|---|---|---|---|---|---|---|---|---|---|---|---|
| | 40–44 | | 45–54 | | 55–64 | NOT REPORTED | TOTAL | | CUMULATIVE PER CENT. OF TOTAL | | |
| | Male | Female | Male | Female | Male | Female | Male | Female | Male | Female | |
| Less than $3 00 | ........ | ........ | ........ | ........ | ........ | ........ | ........ | 3 | ........ | 1.60 | Less than $3 00 |
| $3 00–$3 49 | ........ | ........ | ........ | ........ | ........ | ........ | 2 | 19 | 1.10 | 12.00 | $3 00– 3 49 |
| 3 50– 3 99 | ........ | ........ | ........ | ........ | ........ | ........ | ........ | 16 | ........ | 20.70 | 3 50– 3 99 |
| 4 00– 4 49 | ........ | ........ | ........ | 2 | ........ | ........ | 5 | 20 | 4.00 | 31.50 | 4 00– 4 49 |
| 4 50– 4 99 | ........ | 1 | ........ | 1 | ........ | 1 | 2 | 15 | 5.10 | 39.70 | 4 50– 4 99 |
| 5 00– 5 49 | ........ | ........ | ........ | ........ | ........ | ........ | 15 | 8 | 13.60 | 44.00 | 5 00– 5 49 |
| 5 50– 5 99 | ........ | ........ | ........ | ........ | ........ | ........ | 6 | 11 | 17.00 | 50.00 | 5 50– 5 99 |
| 6 00– 6 49 | ........ | ........ | ........ | 1 | 1 | ........ | 13 | 27 | 24.50 | 64.50 | 6 00– 6 49 |
| 6 50– 6 99 | ........ | ........ | ........ | ........ | ........ | ........ | 5 | 7 | 27.20 | 68.50 | 6 50– 6 99 |
| 7 00– 7 49 | ........ | 1 | ........ | ........ | ........ | ........ | 4 | 13 | 29.50 | 75.50 | 7 00– 7 49 |
| 7 50– 7 99 | ........ | ........ | 1 | ........ | ........ | ........ | 2 | 8 | 30.70 | 80.00 | 7 50– 7 99 |
| 8 00– 8 99 | ........ | ........ | 4 | ........ | ........ | ........ | 27 | 15 | 46.00 | 88.00 | 8 00– 8 99 |
| 9 00– 9 99 | 1 | ........ | ........ | ........ | ........ | ........ | 10 | 11 | 51.80 | 94.00 | 9 00– 9 99 |
| 10 00–10 99 | ........ | ........ | 1 | ........ | 1 | ........ | 10 | 7 | 57.50 | 98.00 | 10 00–10 99 |
| 11 00–11 99 | 2 | ........ | ........ | ........ | ........ | ........ | 8 | 3 | 62 00 | 99.50 | 11 00–11 99 |
| 12 00–12 99 | 2 | ........ | 1 | ........ | ........ | ........ | 11 | 1 | 68.00 | 100.00 | 12 00–12 99 |
| 13 00–13 99 | 3 | ........ | ........ | ........ | ........ | ........ | 12 | ........ | 75.00 | ........ | 13 00–13 99 |
| 14 00–14 99 | ........ | ........ | ........ | ........ | ........ | ........ | 11 | ........ | 81.50 | ........ | 14 00–14 99 |
| 15 00–15 99 | ........ | ........ | ........ | ........ | ........ | ........ | 3 | ........ | 83.00 | ........ | 15 00–15 99 |
| 16 00–17 99 | 1 | ........ | ........ | ........ | ........ | ........ | 8 | ........ | 87.50 | ........ | 16 00–17 99 |
| 18 00–19 99 | ........ | ........ | ........ | ........ | ........ | ........ | 10 | ........ | 93.00 | ........ | 18 00–19 99 |
| 20 00–24 99 | 2 | ........ | ........ | ........ | ........ | ........ | 8 | ........ | 97.50 | ........ | 20 00–24 99 |
| 25 00–29 99 | ........ | ........ | ........ | ........ | ........ | ........ | 3 | ........ | 99.40 | ........ | 25 00–29 99 |
| 30 00–34 99 | ........ | ........ | ........ | ........ | ........ | ........ | 1 | ........ | 100.00 | ........ | 30 00–34 99 |
| Total | 11 | 2 | 7 | 4 | 2 | 1 | 176 | 185 | ........ | ........ | Total |

248. TABLE VIII, B, 2, a

NEW YORK CITY

THE MEN'S SHIRT INDUSTRY — WORKING SHIRTS — FACTORY WORKERS

NUMBER AND PER CENT. OF EMPLOYEES EARNING SPECIFIED WEEKLY RATES, BY OCCUPATION AND SEX

| WEEKLY RATES IN DOLLARS | OCCUPATION | | | | | | | | | | | WEEKLY RATES IN DOLLARS |
|---|---|---|---|---|---|---|---|---|---|---|---|---|
| | MARKERS | CUTTERS | TRIMMERS | CUTTERS' HELPERS | | FOREMEN AND FOREWOMEN | | OPERATORS | | FLOOR WORK | | |
| | Male | Male | Male | Male | Female | Male | Female | Male | Female | Male | Female | |
| Less than $3 00 | ........ | ........ | ........ | ........ | ........ | ........ | ........ | ........ | ........ | ........ | 1 | Less than $3 00 |
| $3 00–$3 49... | ........ | ........ | ........ | ........ | 1 | ........ | ........ | 2 | 3 | ........ | 1 | ...$3 00– 3 49 |
| 3 50– 3 99... | ........ | ........ | ........ | ........ | ........ | ........ | ........ | ........ | 1 | ........ | 5 | ... 3 50– 3 99 |
| 4 00– 4 49... | ........ | ........ | ........ | 1 | ........ | ........ | ........ | 3 | 2 | 1 | 1 | ... 4 00– 4 49 |
| 4 50– 4 99... | ........ | ........ | ........ | 2 | ........ | ........ | ........ | ........ | 3 | ........ | 3 | ... 4 50– 4 99 |
| 5 00– 5 49... | ........ | 2 | ........ | 8 | ........ | ........ | ........ | 1 | 3 | 1 | 2 | ... 5 00– 5 49 |
| 5 50– 5 99... | ........ | ........ | ........ | 3 | ........ | ........ | ........ | ........ | 3 | 1 | 3 | ... 5 50– 5 99 |
| 6 00– 6 49... | ........ | ........ | 1 | 4 | ........ | ........ | ........ | 1 | 8 | 3 | 5 | ... 6 00– 6 49 |
| 6 50– 6 99... | ........ | ........ | ........ | ........ | ........ | ........ | ........ | 1 | ........ | ........ | 2 | ... 6 50– 6 99 |
| 7 00– 7 49... | ........ | 1 | 1 | ........ | ........ | ........ | ........ | ........ | 5 | 1 | 3 | ... 7 00– 7 49 |
| 7 50– 7 99... | ........ | 1 | ........ | ........ | ........ | ........ | ........ | ........ | 1 | ........ | 3 | ... 7 50– 7 99 |
| 8 00– 8 99... | ........ | ........ | 1 | 14 | ........ | ........ | 2 | 3 | 8 | 1 | 2 | ... 8 00– 8 99 |
| 9 00– 9 99... | 1 | 3 | ........ | 2 | ........ | 1 | 4 | ........ | 3 | 1 | ........ | ... 9 00– 9 99 |
| 10 00–10 99... | 1 | 4 | ........ | ........ | ........ | ........ | ........ | 3 | 6 | ........ | ........ | ...10 00–10 99 |
| 11 00–11 99... | ........ | 3 | 1 | ........ | ........ | 1 | 1 | ........ | 2 | ........ | ........ | ...11 00–11 99 |
| 12 00–12 99... | ........ | 3 | 1 | ........ | ........ | 2 | 1 | 4 | ........ | ........ | ........ | ...12 00–12 99 |
| 13 00–13 99... | 1 | 6 | 1 | ........ | ........ | 1 | ........ | 2 | ........ | ........ | ........ | ...13 00–13 99 |
| 14 00–14 99... | 2 | 5 | ........ | ........ | ........ | 2 | ........ | ........ | ........ | 1 | ........ | ...14 00–14 99 |
| 15 00–15 99... | ........ | ........ | ........ | ........ | ........ | 2 | ........ | ........ | ........ | ........ | ........ | ...15 00–15 99 |
| 16 00–17 99... | 1 | 4 | ........ | ........ | ........ | 3 | ........ | ........ | ........ | ........ | ........ | ...16 00–17 99 |
| 18 00–19 99... | 2 | 6 | ........ | ........ | ........ | 2 | ........ | ........ | ........ | ........ | ........ | ...18 00–19 99 |
| 20 00–24 99... | 2 | 3 | ........ | ........ | ........ | 3 | ........ | ........ | ........ | ........ | ........ | ...20 00–24 99 |
| 25 00–29 99... | 1 | ........ | ........ | ........ | ........ | 2 | ........ | ........ | ........ | ........ | ........ | ...25 00–29 99 |
| 30 00–34 99... | ........ | ........ | ........ | ........ | ........ | 1 | ........ | ........ | ........ | ........ | ........ | ...30 00–34 99 |
| Not reported.. | ........ | ........ | ........ | ........ | ........ | ........ | ........ | ........ | 1 | ........ | ........ | ..Not reported |
| Total..... | 11 | 41 | 6 | 34 | 1 | 20 | 8 | 20 | 49 | 10 | 31 | .....Total |

248. TABLE VIII, B, 2, a — (*concluded*)

NEW YORK CITY

THE MEN'S SHIRT INDUSTRY — WORKING SHIRTS — FACTORY WORKERS

NUMBER AND PER CENT. OF EMPLOYEES EARNING SPECIFIED WEEKLY RATES, BY OCCUPATION AND SEX

| WEEKLY RATES IN DOLLARS | OCCUPATION (*concluded*) | | | | | | | | | | | | | WEEKLY RATES IN DOLLARS |
|---|---|---|---|---|---|---|---|---|---|---|---|---|---|---|
| | IRONERS AND PRESSERS | | EXAMINERS | | FOLDERS | | PACKERS | | NOT REPORTED | TOTAL | | CUMULATIVE PER CENT. OF TOTAL | | |
| | Male | Female | Male | Female | Male | Female | Male | Female | Female | Male | Female | Male | Female | |
| Less than $3 00 | ...... | ...... | ...... | ...... | ...... | 2 | ...... | ...... | ...... | ...... | 3 | ...... | 1.60 | Less than $3 00 |
| $3 00–$3 49 | ...... | ...... | ...... | 1 | ...... | 13 | ...... | ...... | ...... | 2 | 19 | 1.10 | 12.00 | $3 00– 3 49 |
| 3 50– 3 99 | ...... | ...... | ...... | 1 | ...... | 4 | ...... | 5 | ...... | ...... | 16 | ...... | 20.70 | 3 50– 3 99 |
| 4 00– 4 49 | ...... | 2 | ...... | 2 | ...... | 4 | ...... | 9 | ...... | 5 | 20 | 4.00 | 31.50 | 4 00– 4 49 |
| 4 50– 4 99 | ...... | 1 | ...... | 3 | ...... | ...... | ...... | 5 | ...... | 2 | 15 | 5.10 | 39.70 | 4 50– 4 99 |
| 5 00– 5 49 | ...... | 1 | ...... | ...... | 1 | ...... | 2 | 2 | ...... | 15 | 8 | 13.60 | 44.00 | 5 00– 5 49 |
| 5 50– 5 99 | ...... | 3 | 1 | ...... | ...... | ...... | 1 | 2 | ...... | 6 | 11 | 17.00 | 50.00 | 5 50– 5 99 |
| 6 00– 6 49 | 1 | 9 | ...... | 4 | 2 | 1 | 1 | ...... | ...... | 13 | 27 | 24.50 | 64.50 | 6 00– 6 49 |
| 6 50– 6 99 | ...... | 2 | 1 | 1 | ...... | 1 | 3 | 1 | ...... | 5 | 7 | 27.20 | 68.50 | 6 50– 6 99 |
| 7 00– 7 49 | ...... | 1 | ...... | 2 | ...... | ...... | 1 | 2 | ...... | 4 | 13 | 29.50 | 75.50 | 7 00– 7 49 |
| 7 50– 7 99 | 1 | 3 | ...... | ...... | ...... | ...... | ...... | 1 | ...... | 2 | 8 | 30.70 | 80.00 | 7 50– 7 99 |
| 8 00– 8 99 | 6 | 1 | ...... | 2 | 1 | ...... | 1 | ...... | ...... | 27 | 15 | 46.00 | 88.00 | 8 00– 8 99 |
| 9 00– 9 99 | ...... | 1 | ...... | 1 | ...... | 1 | 2 | ...... | 1 | 10 | 11 | 51.80 | 94.00 | 9 00– 9 99 |
| 10 00–10 99 | ...... | ...... | 1 | 1 | ...... | ...... | 1 | ...... | ...... | 10 | 7 | 57.50 | 98.00 | 10 00–10 99 |
| 11 00–11 99 | ...... | ...... | 1 | ...... | 2 | ...... | ...... | ...... | ...... | 8 | 3 | 62.00 | 99.50 | 11 00–11 99 |
| 12 00–12 99 | ...... | ...... | 1 | ...... | ...... | ...... | ...... | ...... | ...... | 11 | 1 | 68.00 | 100.00 | 12 00–12 99 |
| 13 00–13 99 | ...... | ...... | ...... | ...... | 1 | ...... | ...... | ...... | ...... | 12 | ...... | 75.00 | ...... | 13 00–13 99 |
| 14 00–14 99 | ...... | ...... | ...... | ...... | 1 | ...... | ...... | ...... | ...... | 11 | ...... | 81.50 | ...... | 14 00–14 99 |
| 15 00–15 99 | ...... | ...... | ...... | ...... | 1 | ...... | ...... | ...... | ...... | 3 | ...... | 83.00 | ...... | 15 00–15 99 |
| 16 00–17 99 | ...... | ...... | ...... | ...... | ...... | ...... | ...... | ...... | ...... | 8 | ...... | 87.50 | ...... | 16 00–17 99 |
| 18 00–19 99 | ...... | ...... | ...... | ...... | ...... | ...... | ...... | ...... | ...... | 10 | ...... | 93.00 | ...... | 18 00–19 99 |
| 20 00–24 99 | ...... | ...... | ...... | ...... | ...... | ...... | ...... | ...... | ...... | 8 | ...... | 97.50 | ...... | 20 00–24 99 |
| 25 00–29 99 | ...... | ...... | ...... | ...... | ...... | ...... | ...... | ...... | ...... | 3 | ...... | 99.40 | ...... | 25 00–29 99 |
| 30 00–34 99 | ...... | ...... | ...... | ...... | ...... | ...... | ...... | ...... | ...... | 1 | ...... | 100.00 | ...... | 30 00–34 99 |
| Not reported | ...... | ...... | ...... | ...... | ...... | ...... | ...... | ...... | ...... | ...... | 1 | ...... | ...... | Not reported |
| Total | 8 | 24 | 5 | 18 | 9 | 26 | 12 | 27 | 1 | 176 | 185 | ...... | ...... | Total |

249. TABLE VI, B, 2, a

NEW YORK CITY

**THE MEN'S SHIRT INDUSTRY — WORKING SHIRTS — FACTORY WORKERS**

NUMBER AND PER CENT. OF EMPLOYEES CLASSIFIED ACCORDING TO ACTUAL WEEKLY EARNINGS, BY AGE GROUPS AND SEX

| ACTUAL WEEKLY EARNINGS IN DOLLARS | AGE GROUPS IN YEARS | | | | | | | | | | | | | | ACTUAL WEEKLY EARNINGS IN DOLLARS |
|---|---|---|---|---|---|---|---|---|---|---|---|---|---|---|---|
| | 14–15 | | 16–17 | | 18–20 | | 21–24 | | 25–29 | | 30–34 | | 35–39 | | |
| | Male | Female | Male | Female | Male | Female | Male | Female | Male | Female | Male | Female | Male | Female | |
| Less than $3 00 | .... | 11 | .... | 24 | 3 | 25 | 2 | 10 | ...... | 3 | ...... | 2 | ...... | 1 | Less than $3 00 |
| $3 00–$3 49... | 1 | 21 | 1 | 20 | 1 | 18 | ...... | 6 | ...... | 1 | ...... | ...... | ...... | 3 | ...$3 00– 3 49 |
| 3 50– 3 99... | .... | 10 | 1 | 18 | 1 | 16 | 1 | 8 | ...... | 2 | ...... | ...... | 1 | 1 | ... 3 50– 3 99 |
| 4 00– 4 49... | .... | 3 | 1 | 23 | 1 | 29 | ...... | 6 | 2 | 6 | ...... | 2 | ...... | 1 | ... 4 00– 4 49 |
| 4 50– 4 99... | 2 | 6 | 1 | 20 | ...... | 25 | ...... | 9 | ...... | 1 | ...... | 3 | ...... | 2 | ... 4 50– 4 99 |
| 5 00– 5 49... | .... | 7 | 9 | 26 | 3 | 26 | 2 | 10 | ...... | 5 | ...... | 1 | ...... | 1 | ... 5 00– 5 49 |
| 5 50– 5 99... | .... | 5 | 2 | 21 | 2 | 32 | 3 | 6 | ...... | 4 | ...... | 2 | ...... | 2 | ... 5 50– 5 99 |
| 6 00– 6 49... | .... | 2 | 4 | 14 | 7 | 51 | ...... | 16 | ...... | 6 | ...... | 3 | ...... | 2 | ... 6 00– 6 49 |
| 6 50– 6 99... | .... | ...... | 1 | 15 | 4 | 38 | ...... | 17 | ...... | 2 | ...... | ...... | ...... | 1 | ... 6 50– 6 90 |
| 7 00– 7 49... | .... | ...... | .... | 15 | 5 | 44 | 2 | 21 | 1 | 5 | 1 | 2 | ...... | 2 | ... 7 00– 7 49 |
| 7 50– 7 99... | .... | ...... | 3 | 10 | 2 | 39 | ...... | 8 | ...... | 4 | 1 | 2 | ...... | 2 | ... 7 50– 7 99 |
| 8 00– 8 99... | .... | ...... | 4 | 22 | 11 | 62 | 6 | 36 | 2 | 6 | 1 | 3 | 2 | 1 | ... 8 00– 8 99 |
| 9 00– 9 99... | .... | ...... | 1 | 6 | 7 | 32 | ...... | 19 | 2 | 5 | 1 | 1 | 1 | 2 | ... 9 00– 9 99 |
| 10 00–10 99... | .... | ...... | .... | 4 | 3 | 34 | 4 | 13 | 1 | 5 | 1 | 2 | 1 | ...... | ...10 00–10 99 |
| 11 00–11 99... | .... | ...... | .... | 1 | 2 | 6 | 2 | 3 | 3 | 5 | 2 | ...... | 2 | 1 | ...11 00–11 99 |
| 12 00–12 99... | .... | ...... | .... | 2 | 2 | 7 | 2 | 1 | 6 | 1 | ...... | ...... | 2 | ...... | ...12 00–12 99 |
| 13 00–13 99... | .... | ...... | .... | 1 | 1 | 2 | 3 | 1 | 3 | 1 | 1 | ...... | 2 | ...... | ...13 00–13 99 |
| 14 00–14 99... | .... | ...... | .... | ...... | 3 | 2 | 5 | 1 | 4 | ...... | ...... | ...... | 2 | ...... | ...14 00–14 99 |
| 15 00–15 99... | .... | ...... | .... | ...... | ...... | ...... | 1 | ...... | 2 | ...... | ...... | 1 | 1 | ...... | ...15 00–15 99 |
| 16 00–17 99... | .... | ...... | .... | ...... | ...... | 1 | 2 | ...... | 2 | ...... | 4 | ...... | 1 | ...... | ...16 00–17 99 |
| 18 00–19 99... | .... | ...... | .... | ...... | 1 | ...... | 2 | 1 | 3 | ...... | 1 | ...... | 4 | ...... | ...18 00–19 99 |
| 20 00–24 99... | .... | ...... | .... | ...... | ...... | ...... | 3 | ...... | 4 | ...... | ...... | ...... | 1 | ...... | ...20 00–24 99 |
| 25 00–29 99... | .... | ...... | .... | ...... | ...... | ...... | ...... | ...... | 1 | ...... | 2 | ...... | 1 | ...... | ...25 00–29 99 |
| 30 00–34 99... | .... | ...... | .... | ...... | ...... | ...... | ...... | ...... | ...... | ...... | 1 | ...... | ...... | ...... | ...30 00–34 99 |
| Not reported.. | .... | ...... | .... | ...... | ...... | 1 | ...... | ...... | ...... | ...... | ...... | ...... | ...... | ...... | ..Not reported |
| Total..... | 3 | 65 | 28 | 242 | 59 | 490 | 40 | 192 | 36 | 62 | 16 | 24 | 21 | 22 | .....Total |

249. TABLE VI, B, 2, a — (*concluded*)

NEW YORK CITY

**THE MEN'S SHIRT INDUSTRY — WORKING SHIRTS — FACTORY WORKERS**

NUMBER AND PER CENT. OF EMPLOYEES CLASSIFIED ACCORDING TO ACTUAL WEEKLY EARNINGS, BY AGE GROUPS AND SEX

| Actual Weekly Rates in Dollars | Age Groups in Years (*concluded*) 40–44 | | 45–54 | | 55–64 | | 65 and over | Not reported | | Total | | Cumulative per cent. of total | | Actual Weekly Rates in Dollars |
|---|---|---|---|---|---|---|---|---|---|---|---|---|---|---|
| | Male | Female | Male | Female | Male | Female | Male | Male | Female | Male | Female | Male | Female | |
| Less than $3 00 | ...... | ...... | ...... | ...... | 2 | ...... | ...... | ...... | ...... | 7 | 76 | 2.90 | 6.70 | Not reported |
| $3 00–$3 49 | ...... | ...... | 2 | ...... | ...... | 1 | ...... | ...... | ...... | 5 | 70 | 5.00 | 13.00 | $3 00–$3 49 |
| 3 50– 3 99 | ...... | ...... | 4 | ...... | ...... | ...... | ...... | ...... | 2 | 8 | 57 | 8.40 | 18.00 | 3 50– 3 99 |
| 4 00– 4 49 | ...... | 1 | 1 | 2 | ...... | ...... | ...... | ...... | 1 | 5 | 74 | 10.40 | 24.70 | 4 00– 4 49 |
| 4 50– 4 99 | ...... | 1 | ...... | 2 | ...... | ...... | ...... | ...... | ...... | 3 | 69 | 11.70 | 30.70 | 4 50– 4 99 |
| 5 00– 5 49 | ...... | 1 | ...... | 1 | ...... | 1 | ...... | ...... | 1 | 14 | 80 | 17.50 | 37.80 | 5 00– 5 49 |
| 5 50– 5 99 | ...... | ...... | ...... | ...... | ...... | ...... | ...... | ...... | 1 | 7 | 73 | 20.50 | 44.20 | 5 50– 5 99 |
| 6 00– 6 49 | ...... | ...... | ...... | 2 | 1 | ...... | 1 | ...... | ...... | 13 | 96 | 26.00 | 52.70 | 6 00– 6 49 |
| 6 50– 6 99 | ...... | 3 | ...... | 1 | ...... | ...... | ...... | ...... | 1 | 5 | 78 | 28.00 | 59.70 | 6 50– 6 99 |
| 7 00– 7 49 | 1 | 2 | 1 | 1 | 1 | ...... | ...... | ...... | 1 | 12 | 93 | 33.00 | 68.00 | 7 00– 7 49 |
| 7 50– 7 99 | ...... | ...... | 1 | ...... | 1 | ...... | ...... | ...... | ...... | 8 | 65 | 36.50 | 73.70 | 7 50– 7 99 |
| 8 00– 8 99 | ...... | ...... | 1 | ...... | ...... | ...... | ...... | ...... | ...... | 27 | 130 | 47.50 | 85.40 | 8 00– 8 99 |
| 9 00– 9 99 | 1 | ...... | ...... | 1 | ...... | ...... | ...... | ...... | 1 | 13 | 67 | 53.00 | 91.20 | 9 00– 9 99 |
| 10 00–10 99 | 1 | ...... | 1 | ...... | ...... | ...... | ...... | ...... | ...... | 12 | 58 | 58.00 | 96.50 | 10 00–10 99 |
| 11 00–11 99 | 2 | 1 | ...... | ...... | 1 | ...... | ...... | ...... | ...... | 14 | 17 | 64.00 | 98.00 | 11 00–11 99 |
| 12 00–12 99 | 3 | ...... | 1 | ...... | ...... | ...... | ...... | ...... | 1 | 16 | 12 | 70.70 | 99.10 | 12 00–12 99 |
| 13 00–13 99 | 2 | ...... | ...... | ...... | ...... | ...... | ...... | ...... | ...... | 12 | 5 | 75.50 | 99.50 | 13 00–13 99 |
| 14 00–14 99 | ...... | ...... | ...... | ...... | ...... | ...... | ...... | ...... | ...... | 14 | 3 | 81.50 | 99.70 | 14 00–14 99 |
| 15 00–15 99 | ...... | ...... | ...... | ...... | ...... | ...... | ...... | ...... | ...... | 4 | 1 | 83.30 | 99.80 | 15 00–15 99 |
| 16 00–17 99 | 2 | ...... | ...... | ...... | ...... | ...... | ...... | ...... | ...... | 11 | 1 | 88.00 | 99.90 | 16 00–17 99 |
| 18 00–19 99 | ...... | ...... | 1 | ...... | ...... | ...... | ...... | ...... | ...... | 12 | 1 | 93.00 | 100.00 | 18 00–19 99 |
| 20 00–24 99 | 2 | ...... | 1 | ...... | ...... | ...... | ...... | 1 | ...... | 12 | ...... | 98.00 | ...... | 20 00–24 99 |
| 25 00–29 99 | ...... | ...... | ...... | ...... | ...... | ...... | ...... | ...... | ...... | 4 | ...... | 99.60 | ...... | 25 00–29 99 |
| 30 00–34 99 | ...... | ...... | ...... | ...... | ...... | ...... | ...... | ...... | ...... | 1 | ...... | 100.00 | ...... | 30 00–34 99 |
| Not reported | ...... | ...... | ...... | ...... | ...... | ...... | ...... | ...... | ...... | ...... | 1 | ...... | ...... | Not reported |
| Total | 14 | 9 | 14 | 10 | 6 | 2 | 1 | 1 | 9 | 239 | 1,127 | ...... | ...... | Total |

250. TABLE IX, B, 2, a

## NEW YORK CITY
## THE MEN'S SHIRT INDUSTRY — WORKING SHIRTS — FACTORY WORKERS

NUMBER AND PER CENT. OF EMPLOYEES CLASSIFIED ACCORDING TO ACTUAL WEEKLY EARNINGS, BY OCCUPATION AND SEX

| ACTUAL WEEKLY EARNINGS IN DOLLARS | OCCUPATION | | | | | | | | | | | ACTUAL WEEKLY EARNINGS IN DOLLARS |
|---|---|---|---|---|---|---|---|---|---|---|---|---|
| | MARKERS | CUTTERS | TRIMMERS | CUTTERS' HELPERS | | FOREMEN AND FOREWOMEN | | OPERATORS | | FLOOR WORK | | |
| | Male | Male | Male | Male | Female | Male | Female | Male | Female | Male | Female | |
| Less than $3 00 | | 1 | | | | | | 3 | 54 | | 11 | Less than $3 00 |
| $3 00–$3 49 | | | | | 1 | | | 2 | 39 | 1 | 12 | $3 00– 3 49 |
| 3 50– 3 99 | | | | 2 | | | | 1 | 31 | 2 | 12 | 3 50– 3 99 |
| 4 00– 4 49 | | | | 1 | | | | 2 | 39 | 1 | 11 | 4 00– 4 49 |
| 4 50– 4 99 | | | | 3 | | | | | 43 | | 10 | 4 50– 4 99 |
| 5 00– 5 49 | | 2 | | 7 | | | | 2 | 60 | 1 | 9 | 5 00– 5 49 |
| 5 50– 5 99 | | | | 2 | | | | 1 | 56 | 2 | 7 | 5 50– 5 99 |
| 6 00– 6 49 | | | 1 | 3 | | | | 2 | 73 | 3 | 7 | 6 00– 6 49 |
| 6 50– 6 99 | | | | | | | | 1 | 58 | | 6 | 6 50– 6 99 |
| 7 00– 7 49 | | 1 | 1 | 2 | | | | 4 | 79 | 2 | 4 | 7 00– 7 49 |
| 7 50– 7 99 | | 1 | | 2 | | | 1 | 3 | 45 | | 6 | 7 50– 7 99 |
| 8 00– 8 99 | | | 1 | 10 | | | 1 | 9 | 108 | 1 | 6 | 8 00– 8 99 |
| 9 00– 9 99 | 1 | 4 | | 2 | | 1 | 4 | 3 | 51 | 1 | 2 | 9 00– 9 99 |
| 10 00–10 99 | 1 | 3 | | | | | | 8 | 49 | | | 10 00–10 99 |
| 11 00–11 99 | | 3 | 1 | | | 2 | 1 | 6 | 14 | | | 11 00–11 99 |
| 12 00–12 99 | | 3 | 2 | | | 1 | 1 | 7 | 11 | | | 12 00–12 99 |
| 13 00–13 99 | 1 | 7 | | | | 1 | | 3 | 5 | | | 13 00–13 99 |
| 14 00–14 99 | 2 | 4 | | | | 2 | | 4 | 3 | 1 | | 14 00–14 99 |
| 15 00–15 99 | | | | | | 2 | | 1 | 1 | | | 15 00–15 99 |
| 16 00–17 99 | 1 | 4 | | | | 3 | | 2 | 1 | | | 16 00–17 99 |
| 18 00–19 99 | 2 | 5 | | | | 2 | | 2 | 1 | | | 18 00–19 99 |
| 20 00–24 99 | 2 | 3 | | | | 3 | | | | | | 20 00–24 99 |
| 25 00–29 99 | 1 | | | | | 2 | | 1 | | | | 25 00–29 99 |
| 30 00–34 99 | | | | | | 1 | | | | | | 30 00–34 99 |
| Not reported | | | | | | | | | 1 | | | Not reported |
| Total | 11 | 41 | 6 | 34 | 1 | 20 | 8 | 67 | 822 | 15 | 103 | Total |

250. TABLE IX, B, 2, a — (concluded) NEW YORK CITY

THE MEN'S SHIRT INDUSTRY — WORKING SHIRTS — FACTORY WORKERS

NUMBER AND PER CENT. OF EMPLOYEES CLASSIFIED ACCORDING TO ACTUAL WEEKLY EARNINGS, BY OCCUPATION AND SEX

| WEEKLY RATES IN DOLLARS | OCCUPATION (concluded) | | | | | | | | | | | | | | WEEKLY RATES IN DOLLARS |
|---|---|---|---|---|---|---|---|---|---|---|---|---|---|---|---|
| | IRONERS AND PRESSERS | | EXAMINERS | | FOLDERS | | PACKERS | | NOT RE-PORTED | TOTAL | | CUMULATIVE PER CENT. OF TOTAL | | | |
| | Male | Female | Male | Female | Male | Female | Male | Female | Female | Male | Female | Male | Female | | |
| Less than $3 00 | 1 | 1 | | 3 | | 5 | 2 | 1 | 1 | 7 | 76 | 2.90 | 6.70 | Less than $3 00 |
| $3 00-$3 49 | 2 | 3 | | 1 | | 11 | | 3 | | 5 | 70 | 5.00 | 13.00 | $3 00- 3 49 |
| 3 50- 3 99 | 3 | 1 | | | | 7 | | 5 | 1 | 8 | 57 | 8.40 | 18.00 | 3 50- 3 99 |
| 4 00- 4 49 | | 6 | | 4 | | 3 | 1 | 11 | | 5 | 74 | 10.40 | 24.70 | 4 00- 4 49 |
| 4 50- 4 99 | | 6 | | 4 | | 1 | | 5 | | 3 | 69 | 11.70 | 30.70 | 4 50- 4 99 |
| 5 00- 5 49 | | 3 | | | 1 | 1 | 1 | 6 | 1 | 14 | 80 | 17.50 | 37.80 | 5 00- 5 49 |
| 5 50- 5 99 | | 7 | 1 | | | 2 | 1 | 1 | | 7 | 73 | 20.50 | 44.20 | 5 50- 5 99 |
| 6 00- 6 49 | | 12 | | 3 | 2 | 1 | 2 | | | 13 | 96 | 26.00 | 52.70 | 6 00- 6 49 |
| 6 50- 6 99 | | 12 | 1 | | | 1 | 3 | 1 | | 5 | 78 | 28.00 | 59.70 | 6 50- 6 99 |
| 7 00- 7 49 | 1 | 5 | | 2 | | | 1 | 2 | 1 | 12 | 93 | 33.00 | 68.00 | 7 00- 7 49 |
| 7 50- 7 99 | | 9 | 1 | 3 | | | 1 | 1 | | 8 | 65 | 36.50 | 73.70 | 7 50- 7 99 |
| 8 00- 8 99 | 2 | 12 | | 2 | 1 | 1 | 3 | | | 27 | 130 | 47.50 | 85.40 | 8 00- 8 99 |
| 9 00- 9 99 | | 5 | | 3 | | | 1 | 1 | 1 | 13 | 67 | 53.00 | 91.20 | 9 00- 9 99 |
| 10 00-10 99 | | 6 | | 3 | | | | | | 12 | 58 | 58.00 | 96.50 | 10 00-10 99 |
| 11 00-11 99 | 1 | 2 | 1 | | | | | | | 14 | 17 | 64.00 | 98.00 | 11 00-11 99 |
| 12 00-12 99 | | | 1 | | 2 | | | | | 16 | 12 | 70.70 | 99.10 | 12 00-12 99 |
| 13 00-13 99 | | | | | | | | | | 12 | 5 | 75.50 | 99.50 | 13 00-13 99 |
| 14 00-14 99 | | | | | 1 | | | | | 14 | 3 | 81.50 | 99.70 | 14 00-14 99 |
| 15 00-15 99 | | | | | 1 | | | | | 4 | 1 | 83.30 | 99.80 | 15 00-15 99 |
| 16 00-17 99 | | | | | 1 | | | | | 11 | 1 | 88.00 | 99.90 | 16 00-17 99 |
| 18 00-19 99 | 1 | | | | | | | | | 12 | 1 | 93.00 | 100.00 | 18 00-19 99 |
| 20 00-24 99 | 4 | | | | | | | | | 12 | | 98.00 | | 20 00-24 99 |
| 25 00-29 99 | | | | | | | | | | 4 | | 99.60 | | 25 00-29 99 |
| 30 00-34 99 | | | | | | | | | | 1 | | 100.00 | | 30 00-34 99 |
| Not reported | | | | | | | | | | | 1 | | | Not reported |
| Total.....1,014 | 15 | 90 | 5 | 28 | 9 | 33 | 16 | 37 | 5 | 239 | 1,127 | | | Total |

251. TABLE V, C, a

NEW YORK CITY

**THE PAPER BOX INDUSTRY — FACTORY WORKERS**

NUMBER AND PER CENT. OF EMPLOYEES EARNING SPECIFIED WEEKLY RATES, BY AGE GROUPS AND SEX

| WEEKLY RATES IN DOLLARS | AGE GROUPS IN YEARS | | | | | | | | | | | | | | WEEKLY RATES IN DOLLARS |
|---|---|---|---|---|---|---|---|---|---|---|---|---|---|---|---|
| | 14–15 | | 16–17 | | 18–20 | | 21–24 | | 25–29 | | 30–34 | | 35–39 | | |
| | Male | Female | Male | Female | Male | Female | Male | Female | Male | Female | Male | Female | Male | Female | |
| Less than $3 00 | 1 | 3 | .... | 1 | ...... | ...... | ...... | ...... | ...... | ...... | ...... | ...... | ...... | ...... | Less than $3 00 |
| $3 00–$3 49... | .... | 19 | 2 | 17 | ...... | 3 | ...... | ...... | ...... | ...... | ...... | ...... | ...... | ...... | ...$3 00– 3 49 |
| 3 50– 3 99... | 3 | 31 | 4 | 27 | ...... | 3 | ...... | 1 | 1 | ...... | 1 | ...... | ...... | ...... | ... 3 50– 3 99 |
| 4 00– 4 49... | 8 | 52 | 10 | 89 | 2 | 24 | 4 | 5 | 1 | 1 | ...... | ...... | 1 | ...... | ... 4 00– 4 49 |
| 4 50– 4 99... | 6 | 49 | 9 | 151 | 1 | 50 | ...... | 8 | ...... | 2 | ...... | ...... | ...... | 2 | ... 4 50– 4 99 |
| 5 00– 5 49... | 10 | 43 | 47 | 222 | 24 | 141 | 8 | 31 | 1 | 9 | 1 | 10 | ...... | 4 | ... 5 00– 5 49 |
| 5 50– 5 99... | 2 | 27 | 16 | 144 | 12 | 82 | 5 | 24 | 1 | 5 | ...... | 5 | 1 | 1 | ... 5 50– 5 99 |
| 6 00– 6 49... | 6 | 13 | 42 | 175 | 39 | 203 | 11 | 85 | 6 | 17 | 4 | 5 | 5 | ...... | ... 6 00– 6 49 |
| 6 50– 6 99... | 1 | ...... | 14 | 49 | 18 | 62 | 8 | 20 | 2 | 6 | 1 | 2 | 1 | 2 | ... 6 50– 6 99 |
| 7 00– 7 49... | .... | 1 | 23 | 28 | 50 | 96 | 17 | 34 | 2 | 4 | 3 | 4 | 3 | 5 | ... 7 00– 7 49 |
| 7 50– 7 99... | .... | ...... | 7 | 22 | 14 | 54 | 3 | 26 | ...... | 7 | ...... | 6 | ...... | 3 | ... 7 50– 7 99 |
| 8 00– 8 99... | .... | ...... | 10 | 28 | 50 | 170 | 25 | 83 | 11 | 58 | 6 | 18 | 4 | 20 | ... 8 00– 8 99 |
| 9 00– 9 99... | .... | ...... | 12 | 17 | 42 | 106 | 27 | 98 | 14 | 45 | 8 | 29 | 2 | 24 | ... 9 00– 9 99 |
| 10 00–10 99... | .... | ...... | 1 | 7 | 37 | 82 | 31 | 75 | 26 | 41 | 19 | 22 | 5 | 16 | ...10 00–10 99 |
| 11 00–11 99... | .... | ...... | 1 | ...... | 16 | 9 | 31 | 25 | 17 | 21 | 14 | 2 | 8 | 7 | ...11 00–11 99 |
| 12 00–12 99... | .... | ...... | 1 | 1 | 18 | 3 | 37 | 23 | 24 | 12 | 18 | 6 | 18 | 5 | ...12 00–12 99 |
| 13 00–13 99... | .... | ...... | .... | ...... | 12 | 2 | 42 | 2 | 24 | 4 | 15 | 2 | 13 | 2 | ...13 00–13 99 |
| 14 00–14 99... | .... | ...... | .... | ...... | 7 | ...... | 34 | 1 | 30 | ...... | 13 | ...... | 10 | 2 | ...14 00–14 99 |
| 15 00–15 99... | .... | ...... | .... | ...... | 7 | 1 | 40 | ...... | 38 | 1 | 29 | 2 | 15 | 1 | ...15 00–15 99 |
| 16 00–17 99... | .... | ...... | .... | ...... | 2 | ...... | 20 | 1 | 60 | 1 | 30 | 1 | 18 | 1 | ...16 00–17 99 |
| 18 00–19 99... | .... | ...... | .... | ...... | 2 | ...... | 17 | ...... | 24 | ...... | 13 | ...... | 19 | ...... | ...18 00–19 99 |
| 20 00–24 99... | .... | ...... | .... | ...... | ...... | ...... | 9 | ...... | 20 | 1 | 30 | ...... | 10 | ...... | ...20 00–24 99 |
| 25 00–29 99... | .... | ...... | .... | ...... | ...... | ...... | ...... | ...... | 5 | ...... | 3 | ...... | 6 | ...... | ...25 00–29 99 |
| 30 00–34 99... | .... | ...... | .... | ...... | ...... | ...... | ...... | ...... | 1 | ...... | 2 | ...... | 5 | ...... | ...30 00–34 99 |
| 35 00–39 99... | .... | ...... | .... | ...... | ...... | ...... | ...... | ...... | ...... | ...... | 1 | ...... | 2 | ...... | ...35 00–39 99 |
| Not reported.. | 3 | 4 | 2 | 6 | 1 | 7 | 2 | 1 | 2 | 4 | 1 | 3 | 1 | 1 | ..Not reported |
| Total..... | 40 | 242 | 201 | 984 | 354 | 1,098 | 371 | 543 | 310 | 239 | 212 | 117 | 147 | 96 | .....Total |

251. TABLE V, C, a — (*continued*)

NEW YORK CITY

THE PAPER BOX INDUSTRY — FACTORY WORKERS

NUMBER AND PER CENT. OF EMPLOYEES EARNING SPECIFIED WEEKLY RATES, BY AGE GROUPS AND SEX

| WEEKLY RATES IN DOLLARS | AGE GROUPS IN YEARS (*concluded*) | | | | | | | | | | | | | | WEEKLY RATES IN DOLLARS |
|---|---|---|---|---|---|---|---|---|---|---|---|---|---|---|---|
| | 40–44 | | 45–54 | | 55–64 | | 65 AND OVER | | NOT REPORTED | | TOTL | | CUMULATIVE PER CENT. OF TOTAL | | |
| | Male | Female | Male | Female | Male | Female | Male | Female | Male | Female | Male | Female | Male | Female | |
| Less than $3 00 | .... | ...... | .... | ...... | ...... | ...... | ...... | ...... | ...... | ...... | 1 | 4 | .05 | .12 | Less than $3 00 |
| $3 00–$3 49... | .... | ...... | .... | ...... | ...... | ...... | ...... | ...... | ...... | 6 | 2 | 45 | .16 | 1.43 | ...$3 00– 3 49 |
| 3 50– 3 99... | .... | ...... | .... | ...... | ...... | ...... | ...... | ...... | ...... | ...... | 9 | 62 | .64 | 3.24 | ... 3 50– 3 99 |
| 4 00– 4 49... | .... | ...... | .... | ...... | ...... | ...... | ...... | ...... | 2 | 1 | 28 | 172 | 2.12 | 8.26 | ... 4 00– 4 49 |
| 4 50– 4 99... | .... | ...... | .... | ...... | ...... | ...... | ...... | ...... | 1 | ...... | 17 | 262 | 3.03 | 15.90 | ... 4 50– 4 99 |
| 5 00– 5 49... | .... | 1 | .... | ...... | 1 | ...... | ...... | ...... | ...... | ...... | 92 | 461 | 8.44 | 31.00 | ... 5 00– 5 49 |
| 5 50– 5 99... | .... | ...... | .... | 1 | ...... | ...... | ...... | ...... | ...... | 5 | 37 | 294 | 9.87 | 38.00 | ... 5 50– 5 99 |
| 6 00– 6 49... | 2 | ...... | 2 | 2 | 4 | 1 | 1 | ...... | ...... | ...... | 122 | 501 | 16.35 | 52.60 | ... 6 00– 6 49 |
| 6 50– 6 99... | .... | 1 | .... | ...... | ...... | 1 | ...... | ...... | ...... | ...... | 45 | 143 | 18.75 | 56.80 | ... 6 50– 6 99 |
| 7 00– 7 49... | 1 | 1 | 4 | 2 | 2 | 1 | ...... | 1 | ...... | ...... | 105 | 177 | 24.35 | 62.00 | ... 7 00– 7 49 |
| 7 50– 7 99... | 1 | 5 | 1 | 2 | ...... | ...... | ...... | ...... | 8 | 2 | 34 | 127 | 26.10 | 65.60 | ... 7 50– 7 99 |
| 8 00– 8 99... | 3 | 12 | 5 | 14 | 4 | 1 | ...... | ...... | 1 | ...... | 119 | 404 | 32.40 | 77.40 | ... 8 00– 8 99 |
| 9 00– 9 99... | 3 | 18 | 1 | 8 | 3 | 6 | ...... | ...... | 1 | 1 | 113 | 352 | 38.40 | 88.90 | ... 9 00– 9 99 |
| 10 00–10 99... | 4 | 6 | 12 | 9 | ...... | 1 | 1 | ...... | ...... | 3 | 136 | 264 | 45.60 | 95.50 | ...10 00–10 99 |
| 11 00–11 99... | 4 | 3 | 9 | 1 | 4 | ...... | ...... | ...... | ...... | ...... | 104 | 68 | 51.10 | 97.30 | ...11 00–11 99 |
| 12 00–12 99... | 13 | 4 | 10 | 3 | 4 | ...... | ...... | ...... | 3 | ...... | 146 | 57 | 59.00 | 99.10 | ...12 00–12 99 |
| 13 00–13 99... | 5 | 1 | 3 | ...... | 3 | ...... | ...... | ...... | ...... | ...... | 117 | 13 | 65.10 | 99.50 | ...13 00–13 99 |
| 14 00–14 99... | 2 | ...... | 6 | 1 | 2 | ...... | ...... | ...... | ...... | 1 | 104 | 5 | 70.60 | 99.65 | ...14 00–14 99 |
| 15 00–15 99... | 8 | ...... | 9 | 1 | 5 | ...... | 1 | ...... | ...... | ...... | 152 | 6 | 78.70 | 99.90 | ...15 00–15 99 |
| 16 00–17 99... | 11 | ...... | 14 | ...... | 2 | ...... | 1 | ...... | ...... | ...... | 158 | 4 | 87.10 | 99.97 | ...16 00–17 99 |
| 18 00–19 99... | 5 | ...... | 8 | ...... | 3 | ...... | ...... | ...... | ...... | ...... | 91 | ...... | 92.00 | ...... | ...18 00–19 99 |
| 20 00–24 99... | 18 | ...... | 16 | ...... | 3 | ...... | ...... | ...... | ...... | ...... | 106 | 1 | 97.50 | 100.00 | ...20 00–24 99 |
| 25 00–29 99... | 5 | ...... | 7 | ...... | ...... | ...... | ...... | ...... | ...... | ...... | 26 | ...... | 99.00 | ...... | ...25 00–29 99 |
| 30 00–34 99... | 2 | ...... | 3 | ...... | 1 | ...... | ...... | ...... | ...... | ...... | 14 | ...... | 99.60 | ...... | ...30 00–34 99 |
| 35 00–39 99... | 1 | ...... | 2 | ...... | ...... | ...... | ...... | ...... | ...... | ...... | 6 | ...... | 100.00 | ...... | ...35 00–39 99 |
| Not reported.. | 2 | 3 | .... | ...... | ...... | 1 | ...... | ...... | ...... | ...... | 14 | 30 | ...... | ...... | ..Not reported |
| Total..... | 90 | 57 | 112 | 44 | 41 | 12 | 4 | 1 | 16 | 19 | 1,898 | 3,452 | ...... | ...... | .....Total |

NEW YORK CITY

THE PAPER BOX INDUSTRY — FACTORY WORKERS

252. TABLE VIII, C, a — NUMBER AND PER CENT. OF EMPLOYEES EARNING SPECIFIED WEEKLY RATES, BY AGE GROUPS AND SEX

| Weekly Rates in Dollars | Occupation | | | | | | | | | | | | Weekly Rates in Dollars |
|---|---|---|---|---|---|---|---|---|---|---|---|---|---|
| | Foremen and Forewomen | | Cutters | | Glue Makers | Setters Up | | General Machine Work | | Glue Table Work | Turners-In | | |
| | Male | Female | Male | Female | Male | Male | Female | Male | Female | Male | Male | Female | |
| Less than $3 00 | ....... | ....... | ....... | ....... | ....... | ....... | ....... | ....... | ....... | ....... | ....... | 1 | Less than $3 00 |
| $3 00–$3 49 | ....... | ....... | ....... | ....... | ....... | ....... | 3 | ....... | ....... | ....... | ....... | 16 | $3 00– 3 49 |
| 3 50– 3 99 | ....... | ....... | 1 | 1 | ....... | 1 | 7 | ....... | ....... | ....... | ....... | 24 | 3 50– 3 99 |
| 4 00– 4 49 | ....... | ....... | 2 | ....... | ....... | 2 | 7 | ....... | 9 | 4 | ....... | 84 | 4 00– 4 49 |
| 4 50– 4 99 | ....... | ....... | 1 | 1 | ....... | 7 | 12 | 1 | 7 | 1 | ....... | 114 | 4 50– 4 99 |
| 5 00– 5 49 | ....... | ....... | 12 | 3 | ....... | 17 | 14 | 11 | 42 | 4 | ....... | 177 | 5 00– 5 49 |
| 5 50– 5 99 | ....... | ....... | ....... | 1 | ....... | 3 | 7 | 6 | 25 | ....... | ....... | 160 | 5 50– 5 99 |
| 6 00– 6 49 | ....... | 1 | 26 | 4 | ....... | 16 | 15 | 24 | 49 | 2 | 1 | 222 | 6 00– 6 49 |
| 6 50– 6 99 | ....... | 2 | 13 | ....... | ....... | | 5 | 14 | 3 | 1 | ....... | 41 | 6 50– 6 99 |
| 7 00– 7 49 | ....... | 2 | 14 | 1 | 1 | 15 | 5 | 15 | 16 | 3 | ....... | 6 | 7 00– 7 49 |
| 7 50– 7 99 | ....... | 3 | 13 | 1 | ....... | 2 | ....... | 6 | 9 | 1 | ....... | ....... | 7 50– 7 99 |
| 8 00– 8 99 | 1 | 3 | 29 | 1 | ....... | 11 | 16 | 17 | 8 | 5 | ....... | 4 | 8 00– 8 99 |
| 9 00– 9 99 | ....... | 4 | 30 | 1 | 2 | 10 | 9 | 12 | 5 | 6 | ....... | 1 | 9 00– 9 99 |
| 10 00–10 99 | ....... | 17 | 30 | ....... | 2 | 13 | 20 | 27 | 3 | 10 | ....... | 1 | 10 00–10 99 |
| 11 00–11 99 | 1 | 9 | 25 | ....... | 4 | 9 | 8 | 16 | ....... | 9 | ....... | ....... | 11 00–11 99 |
| 12 00–12 99 | 3 | 18 | 46 | ....... | 1 | 20 | 7 | 23 | 3 | 25 | ....... | ....... | 12 00–12 99 |
| 13 00–13 99 | 3 | 5 | 29 | ....... | ....... | 42 | 4 | 3 | ....... | 29 | ....... | ....... | 13 00–13 99 |
| 14 00–14 99 | 3 | 4 | 36 | ....... | ....... | 42 | ....... | 3 | ....... | 16 | ....... | ....... | 14 00–14 99 |
| 15 00–15 99 | 3 | 2 | 58 | ....... | 1 | 56 | 1 | 4 | ....... | 17 | ....... | ....... | 15 00–15 99 |
| 16 00–17 99 | 17 | 3 | 103 | ....... | ....... | 27 | ....... | 1 | ....... | 6 | ....... | ....... | 16 00–17 99 |
| 18 00–19 99 | 13 | ....... | 68 | ....... | ....... | 3 | ....... | 4 | ....... | ....... | ....... | ....... | 18 00–19 99 |
| 20 00–24 99 | 48 | 1 | 52 | ....... | ....... | 2 | ....... | ....... | ....... | ....... | ....... | ....... | 20 00–24 99 |
| 25 00–29 99 | 20 | ....... | 6 | ....... | ....... | ....... | ....... | ....... | ....... | ....... | ....... | ....... | 25 00–29 99 |
| 30 00–34 99 | 13 | ....... | ....... | ....... | ....... | ....... | ....... | ....... | ....... | ....... | ....... | ....... | 30 00–34 99 |
| 35 00–39 99 | 6 | ....... | ....... | ....... | ....... | ....... | ....... | ....... | ....... | ....... | ....... | ....... | 35 00–39 99 |
| Not reported | 2 | 1 | 2 | ....... | ....... | 2 | 1 | ....... | 1 | 1 | ....... | 1 | Not reported |
| Total | 133 | 75 | 596 | 14 | 11 | 303 | 141 | 187 | 180 | 140 | 1 | 852 | Total |

NEW YORK CITY

252. TABLE VIII, C, a — (*concluded*)

THE PAPER BOX INDUSTRY — FACTORY WORKERS

NUMBER AND PER CENT. OF EMPLOYEES EARNING SPECIFIED WEEKLY RATES, BY OCCUPATION AND SEX

| WEEKLY RATES IN DOLLARS | OCCUPATION (*concluded*) | | | | | | | | | | | | | | WEEKLY RATES IN DOLLARS |
|---|---|---|---|---|---|---|---|---|---|---|---|---|---|---|---|
| | STRIPPERS AND TOP-LABELERS | | TABLE WORK | | CLOSING AND TYING | | FLOOR WORK | | NOT REPORTED | | TOTAL | | CUMULATIVE PER CENT. OF TOTAL | | |
| | Male | Female | Male | Female | Male | Female | Male | Female | Male | Female | Male | Female | Male | Female | |
| Less than $3 00 | .... | ...... | .... | 1 | ...... | 2 | 1 | ...... | ...... | ...... | 1 | 4 | .05 | .12 | Less than $3 00 |
| $3 00–$3 49... | .... | 1 | 1 | 13 | ...... | 10 | 1 | 2 | ...... | ...... | 2 | 45 | .16 | 1.43 | ...$3 00– 3 49 |
| 3 50– 3 99... | .... | 3 | 1 | 10 | ...... | 6 | 4 | 6 | 2 | 5 | 9 | 62 | .64 | 3.24 | ....3 50– 3 99 |
| 4 00– 4 49... | 1 | 16 | 7 | 30 | 4 | 8 | 8 | 18 | ...... | ...... | 28 | 172 | 2.12 | 8.26 | ....4 00– 4 49 |
| 4 50– 4 99... | .... | 11 | .... | 77 | 2 | 9 | 5 | 26 | ...... | 5 | 17 | 262 | 3.03 | 15.90 | ....4 50– 4 99 |
| 5 00– 5 49... | 2 | 48 | 10 | 123 | 11 | 16 | 23 | 34 | 2 | 4 | 92 | 461 | 8.44 | 31.00 | ....5 00– 5 49 |
| 5 50– 5 99... | 5 | 43 | 5 | 36 | 4 | 11 | 14 | 11 | ...... | ...... | 37 | 294 | 9.87 | 38.00 | ....5 50– 5 99 |
| 6 00– 6 49... | 1 | 99 | 9 | 74 | 20 | 14 | 23 | 18 | ...... | 5 | 122 | 501 | 16.35 | 52.60 | ....6 00– 6 49 |
| 6 50– 6 99... | 1 | 40 | 4 | 42 | 2 | ...... | 6 | 10 | 1 | ...... | 45 | 143 | 18.75 | 56.80 | ....6 50– 6 99 |
| 7 00– 7 49... | 3 | 66 | 8 | 58 | 14 | 5 | 24 | 17 | 8 | 1 | 105 | 177 | 24.35 | 62.00 | ....7 00– 7 49 |
| 7 50– 7 99... | .... | 61 | 3 | 42 | 2 | 1 | 7 | 9 | ...... | 1 | 34 | 127 | 26.10 | 65.60 | ....7 50– 7 99 |
| 8 00– 8 99... | 4 | 159 | 12 | 175 | 23 | 8 | 17 | 27 | ...... | 3 | 119 | 404 | 32.40 | 77.40 | ....8 00– 8 99 |
| 9 00– 9 99... | 3 | 167 | 11 | 156 | 21 | 1 | 18 | 7 | ...... | 1 | 113 | 352 | 38.40 | 88.90 | ....9.00– 9.99 |
| 10 00–10 99... | 1 | 138 | 17 | 83 | 12 | ...... | 22 | 2 | 2 | ...... | 136 | 264 | 45.60 | 99.50 | ...10 00–10.99 |
| 11 00–11 99... | 8 | 28 | 8 | 23 | 8 | ...... | 13 | ...... | 3 | ...... | 104 | 68 | 51.10 | 97.30 | ...11 00–11 99 |
| 12 00–12 99... | 5 | 13 | 14 | 16 | 3 | ...... | 6 | ...... | ...... | ...... | 146 | 57 | 59.00 | 99.10 | ...12 00–12 99 |
| 13 00–13 99... | 1 | 1 | 3 | 1 | 1 | ...... | 5 | ...... | 1 | 2 | 117 | 13 | 65.10 | 99.50 | ...13 00–13 99 |
| 14 00–14 99... | 1 | ...... | 3 | 1 | ...... | ...... | ...... | ...... | ...... | ...... | 104 | 5 | 70.60 | 99.65 | ...14 00–14 99 |
| 15 00–15 99... | 1 | 1 | 7 | 2 | 1 | ...... | 3 | ...... | 1 | ...... | 152 | 6 | 78.70 | 99.90 | ...15 00–15 99 |
| 16 00–17 99... | .... | ...... | 1 | ...... | 1 | ...... | 1 | 1 | 1 | ...... | 158 | 4 | 87.10 | 99.97 | ...16 00–17 99 |
| 18 00–19 99... | 1 | ...... | 1 | ...... | ...... | ...... | ...... | ...... | 1 | ...... | 91 | ...... | 92.00 | ...... | ...18 00–19 99 |
| 20 00–24 99... | .... | ...... | 1 | ...... | ...... | ...... | 1 | ...... | 2 | ...... | 106 | 1 | 97.50 | 100.00 | ...20 00–24 99 |
| 25 00–29 99... | .... | ...... | .... | ...... | ...... | ...... | ...... | ...... | ...... | ...... | 26 | ...... | 99.00 | ...... | ...25 00–29 99 |
| 30 00–34 99... | .... | ...... | .... | ...... | ...... | ...... | 1 | ...... | ...... | ...... | 14 | ...... | 99.60 | ...... | ...30 00–34 99 |
| 35 00–39 99... | .... | ...... | .... | ...... | ...... | ...... | ...... | ...... | ...... | ...... | 6 | ...... | 100.00 | ...... | ...35 00–39 99 |
| Not reported... | .... | 7 | 2 | 13 | 1 | 2 | 3 | 1 | 1 | 3 | 14 | 30 | ...... | ...... | ...Not reported |
| Total..... | 38 | 902 | 128 | 976 | 130 | 93 | 206 | 189 | 25 | 30 | 1,898 | 3,452 | ...... | ...... | .....Total |

253. TABLE VI, C, a

NEW YORK CITY

THE PAPER BOX INDUSTRY — FACTORY WORKERS

Number and Per Cent. of Employees Classified According to Actual Weekly Earnings, by Age Groups and Sex

| Actual Weekly Earnings in Dollars | 14–15 | | 16–17 | | 18–20 | | 21–24 | | 25–29 | | 30–34 | | 35–39 | | Actual Weekly Earnings in Dollars |
|---|---|---|---|---|---|---|---|---|---|---|---|---|---|---|---|
| | Male | Female | Male | Female | Male | Female | Male | Female | Male | Female | Male | Female | Male | Female | |
| Less than $3 00 | 2 | 30 | 6 | 54 | 5 | 46 | 3 | 12 | 1 | 2 | ...... | 4 | 4 | 2 | Less than $3 00 |
| $3 00–$3 49... | 1 | 43 | 6 | 65 | 5 | 21 | 2 | 10 | 2 | 2 | 2 | 4 | 1 | 3 | ...$3 00– 3 49 |
| 3 50– 3 99... | 4 | 37 | 6 | 78 | 3 | 36 | 4 | 8 | ...... | 5 | ...... | 2 | ...... | 3 | ... 3 50– 3 99 |
| 4 00– 4 49... | 9 | 67 | 19 | 132 | 2 | 69 | 5 | 19 | 1 | 6 | 1 | 2 | 1 | 5 | ... 4 00– 4 49 |
| 4 50– 4 99... | 7 | 52 | 17 | 153 | 6 | 98 | 2 | 31 | 2 | 8 | ...... | 6 | ...... | 5 | ... 4 50– 4 99 |
| 5 00– 5 49... | 8 | 54 | 35 | 191 | 20 | 156 | 14 | 58 | 2 | 23 | 2 | 11 | 2 | 9 | ... 5 00– 5 49 |
| 5 50– 5 99... | 4 | 42 | 18 | 153 | 23 | 139 | 6 | 49 | 2 | 9 | 1 | 13 | 1 | 4 | ... 5 50– 5 99 |
| 6 00– 6 49... | 7 | 17 | 33 | 154 | 37 | 188 | 14 | 75 | 11 | 19 | 2 | 15 | 3 | 5 | ... 6 00– 6 49 |
| 6 50– 6 99... | 2 | 7 | 14 | 76 | 23 | 103 | 12 | 47 | 4 | 17 | 1 | 8 | 3 | 8 | ... 6 50– 6 99 |
| 7 00– 7 49... | .... | 7 | 16 | 53 | 37 | 137 | 12 | 80 | 7 | 28 | 4 | 14 | 2 | 15 | ... 7 00– 7 49 |
| 7 50– 7 99... | .... | 3 | 11 | 42 | 30 | 102 | 7 | 70 | 5 | 34 | 1 | 20 | 1 | 7 | ... 7 50– 7 99 |
| 8 00– 8 99... | 1 | 1 | 12 | 55 | 58 | 222 | 31 | 146 | 11 | 87 | 8 | 30 | 4 | 28 | ... 8 00– 8 99 |
| 9 00– 9 99... | .... | ...... | 12 | 27 | 52 | 167 | 35 | 147 | 21 | 76 | 8 | 43 | 3 | 32 | ... 9 00– 9 99 |
| 10 00–10 99... | .... | ...... | 4 | 18 | 34 | 101 | 37 | 105 | 23 | 69 | 16 | 28 | 10 | 27 | ...10 00–10 99 |
| 11 00–11 99... | .... | ...... | 2 | 4 | 21 | 46 | 38 | 71 | 27 | 26 | 15 | 12 | 7 | 13 | ...11 00–11 99 |
| 12 00–12 99... | .... | ...... | 2 | 3 | 15 | 23 | 54 | 60 | 27 | 27 | 20 | 10 | 16 | 8 | ...12 00–12 99 |
| 13 00–13 99... | .... | ...... | .... | ...... | 17 | 15 | 44 | 17 | 24 | 9 | 17 | 3 | 11 | 2 | ...13 00–13 99 |
| 14 00–14 99... | .... | ...... | .... | ...... | 8 | 3 | 39 | 8 | 33 | 3 | 13 | 3 | 13 | 3 | ...14 00–14 99 |
| 15 00–15 99... | .... | ...... | .... | ...... | 13 | 2 | 32 | 2 | 29 | 2 | 26 | 3 | 13 | 1 | ...15 00–15 99 |
| 16 00–17 99... | .... | ...... | .... | ...... | 5 | 2 | 34 | 2 | 63 | 3 | 38 | 1 | 21 | 2 | ...16 00–17 99 |
| 18 00–19 99... | .... | ...... | .... | ...... | 4 | ...... | 26 | ...... | 41 | ...... | 17 | 1 | 19 | 1 | ...18 00–19 99 |
| 20 00–24 99... | .... | ...... | .... | ...... | ...... | ...... | 12 | 1 | 34 | 1 | 35 | ...... | 15 | ...... | ...20 00–24 99 |
| 25 00–29 99... | .... | ...... | .... | ...... | ...... | ...... | ...... | ...... | 9 | ...... | 4 | ...... | 6 | ...... | ...25 00–29 99 |
| 30 00–34 99... | .... | ...... | .... | ...... | ...... | ...... | 1 | ...... | 1 | ...... | 2 | ...... | 6 | ...... | ...30 00–34 99 |
| 35 00–39 99... | .... | ...... | .... | ...... | ...... | ...... | ...... | ...... | ...... | ...... | 2 | ...... | 2 | ...... | ...35 00–39 99 |
| Not reported... | 2 | 2 | 5 | 11 | 4 | 37 | 2 | 6 | ...... | 2 | 1 | 1 | 3 | 2 | ...Nor reported |
| Total..... | 47 | 362 | 218 | 1,269 | 422 | 1,713 | 466 | 1,024 | 380 | 458 | 236 | 234 | 167 | 185 | .....Total |

NEW YORK CITY

253. TABLE VI, C, a — (*concluded*) THE PAPER BOX INDUSTRY — FACTORY WORKERS

NUMBER AND PER CENT. OF EMPLOYEES CLASSIFIED ACCORDING TO ACTUAL WEEKLY EARNINGS, BY AGE GROUPS AND SEX

| ACTUAL WEEKLY EARNINGS IN DOLLARS | AGE GROUPS IN YEARS (*concluded*) 40–44 | | 45–54 | | 55–64 | | 65 AND OVER | NOT REPORTED | | TOTAL | | CUMULATIVE PER CENT. OF TOTAL | | ACTUAL WEEKLY EARNINGS IN DOLLARS |
|---|---|---|---|---|---|---|---|---|---|---|---|---|---|---|
| | Male | Female | Male | Female | Male | Female | Male | Male | Female | Male | Female | Male | Female | |
| Less than $3 00 | ...... | 1 | ...... | 3 | 1 | ...... | 1 | 1 | ...... | 24 | 154 | 1.08 | 2.82 | Less than $3 00 |
| $3 00–$3 49 | ...... | 4 | 1 | 1 | ...... | ...... | ...... | 1 | ...... | 21 | 153 | 2.04 | 5.51 | $3 00– 3 49 |
| 3 50– 3 99 | ...... | ...... | ...... | 4 | ...... | ...... | ...... | ...... | ...... | 17 | 173 | 2.80 | 8.79 | 3 50– 3 99 |
| 4 00– 4 49 | 1 | 2 | ...... | 2 | ...... | ...... | ...... | 1 | ...... | 40 | 304 | 4.62 | 14.35 | 4 00– 4 49 |
| 4 50– 4 99 | ...... | 4 | ...... | 3 | 1 | 2 | ...... | ...... | 1 | 35 | 363 | 6.20 | 21.00 | 4 50– 4 99 |
| 5 00– 5 49 | 1 | 6 | ...... | 8 | 1 | 1 | ...... | ...... | ...... | 85 | 517 | 10.05 | 30.45 | 5 00– 5 49 |
| 5 50– 5 99 | 1 | 1 | 1 | 2 | 2 | 4 | ...... | ...... | ...... | 59 | 416 | 12.70 | 38.05 | 5 50– 5 99 |
| 6 00– 6 49 | 3 | 8 | ...... | 13 | 2 | 1 | 1 | ...... | ...... | 113 | 495 | 17.80 | 47.10 | 6 00– 6 49 |
| 6 50– 6 99 | ...... | 3 | 1 | 6 | 1 | 3 | ...... | ...... | 2 | 61 | 280 | 20.60 | 52.25 | 6 50– 6 99 |
| 7 00– 7 49 | 2 | 9 | 7 | 9 | 1 | 1 | ...... | 3 | ...... | 91 | 353 | 24.75 | 60.00 | 7 00– 7 49 |
| 7 50– 7 99 | 2 | 9 | 2 | 3 | ...... | 4 | ...... | 1 | 1 | 60 | 295 | 27.40 | 64.20 | 7 50– 7 99 |
| 8 00– 8 99 | 4 | 22 | 7 | 16 | 3 | 2 | ...... | ...... | 2 | 139 | 611 | 33.75 | 75.40 | 8 00– 8 99 |
| 9 00– 9 99 | 5 | 29 | 2 | 16 | 3 | 6 | ...... | ...... | 2 | 141 | 545 | 40.10 | 85.50 | 9 00– 9 99 |
| 10 00–10 99 | 7 | 15 | 12 | 13 | 2 | 2 | 1 | ...... | 1 | 146 | 379 | 46.75 | 92.00 | 10 00–10 99 |
| 11 00–11 99 | 8 | 3 | 13 | 3 | 6 | 2 | ...... | ...... | 1 | 137 | 181 | 52.80 | 95.50 | 11 00–11 99 |
| 12 00–12 99 | 7 | 5 | 8 | 4 | 6 | ...... | ...... | ...... | 1 | 155 | 141 | 59.90 | 98.00 | 12 00–12 99 |
| 13 00–13 99 | 8 | 1 | 5 | 1 | 2 | 1 | ...... | ...... | ...... | 128 | 49 | 65.75 | 99.00 | 13 00–13 99 |
| 14 00–14 99 | 7 | 4 | 5 | 1 | 3 | ...... | ...... | 1 | ...... | 122 | 25 | 71.20 | 99.50 | 14 00–14 99 |
| 15 00–15 99 | 6 | ...... | 9 | ...... | 3 | ...... | ...... | ...... | ...... | 131 | 10 | 77.10 | 99.70 | 15 00–15 99 |
| 16 00–17 99 | 12 | ...... | 15 | 1 | 2 | ...... | 2 | ...... | ...... | 192 | 11 | 85.75 | 99.95 | 16 00–17 99 |
| 18 00–19 99 | 5 | ...... | 10 | ...... | 2 | ...... | ...... | ...... | ...... | 124 | 2 | 91.50 | 99.97 | 18 00–19 99 |
| 20 00–24 99 | 19 | ...... | 14 | ...... | 4 | ...... | ...... | ...... | ...... | 133 | 2 | 92.40 | 100.00 | 20 00–24 99 |
| 25 00–29 99 | 5 | ...... | 8 | ...... | ...... | ...... | ...... | ...... | ...... | 32 | ...... | 99.00 | ...... | 25 00–29 99 |
| 30 00–34 99 | 2 | ...... | 3 | ...... | 1 | ...... | ...... | ...... | ...... | 16 | ...... | 99.60 | ...... | 30 00–34 99 |
| 35 00–39 99 | 2 | ...... | 2 | ...... | ...... | ...... | ...... | ...... | ...... | 8 | ...... | 100.00 | ...... | 35 00–39 99 |
| Not reported | 1 | 1 | ...... | ...... | ...... | 1 | ...... | 5 | ...... | 23 | 63 | ...... | ...... | Not reported |
| Total | 108 | 127 | 125 | 109 | 43 | 30 | 5 | 13 | 11 | 2,233 | 5,522 | ...... | ...... | Total |

**254. TABLE IX, C, a**

NEW YORK CITY

**THE PAPER BOX INDUSTRY — FACTORY WORKERS**

NUMBER AND PER CENT. OF EMPLOYEES CLASSIFIED ACCORDING TO ACTUAL WEEKLY EARNINGS, BY OCCUPATION AND SEX

| ACTUAL WEEKLY EARNINGS IN DOLLARS | OCCUPATION | | | | | | | | | | | | ACTUAL WEEKLY EARNINGS IN DOLLARS |
|---|---|---|---|---|---|---|---|---|---|---|---|---|---|
| | FOREMEN AND FOREWOMEN | | CUTTERS | | GLUE MAKERS | SETTERS-UP | | GENERAL MACHINE WORK | | GLUE TABLE WORK | TURNERS-IN | | |
| | Male | Female | Male | Female | Male | Male | Female | Male | Female | Male | Male | Female | |
| Less than $3 00 | ....... | ....... | 3 | 1 | ....... | 3 | 9 | 5 | 5 | ....... | ....... | 43 | Less than $3 00 |
| $3 00–$3 49 | ....... | ....... | 4 | 1 | ....... | ....... | 8 | 2 | 5 | 1 | ....... | 52 | $3 00– 3 49 |
| 3 50– 3 99 | ....... | ....... | 3 | ....... | ....... | 2 | 4 | 2 | 6 | ....... | ....... | 54 | 3 50– 3 99 |
| 4 00– 4 49 | ....... | 1 | 6 | ....... | ....... | 3 | 10 | 3 | 22 | 7 | ....... | 97 | 4 00– 4 49 |
| 4 50– 4 99 | ....... | ....... | 4 | 3 | ....... | 10 | 12 | 6 | 26 | ....... | ....... | 123 | 4 50– 4 99 |
| 5 00– 5 49 | ....... | ....... | 10 | 3 | ....... | 13 | 16 | 9 | 44 | 3 | ....... | 179 | 5 00– 5 49 |
| 5 50– 5 99 | ....... | ....... | 9 | 4 | ....... | 6 | 9 | 15 | 36 | 1 | ....... | 132 | 5 50– 5 99 |
| 6 00– 6 49 | ....... | ....... | 21 | 3 | ....... | 16 | 17 | 24 | 45 | 2 | 1 | 134 | 6 00– 6 49 |
| 6 50– 6 99 | ....... | 3 | 19 | ....... | ....... | 8 | 5 | 10 | 20 | 4 | ....... | 33 | 6 50– 6 99 |
| 7 00– 7 49 | ....... | 3 | 20 | 4 | 1 | 12 | 14 | 10 | 22 | 4 | ....... | 20 | 7 00– 7 49 |
| 7 50– 7 99 | ....... | 1 | 17 | 1 | ....... | 5 | 9 | 9 | 12 | 1 | ....... | 1 | 7 50– 7 99 |
| 8 00– 8 99 | 2 | 4 | 24 | 2 | ....... | 12 | 25 | 13 | 18 | 7 | ....... | 4 | 8 00– 8 99 |
| 9 00– 9 99 | 1 | 5 | 34 | 5 | 2 | 13 | 16 | 22 | 10 | 8 | ....... | 2 | 9 00– 9 99 |
| 10 00–10 99 | ....... | 16 | 35 | 3 | 1 | 14 | 24 | 22 | 1 | 11 | ....... | 1 | 10 00–10 99 |
| 11 00–11 99 | 1 | 9 | 38 | 2 | 4 | 18 | 9 | 17 | 4 | 10 | ....... | ....... | 11 00–11 99 |
| 12 00–12 99 | 1 | 17 | 43 | ....... | 1 | 20 | 10 | 25 | 4 | 21 | ....... | ....... | 12 00–12 99 |
| 13 00–13 99 | 4 | 6 | 30 | ....... | 1 | 36 | 8 | 9 | ....... | 25 | ....... | ....... | 13 00–13 99 |
| 14 00–14 99 | 2 | 7 | 35 | ....... | ....... | 38 | ....... | 10 | ....... | 15 | ....... | ....... | 14 00–14 99 |
| 15 00–15 99 | 3 | 1 | 52 | ....... | ....... | 39 | 1 | 3 | ....... | 15 | ....... | ....... | 15 00–15 99 |
| 16 00–17 99 | 14 | 4 | 102 | ....... | ....... | 38 | ....... | 5 | ....... | 9 | ....... | ....... | 16 00–17 99 |
| 18 00–19 99 | 14 | ....... | 77 | ....... | 1 | 11 | ....... | 3 | ....... | 2 | ....... | ....... | 18 00–19 99 |
| 20 00–24 99 | 47 | 1 | 59 | ....... | ....... | 4 | ....... | ....... | ....... | ....... | ....... | ....... | 20 00–24 99 |
| 25 00–29 99 | 21 | ....... | 6 | ....... | ....... | ....... | ....... | ....... | ....... | ....... | ....... | ....... | 25 00–29 99 |
| 30 00–34 99 | 14 | ....... | ....... | ....... | ....... | ....... | ....... | 1 | ....... | ....... | ....... | ....... | 30 00–34 99 |
| 35 00–39 99 | 6 | ....... | ....... | ....... | ....... | ....... | ....... | ....... | ....... | ....... | ....... | ....... | 35 00–39 99 |
| Not reported | 3 | ....... | 3 | ....... | ....... | 1 | 2 | 2 | 1 | ....... | ....... | 1 | Not reported |
| Total | 133 | 78 | 654 | 32 | 11 | 322 | 208 | 227 | 281 | 146 | 1 | 876 | Total |

NEW YORK CITY

254. TABLE IX, C, a — (*concluded*) **THE PAPER BOX INDUSTRY — FACTORY WORKERS**

Number and Per Cent. of Employees Classified According to Actual Weekly Earnings, by Occupation and Sex

| Actual Weekly Earnings in Dollars | Occupation (*concluded*) | | | | | | | | | | | | | | Actual Weekly Earnings in Dollars |
|---|---|---|---|---|---|---|---|---|---|---|---|---|---|---|---|
| | Strippers and Top Labelers | | Table Work | | Closing and Tying | | Floor Work | | Not Reported | | Total | | Cumulative Per Cent. of Total | | |
| | Male | Female | Male | Female | Male | Female | Male | Female | Male | Female | Male | Female | Male | Female | |
| Less than $3 00 | .... | 13 | 4 | 47 | 3 | 16 | 6 | 20 | ...... | ...... | 24 | 154 | 1.08 | 2.82 | Less than $3 00 |
| $3 00–$3 49... | .... | 8 | 5 | 46 | 2 | 21 | 6 | 11 | 1 | 1 | 21 | 153 | 2.04 | 5.51 | ...$3 00– 3 49 |
| 3 50– 3 99... | .... | 24 | 2 | 63 | 1 | 9 | 6 | 12 | 1 | 1 | 17 | 173 | 2.80 | 8.79 | ... 3 50– 3 99 |
| 4 00– 4 49... | 1 | 37 | 6 | 101 | 7 | 13 | 7 | 22 | ...... | 1 | 40 | 304 | 4.62 | 14.35 | ... 4 00– 4 49 |
| 4 50– 4 99... | 1 | 44 | 5 | 118 | 3 | 14 | 6 | 22 | ...... | 1 | 35 | 363 | 6.20 | 21.00 | ... 4 50– 4 99 |
| 5 00– 5 49... | 2 | 79 | 8 | 155 | 14 | 21 | 25 | 19 | 1 | 1 | 85 | 517 | 10.05 | 30.45 | ... 5 00– 5 49 |
| 5 50– 5 99... | 6 | 80 | 8 | 124 | 5 | 25 | 9 | 5 | ...... | 1 | 59 | 416 | 12.70 | 38.05 | ... 5 50– 5 99 |
| 6 00– 6 49... | 2 | 127 | 10 | 139 | 18 | 15 | 18 | 14 | 1 | 1 | 113 | 495 | 17.80 | 47.10 | ... 6 00– 6 49 |
| 6 50– 6 99... | 1 | 91 | 6 | 112 | 4 | 7 | 8 | 9 | 1 | ...... | 61 | 280 | 20.60 | 52.25 | ... 6 50– 6 99 |
| 7 00– 7 49... | 3 | 127 | 17 | 144 | 7 | 6 | 17 | 12 | ...... | 1 | 91 | 353 | 24.75 | 60.00 | ... 7 00– 7 49 |
| 7 50– 7 99... | 3 | 117 | 9 | 135 | 7 | 11 | 7 | 8 | 2 | ...... | 60 | 295 | 27.40 | 64.20 | ... 7 50– 7 99 |
| 8 00– 8 99... | 16 | 233 | 23 | 311 | 24 | 8 | 17 | 4 | 1 | 2 | 139 | 611 | 33.75 | 75.40 | ... 8 00– 8 99 |
| 9 00– 9 99... | 6 | 227 | 22 | 268 | 18 | 7 | 15 | 3 | ...... | 2 | 141 | 545 | 40.10 | 85.50 | ... 9 00– 9 99 |
| 10 00–10 99... | 2 | 171 | 29 | 158 | 11 | ...... | 19 | 4 | 2 | 1 | 146 | 379 | 46.75 | 92.00 | ...10 00–10 99 |
| 11 00–11 99... | 9 | 78 | 21 | 77 | 5 | 2 | 12 | ...... | 2 | ...... | 137 | 181 | 52.80 | 95.50 | ...11 00–11 99 |
| 12 00–12 99... | 5 | 57 | 27 | 50 | 6 | 2 | 6 | ...... | ...... | 1 | 155 | 141 | 59.90 | 98.00 | ...12 00–12 99 |
| 13 00–13 99... | 2 | 23 | 13 | 11 | 2 | ...... | 5 | ...... | 1 | 1 | 128 | 49 | 65.75 | 99.00 | ...13 00–13 99 |
| 14 00–14 99... | .... | 8 | 17 | 10 | ...... | ...... | 5 | ...... | ...... | ...... | 122 | 25 | 71.20 | 99.50 | ...14 00–14 99 |
| 15 00–15 99... | 17 | 6 | 12 | 2 | 1 | ...... | 2 | ...... | 3 | ...... | 131 | 10 | 77.10 | 99.70 | ...15 00–15 99 |
| 16 00–17 99... | 1 | 4 | 19 | 2 | 1 | ...... | 3 | 1 | ...... | ...... | 192 | 11 | 85.75 | 99.95 | ...16 00–17 99 |
| 18 00–19 99... | 1 | ...... | 15 | 2 | ...... | ...... | ...... | ...... | ...... | ...... | 124 | 2 | 91.50 | 99.97 | ...18 00–19 99 |
| 20 00–24 99... | 1 | ...... | 21 | 1 | ...... | ...... | 1 | ...... | ...... | ...... | 133 | 2 | 92.40 | 100.00 | ...20 00–24 99 |
| 25 00–29 99... | .... | ...... | 5 | ...... | ...... | ...... | ...... | ...... | ...... | ...... | 32 | ...... | 99.00 | ...... | ...25 00–29 99 |
| 30 00–34 99... | .... | ...... | .... | ...... | ...... | ...... | 1 | ...... | ...... | ...... | 16 | ...... | 99.60 | ...... | ...30 00–34 99 |
| 35 00–39 99... | .... | ...... | 2 | ...... | ...... | ...... | ...... | ...... | ...... | ...... | 8 | ...... | 100.00 | ...... | ...35 00–39 99 |
| Not reported.. | .... | 1 | .... | 13 | ...... | 1 | 9 | 44 | 5 | ...... | 23 | 63 | ...... | ...... | ..Not reported |
| Total..... | 63 | 1,555 | 306 | 2,089 | 139 | 178 | 210 | 210 | 21 | 15 | 2,233 | 5,522 | ...... | ...... | .....Total |

255. TABLE V, D, a

NEW YORK CITY

THE CONFECTIONERY INDUSTRY — FACTORY WORKERS

NUMBER AND PER CENT. OF EMPLOYEES EARNING SPECIFIED WEEKLY RATES, BY AGE GROUPS AND SEX

| WEEKLY RATES IN DOLLARS | AGE GROUPS IN YEARS | | | | | | | | | | | | | | WEEKLY RATES IN DOLLARS |
|---|---|---|---|---|---|---|---|---|---|---|---|---|---|---|---|
| | 14–15 | | 16–17 | | 18–20 | | 21–24 | | 25–29 | | 30–34 | | 35–39 | | |
| | Male | Female | Male | Female | Male | Female | Male | Female | Male | Female | Male | Female | Male | Female | |
| Less than $3 00 | 3 | 69 | .... | 33 | ...... | 14 | ...... | 6 | ...... | 2 | ...... | ...... | ...... | 2 | Less than $3 00 |
| $4 00–$4 49... | 5 | 68 | 1 | 78 | ...... | 22 | ...... | 10 | ...... | 5 | ...... | 2 | ...... | 8 | ...$4 00– 4 49 |
| 4 50– 4 99... | 2 | 67 | 6 | 197 | 1 | 97 | ...... | 29 | ...... | 19 | ...... | 15 | ...... | 10 | ... 4 50– 4 99 |
| 5 00– 5 49... | 2 | 12 | 21 | 371 | 9 | 251 | 2 | 72 | 1 | 56 | ...... | 26 | ...... | 34 | ... 5 00– 5 49 |
| 5 50– 5 99... | 2 | 7 | 10 | 153 | 18 | 148 | 5 | 47 | ...... | 31 | ...... | 13 | ...... | 18 | ... 5 50– 5 99 |
| 6 00– 6 49... | .... | 3 | 22 | 143 | 58 | 213 | 18 | 90 | 13 | 39 | 3 | 23 | 2 | 18 | ... 6 00– 6 49 |
| 6 50– 6 99... | .... | ...... | 6 | 19 | 9 | 103 | 4 | 48 | 2 | 26 | ...... | 5 | 2 | 7 | ... 6 50– 6 99 |
| 7 00– 7 49... | .... | ...... | 15 | 38 | 70 | 144 | 48 | 71 | 37 | 37 | 20 | 14 | 14 | 8 | ... 7 00– 7 49 |
| 7 50– 7 99... | .... | ...... | 2 | 17 | 26 | 44 | 26 | 57 | 15 | 37 | 11 | 10 | 10 | 5 | ... 7 50– 7 99 |
| 8 00– 8 99... | .... | ...... | 3 | 16 | 82 | 57 | 61 | 96 | 52 | 44 | 23 | 21 | 25 | 15 | ... 8 00– 8 99 |
| 9 00– 9 99... | .... | ...... | 2 | 7 | 46 | 43 | 88 | 43 | 64 | 34 | 42 | 21 | 24 | 12 | ... 9 00– 9 99 |
| 10 00–10 99... | .... | ...... | 1 | ...... | 15 | 12 | 43 | 32 | 46 | 27 | 35 | 22 | 22 | 11 | ...10 00–10 99 |
| 11 00–11 99... | .... | ...... | .... | ...... | 6 | 2 | 26 | 12 | 42 | 15 | 22 | 5 | 19 | 8 | ...11 00–11 99 |
| 12 00–12 99... | .... | ...... | 1 | ...... | 7 | 2 | 27 | 5 | 50 | 11 | 31 | 5 | 37 | 3 | ...12 00–12 99 |
| 13 00–13 99... | .... | ...... | .... | ...... | 1 | ...... | 16 | 1 | 19 | ...... | 21 | 1 | 22 | 1 | ...13 00–13 99 |
| 14 00–14 99... | .... | ...... | .... | ...... | 1 | ...... | 17 | ...... | 37 | 2 | 28 | 1 | 18 | 1 | ...14 00–14 99 |
| 15 00–15 99... | .... | ...... | 1 | ...... | 4 | 1 | 7 | ...... | 11 | 1 | 16 | 1 | 24 | 2 | ...15 00–15 99 |
| 16 00–17 99... | .... | ...... | .... | ...... | ...... | ...... | 4 | ...... | 18 | 1 | 19 | 2 | 17 | 3 | ...16 00–17 99 |
| 18 00–19 99... | .... | ...... | .... | ...... | ...... | ...... | 4 | ...... | 7 | 3 | 12 | 2 | 11 | 2 | ...18 00–19 99 |
| 20 00–24 99... | .... | ...... | .... | ...... | ...... | ...... | 1 | ...... | 5 | 1 | 11 | 1 | 11 | 1 | ...20 00–24 99 |
| 25 00–29 99... | .... | ...... | .... | ...... | ...... | ...... | ...... | ...... | 1 | ...... | 3 | ...... | 5 | ...... | ...25 00–29 99 |
| 30 00–34 99... | .... | ...... | .... | ...... | ...... | ...... | ...... | ...... | 1 | ...... | 3 | 1 | 1 | ...... | ...30 00–34 99 |
| 35 00–39 99... | .... | ...... | .... | ...... | ...... | ...... | ...... | ...... | 1 | ...... | 2 | ...... | 2 | ...... | ...35 00–39 99 |
| 40 00 and over. | .... | ...... | .... | ...... | ...... | ...... | ...... | ...... | ...... | ...... | 1 | ...... | 1 | ...... | .40 00 and over |
| Not reported.. | .... | ...... | .... | 4 | ...... | 5 | 1 | 5 | ...... | 1 | 2 | ...... | ...... | 2 | ..Not reported |
| Total..... | 14 | 226 | 91 | 1,076 | 353 | 1,158 | 398 | 624 | 422 | 392 | 305 | 191 | 267 | 171 | .....Total |

255. TABLE V, D, a — (*concluded*)

NEW YORK CITY

THE CONFECTIONERY INDUSTRY — FACTORY WORKERS

NUMBER AND PER CENT. OF EMPLOYEES EARNING SPECIFIED WEEKLY RATES, BY AGE GROUPS AND SEX

| WEEKLY RATES IN DOLLARS | AGE GROUPS IN YEARS (*concluded*) 40–44 | | 45–54 | | 55–64 | | 65 AND OVER | | NOT REPORTED | | TOTAL | | CUMULATIVE PER CENT. OF TOTAL | | WEEKLY RATES IN DOLLARS |
|---|---|---|---|---|---|---|---|---|---|---|---|---|---|---|---|
| | Male | Female | Male | Female | Male | Female | Male | Female | Male | Female | Male | Female | Male | Female | |
| Less than $3 90 | .... | ...... | .... | 3 | ...... | ...... | ...... | ...... | ...... | ...... | 3 | 129 | .12 | 3.14 | Less than $4 00 |
| $4 00–$4 49... | .... | 3 | .... | 13 | ...... | 3 | ...... | 1 | ...... | ...... | 6 | 213 | .36 | 8.32 | ...$4 00– 4 49 |
| 4 50– 4 99... | .... | 16 | .... | 22 | ...... | 2 | ...... | 1 | 1 | 2 | 10 | 477 | .77 | 19.90 | ... 4 50– 4 99 |
| 5 00– 5 49... | .... | 22 | .... | 24 | 1 | 13 | ...... | 1 | 1 | 5 | 37 | 887 | 2.26 | 41.50 | ... 5 00– 5 49 |
| 5 50– 5 99... | .... | 15 | 1 | 12 | ...... | 3 | ...... | ...... | ...... | 11 | 36 | 458 | 3.70 | 52.70 | ... 5 50– 5 99 |
| 6 00– 6 49... | 1 | 11 | 2 | 15 | 1 | 7 | ...... | ...... | 1 | 3 | 121 | 565 | 8.60 | 66.50 | ... 6 00– 6 49 |
| 6 50– 6 99... | .... | 6 | .... | 8 | ...... | 1 | ...... | ...... | 2 | ...... | 25 | 223 | 9.60 | 71.80 | ... 6 50– 6 99 |
| 7 00– 7 49... | 6 | 3 | 15 | 3 | 5 | 1 | ...... | ...... | 2 | ...... | 232 | 319 | 19.00 | 79.80 | ... 7 00– 7 49 |
| 7 50– 7 99... | 6 | 1 | 12 | ...... | ...... | ...... | 2 | ...... | ...... | 1 | 110 | 172 | 23.40 | 83.80 | ... 7 50– 7 99 |
| 8 00– 8 99... | 26 | 11 | 32 | 6 | 13 | ...... | 3 | ...... | 2 | ...... | 322 | 266 | 36.40 | 90.20 | ... 8 00– 8 99 |
| 9 00– 9 99... | 17 | 7 | 29 | 1 | 15 | 1 | 3 | ...... | 1 | 2 | 331 | 171 | 49.20 | 94.50 | ... 9 00– 9 99 |
| 10 00–10 99... | 24 | 6 | 37 | 4 | 7 | 2 | 2 | ...... | ...... | 1 | 232 | 117 | 59.20 | 97.20 | ...10 00–10 99 |
| 11 00–11 99... | 9 | 1 | 13 | 2 | 7 | ...... | ...... | ...... | ...... | 1 | 144 | 46 | 64.80 | 98.30 | ...11 00–11 99 |
| 12 00–12 99... | 18 | 3 | 42 | 1 | 11 | ...... | 5 | ...... | ...... | ...... | 229 | 30 | 74.20 | 99.30 | ...12 00–12 99 |
| 13 00–13 99... | 13 | ...... | 13 | 1 | 6 | ...... | 3 | ...... | ...... | ...... | 114 | 4 | 78.90 | 99.40 | ...13 00–13 99 |
| 14 00–14 99... | 13 | ...... | 11 | ...... | 3 | 1 | 2 | ...... | 2 | 1 | 132 | 6 | 84.20 | 99.50 | ...14 00–14 99 |
| 15 00–15 99... | 17 | ...... | 20 | ...... | 5 | ...... | ...... | ...... | ...... | 1 | 105 | 6 | 88.40 | 99.60 | ...15 00–15 99 |
| 16 00–17 99... | 15 | ...... | 14 | 2 | 8 | ...... | 4 | ...... | 1 | ...... | 100 | 8 | 92.50 | 99.70 | ...16 00–17 99 |
| 18 00–19 99... | 9 | ...... | 21 | 1 | 8 | ...... | ...... | ...... | 1 | ...... | 73 | 8 | 95.50 | 99.80 | ...18 00–19 99 |
| 20 00–24 99... | 12 | 1 | 20 | 1 | 5 | ...... | ...... | ...... | ...... | ...... | 65 | 5 | 98.00 | 99.90 | ...20 00–24 99 |
| 25 00–29 99... | 6 | ...... | 4 | ...... | 2 | ...... | ...... | ...... | 1 | ...... | 22 | ...... | 98.70 | ...... | ...25 00–29 99 |
| 30 00–34 99... | 1 | ...... | 3 | ...... | 3 | ...... | 1 | ...... | ...... | ...... | 13 | 1 | 99.30 | 100.00 | ...30 00–34 99 |
| 35 00–39 99... | 4 | ...... | 1 | ...... | 1 | ...... | ...... | ...... | 1 | ...... | 12 | ...... | 99.90 | ...... | ...35 00–39 99 |
| 40 00 and over. | 1 | ...... | 1 | ...... | 1 | ...... | ...... | ...... | ...... | ...... | 5 | ...... | 100.00 | ...... | .40 00 and over |
| Not reported.. | 1 | 2 | .... | 2 | ...... | ...... | ...... | ...... | 5 | ...... | 9 | 21 | ...... | ...... | ..Not reported |
| Total..... | 199 | 108 | 291 | 121 | 102 | 34 | 25 | 3 | 21 | 28 | 2,488 | 4,132 | ...... | ...... | .....Total |

NEW YORK CITY

THE CONFECTIONERY INDUSTRY — FACTORY WORKERS

256. TABLE VIII, D, a  NUMBER AND PER CENT. OF EMPLOYEES EARNING SPECIFIED WEEKLY RATES, BY OCCUPATION AND SEX

| WEEKLY RATES IN DOLLARS | OCCUPATION: FOREMEN AND FOREWOMEN | | CANDY MAKERS | | DIPPERS | | PACKERS | | WRAPPERS | | MACHINE OPERATORS | | HELPERS | | GENERAL LABORERS | | NOT REPORTED | | TOTAL | | CUMULATIVE PER CENT. OF TOTAL | | WEEKLY RATES IN DOLLARS |
|---|---|---|---|---|---|---|---|---|---|---|---|---|---|---|---|---|---|---|---|---|---|---|---|
| | Male | Female | Male | Female | Male | Female | Male | Female | Male | Female | Male | Female | Male | Female | Male | Female | Male | Female | Male | Female | Male | Female | |
| $3 50–$3 99 | .... | .... | .... | .... | .... | 16 | .... | 55 | .... | 22 | .... | .... | 2 | 35 | 1 | .... | .... | 1 | 3 | 129 | .12 | 3.14 | $3 50–$3 99 |
| 4 00– 4 49 | .... | .... | .... | .... | .... | 22 | .... | 96 | .... | 30 | .... | .... | 6 | 60 | .... | 5 | .... | .... | 6 | 213 | .36 | 8.32 | 4 00– 4 49 |
| 4 50– 4 99 | .... | .... | .... | .... | .... | 50 | .... | 154 | .... | 54 | .... | .... | 7 | 191 | 3 | 21 | .... | 7 | 10 | 477 | .77 | 19.90 | 4 50– 4 99 |
| 5 00– 5 49 | .... | 2 | .... | .... | .... | 56 | 1 | 390 | 1 | 139 | .... | .... | 25 | 281 | 10 | 13 | .... | 6 | 37 | 887 | 2.26 | 41.50 | 5 00– 5 49 |
| 5 50– 5 99 | .... | 1 | .... | .... | .... | 50 | .... | 214 | 1 | 57 | .... | .... | 34 | 128 | .... | 8 | 1 | .... | 36 | 458 | 3.70 | 52.70 | 5 50– 5 99 |
| 6 00– 6 49 | .... | 4 | .... | .... | .... | 63 | 1 | 285 | 2 | 76 | .... | .... | 94 | 128 | 24 | 8 | .... | 1 | 121 | 565 | 8.60 | 66.50 | 6 00– 6 49 |
| 6 50– 6 99 | .... | 1 | .... | 1 | .... | 37 | .... | 112 | .... | 30 | .... | .... | 21 | 35 | 4 | 2 | .... | 5 | 25 | 223 | 9.60 | 71.80 | 6 50– 6 99 |
| 7 00– 7 49 | .... | 6 | 1 | 1 | .... | 45 | 12 | 143 | .... | 49 | .... | 1 | 187 | 68 | 32 | 2 | .... | 4 | 232 | 319 | 19.00 | 79.80 | 7 00– 7 49 |
| 7 50– 7 99 | .... | 4 | 2 | .... | 1 | 44 | 3 | 75 | 1 | 25 | .... | 2 | 92 | 20 | 10 | .... | 1 | 2 | 110 | 172 | 23.40 | 83.80 | 7 50– 7 99 |
| 8 00– 8 99 | .... | 22 | 3 | .... | 1 | 118 | 8 | 63 | .... | 25 | 2 | 2 | 261 | 32 | 47 | 1 | .... | 3 | 322 | 266 | 36.40 | 90.20 | 8 00– 8 99 |
| 9 00– 9 99 | 2 | 24 | 10 | .... | .... | 98 | 1 | 17 | .... | 10 | 4 | 1 | 278 | 20 | 34 | 1 | 2 | .... | 331 | 171 | 49.20 | 94.50 | 9 00– 9 99 |
| 10 00–10 99 | .... | 29 | 18 | .... | .... | 75 | 4 | 6 | .... | .... | 8 | .... | 174 | 5 | 23 | 1 | 5 | 1 | 232 | 117 | 59.20 | 97.20 | 10 00–10 99 |
| 11 00–11 99 | 1 | 17 | 13 | .... | .... | 23 | .... | 5 | .... | .... | 17 | 1 | 91 | .... | 18 | .... | 4 | .... | 144 | 46 | 64.80 | 98.30 | 11 00–11 99 |
| 12 00–12 99 | 5 | 22 | 36 | .... | .... | 3 | 1 | .... | .... | .... | 21 | 1 | 142 | 2 | 24 | .... | .... | 2 | 229 | 30 | 74.20 | 99.30 | 12 00–12 99 |
| 13 00–13 99 | 3 | 4 | 21 | .... | .... | .... | 1 | .... | .... | .... | 20 | .... | 58 | .... | 7 | .... | 4 | .... | 114 | 4 | 78.90 | 99.40 | 13 00–13 99 |
| 14 00–14 99 | 8 | 5 | 32 | .... | .... | 1 | 1 | .... | .... | .... | 23 | .... | 66 | .... | 2 | .... | .... | .... | 132 | 6 | 84.20 | 99.50 | 14 00–14 99 |
| 15 00–15 99 | 12 | 6 | 39 | .... | .... | .... | .... | .... | .... | .... | 15 | .... | 27 | .... | 3 | .... | 9 | .... | 105 | 6 | 88.40 | 99.60 | 15 00–15 99 |
| 16 00–17 99 | 22 | 7 | 42 | .... | .... | .... | 1 | 1 | .... | .... | 10 | .... | 22 | .... | 3 | .... | .... | .... | 100 | 8 | 92.50 | 99.70 | 16 00–17 99 |
| 18 00–19 99 | 24 | 7 | 34 | .... | .... | .... | .... | 1 | .... | .... | 10 | .... | 4 | .... | 1 | .... | .... | .... | 73 | 8 | 95.50 | 99.80 | 18 00–19 99 |
| 20 00–24 99 | 44 | 5 | 13 | .... | .... | .... | .... | .... | .... | .... | 5 | .... | 1 | .... | .... | .... | 2 | .... | 65 | 5 | 98.00 | 99.90 | 20 00–24 99 |
| 25 00–29 99 | 15 | .... | 6 | .... | .... | .... | .... | .... | .... | .... | 1 | .... | .... | .... | .... | .... | .... | .... | 22 | .... | 98.70 | .... | 25 00–29 99 |
| 30 00–34 99 | 11 | 1 | 1 | .... | .... | .... | .... | .... | .... | .... | .... | .... | .... | .... | .... | .... | 1 | .... | 13 | 1 | 99.30 | 100.00 | 30 00–34 99 |
| 35 00–39 99 | 11 | .... | 1 | .... | .... | .... | .... | .... | .... | .... | .... | .... | .... | .... | .... | .... | .... | .... | 12 | .... | 99.90 | .... | 35 00–39 99 |
| 40 00 and over | 3 | .... | 1 | .... | .... | .... | .... | .... | .... | .... | .... | .... | .... | .... | .... | .... | 1 | .... | 5 | .... | 100.00 | .... | 40 00 and over |
| Not reported | .... | 1 | 1 | .... | .... | 3 | 1 | 7 | .... | 2 | 1 | .... | 4 | 6 | 2 | .... | .... | 2 | 9 | 21 | .... | .... | Not reported |
| Total | 161 | 168 | 274 | 2 | 2 | 704 | 35 | 1,624 | 5 | 519 | 137 | 8 | 1,596 | 1,011 | 248 | 62 | 30 | 34 | 2,488 | 4,132 | .... | .... | Total |

257. TABLE VI, D, a

NEW YORK CITY

THE CONFECTIONERY INDUSTRY — FACTORY WORKERS

NUMBER AND PER CENT. OF EMPLOYEES CLASSIFIED ACCORDING TO ACTUAL WEEKLY EARNINGS, BY AGE GROUPS AND SEX

| ACTUAL WEEKLY EARNINGS IN DOLLARS | AGE GROUPS | | | | | | | | | | | | | | ACTUAL WEEKLY EARNINGS IN DOLLARS |
|---|---|---|---|---|---|---|---|---|---|---|---|---|---|---|---|
| | 14–15 | | 16–17 | | 18–20 | | 21–24 | | 25–29 | | 30–34 | | 35–39 | | |
| | Male | Female | Male | Female | Male | Female | Male | Female | Male | Female | Male | Female | Male | Female | |
| Less than $3 00 | 1 | 41 | 6 | 78 | 15 | 63 | 13 | 27 | 5 | 11 | 2 | 11 | 4 | 6 | Less than $3 00 |
| $3 00–$3 49... | 1 | 19 | 2 | 53 | 6 | 34 | 4 | 15 | 1 | 4 | 2 | 1 | ...... | 5 | ...$3 00– 3 49 |
| 3 50– 3 99... | .... | 53 | 7 | 69 | 2 | 36 | 1 | 10 | 2 | 7 | 2 | 8 | ...... | 6 | ... 3 50– 3 99 |
| 4 00– 4 49... | 6 | 66 | 5 | 139 | 5 | 78 | 3 | 31 | 1 | 20 | 1 | 8 | ...... | 9 | ... 4 00– 4 49 |
| 4 50– 4 99... | 3 | 43 | 8 | 192 | 16 | 114 | 9 | 38 | 2 | 22 | 3 | 17 | ...... | 13 | ... 4 50– 4 99 |
| 5 00– 5 49... | 1 | 10 | 17 | 264 | 19 | 201 | 12 | 64 | 6 | 57 | 1 | 16 | 1 | 23 | ... 5 00– 5 49 |
| 5 50– 5 99... | 1 | 11 | 4 | 147 | 19 | 156 | 6 | 56 | 7 | 30 | 4 | 12 | 5 | 18 | ... 5 50– 5 99 |
| 6 00– 6 49... | .... | 8 | 12 | 107 | 31 | 178 | 17 | 80 | 7 | 35 | 8 | 15 | 3 | 13 | ... 6 00– 6 49 |
| 6 50– 6 99... | .... | ...... | 9 | 45 | 26 | 125 | 10 | 53 | 17 | 20 | 2 | 13 | 11 | 9 | ... 6 50– 6 99 |
| 7 00– 7 49... | .... | 2 | 11 | 37 | 41 | 110 | 32 | 62 | 16 | 35 | 16 | 10 | 10 | 11 | ... 7 00– 7 49 |
| 7 50– 7 99... | .... | 1 | 4 | 21 | 34 | 67 | 25 | 59 | 27 | 43 | 11 | 13 | 10 | 9 | ... 7 50– 7 99 |
| 8 00– 8 99... | .... | ...... | 3 | 31 | 64 | 101 | 59 | 98 | 56 | 54 | 20 | 30 | 20 | 8 | ... 8 00– 8 99 |
| 9 00– 9 99... | .... | ...... | 2 | 16 | 39 | 74 | 62 | 59 | 39 | 39 | 35 | 17 | 26 | 15 | ... 9 00– 9 99 |
| 10 00–10 99... | .... | ...... | 1 | 5 | 13 | 35 | 34 | 53 | 41 | 34 | 33 | 17 | 25 | 9 | ...10 00–10 99 |
| 11 00–11 99... | .... | ...... | 1 | ...... | 7 | 19 | 30 | 24 | 41 | 17 | 17 | 4 | 13 | 8 | ...11 00–11 99 |
| 12 00–12 99... | .... | ...... | 1 | 1 | 12 | 7 | 33 | 11 | 44 | 10 | 34 | 6 | 29 | 3 | ...12 00–12 99 |
| 13 00–13 99... | .... | ...... | .... | 1 | 2 | 1 | 21 | 7 | 29 | 1 | 18 | 2 | 13 | 1 | ...13 00–13 99 |
| 14 00–14 99... | .... | ...... | .... | ...... | 1 | ...... | 14 | 2 | 31 | 3 | 25 | 2 | 22 | 2 | ...14 00–14 99 |
| 15 00–15 99... | .... | ...... | 1 | ...... | 4 | 2 | 9 | ...... | 12 | 2 | 16 | 1 | 18 | 2 | ...15 00–15 99 |
| 16 00–17 99... | .... | ...... | .... | ...... | ...... | 1 | 8 | ...... | 20 | 1 | 19 | 4 | 19 | 3 | ...16 00–17 99 |
| 18 00–19 99... | .... | ...... | .... | ...... | ...... | ...... | 2 | 1 | 9 | 3 | 13 | 2 | 16 | 2 | ...18 00–19 99 |
| 20 00–24 99... | .... | ...... | .... | ...... | 1 | ...... | 4 | ...... | 6 | 1 | 13 | 1 | 13 | ...... | ...20 00–24 99 |
| 25 00–29 99... | .... | ...... | .... | ...... | ...... | ...... | ...... | ...... | 2 | ...... | 4 | ...... | 6 | 1 | ...25 00–29 99 |
| 30 00–34 99... | .... | ...... | .... | ...... | ...... | ...... | ...... | ...... | ...... | ...... | 2 | ...... | 3 | ...... | ...30 00–34 99 |
| 35 00–39 99... | .... | ...... | .... | ...... | ...... | ...... | ...... | ...... | 1 | ...... | 2 | ...... | 2 | ...... | ...35 00–39 99 |
| 40 00 and over. | .... | ...... | .... | ...... | ...... | ...... | ...... | ...... | ...... | ...... | 1 | ...... | 1 | ...... | .40 00 and over |
| Not reported... | .... | 2 | .... | 9 | 2 | 12 | 4 | 5 | 3 | 5 | 2 | 1 | 2 | 4 | ...Not reported |
| Total..... | 13 | 256 | 94 | 1,215 | 359 | 1,414 | 412 | 755 | 425 | 454 | 306 | 211 | 272 | 180 | ....Total |

257. TABLE VI, D, a

NEW YORK CITY

THE CONFECTIONERY INDUSTRY — FACTORY WORKERS

NUMBER AND PER CENT. OF EMPLOYEES CLASSIFIED ACCORDING TO ACTUAL WEEKLY EARNINGS, BY AGE GROUPS AND SEX

| ACTUAL WEEKLY EARNINGS IN DOLLARS | AGE GROUPS | | | | | | | | | | | | | | ACTUAL WEEKLY EARNINGS IN DOLLARS |
|---|---|---|---|---|---|---|---|---|---|---|---|---|---|---|---|
| | 40–44 | | 45–54 | | 55–64 | | 65 AND OVER | | NOT REPORTED | | TOTAL | | CUMULATIVE PER CENT. OF TOTAL | | |
| | Male | Female | Male | Female | Male | Female | Male | Female | Male | Female | Male | Female | Male | Female | |
| Less than $3 00 | 1 | 4 | .... | 9 | 1 | 2 | ...... | ...... | 1 | 1 | 49 | 253 | 2.00 | 5.30 | Less than $3 00 |
| $3 00–$3 49... | 1 | ...... | 1 | 2 | 1 | 1 | ...... | ...... | ...... | ...... | 19 | 134 | 2.70 | 8.10 | ...$3 00– 3 49 |
| 3 50– 3 99... | .... | 2 | .... | 7 | ...... | 1 | ...... | ...... | ...... | ...... | 14 | 199 | 3.30 | 12.30 | ... 3 50– 3 99 |
| 4 00– 4 49... | .... | 10 | .... | 5 | 2 | 4 | ...... | 1 | ...... | ...... | 23 | 371 | 4.20 | 20.10 | ... 4 00– 4 49 |
| 4 50– 4 99... | .... | 12 | .... | 16 | ...... | 2 | ...... | 1 | ...... | 4 | 41 | 474 | 5.80 | 30.10 | ... 4 50– 4 99 |
| 5 00– 5 49... | 4 | 20 | 2 | 24 | ...... | 11 | ...... | 1 | 2 | 2 | 65 | 693 | 8.40 | 44.70 | ... 5 00– 5 49 |
| 5 50– 5 99... | .... | 17 | 4 | 16 | ...... | 3 | ...... | 1 | ...... | 1 | 50 | 468 | 10.80 | 54.50 | ... 5 50– 5 99 |
| 6 00– 6 49... | .... | 8 | 4 | 12 | 1 | 5 | ...... | ...... | 3 | 2 | 86 | 463 | 13.80 | 64.30 | ... 6 00– 6 49 |
| 6 50– 6 99... | 7 | 5 | 8 | 10 | 3 | ...... | ...... | ...... | 2 | 1 | 95 | 281 | 17.60 | 70.20 | ... 6 50– 6 99 |
| 7 00– 7 49... | 7 | 2 | 13 | 5 | 3 | ...... | 1 | ...... | 2 | ...... | 152 | 274 | 23.60 | 76.00 | ... 7 00– 7 49 |
| 7 50– 7 99... | 6 | 6 | 18 | 1 | 2 | 1 | 1 | ...... | ...... | ...... | 138 | 221 | 29.10 | 80.60 | ... 7 50– 7 99 |
| 8 00– 8 99... | 22 | 14 | 25 | 3 | 13 | ...... | 5 | ...... | ...... | 3 | 287 | 342 | 40.50 | 87.90 | ... 8 00– 8 99 |
| 9 00– 9 99... | 17 | 7 | 26 | 2 | 12 | 1 | 2 | ...... | ...... | 2 | 260 | 232 | 50.90 | 92.80 | ... 9 00– 9 99 |
| 10 00–10 99... | 16 | 5 | 29 | 5 | 7 | 2 | 3 | ...... | ...... | 1 | 202 | 166 | 58.90 | 96.40 | ...10 00–10 99 |
| 11 00–11 99... | 8 | 3 | 18 | 2 | 5 | ...... | 1 | ...... | 3 | ...... | 144 | 77 | 64.60 | 97.90 | ...11 00–11 99 |
| 12 00–12 99... | 14 | 3 | 27 | 2 | 9 | ...... | 4 | ...... | 2 | ...... | 209 | 43 | 73.00 | 98.90 | ...12 00–12 99 |
| 13 00–13 99... | 15 | ...... | 18 | 1 | 7 | ...... | 4 | ...... | 1 | ...... | 128 | 14 | 7.00 | 99.00 | ...13 00–13 99 |
| 14 00–14 99... | 13 | ...... | 17 | ...... | 4 | 2 | 1 | ...... | ...... | 1 | 128 | 12 | 83.10 | 99.40 | ...14 00–14 99 |
| 15 00–15 99... | 15 | ...... | 10 | ...... | 8 | ...... | 2 | ...... | ...... | 1 | 95 | 8 | 87.00 | 99.50 | ...15 00–15 99 |
| 16 00–17 99... | 18 | ...... | 23 | 2 | 6 | ...... | 2 | ...... | ...... | ...... | 115 | 11 | 91.50 | 99.70 | ...16 00–17 99 |
| 18 00–19 99... | 7 | ...... | 19 | 1 | 9 | ...... | ...... | ...... | ...... | ...... | 75 | 9 | 94.50 | 99.80 | ...18 00–19 99 |
| 20 00–24 99... | 16 | 1 | 20 | 1 | 8 | ...... | ...... | ...... | ...... | ...... | 81 | 4 | 97.50 | 99.90 | ...20 00–24 99 |
| 25 00–29 99... | 6 | ...... | 4 | ...... | 4 | ...... | ...... | ...... | 3 | ...... | 29 | 1 | 98.00 | 100.00 | ...25 00–29 99 |
| 30 00–34 99... | 2 | ...... | 4 | ...... | 1 | ...... | 1 | ...... | ...... | ...... | 13 | ...... | 99.20 | ...... | ...30 00–34 99 |
| 35 00–39 99... | 3 | ...... | 1 | ...... | 2 | ...... | ...... | ...... | 1 | ...... | 12 | ...... | 99.90 | ...... | ...35 00–39 99 |
| 40 00 and over. | 2 | ...... | .... | ...... | 1 | ...... | ...... | ...... | 1 | ...... | 6 | ...... | 100.00 | ...... | .40 00 and over |
| Not reported... | .... | 3 | 1 | 4 | 1 | ...... | 1 | ...... | 1 | 2 | 17 | 47 | ...... | ...... | ...Not reported |
| Total..... | 200 | 122 | 292 | 130 | 110 | 35 | 28 | 4 | 22 | 21 | 2,533 | 4,797 | ...... | ...... | .....Total |

258. TABLE IX, D, a

NEW YORK CITY

THE CONFECTIONERY INDUSTRY — FACTORY WORKERS

NUMBER AND PER CENT. OF EMPLOYEES CLASSIFIED ACCORDING TO ACTUAL WEEKLY EARNINGS, BY OCCUPATION AND SEX

| Actual Weekly Earnings in Dollars | Occupation | | | | | | | | | | | | | | | | | | | | | | Actual Weekly Earnings in Dollars |
|---|---|---|---|---|---|---|---|---|---|---|---|---|---|---|---|---|---|---|---|---|---|---|---|
| | Foremen and Forewomen | | Candy Makers | | Dippers | | Packers | | Wrappers | | Machine Operators | | Helpers | | General Laborers | | Not Reported | | Total | | Cumulative Per Cent. of Total | | |
| | Male | Female | Male | Female | Male | Female | Male | Female | Male | Female | Male | Female | Male | Female | Male | Female | Male | Female | Male | Female | Male | Female | |
| Less than $3 00 | 1 | | | | | 23 | 2 | 125 | | 37 | 1 | | 41 | 65 | 4 | 1 | | 2 | 49 | 253 | 2.00 | 5.30 | Less than $3 00 |
| $3 00–$3 49 | 1 | | 1 | | 1 | 6 | | 65 | | 25 | | | 13 | 37 | 1 | 1 | 2 | | 19 | 134 | 2.70 | 8.10 | $3 00– 3 49 |
| 3 50– 3 99 | | 1 | | | | 28 | | 95 | 1 | 30 | | | 13 | 43 | | 2 | | | 14 | 199 | 3.30 | 12.30 | 3 50– 3 99 |
| 4 00– 4 49 | | | | | | 42 | | 167 | 1 | 61 | | | 19 | 86 | 3 | 12 | | 3 | 23 | 371 | 4.20 | 20.10 | 4 00– 4 49 |
| 4 50– 4 99 | | 1 | | | | 52 | | 182 | 1 | 66 | 1 | | 36 | 161 | 3 | 12 | | | 41 | 474 | 5.80 | 30.10 | 4 50– 4 99 |
| 5 00– 5 49 | | 5 | | | | 50 | 2 | 316 | 2 | 86 | 1 | | 49 | 218 | 11 | 17 | | 1 | 65 | 693 | 8.40 | 44.70 | 5 00– 5 49 |
| 5 50– 5 99 | | 3 | 1 | | | 50 | 1 | 229 | | 67 | | | 46 | 111 | 1 | 6 | 1 | 2 | 50 | 468 | 10.80 | 54.50 | 5 50– 5 99 |
| 6 00– 6 49 | | 4 | 1 | | 1 | 75 | 1 | 221 | | 41 | | | 65 | 110 | 18 | 9 | | 3 | 86 | 463 | 13.80 | 64.30 | 6 00– 6 49 |
| 6 50– 6 99 | 1 | 4 | | 1 | | 52 | | 140 | | 35 | | | 83 | 46 | 11 | 2 | | 1 | 95 | 281 | 17.60 | 70.20 | 6 50– 6 99 |
| 7 00– 7 49 | | 3 | | 1 | | 65 | 9 | 118 | | 43 | | 1 | 113 | 40 | 30 | 2 | | 1 | 152 | 274 | 23.60 | 76.00 | 7 00– 7 49 |
| 7 50– 7 99 | 1 | 6 | 3 | | 2 | 63 | 2 | 94 | | 26 | | | 111 | 31 | 18 | | 1 | 1 | 138 | 221 | 29.10 | 80.60 | 7 50– 7 99 |
| 8 00– 8 99 | | 23 | 8 | | 4 | 121 | 8 | 106 | | 32 | 4 | 3 | 228 | 54 | 35 | 2 | | 1 | 287 | 342 | 40.50 | 87.90 | 8 00– 8 99 |
| 9 00– 9 99 | 1 | 21 | 9 | | 2 | 110 | 1 | 53 | | 11 | 4 | 2 | 208 | 34 | 35 | 1 | | | 260 | 232 | 50.90 | 92.80 | 9 00– 9 99 |
| 10 00–10 99 | | 27 | 17 | | 1 | 98 | 3 | 22 | | 4 | 8 | | 150 | 13 | 19 | 2 | 4 | | 202 | 166 | 58.70 | 96.40 | 10 00–10 99 |
| 11 00–11 99 | 1 | 15 | 15 | | 4 | 48 | | 7 | | 1 | 18 | | 90 | 6 | 16 | | | | 144 | 77 | 64.60 | 97.90 | 11 00–11 99 |
| 12 00–12 99 | 2 | 19 | 31 | | 4 | 13 | 2 | 2 | | | 17 | 2 | 130 | 5 | 23 | | | 2 | 209 | 43 | 73.00 | 98.90 | 12 00–12 99 |
| 13 00–13 99 | 6 | 4 | 20 | | | 8 | 2 | 2 | | | 20 | | 67 | | 7 | | 6 | | 128 | 14 | 78.00 | 99.00 | 13 00–13 99 |
| 14 00–14 99 | 9 | 6 | 26 | | 1 | 5 | | | | | 17 | | 73 | 1 | 1 | | 1 | | 128 | 12 | 83.10 | 99.40 | 14 00–14 99 |
| 15 00–15 99 | 9 | 5 | 33 | | | 3 | | | | | 15 | | 25 | | 3 | | 10 | | 95 | 8 | 87.00 | 99.50 | 15 00–15 99 |
| 16 00–17 99 | 17 | 8 | 43 | | | 2 | 1 | 1 | | | 14 | | 34 | | 6 | | | | 115 | 11 | 91.50 | 99.70 | 16 00–17 99 |
| 18 00–19 99 | 27 | 7 | 29 | | | 1 | | 1 | | | 9 | | 5 | | 3 | | 2 | | 75 | 9 | 94.50 | 99.80 | 18 00–19 99 |
| 20 00–24 99 | 42 | 4 | 25 | | | | | | | | 8 | | 4 | | | | 2 | | 81 | 4 | 97.50 | 99.90 | 20 00–24 99 |
| 25 00–29 99 | 18 | 1 | 10 | | | | | | | | 1 | | | | | | | | 29 | 1 | 98.00 | 100.00 | 25 00–29 99 |
| 30 00–34 99 | 11 | | 1 | | | | | | | | | | | | | | 1 | | 13 | | 99.20 | | 30 00–34 99 |
| 35 00–39 99 | 10 | | 1 | | | | | | | | | | | | | | 1 | | 12 | | 99.90 | | 35 00–39 99 |
| 40 00 and over | 5 | | 1 | | | | | | | | | | | | | | | | 6 | | 100.00 | | 40 00 and over |
| Not reported | | 2 | 4 | | | 6 | 1 | 16 | | 9 | 2 | | 8 | 8 | 1 | | 1 | 6 | 17 | 47 | | | Not reported |
| Total | 162 | 169 | 279 | 2 | 20 | 921 | 35 | 1,962 | 5 | 574 | 140 | 8 | 1,611 | 1,069 | 249 | 69 | 32 | 23 | 2,533 | 4,797 | | | Total |

NEW YORK CITY

259. TABLE XIX, D, a

THE CONFECTIONERY INDUSTRY — FACTORY EMPLOYEES

NUMBER AND PER CENT. OF EMPLOYEES CLASSIFIED ACCORDING TO AVERAGE WEEKLY EARNINGS, BY OCCUPATION AND SEX

| AVERAGE WEEKLY EARNINGS IN DOLLARS | OCCUPATION | | | | | | | | | | | | | | TOTAL | | CUMULATIVE PER CENT. OF TOTAL | | AVERAGE WEEKLY EARNINGS IN DOLLARS |
|---|---|---|---|---|---|---|---|---|---|---|---|---|---|---|---|---|---|---|---|
| | FOREMEN AND FOREWOMEN | | CANDY MAKERS | | MACHINE OPERATORS | | DIPPERS | | PACKERS AND WRAPPERS | | HELPERS | | LABORERS | | | | | | |
| | Male | Female | Male | Female | Male | Female | Male | Female | Male | Female | Male | Female | Male | Female | Male | Female | Male | Female | |
| Less than $3 00 | ..... | ..... | ..... | ..... | ..... | ..... | ..... | ..... | ..... | 19 | 2 | 12 | ..... | ..... | 2 | 31 | .50 | 3.10 | Less than $3 00 |
| $3 00-$3 49 | ..... | ..... | ..... | ..... | ..... | ..... | ..... | ..... | ..... | 21 | 7 | 28 | ..... | ..... | 7 | 49 | 2.40 | 8.10 | $3 00- 3 49 |
| 3 50- 3 99 | ..... | ..... | ..... | ..... | ..... | 3 | ..... | ..... | ..... | 57 | 4 | 27 | 1 | ..... | 5 | 87 | 3.70 | 17.00 | 3 50- 3 99 |
| 4 00- 4 49 | ..... | ..... | ..... | ..... | ..... | ..... | ..... | 1 | ..... | 67 | 3 | 53 | 2 | ..... | 5 | 121 | 5.00 | 28.40 | 4 00- 4 49 |
| 4 50- 4 99 | ..... | ..... | ..... | ..... | ..... | 1 | ..... | 3 | 1 | 121 | 8 | 32 | ..... | ..... | 9 | 157 | 7.50 | 45.00 | 4 50- 4 99 |
| 5 00- 5 49 | ..... | ..... | ..... | ..... | ..... | ..... | 1 | 3 | ..... | 88 | ..... | 19 | 5 | 1 | 6 | 111 | 9.00 | 56.20 | 5 00- 5 49 |
| 5 50- 5 99 | ..... | ..... | ..... | ..... | 1 | ..... | ..... | 11 | 1 | 95 | 8 | 17 | 4 | ..... | 14 | 123 | 12.80 | 69.00 | 5 50- 5 99 |
| 6 00- 6 49 | ..... | ..... | ..... | ..... | 1 | ..... | ..... | 9 | ..... | 52 | 9 | 11 | 4 | 1 | 14 | 73 | 16.50 | 76.30 | 6 00- 6 49 |
| 6 50- 6 99 | ..... | 2 | ..... | ..... | 1 | ..... | ..... | 3 | ..... | 24 | 24 | 8 | 3 | ..... | 28 | 37 | 24.00 | 81.00 | 6 50- 6 99 |
| 7 00- 7 49 | ..... | 1 | 1 | ..... | 1 | ..... | ..... | 7 | 1 | 30 | 14 | 13 | 6 | ..... | 23 | 51 | 30.00 | 85.20 | 7 00- 7 49 |
| 7 50- 7 99 | 1 | 1 | ..... | ..... | 2 | ..... | ..... | 7 | 1 | 22 | 19 | 5 | 3 | ..... | 26 | 35 | 37.30 | 89.00 | 7 50- 7 99 |
| 8 00- 8 99 | ..... | 4 | 2 | ..... | 2 | ..... | ..... | 15 | 3 | 11 | 27 | 20 | 7 | ..... | 41 | 50 | 48.00 | 94.00 | 8 00- 8 99 |
| 9 00- 9 99 | ..... | 4 | ..... | ..... | 4 | ..... | ..... | 16 | 3 | 3 | 26 | 6 | 8 | ..... | 41 | 29 | 59.00 | 97.00 | 9 00- 9 99 |
| 10 00-10 99 | ..... | 2 | 5 | ..... | 1 | ..... | ..... | 3 | 2 | 5 | 14 | 3 | 9 | ..... | 31 | 13 | 67.00 | 98.30 | 10 00-10 99 |
| 11 00-11 99 | ..... | 1 | 4 | ..... | 4 | ..... | ..... | 2 | 1 | 1 | 9 | ..... | 2 | ..... | 20 | 4 | 72.20 | 99.00 | 11 00-11 99 |
| 12 00-12 99 | 2 | ..... | 5 | ..... | 1 | ..... | ..... | ..... | 4 | 1 | 11 | ..... | 3 | ..... | 26 | 1 | 80.00 | 99.10 | 12 00-12 99 |
| 13 00-13 99 | 3 | 4 | 6 | ..... | 4 | ..... | ..... | ..... | ..... | ..... | 2 | ..... | 2 | ..... | 17 | 4 | 84.00 | 99.30 | 13 00-13 99 |
| 14 00-14 99 | ..... | 2 | 2 | 1 | 2 | ..... | ..... | ..... | ..... | ..... | ..... | ..... | 1 | ..... | 5 | 3 | 85.20 | 99.50 | 14 00-14 99 |
| 15 00-15 99 | 2 | 1 | 7 | ..... | ..... | ..... | ..... | ..... | 3 | 1 | 1 | 1 | ..... | ..... | 13 | 3 | 88.30 | 99.70 | 15 00-15 99 |
| 16 00-17 99 | 3 | ..... | 7 | ..... | 3 | ..... | ..... | ..... | 1 | 1 | ..... | ..... | ..... | ..... | 14 | 1 | 93.00 | 99.80 | 16 00-17 99 |
| 18 00-19 99 | 4 | ..... | ..... | ..... | ..... | ..... | ..... | ..... | 1 | 1 | ..... | ..... | 1 | ..... | 6 | 1 | 94.00 | 99.90 | 18 00-19 99 |
| 20 00-24 99 | 7 | ..... | 3 | ..... | 1 | ..... | ..... | ..... | 1 | 1 | ..... | ..... | ..... | ..... | 12 | 1 | 97.50 | 100.00 | 20 00-24 99 |
| 25 00-29 99 | 4 | ..... | 1 | ..... | 1 | ..... | ..... | ..... | 1 | ..... | ..... | ..... | ..... | ..... | 7 | ..... | 99.00 | ..... | 25 00-29 99 |
| 30 00-34 99 | 4 | ..... | ..... | ..... | ..... | ..... | ..... | ..... | ..... | ..... | ..... | ..... | ..... | ..... | 4 | ..... | 100.00 | ..... | 30 00-34 99 |
| Total | 30 | 22 | 43 | 1 | 29 | 4 | 1 | 80 | 24 | 621 | 188 | 255 | 61 | 2 | 376 | 985 | ..... | ..... | Total |

## NEW YORK CITY

## 260. TABLE XX, D, a — THE CONFECTIONERY INDUSTRY — FACTORY EMPLOYEES

NUMBER AND PER CENT. OF EMPLOYEES, WORKING FORTY-THREE WEEKS OR MORE, CLASSIFIED ACCORDING TO ACTUAL ANNUAL EARNINGS, BY OCCUPATION AND SEX

| ACTUAL ANNUAL EARNINGS IN DOLLARS | OCCUPATION | | | | | | | | | | | | | | | | ACTUAL ANNUAL EARNINGS IN DOLLARS |
|---|---|---|---|---|---|---|---|---|---|---|---|---|---|---|---|---|---|
| | FOREMEN AND FOREWOMEN | | CANDY MAKERS | | MACHINE OPERATORS | DIPPERS | PACKERS AND WRAPPERS | | HELPERS | | LABORERS | | TOTAL | | CUMULATIVE PER CENT OF TOTAL | | |
| | Male | Female | Male | Female | Male | Female | Male | Female | Male | Female | Male | Female | Male | Female | Male | Female | |
| Under $200 | .... | .... | .... | .... | .... | .... | .... | 6 | .... | 6 | .... | .... | .... | 12 | .... | 3.10 | Under $200 |
| $200– $249 | .... | .... | .... | .... | .... | 5 | .... | 49 | .... | 17 | .... | .... | .... | 71 | .... | 21.50 | $200– 249 |
| 250– 299 | .... | .... | .... | .... | .... | 10 | .... | 65 | .... | 22 | 1 | 1 | 1 | 98 | .50 | 47.00 | 250– 299 |
| 300– 349 | .... | 2 | .... | .... | .... | 10 | .... | 34 | 9 | 13 | .... | .... | 9 | 59 | 5.00 | 62.50 | 300– 349 |
| 350– 399 | 1 | 1 | .... | .... | .... | 8 | .... | 36 | 13 | 11 | 2 | 1 | 16 | 57 | 13.00 | 77.50 | 350– 399 |
| 400– 449 | .... | 4 | 1 | .... | 1 | 15 | .... | 10 | 15 | 12 | 4 | .... | 21 | 41 | 23.50 | 98.00 | 400– 449 |
| 450– 499 | .... | 4 | 2 | .... | 1 | 13 | 2 | 1 | 14 | 4 | 2 | .... | 21 | 22 | 34.00 | 93.50 | 450– 499 |
| 500– 549 | .... | 3 | .... | .... | 2 | 4 | 1 | 4 | 10 | 3 | 7 | .... | 20 | 14 | 44.00 | 97.00 | 500– 549 |
| 550– 599 | .... | 1 | 5 | .... | 1 | 1 | 1 | .... | 11 | .... | .... | .... | 18 | 2 | 53.00 | 97.50 | 550– 599 |
| 600– 649 | 1 | .... | 2 | .... | 3 | .... | 2 | .... | 8 | .... | 2 | .... | 18 | .... | 62.00 | .... | 600– 649 |
| 650– 699 | 1 | 2 | 4 | .... | 3 | .... | 1 | .... | 3 | .... | 2 | .... | 14 | 2 | 69.00 | 98.00 | 650– 699 |
| 700– 749 | 1 | 2 | 5 | 1 | 3 | .... | .... | .... | .... | .... | .... | .... | 9 | 3 | 73.50 | 99.00 | 700– 749 |
| 750– 799 | 2 | .... | 5 | .... | .... | .... | 3 | .... | .... | .... | .... | .... | 10 | .... | 78.50 | .... | 750– 799 |
| 800– 899 | 1 | 1 | 7 | .... | 1 | .... | 1 | 2 | .... | .... | .... | .... | 10 | 3 | 83.50 | 99.80 | 800– 899 |
| 900– 999 | 4 | .... | 2 | .... | 1 | .... | 1 | 1 | .... | .... | 1 | .... | 9 | 1 | 88.00 | 99.90 | 900– 999 |
| 1,000–1,099 | 5 | .... | .... | .... | .... | .... | 1 | .... | .... | .... | .... | .... | 6 | .... | 91.00 | .... | 1,000–1,099 |
| 1,100–1,199 | 1 | .... | 2 | .... | 1 | .... | .... | 1 | .... | .... | .... | .... | 4 | 1 | 93.00 | 100.00 | 1,100–1,199 |
| 1,200–1,299 | 1 | .... | 1 | .... | .... | .... | .... | .... | .... | .... | .... | .... | 2 | .... | 94.00 | .... | 1,200–1,299 |
| 1,300–1,399 | 4 | .... | .... | .... | .... | .... | 1 | .... | .... | .... | .... | .... | 5 | .... | 96.50 | .... | 1,300–1,399 |
| 1,400–1,499 | .... | .... | 1 | .... | 1 | .... | .... | .... | .... | .... | .... | .... | 2 | .... | 97.50 | .... | 1,400–1,499 |
| 1,500–1,599 | 2 | .... | .... | .... | .... | .... | .... | .... | .... | .... | .... | .... | 2 | .... | 98.50 | .... | 1,500–1,599 |
| 1,600–1,799 | 3 | .... | .... | .... | .... | .... | .... | .... | .... | .... | .... | .... | 3 | .... | 100.00 | .... | 1,600–1,799 |
| Total | 27 | 20 | 37 | 1 | 18 | 66 | 14 | 209 | 83 | 88 | 21 | 2 | 200 | 386 | .... | .... | Total |

261. TABLE VIII, D, 1, a

NEW YORK CITY

THE CONFECTIONERY INDUSTRY — WHOLESALE CANDY FACTORIES — FACTORY WORKERS

NUMBER AND PER CENT. OF EMPLOYEES EARNING SPECIFIED WEEKLY RATES, BY OCCUPATION AND SEX

| WEEKLY RATES IN DOLLARS | OCCUPATION | | | | | | | | | | | | | | | | | | | | WEEKLY RATES IN DOLLARS |
|---|---|---|---|---|---|---|---|---|---|---|---|---|---|---|---|---|---|---|---|---|---|
| | FOREMEN AND FOREWOMEN | | CANDY MAKERS | | MACHINE OPERATORS | | DIPPERS | | PACKERS AND WRAPPERS | | HELPERS | | LABORERS | | NOT REPORTED | | TOTAL | | CUMULATIVE PER CENT. OF TOTAL | | |
| | Male | Female | Male | Female | Male | Female | Male | Female | Male | Female | Male | Female | Male | Female | Male | Female | Male | Female | Male | Female | |
| Less than $3 00 | .... | .... | .... | .... | .... | .... | .... | .... | .... | 4 | .... | 1 | .... | .... | .... | .... | .... | 5 | ..... | .20 | Less than $3 00 |
| $3 00–$3 49 | .... | .... | .... | .... | .... | .... | .... | .... | .... | 26 | 1 | 1 | .... | .... | .... | .... | 1 | 27 | .05 | 1.20 | $3 00– 3 49 |
| 3 50– 3 99 | .... | .... | .... | .... | .... | .... | .... | 16 | .... | 46 | 1 | 31 | 1 | .... | .... | .... | 2 | 93 | .15 | 4.70 | 3 50– 3 99 |
| 4 00– 4 49 | .... | .... | .... | .... | .... | .... | .... | 16 | .... | 120 | 6 | 59 | .... | 5 | .... | .... | 6 | 200 | .44 | 12.30 | 4 00– 4 49 |
| 4 50– 4 99 | .... | .... | .... | .... | .... | .... | .... | 39 | .... | 187 | 7 | 172 | 2 | 21 | .... | 1 | 9 | 420 | .88 | 28.20 | 4 50– 4 99 |
| 5 00– 5 49 | .... | 2 | .... | .... | .... | .... | .... | 34 | 2 | 272 | 20 | 209 | 8 | 8 | .... | 2 | 30 | 527 | 2.35 | 48.00 | 5 00– 5 49 |
| 5 50– 5 99 | .... | 1 | .... | .... | .... | .... | .... | 25 | 1 | 138 | 34 | 105 | .... | 5 | .... | .... | 35 | 274 | 4.05 | 58.20 | 5 50– 5 99 |
| 6 00– 6 49 | .... | 4 | .... | .... | .... | .... | .... | 17 | 3 | 177 | 90 | 103 | 23 | 5 | .... | 2 | 116 | 308 | 9.72 | 70.00 | 6 00– 6 49 |
| 6 50– 6 99 | .... | 1 | .... | 1 | .... | .... | .... | 21 | .... | 80 | 19 | 26 | 4 | 1 | .... | 1 | 23 | 131 | 10.80 | 74.90 | 6 50– 6 99 |
| 7 00– 7 49 | .... | 4 | 1 | 1 | .... | .... | .... | 23 | 12 | 109 | 173 | 57 | 27 | 1 | 1 | .... | 214 | 195 | 21.30 | 82.00 | 7 00– 7 49 |
| 7 50– 7 99 | .... | 2 | 2 | .... | .... | .... | 1 | 23 | 4 | 65 | 82 | 17 | 10 | .... | .... | .... | 99 | 107 | 26.20 | 86.00 | 7 50– 7 99 |
| 8 00– 8 99 | .... | 17 | 3 | .... | 2 | .... | 1 | 70 | 8 | 61 | 223 | 29 | 36 | .... | .... | .... | 273 | 177 | 39.50 | 93.00 | 8 00– 8 99 |
| 9 00– 9 99 | 2 | 16 | 8 | .... | 4 | 1 | .... | 27 | 1 | 15 | 204 | 18 | 30 | .... | .... | .... | 249 | 77 | 51.80 | 96.00 | 9 00– 9 99 |
| 10 00–10 99 | .... | 21 | 17 | .... | 8 | .... | .... | 18 | 4 | 5 | 150 | 4 | 19 | .... | .... | .... | 198 | 48 | 61.40 | 97.80 | 10 00–10 99 |
| 11 00–11 99 | 1 | 13 | 12 | .... | 16 | .... | .... | 8 | .... | 4 | 77 | .... | 11 | .... | .... | .... | 117 | 25 | 67.00 | 98.70 | 11 00–11 99 |
| 12 00–12 99 | 5 | 16 | 31 | .... | 21 | 1 | .... | 1 | .... | .... | 116 | 2 | 18 | .... | .... | .... | 191 | 20 | 76.20 | 99.40 | 12 00–12 99 |
| 13 00–13 99 | 3 | 3 | 16 | .... | 17 | .... | .... | .... | 1 | .... | 53 | .... | 5 | .... | .... | .... | 95 | 3 | 81.00 | 99.50 | 13 00–13 99 |
| 14 00–14 99 | 8 | 1 | 22 | .... | 17 | .... | .... | 1 | 1 | .... | 62 | .... | 1 | .... | .... | .... | 111 | 2 | 86.50 | 99.60 | 14 00–14 99 |
| 15 00–15 99 | 11 | 4 | 25 | .... | 12 | .... | .... | .... | .... | .... | 21 | .... | 3 | .... | .... | .... | 72 | 4 | 90.00 | 99.70 | 15 00–15 99 |
| 16 00–17 99 | 19 | 4 | 24 | .... | 6 | .... | .... | .... | .... | .... | 18 | .... | 2 | .... | .... | .... | 69 | 4 | 93.40 | 99.80 | 16 00–17 99 |
| 18 00–19 99 | 23 | 2 | 23 | .... | 7 | .... | .... | .... | .... | .... | 4 | .... | .... | .... | .... | .... | 57 | 2 | 97.00 | 99.90 | 18 00–19 99 |
| 20 00–24 99 | 36 | 2 | 8 | .... | 4 | .... | .... | .... | .... | .... | 1 | .... | .... | .... | .... | .... | 49 | 2 | 98.70 | 99.90 | 20 00–24 99 |
| 25 00–29 99 | 9 | .... | 5 | .... | 1 | .... | .... | .... | .... | .... | .... | .... | .... | .... | .... | .... | 15 | .... | 99.40 | ..... | 25 00–29 99 |
| 30 00–34 99 | 5 | 1 | .... | .... | .... | .... | .... | .... | .... | .... | .... | .... | .... | .... | .... | .... | 5 | 1 | 99.60 | 100.00 | 30 00–34 99 |
| 35 00–39 99 | 9 | .... | .... | .... | .... | .... | .... | .... | .... | .... | .... | .... | .... | .... | .... | .... | 9 | .... | 100.00 | ..... | 35 00–39 99 |
| Not reported | .... | 1 | 1 | .... | 1 | .... | .... | .... | .... | 8 | 4 | 3 | 2 | .... | .... | .... | 8 | 12 | ..... | ..... | Not reported |
| Total | 131 | 115 | 198 | 2 | 116 | 2 | 2 | 339 | 37 | 1,317 | 1,366 | 837 | 202 | 46 | 1 | 6 | 2,053 | 2,664 | ..... | ..... | Total |

NEW YORK CITY

262. TABLE IX, D, 1, a THE CONFECTIONERY INDUSTRY — WHOLESALE FACTORIES — FACTORY WORKERS

NUMBER AND PER CENT. OF EMPLOYEES CLASSIFIED ACCORDING TO ACTUAL WEEKLY EARNINGS, BY OCCUPATION AND SEX

| Actual Weekly Earnings in Dollars | Occupation: Foremen and Forewomen | | Candy Makers | | Machine Operators | | Dippers | | Packers and Wrappers | | Helpers | | Laborers | | Not Reported | | Total | | Cumulative Per Cent. of Total | | Actual Weekly Earnings in Dollars |
|---|---|---|---|---|---|---|---|---|---|---|---|---|---|---|---|---|---|---|---|---|---|
| | Male | Female | Male | Female | Male | Female | Male | Female | Male | Female | Male | Female | Male | Female | Male | Female | Male | Female | Male | Female | |
| Less than $3 00.. | 1 | .... | .... | .... | 1 | .... | .... | 18 | 2 | 114 | 37 | 60 | 4 | .... | .... | 2 | 45 | 194 | 2.10 | 5.90 | ...Less than $3 00 |
| $3 00-$3 49..... | 1 | .... | 1 | .... | .... | .... | 1 | 6 | .... | 72 | 13 | 32 | 1 | 1 | .... | .... | 17 | 111 | 3.00 | 9.30 | ......$3 00- 3 49 |
| 3 50- 3 99..... | .... | 1 | .... | .... | .... | .... | .... | 26 | 1 | 98 | 12 | 41 | .... | 2 | .... | .... | 13 | 168 | 3.60 | 14.30 | ...... 3 50- 3 99 |
| 4 00- 4 49..... | .... | .... | .... | .... | .... | .... | .... | 28 | 1 | 188 | 19 | 81 | 2 | 11 | .... | .... | 22 | 308 | 4.60 | 23.70 | ...... 4 00- 4 49 |
| 4 50- 4 99..... | .... | 1 | .... | .... | 1 | .... | .... | 31 | 1 | 176 | 32 | 133 | 2 | 12 | .... | 1 | 36 | 354 | 6.40 | 34.50 | ...... 4 50- 4 99 |
| 5 00- 5 49..... | .... | 5 | .... | .... | 1 | .... | .... | 31 | 4 | 224 | 45 | 163 | 9 | 12 | .... | 1 | 59 | 436 | 9.20 | 47.70 | ...... 5 00- 5 49 |
| 5 50- 5 99..... | .... | 3 | 1 | .... | .... | .... | .... | 20 | 1 | 152 | 43 | 92 | 1 | 4 | .... | 2 | 46 | 273 | 11.40 | 56.00 | ...... 5 50- 5 99 |
| 6 00- 6 49..... | .... | 4 | 1 | .... | .... | .... | 1 | 33 | 1 | 150 | 58 | 87 | 18 | 7 | .... | .... | 79 | 281 | 15.20 | 64.50 | ...... 6 00- 6 49 |
| 6 50- 6 99..... | 1 | 3 | .... | 1 | .... | .... | .... | 33 | .... | 108 | 74 | 36 | 11 | 1 | .... | 1 | 86 | 183 | 19.30 | 70.10 | ...... 6 50- 6 99 |
| 7 00- 7 49..... | .... | 2 | .... | 1 | .... | .... | .... | 42 | 9 | 116 | 98 | 32 | 24 | 1 | 1 | .... | 132 | 194 | 25.70 | 76.00 | ...... 7 00- 7 49 |
| 7 50- 7 99..... | 1 | 2 | 2 | .... | .... | .... | 2 | 41 | 2 | 83 | 96 | 28 | 14 | .... | .... | .... | 117 | 154 | 31.30 | 80.70 | ...... 7 50- 7 99 |
| 8 00- 8 99..... | .... | 17 | 7 | .... | 4 | .... | 4 | 65 | 8 | 107 | 196 | 50 | 29 | 1 | .... | .... | 248 | 240 | 43.00 | 88.00 | ...... 8 00- 8 99 |
| 9 00- 9 99..... | 1 | 14 | 7 | .... | 4 | 1 | 2 | 60 | 1 | 49 | 153 | 32 | 27 | .... | .... | .... | 195 | 156 | 52.40 | 92.80 | ...... 9 00- 9 99 |
| 10 00-10 99..... | .... | 20 | 16 | .... | 8 | .... | 1 | 57 | 3 | 23 | 134 | 12 | 17 | 1 | .... | .... | 179 | 113 | 60.80 | 96.20 | ......10 00-10 99 |
| 11 00-11 99..... | 1 | 11 | 12 | .... | 17 | .... | 4 | 30 | .... | 6 | 75 | 6 | 11 | .... | .... | .... | 120 | 53 | 66.50 | 97.80 | ......11 00-11 99 |
| 12 00-12 99..... | 2 | 14 | 27 | .... | 17 | 1 | 4 | 9 | 1 | 2 | 110 | 5 | 20 | .... | .... | .... | 181 | 31 | 75.20 | 98.80 | ......12 00-12 99 |
| 13 00-13 99..... | 6 | 3 | 12 | .... | 18 | .... | .... | 7 | 2 | 2 | 61 | .... | 4 | .... | .... | .... | 103 | 12 | 80.20 | 99.10 | ......13 00-13 99 |
| 14 00-14 99..... | 9 | 2 | 19 | .... | 12 | .... | 1 | 5 | .... | .... | 61 | 1 | .... | .... | .... | .... | 102 | 8 | 85.10 | 99.40 | ......14 00-14 99 |
| 15 00-15 99..... | 8 | 4 | 25 | .... | 10 | .... | .... | 3 | .... | .... | 17 | .... | 2 | .... | .... | .... | 62 | 7 | 88.20 | 99.70 | ......15 00-15 99 |
| 16 00-17 99..... | 15 | 4 | 24 | .... | 11 | .... | .... | 1 | .... | .... | 32 | .... | 4 | .... | .... | .... | 86 | 5 | 92.50 | 99.80 | ......16 00-17 99 |
| 18 00-19 99..... | 25 | 2 | 19 | .... | 5 | .... | .... | 1 | .... | .... | 5 | .... | 2 | .... | .... | .... | 56 | 3 | 95.10 | 99.90 | ......18 00-19 99 |
| 20 00-24 99..... | 33 | 2 | 18 | .... | 7 | .... | .... | .... | .... | .... | 3 | .... | .... | .... | .... | .... | 61 | 2 | 98.00 | 100.00 | ......20 00-24 99 |
| 25 00-29 99..... | 13 | .... | 7 | .... | 1 | .... | .... | .... | .... | .... | .... | .... | .... | .... | .... | .... | 21 | .... | 99.10 | ..... | ......25 00-29 99 |
| 30 00-34 99..... | 5 | .... | 1 | .... | .... | .... | .... | .... | .... | .... | .... | .... | .... | .... | .... | .... | 6 | .... | 99.40 | ..... | ......30 00-34 99 |
| 35 00-39 99..... | 8 | .... | .... | .... | .... | .... | .... | .... | .... | .... | .... | .... | .... | .... | .... | .... | 8 | .... | 99.90 | ..... | ......35 00-39 99 |
| 40 00 and over... | 2 | .... | .... | .... | .... | .... | .... | .... | .... | .... | .... | .... | .... | .... | .... | .... | 2 | .... | 100.00 | ..... | ....40 00 and over |
| Not reported.... | .... | 2 | 5 | .... | 2 | .... | .... | 2 | .... | 16 | 7 | 4 | 1 | .... | .... | .... | 15 | 24 | ..... | ..... | .....Not reported |
| Total....... | 132 | 116 | 204 | 2 | 119 | 2 | 20 | 549 | 37 | 1,686 | 1,381 | 895 | 203 | 53 | 1 | 7 | 2,097 | 3,310 | ..... | ..... | ........Total |

NEW YORK CITY

THE CONFECTIONERY INDUSTRY — FACTORIES WITH A RETAIL OUTLET — FACTORY WORKERS

263. TABLE VIII, D, 2, a NUMBER AND PER CENT. OF EMPLOYEES EARNING SPECIFIED WEEKLY RATES, BY OCCUPATION AND SEX

| WEEKLY RATES IN DOLLARS | OCCUPATION: FOREMEN AND FOREWOMEN | | CANDY MAKERS | MACHINE OPERATORS | | DIPPERS | PACKERS AND WRAPPERS | | HELPERS | | LABORERS | | NOT REPORTED | TOTAL | | CUMULATIVE PER CENT. OF TOTAL | | WEEKLY RATES IN DOLLARS |
|---|---|---|---|---|---|---|---|---|---|---|---|---|---|---|---|---|---|---|
| | Male | Female | Male | Male | Female | Female | Male | Female | Male | Female | Male | Female | Female | Male | Female | Male | Female | |
| $3 50-$3 99 | .... | .... | .... | .... | .... | .... | .... | 1 | .... | 2 | .... | .... | .... | .... | 3 | .... | .21 | $3 50-$3 99 |
| 4 00- 4 49 | .... | .... | .... | .... | .... | 6 | .... | 6 | .... | 1 | .... | .... | .... | .... | 13 | .... | 1.10 | 4 00- 4 49 |
| 4 50- 4 99 | .... | .... | .... | .... | .... | 11 | .... | 21 | .... | 19 | 1 | .... | .... | 1 | 51 | .25 | 4.70 | 4 50- 4 99 |
| 5 00- 5 49 | .... | .... | .... | .... | .... | 22 | .... | 257 | 5 | 72 | 2 | 5 | .... | 7 | 356 | 2.00 | 29.50 | 5 00- 5 49 |
| 5 50- 5 99 | .... | .... | .... | .... | .... | 25 | .... | 133 | .... | 23 | .... | 3 | .... | .... | 184 | .... | 42.50 | 5 50- 5 99 |
| 6 00- 6 49 | .... | .... | .... | .... | .... | 46 | .... | 184 | 4 | 25 | 1 | 3 | 1 | 5 | 259 | 3.20 | 60.40 | 6 00- 6 49 |
| 6 50- 6 99 | .... | .... | .... | .... | .... | 16 | .... | 62 | 2 | 9 | .... | 1 | .... | 2 | 88 | 3.70 | 66.50 | 6 50- 6 99 |
| 7 00- 7 49 | .... | 2 | .... | .... | 1 | 22 | .... | 83 | 14 | 11 | 5 | 1 | .... | 19 | 120 | 8.40 | 75.00 | 7 00- 7 49 |
| 7 50- 7 99 | .... | 2 | .... | .... | 2 | 21 | .... | 35 | 10 | 3 | .... | .... | .... | 10 | 63 | 10.80 | 79.80 | 7 50- 7 99 |
| 8 00- 8 99 | .... | 5 | .... | .... | 2 | 48 | .... | 27 | 38 | 3 | 11 | 1 | .... | 49 | 86 | 23.00 | 85.80 | 8 00- 8 99 |
| 9 00- 9 99 | .... | 8 | 2 | .... | .... | 71 | .... | 12 | 74 | 2 | 4 | 1 | .... | 80 | 94 | 42.70 | 92.00 | 9 00- 9 99 |
| 10 00-10 99 | .... | 8 | 1 | .... | .... | 57 | .... | 1 | 24 | 1 | 4 | 1 | .... | 29 | 68 | 50.00 | 96.80 | 10 00-10 99 |
| 11 00-11 99 | .... | 4 | 1 | 1 | 1 | 15 | .... | 1 | 14 | .... | 7 | .... | .... | 23 | 21 | 55.50 | 98.30 | 11 00-11 99 |
| 12 00-12 99 | .... | 6 | 5 | .... | .... | 2 | 1 | .... | 26 | .... | 6 | .... | .... | 38 | 8 | 65.00 | 98.80 | 12 00-12 99 |
| 13 00-13 99 | .... | 1 | 5 | 3 | .... | .... | .... | .... | 5 | .... | 2 | .... | .... | 15 | 1 | 68.70 | 98.90 | 13 00-13 99 |
| 14 00-14 99 | .... | 4 | 10 | 6 | .... | .... | .... | .... | 4 | .... | 1 | .... | .... | 21 | 4 | 74.00 | 99.20 | 14 00-14 99 |
| 15 00-15 99 | 1 | 2 | 14 | 3 | .... | .... | .... | .... | 6 | .... | .... | .... | .... | 24 | 2 | 79.80 | 99.30 | 15 00-15 99 |
| 16 00-17 99 | 3 | 3 | 18 | 4 | .... | .... | 1 | 1 | 4 | .... | 1 | .... | .... | 31 | 4 | 87.40 | 99.50 | 16 00-17 99 |
| 18 00-19 99 | 1 | 5 | 11 | 3 | .... | .... | .... | 1 | .... | .... | 1 | .... | .... | 16 | 6 | 91.40 | 99.90 | 18 00-19 99 |
| 20 00-24 99 | 8 | 3 | 5 | 1 | .... | .... | .... | .... | .... | .... | .... | .... | .... | 14 | 3 | 94.80 | 100.00 | 20 00-24 99 |
| 25 00-29 99 | 6 | .... | 1 | .... | .... | .... | .... | .... | .... | .... | .... | .... | .... | 7 | .... | 96.50 | .... | 25 00-29 99 |
| 30 00-34 99 | 6 | .... | 1 | .... | .... | .... | .... | .... | .... | .... | .... | .... | .... | 7 | .... | 98.20 | .... | 30 00-34 99 |
| 35 00-39 99 | 2 | .... | 1 | .... | .... | .... | .... | .... | .... | .... | .... | .... | .... | 3 | .... | 99.00 | .... | 35 00-39 99 |
| 40 00 and over | 3 | .... | 1 | .... | .... | .... | .... | .... | .... | .... | .... | .... | .... | 4 | .... | 100.00 | .... | 40 00 and over |
| Not reported | .... | .... | .... | .... | .... | 3 | 1 | 1 | .... | 3 | .... | .... | .... | 1 | 7 | .... | .... | Not reported |
| Total | 30 | 53 | 76 | 21 | 6 | 365 | 3 | 826 | 230 | 174 | 46 | 16 | 1 | 406 | 1,441 | .... | .... | Total |

264. TABLE IX, D, 2, a

NEW YORK CITY

THE CONFECTIONERY INDUSTRY — FACTORIES WITH A RETAIL OUTLET — FACTORY WORKERS

NUMBER AND PER CENT. OF EMPLOYEES CLASSIFIED ACCORDING TO ACTUAL WEEKLY EARNINGS, BY OCCUPATION AND SEX

| ACTUAL WEEKLY EARNINGS IN DOLLARS | OCCUPATION | | | | | | | | | | | | | | | | | ACTUAL WEEKLY EARNINGS IN DOLLARS |
|---|---|---|---|---|---|---|---|---|---|---|---|---|---|---|---|---|---|---|
| | FOREMEN AND FOREWOMEN | | CANDY MAKERS | MACHINE OPERATORS | | DIPPERS | PACKERS AND WRAPPERS | | HELPERS | | LABORERS | | NOT REPORTED | TOTAL | | CUMULATIVE PER CENT. OF TOTAL | | |
| | Male | Female | Male | Male | Female | Female | Male | Female | Male | Female | Male | Female | Female | Male | Female | Male | Female | |
| Less than $3 00 | .... | .... | .... | .... | .... | 5 | .... | 48 | 4 | 5 | .... | 1 | .... | 4 | 59 | 1.00 | 4.05 | Less than $3 00 |
| $3 00–$3 49 | .... | .... | .... | .... | .... | .... | .... | 18 | .... | 5 | .... | .... | .... | .... | 23 | .... | 5.60 | $3 00– 3 49 |
| 3 50– 3 99 | .... | .... | .... | .... | .... | 2 | .... | 27 | 1 | 2 | .... | .... | .... | 1 | 31 | 1.24 | 7.80 | 3 50– 3 99 |
| 4 00– 4 49 | .... | .... | .... | .... | .... | 14 | .... | 40 | .... | 5 | 1 | 1 | .... | 1 | 60 | 1.48 | 11.90 | 4 00– 4 49 |
| 4 50– 4 99 | .... | .... | .... | .... | .... | 21 | .... | 72 | 4 | 28 | 1 | .... | .... | 5 | 121 | 2.70 | 20.20 | 4 50– 4 99 |
| 5 00– 5 49 | .... | .... | .... | .... | .... | 19 | .... | 178 | 4 | 55 | 2 | 5 | .... | 6 | 257 | 4.20 | 38.00 | 5 00– 5 49 |
| 5 50– 5 99 | .... | .... | .... | .... | .... | 30 | .... | 144 | 3 | 19 | .... | 2 | .... | 3 | 195 | 4.95 | 51.30 | 5 50– 5 99 |
| 6 00– 6 49 | .... | .... | .... | .... | .... | 42 | .... | 112 | 7 | 23 | .... | 2 | 1 | 7 | 180 | 6.70 | 63.80 | 6 00– 6 49 |
| 6 50– 6 99 | .... | 1 | .... | .... | .... | 19 | .... | 67 | 9 | 10 | .... | 1 | .... | 9 | 98 | 8.90 | 70.50 | 6 50– 6 99 |
| 7 00– 7 49 | .... | 1 | .... | .... | 1 | 23 | .... | 45 | 15 | 8 | 6 | 1 | .... | 21 | 79 | 14.10 | 76.00 | 7 00– 7 49 |
| 7 50– 7 99 | .... | 4 | 1 | .... | .... | 22 | .... | 37 | 15 | 3 | 4 | .... | .... | 20 | 66 | 19.00 | 80.50 | 7 50– 7 99 |
| 8 00– 8 99 | .... | 6 | 1 | .... | 3 | 56 | .... | 31 | 32 | 4 | 6 | 1 | .... | 39 | 101 | 28.70 | 87.00 | 8 00– 8 99 |
| 9 00– 9 99 | .... | 7 | 2 | .... | 1 | 50 | .... | 15 | 55 | 2 | 8 | 1 | .... | 65 | 76 | 44.80 | 92.20 | 9 00– 9 99 |
| 10 00–10 99 | .... | 7 | 1 | .... | .... | 41 | .... | 3 | 16 | 1 | 2 | 1 | .... | 19 | 53 | 49.50 | 96.00 | 10 00–10 99 |
| 11 00–11 99 | .... | 4 | 3 | 1 | .... | 18 | .... | 2 | 15 | .... | 5 | .... | .... | 24 | 24 | 55.50 | 98.30 | 11 00–11 99 |
| 12 00–12 99 | .... | 5 | 4 | .... | 1 | 4 | 1 | .... | 20 | .... | 3 | .... | .... | 28 | 10 | 62.40 | 99.00 | 12 00–12 99 |
| 13 00–13 99 | .... | 1 | 8 | 2 | .... | 1 | .... | .... | 6 | .... | 3 | .... | .... | 19 | 2 | 67.10 | 99.10 | 13 00–13 99 |
| 14 00–14 99 | .... | 4 | 7 | 5 | .... | .... | .... | .... | 12 | .... | 1 | .... | .... | 25 | 4 | 73.20 | 99.30 | 14 00–14 99 |
| 15 00–15 99 | 1 | 1 | 8 | 5 | .... | .... | .... | .... | 8 | .... | 1 | .... | .... | 23 | 1 | 78.90 | 99.40 | 15 00–15 99 |
| 16 00–17 99 | 2 | 4 | 19 | 3 | .... | 1 | 1 | 1 | 2 | .... | 2 | .... | .... | 29 | 6 | 86.00 | 99.60 | 16 00–17 99 |
| 18 00–19 99 | 2 | 5 | 10 | 4 | .... | .... | .... | 1 | .... | .... | 1 | .... | .... | 17 | 6 | 90.00 | 99.80 | 18 00–19 99 |
| 20 00–24 99 | 9 | 2 | 7 | 1 | .... | .... | .... | .... | 1 | .... | .... | .... | .... | 18 | 2 | 94.50 | 99.90 | 20 00–24 99 |
| 25 00–29 99 | 5 | 1 | 3 | .... | .... | .... | .... | .... | .... | .... | .... | .... | .... | 8 | 1 | 96.50 | 100.00 | 25 00–29 99 |
| 30 00–34 99 | 6 | .... | .... | .... | .... | .... | .... | .... | .... | .... | .... | .... | .... | 6 | .... | 98.20 | .... | 30 00–34 99 |
| 35 00–39 99 | 2 | .... | 1 | .... | .... | .... | .... | .... | .... | .... | .... | .... | .... | 3 | .... | 99.00 | .... | 35 00–39 99 |
| 40 00 and over | 3 | .... | 1 | .... | .... | .... | .... | .... | .... | .... | .... | .... | .... | 4 | .... | 100.00 | .... | 40 00 and over |
| Not reported | .... | .... | .... | .... | .... | 4 | 1 | 9 | 1 | 4 | .... | .... | .... | 2 | 17 | .... | .... | Not reported |
| Total | 30 | 53 | 76 | 21 | 6 | 372 | 3 | 850 | 230 | 174 | 46 | 16 | 1 | 406 | 1,472 | .... | .... | Total |

BUFFALO

DEPARTMENT STORES — STOCK AND SALES

265. TABLE V, A,1, a NUMBER AND PER CENT. OF EMPLOYEES EARNING SPECIFIED WEEKLY RATES, BY AGE GROUPS AND SEX

| WEEKLY RATES IN DOLLARS | AGE GROUPS IN YEARS 14–15 | | 16–17 | | 18–20 | | 21–24 | | 25–29 | | 30–34 | | 35–39 | | WEEKLY RATES IN DOLLARS |
|---|---|---|---|---|---|---|---|---|---|---|---|---|---|---|---|
| | Male | Female | Male | Female | Male | Female | Male | Female | Male | Female | Male | Female | Male | Female | |
| $3 00–$3 49 | 15 | 17 | .... | 7 | ...... | ...... | ...... | 1 | ...... | 1 | ...... | ...... | ...... | ...... | $3 00–$3 49 |
| 3 50– 3 99 | 11 | 36 | 2 | 34 | ...... | 5 | ...... | ...... | ...... | ...... | ...... | ...... | ...... | ...... | 3 50– 3 99 |
| 4 00– 4 49 | 28 | 15 | 12 | 47 | ...... | 11 | 1 | 2 | ...... | ...... | ...... | 1 | ...... | ...... | 4 00– 4 49 |
| 4 50– 4 99 | 6 | 8 | 1 | 14 | ...... | 8 | 1 | ...... | ...... | ...... | ...... | 1 | ...... | ...... | 4 50– 4 99 |
| 5 00– 5 49 | 9 | 4 | 14 | 39 | 2 | 49 | ...... | 13 | ...... | 2 | ...... | 1 | ...... | 2 | 5 00– 5 49 |
| 5 50– 5 99 | 1 | ...... | 3 | ...... | ...... | 5 | ...... | ...... | ...... | 1 | ...... | 1 | ...... | ...... | 5 50– 5 99 |
| 6 00– 6 49 | 1 | ...... | 12 | 22 | 6 | 183 | 1 | 146 | ...... | 56 | ...... | 20 | ...... | 6 | 6 00– 6 49 |
| 6 50– 6 99 | .... | ...... | 1 | ...... | ...... | 4 | ...... | 4 | ...... | 2 | ...... | 2 | ...... | ...... | 6 50– 6 99 |
| 7 00– 7 49 | .... | ...... | 2 | 1 | 12 | 29 | 1 | 121 | 1 | 88 | 1 | 24 | ...... | 9 | 7 00– 7 49 |
| 7 50– 7 99 | .... | 1 | 1 | ...... | 1 | 3 | ...... | 9 | ...... | 8 | ...... | 2 | ...... | 1 | 7 50– 7 99 |
| 8 00– 8 99 | .... | ...... | 2 | ...... | 12 | 9 | 3 | 47 | 1 | 68 | ...... | 27 | ...... | 19 | 8 00– 8 99 |
| 9 00– 9 99 | .... | ...... | 1 | ...... | 17 | ...... | 1 | 12 | 2 | 25 | 2 | 18 | ...... | 12 | 9 00– 9 99 |
| 10 00–10 99 | .... | ...... | .... | ...... | 8 | 2 | 20 | 12 | 5 | 32 | 4 | 25 | 2 | 19 | 10 00–10 99 |
| 11 00–11 99 | .... | ...... | .... | ...... | 1 | ...... | 8 | 1 | 1 | 6 | 1 | 6 | ...... | 1 | 11 00–11 99 |
| 12 00–12 99 | .... | ...... | 1 | ...... | 5 | 1 | 33 | 3 | 26 | 13 | 12 | 25 | 6 | 16 | 12 00–12 99 |
| 13 00–13 99 | .... | ...... | .... | ...... | ...... | ...... | 4 | ...... | 5 | 1 | 3 | 2 | ...... | 5 | 13 00–13 99 |
| 14 00–14 99 | .... | ...... | .... | ...... | ...... | ...... | 13 | ...... | 18 | 1 | 11 | 9 | 11 | 1 | 14 00–14 99 |
| 15 00–15 99 | .... | ...... | .... | ...... | 1 | ...... | 10 | 1 | 18 | 7 | 11 | 3 | 12 | 6 | 15 00–15 99 |
| 16 00–17 99 | .... | ...... | .... | ...... | ...... | ...... | 3 | ...... | 14 | 1 | 17 | ...... | 10 | ...... | 16 00–17 99 |
| 18 00–19 99 | .... | ...... | .... | ...... | ...... | ...... | 1 | ...... | 7 | 3 | 16 | 3 | 9 | 3 | 18 00–19 99 |
| 20 00–24 99 | .... | ...... | .... | ...... | ...... | ...... | ...... | ...... | 5 | ...... | 12 | 1 | 7 | ...... | 20 00–24 99 |
| 25 00–29 99 | .... | ...... | .... | ...... | ...... | ...... | ...... | ...... | 1 | ...... | 6 | ...... | 3 | ...... | 25 00–29 99 |
| 30 00–34 99 | .... | ...... | .... | ...... | ...... | ...... | ...... | ...... | ...... | ...... | 1 | ...... | 2 | ...... | 30 00–34 99 |
| 40 00 and over | .... | ...... | .... | ...... | ...... | ...... | ...... | ...... | 1 | ...... | 1 | ...... | 3 | ...... | 40 00 and over |
| Not reported | .... | ...... | .... | ...... | 1 | ...... | 1 | 1 | ...... | ...... | ...... | ...... | ...... | ...... | Not reported |
| Total | 71 | 81 | 52 | 164 | 66 | 309 | 101 | 373 | 105 | 315 | 98 | 171 | 65 | 100 | Total |

265. TABLE V, A,1, a — (*concluded*)

BUFFALO

## DEPARTMENT STORES — STOCK AND SALES

NUMBER AND PER CENT. OF EMPLOYEES EARNING SPECIFIED WEEKLY RATES, BY AGE GROUPS AND SEX

| WEEKLY RATES IN DOLLARS | AGE GROUPS IN YEARS—(*concluded*) 40–44 | | 45–54 | | 55–64 | | 65 AND OVER | NOT REPORTED | | TOTAL | | CUMULATIVE PER CENT OF TOTAL | | WEEKLY RATES IN DOLLARS |
|---|---|---|---|---|---|---|---|---|---|---|---|---|---|---|
| | Male | Female | Male | Female | Male | Female | Male | Male | Female | Male | Female | Male | Female | |
| $3 00–$3 49 | ...... | ...... | ...... | ...... | ...... | ...... | ...... | ...... | ...... | 15 | 26 | 2.00 | 1.60 | $3 00–$3 49 |
| 3 50– 3 99 | 1 | ...... | ...... | ...... | ...... | ...... | ...... | ...... | 1 | 14 | 76 | 3.90 | 6.40 | 3 50– 3 99 |
| 4 00– 4 49 | ...... | ...... | ...... | ...... | ...... | ...... | ...... | ...... | ...... | 41 | 76 | 9.40 | 11.10 | 4 00– 4 49 |
| 4 50– 4 99 | ...... | ...... | ...... | ...... | ...... | ...... | ...... | ...... | ...... | 8 | 31 | 10.40 | 13 00 | 4 50– 4 99 |
| 5 00– 5 49 | ...... | ...... | ...... | ...... | ...... | ...... | ...... | 1 | ...... | 26 | 110 | 13.90 | 19.90 | 5 00– 5 49 |
| 5 50– 5 99 | ...... | ...... | ...... | ...... | ...... | ...... | ...... | ...... | 1 | 4 | 8 | 14.50 | 20.40 | 5 50– 5 99 |
| 6 00– 6 49 | ...... | 1 | ...... | 1 | ...... | ...... | ...... | ...... | 1 | 20 | 436 | 17 10 | 47.60 | 6 00– 6 49 |
| 6 50– 6 99 | ...... | ...... | ...... | ...... | ...... | ...... | ...... | ...... | ...... | 1 | 12 | 17.30 | 48.40 | 6 50– 6 99 |
| 7 00– 7 49 | ...... | 9 | ...... | 2 | ...... | ...... | ...... | 1 | 3 | 18 | 286 | 19.70 | 66.20 | 7 00– 7 49 |
| 7 50– 7 99 | ...... | ...... | ...... | ...... | ...... | ...... | ...... | ...... | ...... | 2 | 24 | 19.90 | 68.70 | 7 50– 7 99 |
| 8 00– 8 99 | ...... | 9 | ...... | 6 | ...... | ...... | ...... | 1 | 2 | 19 | 187 | 22.50 | 79.40 | 8 00– 8 99 |
| 9 00– 9 99 | ...... | 5 | ...... | 1 | ...... | ...... | ...... | ...... | 1 | 23 | 74 | 25.60 | 84.00 | 9 00– 9 99 |
| 10 00–10 99 | ...... | 11 | 2 | 6 | ...... | 1 | ...... | ...... | 4 | 41 | 112 | 31.00 | 91.00 | 10 00–10 99 |
| 11 00–11 99 | ...... | 1 | ...... | ...... | 1 | ...... | 1 | ...... | 1 | 13 | 16 | 32.80 | 92.00 | 11 00–11 99 |
| 12 00–12 99 | 3 | 6 | 4 | 3 | 5 | ...... | ...... | 1 | ...... | 96 | 67 | 45.60 | 96.10 | 12 00–12 99 |
| 13 00–13 99 | 2 | ...... | 1 | 1 | ...... | ...... | ...... | ...... | ...... | 15 | 9 | 47.70 | 96.80 | 13 00–15 99 |
| 14 00–14 99 | 6 | 2 | 10 | ...... | 4 | ...... | ...... | 1 | ...... | 74 | 13 | 57.50 | 97.50 | 14 00–14 99 |
| 15 00–15 99 | 8 | 3 | 19 | 2 | 5 | ...... | 2 | 1 | ...... | 87 | 22 | 69.20 | 98.90 | 15 00–15 99 |
| 16 00–17 99 | 10 | 2 | 6 | 4 | 4 | ...... | 2 | ...... | ...... | 66 | 7 | 78.00 | 99.40 | 16 00–17 99 |
| 18 00–19 99 | 10 | ...... | 9 | ...... | 2 | ...... | 2 | ...... | ...... | 56 | 9 | 85.50 | 99.90 | 18 00–19 99 |
| 20 00–24 99 | 17 | ...... | 19 | ...... | 3 | ...... | 1 | ...... | ...... | 64 | 1 | 94.10 | 99.90 | 20 00–24 99 |
| 25 00–29 99 | 5 | ...... | 8 | ...... | 2 | ...... | ...... | ...... | ...... | 25 | ...... | 97.50 | ...... | 25 00–29 99 |
| 30 00–34 99 | 3 | 1 | 2 | ...... | 1 | ...... | ...... | ...... | ...... | 9 | 1 | 98.60 | 100.00 | 30 00–34 99 |
| 35 00–39 99 | 1 | ...... | ...... | ...... | 1 | ...... | ...... | ...... | ...... | 2 | ...... | 98.00 | ...... | 35 00–39 99 |
| 40 00 and over | ...... | ...... | 2 | ...... | ...... | ...... | 1 | ...... | ...... | 8 | ...... | 100.00 | ...... | 40 00 and over |
| Not reported | ...... | ...... | ...... | ...... | ...... | ...... | ...... | ...... | ...... | 2 | 1 | ...... | ...... | Not reported |
| Total | 66 | 50 | 82 | 26 | 28 | 1 | 9 | 6 | 14 | 749 | 1,604 | ...... | ...... | Total |

266. TABLE VIII, A, 1, a

## BUFFALO
## DEPARTMENT STORES — STOCK AND SALES

NUMBER AND PER CENT. OF EMPLOYEES EARNING SPECIFIED WEEKLY RATES, BY OCCUPATION AND SEX

| WEEKLY RATES IN DOLLARS | OCCUPATION | | | | | | | | | | | | | | | | | | | | WEEKLY RATES IN DOLLARS |
|---|---|---|---|---|---|---|---|---|---|---|---|---|---|---|---|---|---|---|---|---|---|
| | BUYERS | | ASSISTANT BUYERS AND HEADS OF STOCK | | RECEIVING AND STOCK CLERKS | | STOCK PEOPLE | | FLOOR MANAGERS | | SALES PEOPLE | | MESSENGERS, WRAPPERS, ERRAND BOYS | | TOTAL | | CUMULATIVE PER CENT. OF TOTAL | | | | |
| | Male | Female | Male | Female | Male | Female | Male | Female | Male | Female | Male | Female | Male | Female | Male | Female | Male | Female | | | |
| $3 00-$3 49 | ..... | ..... | ..... | ..... | ..... | ..... | 1 | 3 | ..... | ..... | ..... | 3 | 14 | 20 | 15 | 26 | 2.00 | 1.60 | | | $3 00-$3 49 |
| 3 50- 3 99 | ..... | ..... | ..... | ..... | 1 | ..... | 4 | 26 | ..... | ..... | 1 | 4 | 8 | 46 | 14 | 76 | 3.90 | 6.40 | | | 3 50- 3 99 |
| 4 00- 4 49 | ..... | ..... | ..... | ..... | 1 | 1 | 21 | 14 | ..... | ..... | ..... | 18 | 19 | 43 | 41 | 76 | 9.40 | 11.10 | | | 4 00- 4 49 |
| 4 50- 4 99 | ..... | ..... | ..... | ..... | ..... | 1 | 6 | 2 | ..... | ..... | ..... | 8 | 2 | 20 | 8 | 31 | 10.40 | 13.00 | | | 4 50- 4 99 |
| 5 00- 5 49 | ..... | ..... | ..... | ..... | ..... | 1 | 15 | 4 | ..... | ..... | ..... | 70 | 11 | 35 | 26 | 110 | 13.90 | 19.90 | | | 5 00- 5 49 |
| 5 50- 5 99 | ..... | ..... | ..... | ..... | ..... | ..... | ..... | ..... | ..... | ..... | ..... | 7 | 4 | 1 | 4 | 8 | 14.50 | 20.40 | | | 5 50- 5 99 |
| 6 00- 6 49 | ..... | ..... | ..... | ..... | ..... | 3 | 7 | 10 | ..... | ..... | 7 | 418 | 6 | 5 | 20 | 436 | 17.10 | 47.60 | | | 6 00- 6 49 |
| 6 50- 6 99 | ..... | ..... | ..... | ..... | ..... | ..... | ..... | ..... | ..... | ..... | ..... | 12 | 1 | ..... | 1 | 12 | 17.30 | 48.40 | | | 6 50- 6 99 |
| 7 00- 7 49 | ..... | ..... | ..... | ..... | ..... | 1 | 7 | 8 | ..... | ..... | 6 | 277 | 5 | ..... | 18 | 286 | 19.70 | 66.20 | | | 7 00- 7 49 |
| 7 50- 7 99 | ..... | ..... | ..... | ..... | ..... | ..... | 2 | 1 | ..... | ..... | ..... | 23 | ..... | ..... | 2 | 24 | 19.90 | 68.70 | | | 7 50- 7 99 |
| 8 00- 8 99 | ..... | ..... | ..... | ..... | 1 | ..... | 6 | 1 | ..... | ..... | 8 | 186 | 4 | ..... | 19 | 187 | 22.50 | 79.40 | | | 8 00- 8 99 |
| 9 00- 9 99 | ..... | ..... | ..... | ..... | 2 | ..... | 6 | 1 | ..... | ..... | 9 | 73 | 6 | ..... | 23 | 74 | 25.60 | 84.00 | | | 9 00- 9 99 |
| 10 00-10 99 | ..... | ..... | ..... | 4 | 5 | ..... | 12 | ..... | ..... | ..... | 19 | 108 | 5 | ..... | 41 | 112 | 31.00 | 91.00 | | | 10 00-10 99 |
| 11 00-11 99 | ..... | ..... | ..... | 1 | ..... | ..... | 3 | ..... | ..... | ..... | 10 | 15 | ..... | ..... | 13 | 16 | 32.80 | 92.00 | | | 11 00-11 99 |
| 12 00-12 99 | 1 | 1 | 2 | 5 | 11 | ..... | 20 | ..... | ..... | 1 | 60 | 59 | 2 | 1 | 96 | 67 | 45.60 | 96.10 | | | 12 00-12 99 |
| 13 00-13 99 | ..... | ..... | 2 | 1 | ..... | ..... | 2 | ..... | ..... | ..... | 10 | 8 | 1 | ..... | 15 | 9 | 47.70 | 96.80 | | | 13 00-13 99 |
| 14 00-14 99 | ..... | ..... | 1 | 2 | 2 | ..... | 3 | ..... | 4 | ..... | 62 | 11 | 2 | ..... | 74 | 13 | 57.50 | 97.50 | | | 14 00-14 99 |
| 15 00-15 99 | 1 | ..... | ..... | 6 | 6 | ..... | 7 | ..... | 9 | ..... | 62 | 16 | 2 | ..... | 87 | 22 | 69.20 | 98.90 | | | 15 00-15 99 |
| 16 00-17 99 | 3 | ..... | 1 | 1 | 1 | ..... | 3 | ..... | 10 | ..... | 48 | 6 | ..... | ..... | 66 | 7 | 78.00 | 99.40 | | | 16 00-17 99 |
| 18 00-19 99 | 1 | ..... | 2 | 2 | 1 | ..... | ..... | ..... | 12 | ..... | 40 | 7 | ..... | ..... | 56 | 9 | 85.50 | 99.90 | | | 18 00-19 99 |
| 20 00-24 99 | ..... | ..... | 8 | ..... | 1 | ..... | 1 | ..... | 12 | 1 | 42 | ..... | ..... | ..... | 64 | 1 | 94.10 | 99.90 | | | 20 00-24 99 |
| 25 00-29 99 | 1 | ..... | 4 | ..... | 1 | ..... | ..... | ..... | 7 | ..... | 12 | ..... | ..... | ..... | 25 | ..... | 97.50 | ..... | | | 25 00-29 99 |
| 30 00-34 99 | 2 | 1 | 1 | ..... | 1 | ..... | ..... | ..... | 1 | ..... | 4 | ..... | ..... | ..... | 9 | 1 | 98.60 | 100.00 | | | 30 00-34 99 |
| 35 00-39 99 | 2 | ..... | ..... | ..... | ..... | ..... | ..... | ..... | ..... | ..... | ..... | ..... | ..... | ..... | 2 | ..... | 98.00 | ..... | | | 35 00-39 99 |
| 40 00 and over | 7 | ..... | ..... | ..... | ..... | ..... | ..... | ..... | 1 | ..... | ..... | ..... | ..... | ..... | 8 | ..... | 100.00 | ..... | | | 40 00 and over |
| Not reported | ..... | ..... | ..... | ..... | ..... | ..... | ..... | ..... | ..... | ..... | ..... | 1 | 2 | ..... | 2 | 1 | ..... | ..... | | | Not reported |
| Total | 18 | 2 | 21 | 22 | 34 | 7 | 126 | 70 | 56 | 2 | 400 | 1,330 | 94 | 171 | 749 | 1,604 | ..... | ..... | | | Total |

26 . TABLE VI, A, 1, a

**BUFFALO**

**DEPARTMENT STORES — STOCK AND SALES**

NUMBER AND PER CENT. OF EMPLOYEES CLASSIFIED ACCORDING TO ACTUAL WEEKLY EARNINGS, BY AGE GROUPS AND SEX

| ACTUAL WEEKLY EARNINGS IN DOLLARS | AGE GROUPS IN YEARS | | | | | | | | | | | | | | ACTUAL WEEKLY EARNINGS IN DOLLARS |
|---|---|---|---|---|---|---|---|---|---|---|---|---|---|---|---|
| | 14–15 | | 16–17 | | 18–20 | | 21–24 | | 25–29 | | 30–34 | | 35–39 | | |
| | Male | Female | Male | Female | Male | Female | Male | Female | Male | Female | Male | Female | Male | Female | |
| Less than $3 00 | 6 | 9 | .... | 4 | ...... | 9 | 1 | 9 | ...... | 7 | ...... | 4 | ...... | ...... | Less than $3 00 |
| $3 00–$3 49... | 12 | 14 | .... | 10 | 1 | 4 | 1 | 2 | ...... | 1 | ...... | 1 | ...... | ...... | ...$3 00– 3 49 |
| 3 50– 3 99... | 14 | 31 | 3 | 33 | ...... | 8 | ...... | 1 | ...... | 2 | ...... | ...... | ...... | ...... | ... 3 50– 3 99 |
| 4 00– 4 49... | 23 | 14 | 11 | 47 | ...... | 22 | 1 | 1 | ...... | 2 | ...... | 2 | ...... | 1 | ... 4 00– 4 49 |
| 4 50– 4 99... | 6 | 8 | 2 | 13 | 2 | 8 | ...... | 7 | ...... | 3 | ...... | 1 | ...... | 1 | ... 4 50– 4 99 |
| 5 00– 5 49... | 9 | 4 | 13 | 39 | 2 | 53 | ...... | 25 | ...... | 8 | ...... | 2 | ...... | 3 | ... 5 00– 5 49 |
| 5 50– 5 99... | 1 | ...... | 3 | ...... | ...... | 11 | 1 | 14 | ...... | 5 | ...... | 4 | ...... | 1 | ... 5 50– 5 99 |
| 6 00– 6 49... | .... | ...... | 12 | 14 | 5 | 126 | 2 | 104 | 1 | 46 | 1 | 17 | ...... | 4 | ... 6 00– 6 49 |
| 6 50– 6 99... | .... | ...... | 1 | 2 | ...... | 19 | ...... | 16 | ...... | 12 | ...... | 2 | ...... | 6 | ... 6 50– 6 99 |
| 7 00– 7 49... | .... | ...... | 2 | 2 | 11 | 24 | 1 | 91 | | 68 | 1 | 17 | ...... | 5 | ... 7 00– 7 49 |
| 7 50– 7 99... | .... | ...... | 1 | ...... | 1 | 9 | ...... | 11 | ...... | 15 | ...... | 5 | ...... | 7 | ... 7 50– 7 99 |
| 8 00– 8 99... | .... | 1 | 2 | ...... | 12 | 13 | 4 | 46 | 2 | 56 | ...... | 23 | ...... | 15 | ... 8 00– 8 99 |
| 9 00– 9 99... | .... | ...... | 1 | ...... | 15 | 1 | 1 | 14 | 2 | 24 | 2 | 18 | ...... | 11 | ... 9 00– 9 99 |
| 10 00–10 99... | .... | ...... | .... | ...... | 9 | 1 | 20 | 10 | 6 | 32 | 4 | 19 | 3 | 19 | ...10 00–10 99 |
| 11 00–11 99... | .... | ...... | .... | ...... | 1 | ...... | 6 | 5 | 4 | 7 | 2 | 12 | ...... | 1 | ...11 00–11 99 |
| 12 00–12 99... | .... | ...... | 1 | ...... | 5 | 1 | 28 | 5 | 22 | 12 | 12 | 23 | 5 | 9 | ...12 00–12 99 |
| 13 00–13 99... | .... | ...... | .... | ...... | ...... | ...... | 6 | 1 | 4 | 1 | 1 | 2 | 1 | 6 | ...13 00–13 99 |
| 14 00–14 99... | .... | ...... | .... | ...... | ...... | ...... | 13 | ...... | 15 | 3 | 9 | 10 | 8 | 2 | ...14 00–14 99 |
| 15 00–15 99... | .... | ...... | .... | ...... | | ...... | 11 | 1 | 18 | 4 | 12 | 3 | 9 | 7 | ...15 00–15 99 |
| 16 00–17 99... | .... | ...... | .... | ...... | ...... | ...... | 3 | ...... | 14 | 4 | 11 | 1 | 11 | ...... | ...16 00–17 99 |
| 18 00–19 99... | .... | ...... | .... | ...... | ...... | ...... | 1 | ...... | 8 | 3 | 19 | 3 | 11 | 2 | ...18 00–19 99 |
| 20 00–24 99... | .... | ...... | .... | ...... | ...... | ...... | ...... | ...... | 6 | ...... | 15 | 1 | 7 | ...... | ...20 00–24 99 |
| 25 00–29 99... | .... | ...... | .... | ...... | ...... | ...... | ...... | ...... | 1 | ...... | 7 | ...... | 4 | ...... | ...25 00–29 99 |
| 30 00–34 99... | .... | ...... | .... | ...... | ...... | ...... | ...... | ...... | ...... | ...... | 1 | ...... | 3 | ...... | ...30 00–34 99 |
| 35 00–39 99... | .... | ...... | .... | ...... | ...... | ...... | ...... | ...... | ...... | ...... | ...... | ...... | ...... | ...... | ...35 00–39 99 |
| 40 00 and over. | .... | ...... | .... | ...... | ...... | ...... | ...... | ...... | 1 | ...... | 1 | ...... | 3 | ...... | .40 00 and over |
| Not reported... | .... | ...... | .... | ...... | 1 | ...... | 1 | 1 | ...... | ...... | ...... | 1 | ...... | ...... | ...Not reported |
| Total..... | 71 | 81 | 52 | 164 | 66 | 309 | 101 | 373 | 105 | 315 | 98 | 171 | 65 | 100 | ....Total |

267. TABLE VI, A, 1, a — (*concluded*)

BUFFALO

**DEPARTMENT STORES — STOCK AND SALES**

NUMBER AND PER CENT. OF EMPLOYEES CLASSIFIED ACCORDING TO ACTUAL WEEKLY EARNINGS, BY AGE GROUPS AND SEX

| ACTUAL WEEKLY EARNINGS IN DOLLARS | AGE GROUPS IN YEARS (*concluded*) 40–44 | | 45–54 | | 55–64 | | 65 AND OVER | NOT REPORTED | | TOTAL | | CUMULATIVE PER CENT. OF TOTAL | | ACTUAL WEEKLY EARNINGS IN DOLLARS |
|---|---|---|---|---|---|---|---|---|---|---|---|---|---|---|
| | Male | Female | Male | Female | Male | Female | Male | Male | Female | Male | Female | Male | Female | |
| Less than $3 00 | ..... | ..... | ..... | ..... | ..... | ..... | ..... | ..... | 1 | 7 | 43 | .9 | 2.7 | Less than $3 00 |
| $3 00–$3 49 | ..... | ..... | ..... | ..... | ..... | ..... | ..... | ..... | ..... | 14 | 32 | 2.8 | 4.7 | $3 00– 3 49 |
| 3 50– 3 99 | 1 | ..... | ..... | ..... | ..... | ..... | ..... | ..... | 1 | 18 | 76 | 5. | 9.4 | 3 50– 3 99 |
| 4 00– 4 49 | ..... | ..... | ..... | ..... | ..... | ..... | ..... | ..... | ..... | 35 | 98 | 9.9 | 15.5 | 4 00– 4 49 |
| 4 50– 4 99 | ..... | ..... | ..... | ..... | ..... | ..... | ..... | ..... | ..... | 10 | 41 | 11.2 | 18.1 | 4 50– 4 99 |
| 5 00– 5 49 | ..... | 2 | ..... | 1 | ..... | ..... | ..... | 1 | 1 | 25 | 138 | 14.6 | 26.8 | 5 00– 5 49 |
| 5 50– 5 99 | ..... | 1 | ..... | 1 | ..... | ..... | ..... | ..... | ..... | 5 | 37 | 15.3 | 29.0 | 5 50– 5 99 |
| 6 00 6 49 | ..... | 2 | ..... | 1 | ..... | ..... | ..... | ..... | 1 | 21 | 315 | 18.1 | 48.7 | 6 00– 6 49 |
| 6 50– 6 99 | ..... | ..... | ..... | ..... | ..... | ..... | ..... | ..... | 1 | 1 | 58 | 18.2 | 52.4 | 6 50– 6 99 |
| 7 00– 7 49 | ..... | 7 | ..... | 1 | ..... | ..... | ..... | 1 | 2 | 17 | 217 | 20.5 | 65.9 | 7 00– 7 49 |
| 7 50– 7 99 | ..... | 2 | ..... | | 1 | ..... | ..... | ..... | ..... | 3 | 50 | 20.9 | 69.0 | 7 50– 7 99 |
| 8 00– 8 99 | ..... | 8 | ..... | 6 | ..... | ..... | ..... | 1 | 3 | 21 | 171 | 23.7 | 79.6 | 8 00– 8 99 |
| 9 00– 9 99 | ..... | 2 | 1 | 2 | ..... | ..... | ..... | ..... | 1 | 22 | 73 | 26.6 | 84.3 | 9 00– 9 99 |
| 10 00–10 99 | ..... | 9 | 2 | 4 | ..... | 1 | ..... | ..... | 2 | 44 | 97 | 32.5 | 90.4 | 10 00–10 99 |
| 11 00–11 99 | ..... | 2 | ..... | ..... | ..... | ..... | 1 | ..... | 1 | 14 | 28 | 34.4 | 92.1 | 11 00–11 99 |
| 12 00–12 99 | 3 | 6 | 6 | ..... | 5 | ..... | ..... | 1 | ..... | 88 | 56 | 46.2 | 95.6 | 12 00–12 99 |
| 13 00–13 99 | 2 | ..... | 2 | 2 | ..... | ..... | ..... | ..... | ..... | 16 | 12 | 48.3 | 96.3 | 13 00–13 99 |
| 14 00–14 99 | 5 | 3 | 6 | 1 | 5 | ..... | ..... | 1 | ..... | 62 | 19 | 56.6 | 97.5 | 14 00–14 99 |
| 15 00–15 99 | 8 | 3 | 18 | 1 | 2 | ..... | 1 | 1 | ..... | 81 | 19 | 67.5 | 98.6 | 15 00–15 99 |
| 16 00–17 99 | 10 | 2 | 8 | 5 | 5 | ..... | 2 | ..... | ..... | 64 | 12 | 76.1 | 99.5 | 16 00–17 99 |
| 18 00–19 99 | 10 | ..... | 7 | ..... | 2 | ..... | 3 | ..... | ..... | 61 | 8 | 84.2 | 99.9 | 18 00–19 99 |
| 20 00–24 99 | 18 | ..... | 18 | ..... | 4 | ..... | 1 | ..... | ..... | 69 | 1 | 93.5 | 99.9 | 20 00–24 99 |
| 25 00–29 99 | 5 | ..... | 10 | ..... | 2 | ..... | ..... | ..... | ..... | 29 | ..... | 97.4 | ..... | 25 00–29 99 |
| 30 00–34 99 | 3 | 1 | 2 | ..... | 1 | ..... | ..... | ..... | ..... | 10 | 1 | 98.6 | 100.0 | 30 00–34 99 |
| 35 00–39 99 | 1 | ..... | ..... | ..... | 1 | ..... | ..... | ..... | ..... | 2 | ..... | 99.0 | ..... | 35 00–39 99 |
| 40 00 and over | ..... | ..... | 2 | ..... | ..... | ..... | 1 | ..... | ..... | 8 | ..... | 100.0 | ..... | 40 00 and over |
| Not reported | ..... | ..... | ..... | ..... | ..... | ..... | ..... | ..... | ..... | 2 | 2 | ..... | ..... | Not reported |
| Total | 66 | 50 | 82 | 26 | 28 | 1 | 9 | 6 | 14 | 749 | 1,604 | ..... | ..... | Total |

BUFFALO

DEPARTMENT STORES — STOCK AND SALES

268. TABLE IX, A, 1, a NUMBER AND PER CENT. OF EMPLOYEES CLASSIFIED ACCORDING TO ACTUAL WEEKLY EARNINGS, BY OCCUPATION AND SEX

| ACTUAL WEEKLY EARNINGS IN DOLLARS | OCCUPATION | | | | | | | | | | | | | | TOTAL | | CUMULATIVE PER CENT. OF TOTAL | | ACTUAL WEEKLY EARNINGS IN DOLLARS |
|---|---|---|---|---|---|---|---|---|---|---|---|---|---|---|---|---|---|---|---|
| | BUYERS | | ASSISTANT BUYERS AND HEADS OF STOCK | | RECEIVING AND STOCK CLERKS | | STOCK PEOPLE | | FLOOR MANAGERS | | SALES PEOPLE | | MESSENGERS, WRAPPERS, ERRAND BOYS | | | | | | |
| | Male | Female | Male | Female | Male | Female | Male | Female | Male | Female | Male | Female | Male | Female | Male | Female | Male | Female | |
| Less than $3 00 | ..... | ..... | ..... | ..... | ..... | ..... | 3 | 3 | ..... | ..... | ..... | 29 | 4 | 11 | 7 | 43 | .90 | 2.70 | Less than $3 00 |
| 3 00– 3 49 | ..... | ..... | ..... | ..... | ..... | ..... | 1 | 4 | ..... | ..... | 2 | 9 | 11 | 19 | 14 | 32 | 2.80 | 4.70 | 3 00– 3 49 |
| 3 50– 3 99 | ..... | ..... | ..... | ..... | 2 | ..... | 5 | 25 | ..... | ..... | 1 | 9 | 10 | 42 | 18 | 76 | 5.20 | 9.40 | 3 50– 3 99 |
| 4 00– 4 49 | ..... | ..... | ..... | ..... | ..... | 1 | 19 | 13 | ..... | ..... | ..... | 44 | 16 | 40 | 35 | 98 | 9.90 | 15.50 | 4 00– 4 49 |
| 4 50– 4 99 | ..... | ..... | ..... | ..... | ..... | 1 | 6 | 2 | ..... | ..... | ..... | 19 | 4 | 19 | 10 | 41 | 11.20 | 18.10 | 4 50– 4 99 |
| 5 00– 5 49 | ..... | ..... | ..... | 1 | ..... | 1 | 15 | 4 | ..... | ..... | ..... | 97 | 10 | 35 | 25 | 138 | 14.60 | 26.80 | 5 00– 5 49 |
| 5 50– 5 99 | ..... | ..... | ..... | ..... | ..... | ..... | 1 | ..... | ..... | ..... | ..... | 36 | 4 | 1 | 5 | 37 | 15.30 | 29.00 | 5 50– 5 99 |
| 6 00– 6 49 | ..... | ..... | ..... | ..... | ..... | 3 | 7 | 8 | ..... | ..... | 8 | 301 | 6 | 3 | 21 | 315 | 18.10 | 48.70 | 6 00– 6 49 |
| 6 50– 6 99 | ..... | ..... | ..... | 1 | ..... | ..... | ..... | ..... | ..... | ..... | ..... | 57 | 1 | ..... | 1 | 58 | 18.20 | 52.40 | 6 50– 6 99 |
| 7 00– 7 49 | ..... | ..... | ..... | ..... | ..... | 1 | 6 | 8 | ..... | ..... | 6 | 208 | 5 | ..... | 17 | 217 | 20.50 | 65.90 | 7 00– 7 49 |
| 7 50– 7 99 | ..... | ..... | ..... | ..... | ..... | ..... | 2 | 1 | ..... | ..... | 1 | 49 | ..... | ..... | 3 | 50 | 20.90 | 69.00 | 7 50– 7 99 |
| 8 00– 8 99 | ..... | ..... | ..... | ..... | 1 | ..... | 6 | 1 | ..... | ..... | 10 | 170 | 4 | ..... | 21 | 171 | 23.70 | 79.60 | 8 00– 8 99 |
| 9 00– 9 99 | ..... | ..... | ..... | ..... | 2 | ..... | 6 | 1 | 1 | ..... | 8 | 72 | 5 | ..... | 22 | 73 | 26.60 | 84.30 | 9 00– 9 99 |
| 10 00–10 99 | ..... | ..... | ..... | 3 | 5 | ..... | 12 | ..... | ..... | ..... | 22 | 94 | 5 | ..... | 44 | 97 | 32.50 | 90.40 | 10 00–10 99 |
| 11 00–11 99 | ..... | ..... | ..... | 1 | ..... | ..... | 3 | ..... | ..... | ..... | 11 | 27 | ..... | ..... | 14 | 28 | 34.40 | 92.10 | 11 00–11 99 |
| 12 00–12 99 | 1 | 1 | 1 | 5 | 11 | ..... | 18 | ..... | ..... | 1 | 55 | 48 | 2 | 1 | 88 | 56 | 46.20 | 95.60 | 12 00–12 99 |
| 13 00–13 99 | ..... | ..... | 2 | 1 | ..... | ..... | 3 | ..... | ..... | ..... | 10 | 11 | 1 | ..... | 16 | 12 | 48.30 | 96.30 | 13 00–13 99 |
| 14 00–14 99 | ..... | ..... | 2 | 1 | 2 | ..... | 3 | ..... | 3 | ..... | 50 | 18 | 2 | ..... | 62 | 19 | 56.60 | 97.50 | 14 00–14 99 |
| 15 00–15 99 | 1 | ..... | ..... | 5 | 6 | ..... | 6 | ..... | 9 | ..... | 57 | 14 | 2 | ..... | 81 | 19 | 67.50 | 98.60 | 15 00–15 99 |
| 16 00–17 99 | 3 | ..... | ..... | 2 | 1 | ..... | 3 | ..... | 10 | ..... | 47 | 10 | ..... | ..... | 64 | 12 | 76.10 | 99.50 | 16 00–17 99 |
| 18 00–19 99 | 1 | ..... | 1 | 2 | 1 | ..... | ..... | ..... | 12 | ..... | 46 | 6 | ..... | ..... | 61 | 8 | 84.20 | 99.90 | 18 00–19 99 |
| 20 00–24 99 | ..... | ..... | 9 | ..... | 1 | ..... | 1 | ..... | 12 | 1 | 46 | ..... | ..... | ..... | 69 | 1 | 93.50 | 99.90 | 20 00–24 99 |
| 25 00–29 99 | 1 | ..... | 4 | ..... | 1 | ..... | ..... | ..... | 7 | ..... | 16 | ..... | ..... | ..... | 29 | ..... | 97.40 | ..... | 25 00–29 99 |
| 30 00–34 99 | 2 | 1 | 2 | ..... | 1 | ..... | ..... | ..... | 1 | ..... | 4 | ..... | ..... | ..... | 10 | 1 | 98.60 | 100.00 | 30 00–34 99 |
| 35 00–39 99 | 2 | ..... | ..... | ..... | ..... | ..... | ..... | ..... | ..... | ..... | ..... | ..... | ..... | ..... | 2 | ..... | 99.00 | ..... | 35 00–39 99 |
| 40 00 and over | 7 | ..... | ..... | ..... | ..... | ..... | ..... | ..... | 1 | ..... | ..... | ..... | ..... | ..... | 8 | ..... | 100.00 | ..... | 40 00 and over |
| Not reported | ..... | ..... | ..... | ..... | ..... | ..... | ..... | ..... | ..... | ..... | ..... | 2 | 2 | ..... | 2 | 2 | ..... | ..... | Not reported |
| Total | 18 | 2 | 21 | 22 | 34 | 7 | 126 | 70 | 56 | 2 | 400 | 1,330 | 94 | 171 | 749 | 1,604 | ..... | ..... | Total |

## BUFFALO
## DEPARTMENT STORES — OFFICE

269. TABLE V, A,1, b NUMBER AND PER CENT. OF EMPLOYEES EARNING SPECIFIED WEEKLY RATES, BY AGE GROUPS AND SEX

| Weekly Rates in Dollars | Age Groups in Years | | | | | | | | | | | | | | Weekly Rates in Dollars |
|---|---|---|---|---|---|---|---|---|---|---|---|---|---|---|---|
| | 14–15 | | 16–17 | | 18–20 | | 21–24 | | 25–29 | | 30–34 | | 35–39 | | |
| | Male | Female | Male | Female | Male | Female | Male | Female | Male | Female | Male | Female | Male | Female | |
| $3 00–$3 49... | .... | 2 | .... | ...... | ...... | ...... | ...... | ...... | ...... | ...... | ...... | ...... | ...... | ...... | ...$3 00–$3 49 |
| 3 50– 3 99... | .... | 7 | .... | 4 | ...... | 2 | ...... | 1 | ...... | ...... | ...... | ...... | ...... | ...... | ... 3 50– 3 99 |
| 4 00– 4 49... | 9 | 10 | 4 | 18 | ...... | 4 | ...... | ...... | ...... | ...... | ...... | ...... | ...... | ...... | ... 4 00– 4 49 |
| 4 50– 4 99... | 1 | 1 | 2 | 6 | ...... | 3 | ...... | ...... | ...... | 1 | ...... | 1 | ...... | ...... | ... 4 50– 4 99 |
| 5 00– 5 49... | 3 | 1 | 9 | 34 | ...... | 27 | ...... | 2 | ...... | ...... | ...... | ...... | ...... | ...... | ... 5 00– 5 49 |
| 5 50– 5 99... | .... | ...... | 2 | 1 | ...... | 3 | ...... | 1 | ...... | ...... | ...... | ...... | ...... | ...... | ... 5 50– 5 99 |
| 6 00– 6 49... | 1 | 1 | 8 | 16 | 4 | 66 | ...... | 24 | 1 | 3 | ...... | 2 | ...... | 1 | ... 6 00– 6 49 |
| 6 50– 6 99... | .... | ...... | 1 | ...... | 2 | 6 | ...... | 3 | ...... | ...... | ...... | ...... | ...... | ...... | ... 6 50– 6 99 |
| 7 00– 7 49... | .... | ...... | .... | 3 | 4 | 24 | ...... | 25 | ...... | 10 | ...... | 3 | ...... | ...... | ... 7 00– 7 49 |
| 7 50– 7 99... | .... | ...... | 1 | ...... | ...... | ...... | ...... | 1 | ...... | 1 | ...... | ...... | ...... | ...... | ... 7 50– 7 99 |
| 8 00– 8 99... | .... | ...... | 1 | 2 | 8 | 11 | ...... | 25 | ...... | 8 | ...... | ...... | ...... | 1 | ... 8 00– 8 99 |
| 9 00– 9 99... | .... | ...... | .... | ...... | 6 | 1 | 2 | 8 | ...... | 5 | ...... | 2 | ...... | ...... | ... 9 00– 9 99 |
| 10 00–10 99... | .... | ...... | .... | ...... | 4 | 5 | 1 | 15 | 1 | 9 | 2 | 2 | 1 | 2 | ...10 00–10 99 |
| 11 00–11 99... | .... | ...... | .... | ...... | ...... | ...... | ...... | 2 | ...... | 2 | ...... | ...... | ...... | 1 | ...11 00–11 99 |
| 12 00–12 99... | .... | ...... | .... | ...... | 3 | ...... | 14 | 3 | 3 | 5 | 2 | 3 | ...... | 2 | ...12 00–12 99 |
| 13 00–13 99... | .... | ...... | .... | ...... | 1 | ...... | 4 | ...... | 1 | 4 | 1 | 1 | 2 | ...... | ...13 00–13 99 |
| 14 00–14 99... | .... | ...... | .... | ...... | ...... | ...... | 1 | ...... | ...... | 1 | 1 | ...... | 2 | 2 | ...14 00–14 99 |
| 15 00–15 99... | .... | ...... | .... | ...... | ...... | ...... | 5 | 2 | ...... | 2 | 3 | 2 | ...... | 2 | ...15 00–15 99 |
| 16 00–17 99... | .... | ...... | .... | ...... | ...... | ...... | 1 | ...... | 3 | ...... | 5 | ...... | 3 | ...... | ...16 00–17 99 |
| 18 00–19 99... | .... | ...... | .... | ...... | ...... | ...... | ...... | 1 | 4 | ...... | 2 | ...... | 2 | 1 | ...18 00–19 99 |
| 20 00–24 99... | .... | ...... | .... | ...... | ...... | ...... | ...... | ...... | 2 | 1 | 1 | 1 | 1 | ...... | ...20 00–24 99 |
| 25 00–29 99... | .... | ...... | .... | ...... | ...... | ...... | ...... | ...... | 1 | ...... | 1 | ...... | 1 | ...... | ...25 00–29 99 |
| 30 00–34 99... | .... | ...... | .... | ...... | ...... | ...... | ...... | ...... | ...... | ...... | 2 | ...... | 1 | ...... | ...30 00–34 99 |
| Total..... | 14 | 22 | 28 | 84 | 32 | 152 | 28 | 113 | 16 | 52 | 20 | 17 | 13 | 12 | .....Total |

269. TABLE V, A,1, b — (*concluded*)

BUFFALO

DEPARTMENT STORES — OFFICE

NUMBER AND PER CENT. OF EMPLOYEES EARNING SPECIFIED WEEKLY RATES, BY AGE GROUPS AND SEX

| WEEKLY RATES IN DOLLARS | AGE GROUPS IN YEARS (*concluded*) | | | | | | | | | | | | WEEKLY RATES IN DOLLARS |
|---|---|---|---|---|---|---|---|---|---|---|---|---|---|
| | 40–44 | | 45–54 | | 55–64 | 65 AND OVER | NOT REPORTED | | TOTAL | | CUMULATIVE PER CENT. OF TOTAL | | |
| | Male | Female | Male | Female | Male | Male | Male | Female | Male | Female | Male | Female | |
| $3 00–$3 49.... | ....... | ....... | ....... | ....... | ....... | ....... | ....... | ....... | ....... | 2 | ....... | .44 | ...$3 00–$3 49 |
| 3 50– 3 99.... | ....... | ....... | ....... | ....... | ....... | ....... | ....... | ....... | ....... | 14 | ....... | 3.50 | ... 3 50– 3 99 |
| 4 00– 4 49.... | ....... | ....... | ....... | ....... | ....... | ....... | ....... | ....... | 13 | 32 | 7.28 | 10.50 | ... 4 00– 4 49 |
| 4 50– 4 99.... | ....... | ....... | ....... | ....... | ....... | ....... | ....... | ....... | 3 | 12 | 9.00 | 13.10 | ... 4 50– 4 99 |
| 5 00– 5 49.... | ....... | ....... | ....... | ....... | ....... | ....... | ....... | ....... | 12 | 64 | 15.72 | 27.15 | ... 5 00– 5 49 |
| 5 50– 5 99.... | ....... | ....... | ....... | ....... | ....... | ....... | ....... | ....... | 2 | 5 | 16.85 | 28.20 | ... 5 50– 5 99 |
| 6 00– 6 49.... | ....... | ....... | ....... | ....... | ....... | ....... | ....... | ....... | 14 | 113 | 24.75 | 53.00 | ... 6 00– 6 49 |
| 6 50– 6 99.... | ....... | ....... | ....... | ....... | ....... | ....... | ....... | ....... | 3 | 9 | 26.40 | 54.95 | ... 6 50– 6 99 |
| 7 00– 7 49.... | ....... | ....... | ....... | ....... | ....... | ....... | ....... | ....... | 4 | 65 | 28.65 | 69.10 | ... 7 00– 7 49 |
| 7 50– 7 99.... | ....... | ....... | ....... | ....... | ....... | ....... | ....... | ....... | 1 | 2 | 29.20 | 69.60 | ... 7 50– 7 99 |
| 8 00– 8 99.... | ....... | 1 | ....... | ....... | ....... | ....... | ....... | ....... | 9 | 48 | 34.25 | 80.00 | ... 8 00– 8 99 |
| 9 00– 9 99.... | ....... | ....... | ....... | ....... | ....... | ....... | ....... | ....... | 8 | 16 | 38.80 | 83.50 | ... 9 00– 9 99 |
| 10 00–10 99.... | ....... | 1 | 1 | ....... | ....... | ....... | ....... | ....... | 10 | 34 | 44.40 | 91.00 | ...10 00–10 99 |
| 11 00–11 99.... | 1 | ....... | 1 | ....... | ....... | ....... | ....... | ....... | 2 | 5 | 45.50 | 92.00 | ...11 00–11 99 |
| 12 00–12 99.... | 2 | ....... | ....... | ....... | ....... | 1 | ....... | ....... | 25 | 13 | 59.50 | 95.00 | ...12 00–12 99 |
| 13 00–13 99.... | ....... | ....... | ....... | 1 | 1 | ....... | ....... | ....... | 10 | 6 | 65.10 | 96.25 | ...13 00–13 99 |
| 14 00–14 99.... | ....... | ....... | ....... | ....... | ....... | ....... | ....... | 1 | 4 | 4 | 67.50 | 97.10 | ...14 00–14 99 |
| 15 00–15 99.... | 1 | ....... | 4 | ....... | 2 | ....... | ....... | ....... | 15 | 8 | 75.90 | 99.00 | ...15 00–15 99 |
| 16 00–17 99.... | ....... | ....... | 1 | ....... | 1 | ....... | 2 | ....... | 16 | ....... | 85.00 | ....... | ...16 00–17 99 |
| 18 00–19 99.... | ....... | ....... | 2 | ....... | 1 | ....... | ....... | ....... | 11 | 2 | 91.00 | 99.45 | ...18 00–19 99 |
| 20 00–24 99.... | 1 | ....... | ....... | 1 | 1 | ....... | ....... | ....... | 6 | 3 | 94.50 | 100.00 | ...20 00–24 99 |
| 25 00–29 99.... | 2 | ....... | ....... | ....... | ....... | ....... | ....... | ....... | 5 | ....... | 97.20 | ....... | ...25 00–29 00 |
| 30 00–34 99.... | ....... | ....... | ....... | ....... | ....... | ....... | ....... | ....... | 3 | ....... | 99.00 | ....... | ...30 00–34 99 |
| 35 00–39 99.... | 1 | ....... | 1 | ....... | ....... | ....... | ....... | ....... | 2 | ....... | 100.00 | ....... | ...35 00–39 99 |
| Total...... | 8 | 2 | 10 | 2 | 6 | 1 | 2 | 1 | 178 | 457 | ....... | ....... | .....Total |

BUFFALO
DEPARTMENT STORES — OFFICE

270. TABLE VIII, A, 1, b — NUMBER AND PER CENT. OF EMPLOYEES EARNING SPECIFIED WEEKLY RATES, BY OCCUPATION AND SEX

| WEEKLY RATES IN DOLLARS | OCCUPATION | | | | | | | | | | | | | | | | | | | | | WEEKLY RATES IN DOLLARS |
|---|---|---|---|---|---|---|---|---|---|---|---|---|---|---|---|---|---|---|---|---|---|---|
| | SUPERINTENDENTS | BOOKKEEPERS | | CLERKS | | STENOGRAPHERS | | OFFICE BOYS AND GIRLS | | CASHIERS | | TELEPHONE OPERATORS | AUDITORS | | DETECTIVES | ADVERTISERS AND WINDOW DRESSERS | | TOTAL | | CUMULATIVE PER CENT. OF TOTAL | | |
| | Male | Male | Female | Male | Female | Male | Female | Male | Female | Male | Female | Female | Male | Female | Female | Male | Female | Male | Female | Male | Female | |
| $3 00–$3 49 | | | | | 1 | | | | | | 1 | | | | | | | | 2 | | .44 | $3 00–$3 49 |
| 3 50– 3 99 | | | | | 2 | | | | 1 | | 10 | | | 1 | | | | | 14 | | 3.50 | 3 50– 3 99 |
| 4 00– 4 49 | | | | 7 | 6 | | | 6 | 3 | | 18 | | | 5 | | | | 13 | 32 | 7.28 | 10.50 | 4 00– 4 49 |
| 4 50– 4 99 | | | | | 4 | | | 3 | | | 7 | 1 | | | | | | 3 | 12 | 9.00 | 13.10 | 4 50– 4 99 |
| 5 00– 5 49 | | | 3 | 5 | 25 | | | 4 | 11 | | 15 | | | 10 | | 3 | | 12 | 64 | 15.72 | 27.15 | 5 00– 5 49 |
| 5 50– 5 99 | | | 1 | 2 | 3 | | | | | | | 1 | | | | | | 2 | 5 | 16.85 | 28.20 | 5 50– 5 99 |
| 6 00– 6 49 | | | 9 | 13 | 46 | | 1 | | 7 | 1 | 41 | 2 | | 7 | | | | 14 | 113 | 24.75 | 53.00 | 6 00– 6 49 |
| 6 50– 6 99 | | | 2 | 3 | 7 | | | | | | | | | | | | | 3 | 9 | 26.40 | 54.95 | 6 50– 6 99 |
| 7 00– 7 49 | | | 9 | 4 | 21 | | 1 | | 2 | | 18 | 7 | | 7 | | | | 4 | 65 | 28.65 | 69.10 | 7 00– 7 49 |
| 7 50– 7 99 | | | 1 | | | | | | | | 1 | | 1 | | | | | 1 | 2 | 29.20 | 69.60 | 7 50– 7 99 |
| 8 00– 8 99 | | 1 | 15 | 5 | 19 | | 2 | | 1 | 1 | 6 | 3 | | 2 | | 2 | | 9 | 48 | 34.25 | 80.00 | 8 00– 8 99 |
| 9 00– 9 99 | | 1 | 7 | 4 | 5 | 1 | 1 | | | 1 | 2 | 1 | | | | 1 | | 8 | 16 | 38.80 | 83.50 | 9 00– 9 99 |
| 10 00–10 99 | | 1 | 10 | 7 | 7 | | 9 | | | 1 | 5 | 2 | | 1 | | 1 | | 10 | 34 | 44.40 | 91.00 | 10 00–10 99 |
| 11 00–11 99 | | | 2 | 2 | 3 | | | | | | | | | | | | | 2 | 5 | 45.50 | 92.00 | 11 00–11 99 |
| 12 00–12 99 | | 10 | 3 | 12 | 3 | | 3 | | | 1 | 2 | | 1 | | 1 | 1 | 1 | 25 | 13 | 59.50 | 95.00 | 12 00–12 99 |
| 13 00–13 99 | | 5 | 1 | 4 | 1 | | 2 | | | 1 | 2 | | | | | | | 10 | 6 | 65.10 | 96.25 | 13 00–13 99 |
| 14 00–14 99 | | 1 | 2 | 3 | 1 | | | | | | | | | | | | 1 | 4 | 4 | 67.50 | 97.10 | 14 00–14 99 |
| 15 00–15 99 | | 6 | 3 | 7 | 2 | | | | | | 3 | | 1 | | | 1 | | 15 | 8 | 75.90 | 99.00 | 15 00–15 99 |
| 16 00–17 99 | | 5 | | 8 | | | | | | 1 | | | | | | 2 | | 16 | | 85.00 | | 16 00–17 99 |
| 18 00–19 99 | | | 1 | 8 | | | | | | | | | | | | 3 | 1 | 11 | 2 | 91.00 | 99.45 | 18 00–19 99 |
| 20 00–24 99 | 1 | | | 3 | 1 | | 1 | | | | | | | | | 2 | 1 | 6 | 3 | 94.50 | 100.00 | 20 00–24 99 |
| 25 00–29 99 | | | | 3 | | | | | | | | | 1 | | | 1 | | 5 | | 97.20 | | 25 00–29 99 |
| 30 00–34 99 | | | | | | | | | | | | | 1 | | | 2 | | 3 | | 99.00 | | 30 00–34 99 |
| 35 00–39 99 | | | | 1 | | | | | | 1 | | | | | | | | 2 | | 100.00 | | 35 00–39 99 |
| Total | 1 | 30 | 69 | 101 | 157 | 1 | 20 | 13 | 25 | 8 | 131 | 17 | 5 | 33 | 1 | 19 | 4 | 178 | 457 | | | Total |

271 TABLE VI, A, 1, b.

BUFFALO
DEPARTMENT STORES — OFFICE

NUMBER AND PER CENT. OF EMPLOYEES CLASSIFIED ACCORDING TO ACTUAL WEEKLY EARNINGS, BY AGE GROUPS AND SEX

| ACTUAL WEEKLY EARNINGS IN DOLLARS | Age Groups in Years | | | | | | | | | | | | | | ACTUAL WEEKLY EARNINGS IN DOLLARS |
|---|---|---|---|---|---|---|---|---|---|---|---|---|---|---|---|
| | 14–15 | | 16–17 | | 18–20 | | 21–24 | | 25–29 | | 30–34 | | 35–39 | | |
| | Male | Female | Male | Female | Male | Female | Male | Female | Male | Female | Male | Female | Male | Female | |
| Less than $3 00 | .... | 1 | .... | 2 | ...... | ...... | ...... | ...... | ...... | ...... | ...... | ...... | ...... | ...... | Less than $3 00 |
| $3 00–$3 49... | .... | 2 | .... | ...... | ...... | 2 | ...... | ...... | ...... | ...... | ...... | ...... | ...... | 1 | ...$3 00– 3 49 |
| 3 50– 3 99... | .... | 7 | .... | 5 | ...... | 2 | ...... | 1 | ...... | ...... | ...... | ...... | ...... | ...... | ....3 50– 3 99 |
| 4 00– 4 49... | 9 | 9 | 4 | 19 | ...... | 5 | ...... | 2 | ...... | ...... | ...... | ...... | ...... | ...... | ....4 00– 4 49 |
| 4 50– 4 99... | 1 | 1 | 3 | 6 | ...... | 4 | ...... | 1 | ...... | 1 | ...... | 1 | ...... | ...... | ....4 50– 4 99 |
| 5 00– 5 49... | 3 | 1 | 9 | 33 | ...... | 28 | ...... | 3 | ...... | ...... | ...... | ...... | ...... | ...... | ....5 00– 5 49 |
| 5 50– 5 99... | .... | ...... | 1 | 1 | ...... | 5 | ...... | 2 | ...... | 2 | ...... | ...... | ...... | ...... | ....5 50– 5 99 |
| 6 00– 6 49... | 1 | 1 | 8 | 14 | 4 | 60 | ...... | 23 | 1 | 3 | ...... | 2 | ...... | 1 | ....6 00– 6 49 |
| 6 50– 6 99... | .... | ...... | 1 | ...... | 2 | 5 | ...... | 4 | ...... | ...... | ...... | ...... | ...... | ...... | ....6 50– 6 99 |
| 7 00– 7 49... | .... | ...... | .... | 2 | 4 | 26 | ...... | 23 | ...... | 8 | ...... | 3 | ...... | ...... | ....7 00– 7 49 |
| 7 50– 7 99... | .... | ...... | 1 | ...... | ...... | ...... | ...... | 1 | ...... | 1 | ...... | ...... | ...... | ...... | ....7 50– 7 99 |
| 8 00– 8 99... | .... | ...... | 1 | 2 | 8 | 11 | ...... | 23 | ...... | 9 | ...... | ...... | ...... | 1 | ....8 00– 8 99 |
| 9 00– 9 99... | .... | ...... | .... | ...... | 6 | 1 | 2 | 7 | ...... | 5 | ...... | 2 | ...... | ...... | ....9 00– 9 99 |
| 10 00–10 99... | .... | ...... | .... | ...... | 4 | 3 | 1 | 15 | 1 | 9 | 2 | 2 | 2 | 2 | ...10 00–10 99 |
| 11 00–11 99... | .... | ...... | .... | ...... | ...... | ...... | ...... | 2 | ...... | 2 | ...... | ...... | ...... | 1 | ...11 00–11 99 |
| 12 00–12 99... | .... | ...... | .... | ...... | 3 | ...... | 15 | 3 | 3 | 4 | 2 | 3 | ...... | 1 | ...12 00–12 99 |
| 13 00–13 99... | .... | ...... | .... | ...... | 1 | ...... | 4 | ...... | 1 | 4 | 1 | 1 | 1 | ...... | ...13 00–13 99 |
| 14 00–14 99... | .... | ...... | .... | ...... | ...... | ...... | 1 | ...... | ...... | 1 | 1 | ...... | 2 | 2 | ...14 00–14 99 |
| 15 00–15 99... | .... | ...... | .... | ...... | ...... | ...... | 4 | 2 | ...... | 2 | 3 | 2 | ...... | 2 | ...15 00–15 99 |
| 16 00–17 99... | .... | ...... | .... | ...... | ...... | ...... | 1 | ...... | 3 | ...... | 5 | ...... | 3 | ...... | ...16 00–17 99 |
| 18 00–19 99... | .... | ...... | .... | ...... | ...... | ...... | ...... | 1 | 4 | ...... | 2 | ...... | 2 | 1 | ...18 00–19 99 |
| 20 00–24 99... | .... | ...... | .... | ...... | ...... | ...... | ...... | ...... | 2 | 1 | 1 | 1 | 1 | ...... | ...20 00–24 99 |
| 25 00–29 99... | .... | ...... | .... | ...... | ...... | ...... | ...... | ...... | 1 | ...... | 1 | ...... | 1 | ...... | ...25 00–29 99 |
| 30 00–34 99... | .... | ...... | .... | ...... | ...... | ...... | ...... | ...... | ...... | ...... | 2 | ...... | 1 | ...... | ...30 00–34 99 |
| Total..... | 14 | 22 | 28 | 84 | 32 | 152 | 28 | 113 | 16 | 52 | 20 | 17 | 13 | 12 | .....Total |

BUFFALO

271. TABLE VI, A, 1, b — (*concluded*)

DEPARTMENT STORES — OFFICE

NUMBER AND PER CENT. OF EMPLOYEES CLASSIFIED ACCORDING TO ACTUAL WEEKLY EARNINGS, BY AGE GROUPS AND SEX

| ACTUAL WEEKLY EARNINGS IN DOLLARS | AGE GROUPS IN YEARS — (*concluded*) 40–44 | | 45–54 | | 55–64 | 65 AND OVER | NOT REPORTED | | TOTAL | | CUMULATIVE PER CENT. OF TOTAL | | ACTUAL WEEKLY EARNINGS IN DOLLARS |
|---|---|---|---|---|---|---|---|---|---|---|---|---|---|
| | Male | Female | Male | Female | Male | Male | Male | Female | Male | Female | Male | Female | |
| Less than $3 00 | ....... | ....... | ....... | ....... | ....... | ....... | ....... | ....... | ....... | 3 | ....... | .70 | Less than $3 00 |
| $3 00–$3 49 | ....... | ....... | ....... | ....... | ....... | ....... | ....... | ....... | ....... | 5 | ....... | 1.70 | $3 00– 3 49 |
| 3 50– 3 99 | ....... | ....... | ....... | ....... | ....... | ....... | ....... | ....... | ....... | 15 | ....... | 5.00 | 3 50– 3 99 |
| 4 00– 4 49 | ....... | ....... | ....... | ....... | ....... | ....... | ....... | ....... | 13 | 35 | 7.30 | 12.70 | 4 00– 4 49 |
| 4 50– 4 99 | ....... | ....... | ....... | ....... | ....... | ....... | ....... | ....... | 4 | 14 | 9.60 | 15.70 | 4 50– 4 99 |
| 5 00– 5 49 | ....... | ....... | ....... | ....... | ....... | ....... | ....... | ....... | 12 | 65 | 16.30 | 29.90 | 5 00– 5 49 |
| 5 50– 5 99 | ....... | ....... | ....... | ....... | ....... | ....... | ....... | ....... | 1 | 10 | 16.90 | 32.20 | 5 59– 5 99 |
| 6 00– 6 49 | ....... | ....... | ....... | ....... | ....... | ....... | ....... | ....... | 14 | 104 | 24.70 | 54.80 | 6 00– 6 49 |
| 6 50– 6 99 | ....... | ....... | ....... | ....... | ....... | ....... | ....... | ....... | 3 | 9 | 25.40 | 56.80 | 6 50– 6 99 |
| 7 00– 7 49 | 1 | ....... | ....... | ....... | ....... | ....... | ....... | ....... | 5 | 62 | 29.20 | 70.40 | 7 00– 7 49 |
| 7 50– 7 99 | ....... | ....... | ....... | ....... | ....... | ....... | ....... | ....... | 1 | 2 | 29.80 | 70.90 | 7 50– 7 99 |
| 8 00– 8 99 | ....... | 1 | ....... | ....... | ....... | ....... | ....... | ....... | 9 | 47 | 34.80 | 81.10 | 8 00– 8 99 |
| 9 00– 9 99 | ....... | ....... | ....... | ....... | ....... | ....... | ....... | ....... | 8 | 15 | 39.40 | 84.50 | 9 00– 9 99 |
| 10 00–10 99 | ....... | 1 | 1 | ....... | ....... | ....... | 1 | ....... | 12 | 32 | 46.10 | 91.50 | 10 00–10 99 |
| 11 00–11 99 | 1 | ....... | 1 | ....... | ....... | ....... | ....... | ....... | 2 | 5 | 47.20 | 92.50 | 11 00–11 99 |
| 12 00–12 99 | 1 | ....... | ....... | ....... | ....... | 1 | ....... | ....... | 25 | 11 | 61.30 | 95.00 | 12 00–12 99 |
| 13 00–13 99 | ....... | ....... | ....... | 1 | 1 | ....... | ....... | ....... | 9 | 6 | 66.40 | 96.30 | 13 00–13 99 |
| 14 00–14 99 | ....... | ....... | ....... | ....... | ....... | ....... | ....... | 1 | 4 | 4 | 63.60 | 97.10 | 14 00–14 99 |
| 15 00–15 99 | 1 | ....... | 4 | ....... | 2 | ....... | ....... | ....... | 14 | 8 | 76.50 | 98.90 | 15 00–15 99 |
| 16 00–17 99 | ....... | ....... | 1 | ....... | 1 | ....... | 1 | ....... | 15 | ....... | 84.90 | ....... | 16 00–17 99 |
| 18 00–19 99 | ....... | ....... | 2 | ....... | 1 | ....... | ....... | ....... | 11 | 2 | 91.00 | 99.40 | 18 00–19 99 |
| 20 00–24 99 | 1 | ....... | ....... | 1 | 1 | ....... | ....... | ....... | 6 | 3 | 94.50 | 100.00 | 20 00–24 99 |
| 25 00–29 99 | 2 | ....... | ....... | ....... | ....... | ....... | ....... | ....... | 5 | ....... | 97.30 | ....... | 25 00–29 99 |
| 30 00–34 99 | ....... | ....... | ....... | ....... | ....... | ....... | ....... | ....... | 3 | ....... | 99.00 | ....... | 30 00–34 99 |
| 35 00–39 99 | 1 | ....... | 1 | ....... | ....... | ....... | ....... | ....... | 2 | ....... | 100.00 | ....... | 35 00–39 99 |
| Total | 8 | 2 | 10 | 2 | 6 | 1 | 2 | 1 | 178 | 457 | ....... | ....... | Total |

BUFFALO
DEPARTMENT STORES — OFFICE

272. TABLE IX, A, 1, b NUMBER AND PER CENT. OF EMPLOYEES CLASSIFIED ACCORDING TO ACTUAL WEEKLY EARNINGS, BY OCCUPATION AND SEX

| ACTUAL WEEKLY EARNINGS IN DOLLARS | OCCUPATION | | | | | | | | | | | | | | | | | | | | | ACTUAL WEEKLY EARNINGS IN DOLLARS |
|---|---|---|---|---|---|---|---|---|---|---|---|---|---|---|---|---|---|---|---|---|---|---|
| | SUPERINTENDENTS | BOOKKEEPERS | | CLERKS | | STENOGRAPHERS | | OFFICE BOYS AND GIRLS | | CASHIERS | | TELEPHONE OPERATORS | AUDITORS | | DETECTIVES | ADVERTISERS AND WINDOW DRESSERS | | TOTAL | | CUMULATIVE PER CENT. OF TOTAL | | |
| | Male | Male | Female | Male | Female | Male | Female | Male | Female | Male | Female | Female | Male | Female | Female | Male | Female | Male | Female | Male | Female | |
| Less than $3 00 | | | | | | | | | 1 | | 1 | | | 1 | | | | | 3 | | .70 | Less than $3 00 |
| $3 00-$3 49 | | | | | 3 | | | | | | | | | 1 | 1 | | | | 5 | | 1.70 | $3 00- 3 49 |
| 3 50- 3 99 | | | | | 3 | | | | | | 11 | | | 1 | | | | | 15 | | 5.00 | 3 50- 3 99 |
| 4 00- 4 49 | | | 1 | 7 | 6 | | | 6 | 3 | | 21 | | | 4 | | | | 13 | 35 | 7.30 | 12.70 | 4 00- 4 49 |
| 4 50- 4 99 | | | | 1 | 5 | | | 3 | | | 7 | 1 | | 1 | | | | 4 | 14 | 9.60 | 15.70 | 4 50- 4 99 |
| 5 00- 5 49 | | | 4 | 5 | 23 | | | 4 | 11 | | 19 | | | 8 | | 3 | | 12 | 65 | 16.30 | 29.90 | 5 00- 5 49 |
| 5 50- 5 99 | | | 1 | 1 | 4 | | | | 1 | | 2 | 2 | | | | | | 1 | 10 | 16.90 | 32.20 | 5 50- 5 99 |
| 6 00- 6 49 | | | 9 | 13 | 45 | | 1 | | 7 | 1 | 33 | 2 | | 7 | | | | 14 | 104 | 24.70 | 54.80 | 6 00- 6 49 |
| 6 50- 6 99 | | | 1 | 3 | 7 | | | | | | 1 | | | | | | | 3 | 9 | 25.40 | 56.80 | 6 50- 6 99 |
| 7 00- 7 49 | | | 10 | 5 | 20 | | 2 | | 1 | | 16 | 6 | | 7 | | | | 5 | 62 | 29.20 | 70.40 | 7 00- 7 49 |
| 7 50- 7 99 | | | 1 | | | | | | | | 1 | | 1 | | | | | 1 | 2 | 29.80 | 70.90 | 7 50- 7 99 |
| 8 00- 8 99 | | 1 | 14 | 5 | 19 | | 2 | | 1 | 1 | 6 | 3 | | 2 | | 2 | | 9 | 47 | 34.80 | 81.10 | 8 00- 8 99 |
| 9 00- 9 99 | | 1 | 7 | 4 | 5 | 1 | 1 | | | 1 | 1 | 1 | | | | 1 | | 8 | 15 | 39.40 | 84.50 | 9 00- 9 99 |
| 10 00-10 99 | | 1 | 9 | 8 | 7 | | 8 | | | 1 | 5 | 2 | | 1 | | 2 | | 12 | 32 | 46.10 | 91.50 | 10 00-10 99 |
| 11 00-11 99 | | | 2 | 2 | 3 | | | | | | | | | | | | | 2 | 5 | 47.20 | 92.50 | 11 00-11 99 |
| 12 00-12 99 | | 11 | 3 | 11 | 2 | | 3 | | | 1 | 2 | | 1 | | | 1 | 1 | 25 | 11 | 61.30 | 95.00 | 12 00-12 99 |
| 13 00-13 99 | | 5 | 1 | 3 | 1 | | 2 | | | 1 | 2 | | | | | | | 9 | 6 | 66.40 | 96.30 | 13 00-13 99 |
| 14 00-14 99 | | 1 | 2 | 3 | 1 | | | | | | | | | | | | 1 | 4 | 4 | 68.50 | 97.10 | 14 00-14 99 |
| 15 00-15 99 | | 5 | 3 | 7 | 2 | | | | | | 3 | | 1 | | | 1 | | 14 | 8 | 76.50 | 98.90 | 15 00-15 99 |
| 16 00-17 99 | | 5 | | 8 | | | | | | 1 | | | | | | 1 | | 15 | | 84.90 | | 16 00-17 99 |
| 18 00-19 99 | | | 1 | 8 | | | | | | | | | | | | 3 | 1 | 11 | 2 | 91.00 | 99.40 | 18 00-19 99 |
| 20 00-24 99 | 1 | | | 3 | 1 | | 1 | | | | | | | | | 2 | 1 | 6 | 3 | 94.50 | 100.00 | 20 00-24 99 |
| 25 00-29 99 | | | | 3 | | | | | | | | | 1 | | | 1 | | 5 | | 97.30 | | 25 00-29 99 |
| 30 00-34 99 | | | | | | | | | | | | | 1 | | | 2 | | 3 | | 99.00 | | 30 0-34 99 |
| 35 00-39 99 | | | | 1 | | | | | | 1 | | | | | | | | 2 | | 100.00 | | 35 00-39 99 |
| Total | 1 | 30 | 69 | 101 | 157 | 1 | 20 | 13 | 25 | 8 | 131 | 17 | 5 | 33 | 1 | 19 | 4 | 178 | 457 | | | Total |

BUFFALO

DEPARTMENT STORES — SHIPPING AND DELIVERY

273. TABLE V, A, 1, c. NUMBER AND PER CENT. OF EMPLOYEES EARNING SPECIFIED WE KLY RATES, BY AGE GROUPS AND SEX

| WEEKLY RATES IN DOLLARS | AGE GROUPS IN YEARS | | | | | | | | | | | | | | WEEKLY RATES IN DOLLARS |
|---|---|---|---|---|---|---|---|---|---|---|---|---|---|---|---|
| | 14–15 | 16–17 | 18–20 | 21–24 | 25–29 | 30–34 | 35–39 | 40–44 | 45–54 | 55–64 | 65 AND OVER | NOT REPORTED | TOTAL | CUMULATIVE PER CENT. OF TOTAL | |
| | Male | Male | Male | Male | Male | Male | Male | Male | Male | Male | Male | Male | Male | Male | |
| $3 50–$3 99... | 6 | .... | .... | .... | .... | .... | .... | .... | .... | .... | .... | .... | 6 | 1.80 | ...$3 50–$3 99 |
| 4 00– 4 49... | 11 | 1 | .... | .... | .... | .... | .... | .... | .... | .... | .... | .... | 12 | 5.30 | ....4 00– 4 49 |
| 4 50– 4 99... | 1 | .... | .... | .... | .... | .... | .... | .... | .... | .... | .... | .... | 1 | 5.60 | ....4 50– 4 99 |
| 5 00– 5 49... | 15 | 68 | 6 | .... | .... | .... | .... | .... | .... | .... | .... | 1 | 90 | 31.90 | ....5 00– 5 49 |
| 6 00– 6 49... | .... | 5 | 1 | .... | .... | .... | .... | .... | .... | .... | .... | .... | 6 | 33.70 | ....6 00– 6 49 |
| 7 00– 7 49... | .... | .... | 4 | 1 | .... | .... | 1 | .... | .... | .... | .... | .... | 6 | 35.40 | ....7 00– 7 49 |
| 8 00– 8 99... | 1 | 1 | 4 | .... | .... | .... | .... | .... | .... | .... | .... | .... | 6 | 37.20 | ....8 00– 8 99 |
| 9 00– 9 99... | .... | .... | 2 | 1 | 1 | .... | .... | .... | .... | 1 | .... | .... | 5 | 38.60 | ....9 00– 9 99 |
| 10 00–10 99... | .... | .... | 1 | 2 | 2 | .... | .... | .... | 2 | .... | 1 | .... | 8 | 41.00 | ...10 00–10 99 |
| 11 00–11 99... | .... | .... | .... | 1 | .... | .... | .... | 2 | 2 | 1 | .... | .... | 6 | 42.70 | ...11 00–11 99 |
| 12 00–12 99... | .... | .... | 1 | 8 | 2 | 5 | 6 | 9 | 9 | 5 | 1 | .... | 46 | 56.20 | ...12 00–12 99 |
| 13 00–13 99... | .... | .... | 1 | 7 | 2 | 1 | .... | 1 | 3 | .... | .... | .... | 15 | 60.60 | ...13 00–13 99 |
| 14 00–14 99... | .... | .... | .... | 1 | 2 | 2 | 2 | .... | .... | .... | 1 | .... | 8 | 62.90 | ...14 00–14 99 |
| 15 00–15 99... | .... | 1 | 1 | 23 | 23 | 16 | 9 | 6 | 8 | .... | .... | .... | 87 | 88.40 | ...15 00–15 99 |
| 16 00–17 99... | .... | .... | .... | 2 | 6 | 10 | 7 | .... | 4 | 1 | .... | .... | 30 | 94.30 | ...16 00–17 99 |
| 18 00–19 99... | .... | .... | .... | 1 | .... | 1 | .... | 2 | 2 | .... | .... | .... | 6 | 99.00 | ...18 00–19 99 |
| 20 00–24 99... | .... | .... | .... | .... | 1 | 1 | 1 | .... | 1 | .... | .... | .... | 4 | 100.00 | ...20 00–24 99 |
| Total..... | 34 | 76 | 21 | 47 | 39 | 36 | 26 | 20 | 31 | 8 | 3 | 1 | 342 | .... | .....Total |

274. TABLE VIII, c

BUFFALO

DEPARTMENT STORES — SHIPPING AND DELIVERY

NUMBER AND PER CENT. OF EMPLOYEES EARNING SPECIFIED WEEKLY RATES, BY OCCUPATION AND SEX

| WEEKLY RATES IN DOLLARS | OCCUPATION | | | | | | | | | WEEKLY RATES IN DOLLARS |
|---|---|---|---|---|---|---|---|---|---|---|
| | FOREMEN | CLERKS AND ROUTERS | DRIVERS | WAGON BOYS AND HELPERS | CHAUFFEURS | PACKING | STABLEMEN | TOTAL | CUMULATIVE PER CENT. OF TOTAL | |
| | Male | Male | Male | Male | Male | Male | Male | Male | Male | |
| $3 50-$3 99 | | | | 6 | | | | 6 | 1.80 | $3 50-$3 99 |
| 4 00- 4 49 | | | | 12 | | | | 12 | 5.30 | 4 00- 4 49 |
| 4 50- 4 99 | | | | 1 | | | | 1 | 5.60 | 4 50- 4 99 |
| 5 00- 5 49 | | 1 | | 89 | | | | 90 | 31.90 | 5 00- 5 49 |
| 6 00- 6 49 | | 2 | | 4 | | | | 6 | 33.70 | 6 00- 6 49 |
| 7 00- 7 49 | | | | 1 | 1 | 4 | | 6 | 35.40 | 7 00- 7 49 |
| 8 00- 8 99 | | 1 | | 1 | | 4 | | 6 | 37.20 | 8 00- 8 99 |
| 9 00- 9 99 | | 4 | | | | 1 | | 5 | 38.60 | 9 00- 9 99 |
| 10 00-10 99 | | 4 | 1 | | | 2 | 1 | 8 | 41.00 | 10 00-10 99 |
| 11 00-11 99 | | | | | | 3 | 3 | 6 | 42.70 | 11 00-11 99 |
| 12 00-12 99 | | 2 | 10 | 4 | | 10 | 20 | 46 | 56.20 | 12 00-12 99 |
| 13 00-13 99 | | | 10 | 1 | | 2 | 2 | 15 | 60.60 | 13 00-13 99 |
| 14 00-14 99 | | 2 | 2 | | | 4 | | 8 | 62.90 | 14 00-14 99 |
| 5 00-15 99 | | 5 | 76 | 1 | 2 | 2 | 1 | 87 | 88.40 | 15 00-15 99 |
| 16 0-17 99 | | 2 | 23 | | 5 | | | 30 | 94.30 | 16 00-17 99 |
| 18 00-19 99 | 1 | 1 | 3 | | | 1 | | 6 | 99.00 | 18 00-19 99 |
| 20 00-24 99 | 1 | 2 | | | | | 1 | 4 | 100.00 | 20 00-24 99 |
| Total | 2 | 26 | 125 | 120 | 8 | 33 | 28 | 342 | ........ | Total |

275. TABLE VI, A, 1, c

BUFFALO

DEPARTMENT STORES — SHIPPING AND DELIVERY

NUMBER AND PER CENT. OF EMPLOYEES CLASSIFIED ACCORDING TO ACTUAL WEEKLY EARNINGS, BY AGE GROUPS AND SEX

| ACTUAL WEEKLY EARNINGS IN DOLLARS | AGE GROUPS IN YEARS | | | | | | | | | | | | | | |
|---|---|---|---|---|---|---|---|---|---|---|---|---|---|---|---|
| | 14–15 | 16–17 | 18–20 | 21–24 | 25–29 | 30–34 | 35–39 | 40–44 | 45–54 | 55–64 | 65 AND OVER | NOT REPORTED | TOTAL | CUMULATIVE PER CENT. OF TOTAL | ACTUAL WEEKLY EARNINGS IN DOLLARS |
| | Male | Male | Male | Male | Male | Male | Male | Male | Male | Male | Male | Male | Male | Male | |
| Less than $3 00 | .... | .... | .... | .... | .... | .... | .... | .... | .... | .... | ...... | 1 | 1 | .30 | Less than $3 00 |
| $3 00–$3 49 | 2 | 1 | .... | .... | .... | .... | .... | .... | .... | .... | ...... | .......... | 3 | 1.20 | $3 00– 3 49 |
| 3 50– 3 99 | 6 | .... | .... | .... | .... | .... | .... | .... | .... | .... | ...... | .......... | 6 | 2.90 | 3 50– 3 99 |
| 4 00– 4 49 | 11 | 4 | 1 | .... | .... | .... | .... | .... | .... | 1 | ...... | .......... | 17 | 7.90 | 4 00– 4 49 |
| 4 50– 4 99 | 1 | .... | .... | .... | .... | .... | .... | .... | .... | .... | ...... | .......... | 1 | 8.20 | 4 50– 4 99 |
| 5 00– 5 49 | 13 | 64 | 5 | .... | .... | .... | .... | .... | .... | .... | ...... | .......... | 82 | 32.20 | 5 00– 5 49 |
| 6 00– 6 49 | .... | 5 | 1 | .... | .... | 1 | .... | .... | .... | .... | ...... | .......... | 7 | 34.20 | 6 00– 6 49 |
| 6 50– 6 99 | .... | .... | .... | 1 | 1 | .... | .... | .... | .... | .... | ...... | .......... | 2 | 34.80 | 6 50– 6 99 |
| 7 00– 7 49 | .... | .... | 4 | 1 | .... | .... | 1 | .... | .... | .... | ...... | .......... | 6 | 36.60 | 7 00– 7 49 |
| 8 00– 8 99 | 1 | 1 | 4 | .... | .... | .... | .... | .... | .... | .... | ...... | .......... | 6 | 38.40 | 8 00– 8 99 |
| 9 00– 9 99 | .... | .... | 2 | 1 | 1 | .... | .... | .... | .... | 1 | ...... | .......... | 5 | 39.80 | 9 00– 9 99 |
| 10 00–10 99 | .... | .... | 1 | 2 | 2 | .... | .... | .... | 2 | .... | 1 | .......... | 8 | 42.20 | 10 00–10 99 |
| 11 00–11 99 | .... | .... | .... | 3 | .... | .... | .... | 2 | 2 | 1 | ...... | .......... | 8 | 44.50 | 11 00–11 99 |
| 12 00–12 99 | .... | .... | 1 | 8 | 2 | 4 | 6 | 9 | 9 | 4 | 1 | .......... | 44 | 57.40 | 12 00–12 99 |
| 13 00–13 99 | .... | .... | 1 | 6 | 1 | 1 | .... | 1 | 2 | .... | ...... | .......... | 12 | 60.90 | 13 00–13 99 |
| 14 00–14 99 | .... | .... | .... | 1 | 2 | 2 | 2 | .... | .... | .... | 1 | .......... | 8 | 63.20 | 14 00–14 99 |
| 15 00–15 99 | .... | 1 | 1 | 21 | 23 | 16 | 10 | 6 | 9 | .... | ...... | .......... | 87 | 87.70 | 15 00–15 99 |
| 16 00–17 99 | .... | .... | .... | 2 | 6 | 10 | 6 | .... | 4 | 1 | ...... | .......... | 29 | 97.20 | 16 00–17 99 |
| 18 00–19 99 | .... | .... | .... | 1 | .... | 1 | .... | 2 | 2 | .... | ...... | .......... | 6 | 99.00 | 18 00–19 99 |
| 20 00–24 99 | .... | .... | .... | .... | 1 | 1 | 1 | .... | 1 | .... | ...... | .......... | 4 | 100.00 | 20 00–24 99 |
| Total | 34 | 76 | 21 | 47 | 39 | 36 | 26 | 20 | 31 | 8 | 3 | 1 | 342 | .......... | Total |

BUFFALO

276. TABLE IX, A, 1, c DEPARTMENT STORES — SHIPPING AND DELIVERY

Number and Per Cent. of Employees Classified According to Actual Weekly Earnings, by Occupation and Sex

| Actual Weekly Earnings in Dollars | Occupation | | | | | | | | | Actual Weekly Earnings in Dollars |
|---|---|---|---|---|---|---|---|---|---|---|
| | Foremen | Clerks and Routers | Drivers | Wagon Boys and Helpers | Chauffeurs | Packing | Stablemen | Total | Cumulative Per Cent. of Total | |
| | Male | Male | Male | Male | Male | Male | Male | Male | Male | |
| Less than $3 00 | ........ | ........ | ........ | 1 | ........ | ........ | ........ | 1 | .30 | Less than $3 00 |
| $3 00–$3 49 | ........ | ........ | ........ | 3 | ........ | ........ | ........ | 3 | 1.20 | $3 00– 3 49 |
| 3 50– 3 99 | ........ | ........ | ........ | 6 | ........ | ........ | ........ | 6 | 2.90 | 3 50– 3 99 |
| 4 00– 4 49 | ........ | ........ | ........ | 16 | ........ | ........ | 1 | 17 | 7.90 | 4 00– 4 49 |
| 4 50– 4 99 | ........ | ........ | ........ | 1 | ........ | ........ | ........ | 1 | 8.20 | 4 50– 4 99 |
| 5 00– 5 49 | ........ | 1 | ........ | 81 | ........ | ........ | ........ | 82 | 32.20 | 5 00– 5 49 |
| 6 00– 6 49 | ........ | 2 | ........ | 5 | ........ | ........ | ........ | 7 | 34.20 | 6 00– 6 49 |
| 6 50– 6 99 | ........ | ........ | 1 | 1 | ........ | ........ | ........ | 2 | 34.80 | 6 50– 6 99 |
| 7 00– 7 49 | ........ | ........ | ........ | 1 | 1 | 4 | ........ | 6 | 36.60 | 7 00– 7 49 |
| 8 00– 8 99 | ........ | 1 | ........ | 1 | ........ | 4 | ........ | 6 | 38.40 | 8 00– 8 99 |
| 9 00– 9 99 | ........ | 4 | ........ | ........ | ........ | 1 | ........ | 5 | 39.80 | 9 00– 9 99 |
| 10 00–10 99 | ........ | 4 | 1 | ........ | ........ | 2 | 1 | 8 | 42.20 | 10 00–10 99 |
| 11 00–11 99 | ........ | ........ | 2 | ........ | ........ | 3 | 3 | 8 | 44.50 | 11 00–11 99 |
| 12 00–12 99 | ........ | 2 | 10 | 3 | ........ | 10 | 19 | 44 | 57.40 | 12 00–12 99 |
| 13 00–13 99 | ........ | ........ | 8 | ........ | 1 | 2 | 1 | 12 | 60.90 | 13 00–13 99 |
| 14 00–14 99 | ........ | 2 | 2 | ........ | ........ | 4 | ........ | 8 | 63.20 | 14 00–14 99 |
| 15 00–15 99 | ........ | 5 | 75 | 1 | 2 | 2 | 2 | 87 | 87.70 | 15 00–15 99 |
| 16 00–17 99 | ........ | 2 | 23 | ........ | 4 | ........ | ........ | 29 | 97.20 | 16 00–17 99 |
| 18 00–19 99 | 1 | 1 | 3 | ........ | ........ | 1 | ........ | 6 | 99.00 | 18 00–19 99 |
| 20 00–24 99 | 1 | 2 | ........ | ........ | ........ | ........ | 1 | 4 | 100.00 | 20 00–24 99 |
| Total | 2 | 26 | 125 | 120 | 8 | 33 | 28 | 342 | .......... | Total |

277. TABLE V, A, 1, d

BUFFALO

**DEPARTMENT STORES — MANUFACTURING**

NUMBER AND PER CENT. OF EMPLOYEES EARNING SPECIFIED WEEKLY RATES, BY AGE GROUPS AND SEX

| Weekly Rates in Dollars | Age Groups in Years | | | | | | | | | | | | | Weekly Rates in Dollars |
|---|---|---|---|---|---|---|---|---|---|---|---|---|---|---|
| | 14–15 | 16–17 | | 18–20 | | 21–24 | | 25–29 | | 30–34 | | 35–39 | | |
| | Male | Male | Female | Male | Female | Male | Female | Male | Female | Male | Female | Male | Female | |
| Less than $3 00 | | | 3 | | | | | | | | | | 1 | Less than $3 00 |
| $3 00–$3 49 | 2 | | 4 | | | | | | | | | | | $3 00– 3 49 |
| 4 00– 4 49 | | | 2 | | | | | | | | | | | 4 00– 4 49 |
| 4 50– 4 99 | | | 1 | | 1 | | | | | | | | | 4 50– 4 99 |
| 5 00– 5 49 | | | 2 | | 10 | | 4 | | | | | | | 5 00– 5 49 |
| 5 50– 5 99 | | | 1 | | 1 | | | | | | | | | 5 50– 5 99 |
| 6 00– 6 49 | | | 1 | | 14 | | 5 | | 5 | | 1 | | 3 | 6 00– 6 49 |
| 6 50– 6 99 | | | | | 1 | | 2 | | | | | | | 6 50– 6 99 |
| 7 00– 7 49 | | 1 | | | 5 | | 22 | 1 | 14 | | 7 | | 11 | 7 00– 7 49 |
| 7 50– 7 99 | | | | | 2 | | 1 | 1 | 3 | 1 | 2 | | 4 | 7 50– 7 99 |
| 8 00– 8 99 | | | | | 3 | 2 | 12 | | 8 | | 7 | | 13 | 8 00– 8 99 |
| 9 00– 9 99 | | | | | | 1 | 4 | | 9 | | 3 | | 5 | 9 00– 9 99 |
| 10 00–10 99 | | | | 1 | | | 3 | | 5 | | 3 | | 4 | 10 00–10 99 |
| 11 00–11 99 | | | | | | | | | 2 | | | 1 | | 11 00–11 99 |
| 12 00–12 99 | | | | | | 4 | 2 | 2 | 5 | | 2 | | 4 | 12 00–12 99 |
| 13 00–13 99 | | | | 1 | | 1 | | 2 | 1 | 3 | 2 | 1 | | 13 00–13 99 |
| 14 00–14 99 | | | | | | 2 | | 1 | 1 | | 2 | 2 | 3 | 14 00–14 99 |
| 15 00–15 99 | | | | | | 2 | | 3 | 1 | 1 | 1 | 2 | 2 | 15 00–15 99 |
| 16 00–17 99 | | | | | | | | | | 4 | | 3 | 1 | 16 00–17 99 |
| 18 00–19 99 | | | | | | 4 | 1 | 5 | | 6 | | 2 | | 18 00–19 99 |
| 20 00–24 99 | | | | | | | | | 1 | | | | 2 | 20 00–24 99 |
| 25 00–29 99 | | | | | | | | | | | 1 | | 1 | 25 00–29 99 |
| 30 00–34 99 | | | | | | | | | | | 1 | | | 30 00–34 99 |
| 35 00–39 99 | | | | | | | | 1 | | | | | 1 | 35 00–39 99 |
| 40 00 and over | | | | | | | | | | | 1 | | | 40 00 and over |
| Total | 2 | 1 | 14 | 2 | 37 | 16 | 56 | 16 | 55 | 15 | 33 | 11 | 55 | Total |

277. TABLE V, A, 1, d — (*concluded*)

BUFFALO

DEPARTMENT STORES — MANUFACTURING

NUMBER AND PER CENT. OF EMPLOYEES EARNING SPECIFIED WEEKLY RATES, BY AGE GROUPS AND SEX

| WEEKLY RATES IN DOLLARS | AGE GROUPS IN YEARS (*concluded*) 40–44 | | 45–54 | | 55–64 | | 65 AND OVER | | NOT REPORTED | | TOTAL | | CUMULATIVE PER CENT. OF TOTAL | | WEEKLY RATES IN DOLLARS |
|---|---|---|---|---|---|---|---|---|---|---|---|---|---|---|---|
| | Male | Female | Male | Female | Male | Female | Male | Female | Male | Female | Male | Female | Male | Female | |
| Less than $3 00 | .... | .... | .... | .... | .... | .... | .... | .... | .... | .... | .... | 4 | .... | 1.30 | Less than $3 00 |
| $3 00–$3 49 | .... | .... | .... | .... | .... | .... | .... | .... | .... | .... | .... | 6 | .... | 3.20 | $3 00– 3 49 |
| 4 00– 4 49 | .... | .... | .... | .... | .... | .... | .... | .... | .... | .... | .... | 2 | .... | 3.90 | 4 00– 4 49 |
| 4 50– 4 99 | .... | .... | .... | .... | .... | .... | .... | .... | .... | .... | .... | 2 | .... | 4.50 | 4 50– 4 99 |
| 5 00– 5 49 | .... | .... | .... | .... | .... | .... | .... | .... | .... | .... | .... | 16 | .... | 9.70 | 5 00– 5 49 |
| 5 50– 5 99 | .... | .... | .... | .... | .... | .... | .... | .... | .... | .... | .... | 2 | .... | 10.30 | 5 50– 5 99 |
| 6 00– 6 49 | .... | .... | .... | 2 | .... | .... | .... | 1 | .... | 1 | .... | 33 | .... | 21.10 | 6 00– 6 49 |
| 6 50– 6 99 | .... | .... | .... | .... | .... | .... | .... | .... | .... | .... | .... | 3 | .... | 21.90 | 6 50– 6 99 |
| 7 00– 7 49 | 1 | 3 | 1 | 5 | .... | .... | .... | .... | .... | 1 | 4 | 68 | 3.70 | 43.90 | 7 00– 7 49 |
| 7 50– 7 99 | .... | .... | .... | 1 | .... | .... | .... | .... | .... | .... | 2 | 13 | 5.50 | 48.10 | 7 50– 7 99 |
| 8 00– 8 99 | 1 | 4 | .... | 5 | .... | 1 | .... | .... | .... | 6 | 3 | 59 | 8.30 | 67.10 | 8 00– 8 99 |
| 9 00– 9 99 | .... | .... | .... | 1 | .... | .... | .... | .... | .... | 2 | 1 | 24 | 9.20 | 75.00 | 9 00– 9 99 |
| 10 00–10 99 | .... | 2 | .... | 5 | .... | 1 | .... | .... | .... | 3 | 1 | 26 | 10.10 | 83.40 | 10 00–10 99 |
| 11 00–11 99 | 1 | .... | .... | 1 | 1 | .... | .... | .... | .... | .... | 3 | 3 | 12.90 | 84.20 | 11 00–11 99 |
| 12 00–12 99 | .... | 1 | 1 | 1 | 1 | 1 | 1 | .... | .... | .... | 9 | 16 | 21.10 | 89.50 | 12 00–12 99 |
| 13 00–13 99 | .... | 1 | .... | .... | .... | .... | .... | .... | .... | .... | 8 | 4 | 28.50 | 98.80 | 13 00–13 99 |
| 14 00–14 99 | 1 | .... | 2 | 2 | .... | .... | .... | .... | 1 | .... | 9 | 8 | 36.80 | 93.30 | 14 00–14 99 |
| 15 00–15 99 | 2 | 3 | 3 | 1 | 1 | .... | 1 | .... | 1 | 2 | 16 | 10 | 51.40 | 96.50 | 15 00–15 99 |
| 16 00–17 99 | 4 | .... | 3 | .... | 3 | .... | .... | .... | .... | .... | 17 | 1 | 67.00 | 96.90 | 16 00–17 99 |
| 18 00–19 99 | 2 | .... | 5 | .... | 2 | .... | .... | .... | .... | .... | 26 | 1 | 90.90 | 97.20 | 18 00–19 99 |
| 20 00–24 99 | 1 | 1 | 5 | .... | .... | .... | .... | .... | .... | .... | 6 | 4 | 96.30 | 98.50 | 20 00–24 99 |
| 25 00–29 99 | .... | .... | 1 | .... | 1 | .... | .... | .... | .... | .... | 2 | 2 | 98.20 | 99.10 | 25 00–29 99 |
| 30 00–34 99 | .... | .... | .... | .... | .... | .... | .... | .... | .... | .... | .... | 1 | .... | 99.50 | 30 00–34 99 |
| 35 00–39 99 | 1 | .... | .... | .... | .... | .... | .... | .... | .... | .... | 2 | 1 | 100.00 | 99.80 | 35 00–39 99 |
| 40 00 and over | .... | .... | .... | .... | .... | .... | .... | .... | .... | .... | .... | 1 | .... | 100.00 | 40 00 and over |
| Total | 14 | 15 | 21 | 24 | 9 | 3 | 2 | 1 | 2 | 15 | 109 | 310 | .... | .... | Total |

278. TABLE VIII, A, 1, d

BUFFALO

DEPARTMENT STORES — MANUFACTURING

NUMBER AND PER CENT. OF EMPLOYEES EARNING SPECIFIED WEEKLY RATES, BY OCCUPATION AND SEX

| WEEKLY RATES IN DOLLARS | OCCUPATION | | | | | | | | | | | | | WEEKLY RATES IN DOLLARS |
|---|---|---|---|---|---|---|---|---|---|---|---|---|---|---|
| | SEWING | | HOUSE FURNISHING | | CABINET WORK, FRAMING | PHOTO-GRAVURES, PRINTING | METAL WORK, JEWELRY, GLASS WORK | SHOE REPAIRING, BUCKLES, ETC. | | TOTAL | | CUMULATIVE PER CENT. OF TOTAL | | |
| | Male | Female | Male | Female | Male | Female | Male | Male | Female | Male | Female | Male | Female | |
| Less than $3 00 | .... | 4 | .... | ...... | ........ | ......... | ......... | ...... | ...... | .... | 4 | ...... | 1.30 | Less than $3 00 |
| $3 00–$3 49 | .... | 6 | .... | ...... | ........ | ......... | ......... | ...... | ...... | .... | 6 | ...... | 3.20 | $3 00– 3 49 |
| 4 00– 4 49 | .... | 2 | .... | ...... | ........ | ......... | ......... | ...... | ...... | .... | 2 | ...... | 3.90 | 4 00– 4 49 |
| 4 50– 4 99 | .... | 2 | .... | ...... | ........ | ......... | ......... | ...... | ...... | .... | 2 | ...... | 4.50 | 4 50– 4 99 |
| 5 00– 5 49 | .... | 16 | .... | ...... | ........ | ......... | ......... | ...... | ...... | .... | 16 | ...... | 9.70 | 5 00– 5 49 |
| 5 50– 5 99 | .... | 2 | .... | ...... | ........ | ......... | ......... | ...... | ...... | .... | 2 | ...... | 10.30 | 5 50– 5 99 |
| 6 00– 6 49 | .... | 33 | .... | ...... | ........ | ......... | ......... | ...... | ...... | .... | 33 | ...... | 21.00 | 6 00– 6 49 |
| 6 50– 6 99 | .... | 3 | .... | ...... | ........ | ......... | ......... | ...... | ...... | .... | 3 | ...... | 21.90 | 6 50– 6 99 |
| 7 00– 7 49 | .... | 66 | 4 | 2 | ........ | ......... | ......... | ...... | ...... | 4 | 68 | 3.70 | 43.90 | 7 00– 7 49 |
| 7 50– 7 99 | .... | 10 | 2 | 3 | ........ | ......... | ......... | ...... | ...... | 2 | 13 | 5.50 | 48.10 | 7 50– 7 99 |
| 8 00– 8 99 | 1 | 59 | 1 | ...... | 1 | ......... | ......... | ...... | ...... | 3 | 59 | 8.30 | 67.10 | 8 00– 8 99 |
| 9 00– 9 99 | .... | 24 | .... | ...... | 1 | ......... | ......... | ...... | ...... | 1 | 24 | 9.20 | 75.00 | 9 00– 9 99 |
| 10 00–10 99 | .... | 23 | .... | 2 | 1 | 1 | ......... | ...... | ...... | 1 | 26 | 10.10 | 83.40 | 10 00–10 99 |
| 11 00–11 99 | 1 | 3 | 1 | ...... | ........ | ......... | ......... | 1 | ...... | 3 | 3 | 12.90 | 84.20 | 11 00–11 99 |
| 12 00–12 99 | 1 | 15 | 2 | 1 | 3 | ......... | 1 | 2 | ...... | 9 | 16 | 21.10 | 89.50 | 12 00–12 99 |
| 13 00–13 99 | 2 | 4 | 3 | ...... | 3 | ......... | ......... | ...... | ...... | 8 | 4 | 28.50 | 90.80 | 13 00–13 99 |
| 14 00–14 99 | 4 | 8 | 3 | ...... | 1 | ......... | ......... | 1 | ...... | 9 | 8 | 36.80 | 93.30 | 14 00–14 99 |
| 15 00–15 99 | 5 | 10 | 7 | ...... | 3 | ......... | ......... | 1 | ...... | 16 | 10 | 51.40 | 96.50 | 15 00–15 99 |
| 16 00–17 99 | 4 | 1 | 6 | ...... | 7 | ......... | ......... | ...... | ...... | 17 | 1 | 67.00 | 96.90 | 16 00–17 99 |
| 18 00–19 99 | 2 | 1 | 23 | ...... | 1 | ......... | ......... | ...... | ...... | 26 | 1 | 90.90 | 97.20 | 18 00–19 99 |
| 20 00–24 99 | 1 | 4 | 5 | ...... | ........ | ......... | ......... | ...... | ...... | 6 | 4 | 96.30 | 98.50 | 20 00–24 99 |
| 25 00–29 99 | .... | 2 | 2 | ...... | ........ | ......... | ......... | ...... | ...... | 2 | 2 | 98.20 | 99.10 | 25 00–29 99 |
| 30 00–34 99 | .... | 1 | .... | ...... | ........ | ......... | ......... | ...... | ...... | .... | 1 | ...... | 99.50 | 30 00–34 99 |
| 35 00–39 99 | 1 | 1 | 1 | ...... | ........ | ......... | ......... | ...... | ...... | 2 | 1 | 100.00 | 99.80 | 35 00–39 99 |
| 40 00 and over | .... | 1 | .... | ...... | ........ | ......... | ......... | ...... | ...... | .... | 1 | ...... | 100.00 | 40 00 and over |
| Total | 22 | 301 | 60 | 8 | 21 | 1 | 1 | 5 | ...... | 109 | 310 | ...... | ...... | Total |

279. TABLE VI, A, 1, d

BUFFALO

**DEPARTMENT STORES — MANUFACTURING**

NUMBER AND PER CENT. OF EMPLOYEES CLASSIFIED ACCORDING TO ACTUAL WEEKLY EARNINGS, BY AGE GROUPS AND SEX

| ACTUAL WEEKLY EARNINGS IN DOLLARS | AGE GROUPS IN YEARS | | | | | | | | | | | | | ACTUAL WEEKLY EARNINGS IN DOLLARS |
|---|---|---|---|---|---|---|---|---|---|---|---|---|---|---|
| | 14–15 | 16–17 | | 18–20 | | 21–24 | | 25–29 | | 30–34 | | 35–39 | | |
| | Female | Male | Female | Male | Female | Male | Female | Male | Female | Male | Female | Male | Female | |
| Less than $3 00 | ...... | ...... | 3 | ...... | ...... | ...... | ...... | ...... | ...... | ...... | ...... | ...... | 1 | Less than $3 00 |
| $3 00–$3 49 | 2 | ...... | 4 | ...... | 1 | ...... | ...... | ...... | ...... | ...... | ...... | ...... | ...... | $3 00– 3 49 |
| 4 00– 4 49 | ...... | ...... | 2 | ...... | 1 | ...... | 1 | ...... | ...... | ...... | ...... | ...... | ...... | 4 00– 4 49 |
| 4 50– 4 99 | ...... | ...... | 1 | ...... | 1 | ...... | ...... | ...... | ...... | ...... | ...... | ...... | ...... | 4 50– 4 99 |
| 5 00– 5 49 | ...... | ...... | 2 | ...... | 12 | ...... | 5 | ...... | ...... | ...... | 1 | ...... | ...... | 5 00– 5 49 |
| 5 50– 5 99 | ...... | ...... | 1 | ...... | 3 | ...... | 3 | ...... | 1 | ...... | ...... | ...... | 3 | 5 50– 5 99 |
| 6 00– 6 49 | ...... | ...... | 1 | ...... | 10 | 1 | 2 | ...... | 5 | ...... | 1 | ...... | 4 | 6 00– 6 49 |
| 6 50– 6 99 | ...... | ...... | ...... | ...... | ...... | ...... | 2 | ...... | 1 | ...... | ...... | ...... | ...... | 6 50– 6 99 |
| 7 00– 7 49 | ...... | 1 | ...... | ...... | 5 | ...... | 20 | 1 | 13 | ...... | 7 | ...... | 9 | 7 00– 7 49 |
| 7 50– 7 99 | ...... | ...... | ...... | ...... | 2 | ...... | 1 | 1 | 3 | 1 | 2 | ...... | 4 | 7 50– 7 99 |
| 8 00– 8 99 | ...... | ...... | ...... | ...... | 2 | 2 | 12 | ...... | 9 | ...... | 6 | ...... | 11 | 8 00– 8 99 |
| 9 00– 9 99 | ...... | ...... | ...... | ...... | ...... | 1 | 4 | ...... | 9 | ...... | 3 | ...... | 5 | 9 00– 9 99 |
| 10 00–10 99 | ...... | ...... | ...... | 1 | ...... | ...... | 3 | ...... | 4 | ...... | 3 | ...... | 4 | 10 00–10 99 |
| 11 00–11 99 | ...... | ...... | ...... | ...... | ...... | ...... | ...... | ...... | 2 | ...... | ...... | 1 | ...... | 11 00–11 99 |
| 12 00–12 99 | ...... | ...... | ...... | ...... | ...... | 3 | 2 | 3 | 4 | ...... | 2 | ...... | 4 | 12 00–12 99 |
| 13 00–13 99 | ...... | ...... | ...... | 1 | ...... | 2 | ...... | 2 | 1 | 3 | 2 | 1 | ...... | 13 00–13 99 |
| 14 00–14 99 | ...... | ...... | ...... | ...... | ...... | 2 | ...... | 1 | 1 | ...... | 2 | 2 | 3 | 14 00–14 99 |
| 15 00–15 99 | ...... | ...... | ...... | ...... | ...... | 2 | ...... | 2 | 1 | 1 | 1 | 2 | 2 | 15 00–15 99 |
| 16 00–17 99 | ...... | ...... | ...... | ...... | ...... | ...... | ...... | ...... | ...... | 4 | ...... | 3 | 1 | 16 00–17 99 |
| 18 00–19 99 | ...... | ...... | ...... | ...... | ...... | 3 | 1 | 5 | ...... | 5 | ...... | 2 | ...... | 18 00–19 99 |
| 20 00–24 99 | ...... | ...... | ...... | ...... | ...... | ...... | ...... | ...... | 1 | 1 | ...... | ...... | 2 | 20 00–24 99 |
| 25 00–29 99 | ...... | ...... | ...... | ...... | ...... | ...... | ...... | ...... | ...... | ...... | 1 | ...... | 1 | 25 00–29 99 |
| 30 00–34 99 | ...... | ...... | ...... | ...... | ...... | ...... | ...... | ...... | ...... | ...... | 1 | ...... | ...... | 30 00–34 99 |
| 35 00–39 99 | ...... | ...... | ...... | ...... | ...... | ...... | ...... | 1 | ...... | ...... | ...... | ...... | 1 | 35 00–39 99 |
| 40 00 and over | ...... | ...... | ...... | ...... | ...... | ...... | ...... | ...... | ...... | ...... | 1 | ...... | ...... | 40 00 and over |
| Total | 2 | 1 | 14 | 2 | 37 | 16 | 56 | 16 | 55 | 15 | 33 | 11 | 55 | Total |

BUFFALO

279. TABLE VI, A, 1, d

DEPARTMENT STORES — MANUFACTURING

NUMBER AND PER CENT. OF EMPLOYEES CLASSIFIED ACCORDING TO ACTUAL WEEKLY EARNINGS, BY AGE GROUPS AND SEX

| ACTUAL WEEKLY EARNINGS IN DOLLARS | AGE GROUPS IN YEARS (concluded) | | | | | | | | | | | | | | ACTUAL WEEKLY EARNINGS IN DOLLARS |
|---|---|---|---|---|---|---|---|---|---|---|---|---|---|---|---|
| | 40–44 | | 45–54 | | 55–64 | | 65 AND OVER | | NOT REPORTED | | TOTAL | | CUMULATIVE PER CENT. OF TOTAL | | |
| | Male | Female | Male | Female | Male | Female | Male | Female | Male | Female | Male | Female | Male | Female | |
| Less than $3 00 | .... | ...... | .... | ...... | ...... | ...... | ...... | ...... | ...... | ...... | ...... | 4 | ...... | 1.29 | Less than $3 00 |
| $3 00–$3 49... | .... | ...... | .... | ...... | ...... | ...... | ...... | ...... | ...... | ...... | ...... | 7 | ...... | 3.54 | ...$3 00– 3 49 |
| 3 50– 3 99... | .... | ...... | 1 | ...... | ...... | ...... | ...... | ...... | ...... | ...... | 1 | ...... | .92 | ...... | ... 3 50– 3 99 |
| 4 00– 4 49... | .... | ...... | .... | ...... | ...... | ...... | ...... | ...... | ...... | ...... | ...... | 4 | ...... | 4.84 | ... 4 00– 4 49 |
| 4 50– 4 99... | .... | ...... | .... | ...... | ...... | ...... | ...... | ...... | ...... | ...... | ...... | 2 | ...... | 5.48 | ... 4 50– 4 99 |
| 5 00– 5 49... | .... | ...... | .... | ...... | ...... | ...... | ...... | ...... | ...... | ...... | ...... | 20 | ...... | 11.94 | ... 5 00– 5 49 |
| 5 50– 5 99... | .... | ...... | .... | 2 | ...... | ...... | ...... | ...... | ...... | ...... | ...... | 13 | ...... | 16.30 | ... 5 50– 5 99 |
| 6 00– 6 49... | .... | ...... | .... | 2 | ...... | ...... | ...... | 1 | ...... | 1 | 1 | 27 | 1.84 | 24.85 | ... 6 00– 6 49 |
| 6 50– 6 99... | .... | ...... | .... | 1 | ...... | ...... | ...... | ...... | ...... | ...... | ...... | 4 | ...... | 26.15 | ... 6 50– 6 99 |
| 7 00– 7 49... | 1 | 3 | .... | 3 | ...... | ...... | ...... | ...... | ...... | 1 | 3 | 61 | 4.60 | 45.80 | ... 7 00– 7 49 |
| 7 50– 7 99... | .... | ...... | .... | 1 | ...... | ...... | ...... | ...... | ...... | ...... | 2 | 13 | 6.43 | 50.00 | ... 7 50– 7 99 |
| 8 00– 8 99... | 1 | 4 | .... | 4 | ...... | 1 | ...... | ...... | ...... | 6 | 3 | 55 | 9.18 | 67.80 | ... 8 00– 8 99 |
| 9 00– 9 99... | .... | ...... | .... | 1 | ...... | ...... | ...... | ...... | ...... | 2 | 1 | 24 | 10.10 | 76.90 | ... 9 00– 9 99 |
| 10 00–10 99... | .... | 2 | .... | 5 | ...... | 1 | ...... | ...... | ...... | 3 | 1 | 25 | 11 00 | 83.50 | ...10 00–10 99 |
| 11 00–11 99... | 1 | ...... | .... | 1 | 1 | ...... | ...... | ...... | 1 | ...... | 4 | 3 | 14.70 | 84.50 | ...11 00–11 99 |
| 12 00–12 99... | .... | 1 | 1 | 1 | 1 | 1 | 1 | ...... | 1 | ...... | 10 | 15 | 23.85 | 89.50 | ...12 00–12 99 |
| 13 00–13 99... | .... | 1 | .... | 1 | ...... | ...... | ...... | ...... | ...... | ...... | 9 | 5 | 32.18 | 91.00 | ...13 00–13 99 |
| 14 00–14 99... | 1 | ...... | 2 | 1 | ...... | ...... | ...... | ...... | ...... | ...... | 8 | 7 | 39.50 | 93.30 | ...14 00–14 99 |
| 15 00–15 99... | 2 | 3 | 3 | 1 | 1 | ...... | 1 | ...... | ...... | 2 | 14 | 10 | 52.30 | 96.50 | ...15 00–15 99 |
| 16 00–17 99... | 4 | ...... | 3 | ...... | 3 | ...... | ...... | ...... | ...... | ...... | 17 | 1 | 68 00 | 96.95 | ...16 00–17 99 |
| 18 00–19 99... | 2 | ...... | 5 | ...... | 2 | ...... | ...... | ...... | ...... | ...... | 24 | 1 | 90.00 | 97.00 | ...18 00–19 99 |
| 20 00–24 99... | 1 | 1 | 5 | ...... | ...... | ...... | ...... | ...... | ...... | ...... | 7 | 4 | 96.40 | 98.50 | ...20 00–24 99 |
| 25 00–29 99... | .... | ...... | 1 | ...... | 1 | ...... | ...... | ...... | ...... | ...... | 2 | 2 | 98.20 | 99.00 | ...25 00–29 99 |
| 30 00–34 99... | .... | ...... | .... | ...... | ...... | ...... | ...... | ...... | ...... | ...... | ...... | 1 | ...... | 99.40 | ...30 00–34 99 |
| 35 00–39 99... | 1 | ...... | .... | ...... | ...... | ...... | ...... | ...... | ...... | ...... | 2 | 1 | 100.00 | 99.70 | ...35 00–39 99 |
| 40 00 and over. | .... | ...... | .... | ...... | ...... | ...... | ...... | ...... | ...... | ...... | ...... | 1 | ...... | 100.00 | .40 00 and over |
| Total.... | 14 | 15 | 21 | 24 | 9 | 3 | 2 | 1 | 2 | 15 | 109 | 310 | ...... | ...... | .....Total |

280. TABLE IX, A, 1, d

BUFFALO

**DEPARTMENT STORES — MANUFACTURING**

NUMBER AND PER CENT. OF EMPLOYEES CLASSIFIED ACCORDING TO ACTUAL WEEKLY EARNINGS, BY OCCUPATION AND SEX

| ACTUAL WEEKLY EARNINGS IN DOLLARS | OCCUPATION | | | | | | | | | | | | | ACTUAL WEEKLY EARNINGS IN DOLLARS |
|---|---|---|---|---|---|---|---|---|---|---|---|---|---|---|
| | SEWING | | HOUSE FURNISHING | | CABINET WORK, FRAMING | PHOTO-GRAVURES, PRINTING | METAL WORK, JEWELRY, GLASS WORK | SHOE REPAIRING, BUCKLES | CANDY MAKING | TOTAL | | CUMULATIVE PER CENT. OF TOTAL | | |
| | Male | Female | Male | Female | Male | Female | Male | Male | Male | Male | Female | Male | Female | |
| Less than $3 00 | | 4 | | | | | | | | | 4 | | 1.29 | Less than $3 00 |
| $3 00–$3 49 | | 7 | | | | | | | | | 7 | | 3.54 | $3 00– 3 49 |
| 3 50– 3 99 | | | 1 | | | | | | | 1 | | .92 | | 3 50– 3 99 |
| 4 00– 4 49 | | 4 | | | | | | | | | 4 | | 4.84 | 4 00– 4 49 |
| 4 50– 4 99 | | 2 | | | | | | | | | 2 | | 5.48 | 4 50– 4 99 |
| 5 00– 5 49 | | 20 | | | | | | | | | 20 | | 11.94 | 5 00– 5 49 |
| 5 50– 5 99 | | 13 | | | | | | | | | 13 | | 16.30 | 5 50– 5 99 |
| 6 00– 6 49 | | 27 | 1 | | | | | | | 1 | 27 | 1.84 | 24.85 | 6 00– 6 49 |
| 6 50– 6 99 | | 4 | | | | | | | | | 4 | | 26.15 | 6 50– 6 99 |
| 7 00– 7 49 | | 59 | 3 | 2 | | | | | | 3 | 61 | 4.60 | 45.80 | 7 00– 7 49 |
| 7 50– 7 99 | | 10 | 2 | 3 | | | | | | 2 | 13 | 6.43 | 50.00 | 7 50– 7 99 |
| 8 00– 8 99 | 1 | 55 | 1 | | 1 | | | | | 3 | 55 | 9.18 | 67.80 | 8 00– 8 99 |
| 9 00– 9 99 | | 24 | | | 1 | | | | | 1 | 24 | 10.10 | 76.90 | 9 00– 9 99 |
| 10 00–10 99 | | 22 | | 2 | 1 | 1 | | | | 1 | 25 | 11.00 | 83.50 | 10 00–10 99 |
| 11 00–11 99 | 1 | 3 | 2 | | | | | 1 | | 4 | 3 | 14.70 | 84.50 | 11 00–11 99 |
| 12 00–12 99 | 2 | 14 | 1 | 1 | 3 | | 1 | 2 | 1 | 10 | 15 | 23.85 | 89.50 | 12 00–12 99 |
| 13 00–13 99 | 2 | 5 | 4 | | 3 | | | | | 9 | 5 | 32.18 | 91.00 | 13 00–13 99 |
| 14 00–14 99 | 4 | 7 | 2 | | 1 | | | 1 | | 8 | 7 | 39.50 | 93.30 | 14 00–14 99 |
| 15 00–15 99 | 4 | 10 | 7 | | 3 | | | | | 14 | 10 | 52.30 | 96.50 | 15 00–15 99 |
| 16 00–17 99 | 4 | 1 | 6 | | 7 | | | | | 17 | 1 | 68.00 | 96.95 | 16 00–17 99 |
| 18 00–19 99 | 2 | 1 | 21 | | 1 | | | | | 24 | 1 | 90 00 | 97.00 | 18 00–19 99 |
| 20 00–24 99 | 1 | 4 | 6 | | | | | | | 7 | 4 | 96.40 | 98.50 | 20 00–24 99 |
| 25 00–29 99 | | 2 | 2 | | | | | | | 2 | 2 | 98.20 | 99.00 | 25 00–29 99 |
| 30 00–34 99 | | 1 | | | | | | | | | 1 | | 99.40 | 30 00–34 99 |
| 35 00–39 99 | 1 | 1 | 1 | | | | | | | 2 | 1 | 100.00 | 99.70 | 35 00–39 99 |
| 40 00 and over | | 1 | | | | | | | | | 1 | | 100.00 | 40 00 and over |
| Total | 22 | 301 | 60 | 8 | 21 | 1 | 1 | 4 | 1 | 109 | 310 | | | Total |

BUFFALO

DEPARTMENT STORES — PLANT

281. TABLE V, A, 1, c — NUMBER AND PER CENT. OF EMPLOYEES EARNING SPECIFIED WEEKLY RATES, BY AGE GROUPS AND SEX

| WEEKLY RATES IN DOLLARS | AGE GROUPS IN YEARS | | | | | | | | | | | | | WEEKLY RATES IN DOLLARS |
|---|---|---|---|---|---|---|---|---|---|---|---|---|---|---|
| | 14–15 | 16–17 | | 18–20 | | 21–24 | | 25–29 | | 30–34 | | 35–39 | | |
| | Female | Male | Female | Male | Female | Male | Female | Male | Female | Male | Female | Male | Female | |
| $3 00–$3 49 | ...... | ...... | 1 | ...... | 4 | ...... | 13 | ...... | 11 | ...... | 9 | ...... | 9 | $3 00–$3 49 |
| 3 50– 3 99 | 1 | ...... | ...... | ...... | 2 | ...... | 2 | ...... | 2 | ...... | 1 | ...... | 2 | 3 50– 3 99 |
| 4 00– 4 49 | ...... | 1 | ...... | ...... | ...... | ...... | ...... | 1 | ...... | ...... | 1 | ...... | ...... | 4 00– 4 49 |
| 4 50– 4 99 | ...... | ...... | ...... | ...... | 1 | ...... | ...... | ...... | ...... | ...... | ...... | ...... | ...... | 4 50– 4 99 |
| 5 00– 5 49 | ...... | 1 | 2 | ...... | 8 | ...... | 11 | ...... | 8 | ...... | 6 | ...... | 4 | 5 00– 5 49 |
| 6 00– 6 49 | ...... | 1 | 1 | ...... | 11 | ...... | 11 | ...... | 5 | ...... | 8 | ...... | 5 | 6 00– 6 49 |
| 7 00– 7 49 | ...... | 1 | ...... | 1 | ...... | ...... | 1 | ...... | 3 | ...... | 3 | ...... | 2 | 7 00– 7 49 |
| 7 50– 7 99 | ...... | ...... | ...... | ...... | ...... | ...... | ...... | ...... | 1 | ...... | 1 | ...... | ...... | 7 50– 7 99 |
| 8 00– 8 99 | ...... | 2 | ...... | ...... | ...... | ...... | 1 | ...... | ...... | ...... | 2 | ...... | 1 | 8 00– 8 99 |
| 9 00– 9 99 | ...... | ...... | ...... | 3 | ...... | 1 | 2 | 1 | 1 | 1 | 1 | ...... | 1 | 9 00– 9 99 |
| 10 00–10 99 | ...... | ...... | ...... | 1 | ...... | 7 | ...... | 4 | 1 | 1 | 1 | 2 | ...... | 10 00–10 99 |
| 11 00–11 99 | ...... | ...... | ...... | ...... | ...... | 3 | ...... | ...... | ...... | 1 | 1 | 1 | 1 | 11 00–11 99 |
| 12 00–12 99 | ...... | ...... | ...... | 2 | ...... | 17 | ...... | 12 | ...... | 10 | ...... | 6 | ...... | 12 00–12 99 |
| 13 00–13 99 | ...... | ...... | ...... | ...... | ...... | 1 | ...... | 1 | ...... | 1 | ...... | 1 | ...... | 13 00–13 99 |
| 14 00–14 99 | ...... | ...... | ...... | ...... | ...... | ...... | ...... | ...... | ...... | ...... | ...... | 2 | ...... | 14 00–14 99 |
| 15 00–15 99 | ...... | ...... | ...... | ...... | ...... | ...... | ...... | 4 | ...... | 6 | ...... | 1 | 1 | 15 00–15 99 |
| 16 00–17 99 | ...... | ...... | ...... | ...... | ...... | ...... | ...... | 4 | ...... | 3 | ...... | 1 | ...... | 16 00–17 99 |
| 18 00–19 00 | ...... | ...... | ...... | ...... | ...... | ...... | ...... | 1 | ...... | 3 | ...... | 2 | ...... | 18 00–19 99 |
| 20 00–24 99 | ...... | ...... | ...... | ...... | ...... | ...... | ...... | 2 | ...... | ...... | ...... | 2 | ...... | 20 00–24 99 |
| 25 00–29 99 | ...... | ...... | ...... | ...... | ...... | ...... | ...... | ...... | ...... | 1 | ...... | ...... | ...... | 25 00–29 99 |
| Not reported | ...... | ...... | ...... | ...... | ...... | ...... | ...... | 1 | ...... | 2 | ...... | ...... | ...... | Not reported |
| Total | 1 | 6 | 4 | 7 | 26 | 29 | 41 | 31 | 32 | 29 | 34 | 18 | 26 | Total |

281. TABLE V, A, 1, c — (*concluded*)

BUFFALO

**DEPARTMENT STORES — PLANT**

NUMBER AND PER CENT. OF EMPLOYEES EARNING SPECIFIED WEEKLY RATES, BY AGE GROUPS AND SEX

| Weekly Rates in Dollars | Age Groups in Years (*concluded*) | | | | | | | | | | | | Weekly Rates in Dollars |
|---|---|---|---|---|---|---|---|---|---|---|---|---|---|
| | 40–44 | | 45–54 | | 55–64 | | 65 and over | Not reported | Total | | Cumulative per cent. of total | | |
| | Male | Female | Male | Female | Male | Female | Male | Male | Male | Female | Male | Female | |
| $3 00–$3 49.... | ....... | 2 | ....... | 1 | ....... | ....... | ....... | ....... | ....... | 50 | ....... | 23.50 | ...$3 00–$3 49 |
| 3 50– 3 99.... | ....... | ....... | ....... | ....... | ....... | ....... | ....... | ....... | ....... | 10 | ....... | 28.20 | ... 3 50– 3 99 |
| 4 00– 4 49.... | ....... | ....... | ....... | ....... | ....... | ....... | ....... | ....... | 2 | 1 | .80 | 28.60 | ... 4 00– 4 49 |
| 4 50– 4 99.... | ....... | ....... | ....... | ....... | ....... | ....... | ....... | ....... | ....... | 1 | ....... | 29.10 | ... 4 50– 4 99 |
| 5 00– 5 49.... | ....... | 4 | ....... | 6 | ....... | ....... | ....... | ....... | 1 | 49 | 1.20 | 52.10 | ... 5 00– 5 49 |
| 6 00– 6 49.... | ....... | 3 | ....... | 8 | ....... | ....... | ....... | ....... | 1 | 52 | 1.60 | 71.50 | ... 6 00– 6 49 |
| 7 00– 7 49.... | 1 | 6 | ....... | 5 | ....... | 2 | ....... | ....... | 3 | 22 | 2.80 | 87.00 | ... 7 00– 7 49 |
| 7 50– 7 99.... | ....... | 1 | ....... | 1 | ....... | ....... | ....... | ....... | ....... | 4 | ....... | 88.60 | ... 7 50– 7 99 |
| 8 00– 8 99.... | ....... | 1 | ....... | 1 | ....... | 1 | ....... | ....... | 2 | 7 | 3.60 | 92.00 | ... 8 00– 8 99 |
| 9 00– 9 99.... | ....... | 3 | ....... | 1 | ....... | ....... | ....... | ....... | 6 | 9 | 6.00 | 96.30 | ... 9 00– 9 99 |
| 10 00–10 99.... | 3 | ....... | 3 | 2 | 11 | ....... | 2 | ....... | 34 | 4 | 17.60 | 98.00 | ...10 00–10 99 |
| 11 00–11 99.... | 2 | ....... | 4 | ....... | 4 | ....... | 1 | ....... | 16 | 2 | 26.00 | 99.00 | ...11 00–11 99 |
| 12 00–12 99.... | 11 | ....... | 17 | ....... | 21 | ....... | 2 | ....... | 98 | ....... | 65.20 | ....... | ...12 00–12 99 |
| 13 00–13 99.... | ....... | ....... | 4 | ....... | ....... | ....... | ....... | ....... | 8 | ....... | 68.40 | ....... | ...13 00–13 99 |
| 14 00–14 99.... | 2 | ....... | 4 | 1 | 6 | ....... | 1 | ....... | 15 | 1 | 74.40 | 99.50 | ...14 00–14 99 |
| 15 00–15 99.... | 2 | ....... | 7 | ....... | 2 | ....... | ....... | 1 | 23 | 1 | 83.60 | 100.00 | ...15 00–15 99 |
| 16 00–17 99.... | 4 | ....... | 2 | ....... | ....... | ....... | 1 | ....... | 15 | ....... | 89.60 | ....... | ...16 00–17 99 |
| 18 00–19 99.... | 1 | ....... | 1 | ....... | 4 | ....... | ....... | 1 | 13 | ....... | 94.80 | ....... | ...18 00–19 99 |
| 20 00–24 99.... | ....... | ....... | 4 | ....... | ....... | ....... | 1 | ....... | 9 | ....... | 98.40 | ....... | ...20 00–24 99 |
| 25 00–29 99.... | 1 | ....... | 1 | ....... | ....... | ....... | ....... | ....... | 3 | ....... | 99.60 | ....... | ...25 00–29 99 |
| 30 00–34 99.... | ....... | ....... | 1 | ....... | ....... | ....... | ....... | ....... | 1 | ....... | 100.00 | ....... | 30 00–34 99 |
| Not reported.... | 1 | ....... | 2 | ....... | ....... | ....... | ....... | ....... | 6 | ....... | ....... | ....... | ...Not reported |
| Total...... | 28 | 20 | 50 | 26 | 48 | 3 | 8 | 2 | 256 | 213 | ....... | ....... | .....Total |

BUFFALO

DEPARTMENT STORES — PLANT

282. TABLE VIII, A, 1, e NUMBER AND PER CENT. OF EMPLOYEES EARNING SPECIFIED WEEKLY RATES, BY OCCUPATION AND SEX

| WEEKLY RATES IN DOLLARS | OCCUPATION | | | | | | | | | | WEEKLY RATES IN DOLLARS |
|---|---|---|---|---|---|---|---|---|---|---|---|
| | FOREMAN | MECHANICS | JANITORIAL FORCE | | PERSONAL SERVICE | | TOTAL | | CUMULATIVE PER CENT. OF TOTAL | | |
| | Male | Male | Male | Female | Male | Female | Male | Female | Male | Female | |
| $3 00–$3 49 | ........ | ........ | ........ | ........ | ........ | 50 | ........ | 50 | ........ | 23.50 | $3 00–$3 49 |
| 3 50– 3 99 | ........ | ........ | ........ | ........ | ........ | 10 | ........ | 10 | ........ | 28.20 | 3 50– 3 99 |
| 4 00– 4 49 | ........ | 1 | 1 | ........ | ........ | 1 | 2 | 1 | .80 | 28.60 | 4 00– 4 49 |
| 4 50– 4 99 | ........ | ........ | ........ | ........ | ........ | 1 | ........ | 1 | ........ | 29.10 | 4 50– 4 99 |
| 5 00– 5 49 | ........ | ........ | 1 | ........ | ........ | 49 | 1 | 49 | 1.20 | 52.10 | 5 00– 5 49 |
| 6 00– 6 49 | ........ | 1 | ........ | 6 | ........ | 46 | 1 | 52 | 1.60 | 71.50 | 6 00– 6 49 |
| 7 00– 7 49 | ........ | ........ | 3 | 7 | ........ | 15 | 3 | 22 | 2.80 | 87.00 | 7 00– 7 49 |
| 7 50– 7 99 | ........ | ........ | ........ | 4 | ........ | ........ | ........ | 4 | ........ | 88.60 | 7 50– 7 99 |
| 8 00– 8 99 | ........ | ........ | 2 | 2 | ........ | 5 | 2 | 7 | 3.60 | 92.00 | 8 00– 8 99 |
| 9 00– 9 99 | ........ | ........ | 6 | 2 | ........ | 7 | 6 | 9 | 6.00 | 96.30 | 9 00– 9 99 |
| 10 00–10 99 | ........ | 2 | 31 | 1 | 1 | 3 | 34 | 4 | 17.60 | 98.00 | 10 00–10 99 |
| 11 00–11 99 | ........ | ........ | 16 | ........ | ........ | 2 | 16 | 2 | 26.00 | 99.00 | 11 00–11 99 |
| 12 00–12 99 | ........ | 6 | 91 | ........ | 1 | ........ | 98 | ........ | 65.20 | ........ | 12 00–12 99 |
| 13 00–13 99 | ........ | 3 | 5 | ........ | ........ | ........ | 8 | ........ | 68.40 | ........ | 13 00–13 99 |
| 14 00–14 99 | ........ | 1 | 12 | ........ | 2 | 1 | 15 | 1 | 74.40 | 99.50 | 14 00–14 99 |
| 15 00–15 99 | ........ | 15 | 7 | ........ | 1 | 1 | 23 | 1 | 83.60 | 100.00 | 15 00–15 99 |
| 16 00–17 99 | 1 | 7 | 6 | ........ | 1 | ........ | 15 | ........ | 89.60 | ........ | 16 00–17 99 |
| 18 00–19 99 | 2 | 6 | 2 | ........ | 3 | ........ | 13 | ........ | 94.80 | ........ | 18 00–19 99 |
| 20 00–24 99 | 1 | 6 | ........ | ........ | 2 | ........ | 9 | ........ | 98.40 | ........ | 20 00–24 99 |
| 25 00–29 99 | ........ | 2 | 1 | ........ | ........ | ........ | 3 | ........ | 99.60 | ........ | 25 00–29 99 |
| 30 00–34 99 | 1 | ........ | ........ | ........ | ........ | ........ | ........ | 1 | ........ | 100.00 | 30 00–34 99 |
| Not reported | ........ | 6 | ........ | ........ | ........ | ........ | 6 | ........ | ........ | ........ | Not reported |
| Total | 5 | 56 | 184 | 22 | 11 | 191 | 256 | 213 | ........ | ........ | Total |

283. TABLE VI, A, 1, e

BUFFALO

DEPARTMENT STORES — PLANT

Number and Per Cent. of Employees Classified According to Actual Weekly Earnings, by Age Groups and Sex

| Actual Weekly Earnings in Dollars | Age Groups in Years | | | | | | | | | | | | | | | Actual Weekly Earnings in Dollars |
|---|---|---|---|---|---|---|---|---|---|---|---|---|---|---|---|---|
| | 14–15 | 16–17 | | 18–20 | | 21–24 | | 25–29 | | 30–34 | | 35–39 | | 40–44 | | |
| | Female | Male | Female | Male | Female | Male | Female | Male | Female | Male | Female | Male | Female | Male | Female | |
| Less than $3 00 | ...... | .... | ...... | .... | 1 | .... | 2 | .... | 4 | .... | 1 | .... | 3 | ...... | ...... | Less than $3 00 |
| $3 00–$3 49... | ...... | .... | 1 | .... | 4 | .... | 9 | 1 | 6 | .... | 8 | .... | 6 | ...... | 2 | ...$3 00– 3 49 |
| 3 50– 3 99... | 1 | .... | ...... | .... | 1 | .... | 3 | .... | 3 | .... | 2 | .... | 2 | ...... | 1 | ... 3 50– 3 99 |
| 4 00– 4 49... | ...... | 1 | ...... | .... | ...... | .... | 2 | 2 | ...... | .... | 2 | .... | 1 | ...... | ...... | ... 4 00– 4 49 |
| 4 50– 4 99... | ...... | .... | ...... | .... | 1 | .... | ...... | .... | ...... | .... | ...... | 1 | ...... | ...... | ...... | ... 4 50– 4 99 |
| 5 00– 5 49... | ...... | 1 | 2 | .... | 10 | .... | 10 | .... | 8 | .... | 4 | .... | 4 | ...... | 3 | ... 5 00– 5 49 |
| 5 50– 5 99... | ...... | .... | ...... | .... | ...... | .... | ...... | .... | 1 | .... | ...... | .... | 1 | ...... | ...... | ... 5 50– 5 99 |
| 6 00– 6 49... | ...... | 1 | 1 | .... | 9 | .... | 11 | .... | 4 | .... | 8 | .... | 4 | ...... | 4 | ... 6 00– 6 49 |
| 6 50– 6 99... | ...... | .... | ...... | .... | ...... | .... | ...... | .... | ...... | .... | ...... | .... | ...... | ...... | ...... | ... 6 50– 6 99 |
| 7 00– 7 49... | ...... | 1 | ...... | 1 | ...... | .... | 1 | .... | 3 | .... | 3 | .... | 1 | 1 | 5 | ... 7 00– 7 49 |
| 7 50– 7 99... | ...... | .... | ...... | 1 | ...... | .... | ...... | .... | 1 | .... | 1 | .... | ...... | ...... | 1 | ... 7 50– 7 99 |
| 8 00– 8 99... | ...... | 2 | ...... | .... | ...... | 1 | 1 | .... | ...... | .... | 2 | .... | 1 | ...... | 1 | ... 8 00– 8 99 |
| 9 00– 9 99... | ...... | .... | ...... | 2 | ...... | 1 | 2 | 1 | 1 | 1 | 1 | .... | 1 | ...... | 3 | ... 9 00– 9 99 |
| 10 00–10 99... | ...... | .... | ...... | 1 | ...... | 9 | ...... | 3 | 1 | 1 | 1 | 2 | ...... | 4 | ...... | ...10 00–10 99 |
| 11 00–11 99... | ...... | .... | ...... | .... | ...... | 3 | ...... | .... | ...... | 1 | 1 | 1 | 1 | 2 | ...... | ...11 00–11 99 |
| 12 00–12 99... | ...... | .... | ...... | 2 | ...... | 14 | ...... | 11 | ...... | 10 | ...... | 6 | ...... | 9 | ...... | ...12 00–12 99 |
| 13 00–13 99... | ...... | .... | ...... | .... | ...... | 1 | ...... | 1 | ...... | 1 | ...... | 1 | ...... | 1 | ...... | ...13 00–13 99 |
| 14 00–14 99... | ...... | .... | ...... | .... | ...... | .... | ...... | .... | ...... | .... | ...... | 1 | ...... | 2 | ...... | ...14 00–14 99 |
| 15 00–15 99... | ...... | .... | ...... | .... | ...... | .... | ...... | 4 | ...... | 5 | ...... | 1 | 1 | 2 | ...... | ...15 00–15 99 |
| 16 00–17 99... | ...... | .... | ...... | .... | ...... | .... | ...... | 4 | ...... | 3 | ...... | 1 | ...... | 4 | ...... | ...16 00–17 99 |
| 18 00–19 99... | ...... | .... | ...... | .... | ...... | .... | ...... | 1 | ...... | 4 | ...... | 2 | ...... | 1 | ...... | ...18 00–19 99 |
| 20 00–24 99... | ...... | .... | ...... | .... | ...... | .... | ...... | 3 | ...... | 1 | ...... | 2 | ...... | 1 | ...... | ...20 00–24 99 |
| 25 00–29 99... | ...... | .... | ...... | .... | ...... | .... | ...... | .... | ...... | 2 | ...... | .... | ...... | 1 | ...... | ...25 00–29 99 |
| Total..... | 1 | 6 | 4 | 7 | 26 | 29 | 41 | 31 | 32 | 29 | 34 | 18 | 26 | 28 | 20 | .....Total |

BUFFALO

283. TABLE VI, A, 1, e — (*concluded*) DEPARTMENT STORES — PLANT

NUMBER AND PER CENT. OF EMPLOYEES CLASSIFIED ACCORDING TO ACTUAL WEEKLY EARNINGS, BY AGE GROUPS AND SEX

| Actual Weekly Earnings in Dollars | Age Groups in Years (*concluded*): 45–54 | | 55–64 | | 65 and over | Not reported | Total | | Cumulative per cent. of total | | Actual Weekly Earnings in Dollars |
|---|---|---|---|---|---|---|---|---|---|---|---|
| | Male | Female | Male | Female | Male | Male | Male | Female | Male | Female | |
| Less than $3 00 | ........ | ........ | ........ | ........ | ........ | ........ | ........ | 11 | ........ | 5.17 | Less than $3 00 |
| $3 00–$3 49 | ........ | 1 | 1 | ........ | ........ | ........ | 2 | 37 | .78 | 22.50 | $3 00– 3 49 |
| 3 50– 3 99 | 1 | ........ | ........ | ........ | ........ | ........ | 1 | 13 | 1.17 | 28.60 | 3 50– 3 99 |
| 4 00– 4 49 | ........ | ........ | ........ | ........ | ........ | ........ | 3 | 5 | 2.34 | 31.00 | 4 00– 4 49 |
| 4 50– 4 99 | ........ | ........ | ........ | ........ | ........ | ........ | 1 | 1 | 2.74 | 31.45 | 4 50– 4 99 |
| 5 00– 5 49 | ........ | 6 | ........ | ........ | ........ | ........ | 1 | 47 | 3.12 | 53.50 | 5 00– 5 49 |
| 5 50– 5 99 | ........ | ........ | ........ | ........ | ........ | ........ | ........ | 2 | ........ | 75.00 | 5 50– 5 99 |
| 6 00– 6 49 | ........ | 8 | ........ | ........ | ........ | ........ | 1 | 49 | 3.52 | 77.50 | 6 00– 6 49 |
| 6 50– 6 99 | ........ | ........ | ........ | ........ | ........ | ........ | ........ | ........ | ........ | ........ | 6 50– 6 99 |
| 7 00– 7 49 | ........ | 5 | ........ | 2 | ........ | ........ | 3 | 20 | 4.68 | 87.00 | 7 00– 7 49 |
| 7 50– 7 99 | ........ | 1 | ........ | ........ | ........ | ........ | 1 | 4 | 5.08 | 88.80 | 7 50– 7 99 |
| 8 00– 8 99 | ........ | 1 | ........ | 1 | ........ | ........ | 3 | 7 | 6.25 | 92.00 | 8 00– 8 99 |
| 9 00– 9 99 | ........ | 2 | 1 | ........ | ........ | ........ | 6 | 10 | 8.60 | 96.80 | 9 00– 9 99 |
| 10 00–10 99 | 5 | 2 | 10 | ........ | 2 | ........ | 37 | 4 | 23.05 | 98.60 | 10 00–10 99 |
| 11 00–11 99 | 4 | ........ | 3 | ........ | 1 | ........ | 15 | 2 | 28.90 | 99.50 | 11 00–11 99 |
| 12 00–12 99 | 16 | ........ | 20 | ........ | 2 | ........ | 90 | ........ | 64.00 | ........ | 12 00–12 99 |
| 13 00–13 99 | 4 | ........ | ........ | ........ | ........ | ........ | 9 | ........ | 66.60 | ........ | 13 00–13 99 |
| 14 00–14 99 | 3 | ........ | 7 | ........ | 1 | ........ | 14 | ........ | 73.00 | ........ | 14 00–14 99 |
| 15 00–15 99 | 7 | ........ | 2 | ........ | ........ | 1 | 22 | 1 | 81.60 | 100.00 | 15 00–15 99 |
| 16 00–17 99 | 2 | ........ | ........ | ........ | 1 | ........ | 15 | ........ | 87.50 | ........ | 16 00–17 99 |
| 18 00–19 99 | 1 | ........ | 3 | ........ | ........ | 1 | 13 | ........ | 92.50 | ........ | 18 00–19 99 |
| 20 00–24 99 | 4 | ........ | 1 | ........ | 1 | ........ | 13 | ........ | 97.60 | ........ | 20 00–24 99 |
| 25 00–29 99 | 2 | ........ | ........ | ........ | ........ | ........ | 5 | ........ | 99.60 | ........ | 25 00–29 99 |
| 30 00–34 99 | 1 | ........ | ........ | ........ | ........ | ........ | 1 | ........ | 100.00 | ........ | 30 00–34 99 |
| Total | 50 | 26 | 48 | 3 | 8 | 2 | 256 | 213 | ........ | ........ | Total |

284. TABLE IX, A, 1, e

## BUFFALO
## DEPARTMENT STORES — PLANT

Number and Per Cent. of Employees Classified According to Actual Weekly Earnings, by Occupation and Sex

| Actual Weekly Earnings in Dollars | Occupation | | | | | | | | | | | Actual Weekly Earnings in Dollars |
|---|---|---|---|---|---|---|---|---|---|---|---|---|
| | Foreman | Mechanics | | Janitorial Force | | Personal Service | | Total | | Cumulative Per Cent. of Total | | |
| | Male | Male | Female | Male | Female | Male | Female | Male | Female | Male | Female | |
| Less than $3 00 | ........ | ........ | ........ | ........ | ........ | ........ | 11 | ........ | 11 | ........ | 5.17 | Less than $3 00 |
| $3 00–$3 49... | ........ | 1 | ........ | 1 | ........ | ........ | 37 | 2 | 37 | .78 | 22.50 | ...$3 00– 3 49 |
| 3 50– 3 99... | ........ | 1 | ........ | ........ | ........ | ........ | 13 | 1 | 13 | 1.17 | 28.60 | ... 3 50– 3 99 |
| 4 00– 4 49... | ........ | 1 | ........ | 2 | ........ | ........ | 5 | 3 | 5 | 2.34 | 31.00 | ... 4 00– 4 49 |
| 4 50– 4 99... | ........ | ........ | ........ | ........ | ........ | 1 | 1 | 1 | 1 | 2.74 | 31.45 | ... 4 50– 4 99 |
| 5 00– 5 49... | ........ | ........ | ........ | 1 | ........ | ........ | 47 | 1 | 47 | 3.12 | 53.50 | ... 5 00– 5 49 |
| 5 50– 5 99... | ........ | ........ | ........ | ........ | ........ | ........ | 2 | ........ | 2 | ........ | 75.00 | ... 5 50– 5 99 |
| 6 00– 6 49... | ........ | 1 | ........ | ........ | 7 | ........ | 42 | 1 | 49 | 3.52 | 77.50 | ... 6 00– 6 49 |
| 6 50– 6 99... | ........ | ........ | ........ | ........ | ........ | ........ | ........ | ........ | ........ | ........ | ........ | ... 6 50– 6 99 |
| 7 00– 7 49... | ........ | ........ | ........ | 3 | 6 | ........ | 14 | 3 | 20 | 4.68 | 87.00 | ... 7 00– 7 49 |
| 7 50– 7 99... | ........ | ........ | ........ | 1 | 4 | ........ | ........ | 1 | 4 | 5.08 | 88.80 | ... 7 50– 7 99 |
| 8 00– 8 99... | ........ | ........ | ........ | 3 | 2 | ........ | 5 | 3 | 7 | 6.25 | 92.00 | ... 8 00– 8 99 |
| 9 00– 9 99... | ........ | ........ | ........ | 6 | 2 | ........ | 8 | 6 | 10 | 8.60 | 96.80 | ... 9 00– 9 99 |
| 10 00–10 99... | ........ | 1 | ........ | 35 | 1 | 1 | 3 | 37 | 4 | 23.05 | 98.60 | ...10.00–10 99 |
| 11 00–11 99... | ........ | ........ | ........ | 15 | ........ | ........ | 2 | 15 | 2 | 28.90 | 99.50 | ...11 00–11 99 |
| 12 00–12 99... | ........ | 6 | ........ | 83 | ........ | 1 | ........ | 90 | ........ | 64.00 | ........ | ...12 00–12 99 |
| 13 00–13 99... | ........ | 3 | ........ | 6 | ........ | ........ | ........ | 9 | ........ | 66.60 | ........ | ...13 00–13 99 |
| 14 00–14 99... | ........ | 1 | ........ | 12 | ........ | 1 | ........ | 14 | ........ | 73.00 | ........ | ...14 00–14 99 |
| 15 00–15 99... | ........ | 14 | ........ | 7 | ........ | 1 | 1 | 22 | 1 | 81.60 | 100.00 | ...15 00–15 99 |
| 16 00–17 99... | 1 | 7 | ........ | 6 | ........ | 1 | ........ | 15 | ........ | 87.50 | ........ | ...16 00–17 99 |
| 18 00–19 99... | 2 | 6 | ........ | 2 | ........ | 3 | ........ | 13 | ........ | 92.50 | ........ | ...18 00–19 99 |
| 20 00–24 99... | 1 | 10 | ........ | ........ | ........ | 2 | ........ | 13 | ........ | 97.60 | ........ | ...20 00–24 99 |
| 25 00–29 00... | ........ | 4 | ........ | 1 | ........ | ........ | ........ | 5 | ........ | 99.60 | ........ | ...25 00–29 99 |
| 30 00–34 99... | 1 | ........ | ........ | ........ | ........ | ........ | ........ | 1 | ........ | 100.00 | ........ | ...30 00–34 99 |
| Total..... | 5 | 56 | ........ | 184 | 22 | 11 | 191 | 256 | 213 | ........ | ........ | .....Total |

285. TABLE V, A, 2, a

BUFFALO

NEIGHBORHOOD STORES — STOCK AND SALES

Number and Per Cent. of Employees Earning Specified Weekly Rates, by Age Groups and Sex

| Weekly Rates in Dollars | Age Groups in Years | | | | | | | | | | | | | | Weekly Rates in Dollars |
|---|---|---|---|---|---|---|---|---|---|---|---|---|---|---|---|
| | 14–15 | | 16–17 | | 18–20 | | 21–24 | | 25–29 | | 30–34 | | 35–39 | | |
| | Male | Female | Male | Female | Male | Female | Male | Female | Male | Female | Male | Female | Male | Female | |
| Less than $3 00 | .... | 2 | .... | .... | .... | .... | .... | .... | .... | .... | .... | .... | .... | .... | Less than $3 00 |
| $3 00–$3 49... | 4 | .... | .... | 3 | .... | .... | .... | .... | .... | .... | .... | .... | .... | .... | ...$3 00– 3 49 |
| 3 50– 3 99... | 2 | 1 | 1 | 2 | .... | .... | .... | .... | .... | .... | .... | .... | .... | .... | ... 3 50– 3 99 |
| 4 00– 4 49... | 1 | 1 | 2 | 5 | .... | 1 | .... | .... | .... | .... | .... | .... | .... | .... | ... 4 00– 4 49 |
| 4 50– 4 99... | .... | 1 | .... | 13 | .... | 10 | .... | 1 | .... | .... | .... | .... | .... | .... | ... 4 50– 4 99 |
| 5 00– 5 49... | 1 | .... | .... | 14 | 1 | 40 | .... | 12 | .... | 1 | .... | .... | .... | .... | ... 5 00– 5 49 |
| 5 50– 5 99... | .... | .... | .... | 2 | .... | 29 | .... | 10 | .... | 2 | .... | .... | .... | .... | ... 5 50– 5 99 |
| 6 00– 6 49... | .... | .... | 1 | 1 | .... | 15 | 1 | 23 | .... | 4 | .... | .... | .... | .... | ... 6 00– 6 49 |
| 6 50– 6 99... | .... | .... | .... | .... | .... | 6 | .... | 13 | .... | 3 | .... | .... | .... | 1 | ... 6 50– 6 99 |
| 7 00– 7 49... | .... | .... | .... | .... | 2 | 3 | .... | 16 | .... | 6 | .... | 1 | .... | .... | ... 7 00– 7 49 |
| 7 50– 7 99... | .... | .... | .... | .... | .... | .... | .... | 5 | .... | 2 | .... | .... | .... | .... | ... 7 50– 7 99 |
| 8 00– 8 99... | .... | .... | .... | .... | 1 | 2 | .... | 10 | .... | 3 | .... | 5 | .... | 3 | ... 8 00– 8 99 |
| 9 00– 9 99... | .... | .... | .... | .... | 1 | 1 | .... | 6 | .... | 3 | .... | 3 | .... | 1 | ... 9 00– 9 99 |
| 10 00–10 99... | .... | .... | .... | .... | 1 | .... | 1 | .... | 2 | 3 | .... | 3 | .... | 1 | ...10 00–10 99 |
| 11 00–11 99... | .... | .... | .... | .... | 1 | .... | 1 | .... | 1 | 1 | .... | .... | 1 | .... | ...11 00–11 99 |
| 12 00–12 99... | .... | .... | .... | .... | .... | .... | 3 | .... | 2 | 3 | .... | 1 | 1 | 1 | ...12 00–12 99 |
| 13 00–13 99... | .... | .... | .... | .... | .... | .... | 1 | .... | .... | .... | .... | .... | .... | .... | ...13 00–13 99 |
| 14 00–14 99... | .... | .... | .... | .... | .... | 1 | .... | .... | .... | .... | .... | 1 | .... | .... | ...14 00–14 99 |
| 15 00–15 99... | .... | .... | .... | .... | .... | .... | .... | .... | 1 | .... | .... | .... | 1 | .... | ...15 00–15 99 |
| 16 00–17 99... | .... | .... | .... | .... | .... | .... | 1 | 1 | .... | .... | 3 | .... | 1 | .... | ...16 00–17 99 |
| 18 00–19 99... | .... | .... | .... | .... | .... | .... | .... | .... | 1 | .... | .... | .... | 5 | .... | ...18 00–19 99 |
| 20 00–24 99... | .... | .... | .... | .... | .... | .... | .... | .... | .... | .... | .... | 1 | 1 | .... | ...20 00–24 99 |
| 25 00–29 99... | .... | .... | .... | .... | .... | .... | .... | .... | .... | .... | .... | .... | .... | .... | ...25 00–29 99 |
| Total..... | 8 | 5 | 4 | 40 | 7 | 108 | 8 | 97 | 7 | 31 | 3 | 15 | 10 | 7 | .....Total |

285. TABLE V, A, 2, a — (*concluded*)

BUFFALO

NEIGHBORHOOD STORES — STOCK AND SALES

NUMBER AND PER CENT. OF EMPLOYEES EARNING SPECIFIED WEEKLY RATES, BY AGE GROUPS AND SEX

| WEEKLY RATES IN DOLLARS | AGE GROUPS IN YEARS—(*concluded*) | | | | | | | | | | | | WEEKLY RATES IN DOLLARS |
|---|---|---|---|---|---|---|---|---|---|---|---|---|---|
| | 40–44 | | 45–54 | | 55–64 | | 65 AND OVER | | TOTAL | | CUMULATIVE PER CENT OF TOTAL | | |
| | Male | Female | Male | Female | Male | Female | Male | Female | Male | Female | Male | Female | |
| Less than $3 00 | ....... | ....... | ....... | ....... | ....... | ....... | ....... | ....... | ....... | 2 | ....... | .60 | Less than $3 00 |
| $3 00–$3 49 | ....... | ....... | ....... | ....... | ....... | ....... | ....... | ....... | 4 | 3 | 6.70 | 1.60 | $3 00– 3 49 |
| 3 50– 3 99 | ....... | ....... | ....... | ....... | ....... | ....... | ....... | ....... | 3 | 3 | 11.70 | 2.60 | 3 50– 3 99 |
| 4 00– 4 49 | ....... | ....... | ....... | ....... | ....... | ....... | ....... | ....... | 3 | 7 | 16.70 | 4.80 | 4 00– 4 49 |
| 4 50– 4 99 | ....... | ....... | ....... | ....... | ....... | ....... | ....... | ....... | ....... | 25 | ....... | 12.80 | 4 50– 4 99 |
| 5 00– 5 49 | ....... | ....... | ....... | 1 | ....... | ....... | ....... | ....... | 2 | 68 | 20.00 | 34.60 | 5 00– 5 49 |
| 5 50– 5 99 | ....... | ....... | ....... | ....... | ....... | ....... | ....... | ....... | ....... | 43 | ....... | 48.40 | 5 50– 5 99 |
| 6 00– 6 49 | ....... | ....... | ....... | ....... | ....... | ....... | ....... | ....... | 2 | 43 | 23.30 | 62.20 | 6 00– 6 49 |
| 6 50– 6 99 | ....... | ....... | ....... | ....... | ....... | 1 | ....... | ....... | ....... | 24 | ....... | 70.00 | 6 50– 6 99 |
| 7 00– 7 49 | ....... | ....... | ....... | ....... | ....... | ....... | ....... | ....... | 2 | 26 | 26.60 | 78.20 | 7 00– 7 49 |
| 7 50– 7 99 | ....... | ....... | ....... | ....... | ....... | ....... | ....... | ....... | ....... | 7 | ....... | 80.50 | 7 50– 7 99 |
| 8 00– 8 99 | ....... | ....... | ....... | ....... | ....... | ....... | ....... | ....... | 1 | 23 | 28.30 | 87.90 | 8 00– 8 99 |
| 9 00– 9 99 | ....... | 1 | ....... | ....... | ....... | ....... | ....... | ....... | 1 | 15 | 30.00 | 92.60 | 9 00– 9 99 |
| 10 00–10 99 | ....... | ....... | ....... | 1 | ....... | ....... | ....... | ....... | 4 | 8 | 36.60 | 95.20 | 10 00–10 99 |
| 11 00–11 99 | ....... | ....... | 2 | ....... | 1 | ....... | ....... | ....... | 7 | 1 | 48.30 | 95.60 | 11 00–11 99 |
| 12 00–12 99 | ....... | ....... | 2 | ....... | 1 | 1 | ....... | ....... | 9 | 6 | 63.30 | 97.50 | 12 00–12 99 |
| 13 00–13 99 | 1 | ....... | ....... | ....... | ....... | ....... | ....... | 1 | 2 | 1 | 66.20 | 97.80 | 13 00–13 99 |
| 14 00–14 99 | ....... | ....... | 1 | 1 | ....... | ....... | ....... | 2 | 1 | 5 | 68.30 | 99.50 | 14 00–14 99 |
| 15 00–15 99 | ....... | ....... | 1 | ....... | ....... | ....... | ....... | ....... | 3 | ....... | 73.40 | ....... | 15 00–15 99 |
| 16 00–17 99 | ....... | ....... | ....... | ....... | 1 | ....... | 1 | ....... | 7 | 1 | 85.00 | 99.80 | 16 00–17 99 |
| 18 00–19 99 | ....... | ....... | 1 | ....... | ....... | ....... | ....... | ....... | 7 | ....... | 96.60 | ....... | 18 00–19 99 |
| 20 00–24 99 | ....... | ....... | ....... | ....... | ....... | ....... | ....... | ....... | 1 | 1 | 98.40 | 100.00 | 20 00–24 99 |
| 25 00–29 99 | 1 | ....... | ....... | ....... | ....... | ....... | ....... | ....... | 1 | ....... | 100.00 | ....... | 25 00–29 99 |
| Total | 2 | 1 | 7 | 3 | 3 | 2 | 1 | 3 | 60 | 312 | ....... | ....... | Total |

BUFFALO

NEIGHBORHOOD STORES — STOCK AND SALES

286. TABLE VIII, A, 2, a  NUMBER AND PER CENT. OF EMPLOYEES EARNING SPECIFIED WEEKLY RATES, BY OCCUPATION AND SEX

| WEEKLY RATES IN DOLLARS | OCCUPATION: BUYERS | ASSISTANT BUYERS AND HEADS OF STOCK | | RECEIVING AND STOCK CLERKS | STOCK PEOPLE | | FLOOR MANAGERS | | SALES PEOPLE | | MESSENGERS, WRAPPERS, ERRAND BOYS | | TOTAL | | CUMULATIVE PER CENT. OF TOTAL | | WEEKLY RATES IN DOLLARS |
|---|---|---|---|---|---|---|---|---|---|---|---|---|---|---|---|---|---|
| | Male | Male | Female | Male | Male | Female | Male | Female | Male | Female | Male | Female | Male | Female | Male | Female | |
| Less than $3 00 | | | | | | | | | | | | 2 | | 2 | | .60 | Less than $3 00 |
| $3 00–$3 49 | | | | | | | | | | 2 | 4 | 1 | 4 | 3 | 6.70 | 1.60 | $3 00– 3 49 |
| 3 50– 3 99 | | | | | 1 | | | | | 2 | 2 | 1 | 3 | 3 | 11.70 | 2.60 | 3 50– 3 99 |
| 4 00– 4 49 | | | | 1 | 1 | | | | | 7 | 1 | | 3 | 7 | 16.70 | 4.80 | 4 00– 4 49 |
| 4 50– 4 99 | | | | | | | | | | 25 | | | | 25 | | 12.80 | 4 50– 4 99 |
| 5 00– 5 49 | | | | 1 | 1 | | | | | 67 | | 1 | 2 | 68 | 20.00 | 34.60 | 5 00– 5 49 |
| 5 50– 5 99 | | | | | | | | | | 43 | | | | 43 | | 48.40 | 5 50– 5 99 |
| 6 00– 6 49 | | | | | 1 | 1 | | | | 42 | 1 | | 2 | 43 | 23.30 | 62.20 | 6 00– 6 49 |
| 6 50– 6 99 | | | | | | | | | | 24 | | | | 24 | | 70.00 | 6 50– 6 99 |
| 7 00– 7 49 | | | | | | 1 | | | 2 | 25 | | | 2 | 26 | 26.60 | 78.20 | 7 00– 7 49 |
| 7 50– 7 99 | | | | | | | | | | 7 | | | | 7 | | 80.50 | 7 50– 7 99 |
| 8 00– 8 99 | | | | | | 1 | | | 1 | 22 | | | 1 | 23 | 28.30 | 87.90 | 8 00– 8 99 |
| 9 00– 9 99 | | | | | | | | | 1 | 15 | | | 1 | 15 | 30.00 | 92.60 | 9 00– 9 99 |
| 10 00–10 99 | 1 | | | | | | | | 2 | 8 | 1 | | 4 | 8 | 36.60 | 95.20 | 10 00–10 99 |
| 11 00–11 99 | | 3 | | | 1 | | 1 | | 2 | 1 | | | 7 | 1 | 48.30 | 95.60 | 11 00–11 99 |
| 12 00–12 99 | | 4 | | | 1 | | 1 | 1 | 3 | 5 | | | 9 | 6 | 63.30 | 97.50 | 12 00–12 99 |
| 13 00–13 99 | | 1 | | | | | | | 1 | 1 | | | 2 | 1 | 66.20 | 97.80 | 13 00–13 99 |
| 14 00–14 99 | 1 | | | | | | | 1 | | 4 | | | 1 | 5 | 68.30 | 99.50 | 14 00–14 99 |
| 15 00–15 99 | | | | | | | 1 | | 2 | | | | 3 | | 73.40 | | 15 00–15 99 |
| 16 00–17 99 | | 1 | 1 | 1 | | | 1 | | 3 | | 1 | | 7 | 1 | 85.00 | 99.80 | 16 00–17 99 |
| 18 00–19 99 | 1 | | | 1 | | | 2 | | 3 | | | | 7 | | 96.60 | | 18 00–19 99 |
| 20 00–24 99 | | | 1 | | | | | | 1 | | | | 1 | 1 | 98.40 | 100.00 | 20 00–24 99 |
| 25 00–29 99 | | 1 | | | | | | | | | | | 1 | | 100.00 | | 25 00–29 99 |
| Total | 3 | 10 | 2 | 4 | 6 | 3 | 6 | 2 | 21 | 300 | 10 | 5 | 60 | 312 | | | Total |

BUFFALO

287. TABLE VI, A, 2, a

## NEIGHBORHOOD STORES — STOCK AND SALES

Number and Per Cent. of Employees Classified According to Actual Weekly Earnings, by Age Groups and Sex

| Actual Weekly Earnings in Dollars | Age Groups in Years | | | | | | | | | | | | | | Actual Weekly Earnings in Dollars |
|---|---|---|---|---|---|---|---|---|---|---|---|---|---|---|---|
| | 14–15 | | 16–17 | | 18–20 | | 21–24 | | 25–29 | | 30–34 | | 35–39 | | |
| | Male | Female | Male | Female | Male | Female | Male | Female | Male | Female | Male | Female | Male | Female | |
| Less than $3 00 | 1 | 2 | .... | ...... | ...... | 1 | ...... | 1 | ...... | ...... | ...... | 1 | ...... | 1 | Less than $3 00 |
| $3 00–$3 49... | 3 | 1 | .... | 3 | ...... | 1 | ...... | 1 | ...... | ...... | ...... | ...... | ...... | ...... | ...$3 00– 3 49 |
| 3 50– 3 99... | 2 | ...... | 1 | 5 | ...... | ...... | ...... | ...... | ...... | ...... | ...... | ...... | ...... | ...... | ....3 50– 3 99 |
| 4 00– 4 49... | 1 | 1 | 2 | 4 | ...... | 3 | ...... | 1 | ...... | ...... | ...... | ...... | ...... | ...... | ....4 00– 4 49 |
| 4 50– 4 99... | .... | 1 | .... | 14 | ...... | 11 | ...... | 3 | ...... | 1 | ...... | ...... | ...... | ...... | ....4 50– 4 99 |
| 5 00– 5 49... | 1 | ...... | .... | 12 | 1 | 39 | ...... | 12 | ...... | ...... | ...... | ...... | ...... | ...... | ....5 00– 5 49 |
| 5 50– 5 99... | .... | ...... | .... | 1 | ...... | 20 | ...... | 8 | ...... | ...... | ...... | ...... | ...... | ...... | ....5 50– 5 99 |
| 6 00– 6 49... | .... | ...... | 1 | 1 | ...... | 20 | 1 | 19 | ...... | 2 | ...... | ...... | ...... | 1 | ....6 00– 6 49 |
| 6 50– 6 99... | .... | ...... | .... | ...... | ...... | 5 | ...... | 10 | ...... | 5 | ...... | ...... | ...... | ...... | ....6 50– 6 99 |
| 7 00– 7 49... | .... | ...... | .... | ...... | 2 | 3 | ...... | 14 | ...... | 6 | ...... | 1 | ...... | 1 | ....7 00– 7 49 |
| 7 50– 7 99... | .... | ...... | .... | ...... | ...... | 1 | ...... | 11 | ...... | 3 | ...... | ...... | ...... | ...... | ....7 50– 7 99 |
| 8 00– 8 99... | .... | ...... | .... | ...... | 1 | 2 | ...... | 10 | ...... | 4 | ...... | 4 | ...... | 2 | ....8 00– 8 99 |
| 9 00– 9 99... | .... | ...... | .... | ...... | 1 | 1 | ...... | 6 | ...... | 2 | ...... | 4 | ...... | 1 | ....9 00– 9 99 |
| 10 00–10 99... | .... | ...... | .... | ...... | 1 | ...... | 1 | ...... | 2 | 4 | ...... | 2 | ...... | 1 | ...10 00–10 99 |
| 11 00–11 99... | .... | ...... | .... | ...... | 1 | ...... | 1 | ...... | 1 | 2 | ...... | ...... | 1 | ...... | ...11 00–11 99 |
| 12 00–12 99... | .... | ...... | .... | ...... | ...... | ...... | 3 | ...... | 2 | 2 | ...... | 1 | 1 | ...... | ...12 00–12 99 |
| 13 00–13 99... | .... | ...... | .... | ...... | ...... | ...... | 1 | ...... | ...... | ...... | ...... | ...... | ...... | ...... | ...13 00–13 99 |
| 14 00–14 99... | .... | ...... | .... | ...... | ...... | ...... | ...... | ...... | ...... | ...... | ...... | 1 | ...... | ...... | ...14 00–14 99 |
| 15 00–15 99... | .... | ...... | .... | ...... | ...... | 1 | ...... | ...... | 1 | ...... | ...... | ...... | ...... | ...... | ...15 00–15 99 |
| 16 00–17 99... | .... | ...... | .... | ...... | ...... | ...... | 1 | 1 | ...... | ...... | 2 | ...... | 1 | ...... | ...16 00–17 99 |
| 18 00–19 99... | .... | ...... | .... | ...... | ...... | ...... | ...... | ...... | ...... | ...... | 1 | ...... | 5 | ...... | ...18 00–19 99 |
| 20 00–24 99... | .... | ...... | .... | ...... | ...... | ...... | ...... | ...... | 1 | ...... | ...... | 1 | 2 | ...... | ...20 00–24 99 |
| Total..... | 8 | 5 | 4 | 40 | 7 | 108 | 8 | 97 | 7 | 31 | 3 | 15 | 10 | 7 | .....Total |

BUFFALO

287. TABLE VI, A, 2, a — (*concluded*) NEIGHBORHOOD STORES — STOCK AND SALES

NUMBER AND PER CENT. OF EMPLOYEES CLASSIFIED ACCORDING TO ACTUAL WEEKLY EARNINGS, BY AGE GROUPS AND SEX

| ACTUAL WEEKLY EARNINGS IN DOLLARS | AGE GROUPS IN YEARS (*concluded*) | | | | | | | | | | | | ACTUAL WEEKLY EARNINGS IN DOLLARS |
|---|---|---|---|---|---|---|---|---|---|---|---|---|---|
| | 40–44 | | 45–54 | | 55–64 | | 65 AND OVER | NOT REPORTED | TOTAL | | CUMULATIVE PER CENT. OF TOTAL | | |
| | Male | Female | Male | Female | Male | Female | Male | Female | Male | Female | Male | Female | |
| Less than $3 00 | ....... | ....... | ....... | ....... | ....... | ....... | ....... | ....... | 1 | 6 | 1.70 | 1.90 | Less than $3 00 |
| $3 00–$3 49 | ....... | ....... | ....... | ....... | ....... | ....... | ....... | ....... | 3 | 6 | 6.60 | 3.80 | $3 00– 3 49 |
| 3 50– 3 99 | ....... | ....... | ....... | ....... | ....... | ....... | ....... | ....... | 3 | 5 | 11.70 | 5.50 | 3 50– 3 99 |
| 4 00– 4 49 | ....... | ....... | ....... | ....... | ....... | ....... | ....... | ....... | 3 | 9 | 16.60 | 8.30 | 4 00– 4 49 |
| 4 50– 4 99 | ....... | ....... | ....... | ....... | ....... | ....... | ....... | ....... | ....... | 30 | ....... | 17.90 | 4 50– 4 99 |
| 5 00– 5 49 | ....... | ....... | ....... | 1 | ....... | ....... | ....... | ....... | 2 | 64 | 20.00 | 38.50 | 5 00– 5 49 |
| 5 50– 5 99 | ....... | ....... | ....... | ....... | ....... | ....... | ....... | ....... | ....... | 29 | ....... | 47.80 | 5 50– 5 99 |
| 6 00– 6 49 | ....... | ....... | ....... | ....... | ....... | ....... | ....... | ....... | 2 | 43 | 23.30 | 61.50 | 6 00– 6 49 |
| 6 50– 6 99 | ....... | ....... | ....... | ....... | ....... | 1 | ....... | ....... | ....... | 21 | ....... | 68.30 | 6 50– 6 99 |
| 7 00– 7 49 | ....... | ....... | ....... | 1 | ....... | ....... | ....... | ....... | 2 | 26 | 26.60 | 76.60 | 7 00– 7 49 |
| 7 50– 7 99 | ....... | ....... | ....... | ....... | ....... | ....... | ....... | ....... | ....... | 15 | ....... | 81.50 | 7 50– 7 99 |
| 8 00– 8 99 | ....... | ....... | ....... | ....... | ....... | ....... | ....... | ....... | 1 | 22 | 28.30 | 88.50 | 8 00– 8 99 |
| 9 00– 9 99 | ....... | 1 | ....... | ....... | ....... | ....... | ....... | ....... | 1 | 15 | 30.00 | 93.30 | 9 00– 9 99 |
| 10 00–10 99 | ....... | ....... | ....... | 1 | ....... | ....... | ....... | ....... | 4 | 8 | 36.60 | 95.90 | 10 00–10 99 |
| 11 00–11 99 | ....... | ....... | 2 | ....... | 1 | ....... | ....... | ....... | 7 | 2 | 48.30 | 96.50 | 11 00–11 99 |
| 12 00–12 99 | ....... | ....... | 2 | ....... | 1 | 1 | ....... | 1 | 9 | 5 | 63.30 | 98.10 | 12 00–12 99 |
| 13 00–13 99 | 1 | ....... | ....... | ....... | ....... | ....... | ....... | ....... | 2 | ....... | 66.60 | ....... | 13 00–13 99 |
| 14 00–14 99 | ....... | ....... | 1 | ....... | ....... | ....... | ....... | 2 | 1 | 3 | 68.30 | 99.10 | 14 00–14 99 |
| 15 00–15 99 | ....... | ....... | 1 | ....... | ....... | ....... | ....... | ....... | 2 | 1 | 71.60 | 99.40 | 15 00–15 99 |
| 16 00–17 99 | ....... | ....... | ....... | ....... | 1 | ....... | 1 | ....... | 6 | 1 | 81.60 | 99.70 | 16 00–17 99 |
| 18 00–19 99 | ....... | ....... | 1 | ....... | ....... | ....... | ....... | ....... | 7 | ....... | 93.30 | ....... | 18 00–19 99 |
| 20 00–24 99 | ....... | ....... | ....... | ....... | ....... | ....... | ....... | ....... | 3 | 1 | 98.30 | 100.00 | 20 00–24 99 |
| 25 00–29 99 | 1 | ....... | ....... | ....... | ....... | ....... | ....... | ....... | 1 | ....... | 100.00 | ....... | 25 00–29 99 |
| Total | 2 | 1 | 7 | 3 | 3 | 2 | 1 | 3 | 60 | 312 | ....... | ....... | Total |

288. TABLE IX, A, 2, a

BUFFALO

NEIGHBORHOOD STORES — STOCK AND SALES

NUMBER AND PER CENT. OF EMPLOYEES CLASSIFIED ACCORDING TO ACTUAL WEEKLY EARNINGS, BY OCCUPATION AND SEX

| ACTUAL WEEKLY EARNINGS IN DOLLARS | OCCUPATION | | | | | | | | | | | | | | | | ACTUAL WEEKLY EARNINGS IN DOLLARS |
|---|---|---|---|---|---|---|---|---|---|---|---|---|---|---|---|---|---|
| | BUYERS | ASSISTANT BUYERS AND HEADS OF STOCK | | RECEIVING AND STOCK CLERKS | STOCK PEOPLE | | FLOOR MANAGERS | | SALES PEOPLE | | MESSENGERS, WRAPPERS, ERRAND BOYS | | TOTAL | | CUMULATIVE PER CENT. OF TOTAL | | |
| | Male | Male | Female | Male | Male | Female | Male | Female | Male | Female | Male | Female | Male | Female | Male | Female | |
| Less than $3 00 | | | | | | 1 | | | | 3 | 1 | 2 | 1 | 6 | 1.70 | 1.90 | Less than $3 00 |
| $3 00–$3 49 | | | | | | | | | | 5 | 3 | 1 | 3 | 6 | 6.60 | 3.80 | $3 00– 3 49 |
| 3 50– 3 99 | | | | | 1 | | | | | 4 | 2 | 1 | 3 | 5 | 11.70 | 5.50 | 3 50– 3 99 |
| 4 00– 4 49 | | | | 1 | 1 | | | | | 9 | 1 | | 3 | 9 | 16.60 | 8.30 | 4 00– 4 49 |
| 4 50– 4 99 | | | | | | 1 | | | | 28 | | 1 | | 30 | | 17.90 | 4 50– 4 99 |
| 5 00– 5 49 | | | | 1 | 1 | | | | | 64 | | | 2 | 64 | 20.00 | 38.50 | 5 00– 5 49 |
| 5 50– 5 99 | | | | | | | | | | 29 | | | | 29 | | 47.80 | 5 50– 5 99 |
| 6 00– 6 49 | | | | | 1 | | | 1 | | 42 | 1 | | 2 | 43 | 23.30 | 61.50 | 6 00– 6 49 |
| 6 50– 6 99 | | | | | | | | | | 21 | | | | 21 | | 68.30 | 6 50– 6 99 |
| 7 00– 7 49 | | | | | | | | 1 | 2 | 25 | | | 2 | 26 | 26.60 | 76.60 | 7 00– 7 49 |
| 7 50– 7 99 | | | | | | | | | | 15 | | | | 15 | | 81.50 | 7 50– 7 99 |
| 8 00– 8 99 | | | | | | 1 | | | 1 | 21 | | | 1 | 22 | 28.30 | 88.50 | 8 00– 8 99 |
| 9 00– 9 99 | | | | | | | | | 1 | 15 | | | 1 | 15 | 30.00 | 93.30 | 9 00– 9 99 |
| 10 00–10 99 | 1 | | | | | | | | 2 | 8 | 1 | | 4 | 8 | 36.60 | 95.90 | 10 00–10 99 |
| 11 00–11 99 | | 3 | | | 1 | | 1 | | 2 | 2 | | | 7 | 2 | 48.30 | 96.50 | 11 00–11 99 |
| 12 00–12 99 | | 4 | | | 1 | | 1 | | 3 | 5 | | | 9 | 5 | 63.30 | 98.10 | 12 00–12 99 |
| 13 00–13 99 | | 1 | | | | | | | 1 | | | | 2 | | 66.60 | | 13 00–13 99 |
| 14 00–14 99 | 1 | | | | | | | | | 3 | | | 1 | 3 | 68.30 | 99.10 | 14 00–14 99 |
| 15 00–15 99 | | | | | | | 1 | | 1 | 1 | | | 2 | 1 | 71.60 | 99.40 | 15 00–15 99 |
| 16 00–17 99 | | 1 | 1 | | | | 1 | | 3 | | 1 | | 6 | 1 | 81.60 | 99.70 | 16 00–17 99 |
| 18 00–19 99 | | | | 2 | | | 2 | | 3 | | | | 7 | | 93.30 | | 18 00–19 99 |
| 20 00–24 99 | 1 | | 1 | | | | | | 2 | | | | 3 | 1 | 98.30 | 100.00 | 20 00–24 99 |
| 25 00–29 99 | | 1 | | | | | | | | | | | 1 | | 100.00 | | 25 00–29 99 |
| Total | 3 | 10 | 2 | 4 | 6 | 3 | 6 | 2 | 21 | 300 | 10 | 5 | 60 | 312 | | | Total |

289. TABLE XV, A, 2, b, c, d, e

BUFFALO

**NEIGHBORHOOD STORES — OFFICE, SHIPPING AND DELIVERY, MANUFACTURING AND PLANT**

NUMBER OF EMPLOYEES EARNING SPECIFIED WEEKLY RATES, ACCORDING TO DEPARTMENT AND SEX

| WEEKLY RATES IN DOLLARS | DEPARTMENT | | | | | | | | | | | WEEKLY RATES IN DOLLARS |
|---|---|---|---|---|---|---|---|---|---|---|---|---|
| | OFFICE | | SHIPPING AND DELIVERY | MANUFACTURING | | PLANT | | TOTAL | | CUMULATIVE PER CENT. OF TOTAL | | |
| | Male | Female | Male | Male | Female | Male | Female | Male | Female | Male | Female | |
| Less than $3 00 | ........ | ........ | ........ | ........ | 2 | ........ | ........ | ........ | 2 | ........ | 3.00 | Less than $3 00 |
| $3 00–$3 49 | ........ | ........ | 1 | ........ | ........ | ........ | ........ | 1 | ........ | 2.10 | ........ | $3 00– 3 49 |
| 3 50– 3 99 | ........ | ........ | 1 | ........ | ........ | ........ | ........ | 1 | ........ | 4.30 | ........ | 3 50– 3 99 |
| 4 00– 4 49 | ........ | 1 | 3 | ........ | 1 | ........ | ........ | 3 | 2 | 10.60 | 6.00 | 4 00– 4 49 |
| 4 50– 4 99 | ........ | 1 | ........ | ........ | ........ | ........ | ........ | ........ | 1 | ........ | 7.60 | 4 50– 4 99 |
| 5 00– 5 49 | ........ | 6 | 1 | ........ | 3 | 2 | ........ | 3 | 9 | 17.00 | 21.20 | 5 00– 5 49 |
| 5 50– 5 99 | ........ | 6 | ........ | ........ | 2 | ........ | ........ | ........ | 8 | ........ | 33.30 | 5 50– 5 99 |
| 6 00– 6 49 | ........ | 5 | ........ | ........ | 5 | 1 | ........ | 1 | 10 | 19.10 | 48.50 | 6 00– 6.49 |
| 6 50– 6 99 | ........ | 2 | ........ | ........ | 1 | ........ | ........ | ........ | 3 | ........ | 53.00 | 6 50– 6 99 |
| 7 00– 7 49 | ........ | 2 | ........ | ........ | ........ | ........ | ........ | ........ | 2 | ........ | 56.00 | 7 00– 7 49 |
| 7 50– 7 99 | ........ | ........ | ........ | ........ | 3 | ........ | ........ | ........ | 3 | ........ | 60.60 | 7 50– 7 99 |
| 8 00– 8 99 | ........ | 3 | 1 | ........ | 2 | ........ | ........ | 1 | 5 | 21.30 | 68.20 | 8 00– 8 99 |
| 9 00– 9 99 | ........ | 3 | ........ | ........ | 3 | ........ | ........ | ........ | 6 | ........ | 77.30 | 9 00– 9 99 |
| 10 00–10 99 | ........ | 2 | 3 | ........ | 3 | 1 | ........ | 4 | 5 | 29.80 | 84.90 | 10 00–10 99 |
| 11 00–11 99 | ........ | 1 | ........ | ........ | 1 | 3 | ........ | 3 | 2 | 36.20 | 87.90 | 11 00–11 99 |
| 12 00–12 99 | ........ | 1 | 1 | ........ | ........ | 4 | 1 | 5 | 2 | 48.80 | 91.00 | 12 00–12 99 |
| 13 00–13 99 | ........ | 1 | ........ | 3 | 2 | 1 | ........ | 4 | 3 | 55.30 | 95.50 | 13 00–13 99 |
| 14 00–14 99 | 1 | ........ | 1 | ........ | 1 | 1 | 1 | 3 | 2 | 61.70 | 98.50 | 14 00–14 99 |
| 15 00–15 99 | ........ | ........ | 5 | 1 | ........ | ........ | ........ | 6 | ........ | 74.50 | ........ | 15 00–15 99 |
| 16 00–17 99 | 1 | 1 | 2 | 4 | ........ | 1 | ........ | 8 | 1 | 91.50 | 100.00 | 16 00–17 99 |
| 18 00–19 99 | ........ | ........ | ........ | ........ | ........ | 1 | ........ | 1 | ........ | 93.60 | ........ | 18 00–19 99 |
| 20 00–24 99 | 1 | ........ | ........ | 1 | ........ | ........ | ........ | 2 | ........ | 97.90 | ........ | 20 00–24 99 |
| 25 00–29 99 | 1 | ........ | ........ | ........ | ........ | ........ | ........ | 1 | ........ | 100.00 | ........ | 25 00–29 99 |
| Total | 4 | 35 | 19 | 9 | 29 | 15 | 2 | 47 | 66 | ........ | ........ | Total |

290. TABLE XVI, A, 2, b, c, d, e

BUFFALO

**NEIGHBORHOOD STORES — OFFICE, SHIPPING AND DELIVERY, MANUFACTURING AND PLANT**

NUMBER OF EMPLOYEES CLASSIFIED ACCORDING TO ACTUAL WEEKLY EARNINGS, BY DEPARTMENT AND SEX

| ACTUAL WEEKLY EARNINGS IN DOLLARS | DEPARTMENT | | | | | | | | | | | ACTUAL WEEKLY EARNINGS IN DOLLARS |
|---|---|---|---|---|---|---|---|---|---|---|---|---|
| | OFFICE | | SHIPPING AND DELIVERY | MANUFACTURING | | PLANT | | TOTAL | | CUMULATIVE PER CENT. OF TOTAL | | |
| | Male | Female | Male | Male | Female | Male | Female | Male | Female | Male | Female | |
| Less than $3 00. | ........ | ........ | ........ | ........ | 2 | ........ | ........ | ........ | 2 | ........ | 3.00 | Less than $3 00 |
| $3 00– 3 49.... | ........ | 1 | 2 | ........ | ........ | ........ | ........ | 2 | 1 | 4.30 | 4.50 | ...$3 00– 3 49 |
| 3 50– 3 99.... | ........ | ........ | 1 | ........ | ........ | ........ | ........ | 1 | ........ | 6.40 | ........ | ....3 50– 3 99 |
| 4 00– 4 49.... | ........ | 2 | 2 | ........ | ........ | ........ | ........ | 2 | 2 | 10.60 | 7.60 | ....4 00– 4 49 |
| 4 50– 4 99.... | ........ | 1 | ........ | ........ | 2 | ........ | ........ | ........ | 3 | ........ | 12.10 | ....4 50– 4 99 |
| 5 00– 5 49.... | ........ | 5 | 1 | ........ | 4 | 2 | ........ | 3 | 9 | 17.00 | 25.80 | ....5 00– 5 49 |
| 5 50– 5 99.... | ........ | 2 | ........ | ........ | 1 | ........ | ........ | ........ | 3 | ........ | 30.30 | ....5 50– 5 99 |
| 6 00– 6 49.... | ........ | 8 | ........ | ........ | | 1 | 1 | 1 | 13 | 19.10 | 50.00 | ....6 00– 6 49 |
| 6 50– 6 99.... | ........ | 1 | ........ | ........ | 2 | ........ | ........ | ........ | 3 | ........ | 54.50 | ....6 50– 6 99 |
| 7 00– 7 49.... | ........ | 2 | ........ | ........ | ........ | ........ | 1 | ........ | 3 | ........ | 59.10 | ....7 00– 7 49 |
| 7 50– 7 99.... | ........ | 1 | ........ | ........ | 1 | ........ | ........ | ........ | 2 | ........ | 62.10 | ....7 50– 7 99 |
| 8 00– 8 99.... | ........ | 3 | 1 | ........ | 5 | ........ | ........ | 1 | 8 | 21.3 | 74.30 | ....8 00– 8 99 |
| 9 00– 9 99.... | ........ | 3 | ........ | ........ | 2 | ........ | ........ | ........ | 5 | ........ | 81.40 | ....9 00– 9 99 |
| 10 00–10 99.... | ........ | 2 | 3 | ........ | 2 | 1 | ........ | 4 | 4 | 29.80 | 87.90 | ...10 00–10 99 |
| 11 00–11 99.... | ........ | 1 | ........ | ........ | 1 | 3 | ........ | 3 | 2 | 36.20 | 91.00 | ...11 00–11 99 |
| 12 00–12 99.... | ........ | 1 | 1 | ........ | ........ | 4 | ........ | 5 | 1 | 46.80 | 92.50 | ...12 00–12 99 |
| 13 00–13 99.... | ........ | 1 | ........ | 3 | 1 | 1 | ........ | 4 | 2 | 55.30 | 95.50 | ...13 00–13 99 |
| 14 00–14 99.... | 1 | ........ | 1 | ........ | 2 | 1 | ........ | 3 | 2 | 61.70 | 98.50 | ...14 00–14 99 |
| 15 00–15 99.... | ........ | ........ | 5 | 1 | ........ | ........ | ........ | 6 | ........ | 74.50 | ........ | ...15 00–15 99 |
| 16 00–17 99.... | 1 | 1 | 2 | 4 | ........ | 1 | ........ | 8 | 1 | 91.50 | 100.00 | ...16 00–17 99 |
| 20 00–24 99.... | 1 | ........ | ........ | 1 | ........ | 1 | ........ | 3 | ........ | 97.90 | ........ | ...20 00–24 99 |
| 25 00–29 99.... | 1 | ........ | ........ | ........ | ........ | ........ | ........ | 1 | ........ | 100.00 | ........ | ...25 00–29 99 |
| Total..... | 4 | 35 | 19 | 9 | 29 | 15 | 2 | 47 | 66 | ........ | ........ | .....Total |

BUFFALO

NEIGHBORHOOD STORES — OFFICE, SHIPPING AND DELIVERY, MANUFACTURING AND PLANT

291. TABLE XVII, A, 2, b, c, d, e NUMBER OF EMPLOYEES CLASSIFIED BY AGE GROUPS, ACCORDING TO D PARTMENT AND SEX

| AGE GROUPS IN YEARS | DEPARTMENT | | | | | | | | | | | AGE GROUPS IN YEARS |
|---|---|---|---|---|---|---|---|---|---|---|---|---|
| | OFFICE | | SHIPPING AND DELIVERY | MANUFACTURING- | | PLANT | | TOTAL | | PER CENT. OF TOTAL | | |
| | Male | Female | Male | Male | Female | Male | Female | Male | Female | Male | Female | |
| 14–15 | ........ | ........ | 4 | ........ | ........ | ........ | ........ | 4 | ........ | 8.50 | ........ | 14–15 |
| 16–17 | ........ | 4 | 3 | ........ | 5 | 1 | ........ | 4 | 9 | 8.50 | 14.10 | 16–17 |
| 18–20 | ........ | 12 | 2 | ........ | 6 | 2 | ........ | 4 | 18 | 8.50 | 28.20 | 18–20 |
| 21–24 | 1 | 10 | 4 | ........ | 10 | 1 | ........ | 6 | 20 | 12.80 | 31.20 | 21–24 |
| 25–29 | ........ | 7 | 1 | 1 | 3 | 1 | ........ | 3 | 10 | 6.40 | 15.60 | 25–29 |
| 30–34 | 1 | ........ | 3 | ........ | 1 | ........ | ........ | 4 | 1 | 8.50 | 1.60 | 30–34 |
| 35–39 | 1 | ........ | ........ | 1 | 1 | 3 | 1 | 5 | 2 | 10.60 | 3.10 | 35–39 |
| 40–44 | ........ | ........ | 1 | 4 | 2 | 1 | ........ | 6 | 2 | 12.80 | 3.10 | 40–44 |
| 45–54 | 1 | 1 | | 3 | ........ | 4 | 1 | 9 | 2 | 19.20 | 3.10 | 45–54 |
| 55–64 | ........ | ........ | ........ | ........ | ........ | 1 | ........ | 1 | ........ | 2.10 | ........ | 55–64 |
| 65 and ove | ........ | ........ | ........ | ........ | ........ | 1 | ........ | 1 | ........ | 2.10 | ........ | 65 and over |
| Not reported | ........ | 1 | ........ | ........ | 1 | ........ | ........ | ........ | 2 | ........ | ........ | Not reported |
| Total | 4 | 35 | 19 | 9 | 29 | 15 | 2 | 47 | 66 | 100.00 | 100.00 | Total |

BUFFALO

THE PAPER BOX INDUSTRY — FACTORY WORKERS

292. TABLE V, C, a — NUMBER AND PER CENT. OF EMPLOYEES EARNING SPECIFIED WEEKLY RATES, BY AGE GROUPS AND SEX

| WEEKLY RATES IN DOLLARS | AGE GROUPS IN YEARS | | | | | | | | | | | | | | WEEKLY RATES IN DOLLARS |
|---|---|---|---|---|---|---|---|---|---|---|---|---|---|---|---|
| | 14–15 | | 16–17 | | 18–20 | | 21–24 | | 25–29 | | 30–34 | | 35–39 | | |
| | Male | Female | Male | Female | Male | Female | Male | Female | Male | Female | Male | Female | Male | Female | |
| Less than $3 00 | .... | 5 | .... | ...... | ...... | ...... | ...... | ...... | ...... | ...... | ...... | ...... | ...... | ...... | Less than $3 00 |
| $3 00–$3 49... | .... | 3 | .... | 2 | ...... | ...... | ...... | ...... | ...... | ...... | ...... | ...... | ...... | ...... | ...$3 00– 3 49 |
| 3 50– 3 99... | .... | 4 | .... | 1 | ...... | ...... | ...... | ...... | ...... | ...... | ...... | ...... | ...... | ...... | ... 3 50– 3 99 |
| 4 00– 4 49... | 2 | ...... | .... | 7 | ...... | 1 | ...... | 1 | ...... | ...... | ...... | ...... | ...... | ...... | ... 4 00– 4 49 |
| 4 50– 4 99... | 1 | 1 | .... | 7 | ...... | ...... | ...... | ...... | ...... | ...... | ...... | ...... | ...... | ...... | ... 4 50– 4 99 |
| 5 00– 5 49... | .... | ...... | 1 | 12 | ...... | 21 | ...... | 10 | ...... | 4 | ...... | 2 | ...... | ...... | ... 5 00– 5 49 |
| 5 50– 5 99... | .... | ...... | 1 | 1 | ...... | 9 | ...... | 3 | ...... | ...... | ...... | ...... | ...... | ...... | ... 5 50– 5 99 |
| 6 00– 6 49... | .... | ...... | 6 | 10 | ...... | 25 | ...... | 22 | ...... | 2 | ...... | ...... | ...... | 1 | ... 6 00– 6 49 |
| 6 50– 6 99... | .... | ...... | .... | 1 | ...... | 3 | ...... | 1 | ...... | 1 | ...... | 1 | ...... | 1 | ... 6 50– 6 99 |
| 7 00– 7 49... | .... | ...... | 4 | 4 | 3 | 15 | ...... | 17 | ...... | 4 | ...... | 2 | ...... | 2 | ... 7 00– 7 49 |
| 7 50– 7 99... | .... | ...... | .... | 1 | 5 | 1 | 1 | 3 | ...... | ...... | ...... | 1 | ...... | ...... | ... 7 50– 7 99 |
| 8 00– 8 99... | .... | 1 | 3 | ...... | 2 | 3 | 1 | 8 | 1 | 5 | ...... | 1 | ...... | 1 | ... 8 00– 8 99 |
| 9 00– 9 99... | .... | ...... | .... | ...... | 7 | ...... | 3 | 8 | ...... | 1 | 1 | ...... | ...... | ...... | ... 9 00– 9 99 |
| 10 00–10 99... | .... | ...... | .... | ...... | 2 | 1 | 7 | 2 | ...... | 4 | ...... | ...... | ...... | ...... | ...10 00–10 99 |
| 11 00–11 99... | .... | ...... | .... | ...... | ...... | ...... | 1 | ...... | 2 | 2 | 1 | ...... | ...... | ...... | ...11 00–11 99 |
| 12 00–12 99... | .... | ...... | .... | ...... | ...... | ...... | 8 | 1 | 2 | 1 | 1 | ...... | 1 | ...... | ...12 00–12 99 |
| 13 00–13 99... | .... | ...... | .... | ...... | ...... | ...... | 1 | ...... | 1 | ...... | ...... | ...... | ...... | ...... | ...13 00–13 99 |
| 14 00–14 99... | .... | ...... | .... | ...... | ...... | ...... | 1 | ...... | 1 | ...... | 1 | 1 | ...... | ...... | ...14 00–14 99 |
| 15 00–15 99... | .... | ...... | .... | ...... | ...... | ...... | 2 | ...... | 3 | ...... | 1 | ...... | ...... | ...... | ...15 00–15 99 |
| 16 00–17 99... | .... | ...... | .... | ...... | ...... | ...... | 2 | ...... | 3 | ...... | 1 | ...... | ...... | ...... | ...16 00–17 99 |
| 18 00–19 99... | .... | ...... | .... | ...... | ...... | ...... | ...... | ...... | 1 | ...... | 3 | ...... | ...... | ...... | ...18 00–19 99 |
| 20 00–24 99... | .... | ...... | .... | ...... | ...... | ...... | ...... | ...... | 1 | ...... | 5 | ...... | ...... | ...... | ...20 00–24 99 |
| 25 00–29 99... | .... | ...... | .... | ...... | ...... | ...... | ...... | ...... | 1 | ...... | 1 | ...... | ...... | ...... | ...25 00–29 99 |
| 30 00–34 99... | .... | ...... | .... | ...... | ...... | ...... | ...... | ...... | ...... | ...... | ...... | ...... | 1 | ...... | ...30 00–34 99 |
| Not reported... | .... | ...... | 1 | 1 | ...... | 2 | 2 | 2 | ...... | ...... | 1 | ...... | ...... | ...... | ...Not reported |
| **Total**..... | **3** | **14** | **16** | **47** | **19** | **81** | **29** | **78** | **16** | **24** | **16** | **8** | **2** | **5** | .....**Total** |

292. TABLE V, C, a — *(concluded)*

BUFFALO

**THE PAPER BOX INDUSTRY — FACTORY WORKERS**

NUMBER AND PER CENT. OF EMPLOYEES EARNING SPECIFIED WEEKLY RATES, BY AGE GROUPS AND SEX

| WEEKLY RATES IN DOLLARS | AGE GROUPS IN YEARS | | | | | | | | | | | WEEKLY RATES IN DOLLARS |
|---|---|---|---|---|---|---|---|---|---|---|---|---|
| | 40–44 | | 45–54 | | 55–64 | | NOT REPORTED | TOTAL | | CUMULATIVE PER CENT. OF TOTAL | | |
| | Male | Female | Male | Female | Male | Female | Female | Male | Female | Male | Female | |
| Less than $3 00 | | | | | | | | | 5 | | 1.90 | Less than $3 00 |
| $3 00–$3 49 | | | | | | | | | 5 | | 3.80 | $3 00– 3 49 |
| 3 50– 3 99 | | | | | | | | | 5 | | 5.60 | 3 50– 3 99 |
| 4 00– 4 49 | | | | | | | | 2 | 9 | 1.80 | 9.00 | 4 00– 4 49 |
| 4 50– 4 99 | | | | | | | | 1 | 8 | 2.70 | 12.10 | 4 50– 4 99 |
| 5 00– 5 49 | | 1 | | | | 1 | | 1 | 51 | 3.60 | 31.20 | 5 00– 5 49 |
| 5 50– 5 99 | | | | 1 | | | | 1 | 14 | 4.50 | 36.50 | 5 50– 5 99 |
| 6 00– 6 49 | | 2 | | 1 | | | 2 | 6 | 65 | 9.90 | 60.50 | 6 00– 6 49 |
| 6 50– 6 99 | | | | | | | | | 8 | | 64.00 | 6 50– 6 99 |
| 7 00– 7 49 | | | | 3 | | | 1 | 7 | 48 | 16.20 | 82.00 | 7 00– 7 49 |
| 7 50– 7 99 | | | | | | | | 6 | 6 | 21.60 | 84.20 | 7 50– 7 99 |
| 8 00– 8 99 | | | | | | | | 7 | 19 | 27.90 | 91.40 | 8 00– 8 99 |
| 9 00– 9 99 | | 1 | | | 1 | | | 12 | 10 | 38.80 | 95.20 | 9 00– 9 99 |
| 10 00–10 99 | 1 | | | | 2 | | | 12 | 7 | 49.60 | 97.80 | 10 00–10 99 |
| 11 00–11 99 | | | | | | | | 4 | 2 | 53.20 | 98.50 | 11 00–11 99 |
| 12 00–12 99 | | | | | 1 | | | 13 | 2 | 64.90 | 99.40 | 12 00–12 99 |
| 13 00–13 99 | | | | | | | | 2 | | 66.70 | | 13 00–13 99 |
| 14 00–14 99 | | | | | | | | 3 | 1 | 69.40 | 99.70 | 14 00–14 99 |
| 15 00–15 99 | 1 | | | | | | | 7 | | 75.70 | | 15 00–15 99 |
| 16 00–17 99 | 1 | 1 | 1 | | 1 | | | 9 | 1 | 83.80 | 100.00 | 16 00–17 99 |
| 18 00–19 99 | | | | | | | | 4 | | 87.50 | | 18 00–19 99 |
| 20 00–24 99 | 1 | | | | 1 | | | 8 | | 94.50 | | 20 00–24 99 |
| 25 00–29 99 | 1 | | 1 | | | | | 4 | | 98.20 | | 25 00–29 99 |
| 30 00–34 99 | 1 | | | | | | | 2 | | 100.00 | | 30 00–34 99 |
| Not reported | | | | | | | | 4 | 5 | | | Not reported |
| Total | 6 | 5 | 2 | 5 | 6 | 1 | 3 | 115 | 271 | | | Total |

BUFFALO

THE PAPER BOX INDUSTRY — FACTORY WORKERS

293. TABLE VIII, C, a NUMBER AND PER CENT. OF EMPLOYEES EARNING SPECIFIED WEEKLY RATES, BY OCCUPATION AND SEX

| WEEKLY RATES IN DOLLARS | OCCUPATION: FOREMEN AND FOREWOMEN | | CUTTERS | | SETTERS-UP | | GENERAL MACHINE WORK | | TURNERS-IN | STRIPPERS AND TOP LABELERS | TABLE WORK | | CLOSING AND TYING | FLOOR WORK | | TOTAL | | CUMULATIVE PER CENT. OF TOTAL | | WEEKLY RATES IN DOLLARS |
|---|---|---|---|---|---|---|---|---|---|---|---|---|---|---|---|---|---|---|---|---|
| | Male | Female | Male | Female | Male | Female | Male | Female | Female | Female | Male | Female | Female | Male | Female | Male | Female | Male | Female | |
| Less than $3 00 | | | | | | 2 | | | | 2 | | 1 | | | | | 5 | | 1.90 | Less than $3 00 |
| $3 00-$3 49 | | | | | | | | | 1 | 1 | | 2 | | | 1 | | 5 | | 3.80 | $3 00- 3 49 |
| 3 50- 3 99 | | | | | | | | | | | | 3 | | | 2 | | 5 | | 5.60 | 3 50- 3 99 |
| 4 00- 4 49 | | | | 1 | | | | 3 | 1 | | | 1 | 1 | 2 | 2 | 2 | 9 | 1.80 | 9.00 | 4 00- 4 49 |
| 4 50- 4 99 | | | | | | | | 1 | 1 | 1 | | 2 | 2 | 1 | 1 | 1 | 8 | 2.70 | 12.10 | 4 50- 4 99 |
| 5 00- 5 49 | | | 1 | 1 | | 3 | | 11 | 1 | 8 | | 6 | 7 | | 14 | 1 | 51 | 3.60 | 31.20 | 5 00- 5 49 |
| 5 50- 5 99 | | | | | | | | 4 | | 4 | | 2 | 4 | 1 | | 1 | 14 | 4.50 | 36.50 | 5 50- 5 99 |
| 6 00- 6 49 | | | | 3 | | 3 | 2 | 29 | | 3 | | 2 | 12 | 4 | 13 | 6 | 65 | 9.90 | 60.50 | 6 00- 6 49 |
| 6 50- 6 99 | | | | | | 2 | | 2 | | | | | | | 4 | | 8 | | 64.00 | 6 50- 6 99 |
| 7 00- 7 49 | | 4 | 4 | 2 | | 1 | 1 | 23 | | 1 | | 1 | 6 | 2 | 10 | 7 | 48 | 16.20 | 82.00 | 7 00- 7 49 |
| 7 50- 7 99 | | 1 | 3 | 2 | | | 2 | 2 | | | 1 | | | | 1 | 6 | 6 | 21.60 | 84.20 | 7 50- 7 99 |
| 8 00- 8 99 | 1 | 9 | 3 | | 1 | 1 | 1 | 2 | | | | 2 | | 1 | 5 | 7 | 19 | 27.90 | 91.40 | 8 00- 8 99 |
| 9 00- 9 99 | | 8 | 7 | | | | 5 | 1 | | | | | | | 1 | 12 | 10 | 38.80 | 95.20 | 9 00- 9 99 |
| 10 00-10 99 | | 5 | 6 | 1 | | | 3 | 1 | | | 1 | | | 2 | | 12 | 7 | 49.60 | 97.80 | 10 00-10 99 |
| 11 00-11 99 | | 2 | 2 | | | | 2 | | | | | | | | | 4 | 2 | 53.20 | 98.50 | 11 00-11 99 |
| 12 00-12 99 | | 2 | 7 | | | | 4 | | | | | | | 2 | | 13 | 2 | 64.90 | 99.40 | 12 00-12 99 |
| 13 00-13 99 | | | 1 | | | | 1 | | | | | | | | | 2 | | 66.70 | | 13 00-13 99 |
| 14 00-14 99 | | 1 | 1 | | | | 2 | | | | | | | | | 3 | 1 | 69.40 | 99.70 | 14 00-14 99 |
| 15 00-15 99 | 2 | | 3 | | | | 1 | | | | 1 | | | | | 7 | | 75.70 | | 15 00-15 99 |
| 16 00-17 99 | 5 | | 4 | 1 | | | | | | | | | | | | 9 | 1 | 83.80 | 100.00 | 16 00-17 99 |
| 18 00-19 99 | 3 | | 1 | | | | | | | | | | | | | 4 | | 87.50 | | 18 00-19 99 |
| 20 00-24 99 | 8 | | | | | | | | | | | | | | | 8 | | 94.50 | | 20 00-24 99 |
| 25 00-29 99 | 4 | | | | | | | | | | | | | | | 4 | | 98.20 | | 25 00-29 99 |
| 30 00-34 99 | 2 | | | | | | | | | | | | | | | 2 | | 100.00 | | 30 00-34 99 |
| Not reported | 1 | 1 | 1 | | | | 2 | 1 | | 1 | | 1 | | | 1 | 4 | 5 | | | Not reported |
| Total | 26 | 33 | 44 | 11 | 1 | 12 | 26 | 80 | 4 | 21 | 3 | 23 | 32 | 15 | 55 | 115 | 271 | | | Total |

BUFFALO

294. TABLE VI, C, a

## THE PAPER BOX INDUSTRY — FACTORY WORKERS

NUMBER AND PER CENT. OF EMPLOYEES CLASSIFIED ACCORDING TO ACTUAL WEEKLY EARNINGS, BY AGE GROUPS AND SEX

| Actual Weekly Earnings in Dollars | Age Groups in Years | | | | | | | | | | | | | | Actual Weekly Earnings in Dollars |
|---|---|---|---|---|---|---|---|---|---|---|---|---|---|---|---|
| | 14–15 | | 16–17 | | 18–20 | | 21–24 | | 25–29 | | 30–34 | | 35–39 | | |
| | Male | Female | Male | Female | Male | Female | Male | Female | Male | Female | Male | Female | Male | Female | |
| Less than $3 00 | .... | 14 | 2 | 7 | 1 | 8 | .... | 3 | .... | .... | .... | .... | .... | 1 | Less than $3 00 |
| $3 00–$3 49... | .... | 5 | .... | 8 | .... | 3 | .... | 2 | .... | .... | .... | .... | .... | .... | ...$3 00– 3 49 |
| 3 50– 3 99... | 1 | 11 | .... | 9 | .... | 6 | .... | 2 | .... | 1 | .... | .... | .... | 1 | ... 3 50– 3 99 |
| 4 00– 4 49... | 2 | 4 | .... | 19 | .... | 10 | .... | 8 | .... | 2 | .... | .... | .... | .... | ... 4 00– 4 49 |
| 4 50– 4 99... | .... | 6 | .... | 10 | .... | 19 | .... | 11 | .... | 1 | .... | 1 | .... | .... | ... 4 50– 4 99 |
| 5 00– 5 49... | 1 | 1 | 3 | 24 | .... | 28 | .... | 21 | .... | 3 | .... | 1 | .... | .... | ... 5 00– 5 49 |
| 5 50– 5 99... | .... | 2 | 2 | 20 | 2 | 24 | .... | 18 | .... | 3 | .... | 1 | .... | .... | ... 5 50– 5 99 |
| 6 00– 6 49... | .... | 5 | 4 | 13 | .... | 29 | .... | 17 | .... | 5 | .... | .... | .... | 1 | ... 6 00– 6 49 |
| 6 50– 6 99... | .... | .... | .... | 5 | .... | 29 | 1 | 22 | .... | 1 | .... | 1 | .... | 2 | ... 6 50– 6 99 |
| 7 00– 7 49... | .... | .... | 2 | 9 | 4 | 17 | 1 | 25 | .... | 6 | .... | 2 | .... | 2 | ... 7 00– 7 49 |
| 7 50– 7 99... | .... | .... | 1 | 4 | 1 | 12 | 1 | 7 | .... | 1 | .... | 1 | .... | .... | ... 7 50– 7 99 |
| 8 00– 8 99... | .... | 1 | 2 | 7 | 6 | 22 | 1 | 20 | 1 | 4 | .... | 1 | .... | 2 | ... 8 00– 8 99 |
| 9 00– 9 99... | .... | .... | 1 | 4 | 2 | 10 | 4 | 11 | 1 | 3 | .... | .... | .... | .... | ... 9 00– 9 99 |
| 10 00–10 99... | .... | .... | .... | .... | 4 | 4 | 4 | 1 | 1 | 3 | 1 | 1 | .... | .... | ...10 00–10 99 |
| 11 00–11 99... | .... | .... | .... | 1 | 1 | 1 | 4 | .... | .... | 3 | 1 | .... | .... | .... | ...11 00–11 99 |
| 12 00–12 99... | .... | .... | .... | .... | .... | .... | 4 | 1 | 3 | 1 | .... | .... | 1 | .... | ...12 00–12 99 |
| 13 00–13 99... | .... | .... | .... | .... | 1 | .... | 2 | .... | .... | .... | 1 | .... | .... | .... | ...13 00–13 99 |
| 14 00–14 99... | .... | .... | .... | .... | 1 | .... | 4 | .... | .... | .... | 2 | 1 | .... | .... | ...14 00–14 99 |
| 15 00–15 99... | .... | .... | .... | .... | .... | .... | 2 | .... | 5 | .... | 1 | .... | .... | .... | ...15 00–15 99 |
| 16 00–17 99... | .... | .... | .... | .... | 1 | .... | 2 | .... | 1 | 1 | 2 | .... | .... | .... | ...16 00–17 99 |
| 18 00–19 99... | .... | .... | .... | .... | .... | .... | .... | .... | .... | .... | 2 | .... | .... | .... | ...18 00–19 99 |
| 20 00–24 99... | .... | .... | .... | .... | .... | .... | .... | .... | 1 | .... | 3 | .... | .... | .... | ...20 00–24 99 |
| 25 00–29 99... | .... | .... | .... | .... | .... | .... | .... | .... | 1 | .... | .... | .... | .... | .... | ...25 00–29 99 |
| 30 00–34 99... | .... | .... | .... | .... | .... | .... | .... | .... | .... | .... | .... | .... | .... | .... | ...30 00–34 99 |
| Not reported.. | .... | .... | .... | .... | .... | .... | 1 | .... | 2 | .... | 5 | .... | 1 | .... | ..Not reported |
| Total..... | 4 | 49 | 17 | 140 | 24 | 222 | 31 | 169 | 16 | 38 | 18 | 10 | 2 | 9 | .....Total |

BUFFALO

294. TABLE VI, C, a — (*concluded*) THE PAPER BOX INDUSTRY — FACTORY WORKERS

NUMBER AND PER CENT. OF EMPLOYEES CLASSIFIED ACCORDING TO ACTUAL WEEKLY EARNINGS, BY AGE GROUPS AND SEX

| ACTUAL WEEKLY EARNINGS IN DOLLARS | AGE GROUPS IN YEARS (*concluded*) | | | | | | | | | | | ACTUAL WEEKLY EARNINGS IN DOLLARS |
|---|---|---|---|---|---|---|---|---|---|---|---|---|
| | 40–44 | | 45–54 | | 55–64 | | NOT REPORTED | TOTAL | | CUMULATIVE PER CENT. OF TOTAL | | |
| | Male | Female | Male | Female | Male | Female | Female | Male | Female | Male | Female | |
| Less than $3 00 | ........ | ........ | ........ | ........ | ........ | ........ | ........ | 3 | 33 | 2.50 | 5.00 | Less than $3 00 |
| $3 00–$3 49... | ........ | ........ | ........ | ........ | ........ | ........ | ........ | ........ | 18 | ........ | 7.80 | ...$3 00– 3 49 |
| 3 50– 3 99... | ........ | ........ | ........ | ........ | ........ | ........ | ........ | 1 | 30 | 3.40 | 12.40 | ... 3 50– 3 99 |
| 4 00– 4 49... | ........ | ........ | ........ | ........ | ........ | ........ | ........ | 2 | 43 | 5.00 | 18.90 | ... 4 00– 4 49 |
| 4 50– 4 99... | ........ | ........ | ........ | 2 | ........ | ........ | 1 | ........ | 51 | ........ | 26.70 | ... 4 50– 4 99 |
| 5 00– 5 49... | ........ | 3 | ........ | ........ | ........ | 1 | ........ | 4 | 82 | 8.40 | 39.20 | ... 5 00– 5 49 |
| 5 50– 5 99... | ........ | 1 | ........ | 1 | ........ | ........ | ........ | 4 | 70 | 11.80 | 49.90 | ... 5 50– 5 99 |
| 6 00– 6 49... | ........ | 1 | ........ | 1 | 1 | ........ | 1 | 5 | 73 | 15.90 | 61.00 | ... 6 00– 6 49 |
| 6 50– 6 99... | ........ | ........ | ........ | 1 | ........ | ........ | ........ | 1 | 61 | 16.80 | 70.40 | ... 6 50– 6 99 |
| 7 00– 7 49... | ........ | ........ | ........ | 2 | ........ | ........ | 1 | 7 | 64 | 22.70 | 80.20 | ... 7 00– 7 49 |
| 7 50– 7 99... | ........ | ........ | ........ | ........ | ........ | ........ | ........ | 3 | 25 | 25.20 | 84.00 | ... 7 50– 7 99 |
| 8 00– 8 99... | ........ | 1 | ........ | ........ | ........ | ........ | ........ | 10 | 58 | 33.60 | 92.80 | ... 8 00– 8 99 |
| 9 00– 9 99... | 1 | ........ | 1 | ........ | ........ | ........ | ........ | 10 | 28 | 42.00 | 97.10 | ... 9 00– 9 99 |
| 10 00–10 99... | ........ | ........ | ........ | ........ | 2 | ........ | ........ | 12 | 9 | 52.10 | 98.50 | ...10 00–10 99 |
| 11 00–11 99... | ........ | ........ | ........ | ........ | ........ | ........ | ........ | 6 | 5 | 57.20 | 99.20 | ...11 00–11 99 |
| 12 00–12 99... | ........ | ........ | ........ | ........ | 1 | ........ | ........ | 9 | 2 | 64.70 | 99.50 | ...12 00–12 99 |
| 13 00–13 99... | ........ | ........ | ........ | ........ | ........ | ........ | ........ | 4 | ........ | 68.10 | ........ | ...13 00–13 99 |
| 14 00–14 99... | ........ | ........ | ........ | ........ | ........ | ........ | ........ | 7 | 1 | 74.00 | 99.70 | ...14 00–14 99 |
| 15 00–15 99... | 1 | ........ | 2 | ........ | ........ | ........ | ........ | 11 | ........ | 83.20 | ........ | ...15 00–15 99 |
| 16 00–17 99... | 1 | 1 | ........ | ........ | 1 | ........ | ........ | 8 | 2 | 90.00 | 100.00 | ...16 00–17 99 |
| 18 00–19 99... | ........ | ........ | ........ | ........ | 1 | ........ | ........ | 3 | ........ | 92.50 | ........ | ...18 00–19 99 |
| 20 00–24 99... | 1 | ........ | 1 | ........ | ........ | ........ | ........ | 6 | ........ | 97.50 | ........ | ...20 00–24 99 |
| 25 00–29 99... | ........ | ........ | ........ | ........ | ........ | ........ | ........ | 1 | ........ | 98.40 | ........ | ...25 00–29 99 |
| 30 00–34 99... | 1 | ........ | ........ | ........ | ........ | ........ | ........ | 1 | ........ | 100.00 | ........ | ...30 00–34 99 |
| Not reported... | 1 | ........ | 1 | ........ | ........ | ........ | ........ | 11 | ........ | ........ | ........ | ...Not reported |
| Total..... | 6 | 7 | 5 | 7 | 6 | 1 | 3 | 129 | 655 | ........ | ........ | .....Total |

BUFFALO

THE PAPER BOX INDUSTRY — FACTORY WORKERS

295. TABLE IX, C, a NUMBER AND PER CENT. OF EMPLOYEES CLASSIFIED ACCORDING TO ACTUAL WEEKLY EARNINGS, BY OCCUPATION AND SEX

| ACTUAL WEEKLY EARNING IN DOLLARS | OCCUPATION | | | | | | | | | | | | | | | | | CUMULATIVE PER CENT. OF TOTAL | | ACTUAL WEEKLY EARNINGS IN DOLLARS |
|---|---|---|---|---|---|---|---|---|---|---|---|---|---|---|---|---|---|---|---|---|
| | FOREMEN AND FOREWOMEN | | CUTTERS | | SETTERS-UP | | GENERAL MACHINE WORK | | TURNERS-IN | STRIPPERS AND TOP LABELERS | TABLE WORK | | CLOSING AND TYING | FLOOR WORK | | TOTAL | | | | |
| | Male | Female | Male | Female | Male | Female | Male | Female | Female | Female | Male | Female | Female | Male | Female | Male | Female | Male | Female | |
| Less than $3 00 | | | 3 | | | 3 | | 5 | 6 | 6 | | 4 | 3 | | 6 | 3 | 33 | 2.50 | 5.00 | Less than $3 00 |
| $3 00-$3 49 | | | | | | 2 | | 1 | 3 | 2 | | 9 | | | 1 | | 18 | | 7.80 | $3 00- 3 49 |
| 3 50- 3 99 | | | | 1 | | | | 5 | 7 | 3 | | 7 | 3 | 1 | 4 | 1 | 30 | 3.40 | 12.40 | 3 50- 3 99 |
| 4 00- 4 49 | | 1 | | 2 | | | | 3 | 5 | 7 | | 13 | 6 | 2 | 6 | 2 | 43 | 5.00 | 18.90 | 4 00- 4 49 |
| 4 50- 4 99 | | | | | | | | 11 | 5 | 7 | | 16 | 9 | | 3 | | 51 | | 26.70 | 4 0- 4 99 |
| 5 00- 5 49 | | | 1 | | | 6 | 1 | 25 | 2 | 9 | | 15 | 5 | 2 | 20 | 4 | 82 | 8.40 | 39.20 | 5 00- 5 49 |
| 5 50- 5 99 | | 1 | 1 | 1 | | 1 | 1 | 19 | 1 | 12 | 1 | 20 | 9 | 1 | 6 | 4 | 70 | 11.80 | 49.90 | 5 50- 5 99 |
| 6 00- 6 49 | | 2 | | 2 | | 2 | 2 | 25 | 2 | 9 | | 18 | 9 | 3 | 4 | 5 | 73 | 15.90 | 61.00 | 6 00- 6 49 |
| 6 50- 6 99 | | 2 | | 1 | | 4 | 1 | 17 | 1 | 5 | | 20 | 7 | | 4 | 1 | 61 | 16.80 | 70.40 | 6 50- 6 99 |
| 7 00- 7 49 | | 4 | 3 | 2 | | 3 | 2 | 24 | | 2 | | 14 | 4 | 2 | 11 | 7 | 64 | 22.70 | 80.20 | 7 00- 7 49 |
| 7 50- 7 99 | | 3 | 2 | 1 | | 1 | 1 | 7 | | 8 | | 5 | | | | 3 | 25 | 25.20 | 84.00 | 7 50- 7 99 |
| 8 00- 8 99 | 1 | 7 | 4 | | 1 | 3 | 3 | 20 | | 7 | | 17 | 1 | 1 | 3 | 10 | 58 | 33.60 | 92.80 | 8 00- 8 99 |
| 9 00- 9 99 | | 6 | 4 | | | 1 | 3 | 9 | | 3 | | 7 | 2 | 3 | | 10 | 28 | 42.00 | 97.10 | 9 00- 9 99 |
| 10 00-10 99 | | 2 | 8 | 1 | | 1 | 2 | 1 | | 2 | | 2 | | 2 | | 12 | 9 | 52.10 | 98.50 | 10 00-10 99 |
| 11 00-11 99 | | 2 | 3 | | | 1 | 1 | 1 | | | 1 | | 1 | 1 | | 6 | 5 | 57.20 | 99.20 | 11 00-11 99 |
| 12 00-12 99 | | 2 | 7 | | | | 2 | | | | | | | | | 9 | 2 | 64.70 | 99.50 | 12 00-12 99 |
| 13 00-13 99 | | | | | | | 4 | | | | | | | | | 4 | | 68.10 | | 13 00-13 99 |
| 14 00-14 99 | | 1 | 4 | | | | 3 | | | | | | | | | 7 | 1 | 74.00 | 99.70 | 14 00-14 99 |
| 15 00-15 99 | 3 | | 4 | | | | 3 | | | | 1 | | | | | 11 | | 83.20 | | 15 00-15 99 |
| 16 00-17 99 | 3 | | 1 | 1 | | | 4 | 1 | | | | | | | | 8 | 2 | 90.00 | 100.00 | 16 00-17 99 |
| 18 00-19 99 | 2 | | 1 | | | | | | | | | | | | | 3 | | 92.50 | | 18 00-19 99 |
| 20 00-24 99 | 5 | | | | | | 1 | | | | | | | | | 6 | | 97.50 | | 20 00-24 99 |
| 25 00-29 99 | 1 | | | | | | | | | | | | | | | 1 | | 98.40 | | 25 00-29 99 |
| 30 00-34 99 | 1 | | | | | | | | | | | | | | | 1 | | 100.00 | | 30 00-34 99 |
| Not reported | 10 | | 1 | | | | | | | | | | | | | 11 | | | | Not reported |
| Total | 26 | 33 | 47 | 12 | 1 | 28 | 34 | 174 | 32 | 82 | 3 | 167 | 59 | 18 | 68 | 129 | 655 | | | Total |

BUFFALO

THE CONFECTIONERY INDUSTRY — FACTORY WORKERS

296. TABLE V, D, a — NUMBER AND PER CENT. OF EMPLOYEES EARNING SPECIFIED WEEKLY RATES, BY AGE GROUPS AND SEX

| WEEKLY RATES IN DOLLARS | AGE GROUPS IN YEARS | | | | | | | | | | | WEEKLY RATES IN DOLLARS |
|---|---|---|---|---|---|---|---|---|---|---|---|---|
| | 14–15 | 16–17 | | 18–20 | | 21–24 | | 25–29 | | 30–34 | | |
| | Female | Male | Female | Male | Female | Male | Female | Male | Female | Male | Female | |
| $3 50–$3 99... | 1 | ........ | 2 | ........ | ........ | ........ | ........ | ........ | ........ | ........ | ........ | ...$3 50–$3 99 |
| 4 00– 4 49... | 1 | ........ | 31 | ........ | 11 | ........ | 3 | ........ | ........ | ........ | ........ | ... 4 00– 4 49 |
| 4 50– 4 99... | ........ | ........ | 11 | ........ | 15 | ........ | 1 | ........ | 1 | ........ | ........ | ... 4 50– 4 99 |
| 5 00– 5 49... | ........ | ........ | 2 | ........ | 8 | ........ | 6 | ........ | 2 | ........ | 1 | ... 5 00– 5 49 |
| 5 50– 5 99... | ........ | ........ | ........ | ........ | 3 | ........ | 1 | ........ | ........ | ........ | ........ | ... 5 50– 5 99 |
| 6 00– 6 49... | ........ | 2 | ........ | ........ | 6 | 1 | 5 | ........ | 4 | ........ | 1 | ... 6 00– 6 49 |
| 6 50– 6 99... | ........ | ........ | ........ | ........ | 1 | ........ | 2 | ........ | 2 | ........ | 1 | ... 6 50– 6 99 |
| 7 00– 7 49... | ........ | ........ | ........ | 3 | 2 | 2 | 4 | ........ | 1 | ........ | 1 | ... 7 00– 7 49 |
| 7 50– 7 99... | ........ | ........ | ........ | 2 | ........ | 1 | 1 | 1 | 1 | ........ | ........ | ... 7 50– 7 99 |
| 8 00– 8 99... | ........ | 1 | ........ | 5 | 1 | 3 | 1 | 2 | 3 | ........ | ........ | ... 8 00– 8 99 |
| 9 00– 9 99... | ........ | ........ | ........ | 3 | ........ | 1 | 1 | 3 | 1 | 1 | ........ | ... 9 00– 9 99 |
| 10 00–10 99... | ........ | ........ | ........ | 1 | ........ | 3 | ........ | ........ | 1 | ........ | ........ | ...10 00–10 99 |
| 11 00–11 99... | ........ | ........ | ........ | ........ | ........ | 1 | ........ | ........ | ........ | ........ | ........ | ...11 00–11 99 |
| 12 00–12 99... | ........ | ........ | ........ | 1 | ........ | 6 | ........ | 1 | ........ | ........ | ........ | ...12 00–12 99 |
| 14 00–14 99... | ........ | ........ | ........ | ........ | ........ | 1 | ........ | ........ | ........ | 1 | ........ | ...14 00–14 99 |
| 15 00–15 99... | ........ | ........ | ........ | ........ | ........ | 1 | ........ | 2 | ........ | 1 | ........ | ...15 00–15 99 |
| 18 00–19 99... | ........ | ........ | ........ | ........ | ........ | 1 | ........ | ........ | ........ | 1 | ........ | ...18 00–19 99 |
| 20 00–24 99... | ........ | ........ | ........ | ........ | ........ | ........ | ........ | 1 | ........ | 1 | ........ | ...20 00–24 99 |
| Total..... | 2 | 3 | 46 | 15 | 47 | 21 | 25 | 10 | 16 | 5 | 4 | .....Total |

296. TABLE V, D, a — (*concluded*)

BUFFALO

**THE CONFECTIONERY INDUSTRY — FACTORY WORKERS**

NUMBER AND PER CENT. OF EMPLOYEES EARNING SPECIFIED WEEKLY RATES, BY AGE GROUPS AND SEX

| WEEKLY RATES IN DOLLARS | AGE GROUPS IN YEARS (*concluded*) 35–39 | | 40–44 | | 45–54 | 55–64 | 65 AND OVER | TOTAL | | CUMULATIVE PER CENT OF TOTAL | | WEEKLY RATES IN DOLLARS |
|---|---|---|---|---|---|---|---|---|---|---|---|---|
| | Male | Female | Male | Female | Male | Male | Male | Male | Female | Male | Female | |
| $3 50–$3 99... | ........ | ........ | ........ | ........ | ........ | ........ | ........ | ........ | 3 | ........ | 2.10 | ...$3 50–$3 99 |
| 4 00– 4 49... | ........ | 1 | ........ | ........ | ........ | ........ | ........ | ........ | 47 | ........ | 35.00 | ... 4 00– 4 49 |
| 4 50– 4 99... | ........ | ........ | ........ | ........ | ........ | ........ | ........ | ........ | 28 | ........ | 54.50 | ... 4 50– 4 99 |
| 5 00– 5 49... | ........ | ........ | ........ | ........ | ........ | ........ | ........ | ........ | 19 | ........ | 67.80 | ... 5 00– 5 49 |
| 5 50– 5 99... | ........ | ........ | ........ | ........ | ........ | ........ | ........ | ........ | 4 | ........ | 70 60 | ... 5 50– 5 99 |
| 6 00– 6 49... | ........ | ........ | ........ | ........ | ........ | ........ | ........ | 3 | 16 | 3.70 | 81.90 | ... 6 00– 6 49 |
| 6 50– 6 99... | ........ | ........ | ........ | ........ | ........ | ........ | ........ | ........ | 6 | ........ | 86.10 | ... 6 50– 6 99 |
| 7 00– 7 49... | ........ | ........ | ........ | ........ | ........ | ........ | ........ | 5 | 8 | 10 00 | 91.60 | ... 7 00– 7 49 |
| 7 50– 7 99... | ........ | ........ | ........ | ........ | ........ | ........ | ........ | 4 | 2 | 15 00 | 93.10 | ... 7 50– 7 99 |
| 8 00– 8 99... | ........ | ........ | ........ | ........ | ........ | 2 | ........ | 13 | 5 | 31.20 | 96.60 | ... 8 00– 8 99 |
| 9 00– 9 99... | 1 | ........ | 1 | ........ | ........ | ........ | ........ | 10 | 2 | 43.70 | 98.00 | ... 9 00– 9 99 |
| 10 00–10 99... | 1 | 1 | ........ | ........ | ........ | ........ | 1 | 6 | 2 | 51.[illegible]0 | 99.40 | ...10 00–10 99 |
| 11 00–11 99... | 1 | ........ | ........ | ........ | ........ | ........ | ........ | 2 | ........ | 53.70 | ........ | ...11 00–11 99 |
| 12 00–12 99... | ........ | ........ | ........ | ........ | 1 | ........ | ........ | 9 | ........ | 65 00 | ........ | ...12 00–12 99 |
| 13 00–13 99... | ........ | ........ | ........ | 1 | 1 | ........ | ........ | 1 | 1 | 66.20 | 100.00 | ...13 00–13 99 |
| 14 00–14 99... | ........ | ........ | ........ | ........ | 1 | ........ | ........ | 3 | ........ | 70.00 | ........ | ...14 00–14 99 |
| 15 00–15 99... | 2 | ........ | 1 | ........ | ........ | ........ | ........ | 7 | ........ | 78.70 | ........ | ...15 00–15 99 |
| 18 00–19 99... | 2 | ........ | 1 | ........ | 2 | 1 | ........ | 8 | ........ | 88.70 | ........ | ...18 00–19 99 |
| 20 00–24 99... | 1 | ........ | 2 | ........ | 4 | ........ | ........ | 9 | ........ | 100.00 | ........ | ...20 00–24 99 |
| Total..... | 8 | 2 | 5 | 1 | 9 | 3 | 1 | 80 | 143 | ........ | ........ | .....Total |

BUFFALO

THE CONFECTIONERY INDUSTRY — FACTORY WORKERS

297. TABLE VIII, D, a Number and Per Cent. of Employees Earning Specified Weekly Rates, by Occupations and Sex

| Weekly Rates in Dollars | Occupation: Foremen and Forewomen | | Candy Makers | Dippers | Packers | | Wrappers | Machine Operators | Helpers | | Total | | Cumulative Per Cent. of Total | | Weekly Rates in Dollars |
|---|---|---|---|---|---|---|---|---|---|---|---|---|---|---|---|
| | Male | Female | Male | Female | Male | Female | Male | Male | Male | Female | Male | Female | Male | Female | |
| $3 50–$3 99 | | | | | | 2 | | | | 1 | | 3 | | 2.1 | $3 50–$3 99 |
| 4 00– 4 49 | | | | 2 | | 34 | | | | 11 | | 47 | | 35.0 | 4 00– 4 49 |
| 4 50– 4 99 | | | | 2 | | 18 | 3 | | | 5 | | 28 | | 54.5 | 4 50– 4 99 |
| 5 00– 5 49 | | | | 2 | | 11 | 4 | | | 2 | | 19 | | 67.8 | 5 00– 5 49 |
| 5 50– 5 99 | | | | 2 | | 1 | 1 | | | | | 4 | | 70.6 | 5 50– 5 99 |
| 6 00– 6 49 | | 2 | | 1 | | 12 | 1 | | 3 | | 3 | 16 | 3.7 | 81.9 | 6 00– 6 49 |
| 6 50– 6 99 | | 1 | | 1 | | 2 | 1 | | | 1 | | 6 | | 86.1 | 6 50– 6 99 |
| 7 00– 7 49 | | 2 | | 3 | | 2 | 1 | | 5 | | 5 | 8 | 10.0 | 91.6 | 7 00– 7 49 |
| 7 50– 7 99 | | | | 1 | | | | | 4 | 1 | 4 | 2 | 15.0 | 93.1 | 7 50– 7 99 |
| 8 00– 8 99 | | 2 | | | | 2 | | 1 | 12 | 1 | 13 | 5 | 31.2 | 96.6 | 8 00– 8 99 |
| 9 00– 9 99 | | 1 | 3 | | 1 | 1 | | | 6 | | 10 | 2 | 43.7 | 98.0 | 9 00– 9 99 |
| 10 00–10 99 | | 2 | 1 | | | | | | 5 | | 6 | 2 | 51.3 | 99.4 | 10 00–10 99 |
| 11 00–11 99 | | | | | 1 | | | | 1 | | 2 | | 53.7 | | 11 00–11 99 |
| 12 00–12 99 | | | 8 | | | | | | 1 | | 9 | | 65.0 | | 12 00–12 99 |
| 13 00–13 99 | 1 | | | 1 | | | | | | | 1 | 1 | 66.2 | 100.0 | 13 00–13 99 |
| 14 00–14 99 | | | 2 | | | | | | 1 | | 3 | | 70.0 | | 14 00–14 99 |
| 15 00–15 99 | | | 7 | | | | | | | | 7 | | 78.7 | | 15 00–15 99 |
| 16 00–17 99 | | | | | | | | | | | | | | | 16 00–17 99 |
| 18 00–19 99 | 1 | | 7 | | | | | | | | 8 | | 88.7 | | 18 00–19 99 |
| 20 00–24 99 | 1 | | 8 | | | | | | | | 9 | | 100.0 | | 20 00–24 99 |
| Total | 3 | 10 | 36 | 15 | 2 | 85 | 11 | 1 | 38 | 22 | 80 | 143 | | | Total |

298. TABLE VI, D, a

## BUFFALO
## THE CONFECTIONERY INDUSTRY — FACTORY WORKERS

NUMBER AND PER CENT. OF EMPLOYEES CLASSIFIED ACCORDING TO ACTUAL WEEKLY EARNINGS, BY AGE GROUPS AND SEX

| ACTUAL WEEKLY EARNINGS IN DOLLARS | AGE GROUPS IN YEARS: 14–15 | 16–17 | | 18–20 | | 21–24 | | 25–29 | | 30–34 | | 35–39 | | 40–44 | | 45–54 | 55–64 | 65 AND OVER | TOTAL | | CUMULATIVE PER CENT. OF TOTAL | | ACTUAL WEEKLY EARNINGS IN DOLLARS |
|---|---|---|---|---|---|---|---|---|---|---|---|---|---|---|---|---|---|---|---|---|---|---|---|
| | Female | Male | Female | Male | Female | Male | Female | Male | Female | Male | Female | Male | Female | Male | Female | Male | Male | Male | Male | Female | Male | Female | |
| Less than $3 00 | 1 | ..... | 14 | 1 | 4 | 1 | 2 | 1 | 1 | ..... | ..... | ..... | ..... | ..... | ..... | ..... | 1 | ..... | 4 | 22 | 5.00 | 12.00 | Less than $3 00 |
| $3 00–$3 49 | 1 | ..... | 11 | 2 | 12 | ..... | 2 | ..... | ..... | ..... | ..... | ..... | ..... | ..... | ..... | ..... | ..... | ..... | 2 | 26 | 7.50 | 28.8 | $3 00– 3 49 |
| 3 50– 3 99 | 1 | ..... | 9 | 1 | 7 | 2 | ..... | ..... | 1 | ..... | ..... | ..... | ..... | ..... | ..... | ..... | ..... | ..... | 3 | 18 | 11.20 | 39.60 | 3 50– 3 99 |
| 4 00– 4 49 | ..... | ..... | 10 | ..... | 2 | ..... | 3 | 1 | 1 | ..... | ..... | ..... | 1 | ..... | ..... | ..... | ..... | ..... | 1 | 17 | 12.50 | 49.70 | 4 00– 4 49 |
| 4 50– 4 99 | ..... | ..... | 5 | 3 | 12 | 1 | 1 | ..... | 1 | ..... | ..... | ..... | ..... | ..... | ..... | ..... | ..... | ..... | 4 | 19 | 17.50 | 61.10 | 4 50– 4 99 |
| 5 00– 5 49 | ..... | 1 | 5 | 1 | 3 | 2 | 6 | 2 | 2 | ..... | 1 | 1 | ..... | ..... | ..... | ..... | ..... | ..... | 7 | 17 | 26.20 | 71.40 | 5 00– 5 49 |
| 5 50– 5 99 | ..... | ..... | 2 | 1 | 3 | 1 | 7 | ..... | 3 | ..... | ..... | ..... | ..... | ..... | ..... | ..... | ..... | ..... | 2 | 15 | 28.80 | 80.30 | 5 50– 5 99 |
| 6 00– 6 49 | ..... | 1 | ..... | ..... | 7 | 1 | 2 | 1 | 3 | ..... | 1 | ..... | ..... | ..... | ..... | ..... | ..... | ..... | 3 | 13 | 32.50 | 88.00 | 6 00– 6 49 |
| 6 50– 6 99 | ..... | ..... | ..... | 2 | 1 | 1 | ..... | ..... | 1 | ..... | 1 | ..... | ..... | ..... | ..... | ..... | 1 | ..... | 4 | 3 | 37.50 | 89.90 | 6 50– 6 99 |
| 7 00– 7 49 | ..... | ..... | ..... | 1 | 1 | 1 | 2 | ..... | 1 | ..... | 2 | ..... | ..... | ..... | ..... | ..... | ..... | ..... | 2 | 6 | 40.00 | 93.50 | 7 00– 7 49 |
| 7 50– 7 99 | ..... | ..... | ..... | ..... | ..... | ..... | 2 | 1 | ..... | ..... | ..... | ..... | ..... | 1 | ..... | ..... | ..... | ..... | 2 | 2 | 42.50 | 94.70 | 7 50– 7 99 |
| 8 00– 8 99 | ..... | 1 | ..... | 2 | 1 | 2 | 2 | ..... | 2 | ..... | ..... | ..... | ..... | ..... | ..... | ..... | ..... | ..... | 5 | 5 | 48.70 | 97.70 | 8 00– 8 99 |
| 9 00– 9 99 | ..... | ..... | ..... | ..... | ..... | ..... | ..... | 1 | 1 | 2 | ..... | 2 | ..... | ..... | ..... | ..... | ..... | ..... | 5 | 1 | 55.00 | 98.30 | 9 00– 9 99 |
| 10 00–10 99 | ..... | ..... | ..... | 1 | ..... | 4 | ..... | 1 | 1 | ..... | ..... | ..... | 1 | ..... | 1 | ..... | ..... | 1 | 7 | 3 | 63.80 | 100.00 | 10 00–10 99 |
| 11 00–11 99 | ..... | ..... | ..... | ..... | ..... | 3 | ..... | ..... | ..... | ..... | ..... | ..... | ..... | 1 | ..... | ..... | ..... | ..... | 4 | ..... | 68.70 | ..... | 11 00–11 99 |
| 12 00–12 99 | ..... | ..... | ..... | ..... | ..... | 1 | ..... | ..... | ..... | ..... | ..... | 1 | ..... | ..... | ..... | 2 | ..... | ..... | 4 | ..... | 73.70 | ..... | 12 00–12 99 |
| 13 00–13 99 | ..... | ..... | ..... | ..... | ..... | ..... | ..... | ..... | ..... | ..... | ..... | ..... | ..... | ..... | ..... | 1 | ..... | ..... | 1 | ..... | 75.00 | ..... | 13 00–13 99 |
| 14 00–14 99 | ..... | ..... | ..... | ..... | ..... | ..... | ..... | ..... | ..... | ..... | ..... | ..... | ..... | 1 | ..... | ..... | ..... | ..... | 1 | ..... | 76.20 | ..... | 14 00–14 99 |
| 15 00–15 99 | ..... | ..... | ..... | ..... | ..... | ..... | ..... | 1 | ..... | 1 | ..... | 2 | ..... | ..... | ..... | 2 | 1 | ..... | 7 | ..... | 85.00 | ..... | 15 00–15 99 |
| 16 00–17 99 | ..... | ..... | ..... | ..... | ..... | ..... | ..... | ..... | ..... | ..... | ..... | 1 | ..... | ..... | ..... | 2 | ..... | ..... | 3 | ..... | 88.70 | ..... | 16 00–17 99 |
| 18 00–19 99 | ..... | ..... | ..... | ..... | ..... | 1 | ..... | ..... | ..... | 1 | ..... | ..... | ..... | 1 | ..... | 1 | ..... | ..... | 4 | ..... | 93.80 | ..... | 18 00–19 99 |
| 20 00–24 99 | ..... | ..... | ..... | ..... | ..... | ..... | ..... | 1 | ..... | 1 | ..... | 1 | ..... | 1 | ..... | 1 | ..... | ..... | 5 | ..... | 100.00 | ..... | 20 00–24 99 |
| Total | 3 | 3 | 56 | 15 | 53 | 21 | 29 | 10 | 18 | 5 | 5 | 8 | 2 | 5 | 1 | 9 | 3 | 1 | 80 | 167 | ..... | ..... | Total |

299. TABLE IX, D, a

BUFFALO

**THE CONFECTIONERY INDUSTRY — FACTORY WORKERS**

NUMBER AND PER CENT. OF EMPLOYEES CLASSIFIED ACCORDING TO ACTUAL WEEKLY EARNINGS, BY OCCUPATION AND SEX

| Actual Weekly Earnings in Dollars | Occupation: Foremen and Forewomen | | Candy Makers | Dippers | Packers | | Wrappers | Machine Operators | Helpers | | Total | | Cumulative Per Cent. of Total | | Actual Weekly Earnings in Dollars |
|---|---|---|---|---|---|---|---|---|---|---|---|---|---|---|---|
| | Male | Female | Male | Female | Male | Female | Female | Male | Male | Female | Male | Female | Male | Female | |
| Less than $3 00 | | | | 1 | | 15 | | | 4 | 6 | 4 | 22 | 5.0 | 12.0 | Less than $3 00 |
| $3 00–$3 49 | | | | 1 | | 18 | 1 | | 2 | 6 | 2 | 26 | 7.5 | 28.8 | $3 00– 3 49 |
| 3 50– 3 99 | | | 1 | 2 | | 14 | | | 2 | 2 | 3 | 18 | 11.2 | 39.6 | 3 50– 3 99 |
| 4 00– 4 49 | | | | 1 | | 13 | 1 | | 1 | 2 | 1 | 17 | 12.5 | 49.7 | 4 00– 4 49 |
| 4 50– 4 99 | | | 1 | 2 | | 12 | 3 | | 3 | 2 | 4 | 19 | 17.5 | 61.1 | 4 50– 4 99 |
| 5 00– 5 49 | | 1 | | 3 | | 10 | 2 | | 7 | 1 | 7 | 17 | 26.2 | 71.4 | 5 00– 5 49 |
| 5 50– 5 99 | | 1 | | 5 | | 5 | 3 | | 2 | 1 | 2 | 15 | 28.8 | 80.3 | 5 50– 5 99 |
| 6 00– 6 49 | | 1 | | 6 | | 6 | | | 3 | | 3 | 13 | 32.5 | 88.0 | 6 00– 6 49 |
| 6 50– 6 99 | | | | | | 1 | 1 | 1 | 3 | 1 | 4 | 3 | 37.5 | 89.9 | 6 50– 6 99 |
| 7 00– 7 49 | | 2 | | 3 | | 1 | | | 2 | | 2 | 6 | 40.0 | 93.5 | 7 00– 7 49 |
| 7 50– 7 99 | | | 1 | | | 1 | | | 1 | 1 | 2 | 2 | 42.5 | 94.7 | 7 50– 7 99 |
| 8 00– 8 99 | | 2 | 1 | | | 3 | | | 4 | | 5 | 5 | 48.7 | 97.7 | 8 00– 8 99 |
| 9 00– 9 99 | | 1 | 2 | | 1 | | | | 2 | | 5 | 1 | 55.0 | 98.3 | 9 00– 9 99 |
| 10 00–10 99 | | 2 | 5 | 1 | | | | | 2 | | 7 | 3 | 63.8 | 100.0 | 10 00–10 99 |
| 11 00–11 99 | | | 3 | | 1 | | | | | | 4 | | 68.7 | | 11 00–11 99 |
| 12 00–12 99 | | | 4 | | | | | | | | 4 | | 73.7 | | 12 00–12 99 |
| 13 00–13 99 | 1 | | | | | | | | | | 1 | | 75.0 | | 13 00–13 99 |
| 14 00–14 99 | | | 1 | | | | | | | | 1 | | 76.2 | | 14 00–14 99 |
| 15 00–15 99 | | | 7 | | | | | | | | 7 | | 85.0 | | 15 00–15 99 |
| 16 00–17 99 | | | 3 | | | | | | | | 3 | | 88.7 | | 16 00–17 99 |
| 18 00–19 99 | 1 | | 3 | | | | | | | | 4 | | 93.8 | | 18 00–19 99 |
| 20 00–24 99 | 1 | | 4 | | | | | | | | 5 | | 100.0 | | 20 00–24 99 |
| Total | 3 | 10 | 36 | 25 | 2 | 99 | 11 | 1 | 38 | 22 | 80 | 167 | | | Total |

300. TABLE V, A, 1, a

ROCHESTER

DEPARTMENT STORES — STOCK AND SALES

NUMBER AND PER CENT. OF EMPLOYEES EARNING SPECIFIED WEEKLY RATES, BY AGE GROUPS AND SEX

| Weekly Rates in Dollars | Age Groups in Years | | | | | | | | | | | | | | Weekly Rates in Dollars |
|---|---|---|---|---|---|---|---|---|---|---|---|---|---|---|---|
| | 14–15 | | 16–17 | | 18–20 | | 21–24 | | 25–29 | | 30–34 | | 35–39 | | |
| | Male | Female | Male | Female | Male | Female | Male | Female | Male | Female | Male | Female | Male | Female | |
| $3 50–$3 99... | 11 | 78 | .... | 11 | ...... | ...... | ...... | ...... | ...... | ...... | ...... | ...... | ...... | ...... | ...$3 50–$3 99 |
| 4 00– 4 49... | 23 | 13 | 3 | 17 | 2 | 4 | ...... | ...... | ...... | ...... | ...... | ...... | ...... | ...... | ... 4 00– 4 49 |
| 4 50– 4 99... | 4 | 4 | 1 | 15 | ...... | ...... | ...... | ...... | ...... | ...... | ...... | 1 | ...... | ...... | ... 4 50– 4 99 |
| 5 00– 5 49... | 8 | 2 | 7 | 28 | 1 | 11 | ...... | 3 | ...... | 2 | ...... | 1 | ...... | 1 | ... 5 00– 5 49 |
| 5 50– 5 99... | .... | 2 | 1 | 1 | ...... | ...... | ...... | ...... | ...... | ...... | ...... | 1 | ...... | ...... | ... 5 50– 5 99 |
| 6 00– 6 49... | 1 | ...... | 7 | 16 | ...... | 51 | 1 | 23 | ...... | 7 | ...... | ...... | ...... | 2 | ... 6 00– 6 49 |
| 6 50– 6 99... | .... | ...... | .... | 1 | ...... | 3 | ...... | 2 | ...... | 2 | ...... | ...... | ...... | 1 | ... 6 50– 6 99 |
| 7 00– 7 49... | .... | ...... | 4 | 4 | 3 | 56 | ...... | 70 | ...... | 49 | ...... | 21 | ...... | 13 | ... 7 00– 7 49 |
| 7 50– 7 99... | .... | ...... | 1 | ...... | 1 | 2 | ...... | 9 | ...... | 8 | ...... | 2 | ...... | 2 | ... 7 50– 7 99 |
| 8 00– 8 99... | .... | ...... | 2 | ...... | 5 | 14 | 5 | 69 | 2 | 49 | 1 | 25 | ...... | 23 | ... 8 00– 8 99 |
| 9 00– 9 99... | .... | ...... | .... | ...... | 8 | 5 | 6 | 16 | ...... | 29 | ...... | 14 | ...... | 8 | ... 9 00– 9 99 |
| 10 00–10 99... | .... | ...... | 1 | ...... | 8 | 4 | 21 | 7 | 4 | 20 | 2 | 19 | 1 | 10 | ...10 00–10 99 |
| 11 00–11 99... | .... | ...... | 1 | ...... | ...... | ...... | 3 | 2 | 2 | 7 | ...... | 11 | ...... | 4 | ...11 00–11 99 |
| 12 00–12 99... | .... | ...... | .... | ...... | 3 | ...... | 19 | 8 | 12 | 10 | 5 | 9 | 2 | 15 | ...12 00–12 99 |
| 13 00–13 99... | .... | ...... | .... | ...... | ...... | ...... | 4 | 2 | 3 | 4 | 4 | 3 | 2 | 3 | ...13 00–13 99 |
| 14 00–14 99... | .... | ...... | .... | ...... | ...... | ...... | 3 | ...... | 10 | 3 | 3 | 2 | 1 | 8 | ...14 00–14 99 |
| 15 00–15 99... | .... | ...... | .... | ...... | ...... | ...... | 6 | 1 | 16 | 2 | 15 | 13 | 12 | 4 | ...15 00–15 99 |
| 16 00–17 99... | .... | ...... | .... | ...... | ...... | ...... | ...... | 1 | 8 | 2 | 6 | 4 | 3 | 2 | ...16 00–17 99 |
| 18 00–19 99... | .... | ...... | .... | ...... | ...... | ...... | 1 | ...... | 4 | 1 | 7 | 1 | 6 | 1 | ...18 00–19 99 |
| 20 00–24 99... | .... | ...... | .... | ...... | ...... | ...... | ...... | 1 | 10 | 1 | 9 | 1 | 7 | 2 | ...20 00–24 99 |
| 25 00–29 99... | .... | ...... | .... | ...... | ...... | ...... | ...... | ...... | ...... | ...... | 2 | 1 | 3 | 1 | ...25 00–29 99 |
| 30 00–34 99... | .... | ...... | .... | ...... | ...... | ...... | ...... | ...... | 1 | ...... | ...... | ...... | ...... | ...... | ...30 00–34 99 |
| 40 00 and over. | .... | ...... | .... | ...... | ...... | ...... | ...... | ...... | ...... | ...... | 1 | ...... | 1 | ...... | 40 00 and over. |
| Total..... | 47 | 99 | 28 | 93 | 31 | 150 | 69 | 214 | 72 | 196 | 55 | 129 | 38 | 100 | ....Total. |

300. TABLE V, A, 1, a — (*concluded*)

ROCHESTER

DEPARTMENT STORES — STOCK AND SALES

NUMBER AND PER CENT. OF EMPLOYEES EARNING SPECIFIED WEEKLY RATES, BY AGE GROUPS AND SEX

| WEEKLY RATES IN DOLLARS | AGE GROUPS IN YEARS—(*concluded*) | | | | | | | | | | | | | WEEKLY RATES IN DOLLARS |
|---|---|---|---|---|---|---|---|---|---|---|---|---|---|---|
| | 40–44 | | 45–54 | | 55–64 | | 65 AND OVER | NOT REPORTED | | TOTAL | | CUMULATIVE PER CENT. OF TOTAL | | |
| | Male | Female | Male | Female | Male | Female | Male | Male | Female | Male | Female | Male | Female | |
| $3 50–$3 99 | ...... | ...... | ...... | ...... | ...... | ...... | ...... | ...... | ...... | 11 | 89 | 2.60 | 8.00 | $3 50–$3 99 |
| 4 00– 4 49 | ...... | ...... | ...... | ...... | ...... | ...... | ...... | ...... | ...... | 28 | 34 | 9.20 | 11.00 | 4 00– 4 49 |
| 4 50– 4 99 | ...... | ...... | ...... | ...... | ...... | ...... | ...... | ...... | ...... | 5 | 20 | 10.40 | 12.90 | 4 50– 4 99 |
| 5 00– 5 49 | ...... | 1 | ...... | 1 | ...... | ...... | ...... | ...... | ...... | 16 | 50 | 14.10 | 17.40 | 5 00– 5 49 |
| 5 50– 5 99 | ...... | ...... | ...... | ...... | ...... | ...... | ...... | ...... | ...... | 1 | 4 | 14.40 | 17.80 | 5 50– 5 99 |
| 6 00– 6 49 | ...... | 2 | ...... | 1 | ...... | ...... | ...... | ...... | 1 | 9 | 103 | 16.50 | 27.10 | 6 00– 6 49 |
| 6 50– 6 99 | ...... | ...... | ...... | ...... | ...... | ...... | ...... | ...... | ...... | ...... | 9 | ...... | 27.90 | 6 50– 6 99 |
| 7 00– 7 49 | ...... | 6 | ...... | 4 | ...... | ...... | ...... | ...... | 3 | 7 | 226 | 18.10 | 48.30 | 7 00– 7 49 |
| 7 50– 7 99 | ...... | 2 | ...... | 1 | ...... | ...... | ...... | ...... | ...... | 2 | 26 | 18.60 | 50.60 | 7 50– 7 99 |
| 8 00– 8 99 | ...... | 4 | ...... | 7 | ...... | ...... | ...... | ...... | 3 | 15 | 194 | 22.10 | 68.20 | 8 00– 8 99 |
| 9 00– 9 99 | ...... | 4 | ...... | 5 | ...... | ...... | ...... | ...... | 8 | 14 | 89 | 25.40 | 76.20 | 9 00– 9 99 |
| 10 00–10 99 | ...... | 6 | 2 | 6 | 2 | 1 | ...... | 1 | 3 | 42 | 76 | 35.30 | 83.00 | 10 00–10 99 |
| 11 00–11 99 | ...... | 3 | ...... | ...... | ...... | ...... | ...... | 1 | 3 | 7 | 30 | 36.90 | 85.70 | 11 00–11 99 |
| 12 00–12 99 | 1 | 13 | 4 | 6 | ...... | 2 | 1 | ...... | 2 | 47 | 65 | 48.00 | 91.50 | 12 00–12 99 |
| 13 00–13 99 | 1 | 4 | 3 | 1 | 1 | ...... | 1 | ...... | 1 | 19 | 18 | 52.50 | 93.30 | 13 00–13 99 |
| 14 00–14 99 | 3 | 1 | 5 | ...... | 1 | ...... | ...... | 1 | 1 | 27 | 15 | 58.90 | 94.60 | 14 00–14 99 |
| 15 00–15 99 | 4 | 5 | 8 | 4 | 2 | ...... | ...... | ...... | 2 | 63 | 31 | 73.70 | 97.50 | 15 00–15 99 |
| 16 00–17 99 | 3 | ...... | 6 | 2 | 3 | ...... | ...... | ...... | 1 | 29 | 12 | 80.50 | 98.50 | 16 00–17 99 |
| 18 00–19 99 | 7 | 3 | 3 | 2 | 1 | ...... | ...... | ...... | ...... | 29 | 8 | 87.40 | 99.10 | 18 00–19 99 |
| 20 00–24 99 | 5 | ...... | 1 | 1 | 2 | ...... | ...... | 1 | ...... | 35 | 6 | 95.60 | 99.70 | 20 00–24 99 |
| 25 00–29 99 | 2 | ...... | 3 | ...... | ...... | ...... | ...... | ...... | 1 | 10 | 3 | 97.80 | 99.90 | 25 00–29 99 |
| 30 00–34 99 | ...... | ...... | ...... | 1 | ...... | ...... | ...... | ...... | ...... | 1 | 1 | 98.20 | 100.00 | 30 00–34 99 |
| 35 00–39 99 | 1 | ...... | ...... | ...... | ...... | ...... | ...... | ...... | ...... | 1 | ...... | 98.50 | ...... | 35 00–39 99 |
| 40 00 and over | 2 | ...... | 2 | ...... | 1 | ...... | ...... | ...... | ...... | 7 | ...... | 100.00 | ...... | 40 00 and over |
| Total | 29 | 54 | 37 | 42 | 13 | 3 | 2 | 4 | 29 | 425 | 1,109 | ...... | ...... | Total |

301. TABLE VIII, A, 1, a

ROCHESTER

DEPARTMENT STORES — STOCK AND SALES

NUMBER AND PER CENT. OF EMPLOYEES EARNING SPECIFIED WEEKLY RATES, BY OCCUPATION AND SEX

| WEEKLY RATES IN DOLLARS | OCCUPATION: SUPERINTENDENTS | BUYERS | | ASSISTANT BUYERS AND HEADS OF STOCK | | RECEIVING AND STOCK CLERKS | | STOCK PEOPLE | | FLOOR MANAGERS | | SALES PEOPLE | | MESSENGERS, WRAPPERS, ERRAND BOYS | | TOTAL | | CUMULATIVE PER CENT. OF TOTAL | | WEEKLY RATES IN DOLLARS |
|---|---|---|---|---|---|---|---|---|---|---|---|---|---|---|---|---|---|---|---|---|
| | Male | Male | Female | Male | Female | Male | Female | Male | Female | Male | Female | Male | Female | Male | Female | Male | Female | Male | Female | |
| $3 50–$3 99 | .... | .... | .... | .... | .... | .... | .... | 1 | 1 | .... | .... | .... | .... | 10 | 88 | 11 | 89 | 2.60 | 8.00 | $3 50–$3 99 |
| 4 00– 4 49 | .... | .... | .... | .... | .... | .... | .... | 9 | 9 | .... | .... | .... | 2 | 19 | 23 | 28 | 34 | 9.20 | 11.10 | 4 00– 4 49 |
| 4 50– 4 99 | .... | .... | .... | .... | .... | .... | 1 | 2 | 4 | .... | .... | .... | 3 | 3 | 12 | 5 | 20 | 10.40 | 12.90 | 4 50– 4 99 |
| 5 00– 5 49 | .... | .... | .... | .... | .... | .... | 1 | 7 | 15 | .... | .... | 3 | 30 | 6 | 4 | 16 | 50 | 14.10 | 17.40 | 5 00– 5 49 |
| 5 50– 5 99 | .... | .... | .... | .... | .... | .... | .... | 1 | 1 | .... | .... | .... | 3 | .... | .... | 1 | 4 | 14.40 | 17.80 | 5 50– 5 99 |
| 6 00– 6 49 | .... | .... | .... | .... | .... | 1 | 1 | 1 | 4 | .... | .... | 6 | 94 | 1 | 4 | 9 | 103 | 16.50 | 27.10 | 6 00– 6 49 |
| 6 50– 6 99 | .... | .... | .... | .... | .... | .... | .... | .... | .... | .... | .... | .... | 9 | .... | .... | .... | 9 | .... | 27.90 | 6 50– 6 99 |
| 7 00– 7 49 | .... | .... | .... | .... | .... | .... | 1 | 3 | 2 | .... | .... | 4 | 223 | .... | .... | 7 | 226 | 18.10 | 48.30 | 7 00– 7 49 |
| 7 50– 7 99 | .... | .... | .... | .... | .... | .... | .... | .... | .... | .... | .... | 1 | 26 | 1 | .... | 2 | 26 | 18.60 | 50.60 | 7 50– 7 99 |
| 8 00– 8 99 | .... | .... | .... | .... | .... | .... | 1 | 2 | 1 | .... | .... | 13 | 191 | .... | 1 | 15 | 194 | 22.10 | 68.20 | 8 00– 8 99 |
| 9 00– 9 99 | .... | .... | .... | .... | .... | 1 | 2 | 3 | .... | .... | .... | 10 | 87 | .... | .... | 14 | 89 | 25.40 | 76.20 | 9 00– 9 99 |
| 10 00–10 99 | .... | .... | .... | .... | .... | 2 | 1 | 4 | 1 | .... | .... | 34 | 74 | 2 | .... | 42 | 76 | 35.30 | 83.00 | 10 00–10 99 |
| 11 00–11 99 | .... | .... | .... | .... | .... | 1 | 1 | 2 | .... | .... | .... | 4 | 29 | .... | .... | 7 | 30 | 36.90 | 85.70 | 11 00–11 99 |
| 12 00–12 99 | .... | 1 | .... | .... | 1 | 6 | .... | 3 | .... | .... | .... | 37 | 64 | .... | .... | 47 | 65 | 48.00 | 91.50 | 12 00–12 99 |
| 13 00–13 99 | .... | .... | .... | .... | .... | 2 | 1 | 1 | .... | .... | .... | 16 | 17 | .... | .... | 19 | 18 | 52.50 | 93.30 | 13 00–13 99 |
| 14 00–14 99 | .... | .... | .... | .... | .... | 3 | 1 | 1 | .... | .... | .... | 23 | 14 | .... | .... | 27 | 15 | 58.90 | 94.60 | 14 00–14 99 |
| 15 00–15 99 | .... | .... | .... | 1 | 1 | 1 | 1 | .... | .... | 2 | .... | 59 | 29 | .... | .... | 63 | 31 | 73.70 | 97.50 | 15 00–15 99 |
| 16 00–17 99 | .... | .... | .... | .... | 1 | 2 | .... | 2 | .... | .... | .... | 25 | 11 | .... | .... | 29 | 12 | 80.50 | 98.50 | 16 00–17 99 |
| 18 00–19 99 | .... | 1 | .... | 1 | .... | 1 | .... | .... | .... | 2 | 1 | 24 | 7 | .... | .... | 29 | 8 | 87.40 | 99.10 | 18 00–19 99 |
| 20 00–24 99 | .... | 1 | .... | 4 | 1 | .... | .... | .... | .... | 8 | .... | 22 | 5 | .... | .... | 35 | 6 | 95.60 | 99.70 | 20 00–24 99 |
| 25 00–29 99 | 1 | .... | 1 | .... | 1 | .... | .... | .... | .... | 2 | .... | 7 | 1 | .... | .... | 10 | 3 | 97.80 | 99.90 | 25 00–29 99 |
| 30 00–34 99 | .... | .... | .... | .... | .... | .... | .... | .... | .... | 1 | .... | .... | 1 | .... | .... | 1 | 1 | 98.20 | 100.00 | 30 00–34 99 |
| 35 00–39 99 | .... | .... | .... | .... | .... | .... | .... | .... | .... | 1 | .... | .... | .... | .... | .... | 1 | .... | 98.50 | .... | 35 00–39 99 |
| 40 00 and over | .... | 7 | .... | .... | .... | .... | .... | .... | .... | .... | .... | .... | .... | .... | .... | 7 | .... | 100.00 | .... | 40 00 and over |
| Total | 1 | 10 | 1 | 6 | 5 | 20 | 12 | 42 | 38 | 16 | 1 | 288 | 920 | 42 | 132 | 425 | 1,109 | .... | .... | Total |

302. TABLE VI, A, 1, a

ROCHESTER

DEPARTMENT STORES — STOCK AND SALES

NUMBER AND PER CENT. OF EMPLOYEES CLASSIFIED ACCORDING TO ACTUAL WEEKLY EARNINGS, BY AGE GROUPS AND SEX

| ACTUAL WEEKLY EARNINGS IN DOLLARS | AGE GROUPS IN YEARS | | | | | | | | | | | | | | ACTUAL WEEKLY EARNINGS IN DOLLARS |
|---|---|---|---|---|---|---|---|---|---|---|---|---|---|---|---|
| | 14–15 | | 16–17 | | 18–20 | | 21–24 | | 25–29 | | 30–34 | | 35–39 | | |
| | Male | Female | Male | Female | Male | Female | Male | Female | Male | Female | Male | Female | Male | Female | |
| Less than $3 00 | 2 | 6 | .... | 3 | ...... | 3 | ...... | 2 | ...... | 3 | ...... | ...... | ...... | ...... | Less than $3 00 |
| $3 00–$3 49... | 2 | 5 | 1 | 1 | ...... | 1 | 1 | ...... | ...... | ...... | ...... | ...... | ...... | ...... | ...$3 00– 3 49 |
| 3 50– 3 99... | 10 | 67 | .... | 11 | ...... | 2 | ...... | 1 | ...... | 1 | ...... | 3 | ...... | ...... | ... 3 50– 3 99 |
| 4 00– 4 49... | 21 | 13 | 4 | 20 | 3 | 7 | ...... | ...... | ...... | 3 | ...... | ...... | ...... | ...... | ... 4 00– 4 49 |
| 4 50– 4 99... | 4 | 4 | 1 | 13 | ...... | 2 | 1 | 1 | ...... | 5 | ...... | 1 | ...... | 1 | ... 4 50– 4 99 |
| 5 00– 5 49... | 7 | 2 | 6 | 22 | 1 | 15 | ...... | 7 | ...... | 4 | ...... | 3 | ...... | 3 | ... 5 00– 5 49 |
| 5 50– 5 99... | .... | 2 | 1 | 3 | ...... | 8 | ...... | 4 | ...... | 7 | ...... | 2 | ...... | 1 | ... 5 50– 5 99 |
| 6 00– 6 49... | 1 | ...... | 7 | 14 | ...... | 44 | 1 | 28 | 1 | 8 | ...... | 3 | ...... | 2 | ... 6 00– 6 49 |
| 6 50– 6 99... | .... | ...... | .... | 1 | 1 | 3 | ...... | 10 | ...... | 6 | ...... | 2 | ...... | 1 | ... 6 50– 6 99 |
| 7 00– 7 49... | .... | ...... | 3 | 3 | 4 | 44 | ...... | 63 | ...... | 34 | ...... | 14 | ...... | 10 | ... 7 00– 7 49 |
| 7 50– 7 99... | .... | ...... | 1 | ...... | 1 | 3 | ...... | 8 | ...... | 11 | ...... | 2 | ...... | 4 | ... 7 50– 7 99 |
| 8 00– 8 99... | .... | ...... | 2 | ...... | 6 | 14 | 6 | 54 | 1 | 46 | 1 | 24 | ...... | 23 | ... 8 00– 8 99 |
| 9 00– 9 99... | .... | ...... | .... | ...... | 7 | 2 | 5 | 16 | 2 | 24 | 1 | 13 | ...... | 8 | ... 9 00– 9 99 |
| 10 00–10 99... | .... | ...... | 1 | ...... | 5 | 2 | 21 | 7 | 3 | 16 | 2 | 18 | 1 | 9 | ...10 00–10 99 |
| 11 00–11 99... | .... | ...... | 1 | ...... | 1 | ...... | 4 | 3 | 3 | 7 | 3 | 10 | ...... | 4 | ...11 00–11–99 |
| 12 00–12 99... | .... | ...... | .... | ...... | 2 | ...... | 15 | 4 | 10 | 8 | 3 | 9 | 1 | 12 | ...12 00–12 99 |
| 13 00–13 99... | .... | ...... | .... | ...... | ...... | ...... | 5 | 3 | 3 | 4 | 3 | 5 | 1 | 5 | ...13 00–13 99 |
| 14 00–14 99... | .... | ...... | .... | ...... | ...... | ...... | 4 | ...... | 10 | 2 | 4 | 3 | 2 | 6 | ...14 00–14 99 |
| 15 00–15 99... | .... | ...... | .... | ...... | ...... | ...... | 5 | 1 | 16 | 3 | 13 | 9 | 12 | 5 | ...15 00–15 99 |
| 16 00–17 99... | .... | ...... | .... | ...... | ...... | ...... | ...... | 1 | 8 | 2 | 7 | 2 | 5 | 3 | ...16 00–17 99 |
| 18 00–19 99... | .... | ...... | .... | ...... | ...... | ...... | 1 | ...... | 4 | 1 | 6 | 3 | 4 | 1 | ...18 00–19 99 |
| 20 00–24 99... | .... | ...... | .... | ...... | ...... | ...... | ...... | 1 | 10 | 1 | 9 | 1 | 8 | 1 | ...20 00–24 99 |
| 25 00–29 99... | .... | ...... | .... | ...... | ...... | ...... | ...... | ...... | ...... | ...... | 2 | 1 | 3 | 1 | ...25 00–29 99 |
| 30 00–34 99... | .... | ...... | .... | ...... | ...... | ...... | ...... | ...... | 1 | ...... | ...... | ...... | ...... | ...... | ...30 00–34 99 |
| 40 00 and over. | .... | ...... | .... | ...... | ...... | ...... | ...... | ...... | ...... | ...... | 1 | ...... | 1 | ...... | .40 00 and over |
| Not reported... | .... | ...... | .... | 2 | ...... | ...... | ...... | ...... | ...... | ...... | ...... | 1 | ...... | ...... | ...Not reported |
| Total..... | 47 | 99 | 28 | 93 | 31 | 150 | 69 | 214 | 72 | 196 | 55 | 129 | 38 | 100 | .....Total |

302. TABLE VI, A, 1, a — *(concluded)*

ROCHESTER

DEPARTMENT STORES — STOCK AND SALES

NUMBER AND PER CENT. OF EMPLOYEES CLASSIFIED ACCORDING TO ACTUAL WEEKLY EARNINGS, BY AGE GROUPS AND SEX

| ACTUAL WEEKLY EARNINGS IN DOLLARS | AGE GROUPS IN YEARS—*(concluded)* 40–44 | | 45–54 | | 55–64 | | 65 AND OVER | NOT REPORTED | | TOTAL | | CUMULATIVE PER CENT. OF TOTAL | | ACTUAL WEEKLY EARNINGS IN DOLLARS |
|---|---|---|---|---|---|---|---|---|---|---|---|---|---|---|
| | Male | Female | Male | Female | Male | Female | Male | Male | Female | Male | Female | Male | Female | |
| Less than $3 00... | ...... | ...... | ...... | ...... | ...... | ...... | ...... | ...... | ...... | 2 | 17 | .50 | 1.50 | ..Less than $3 00 |
| $3 00–$3 49...... | ...... | ...... | ...... | ...... | ...... | ...... | ...... | 1 | ...... | 5 | 7 | 1.60 | 2.20 | .....$3 00– 3 49 |
| 3 50– 3 99...... | ...... | ...... | ...... | ...... | ...... | ...... | ...... | ...... | ...... | 10 | 85 | 4.00 | 9.90 | ..... 3 50– 3 99 |
| 4 00– 4 49...... | ...... | 1 | ...... | ...... | ...... | ...... | ...... | ...... | ...... | 28 | 44 | 10.60 | 13.80 | ..... 4 00– 4 49 |
| 4 50– 4 99...... | ...... | ...... | ...... | ...... | ...... | ...... | ...... | ...... | ...... | 6 | 27 | 12.00 | 16.30 | ..... 4 50– 4 99 |
| 5 00– 5 49...... | ...... | ...... | ...... | 3 | ...... | ...... | ...... | ...... | ...... | 14 | 59 | 15.30 | 21.60 | ..... 5 00– 5 49 |
| 5 50– 5 99...... | ...... | ...... | ...... | 1 | ...... | ...... | ...... | ...... | ...... | 1 | 28 | 15.50 | 24.20 | ..... 5 50– 5 99 |
| 6 00– 6 49...... | ...... | 2 | ...... | ...... | ...... | ...... | ...... | ...... | 1 | 10 | 102 | 17.90 | 33.40 | ..... 6 00– 6 49 |
| 6 50– 6 99...... | ...... | ...... | ...... | ...... | ...... | ...... | ...... | ...... | 1 | 1 | 24 | 18.10 | 35.60 | ..... 6 50– 6 99 |
| 7 00– 7 49...... | ...... | 6 | ...... | 4 | ...... | ...... | ...... | ...... | 4 | 7 | 182 | 19.80 | 52.00 | ..... 7 00– 7 49 |
| 7 50– 7 99...... | ...... | 4 | ...... | 1 | ...... | ...... | ...... | ...... | ...... | 2 | 33 | 20.20 | 55.00 | ..... 7 50– 7 99 |
| 8 00– 8 99...... | ...... | 4 | ...... | 7 | ...... | ...... | ...... | ...... | 4 | 16 | 176 | 24.00 | 70.90 | ..... 8 00– 8 99 |
| 9 00– 9 99...... | ...... | 4 | 1 | 5 | ...... | ...... | ...... | ...... | 7 | 16 | 79 | 27.80 | 78.00 | ..... 9 00– 9 99 |
| 10 00–10 99...... | 1 | 7 | 1 | 4 | 2 | 1 | ...... | 1 | 2 | 38 | 66 | 36.70 | 84.00 | .....10 00–10 99 |
| 11 00–11 99...... | ...... | 3 | ...... | 1 | ...... | ...... | ...... | ...... | 2 | 12 | 30 | 39.50 | 86.70 | .....11 00–11 99 |
| 12 00–12 99...... | ...... | 10 | 4 | 5 | ...... | 2 | 1 | ...... | 3 | 36 | 53 | 48.00 | 91.50 | .....12 00–12 99 |
| 13 00–13 99...... | 1 | 4 | 4 | 2 | ...... | ...... | 1 | ...... | ...... | 18 | 23 | 52.20 | 93.60 | .....13 00–13 99 |
| 14 00–14 99...... | 3 | 4 | 5 | ...... | 1 | ...... | ...... | 1 | 1 | 30 | 16 | 59.30 | 95.10 | .....14 00–14 99 |
| 15 00–15 99...... | 3 | 2 | 6 | 4 | 2 | ...... | ...... | ...... | 3 | 57 | 27 | 72.70 | 97.50 | .....15 00–15 99 |
| 16 00–17 99...... | 3 | ...... | 6 | 2 | 4 | ...... | ...... | ...... | ...... | 33 | 10 | 80.50 | 98.50 | .....16 00–17 99 |
| 18 00–19 99...... | 6 | 2 | 4 | 1 | ...... | ...... | ...... | ...... | ...... | 25 | 8 | 86.40 | 99.30 | .....18 00–19 99 |
| 20 00–24 99...... | 5 | 1 | 1 | 1 | 3 | ...... | ...... | 1 | ...... | 37 | 6 | 95.00 | 99.70 | .....20 00–24 99 |
| 25 00–29 99...... | 4 | ...... | 3 | ...... | ...... | ...... | ...... | ...... | 1 | 12 | 3 | 98.00 | 99.90 | .....25 00–29 99 |
| 30 00–34 99...... | ...... | ...... | ...... | 1 | ...... | ...... | ...... | ...... | ...... | 1 | 1 | 98.10 | 100.00 | .....30 00–34 99 |
| 35 00–39 99...... | 1 | ...... | ...... | ...... | ...... | ...... | ...... | ...... | ...... | 1 | ...... | 98.90 | ...... | .....35 00–39 99 |
| 40 00 and over.... | 2 | ...... | 2 | ...... | 1 | ...... | ...... | ...... | ...... | 7 | ...... | 100.00 | ...... | ...40 00 and over |
| Not reported...... | ...... | ...... | ...... | ...... | ...... | ...... | ...... | ...... | ...... | ...... | 3 | ...... | ...... | .....Not reported |
| Total........ | 29 | 54 | 37 | 42 | 13 | 3 | 2 | 4 | 29 | 425 | 1,109 | ...... | ...... | .......Total |

303. TABLE IX, A, 1, a

ROCHESTER

DEPARTMENT STORES — STOCK AND SALES

Number and Per Cent. of Employees Classified According to Actual Weekly Earnings, by Occupation and Sex

| Actual Weekly Earnings in Dollars | Occupation | | | | | | | | | | | | | | | Total | | Cumulative Per Cent. of Total | | Actual Weekly Earnings in Dollars |
|---|---|---|---|---|---|---|---|---|---|---|---|---|---|---|---|---|---|---|---|---|
| | Superintendents | Buyers | | Assistant Buyers and Heads of Stock | | Receiving and Stock Clerks | | Stock People | | Floor Managers | | Sales People | | Messengers, Wrappers, Errand Boys | | | | | | |
| | Male | Male | Female | Male | Female | Male | Female | Male | Female | Male | Female | Male | Female | Male | Female | Male | Female | Male | Female | |
| Less than $3 00 | ... | ... | ... | ... | ... | ... | ... | 1 | ... | ... | ... | ... | 11 | 1 | 6 | 2 | 17 | .50 | 1.50 | Less than $3 00 |
| $3 00–$3 49 | ... | ... | ... | ... | ... | ... | ... | 2 | ... | ... | ... | 1 | 1 | 2 | 6 | 5 | 7 | 1.60 | 2.20 | $3 00– 3 49 |
| 3 50– 3 99 | ... | ... | ... | ... | ... | ... | ... | ... | 2 | ... | ... | 1 | 7 | 9 | 76 | 10 | 85 | 4.00 | 9.90 | 3 50– 3 99 |
| 4 00– 4 49 | ... | ... | ... | ... | ... | ... | 1 | 8 | 8 | ... | ... | 1 | 10 | 19 | 25 | 28 | 44 | 10.60 | 13.80 | 4 00– 4 49 |
| 4 50– 4 99 | ... | ... | ... | ... | ... | ... | 1 | 3 | 5 | ... | ... | 1 | 11 | 2 | 10 | 6 | 27 | 12.00 | 16.30 | 4 50– 4 99 |
| 5 00– 5 49 | ... | ... | ... | ... | ... | ... | 1 | 6 | 15 | ... | ... | 2 | 38 | 6 | 5 | 14 | 59 | 15.30 | 21.60 | 5 00– 5 49 |
| 5 50– 5 99 | ... | ... | ... | ... | ... | ... | ... | 1 | 1 | ... | ... | ... | 26 | ... | 1 | 1 | 28 | 15.50 | 24.20 | 5 50– 5 99 |
| 6 00– 6 49 | ... | ... | ... | ... | ... | 1 | ... | 1 | 5 | ... | ... | 7 | 96 | 1 | 1 | 10 | 102 | 17.90 | 33.40 | 6 00– 6 49 |
| 6 50– 6 99 | ... | ... | ... | ... | ... | ... | 1 | ... | ... | ... | ... | 1 | 23 | ... | ... | 1 | 24 | 18.10 | 35.60 | 6 50– 6 99 |
| 7 00– 7 49 | ... | ... | ... | ... | ... | ... | ... | 2 | 1 | ... | ... | 5 | 181 | ... | ... | 7 | 182 | 19.80 | 52.00 | 7 00– 7 49 |
| 7 50– 7 99 | ... | ... | ... | ... | ... | ... | ... | ... | ... | ... | ... | 1 | 33 | 1 | ... | 2 | 33 | 20.20 | 55.00 | 7 50– 7 99 |
| 8 00– 8 99 | ... | ... | ... | ... | ... | ... | 2 | 2 | 1 | ... | ... | 14 | 172 | ... | 1 | 16 | 176 | 24.00 | 70.90 | 8 00– 8 99 |
| 9 00– 9 99 | ... | ... | ... | ... | ... | 1 | 2 | 4 | ... | 1 | ... | 10 | 77 | ... | ... | 16 | 79 | 27.80 | 78.00 | 9 00– 9 99 |
| 10 00–10 99 | ... | ... | ... | ... | 1 | 2 | 1 | 3 | ... | ... | ... | 32 | 64 | 1 | ... | 38 | 66 | 36.70 | 84.00 | 10 00–10 99 |
| 11 00–11 99 | ... | ... | ... | ... | ... | 2 | ... | 3 | ... | ... | ... | 7 | 30 | ... | ... | 12 | 30 | 39.50 | 86.70 | 11 00–11 99 |
| 12 00–12 99 | ... | 1 | ... | ... | ... | 6 | ... | 2 | ... | ... | ... | 27 | 53 | ... | ... | 36 | 53 | 48.00 | 91.50 | 12 00–12 99 |
| 13 00–13 99 | ... | ... | ... | ... | ... | 1 | 1 | 1 | ... | ... | ... | 16 | 22 | ... | ... | 18 | 23 | 52.20 | 93.60 | 13 00–13 99 |
| 14 00–14 99 | ... | ... | ... | ... | ... | 3 | 1 | 1 | ... | ... | ... | 26 | 15 | ... | ... | 30 | 16 | 59.30 | 95.10 | 14 00–14 99 |
| 15 00–15 99 | ... | ... | ... | 1 | 1 | 1 | 1 | ... | ... | 2 | ... | 53 | 25 | ... | ... | 57 | 27 | 72.70 | 97.50 | 15 00–15 99 |
| 16 00–17 99 | ... | ... | ... | ... | 1 | 2 | ... | 2 | ... | ... | ... | 29 | 9 | ... | ... | 33 | 10 | 80.50 | 98.50 | 16 00–17 99 |
| 18 00–19 99 | ... | 1 | ... | 1 | ... | 1 | ... | ... | ... | 1 | 1 | 21 | 7 | ... | ... | 25 | 8 | 86.40 | 99.30 | 18 00–19 99 |
| 20 00–24 99 | ... | 1 | ... | 4 | 1 | ... | ... | ... | ... | 8 | ... | 24 | 5 | ... | ... | 37 | 6 | 95.00 | 99.70 | 20 00–24 99 |
| 25 00–29 99 | 1 | ... | 1 | ... | 1 | ... | ... | ... | ... | 2 | ... | 9 | 1 | ... | ... | 12 | 3 | 98.00 | 90.90 | 25 00–29 99 |
| 30 00–34 99 | ... | ... | ... | ... | ... | ... | ... | ... | ... | 1 | ... | ... | 1 | ... | ... | 1 | 1 | 98.10 | 100.00 | 30 00–34 99 |
| 35 00–39 99 | ... | ... | ... | ... | ... | ... | ... | ... | ... | 1 | ... | ... | ... | ... | ... | 1 | ... | 98.90 | ... | 35 00–39 99 |
| 40 00 and over | ... | 7 | ... | ... | ... | ... | ... | ... | ... | ... | ... | ... | ... | ... | ... | 7 | ... | 100.00 | ... | 40 00 and over |
| Not reported | ... | ... | ... | ... | ... | ... | ... | ... | ... | ... | ... | ... | 2 | ... | 1 | ... | 3 | ... | ... | Not reported |
| Total | 1 | 10 | 1 | 6 | 5 | 20 | 12 | 42 | 38 | 16 | 1 | 288 | 920 | 42 | 132 | 425 | 1,109 | ... | ... | Total |

ROCHESTER
DEPARTMENT STORES — OFFICE

304. TABLE V, A, 1, b  NUMBER AND PER CENT. OF EMPLOYEES EARNING SPECIFIED WEEKLY RATES, BY AGE GROUPS AND SEX

| WEEKLY RATES IN DOLLARS | AGE GROUPS IN YEARS | | | | | | | | | | | | | | WEEKLY RATES IN DOLLARS |
|---|---|---|---|---|---|---|---|---|---|---|---|---|---|---|---|
| | 14–15 | | 16–17 | | 18–20 | | 21–24 | | 25–29 | | 30–34 | | 35–39 | | |
| | Male | Female | Male | Female | Male | Female | Male | Female | Male | Female | Male | Female | Male | Female | |
| $3 50–$3 99 | .... | 2 | .... | .... | 1 | .... | .... | .... | .... | .... | .... | .... | .... | .... | $3 50–$3 99 |
| 4 00– 4 49 | 3 | 5 | .... | 5 | .... | .... | .... | .... | .... | .... | .... | .... | .... | .... | 4 00– 4 49 |
| 4 50– 4 99 | .... | 1 | .... | 2 | .... | .... | .... | .... | .... | .... | .... | .... | .... | .... | 4 50– 4 99 |
| 5 00– 5 49 | 1 | 2 | 1 | 19 | .... | 12 | .... | .... | .... | .... | .... | 1 | .... | .... | 5 00– 5 49 |
| 5 50– 5 99 | .... | .... | .... | 5 | .... | 2 | .... | .... | .... | .... | .... | .... | .... | .... | 5 50– 5 99 |
| 6 00– 6 49 | .... | 1 | 4 | 18 | 2 | 35 | .... | 11 | .... | 2 | .... | 2 | .... | 1 | 6 00– 6 49 |
| 6 50– 6 99 | .... | .... | .... | 1 | .... | 3 | .... | 2 | .... | .... | .... | .... | .... | .... | 6 50– 6 99 |
| 7 00– 7 49 | .... | .... | 1 | 6 | 4 | 23 | .... | 21 | .... | 9 | .... | 5 | .... | .... | 7 00– 7 49 |
| 7 50– 7 99 | .... | .... | .... | .... | .... | 3 | 1 | .... | .... | .... | .... | .... | .... | .... | 7 50– 7 99 |
| 8 00– 8 99 | .... | .... | 1 | 2 | 3 | 7 | 1 | 19 | .... | 8 | .... | 2 | .... | 2 | 8 00– 8 99 |
| 9 00– 9 99 | .... | .... | 1 | .... | 6 | 7 | 2 | 11 | .... | 1 | .... | 4 | .... | .... | 9 00– 9 99 |
| 10 00–10 99 | .... | .... | .... | .... | 1 | 4 | 1 | 12 | 2 | 5 | .... | 1 | .... | .... | 10 00–10 99 |
| 11 00–11 99 | .... | .... | .... | .... | 1 | .... | 1 | 2 | .... | 4 | .... | 1 | .... | .... | 11 00–11 99 |
| 12 00–12 99 | .... | .... | .... | .... | 1 | 2 | 7 | 6 | 4 | 8 | 2 | 1 | 5 | 1 | 12 00–12 99 |
| 13 00–13 99 | .... | .... | .... | .... | 2 | .... | 4 | .... | 1 | .... | 1 | 1 | 1 | .... | 13 00–13 99 |
| 14 00–14 99 | .... | .... | .... | .... | .... | 1 | 2 | .... | 1 | 2 | .... | .... | .... | 1 | 14 00–14 99 |
| 15 00–15 99 | .... | .... | .... | .... | .... | .... | 2 | 1 | 2 | .... | 1 | 1 | 1 | .... | 15 00–15 99 |
| 16 00–17 99 | .... | .... | .... | .... | .... | .... | 2 | 1 | 1 | .... | 4 | 1 | 1 | .... | 16 00–17 99 |
| 18 00–19 99 | .... | .... | .... | .... | .... | .... | .... | .... | 1 | 1 | 1 | .... | .... | .... | 18 00–19 99 |
| 20 00–24 99 | .... | .... | .... | .... | .... | .... | .... | .... | 2 | .... | 1 | .... | 1 | 1 | 20 00–24 99 |
| 30 00–34 99 | .... | .... | .... | .... | .... | .... | .... | .... | .... | .... | 1 | .... | .... | .... | 30 00–34 99 |
| 35 00–39 99 | .... | .... | .... | .... | .... | .... | .... | .... | .... | .... | 1 | .... | .... | .... | 35 00–39 99 |
| 40 00 and over | .... | .... | .... | .... | .... | .... | 1 | .... | .... | .... | 2 | .... | .... | .... | 40 00 and over |
| Not reported | .... | 1 | .... | .... | .... | .... | .... | .... | .... | .... | .... | .... | .... | .... | Not reported |
| Total | 4 | 12 | 8 | 58 | 21 | 99 | 24 | 86 | 14 | 40 | 14 | 20 | 9 | 6 | Total |

304. TABLE V, A, 1, b — (*concluded*)

ROCHESTER
DEPARTMENT STORES — OFFICE
NUMBER AND PER CENT. OF EMPLOYEES EARNING SPECIFIED WEEKLY RATES, BY AGE GROUPS AND SEX

| WEEKLY RATES IN DOLLARS | AGE GROUPS IN YEARS (*concluded*) | | | | | | | | | | | | | WEEKLY RATES IN DOLLARS |
|---|---|---|---|---|---|---|---|---|---|---|---|---|---|---|
| | 40–44 | | 45–54 | | 55–64 | 65 AND OVER | NOT REPORTED | | TOTAL | | CUMULATIVE PER CENT. OF TOTAL | | |
| | Male | Female | Male | Female | Male | Male | Male | Female | Male | Female | Male | Female | |
| $3 50–$3 99 | ....... | ....... | ....... | ....... | ....... | ....... | ....... | ....... | 1 | 2 | .89 | .61 | $3 50–$3 99 |
| 4 00– 4 49 | ....... | ....... | ....... | ....... | ....... | ....... | ....... | ....... | 3 | 10 | 3.54 | 3.67 | 4 00– 4 49 |
| 4 50– 4 99 | ....... | ....... | ....... | ....... | ....... | ....... | ....... | ....... | ....... | 3 | ....... | 4.59 | 4 50– 4 99 |
| 5 00– 5 49 | ....... | ....... | ....... | ....... | ....... | ....... | ....... | 1 | 2 | 35 | 5.32 | 15.30 | 5 00– 5 49 |
| 5 50– 5 99 | ....... | ....... | ....... | ....... | ....... | ....... | ....... | ....... | ....... | 7 | ....... | 16.90 | 5 50– 5 99 |
| 6 00– 6 49 | ....... | ....... | ....... | 2 | ....... | ....... | ....... | 1 | 6 | 73 | 10.62 | 39.75 | 6 00– 6 49 |
| 6 50– 6 99 | ....... | ....... | ....... | ....... | ....... | ....... | ....... | ....... | ....... | 6 | ....... | 41.60 | 6 50– 6 99 |
| 7 00– 7 49 | ....... | ....... | ....... | ....... | ....... | ....... | ....... | ....... | 5 | 64 | 15.05 | 61.10 | 7 00– 7 49 |
| 7 50– 7 99 | ....... | ....... | ....... | ....... | ....... | ....... | ....... | ....... | 1 | 3 | 15.95 | 63.00 | 7 50– 7 99 |
| 8 00– 8 99 | ....... | 1 | ....... | ....... | ....... | ....... | ....... | ....... | 5 | 41 | 20.40 | 74.60 | 8 00– 8 99 |
| 9 00– 9 99 | ....... | ....... | ....... | ....... | ....... | 1 | ....... | ....... | 10 | 23 | 29.20 | 81.60 | 9 00– 9 99 |
| 10 00–10 99 | ....... | ....... | ....... | ....... | ....... | ....... | ....... | ....... | 4 | 22 | 32.80 | 88.56 | 10 00–10 99 |
| 11 00–11 99 | ....... | ....... | 1 | ....... | ....... | ....... | ....... | ....... | 3 | 7 | 35.40 | 91.50 | 11 00–11 99 |
| 12 00–12 99 | 1 | ....... | 3 | ....... | 2 | ....... | ....... | ....... | 25 | 18 | 57.50 | 96.00 | 12 00–12 99 |
| 13 00–13 99 | ....... | ....... | 1 | ....... | ....... | ....... | ....... | 1 | 10 | 2 | 66.50 | 96.60 | 13 00–13 99 |
| 14 00–14 99 | ....... | ....... | 2 | ....... | 1 | ....... | ....... | ....... | 6 | 4 | 70.90 | 98.00 | 14 00–14 99 |
| 15 00–15 99 | 2 | ....... | ....... | ....... | 1 | ....... | 1 | ....... | 10 | 2 | 80.50 | 98.50 | 15 00–15 99 |
| 16 00–17 99 | ....... | ....... | ....... | ....... | ....... | ....... | ....... | ....... | 8 | 2 | 87.70 | 99.00 | 16 00–17 99 |
| 18 00–19 99 | 1 | ....... | 1 | ....... | ....... | ....... | ....... | ....... | 4 | 1 | 91.25 | 99.50 | 18 00–19 99 |
| 20 00–24 99 | ....... | ....... | ....... | ....... | 1 | ....... | ....... | ....... | 5 | 1 | 95.55 | 100.00 | 20 00–24 99 |
| 30 00–34 99 | ....... | ....... | ....... | ....... | ....... | ....... | ....... | ....... | 1 | ....... | 96.50 | ....... | 30 00–34 99 |
| 35 00–39 99 | ....... | ....... | ....... | ....... | ....... | ....... | ....... | ....... | 1 | ....... | 97.50 | ....... | 35 00–39 99 |
| 40 00 and over | ....... | ....... | ....... | ....... | ....... | ....... | ....... | ....... | 3 | ....... | 100.00 | ....... | 40 00 and over |
| Not reported | ....... | ....... | ....... | ....... | 1 | ....... | ....... | ....... | 1 | 1 | ....... | ....... | Not reported |
| Total | 4 | 1 | 8 | 2 | 6 | 1 | 1 | 3 | 114 | 327 | ....... | ....... | Total |

305. TABLE VIII, A, 1, b

ROCHESTER

DEPARTMENT STORES — OFFICE

NUMBER AND PER CENT. OF EMPLOYEES EARNING SPECIFIED WEEKLY RATES, BY OCCUPATION AND SEX

| WEEKLY RATES IN DOLLARS | OCCUPATION | | | | | | | | | | | | | | | | | | WEEKLY RATES IN DOLLARS |
|---|---|---|---|---|---|---|---|---|---|---|---|---|---|---|---|---|---|---|---|
| | BOOK-KEEPERS | | CLERKS | | STENOG-RAPHERS | | OFFICE BOYS AND GIRLS | | CASHIERS | | TELEPHONE OPERATORS | AUDITORS | | ADVERTISERS AND WINDOW DRESSERS | TOTAL | | CUMULATIVE PER CENT. OF TOTAL | | |
| | Male | Female | Male | Female | Male | Female | Male | Female | Male | Female | Female | Male | Female | Male | Male | Female | Male | Female | |
| $3 50-$3 99 | .... | .... | 1 | 2 | .... | .... | .... | .... | .... | .... | .... | .... | .... | .... | 1 | 2 | .89 | .61 | $3 50-$3 99 |
| 4 00- 4 49 | .... | .... | 2 | 6 | .... | .... | 1 | .... | .... | .... | 3 | .... | 1 | .... | 3 | 10 | 3.54 | 3.67 | 4 00- 4 49 |
| 4 50- 4 99 | .... | .... | .... | 1 | .... | .... | .... | .... | .... | 1 | .... | .... | 1 | .... | .... | 3 | .... | 4.59 | 4 50- 4 99 |
| 5 00- 5 49 | .... | .... | 1 | 25 | .... | .... | 1 | 1 | .... | 4 | .... | .... | 5 | .... | 2 | 35 | 5.32 | 15.30 | 5 00- 5 49 |
| 5 50- 5 99 | .... | .... | .... | 2 | .... | .... | .... | .... | .... | 3 | .... | .... | 2 | .... | .... | 7 | .... | 16.90 | 5 50- 5 99 |
| 6 00- 6 49 | .... | 1 | 3 | 28 | .... | .... | 1 | .... | .... | 37 | 1 | .... | 6 | 2 | 6 | 73 | 10.62 | 39.75 | 6 00- 6 49 |
| 6 50- 6 99 | .... | .... | .... | 3 | .... | .... | .... | .... | .... | 1 | .... | .... | 2 | .... | .... | 6 | .... | 41.60 | 6 50- 6 99 |
| 7 00- 7 49 | .... | 2 | 5 | 21 | .... | 2 | .... | .... | .... | 31 | 3 | .... | 5 | .... | 5 | 64 | 15.05 | 61.10 | 7 00- 7 49 |
| 7 50- 7 99 | .... | .... | 1 | .... | .... | .... | .... | .... | .... | 2 | 1 | .... | .... | .... | 1 | 3 | 15.95 | 63.00 | 7 50- 7 99 |
| 8 00- 8 99 | .... | 3 | 2 | 21 | .... | 3 | .... | .... | .... | 9 | 4 | .... | 1 | 3 | 5 | 41 | 20.40 | 74.60 | 8 00- 8 99 |
| 9 00- 9 99 | 2 | 2 | 6 | 16 | .... | 1 | .... | .... | .... | 2 | 1 | .... | 1 | 2 | 10 | 23 | 29.20 | 81.60 | 9 00- 9 99 |
| 10 00-10 99 | .... | 5 | 1 | 10 | .... | 1 | .... | .... | .... | 5 | 1 | 2 | .... | 1 | 4 | 22 | 32.80 | 88.56 | 10 00-10 99 |
| 11 00-11 99 | .... | 2 | 3 | 1 | .... | 3 | .... | .... | .... | .... | .... | .... | 1 | .... | 3 | 7 | 35.40 | 91.50 | 11 00-11 99 |
| 12 00-12 99 | 2 | 3 | 20 | 8 | .... | 3 | .... | .... | .... | 3 | 1 | 1 | .... | 2 | 25 | 18 | 57.50 | 96.00 | 12 00-12 99 |
| 13 00-13 99 | 2 | .... | 6 | .... | 1 | 1 | .... | .... | .... | 1 | .... | .... | .... | 1 | 10 | 2 | 66.50 | 96.60 | 13 00-13 99 |
| 14 00-14 99 | .... | 1 | 5 | .... | .... | 1 | .... | .... | .... | 2 | .... | .... | .... | 1 | 6 | 4 | 70.90 | 98.00 | 14 00-14 99 |
| 15 00-15 99 | 3 | .... | 4 | 1 | .... | 1 | .... | .... | .... | .... | .... | .... | .... | 3 | 10 | 2 | 80.50 | 98.50 | 15 00-15 99 |
| 16 00-17 99 | 6 | 1 | 2 | .... | .... | 1 | .... | .... | .... | .... | .... | .... | .... | .... | 8 | 2 | 87.70 | 99.00 | 16 00-17 99 |
| 18 00-19 99 | 2 | .... | 1 | .... | .... | 1 | .... | .... | .... | .... | .... | .... | .... | 1 | 4 | 1 | 91.25 | 99.50 | 18 00-19 99 |
| 20 00-24 99 | .... | .... | 4 | .... | .... | 1 | .... | .... | 1 | .... | .... | .... | .... | .... | 5 | 1 | 95.55 | 100.00 | 20 00-24 99 |
| 30 00 34 99 | .... | .... | .... | .... | .... | .... | .... | .... | .... | .... | .... | .... | .... | 1 | 1 | .... | 96.50 | .... | 30 00 34 99 |
| 35 00 39 99 | .... | .... | 1 | .... | .... | .... | .... | .... | .... | .... | .... | .... | .... | .... | 1 | .... | 97.50 | .... | 35 00-39 99 |
| 40 00 and over | .... | .... | .... | .... | .... | .... | .... | .... | .... | .... | .... | 1 | .... | 2 | 3 | .... | 100.00 | .... | 40 00 and over |
| Not reported | .... | .... | 1 | .... | .... | .... | .... | .... | .... | 1 | .... | .... | .... | .... | 1 | 1 | .... | .... | Not reported |
| Total | 17 | 20 | 69 | 145 | 1 | 19 | 3 | 1 | 1 | 102 | 15 | 4 | 25 | 19 | 114 | 327 | .... | .... | Total |

306. TABLE VI, A, 1, b

## ROCHESTER
## DEPARTMENT STORES — OFFICE

NUMBER AND PER CENT. OF EMPLOYEES CLASSIFIED ACCORDING TO ACTUAL WEEKLY EARNINGS, BY AGE GROUPS AND SEX

| ACTUAL WEEKLY EARNINGS IN DOLLARS | AGE GROUPS IN YEARS | | | | | | | | | | | | | | ACTUAL WEEKLY EARNINGS IN DOLLARS |
|---|---|---|---|---|---|---|---|---|---|---|---|---|---|---|---|
| | 14–15 | | 16–17 | | 18–20 | | 21–24 | | 25–29 | | 30–34 | | 35–39 | | |
| | Male | Female | Male | Female | Male | Female | Male | Female | Male | Female | Male | Female | Male | Female | |
| Less than $3 00 | .... | ...... | .... | 1 | 1 | ...... | ...... | ...... | ...... | ...... | ...... | ...... | ...... | ...... | Less than $3 00 |
| $3 00–$3 49 | 1 | ...... | .... | 1 | ...... | ...... | ...... | ...... | ...... | ...... | ...... | 1 | ...... | ...... | $3 00– 3 49 |
| 3 50– 3 99 | .... | 3 | .... | ...... | ...... | 1 | ...... | ...... | ...... | ...... | ...... | ...... | ...... | ...... | 3 50– 3 99 |
| 4 00– 4 49 | 2 | 4 | .... | 8 | ...... | 2 | ...... | ...... | ...... | ...... | ...... | ...... | ...... | ...... | 4 00– 4 49 |
| 4 50– 4 99 | .... | 1 | .... | 2 | ...... | 2 | ...... | 2 | ...... | ...... | ...... | ...... | ...... | ...... | 4 50– 4 99 |
| 5 00– 5 49 | 1 | 2 | 1 | 15 | ...... | 12 | ...... | 1 | ...... | ...... | ...... | 1 | ...... | ...... | 5 00– 5 49 |
| 5 50– 5 99 | .... | ...... | .... | 8 | ...... | 6 | ...... | 4 | ...... | ...... | ...... | ...... | ...... | ...... | 5 50– 5 99 |
| 6 00– 6 49 | .... | 1 | 4 | 14 | 4 | 33 | ...... | 7 | ...... | 2 | ...... | 3 | ...... | 1 | 6 00– 6 49 |
| 6 50– 6 99 | .... | ...... | .... | 1 | ...... | 1 | 1 | 4 | ...... | 1 | ...... | ...... | ...... | ...... | 6 50– 6 99 |
| 7 00– 7 49 | .... | ...... | 1 | 6 | 3 | 19 | ...... | 18 | ...... | 8 | ...... | 5 | ...... | ...... | 7 00– 7 49 |
| 7 50– 7 99 | .... | ...... | .... | ...... | ...... | 3 | 1 | ...... | ...... | ...... | ...... | ...... | ...... | ...... | 7 50– 7 99 |
| 8 00– 8 99 | .... | ...... | 1 | 2 | 4 | 6 | 2 | 20 | ...... | 8 | ...... | 2 | ...... | 2 | 8 00– 8 99 |
| 9 00– 9 99 | .... | ...... | 1 | ...... | 5 | 8 | 2 | 14 | ...... | 1 | ...... | 2 | ...... | ...... | 9 00– 9 99 |
| 10 00–10 99 | .... | ...... | .... | ...... | 2 | 3 | ...... | 7 | 2 | 5 | ...... | 1 | ...... | ...... | 10 00–10 99 |
| 11 00–11 99 | .... | ...... | .... | ...... | 1 | 1 | 1 | 2 | 1 | 4 | ...... | 1 | ...... | ...... | 11 00–11 99 |
| 12 00–12 99 | .... | ...... | .... | ...... | ...... | 1 | 6 | 5 | 3 | 8 | 2 | 1 | 5 | 1 | 12 00–12 99 |
| 13 00–13 99 | .... | ...... | .... | ...... | 1 | ...... | 4 | ...... | 1 | ...... | 1 | 1 | 1 | ...... | 13 00–13 99 |
| 14 00–14 99 | .... | ...... | .... | ...... | ...... | 1 | 2 | ...... | 1 | 2 | ...... | ...... | ...... | 1 | 14 00–14 99 |
| 15 00–15 99 | .... | ...... | .... | ...... | ...... | ...... | 2 | 1 | 2 | ...... | 1 | 1 | 1 | ...... | 15 00–15 99 |
| 16 00–17 99 | .... | ...... | .... | ...... | ...... | ...... | 2 | 1 | 1 | ...... | 4 | 1 | 1 | ...... | 16 00–17 99 |
| 18 00–19 99 | .... | ...... | .... | ...... | ...... | ...... | ...... | ...... | 1 | 1 | 1 | ...... | ...... | ...... | 18 00–19 99 |
| 20 00–24 99 | .... | ...... | .... | ...... | ...... | ...... | 1 | ...... | 2 | ...... | 1 | ...... | 1 | 1 | 20 00–24 99 |
| 30 00–34 99 | .... | ...... | .... | ...... | ...... | ...... | ...... | ...... | ...... | ...... | 1 | ...... | ...... | ...... | 30 00–34 99 |
| 35 00–39 99 | .... | ...... | .... | ...... | ...... | ...... | ...... | ...... | ...... | ...... | 1 | ...... | ...... | ...... | 35 00–39 99 |
| 40 00 and over | .... | ...... | .... | ...... | ...... | ...... | ...... | ...... | ...... | ...... | 2 | ...... | ...... | ...... | 40 00 and over |
| Not reported | .... | 1 | .... | ...... | ...... | ...... | ...... | ...... | ...... | ...... | ...... | ...... | ...... | ...... | Not reported |
| Total | 4 | 12 | 8 | 58 | 21 | 99 | 24 | 86 | 14 | 40 | 14 | 20 | 9 | 6 | Total |

306. TABLE VI, A, 1, b — (*concluded*)

ROCHESTER

DEPARTMENT STORES — OFFICE

Number and Per Cent. of Employees Classified According to Actual Weekly Earnings, by Age Groups and Sex

| Actual Weekly Earnings Dollars | Age Groups in Years (*concluded*) | | | | | | | | | | | | Actual Weekly Earnings in Dollars |
|---|---|---|---|---|---|---|---|---|---|---|---|---|---|
| | 40–44 | | 45–54 | | 55–64 | 65 and over | Not reported | | Total | | Cumulative per cent. of total | | |
| | Male | Female | Male | Female | Male | Male | Male | Female | Male | Female | Male | Female | |
| Less than $3 00 | ... | ... | ... | ... | ... | ... | ... | 1 | 1 | 2 | .89 | .61 | Less than $3 00 |
| $3 00–$3 49 | ... | ... | ... | ... | ... | ... | ... | ... | 1 | 2 | 1.77 | 1.12 | $3 00– 3 49 |
| 3 50– 3 99 | ... | ... | ... | ... | ... | ... | ... | ... | ... | 4 | ... | 2.41 | 3 50– 3 99 |
| 4 00– 4 49 | ... | ... | ... | ... | ... | ... | ... | ... | 2 | 14 | 3.54 | 6.75 | 4 00– 4 49 |
| 4 50– 4 99 | ... | ... | ... | ... | ... | ... | ... | ... | ... | 7 | ... | 8.90 | 4 50– 4 99 |
| 5 00– 5 49 | ... | ... | ... | ... | ... | ... | ... | 1 | 2 | 32 | 5.32 | 18.70 | 5 00– 5 49 |
| 5 50– 5 99 | ... | ... | ... | ... | ... | ... | ... | ... | ... | 18 | ... | 24.95 | 5 50– 5 99 |
| 6 00– 6 49 | ... | ... | ... | 2 | ... | ... | ... | ... | 8 | 63 | 12.80 | 43.60 | 6 00– 6 49 |
| 6 50– 6 99 | ... | ... | ... | ... | ... | ... | ... | ... | 1 | 7 | 13.28 | 45.75 | 6 50– 6 99 |
| 7 00– 7 49 | ... | ... | ... | ... | ... | ... | ... | ... | 4 | 56 | 16.80 | 63.00 | 7 00– 7 49 |
| 7 50– 7 99 | ... | ... | ... | ... | ... | ... | ... | ... | 1 | 3 | 17.70 | 64.00 | 7 50– 7 99 |
| 8 00– 8 99 | ... | 1 | ... | ... | ... | ... | ... | ... | 7 | 41 | 18.95 | 76.25 | 8 00– 8 99 |
| 9 00– 9 99 | ... | ... | ... | ... | ... | 1 | ... | ... | 9 | 25 | 31.85 | 84.00 | 9 00– 9 99 |
| 10 00–10 99 | ... | ... | ... | ... | ... | ... | ... | ... | 4 | 16 | 35.40 | 89.00 | 10 00–10 99 |
| 11 00–11 99 | ... | ... | 1 | ... | ... | ... | ... | ... | 4 | 8 | 39.00 | 91.50 | 11 00–11 99 |
| 12 00–12 99 | 1 | ... | 3 | ... | 2 | ... | ... | ... | 22 | 16 | 58.50 | 96.50 | 12 00–12 99 |
| 13 00–13 99 | ... | ... | 1 | ... | ... | ... | ... | 1 | 9 | 2 | 66.40 | 97.00 | 13 00–13 99 |
| 14 00–14 99 | ... | ... | 2 | ... | 1 | ... | ... | ... | 6 | 4 | 71.75 | 98.25 | 14 00–14 99 |
| 15 00–15 99 | 2 | ... | ... | ... | 1 | ... | 1 | ... | 10 | 2 | 80.50 | 98.75 | 15 00–15 99 |
| 16 00–17 99 | ... | ... | ... | ... | ... | ... | ... | ... | 8 | 2 | 87.60 | 99.40 | 16 00–17 99 |
| 18 00–19 99 | 1 | ... | 1 | ... | ... | ... | ... | ... | 4 | 1 | 91.20 | 99.70 | 18 00–19 99 |
| 20 00–24 99 | ... | ... | ... | ... | 1 | ... | ... | ... | 6 | 1 | 96.50 | 100.00 | 20 00–24 99 |
| 30 00–34 99 | ... | ... | ... | ... | ... | ... | ... | ... | 1 | ... | 97.50 | ... | 30 00–34 99 |
| 35 00–39 99 | ... | ... | ... | ... | ... | ... | ... | ... | 1 | ... | 98.25 | ... | 35 00–39 99 |
| 40 00 and over | ... | ... | ... | ... | ... | ... | ... | ... | 2 | ... | 100.00 | ... | 40 00 and over |
| Not reported | ... | ... | ... | ... | 1 | ... | ... | ... | 1 | 1 | ... | ... | Not reported |
| Total | 4 | 1 | 8 | 2 | 6 | 1 | 1 | 3 | 114 | 327 | ... | ... | Total |

307. TABLE IX, A, 1, b

ROCHESTER
DEPARTMENT STORES — OFFICE

NUMBER AND PER CENT. OF EMPLOYEES CLASSIFIED ACCORDING TO ACTUAL WEEKLY EARNINGS, BY OCCUPATION AND SEX

| ACTUAL WEEKLY EARNINGS IN DOLLARS | OCCUPATION | | | | | | | | | | | | | | | | | | ACTUAL WEEKLY EARNINGS IN DOLLARS |
|---|---|---|---|---|---|---|---|---|---|---|---|---|---|---|---|---|---|---|---|
| | BOOK-KEEPERS | | CLERKS | | STENOG-RAPHERS | | OFFICE BOYS AND GIRLS | | CASHIERS | | TELEPHONE OPERATORS | AUDITORS | | ADVERTISERS AND WINDOW DRESSERS | TOTAL | | CUMULATIVE PER CENT. OF TOTAL | | |
| | Male | Female | Male | Female | Male | Female | Male | Female | Male | Female | Female | Male | Female | Male | Male | Female | Male | Female | |
| Less than $3 00 | .... | .... | 1 | 1 | .... | .... | .... | .... | .... | 1 | .......... | .... | .... | .......... | 1 | 2 | .89 | .61 | Less than $3 00 |
| $3 00–$3 49 | .... | .... | .... | 1 | .... | .... | 1 | .... | .... | 1 | .......... | .... | .... | .......... | 1 | 2 | 1.77 | 1.12 | $3 00– 3 49 |
| 3 50– 3 99 | .... | .... | .... | 3 | .... | .... | .... | .... | .... | 1 | .......... | .... | .... | .......... | .... | 4 | ..... | 2.41 | 3 50 3 99 |
| 4 00– 4 49 | .... | .... | 2 | 8 | .... | .... | .... | .... | .... | .... | 3 | .... | 3 | .......... | 2 | 14 | 3.54 | 6.75 | 4 00– 4 49 |
| 4 50– 4 99 | .... | .... | .... | 1 | .... | .... | .... | .... | .... | 4 | .......... | .... | 2 | .......... | .... | 7 | ..... | 8.90 | 4 50– 4 99 |
| 5 00– 5 49 | .... | .... | 1 | 22 | .... | .... | 1 | 1 | .... | 6 | .......... | .... | 3 | .......... | 2 | 32 | 5.32 | 18.70 | 5 00– 5 49 |
| 5 50– 5 99 | .... | .... | .... | 7 | .... | .... | .... | .... | .... | 7 | .......... | .... | 4 | .......... | .... | 18 | ..... | 24.95 | 5 50– 5 99 |
| 6 00– 6 49 | .... | 2 | 4 | 24 | .... | .... | 1 | .... | .... | 31 | 1 | .... | 5 | 3 | 8 | 63 | 12.80 | 43.60 | 6 00– 6 49 |
| 6 50– 6 99 | .... | 1 | .... | 2 | .... | .... | .... | .... | .... | 1 | .......... | 1 | 3 | .......... | 1 | 7 | 13.28 | 45.75 | 6 50– 6 99 |
| 7 00– 7 49 | .... | 2 | 4 | 20 | .... | 2 | .... | .... | .... | 26 | 3 | .... | 3 | .......... | 4 | 56 | 16.80 | 63.00 | 7 00– 7 49 |
| 7 50– 7 99 | .... | .... | 1 | .... | .... | .... | .... | .... | .... | 2 | 1 | .... | .... | .......... | 1 | 3 | 17.70 | 64.00 | 7 50– 7 99 |
| 8 00 8 99 | .... | 3 | 3 | 22 | .... | 3 | .... | .... | .... | 8 | 4 | .... | 1 | 4 | 7 | 41 | 18.95 | 76.25 | 8 00 8 99 |
| 9 00– 9 99 | 2 | 1 | 6 | 18 | .... | 1 | .... | .... | .... | 3 | 2 | .... | .... | 1 | 9 | 25 | 31.85 | 84.00 | 9 00– 9 99 |
| 10 00–10 99 | 1 | 4 | 1 | 6 | .... | 1 | .... | .... | .... | 4 | 1 | 1 | .... | 1 | 4 | 16 | 35.40 | 89.00 | 10 00–10 99 |
| 11 00–11 99 | .... | 3 | 4 | 1 | .... | 3 | .... | .... | .... | .... | .......... | .... | 1 | .......... | 4 | 8 | 39.00 | 91.50 | 11 00–11 99 |
| 12 00–12 99 | 2 | 2 | 18 | 8 | .... | 3 | .... | .... | .... | 3 | .......... | 1 | .... | 1 | 22 | 16 | 58.50 | 96.50 | 12 00–12 99 |
| 13 00–13 99 | 1 | .... | 6 | .... | 1 | 1 | .... | .... | .... | 1 | .......... | .... | .... | 1 | 9 | 2 | 66.40 | 97.00 | 13 00–13 99 |
| 14 00–14 99 | .... | 1 | 5 | .... | .... | 1 | .... | .... | .... | 2 | .......... | .... | .... | 1 | 6 | 4 | 71.75 | 98.25 | 14 00–14 99 |
| 15 00–15 99 | 3 | .... | 4 | 1 | .... | 1 | .... | .... | .... | .... | .......... | .... | .... | 3 | 10 | 2 | 80.50 | 98.75 | 15 00–15 99 |
| 16 00–17 99 | 6 | 1 | 2 | .... | .... | 1 | .... | .... | .... | .... | .......... | .... | .... | .......... | 8 | 2 | 87.60 | 99.40 | 16 00–17 99 |
| 18 00–19 99 | 2 | .... | 1 | .... | .... | 1 | .... | .... | .... | .... | .......... | .... | .... | 1 | 4 | 1 | 91.20 | 99.70 | 18 00–19 99 |
| 20 00–24 99 | .... | .... | 4 | .... | .... | 1 | .... | .... | 1 | .... | .......... | .... | .... | 1 | 6 | 1 | 96.50 | 100.00 | 20 00–24 99 |
| 30 00–34 99 | .... | .... | .... | .... | .... | .... | .... | .... | .... | .... | .......... | .... | .... | 1 | 1 | .... | 97.50 | ..... | 30 00–34 99 |
| 35 00–39 99 | .... | .... | 1 | .... | .... | .... | .... | .... | .... | .... | .......... | .... | .... | .......... | 1 | .... | 98.25 | ..... | 35 00–39 99 |
| 40 00 and over | .... | .... | .... | .... | .... | .... | .... | .... | .... | .... | .......... | 1 | .... | 1 | 2 | .... | 100.00 | ..... | 40 00 and over |
| Not reported | .... | .... | 1 | .... | .... | .... | .... | .... | .... | 1 | .......... | .... | .... | .......... | 1 | 1 | ..... | ..... | Not reported |
| Total | 17 | 20 | 69 | 145 | 1 | 19 | 3 | 1 | 1 | 102 | 15 | 4 | 25 | 19 | 114 | 327 | ..... | ..... | Total |

308. TABLE XV, A, 1, c, d, e

ROCHESTER

DEPARTMENT STORES — SHIPPING AND DELIVERY, MANUFACTURING, PLANT

NUMBER OF EMPLOYEES EARNING SPECIFIED WEEKLY RATES, ACCORDING TO DEPARTMENT AND SEX

| WEEKLY RATES IN DOLLARS | DEPARTMENT | | | | | | | | | WEEKLY RATES IN DOLLARS |
|---|---|---|---|---|---|---|---|---|---|---|
| | PLANT | | SHIPPING AND DELIVERY | MANUFACTURING | | TOTAL | | CUMULATIVE PER CENT. OF TOTAL | | |
| | Male | Female | Male | Male | Female | Male | Female | Male | Female | |
| Less than $3 00 | ........ | ........ | ........ | ........ | 8 | ........ | 8 | ........ | 2.16 | Less than $3 00 |
| $3 00–$3 49 | ........ | 1 | ........ | ........ | 3 | ........ | 4 | ........ | 3.24 | $3 00– 3 49 |
| 4 00– 4 49 | ........ | 22 | 1 | ........ | 5 | 1 | 27 | .25 | 10.52 | 4 00– 4 49 |
| 4 50– 4 99 | ........ | 10 | ........ | ........ | ........ | ........ | 10 | ........ | 13.22 | 4 50– 4 99 |
| 5 00– 5 49 | 1 | 36 | 2 | ........ | 9 | 3 | 45 | 1.15 | 25.35 | 5 00– 5 49 |
| 5 50– 5 99 | ........ | 2 | ........ | ........ | 1 | ........ | 3 | ........ | 26.20 | 5 50– 5 99 |
| 6 00– 6 49 | 2 | 16 | 2 | ........ | 15 | 4 | 31 | 2.30 | 34.60 | 6 00– 6 49 |
| 6 50– 6 99 | ........ | ........ | ........ | ........ | 1 | ........ | 1 | ........ | 34.80 | 6 50– 6 99 |
| 7 00– 7 49 | 4 | 26 | 1 | 1 | 16 | 6 | 42 | 3.55 | 46.20 | 7 00– 7 49 |
| 7 50– 7 99 | ........ | 1 | ........ | ........ | 1 | ........ | 2 | ........ | 41.70 | 7 50– 7 99 |
| 8 00– 8 99 | 3 | 4 | 3 | 1 | 36 | 7 | 40 | 5.33 | 57.50 | 8 00– 8 99 |
| 9 00– 9 99 | 6 | 1 | 4 | ........ | 62 | 10 | 63 | 7.86 | 74.50 | 9 00– 9 99 |
| 10 00–10 99 | 21 | 2 | 14 | 2 | 23 | 37 | 25 | 17.28 | 81.00 | 10 00–10 99 |
| 11 00–11 99 | 8 | ........ | 6 | 1 | 9 | 15 | 9 | 21.50 | 83.60 | 11 00–11 99 |
| 12 00–12 99 | 54 | 2 | 56 | 5 | 27 | 115 | 29 | 50.25 | 91.50 | 12 00–12 99 |
| 13 00–13 99 | 7 | ........ | 37 | 2 | 5 | 46 | 5 | 61.50 | 92.75 | 13 00–13 99 |
| 14 00–14 99 | 17 | ........ | 6 | 2 | 4 | 25 | 4 | 68.25 | 94.00 | 14 00–14 99 |
| 15 00–15 99 | 10 | ........ | 24 | 10 | 8 | 44 | 8 | 79.50 | 96.00 | 15 00–15 99 |
| 16 00–17 99 | 13 | ........ | 7 | 15 | 1 | 35 | 1 | 88.40 | 96.25 | 16 00–17 99 |
| 18 00–19 99 | 8 | ........ | 4 | 6 | 2 | 18 | 2 | 93.00 | 96.90 | 18 00–19 99 |
| 20 00–24 99 | 15 | ........ | ........ | 8 | 3 | 23 | 3 | 98.75 | 97.70 | 20 00–24 99 |
| 25 00–29 99 | 1 | ........ | 1 | ........ | 4 | 2 | 4 | 99.25 | 98.75 | 25 00–29 99 |
| 30 00–34 99 | ........ | ........ | ........ | 1 | 1 | 1 | 1 | 99.50 | 99.00 | 30 00–34 99 |
| 35 00–39 99 | 1 | ........ | ........ | 1 | 3 | 2 | 3 | 100.00 | 99.75 | 35 00–39 99 |
| 40 00 and over | ........ | ........ | ........ | ........ | 1 | ........ | 1 | ........ | 100.00 | 40 00 and over |
| Not reported | 2 | ........ | 1 | ........ | ........ | 3 | ........ | ........ | ........ | Not reported |
| Total | 173 | 123 | 169 | 55 | 248 | 397 | 371 | ........ | ........ | Total |

309. TABLE XVI, A, 1, c, d, e

ROCHESTER

**DEPARTMENT STORES — SHIPPING AND DELIVERY, MANUFACTURING, PLANT**

Number of Employees Classified According to Actual Weekly Earnings, by Department and Sex

| Actual Weekly Earnings in Dollars | Department | | | | | | | | | Actual Weekly Earnings in Dollars |
|---|---|---|---|---|---|---|---|---|---|---|
| | Plant | | Shipping and Delivery | Manufacturing | | Total | | Cumulative per cent of total | | |
| | Male | Female | Male | Male | Female | Male | Female | Male | Female | |
| Less than $3 00 | | 1 | | | 8 | | 9 | | 2.43 | Less than $3 00 |
| $3 00–$3 49 | | | | | 6 | | 6 | | 4.04 | $3 00– 3 49 |
| 3 50– 3 99 | | 1 | | | | | 1 | | 4.31 | 3 50– 3 99 |
| 4 00– 4 49 | | 22 | 1 | | 6 | 1 | 28 | .25 | 11.88 | 4 00– 4 49 |
| 4 50– 4 99 | 1 | 10 | | | 6 | 1 | 16 | .51 | 16.20 | 4 50– 4 99 |
| 5 00– 5 49 | 1 | 37 | 2 | | 11 | 3 | 48 | 1.27 | 29.15 | 5 00– 5 49 |
| 5 50– 5 99 | | 4 | | | 5 | | 9 | | 31.35 | 5 50– 5 99 |
| 6 00– 6 49 | 2 | 14 | 2 | | 17 | 4 | 31 | 2.28 | 39.90 | 6 00– 6 49 |
| 6 50– 6 99 | | 2 | | | 6 | | 8 | | 42.00 | 6 50– 6 99 |
| 7 00– 7 49 | 4 | 24 | 1 | 1 | 15 | 6 | 39 | 3.80 | 52.60 | 7 00– 7 49 |
| 7 50– 7 99 | | 1 | | | 3 | | 4 | | 53.70 | 7 50– 7 99 |
| 8 00– 8 99 | 4 | 2 | 4 | 1 | 32 | 9 | 34 | 6.08 | 62.90 | 8 00– 8 99 |
| 9 00– 9 99 | 4 | 1 | 4 | | 51 | 8 | 52 | 8.11 | 76.80 | 9 00– 9 99 |
| 10 00–10 99 | 17 | 2 | 17 | 2 | 22 | 36 | 24 | 17.22 | 83.40 | 10 00–10 99 |
| 11 00–11 99 | 13 | | 9 | 2 | 9 | 24 | 9 | 23.30 | 86.75 | 11 00–11 99 |
| 12 00–12 99 | 52 | 2 | 50 | 5 | 19 | 107 | 21 | 50.50 | 91.50 | 12 00–12 99 |
| 13 00–13 99 | 7 | | 37 | 1 | 5 | 45 | 5 | 61.90 | 92.75 | 13 00–13 99 |
| 14 00–14 99 | 17 | | 6 | 3 | 5 | 26 | 5 | 68.50 | 94.00 | 14 00–14 99 |
| 15 00–15 99 | 10 | | 24 | 9 | 7 | 43 | 7 | 79.35 | 96.00 | 15 00–15 99 |
| 16 00–17 99 | 14 | | 6 | 15 | 1 | 35 | 1 | 88.20 | 96.25 | 16 00–17 99 |
| 18 00–19 99 | 10 | | 3 | 6 | 3 | 19 | 3 | 93.00 | 97.00 | 18 00–19 99 |
| 20 00–24 99 | 15 | | | 8 | 3 | 23 | 3 | 98.90 | 97.85 | 20 00–24 99 |
| 25 00–29 99 | 1 | | 1 | | 3 | 2 | 3 | 99.40 | 98.75 | 25 00–29 99 |
| 30 00–34 99 | | | | 1 | 1 | 1 | 1 | 99.60 | 99.00 | 30 00–34 99 |
| 35 00–39 99 | 1 | | | 1 | 3 | 2 | 3 | 100.00 | 99.75 | 35 00–39 99 |
| 40 00 and over | | | | | 1 | | 1 | | 100.00 | 40 00 and over |
| Not reported | | | 2 | | | 2 | | | | Not reported |
| Total | 173 | 123 | 169 | 55 | 248 | 397 | 371 | | | Total |

ROCHESTER

**DEPARTMENT STORES — SHIPPING AND DELIVERY, MANUFACTURING, PLANT**

**310. TABLE XVII, A, 1, c, d, e.** NUMBER OF EMPLOYEES CLASSIFIED BY AGE GROUPS ACCORDING TO DEPARTMENT AND SEX

| AGE GROUPS IN YEARS | DEPARTMENT | | | | | | | | | AGE GROUPS IN YEARS |
|---|---|---|---|---|---|---|---|---|---|---|
| | SHIPPERS AND DELIVERY | PLANT | | MANUFACTURING | | TOTAL | | PER CENT. OF TOTAL | | |
| | Male | Male | Female | Male | Female | Male | Female | Male | Female | |
| 14–15 | ........ | 1 | ........ | ........ | 3 | 1 | 3 | .25 | .80 | 14–15 |
| 16–17 | 6 | 5 | 3 | ........ | 12 | 11 | 15 | 2.77 | 4.03 | 16–17 |
| 18–20 | 16 | 10 | 9 | 3 | 32 | 29 | 41 | 7.31 | 11.15 | 18–20 |
| 21–24 | 33 | 14 | 22 | 5 | 28 | 52 | 50 | 13.10 | 13.47 | 21–24 |
| 25–29 | 32 | 32 | 21 | 9 | 43 | 73 | 64 | 18.40 | 17.24 | 25–29 |
| 30–34 | 14 | 28 | 20 | 11 | 25 | 53 | 45 | 13.35 | 12.11 | 30–34 |
| 35–39 | 17 | 15 | 12 | 7 | 31 | 39 | 43 | 9.83 | 11.60 | 35–39 |
| 40–44 | 13 | 16 | 9 | 4 | 15 | 33 | 24 | 8.31 | 6.46 | 40–44 |
| 45–54 | 21 | 27 | 16 | 9 | 35 | 57 | 51 | 14.35 | 13.74 | 45–54 |
| 55–64 | 16 | 19 | 10 | 3 | 10 | 38 | 20 | 9.57 | 5.37 | 55–64 |
| 65 and over | 1 | 4 | ........ | 2 | ........ | 7 | ........ | 1.76 | ........ | 65 and over |
| Not reported | ........ | 2 | 1 | 2 | 14 | 4 | 15 | 1.00 | 4.03 | Not reported |
| Total | 169 | 173 | 123 | 55 | 248 | 397 | 371 | 100.00 | 100.00 | Total |

ROCHESTER

**THE PAPER BOX INDUSTRY — FACTORY WORKERS**

311. TABLE V, c, a — NUMBER AND PER CENT. OF EMPLOYEES EARNING SPECIFIED WEEKLY RATES, BY AGE GROUPS AND SEX

| WEEKLY RATES IN DOLLARS | AGE GROUPS IN YEARS | | | | | | | | | | | | | | WEEKLY RATES IN DOLLARS |
|---|---|---|---|---|---|---|---|---|---|---|---|---|---|---|---|
| | 14–15 | | 16–17 | | 18–20 | | 21–24 | | 25–29 | | 30–34 | | 35–39 | | |
| | Male | Female | Male | Female | Male | Female | Male | Female | Male | Female | Male | Female | Male | Female | |
| $3 00–$3 49... | .... | 2 | .... | ...... | ...... | ...... | ...... | ...... | ...... | ...... | ...... | ...... | ...... | ...... | ...$3 00–$3 49 |
| 3 50– 3 99... | .... | 3 | .... | ...... | ...... | ...... | ...... | ...... | ...... | ...... | ...... | ...... | ...... | ...... | ...3 50– 3 99 |
| 4 00– 4 49... | .... | 3 | .... | 1 | ...... | ...... | ...... | ...... | ...... | ...... | ...... | ...... | ...... | ...... | ...4 00– 4 49 |
| 4 50– 4 99... | .... | 7 | 1 | 2 | ...... | ...... | ...... | ...... | ...... | ...... | ...... | ...... | ...... | ...... | ...4 50– 4 99 |
| 5 00– 5 49... | .... | 3 | .... | 12 | ...... | 3 | ...... | ...... | ...... | ...... | ...... | ...... | ...... | ...... | ...5 00– 5 49 |
| 5 50– 5 99... | .... | 1 | .... | 3 | ...... | 1 | ...... | 2 | ...... | 2 | ...... | 1 | ...... | ...... | ...5 50– 5 99 |
| 6 00– 6 49... | .... | ...... | .... | 11 | ...... | 10 | ...... | 9 | ...... | 1 | ...... | ...... | ...... | ...... | ...6 00– 6 49 |
| 6 50– 6 99... | .... | ...... | .... | 7 | ...... | 3 | ...... | 1 | ...... | ...... | ...... | ...... | ...... | ...... | ...6 50– 6 99 |
| 7 00– 7 49... | .... | ...... | .... | ...... | 1 | 6 | ...... | 3 | ...... | 5 | ...... | 1 | ...... | ...... | ...7 00– 7 49 |
| 7 50– 7 99... | .... | ...... | .... | 1 | ...... | 5 | 1 | 3 | ...... | 4 | ...... | 1 | ...... | ...... | ...7 50– 7 99 |
| 8 00– 8 99... | .... | ...... | 3 | 2 | 1 | 3 | 1 | 10 | 1 | 3 | ...... | 4 | ...... | 1 | ...8 00– 8 99 |
| 9 00– 9 99... | .... | ...... | .... | ...... | ...... | 3 | 1 | 6 | ...... | 3 | 1 | 3 | ...... | ...... | ...9 00– 9 99 |
| 10 00–10 99... | .... | ...... | .... | 1 | 2 | ...... | 2 | 3 | 1 | 3 | ...... | 4 | ...... | 1 | ...10 00–10 99 |
| 11 00–11 99... | .... | ...... | .... | ...... | 2 | ...... | 2 | 1 | ...... | ...... | ...... | ...... | ...... | ...... | ...11 00–11 99 |
| 12 00–12 99... | .... | ...... | .... | ...... | 2 | ...... | 4 | 1 | 2 | 1 | 1 | 1 | ...... | ...... | ...12 00–12 99 |
| 13 00–13 99... | .... | ...... | .... | ...... | ...... | ...... | 2 | ...... | 1 | ...... | ...... | ...... | ...... | 1 | ...13 00–13 99 |
| 14 00–14 99... | .... | ...... | .... | ...... | ...... | ...... | 1 | ...... | 1 | ...... | ...... | ...... | ...... | ...... | ...14 00–14 99 |
| 15 00–15 99... | .... | ...... | .... | ...... | ...... | ...... | 2 | ...... | 1 | ...... | 3 | ...... | 1 | ...... | ...15 00–15 99 |
| 16 00–17 99... | .... | ...... | .... | ...... | ...... | ...... | 3 | ...... | 3 | ...... | 2 | 1 | 1 | ...... | ...16 00–17 99 |
| 18 00–19 99... | .... | ...... | .... | ...... | ...... | ...... | ...... | ...... | 2 | ...... | 1 | 1 | 1 | ...... | ...18 00–19 99 |
| 20 00–24 99... | .... | ...... | .... | ...... | ...... | ...... | ...... | ...... | ...... | ...... | 4 | ...... | 1 | ...... | ...20 00–24 99 |
| 25 00–29 99... | .... | ...... | .... | ...... | ...... | ...... | ...... | ...... | 1 | ...... | ...... | ...... | ...... | 1 | ...25 00–29 99 |
| Not reported... | 1 | ...... | 2 | 11 | 4 | 11 | 2 | 12 | 8 | 7 | 1 | 5 | 6 | ...... | ...Not reported |
| Total..... | 1 | 19 | 6 | 51 | 12 | 45 | 21 | 51 | 21 | 29 | 13 | 22 | 10 | 4 | .....Total |

311. TABLE V, c, a — (*concluded*)

ROCHESTER

**THE PAPER BOX INDUSTRY — FACTORY WORKERS**

NUMBER AND PER CENT. OF EMPLOYEES EARNING SPECIFIED WEEKLY RATES, BY AGE GROUPS AND SEX

| WEEKLY RATES IN DOLLARS | AGE GROUPS IN YEARS (*concluded*) 40–44 | | 45–54 | | 55–64 | 65 AND OVER | NOT REPORTED | TOTAL | | CUMULATIVE PER CENT. OF TOTAL | | WEEKLY RATES IN DOLLARS |
|---|---|---|---|---|---|---|---|---|---|---|---|---|
| | Male | Female | Male | Female | Male | Male | Female | Male | Female | Male | Female | |
| $3 00–$3 49 | | | | | | | | | 2 | | 1.92 | $3 00–$3 49 |
| 3 50– 3 99 | | | | | | | | | 3 | | 2.73 | 3 50– 3 99 |
| 4 00– 4 49 | | | | | | | | | 4 | | 4.92 | 4 00– 4 49 |
| 4 50– 4 99 | | | | | | | | 1 | 9 | 1.37 | 9.84 | 4 50– 4 99 |
| 5 00– 5 49 | | | | | | | | | 18 | | 19.68 | 5 00– 5 49 |
| 5 50– 5 99 | | | | | | | | | 10 | | 25.40 | 5 50– 5 99 |
| 6 00– 6 49 | | | | 1 | | | | | 32 | | 42.60 | 6 00– 6 49 |
| 6 50– 6 99 | | | | | | | | | 11 | | 48.60 | 6 50– 6 99 |
| 7 00– 7 49 | | | | | | | | 1 | 15 | 2.74 | 56.80 | 7 00– 7 49 |
| 7 50– 7 99 | | 1 | | | | | | 1 | 15 | 4.10 | 65.00 | 7 50– 7 99 |
| 8 00– 8 99 | 1 | | | 1 | | | | 7 | 24 | 13.70 | 78.10 | 8 00– 8 99 |
| 9 00– 9 99 | | | | 1 | 1 | 1 | | 4 | 16 | 19.20 | 87.00 | 9 00– 9 99 |
| 10 00–10 99 | 2 | 3 | | | | | | 7 | 15 | 28.80 | 95.00 | 10 00–10 99 |
| 11 00–11 99 | | | | | | | | 4 | 1 | 34.25 | 95.50 | 11 00–11 99 |
| 12 00–12 99 | | 1 | | | 1 | | | 10 | 4 | 48.00 | 97.80 | 12 00–12 99 |
| 13 00–13 99 | | | | | | | | 3 | 1 | 52.00 | 98.30 | 13 00–13 99 |
| 14 00–14 99 | | | | | 1 | | | 3 | | 56.20 | | 14 00–14 99 |
| 15 00–15 99 | | | | | | | | 7 | | 65.80 | | 15 00–15 99 |
| 16 00–17 99 | 1 | | 1 | | 1 | | | 12 | 1 | 82.20 | 99.00 | 16 00–17 99 |
| 18 00–19 99 | | | 2 | | | | | 6 | 1 | 90.50 | 99.50 | 18 00–19 99 |
| 20 00–24 99 | 1 | | | | | | | 6 | | 98.50 | | 20 00–24 99 |
| 25 00–29 99 | | | | | | | | 1 | 1 | 100.00 | 100.00 | 25 00–29 99 |
| Not reported | 1 | | 2 | 1 | | 2 | 1 | 29 | 48 | | | Not reported |
| Total | 6 | 5 | 5 | 4 | 4 | 3 | 1 | 102 | 231 | | | Total |

ROCHESTER

THE PAPER BOX INDUSTRY — FACTORY WORKERS

312. TABLE VIII, C, a NUMBER AND PER CENT. OF EMPLOYEES EARNING SPECIFIED WEEKLY RATES, BY OCCUPATION AND SEX

| WEEKLY RATES IN DOLLARS | OCCUPATION: Foremen and forewomen | | Cutters | | Setters-up | | General machine work | | Turners-in | Strippers and top labelers | | Table work | | Closing and tying | | Floor work | | Total | | Cumulative per cent. of total | | WEEKLY RATES IN DOLLARS |
|---|---|---|---|---|---|---|---|---|---|---|---|---|---|---|---|---|---|---|---|---|---|---|
| | Male | Female | Male | Female | Male | Female | Male | Female | Female | Male | Female | Male | Female | Male | Female | Male | Female | Male | Female | Male | Female | |
| $3 00-$3 49... | .... | .... | ... | ... | .... | .... | .... | .... | ........ | .... | .... | .... | .... | .... | .... | ... | 2 | ... | 2 | ..... | 1.92 | ...$3 00-$3 49 |
| 3 50- 3 99... | .... | .... | ... | ... | .... | .... | .... | .... | ........ | .... | .... | .... | 1 | .... | .... | ... | 2 | ... | 3 | ..... | 2.73 | ... 3 50- 3 99 |
| 4 00- 4 49... | .... | .... | ... | ... | .... | .... | .... | .... | 3 | .... | .... | .... | 1 | .... | .... | ... | ... | ... | 4 | ..... | 4.92 | ... 4 00- 4 49 |
| 4 50- 4 99... | .... | .... | ... | ... | .... | .... | .... | .... | 6 | .... | .... | .... | .... | .... | 1 | 1 | 2 | 1 | 9 | 1.37 | 9.84 | ... 4 50- 4 99 |
| 5 00- 5 49... | .... | .... | ... | ... | .... | .... | .... | 1 | 7 | .... | .... | .... | 4 | .... | .... | ... | 6 | ... | 18 | ..... | 19.68 | ... 5 00- 5 49 |
| 5 50- 5 99... | .... | .... | ... | ... | .... | 1 | .... | 2 | 3 | .... | .... | .... | 3 | .... | 1 | ... | ... | ... | 10 | ..... | 25.40 | ... 5 50- 5 99 |
| 6 00- 6 49... | .... | .... | ... | ... | .... | 2 | .... | 2 | 1 | .... | 7 | .... | 16 | .... | 2 | ... | 2 | ... | 32 | ..... | 42.60 | ... 6 00- 6 49 |
| 6 50- 6 99... | .... | .... | ... | ... | .... | .... | .... | 3 | 1 | .... | 3 | .... | 1 | .... | 1 | ... | 2 | ... | 11 | ..... | 48.60 | ... 6 50- 6 99 |
| 7 00- 7 49... | .... | .... | ... | ... | .... | 3 | .... | 2 | 1 | .... | 1 | .... | 7 | .... | 1 | 1 | ... | 1 | 15 | 2.74 | 56.80 | ... 7 00- 7 49 |
| 7 50- 7 99... | .... | .... | ... | ... | .... | 1 | .... | 5 | ........ | .... | .... | .... | 4 | .... | 2 | 1 | 3 | 1 | 15 | 4.10 | 65.00 | ... 7 50- 7 99 |
| 8 00- 8 99... | .... | 1 | 1 | ... | .... | 4 | .... | 1 | ........ | .... | 5 | .... | 10 | 1 | .... | 5 | 3 | 7 | 24 | 13.70 | 78.10 | ... 8 00- 8 99 |
| 9 00- 9 99... | .... | 2 | 2 | 1 | .... | 3 | 1 | 1 | ........ | .... | 1 | 1 | 5 | .... | .... | ... | 3 | 4 | 16 | 19.20 | 87.00 | ... 9 00- 9 99 |
| 10 00-10 99... | .... | 2 | 2 | 1 | .... | 4 | 1 | .... | ........ | 1 | 1 | .... | 5 | .... | 1 | 3 | 1 | 7 | 15 | 28.80 | 95.00 | ...10 00-10 99 |
| 11 00-11 99... | .... | .... | 1 | ... | 1 | .... | .... | 1 | ........ | .... | .... | .... | .... | .... | .... | 2 | ... | 4 | 1 | 34.25 | 95.50 | ...11 00-11 99 |
| 12 00-12 99... | 2 | 3 | 3 | ... | 2 | .... | 2 | .... | ........ | .... | .... | 1 | 1 | .... | .... | ... | ... | 10 | 4 | 48.00 | 97.80 | ...12 00-12 99 |
| 13 00-13 99... | .... | .... | 2 | ... | 1 | .... | .... | .... | ........ | .... | .... | .... | 1 | .... | .... | ... | ... | 3 | 1 | 52.00 | 98.30 | ...13 00-13 99 |
| 14 00-14 99... | .... | .... | 3 | ... | .... | .... | .... | .... | ........ | .... | .... | .... | .... | .... | .... | ... | ... | 3 | ... | 56.20 | ..... | ...14 00-14 99 |
| 15 00-15 99... | 1 | .... | 6 | ... | .... | .... | .... | .... | ........ | .... | .... | .... | .... | .... | .... | ... | ... | 7 | ... | 65.80 | ..... | ...15 00-15 99 |
| 16 00-17 99... | 2 | .... | 10 | ... | .... | .... | .... | .... | ........ | .... | .... | .... | 1 | .... | .... | ... | ... | 12 | 1 | 82.20 | 99.00 | ...16 00-17 99 |
| 18 00-19 99... | 5 | 1 | 1 | ... | .... | .... | .... | .... | ........ | .... | .... | .... | .... | .... | .... | ... | ... | 6 | 1 | 90.50 | 99.50 | ...18 00-19 99 |
| 20 00-24 99... | 6 | .... | ... | ... | .... | .... | .... | .... | ........ | .... | .... | .... | .... | .... | .... | ... | ... | 6 | ... | 98.50 | ..... | ...20 00-24 99 |
| 25 00-29 99... | 1 | 1 | ... | ... | .... | .... | .... | .... | ........ | .... | .... | .... | .... | .... | .... | ... | ... | 1 | 1 | 100.00 | 100.00 | ...25 00-29 99 |
| Not reported.. | .... | .... | 15 | 9 | .... | 4 | 7 | 2 | ........ | 1 | 1 | .... | 27 | .... | .... | 6 | 5 | 29 | 48 | ..... | ..... | ..Not reported |
| Total..... | 17 | 10 | 46 | 11 | 4 | 22 | 11 | 20 | 22 | 2 | 19 | 2 | 87 | 1 | 9 | 19 | 31 | 102 | 231 | ..... | ..... | ......Total |

313. TABLE VI, c, a.

ROCHESTER

THE PAPER BOX INDUSTRY — FACTORY WORKERS

NUMBER AND PER CENT. OF EMPLOYEES CLASSIFIED ACCORDING TO ACTUAL WEEKLY EARNINGS, BY AGE GROUPS AND SEX

| Actual Weekly Earnings in Dollars | Age Groups in Years | | | | | | | | | | | | | | Actual Weekly Earnings in Dollars |
|---|---|---|---|---|---|---|---|---|---|---|---|---|---|---|---|
| | 14–15 | | 16–17 | | 18–20 | | 21–24 | | 25–29 | | 30–34 | | 35–39 | | |
| | Male | Female | Male | Female | Male | Female | Male | Female | Male | Female | Male | Female | Male | Female | |
| Less than $3 00 | .... | 1 | .... | 6 | ...... | 2 | 1 | 1 | ...... | ...... | ...... | 1 | ...... | 1 | Less than $3 00 |
| $3 00–$3 49... | .... | 6 | .... | 1 | ...... | 1 | ...... | 4 | ...... | ...... | ...... | ...... | ...... | ...... | ...$3 00– 3 49 |
| 3 50– 3 99... | .... | 3 | .... | 3 | ...... | 1 | ...... | 1 | ...... | 2 | ...... | ...... | ...... | ...... | ...3 50– 3 99 |
| 4 00– 4 49... | .... | 6 | .... | 6 | ...... | 3 | ...... | 3 | ...... | 1 | ...... | 1 | ...... | ...... | ...4 00– 4 49 |
| 4 50– 4 99... | .... | 6 | 1 | 4 | ...... | 8 | ...... | 5 | ...... | 1 | ...... | 1 | ...... | 1 | ...4 50– 4 99 |
| 5 00– 5 49... | .... | 4 | .... | 23 | ...... | 6 | ...... | 8 | 1 | 2 | ...... | 1 | ...... | ...... | ...5 00– 5 49 |
| 5 50– 5 99... | 1 | 1 | .... | 11 | ...... | 6 | ...... | 4 | ...... | 3 | ...... | ...... | ...... | 3 | ...5 50– 5 99 |
| 6 00– 6 49... | .... | ...... | 1 | 15 | ...... | 10 | ...... | 8 | ...... | 4 | ...... | 1 | ...... | ...... | ...6 00– 6 49 |
| 6 50– 6 99... | .... | ...... | 2 | 13 | 3 | 14 | ...... | 6 | ...... | 7 | ...... | ...... | ...... | 1 | ...6 50– 6 99 |
| 7 00– 7 49... | .... | 2 | .... | 4 | ...... | 10 | ...... | 12 | 1 | 11 | ...... | 4 | ...... | 1 | ...7 00– 7 49 |
| 7 50– 7 99... | .... | ...... | 1 | 4 | 1 | 9 | 1 | 6 | 1 | 4 | ...... | 2 | ...... | ...... | ...7 50– 7 99 |
| 8 00– 8 99... | .... | 1 | 3 | 8 | 3 | 20 | ...... | 19 | 1 | 5 | 1 | 11 | 1 | 2 | ...8 00– 8 99 |
| 9 00– 9 99... | .... | ...... | .... | 2 | 2 | 15 | 2 | 12 | 3 | 9 | 1 | 8 | 1 | 1 | ...9 00– 9 99 |
| 10 00–10 99... | .... | ...... | .... | 3 | 2 | 4 | 3 | 6 | 3 | 6 | ...... | 4 | ...... | 1 | ...10 00–10 99 |
| 11 00–11 99... | .... | ...... | .... | 2 | 1 | 7 | 3 | 15 | 1 | 4 | ...... | 2 | ...... | 1 | ...11 00–11 99 |
| 12 00–12 99... | .... | ...... | .... | ...... | 2 | 1 | 4 | 2 | 3 | 4 | 1 | 4 | 2 | ...... | ...12 00–12 99 |
| 13 00–13 99... | .... | ...... | .... | ...... | ...... | 1 | 3 | 1 | 1 | ...... | ...... | 1 | ...... | 1 | ...13 00–13 99 |
| 14 00–14 99... | .... | ...... | .... | ...... | ...... | ...... | ...... | ...... | 1 | ...... | 1 | ...... | 1 | ...... | ...14 00–14 99 |
| 15 00–15 99... | .... | ...... | .... | ...... | ...... | ...... | 2 | ...... | 2 | ...... | 3 | ...... | 1 | ...... | ...15 00–15 99 |
| 16 00–17 99... | .... | ...... | .... | ...... | ...... | ...... | 3 | 1 | 1 | ...... | 2 | 1 | 2 | ...... | ...16 00–17 99 |
| 18 00–19 99... | .... | ...... | .... | ...... | ...... | ...... | ...... | ...... | 2 | ...... | 1 | 1 | 1 | ...... | ...18 00–19 99 |
| 20 00–24 99... | .... | ...... | .... | ...... | ...... | ...... | ...... | ...... | ...... | ...... | 3 | ...... | 1 | ...... | ...20 00–24 99 |
| 25 00–29 99... | .... | ...... | .... | ...... | ...... | ...... | ...... | ...... | 1 | ...... | ...... | ...... | ...... | 1 | ...25 00–29 99 |
| Total..... | 1 | 30 | 8 | 105 | 14 | 118 | 22 | 114 | 22 | 63 | 13 | 43 | 10 | 14 | .....Total |

ROCHESTER

313. TABLE VI, c, a — (*concluded*)

**THE PAPER BOX INDUSTRY — FACTORY WORKERS**

Number and Per Cent. of Employees Classified According to Actual Weekly Earnings, by Age Groups and Sex

| Actual Weekly Earnings in Dollars | Age Groups in Years | | | | | | | | | | | | Actual Weekly Earnings in Dollars |
|---|---|---|---|---|---|---|---|---|---|---|---|---|---|
| | 40–44 | | 45–54 | | 55–64 | | 65 and over | Not reported | Total | | Cumulative per cent. of total | | |
| | Male | Female | Male | Female | Male | Female | Male | Female | Male | Female | Male | Female | |
| Less than $3 00 | | | | | | | | 1 | 1 | 13 | .90 | 2.50 | Less than $3 00 |
| $3 00–$3 49 | | | | | | | | | | 12 | | 4.90 | $3 00– 3 49 |
| 3 50– 3 99 | | | | | | | | | | 10 | | 6.90 | 3 50– 3 99 |
| 4 00– 4 49 | | | | | | | | | | 20 | | 10.80 | 4 00– 4 49 |
| 4 50– 4 99 | | | | | | | | 3 | 1 | 29 | 1.90 | 16.50 | 4 50– 4 99 |
| 5 00– 5 49 | | | | | | | | | 1 | 44 | 2.80 | 25.10 | 5 00– 5 49 |
| 5 50– 5 99 | | | | | | | | | 1 | 28 | 3.70 | 30.60 | 5 50– 5 99 |
| 6 00– 6 49 | | | | 1 | | 1 | | | 1 | 40 | 4.60 | 53.40 | 6 00– 6 49 |
| 6 50– 6 99 | | | | 1 | | | | | 5 | 42 | 9.30 | 46.70 | 6 50– 6 99 |
| 7 00– 7 49 | | | | 2 | | | | | 1 | 46 | 10.20 | 55.70 | 7 00– 7 49 |
| 7 50– 7 99 | | 1 | | 2 | | | 1 | | 5 | 28 | 14.80 | 61.10 | 7 50– 7 99 |
| 8 00– 8 99 | 1 | 1 | 1 | 2 | | | | | 11 | 69 | 25.00 | 74.60 | 8 00– 8 99 |
| 9 00– 9 99 | | 1 | | | 1 | | 2 | | 12 | 48 | 36.10 | 84.10 | 9 00– 9 99 |
| 10 00–10 99 | 3 | 4 | | | | | | 1 | 11 | 29 | 46.30 | 89.80 | 10 00–10 99 |
| 11 00–11 99 | | | | | | | | | 5 | 31 | 51.00 | 95.90 | 11 00–11 99 |
| 12 00–12 99 | | 1 | 1 | 1 | 1 | | | | 14 | 13 | 63.90 | 98.50 | 12 00–12 99 |
| 13 00–13 99 | | | | | | | | | 4 | 4 | 67.60 | 99.20 | 13 00–13 99 |
| 14 00–14 99 | | | | | 1 | | | | 4 | | 71.30 | | 14 00–14 99 |
| 15 00–15 99 | | | | | | | | | 8 | | 78.60 | | 15 00–15 99 |
| 16 00–17 99 | 1 | | 2 | | 1 | | | | 12 | 2 | 89.80 | 99.60 | 16 00–17 99 |
| 18 00–19 99 | | | 1 | | | | | | 5 | 1 | 94.50 | 99.80 | 18 00–19 99 |
| 20 00–24 99 | 1 | | | | | | | | 5 | | 99.00 | | 20 00–24 99 |
| 25 00–29 99 | | | | | | | | | 1 | 1 | 100.00 | 100.00 | 25 00–29 99 |
| Total | 6 | 8 | 5 | 9 | 4 | 1 | 3 | 5 | 108 | 510 | | | Total |

ROCHESTER

314. TABLE IX, C, a

THE PAPER BOX INDUSTRY — FACTORY WORKERS

NUMBER AND PER CENT. OF EMPLOYEES CLASSIFIED ACCORDING TO ACTUAL WEEKLY EARNINGS, BY OCCUPATION AND SEX

| ACTUAL WEEKLY EARNINGS IN DOLLARS | OCCUPATION: FOREMEN AND FOREWOMEN | | CUTTERS | | SETTERS-UP | | GENERAL MACHINE WORK | | TURNERS-IN | STRIPPERS AND TOP LABELERS | | TABLE WORK | | CLOSING AND TYING | | FLOOR WORK | | TOTAL | | CUMULATIVE PER CENT. OF TOTAL | | ACTUAL WEEKLY EARNINGS IN DOLLARS |
|---|---|---|---|---|---|---|---|---|---|---|---|---|---|---|---|---|---|---|---|---|---|---|
| | Male | Female | Male | Female | Male | Female | Male | Female | Female | Male | Female | Male | Female | Male | Female | Male | Female | Male | Female | Male | Female | |
| Less than $3 00 | | | | | | 1 | | 1 | 2 | | | | 6 | 1 | 1 | | 2 | 1 | 13 | .90 | 2.50 | Less than $3 00 |
| $3 00–$3 49 | | | | | | 1 | | 1 | 2 | | | | 5 | | | | 3 | | 12 | | 4.90 | $3 00– 3 49 |
| 3 50– 3 99 | | | | | | | | | 1 | | 2 | | 5 | | | | 2 | | 10 | | 6.90 | 3 50– 3 99 |
| 4 00– 4 49 | | | | | | 1 | | 1 | 5 | | 2 | | 9 | | | | 2 | | 20 | | 10.80 | 4 00– 4 49 |
| 4 50– 4 99 | | | | | | 2 | | | 7 | | 2 | | 11 | | 2 | 1 | 5 | 1 | 29 | 1.90 | 16.50 | 4 50– 4 99 |
| 5 00– 5 49 | | | | | 1 | 4 | | 3 | 9 | | 7 | | 18 | | | | 3 | 1 | 44 | 2.80 | 25.10 | 5 00– 5 49 |
| 5 50– 5 99 | | | | | | 1 | | 3 | 2 | | 6 | | 13 | | | 1 | 3 | 1 | 28 | 3.70 | 30.60 | 5 50– 5 99 |
| 6 00– 6 49 | | | 1 | 1 | | 6 | | 4 | | | 9 | | 17 | | 1 | | 2 | 1 | 40 | 4.60 | 53.40 | 6 00– 6 49 |
| 6 50– 6 99 | | | 1 | 3 | | 5 | 1 | 5 | 1 | | 9 | | 15 | | 1 | 3 | 3 | 5 | 42 | 9.30 | 46.70 | 6 50– 6 99 |
| 7 00– 7 49 | | 1 | 1 | 2 | | 4 | | 3 | 1 | | 8 | | 21 | | 1 | | 5 | 1 | 46 | 10.20 | 55.70 | 7 00– 7 49 |
| 7 50– 7 99 | | | 1 | 3 | | 5 | 2 | 3 | | | 2 | | 11 | | 2 | 2 | 2 | 5 | 28 | 14.80 | 61.10 | 7 50– 7 99 |
| 8 00– 8 99 | | 2 | 3 | | | 6 | | 3 | | 1 | 16 | 1 | 35 | | 1 | 6 | 6 | 11 | 69 | 25.00 | 74.60 | 8 00– 8 99 |
| 9 00– 9 99 | | 2 | 6 | 1 | | 4 | 2 | 6 | | 1 | 8 | 1 | 25 | | | 2 | 2 | 12 | 48 | 36.10 | 84.10 | 9 00– 9 99 |
| 10 00–10 99 | | 3 | 4 | 1 | | 4 | 2 | 1 | | | 3 | | 14 | | 2 | 5 | 1 | 11 | 29 | 46.30 | 89.80 | 10 00–10 99 |
| 11 00–11 99 | | 1 | 3 | | 1 | 2 | | 4 | | | 9 | 1 | 13 | | 1 | | 1 | 5 | 31 | 51.00 | 95.90 | 11 00–11 99 |
| 12 00–12 99 | 2 | 3 | 6 | | 2 | 1 | 3 | | 1 | | 1 | | 7 | | | 1 | | 14 | 13 | 63.90 | 98.50 | 12 00–12 99 |
| 13 00–13 99 | | | 3 | | 1 | 1 | | | | | 1 | | 2 | | | | | 4 | 4 | 67.60 | 99.20 | 13 00–13 99 |
| 14 00–14 99 | | | 3 | | | | 1 | | | | | | | | | | | 4 | | 71.30 | | 14 00–14 99 |
| 15 00–15 99 | 1 | | 7 | | | | | | | | | | | | | | | 8 | | 78.60 | | 15 00–15 99 |
| 16 00–17 99 | 3 | | 9 | | | | | | | | | | 2 | | | | | 12 | 2 | 89.80 | 99.60 | 16 00–17 99 |
| 18 00–19 99 | 5 | 1 | | | | | | | | | | | | | | | | 5 | 1 | 94.50 | 99.80 | 18 00–19 99 |
| 20 00–24 99 | 5 | | | | | | | | | | | | | | | | | 5 | | 99.00 | | 20 00–24 99 |
| 25 00–29 99 | 1 | 1 | | | | | | | | | | | | | | | | 1 | 1 | 100.00 | 100.00 | 25 00–29 99 |
| Total | 17 | 14 | 48 | 11 | 5 | 48 | 11 | 38 | 31 | 2 | 85 | 3 | 229 | 1 | 12 | 21 | 42 | 108 | 510 | | | Total |

ROCHESTER

315. TABLE V, D, a

**THE CONFECTIONERY INDUSTRY — FACTORY WORKERS**

Number and Per Cent. of Employees Earning Specified Weekly Rates, by Age Groups and Sex

| Weekly Rates in Dollars | Age Groups in Years | | | | | | | | | | | | | Weekly Rates in Dollars |
|---|---|---|---|---|---|---|---|---|---|---|---|---|---|---|
| | 14–15 | 16–17 | | 18–20 | | 21–24 | | 25–29 | | 30–34 | | 35–39 | | |
| | Female | Male | Female | Male | Female | Male | Female | Male | Female | Male | Female | Male | Female | |
| $5 00–$5 49 | ...... | ...... | 1 | ...... | ...... | ...... | ...... | ...... | ...... | ...... | ...... | ...... | ...... | $5 00–$5 49 |
| 5 50– 5 99 | ...... | ...... | 1 | ...... | ...... | ...... | ...... | ...... | ...... | ...... | ...... | ...... | ...... | 5 50– 5 99 |
| 6 00– 6 49 | ...... | ...... | 3 | ...... | 5 | ...... | 1 | ...... | 2 | ...... | ...... | ...... | ...... | 6 00– 6 49 |
| 6 50– 6 99 | ...... | ...... | 2 | ...... | 2 | ...... | 1 | ...... | ...... | ...... | ...... | ...... | ...... | 6 50– 6 99 |
| 7 00– 7 49 | ...... | ...... | ...... | 2 | 3 | 1 | 1 | ...... | ...... | ...... | 1 | ...... | ...... | 7 00– 7 49 |
| 7 50– 7 99 | ...... | 1 | ...... | 6 | ...... | 1 | ...... | 1 | 1 | ...... | 1 | 1 | ...... | 7 50– 7 99 |
| 8 00– 8 99 | ...... | 1 | 1 | 4 | 5 | 2 | 5 | 3 | 5 | 4 | ...... | ...... | 1 | 8 00– 8 99 |
| 9 00– 9 99 | ...... | ...... | ...... | 1 | 2 | 4 | 8 | 1 | 1 | ...... | 2 | ...... | 5 | 9 00– 9 99 |
| 10 00–10 99 | ...... | ...... | ...... | 2 | ...... | 2 | 3 | 1 | 5 | ...... | 4 | ...... | 3 | 10 00–10 99 |
| 11 00–11 99 | ...... | ...... | ...... | ...... | ...... | 2 | ...... | 1 | ...... | 2 | 1 | 1 | 1 | 11 00–11 99 |
| 12 00–12 99 | ...... | ...... | ...... | ...... | ...... | 2 | ...... | 3 | ...... | ...... | ...... | ...... | ...... | 12 00–12 99 |
| 13 00–13 99 | ...... | ...... | ...... | ...... | ...... | ...... | ...... | 2 | ...... | 4 | ...... | 2 | ...... | 13 00–13 99 |
| 14 00–14 99 | ...... | ...... | ...... | ...... | ...... | ...... | 1 | 1 | ...... | 1 | ...... | ...... | ...... | 14 00–14 99 |
| 15 00–15 99 | ...... | ...... | ...... | ...... | ...... | ...... | ...... | ...... | ...... | 2 | ...... | 3 | ...... | 15 00–15 99 |
| 16 00–17 99 | ...... | ...... | ...... | ...... | ...... | 1 | ...... | 1 | ...... | 1 | ...... | 1 | ...... | 16 00–17 99 |
| 18 00–19 99 | ...... | ...... | ...... | ...... | ...... | ...... | ...... | 1 | ...... | 1 | ...... | 1 | ...... | 18 00–19 99 |
| 20 00–24 99 | ...... | ...... | ...... | ...... | ...... | ...... | ...... | 1 | ...... | 1 | ...... | 2 | ...... | 20 00–24 99 |
| 25 00–29 99 | ...... | ...... | ...... | ...... | ...... | ...... | ...... | ...... | ...... | ...... | ...... | ...... | ...... | 25 00–29 99 |
| Not reported | 1 | ...... | 1 | ...... | 5 | 1 | 1 | ...... | ...... | ...... | ...... | ...... | ...... | Not reported |
| Total | 1 | 2 | 9 | 15 | 22 | 16 | 21 | 16 | 14 | 16 | 9 | 11 | 10 | Total |

ROCHESTER

815. TABLE V, D, a — (*concluded*) THE CONFECTIONERY INDUSTRY — FACTORY WORKERS

NUMBER AND PER CENT. OF EMPLOYEES EARNING SPECIFIED WEEKLY RATES, BY AGE GROUPS AND SEX

| WEEKLY RATES IN DOLLARS | AGE GROUPS IN YEARS (*concluded*) 40–44 | | 45–54 | | 55–64 | | NOT REPORTED | TOTAL | | CUMULATIVE PER CENT. OF TOTAL | | WEEKLY RATES IN DOLLARS |
|---|---|---|---|---|---|---|---|---|---|---|---|---|
| | Male | Female | Male | Female | Male | Female | Female | Male | Female | Male | Female | |
| $5 00–$5 49... | ........ | ........ | ........ | ........ | ........ | ........ | ........ | ........ | 1 | ........ | 1.10 | ...$5 00–$5 49 |
| 5 50– 5 99... | ........ | ........ | ........ | ........ | ........ | ........ | ........ | ........ | 1 | ........ | 2.20 | ... 5 50– 5 99 |
| 6 00– 6 49... | ........ | ........ | ........ | ........ | ........ | ........ | ........ | ........ | 11 | ........ | 14.60 | ... 6 00– 6 49 |
| 6 50– 6 99... | ........ | ........ | ........ | ........ | ........ | ........ | ........ | ........ | 5 | ........ | 19.80 | ... 6 50– 6 99 |
| 7 00– 7 49... | ........ | ........ | ........ | 1 | ........ | ........ | ........ | 3 | 6 | 3.10 | 25.70 | ... 7 00– 7 49 |
| 7 50– 7 99... | 1 | 1 | ........ | ........ | ........ | ........ | ........ | 11 | 3 | 14.45 | 29.70 | ... 7 50– 7 99 |
| 8 00– 8 99... | ........ | 1 | 1 | ........ | 1 | 1 | ........ | 16 | 19 | 31.00 | 50.50 | ... 8 00– 8 99 |
| 9 00– 9 99... | 2 | 1 | 1 | 4 | 1 | ........ | 1 | 10 | 24 | 41.25 | 81.40 | ... 9 00– 9 99 |
| 10 00–10 99... | ........ | 2 | ........ | ........ | 1 | ........ | ........ | 6 | 17 | 47.50 | 95.50 | ...10 00–10 99 |
| 11 00–11 99... | ........ | ........ | 1 | ........ | ........ | ........ | ........ | 7 | 2 | 54.60 | 97.75 | ...11 00–11 99 |
| 12 00–12 99... | 1 | ........ | 2 | 1 | 1 | ........ | ........ | 9 | 1 | 64.00 | 99.00 | ...12 00–12 99 |
| 13 00–13 99... | ........ | ........ | ........ | ........ | ........ | ........ | ........ | 8 | ........ | 72.25 | ........ | ...13 00–13 99 |
| 14 00–14 99... | 1 | ........ | 1 | ........ | ........ | ........ | ........ | 4 | 1 | 76.40 | 100.00 | ...14 00–14 99 |
| 15 00–15 99... | 2 | ........ | ........ | ........ | ........ | ........ | ........ | 7 | ........ | 83.50 | ........ | ...15 00–15 99 |
| 16 00–17 99... | 1 | ........ | 1 | ........ | ........ | ........ | ........ | 6 | ........ | 89.60 | ........ | ...16 00–17 99 |
| 18 00–19 99... | ........ | ........ | ........ | ........ | ........ | ........ | ........ | 3 | ........ | 93.00 | ........ | ...18 00–19 99 |
| 20 00–24 99... | 1 | ........ | 1 | ........ | ........ | ........ | ........ | 6 | ........ | 99.00 | ........ | ...20 00–24 99 |
| 25 00–29 99... | ........ | ........ | 1 | ........ | ........ | ........ | ........ | 1 | ........ | 100.00 | ........ | ...25 00–29 99 |
| Not reported.. | ........ | ........ | ........ | ........ | ........ | ........ | ........ | 1 | 8 | ........ | ........ | ..Not reported |
| Total..... | 9 | 5 | 9 | 6 | 4 | 1 | 1 | 98 | 99 | ........ | ........ | .....Total |

ROCHESTER

THE CONFECTIONERY INDUSTRY — FACTORY WORKERS

316. TABLE VIII, D, a — NUMBER AND PER CENT. OF EMPLOYEES EARNING SPECIFIED WEEKLY RATES, BY OCCUPATION AND SEX

| Weekly Rates in Dollars | Foremen and Forewomen | | Candy Makers | Dippers | Packers | | Wrappers | | Machine Operators | | Helpers | | General Laborers | Total | | Cumulative Per Cent. of Total | | Weekly Rates in Dollars |
|---|---|---|---|---|---|---|---|---|---|---|---|---|---|---|---|---|---|---|
| | Male | Female | Male | Female | Male | Female | Male | Female | Male | Female | Male | Female | Male | Male | Female | Male | Female | |
| $5 00-$5 49 | | | | | | | | | | | | 1 | | | 1 | | 1.10 | $5 00-$5 49 |
| 5 50- 5 99 | | | | | | 1 | | | | | | | | | 1 | | 2.20 | 5 50- 5 99 |
| 6 00- 6 49 | | | | | | 8 | | | | | | 3 | | | 11 | | 14.60 | 6 00- 6 49 |
| 6 50- 6 99 | | | | 2 | | 3 | | | | | | | | | 5 | | 19.80 | 6 50- 6 99 |
| 7 00- 7 49 | | 1 | | | | 4 | | | | | 3 | 1 | | 3 | 6 | 3.10 | 25.70 | 7 00- 7 49 |
| 7 50- 7 99 | | | | | | 3 | | | | | 11 | | | 11 | 3 | 14.45 | 29.70 | 7 50- 7 99 |
| 8 00- 8 99 | | | | 1 | 1 | 7 | 2 | | | | 13 | 11 | | 16 | 19 | 31.00 | 50.50 | 8 00- 8 99 |
| 9 00- 9 99 | | 5 | | | | 8 | | 1 | | | 10 | 10 | | 10 | 24 | 41.25 | 81.40 | 9 00- 9 99 |
| 10 00-10 99 | | 6 | | | | 2 | | | | 9 | 6 | | | 6 | 17 | 47.50 | 95.50 | 10 00-10 99 |
| 11 00-11 99 | | 2 | 1 | | | | | | | | 6 | | | 7 | 2 | 54.60 | 97.75 | 11 00-11 99 |
| 12 00-12 99 | 1 | 1 | | | | | | | | | 7 | | 1 | 9 | 1 | 64.00 | 99.00 | 12 00-12 99 |
| 13 00-13 99 | 2 | | 3 | | | | | | 1 | | 2 | | | 8 | | 72.25 | | 13 00-13 99 |
| 14 00-14 99 | 3 | 1 | | | | | | | | | 1 | | | 4 | 1 | 76.40 | 100.00 | 14 00-14 99 |
| 15 00-15 99 | 3 | | 4 | | | | | | | | | | | 7 | | 83.50 | | 15 00-15 99 |
| 16 00-17 99 | 2 | | 3 | | | | | | | | 1 | | | 6 | | 89.60 | | 16 00-17 99 |
| 18 00-19 99 | | | 2 | | | | | | | | 1 | | | 3 | | 93.00 | | 18 00-19 99 |
| 20 00-24 99 | 5 | | 1 | | | | | | | | | | | 6 | | 99.00 | | 20 00-24 99 |
| 25 00-29 99 | 1 | | | | | | | | | | | | | 1 | | 100.00 | | 25 00-29 99 |
| Not reported | | | | 1 | | 3 | | | | | 1 | 4 | | 1 | 8 | | | Not reported |
| Total | 17 | 16 | 14 | 4 | 1 | 39 | 2 | 1 | 1 | 9 | 62 | 30 | 1 | 98 | 99 | | | Total |

ROCHESTER

317. TABLE VI, D, a

**THE CONFECTIONERY INDUSTRY — FACTORY WORKERS**

NUMBER AND PER CENT. OF EMPLOYEES CLASSIFIED ACCORDING TO ACTUAL WEEKLY EARNINGS, BY AGE GROUPS AND SEX

| Actual Weekly Earnings in Dollars | Age Groups in Years | | | | | | | | | | | | | Actual Weekly Earnings in Dollars |
|---|---|---|---|---|---|---|---|---|---|---|---|---|---|---|
| | 14–15 | 16–17 | | 18–20 | | 21–24 | | 25–29 | | 30–34 | | 35–39 | | |
| | Female | Male | Female | Male | Female | Male | Female | Male | Female | Male | Female | Male | Female | |
| Less than $3 00 | ...... | ...... | 3 | 2 | 1 | 1 | ...... | 1 | ...... | ...... | ...... | ...... | ...... | Less than $3 00 |
| $3 00–$3 49 | ...... | ...... | 2 | ...... | 1 | ...... | 1 | ...... | ...... | ...... | ...... | ...... | ...... | $3 00–$3 49 |
| 3 50– 3 99 | ...... | ...... | 1 | 1 | 1 | 1 | 1 | ...... | ...... | ...... | ...... | ...... | ...... | 3 50– 3 99 |
| 4 00– 4 49 | 1 | ...... | 1 | ...... | 5 | ...... | ...... | ...... | 1 | 1 | ...... | ...... | ...... | 4 00– 4 49 |
| 4 50– 4 99 | ...... | ...... | 2 | ...... | 9 | ...... | 1 | ...... | 1 | ...... | ...... | ...... | 1 | 4 50– 4 99 |
| 5 00– 5 49 | ...... | ...... | 2 | ...... | 4 | 1 | 2 | ...... | ...... | 1 | ...... | ...... | ...... | 5 00– 5 49 |
| 5 50– 5 99 | ...... | ...... | 2 | ...... | 4 | 1 | 5 | 1 | 1 | ...... | 1 | 1 | ...... | 5 50– 5 99 |
| 6 00– 6 49 | ...... | ...... | 1 | 4 | 3 | ...... | ...... | 1 | 1 | 1 | ...... | ...... | ...... | 6 00– 6 49 |
| 6 50– 6 99 | ...... | 1 | ...... | 3 | 4 | 1 | 3 | ...... | 2 | ...... | 1 | 1 | 2 | 6 50– 6 99 |
| 7 00– 7 49 | ...... | 1 | ...... | 1 | 6 | 1 | 3 | 1 | ...... | ...... | 1 | ...... | 1 | 7 00– 7 49 |
| 7 50– 7 99 | ...... | ...... | 2 | 2 | 3 | ...... | 5 | 2 | 1 | ...... | ...... | ...... | ...... | 7 50– 7 99 |
| 8 00– 8 99 | 1 | ...... | ...... | 2 | 5 | 6 | 5 | ...... | 6 | 1 | 2 | ...... | 4 | 8 00– 8 99 |
| 9 00– 9 99 | ...... | ...... | ...... | 1 | 2 | 2 | 6 | 3 | 3 | 1 | 4 | ...... | 3 | 9 00– 9 99 |
| 10 00–10 99 | ...... | ...... | ...... | ...... | ...... | ...... | 2 | 1 | 6 | 3 | 3 | 1 | 3 | 10 00–10 99 |
| 11 00–11 99 | ...... | ...... | ...... | ...... | ...... | 1 | 1 | 2 | 2 | 2 | ...... | 2 | 1 | 11 00–11 99 |
| 12 00–12 99 | ...... | ...... | ...... | ...... | ...... | ...... | ...... | ...... | ...... | 1 | ...... | ...... | 1 | 12 00–12 99 |
| 13 00–13 99 | ...... | ...... | ...... | ...... | ...... | ...... | ...... | ...... | ...... | 1 | ...... | 3 | ...... | 13 00–13 99 |
| 14 00–14 99 | ...... | ...... | ...... | ...... | ...... | ...... | 1 | 1 | ...... | 1 | ...... | ...... | ...... | 14 00–14 99 |
| 15 00–15 99 | ...... | ...... | ...... | ...... | ...... | ...... | ...... | 2 | ...... | 1 | ...... | ...... | ...... | 15 00–15 99 |
| 16 00–17 99 | ...... | ...... | ...... | ...... | ...... | 1 | ...... | ...... | ...... | ...... | ...... | 1 | ...... | 16 00–17 99 |
| 18 00–19 99 | ...... | ...... | ...... | ...... | ...... | ...... | ...... | 1 | ...... | ...... | ...... | 1 | ...... | 18 00–19 99 |
| 20 00–24 9 | ...... | ...... | ...... | ...... | ...... | ...... | ...... | ...... | ...... | 2 | ...... | 1 | ...... | 20 00–24 99 |
| 25 00–29 99 | ...... | ...... | ...... | ...... | ...... | ...... | ...... | ...... | ...... | ...... | ...... | ...... | ...... | 25 00–29 99 |
| Total | 2 | 2 | 16 | 16 | 48 | 16 | 36 | 16 | 24 | 16 | 12 | 11 | 16 | Total |

ROCHESTER

317. TABLE VI, D, a — (*concluded*) **THE CONFECTIONERY INDUSTRY — FACTORY WORKERS**

Number and Per Cent. of Employees Classified According to Actual Weekly Earnings, by Age Groups and Sex

| Actual Weekly Earnings in Dollars | Age Groups in Years (*concluded*) 40–44 | | 45–54 | | 55–64 | | Not Reported | Total | | Cumulative Per Cent. of Total | | Actual Weekly Earnings in Dollars |
|---|---|---|---|---|---|---|---|---|---|---|---|---|
| | Male | Female | Male | Female | Male | Female | Female | Male | Female | Male | Female | |
| Less than $3 00 | ........ | ........ | ........ | ........ | ........ | ........ | ........ | 4 | 4 | 4.30 | 2.36 | Less than $3 00 |
| $3 00–$3 49... | ........ | ........ | ........ | ........ | ........ | ........ | ........ | ........ | 4 | ........ | 4.70 | ...$3 00– 3 49 |
| 3 50– 3 99... | ........ | ........ | ........ | ........ | ........ | ........ | ........ | 2 | 3 | 6.50 | 6.47 | ... 3 50– 3 99 |
| 4 00– 4 49... | ........ | ........ | ........ | ........ | ........ | ........ | ........ | 1 | 8 | 7.70 | 11.20 | ... 4 00– 4 49 |
| 4 50– 4 99... | ........ | ........ | ........ | ........ | 1 | ........ | ........ | 1 | 14 | 8.80 | 19.40 | ... 4 50– 4 99 |
| 5 00– 5 49... | ........ | ........ | ........ | ........ | ........ | ........ | ........ | 2 | 8 | 10.10 | 24.10 | ... 5 00– 5 49 |
| 5 50– 5 99... | ........ | ........ | ........ | ........ | ........ | ........ | ........ | 3 | 13 | 13.12 | 31.80 | ... 5 50– 5 99 |
| 6 00– 6 49... | ........ | 1 | ........ | 1 | ........ | ........ | ........ | 6 | 7 | 19.20 | 35.90 | ... 6 00– 6 49 |
| 6 50– 6 99... | 1 | ........ | ........ | 1 | ........ | ........ | ........ | 7 | 13 | 26.25 | 43.50 | ... 6 50– 6 99 |
| 7 00– 7 49... | ........ | ........ | 1 | 1 | ........ | 1 | ........ | 5 | 13 | 31.18 | 51.20 | ... 7 00– 7 49 |
| 7 50– 7 99... | ........ | ........ | ........ | ........ | 1 | ........ | ........ | 5 | 11 | 36.40 | 57.60 | ... 7 50– 7 99 |
| 8 00– 8 99... | 2 | 1 | 3 | ........ | 1 | 1 | ........ | 15 | 25 | 51.50 | 72.40 | ... 8 00– 8 99 |
| 9 00– 9 99... | ........ | 1 | 1 | 4 | ........ | ........ | 1 | 8 | 24 | 59.60 | 86.50 | ... 9 00– 9 99 |
| 10 00–10 99... | ........ | 2 | ........ | ........ | ........ | ........ | ........ | 5 | 16 | 64.65 | 96.00 | ...10 00–10 99 |
| 11 00–11 99... | 2 | ........ | 1 | ........ | ........ | ........ | ........ | 10 | 4 | 74.75 | 98.30 | ...11 00–11 99 |
| 12 00–12 99... | ........ | ........ | ........ | 1 | 1 | ........ | ........ | 2 | 2 | 76.80 | 99.50 | ...12 00–12 99 |
| 13 00–13 99... | 2 | ........ | ........ | ........ | ........ | ........ | ........ | 6 | ........ | 82.90 | ........ | ...13 00–13 99 |
| 14 00–14 99... | ........ | ........ | 1 | ........ | ........ | ........ | ........ | 3 | 1 | 85.95 | 100.00 | ...14 00–14 99 |
| 15 00–15 99... | 1 | ........ | 1 | ........ | ........ | ........ | ........ | 5 | ........ | 90.95 | ........ | ...15 00–15 99 |
| 16 00–17 99... | ........ | ........ | ........ | ........ | ........ | ........ | ........ | 2 | ........ | 92.80 | ........ | ...16 00–17 99 |
| 18 00–19 99... | ........ | ........ | ........ | ........ | ........ | ........ | ........ | 2 | ........ | 95.00 | ........ | ...18 00–19 99 |
| 20 00–24 99... | 1 | ........ | ........ | ........ | ........ | ........ | ........ | 4 | ........ | 99.00 | ........ | ...20 00–24 99 |
| 25 00–29 99... | ........ | ........ | 1 | ........ | ........ | ........ | ........ | 1 | ........ | 100.00 | ........ | ...25 00–29 99 |
| Total..... | 9 | 5 | 9 | 8 | 4 | 2 | 1 | 99 | 170 | ........ | ........ | .....Total |

ROCHESTER

318. TABLE IX, D, a — THE CONFECTIONERY INDUSTRY — FACTORY WORKERS

NUMBER AND PER CENT. OF EMPLOYEES CLASSIFIED ACCORDING TO ACTUAL WEEKLY EARNINGS, BY OCCUPATION AND SEX

| ACTUAL WEEKLY EARNINGS IN DOLLARS | OCCUPATION | | | | | | | | | | | | | | | | | ACTUAL WEEKLY EARNINGS IN DOLLARS |
|---|---|---|---|---|---|---|---|---|---|---|---|---|---|---|---|---|---|---|
| | FOREMEN AND FOREWOMEN | | CANDY MAKERS | DIPPERS | PACKERS | | WRAPPERS | | MACHINE OPERATORS | | HELPERS | | GENERAL LABORERS | TOTAL | | CUMULATIVE PER CENT. OF TOTAL | | |
| | Male | Female | Male | Female | Male | Female | Male | Female | Male | Female | Male | Female | Male | Male | Female | Male | Female | |
| Less than $3 00 | ..... | ..... | ..... | ..... | ..... | 3 | ..... | ..... | ..... | ..... | 4 | 1 | ..... | 4 | 4 | 4.30 | 2.36 | Less than $3 00 |
| $3 00-$3 49 | ..... | ..... | ..... | ..... | ..... | 3 | ..... | ..... | ..... | ..... | ..... | 1 | ..... | ..... | 4 | ..... | 4.70 | $3 00- 3 49 |
| 3 50- 3 99 | ..... | ..... | ..... | 1 | ..... | 1 | ..... | ..... | ..... | 1 | 2 | ..... | ..... | 2 | 3 | 6.50 | 6.47 | 3 50- 3 99 |
| 4 00- 4 49 | ..... | ..... | ..... | 1 | ..... | 6 | ..... | ..... | ..... | ..... | 1 | 1 | ..... | 1 | 8 | 7.70 | 11.20 | 4 00- 4 49 |
| 4 50- 4 99 | ..... | ..... | ..... | 2 | ..... | 8 | ..... | ..... | ..... | ..... | 1 | 4 | ..... | 1 | 14 | 8.80 | 19.40 | 4 50- 4 99 |
| 5 00- 5 49 | ..... | 1 | ..... | 1 | ..... | 4 | ..... | ..... | ..... | ..... | 2 | 2 | ..... | 2 | 8 | 10.10 | 24.10 | 5 00- 5 49 |
| 5 50- 5 99 | ..... | ..... | ..... | 5 | ..... | 6 | ..... | ..... | ..... | ..... | 3 | 2 | ..... | 3 | 13 | 13.12 | 31.80 | 5 50- 5 99 |
| 6 00- 6 49 | ..... | ..... | ..... | 2 | ..... | 5 | 1 | ..... | ..... | ..... | 5 | ..... | ..... | 6 | 7 | 19.20 | 35.90 | 6 00- 6 49 |
| 6 50- 6 99 | ..... | ..... | ..... | 5 | ..... | 6 | ..... | 1 | ..... | ..... | 7 | 1 | ..... | 7 | 13 | 26.25 | 43.50 | 6 50- 6 99 |
| 7 00- 7 49 | ..... | 1 | ..... | ..... | 1 | 8 | 1 | 1 | ..... | ..... | 3 | 3 | ..... | 5 | 13 | 31.18 | 51.20 | 7 00- 7 49 |
| 7 50- 7 99 | ..... | 2 | ..... | 2 | ..... | 6 | ..... | 1 | ..... | ..... | 5 | ..... | ..... | 5 | 11 | 36.40 | 57.60 | 7 50- 7 99 |
| 8 00- 8 99 | ..... | 2 | ..... | 5 | ..... | 8 | ..... | 1 | ..... | 1 | 15 | 8 | ..... | 15 | 25 | 51.50 | 72.40 | 8 00- 8 99 |
| 9 00- 9 99 | ..... | 4 | 1 | 1 | ..... | 9 | ..... | ..... | ..... | 1 | 7 | 9 | ..... | 8 | 24 | 59.60 | 86.50 | 9 00- 9 99 |
| 10 00-10 99 | 1 | 4 | 2 | 2 | ..... | 4 | ..... | ..... | ..... | 6 | 2 | ..... | ..... | 5 | 16 | 64.65 | 96.00 | 10 00-10 99 |
| 11 00-11 99 | 3 | ..... | 2 | 1 | ..... | 2 | ..... | 1 | 1 | ..... | 4 | ..... | ..... | 10 | 4 | 74.75 | 98.30 | 11 00-11 99 |
| 12 00-12 99 | 1 | 1 | ..... | ..... | ..... | 1 | ..... | ..... | ..... | ..... | ..... | ..... | 1 | 2 | 2 | 76.80 | 99.50 | 12 00-12 99 |
| 13 00-13 99 | 3 | ..... | 3 | ..... | ..... | ..... | ..... | ..... | ..... | ..... | ..... | ..... | ..... | 6 | ..... | 82.90 | ..... | 13 00-13 99 |
| 14 00-14 99 | 2 | 1 | ..... | ..... | ..... | ..... | ..... | ..... | ..... | ..... | 1 | ..... | ..... | 3 | 1 | 85.95 | 100.00 | 14 00-14 99 |
| 15 00-15 99 | 3 | ..... | 2 | ..... | ..... | ..... | ..... | ..... | ..... | ..... | ..... | ..... | ..... | 5 | ..... | 90.50 | ..... | 15 00-15 99 |
| 16 00-17 99 | ..... | ..... | 2 | ..... | ..... | ..... | ..... | ..... | ..... | ..... | ..... | ..... | ..... | 2 | ..... | 92.98 | ..... | 16 00-17 99 |
| 18 00-19 99 | ..... | ..... | 1 | ..... | ..... | ..... | ..... | ..... | ..... | ..... | 1 | ..... | ..... | 2 | ..... | 95.00 | ..... | 18 00-19 99 |
| 20 00-24 99 | 3 | ..... | 1 | ..... | ..... | ..... | ..... | ..... | ..... | ..... | ..... | ..... | ..... | 4 | ..... | 99.00 | ..... | 20 00-24 99 |
| 25 00-29 99 | 1 | ..... | ..... | ..... | ..... | ..... | ..... | ..... | ..... | ..... | ..... | ..... | ..... | 1 | ..... | 100.00 | ..... | 25 00-29 99 |
| Total | 17 | 16 | 14 | 28 | 1 | 80 | 2 | 5 | 1 | 9 | 63 | 32 | 1 | 99 | 170 | ..... | ..... | Total |

319. TABLE V, A, 1, a

SYRACUSE

DEPARTMENT STORES — STOCK AND SALES

NUMBER AND PER CENT. OF EMPLOYEES EARNING SPECIFIED WEEKLY RATES, BY AGE GROUPS AND SEX

| WEEKLY RATES IN DOLLARS | AGE GROUPS IN YEARS | | | | | | | | | | | | | | WEEKLY RATES IN DOLLARS |
|---|---|---|---|---|---|---|---|---|---|---|---|---|---|---|---|
| | 14–15 | | 16–17 | | 18–20 | | 21–24 | | 25–29 | | 30–34 | | 35–39 | | |
| | Male | Female | Male | Female | Male | Female | Male | Female | Male | Female | Male | Female | Male | Female | |
| Less than $3 00 | 1 | 27 | .... | 1 | .... | .... | .... | .... | .... | .... | .... | .... | .... | .... | Less than $3 00 |
| $3 00–$3 49... | 7 | 21 | 1 | 23 | .... | 3 | .... | .... | .... | .... | .... | .... | .... | .... | ...$3 00– 3 49 |
| 3 50– 3 99... | 6 | .... | 2 | 17 | .... | 3 | .... | .... | .... | .... | .... | .... | .... | .... | ... 3 50– 3 99 |
| 4 00– 4 49... | 4 | 1 | 1 | 26 | .... | 16 | .... | .... | .... | .... | .... | .... | .... | .... | ... 4 00– 4 49 |
| 4 50– 4 99... | 1 | .... | 1 | 2 | .... | 10 | .... | .... | .... | .... | .... | .... | .... | .... | ... 4 50– 4 99 |
| 5 00– 5 49... | 2 | .... | 4 | 10 | 2 | 29 | .... | 10 | .... | 3 | .... | 2 | .... | .... | ... 5 00– 5 49 |
| 5 50– 5 99... | .... | .... | .... | .... | .... | 2 | .... | 1 | .... | 1 | .... | .... | .... | .... | ... 5 50– 5 99 |
| 6 00– 6 49... | .... | .... | 3 | 5 | .... | 30 | .... | 21 | .... | 8 | .... | 2 | .... | 1 | ... 6 00– 6 49 |
| 6 50– 6 99... | .... | .... | .... | .... | .... | .... | .... | 2 | .... | .... | .... | 2 | .... | .... | ... 6 50– 6 99 |
| 7 00– 7 49... | .... | .... | .... | .... | 5 | 12 | .... | 19 | .... | 12 | .... | 5 | .... | 6 | ... 7 00– 7 49 |
| 7 50– 7 99... | .... | .... | .... | .... | .... | .... | .... | 3 | .... | 1 | .... | .... | .... | 1 | ... 7 50– 7 99 |
| 8 00– 8 99... | .... | .... | 3 | .... | 3 | 7 | 2 | 22 | .... | 19 | .... | 12 | .... | 4 | ... 8 00– 8 99 |
| 9 00– 9 99... | .... | .... | .... | .... | 1 | 1 | .... | 8 | 1 | 15 | .... | 11 | .... | 3 | ... 9 00– 9 99 |
| 10 00–10 99... | .... | .... | .... | .... | 2 | .... | 5 | 3 | 1 | 8 | .... | 8 | .... | 4 | ...10 00–10 99 |
| 11 00–11 99... | .... | .... | .... | .... | 1 | .... | 4 | 2 | 1 | 8 | .... | 3 | 1 | 2 | ...11 00–11 99 |
| 12 00–12 99... | .... | .... | .... | .... | .... | .... | 6 | 1 | 3 | 4 | 1 | 10 | 1 | 6 | ...12 00–12 99 |
| 13 00–13 99... | .... | .... | .... | .... | .... | .... | .... | .... | 2 | .... | .... | 5 | .... | .... | ...13 00–13 99 |
| 14 00–14 99... | .... | .... | .... | .... | .... | .... | 2 | 1 | 3 | 2 | 3 | 1 | 1 | 2 | ...14 00–14 99 |
| 15 00–15 99... | .... | .... | .... | 1 | .... | .... | 3 | .... | 4 | 3 | 3 | 2 | 3 | 5 | ...15 00–15 99 |
| 16 00–17 99... | .... | .... | .... | .... | .... | .... | .... | .... | 4 | 1 | 5 | 1 | 3 | 3 | ...16 00–17 99 |
| 18 00–19 99... | .... | .... | .... | .... | .... | .... | 1 | .... | 2 | .... | 4 | .... | 3 | 1 | ...18 00–19 99 |
| 20 00–24 99... | .... | .... | .... | .... | .... | .... | 2 | .... | 4 | .... | 6 | 1 | 5 | 2 | ...20 00–24 99 |
| 25 00–29 99... | .... | .... | .... | .... | .... | .... | .... | .... | 1 | .... | .... | .... | 3 | .... | ...25 00–29 99 |
| 30 00–34 99... | .... | .... | .... | .... | .... | .... | .... | .... | .... | .... | 3 | .... | 4 | 1 | ...30 00–34 99 |
| 35 00–39 99... | .... | .... | .... | .... | .... | .... | .... | .... | .... | .... | .... | .... | 2 | 2 | ...35 00–39 99 |
| 40 00 and over. | .... | .... | .... | .... | .... | .... | .... | .... | .... | .... | 1 | .... | 2 | .... | .40 00 and over |
| Not reported.. | .... | .... | 1 | .... | .... | 1 | .... | .... | .... | .... | .... | .... | .... | .... | ..Not reported |
| Total.... | 21 | 49 | 16 | 85 | 14 | 114 | 25 | 93 | 26 | 85 | 26 | 65 | 28 | 43 | .....Total |

SYRACUSE

319. TABLE V, A, 1, a — (*concluded*) DEPARTMENT STORES — STOCK AND SALES

Number and Per Cent. of Employees Earning Specified Weekly Rates, by Age Groups and Sex

| Weekly Rates in Dollars | Age Groups in Years (*concluded*) 40–44 | | 45–54 | | 55–64 | | 65 and over | | Not reported | | Total | | Cumulative per cent. of total | | Weekly Rates in Dollars |
|---|---|---|---|---|---|---|---|---|---|---|---|---|---|---|---|
| | Male | Female | Male | Female | Male | Female | Male | Female | Male | Female | Male | Female | Male | Female | |
| Less than $3 00 | .... | ...... | .... | ...... | ...... | ...... | ...... | ...... | ...... | ...... | 1 | 28 | .40 | 4.70 | Less than $3 00 |
| $3 00–$3 49... | .... | ...... | .... | ...... | ...... | ...... | ...... | ...... | ...... | ...... | 8 | 47 | 3.80 | 12.50 | ...$3 00– 3 49 |
| 3 50– 3 99... | .... | ...... | .... | ...... | ...... | ...... | ...... | ...... | ...... | ...... | 8 | 20 | 7.10 | 15.90 | ... 3 50– 3 99 |
| 4 00– 4 49... | .... | ...... | .... | ...... | ...... | ...... | ...... | ...... | ...... | ...... | 5 | 43 | 9.20 | 23.00 | ... 4 00– 4 49 |
| 4 50– 4 99... | .... | ...... | .... | ...... | ...... | ...... | ...... | ...... | ...... | ...... | 2 | 12 | 10.00 | 25.00 | ... 4 50– 4 99 |
| 5 00– 5 49... | .... | ...... | .... | ...... | ...... | ...... | ...... | ...... | ...... | 1 | 8 | 55 | 13.30 | 34.20 | ... 5 00– 5 49 |
| 5 50– 5 99... | .... | ...... | .... | ...... | ...... | ...... | ...... | ...... | ...... | ...... | ...... | 4 | ...... | 34.80 | ... 5 50– 5 99 |
| 6 00– 6 49... | .... | 2 | .... | 1 | ...... | ...... | ...... | ...... | ...... | ...... | 3 | 70 | 14.60 | 46.50 | ... 6 00– 6 49 |
| 6 50– 6 99... | .... | 1 | .... | ...... | ...... | ...... | ...... | ...... | ...... | ...... | ...... | 5 | ...... | 47.40 | ... 6 50– 6 99 |
| 7 00– 7 49... | .... | 2 | .... | 2 | ...... | ...... | ...... | ...... | ...... | 2 | 5 | 60 | 16.70 | 57.40 | ... 7 00– 7 49 |
| 7 50– 7 99... | .... | ...... | .... | ...... | ...... | ...... | ...... | ...... | ...... | ...... | ...... | 5 | ...... | 58.20 | ... 7 50– 7 99 |
| 8 00– 8 99... | .... | 1 | .... | 7 | 1 | ...... | ...... | 1 | ...... | 2 | 9 | 75 | 20.40 | 70.80 | ... 8 00– 8 99 |
| 9 00– 9 99... | .... | ...... | 1 | 1 | ...... | ...... | ...... | ...... | ...... | 1 | 3 | 40 | 21.70 | 77.50 | ... 9 00– 9 99 |
| 10 00–10 99... | .... | ...... | 1 | 2 | ...... | ...... | 1 | ...... | ...... | 5 | 10 | 30 | 25.80 | 82.50 | ...10 00–10 99 |
| 11 00–11 99... | .... | 1 | .... | ...... | ...... | ...... | ...... | ...... | ...... | ...... | 7 | 16 | 28.80 | 85.10 | ...11 00–11 99 |
| 12 00–12 99... | .... | 4 | 2 | 3 | 2 | ...... | ...... | ...... | ...... | 5 | 15 | 33 | 35.00 | 90.60 | ...12 00–12 99 |
| 13 00–13 99... | .... | ...... | 2 | 2 | 1 | ...... | ...... | ...... | ...... | 1 | 5 | 8 | 37.10 | 92.00 | ...13 00–13 99 |
| 14 00–14 99... | 3 | 2 | 4 | ...... | 1 | ...... | 2 | ...... | ...... | 1 | 19 | 9 | 45.00 | 93.50 | ...14 00–14 99 |
| 15 00–15 99... | .... | 3 | 5 | 1 | 3 | ...... | ...... | ...... | 1 | 4 | 22 | 19 | 54.20 | 96.70 | ...15 00–15 99 |
| 16 00–17 99... | .... | ...... | 6 | ...... | 4 | ...... | 1 | ...... | ...... | ...... | 23 | 5 | 63.80 | 97.50 | ...16 00–17 99 |
| 18 00–19 99... | .... | 1 | 3 | ...... | 1 | ...... | ...... | ...... | ...... | 1 | 14 | 3 | 69.60 | 98.00 | ...18 00–19 99 |
| 20 00–24 99... | 6 | ...... | 4 | ...... | 1 | 1 | 1 | ...... | ...... | ...... | 29 | 4 | 81.60 | 98.60 | ...20 00–24 99 |
| 25 00–29 99... | 4 | ...... | 3 | 1 | 3 | ...... | ...... | ...... | ...... | 1 | 14 | 2 | 87.50 | 98.90 | ...25 00–29 99 |
| 30 00–34 99... | 1 | ...... | 6 | ...... | 2 | ...... | ...... | ...... | ...... | 1 | 16 | 2 | 94.20 | 99.30 | ...30 00–34 99 |
| 35 00–39 99... | .... | ...... | 1 | ...... | 1 | ...... | ...... | ...... | ...... | ...... | 4 | 2 | 95.90 | 99.60 | ...35 00–39 99 |
| 40 00 and over. | 2 | ...... | 5 | 1 | ...... | 1 | ...... | ...... | ...... | ...... | 10 | 2 | 100.00 | 100.00 | .40 00 and over |
| Not reported.. | .... | ...... | .... | ...... | ...... | ...... | ...... | ...... | ...... | ...... | 1 | 1 | ...... | ...... | ..Not reported |
| Total..... | 16 | 17 | 43 | 21 | 20 | 2 | 5 | 1 | 1 | 25 | 241 | 600 | ...... | ...... | .....Total |

SYRACUSE

DEPARTMENT STORES — STOCK AND SALES

320. TABLE VIII, A, 1, a  NUMBER AND PER CENT. OF EMPLOYEES EARNING SPECIFIED WEEKLY RATES, BY OCCUPATION AND SEX

| WEEKLY RATES IN DOLLARS | OCCUPATION: SUPERINTENDENTS | BUYERS | | ASSISTANT BUYERS AND HEADS OF STOCK | | RECEIVING AND STOCK CLERKS | | STOCK PEOPLE | | FLOOR MANAGERS | | SALES PEOPLE | | MESSENGERS, WRAPPERS AND ERRAND BOYS | | TOTAL | | CUMULATIVE PER CENT. OF TOTAL | WEEKLY RATES IN DOLLARS |
|---|---|---|---|---|---|---|---|---|---|---|---|---|---|---|---|---|---|---|---|
| | Male | Male | Female | Male | Female | Male | Female | Male | Female | Male | Female | Male | Female | Male | Female | Male | Female | Male | |
| Less than $3 00 | ... | ... | ... | ... | ... | ... | ... | ... | 2 | ... | ... | ... | ... | 1 | 26 | 1 | 28 | .40 | Less than $3 00 |
| $3 00–$3 49 | ... | ... | ... | ... | ... | ... | ... | 1 | 6 | ... | ... | ... | 4 | 7 | 37 | 8 | 47 | 3.80 | $3 00– 3 49 |
| 3 50– 3 99 | ... | ... | ... | ... | ... | ... | ... | 3 | 6 | ... | ... | ... | 4 | 5 | 10 | 8 | 20 | 7.10 | 3 50– 3 99 |
| 4 00– 4 49 | ... | ... | ... | ... | ... | ... | ... | ... | 9 | ... | ... | ... | 17 | 5 | 17 | 5 | 43 | 9.20 | 4 00– 4 49 |
| 4 50– 4 99 | ... | ... | ... | ... | ... | ... | ... | 1 | 5 | ... | ... | ... | 4 | 1 | 3 | 2 | 12 | 10.00 | 4 50– 4 99 |
| 5 00– 5 49 | ... | ... | ... | ... | ... | ... | ... | 3 | 14 | ... | ... | 1 | 38 | 4 | 3 | 8 | 55 | 13.30 | 5 00– 5 49 |
| 5 50– 5 99 | ... | ... | ... | ... | ... | ... | ... | ... | ... | ... | ... | ... | 4 | ... | ... | ... | 4 | ... | 5 50– 5 99 |
| 6 00– 6 49 | ... | ... | ... | ... | ... | ... | ... | 2 | 6 | ... | ... | 1 | 59 | ... | 5 | 3 | 70 | 14.60 | 6 00– 6 49 |
| 6 50– 6 99 | ... | ... | ... | ... | ... | ... | ... | ... | ... | ... | ... | ... | 5 | ... | ... | ... | 5 | ... | 6 50– 6 99 |
| 7 00– 7 49 | ... | ... | ... | ... | ... | 1 | ... | 1 | ... | ... | ... | 2 | 58 | 1 | 2 | 5 | 60 | 16.70 | 7 00– 7 49 |
| 7 50– 7 99 | ... | ... | ... | ... | ... | ... | ... | ... | ... | ... | ... | ... | 5 | ... | ... | ... | 5 | ... | 7 50– 7 99 |
| 8 00– 8 99 | ... | ... | ... | ... | ... | 2 | ... | 2 | ... | ... | ... | 5 | 74 | ... | 1 | 9 | 75 | 20.40 | 8 00– 8 99 |
| 9 00– 9 99 | ... | ... | ... | ... | ... | 1 | 1 | ... | ... | ... | ... | 1 | 39 | 1 | ... | 3 | 40 | 21.70 | 9 00– 9 99 |
| 10 00–10 99 | ... | ... | ... | 1 | ... | ... | ... | ... | ... | ... | 1 | 8 | 29 | 1 | ... | 10 | 30 | 25.80 | 10 00–10 99 |
| 11 00–11 99 | ... | ... | ... | ... | 1 | 1 | ... | ... | ... | ... | ... | 6 | 15 | ... | ... | 7 | 16 | 28.80 | 11 00–11 99 |
| 12 00–12 99 | ... | ... | ... | ... | ... | ... | ... | ... | ... | ... | 1 | 15 | 32 | ... | ... | 15 | 23 | 35.00 | 12 00–12 99 |
| 13 00–13 99 | ... | ... | ... | ... | 1 | 3 | ... | ... | ... | ... | ... | 2 | 7 | ... | ... | 5 | 8 | 37.10 | 13 00–13 99 |
| 14 00–14 99 | ... | ... | ... | ... | 2 | 2 | ... | ... | ... | ... | ... | 17 | 7 | ... | ... | 19 | 9 | 45.00 | 14 00–14 99 |
| 15 00–15 99 | ... | ... | 2 | ... | ... | ... | ... | ... | ... | 2 | ... | 20 | 17 | ... | ... | 22 | 19 | 54.20 | 15 00–15 99 |
| 16 00–17 99 | ... | ... | ... | ... | 1 | ... | ... | ... | ... | 2 | 1 | 21 | 3 | ... | ... | 23 | 5 | 63.80 | 16 00–17 99 |
| 18 00–19 99 | ... | ... | ... | 2 | ... | ... | ... | ... | ... | ... | ... | 12 | 3 | ... | ... | 14 | 3 | 69.60 | 18 00–19 99 |
| 20 00–24 99 | ... | ... | ... | 5 | 2 | ... | ... | ... | ... | 5 | ... | 19 | 2 | ... | ... | 29 | 4 | 81.60 | 20 00–24 99 |
| 25 00–29 99 | 1 | 2 | 1 | 5 | ... | ... | ... | ... | ... | 1 | ... | 5 | 1 | ... | ... | 14 | 2 | 87.50 | 25 00–29 99 |
| 30 00–34 99 | 1 | 8 | 2 | ... | ... | ... | ... | ... | ... | 3 | ... | 4 | ... | ... | ... | 16 | 2 | 94.20 | 30 00–34 99 |
| 35 00–39 99 | ... | 1 | 2 | 1 | ... | ... | ... | ... | ... | 1 | ... | 1 | ... | ... | ... | 4 | 2 | 95.90 | 35 00–39 99 |
| 40 00 and over | 2 | 8 | 2 | ... | ... | ... | ... | ... | ... | ... | ... | ... | ... | ... | ... | 10 | 2 | 100 00 | 40 00 and over |
| Not reported | ... | ... | ... | ... | ... | ... | ... | ... | ... | ... | ... | 1 | 1 | ... | ... | 1 | 1 | ... | Not reported |
| Total | 4 | 19 | 9 | 14 | 7 | 10 | 1 | 13 | 48 | 14 | 3 | 141 | 424 | 26 | 104 | 241 | 600 | ... | Total |

321. TABLE VI, A, 1, a

SYRACUSE

DEPARTMENT STORES — STOCK AND SALES

NUMBER AND PER CENT. OF EMPLOYEES CLASSIFIED ACCORDING TO ACTUAL WEEKLY EARNINGS, BY AGE GROUPS AND SEX

| ACTUAL WEEKLY EARNINGS IN DOLLARS | AGE GROUPS IN YEARS | | | | | | | | | | | | | | ACTUAL WEEKLY EARNINGS IN DOLLARS |
|---|---|---|---|---|---|---|---|---|---|---|---|---|---|---|---|
| | 14–15 | | 16–17 | | 18–20 | | 21–24 | | 25–29 | | 30–34 | | 35–39 | | |
| | Male | Female | Male | Female | Male | Female | Male | Female | Male | Female | Male | Female | Male | Female | |
| Less than $3 00 | 2 | 29 | 1 | 8 | ...... | 3 | ...... | ...... | ...... | 1 | ...... | ...... | ...... | ...... | Less than $3 00 |
| $3 00–$3 49... | 6 | 19 | 1 | 20 | ...... | 4 | ...... | 2 | ...... | ...... | ...... | ...... | ...... | ...... | ...$3 00– 3 49 |
| 3 50– 3 99... | 6 | 1 | 2 | 16 | ...... | 6 | ...... | 1 | ...... | ...... | ...... | 1 | ...... | ...... | ... 3 50– 3 99 |
| 4 00– 4 49... | 4 | ...... | 1 | 28 | ...... | 17 | ...... | 1 | ...... | ...... | ...... | 2 | ...... | ...... | ... 4 00– 4 49 |
| 4 50– 4 99... | 1 | ...... | 1 | 2 | 1 | 9 | ...... | 1 | ...... | ...... | ...... | ...... | ...... | ...... | ... 4 50– 4 99 |
| 5 00– 5 49... | 2 | ...... | 4 | 7 | 1 | 26 | ...... | 9 | ...... | 6 | ...... | 2 | ...... | 1 | ... 5 00– 5 49 |
| 5 50– 5 99... | .... | ...... | .... | ...... | ...... | 5 | ...... | 4 | ...... | 4 | ...... | ...... | ...... | ...... | ... 5 50– 5 99 |
| 6 00– 6 49... | .... | ...... | 3 | 4 | ...... | 24 | ...... | 18 | ...... | 6 | ...... | 1 | ...... | 2 | ... 6 00– 6 49 |
| 6 50– 6 99... | .... | ...... | .... | ...... | 1 | ...... | ...... | 2 | ...... | 1 | ...... | 3 | ...... | 1 | ... 6 50– 6 99 |
| 7 00– 7 49... | .... | ...... | .... | ...... | 5 | 12 | ...... | 20 | ...... | 12 | ...... | 4 | ...... | 6 | ... 7 00– 7 49 |
| 7 50– 7 99... | .... | ...... | .... | ...... | ...... | ...... | ...... | 2 | ...... | 1 | ...... | 1 | ...... | 1 | ... 7 50– 7 99 |
| 8 00– 8 99... | .... | ...... | 3 | ...... | 2 | 7 | 2 | 18 | 1 | 17 | ...... | 12 | ...... | 2 | ... 8 00– 8 99 |
| 9 00– 9 99... | .... | ...... | .... | ...... | 1 | 1 | ...... | 9 | ...... | 12 | ...... | 11 | ...... | 3 | ... 9 00– 9 99 |
| 10 00–10 99... | .... | ...... | .... | ...... | 2 | ...... | 8 | 2 | 1 | 10 | ...... | 8 | ...... | 5 | ...10 00–10 99 |
| 11 00–11 99... | .... | ...... | .... | ...... | 1 | ...... | 4 | 2 | 3 | 7 | 1 | 2 | 1 | 5 | ...11 00–11 99 |
| 12 00–12 99... | .... | ...... | .... | ...... | ...... | ...... | 3 | 1 | 2 | 3 | 1 | 8 | 2 | 2 | ...12 00–12 99 |
| 13 00–13 99... | .... | ...... | .... | ...... | ...... | ...... | 1 | ...... | 2 | 1 | ...... | 5 | ...... | ...... | ...13 00–13 99 |
| 14 00–14 99... | .... | ...... | .... | ...... | ...... | ...... | 2 | 1 | 3 | 1 | 2 | 1 | ...... | 2 | ...14 00–14 99 |
| 15 00–15 99... | .... | ...... | .... | ...... | ...... | ...... | 2 | ...... | 4 | 2 | 3 | 2 | 3 | 4 | ...15 00–15 99 |
| 16 00–17 99... | .... | ...... | .... | ...... | ...... | ...... | ...... | ...... | 3 | 1 | 5 | 1 | 4 | 3 | ...16 00–17 99 |
| 18 00–19 99... | .... | ...... | .... | ...... | ...... | ...... | 1 | ...... | 2 | ...... | 3 | ...... | 3 | 1 | ...18 00–19 99 |
| 20 00–24 99... | .... | ...... | .... | ...... | ...... | ...... | 2 | ...... | 4 | ...... | 6 | 1 | 4 | 2 | ...20 00–24 99 |
| 25 00–29 99... | .... | ...... | .... | ...... | ...... | ...... | ...... | ...... | 1 | ...... | ...... | ...... | 3 | ...... | ...25 00–29 99 |
| 30 00–34 99... | .... | ...... | .... | ...... | ...... | ...... | ...... | ...... | ...... | ...... | 3 | ...... | 4 | 1 | ...30 00–34 99 |
| 35 00–39 99... | .... | ...... | .... | ...... | ...... | ...... | ...... | ...... | ...... | ...... | ...... | ...... | 2 | 2 | ...35 00–39 99 |
| 40 00 and over. | .... | ...... | .... | ...... | ...... | ...... | ...... | ...... | ...... | ...... | 1 | ...... | 2 | ...... | .40 00 and over |
| Not reported.. | .... | ...... | .... | ...... | ...... | ...... | ...... | ...... | ...... | ...... | 1 | ...... | ...... | ...... | ..Not reported |
| Total..... | 21 | 49 | 16 | 85 | 14 | 114 | 25 | 93 | 26 | 85 | 26 | 65 | 28 | 33 | .....Total |

321. TABLE VI, A, 1, a — *(concluded)*

SYRACUSE
**DEPARTMENT STORES — STOCK AND SALES**
Number and Per Cent. of Employees Classified According to Actual Weekly Earnings, by Age Groups and Sex

| Actual Weekly Earnings in Dollars | Age Groups in Years *(concluded)* 40–44 | | 45–54 | | 55–64 | | 65 and over | | Not reported | | Total | | Cumulative per cent. of total | | Actual Weekly Earnings in Dollars |
|---|---|---|---|---|---|---|---|---|---|---|---|---|---|---|---|
| | Male | Female | Male | Female | Male | Female | Male | Female | Male | Female | Male | Female | Male | Female | |
| Less than $3 00 | .... | ...... | .... | ...... | ...... | ...... | ...... | ...... | ...... | ...... | 3 | 41 | 1.30 | 6.80 | Less than $3 00 |
| $3 00–$3 49 | .... | ...... | .... | ...... | ...... | ...... | ...... | ...... | ...... | ...... | 7 | 45 | 4.20 | 14.30 | $3 00– 3 49 |
| 3 50– 3 99 | .... | ...... | .... | ...... | ...... | ...... | ...... | ...... | ...... | ...... | 8 | 25 | 7.50 | 18.50 | 3 50– 3 99 |
| 4 00– 4 49 | .... | 1 | .... | ...... | ...... | ...... | ...... | ...... | ...... | ...... | 5 | 49 | 9.60 | 25.80 | 4 00– 4 49 |
| 4 50– 4 99 | .... | ...... | .... | ...... | ...... | ...... | ...... | ...... | ...... | ...... | 3 | 12 | 10.80 | 28.70 | 4 50– 4 99 |
| 5 00– 5 49 | .... | 1 | .... | ...... | ...... | ...... | ...... | ...... | ...... | 1 | 7 | 53 | 13.80 | 37.50 | 5 00– 5 49 |
| 5 50– 5 99 | .... | ...... | .... | ...... | ...... | ...... | ...... | ...... | ...... | ...... | ...... | 13 | ...... | 39.70 | 5 50– 5 99 |
| 6 00– 6 49 | .... | 2 | .... | 2 | ...... | ...... | ...... | ...... | ...... | 1 | 3 | 60 | 15.00 | 49.70 | 6 00– 6 49 |
| 6 50– 6 99 | .... | ...... | .... | ...... | ...... | ...... | ...... | ...... | ...... | ...... | 1 | 7 | 15.40 | 50.80 | 6 50– 6 99 |
| 7 00– 7 49 | .... | 2 | 1 | 1 | ...... | ...... | ...... | ...... | ...... | 1 | 6 | 58 | 17.90 | 60.50 | 7 00– 7 49 |
| 7 50– 7 99 | .... | ...... | .... | ...... | ...... | ...... | ...... | ...... | ...... | 1 | ...... | 6 | ...... | 61.50 | 7 50– 7 99 |
| 8 00– 8 99 | .... | ...... | .... | 7 | 1 | ...... | ...... | 1 | ...... | 2 | 9 | 66 | 21.70 | 72.50 | 8 00– 8 99 |
| 9 00– 9 99 | .... | ...... | 1 | 1 | ...... | ...... | ...... | ...... | ...... | 1 | 2 | 38 | 22.50 | 78.80 | 9 00– 9 99 |
| 10 00–10 99 | .... | 1 | 1 | 2 | ...... | ...... | 1 | ...... | ...... | 5 | 13 | 33 | 23.90 | 84.40 | 10 00–10 99 |
| 11 00–11 99 | .... | 1 | .... | 1 | ...... | ...... | ...... | ...... | ...... | ...... | 10 | 18 | 32.10 | 87.30 | 11 00–11 99 |
| 12 00–12 99 | .... | 3 | 2 | 2 | 3 | ...... | ...... | ...... | ...... | 5 | 13 | 24 | 37.50 | 91.30 | 12 00–12 99 |
| 13 00–13 99 | .... | ...... | 2 | 2 | 1 | ...... | ...... | ...... | ...... | 1 | 6 | 9 | 40.00 | 92.90 | 13 00–13 99 |
| 14 00–14 99 | 3 | 2 | 4 | ...... | 1 | ...... | 2 | ...... | ...... | 1 | 17 | 8 | 47.10 | 94.10 | 14 00–14 99 |
| 15 00–15 99 | .... | 3 | 5 | 1 | 3 | ...... | ...... | ...... | 1 | 3 | 21 | 15 | 55.90 | 96.60 | 15 00–15 99 |
| 16 00–17 99 | .... | ...... | 6 | ...... | 3 | ...... | 1 | ...... | ...... | ...... | 22 | 5 | 65.00 | 97.50 | 16 00–17 99 |
| 18 00–19 99 | .... | 1 | 3 | ...... | 1 | ...... | ...... | ...... | ...... | 1 | 13 | 3 | 70.50 | 98.00 | 18 00–19 99 |
| 20 00–24 99 | 6 | ...... | 3 | ...... | 1 | 1 | 1 | ...... | ...... | ...... | 27 | 4 | 81.70 | 98.60 | 20 00–24 99 |
| 25 00–29 99 | 4 | ...... | 3 | 1 | 3 | ...... | ...... | ...... | ...... | 1 | 14 | 2 | 87.50 | 99.00 | 25 00–29 99 |
| 30 00–34 99 | 1 | ...... | 6 | ...... | 2 | ...... | ...... | ...... | ...... | 1 | 16 | 2 | 94.30 | 99.40 | 30 00–34 99 |
| 35 00–39 99 | .... | ...... | 1 | ...... | 1 | ...... | ...... | ...... | ...... | ...... | 4 | 2 | 95.90 | 99.80 | 35 00–39 99 |
| 40 00 and under | 2 | ...... | 5 | 1 | ...... | 1 | ...... | ...... | ...... | ...... | 10 | 2 | 100.00 | 100.00 | 40 00 and over |
| Not reported | .... | ...... | .... | ...... | ...... | ...... | ...... | ...... | ...... | ...... | 1 | ...... | ...... | ...... | Not reported |
| Total | 16 | 17 | 43 | 21 | 20 | 2 | 5 | 1 | 1 | 25 | 241 | 600 | ...... | ...... | Total |

## SYRACUSE
## DEPARTMENT STORES — STOCK AND SALES

322. TABLE IX, A, 1, a    NUMBER AND PER CENT. OF EMPLOYEES CLASSIFIED ACCORDING TO ACTUAL WEEKLY EARNINGS, BY OCCUPATION AND SEX

| ACTUAL WEEKLY EARNINGS IN DOLLARS | OCCUPATION | | | | | | | | | | | | | | | | | | | ACTUAL WEEKLY EARNINGS IN DOLLARS |
|---|---|---|---|---|---|---|---|---|---|---|---|---|---|---|---|---|---|---|---|---|
| | SUPERINTENDENTS | BUYERS | | ASSISTANT BUYERS AND HEADS OF STOCK | | RECEIVING AND STOCK CLERKS | | STOCK PEOPLE | | FLOOR MANAGERS | | SALES PEOPLE | | MESSENGERS, WRAPPERS AND ERRAND BOYS | | TOTAL | | CUMULATIVE PER CENT. OF TOTAL | | |
| | Male | Male | Female | Male | Female | Male | Female | Male | Female | Male | Female | Male | Female | Male | Female | Male | Female | Male | Female | |
| Less than $3 00 | ... | ... | ... | ... | 1 | ... | ... | ... | 3 | ... | ... | 1 | 4 | 2 | 33 | 3 | 41 | 1.30 | 6.80 | Less than $3 00 |
| $3 00-$3 49 | ... | ... | ... | ... | ... | ... | ... | 1 | 6 | ... | ... | ... | 6 | 6 | 33 | 7 | 45 | 4.20 | 14.30 | $3 00- 3 49 |
| 3 50- 3 99 | ... | ... | ... | ... | ... | ... | ... | 3 | 5 | ... | ... | ... | 10 | 5 | 10 | 8 | 25 | 7.50 | 18.50 | 3 50- 3 99 |
| 4 00- 4 49 | ... | ... | ... | ... | ... | ... | ... | ... | 10 | ... | ... | ... | 24 | 5 | 15 | 5 | 49 | 9.60 | 25.80 | 4 00- 4 49 |
| 4 50- 4 99 | ... | ... | ... | ... | ... | ... | ... | 1 | 5 | ... | ... | 1 | 5 | 1 | 2 | 3 | 12 | 10.80 | 28.70 | 4 50- 4 99 |
| 5 00- 5 49 | ... | ... | 1 | ... | ... | ... | ... | 3 | 13 | ... | ... | ... | 36 | 4 | 3 | 7 | 53 | 13.80 | 37.50 | 5 00- 5 49 |
| 5 50- 5 99 | ... | ... | ... | ... | ... | ... | ... | ... | ... | ... | ... | ... | 13 | ... | ... | ... | 13 | ... | 39.70 | 5 50- 5 99 |
| 6 00- 6 49 | ... | ... | ... | ... | ... | ... | ... | 2 | 6 | ... | ... | 1 | 49 | ... | 5 | 3 | 60 | 15.00 | 49.70 | 6 00- 6 49 |
| 6 50- 6 99 | ... | ... | ... | ... | ... | ... | ... | ... | ... | ... | ... | 1 | 7 | ... | ... | 1 | 7 | 15.40 | 50.80 | 6 50- 6 99 |
| 7 00- 7 49 | ... | ... | ... | 1 | ... | 1 | ... | 1 | ... | ... | ... | 2 | 56 | 1 | 2 | 6 | 58 | 17.90 | 60.50 | 7 00- 7 49 |
| 7 50- 7 99 | ... | ... | ... | ... | ... | ... | ... | ... | ... | ... | ... | ... | 6 | ... | ... | ... | 6 | ... | 61.50 | 7 50- 7 99 |
| 8 00- 8 99 | ... | ... | ... | ... | ... | 2 | ... | 2 | ... | ... | ... | 4 | 65 | 1 | 1 | 9 | 66 | 21.70 | 72.50 | 8 00- 8 99 |
| 9 00- 9 99 | ... | ... | ... | ... | ... | 1 | 1 | ... | ... | ... | ... | 1 | 37 | ... | ... | 2 | 38 | 22.50 | 78.80 | 9 00- 9 99 |
| 10 00-10 99 | ... | ... | ... | 1 | ... | ... | ... | ... | ... | ... | 2 | 11 | 31 | 1 | ... | 13 | 33 | 23.90 | 84.40 | 10 00-10 99 |
| 11 00-11 99 | ... | ... | ... | ... | 1 | 2 | ... | ... | ... | ... | ... | 8 | 17 | ... | ... | 10 | 18 | 32.10 | 87.30 | 11 00-11 99 |
| 12 00-12 99 | ... | ... | ... | ... | ... | ... | ... | ... | ... | ... | ... | 13 | 24 | ... | ... | 13 | 24 | 37.50 | 91.30 | 12 00-12 99 |
| 13 00-13 99 | ... | ... | ... | ... | 1 | 3 | ... | ... | ... | ... | ... | 3 | 8 | ... | ... | 6 | 9 | 40.00 | 92.90 | 13 00-13 99 |
| 14 00-14 99 | ... | ... | ... | ... | 1 | 1 | ... | ... | ... | ... | ... | 16 | 7 | ... | ... | 17 | 8 | 47.10 | 94.10 | 14 00-14 99 |
| 15 00-15 99 | ... | ... | 1 | ... | ... | ... | ... | ... | ... | 2 | ... | 19 | 14 | ... | ... | 21 | 15 | 55.90 | 96.60 | 15 00-15 99 |
| 16 00-17 99 | ... | ... | ... | ... | 1 | ... | ... | ... | ... | 3 | 1 | 19 | 3 | ... | ... | 22 | 5 | 65.00 | 97.50 | 16 00-17 99 |
| 18 00-19 99 | ... | ... | ... | 2 | ... | ... | ... | ... | ... | ... | ... | 11 | 3 | ... | ... | 13 | 3 | 70.50 | 98.00 | 18 00-19 99 |
| 20 00-24 99 | ... | ... | ... | 4 | 2 | ... | ... | ... | ... | 4 | ... | 19 | 2 | ... | ... | 27 | 4 | 81.70 | 98.60 | 20 00-24 99 |
| 25 00-29 99 | 1 | 2 | 1 | 5 | ... | ... | ... | ... | ... | 1 | ... | 5 | 1 | ... | ... | 14 | 2 | 87.50 | 99.00 | 25 00-29 99 |
| 30 00-34 99 | 1 | 8 | 2 | ... | ... | ... | ... | ... | ... | 3 | ... | 4 | ... | ... | ... | 16 | 2 | 94.30 | 99.40 | 30 00-34 99 |
| 35 00-39 99 | ... | 1 | 2 | 1 | ... | ... | ... | ... | ... | 1 | ... | 1 | ... | ... | ... | 4 | 2 | 95.90 | 99.80 | 35 00-39 99 |
| 40 00 and over | 2 | 8 | 2 | ... | ... | ... | ... | ... | ... | ... | ... | ... | ... | ... | ... | 10 | 2 | 100.00 | 100.00 | 40 00 and over |
| Not reported | ... | ... | ... | ... | ... | ... | ... | ... | ... | ... | ... | 1 | ... | ... | ... | 1 | ... | ... | ... | Not reported |
| Total | 4 | 19 | 9 | 14 | 7 | 10 | 1 | 13 | 48 | 14 | 3 | 141 | 428 | 26 | 104 | 241 | 660 | ... | ... | Total |

323. TABLE XV, A, 1, b, c, d, e

SYRACUSE

**DEPARTMENT STORES — OFFICE, SHIPPING AND DELIVERY, MANUFACTURING, PLANT**

NUMBER OF EMPLOYEES EARNING SPECIFIED WEEKLY RATES, ACCORDING TO DEPARTMENT AND SEX

| WEEKLY RATES IN DOLLARS | DEPARTMENT | | | | | | | | | | | | WEEKLY RATES IN DOLLARS |
|---|---|---|---|---|---|---|---|---|---|---|---|---|---|
| | OFFICE | | SHIPPING AND DELIVERY | | MANUFACTURING | | PLANT | | TOTAL | | CUMULATIVE PER CENT. OF TOTAL | | |
| | Male | Female | Male | Female | Male | Female | Male | Female | Male | Female | Male | Female | |
| Less than $3 00 | ....... | 1 | ....... | ....... | ....... | 6 | ....... | ....... | ....... | 7 | ....... | 1.70 | Less than $3 00 |
| $3 00–$3 49 | ....... | 1 | ....... | ....... | ....... | 3 | ....... | 1 | ....... | 5 | ....... | 2.90 | $3 00– 3 49 |
| 3 50– 3 99 | ....... | 2 | 1 | ....... | ....... | 1 | ....... | ....... | 1 | 3 | .50 | 3.60 | 3 50– 3 99 |
| 4 00– 4 49 | 1 | 12 | 5 | ....... | ....... | 3 | ....... | 1 | 6 | 16 | 3.50 | 7.50 | 4 00– 4 49 |
| 4 50– 4 99 | ....... | 10 | 1 | ....... | ....... | ....... | ....... | 3 | 1 | 13 | 4.00 | 10.70 | 4 50– 4 99 |
| 5 00– 5 49 | ....... | 34 | 6 | 1 | ....... | 4 | ....... | 2 | 6 | 41 | 7.10 | 20.60 | 5 00– 5 49 |
| 5 50– 5 99 | ....... | ....... | ....... | ....... | ....... | 2 | ....... | 1 | ....... | 3 | ....... | 21.40 | 5 50– 5 99 |
| 6 00– 6 49 | 1 | 29 | 2 | 1 | ....... | 10 | 1 | 14 | 4 | 54 | 9.10 | 34.40 | 6 00– 6 49 |
| 6 50– 6 99 | 1 | 3 | ....... | ....... | ....... | 1 | ....... | ....... | 1 | 4 | 9.60 | 35.40 | 6 50– 6 99 |
| 7 00– 7 49 | 2 | 22 | ....... | 1 | ....... | 16 | 1 | 1 | 3 | 40 | 11.10 | 45.20 | 7 00– 7 49 |
| 7 50– 7 99 | 1 | 3 | ....... | ....... | ....... | 4 | ....... | ....... | 1 | 7 | 11.60 | 46.80 | 7 50– 7 99 |
| 8 00– 8 99 | 1 | 16 | ....... | ....... | 1 | 28 | 1 | 2 | 3 | 46 | 13.10 | 58.00 | 8 00– 8 99 |
| 9 00– 9 99 | ....... | 13 | 2 | ....... | ....... | 27 | 2 | ....... | 4 | 40 | 15.20 | 67.70 | 9 00– 9 99 |
| 10 00–10 99 | 4 | 20 | 3 | ....... | 1 | 16 | 7 | 2 | 15 | 38 | 22.80 | 77.00 | 10 00–10 99 |
| 11 00–11 99 | ....... | 11 | 2 | ....... | ....... | 7 | 5 | ....... | 7 | 18 | 26.20 | 81.30 | 11 00–11 99 |
| 12 00–12 99 | 5 | 8 | 18 | ....... | ....... | 15 | 24 | 3 | 47 | 26 | 50.00 | 87.60 | 12 00–12 99 |
| 13 00–13 99 | 2 | 1 | 3 | ....... | 1 | 4 | 2 | ....... | 8 | 5 | 54.00 | 88.80 | 13 00–13 99 |
| 14 00–14 99 | 2 | 4 | 6 | ....... | ....... | 4 | 3 | ....... | 11 | 8 | 59.60 | 90.80 | 14 00–14 99 |
| 15 00–15 99 | 7 | 4 | 3 | ....... | 7 | 6 | 4 | ....... | 21 | 10 | 70.00 | 93.20 | 15 00–15 99 |
| 16 00–17 99 | 4 | 2 | 4 | ....... | 3 | 5 | ....... | 1 | 11 | 8 | 75.80 | 95.10 | 16 00–17 99 |
| 18 00–19 99 | ....... | 3 | 4 | ....... | 6 | 4 | 2 | ....... | 12 | 7 | 81.80 | 96.90 | 18 00–19 99 |
| 20 00–24 99 | 10 | 2 | ....... | ....... | 3 | 2 | 5 | ....... | 18 | 4 | 91.00 | 97.90 | 20 00–24 99 |
| 25 00–29 99 | 2 | 2 | 1 | ....... | 1 | 2 | 2 | ....... | 6 | 4 | 94.00 | 98.80 | 25 00–29 99 |
| 30 00–34 99 | 2 | ....... | ....... | ....... | 2 | ....... | ....... | ....... | 4 | ....... | 96.00 | ....... | 30 00–34 99 |
| 35 00–39 99 | 2 | ....... | ....... | ....... | 2 | ....... | ....... | ....... | 4 | ....... | 98.00 | ....... | 35 00–39 99 |
| 40 and over | 1 | 1 | ....... | ....... | 3 | 4 | ....... | ....... | 4 | 5 | 100.00 | 100.00 | 40 and over |
| Not reported | ....... | ....... | 1 | ....... | 3 | 3 | ....... | ....... | 4 | 3 | ....... | ....... | Not reported |
| Total | 48 | 204 | 62 | 3 | 33 | 177 | 59 | 31 | 202 | 415 | ....... | ....... | Total |

324. TABLE XVI, A, 1, b, c, d, e

## SYRACUSE

### DEPARTMENT STORES — OFFICE, SHIPPING AND DELIVERY, MANUFACTURING, PLANT

Number of Employees Classified According to Actual Weekly Earnings, by Department and Sex

| Actual Weekly Earnings in Dollars | Department | | | | | | | | | | | | Actual Weekly Earnings in Dollars |
|---|---|---|---|---|---|---|---|---|---|---|---|---|---|
| | Office | | Shipping and Delivery | | Manufacturing | | Plant | | Total | | Cumulative per cent. of total | | |
| | Male | Female | Male | Female | Male | Female | Male | Female | Male | Female | Male | Female | |
| Less than $3 00. | 1 | 1 | 1 | ....... | ....... | 11 | ....... | ....... | 2 | 12 | .99 | 2.86 | Less than $3 00 |
| $3 00–$3 49.... | ....... | 2 | 2 | ....... | ....... | 5 | ....... | 2 | 2 | 9 | 1.98 | 5.02 | ...$3 00– 3 49 |
| 3 50– 3 99.... | ....... | 6 | ....... | ....... | ....... | 1 | ....... | ....... | ....... | 7 | ....... | 6.68 | ....3 50– 3 99 |
| 4 00– 4 49.... | 1 | 11 | 5 | ....... | ....... | 4 | ....... | 2 | 6 | 17 | 4.95 | 10.75 | ....4 00– 4 49 |
| 4 50– 4 99.... | ....... | 11 | 1 | ....... | ....... | ....... | ....... | 2 | 1 | 13 | 5.45 | 13.85 | ....4 50– 4 99 |
| 5 00– 5 49.... | ....... | 32 | 6 | 1 | ....... | 6 | ....... | 3 | 6 | 42 | 8.42 | 23.90 | ....5 00– 5 49 |
| 5 50– 5 99.... | ....... | 2 | ....... | ....... | 1 | 8 | ....... | 2 | 1 | 12 | 8.81 | 26.78 | ....5 50– 5 99 |
| 6 00– 6 49.... | 1 | 30 | 2 | 1 | ....... | 8 | 1 | 12 | 4 | 51 | 10.90 | 38.90 | ....6 00– 6 49 |
| 6 50– 6 99.... | 1 | 4 | ....... | ....... | 1 | 2 | ....... | ....... | 2 | 6 | 11.90 | 40.40 | ....6 50– 6 99 |
| 7 00– 7 49.... | 2 | 20 | ....... | 1 | ....... | 13 | 1 | 1 | 3 | 35 | 13.38 | 48.75 | ....7 00– 7 49 |
| 7 50– 7 99.... | 1 | 1 | ....... | ....... | ....... | 6 | ....... | ....... | 1 | 7 | 13.88 | 50.40 | ....7 50– 7 99 |
| 8 00– 8 99.... | ....... | 15 | 1 | ....... | 2 | 27 | 1 | 1 | 4 | 43 | 15.85 | 60.60 | ....8 00– 8 99 |
| 9 00– 9 99.... | ....... | 19 | 2 | ....... | ....... | 24 | 2 | ....... | 4 | 43 | 17.80 | 71.00 | ....9 00– 9 99 |
| 10 00–10 99.... | 4 | 15 | 3 | ....... | 1 | 16 | 8 | 2 | 16 | 33 | 25.75 | 78 00 | ...10 00–10 99 |
| 11 00–11 99.... | 1 | 12 | 2 | ....... | 1 | 7 | 5 | ....... | 9 | 19 | 30.20 | 83.40 | ...11 00–11 99 |
| 12 00–12 99.... | 4 | 5 | 16 | ....... | ....... | 15 | 23 | 3 | 43 | 23 | 51.50 | 88.80 | ...12 00–12 99 |
| 13 00–13 99.... | 2 | 1 | 3 | ....... | 1 | 3 | 2 | ....... | 8 | 4 | 55.50 | 89.75 | ...13 00–13 99 |
| 14 00–14 99.... | 2 | 3 | 6 | ....... | ....... | 3 | 3 | ....... | 11 | 6 | 60.90 | 91.25 | ...14 00–14 99 |
| 15 00–15 99.... | 6 | 4 | 3 | ....... | 7 | 4 | 4 | ....... | 20 | 8 | 70.90 | 93.10 | ...15 00–15 99 |
| 16 00–17 99.... | 5 | 2 | 4 | ....... | 3 | 6 | ....... | 1 | 12 | 9 | 76.75 | 95.25 | ...16 00–17 99 |
| 18 00–19 99.... | ....... | 3 | 3 | ....... | 6 | 4 | 2 | ....... | 11 | 7 | 82.25 | 97.00 | ...18 00–19 99 |
| 20 00–24 99.... | 11 | 3 | 1 | ....... | 3 | 2 | 5 | ....... | 20 | 5 | 92.00 | 98.00 | ...20 00–24 99 |
| 25 00–29 99.... | 1 | 1 | 1 | ....... | 1 | 2 | 2 | ....... | 5 | 3 | 94.50 | 99.00 | ...25 00–29 99 |
| 30 00–34 99.... | 2 | ....... | ....... | ....... | 2 | ....... | ....... | ....... | 4 | ....... | 96.50 | ....... | ...30 00–34 99 |
| 35 00–39 99.... | 2 | ....... | ....... | ....... | 2 | ....... | ....... | ....... | 4 | ....... | 98.50 | ....... | ...35 00–39 99 |
| 40 00 and over.. | 1 | 1 | ....... | ....... | 2 | 4 | ....... | ....... | 3 | 5 | 100.00 | 100.00 | .40 00 and over |
| Total...... | 48 | 204 | 62 | 3 | 33 | 181 | 59 | 31 | 202 | 419 | ....... | ....... | .....Total |

SYRACUSE

DEPARTMENT STORES — OFFICE, SHIPPING AND DELIVERY, MANUFACTURING, PLANT

325. TABLE XVII, A, 1, b, c, d, e — Number of Employees Classified by Age Groups, According to Department and Sex

| Age Group in Years | Department | | | | | | | | | | | | Age Group in Years |
|---|---|---|---|---|---|---|---|---|---|---|---|---|---|
| | Office | | Shipping and Delivery | | Manufacturing | | Plant | | Total | | Per cent. of Total | | |
| | Male | Female | Male | Female | Male | Female | Male | Female | Male | Female | Male | Female | |
| 14–15 | ....... | 2 | 7 | ....... | ....... | 2 | ....... | ....... | 7 | 4 | 3.46 | .95 | 14–15 |
| 16–17 | 2 | 14 | 7 | 2 | ....... | 9 | ....... | 3 | 9 | 28 | 4.45 | 6.68 | 16–17 |
| 18–20 | 4 | 70 | 3 | 1 | 2 | 26 | 7 | 3 | 16 | 100 | 7.92 | 23.85 | 18–20 |
| 21–24 | 6 | 54 | 11 | ....... | 2 | 31 | 5 | 3 | 24 | 88 | 11.90 | 21.00 | 21–24 |
| 25–29 | 7 | 26 | 11 | ....... | 4 | 30 | 7 | 4 | 29 | 60 | 14.37 | 14.30 | 25–29 |
| 30–34 | 7 | 6 | 5 | ....... | 7 | 16 | 6 | 5 | 25 | 27 | 12.38 | 6.49 | 30–34 |
| 35–39 | 4 | 9 | 6 | ....... | 4 | 18 | 5 | 3 | 19 | 30 | 9.40 | 7.15 | 35–39 |
| 40–44 | 4 | 7 | 5 | ....... | 6 | 10 | 6 | 1 | 21 | 18 | 10.40 | 4.29 | 40–44 |
| 45–54 | 6 | 2 | 4 | ....... | 4 | 18 | 11 | 7 | 25 | 27 | 12.37 | 6.48 | 45–54 |
| 55–64 | 4 | ....... | 1 | ....... | 3 | 7 | 12 | 1 | 20 | 8 | 9.90 | 1.90 | 55–64 |
| 65 and over | 2 | ....... | 2 | ....... | 1 | 2 | ....... | 1 | 5 | 3 | 2.41 | .71 | 65 and over |
| Not reported | 2 | 14 | ....... | ....... | ....... | 12 | ....... | ....... | 2 | 26 | .98 | 6.20 | Not reported |
| Total | 48 | 204 | 62 | 3 | 33 | 181 | 59 | 31 | 202 | 419 | 100.00 | 100.00 | Total |

ALBANY

DEPARTMENT STORES — STOCK AND SALES

326. TABLE V, A, 1, a — NUMBER AND PER CENT. OF EMPLOYEES EARNING SPECIFIED WEEKLY RATES, BY AGE GROUPS AND SEX

| Weekly Rates in Dollars | Age Groups in Years | | | | | | | | | | | | | | Weekly Rates in Dollars |
|---|---|---|---|---|---|---|---|---|---|---|---|---|---|---|---|
| | 14–15 | | 16–17 | | 18–20 | | 21–24 | | 25–29 | | 30–34 | | 35–39 | | |
| | Male | Female | Male | Female | Male | Female | Male | Female | Male | Female | Male | Female | Male | Female | |
| Less than $3 00 | 1 | 10 | .... | .... | .... | 1 | .... | .... | .... | 1 | .... | .... | .... | .... | Less than $3 00 |
| $3 00–$3 49... | 1 | 2 | 1 | 14 | .... | .... | .... | .... | .... | .... | .... | .... | .... | .... | ...$3 00– 3 49 |
| 3 50– 3 99... | 1 | .... | .... | 30 | .... | 4 | .... | .... | .... | .... | .... | .... | .... | .... | ... 3 50– 3 99 |
| 4 00– 4 49... | .... | .... | 1 | 2 | .... | 2 | .... | .... | .... | .... | .... | .... | .... | .... | ... 4 00– 4 49 |
| 4 50– 4 99... | .... | .... | .... | 10 | .... | 12 | .... | 4 | .... | .... | .... | .... | .... | .... | ... 4 50– 4 99 |
| 5 00– 5 49... | .... | .... | 2 | 1 | 2 | 29 | .... | 20 | .... | 17 | .... | 5 | .... | .... | ... 5 00– 5 49 |
| 5 50– 5 99... | .... | .... | .... | .... | .... | 1 | .... | .... | .... | 5 | .... | 1 | .... | .... | ... 5 50– 5 99 |
| 6 00– 6 49... | .... | .... | 2 | .... | 1 | 8 | .... | 19 | .... | 20 | .... | 11 | .... | 5 | ... 6 00– 6 49 |
| 6 50– 6 99... | .... | .... | .... | .... | .... | .... | .... | .... | .... | .... | .... | 1 | .... | .... | ... 6 50– 6 99 |
| 7 00– 7 49... | .... | .... | .... | .... | 6 | .... | .... | 10 | 1 | 12 | .... | 7 | .... | 6 | ... 7 00– 7 49 |
| 8 00– 8 99... | .... | .... | .... | .... | 1 | 1 | .... | 2 | .... | 8 | 1 | 3 | .... | 2 | ... 8 00– 8 99 |
| 9 00– 9 99... | .... | .... | .... | .... | 1 | .... | 1 | 4 | 1 | 3 | .... | 2 | 1 | 2 | ... 9 00– 9 99 |
| 10 00–10 99... | .... | .... | .... | .... | 1 | .... | 4 | 2 | 1 | 4 | .... | 3 | 2 | 4 | ...10 00–10 99 |
| 11 00–11 99... | .... | .... | .... | .... | .... | .... | .... | .... | .... | 1 | .... | .... | .... | .... | ...11 00–11 99 |
| 12 00–12 99... | .... | .... | .... | .... | .... | .... | 3 | .... | 3 | 2 | 2 | 6 | .... | 7 | ...12 00–12 99 |
| 13 00–13 99... | .... | .... | .... | .... | .... | .... | .... | .... | 1 | .... | 1 | .... | .... | .... | ...13 00–13 99 |
| 14 00–14 99... | .... | .... | .... | .... | .... | .... | 3 | .... | 4 | .... | 1 | .... | 2 | .... | ...14 00–14 99 |
| 15 00–15 99... | .... | .... | .... | .... | .... | .... | .... | .... | 1 | .... | .... | .... | .... | 2 | ...15 00–15 99 |
| 16 00–17 99... | .... | .... | .... | .... | .... | .... | 1 | .... | 1 | 1 | 4 | .... | 1 | .... | ...16 00–17 99 |
| 18 00–19 99... | .... | .... | .... | .... | .... | .... | .... | .... | 1 | 1 | .... | .... | 4 | .... | ...18 00–19 99 |
| 20 00–24 99... | .... | .... | .... | .... | .... | .... | .... | .... | .... | .... | 2 | 2 | 2 | .... | ...20 00–24 99 |
| 25 00–29 99... | .... | .... | .... | .... | .... | .... | .... | .... | .... | .... | 1 | .... | 1 | 1 | ...25 00–29 99 |
| 30 00–34 99... | .... | .... | .... | .... | .... | .... | .... | .... | .... | .... | .... | .... | .... | 1 | ...30 00–34 99 |
| 35 00–39 99... | .... | .... | .... | .... | .... | .... | .... | .... | .... | .... | 1 | .... | .... | .... | ...35 00–39 99 |
| 40 00 and over. | .... | .... | .... | .... | .... | .... | .... | .... | .... | .... | .... | .... | 1 | .... | .40 00 and over |
| Total..... | 3 | 12 | 6 | 57 | 12 | 58 | 12 | 61 | 14 | 75 | 13 | 41 | 14 | 30 | .....Total |

326. TABLE V, A, 1, a — (*concluded*)

ALBANY

**DEPARTMENT STORES — STOCK AND SALES**

NUMBER AND PER CENT. OF EMPLOYEES EARNING SPECIFIED WEEKLY RATES, BY AGE GROUPS AND SEX

| WEEKLY RATES IN DOLLARS | AGE GROUPS IN YEARS (*concluded*) | | | | | | | | | | | | WEEKLY RATES IN DOLLARS |
|---|---|---|---|---|---|---|---|---|---|---|---|---|---|
| | 40–44 | | 45–54 | | 55–64 | 65 AND OVER | NOT REPORTED | | TOTAL | | CUMULATIVE PER CENT. OF TOTAL | | |
| | Male | Female | Male | Female | Male | Male | Male | Female | Male | Female | Male | Female | |
| Less than $3 00. | ....... | ....... | ....... | ....... | ....... | ....... | 1 | ....... | 2 | 12 | 1.54 | 3.32 | Less than $3 00 |
| $3 00–$3 49.... | ....... | ....... | ....... | ....... | ....... | ....... | ....... | ....... | 2 | 16 | 3.08 | 7.75 | ...$3 00– 3 49 |
| 3 50– 3 99.... | ....... | ....... | ....... | ....... | ....... | ....... | ....... | ....... | 1 | 34 | 3.84 | 17.20 | ... 3 50– 3 99 |
| 4 00– 4 49.... | ....... | ....... | ....... | ....... | ....... | ....... | ....... | ....... | 1 | 4 | 4.62 | 18.30 | ... 4 00– 4 49 |
| 4 50– 4 99.... | ....... | ....... | ....... | ....... | ....... | ....... | ....... | ....... | ....... | 26 | ....... | 25.50 | ... 4 50– 4 99 |
| 5 00– 5 49.... | ....... | 1 | ....... | ....... | ....... | ....... | ....... | ....... | 4 | 73 | 7.70 | 45.70 | ... 5 00– 5 49 |
| 5 50– 5 99.... | ....... | 1 | ....... | ....... | ....... | ....... | ....... | ....... | ....... | 8 | ....... | 48.00 | ... 5 50– 5 99 |
| 6 00– 6 49.... | ....... | 2 | ....... | 1 | ....... | ....... | ....... | 2 | 3 | 68 | 10.00 | 66.75 | ... 6 00– 6 49 |
| 6 50– 6 99.... | ....... | ....... | ....... | ....... | ....... | ....... | ....... | ....... | ....... | 1 | ....... | 67.00 | ... 6 50– 6 99 |
| 7 00– 7 49.... | ....... | 2 | ....... | 2 | ....... | ....... | ....... | ....... | 7 | 39 | 15.75 | 77.75 | ... 7 00– 7 49 |
| 8 00– 8 99.... | ....... | 3 | ....... | 1 | ....... | ....... | ....... | 1 | 2 | 21 | 16.85 | 83.75 | ... 8 00– 8 99 |
| 9 00– 9 99.... | ....... | ....... | ....... | ....... | ....... | ....... | ....... | ....... | 4 | 11 | 20.00 | 86.75 | ... 9 00– 9 99 |
| 10 00–10 99.... | ....... | 1 | ....... | 1 | ....... | ....... | ....... | 1 | 8 | 16 | 26.15 | 91.25 | ...10 00–10 99 |
| 11 00–11 99.... | ....... | ....... | ....... | ....... | ....... | ....... | ....... | ....... | ....... | 1 | ....... | 91.50 | ...11 00–11 99 |
| 12 00–12 99.... | ....... | 4 | 1 | 2 | ....... | ....... | ....... | ....... | 9 | 21 | 33.05 | 97.25 | ...12 00–12 99 |
| 13 00–13 99.... | ....... | ....... | ....... | ....... | ....... | ....... | ....... | ....... | 2 | ....... | 34.60 | ....... | ...13 00–13 99 |
| 14 00–14 99.... | 1 | ....... | ....... | ....... | 1 | ....... | ....... | ....... | 12 | ....... | 43.80 | ....... | ...14 00–14 99 |
| 15 00–15 99.... | 2 | ....... | 1 | ....... | ....... | 1 | ....... | ....... | 5 | 2 | 47.70 | 97.75 | ...15 00–15 99 |
| 16 00–17 99.... | 5 | ....... | 6 | ....... | ....... | ....... | ....... | 1 | 18 | 2 | 61.50 | 98.40 | ...16 00–17 99 |
| 18 00–19 99.... | ....... | ....... | 3 | ....... | ....... | ....... | ....... | ....... | 8 | 1 | 62.70 | 98.60 | ...18 00–19 99 |
| 20 00–24 99.... | 4 | ....... | 9 | 1 | 1 | 1 | ....... | ....... | 19 | 3 | 82.30 | 99.50 | ...20 00–24 99 |
| 25 00–29 99.... | 4 | ....... | 5 | ....... | ....... | ....... | ....... | ....... | 11 | 1 | 90.75 | 99.75 | ...25 00–29 99 |
| 30 00–34 99.... | ....... | ....... | 2 | ....... | 2 | ....... | ....... | ....... | 4 | 1 | 93.80 | 100.00 | ...30 00–34 99 |
| 35 00–39 99.... | 1 | ....... | 1 | ....... | ....... | 1 | ....... | ....... | 4 | ....... | 97.00 | ....... | ...35 00–39 99 |
| 40 00 and over.. | ....... | ....... | 1 | ....... | 1 | 1 | ....... | ....... | 4 | ....... | 100.00 | ....... | .40 00 and over |
| Total...... | 17 | 14 | 29 | 8 | 5 | 4 | 1 | 5 | 130 | 361 | ....... | ....... | .....Total |

327. TABLE VIII, A, 1, a

## ALBANY
## DEPARTMENT STORES — STOCK AND SALES

Number and Per Cent. of Employees Earning Specified Weekly Rates, by Occupation and Sex

| Weekly Rates in Dollars | Superintendents | Buyers | Assistant Buyers and Heads of Stock | | Receiving and Stock Clerks | | Stock People | | Floor Managers | | Sales People | | Messengers, Wrappers and Errand Boys | | Total | | Cumulative Per Cent. of Total | | Weekly Rates in Dollars |
|---|---|---|---|---|---|---|---|---|---|---|---|---|---|---|---|---|---|---|---|
| | Male | Male | Male | Female | Male | Female | Male | Female | Male | Female | Male | Female | Male | Female | Male | Female | Male | Female | |
| Less than $3 00 | .... | .... | .... | .... | 1 | .... | 1 | 1 | .... | .... | .... | 2 | .... | 9 | 2 | 12 | 1.54 | 3.32 | Less than $3 00 |
| $3 00- 3 49 | .... | .... | .... | .... | .... | .... | .... | 3 | .... | .... | .... | 1 | 2 | 12 | 2 | 16 | 3.08 | 7.75 | $3 00- 3 49 |
| 3 50- 3 99 | .... | .... | .... | .... | .... | .... | .... | 1 | .... | .... | .... | 2 | 1 | 31 | 1 | 34 | 3.84 | 17.20 | 3 50- 3 99 |
| 4 00- 4 49 | .... | .... | .... | .... | .... | .... | 1 | 2 | .... | .... | .... | 2 | .... | .... | 1 | 4 | 4.62 | 18.30 | 4 00- 4 49 |
| 4 50- 4 99 | .... | .... | .... | .... | .... | .... | .... | 1 | .... | .... | .... | 17 | .... | 8 | .... | 26 | .... | 25.50 | 4 50- 4 99 |
| 5 00- 5 49 | .... | .... | .... | .... | .... | .... | 3 | .... | .... | .... | 1 | 70 | .... | 3 | 4 | 73 | 7.70 | 45.70 | 5 00- 5 49 |
| 5 50- 5 99 | .... | .... | .... | .... | .... | .... | .... | .... | .... | .... | .... | 7 | .... | 1 | .... | 8 | .... | 48.00 | 5 50- 5 99 |
| 6 00- 6 49 | .... | .... | .... | .... | .... | .... | .... | .... | .... | .... | .... | 67 | 3 | 1 | 3 | 68 | 10.00 | 66.75 | 6 00- 6 49 |
| 6 50- 6 99 | .... | .... | .... | .... | .... | .... | .... | .... | .... | .... | .... | 1 | .... | .... | .... | 1 | .... | 67.00 | 6 50- 6 99 |
| 7 00- 7 49 | .... | .... | .... | 1 | .... | 1 | .... | .... | .... | .... | 2 | 36 | 5 | 1 | 7 | 39 | 15.75 | 77.75 | 7 00- 7 49 |
| 8 00- 8 99 | .... | .... | .... | 1 | .... | .... | .... | .... | .... | .... | 1 | 20 | 1 | .... | 2 | 21 | 16.85 | 83.75 | 8 00- 8 99 |
| 9 00- 9 99 | .... | .... | .... | .... | .... | .... | 1 | .... | .... | .... | 1 | 11 | 2 | .... | 4 | 11 | 20.00 | 86.75 | 9 00- 9 99 |
| 10 00-10 99 | .... | .... | 1 | 2 | .... | .... | 1 | .... | .... | .... | 5 | 14 | 1 | .... | 8 | 16 | 26.15 | 91.25 | 10 00-10 99 |
| 11 00-11 99 | .... | .... | .... | .... | .... | .... | .... | .... | .... | .... | .... | 1 | .... | .... | .... | 1 | .... | 91.50 | 11 00-11 99 |
| 12 00-12 99 | .... | .... | .... | 3 | .... | .... | 1 | .... | .... | .... | 6 | 18 | 2 | .... | 9 | 21 | 33.05 | 97.25 | 12 00-12 99 |
| 13 00-13 99 | .... | .... | .... | .... | .... | .... | .... | .... | .... | .... | 2 | .... | .... | .... | 2 | .... | 34.60 | .... | 13 00-13 99 |
| 14 00-14 99 | .... | .... | 1 | .... | 1 | .... | .... | .... | .... | .... | 10 | .... | .... | .... | 12 | .... | 43.80 | .... | 14 00-14 99 |
| 15 00-15 99 | .... | .... | .... | 1 | .... | .... | .... | .... | .... | .... | 5 | 1 | .... | .... | 5 | 2 | 47.70 | 97.75 | 15 00-15 99 |
| 16 00-17 99 | .... | .... | .... | 2 | 1 | .... | 2 | .... | 1 | .... | 14 | .... | .... | .... | 18 | 2 | 61.50 | 98.40 | 16 00-17 99 |
| 18 00-19 99 | .... | .... | 2 | .... | .... | .... | .... | .... | .... | .... | 6 | 1 | .... | .... | 8 | 1 | 62.70 | 98.60 | 18 00-19 99 |
| 20 00-24 99 | 1 | 4 | .... | 1 | .... | .... | .... | .... | 2 | 1 | 12 | 1 | .... | .... | 19 | 3 | 82.30 | 99.50 | 20 00-24 99 |
| 25 00-29 99 | 1 | 1 | .... | 1 | .... | .... | .... | .... | 2 | .... | 7 | .... | .... | .... | 11 | 1 | 90.75 | 99.75 | 25 00-29 99 |
| 30 00-34 99 | .... | 3 | .... | 1 | .... | .... | .... | .... | .... | .... | 1 | .... | .... | .... | 4 | 1 | 93.80 | 100.00 | 30 00-34 99 |
| 35 00-39 99 | .... | 3 | .... | .... | .... | .... | .... | .... | 1 | .... | .... | .... | .... | .... | 4 | .... | 97.00 | .... | 35 00-39 99 |
| 40 00 and over | .... | 4 | .... | .... | .... | .... | .... | .... | .... | .... | .... | .... | .... | .... | 4 | .... | 100.00 | .... | 40 00 and over |
| Total | 2 | 15 | 4 | 13 | 3 | 1 | 10 | 8 | 6 | 1 | 73 | 272 | 17 | 66 | 130 | 361 | .... | .... | Total |

ALBANY

328. TABLE VI, A, 1, a

DEPARTMENT STORES — STOCK AND SALES

NUMBER AND PER CENT. OF EMPLOYEES CLASSIFIED ACCORDING TO ACTUAL WEEKLY EARNINGS, BY AGE GROUPS AND SEX

| Actual Weekly Earnings in Dollars | Age Groups in Years | | | | | | | | | | | | | | Actual Weekly Earnings in Dollars |
|---|---|---|---|---|---|---|---|---|---|---|---|---|---|---|---|
| | 14–15 | | 16–17 | | 18–20 | | 21–24 | | 25–29 | | 30–34 | | 35–39 | | |
| | Male | Female | Male | Female | Male | Female | Male | Female | Male | Female | Male | Female | Male | Female | |
| Less than $3 00 | 1 | 10 | .... | 3 | .... | 1 | .... | .... | .... | 1 | .... | .... | .... | .... | Less than $3 00 |
| $3 00–$3 49 | 1 | 2 | 1 | 17 | .... | .... | .... | .... | .... | .... | .... | .... | .... | .... | $3 00– 3 49 |
| 3 50– 3 99 | 1 | .... | .... | 26 | .... | 6 | .... | 3 | .... | .... | .... | .... | .... | .... | 3 50– 3 99 |
| 4 00– 4 49 | .... | .... | 1 | 2 | .... | 3 | .... | 1 | .... | 2 | .... | .... | .... | .... | 4 00– 4 49 |
| 4 50– 4 99 | .... | .... | 1 | 8 | .... | 15 | .... | 2 | .... | .... | .... | 1 | .... | .... | 4 50– 4 99 |
| 5 00– 5 49 | .... | .... | 1 | 1 | 2 | 24 | .... | 20 | .... | 16 | .... | 3 | .... | .... | 5 00– 5 49 |
| 5 50– 5 99 | .... | .... | .... | .... | .... | 1 | .... | 1 | .... | 9 | .... | 1 | .... | .... | 5 50– 5 99 |
| 6 00– 6 49 | .... | .... | 2 | .... | 1 | 5 | .... | 17 | .... | 18 | .... | 13 | .... | 5 | 6 00– 6 49 |
| 6 50– 6 99 | .... | .... | .... | .... | .... | 1 | .... | .... | .... | 2 | .... | 1 | .... | .... | 6 50– 6 99 |
| 7 00– 7 49 | .... | .... | .... | .... | 7 | .... | 1 | 9 | 1 | 8 | .... | 5 | .... | 6 | 7 00– 7 49 |
| 7 50– 7 99 | .... | .... | .... | .... | .... | .... | .... | .... | .... | 1 | .... | .... | .... | .... | 7 50– 7 99 |
| 8 00– 8 99 | .... | .... | .... | .... | .... | 1 | .... | 3 | .... | 7 | 1 | 5 | .... | 3 | 8 00– 8 99 |
| 9 00– 9 99 | .... | .... | .... | .... | 1 | .... | 2 | 3 | 1 | 2 | .... | 3 | 1 | 1 | 9 00– 9 99 |
| 10 00–10 99 | .... | .... | .... | .... | 1 | .... | 3 | 2 | 1 | 4 | .... | 3 | 1 | 4 | 10 00–10 99 |
| 11 00–11 99 | .... | .... | .... | .... | .... | .... | .... | .... | .... | 1 | .... | .... | 1 | 1 | 11 00–11 99 |
| 12 00–12 99 | .... | .... | .... | .... | .... | .... | 3 | .... | 3 | 1 | 2 | 3 | .... | 2 | 12 00–12 99 |
| 13 00–13 99 | .... | .... | .... | .... | .... | .... | .... | .... | 1 | .... | 1 | .... | .... | .... | 13 00–13 99 |
| 14 00–14 99 | .... | .... | .... | .... | .... | .... | 2 | .... | 2 | 1 | 1 | 1 | 2 | 2 | 14 00–14 99 |
| 15 00–15 99 | .... | .... | .... | .... | .... | .... | .... | .... | 3 | .... | 1 | .... | .... | 2 | 15 00–15 99 |
| 16 00–17 99 | .... | .... | .... | .... | .... | .... | 1 | .... | 1 | 1 | 3 | .... | 1 | 2 | 16 00–17 99 |
| 18 00–19 99 | .... | .... | .... | .... | .... | .... | .... | .... | 1 | 1 | .... | .... | 4 | .... | 18 00–19 99 |
| 20 00–24 99 | .... | .... | .... | .... | .... | .... | .... | .... | .... | .... | 2 | 2 | 2 | .... | 20 00–24 99 |
| 25 00–29 99 | .... | .... | .... | .... | .... | .... | .... | .... | .... | .... | 1 | .... | 1 | 1 | 25 00–29 99 |
| 30 00–34 99 | .... | .... | .... | .... | .... | .... | .... | .... | .... | .... | .... | .... | .... | 1 | 30 00–34 99 |
| 35 00–39 99 | .... | .... | .... | .... | .... | .... | .... | .... | .... | .... | 1 | .... | .... | .... | 35 00–39 99 |
| 40 00 and over | .... | .... | .... | .... | .... | .... | .... | .... | .... | .... | .... | .... | 1 | .... | 40 00 and over |
| Not reported | .... | .... | .... | .... | .... | 1 | .... | .... | .... | .... | .... | .... | .... | .... | Not reported |
| Total | 3 | 12 | 6 | 57 | 12 | 58 | 12 | 61 | 14 | 75 | 13 | 41 | 14 | 30 | Total |

328. TABLE VI, A, 1, a (*concluded*)

ALBANY

**DEPARTMENT STORES — STOCK AND SALES**

NUMBER AND PER CENT. OF EMPLOYEES CLASSIFIED ACCORDING TO ACTUAL WEEKLY EARNINGS, BY AGE GROUPS AND SEX

| ACTUAL WEEKLY EARNINGS IN DOLLARS | AGE GROUPS IN YEARS (*concluded*) 40–44 | | 45–54 | | 55–64 | 65 AND OVER | NOT REPORTED | | TOTAL | | CUMULATIVE PER CENT. OF TOTAL | | ACTUAL WEEKLY EARNINGS IN DOLLARS |
|---|---|---|---|---|---|---|---|---|---|---|---|---|---|
| | Male | Female | Male | Female | Male | Male | Male | Female | Male | Female | Male | Female | |
| Less than $3 00. | ....... | ....... | ....... | ....... | ....... | ....... | 1 | ....... | 2 | 15 | 1.54 | 4.17 | Less than $3 00 |
| $3 00–$3 49.... | ....... | ....... | ....... | ....... | ....... | ....... | ....... | ....... | 2 | 19 | 3.08 | 9.45 | ...$3 00– 3 49 |
| 3 50– 3 99.... | ....... | ....... | ....... | ....... | ....... | ....... | ....... | ....... | 1 | 35 | 3.84 | 19.18 | ... 3 50– 3 99 |
| 4 00– 4 99.... | ....... | ....... | ....... | ....... | ....... | ....... | ....... | ....... | 1 | 8 | 4.62 | 21.40 | ... 4 00– 4 49 |
| 4 50– 4 99.... | ....... | ....... | ....... | ....... | ....... | ....... | ....... | ....... | 1 | 26 | 5.39 | 28.60 | ... 4 50– 4 99 |
| 5 00– 5 49.... | ....... | 1 | ....... | ....... | ....... | ....... | ....... | ....... | 3 | 65 | 7.70 | 46.70 | ... 5 00– 5 49 |
| 5 50– 5 99.... | ....... | 1 | ....... | ....... | ....... | ....... | ....... | ....... | ....... | 13 | ....... | 50.30 | ... 5 50– 5 99 |
| 6 00– 6 49.... | ....... | 2 | ....... | 2 | ....... | ....... | ....... | 2 | 3 | 64 | 10.00 | 68.10 | ... 6 00– 6 49 |
| 6 50– 6 99.... | ....... | ....... | ....... | ....... | ....... | ....... | ....... | 2 | ....... | 6 | ....... | 69.75 | ... 6 50– 6 99 |
| 7 00– 7 49.... | ....... | 2 | ....... | 1 | ....... | ....... | ....... | ....... | 9 | 31 | 16.85 | 78.40 | ... 7 00– 7 49 |
| 7 50– 7 99.... | ....... | ....... | ....... | ....... | ....... | ....... | ....... | ....... | ....... | 1 | ....... | 78.70 | ... 7 50– 7 99 |
| 8 00– 8 99.... | ....... | 3 | ....... | 1 | ....... | ....... | ....... | ....... | 1 | 23 | 17.62 | 85.00 | ... 8 00– 8 99 |
| 9 00– 9 99.... | ....... | ....... | ....... | ....... | ....... | ....... | ....... | ....... | 5 | 9 | 21.46 | 87.50 | ... 9 00– 9 99 |
| 10 00–10 99.... | ....... | 1 | ....... | 2 | ....... | ....... | ....... | ....... | 6 | 16 | 26.15 | 92.00 | ...10 00–10 99 |
| 11 00–11 99.... | ....... | ....... | ....... | ....... | ....... | ....... | ....... | ....... | 1 | 2 | 26.92 | 92.50 | ...11 00–11 99 |
| 12 00–12 99.... | ....... | 4 | 1 | 1 | ....... | ....... | ....... | ....... | 9 | 11 | 33.82 | 95.50 | ...12 00–12 99 |
| 13 00–13 99.... | ....... | ....... | ....... | ....... | ....... | ....... | ....... | ....... | 2 | ....... | 35.37 | ....... | ...13 00–13 99 |
| 14 00–14 99.... | 1 | ....... | ....... | ....... | 1 | ....... | ....... | ....... | 9 | 4 | 42.25 | 96.50 | ...14 00–14 99 |
| 15 00–15 99.... | 2 | ....... | 1 | ....... | ....... | ....... | ....... | ....... | 7 | 2 | 47.70 | 97.25 | ...15 00–15 99 |
| 16 00–17 99.... | 4 | ....... | 6 | ....... | ....... | 1 | ....... | 1 | 17 | 4 | 60.73 | 98.40 | ...16 00–17 99 |
| 18 00–19 99.... | 1 | ....... | 3 | ....... | ....... | ....... | ....... | ....... | 9 | 1 | 62.70 | 98.60 | ...18 00–19 99 |
| 20 00–24 99.... | 4 | ....... | 9 | 1 | 1 | 1 | ....... | ....... | 19 | 3 | 82.30 | 99.50 | ...20 00–24 99 |
| 25 00–29 99.... | 4 | ....... | 5 | ....... | ....... | ....... | ....... | ....... | 11 | 1 | 90.75 | 99.75 | ...25 00–29 99 |
| 30 00–34 99.... | ....... | ....... | 2 | ....... | 2 | ....... | ....... | ....... | 4 | 1 | 93.80 | 100.00 | ...30 00–34 99 |
| 35 00–39 99.... | 1 | ....... | 1 | ....... | ....... | 1 | ....... | ....... | 4 | ....... | 97.00 | ....... | ...35 00–39 99 |
| 40 00 and over.. | ....... | ....... | 1 | ....... | 1 | 1 | ....... | ....... | 4 | ....... | 100.00 | ....... | .40 00 and over |
| Not reported.... | ....... | ....... | ....... | ....... | ....... | ....... | ....... | ....... | ....... | 1 | ....... | ....... | ...Not reported |
| Total...... | 17 | 14 | 29 | 8 | 5 | 4 | 1 | 5 | 130 | 361 | ....... | ....... | .....Total |

329. TABLE IX, A, 1, a

ALBANY

DEPARTMENT STORES — STOCK AND SALES

Number and Per Cent. of Employees Classified According to Actual Weekly Earnings, by Occupation and Sex

| Actual Weekly Earnings in Dollars | Occupation | | | | | | | | | | | | | | | | | | Actual Weekly Earnings in Dollars |
|---|---|---|---|---|---|---|---|---|---|---|---|---|---|---|---|---|---|---|---|
| | Superintendents | Buyers | Assistant Buyers and Heads of Stock | | Receiving and Stock Clerks | | Stock People | | Floor Managers | | Sales People | | Messengers, Wrappers and Errand Boys | | Total | | Cumulative Per Cent. of Total | | |
| | Male | Male | Male | Female | Male | Female | Male | Female | Male | Female | Male | Female | Male | Female | Male | Female | Male | Female | |
| Less than $3 00 | | | | | 1 | | 1 | 1 | | | | 2 | | 12 | 2 | 15 | 1.54 | 4.17 | Less than $3 00 |
| $3 00-$3 49 | | | | | | | | 3 | | | | 1 | 2 | 15 | 2 | 19 | 3.08 | 9.45 | $3 00- 3 49 |
| 3 50- 3 99 | | | | | | | | 3 | | | | 5 | 1 | 27 | 1 | 35 | 3.84 | 19.18 | 3 50- 3 99 |
| 4 00- 4 49 | | | | | | | 1 | | | | | 7 | | 1 | 1 | 8 | 4.62 | 21.40 | 4 00- 4 49 |
| 4 50- 4 99 | | | | | | | 1 | 1 | | | | 19 | | 6 | 1 | 26 | 5.39 | 28.60 | 4 50- 4 99 |
| 5 00- 5 49 | | | | | | | 2 | | | | 1 | 62 | | 3 | 3 | 65 | 7.70 | 46.70 | 5 00- 5 49 |
| 5 50- 5 99 | | | | | | | | | | | | 12 | | 1 | | 13 | | 50.30 | 5 50- 5 99 |
| 6 00- 6 49 | | | | | | | | | | | | 64 | 3 | | 3 | 64 | 10.00 | 68.10 | 6 00- 6 49 |
| 6 50- 6 99 | | | | | | | | | | | | 6 | | | | 6 | | 69.75 | 6 50- 6 99 |
| 7 00- 7 49 | | | | 1 | | 1 | | | | | 3 | 28 | 6 | 1 | 9 | 31 | 16.85 | 78.40 | 7 00- 7 49 |
| 7 50- 7 99 | | | | | | | | | | | | 1 | | | | 1 | | 78.70 | 7 50- 7 99 |
| 8 00- 8 99 | | | | 1 | | | | | | | 1 | 22 | | | 1 | 23 | 17.62 | 85.00 | 8 00- 8 99 |
| 9 00- 9 99 | | | | | | | 1 | | | | 2 | 9 | 2 | | 5 | 9 | 21.46 | 87.50 | 9 00- 9 99 |
| 10 00-10 99 | | | 1 | 3 | | | 1 | | | | 3 | 13 | 1 | | 6 | 16 | 26.15 | 92.00 | 10 00-10 99 |
| 11 00-11 99 | | | | | | | | | | | 1 | 2 | | | 1 | 2 | 26.92 | 92.50 | 11 00-11 99 |
| 12 00-12 99 | | | | 2 | | | 1 | | | | 6 | 9 | 2 | | 9 | 11 | 33.82 | 95.50 | 12 00-12 99 |
| 13 00-13 99 | | | | | | | | | | | 2 | | | | 2 | | 35.37 | | 13 00-13 99 |
| 14 00-14 99 | | | 1 | | 1 | | | | | | 7 | 4 | | | 9 | 4 | 42.25 | 96.50 | 14 00-14 99 |
| 15 00-15 99 | | | | | | | | | | | 7 | 2 | | | 7 | 2 | 47.70 | 97.25 | 15 00-15 99 |
| 16 00-17 99 | | | | 3 | 1 | | 2 | | 1 | | 13 | 1 | | | 17 | 4 | 60.73 | 98.40 | 16 00-17 99 |
| 18 00-19 99 | | | 2 | | | | | | | | 7 | 1 | | | 9 | 1 | 62.70 | 98.60 | 18 00-19 99 |
| 20 00-24 99 | 1 | 4 | | 1 | | | | | 2 | 1 | 12 | 1 | | | 19 | 3 | 82.30 | 99.50 | 20 00 24 99 |
| 25 00 29 99 | 1 | 1 | | 1 | | | | | 2 | | 7 | | | | 11 | 1 | 90.75 | 99.75 | 25 00 29 99 |
| 30 00 34 99 | | 3 | | 1 | | | | | | | 1 | | | | 4 | 1 | 93.80 | 100.00 | 30 00 34 99 |
| 35 00 39 99 | | 3 | | | | | | | 1 | | | | | | 4 | | 97.00 | | 35 00 39 99 |
| 40 00 and over | | 4 | | | | | | | | | | | | | 4 | | 100.00 | | 40 00 and over |
| Not reported | | | | | | | | | | | | 1 | | | | 1 | | | Not reported |
| Total | 2 | 15 | 4 | 13 | 3 | 1 | 10 | 8 | 6 | 1 | 73 | 272 | 17 | 66 | 130 | 361 | | | Total |

ALBANY

DEPARTMENT STORES — OFFICE, SHIPPING AND DELIVERY, MANUFACTURING, PLANT

330. TABLE XV, A, 1, b, c, d, e NUMBER OF EMPLOYEES EARNING SPECIFIED WEEKLY RATES BY DEPARTMENT AND SEX

| WEEKLY RATES IN DOLLARS | DEPARTMENT | | | | | | | | | | | WEEKLY RATES IN DOLLARS |
|---|---|---|---|---|---|---|---|---|---|---|---|---|
| | OFFICE | | SHIPPING AND DELIVERY | MANUFACTURING | | PLANT | | TOTAL | | CUMULATIVE PER CENT. OF TOTAL | | |
| | Male | Female | Male | Male | Female | Male | Female | Male | Female | Male | Female | |
| Less than $3 00 | 1 | ........ | 3 | ........ | ........ | ........ | ........ | 4 | ........ | 2.30 | ........ | Less than $3 00 |
| $3 00-$3 49... | ........ | 3 | ........ | 1 | 1 | ........ | ........ | 1 | 4 | 2.90 | 2.20 | ...$3 00- 3.49 |
| 3 50- 3 99... | 4 | 1 | 1 | ........ | ........ | ........ | ........ | 5 | 1 | 5.80 | 2.80 | ... 3 50- 3 99 |
| 4 00- 4 49... | ........ | 3 | 3 | ........ | 2 | ........ | 1 | 3 | 6 | 7.50 | 6.20 | ... 4 00- 4 49 |
| 4 50- 4 99... | 1 | 4 | 12 | 1 | ........ | ........ | ........ | 14 | 4 | 15.60 | 8.40 | ... 4 50- 4 99 |
| 5 00- 5 49... | 2 | 14 | 1 | ........ | 3 | ........ | 1 | 3 | 18 | 17.40 | 18.50 | ... 5 00- 5 49 |
| 5 50- 5 99... | ........ | 1 | ........ | ........ | ........ | ........ | ........ | ........ | 1 | ........ | 19.10 | ... 5 50- 5 99 |
| 6 00- 6 49... | 2 | 34 | 3 | 1 | 15 | ........ | 4 | 6 | 53 | 20.80 | 48.90 | ... 6 00- 6 49 |
| 7 00- 7 49... | ........ | 16 | ........ | 1 | 19 | ........ | 1 | 1 | 36 | 21.40 | 69.10 | ... 7 00- 7 49 |
| 7 50- 7 99... | ........ | 1 | ........ | ........ | ........ | ........ | ........ | ........ | 1 | ........ | 69.70 | ... 7 50- 7 99 |
| 8 00- 8 99... | 1 | 10 | 1 | ........ | 18 | 9 | ........ | 1 | 28 | 27.80 | 85.50 | ... 8 00- 8 99 |
| 9 00- 9 99... | 3 | 4 | 3 | 2 | 4 | 2 | ........ | 10 | 8 | 33.60 | 89.90 | ... 9 00- 9 99 |
| 10 00-10 99... | 1 | 4 | 2 | ........ | 2 | 2 | 1 | 5 | 7 | 36.40 | 93.90 | ...10 00-10 99 |
| 11 00-11 99... | ........ | 1 | 3 | 1 | ........ | 1 | ........ | 5 | 1 | 39.40 | 94.40 | ...11 00-11 99 |
| 12 00-12 99... | 4 | ........ | 6 | 2 | 3 | 7 | ........ | 19 | 3 | 50.30 | 96.00 | ...12 00-12 99 |
| 13 00-13 99... | 2 | ........ | 1 | 1 | ........ | 1 | ........ | 5 | ........ | 53.20 | ........ | ...13 00-13 99 |
| 14 00-14 99... | 3 | ........ | 2 | 2 | 1 | 2 | ........ | 9 | 1 | 58 40 | 96.60 | ...14 00-14 99 |
| 15 00-15 99... | 2 | 1 | 14 | 3 | 2 | 3 | ........ | 22 | 3 | 71.10 | 98.40 | ...15 00-15 99 |
| 16 00-17 99... | 1 | 1 | 1 | 12 | ........ | 1 | ........ | 15 | 1 | 79.80 | 98.90 | ...16 00-17 99 |
| 18 00-19 99... | 2 | ........ | 1 | 7 | 1 | 1 | ........ | 11 | 1 | 81.10 | 99.50 | ...18 00-19 99 |
| 20 00-24 99... | 1 | ........ | 2 | 7 | 1 | 4 | ........ | 14 | 1 | 94.30 | 100.00 | ...20 00-24 99 |
| 25 00-29 99... | 2 | ........ | ........ | ........ | ........ | 1 | ........ | 3 | ........ | 96.00 | ........ | ...25 00-29 99 |
| 30 00-34 99... | 2 | ........ | ........ | ........ | ........ | ........ | ........ | 2 | ........ | 97.20 | ........ | ...30 00-34 99 |
| 35 00-39 99... | 2 | ........ | ........ | ........ | ........ | ........ | ........ | 2 | ........ | 98.40 | ........ | ...35 00-39 99 |
| 40 00 and over. | 3 | ........ | ........ | ........ | ........ | ........ | ........ | 3 | ........ | 100.00 | ........ | .40 00 and over |
| Total..... | 39 | 98 | 59 | 41 | 72 | 34 | 8 | 173 | 178 | ........ | ........ | .....Total |

331. TABLE XVI, A, 1, b, c, d, e

ALBANY

**DEPARTMENT STORES — OFFICE, SHIPPING AND DELIVERY, MANUFACTURING, PLANT**

Number of Employees Classified According to Actual Weekly Earnings, by Department and Sex

| Actual Weekly Earnings in Dollars | Department: Office | | Department: Shipping and Delivery | Department: Manufacturing | | Department: Plant | | Department: Total | | Department: Cumulative Per Cent. of Total | | Actual Weekly Earnings in Dollars |
|---|---|---|---|---|---|---|---|---|---|---|---|---|
| | Male | Female | Male | Male | Female | Male | Female | Male | Female | Male | Female | |
| Less than $3 00 | 1 | 2 | 4 | ........ | ........ | ........ | ........ | 5 | 2 | 2.90 | 1.10 | Less than $3 00 |
| $3 00–$3 49... | ........ | 2 | ........ | 1 | 1 | ........ | ........ | 1 | 3 | 3.50 | 2.80 | ...$3 00– 3 49 |
| 3 50– 3 99... | 4 | 3 | 1 | ........ | ........ | ........ | ........ | 5 | 3 | 6.40 | 4.50 | ... 3 50– 3 99 |
| 4 00– 4 49... | ........ | 2 | 3 | ........ | 3 | ........ | 1 | 3 | 6 | 8.10 | 7.90 | ... 4 00– 4 49 |
| 4 50– 4 99... | 1 | 6 | 12 | 1 | ........ | ........ | ........ | 14 | 6 | 16.20 | 11.20 | ... 4 50– 4 99 |
| 5 00– 5 49... | 2 | 12 | 1 | ........ | 4 | ........ | 1 | 3 | 17 | 17.90 | 20.80 | ... 5 00– 5 49 |
| 5 50– 5 99... | ........ | 4 | ........ | ........ | 3 | ........ | ........ | ........ | 7 | ........ | 24.70 | ... 5 50– 5 99 |
| 6 00– 6 49... | 3 | 31 | 3 | 1 | 13 | ........ | 4 | 7 | 48 | 22.00 | 51.70 | ... 6 00– 6 49 |
| 6 50– 6 99... | ........ | ........ | ........ | ........ | ........ | 1 | ........ | 1 | ........ | 22.60 | ........ | ... 6 50– 6 99 |
| 7 00– 7 49... | ........ | 15 | ........ | 1 | 16 | ........ | 1 | 1 | 32 | 23.10 | 69.70 | ... 7 00– 7 49 |
| 7 50– 7 99... | ........ | 1 | ........ | ........ | ........ | ........ | ........ | ........ | 1 | ........ | 70.30 | ... 7 50– 7 99 |
| 8 00– 8 99... | 1 | 10 | 2 | ........ | 19 | 8 | ........ | 11 | 29 | 29.50 | 86.50 | ... 8 00– 8 99 |
| 9 00– 9 99... | 3 | 4 | 4 | 2 | 3 | 2 | ........ | 11 | 7 | 35.80 | 90.50 | ... 9 00– 9 99 |
| 10 00–10 99... | 1 | 3 | 2 | ........ | 2 | 2 | 1 | 5 | 6 | 38.70 | 93.90 | ...10 00–10 99 |
| 11 00–11 99... | 1 | 1 | 2 | 1 | ........ | ........ | ........ | 4 | 1 | 41 00 | 94.50 | ...11 00–11 99 |
| 12 00–12 99... | 3 | ........ | 5 | 2 | 3 | 7 | ........ | 17 | 3 | 50.90 | 96.10 | ...12 00–12 99 |
| 13 00–13 99... | 1 | ........ | 1 | 1 | ........ | 2 | ........ | 5 | ........ | 53.80 | ........ | ...13 00–13 99 |
| 14 00–14 99... | 3 | ........ | 1 | 2 | 1 | 3 | ........ | 9 | 1 | 59.00 | 96.60 | ...14 00–14 99 |
| 15 00–15 99... | 2 | 1 | 14 | 4 | 2 | 2 | ........ | 22 | 3 | 71.70 | 98.50 | ...15 00–15 99 |
| 16 00–17 99... | 1 | 1 | 1 | 12 | ........ | 1 | ........ | 15 | 1 | 80.40 | 99.00 | ...16 00–17 99 |
| 18 00–19 99... | 2 | ........ | 1 | 6 | 1 | 1 | ........ | 10 | 1 | 86.10 | 99.50 | ...18 00–19 99 |
| 20 00–24 99... | 1 | ........ | 2 | 7 | 1 | 4 | ........ | 14 | 1 | 94.30 | 100.00 | ...20 00–24 99 |
| 25 00–29 99... | 2 | ........ | ........ | ........ | ........ | 1 | ........ | 3 | ........ | 97.00 | ........ | ...25 00–29 99 |
| 30 00–34 99... | 2 | ........ | ........ | ........ | ........ | ........ | ........ | 2 | ........ | 97.20 | ........ | ...30 00–34 99 |
| 35 00–39 99... | 2 | ........ | ........ | ........ | ........ | ........ | ........ | 2 | ........ | 98.30 | ........ | ...35 00–39 99 |
| 40 00 and over. | 3 | ........ | ........ | ........ | ........ | ........ | ........ | 3 | ........ | 100.00 | ........ | .40 00 and over |
| Total..... | 39 | 98 | 59 | 41 | 72 | 34 | 8 | 173 | 178 | ........ | ........ | .....Total |

332. TABLE XVII, A, 1, b, c, d, e

ALBANY

**DEPARTMENT STORES — OFFICE, SHIPPING AND DELIVERY, MANUFACTURING. PLANT,**

NUMBER OF EMPLOYEES CLASSIFIED BY AGE GROUPS ACCORDING TO DEPARTMENT AND SEX

| AGE GROUPS IN YEARS | DEPARTMENT | | | | | | | | | | | AGE GROUPS IN YEARS |
|---|---|---|---|---|---|---|---|---|---|---|---|---|
| | OFFICE | | SHIPPING AND DELIVERY | MANUFACTURING | | PLANT | | TOTAL | | CUMULATIVE PER CENT. OF TOTAL | | |
| | Male | Female | Male | Male | Female | Male | Female | Male | Female | Male | Female | |
| 14–15........ | 4 | ........ | 11 | ........ | ........ | ........ | ........ | 15 | ........ | 8.70 | ........ | .........14–15 |
| 16–17........ | 2 | 10 | 11 | 3 | 1 | ........ | 1 | 16 | 12 | 9.30 | 7.10 | .........16–17 |
| 18–20........ | 4 | 27 | 2 | 2 | 5 | 4 | ........ | 12 | 32 | 7.00 | 18.18 | .........18–20 |
| 21–24........ | 6 | 32 | 11 | 1 | 9 | 6 | ........ | 24 | 41 | 13.90 | 24.10 | .........21–24 |
| 25–29........ | 5 | 17 | 6 | 6 | 7 | 4 | ........ | 21 | 24 | 12.20 | 14.10 | .........25–29 |
| 30–34........ | 2 | 4 | 6 | 9 | 5 | 2 | 1 | 19 | 10 | 11.10 | 5.90 | .........30–34 |
| 35–39........ | 5 | 5 | 3 | 3 | 10 | 4 | 2 | 15 | 17 | 8.70 | 10.00 | .........35–39 |
| 40–44........ | 1 | 2 | 2 | 6 | 11 | 4 | 3 | 13 | 16 | 7.60 | 9.40 | .........40–44 |
| 45–54........ | 6 | 1 | 4 | 8 | 8 | 5 | 1 | 23 | 10 | 13.40 | 5.90 | .........45–54 |
| 55–64........ | 3 | ........ | 2 | 2 | 8 | 4 | ........ | 11 | 8 | 6.40 | 4.70 | .........55–64 |
| 65 and over.... | 1 | ........ | ........ | 1 | ........ | 1 | ........ | 3 | ........ | 1.70 | ........ | ....65 and over |
| Not reported... | ........ | ........ | 1 | ........ | 8 | ........ | ........ | 1 | 8 | ........ | ........ | ...Not reported |
| Total..... | 39 | 98 | 59 | 41 | 72 | 34 | 8 | 173 | 178 | 100.00 | 100.00 | .....Total |

ALBANY

THE MEN'S SHIRT INDUSTRY — FACTORY WORKERS

333. TABLE V, B, a NUMBER AND PER CENT. OF EMPLOYEES EARNING SPECIFIED WEEKLY RATES, BY AGE GROUPS AND SEX

| WEEKLY RATES IN DOLLARS | AGE GROUPS IN YEARS | | | | | | | | | | | WEEKLY RATES IN DOLLARS |
|---|---|---|---|---|---|---|---|---|---|---|---|---|
| | 14–15 | | 16–17 | | 18–20 | | 21–24 | | 25–29 | | 30–34 | |
| | Male | Female | Male | Female | Male | Female | Male | Female | Male | Female | Female | |
| $4 00–$4 49 | | 3 | | 7 | | 1 | | | | | | $4 00–$4 49 |
| 4 50– 4 99 | | | 1 | 7 | | 5 | | | | | | 4 50– 4 99 |
| 5 00– 5 49 | | 1 | | 9 | | 10 | | 4 | | 1 | | 5 00– 5 49 |
| 5 50– 5 99 | | | | 1 | | | | 1 | | | | 5 50– 5 99 |
| 6 00– 6 49 | 1 | | | 4 | | 14 | | 9 | | 4 | | 6 00– 6 49 |
| 6 50– 6 99 | | | | | | 2 | | 2 | | 2 | | 6 50– 6 99 |
| 7 00– 7 49 | | | | | 1 | 7 | | 2 | | 2 | 5 | 7 00– 7 49 |
| 7 50– 7 99 | | | | | | 1 | | 1 | | | | 7 50– 7 99 |
| 8 00– 8 99 | | | | | | 2 | | 1 | | 2 | 2 | 8 00– 8 99 |
| 9 00– 9 99 | | | 1 | | 1 | | | 4 | | 4 | 3 | 9 00– 9 99 |
| 10 00–10 99 | | | | | 1 | 1 | | 5 | | 2 | 3 | 10 00–10 99 |
| 11 00–11 99 | | | | | | | | | | 2 | 1 | 11 00–11 99 |
| 12 00–12 99 | | | | | | | 1 | | | 1 | | 12 00–12 99 |
| 13 00–13 99 | | | | | | | | | | 2 | 1 | 13 00–13 99 |
| 15 00–15 99 | | | | | | | 1 | | | | | 15 00–15 99 |
| 16 00–17 99 | | | | | | | | | 1 | | | 16 00–17 99 |
| 18 00–19 99 | | | | | | | | | | 1 | | 18 00–19 99 |
| 20 00–24 99 | | | | | | | | | 1 | | | 20 00–24 99 |
| Not reported | | | | | | | | 1 | | | | Not reported |
| Total | 1 | 4 | 2 | 28 | 3 | 43 | 2 | 30 | 2 | 23 | 15 | Total |

ALBANY

333. TABLE V, B, a — (*concluded*) THE MEN'S SHIRT INDUSTRY — FACTORY WORKERS

Number and Per Cent. of Employees Earning Specified Weekly Rates, by Age Groups and Sex

| Weekly Rates in Dollars | Age Groups in Years (*concluded*) | | | | | | | | | | | | Weekly Rates in Dollars |
|---|---|---|---|---|---|---|---|---|---|---|---|---|---|
| | 35–39 | | 40–44 | | 45–54 | | 55–64 | Not reported | Total | | Cumulative per cent. of total | | |
| | Male | Female | Male | Female | Male | Female | Female | Female | Male | Female | Male | Female | |
| 4 00–$4 49 | ....... | ....... | ....... | ....... | ....... | ....... | ....... | ....... | ....... | 11 | ....... | 7.0 | $4 00–$4 49 |
| 4 50– 4 99 | ....... | ....... | ....... | ....... | ....... | ....... | ....... | ....... | 1 | 12 | 7.7 | 14.6 | 4 50– 4 99 |
| 5 00– 5 49 | ....... | 1 | ....... | ....... | ....... | ....... | ....... | ....... | ....... | 26 | ....... | 31.2 | 5 00– 5 49 |
| 5 50– 5 99 | ....... | ....... | ....... | ....... | ....... | ....... | ....... | ....... | ....... | 2 | ....... | 32.5 | 5 50– 5 99 |
| 6 00– 6 49 | ....... | 2 | ....... | ....... | ....... | 1 | ....... | 1 | 1 | 35 | 15.4 | 54.8 | 6 00– 6 49 |
| 6 50– 6 99 | ....... | ....... | ....... | ....... | ....... | ....... | ....... | ....... | ....... | 6 | ....... | 58.6 | 6 50– 6 99 |
| 7 00– 7 49 | ....... | 1 | ....... | ....... | ....... | ....... | 1 | ....... | 1 | 18 | 23.1 | 70.1 | 7 00– 7 49 |
| 7 50– 7 99 | ....... | ....... | ....... | ....... | ....... | ....... | ....... | ....... | ....... | 2 | ....... | 71.4 | 7 50– 7 99 |
| 8 00– 8 99 | ....... | 1 | ....... | ....... | ....... | ....... | ....... | ....... | ....... | 8 | ....... | 76.5 | 8 00– 8 99 |
| 9 00– 9 99 | ....... | 1 | ....... | ....... | ....... | 1 | ....... | ....... | 2 | 13 | 38.5 | 84.7 | 9 00– 9 99 |
| 10 00–10 99 | ....... | 1 | ....... | ....... | ....... | ....... | ....... | 1 | 1 | 13 | 46.2 | 93.0 | 10 00–10 99 |
| 11 00–11 99 | ....... | ....... | ....... | ....... | ....... | ....... | ....... | ....... | ....... | 3 | ....... | 95.0 | 11 00–11 99 |
| 12 00–12 99 | ....... | ....... | ....... | ....... | ....... | ....... | ....... | ....... | 1 | 1 | 53.9 | 95.5 | 12 00–12 99 |
| 13 00–13 99 | ....... | ....... | ....... | ....... | 1 | ....... | ....... | ....... | 1 | 3 | 61.6 | 97.5 | 13 00–13 99 |
| 14 00–14 99 | ....... | 1 | ....... | ....... | ....... | ....... | ....... | ....... | ....... | 1 | ....... | 98.1 | 14 00–14 99 |
| 15 00–15 99 | 1 | 1 | ....... | 1 | ....... | ....... | ....... | ....... | 2 | 2 | 77.0 | 99.4 | 15 00–15 99 |
| 16 00–17 99 | ....... | ....... | ....... | ....... | ....... | ....... | ....... | ....... | 1 | ....... | 84.6 | ....... | 16 00–17 99 |
| 18 00–19 99 | ....... | ....... | ....... | ....... | ....... | ....... | ....... | ....... | ....... | 1 | ....... | 100.0 | 18 00–19 99 |
| 20 00–24 99 | ....... | ....... | ....... | ....... | ....... | ....... | ....... | ....... | 1 | ....... | 92.5 | ....... | 20 00–24 99 |
| 30 00–34 99 | ....... | ....... | 1 | ....... | ....... | ....... | ....... | ....... | 1 | ....... | 100.0 | ....... | 30 00–34 99 |
| Not reported | ....... | ....... | ....... | ....... | ....... | ....... | ....... | ....... | ....... | 1 | ....... | ....... | Not reported |
| Total | 1 | 9 | 1 | 1 | 1 | 2 | 1 | 2 | 13 | 158 | ....... | ....... | Total |

ALBANY
THE MEN'S SHIRT INDUSTRY — FACTORY WORKERS

334. TABLE VIII, B, a NUMBER AND PER CENT. OF EMPLOYEES EARNING SPECIFIED WEEKLY RATES, BY OCCUPATION AND SEX

| WEEKLY RATES IN DOLLARS | OCCUPATION | | | | | | | | | | | | | | | | | | WEEKLY RATES IN DOLLARS |
|---|---|---|---|---|---|---|---|---|---|---|---|---|---|---|---|---|---|---|---|
| | CUTTERS | TRIMMERS | FOREMEN AND FOREWOMEN | | OPERATORS | FLOOR WORK | LAUNDRY HELPERS | STARCHERS AND DAMPNERS | IRONERS AND PRESSERS | EXAMINERS | | FOLDERS | PACKERS | | TOTAL | | CUMULATIVE PER CENT. OF TOTAL | | |
| | Male | Female | Male | Female | Female | Female | Female | Female | Female | Male | Female | Female | Male | Female | Male | Female | Male | Female | |
| $4 00-$4 49 | ........ | 1 | ..... | ..... | 2 | 4 | ........ | 3 | ........ | ..... | 1 | ........ | ..... | ..... | ..... | 11 | ..... | 7.00 | $4 00-$4 49 |
| 4 50- 4 99 | ........ | ........ | ..... | ..... | 2 | 1 | 1 | ........ | ........ | 1 | 6 | ........ | ..... | 1 | 1 | 12 | 7.70 | 14.60 | 4 50- 4 99 |
| 5 00- 5 49 | ........ | ........ | ..... | ..... | 2 | 5 | 1 | ........ | 1 | ..... | 17 | ........ | ..... | ..... | ..... | 26 | ..... | 31.20 | 5 00- 5 49 |
| 5 50- 5 99 | ........ | ........ | ..... | ..... | ........ | ........ | ........ | ........ | ........ | ..... | 2 | ........ | ..... | ..... | ..... | 2 | ..... | 32.50 | 5 50- 5 99 |
| 6 00- 6 49 | ........ | ........ | ..... | ..... | ........ | 2 | 1 | ........ | ........ | ..... | 32 | ........ | 1 | ..... | 1 | 35 | 15.40 | 54.80 | 6 00- 6 49 |
| 6 50- 6 99 | ........ | ........ | ..... | ..... | 1 | ........ | ........ | ........ | ........ | ..... | 5 | ........ | ..... | ..... | ..... | 6 | ..... | 58.60 | 6 50- 6 99 |
| 7 00- 7 49 | ........ | ........ | ..... | ..... | 1 | ........ | ........ | ........ | ........ | 1 | 17 | ........ | ..... | ..... | 1 | 18 | 23.10 | 70.10 | 7 00- 7 49 |
| 7 50- 7 99 | ........ | ........ | ..... | ..... | 1 | ........ | 1 | ........ | ........ | ..... | ..... | ........ | ..... | ..... | ..... | 2 | ..... | 71.40 | 7 50- 7 99 |
| 8 00- 8 99 | ........ | ........ | ..... | ..... | 1 | ........ | ........ | ........ | ........ | ..... | 7 | ........ | ..... | ..... | ..... | 8 | ..... | 76.50 | 8 00- 8 99 |
| 9 00- 9 99 | ........ | ........ | ..... | 1 | 2 | 1 | ........ | ........ | ........ | 2 | 9 | ........ | ..... | ..... | 2 | 13 | 38.50 | 84.70 | 9 00- 9 99 |
| 10 00-10 99 | 1 | ........ | ..... | 3 | 1 | ........ | 2 | ........ | ........ | ..... | 6 | 1 | ..... | ..... | 1 | 13 | 46.20 | 93.00 | 10 00-10 99 |
| 11 00-11 99 | ........ | ........ | ..... | ..... | ........ | ........ | 1 | ........ | ........ | ..... | 2 | ........ | ..... | ..... | ..... | 3 | ..... | 95.00 | 11 00-11 99 |
| 12 00-12 99 | 1 | ........ | ..... | 1 | ........ | ........ | ........ | ........ | ........ | ..... | ..... | ........ | ..... | ..... | 1 | 1 | 53.90 | 95.50 | 12 00-12 99 |
| 13 00-13 99 | ........ | ........ | ..... | 2 | ........ | ........ | 1 | ........ | ........ | 1 | ..... | ........ | ..... | ..... | 1 | 3 | 61.60 | 97.50 | 13 00-13 99 |
| 14 00-14 99 | ........ | ........ | ..... | 1 | ........ | ........ | ........ | ........ | ........ | ..... | ..... | ........ | ..... | ..... | ..... | 1 | ..... | 98.10 | 14 00-14 99 |
| 15 00-15 99 | 1 | ........ | 1 | 2 | ........ | ........ | ........ | ........ | ........ | ..... | ..... | ........ | ..... | ..... | 2 | 2 | 77.00 | 99.40 | 15 00-15 99 |
| 16 00-17 99 | 1 | ........ | ..... | ..... | ........ | ........ | ........ | ........ | ........ | ..... | ..... | ........ | ..... | ..... | 1 | ..... | 84.60 | ........ | 16 00-17.99 |
| 18 00-19 99 | ........ | ........ | ..... | 1 | ........ | ........ | ........ | ........ | ........ | ..... | ..... | ........ | ..... | ..... | ..... | 1 | ..... | 100.00 | 18 001-9 99 |
| 20 00-24 99 | ........ | ........ | 1 | ..... | ........ | ........ | ........ | ........ | ........ | ..... | ..... | ........ | ..... | ..... | 1 | ..... | 92.50 | ........ | 20 002-4 99 |
| 30 00-34 99 | ........ | ........ | 1 | ..... | ........ | ........ | ........ | ........ | ........ | ..... | ..... | ........ | ..... | ..... | 1 | ..... | 100.00 | ........ | 30 003-4 99 |
| Not reported | ........ | ........ | ..... | ..... | 1 | ........ | ........ | ........ | ........ | ..... | ..... | ........ | ..... | ..... | ..... | 1 | ..... | ........ | Not reported |
| Total | 4 | 1 | 3 | 11 | 14 | 14 | 8 | 3 | 1 | 5 | 104 | 1 | 1 | 1 | 13 | 158 | ..... | ........ | Total |

335. TABLE VI, B, a

ALBANY

THE MEN'S SHIRT INDUSTRY — FACTORY WORKERS

NUMBER AND PER CENT. OF EMPLOYEES CLASSIFIED ACCORDING TO ACTUAL WEEKLY EARNINGS, BY AGE GROUPS AND SEX

| ACTUAL WEEKLY EARNINGS IN DOLLARS | AGE GROUPS IN YEARS | | | | | | | | | | | ACTUAL WEEKLY EARNINGS IN DOLLARS |
|---|---|---|---|---|---|---|---|---|---|---|---|---|
| | 14–15 | | 16–17 | | 18–20 | | 21–24 | | 25–29 | | 30–34 | |
| | Male | Female | Male | Female | Male | Female | Male | Female | Male | Female | Female | |
| Less than $3 00 | 1 | 1 | | 12 | | 16 | | 9 | | 1 | 5 | Less than $3 00 |
| $3 00–$3 49 | | | | 4 | | 11 | | 6 | | 4 | 2 | $3 00– 3 49 |
| 3 50– 3 99 | | 2 | | 4 | | 5 | 1 | 9 | | 5 | 2 | 3 50– 3 99 |
| 4 00– 4 49 | | 1 | | 12 | | 9 | | 15 | | 10 | 1 | 4 00– 4 49 |
| 4 50– 4 99 | | | 1 | 17 | | 20 | | 14 | | 5 | 3 | 4 50– 4 99 |
| 5 00– 5 49 | | 2 | | 9 | 1 | 26 | | 23 | | 7 | 5 | 5 00– 5 49 |
| 5 50– 5 99 | | 1 | | 6 | | 20 | | 16 | | 10 | 3 | 5 50– 5 99 |
| 6 00– 6 49 | 1 | | 1 | 6 | | 33 | 1 | 22 | | 16 | 10 | 6 00– 6 49 |
| 6 50– 6 99 | | | | 1 | | 14 | | 18 | | 14 | 7 | 6 50– 6 99 |
| 7 00– 7 49 | | | | 3 | 1 | 17 | | 27 | 1 | 13 | 6 | 7 00– 7 49 |
| 7 50– 7 99 | | | | 4 | | 11 | | 11 | | 5 | 5 | 7 50– 7 99 |
| 8 00– 8 99 | | | | 2 | | 12 | | 28 | | 20 | 14 | 8 00– 8 99 |
| 9 00– 9 99 | | 1 | | 2 | 1 | 13 | | 20 | | 14 | 13 | 9 00– 9 99 |
| 10 00–10 99 | | | | 1 | 1 | 11 | | 17 | | 17 | 9 | 10 00–10 99 |
| 11 00–11 99 | | | | | | 3 | 1 | 5 | 1 | 13 | 3 | 11 00–11 99 |
| 12 00–12 99 | | | | | | 1 | | 7 | | 5 | 4 | 12 00–12 99 |
| 13 00–13 99 | | | | 1 | 1 | | | 1 | | 6 | 2 | 13 00–13 99 |
| 14 00–14 99 | | | | | | 1 | 1 | 4 | | 5 | | 14 00–14 99 |
| 15 00–15 99 | | | | | | | 1 | 1 | | | | 15 00–15 99 |
| 16 00–17 99 | | | | | | | | | 1 | | | 16 00–17 99 |
| 18 00–19 99 | | | | | | | | | | 1 | | 18 00–19 99 |
| 20 00–24 99 | | | | | | | | | 1 | | | 20 00–24 99 |
| Total | 2 | 8 | 2 | 84 | 5 | 223 | 5 | 253 | 4 | 171 | 94 | Total |

ALBANY

335. TABLE VI, B, a — (*concluded*) **THE MEN'S SHIRT INDUSTRY — FACTORY WORKERS**

Number and Per Cent. of Employees Classified According to Actual Weekly Earnings, by Age Groups and Sex

| Actual Weekly Earnings in Dollars | Age Groups in Years (concluded) | | | | | | | | | | | | | Actual Weekly Earnings in Dollars |
|---|---|---|---|---|---|---|---|---|---|---|---|---|---|---|
| | 35–39 | | 40–44 | | 45–54 | | 55–64 | Not reported | Total | | Cumulative per cent. of total | | | |
| | Male | Female | Male | Female | Male | Female | Female | Female | Male | Female | Male | Female | | |
| Less than $3 00 | ....... | 4 | ....... | 4 | ....... | 2 | 2 | ....... | 1 | 56 | 4.5 | 5.9 | Less than $3 00 |
| $3 00–$3 49 | ....... | 1 | ....... | ....... | ....... | ....... | 1 | ....... | ....... | 29 | ....... | 8.9 | $3 00– 3 49 |
| 3 50– 3 99 | ....... | 1 | ....... | ....... | ....... | ....... | ....... | ....... | 1 | 28 | 9.1 | 11.9 | 3 50– 3 99 |
| 4 00– 4 49 | ....... | 3 | ....... | 1 | ....... | 1 | ....... | ....... | ....... | 53 | ....... | 17.4 | 4 00– 4 49 |
| 4 50– 4 99 | ....... | 2 | ....... | ....... | ....... | 2 | 1 | ....... | 1 | 64 | 13.6 | 24.2 | 4 50– 4 99 |
| 5 00– 5 49 | ....... | 3 | 1 | 2 | ....... | 2 | ....... | ....... | 2 | 79 | 22.7 | 32.4 | 5 00– 5 49 |
| 5 50– 5 99 | ....... | 3 | ....... | 2 | ....... | 2 | 1 | ....... | ....... | 64 | ....... | 39.2 | 5 50– 5 99 |
| 6 00– 6 49 | ....... | 7 | ....... | 5 | ....... | 1 | 1 | 2 | 3 | 103 | 36.4 | 50.0 | 6 00– 6 49 |
| 6 50– 6 99 | ....... | 2 | ....... | 1 | ....... | 3 | 1 | ....... | ....... | 61 | ....... | 56.4 | 6 50– 6 99 |
| 7 00– 7 49 | ....... | 3 | ....... | 3 | ....... | ....... | ....... | 1 | 2 | 73 | 45.5 | 64.0 | 7 00– 7 49 |
| 7 50– 7 99 | ....... | 8 | ....... | 3 | ....... | ....... | ....... | 1 | ....... | 48 | ....... | 69.0 | 7 50– 7 99 |
| 8 00– 8 99 | ....... | 9 | ....... | 3 | ....... | 1 | 1 | 1 | ....... | 91 | ....... | 78.6 | 8 00– 8 99 |
| 9 00– 9 99 | ....... | 3 | ....... | 1 | ....... | 2 | ....... | ....... | 1 | 69 | 50.0 | 85.8 | 9 00– 9 99 |
| 10 00–10 99 | ....... | 5 | ....... | 1 | ....... | ....... | ....... | 1 | 1 | 62 | 54.5 | 92.4 | 10 00–10 99 |
| 11 00–11 99 | ....... | ....... | ....... | 1 | ....... | ....... | ....... | ....... | 2 | 25 | 63.6 | 95.0 | 11 00–11 99 |
| 12 00–12 99 | ....... | 4 | ....... | ....... | ....... | ....... | ....... | ....... | ....... | 21 | ....... | 97.2 | 12 00–12 99 |
| 13 00–13 99 | ....... | ....... | ....... | 1 | 1 | ....... | ....... | ....... | 2 | 11 | 72.8 | 98.4 | 13 00–13 99 |
| 14 00–14 99 | ....... | 1 | ....... | 1 | ....... | ....... | ....... | ....... | 1 | 12 | 77.3 | 99.6 | 14 00–14 99 |
| 15 00–15 99 | 1 | 1 | ....... | 1 | ....... | ....... | ....... | ....... | 2 | 3 | 86.5 | 99.9 | 15 00–15 99 |
| 16 00–17 99 | ....... | ....... | ....... | ....... | ....... | ....... | ....... | ....... | 1 | ....... | 91.0 | ....... | 16 00–17 00 |
| 18 00–19 99 | ....... | ....... | ....... | ....... | ....... | ....... | ....... | ....... | ....... | 1 | ....... | 100.0 | 18 00–19 99 |
| 20 00–24 99 | ....... | ....... | ....... | ....... | ....... | ....... | ....... | ....... | 1 | ....... | 95.5 | ....... | 20 00–24 99 |
| 30 00–34 99 | ....... | ....... | 1 | ....... | ....... | ....... | ....... | ....... | 1 | ....... | 100.0 | ....... | 30 00–34 99 |
| Total | 1 | 60 | 2 | 30 | 1 | 16 | 8 | 6 | 22 | 953 | ....... | ....... | Total |

336. TABLE IX, B, a

ALBANY

THE MEN'S SHIRT INDUSTRY — FACTORY WORKERS

NUMBER AND PER CENT. OF EMPLOYEES CLASSIFIED ACCORDING TO ACTUAL WEEKLY EARNINGS, BY OCCUPATION AND SEX

| Actual Weekly Earnings in Dollars | Occupation | | | | | | | | | | | Actual Weekly Earnings in Dollars |
|---|---|---|---|---|---|---|---|---|---|---|---|---|
| | Cutters | Trimmers | Cutters' helpers | | Foremen and forewomen | | Operators | | Floor work | | Laundry helpers | |
| | Male | Female | Male | Female | Male | Female | Male | Female | Male | Female | Female | |
| Less than $3 00 | ........ | ........ | ........ | ........ | ........ | ........ | 1 | 40 | ........ | 9 | ........ | Less than $3 00 |
| $3 00–$3 49... | ........ | ........ | ........ | 2 | ........ | ........ | ........ | 19 | ........ | 2 | ........ | ...$3 00– 3 49 |
| 3 50– 3 99... | ........ | ........ | ........ | ........ | ........ | ........ | ........ | 22 | ........ | 1 | 1 | ... 3 50– 3 99 |
| 4 00– 4 49... | ........ | 1 | ........ | ........ | ........ | ........ | ........ | 37 | ........ | 4 | ........ | ... 4 00– 4 49 |
| 4 50– 4 99... | ........ | ........ | ........ | ........ | ........ | ........ | ........ | 35 | ........ | 4 | 2 | ... 4 50– 4 99 |
| 5 00– 5 49... | ........ | ........ | 1 | ........ | ........ | ........ | ........ | 48 | ........ | 7 | ........ | ... 5 00– 5 49 |
| 5 50– 5 99... | ........ | ........ | ........ | 1 | ........ | ........ | ........ | 36 | ........ | 2 | 2 | ... 5 50– 5 99 |
| 6 00– 6 49... | ........ | 1 | ........ | ........ | ........ | ........ | ........ | 64 | ........ | 4 | 1 | ... 6 00– 6 49 |
| 6 50– 6 99... | ........ | ........ | ........ | ........ | ........ | ........ | ........ | 42 | ........ | 1 | ........ | ... 6 50– 6 99 |
| 7 00– 7 49... | ........ | 1 | ........ | ........ | ........ | ........ | ........ | 50 | 1 | 1 | ........ | ... 7 00– 7 49 |
| 7 50– 7 99... | ........ | ........ | ........ | ........ | ........ | ........ | ........ | 31 | ........ | ........ | 2 | ... 7 50– 7 99 |
| 8 00– 8 99... | ........ | ........ | ........ | ........ | ........ | 1 | ........ | 67 | ........ | 4 | ........ | ... 8 00– 8 99 |
| 9 00– 9 99... | ........ | ........ | ........ | ........ | ........ | 1 | ........ | 47 | ........ | 2 | 1 | ... 9 00– 9 99 |
| 10 00–10 99... | 1 | ........ | ........ | ........ | ........ | 2 | ........ | 46 | ........ | 4 | 2 | ...10 00–10 99 |
| 11 00–11 99... | 1 | ........ | ........ | ........ | ........ | ........ | ........ | 20 | ........ | ........ | 1 | ...11 00–11 99 |
| 12 00–12 99... | ........ | ........ | ........ | ........ | ........ | 1 | ........ | 17 | ........ | ........ | ........ | ...12 00–12 99 |
| 13 00–13 99... | ........ | 1 | ........ | ........ | ........ | 2 | 1 | 5 | ........ | ........ | 1 | ...13 00–13 99 |
| 14 00–14 99... | 1 | ........ | ........ | ........ | ........ | 1 | ........ | 10 | ........ | ........ | ........ | ...14 00–14 99 |
| 15 00–15 99... | 1 | ........ | ........ | ........ | 1 | 2 | ........ | 1 | ........ | ........ | ........ | ...15 00–15 99 |
| 16 00–17 99... | 1 | ........ | ........ | ........ | ........ | ........ | ........ | ........ | ........ | ........ | ........ | ...16 00–17 99 |
| 18 00–19 99... | ........ | ........ | ........ | ........ | ........ | 1 | ........ | ........ | ........ | ........ | ........ | ...18 00–19 99 |
| 20 00–24 99... | ........ | ........ | ........ | ........ | 1 | ........ | ........ | ........ | ........ | ........ | ........ | ...20 00–24 99 |
| 30 00–34 99... | ........ | ........ | ........ | ........ | 1 | ........ | ........ | ........ | ........ | ........ | ........ | ...30 00–34 99 |
| Total..... | 5 | 4 | 1 | 3 | 3 | 11 | 2 | 637 | 1 | 45 | 13 | .....Total |

ALBANY

336. TABLE IX, B, a — (*concluded*) THE MEN'S SHIRT INDUSTRY — FACTORY WORKERS

NUMBER AND PER CENT. OF EMPLOYEES CLASSIFIED ACCORDING TO ACTUAL WEEKLY EARNINGS, BY OCCUPATION AND SEX

| ACTUAL WEEKLY EARNINGS IN DOLLARS | OCCUPATION—(*concluded*) | | | | | | | | | | | | ACTUAL WEEKLY EARNINGS IN DOLLARS |
|---|---|---|---|---|---|---|---|---|---|---|---|---|---|
| | STARCHERS AND DAMPNERS | IRONERS AND PRESSERS | EXAMINERS | | FOLDERS | | PACKERS | | TOTAL | | CUMULATIVE PER CENT OF TOTAL | | |
| | Female | Female | Male | Female | Male | Female | Male | Female | Male | Female | Male | Female | |
| Less than $3 00 | ........ | ........ | ..... | 5 | ....... | 2 | ....... | ....... | 1 | 56 | 4.50 | 5.90 | Less than $3 00 |
| $3 00–$3 49 | 1 | 2 | ..... | ..... | ....... | 3 | ....... | ....... | ....... | 29 | ....... | 8.90 | $3 00– 3 49 |
| 3 50– 3 99 | 2 | ........ | ..... | 2 | 1 | ....... | ....... | ....... | 1 | 28 | 9.10 | 11.90 | 3 50– 3 99 |
| 4 00– 4 49 | ........ | 1 | ..... | 7 | ....... | 3 | ....... | ....... | ....... | 53 | ....... | 17.40 | 4 00– 4 49 |
| 4 50– 4 99 | 3 | 1 | 1 | 12 | ....... | 6 | ....... | 1 | 1 | 64 | 13.60 | 24.20 | 4 50– 4 99 |
| 5 00– 5 49 | ........ | 2 | ..... | 20 | 1 | 2 | ....... | ....... | 2 | 79 | 22.70 | 32.40 | 5 00– 5 49 |
| 5 50– 5 99 | 1 | 3 | ..... | 15 | ....... | 4 | ....... | ....... | ....... | 64 | ....... | 39.20 | 5 50– 5 99 |
| 6 00– 6 49 | ........ | 2 | 1 | 25 | 1 | 6 | 1 | ....... | 3 | 103 | 36.40 | 50.00 | 6 00– 6 49 |
| 6 50– 6 99 | 1 | 2 | ..... | 12 | ....... | 3 | ....... | ....... | ....... | 61 | ....... | 56.40 | 6 50– 6 99 |
| 7 00– 7 49 | ........ | 5 | 1 | 12 | ....... | 4 | ....... | ....... | 2 | 73 | 45.50 | 64.00 | 7 00– 7 49 |
| 7 50– 7 99 | 2 | 3 | ..... | 4 | ....... | 6 | ....... | ....... | ....... | 48 | ....... | 69.00 | 7 50– 7 99 |
| 8 00– 8 99 | ........ | 3 | ..... | 7 | ....... | 9 | ....... | ....... | ....... | 91 | ....... | 78.60 | 8 00– 8 99 |
| 9 00– 9 99 | 2 | 1 | 1 | 10 | ....... | 5 | ....... | ....... | 1 | 69 | 50.00 | 85.80 | 9 00– 9 99 |
| 10 00–10 99 | 1 | ........ | ..... | 5 | ....... | 2 | ....... | ....... | 1 | 62 | 54.50 | 92.40 | 10 00–10 99 |
| 11 00–11 99 | ........ | ........ | ..... | 2 | 1 | 2 | ....... | ....... | 2 | 25 | 63.60 | 95.00 | 11 00–11 99 |
| 12 00–12 99 | ........ | ........ | ..... | 3 | ....... | ....... | ....... | ....... | ....... | 21 | ....... | 97.20 | 12 00–12 99 |
| 13 00–13 99 | ........ | 1 | 1 | ..... | ....... | ....... | ....... | 1 | 2 | 11 | 72.80 | 98.40 | 13 00–13 99 |
| 14 00–14 99 | ........ | 1 | ..... | ..... | ....... | ....... | ....... | ....... | 1 | 12 | 77.30 | 99.60 | 14 00–14 99 |
| 15 00–15 99 | ........ | ........ | ..... | ..... | ....... | ....... | ....... | ....... | 2 | 3 | 86.50 | 99.90 | 15 00–15 99 |
| 16 00–17 99 | ........ | ........ | ..... | ..... | ....... | ....... | ....... | ....... | 1 | ....... | 91.00 | ....... | 16 00–17 99 |
| 18 00–19 99 | ........ | ........ | ..... | ..... | ....... | ....... | ....... | ....... | ....... | 1 | ....... | 100.00 | 18 00–19 99 |
| 20 00–24 99 | ........ | ........ | ..... | ..... | ....... | ....... | ....... | ....... | 1 | ....... | 95.50 | ....... | 20 00–24 99 |
| 30 00–34 99 | ........ | ........ | ..... | ..... | ....... | ....... | ....... | ....... | 1 | ....... | 100.00 | ....... | 30 00–34 99 |
| Total | 13 | 27 | 5 | 141 | 4 | 57 | 1 | 2 | 22 | 953 | ....... | ....... | Total |

337. TABLE V, A, 1, a

SCHENECTADY

DEPARTMENT STORES — STOCK AND SALES

NUMBER AND PER CENT. OF EMPLOYEES EARNING SPECIFIED WEEKLY RATES, BY AGE GROUPS AND SEX

| WEEKLY RATES IN DOLLARS | AGE GROUPS IN YEARS | | | | | | | | | | | | | | WEEKLY RATES IN DOLLARS |
|---|---|---|---|---|---|---|---|---|---|---|---|---|---|---|---|
| | 14–15 | | 16–17 | | 18–20 | | 21–24 | | 25–29 | | 30–34 | | 35–39 | | |
| | Male | Female | Male | Female | Male | Female | Male | Female | Male | Female | Male | Female | Male | Female | |
| Less than $3 00 | 2 | ...... | .... | ...... | ...... | ...... | ...... | ...... | ...... | ...... | ...... | ...... | ...... | ...... | Less than $3 00 |
| $3 00–$3 49... | 1 | 2 | .... | 16 | ...... | ...... | ...... | ...... | ...... | ...... | ...... | ...... | ...... | ...... | ...$3 00– 3 49 |
| 3 50– 3 99... | 1 | 1 | 1 | 5 | ...... | 1 | ...... | ...... | ...... | ...... | ...... | ...... | ...... | ...... | ... 3 50– 3 99 |
| 4 00– 4 49... | .... | ...... | .... | 8 | 1 | 4 | ...... | ...... | ...... | ...... | ...... | ...... | ...... | ...... | ... 4 00– 4 49 |
| 4 50– 4 99... | .... | ...... | .... | 1 | ...... | 1 | ...... | 1 | ...... | ...... | ...... | ...... | ...... | ...... | ... 4 50– 4 99 |
| 5 00– 5 49... | .... | ...... | 2 | 7 | ...... | 20 | ...... | 3 | ...... | ...... | ...... | 1 | ...... | ...... | ... 5 00– 5 49 |
| 6 00– 6 49... | .... | ...... | .... | 1 | 2 | 10 | ...... | 5 | ...... | 8 | ...... | 1 | ...... | 2 | ... 6 00– 6 49 |
| 6 50– 6 99... | .... | ...... | .... | ...... | ...... | ...... | ...... | ...... | ...... | ...... | ...... | ...... | ...... | 1 | ... 6 50– 6 99 |
| 7 00– 7 49... | .... | ...... | .... | ...... | ...... | 7 | ...... | 6 | ...... | 5 | ...... | 4 | ...... | 2 | ... 7 00– 7 49 |
| 7 50– 7 99... | .... | ...... | .... | ...... | ...... | 1 | ...... | ...... | ...... | ...... | ...... | ...... | ...... | ...... | ... 7 50– 7 99 |
| 8 00– 8 99... | .... | ...... | .... | ...... | ...... | ...... | ...... | 10 | ...... | 9 | ...... | 2 | ...... | 3 | ... 8 00– 8 99 |
| 9 00– 9 99... | .... | ...... | .... | ...... | 1 | ...... | 1 | 3 | ...... | 4 | ...... | 4 | ...... | 2 | ... 9 00– 9 99 |
| 10 00–10 99... | .... | ...... | .... | ...... | 1 | ...... | 1 | 3 | ...... | 3 | ...... | 5 | ...... | 3 | ...10 00–10 99 |
| 11 00–11 99... | .... | ...... | .... | ...... | 2 | ...... | ...... | 1 | ...... | 2 | ...... | ...... | ...... | 2 | ...11 00–11 99 |
| 12 00–12 99... | .... | ...... | 1 | ...... | 1 | ...... | 1 | 1 | 1 | 3 | ...... | 3 | ...... | ...... | ...12 00–12 99 |
| 13 00–13 99... | .... | ...... | .... | ...... | ...... | ...... | 1 | ...... | 1 | 1 | ...... | ...... | ...... | ...... | ...13 00–13 99 |
| 14 00–14 99... | .... | ...... | .... | ...... | 1 | ...... | 1 | ...... | 2 | 1 | ...... | ...... | 1 | ...... | ...14 00–14 99 |
| 15 00–15 99... | .... | ...... | .... | ...... | ...... | ...... | 1 | ...... | 1 | 1 | ...... | 3 | 1 | 2 | ...15 00–15 99 |
| 16 00–17 99... | .... | ...... | .... | ...... | ...... | 1 | 1 | ...... | 2 | 2 | 3 | ...... | 2 | 1 | ...16 00–17 99 |
| 18 00–19 99... | .... | ...... | .... | ...... | ...... | ...... | ...... | ...... | 6 | 1 | 1 | 1 | 1 | 1 | ...18 00–19 99 |
| 20 00–24 99... | .... | ...... | .... | ...... | ...... | ...... | 1 | ...... | 2 | ...... | 2 | 1 | ...... | ...... | ...20 00–24 99 |
| 25 00–29 99... | .... | ...... | .... | ...... | ...... | ...... | ...... | ...... | ...... | ...... | 3 | ...... | 1 | 1 | ...25 00–29 99 |
| 30 00–34 99... | .... | ...... | .... | ...... | ...... | ...... | ...... | ...... | ...... | ...... | ...... | ...... | 2 | ...... | ...30 00–34 99 |
| 35 00–39 99... | .... | ...... | .... | ...... | ...... | ...... | ...... | ...... | ...... | ...... | ...... | ...... | ...... | ...... | ...35 00–39 99 |
| 40 00 and over. | .... | ...... | .... | ...... | ...... | ...... | ...... | ...... | ...... | ...... | 1 | ...... | ...... | ...... | 40 00 and over. |
| Not reported.. | .... | ...... | .... | ...... | ...... | ...... | ...... | ...... | ...... | ...... | ...... | 1 | ...... | ...... | ..Not reported |
| Total.... | 4 | 3 | 4 | 38 | 9 | 45 | 8 | 33 | 15 | 40 | 10 | 26 | 8 | 20 | .....Total |

337. TABLE V, A, 1, a — *(concluded)*

SCHENECTADY

**DEPARTMENT STORES — STOCK AND SALES**

NUMBER AND PER CENT. OF EMPLOYEES EARNING SPECIFIED WEEKLY RATES, BY AGE GROUPS AND SEX

| WEEKLY RATES IN DOLLARS | AGE GROUPS IN YEARS—*(concluded)* 40–44 | | 45–54 | | 55–64 | 65 AND OVER | NOT REPORTED | TOTAL | | CUMULATIVE PER CENT OF TOTAL | | WEEKLY RATES IN DOLLARS |
|---|---|---|---|---|---|---|---|---|---|---|---|---|
| | Male | Female | Male | Female | Male | Male | Female | Male | Female | Male | Female | |
| Less than $3 00 | | | | | | | | 2 | | 2.40 | | Less than $3 00 |
| $3 00–$3 49 | | | | | | | | 1 | 18 | 3.60 | 7.90 | $3 00– 3 49 |
| 3 50– 3 99 | | | | | | | | 2 | 7 | 5.90 | 11.00 | 3 50– 3 99 |
| 4 00– 4 49 | | | | | | | | 1 | 12 | 7.10 | 16.30 | 4 00– 4 49 |
| 4 50– 4 99 | | | | | | | | | 3 | | 17.60 | 4 50– 4 99 |
| 5 00– 5 49 | | | | | | | 1 | 2 | 32 | 9.50 | 31.80 | 5 00– 5 49 |
| 6 00– 6 49 | | | | 1 | | | | 2 | 28 | 11.90 | 44.00 | 6 00– 6 49 |
| 6 50– 6 99 | | | | | | | | | 1 | | 44.50 | 6 50– 6 99 |
| 7 00– 7 49 | | | | | | | | | 24 | | 55.10 | 7 00– 7 49 |
| 7 50– 7 99 | | | | 1 | | | | | 2 | | 56.00 | 7 50– 7 99 |
| 8 00– 8 99 | | 3 | | 2 | | | | | 29 | | 68.80 | 8 00– 8 99 |
| 9 00– 9 99 | | 2 | | | | | | 2 | 15 | 14.30 | 75.40 | 9 00– 9 99 |
| 10 00–10 99 | 2 | 2 | | | | | | 4 | 16 | 19.10 | 82.50 | 10 00–10 99 |
| 11 00–11 99 | | | | 1 | | | 1 | 2 | 7 | 21.40 | 85.50 | 11 00–11 99 |
| 12 00–12 99 | | 1 | 1 | | 1 | | | 6 | 8 | 28.60 | 89.00 | 12 00–12 99 |
| 13 00–13 99 | | | | | | | | 2 | 1 | 30.90 | 89.50 | 13 00–13 99 |
| 14 00–14 99 | | | 1 | 1 | | | 1 | 6 | 3 | 38.10 | 98.80 | 14 00–14 99 |
| 15 00–15 99 | | 1 | | 1 | | 1 | | 4 | 8 | 42.80 | 94.40 | 15 00–15 99 |
| 16 00–17 99 | | 1 | | 1 | | | | 8 | 6 | 52.40 | 97.00 | 16 00–17 99 |
| 18 00–19 99 | 3 | | | | | | | 11 | 3 | 65.50 | 98.30 | 18 00–19 99 |
| 20 00–24 99 | 1 | | 3 | | | | | 9 | 1 | 76.20 | 98.80 | 20 00–24 99 |
| 25 00–29 99 | 1 | | 1 | | 2 | | | 8 | 1 | 85.70 | 99.10 | 25 00–29 99 |
| 30 00–34 99 | 1 | 1 | 1 | | | | | 4 | 1 | 90.50 | 99.60 | 30 00–34 99 |
| 35 00–39 99 | 1 | | 3 | 1 | | | | 4 | 1 | 95.20 | 100.00 | 35 00–39 99 |
| 40 00 and over | 3 | | | | | | | 4 | | 100.00 | | 40 00 and over |
| Not reported | | | | | | | | | 1 | | | Not reported |
| Total | 12 | 11 | 10 | 9 | 3 | 1 | 3 | 84 | 228 | | | Total |

338. TABLE VIII, A, 1, a

## SCHENECTADY
## DEPARTMENT STORES — STOCK AND SALES

Number and Per Cent. of Employees Earning Specified Weekly Rates, by Occupation and Sex

| Weekly Rates in Dollars | Superintendents | Buyers | | Assistant Buyers and Heads of Stock | | Receiving and Stock Clerks | | Stock People | | Floor Managers | Sales People | | Messengers, Wrappers and Errand Boys | | Total | | Cumulative Per Cent. of Total | | Weekly Rates in Dollars |
|---|---|---|---|---|---|---|---|---|---|---|---|---|---|---|---|---|---|---|---|
| | Male | Male | Female | Male | Female | Male | Female | Male | Female | Male | Male | Female | Male | Female | Male | Female | Male | Female | |
| Less than $3 00 | .......... | .... | .... | .... | .... | .... | .... | .... | .... | .......... | .... | .... | 2 | .... | 2 | .... | 2.40 | .... | Less than $3 00 |
| $3 00–$3 49 | .......... | .... | .... | .... | .... | .... | .... | .... | 1 | .......... | .... | 3 | 1 | 14 | 1 | 18 | 3.60 | 7.90 | $3 00– 3 49 |
| 3 50– 3 99 | .......... | .... | .... | .... | .... | .... | .... | .... | .... | .......... | .... | .... | 2 | 7 | 2 | 7 | 5.90 | 11.00 | 3 50– 3 99 |
| 4 00– 4 49 | .......... | .... | .... | .... | .... | .... | .... | 1 | .... | .......... | .... | 9 | .... | 3 | 1 | 12 | 7.10 | 16.30 | 4 00– 4 49 |
| 4 50– 4 99 | .......... | .... | .... | .... | .... | .... | .... | .... | .... | .......... | .... | 3 | .... | .... | .... | 3 | .... | 17.60 | 4 50– 4 99 |
| 5 00– 5 49 | .......... | .... | .... | .... | .... | .... | .... | 2 | 2 | .......... | .... | 30 | .... | .... | 2 | 32 | 9.50 | 31.80 | 5 00– 5 49 |
| 6 00– 6 49 | .......... | .... | .... | .... | .... | .... | .... | 1 | .... | .......... | 1 | 28 | .... | .... | 2 | 28 | 11.90 | 44.00 | 6 00– 6 49 |
| 6 50– 6 99 | .......... | .... | .... | .... | .... | .... | .... | .... | .... | .......... | .... | 1 | .... | .... | .... | 1 | .... | 44.50 | 6 50– 6 99 |
| 7 00– 7 49 | .......... | .... | .... | .... | .... | .... | 1 | .... | .... | .......... | .... | 23 | .... | .... | .... | 24 | .... | 55.10 | 7 00– 7 49 |
| 7 50– 7 99 | .......... | .... | .... | .... | .... | .... | .... | .... | .... | .......... | .... | 2 | .... | .... | .... | 2 | .... | 56.00 | 7 50– 7 99 |
| 8 00– 8 99 | .......... | .... | .... | .... | .... | .... | .... | .... | .... | .......... | .... | 29 | .... | .... | .... | 29 | .... | 68.80 | 8 00– 8 99 |
| 9 00– 9 99 | .......... | .... | .... | .... | .... | .... | 1 | .... | .... | .......... | 2 | 14 | .... | .... | 2 | 15 | 14.30 | 75.40 | 9 00– 9 99 |
| 10 00–10 99 | .......... | .... | .... | .... | .... | 2 | .... | .... | .... | .......... | 2 | 16 | .... | .... | 4 | 16 | 19.10 | 82.50 | 10 00–10 99 |
| 11 00–11 99 | .......... | .... | .... | .... | 1 | .... | .... | .... | .... | .......... | 2 | 6 | .... | .... | 2 | 7 | 21.40 | 85.50 | 11 00–11 99 |
| 12 00–12 99 | .......... | .... | .... | .... | .... | .... | .... | .... | .... | .......... | 6 | 8 | .... | .... | 6 | 8 | 28.60 | 89.00 | 12 00–12 99 |
| 13 00–13 99 | .......... | .... | .... | .... | .... | .... | .... | .... | .... | .......... | 2 | 1 | .... | .... | 2 | 1 | 30.90 | 89.50 | 13 00–13 99 |
| 14 00–14 99 | .......... | .... | .... | .... | .... | .... | .... | .... | .... | .......... | 6 | 3 | .... | .... | 6 | 3 | 38.10 | 90.80 | 14 00–14 99 |
| 15 00–15 99 | .......... | .... | 1 | .... | 1 | .... | .... | .... | .... | .......... | 4 | 6 | .... | .... | 4 | 8 | 42.80 | 94.40 | 15 00–15 99 |
| 16 00–17 99 | .......... | .... | 1 | .... | 1 | .... | .... | .... | .... | .......... | 8 | 4 | .... | .... | 8 | 6 | 52.40 | 97.00 | 16 00–17 99 |
| 18 00–19 99 | .......... | .... | .... | 1 | .... | .... | .... | .... | .... | 1 | 9 | 3 | .... | .... | 11 | 3 | 65.50 | 98.30 | 18 00–19 99 |
| 20 00–24 99 | 1 | .... | .... | 2 | .... | .... | .... | .... | .... | 1 | 5 | 1 | .... | .... | 9 | 1 | 76.20 | 98.80 | 20 00–24 99 |
| 25 00–29 99 | .......... | 5 | 1 | .... | .... | .... | .... | .... | .... | .......... | 3 | .... | .... | .... | 8 | 1 | 85.70 | 99.10 | 25 00–29 99 |
| 30 00–34 99 | .......... | 3 | 1 | .... | .... | .... | .... | .... | .... | .......... | 1 | .... | .... | .... | 4 | 1 | 90.50 | 99.60 | 30 00–34 99 |
| 35 00–39 99 | .......... | 2 | 1 | .... | .... | .... | .... | .... | .... | 2 | .... | .... | .... | .... | 4 | 1 | 95.20 | 100.00 | 35 00–39 99 |
| 40 00 and over | .......... | 3 | .... | .... | .... | .... | .... | .... | .... | 1 | .... | .... | .... | .... | 4 | .... | 100.00 | .... | 40 00 and over |
| Not reported | .......... | .... | .... | .... | .... | .... | .... | .... | .... | .......... | .... | 1 | .... | .... | .... | 1 | .... | .... | Not reported |
| Total | 1 | 13 | 5 | 3 | 3 | 2 | 2 | 4 | 3 | 5 | 51 | 191 | 5 | 24 | 84 | 228 | .... | .... | Total |

339. TABLE VI, A, 1, a.

SCHENECTADY

**DEPARTMENT STORES — STOCK AND SALES**

NUMBER AND PER CENT. OF EMPLOYEES CLASSIFIED ACCORDING TO ACTUAL WEEKLY EARNINGS, BY AGE GROUPS AND SEX

| Actual Weekly Earnings in Dollars | Age Groups in Years | | | | | | | | | | | | | | Actual Weekly Earnings in Dollars |
|---|---|---|---|---|---|---|---|---|---|---|---|---|---|---|---|
| | 14–15 | | 16–17 | | 18–20 | | 21–24 | | 25–29 | | 30–34 | | 35–39 | | |
| | Male | Female | Male | Female | Male | Female | Male | Female | Male | Female | Male | Female | Male | Female | |
| Less than $3 00 | 2 | 1 | .... | 2 | .... | 2 | .... | 1 | .... | .... | .... | .... | .... | .... | Less than $3 00 |
| $3 00–$3 49... | 1 | 1 | 1 | 15 | .... | 1 | .... | .... | .... | .... | .... | .... | .... | 1 | ...$3 00– 3 49 |
| 3 50– 3 99... | 1 | 1 | 1 | 4 | .... | 2 | .... | .... | .... | .... | .... | .... | .... | .... | ....3 50– 3 99 |
| 4 00– 4 49... | .... | .... | .... | 9 | 1 | 3 | .... | .... | .... | .... | .... | .... | .... | .... | ....4 00– 4 49 |
| 4 50– 4 99... | .... | .... | .... | 1 | .... | 2 | .... | 1 | .... | .... | .... | .... | .... | .... | ....4 50– 4 99 |
| 5 00– 5 49... | .... | .... | 1 | 6 | .... | 17 | .... | 3 | .... | .... | .... | 1 | .... | .... | ....5 00– 5 49 |
| 5 50– 5 99... | .... | .... | .... | .... | 1 | 1 | .... | .... | .... | 1 | .... | .... | .... | .... | ....5 50– 5 99 |
| 6 00– 6 49... | .... | .... | .... | 1 | 2 | 9 | .... | 5 | .... | 7 | .... | 1 | .... | 1 | ....6 00– 6 49 |
| 6 50– 6 99... | .... | .... | .... | .... | .... | .... | .... | .... | .... | .... | .... | .... | .... | 1 | ....6 50– 6 99 |
| 7 00– 7 49... | .... | .... | .... | .... | .... | 6 | .... | 6 | .... | 5 | .... | 5 | .... | 2 | ....7 00– 7 49 |
| 7 50– 7 99... | .... | .... | .... | .... | .... | 1 | 1 | .... | .... | 1 | .... | .... | .... | .... | ....7 50– 7 99 |
| 8 00– 8 99... | .... | .... | .... | .... | .... | .... | .... | 9 | .... | 8 | .... | 3 | .... | 3 | ....8 00– 8 99 |
| 9 00– 9 99... | .... | .... | .... | .... | 1 | .... | .... | 3 | .... | 5 | .... | 5 | .... | 2 | ....9 00– 9 99 |
| 10 00–10 99... | .... | .... | .... | .... | 1 | .... | 1 | 3 | 1 | 3 | .... | 3 | .... | 3 | ...10 00–10 99 |
| 11 00–11 99... | .... | .... | .... | .... | 2 | .... | .... | 1 | .... | 1 | .... | .... | .... | 1 | ...11 00–11 99 |
| 12 00–12 99... | .... | .... | 1 | .... | 1 | .... | 1 | 1 | 1 | 3 | .... | 3 | .... | 1 | ...12 00–12 99 |
| 13 00–13 99... | .... | .... | .... | .... | .... | .... | 1 | .... | 1 | 1 | .... | .... | .... | .... | ...13 00–13 99 |
| 14 00–14 99... | .... | .... | .... | .... | 1 | .... | 1 | .... | 2 | 1 | .... | .... | 1 | .... | ...14 00–14 99 |
| 15 00–15 99... | .... | .... | .... | .... | .... | .... | 1 | .... | .... | 1 | .... | 3 | 1 | 2 | ...15 00–15 99 |
| 16 00–17 99... | .... | .... | .... | .... | .... | 1 | 1 | .... | 2 | 3 | 3 | .... | 2 | 1 | ...16 00–17 99 |
| 18 00–19 99... | .... | .... | .... | .... | .... | .... | .... | .... | 6 | .... | 1 | 1 | 1 | 1 | ...18 00–19 99 |
| 20 00–24 99... | .... | .... | .... | .... | .... | .... | 1 | .... | 2 | .... | 2 | 1 | .... | .... | ...20 00–24 99 |
| 25 00–29 99... | .... | .... | .... | .... | .... | .... | .... | .... | .... | .... | 3 | .... | 1 | 1 | ...25 00–29 99 |
| 30 00–34 99... | .... | .... | .... | .... | .... | .... | .... | .... | .... | .... | .... | .... | 2 | .... | ...30 00–34 99 |
| 40 00 and over. | .... | .... | .... | .... | .... | .... | .... | .... | .... | .... | 1 | .... | .... | .... | .40 00 and over |
| Total..... | 4 | 3 | 4 | 38 | 10 | 45 | 8 | 33 | 15 | 40 | 10 | 26 | 8 | 20 | .....Total |

339. TABLE VI, A, 1, a — (*concluded*)

SCHENECTADY

DEPARTMENT STORES — STOCK AND SALES

NUMBER AND PER CENT. OF EMPLOYEES CLASSIFIED ACCORDING TO ACTUAL WEEKLY EARNINGS, BY AGE GROUPS AND SEX

| ACTUAL WEEKLY EARNINGS IN DOLLARS | AGE GROUPS IN YEARS (*concluded*) | | | | | | | | | | | ACTUAL WEEKLY EARNINGS IN DOLLARS |
|---|---|---|---|---|---|---|---|---|---|---|---|---|
| | 40–44 | | 45–54 | | 55–64 | 65 AND OVER | NOT REPORTED | TOTAL | | CUMULATIVE PER CENT. OF TOTAL | | |
| | Male | Female | Male | Female | Male | Male | Female | Male | Female | Male | Female | |
| Less than $3 00 | ........ | ........ | ........ | ........ | ........ | ........ | ........ | 2 | 6 | 2.40 | 2.60 | Less than $3 00 |
| $3 00–$3 49... | ........ | ........ | ........ | ........ | ........ | ........ | ........ | 2 | 18 | 4.70 | 10.50 | ...$3 00– 3 49 |
| 3 50– 3 99... | ........ | ........ | ........ | ........ | ........ | ........ | ........ | 2 | 7 | 7.10 | 13.60 | ....3 50– 3 99 |
| 4 00– 4 49... | ........ | ........ | ........ | ........ | ........ | ........ | ........ | 1 | 12 | 8.20 | 18.90 | ....4 00– 4 49 |
| 4 50– 4 99... | ........ | ........ | ........ | ........ | ........ | ........ | ........ | ........ | 4 | ........ | 20.60 | ....4 50– 4 99 |
| 5 00– 5 49... | ........ | ........ | ........ | ........ | ........ | ........ | 1 | 1 | 28 | 9.40 | 32.90 | ....5 00– 5 49 |
| 5 50– 5 99... | ........ | ........ | ........ | ........ | ........ | ........ | ........ | 1 | 2 | 10.60 | 33.80 | ....5 50– 5 99 |
| 6 00– 6 49... | ........ | ........ | ........ | 1 | ........ | ........ | ........ | 2 | 25 | 12.90 | 44.70 | ....6 00– 6 49 |
| 6 50– 6 99... | ........ | ........ | ........ | ........ | ........ | ........ | ........ | ........ | 1 | ........ | 45.20 | ....6 50– 6 99 |
| 7 00– 7 49... | ........ | ........ | ........ | 1 | ........ | ........ | ........ | ........ | 25 | ........ | 56.10 | ....7 00– 7 49 |
| 7 50– 7 99... | ........ | ........ | ........ | 1 | ........ | ........ | ........ | 1 | 3 | 14.10 | 57.50 | ....7 50– 7 99 |
| 8 00– 8 99... | ........ | 3 | ........ | 1 | ........ | ........ | ........ | ........ | 27 | ........ | 69.40 | ....8 00– 8 99 |
| 9 00– 9 99... | ........ | 2 | ........ | ........ | ........ | ........ | ........ | 1 | 17 | 15.30 | 76.80 | ....9 00– 9 99 |
| 10 00–10 99... | 2 | 2 | ........ | ........ | ........ | ........ | ........ | 5 | 14 | 21.20 | 83.00 | ...10 00–10 99 |
| 11 00–11 99... | ........ | ........ | ........ | 1 | ........ | ........ | 1 | 2 | 5 | 23.60 | 85.10 | ...11 00–11 99 |
| 12 00–12 99... | ........ | 1 | 1 | ........ | 1 | ........ | ........ | 6 | 9 | 30.60 | 89.00 | ...12 00–12 99 |
| 13 00–13 99... | ........ | ........ | ........ | ........ | ........ | ........ | ........ | 2 | 1 | 32.00 | 89.50 | ...13 00–13 99 |
| 14 00–14 99... | ........ | ........ | 1 | 1 | ........ | ........ | 1 | 6 | 3 | 40.00 | 90.80 | ...14 00–14 99 |
| 15 00–15 99... | ........ | 1 | ........ | 1 | ........ | 1 | ........ | 3 | 8 | 43.50 | 94.30 | ...15 00–15 99 |
| 16 00–17 99... | 1 | 1 | ........ | 1 | ........ | ........ | ........ | 9 | 7 | 54.10 | 97.40 | ...16 00–17 99 |
| 18 00–19 99... | 3 | ........ | ........ | ........ | ........ | ........ | ........ | 11 | 2 | 67.10 | 98.30 | ...18 00–19 99 |
| 20 00–24 99... | 1 | ........ | 3 | ........ | ........ | ........ | ........ | 9 | 1 | 77.60 | 98.60 | ...20 00–24 99 |
| 25 00–29 99... | ........ | ........ | 1 | ........ | 2 | ........ | ........ | 7 | 1 | 86.00 | 99.10 | ...25 00–29 99 |
| 30 00–34 99... | 1 | 1 | 1 | ........ | ........ | ........ | ........ | 4 | 1 | 90.60 | 99.50 | ...30 00–34 99 |
| 35 00–39 99... | 1 | ........ | 3 | 1 | ........ | ........ | ........ | 4 | 1 | 95.30 | 100.00 | ...35 00–39 99 |
| 40 00 and over. | 3 | ........ | ........ | ........ | ........ | ........ | ........ | 4 | ........ | 100.00 | ........ | .40 00 and over |
| Total.... | 12 | 11 | 10 | 9 | 3 | 1 | 3 | 85 | 228 | ........ | ........ | .....Total |

340. TABLE IX, A, 1, a

SCHENECTADY

DEPARTMENT STORES — STOCK AND SALES

NUMBER AND PER CENT. OF EMPLOYEES CLASSIFIED ACCORDING TO ACTUAL WEEKLY EARNINGS, BY OCCUPATION AND SEX

| WEEKLY RATES IN DOLLARS | OCCUPATION: SUPERINTENDENTS | BUYERS | | ASSISTANT BUYERS AND HEADS OF STOCK | | RECEIVING AND STOCK CLERKS | | STOCK PEOPLE | | FLOOR MANAGERS | SALES PEOPLE | | MESSENGERS, WRAPPERS AND ERRAND BOYS | | TOTAL | | CUMULATIVE PER CENT. OF TOTAL | | WEEKLY RATES IN DOLLARS |
|---|---|---|---|---|---|---|---|---|---|---|---|---|---|---|---|---|---|---|---|
| | Male | Male | Female | Male | Female | Male | Female | Male | Female | Male | Male | Female | Male | Female | Male | Female | Male | Female | |
| Less than $3 00 | | | | | | | | | 1 | | | 3 | 2 | 2 | 2 | 6 | 2.40 | 2.60 | Less than $3 00 |
| $3 00–$3 49 | | | | | | | | 1 | | | | 5 | 1 | 13 | 2 | 18 | 4.70 | 10.50 | $3 00– 3 49 |
| 3 50– 3 99 | | | | | | | | | | | | 1 | 2 | 6 | 2 | 7 | 7.10 | 13.60 | 3 50– 3 99 |
| 4 00– 4 49 | | | | | | | | 1 | | | | 9 | | 3 | 1 | 12 | 8.20 | 18.90 | 4 00– 4 49 |
| 4 50– 4 99 | | | | | | | | | | | | 4 | | | | 4 | | 20.60 | 4 50– 4 99 |
| 5 00– 5 49 | | | | | | | | 1 | 2 | | | 26 | | | 1 | 28 | 9.40 | 32.90 | 5 00– 5 49 |
| 5 50– 5 99 | | | | | | | | | | | 1 | 2 | | | 1 | 2 | 10.60 | 33.80 | 5 50– 5 99 |
| 6 00– 6 49 | | | | | | | | 1 | | | 1 | 25 | | | 2 | 25 | 12.90 | 44.70 | 6 00– 6 49 |
| 6 50– 6 99 | | | | | | | | | | | | 1 | | | | 1 | | 45.20 | 6 50– 6 99 |
| 7 00– 7 49 | | | | | | | 1 | | | | | 24 | | | | 25 | | 56.10 | 7 00– 7 49 |
| 7 50– 7 99 | | | | | | | | | | | 1 | 3 | | | 1 | 3 | 14.10 | 57.50 | 7 50– 7 99 |
| 8 00– 8 99 | | | | | | | | | | | | 27 | | | | 27 | | 69.40 | 8 00– 8 99 |
| 9 00– 9 99 | | | | | 1 | | 1 | | | | 1 | 15 | | | 1 | 17 | 15.30 | 76.80 | 9 00– 9 99 |
| 10 00–10 99 | | | | | | 2 | | | | | 3 | 14 | | | 5 | 14 | 21.20 | 83.00 | 10 00–10 99 |
| 11 00–11 99 | | | | | | | | | | | 2 | 5 | | | 2 | 5 | 23.60 | 85.10 | 11 00–11 99 |
| 12 00–12 99 | | | | | | | | | | | 6 | 9 | | | 6 | 9 | 30.60 | 89.00 | 12 00–12 99 |
| 13 00–13 99 | | | | | | | | | | | 2 | 1 | | | 2 | 1 | 32.90 | 89.50 | 13 00–13 99 |
| 14 00–14 99 | | | | | | | | | | | 6 | 3 | | | 6 | 3 | 40.00 | 90.80 | 14 00–14 99 |
| 15 00–15 99 | | | 1 | | 1 | | | | | | 3 | 6 | | | 3 | 8 | 43.50 | 94.30 | 15 00–15 99 |
| 16 00–17 99 | | 1 | 1 | | 1 | | | | | | 8 | 5 | | | 9 | 7 | 54.10 | 97.40 | 16 00–17 99 |
| 18 00–19 99 | | | | 1 | | | | | | 1 | 9 | 2 | | | 11 | 2 | 67.10 | 98.30 | 18 00–19 99 |
| 20 00–24 99 | 1 | | | 2 | | | | | | 1 | 5 | 1 | | | 9 | 1 | 77.60 | 98.60 | 20 00–24 99 |
| 25 00–29 99 | | 4 | 1 | | | | | | | | 3 | | | | 7 | 1 | 86.00 | 99.10 | 25 00–29 99 |
| 30 00–34 99 | | 3 | 1 | | | | | | | | 1 | | | | 4 | 1 | 90.60 | 99.50 | 30 00–34 99 |
| 35 00–39 99 | | 2 | 1 | | | | | | | 2 | | | | | 4 | 1 | 95.30 | 100.00 | 35 00–39 99 |
| 40 00 and over | | 3 | | | | | | | | 1 | | | | | 4 | | 100.00 | | 40 00 and over |
| Total | 1 | 13 | 5 | 3 | 3 | 2 | 2 | 4 | 3 | 5 | 52 | 191 | 5 | 24 | 85 | 228 | | | Total |

341. TABLE XV, A, 1, b, c, d, e.

SCHENECTADY

**DEPARTMENT STORES — OFFICE, SHIPPING AND DELIVERY, MANUFACTURING, PLANT**

NUMBER OF EMPLOYEES EARNING SPECIFIED WEEKLY RATES, ACCORDING TO DEPARTMENT AND SEX

| WEEKLY RATES IN DOLLARS | DEPARTMENT | | | | | | | | | | | WEEKLY RATES IN DOLLARS |
|---|---|---|---|---|---|---|---|---|---|---|---|---|
| | OFFICE | | SHIPPING AND DELIVERY | MANUFACTURING | | PLANT | | TOTAL | | CUMULATIVE PER CENT. OF TOTAL | | |
| | Male | Female | Male | Male | Female | Male | Female | Male | Female | Male | Female | |
| Less than $3 00 | ........ | ........ | ........ | ........ | 1 | ........ | 2 | ........ | 3 | ........ | 2.10 | Less than $3 00 |
| $3 00–$3 49... | 1 | 2 | ........ | ........ | 4 | ........ | 7 | 1 | 13 | 1.30 | 10.80 | ...$3 00– 3 49 |
| 3 50– 3 99... | ........ | 2 | ........ | ........ | 1 | ........ | ........ | ........ | 3 | ........ | 12.80 | ....3 50– 3 99 |
| 4 00– 4 49... | ........ | 4 | 1 | ........ | 3 | ........ | 1 | 1 | 8 | 2.50 | 18.30 | ....4 00– 4 49 |
| 4 50– 4 99... | ........ | 1 | ........ | ........ | 1 | ........ | ........ | ........ | 2 | ........ | 19.60 | ....4 50– 4 99 |
| 5 00– 5 49... | ........ | 7 | 1 | ........ | 2 | ........ | 8 | 1 | 17 | 3.80 | 31.10 | ....5 00– 5 49 |
| 6 00– 6 49... | 1 | 5 | 2 | ........ | 1 | 1 | 1 | 4 | 7 | 8.80 | 35.80 | ....6 00– 6 49 |
| 7 00– 7 49... | 1 | 11 | 1 | ........ | 5 | 1 | ........ | 3 | 16 | 12.50 | 46.60 | ....7 00– 7 49 |
| 7 50– 7 99... | ........ | ........ | ........ | ........ | 3 | ........ | ........ | ........ | 3 | ........ | 48.70 | ....7 50– 7 99 |
| 8 00– 8 99... | ........ | 4 | ........ | ........ | 11 | 2 | 1 | 2 | 16 | 15.00 | 59.50 | ....8 00– 8 99 |
| 9 00– 9 99... | ........ | 5 | 1 | ........ | 15 | ........ | 1 | 1 | 21 | 16.20 | 73.60 | ....9 00– 9 99 |
| 10 00–10 99... | ........ | 2 | 3 | ........ | 3 | 1 | ........ | 4 | 5 | 21.20 | 77.00 | ...10 00–10 99 |
| 11 00–11 99... | 1 | 3 | 2 | ........ | 1 | 1 | ........ | 4 | 4 | 51.20 | 79.70 | ...11 00–11 99 |
| 12 00–12 99... | ........ | 3 | 4 | 1 | 10 | 2 | ........ | 7 | 13 | 35.00 | 78.50 | ...12 00–12 99 |
| 13 00–13 99... | ........ | ........ | 1 | 1 | ........ | ........ | ........ | 2 | ........ | 37.50 | ........ | ...13 00–13 99 |
| 14 00–14 99... | ........ | 1 | 7 | ........ | 3 | 3 | ........ | 10 | 4 | 50.00 | 91.20 | ...14 00–14 99 |
| 15 00–15 99... | 2 | 2 | 5 | 1 | 3 | 2 | ........ | 10 | 5 | 62.50 | 94.50 | ...15 00–15 99 |
| 16 00–17 99... | ........ | 1 | 1 | 1 | 1 | 3 | ........ | 5 | 2 | 68.70 | 96.00 | ...16 00–17 99 |
| 18 00–19 99... | ........ | ........ | 5 | 2 | 1 | ........ | ........ | 7 | 1 | 77.50 | 96.60 | ...18 00–19 99 |
| 20 00–24 99... | 1 | ........ | ........ | 6 | 1 | 1 | ........ | 8 | 1 | 87.50 | 97.40 | ...20 00–24 99 |
| 25 00–29 99... | 4 | ........ | ........ | 2 | 1 | ........ | ........ | 6 | 1 | 95.00 | 98.00 | ...25 00–29 99 |
| 30 00–34 99... | 2 | 1 | ........ | ........ | 1 | ........ | ........ | 2 | 2 | 97.50 | 99.30 | ...30 00–34 99 |
| 35 00–39 99... | 1 | ........ | ........ | ........ | ........ | ........ | ........ | 1 | ........ | 98.70 | ........ | ...35 00–39 99 |
| 40 00 and over. | 1 | ........ | ........ | ........ | 1 | ........ | ........ | 1 | 1 | 100.00 | 100.00 | .40 00 and over |
| Total..... | 15 | 54 | 34 | 14 | 73 | 17 | 21 | 80 | 148 | ........ | ........ | .....Total |

342. TABLE XVI, A, 1, b, c, d, e.

SCHENECTADY

**DEPARTMENT STORES — OFFICE, SHIPPING AND DELIVERY, MANUFACTURING, PLANT**

NUMBER OF EMPLOYEES CLASSIFIED ACCORDING TO ACTUAL WEEKLY EARNINGS, BY DEPARTMENT AND SEX

| ACTUAL WEEKLY EARNINGS IN DOLLARS | DEPARTMENT | | | | | | | | | | | ACTUAL WEEKLY EARNINGS IN DOLLARS |
|---|---|---|---|---|---|---|---|---|---|---|---|---|
| | OFFICE | | SHIPPING AND DELIVERY | MANUFACTURING | | PLANT | | TOTAL | | CUMULATIVE PER CENT. OF TOTAL | | |
| | Male | Female | Male | Male | Female | Male | Female | Male | Female | Male | Female | |
| Less than $3 00 | ........ | 1 | 1 | ........ | 3 | 1 | 4 | 2 | 8 | 2.50 | 5.40 | Less than $3 00 |
| $3 00–$3 49... | 1 | 2 | ........ | ........ | 4 | ........ | 6 | 1 | 12 | 3.80 | 13.50 | ...$3 00– 3 49 |
| 3 50– 3 99... | ........ | 3 | 1 | ........ | 1 | ........ | 1 | 1 | 5 | 5.00 | 16.90 | ....3 50– 3 99 |
| 4 00– 4 49... | ........ | 4 | ........ | ........ | 1 | ........ | 1 | ........ | 6 | ........ | 21.00 | ....4 00– 4 49 |
| 4 50– 4 99... | ........ | ........ | ........ | ........ | 1 | ........ | ........ | ........ | 1 | ........ | 21.60 | ....4 50– 4 99 |
| 5 00– 5 49... | ........ | 6 | ........ | ........ | 2 | ........ | 7 | ........ | 15 | ........ | 31.80 | ....5 00– 5 49 |
| 5 50– 5 99... | ........ | ........ | ........ | ........ | 1 | ........ | ........ | ........ | 1 | ........ | 32.40 | ....5 50– 5 99 |
| 6 00– 6 49... | 1 | 7 | 2 | ........ | 3 | ........ | 1 | 3 | 11 | 8.80 | 39.80 | ....6 00– 6 49 |
| 6 50– 6 99... | ........ | ........ | ........ | ........ | 2 | ........ | ........ | ........ | 2 | ........ | 41.20 | ....6 50– 6 99 |
| 7 00– 7 49... | 1 | 9 | 1 | ........ | 6 | 1 | ........ | 3 | 15 | 12.50 | 51.40 | ....7 00– 7 49 |
| 7 50– 7 99... | ........ | ........ | 1 | ........ | 5 | ........ | ........ | 1 | 5 | 13.80 | 54.70 | ....7 50– 7 99 |
| 8 00– 8 99... | ........ | 4 | ........ | ........ | 10 | 2 | ........ | 2 | 14 | 16.30 | 64.20 | ....8 00– 8 99 |
| 9 00– 9 99... | ........ | 5 | 1 | ........ | 9 | ........ | 1 | 1 | 15 | 17.50 | 74.40 | ....9 00– 9 99 |
| 10 00–10 99... | ........ | 2 | 3 | ........ | 3 | 1 | ........ | 4 | 5 | 22.50 | 77.80 | ...10 00–10 99 |
| 11 00–11 99... | 1 | 3 | 3 | ........ | 2 | 1 | ........ | 5 | 5 | 28.80 | 81.10 | ...11 00–11 99 |
| 12 00–12 99... | ........ | 3 | 4 | 1 | 8 | 2 | ........ | 7 | 11 | 37.50 | 88.50 | ...12 00–12 99 |
| 13 00–13 99... | ........ | ........ | 1 | 1 | ........ | ........ | ........ | 2 | ........ | 40.00 | ........ | ...13 00–13 99 |
| 14 00–14 99... | ........ | 1 | 7 | 1 | 3 | 2 | ........ | 10 | 4 | 52.50 | 91.20 | ...14 00–14 99 |
| 15 00–15 99... | 2 | 2 | 3 | 2 | 3 | 3 | ........ | 10 | 5 | 65.00 | 94.60 | ...15 00–15 99 |
| 16 00–17 99... | ........ | 1 | 1 | 1 | 1 | 3 | ........ | 5 | 2 | 71.30 | 96.00 | ...16 00–17 99 |
| 18 00–19 99... | ........ | ........ | 5 | 1 | 1 | ........ | ........ | 6 | 1 | 78.70 | 96.60 | ...18 00–19 99 |
| 20 00–24 99... | 2 | ........ | ........ | 6 | 1 | 1 | ........ | 9 | 1 | 90.00 | 97.40 | ...20 00–24 99 |
| 25 00–29 99... | 3 | ........ | ........ | 1 | 1 | ........ | ........ | 4 | 1 | 95.00 | 98.00 | ...25 00–29 99 |
| 30 00–34 99... | 2 | 1 | ........ | ........ | 1 | ........ | ........ | 2 | 2 | 97.50 | 99.40 | ...30 00–34 99 |
| 35 00–39 99... | 1 | ........ | ........ | ........ | ........ | ........ | ........ | 1 | ........ | 98.70 | ........ | ...35 00–39 99 |
| 40 00 and over. | 1 | ........ | ........ | ........ | 1 | ........ | ........ | 1 | 1 | 100.00 | 100.00 | .40 00 and over |
| Total..... | 15 | 54 | 34 | 14 | 73 | 17 | 21 | 80 | 148 | ........ | ........ | .....Total |

343. TABLE XVII, A, 1, b, c, d, e

SCHENECTADY

**DEPARTMENT STORES — OFFICE, SHIPPING AND DELIVERY, MANUFACTURING, PLANT**

NUMBER OF EMPLOYEES CLASSIFIED BY AGE GROUPS ACCORDING TO DEPARTMENT AND SEX

| AGE GROUPS IN YEARS | DEPARTMENT | | | | | | | | | | | AGE GROUPS IN YEARS |
|---|---|---|---|---|---|---|---|---|---|---|---|---|
| | OFFICE | | SHIPPING AND DELIVERY | MANUFACTURING | | PLANT | | TOTAL | | PER CENT. OF TOTAL | | |
| | Male | Female | Male | Male | Female | Male | Female | Male | Female | Male | Female | |
| 16–17 | 1 | 6 | 1 | ........ | 4 | ........ | ........ | 2 | 10 | 2.50 | 6.80 | 16–17 |
| 18–20 | 3 | 22 | 3 | ........ | 11 | 1 | 1 | 7 | 34 | 8.80 | 23.00 | 18–20 |
| 21–24 | 1 | 12 | 7 | 1 | 11 | 1 | 7 | 10 | 30 | 12.70 | 20.20 | 21–24 |
| 25–29 | 1 | 6 | 9 | 1 | 9 | 5 | 8 | 16 | 23 | 20.20 | 15.50 | 25–29 |
| 30–34 | 4 | 2 | 4 | 1 | 13 | 1 | 3 | 10 | 18 | 12.70 | 12.20 | 30–34 |
| 35–39 | 1 | 3 | 4 | 4 | 8 | ........ | ........ | 9 | 11 | 11.40 | 7.40 | 35–39 |
| 40–44 | 1 | 2 | 1 | 4 | 6 | 2 | ........ | 8 | 8 | 10.10 | 5.40 | 40–44 |
| 45–54 | 1 | 1 | 4 | 2 | 10 | 3 | 2 | 10 | 13 | 12.70 | 8.80 | 45–54 |
| 55–64 | 1 | ........ | 1 | 1 | 1 | 3 | ........ | 6 | 1 | 7.60 | .70 | 55–64 |
| 65 and over | ........ | ........ | ........ | ........ | ........ | 1 | ........ | 1 | ........ | 1.30 | ........ | 65 and over |
| Not reported | 1 | ........ | ........ | ........ | ........ | ........ | ........ | 1 | ........ | ........ | ........ | Not reported |
| Total | 15 | 54 | 34 | 14 | 73 | 17 | 21 | 80 | 148 | 100.00 | 100.00 | Total |

UTICA

DEPARTMENT STORES — STOCK AND SALES

344. TABLE V, A, 1, a NUMBER AND PER CENT. OF EMPLOYEES EARNING SPECIFIED WEEKLY RATES, BY AGE GROUPS AND SEX

| WEEKLY RATES IN DOLLARS | AGE GROUPS IN YEARS 14–15 | | 16–17 | | 18–20 | | 21–24 | | 25–29 | | 30–34 | | 35–39 | | WEEKLY RATES IN DOLLARS |
|---|---|---|---|---|---|---|---|---|---|---|---|---|---|---|---|
| | Male | Female | Male | Female | Male | Female | Male | Female | Male | Female | Male | Female | Male | Female | |
| $3 00–$3 49... | .... | 2 | .... | 2 | ...... | ...... | ...... | ...... | ...... | ...... | ...... | ...... | ...... | ...... | ...$3 00–$3 49 |
| 3 50– 3 99... | 9 | ...... | 1 | 2 | ...... | ...... | ...... | ...... | ...... | ...... | ...... | ...... | ...... | ...... | ... 3 50– 3 99 |
| 4 00– 4 49... | 4 | 14 | 6 | 29 | ...... | 5 | ...... | 2 | ...... | ...... | ...... | ...... | ...... | ...... | ... 4 00– 4 49 |
| 4 50– 4 99... | 1 | ...... | 1 | 1 | ...... | 1 | ...... | 1 | ...... | ...... | ...... | ...... | ...... | ...... | ... 4 50– 4 99 |
| 5 00– 5 49... | .... | ...... | 3 | 23 | 1 | 19 | ...... | 6 | ...... | 2 | ...... | 2 | ...... | ...... | ... 5 00– 5 49 |
| 5 50– 5 99... | .... | ...... | 1 | ...... | ...... | 3 | ...... | 1 | ...... | ...... | ...... | ...... | ...... | ...... | ... 5 50– 5 99 |
| 6 00– 6 49... | .... | 1 | 4 | 5 | 1 | 26 | ...... | 19 | 1 | 3 | ...... | 3 | ...... | 3 | ... 6 00– 6 49 |
| 7 00– 7 49... | .... | ...... | 1 | 1 | 4 | 13 | 1 | 18 | ...... | 5 | ...... | 2 | ...... | 4 | ... 7 00– 7 49 |
| 7 50– 7 99... | .... | ...... | .... | ...... | ...... | ...... | ...... | 1 | ...... | ...... | ...... | ...... | ...... | ...... | ... 7 50– 7 99 |
| 8 00– 8 99... | .... | ...... | 1 | 1 | 4 | 4 | ...... | 16 | ...... | 8 | ...... | 4 | ...... | 5 | ... 8 00– 8 99 |
| 9 00– 9 99... | .... | ...... | .... | ...... | 2 | 1 | 1 | 7 | ...... | 11 | ...... | 5 | ...... | 3 | ... 9 00– 9 99 |
| 10 00–10 99... | .... | ...... | .... | ...... | 1 | ...... | 2 | 6 | 2 | 11 | 1 | 2 | ...... | 10 | ...10 00–10 99 |
| 11 00–11 99... | .... | ...... | .... | ...... | ...... | ...... | 2 | 1 | ...... | 1 | ...... | 3 | ...... | ...... | ...11 00–11 99 |
| 12 00–12 99... | .... | ...... | .... | ...... | 4 | ...... | 1 | ...... | 5 | 4 | 1 | 6 | 1 | 6 | ...12 00–12 99 |
| 13 00–13 99... | .... | ...... | .... | ...... | ...... | ...... | ...... | ...... | ...... | ...... | ...... | ...... | ...... | 1 | ...13 00–13 99 |
| 14 00–14 99... | .... | ...... | .... | ...... | ...... | ...... | ...... | ...... | 1 | ...... | 2 | ...... | 2 | ...... | ...14 00–14 99 |
| 15 00–15 99... | .... | ...... | .... | ...... | ...... | ...... | ...... | ...... | 2 | 3 | 1 | 1 | 4 | ...... | ...15 00–15 99 |
| 16 00–17 99... | .... | ...... | .... | ...... | ...... | ...... | ...... | ...... | 3 | ...... | ...... | ...... | 5 | ...... | ...16 00–17 99 |
| 18 00–19 99... | .... | ...... | .... | ...... | ...... | ...... | ...... | ...... | 1 | 1 | 2 | ...... | 1 | 1 | ...18 00–19 99 |
| 20 00–24 99... | .... | ...... | .... | ...... | ...... | ...... | ...... | ...... | 3 | ...... | 3 | 1 | 4 | ...... | ...20 00–24 99 |
| 25 00–29 99... | .... | ...... | .... | ...... | ...... | ...... | ...... | ...... | ...... | ...... | 2 | ...... | 2 | 3 | ...25 00–29 99 |
| 30 00–34 99... | .... | ...... | .... | ...... | ...... | ...... | ...... | ...... | ...... | ...... | 1 | ...... | 3 | ...... | ...30 00–34 99 |
| 35 00–39 99... | .... | ...... | .... | ...... | ...... | ...... | ...... | ...... | ...... | ...... | 1 | ...... | ...... | ...... | ...35 00–39 99 |
| 40 00 and over. | .... | ...... | .... | ...... | ...... | ...... | ...... | ...... | ...... | ...... | 1 | ...... | 2 | ...... | .40 00 and over |
| Not reported.. | .... | ...... | .... | ...... | ...... | ...... | ...... | ...... | ...... | ...... | ...... | ...... | 2 | 1 | ..Not reported |
| Total..... | 14 | 17 | 18 | 64 | 17 | 72 | 7 | 78 | 18 | 49 | 15 | 29 | 26 | 37 | .....Total |

344. TABLE V, A, 1, a — (*concluded*)

UTICA

DEPARTMENT STORES — STOCK AND SALES

NUMBER AND PER CENT. OF EMPLOYEES EARNING SPECIFIED WEEKLY RATES, BY AGE GROUPS AND SEX

| WEEKLY RATES IN DOLLARS | AGE GROUPS IN YEARS (*concluded*) 49–44 | | 45–54 | | 55–64 | | 65 AND OVER | NOT REPORTED | | TOTAL | | CUMULATIVE PER CENT. OF TOTAL | | WEEKLY RATES IN DOLLARS |
|---|---|---|---|---|---|---|---|---|---|---|---|---|---|---|
| | Male | Female | Male | Female | Male | Female | Male | Male | Female | Male | Female | Male | Female | |
| $3 00–$3 49 | ...... | ...... | ...... | ...... | ...... | ...... | ...... | 1 | ...... | 1 | 4 | .60 | 1.10 | $3 00–$3 49 |
| 3 50– 3 99 | ...... | ...... | ...... | ...... | ...... | ...... | ...... | ...... | ...... | 10 | 2 | 6.60 | 1.60 | 3 50– 3 99 |
| 4 00– 4 49 | ...... | ...... | ...... | ...... | ...... | ...... | ...... | ...... | ...... | 10 | 50 | 12.70 | 14.90 | 4 00– 4 49 |
| 4 50– 4 99 | ...... | ...... | ...... | ...... | ...... | ...... | ...... | ...... | ...... | 2 | 3 | 13.90 | 15.70 | 4 50– 4 99 |
| 5 00– 5 49 | ...... | ...... | ...... | ...... | ...... | ...... | ...... | 1 | ...... | 5 | 52 | 16.90 | 29.50 | 5 00– 5 49 |
| 5 50– 5 99 | ...... | ...... | ...... | ...... | ...... | ...... | ...... | ...... | ...... | 1 | 4 | 17.50 | 30.60 | 5 50– 5 99 |
| 6 00– 6 49 | ...... | ...... | ...... | 2 | ...... | ...... | ...... | ...... | 1 | 6 | 63 | 21.10 | 47.30 | 6 00– 6 49 |
| 7 00– 7 49 | ...... | ...... | ...... | 1 | ...... | ...... | ...... | ...... | ...... | 6 | 44 | 24.70 | 59.10 | 7 00– 7 49 |
| 7 50– 7 99 | ...... | 1 | ...... | ...... | ...... | ...... | ...... | ...... | ...... | ...... | 2 | ...... | 59.60 | 7 50– 7 99 |
| 8 00– 8 99 | ...... | 3 | ...... | 2 | ...... | ...... | ...... | ...... | ...... | 5 | 43 | 27.70 | 71.00 | 8 00– 8 99 |
| 9 00– 9 99 | 1 | 1 | ...... | ...... | ...... | ...... | ...... | ...... | ...... | 4 | 28 | 30.10 | 78.50 | 9 00– 9 99 |
| 10 00–10 99 | ...... | 1 | ...... | 2 | 3 | ...... | ...... | ...... | ...... | 9 | 32 | 35.60 | 87.00 | 10 00–10 99 |
| 11 00–11 99 | ...... | ...... | ...... | 1 | ...... | ...... | ...... | ...... | 1 | 2 | 7 | 36.80 | 88.80 | 11 00–11 99 |
| 12 00–12 99 | 2 | ...... | 4 | 4 | 2 | ...... | ...... | ...... | ...... | 20 | 20 | 48.80 | 94.20 | 12 00–12 99 |
| 13 00–13 99 | 1 | ...... | ...... | ...... | ...... | ...... | ...... | ...... | ...... | 1 | 1 | 49.40 | 94.40 | 13 00–13 99 |
| 14 00–14 99 | ...... | 1 | 1 | 1 | 1 | 1 | ...... | ...... | ...... | 7 | 3 | 53.60 | 95.20 | 14 00–14 99 |
| 15 00–15 99 | 2 | 1 | 4 | 1 | ...... | ...... | 1 | ...... | ...... | 14 | 6 | 62.00 | 96.80 | 15 00–15 99 |
| 16 00–17 99 | 2 | 2 | 2 | ...... | ...... | ...... | ...... | ...... | 2 | 12 | 4 | 69.30 | 97.90 | 16 00–17 99 |
| 18 00–19 99 | 2 | ...... | 3 | ...... | 1 | ...... | ...... | ...... | ...... | 10 | 2 | 75.30 | 98.50 | 18 00–19 99 |
| 20 00–24 99 | 4 | ...... | 4 | ...... | 1 | ...... | ...... | ...... | ...... | 19 | 1 | 86.70 | 98.60 | 20 00–24 99 |
| 25 00–29 99 | 5 | ...... | 2 | 1 | 2 | ...... | ...... | ...... | ...... | 13 | 4 | 94.50 | 99.70 | 25 00–29 99 |
| 30 00–34 99 | ...... | ...... | ...... | ...... | ...... | ...... | ...... | ...... | 1 | 4 | 1 | 97.00 | 100.00 | 30 00–34 99 |
| 35 00–39 99 | ...... | ...... | ...... | ...... | ...... | ...... | ...... | ...... | ...... | 1 | ...... | 97.50 | ...... | 35 00–39 99 |
| 40 00 and over | ...... | ...... | 1 | ...... | ...... | ...... | ...... | ...... | ...... | 4 | ...... | 100.00 | ...... | 40 00 and over |
| Not reported | ...... | ...... | ...... | ...... | ...... | ...... | ...... | ...... | ...... | 2 | 1 | ...... | ...... | Not reported |
| Total | 19 | 10 | 21 | 15 | 10 | 1 | 1 | 2 | 5 | 168 | 377 | ...... | ...... | Total |

345. TABLE VIII, A, 1, a

UTICA

DEPARTMENT STORES — STOCK AND SALES

Number and Per Cent. of Employees Earning Specified Weekly Rates, by Occupation and Sex

| Weekly Rates in Dollars | Occupation: Superintendents | Assistant Buyers and Heads of Stock | | Receiving and Stock Clerks | | Stock People | | Floor Managers | | Sales People | | Messengers, Wrappers, Errand Boys | | Total | | Cumulative Per Cent. of Total | | Weekly Rates in Dollars |
|---|---|---|---|---|---|---|---|---|---|---|---|---|---|---|---|---|---|---|
| | Male | Male | Female | Male | Female | Male | Female | Male | Female | Male | Female | Male | Female | Male | Female | Male | Female | |
| $3 00–$3 49 | | | | | | | | | | 1 | | | 4 | 1 | 4 | .60 | 1.10 | $3 00–$3 49 |
| 3 50– 3 99 | | | | | | | | | | | | 10 | 2 | 10 | 2 | 6.60 | 1.60 | 3 50– 3 99 |
| 4 00– 4 49 | | | | | | | 1 | | | 1 | 16 | 9 | 33 | 10 | 50 | 12.70 | 14.90 | 4 00– 4 49 |
| 4 50– 4 99 | | | | | | | 1 | | | | 1 | 2 | 1 | 2 | 3 | 13.90 | 15.70 | 4 50– 4 99 |
| 5 00– 5 49 | | | | | | 2 | | | | | 48 | 3 | 4 | 5 | 52 | 16.90 | 29.50 | 5 00– 5 49 |
| 5 50– 5 99 | | | | | | | | | | | 4 | 1 | | 1 | 4 | 17.50 | 30.60 | 5 50– 5 99 |
| 6 00– 6 49 | | | | | | 1 | | | | 3 | 63 | 2 | | 6 | 63 | 21.10 | 47.30 | 6 00– 6 49 |
| 7 00– 7 49 | | | | | | | | | | 6 | 44 | | | 6 | 44 | 24.70 | 59.10 | 7 00– 7 49 |
| 7 50– 7 99 | | | | | | | | | | | 2 | | | | 2 | | 59.60 | 7 50– 7 99 |
| 8 00– 8 99 | | 1 | | | | | | | | 4 | 42 | | 1 | 5 | 43 | 27.70 | 71.00 | 8 00– 8 99 |
| 9 00– 9 99 | | | 1 | | 1 | | | | | 4 | 26 | | | 4 | 28 | 30.10 | 78.50 | 9 00– 9 99 |
| 10 00–10 99 | | 1 | 2 | | | | | 1 | | 7 | 30 | | | 9 | 32 | 35.60 | 87.00 | 10 00–10 99 |
| 11 00–11 99 | | | | | 1 | | | | | 2 | 6 | | | 2 | 7 | 36.80 | 88.80 | 11 00–11 99 |
| 12 00–12 99 | | | 3 | 2 | | | | | 1 | 18 | 16 | | | 20 | 20 | 48.80 | 94.20 | 12 00–12 99 |
| 13 00–13 99 | | | | | | | | | | 1 | 1 | | | 1 | 1 | 49.40 | 94.40 | 13 00–13 99 |
| 14 00–14 99 | | | | | | | | | | 7 | 3 | | | 7 | 3 | 53.60 | 95.20 | 14 00–14 99 |
| 15 00–15 99 | | | 3 | 1 | | | | 2 | | 11 | 3 | | | 14 | 6 | 62.00 | 96.80 | 15 00–15 99 |
| 16 00–17 99 | | 1 | 1 | | | | | 1 | | 10 | 3 | | | 12 | 4 | 69.30 | 97.90 | 16 00–17 99 |
| 18 00–19 99 | | 2 | | | | | | 2 | 1 | 6 | 1 | | | 10 | 2 | 75.30 | 98.50 | 18 00–19 99 |
| 20 00–24 99 | | 6 | | | | | | 3 | 1 | 10 | | | | 19 | 1 | 86.70 | 98.60 | 20 00–24 99 |
| 25 00–29 99 | | 5 | 3 | | | | | 4 | 1 | 4 | | | | 13 | 4 | 94.50 | 99.70 | 25 00–29 99 |
| 30 00–34 99 | 1 | 2 | 1 | | | | | 1 | | | | | | 4 | 1 | 97.00 | 100.00 | 30 00–34 99 |
| 35 00–39 99 | | | | | | | | 1 | | | | | | 1 | | 97.50 | | 35 00–39 99 |
| 40 00 and over | | 2 | | | | | | 2 | | | | | | 4 | | 100.00 | | 40 00 and over |
| Not reported | | 2 | | | | | | | | | 1 | | | 2 | 1 | | | Not reported |
| Total | 1 | 22 | 14 | 3 | 2 | 3 | 2 | 17 | 4 | 95 | 310 | 27 | 45 | 168 | 377 | | | Total |

346. TABLE VI, A, I, a

UTICA

DEPARTMENT STORES — STOCK AND SALES

Number and Per Cent. of Employees Classified According to Actual Weekly Earnings, by Age Groups and Sex

| Actual Weekly Earnings in Dollars | Age Groups in Years | | | | | | | | | | | | | | Actual Weekly Earnings in Dollars |
|---|---|---|---|---|---|---|---|---|---|---|---|---|---|---|---|
| | 14–15 | | 16–17 | | 18–20 | | 21–24 | | 25–29 | | 30–34 | | 35–39 | | |
| | Male | Female | Male | Female | Male | Female | Male | Female | Male | Female | Male | Female | Male | Female | |
| Less than $3 00 | ... | ... | ... | 1 | ... | ... | ... | ... | ... | ... | ... | 1 | ... | ... | Less than $3 00 |
| $3 00–$3 49 | 1 | 2 | 2 | 5 | ... | 1 | ... | 1 | ... | ... | ... | ... | ... | ... | $3 00– 3 49 |
| 3 50– 3 99 | 9 | 2 | 1 | 7 | ... | 1 | ... | 1 | ... | ... | ... | ... | ... | ... | 3 50– 3 99 |
| 4 00– 4 49 | 3 | 12 | 4 | 23 | 1 | 7 | ... | 2 | ... | ... | ... | ... | ... | ... | 4 00– 4 49 |
| 4 50– 4 99 | 1 | ... | 1 | 7 | ... | 4 | ... | 1 | ... | ... | ... | ... | ... | ... | 4 50– 4 99 |
| 5 50– 5 49 | ... | ... | 3 | 14 | ... | 12 | ... | 8 | ... | 1 | ... | 2 | ... | ... | 5 00– 5 49 |
| 5 50– 5 99 | ... | ... | 2 | 1 | ... | 5 | ... | 1 | 1 | 1 | ... | ... | ... | ... | 5 50– 5 99 |
| 6 00– 6 49 | ... | 1 | 4 | 3 | 3 | 18 | ... | 17 | ... | 3 | ... | 2 | ... | 2 | 6 00– 6 49 |
| 6 50– 6 99 | ... | ... | ... | 1 | ... | 2 | ... | 1 | ... | ... | ... | 1 | ... | 1 | 6 50– 6 99 |
| 7 00– 7 49 | ... | ... | ... | 1 | 4 | 16 | 1 | 15 | ... | 8 | ... | 1 | ... | 3 | 7 00– 7 49 |
| 7 50– 7 99 | ... | ... | ... | ... | ... | ... | ... | 3 | ... | 1 | ... | 2 | ... | ... | 7 50– 7 99 |
| 8 00– 8 99 | ... | ... | 1 | 1 | 3 | 5 | ... | 13 | ... | 2 | ... | 3 | ... | 5 | 8 00– 8 99 |
| 9 00– 9 99 | ... | ... | ... | ... | 1 | ... | 1 | 9 | ... | 11 | ... | 6 | ... | 2 | 9 00– 9 99 |
| 10 00–10 99 | ... | ... | ... | ... | 1 | 1 | 2 | 4 | 2 | 13 | 1 | ... | ... | 11 | 10 00–10 99 |
| 11 00–11 99 | ... | ... | ... | ... | ... | ... | 2 | 1 | 1 | 1 | ... | 3 | ... | 2 | 11 00–11 99 |
| 12 00–12 99 | ... | ... | ... | ... | 4 | ... | 1 | ... | 4 | 4 | 1 | 5 | 1 | 5 | 12 00–12 99 |
| 13 00–13 99 | ... | ... | ... | ... | ... | ... | ... | 1 | ... | ... | ... | 1 | ... | 2 | 13 00–13 99 |
| 14 00–14 99 | ... | ... | ... | ... | ... | ... | ... | ... | 1 | ... | 2 | ... | 2 | ... | 14 00–14 99 |
| 15 00–15 99 | ... | ... | ... | ... | ... | ... | ... | ... | 2 | 3 | 1 | 1 | 4 | ... | 15 00–15 99 |
| 16 00–17 99 | ... | ... | ... | ... | ... | ... | ... | ... | 3 | ... | ... | ... | 5 | 1 | 16 00–17 99 |
| 18 00–19 99 | ... | ... | ... | ... | ... | ... | ... | ... | 1 | 1 | 2 | ... | 1 | 1 | 18 00–19 99 |
| 20 00–24 99 | ... | ... | ... | ... | ... | ... | ... | ... | 3 | ... | 2 | 1 | 4 | ... | 20 00–24 99 |
| 25 00–29 99 | ... | ... | ... | ... | ... | ... | ... | ... | ... | ... | 3 | ... | 2 | 1 | 25 00–29 99 |
| 30 00–34 99 | ... | ... | ... | ... | ... | ... | ... | ... | ... | ... | 1 | ... | 3 | ... | 30 00–34 99 |
| 35 00–39 99 | ... | ... | ... | ... | ... | ... | ... | ... | ... | ... | 1 | ... | 1 | ... | 35 00–39 99 |
| 40 00 and over | ... | ... | ... | ... | ... | ... | ... | ... | ... | ... | 1 | ... | 3 | ... | 40 00 and over |
| Not reported | ... | ... | ... | ... | ... | ... | ... | ... | ... | ... | ... | ... | ... | 1 | Not reported |
| Total | 14 | 17 | 18 | 64 | 17 | 72 | 7 | 78 | 18 | 49 | 15 | 29 | 26 | 37 | Total |

UTICA

346. TABLE VI, A, 1, a — *(concluded)* DEPARTMENT STORES — STOCK AND SALES

NUMBER AND PER CENT. OF EMPLOYEES CLASSIFIED ACCORDING TO ACTUAL WEEKLY EARNINGS, BY AGE GROUPS AND SEX

| ACTUAL WEEKLY EARNINGS IN DOLLARS | AGE GROUPS IN YEARS *(concluded)* | | | | | | | | | | | | | ACTUAL WEEKLY EARNINGS IN DOLLARS |
|---|---|---|---|---|---|---|---|---|---|---|---|---|---|---|
| | 40–44 | | 45–54 | | 55–64 | | 65 AND OVER | NOT REPORTED | | TOTAL | | CUMULATIVE PER CENT. OF TOTAL | | |
| | Male | Female | Male | Female | Male | Female | Male | Male | Female | Male | Female | Male | Female | |
| Less than $3 00 | | | | | | | | | | | 2 | | .50 | Less than $3 00 |
| $3 00–$3 49 | | | | | | | | 1 | | 4 | 9 | 2.40 | 2.90 | $3 00– 3 49 |
| 3 50– 3 99 | | | | | | | | | | 10 | 11 | 8.30 | 5.90 | 3 50– 3 99 |
| 4 00– 4 49 | | | | | | | | | | 8 | 44 | 13.10 | 17.60 | 4 00– 4 49 |
| 4 50– 4 99 | | | | | | | | | | 2 | 12 | 14.30 | 20.80 | 4 50– 4 99 |
| 5 00– 5 49 | | | | | | | | 1 | | 4 | 37 | 16.70 | 30.60 | 5 00– 5 49 |
| 5 50– 5 99 | | | | | | | | | | 3 | 8 | 18.50 | 32.70 | 5 50– 5 99 |
| 6 00– 6 49 | | 1 | | 2 | | | | | 1 | 7 | 50 | 22.60 | 46.00 | 6 00– 6 49 |
| 6 50– 6 99 | | | | | | | | | | | 6 | | 47.60 | 6 50– 6 99 |
| 7 00– 7 49 | | | | 1 | | | | | | 5 | 45 | 25.60 | 59.60 | 7 00– 7 49 |
| 7 50– 7 99 | | | | | | | | | | | 6 | | 61.20 | 7 50– 7 99 |
| 8 00– 8 99 | | 2 | | 2 | | | | | | 4 | 33 | 28.00 | 70.00 | 8 00– 8 99 |
| 9 00– 9 99 | 1 | 2 | | | | | | | | 3 | 30 | 29.80 | 78.00 | 9 00– 9 99 |
| 10 00–10 99 | | 1 | | 3 | 3 | | | | | 9 | 33 | 35.20 | 87.80 | 10 00–10 99 |
| 11 00–11 99 | | | | 2 | | | | | 1 | 3 | 10 | 36.90 | 89.50 | 11 00–11 99 |
| 12 00–12 99 | 2 | | 3 | 4 | 2 | | | | | 18 | 18 | 47.60 | 94.20 | 12 00–12 99 |
| 13 00–13 99 | 1 | | 1 | | | | | | | 2 | 4 | 48.80 | 95.30 | 13 00–13 99 |
| 14 00–14 99 | | 1 | 1 | | 1 | 1 | | | 1 | 7 | 3 | 53.00 | 96.00 | 14 00–14 99 |
| 15 00–15 99 | 2 | 1 | 4 | | | | 1 | | | 14 | 5 | 61.40 | 97.50 | 15 00–15 99 |
| 16 00–17 99 | 2 | 1 | 2 | | | | | | 1 | 12 | 3 | 68.50 | 98.20 | 16 00–17 99 |
| 18 00–19 99 | 2 | 1 | 3 | | 1 | | | | | 10 | 3 | 74.50 | 99.00 | 18 00–19 99 |
| 20 00–24 99 | 4 | | 4 | | 1 | | | | | 18 | 1 | 85.10 | 99.20 | 20 00–24 99 |
| 25 00–29 99 | 5 | | 2 | 1 | 2 | | | | | 14 | 2 | 93.50 | 99.80 | 25 00–29 99 |
| 30 00–34 99 | | | | | | | | | 1 | 4 | 1 | 95.80 | 100.00 | 30 00–34 99 |
| 35 00–39 99 | | | | | | | | | | 2 | | 97.00 | | 35 00–39 99 |
| 40 00 and over | | | 1 | | | | | | | 5 | | 100.00 | | 40 00 and over |
| Not reported | | | | | | | | | | | 1 | | | Not reported |
| Total | 19 | 10 | 21 | 15 | 10 | 1 | 1 | 2 | 5 | 168 | 377 | | | Total |

47. TABLE IX, A, 1, a

UTICA

DEPARTMENT STORES — STOCK AND SALES

NUMBER AND PER CENT. OF EMPLOYEES CLASSIFIED ACCORDING TO ACTUAL WEEKLY EARNINGS, BY OCCUPATION AND SEX

| ACTUAL WEEKLY EARNINGS IN DOLLARS | OCCUPATION | | | | | | | | | | | | | | | | | ACTUAL WEEKLY EARNINGS IN DOLLARS |
|---|---|---|---|---|---|---|---|---|---|---|---|---|---|---|---|---|---|---|
| | SUPERINTENDENTS | ASSISTANT BUYERS AND HEADS OF STOCK | | RECEIVING AND STOCK CLERKS | | STOCK PEOPLE | | FLOOR MANAGERS | | SALES PEOPLE | | MESSENGERS, WRAPPERS, ERRAND BOYS | | TOTAL | | CUMULATIVE PER CENT. OF TOTAL | | |
| | Male | Male | Female | Male | Female | Male | Female | Male | Female | Male | Female | Male | Female | Male | Female | Male | Female | |
| Less than $3 00 | | | | | | | | | | | 2 | | | | 2 | | .50 | Less than $3 00 |
| $3 00–$3 49 | | | | | | | 1 | | | 1 | 2 | 3 | 6 | 4 | 9 | 2.40 | 2.90 | $3 00– 3 49 |
| 3 50– 3 99 | | | | | | | | | | | 6 | 10 | 5 | 10 | 11 | 8.30 | 5.90 | 3 50– 3 99 |
| 4 00– 4 49 | | | | | | 1 | | | | 1 | 16 | 6 | 28 | 8 | 44 | 13.10 | 17.60 | 4 00– 4 49 |
| 4 50– 4 99 | | | | | | | 1 | | | | 11 | 2 | | 2 | 12 | 14.30 | 20.80 | 4 50– 4 99 |
| 5 00– 5 49 | | | | | | 1 | | | | | 32 | 3 | 5 | 4 | 37 | 16.70 | 30.60 | 5 00– 5 49 |
| 5 50– 5 99 | | | | | | | | | | 2 | 8 | 1 | | 3 | 8 | 18.50 | 32.70 | 5 50– 5 99 |
| 6 00– 6 49 | | | | | | 1 | | | | 4 | 50 | 2 | | 7 | 50 | 22.60 | 46.00 | 6 00– 6 49 |
| 6 50– 6 99 | | | | | | | | | | | 6 | | | | 6 | | 47.60 | 6 50– 6 99 |
| 7 00– 7 49 | | | | | | | | | | 5 | 45 | | | 5 | 45 | 25.60 | 59.60 | 7 00– 7 49 |
| 7 50– 7 99 | | | | | | | | | | | 6 | | | | 6 | | 61.20 | 7 50– 7 99 |
| 8 00– 8 99 | | 1 | 1 | | | | | | | 3 | 31 | | 1 | 4 | 33 | 28.00 | 70.00 | 8 00– 8 99 |
| 9 00– 9 99 | | | 1 | | 1 | | | | | 3 | 28 | | | 3 | 30 | 29.80 | 78.00 | 9 00– 9 99 |
| 10 00–10 99 | | 1 | 2 | | | | | 1 | | 7 | 31 | | | 9 | 33 | 35.20 | 87.80 | 10 00–10 99 |
| 11 00–11 99 | | | | | 1 | | | | | 3 | 9 | | | 3 | 10 | 36.90 | 89.50 | 11 00–11 99 |
| 12 00–12 99 | | | 3 | 2 | | | | | 1 | 16 | 14 | | | 18 | 18 | 47.60 | 94.20 | 12 00–12 99 |
| 13 00–13 99 | | | | | | | | | | 2 | 4 | | | 2 | 4 | 48.80 | 95.30 | 13 00–13 99 |
| 14 00–14 99 | | | | | | | | | | 7 | 3 | | | 7 | 3 | 53.00 | 96.00 | 14 00–14 99 |
| 15 00–15 99 | | | 3 | 1 | | | | 2 | | 11 | 2 | | | 14 | 5 | 61.40 | 97.50 | 15 00–15 99 |
| 16 00–17 99 | | 1 | 2 | | | | | 1 | | 10 | 1 | | | 12 | 3 | 68.50 | 98.20 | 16 00–17 99 |
| 18 00–19 99 | | 2 | | | | | | 2 | 1 | 6 | 2 | | | 10 | 3 | 74.50 | 99.00 | 18 00–19 99 |
| 20 00–24 99 | | 6 | | | | | | 3 | 1 | 9 | | | | 18 | 1 | 85.10 | 99.20 | 20 00–24 99 |
| 25 00–29 99 | | 5 | 1 | | | | | 4 | 1 | 5 | | | | 14 | 2 | 93.50 | 99.80 | 25 00–29 99 |
| 30 00–34 99 | 1 | 2 | 1 | | | | | 1 | | | | | | 4 | 1 | 95.80 | 100.00 | 30 00–34 99 |
| 35 00–39 99 | | 1 | | | | | | 1 | | | | | | 2 | | 97.00 | | 35 00–39 99 |
| 40 00 and over | | 3 | | | | | | 2 | | | | | | 5 | | 100.00 | | 40 00 and over |
| Not reported | | | | | | | | | | | 1 | | | | 1 | | | Not reported |
| Total | 1 | 22 | 14 | 3 | 2 | 3 | 2 | 17 | 4 | 95 | 310 | 27 | 45 | 168 | 377 | | | Total |

348. TABLE XV, A, 1, b, c, d, e.

UTICA

**DEPARTMENT STORES — OFFICE, SHIPPING AND DELIVERY, MANUFACTURING, PLANT**

NUMBER OF EMPLOYEES EARNING SPECIFIED WEEKLY RATES, ACCORDING TO DEPARTMENT AND SEX

| WEEKLY RATES IN DOLLARS | DEPARTMENT | | | | | | | | | | | WEEKLY RATES IN DOLLARS |
|---|---|---|---|---|---|---|---|---|---|---|---|---|
| | OFFICE | | SHIPPING AND DELIVERY | MANUFACTURING | | PLANT | | TOTAL | | CUMULATIVE PER CENT. OF TOTAL | | |
| | Male | Female | Male | Male | Female | Male | Female | Male | Female | Male | Female | |
| Less than $3 00 | ........ | ........ | ........ | ........ | 1 | ........ | ........ | ........ | 1 | ........ | .80 | Less than $3 00 |
| $3 50–$3 99... | ........ | 1 | ........ | ........ | ........ | ........ | 10 | ........ | 11 | ........ | 9.30 | ...$3 50– 3 99 |
| 4 00– 4 49... | ........ | 2 | ........ | ........ | ........ | ........ | 1 | ........ | 3 | ........ | 11.60 | ....4 00– 4 49 |
| 4 50– 4 99... | ........ | ........ | 2 | ........ | ........ | 1 | ........ | 3 | ........ | 2.60 | ........ | ....4 50– 4 99 |
| 5 00– 5 49... | ........ | 6 | 1 | ........ | ........ | 1 | 3 | 2 | 9 | 4.40 | 18.60 | ....5 00– 5 49 |
| 5 50– 5 99... | ........ | ........ | ........ | ........ | ........ | ........ | 5 | ........ | 5 | ........ | 22.50 | ....5 50– 5 99 |
| 6 00– 6 49... | 2 | 7 | ........ | ........ | 1 | ........ | ........ | 2 | 8 | 6.10 | 28.70 | ....6 00– 6 49 |
| 7 00– 7 49... | 1 | 8 | 3 | ........ | 1 | 1 | 1 | 5 | 10 | 10.40 | 36.40 | ....7 00– 7 49 |
| 7 50– 7 99... | ........ | ........ | ........ | ........ | 2 | 1 | ........ | 1 | 2 | 11.30 | 38.00 | ....7 50– 7 99 |
| 8 00– 8 99... | ........ | 19 | ........ | ........ | 20 | 5 | 2 | 5 | 41 | 15.70 | 69.80 | ....8 00– 8 99 |
| 9 00– 9 99... | 1 | 6 | 1 | ........ | 3 | 1 | ........ | 3 | 9 | 18.30 | 76.80 | ....9 00– 9 99 |
| 10 00–10 99... | 1 | 5 | 1 | ........ | 4 | 7 | 1 | 9 | 10 | 26.10 | 84.50 | ...10 00–10 99 |
| 11 00–11 99... | 1 | 1 | ........ | 1 | ........ | 1 | ........ | 3 | 1 | 28.70 | 85.30 | ...11 00–11 99 |
| 12 00–12 99... | 6 | 4 | 11 | 1 | 5 | 7 | 1 | 25 | 10 | 50 50 | 93.10 | ...12 00–12 99 |
| 13 00–13 99... | ........ | 1 | 9 | 1 | ........ | ........ | ........ | 10 | 1 | 59.20 | 93.90 | ...13 00–13 99 |
| 14 00–14 99... | 1 | ........ | ........ | 2 | 1 | 2 | ........ | 5 | 1 | 63.50 | 94.60 | ...14 00–14 99 |
| 15 00–15 99... | 8 | 1 | 3 | 2 | 1 | 3 | 1 | 16 | 3 | 77.40 | 97.00 | ...15 00–15 99 |
| 16 00–17 99... | ........ | ........ | 2 | ........ | ........ | 3 | ........ | 5 | ........ | 81.70 | ........ | ...16 00–17 99 |
| 18 00–19 99... | 2 | ........ | ........ | 1 | ........ | 2 | ........ | 5 | ........ | 86.10 | ........ | ...18 00–19 99 |
| 20 00–24 99... | 6 | ........ | ........ | 3 | 2 | 2 | ........ | 11 | 2 | 95.60 | 98.50 | ...20 00–24 99 |
| 25 00–29 99... | 2 | ........ | ........ | ........ | 2 | 1 | ........ | 3 | 2 | 98.30 | 100.00 | ...25 00–29 99 |
| 30 00–34 99... | 1 | ........ | ........ | ........ | ........ | ........ | ........ | 1 | ........ | 99.20 | ........ | ...30 00–34 99 |
| 35 00–39 99... | 1 | ........ | ........ | ........ | ........ | ........ | ........ | 1 | ........ | 100.00 | ........ | ...35 00–39 99 |
| Total..... | 33 | 61 | 33 | 11 | 43 | 38 | 25 | 115 | 129 | ........ | ........ | .....Total |

349. TABLE XVI, A, 1, b, c, d, e.

UTICA

DEPARTMENT STORES — OFFICE, SHIPPING AND DELIVERY, MANUFACTURING, PLANT

NUMBER OF EMPLOYEES CLASSIFIED ACCORDING TO ACTUAL WEEKLY EARNINGS, BY DEPARTMENT AND SEX

| ACTUAL WEEKLY EARNINGS IN DOLLARS | DEPARTMENT | | | | | | | | | | | ACTUAL WEEKLY EARNINGS IN DOLLARS |
|---|---|---|---|---|---|---|---|---|---|---|---|---|
| | OFFICE | | SHIPPING AND DELIVERY | MANUFACTURING | | PLANT | | TOTAL | | CUMULATIVE PER CENT. OF TOTAL | | |
| | Male | Female | Male | Male | Female | Male | Female | Male | Female | Male | Female | |
| Less than $3 00 | ........ | ........ | ........ | ........ | 1 | ........ | 2 | ........ | 3 | ........ | 2.30 | Less than $3 00 |
| $3 50–$3 99... | ........ | 1 | ........ | ........ | ........ | ........ | 8 | ........ | 9 | ........ | 9.30 | ...$3 50– 3 99 |
| 4 00– 4 49... | ........ | 2 | ........ | ........ | ........ | ........ | 1 | ........ | 3 | ........ | 11.60 | ....4 00– 4 49 |
| 4 50– 4 99... | ........ | ........ | 2 | ........ | ........ | 1 | ........ | 3 | ........ | 2.60 | ........ | ....4 50– 4 99 |
| 5 00– 5 49... | ........ | 6 | 1 | ........ | ........ | 1 | 3 | 2 | 9 | 4.30 | 18.60 | ....5 00– 5 49 |
| 5 50– 5 99... | ........ | ........ | ........ | ........ | ........ | ........ | 5 | ........ | 5 | ........ | 22.50 | ....5 50– 5 99 |
| 6 00– 6 49... | 2 | 8 | ........ | ........ | 3 | ........ | ........ | 2 | 11 | 6.00 | 31.00 | ....6 00– 6 49 |
| 6 50– 6 99... | ........ | ........ | ........ | ........ | 1 | ........ | ........ | ........ | 1 | ........ | 31.80 | ....6 50– 6 99 |
| 7 00– 7 49... | 1 | 7 | 3 | 1 | 2 | 1 | 1 | 6 | 10 | 11.20 | 39.50 | ....7 00– 7 49 |
| 7 50– 7 99... | ........ | ........ | 1 | ........ | 1 | 1 | ........ | 2 | 1 | 12.90 | 40.30 | ....7 50– 7 99 |
| 8 00– 8 99... | ........ | 17 | ........ | ........ | 18 | 5 | 2 | 5 | 37 | 17.20 | 69.00 | ....8 00– 8 99 |
| 9 00– 9 99... | 1 | 6 | 1 | ........ | 3 | 2 | ........ | 4 | 9 | 20.70 | 76.00 | ....9 00– 9 99 |
| 10 00–10 99... | 1 | 7 | 1 | ........ | 4 | 6 | 1 | 8 | 12 | 27.60 | 85.30 | ...10 00–10 99 |
| 11 00–11 99... | 1 | 1 | ........ | 1 | ........ | 1 | ........ | 3 | 1 | 30.20 | 86.00 | ...11 00–11 99 |
| 12 00–12 99... | 6 | 4 | 11 | 1 | 4 | 5 | 1 | 23 | 9 | 50.00 | 93.00 | ...12 00–12 99 |
| 13 00–13 99... | ........ | 1 | 8 | 2 | 1 | 1 | ........ | 11 | 2 | 59.50 | 94.60 | ...13 00–13 99 |
| 14 00–14 99... | 1 | ........ | ........ | 1 | 1 | 3 | ........ | 5 | 1 | 63.80 | 95.40 | ...14 00–14 99 |
| 15 00–15 99... | 8 | 1 | 3 | 2 | ........ | 3 | 1 | 16 | 2 | 77.50 | 97.00 | ...15 00–15 99 |
| 16 00–17 99... | ........ | ........ | 2 | ........ | ........ | 3 | ........ | 5 | ........ | 81.90 | ........ | ...16 00–17 99 |
| 18 00–19 99... | 2 | ........ | ........ | 1 | ........ | 2 | ........ | 5 | ........ | 86.20 | ........ | ...18 00–19 99 |
| 20 00–24 99... | 6 | ........ | ........ | 3 | 2 | 2 | ........ | 11 | 2 | 95.70 | 98.50 | ...20 00–24 99 |
| 25 00–29 99... | 2 | ........ | ........ | ........ | 2 | 1 | ........ | 3 | 2 | 98.20 | 100.00 | ...25 00–29 99 |
| 30 00–34 99... | 1 | ........ | ........ | ........ | ........ | ........ | ........ | 1 | ........ | 99.10 | ........ | ...30 00–34 99 |
| 35 00–39 99... | 1 | ........ | ........ | ........ | ........ | ........ | ........ | 1 | ........ | 100.00 | ........ | ...35 00–39 99 |
| Total..... | 33 | 61 | 33 | 12 | 43 | 38 | 25 | 116 | 129 | ........ | ........ | .....Total |

UTICA

DEPARTMENT STORES — OFFICE, SHIPPING AND DELIVERY, MANUFACTURING, PLANT

350. Table XVII, A, 1, b, c, d, e. NUMBER OF EMPLOYEES CLASSIFIED BY AGE GROUPS, ACCORDING TO DEPARTMENT AND SEX

| AGE GROUPS IN YEARS | DEPARTMENT | | | | | | | | | | | AGE GROUPS IN YEARS |
|---|---|---|---|---|---|---|---|---|---|---|---|---|
| | OFFICE | | SHIPPING AND DELIVERY | MANUFACTURING | | PLANT | | TOTAL | | CUMULATIVE PER CENT. OF TOTAL | | |
| | Male | Female | Male | Male | Female | Male | Female | Male | Female | Male | Female | |
| 14–15 | ........ | 1 | 2 | ........ | ........ | ........ | ........ | 2 | 1 | 1.70 | .80 | 14–15 |
| 16–17 | 1 | 3 | ........ | ........ | 1 | 3 | ........ | 4 | 4 | 3.40 | 3.20 | 16–17 |
| 18–20 | 3 | 20 | 9 | 1 | 1 | 4 | 2 | 17 | 23 | 14.70 | 18.30 | 18–20 |
| 21–24 | 6 | 18 | 4 | 2 | 5 | 1 | 2 | 13 | 25 | 11.20 | 19.80 | 21–24 |
| 25–29 | 9 | 11 | 7 | 2 | 6 | 3 | 3 | 21 | 20 | 18.10 | 15.90 | 25–29 |
| 30–34 | 3 | 4 | 3 | 1 | 4 | 2 | 5 | 9 | 13 | 7.70 | 10.30 | 30–34 |
| 35–39 | 6 | 2 | 2 | 3 | 6 | 3 | 6 | 14 | 14 | 12.10 | 11.10 | 35–39 |
| 40–44 | 2 | 2 | 1 | 1 | 7 | 2 | 5 | 6 | 14 | 5.20 | 11.10 | 40–44 |
| 45–54 | 2 | ........ | 4 | ........ | 10 | 13 | 1 | 19 | 11 | 16.40 | 8.70 | 45–54 |
| 55–64 | ........ | ........ | 1 | 2 | ........ | 5 | 1 | 8 | 1 | 6.90 | .80 | 55–64 |
| 65 and over | 1 | ........ | ........ | ........ | ........ | 2 | ........ | 3 | ........ | 2.60 | ........ | 65 and over |
| Not reported | ........ | ........ | ........ | ........ | 3 | ........ | ........ | ........ | 3 | ........ | ........ | Not reported |
| Total | 33 | 61 | 33 | 12 | 43 | 38 | 25 | 116 | 129 | 100.00 | 100.00 | Total |

TROY

DEPARTMENT STORES — STOCK AND SALES

351. TABLE V, A, 1, a. NUMBER AND PER CENT. OF EMPLOYEES EARNING SPECIFIED WEEKLY RATES, BY AGE GROUPS AND SEX

| WEEKLY RATES IN DOLLARS | Age Groups in Years | | | | | | | | | | | | | | WEEKLY RATES IN DOLLARS |
|---|---|---|---|---|---|---|---|---|---|---|---|---|---|---|---|
| | 14–15 | | 16–17 | | 18–20 | | 21–24 | | 25–29 | | 30–34 | | 35–39 | | |
| | Male | Female | Male | Female | Male | Female | Male | Female | Male | Female | Male | Female | Male | Female | |
| Less than $3 00 | 1 | | | | | | | | | | | | | | Less than $3 00 |
| $3 00–$3 49 | 2 | 26 | 4 | 18 | | 1 | | | | | | | | | $3 00– 3 49 |
| 3 50– 3 99 | | | 2 | 7 | | | | | | | | | | | 3 50– 3 99 |
| 4 00– 4 49 | 2 | 1 | 7 | 9 | 1 | 3 | | | | | | | | | 4 00– 4 49 |
| 4 50– 4 99 | | | 7 | 5 | | | | | | | | | | | 4 50– 4 99 |
| 5 00– 5 49 | 1 | | 8 | 2 | | 3 | | 1 | | 1 | | 1 | | | 5 00– 5 49 |
| 5 50– 5 99 | | | 1 | | | 1 | | | | | | | | | 5 50– 5 99 |
| 6 00– 6 49 | | | 1 | 4 | 1 | 17 | | 9 | | 3 | | | | 3 | 6 00– 6 49 |
| 6 50– 6 99 | | | | | | | | 1 | | | | | | | 6 50– 6 99 |
| 7 00– 7 49 | | | 2 | | 4 | 17 | 2 | 17 | 1 | 6 | | 2 | | 1 | 7 00– 7 49 |
| 7 50– 7 99 | | | | | 1 | 1 | | 1 | | 2 | | 1 | | | 7 50– 7 99 |
| 8 00– 8 99 | | | | 2 | 7 | 6 | 1 | 19 | | 11 | | 1 | | 2 | 8 00– 8 99 |
| 9 00– 9 99 | | | | | 1 | 2 | | 5 | | 5 | 1 | 4 | | 2 | 9 00– 9 99 |
| 10 00–10 99 | | | | | | 2 | 5 | 9 | | 12 | | 2 | | 1 | 10 00–10 99 |
| 11 00–11 99 | | | | | | | 1 | | | | | | | 1 | 11 00–11 99 |
| 12 00–12 99 | | | | | | | 5 | 2 | 1 | 2 | 5 | 3 | 2 | 5 | 12 00–12 99 |
| 13 00–13 99 | | | | | | | | | 2 | | 3 | 2 | 1 | 1 | 13 00–13 99 |
| 14 00–14 99 | | | | | | | 4 | | 2 | 1 | 1 | 1 | 2 | 4 | 14 00–14 99 |
| 15 00–15 99 | | | | | | | 1 | | 2 | | 8 | 1 | | 2 | 15 00–15 99 |
| 16 00–17 99 | | | | | | | | 1 | | 1 | 4 | 2 | 2 | 1 | 16 00–17 99 |
| 18 00–19 99 | | | | | | | | | 2 | | 2 | 1 | 1 | | 18 00–19 99 |
| 20 00–24 99 | | | | | | | | | 2 | | 4 | 1 | 7 | 2 | 20 00–24 99 |
| 25 00–29 99 | | | | | | | | | 1 | | 1 | | 3 | | 25 00–29 99 |
| Total | 6 | 27 | 32 | 47 | 15 | 53 | 19 | 65 | 13 | 44 | 29 | 22 | 18 | 25 | Total |

351. TABLE V, A, 1, a — (*concluded*)

TROY

DEPARTMENT STORES — STOCK AND SALES

NUMBER AND PER CENT. OF EMPLOYEES EARNING SPECIFIED WEEKLY RATES, BY AGE GROUPS AND SEX

| WEEKLY RATES IN DOLLARS | AGE GROUPS IN YEARS (*concluded*) | | | | | | | | | | | | WEEKLY RATES IN DOLLARS |
|---|---|---|---|---|---|---|---|---|---|---|---|---|---|
| | 40–44 | | 45–54 | | 55–64 | 65 AND OVER | NOT REPORTED | | TOTAL | | CUMULATIVE PER CENT. OF TOTAL | | |
| | Male | Female | Male | Female | Male | Male | Male | Female | Male | Female | Male | Female | |
| Less than $3 00 | ....... | ....... | ....... | ....... | ....... | ....... | ....... | ....... | 1 | ....... | .50 | ....... | Less than $3 00 |
| $3 00–$3 49 | ....... | ....... | ....... | ....... | ....... | ....... | ....... | ....... | 6 | 45 | 3.20 | 14.60 | $3 00– 3 49 |
| 3 50– 3 99 | ....... | ....... | ....... | ....... | ....... | ....... | ....... | ....... | 2 | 7 | 4.10 | 16.90 | 3 50– 3 99 |
| 4 00– 4 49 | ....... | ....... | ....... | ....... | ....... | ....... | ....... | ....... | 10 | 13 | 8.60 | 21.10 | 4 00– 4 49 |
| 4 50– 4 99 | ....... | ....... | ....... | ....... | ....... | ....... | ....... | ....... | 7 | 5 | 11.80 | 22.70 | 4 50– 4 99 |
| 5 00– 5 49 | ....... | ....... | ....... | ....... | ....... | ....... | ....... | ....... | 9 | 8 | 15.90 | 25.30 | 5 00– 5 49 |
| 5 50– 5 99 | ....... | ....... | ....... | ....... | ....... | ....... | ....... | ....... | 1 | 1 | 16.40 | 25.60 | 5 50– 5 99 |
| 6 00– 6 49 | ....... | 1 | ....... | ....... | 1 | ....... | ....... | ....... | 3 | 37 | 17.70 | 37.60 | 6 00– 6 49 |
| 6 50– 6 99 | ....... | ....... | ....... | ....... | ....... | ....... | ....... | ....... | ....... | 1 | ....... | 38.00 | 6 50– 6 99 |
| 7 00– 7 49 | ....... | 1 | ....... | ....... | ....... | ....... | ....... | ....... | 9 | 44 | 21.80 | 52.30 | 7 00– 7 49 |
| 7 50– 7 99 | ....... | ....... | ....... | 1 | ....... | ....... | ....... | ....... | 1 | 6 | 22.30 | 54.20 | 7 50– 7 99 |
| 8 00– 8 99 | ....... | ....... | ....... | ....... | ....... | ....... | ....... | ....... | 8 | 41 | 25.90 | 67.50 | 8 00– 8 99 |
| 9 00– 9 99 | 1 | 1 | 1 | 2 | ....... | ....... | ....... | ....... | 4 | 21 | 27.80 | 74.40 | 9 00– 9 99 |
| 10 00–10 99 | ....... | 3 | 1 | 2 | ....... | 1 | ....... | 2 | 7 | 33 | 30.90 | 85.00 | 10 00–10 99 |
| 11 00–11 99 | ....... | ....... | 1 | ....... | 1 | ....... | ....... | 1 | 3 | 2 | 32.30 | 85.80 | 11 00–11 99 |
| 12 00–12 99 | 1 | ....... | 1 | 2 | 1 | ....... | ....... | ....... | 16 | 14 | 39.60 | 90.40 | 12 00–12 99 |
| 13 00–13 99 | 1 | ....... | 1 | ....... | ....... | 1 | ....... | ....... | 9 | 3 | 43.60 | 91.30 | 13 00–13 99 |
| 14 00–14 99 | ....... | 2 | 4 | ....... | ....... | ....... | ....... | 2 | 13 | 10 | 49.50 | 94.50 | 14 00–14 99 |
| 15 00–15 99 | 1 | 1 | 2 | ....... | 1 | 1 | 1 | ....... | 17 | 4 | 52.30 | 95.80 | 15 00–15 99 |
| 16 00–17 99 | 3 | ....... | 10 | ....... | 2 | 1 | ....... | 1 | 22 | 6 | 67.30 | 97.70 | 16 00–17 99 |
| 18 00–19 99 | 3 | ....... | 7 | ....... | 2 | ....... | 1 | ....... | 18 | 1 | 75.50 | 98.00 | 18 00–19 99 |
| 20 00–24 99 | 5 | ....... | 11 | 1 | 3 | ....... | ....... | 1 | 32 | 5 | 90.00 | 99.70 | 20 00–24 99 |
| 25 00–29 99 | 1 | ....... | 6 | 1 | ....... | ....... | ....... | ....... | 12 | 1 | 95.50 | 100.00 | 25 00–29 99 |
| 30 00–34 99 | 1 | ....... | 3 | ....... | 2 | ....... | ....... | ....... | 6 | ....... | 98.30 | ....... | 30 00–34 99 |
| 35 00–39 99 | ....... | ....... | 1 | ....... | 1 | ....... | ....... | ....... | 2 | ....... | 99.10 | ....... | 35 00–39 99 |
| 40 00 and over | ....... | ....... | 1 | ....... | 1 | ....... | ....... | ....... | 2 | ....... | 100.0 | ....... | 40 00 and over |
| Total | 17 | 9 | 50 | 9 | 15 | 4 | 2 | 7 | 220 | 308 | ....... | ....... | Total |

352. TABLE VIII, A, 1, a

TROY

DEPARTMENT STORES — STOCK AND SALES

NUMBER AND PER CENT. OF EMPLOYEES EARNING SPECIFIED WEEKLY RATES, BY OCCUPATION AND SEX

| WEEKLY RATES IN DOLLARS | OCCUPATION | | | | | | | | | | | | | | | | | WEEKLY RATES IN DOLLARS |
|---|---|---|---|---|---|---|---|---|---|---|---|---|---|---|---|---|---|---|
| | BUYERS | | ASSISTANT BUYERS AND HEADS OF STOCK | | RECEIVING AND STOCK CLERKS | STOCK PEOPLE | | FLOOR MANAGERS | SALES PEOPLE | | MESSENGERS, WRAPPERS, ERRAND BOYS | | TOTAL | | CUMULATIVE PER CENT. OF TOTAL | | |
| | Male | Female | Male | Female | Male | Male | Female | Male | Male | Female | Male | Female | Male | Female | Male | Female | |
| Less than $3 00 | ..... | ..... | ..... | ..... | .......... | ..... | ..... | .......... | ..... | ..... | 1 | ..... | 1 | ..... | .50 | ..... | Less than $3 00 |
| $3 00–$3 49 | ..... | ..... | ..... | ..... | .......... | ..... | ..... | .......... | ..... | ..... | 6 | 45 | 6 | 45 | 3.20 | 14.60 | $3 00– 3 49 |
| 3 50– 3 99 | ..... | ..... | ..... | ..... | .......... | ..... | ..... | .......... | ..... | ..... | 2 | 7 | 2 | 7 | 4.10 | 16.90 | 3 50– 3 99 |
| 4 00– 4 49 | ..... | ..... | ..... | ..... | .......... | 1 | ..... | .......... | ..... | 2 | 9 | 11 | 10 | 13 | 8.60 | 21.10 | 4 00– 4 49 |
| 4 50– 4 99 | ..... | ..... | ..... | ..... | .......... | ..... | ..... | .......... | ..... | ..... | 7 | 5 | 7 | 5 | 11.80 | 22.70 | 4 50– 4 99 |
| 5 00– 5 49 | ..... | ..... | ..... | ..... | .......... | 3 | ..... | .......... | ..... | 5 | 6 | 3 | 9 | 8 | 15.90 | 25.30 | 5 00– 5 49 |
| 5 50– 5 99 | ..... | ..... | ..... | ..... | .......... | ..... | ..... | .......... | ..... | 1 | 1 | ..... | 1 | 1 | 16.40 | 25.60 | 5 50– 5 99 |
| 6 00– 6 49 | ..... | ..... | ..... | ..... | .......... | 2 | 1 | .......... | 1 | 36 | ..... | ..... | 3 | 37 | 17.70 | 37.60 | 6 00– 6 49 |
| 6 50– 6 99 | ..... | ..... | ..... | ..... | .......... | ..... | ..... | .......... | ..... | 1 | ..... | ..... | ..... | 1 | ..... | 38.00 | 6 50– 6 99 |
| 7 00– 7 49 | ..... | ..... | ..... | ..... | .......... | ..... | ..... | .......... | 5 | 44 | 4 | ..... | 9 | 44 | 21.80 | 52.30 | 7 00– 7 49 |
| 7 50– 7 99 | ..... | ..... | ..... | ..... | .......... | ..... | ..... | .......... | ..... | 6 | 1 | ..... | 1 | 6 | 22.30 | 54.20 | 7 50– 7 99 |
| 8 00– 8 99 | ..... | ..... | ..... | ..... | .......... | ..... | ..... | .......... | 7 | 40 | 1 | 1 | 8 | 41 | 25.90 | 67.50 | 8 00– 8 99 |
| 9 00– 9 99 | ..... | ..... | ..... | ..... | .......... | ..... | ..... | .......... | 4 | 21 | ..... | ..... | 4 | 21 | 27.80 | 74.40 | 9 00– 9 99 |
| 10 00–10 99 | ..... | 1 | ..... | ..... | 1 | ..... | ..... | .......... | 6 | 32 | ..... | ..... | 7 | 33 | 30.90 | 85.00 | 10 00–10 99 |
| 11 00–11 99 | ..... | 1 | ..... | ..... | .......... | 2 | ..... | .......... | 1 | 1 | ..... | ..... | 3 | 2 | 32.30 | 85.80 | 11 00–11 99 |
| 12 00–12 99 | ..... | 1 | 1 | ..... | .......... | ..... | ..... | .......... | 15 | 13 | ..... | ..... | 16 | 14 | 39.60 | 90.40 | 12 00–12 99 |
| 13 00–13 99 | ..... | ..... | ..... | ..... | .......... | ..... | ..... | .......... | 9 | 3 | ..... | ..... | 9 | 3 | 43.60 | 91.30 | 13 00–13 99 |
| 14 00–14 99 | ..... | ..... | ..... | ..... | 1 | ..... | ..... | .......... | 12 | 10 | ..... | ..... | 13 | 10 | 49.50 | 94.50 | 14 00–14 99 |
| 15 00–15 99 | ..... | ..... | ..... | ..... | .......... | 1 | ..... | 1 | 14 | 4 | 1 | ..... | 17 | 4 | 52.30 | 95.80 | 15 00–15 99 |
| 16 00–17 99 | 5 | 2 | ..... | ..... | .......... | ..... | ..... | 1 | 16 | 4 | ..... | ..... | 22 | 6 | 67.30 | 97.70 | 16 00–17 99 |
| 18 00–19 99 | ..... | ..... | 1 | 1 | .......... | ..... | ..... | 1 | 16 | ..... | ..... | ..... | 18 | 1 | 75.50 | 98.00 | 18 00–19 99 |
| 20 00–24 99 | 5 | 2 | 1 | ..... | .......... | ..... | ..... | 5 | 21 | 3 | ..... | ..... | 32 | 5 | 90.00 | 99.70 | 20 00–24 99 |
| 25 00–29 99 | 7 | 1 | ..... | ..... | .......... | ..... | ..... | 2 | 3 | ..... | ..... | ..... | 12 | 1 | 95.50 | 100.00 | 25 00–29 99 |
| 30 00–34 99 | 6 | ..... | ..... | ..... | .......... | ..... | ..... | .......... | ..... | ..... | ..... | ..... | 6 | ..... | 98.30 | ..... | 30 00–34 99 |
| 35 00–39 99 | 2 | ..... | ..... | ..... | .......... | ..... | ..... | .......... | ..... | ..... | ..... | ..... | 2 | ..... | 99.10 | ..... | 35 00–39 99 |
| 40 00 and over | 2 | ..... | ..... | ..... | .......... | ..... | ..... | .......... | ..... | ..... | ..... | ..... | 2 | ..... | 100.00 | ..... | 40 00 and over |
| Total | 27 | 8 | 3 | 1 | 2 | 9 | 1 | 10 | 130 | 226 | 39 | 72 | 220 | 308 | ..... | ..... | Total |

353. TABLE VI, A, 1, a

TROY

DEPARTMENT STORES — STOCK AND SALES

NUMBER AND PER CENT. OF EMPLOYEES CLASSIFIED ACCORDING TO ACTUAL WEEKLY EARNINGS, BY AGE GROUPS AND SEX

| ACTUAL WEEKLY EARNINGS IN DOLLARS | AGE GROUPS IN YEARS | | | | | | | | | | | | | | ACTUAL WEEKLY EARNINGS IN DOLLARS |
|---|---|---|---|---|---|---|---|---|---|---|---|---|---|---|---|
| | 14–15 | | 16–17 | | 18–20 | | 21–24 | | 25–29 | | 30–34 | | 35–39 | | |
| | Male | Female | Male | Female | Male | Female | Male | Female | Male | Female | Male | Female | Male | Female | |
| Less than $3 00 | 1 | 4 | 3 | 7 | ...... | 1 | ...... | ...... | ...... | ...... | ...... | ...... | ...... | ...... | Less than $3 00 |
| $3 00–$3 49... | 2 | 22 | 2 | 11 | ...... | ...... | ...... | ...... | ...... | ...... | ...... | ...... | ...... | ...... | ...$3 00– 3 49 |
| 3 50– 3 99... | .... | ...... | 4 | 8 | ...... | 2 | ...... | ...... | ...... | ...... | ...... | ...... | ...... | ...... | ... 3 50– 3 99 |
| 4 00– 4 49... | 2 | 1 | 5 | 8 | 1 | 1 | ...... | 1 | ...... | 1 | ...... | ...... | ...... | 1 | ... 4 00– 4 49 |
| 4 50– 4 99... | .... | ...... | 6 | 5 | ...... | ...... | ...... | ...... | ...... | ...... | ...... | ...... | ...... | ...... | ... 4 50– 4 99 |
| 5 00– 5 49... | 1 | ...... | 8 | 2 | ...... | 4 | ...... | 2 | ...... | 1 | ...... | 1 | ...... | ...... | ... 5 00– 5 49 |
| 5 50– 5 99... | .... | ...... | 1 | 1 | ...... | 2 | ...... | 1 | ...... | 3 | ...... | ...... | ...... | 1 | ... 5 50– 5 99 |
| 6 00– 6 49... | .... | ...... | 1 | 3 | 1 | 17 | ...... | 11 | ...... | 1 | ...... | ...... | ...... | 3 | ... 6 00– 6 49 |
| 6 50– 6 99... | .... | ...... | .... | ...... | 1 | 2 | ...... | 2 | ...... | ...... | ...... | ...... | ...... | ...... | ... 6 50– 6 99 |
| 7 00– 7 49... | .... | ...... | 2 | ...... | 3 | 14 | 2 | 16 | 1 | 9 | ...... | 2 | ...... | ...... | ... 7 00– 7 49 |
| 7 50– 7 99... | .... | ...... | .... | ...... | 1 | ...... | ...... | 1 | ...... | 1 | ...... | 1 | ...... | ...... | ... 7 50– 7 99 |
| 8 00– 8 99... | .... | ...... | .... | 2 | 7 | 6 | 1 | 16 | ...... | 7 | 1 | 3 | ...... | 2 | ... 8 00– 8 99 |
| 9 00– 9 99... | .... | ...... | .... | ...... | 1 | 4 | ...... | 5 | ...... | 7 | 1 | 3 | ...... | 3 | ... 9 00– 9 99 |
| 10 00–10 99... | .... | ...... | .... | ...... | ...... | ...... | 5 | 7 | ...... | 10 | ...... | 1 | ...... | ...... | ...10 00–10 99 |
| 11 00–11 99... | .... | ...... | .... | ...... | ...... | ...... | 1 | ...... | 1 | 1 | 2 | ...... | ...... | 1 | ...11 00–11 99 |
| 12 00–12 99... | .... | ...... | .... | ...... | ...... | ...... | 5 | 2 | 2 | 2 | 3 | 3 | 2 | 3 | ...12 00–12 99 |
| 13 00–13 99... | .... | ...... | .... | ...... | ...... | ...... | 1 | ...... | 1 | ...... | 3 | 2 | 1 | 2 | ...13 00–13 99 |
| 14 00–14 99... | .... | ...... | .... | ...... | ...... | ...... | 3 | ...... | 2 | ...... | 1 | 2 | 2 | 6 | ...14 00–14 99 |
| 15 00–15 99... | .... | ...... | .... | ...... | ...... | ...... | 1 | ...... | 1 | ...... | 7 | ...... | ...... | ...... | ...15 00–15 99 |
| 16 00–17 99... | .... | ...... | .... | ...... | ...... | ...... | ...... | 1 | ...... | 1 | 4 | 3 | 2 | 1 | ...16 00–17 99 |
| 18 00–19 99... | .... | ...... | .... | ...... | ...... | ...... | ...... | ...... | 2 | ...... | 2 | 1 | 1 | ...... | ...18 00–19 99 |
| 20 00–24 99... | .... | ...... | .... | ...... | ...... | ...... | ...... | ...... | 2 | ...... | 4 | ...... | 7 | 2 | ...20 00–24 99 |
| 25 00–29 99... | .... | ...... | .... | ...... | ...... | ...... | ...... | ...... | 1 | ...... | 1 | ...... | 3 | ...... | ...25 00–29 99 |
| Total..... | 6 | 27 | 32 | 47 | 15 | 53 | 19 | 65 | 13 | 44 | 29 | 22 | 18 | 25 | .....Total |

353. TABLE VI, A, 1, * — (*concluded*)

TROY

DEPARTMENT STORES — STOCK AND SALES

NUMBER AND PER CENT. OF EMPLOYEES CLASSIFIED ACCORDING TO ACTUAL WEEKLY EARNINGS, BY AGE GROUPS AND SEX

| ACTUAL WEEKLY EARNINGS IN DOLLARS | AGE GROUPS IN YEARS (*concluded*) 40–44 | | 45–54 | | 55–64 | 65 AND OVER | NOT REPORTED | | TOTAL | | CUMULATIVE PER CENT. OF TOTAL | | ACTUAL WEEKLY EARNINGS IN DOLLARS |
|---|---|---|---|---|---|---|---|---|---|---|---|---|---|
| | Male | Female | Male | Female | Male | Male | Male | Female | Male | Female | Male | Female | |
| Less than $3 00. | ....... | ....... | ....... | ....... | ....... | ....... | ....... | ....... | 4 | 12 | 1.80 | 3.90 | Less than $3 00 |
| $3 00–$3 49.... | ....... | ....... | ....... | ....... | ....... | ....... | ....... | ....... | 4 | 33 | 3.70 | 14.60 | ...$3 00– 3 49 |
| 3 50– 3 99.... | ....... | ....... | ....... | ....... | ....... | ....... | ....... | ....... | 4 | 10 | 5.50 | 17.90 | ... 3 50– 3 99 |
| 4 00– 4 49.... | ....... | ....... | ....... | ....... | ....... | ....... | ....... | ....... | 8 | 13 | 9.10 | 22.10 | ... 4 00– 4 49 |
| 4 50– 4 99.... | ....... | ....... | ....... | ....... | ....... | ....... | ....... | ....... | 6 | 5 | 11.90 | 23.70 | ... 4 50– 4 99 |
| 5 00– 5 49.... | ....... | ....... | ....... | 1 | ....... | ....... | ....... | ....... | 9 | 11 | 16.00 | 27.30 | ... 5 00– 5 49 |
| 5 50– 5 99.... | ....... | ....... | ....... | ....... | ....... | ....... | ....... | ....... | 1 | 8 | 16.40 | 29.90 | ... 5 50– 5 99 |
| 6 00– 6 49.... | ....... | 1 | ....... | ....... | 1 | ....... | ....... | ....... | 3 | 36 | 17.80 | 41.50 | ... 6 00– 6 49 |
| 6 50– 6 99.... | ....... | ....... | ....... | ....... | ....... | ....... | ....... | ....... | 1 | 4 | 18.30 | 42.80 | ... 6 50– 6 99 |
| 7 00– 7 49.... | ....... | 1 | ....... | ....... | ....... | ....... | ....... | ....... | 8 | 42 | 21.90 | 56.50 | ... 7 00– 7 49 |
| 7 50– 7 99.... | ....... | ....... | ....... | 1 | ....... | ....... | ....... | ....... | 1 | 4 | 24.70 | 57.80 | ... 7 50– 7 99 |
| 8 00– 8 99.... | ....... | ....... | ....... | 1 | ....... | ....... | ....... | ....... | 9 | 37 | 26.70 | 69.80 | ... 8 00– 8 99 |
| 9 00– 9 99.... | 1 | 2 | 2 | 1 | ....... | ....... | ....... | ....... | 5 | 25 | 28.80 | 73.00 | ... 9 00– 9 99 |
| 10 00–10 99.... | ....... | 2 | 1 | 1 | ....... | 1 | ....... | 2 | 7 | 23 | 32.00 | 85.50 | ...10 00–10 99 |
| 11 00–11 99.... | ....... | ....... | 1 | ....... | 1 | ....... | ....... | 1 | 6 | 3 | 34.70 | 86.40 | ...11 00–11 99 |
| 12 00–12 99.... | 1 | ....... | 1 | 2 | 1 | ....... | ....... | ....... | 15 | 12 | 41.60 | 90.30 | ...12 00–12 99 |
| 13 00–13 99.... | ....... | ....... | ....... | ....... | ....... | 1 | ....... | ....... | 7 | 4 | 44.80 | 91.60 | ...13 00–13 99 |
| 14 00–14 99.... | 1 | 2 | 4 | ....... | ....... | ....... | ....... | 2 | 13 | 12 | 50.70 | 95.50 | ...14 00–14 99 |
| 15 00–15 99.... | 2 | 1 | 3 | ....... | 1 | 1 | 1 | ....... | 17 | 1 | 58.50 | 95.80 | ...15 00–15 99 |
| 16 00–17 99.... | 2 | ....... | 7 | ....... | 2 | 1 | ....... | 1 | 18 | 7 | 66.70 | 98.10 | ...16 00–17 99 |
| 18 00–19 99.... | 3 | ....... | 9 | ....... | 2 | ....... | 1 | ....... | 20 | 1 | 75.80 | 98.40 | ...18 00–19 99 |
| 20 00–24 99.... | 5 | ....... | 10 | 1 | 3 | ....... | ....... | 1 | 31 | 4 | 90.00 | 99.70 | ...20 00–24 99 |
| 25 00–29 99.... | 1 | ....... | 6 | 1 | ....... | ....... | ....... | ....... | 12 | 1 | 95.50 | 100.00 | ...25 00–29 99 |
| 30 00–34 99.... | 1 | ....... | 3 | ....... | 3 | ....... | ....... | ....... | 7 | ....... | 98.60 | ....... | ...30 00–34 99 |
| 35 00–39 99.... | ....... | ....... | 1 | ....... | ....... | ....... | ....... | ....... | 1 | ....... | 99.10 | ....... | ...35 00–39 99 |
| 40 00 and over.. | ....... | ....... | 1 | ....... | 1 | ....... | ....... | ....... | 2 | ....... | 100.00 | ....... | .40 00 and over |
| Not reported.... | ....... | ....... | 1 | ....... | ....... | ....... | ....... | ....... | 1 | ....... | ....... | ....... | ...Not reported |
| Total...... | 17 | 9 | 50 | 9 | 15 | 4 | 2 | 7 | 220 | 308 | ....... | ....... | .....Total |

354. TABLE IX, A, 1, a

TROY

DEPARTMENT STORES — STOCK AND SALES

NUMBER AND PER CENT. OF EMPLOYEES CLASSIFIED ACCORDING TO ACTUAL WEEKLY EARNINGS, BY OCCUPATION AND SEX

| ACTUAL WEEKLY EARNINGS IN DOLLARS | OCCUPATION | | | | | | | | | | | | | | | | ACTUAL WEEKLY EARNINGS IN DOLLARS |
|---|---|---|---|---|---|---|---|---|---|---|---|---|---|---|---|---|---|
| | BUYERS | | ASSISTANT BUYERS AND HEADS OF STOCK | | RECEIVING AND STOCK CLERKS | STOCK PEOPLE | | FLOOR MANAGERS | SALES PEOPLE | | MESSENGERS, WRAPPERS, ERRAND BOYS | | TOTAL | | CUMULATIVE PER CENT. OF TOTAL | | |
| | Male | Female | Male | Female | Male | Male | Female | Male | Male | Female | Male | Female | Male | Female | Male | Female | |
| Less than $3 00 | ..... | ..... | ..... | ..... | ..... | ..... | ..... | ..... | ..... | ..... | 4 | 12 | 4 | 12 | 1.80 | 3.90 | Less than $3 00 |
| $3 00–$3 49 | ..... | ..... | ..... | ..... | ..... | ..... | ..... | ..... | ..... | ..... | 4 | 33 | 4 | 33 | 3.70 | 14.60 | $3 00– 3 49 |
| 3 50– 3 99 | ..... | ..... | ..... | ..... | ..... | ..... | ..... | ..... | ..... | ..... | 4 | 10 | 4 | 10 | 5.50 | 17.90 | 3 50– 3 99 |
| 4 00– 4 49 | ..... | ..... | ..... | ..... | ..... | 1 | ..... | ..... | ..... | 5 | 7 | 8 | 8 | 13 | 9.10 | 22.10 | 4 00– 4 49 |
| 4 50– 4 99 | ..... | ..... | ..... | ..... | ..... | ..... | ..... | ..... | ..... | ..... | 6 | 5 | 6 | 5 | 11.90 | 23.70 | 4 50– 4 99 |
| 5 00– 5 49 | ..... | ..... | ..... | ..... | ..... | 3 | ..... | ..... | ..... | 8 | 6 | 3 | 9 | 11 | 16.00 | 27.30 | 5 00– 5 49 |
| 5 50– 5 99 | ..... | ..... | ..... | ..... | ..... | ..... | ..... | ..... | ..... | 8 | 1 | ..... | 1 | 8 | 16.40 | 29.90 | 5 50– 5 99 |
| 6 00– 6 49 | ..... | ..... | ..... | ..... | ..... | 2 | 1 | ..... | 1 | 35 | ..... | ..... | 3 | 36 | 17.80 | 41.50 | 6 00– 6 49 |
| 6 50– 6 99 | ..... | ..... | ..... | ..... | ..... | ..... | ..... | ..... | ..... | 4 | 1 | ..... | 1 | 4 | 18.30 | 42.80 | 6 50– 6 99 |
| 7 00– 7 49 | ..... | ..... | ..... | ..... | ..... | ..... | ..... | ..... | 5 | 42 | 3 | ..... | 8 | 42 | 21.90 | 56.50 | 7 00– 7 49 |
| 7 50– 7 99 | ..... | ..... | ..... | ..... | ..... | ..... | ..... | ..... | ..... | 4 | 1 | ..... | 1 | 4 | 24.70 | 57.80 | 7 50– 7 99 |
| 8 00– 8 99 | ..... | ..... | ..... | ..... | ..... | ..... | ..... | ..... | 8 | 36 | 1 | 1 | 9 | 37 | 26.50 | 69.80 | 8 00– 8 99 |
| 9 00– 9 99 | ..... | ..... | ..... | ..... | ..... | ..... | ..... | ..... | 5 | 25 | ..... | ..... | 5 | 25 | 28.80 | 73.00 | 9 00– 9 99 |
| 10 00–10 99 | ..... | 1 | ..... | ..... | 1 | ..... | ..... | ..... | 6 | 22 | ..... | ..... | 7 | 23 | 32.00 | 85.50 | 10 00–10 99 |
| 11 00–11 99 | ..... | 1 | ..... | ..... | ..... | 2 | ..... | ..... | 4 | 2 | ..... | ..... | 6 | 3 | 34.70 | 86.40 | 11 00–11 99 |
| 12 00–12 99 | ..... | 1 | 1 | ..... | ..... | ..... | ..... | ..... | 14 | 11 | ..... | ..... | 15 | 12 | 41.60 | 90.30 | 12 00–12 99 |
| 13 00–13 99 | ..... | ..... | ..... | ..... | ..... | ..... | ..... | ..... | 7 | 4 | ..... | ..... | 7 | 4 | 44.80 | 91.60 | 13 00–13 99 |
| 14 00–14 99 | ..... | ..... | ..... | ..... | 1 | ..... | ..... | ..... | 12 | 12 | ..... | ..... | 13 | 12 | 50.70 | 95.50 | 14 00–14 99 |
| 15 00–15 99 | ..... | ..... | ..... | ..... | ..... | 1 | ..... | 1 | 14 | 1 | 1 | ..... | 17 | 1 | 58.50 | 95.80 | 15 00–15 99 |
| 16 00–17 99 | 5 | 3 | ..... | ..... | ..... | ..... | ..... | 1 | 12 | 4 | ..... | ..... | 18 | 7 | 66.70 | 98.10 | 16 00–17 99 |
| 18 00–19 99 | ..... | ..... | 1 | 1 | ..... | ..... | ..... | 1 | 18 | ..... | ..... | ..... | 20 | 1 | 75.80 | 98.40 | 18 00–19 99 |
| 20 00–24 99 | 5 | 1 | 1 | ..... | ..... | ..... | ..... | 5 | 20 | 3 | ..... | ..... | 31 | 4 | 90.00 | 99.70 | 20 00–24 99 |
| 25 00–29 99 | 7 | 1 | ..... | ..... | ..... | ..... | ..... | 2 | 3 | ..... | ..... | ..... | 12 | 1 | 95.50 | 100.00 | 25 00–29 99 |
| 30 00–34 99 | 7 | ..... | ..... | ..... | ..... | ..... | ..... | ..... | ..... | ..... | ..... | ..... | 7 | ..... | 98.60 | ..... | 30 00–34 99 |
| 35 00–39 99 | 1 | ..... | ..... | ..... | ..... | ..... | ..... | ..... | ..... | ..... | ..... | ..... | 1 | ..... | 99.10 | ..... | 35 00–39 99 |
| 40 00 and over | 2 | ..... | ..... | ..... | ..... | ..... | ..... | ..... | ..... | ..... | ..... | ..... | 2 | ..... | 100.00 | ..... | 40 00 and over |
| Not reported | ..... | ..... | ..... | ..... | ..... | ..... | ..... | ..... | 1 | ..... | ..... | ..... | 1 | ..... | ..... | ..... | Not reported |
| Total | 27 | 8 | 3 | 1 | 2 | 9 | 1 | 10 | 130 | 226 | 39 | 72 | 220 | 308 | ..... | ..... | Total |

355. TABLE XV, A, 1, b, c, d, e

TROY

**DEPARTMENT STORES — OFFICE, SHIPPING AND DELIVERY, MANUFACTURING, PLANT**

NUMBER OF EMPLOYEES EARNING SPECIFIED WEEKLY RATES ACCORDING TO DEPARTMENT AND SEX

| WEEKLY RATES IN DOLLARS | DEPARTMENT | | | | | | | | | | | WEEKLY RATES IN DOLLARS |
|---|---|---|---|---|---|---|---|---|---|---|---|---|
| | OFFICE | | SHIPPING AND DELIVERY | MANUFACTURING | | PLANT | | TOTAL | | CUMULATIVE PER CENT OF TOTAL | | |
| | Male | Female | Male | Male | Female | Male | Female | Male | Female | Male | Female | |
| $3 00–$3 49... | 1 | ........ | ........ | ........ | 2 | ........ | ........ | 1 | 2 | 1.00 | 1.50 | ...$3 00–$3 49 |
| 4 00– 4 49... | 2 | 1 | 5 | ........ | 1 | ........ | ........ | 7 | 2 | 7.80 | 3.00 | ... 4 00– 4 49 |
| 4 50– 4 99... | ........ | 2 | ........ | ........ | ........ | ........ | ........ | ........ | 2 | ........ | 4.50 | ... 4 50– 4 99 |
| 5 00– 5 49... | ........ | ........ | 2 | ........ | 1 | ........ | ........ | 2 | 1 | 9.70 | 5.30 | ... 5 00– 5 49 |
| 5 50– 5 99... | 1 | 4 | ........ | ........ | ........ | ........ | ........ | 1 | 4 | 10.70 | 8.30 | ... 5 50– 5 99 |
| 6 00– 6 49... | 3 | 11 | ........ | ........ | ........ | ........ | ........ | 3 | 11 | 13.60 | 16.60 | ... 6 00– 6 49 |
| 7 00– 7 49... | 1 | 6 | 2 | ........ | 3 | ........ | ........ | 3 | 9 | 16.50 | 23.30 | ... 7 00– 7 49 |
| 7 50– 7 99... | ........ | ........ | ........ | ........ | 34 | ........ | ........ | ........ | 34 | ........ | 48.90 | ... 7 50– 7 99 |
| 8 00– 8 99... | ........ | 7 | 1 | ........ | 7 | ........ | ........ | 1 | 14 | 17.50 | 59.50 | ... 8 00– 8 99 |
| 9 00– 9 99... | 2 | 4 | 1 | ........ | 8 | 2 | 5 | 5 | 17 | 22.30 | 72.20 | ... 9 00– 9 99 |
| 10 00–10 99... | ........ | 6 | 3 | ........ | 4 | 6 | ........ | 9 | 10 | 31.10 | 79.80 | ...10 00–10 99 |
| 11 00–11 99... | 1 | 1 | ........ | ........ | 2 | ........ | ........ | 1 | 3 | 32.00 | 82.00 | ...11 00–11 99 |
| 12 00–12 99... | 1 | 3 | 2 | 4 | 4 | 5 | ........ | 12 | 7 | 43.70 | 87.30 | ...12 00–12 99 |
| 13 00–13 99... | 2 | 2 | 3 | ........ | 1 | ........ | ........ | 5 | 3 | 48.50 | 89.50 | ...13 00–13 99 |
| 14 00–14 99... | 1 | 1 | 1 | 1 | 6 | ........ | ........ | 3 | 7 | 51.50 | 94.80 | ...14 00–14 99 |
| 15 00–15 99... | 2 | 2 | 9 | 1 | 2 | 2 | ........ | 14 | 4 | 65.00 | 97.80 | ...15 00–15 99 |
| 16 00–17 99... | 1 | 1 | 4 | 2 | 1 | 3 | ........ | 10 | 2 | 74.70 | 99.30 | ...16 00–17 99 |
| 18 00–19 99... | 5 | ........ | 1 | 3 | ........ | 3 | ........ | 12 | ........ | 86.40 | ........ | ...18 00–19 99 |
| 20 00–24 99... | 2 | ........ | ........ | 1 | ........ | 2 | ........ | 5 | ........ | 91.30 | ........ | ...20 00–24 99 |
| 25 00–29 99... | 4 | ........ | ........ | ........ | ........ | ........ | ........ | 4 | ........ | 95.10 | ........ | ...25 00–29 99 |
| 30 00–34 99... | 3 | ........ | ........ | ........ | 1 | ........ | ........ | 3 | 1 | 98.00 | 100.00 | ...30 00–34 99 |
| 35 00–39 99... | 2 | ........ | ........ | ........ | ........ | ........ | ........ | 2 | ........ | 100.00 | ........ | ...35 00–39 99 |
| Total..... | 34 | 51 | 34 | 12 | 77 | 23 | 5 | 103 | 133 | ........ | ........ | .....Total |

356. TABLE XVI, A, 1, b, c, d, e

TROY

**DEPARTMENT STORES — OFFICE, SHIPPING AND DELIVERY, MANUFACTURING, PLANT**

Number of Employees Classified According to Actual Weekly Earnings, by Department and Sex

| Actual Weekly Earnings in Dollars | Department | | | | | | | | | | | Actual Weekly Earnings in Dollars |
|---|---|---|---|---|---|---|---|---|---|---|---|---|
| | Office | | Shipping and Delivery | Manufacturing | | Plant | | Total | | Cumulative per cent of total | | |
| | Male | Female | Male | Male | Female | Male | Female | Male | Female | Male | Female | |
| $3 00–$3 49... | 2 | 1 | ........ | ........ | 3 | ........ | ........ | 2 | 4 | 1.90 | 3.00 | ...$3 00–$3 49 |
| 3 50– 3 99... | ........ | ........ | ........ | ........ | 1 | ........ | ........ | ........ | 1 | ........ | 3.80 | ... 3 50– 3 99 |
| 4 00– 4 49... | 2 | ........ | 5 | ........ | 2 | 1 | ........ | 8 | 2 | 9.70 | 5.30 | ... 4 00– 4 49 |
| 4 50– 4 99... | ........ | 2 | ........ | ........ | 1 | ........ | ........ | ........ | 3 | ........ | 7.50 | ... 4 50– 4 99 |
| 5 00– 5 49... | ........ | ........ | 2 | ........ | ........ | ........ | ........ | 2 | ........ | 11.60 | ........ | ... 5 00– 5 49 |
| 5 50– 5 99... | 2 | 7 | ........ | ........ | ........ | ........ | ........ | 2 | 7 | 13.60 | 12.80 | ... 5 50– 5 99 |
| 6 00– 6 49... | 2 | 11 | ........ | ........ | 1 | ........ | ........ | 2 | 12 | 15.50 | 21.80 | ... 6 00– 6 49 |
| 6 50– 6 99... | ........ | 1 | ........ | ........ | 5 | ........ | ........ | ........ | 6 | ........ | 26.30 | ... 6 50– 6 99 |
| 7 00– 7 49... | 1 | 3 | 2 | ........ | 4 | ........ | ........ | 3 | 7 | 18.40 | 31.60 | ... 7 00– 7 49 |
| 7 50– 7 99... | ........ | 1 | ........ | ........ | 26 | ........ | ........ | ........ | 27 | ........ | 51.90 | ... 7 50– 7 99 |
| 8 00– 8 99... | ........ | 7 | 1 | ........ | 6 | ........ | 2 | 1 | 15 | 19.40 | 63.20 | ... 8 00– 8 99 |
| 9 00– 9 99... | 2 | 3 | 1 | ........ | 7 | 2 | 3 | 5 | 13 | 24.30 | 73.00 | ... 9 00– 9 99 |
| 10 00–10 99... | ........ | 6 | 3 | ........ | 4 | 6 | ........ | 9 | 10 | 33.00 | 80.50 | ...10 00–10 99 |
| 11 00–11 99... | 1 | ........ | ........ | 1 | 2 | ........ | ........ | 2 | 2 | 35.00 | 87.00 | ...11 00–11 99 |
| 12 00–12 99... | ........ | 4 | 2 | 4 | 4 | 4 | ........ | 10 | 8 | 44.60 | 88.00 | ...12 00–12 99 |
| 13 00–13 99... | 2 | 1 | 3 | ........ | 3 | ........ | ........ | 5 | 4 | 49.50 | 91.00 | ...13 00–13 99 |
| 14 00–14 99... | 1 | 1 | 1 | 1 | 4 | ........ | ........ | 3 | 5 | 52.50 | 94.70 | ...14 00–14 99 |
| 15 00–15 99... | 2 | 2 | 9 | 1 | 2 | 2 | ........ | 14 | 4 | 66.00 | 97.70 | ...15 00–15 99 |
| 16 00–17 99... | 1 | 1 | 4 | 1 | 1 | 3 | ........ | 9 | 2 | 74.70 | 99.30 | ...16 00–17 99 |
| 18 00–19 99... | 5 | ........ | 1 | 3 | ........ | 3 | ........ | 12 | ........ | 86.50 | ........ | ...18 00–19 99 |
| 20 00–24 99... | 2 | ........ | ........ | 1 | ........ | 2 | ........ | 5 | ........ | 91.30 | ........ | ...20 00–24 99 |
| 25 00–29 99... | 4 | ........ | ........ | ........ | ........ | ........ | ........ | 4 | ........ | 95.20 | ........ | ...25 00–29 99 |
| 30 00–34 99... | 3 | ........ | ........ | ........ | 1 | ........ | ........ | 3 | 1 | 98.00 | 100.00 | ...30 00–34 99 |
| 35 00–39 99... | 2 | ........ | ........ | ........ | ........ | ........ | ........ | 2 | ........ | 100.00 | ........ | ...35 00–39 99 |
| Total..... | 34 | 51 | 34 | 12 | 77 | 23 | 5 | 103 | 133 | ........ | ........ | .....Total |

357. TABLE XVII, A, 1, b, c, d, e

TROY

**DEPARTMENT STORES — OFFICE, SHIPPING AND DELIVERY, MANUFACTURING, PLANT**

NUMBER OF EMPLOYEES CLASSIFIED BY AGE GROUPS ACCORDING TO DEPARTMENT AND SEX

| AGE GROUPS IN YEARS | DEPARTMENT | | | | | | | | | | | AGE GROUPS IN YEARS |
|---|---|---|---|---|---|---|---|---|---|---|---|---|
| | OFFICE | | SHIPPING AND DELIVERY | MANUFACTURING | | PLANT | | TOTAL | | PER CENT OF TOTAL | | |
| | Male | Female | Male | Male | Female | Male | Female | Male | Female | Male | Female | |
| 14–15 | 1 | ........ | 3 | ........ | ........ | ........ | ........ | 4 | ........ | 3.90 | ........ | 14–15 |
| 16–17 | 3 | 3 | 4 | ........ | ........ | ........ | ........ | 7 | 3 | 6.80 | 2.40 | 16–17 |
| 18–20 | 5 | 19 | 4 | ........ | 4 | 1 | ........ | 10 | 23 | 9.70 | 18.40 | 18–20 |
| 21–24 | 1 | 16 | 3 | 1 | 9 | ........ | ........ | 5 | 25 | 4.90 | 20.00 | 21–24 |
| 25–29 | 6 | 7 | 4 | 2 | 11 | ........ | ........ | 12 | 18 | 11.60 | 14.40 | 25–29 |
| 30–34 | 1 | 4 | 5 | 1 | 6 | 2 | ........ | 9 | 10 | 8.75 | 8.00 | 30–34 |
| 35–39 | 3 | ........ | 3 | ........ | 12 | 6 | 2 | 12 | 14 | 11.60 | 11.20 | 35–39 |
| 40–44 | 3 | ........ | 4 | 1 | 10 | 1 | ........ | 9 | 10 | 8.76 | 8.00 | 40–44 |
| 45–54 | 9 | 1 | 3 | 4 | 12 | 2 | ........ | 18 | 13 | 17.50 | 10.40 | 45–54 |
| 55–64 | 1 | ........ | ........ | 3 | 4 | 10 | 2 | 14 | 6 | 13.60 | 4.80 | 55–64 |
| 65 and over | 1 | ........ | 1 | ........ | 2 | 1 | 1 | 3 | 3 | 2.90 | 2.40 | 65 and over |
| Not reported | ........ | 1 | ........ | ........ | 7 | ........ | ........ | ........ | 8 | ........ | ........ | Not reported |
| Total | 34 | 51 | 34 | 12 | 77 | 23 | 5 | 103 | 133 | 100.00 | 100.00 | Total |

TROY

THE MEN'S SHIRT INDUSTRY — FACTORY WORKERS

358. TABLE V, B, a. Number and Per Cent. of Employees Earning Specified Weekly Rates, by Age Groups and Sex

| Weekly Rates in Dollars | Age Groups in Years: 14–15 | | 16–17 | | 18–20 | | 21–24 | | 25–29 | | 30–34 | | 35–39 | | Weekly Rates in Dollars |
|---|---|---|---|---|---|---|---|---|---|---|---|---|---|---|---|
| | Male | Female | Male | Female | Male | Female | Male | Female | Male | Female | Male | Female | Male | Female | |
| $4 00–$4 49 | .... | 2 | 1 | 2 | ...... | ...... | ...... | ...... | ...... | ...... | ...... | ...... | ...... | ...... | $4 00–$4 49 |
| 4 50– 4 99 | .... | ...... | 1 | ...... | ...... | ...... | ...... | 1 | ...... | ...... | ...... | ...... | ...... | ...... | 4 50– 4 99 |
| 5 00– 5 49 | 1 | 1 | 7 | 7 | ...... | 5 | ...... | ...... | ...... | ...... | ...... | ...... | ...... | ...... | 5 00– 5 49 |
| 5 50– 5 99 | .... | ...... | 1 | 12 | ...... | 4 | ...... | ...... | ...... | ...... | ...... | ...... | ...... | 1 | 5 50– 5 99 |
| 6 00– 6 49 | .... | ...... | 3 | 10 | 1 | 13 | ...... | 1 | ...... | 2 | ...... | ...... | ...... | 1 | 6 00– 6 49 |
| 6 50– 6 99 | .... | ...... | .... | ...... | ...... | 1 | ...... | 1 | ...... | ...... | ...... | ...... | ...... | ...... | 6 50– 6 99 |
| 7 00– 7 49 | .... | ...... | 3 | 3 | ...... | 14 | ...... | 10 | ...... | 6 | ...... | 2 | ...... | 1 | 7 00– 7 49 |
| 7 50– 7 99 | .... | ...... | .... | ...... | 3 | ...... | 1 | 1 | 1 | 1 | 1 | ...... | ...... | ...... | 7 50– 7 99 |
| 8 00– 8 99 | .... | ...... | .... | ...... | 3 | 2 | ...... | 12 | 1 | 5 | 1 | 2 | 1 | 7 | 8 00– 8 99 |
| 9 00– 9 99 | .... | ...... | .... | ...... | 2 | ...... | 1 | 7 | ...... | 8 | ...... | 6 | ...... | 7 | 9 00– 9 99 |
| 10 00–10 99 | .... | ...... | 1 | ...... | 2 | ...... | 1 | 5 | 2 | 1 | 1 | 2 | ...... | 2 | 10 00–10 99 |
| 11 00–11 99 | .... | ...... | .... | ...... | 1 | ...... | ...... | 3 | 1 | 1 | 1 | 1 | ...... | ...... | 11 00–11 99 |
| 12 00–12 99 | .... | ...... | .... | ...... | ...... | ...... | 7 | 2 | 2 | 4 | 1 | 8 | 1 | ...... | 12 00–12 99 |
| 13 00–13 99 | .... | ...... | .... | ...... | ...... | ...... | 2 | 1 | ...... | ...... | 2 | ...... | ...... | 2 | 13 00–13 99 |
| 14 00–14 99 | .... | ...... | .... | ...... | ...... | ...... | 1 | ...... | 4 | ...... | 1 | ...... | 1 | ...... | 14 00–14 99 |
| 15 00–15 99 | .... | ...... | .... | ...... | ...... | ...... | 5 | ...... | 4 | ...... | 3 | ...... | 7 | ...... | 15 00–15 99 |
| 16 00–17 99 | .... | ...... | .... | ...... | ...... | ...... | ...... | ...... | ...... | ...... | 4 | ...... | 3 | 1 | 16 00–17 99 |
| 18 00–19 99 | .... | ...... | .... | ...... | ...... | ...... | ...... | ...... | ...... | ...... | 3 | ...... | 1 | ...... | 18 00–19 99 |
| 20 00–24 99 | .... | ...... | .... | ...... | ...... | ...... | ...... | ...... | ...... | ...... | 2 | ...... | 2 | ...... | 20 00–24 99 |
| 25 00–29 99 | .... | ...... | .... | ...... | ...... | ...... | ...... | ...... | ...... | ...... | 1 | ...... | 2 | ...... | 25 00–29 99 |
| Not reported | .... | ...... | .... | 10 | 2 | 42 | 1 | 58 | ...... | 41 | ...... | 43 | ...... | 26 | Not reported |
| Total | 1 | 3 | 17 | 44 | 14 | 81 | 19 | 102 | 15 | 69 | 21 | 64 | 18 | 48 | Total |

TROY

358. TABLE V, B, a — (*concluded*) THE MEN'S SHIRT INDUSTRY — FACTORY WORKERS

NUMBER AND PER CENT. OF EMPLOYEES EARNING SPECIFIED WEEKLY RATES, BY AGE GROUPS AND SEX

| WEEKLY RATES IN DOLLARS | AGE GROUPS IN YEARS (*concluded*) 40–44 | | 45–54 | | 55–64 | | 65 AND OVER | | NOT REPORTED | TOTAL | | CUMULATIVE PER CENT. OF TOTAL | | WEEKLY RATES IN DOLLARS |
|---|---|---|---|---|---|---|---|---|---|---|---|---|---|---|
| | Male | Female | Male | Female | Male | Female | Male | Female | Female | Male | Female | Male | Female | |
| $4 00–$4 49 | ...... | ...... | ...... | ...... | ...... | ...... | ...... | ...... | ...... | 1 | 4 | .70 | 1.80 | $4 00–$4 49 |
| 4 50– 4 99 | ...... | ...... | ...... | ...... | ...... | ...... | ...... | ...... | ...... | 1 | 1 | 1.50 | 2.20 | 4 50– 4 99 |
| 5 00– 5 49 | ...... | ...... | ...... | ...... | ...... | ...... | ...... | ...... | ...... | 8 | 13 | 7.30 | 8.00 | 5 00– 5 49 |
| 5 50– 5 99 | ...... | ...... | ...... | ...... | ...... | ...... | ...... | ...... | 1 | 1 | 18 | 8.00 | 16.00 | 5 50– 5 99 |
| 6 00– 6 49 | ...... | ...... | ...... | ...... | ...... | ...... | ...... | ...... | ...... | 4 | 27 | 10.90 | 28.00 | 6 00– 6 49 |
| 6 50– 6 99 | ...... | ...... | ...... | ...... | ...... | ...... | ...... | ...... | ...... | ...... | 2 | ...... | 28.90 | 6 50– 6 99 |
| 7 00– 7 49 | ...... | 3 | ...... | 4 | ...... | ...... | ...... | ...... | ...... | 3 | 43 | 13.10 | 48.00 | 7 00– 7 49 |
| 7 50– 7 99 | ...... | ...... | ...... | ...... | ...... | ...... | ...... | ...... | ...... | 6 | 2 | 17.40 | 48.90 | 7 50– 7 99 |
| 8 00– 8 99 | ...... | 2 | ...... | 5 | ...... | ...... | ...... | ...... | ...... | 6 | 35 | 21.80 | 64.50 | 8 00– 8 99 |
| 9 00– 9 99 | 1 | 1 | 2 | 4 | 1 | 1 | 1 | 1 | 2 | 8 | 37 | 27.60 | 81.00 | 9 00– 9 99 |
| 10 00–10 99 | 1 | 1 | 1 | 1 | ...... | 1 | ...... | ...... | ...... | 9 | 13 | 34.10 | 86.70 | 10 00–10 99 |
| 11 00–11 99 | 1 | 1 | 1 | ...... | ...... | 1 | ...... | ...... | ...... | 5 | 7 | 37.70 | 89.80 | 11 00–11 99 |
| 12 00–12 99 | ...... | 1 | 1 | ...... | ...... | ...... | ...... | ...... | ...... | 12 | 15 | 46.40 | 96.50 | 12 00–12 99 |
| 13 00–13 99 | ...... | ...... | 1 | ...... | ...... | ...... | ...... | 1 | ...... | 5 | 4 | 50.00 | 98.30 | 13 00–13 99 |
| 14 00–14 99 | ...... | ...... | 1 | ...... | 1 | ...... | ...... | ...... | ...... | 9 | ...... | 56.50 | ...... | 14 00–14 99 |
| 15 00–15 99 | 3 | ...... | 3 | 2 | 1 | ...... | ...... | ...... | ...... | 26 | 2 | 75.50 | 99.20 | 15 00–15 99 |
| 16 00–17 99 | 1 | ...... | 5 | ...... | ...... | ...... | ...... | ...... | ...... | 13 | 1 | 84.80 | 99.60 | 16 00–17 99 |
| 18 00–19 99 | 2 | ...... | 1 | 1 | 3 | ...... | ...... | ...... | ...... | 10 | 1 | 92.00 | 100.00 | 18 00–19 99 |
| 20 00–24 99 | 1 | ...... | 2 | ...... | ...... | ...... | ...... | ...... | ...... | 7 | ...... | 97.20 | ...... | 20 00–24 99 |
| 25 00–29 99 | ...... | ...... | ...... | ...... | ...... | ...... | ...... | ...... | ...... | 3 | ...... | 99.40 | ...... | 25 00–29 99 |
| 30 00–34 99 | 1 | ...... | ...... | ...... | ...... | ...... | ...... | ...... | ...... | 1 | ...... | 100.00 | ...... | 30 00–34 99 |
| Not reported | ...... | 20 | ...... | 18 | ...... | 1 | ...... | 1 | 8 | 3 | 268 | ...... | ...... | Not reported |
| Total | 11 | 29 | 18 | 35 | 6 | 4 | 1 | 3 | 11 | 141 | 493 | ...... | ...... | Total |

TROY

THE MEN'S SHIRT INDUSTRY — FACTORY WORKERS

359. TABLE VIII, B, a. Number and Per Cent. of Employees Earning Specified Weekly Rates, by Occupation and Sex

| Weekly Rates in Dollars | Occupation | | | | | | | | | | | | | Weekly Rates in Dollars |
|---|---|---|---|---|---|---|---|---|---|---|---|---|---|---|
| | Markers | Cutters | Trimmers | | Cutters' Helpers | | Foremen and Forewomen | | Operators | Floor Work | | Laundry Helpers | | |
| | Male | Male | Male | Female | Male | Female | Male | Female | Female | Male | Female | Male | Female | |
| $4 00–$4 49...... | ...... | ...... | ...... | ...... | ...... | ...... | ...... | ...... | ...... | ...... | 2 | 1 | 1 | ......$4 00–$4 49 |
| 4 50– 4 99...... | ...... | ...... | ...... | ...... | ...... | ...... | ...... | ...... | ...... | ...... | ...... | 1 | 1 | ......4 50– 4 99 |
| 5 00– 5 49...... | ...... | 2 | ...... | ...... | 3 | ...... | ...... | ...... | ...... | 1 | 3 | 1 | 4 | ......5 00– 5 49 |
| 5 50– 5 99...... | ...... | ...... | ...... | ...... | ...... | ...... | ...... | ...... | ...... | ...... | 2 | ...... | 2 | ......5 50– 5 99 |
| 6 00– 6 49...... | ...... | ...... | ...... | ...... | 3 | ...... | ...... | 1 | 2 | ...... | 4 | ...... | 1 | ......6 00– 6 49 |
| 7 00– 7 49...... | ...... | 1 | ...... | ...... | 2 | 1 | ...... | ...... | 2 | ...... | ...... | ...... | 1 | ......7 00– 7 49 |
| 7 50– 7 99...... | ...... | 1 | ...... | ...... | ...... | ...... | ...... | ...... | ...... | ...... | ...... | 2 | ...... | ......7 50– 7 99 |
| 8 00– 8 99...... | ...... | ...... | ...... | ...... | ...... | ...... | ...... | 1 | 16 | ...... | ...... | 2 | 3 | ......8 00– 8 99 |
| 9 00– 9 99...... | ...... | 1 | ...... | ...... | 1 | 1 | ...... | 3 | 16 | ...... | 3 | 6 | ...... | ......9 00– 9 99 |
| 10 00–10 99...... | ...... | ...... | 1 | ...... | ...... | ...... | 1 | 2 | 3 | ...... | 1 | 4 | 1 | .....10 00–10 99 |
| 11 00–11 99...... | ...... | 1 | 1 | 1 | ...... | ...... | 1 | 3 | 2 | ...... | ...... | 1 | 1 | .....11 00–11 99 |
| 12 00–12 99...... | ...... | 6 | ...... | ...... | ...... | ...... | 2 | 9 | ...... | ...... | ...... | 1 | ...... | .....12 00–12 99 |
| 13 00–13 99...... | ...... | 2 | ...... | ...... | ...... | ...... | 2 | 2 | ...... | ...... | ...... | 1 | 1 | .....13 00–13 99 |
| 14 00–14 99...... | ...... | 7 | 1 | ...... | ...... | ...... | ...... | ...... | ...... | ...... | ...... | ...... | ...... | .....14 00–14 99 |
| 15 00–15 99...... | ...... | 18 | ...... | ...... | ...... | ...... | 3 | 2 | ...... | 2 | ...... | 2 | ...... | .....15 00–15 99 |
| 16 00–17 99...... | ...... | 8 | ...... | ...... | ...... | ...... | 4 | 1 | ...... | 1 | ...... | ...... | ...... | .....16 00–17 99 |
| 18 00–19 99...... | ...... | 1 | ...... | ...... | ...... | ...... | 8 | 1 | ...... | ...... | ...... | 1 | ...... | .....18 00–19 99 |
| 20 00–24 99...... | ...... | ...... | ...... | ...... | ...... | ...... | 7 | ...... | ...... | ...... | ...... | ...... | ...... | .....20 00–24 99 |
| 25 00–29 99...... | ...... | ...... | ...... | ...... | ...... | ...... | 2 | ...... | ...... | ...... | ...... | 1 | ...... | .....25 00–29 99 |
| 30 00–34 99...... | ...... | ...... | ...... | ...... | ...... | ...... | 1 | ...... | ...... | ...... | ...... | ...... | ...... | .....30 00–34 99 |
| Not reported...... | 1 | ...... | ...... | ...... | ...... | ...... | ...... | ...... | 236 | ...... | 2 | ...... | ...... | .....Not reported |
| Total........ | 1 | 48 | 3 | 1 | 9 | 2 | 31 | 25 | 277 | 4 | 17 | 24 | 16 | .......Total |

TROY

359. TABLE VIII, B, a — (*concluded*) THE MEN'S SHIRT INDUSTRY — FACTORY WORKERS

NUMBER AND PER CENT. OF EMPLOYEES EARNING SPECIFIED WEEKLY RATES, BY OCCUPATION AND SEX

| WEEKLY RATES IN DOLLARS | OCCUPATION | | | | | | | | | | | | | WEEKLY RATES IN DOLLARS |
|---|---|---|---|---|---|---|---|---|---|---|---|---|---|---|
| | STARCHERS AND DAMPNERS | | IRONERS AND PRESSERS | | EXAMINERS | | FOLDER | PACKERS | | TOTAL | | CUMULATIVE PER CENT. OF TOTAL | | |
| | Male | Female | Male | Female | Male | Female | Female | Male | Female | Male | Female | Male | Female | |
| $4 00–$4 49...... | ...... | ...... | ...... | ...... | ...... | 1 | ...... | ...... | ...... | 1 | 4 | .70 | 1.80 | .....$4 00– 4 49 |
| 4 50– 4 99...... | ...... | ...... | ...... | ...... | ...... | ...... | ...... | ...... | ...... | 1 | 1 | 1.50 | 2.20 | ......4 50– 4 99 |
| 5 00– 5 49...... | ...... | ...... | ...... | 1 | 1 | 3 | ...... | ...... | 2 | 8 | 13 | 7.30 | 8.00 | ......5 00– 5 49 |
| 5 50– 5 99...... | ...... | ...... | ...... | 1 | ...... | 13 | ...... | 1 | ...... | 1 | 18 | 8.00 | 16.00 | ......5 50– 5 99 |
| 6 00– 6 49...... | ...... | ...... | ...... | 2 | 1 | 15 | ...... | ...... | 2 | 4 | 27 | 10.90 | 28.00 | ......6 00– 6 49 |
| 6 50– 6 99...... | ...... | ...... | ...... | ...... | ...... | 2 | ...... | ...... | ...... | ...... | 2 | ...... | 28.90 | ......6 50– 6 99 |
| 7 00– 7 49...... | ...... | ...... | ...... | ...... | ...... | 34 | ...... | ...... | 5 | 3 | 43 | 13.10 | 48.00 | ......7 00– 7 49 |
| 7 50– 7 99...... | ...... | ...... | 1 | ...... | 2 | 2 | ...... | ...... | ...... | 6 | 2 | 17.40 | 48.90 | ......7 50– 7 99 |
| 8 00– 8 99...... | ...... | ...... | 1 | 1 | 1 | 11 | ...... | 2 | 3 | 6 | 35 | 21.80 | 64.50 | ......8 00– 8 99 |
| 9 00– 9 99...... | ...... | ...... | ...... | ...... | ...... | 10 | ...... | ...... | 4 | 8 | 37 | 27.60 | 81.00 | ......9 00– 9 99 |
| 10 00–10 99...... | 1 | ...... | ...... | 1 | 1 | 5 | ...... | 1 | ...... | 9 | 13 | 34.10 | 86.70 | .....10 00–10 99 |
| 11 00–11 99...... | 1 | ...... | ...... | ...... | ...... | ...... | ...... | ...... | ...... | 5 | 7 | 37.70 | 89.80 | .....11 00–11 99 |
| 12 00–12 99...... | ...... | ...... | ...... | ...... | 3 | 5 | 1 | ...... | ...... | 12 | 15 | 46.40 | 96.50 | .....12 00–12 99 |
| 13 00–13 99...... | ...... | ...... | ...... | ...... | ...... | 1 | ...... | ...... | ...... | 5 | 4 | 50.00 | 98.30 | .....13 00–13 99 |
| 14 00–14 99...... | ...... | ...... | ...... | ...... | 1 | ...... | ...... | ...... | ...... | 9 | ...... | 56.50 | ...... | .....14 00–14 99 |
| 15 00–15 99...... | ...... | ...... | ...... | ...... | 1 | ...... | ...... | ...... | ...... | 26 | 2 | 75.50 | 99.20 | .....15 00–15 99 |
| 16 00–17 99...... | ...... | ...... | ...... | ...... | ...... | ...... | ...... | ...... | ...... | 13 | 1 | 84.80 | 99.60 | .....16 00–17 99 |
| 18 00–19 99...... | ...... | ...... | ...... | ...... | ...... | ...... | ...... | ...... | ...... | 10 | 1 | 92.00 | 100.00 | .....18 00–19 99 |
| 20 00–24 99...... | ...... | ...... | ...... | ...... | ...... | ...... | ...... | ...... | ...... | 7 | ...... | 97.20 | ...... | .....20 00–24 99 |
| 25 00–29 99...... | ...... | ...... | ...... | ...... | ...... | ...... | ...... | ...... | ...... | 3 | ...... | 99.40 | ...... | .....25 00–29 99 |
| 30 00–34 99...... | ...... | ...... | ...... | ...... | ...... | ...... | ...... | ...... | ...... | 1 | ...... | 100.00 | ...... | .....30 00–34 99 |
| Not reported...... | ...... | 18 | ...... | 6 | 1 | 4 | ...... | 1 | 2 | 3 | 268 | ...... | ...... | .....Not reported |
| Total........ | 2 | 18 | 2 | 12 | 12 | 106 | 1 | 5 | 18 | 141 | 493 | ...... | ...... | .......Total |

360. TABLE VI, B, a

TROY

**THE MEN'S SHIRT INDUSTRY — FACTORY WORKERS**

Number and Per Cent. of Employees Classified According to Actual Weekly Earnings, by Age Groups and Sex

| Actual Weekly Earnings in Dollars | Age Groups in Years | | | | | | | | | | | | | | Actual Weekly Earnings in Dollars |
|---|---|---|---|---|---|---|---|---|---|---|---|---|---|---|---|
| | 14–15 | | 16–17 | | 18–20 | | 21–24 | | 25–29 | | 30–34 | | 35–39 | | |
| | Male | Female | Male | Female | Male | Female | Male | Female | Male | Female | Male | Female | Male | Female | |
| Less than $3 00 | .... | 1 | 2 | 10 | ...... | 15 | 1 | 4 | 2 | 6 | 1 | 3 | ...... | 5 | Less than $3 00 |
| $3 00–$3 49... | .... | ...... | .... | 5 | ...... | 3 | 1 | 4 | ...... | 1 | ...... | 1 | ...... | 2 | ...$3 00– 3 49 |
| 3 50– 3 99... | .... | ...... | 1 | 2 | 1 | 7 | 4 | 1 | 6 | 1 | 3 | 2 | 1 | 1 | ... 3 50– 3 99 |
| 4 00– 4 49... | .... | 3 | 3 | 3 | ...... | 11 | 3 | 2 | 3 | 5 | ...... | 4 | 5 | 2 | ... 4 00– 4 49 |
| 4 50– 4 99... | .... | 1 | 3 | 3 | ...... | 11 | 3 | 6 | 2 | 5 | 4 | 3 | 1 | 4 | ... 4 50– 4 99 |
| 5 00– 5 49... | 2 | ...... | 2 | 13 | 3 | 20 | 9 | 7 | 9 | 7 | 6 | 5 | 5 | 3 | ... 5 00– 5 49 |
| 5 50– 5 99... | .... | ...... | 1 | 18 | 2 | 23 | ...... | 18 | 1 | 9 | 1 | 9 | 3 | 7 | ... 5 50– 5 99 |
| 6 00– 6 49... | .... | ...... | 3 | 13 | 1 | 19 | 2 | 18 | 5 | 6 | 8 | 6 | 6 | 14 | ... 6 00– 6 49 |
| 6 50– 6 99... | .... | ...... | .... | 2 | ...... | 17 | 4 | 7 | 7 | 11 | 1 | 5 | 1 | 6 | ... 6 50– 6 99 |
| 7 00– 7 49... | .... | ...... | 1 | 5 | ...... | 22 | 3 | 15 | 3 | 14 | 2 | 7 | 4 | 7 | ... 7 00– 7 49 |
| 7 50– 7 99... | .... | ...... | .... | 1 | 4 | 4 | 2 | 20 | 1 | 14 | 5 | 10 | 2 | 8 | ... 7 50– 7 99 |
| 8 00– 8 99... | .... | ...... | 1 | 4 | 4 | 16 | 5 | 34 | 14 | 29 | 14 | 24 | 18 | 28 | ... 8 00– 8 99 |
| 9 00– 9 99... | .... | ...... | .... | 2 | 3 | 13 | 4 | 27 | 2 | 24 | 3 | 28 | ...... | 21 | ... 9 00– 9 99 |
| 10 00–10 99... | .... | ...... | .... | 2 | 2 | 11 | 10 | 19 | 5 | 31 | 5 | 19 | 2 | 16 | ...10 00–10 99 |
| 11 00–11 99... | .... | ...... | .... | ...... | ...... | 8 | 4 | 24 | 7 | 17 | 6 | 11 | 5 | 14 | ...11 00–11 99 |
| 12 00–12 99... | .... | ...... | .... | 1 | 2 | 7 | 8 | 13 | 3 | 17 | 10 | 23 | 8 | 17 | ...12 00–12 99 |
| 13 00–13 99... | .... | ...... | .... | ...... | ...... | 3 | 3 | 17 | 6 | 21 | 3 | 12 | ...... | 12 | ...13 00–13 99 |
| 14 00–14 99... | .... | ...... | .... | ...... | ...... | 8 | 2 | 17 | ...... | 13 | 1 | 6 | 7 | 3 | ...14 00–14 99 |
| 15 00–15 99... | .... | ...... | .... | 1 | ...... | 3 | 4 | 11 | 1 | 6 | 2 | 8 | 8 | 7 | ...15 00–15 99 |
| 16 00–17 99... | .... | ...... | .... | ...... | ...... | 3 | ...... | 7 | 2 | 2 | 4 | 4 | 2 | 7 | ...16 00–17 99 |
| 18 00–19 99... | .... | ...... | .... | ...... | ...... | ...... | ...... | 1 | ...... | 1 | 4 | ...... | 1 | ...... | ...18 00–19 99 |
| 20 00–24 99... | .... | ...... | .... | ...... | ...... | ...... | 1 | ...... | 5 | ...... | 5 | ...... | 4 | ...... | ...20 00–24 99 |
| 25 00–29 99... | .... | ...... | .... | ...... | ...... | ...... | ...... | ...... | ...... | ...... | 3 | ...... | 2 | ...... | ...25 00–29 99 |
| Not reported... | .... | ...... | .... | ...... | 1 | ...... | ...... | ...... | ...... | ...... | ...... | ...... | ...... | ...... | ...Not reported |
| Total..... | 2 | 5 | 17 | 85 | 23 | 224 | 73 | 272 | 84 | 240 | 91 | 190 | 85 | 184 | .....Total |

TROY

360. TABLE VI, B, a.—(*concluded*) THE MEN'S SHIRT INDUSTRY — FACTORY WORKERS

NUMBER AND PER CENT. OF EMPLOYEES CLASSIFIED ACCORDING TO ACTUAL WEEKLY EARNINGS, BY AGE GROUPS AND SEX.—(*concluded*)

| ACTUAL WEEKLY EARNINGS IN DOLLARS | AGE GROUPS IN YEARS—(*concluded*) | | | | | | | | | | TOTAL | | CUMULATIVE PER CENT. OF TOTAL | | ACTUAL WEEKLY EARNINGS IN DOLLARS |
|---|---|---|---|---|---|---|---|---|---|---|---|---|---|---|---|
| | 40–44 | | 45–54 | | 55–64 | | 65 AND OVER | | NOT REPORTED | | | | | | |
| | Male | Female | Male | Female | Male | Female | Male | Female | Male | Female | Male | Female | Male | Female | |
| Less than $3 00 | 1 | 5 | .... | 5 | ...... | ...... | ...... | ...... | 1 | ...... | 8 | 54 | 1.60 | 3.70 | Less than $3 00 |
| $3 00–$3 49... | .... | 2 | 1 | 3 | ...... | 1 | ...... | 1 | ...... | ...... | 2 | 23 | 2.00 | 4.80 | ...$3 00– 3 49 |
| 3 50– 3 99... | .... | 3 | 2 | 2 | ...... | ...... | ...... | ...... | 1 | ...... | 19 | 19 | 5.80 | 6.60 | ... 3 50– 3 99 |
| 4 00– 4 49... | .... | 7 | .... | 2 | ...... | ...... | ...... | ...... | ...... | ...... | 14 | 39 | 8.70 | 9.30 | ... 4 00– 4 49 |
| 4 50– 4 99... | .... | 3 | 1 | 1 | ...... | 1 | 1 | ...... | ...... | ...... | 15 | 38 | 11.70 | 11.90 | ... 4 50– 4 99 |
| 5 00– 5 49... | 1 | 6 | 1 | ...... | ...... | ...... | 1 | ...... | ...... | 1 | 39 | 62 | 19.50 | 16.20 | ... 5 00– 5 49 |
| 5 50– 5 99... | .... | 3 | .... | 4 | 1 | 1 | ...... | ...... | ...... | 2 | 9 | 94 | 21.40 | 22.60 | ... 5 50– 5 99 |
| 6 00– 6 49... | 3 | 5 | 1 | 5 | ...... | 1 | ...... | ...... | 1 | ...... | 30 | 87 | 27.40 | 28.60 | ... 6 00– 6 49 |
| 6 50– 6 99... | .... | 5 | 2 | 3 | ...... | ...... | ...... | ...... | 1 | ...... | 16 | 56 | 30.60 | 32.50 | ... 6 50– 6 99 |
| 7 00– 7 49... | .... | 6 | 1 | 6 | ...... | 1 | ...... | ...... | ...... | 4 | 14 | 87 | 33.40 | 38.40 | ... 7 00– 7 49 |
| 7 50– 7 99... | 4 | 8 | 6 | 6 | 2 | ...... | ...... | ...... | ...... | 1 | 26 | 72 | 38.70 | 43.40 | ... 7 50– 7 99 |
| 8 00– 8 99... | 10 | 16 | 8 | 8 | 1 | 2 | ...... | 1 | ...... | 1 | 75 | 163 | 53.80 | 54.60 | ... 8 00– 8 99 |
| 9 00– 9 99... | 1 | 7 | 2 | 10 | ...... | 4 | ...... | 1 | ...... | 4 | 15 | 141 | 56.80 | 64.40 | ... 9 00– 9 99 |
| 10 00–10 99... | 5 | 12 | 2 | 13 | ...... | 1 | ...... | ...... | ...... | ...... | 31 | 124 | 63.10 | 72.80 | ...10 00–10.99 |
| 11 00–11 99... | 6 | 12 | 1 | 9 | 1 | 2 | ...... | ...... | ...... | 4 | 30 | 101 | 69.10 | 79.80 | ...11 00–11 99 |
| 12 00–12 99... | 2 | 5 | 5 | 5 | 1 | 1 | ...... | ...... | ...... | ...... | 39 | 89 | 77.00 | 85.90 | ...12 00–12 99 |
| 13 00–13 99... | 6 | 5 | 5 | 7 | 1 | ...... | ...... | 1 | ...... | 1 | 24 | 79 | 81.80 | 91.40 | ...13 00–13 99 |
| 14 00–14 99... | 2 | 3 | 8 | 4 | ...... | ...... | ...... | ...... | ...... | 1 | 20 | 55 | 85.80 | 95.20 | ...14 00–14 99 |
| 15 00–15 99... | 7 | ...... | 1 | 4 | ...... | ...... | ...... | ...... | ...... | ...... | 23 | 40 | 90.50 | 97.90 | ...15 00–15 99 |
| 16 00–17 99... | .... | 3 | 3 | ...... | ...... | ...... | ...... | ...... | ...... | ...... | 11 | 26 | 92.70 | 99.70 | ...16 00–17 99 |
| 18 00–19 99... | 4 | ...... | 1 | 2 | 3 | ...... | ...... | ...... | ...... | ...... | 13 | 4 | 95.40 | 99.90 | ...18 00–19 99 |
| 20 00–24 99... | 1 | ...... | 1 | 1 | ...... | ...... | ...... | ...... | ...... | ...... | 17 | 1 | 98.80 | 100.00 | ...20 00–24 99 |
| 25 00–29 99... | .... | ...... | .... | ...... | ...... | ...... | ...... | ...... | ...... | ...... | 5 | ...... | 99.80 | ...... | ...25 00–29 99 |
| 30 00–34 99... | 1 | ...... | .... | ...... | ...... | ...... | ...... | ...... | ...... | ...... | 1 | ...... | 100 00 | ...... | ...30 00–34 99 |
| Not reported... | .... | ...... | .... | ...... | ...... | ...... | ...... | ...... | ...... | ...... | 1 | ...... | ...... | ...... | ...Not reported |
| Total..... | 54 | 116 | 52 | 100 | 10 | 15 | 2 | 4 | 4 | 19 | 497 | 1,454 | ...... | ...... | .....Total |

361. TABLE IV, B, a

TROY

THE MEN'S SHIRT INDUSTRY — FACTORY WORKERS

NUMBER AND PER CENT OF EMPLOYEES CLASSIFIED ACCORDING TO ACTUAL WEEKLY EARNINGS, BY OCCUPATION AND SEX

| ACTUAL WEEKLY EARNINGS IN DOLLARS | OCCUPATION | | | | | | | | | | | | | | ACTUAL WEEKLY EARNINGS IN DOLLARS |
|---|---|---|---|---|---|---|---|---|---|---|---|---|---|---|---|
| | MARKERS | CUTTERS | TRIMMERS | | CUTTERS' HELPERS | | FOREMEN AND FOREWOMEN | | OPERATORS | | FLOOR WORK | | LAUNDRY HELPERS | | |
| | Male | Male | Male | Female | Male | Female | Male | Female | Male | Female | Male | Female | Male | Female | |
| Less than $3 00 | .... | 2 | .... | .... | .... | .... | .... | .... | .... | 17 | .... | 3 | .... | 2 | Less than $3 00 |
| $3 00–$3 49... | .... | 1 | .... | .... | .... | .... | .... | 1 | .... | 13 | .... | .... | .... | .... | ...$3 00– 3 49 |
| 3 50– 3 99... | .... | .... | .... | .... | 1 | .... | .... | .... | .... | 6 | .... | 1 | .... | .... | ... 3 50– 3 99 |
| 4 00– 4 49... | .... | 1 | .... | .... | 1 | .... | .... | .... | .... | 10 | .... | 6 | 2 | 1 | ... 4 00– 4 49 |
| 4 50– 4 99... | .... | 2 | .... | .... | 1 | .... | .... | .... | .... | 15 | .... | 4 | 2 | 3 | ... 4 50– 4 99 |
| 5 00– 5 49... | .... | .... | .... | .... | 2 | .... | .... | .... | .... | 24 | 1 | 6 | 1 | 3 | ... 5 00– 5 49 |
| 5 50– 5 99... | .... | .... | .... | .... | 1 | 1 | .... | .... | .... | 32 | .... | 4 | .... | 2 | ... 5 50– 5 99 |
| 6 00– 6 49... | .... | 1 | .... | .... | 2 | .... | .... | 1 | .... | 38 | .... | 4 | .... | 1 | ... 6 00– 6 49 |
| 6 50– 6 99... | .... | .... | .... | .... | .... | .... | .... | .... | .... | 30 | .... | 1 | 1 | 1 | ... 6 50– 6 99 |
| 7 00– 7 49... | .... | 3 | .... | .... | 1 | .... | .... | .... | .... | 31 | .... | 1 | .... | 2 | ... 7 00– 7 49 |
| 7 50– 7 99... | .... | 4 | .... | .... | .... | 1 | .... | .... | .... | 26 | .... | 3 | 4 | 1 | ... 7 50– 7 99 |
| 8 00– 8 99... | .... | 2 | 1 | .... | 1 | .... | .... | 1 | .... | 110 | 1 | 2 | 1 | 1 | ... 8 00– 8 99 |
| 9 00– 9 99... | .... | 1 | .... | 1 | .... | .... | .... | 3 | 1 | 97 | .... | 7 | 2 | .... | ... 9 00– 9 99 |
| 10 00–10 99... | .... | 7 | 1 | .... | 2 | .... | 1 | 2 | 1 | 88 | .... | 2 | 3 | 7 | ...10 00–10 99 |
| 11 00–11 99... | .... | 9 | .... | .... | .... | .... | 1 | 4 | .... | 63 | .... | 3 | 3 | 2 | ...11 00–11 99 |
| 12 00–12 99... | .... | 13 | 1 | .... | .... | .... | 2 | 8 | .... | 47 | .... | 1 | .... | .... | ...12 00–12 99 |
| 13 00–13 99... | .... | 6 | .... | .... | .... | .... | 2 | 2 | .... | 41 | 1 | .... | 1 | .... | ...13 00–13 99 |
| 14 00–14 99... | .... | 4 | .... | .... | .... | .... | .... | .... | .... | 41 | .... | 1 | .... | .... | ...14 00–14 99 |
| 15 00–15 99... | .... | 6 | .... | .... | .... | .... | 3 | 2 | .... | 14 | 3 | .... | 2 | .... | ...15 00–15 99 |
| 16 00–17 99... | .... | 6 | .... | .... | .... | .... | 4 | 1 | .... | 19 | 1 | .... | .... | .... | ...16 00–17 99 |
| 18 00–19 99... | .... | 2 | .... | .... | .... | .... | 9 | 1 | .... | 2 | .... | .... | 1 | .... | ...18 00–19 99 |
| 20 00–24 99... | 1 | 10 | .... | .... | .... | .... | 6 | .... | .... | 1 | .... | .... | .... | .... | ...20 00–24 99 |
| 25 00–29 99... | .... | 2 | .... | .... | .... | .... | 2 | .... | .... | .... | .... | .... | 1 | .... | ...25 00–29 99 |
| 30 00–34 99... | .... | .... | .... | .... | .... | .... | 1 | .... | .... | .... | .... | .... | .... | .... | ...30 00–34 99 |
| Total..... | 1 | 82 | 3 | 1 | 12 | 2 | 31 | 26 | 2 | 765 | 7 | 49 | 24 | 26 | .....Total |

TROY

361. TABLE IV, B, a.—*(concluded)* **THE MEN'S SHIRT INDUSTRY — FACTORY WORKERS**

NUMBER AND PER CENT OF EMPLOYEES CLASSIFIED ACCORDING TO ACTUAL WEEKLY EARNINGS, BY OCCUPATION AND SEX—*(concluded)*

| ACTUAL WEEKLY EARNINGS IN DOLLARS | OCCUPATION—*(concluded)* | | | | | | | | | | | | | | ACTUAL WEEKLY EARNINGS IN DOLLARS |
|---|---|---|---|---|---|---|---|---|---|---|---|---|---|---|---|
| | STARCHERS AND DAMPNERS | | IRONERS AND PRESSERS | | EXAMINERS | | FOLDERS | | PACKERS | | TOTAL | | CUMULATIVE PER CENT OF TOTAL | | |
| | Male | Female | Male | Female | Male | Female | Male | Female | Male | Female | Male | Female | Male | Female | |
| Less than $3 00 | .... | 19 | 5 | 6 | ...... | 1 | ...... | 5 | 1 | 1 | 8 | 54 | 1.60 | 3.70 | Less than $3 00 |
| $3 00–$3 49... | .... | 5 | 1 | 1 | ...... | ...... | ...... | 3 | ...... | ...... | 2 | 23 | 2.00 | 4.80 | ... 3 00– 3 49 |
| 3 50– 3 99... | .... | 6 | 15 | 4 | ...... | ...... | 3 | 2 | ...... | ...... | 19 | 19 | 5.80 | 6.60 | ... 3 50– 3 99 |
| 4 00– 4 49... | .... | 4 | 8 | 6 | ...... | 4 | 2 | 8 | ...... | ...... | 14 | 39 | 8.70 | 9.30 | ... 4 00– 4 49 |
| 4 50– 4 99... | .... | 2 | 10 | 7 | ...... | 2 | ...... | 4 | ...... | 1 | 15 | 38 | 11.70 | 11.90 | ... 4 50– 4 99 |
| 5 00– 5 49... | .... | 2 | 31 | 12 | 1 | 10 | 3 | 4 | ...... | 1 | 39 | 62 | 19.50 | 16.20 | ... 5 00– 5 49 |
| 5 50– 5 99... | .... | 11 | 5 | 13 | ...... | 21 | 3 | 10 | ...... | ...... | 9 | 94 | 21.40 | 22.60 | ... 5 50– 5 99 |
| 6 00– 6 49... | .... | 6 | 23 | 9 | 1 | 18 | 3 | 6 | ...... | 4 | 30 | 87 | 27.40 | 28.60 | ... 6 00– 6 49 |
| 6 50– 6 99... | .... | 3 | 15 | 7 | ...... | 8 | ...... | 5 | ...... | 1 | 16 | 56 | 30.60 | 32.50 | ... 6 50– 6 99 |
| 7 00– 7 49... | .... | 6 | 10 | 7 | ...... | 27 | ...... | 9 | ...... | 4 | 14 | 87 | 33.40 | 38.40 | ... 7 00– 7 49 |
| 7 50– 7 99... | .... | 20 | 15 | 10 | 3 | 10 | ...... | 1 | ...... | ...... | 26 | 72 | 38.70 | 43.40 | ... 7 50– 7 99 |
| 8 00– 8 99... | .... | 9 | 65 | 13 | ...... | 19 | 1 | 4 | 3 | 4 | 75 | 163 | 53.80 | 54.60 | ... 8 00– 8 99 |
| 9 00– 9 99... | .... | ...... | 9 | 10 | ...... | 14 | 1 | 6 | 1 | 3 | 15 | 141 | 56.80 | 64.40 | ... 9 00– 9 99 |
| 10 00–10 99... | 1 | 1 | 14 | 18 | 1 | 2 | ...... | 4 | ...... | ...... | 31 | 124 | 63.10 | 72.80 | ...10 00–10 99 |
| 11 00–11 99... | .... | ...... | 17 | 21 | ...... | 3 | ...... | 4 | ...... | 1 | 30 | 101 | 69.10 | 79.80 | ...11 00–11 99 |
| 12 00–12 99... | 1 | ...... | 19 | 23 | 3 | 3 | ...... | 7 | ...... | ...... | 39 | 89 | 77.00 | 85.90 | ...12 00–12 99 |
| 13 00–13 99... | .... | ...... | 14 | 30 | ...... | 1 | ...... | 5 | ...... | ...... | 24 | 79 | 81.80 | 91.40 | ...13 00–13 99 |
| 14 00–14 99... | .... | ...... | 15 | 2 | 1 | ...... | ...... | 11 | ...... | ...... | 20 | 55 | 85.80 | 95.20 | ...14 00–14 99 |
| 15 00–15 99... | .... | 10 | 8 | 1 | 1 | ...... | ...... | 13 | ...... | ...... | 23 | 40 | 90.50 | 97.90 | ...15 00–15 99 |
| 16 00–17 99... | .... | 1 | .... | ...... | ...... | 1 | ...... | 4 | ...... | ...... | 11 | 26 | 92.70 | 99.70 | ...16 00–17 99 |
| 18 00–19 99... | .... | ...... | 1 | ...... | ...... | ...... | ...... | 1 | ...... | ...... | 13 | 4 | 95.40 | 99.90 | ...18 00–19 99 |
| 20 00–24 99... | .... | ...... | .... | ...... | ...... | ...... | ...... | ...... | ...... | ...... | 17 | 1 | 98.80 | 100.00 | ...20 00–24 99 |
| 25 00–29 99... | .... | ...... | .... | ...... | ...... | ...... | ...... | ...... | ...... | ...... | 5 | ...... | 99.80 | ...... | ...25 00–29 99 |
| 30 00–34 99... | .... | ...... | .... | ...... | ...... | ...... | ...... | ...... | ...... | ...... | 1 | ...... | 100.00 | ...... | ...30 00–34 99 |
| Not reported.. | .... | ...... | .... | ...... | 1 | ...... | ...... | ...... | ...... | ...... | 1 | ...... | ...... | ...... | ..Not reported |
| Total..... | 2 | 105 | 300 | 200 | 12 | 144 | 16 | 116 | 5 | 20 | 497 | 1,454 | ...... | ...... | .....Total |

TROY

**THE PAPER BOX INDUSTRY — FACTORY WORKERS**

362. TABLE V, C, a. NUMBER AND PER CENT. OF EMPLOYEES EARNING SPECIFIED WEEKLY RATES, BY AGE GROUPS AND SEX

| WEEKLY RATES IN DOLLARS | AGE GROUPS IN YEARS | | | | | | | | | | | | | WEEKLY RATES IN DOLLARS |
|---|---|---|---|---|---|---|---|---|---|---|---|---|---|---|
| | 14–15 | 16–17 | | 18–20 | | 21–24 | | 25–29 | | 30–34 | | 35–39 | | |
| | Male | Male | Female | Male | Female | Male | Female | Male | Female | Male | Female | Male | Female | |
| $3 00–$3 49...... | 1 | ...... | ...... | ...... | ...... | ...... | ...... | ...... | ...... | ...... | ...... | ...... | ...... | ......$3 00–$3 49 |
| 3 50– 3 99...... | 1 | 1 | ...... | ...... | ...... | ...... | ...... | ...... | ...... | ...... | ...... | ...... | ...... | ......3 50– 3 99 |
| 4 00– 4 49...... | 2 | 3 | 2 | ...... | ...... | ...... | ...... | ...... | ...... | ...... | ...... | ...... | ...... | ......4 00– 4 49 |
| 4 50– 4 99...... | 3 | 2 | 1 | 1 | 2 | ...... | ...... | ...... | ...... | ...... | ...... | ...... | ...... | ......4 50– 4 99 |
| 5 00– 5 49...... | 2 | 2 | 4 | ...... | 1 | ...... | ...... | ...... | 1 | ...... | ...... | ...... | ...... | ......5 00– 5 49 |
| 5 50– 5 99...... | ...... | 3 | ...... | ...... | ...... | ...... | ...... | ...... | ...... | ...... | ...... | ...... | ...... | ......5 50– 5 99 |
| 6 00– 6 49...... | ...... | ...... | 2 | 1 | 2 | ...... | 1 | ...... | ...... | ...... | ...... | ...... | ...... | ......6 00– 6 49 |
| 7 00– 7 49...... | ...... | 1 | ...... | 2 | ...... | ...... | 1 | ...... | ...... | 1 | 1 | ...... | ...... | ......7 00– 7 49 |
| 7 50– 7 99...... | ...... | ...... | ...... | 1 | ...... | 1 | 1 | 1 | ...... | ...... | ...... | ...... | ...... | ......7 50– 7 99 |
| 8 00– 8 99...... | ...... | ...... | ...... | 1 | ...... | 2 | 1 | ...... | 2 | ...... | 1 | ...... | ...... | ......8 00– 8 99 |
| 9 00– 9 99...... | ...... | 1 | ...... | 2 | ...... | 5 | 1 | 4 | ...... | 4 | ...... | 2 | 1 | ......9 00– 9 99 |
| 10 00–10 99...... | ...... | 1 | ...... | ...... | ...... | 3 | 1 | 3 | ...... | 2 | ...... | 2 | ...... | .....10 00–10 99 |
| 11 00–11 99...... | ...... | ...... | ...... | ...... | ...... | 1 | ...... | 1 | ...... | 1 | 1 | ...... | ...... | .....11 00–11 99 |
| 12 00–12 99...... | ...... | ...... | ...... | 1 | ...... | 3 | ...... | ...... | ...... | 1 | ...... | 2 | ...... | .....12 00–12 99 |
| 13 00–13 99...... | ...... | ...... | ...... | ...... | ...... | ...... | ...... | 2 | ...... | 1 | ...... | ...... | ...... | .....13 00–13 99 |
| 14 00–14 99...... | ...... | ...... | ...... | ...... | ...... | ...... | ...... | ...... | ...... | 1 | ...... | ...... | ...... | .....14 00–14 99 |
| 15 00–15 99...... | ...... | ...... | ...... | ...... | ...... | 1 | ...... | ...... | ...... | ...... | ...... | 1 | ...... | .....15 00–15 99 |
| 16 00–17 99...... | ...... | ...... | ...... | ...... | ...... | ...... | ...... | 1 | ...... | ...... | ...... | ...... | ...... | .....16 00–17 99 |
| 30 00–34 99...... | ...... | ...... | ...... | ...... | ...... | ...... | ...... | ...... | ...... | 1 | ...... | ...... | ...... | .....30 00–34 99 |
| Not reported...... | ...... | ...... | ...... | ...... | ...... | ...... | ...... | 1 | ...... | ...... | ...... | ...... | ...... | .....Not reported |
| Total........ | 9 | 14 | 9 | 9 | 5 | 16 | 6 | 13 | 3 | 12 | 3 | 7 | 1 | ......Total |

362. TABLE V, C, a — (*concluded*)

TROY

**THE PAPER BOX INDUSTRY — FACTORY WORKERS**

NUMBER AND PER CENT. OF EMPLOYEES EARNING SPECIFIED WEEKLY RATES, BY AGE GROUPS AND SEX

| WEEKLY RATES IN DOLLARS | AGE GROUPS IN YEARS (*concluded*) | | | | | | | | | | | | | | WEEKLY RATES IN DOLLARS |
|---|---|---|---|---|---|---|---|---|---|---|---|---|---|---|---|
| | 40–44 | | 45–54 | | 55–64 | | 65 AND OVER | NOT REPORTED | TOTAL | | ACCUMULATIVE PER CENT OF TOTAL | | | | |
| | Male | Female | Male | Female | Male | Female | Male | Male | Male | Female | Male | Female | | | |
| $3 00–$3 49 | ....... | ....... | ....... | ....... | ....... | ....... | ....... | ....... | 1 | ....... | .90 | ....... | $3 00–$3 49 | | |
| 3 50– 3 99 | ....... | ....... | ....... | ....... | ....... | ....... | ....... | ....... | 2 | ....... | 2.70 | ....... | 3 50– 3 99 | | |
| 4 00– 4 49 | ....... | ....... | ....... | ....... | ....... | ....... | ....... | ....... | 5 | 2 | 7.30 | 5.20 | 4 00– 4 49 | | |
| 4 50– 4 99 | ....... | ....... | ....... | ....... | ....... | ....... | ....... | ....... | 6 | 3 | 12.80 | 13.20 | 4 50– 4 99 | | |
| 5 00– 5 49 | ....... | ....... | ....... | ....... | ....... | ....... | ....... | ....... | 4 | 6 | 16.40 | 29.00 | 5 00– 5 49 | | |
| 5 50– 5 99 | ....... | ....... | ....... | ....... | ....... | ....... | ....... | ....... | 3 | ....... | 19.10 | ....... | 5 50– 5 99 | | |
| 6 00– 6 49 | ....... | ....... | ....... | ....... | ....... | ....... | ....... | ....... | 1 | 5 | 20.00 | 42.00 | 6 00– 6 49 | | |
| 7 00– 7 49 | ....... | ....... | ....... | ....... | ....... | 1 | 1 | ....... | 5 | 3 | 24.50 | 50.00 | 7 00– 7 49 | | |
| 7 50– 7 99 | ....... | ....... | ....... | ....... | ....... | ....... | ....... | ....... | 3 | 1 | 27.20 | 52.50 | 7 50– 7 99 | | |
| 8 00– 8 99 | ....... | ....... | ....... | ....... | 1 | 1 | ....... | ....... | 4 | 5 | 31.00 | 66.00 | 8 00– 8 99 | | |
| 9 00– 9 99 | ....... | 4 | 1 | ....... | ....... | ....... | ....... | ....... | 19 | 6 | 48.00 | 81.70 | 9 00– 9 99 | | |
| 10 00–10 99 | 1 | ....... | ....... | 4 | ....... | 1 | ....... | ....... | 12 | 6 | 59.00 | 97.40 | 10 00–10 99 | | |
| 11 00–11 99 | 2 | ....... | 1 | ....... | ....... | ....... | ....... | ....... | 6 | 1 | 64.50 | 100.00 | 11 00–11 99 | | |
| 12 00–12 99 | 1 | ....... | 1 | ....... | 1 | ....... | ....... | 1 | 11 | ....... | 74.50 | ....... | 12 00–12 99 | | |
| 13 00–13 99 | 2 | ....... | 3 | ....... | ....... | ....... | ....... | ....... | 8 | ....... | 82.00 | ....... | 13 00–13 99 | | |
| 14 00–14 99 | ....... | ....... | ....... | ....... | 1 | ....... | ....... | ....... | 2 | ....... | 83.50 | ....... | 14 00–14 99 | | |
| 15 00–15 99 | 2 | ....... | ....... | ....... | ....... | ....... | ....... | ....... | 4 | ....... | 87.00 | ....... | 15 00–15 99 | | |
| 16 00–17 99 | 1 | ....... | 2 | ....... | ....... | ....... | ....... | ....... | 4 | ....... | 91.00 | ....... | 16 00–17 99 | | |
| 18 00–19 99 | 1 | ....... | ....... | ....... | ....... | ....... | ....... | ....... | 1 | ....... | 92.00 | ....... | 18 00–19 99 | | |
| 20 00–24 99 | 1 | ....... | 5 | ....... | 1 | ....... | ....... | ....... | 7 | ....... | 98.00 | ....... | 20 00–24 99 | | |
| 25 00–29 99 | ....... | ....... | ....... | ....... | 1 | ....... | ....... | ....... | 1 | ....... | 99.00 | ....... | 25 00–29 99 | | |
| 30 00–34 99 | ....... | ....... | ....... | ....... | ....... | ....... | ....... | ....... | 1 | ....... | 100.00 | ....... | 30 00–34 99 | | |
| Not reported | 1 | ....... | ....... | ....... | 1 | ....... | ....... | ....... | 3 | ....... | ....... | ....... | Not reported | | |
| Total | 12 | 4 | 13 | 4 | 6 | 3 | 1 | 1 | 113 | 38 | ....... | ....... | Total | | |

TROY
THE PAPER BOX INDUSTRY — FACTORY WORKERS

363. TABLE VIII, C, a NUMBER AND PER CENT. OF EMPLOYEES EARNING SPECIFIED WEEKLY RATES, BY OCCUPATION AND SEX

| Weekly Rates in Dollars | Foremen and Forewomen | | Cutters | Setters-up | | General Machine Work | | Glue Table Work | Turners-in | | Strippers and Top Labelers | | Table Work | | Closing and Tying | | Floor Work | Total | | Cumulative Per Cent of Total | | Weekly Rates in Dollars |
|---|---|---|---|---|---|---|---|---|---|---|---|---|---|---|---|---|---|---|---|---|---|---|
| | Male | Female | Male | Male | Female | Male | Female | Male | Male | Female | Male | Female | Male | Female | Male | Female | Male | Male | Female | Male | Female | |
| $3 00- 3 49 | | | | | | | | | | | | | | | | | 1 | 1 | | .90 | | $3 00-$3 49 |
| 3 50- 3 99 | | | | 1 | | | | | 1 | | | | | | | | | 2 | | 2.70 | | 3 50- 3 99 |
| 4 00- 4 49 | | | | 4 | | | | | | 2 | | | | | 1 | | | 5 | 2 | 7.30 | 5.20 | 4 00- 4 49 |
| 4 50- 4 99 | | | | 3 | | | | | | 3 | | | | | 3 | | | 6 | 3 | 12.80 | 13.20 | 4 50- 4 99 |
| 5 00- 5 49 | | | 1 | 2 | 1 | | | | | 2 | | 2 | | | | 1 | 1 | 4 | 6 | 16.40 | 29.00 | 5 00- 5 49 |
| 5 50- 5 99 | | | | 2 | | | | | | | | | | | 1 | | | 3 | | 19.10 | | 5 50- 5 99 |
| 6 00- 6 49 | | | | | | | | | | | | 4 | | 1 | 1 | | | 1 | 5 | 20.00 | 42.00 | 6 00- 6 49 |
| 7 00- 7 49 | | | 1 | 1 | | | 3 | | | | | | | | 3 | | | 5 | 3 | 24.50 | 50.00 | 7 00- 7 49 |
| 7 50- 7 99 | | | | 1 | | | | | | | | 1 | | | 2 | | | 3 | 1 | 27.20 | 52.50 | 7 50- 7 99 |
| 8 00- 8 99 | | | | | | | | | | | | 2 | 1 | 2 | 3 | 1 | | 4 | 5 | 31.00 | 66.00 | 8 00- 8 99 |
| 9 00- 9 99 | | | 4 | 3 | | 2 | | | | | 5 | 4 | 1 | 2 | 4 | | | 19 | 6 | 48.00 | 81.70 | 9 00- 9 99 |
| 10 00-10 99 | | | 3 | 2 | | | | 2 | | | 3 | 2 | 1 | 4 | | | 1 | 12 | 6 | 59.00 | 97.40 | 10 00-10 99 |
| 11 00-11 99 | | 1 | 4 | | | | | 1 | | | 1 | | | | | | | 6 | 1 | 64.50 | 100.00 | 11 00-11 99 |
| 12 00-12 99 | | | 9 | | | 1 | | | | | 1 | | | | | | | 11 | | 74.50 | | 12 00-12 99 |
| 13 00-13 99 | 2 | | 6 | | | | | | | | | | | | | | | 8 | | 82.00 | | 13 00-13 99 |
| 14 00-14 99 | 1 | | 1 | | | | | | | | | | | | | | | 2 | | 83.50 | | 14 00-14 99 |
| 15 00-15 99 | 1 | | 2 | | | | | | | | 1 | | | | | | | 4 | | 87.00 | | 15 00-15 99 |
| 16 00-17 99 | 2 | | 2 | | | | | | | | | | | | | | | 4 | | 91.00 | | 16 00-17 99 |
| 18 00-19 99 | 1 | | | | | | | | | | | | | | | | | 1 | | 92.00 | | 18 00-19 99 |
| 20 00-24 99 | 4 | | 3 | | | | | | | | | | | | | | | 7 | | 98.00 | | 20 00-24 99 |
| 25 00-29 99 | 1 | | | | | | | | | | | | | | | | | 1 | | 99.00 | | 25 00-29 99 |
| 30 00-34 99 | 1 | | | | | | | | | | | | | | | | | 1 | | 100 00 | | 30 00-34 99 |
| Not reported | 1 | | 1 | 1 | | | | | | | | | | | | | | 3 | | | | Not reported |
| Total | 14 | 1 | 37 | 20 | 1 | 3 | 3 | 3 | 1 | 7 | 11 | 15 | 3 | 9 | 18 | 2 | 3 | 113 | 38 | | | Total |

364. TABLE VI, C, a

TROY

**THE PAPER BOX INDUSTRY — FACTORY WORKERS**

NUMBER AND PER CENT OF EMPLOYEES CLASSIFIED ACCORDING TO ACTUAL WEEKLY EARNINGS, BY AGE GROUPS AND SEX

| ACTUAL WEEKLY EARNINGS IN DOLLARS | AGE GROUPS IN YEARS | | | | | | | | | | | | | | ACTUAL WEEKLY EARNINGS IN DOLLARS |
|---|---|---|---|---|---|---|---|---|---|---|---|---|---|---|---|
| | 14–15 | | 16–17 | | 18–20 | | 21–24 | | 25–29 | | 30–34 | | 35–39 | | |
| | Male | Female | Male | Female | Male | Female | Male | Female | Male | Female | Male | Female | Male | Female | |
| Less than $3 00 | 3 | ...... | 2 | ...... | 1 | 1 | ...... | 1 | ...... | ...... | ...... | ...... | ...... | ...... | Less than $3 00 |
| $3 00–$3 49... | 3 | ...... | 3 | 1 | ...... | ...... | ...... | ...... | ...... | 1 | ...... | ...... | ...... | ...... | ...$3 00– 3 49 |
| 3 50– 3 99... | 3 | ...... | 1 | 3 | ...... | 1 | ...... | ...... | ...... | ...... | ...... | ...... | ...... | ...... | ....3 50– 3 99 |
| 4 00– 4 49... | 4 | ...... | 3 | 4 | ...... | 3 | ...... | ...... | ...... | ...... | ...... | ...... | ...... | ...... | ....4 00– 4 49 |
| 4 50– 4 99... | 3 | ...... | 3 | 3 | 1 | 2 | ...... | ...... | ...... | 1 | ...... | ...... | ...... | ...... | ....4 50– 4 99 |
| 5 00– 5 49... | 1 | 1 | 3 | 3 | 1 | 5 | ...... | ...... | ...... | 1 | ...... | ...... | ...... | ...... | ....5 00– 5 49 |
| 5 50– 5 99... | 2 | ...... | 6 | 4 | 2 | 7 | ...... | ...... | ...... | ...... | ...... | ...... | ...... | 1 | ....5 50– 5 99 |
| 6 00– 6 49... | .... | ...... | 1 | 2 | 3 | 1 | 1 | 2 | ...... | 1 | ...... | 1 | ...... | 1 | ....6 00– 6 49 |
| 6 50– 6 99... | .... | ...... | 1 | ...... | 1 | 2 | 1 | 1 | ...... | ...... | ...... | ...... | ...... | 1 | ....6 50– 6 99 |
| 7 00– 7 49... | .... | ...... | .... | 1 | ...... | 2 | 3 | 2 | 1 | 1 | 2 | 1 | ...... | ...... | ....7 00– 7 49 |
| 7 50– 7 99... | .... | ...... | 1 | ...... | 3 | 1 | ...... | 2 | 1 | ...... | ...... | ...... | 1 | 3 | ....7 50– 7 99 |
| 8 00– 8 99... | .... | ...... | .... | ...... | 2 | 1 | 5 | 5 | 5 | 3 | 4 | 1 | 2 | ...... | ....8 00– 8 99 |
| 9 00– 9 99... | .... | ...... | 1 | ...... | 1 | 2 | 9 | 3 | 2 | 2 | 3 | 4 | ...... | 1 | ....9 00– 9 99 |
| 10 00–10 99... | .... | ...... | .... | ...... | 1 | ...... | 4 | 8 | 2 | 4 | 2 | 2 | 3 | 2 | ...10 00–10 99 |
| 11 00–11 99... | .... | ...... | .... | ...... | 2 | 1 | 2 | 1 | 3 | ...... | 2 | 2 | 1 | 1 | ...11 00–11 99 |
| 12 00–12 99... | .... | ...... | .... | ...... | 2 | ...... | ...... | ...... | 3 | ...... | 1 | 1 | ...... | 2 | ...12 00–12 99 |
| 13 00–13 99... | .... | ...... | .... | ...... | ...... | ...... | 3 | 1 | 2 | ...... | 2 | ...... | ...... | ...... | ...13 00–13 99 |
| 14 00–14 99... | .... | ...... | .... | ...... | 1 | ...... | 1 | ...... | ...... | ...... | ...... | ...... | 1 | ...... | ...14 00–14 99 |
| 15 00–15 99... | .... | ...... | .... | ...... | ...... | ...... | 2 | ...... | 5 | ...... | 2 | ...... | 4 | ...... | ...15 00–15 99 |
| 16 00–17 99... | .... | ...... | .... | ...... | ...... | ...... | 1 | ...... | 3 | ...... | ...... | 1 | 1 | ...... | ...16 00–17 99 |
| 18 00–19 99... | .... | ...... | .... | ...... | ...... | ...... | ...... | ...... | ...... | ...... | 1 | ...... | ...... | ...... | ...18 00–19 99 |
| 20 00–24 99... | .... | ...... | .... | ...... | ...... | ...... | ...... | ...... | ...... | ...... | 1 | ...... | ...... | ...... | ...20 00–25 99 |
| 30 00–34 99... | .... | ...... | .... | ...... | ...... | ...... | ...... | ...... | ...... | ...... | 1 | ...... | ...... | ...... | ...30 00–34 99 |
| Total..... | 19 | 1 | 25 | 21 | 21 | 29 | 32 | 26 | 27 | 14 | 21 | 13 | 13 | 12 | .....Total |

TROY

364. TABLE VI, C, a — (*concluded*) THE PAPER BOX INDUSTRY — FACTORY WORKERS

NUMBER AND PER CENT. OF EMPLOYEES CLASSIFIED ACCORDING TO ACTUAL WEEKLY EARNINGS, BY AGE GROUPS AND SEX

| ACTUAL WEEKLY EARNINGS IN DOLLARS | AGE GROUPS IN YEARS (*concluded*) | | | | | | | | | | | | | | ACTUAL WEEKLY EARNINGS IN DOLLARS |
|---|---|---|---|---|---|---|---|---|---|---|---|---|---|---|---|
| | 40–44 | | 45–54 | | 55–64 | | 65 AND OVER | NOT REPORTED | | TOTAL | | CUMULATIVE PER CENT OF TOTAL | | |
| | Male | Female | Male | Female | Male | Female | Male | Male | Female | Male | Female | Male | Female | |
| Less than $3 00 | ...... | 1 | ...... | ...... | ...... | ...... | ...... | ...... | ...... | 6 | 3 | 3.05 | 2.1 | Less than $3 00 |
| $3 00–$3 49 | ...... | ...... | ...... | ...... | ...... | ...... | ...... | ...... | ...... | 6 | 2 | 6.1 | 3.5 | $3 00– 3 49 |
| 3 50– 3 99 | ...... | ...... | ...... | ...... | ...... | ...... | ...... | ...... | ...... | 4 | 4 | 8.15 | 6.3 | 3 50– 3 99 |
| 4 00– 4 49 | ...... | ...... | ...... | ...... | ...... | ...... | ...... | ...... | ...... | 7 | 7 | 11.7 | 11.2 | 4 00– 4 49 |
| 4 50– 4 99 | ...... | ...... | ...... | ...... | ...... | ...... | ...... | ...... | ...... | 7 | 6 | 15.3 | 15.4 | 4 50– 4 99 |
| 5 00– 5 49 | ...... | ...... | ...... | ...... | ...... | 1 | ...... | ...... | ...... | 5 | 11 | 17.8 | 23.0 | 5 00– 5 49 |
| 5 50– 5 99 | ...... | ...... | ...... | ...... | ...... | ...... | ...... | ...... | ...... | 10 | 12 | 23.0 | 31.5 | 5 50– 5 99 |
| 6 00– 6 49 | ...... | ...... | 1 | ...... | ...... | 1 | ...... | ...... | ...... | 6 | 9 | 26.0 | 37.8 | 6 00– 6 49 |
| 6 50– 6 99 | ...... | ...... | ...... | ...... | ...... | ...... | ...... | ...... | ...... | 3 | 4 | 27.5 | 40.5 | 6 50– 6 99 |
| 7 00– 7 49 | ...... | 1 | ...... | 1 | ...... | 1 | 1 | ...... | ...... | 7 | 10 | 31.2 | 47.5 | 7 00– 7 49 |
| 7 50– 7 99 | ...... | ...... | 1 | ...... | ...... | ...... | ...... | ...... | 1 | 7 | 7 | 34.9 | 52.5 | 7 50– 7 99 |
| 8 00– 8 99 | 1 | 1 | 1 | 1 | 1 | ...... | ...... | ...... | 1 | 21 | 13 | 45.4 | 61.5 | 8 00– 8 99 |
| 9 00– 9 99 | 1 | 4 | ...... | 4 | ...... | 1 | ...... | ...... | ...... | 17 | 21 | 54.0 | 76.2 | 9 00– 9 99 |
| 10 00–10 99 | 1 | 1 | ...... | 2 | 1 | ...... | ...... | ...... | ...... | 14 | 19 | 61.0 | 89.5 | 10 00–10 99 |
| 11 00–11 99 | 4 | ...... | 1 | ...... | ...... | 1 | ...... | 1 | ...... | 16 | 6 | 69.3 | 93.7 | 11 00–11 99 |
| 12 00–12 99 | 1 | 2 | 2 | 1 | 1 | ...... | ...... | ...... | ...... | 10 | 6 | 74.5 | 97.9 | 12 00–12 99 |
| 13 00–13 99 | 2 | ...... | 2 | ...... | ...... | ...... | ...... | ...... | ...... | 11 | 1 | 80.0 | 98.6 | 13 00–13 99 |
| 14 00–14 99 | ...... | ...... | ...... | ...... | 1 | ...... | ...... | ...... | ...... | 4 | ...... | 82.0 | ...... | 14 00–14 99 |
| 15 00–15 99 | 1 | ...... | ...... | ...... | ...... | ...... | ...... | ...... | ...... | 14 | ...... | 89.3 | ...... | 15 00–15 99 |
| 16 00–17 99 | 1 | 1 | 2 | ...... | ...... | ...... | ...... | ...... | ...... | 8 | 2 | 93.4 | 100.0 | 16 00–17 99 |
| 18 00–19 99 | 1 | ...... | ...... | ...... | ...... | ...... | ...... | ...... | ...... | 2 | ...... | 94.6 | ...... | 18 00–19 99 |
| 20 00–24 99 | 2 | ...... | 5 | ...... | 1 | ...... | ...... | ...... | ...... | 9 | ...... | 99.0 | ...... | 20 00–24 99 |
| 25 00–29 99 | ...... | ...... | ...... | ...... | 1 | ...... | ...... | ...... | ...... | 1 | ...... | 99.5 | ...... | 25 00–29 99 |
| 30 00–34 99 | ...... | ...... | ...... | ...... | ...... | ...... | ...... | ...... | ...... | 1 | ...... | 100.0 | ...... | 30 00–34 99 |
| Total | 15 | 11 | 15 | 9 | 6 | 5 | 1 | 1 | 2 | 196 | 143 | ...... | ...... | Total |

365. TABLE IX, C, a

TROY

THE PAPER BOX INDUSTRY — FACTORY WORKERS

NUMBER AND PER CENT. OF EMPLOYEES CLASSIFIED ACCORDING TO ACTUAL WEEKLY EARNINGS, BY OCCUPATION AND SEX

| ACTUAL WEEKLY EARNINGS IN DOLLARS | OCCUPATION | | | | | | | | | | | | | | | | | | | | | | | | ACTUAL WEEKLY EARNINGS IN DOLLARS |
|---|---|---|---|---|---|---|---|---|---|---|---|---|---|---|---|---|---|---|---|---|---|---|---|---|---|
| | FOREMEN AND FOREWOMEN | | CUTTERS | SETTERS-UP | | GENERAL MACHINE WORK | | GLUE TABLE WORK | TURNERS-IN | | STRIPPERS AND TOP LABELERS | | TABLE WORK | | CLOSING AND TYING | | FLOOR WORK | | TOTAL | | CUMULATIVE PER CENT OF TOTAL | | |
| | Male | Female | Male | Male | Female | Male | Female | Male | Male | Female | Male | Female | Male | Female | Male | Female | Male | Female | Male | Female | Male | Female | |
| Less than $3 00 | | | | 2 | | | 1 | | 3 | 1 | | 1 | | | 1 | | | | 6 | 3 | 3.05 | 2.10 | Less than $3 00 |
| $3 00–$3 49 | | | | 3 | | | | | 2 | 2 | | | | | | | 1 | | 6 | 2 | 6.10 | 3.50 | $3 00– 3 49 |
| 3 50– 3 99 | | | | 1 | | | | | 1 | 4 | | | | | 2 | | | | 4 | 4 | 8.15 | 6.30 | 3 50– 3 99 |
| 4 00– 4 49 | | | | 3 | 1 | | | | 1 | 4 | | 1 | | 1 | 2 | | 1 | | 7 | 7 | 11.70 | 11.20 | 4 00– 4 49 |
| 4 50– 4 99 | | | 1 | 1 | | | 1 | | 5 | 3 | | 1 | | | | | | 1 | 7 | 6 | 15.30 | 15.40 | 4 50– 4 99 |
| 5 00– 5 49 | | | | 2 | | | | | | 8 | 2 | 2 | | 1 | | | 1 | | 5 | 11 | 17.80 | 23.00 | 5 00– 5 49 |
| 5 50– 5 99 | | | | 2 | | | 1 | | 6 | 4 | | 5 | | 1 | 1 | 1 | 1 | | 10 | 12 | 23.00 | 31.50 | 5 50– 5 99 |
| 6 00– 6 49 | | | 1 | 2 | | | 2 | | 2 | 4 | | 2 | | | 1 | 1 | | | 6 | 9 | 26.00 | 37.80 | 6 00– 6 49 |
| 6 50– 6 99 | | | 1 | | | | | | | 1 | 1 | 3 | | | 1 | | | | 3 | 4 | 27.50 | 40.50 | 6 50– 6 99 |
| 7 00– 7 49 | | | 1 | 2 | | | 1 | | | 1 | 1 | 4 | | 3 | 3 | 1 | | | 7 | 10 | 31.20 | 47.50 | 7 00– 7 49 |
| 7 50– 7 99 | | | | 2 | | | | | | | 2 | 3 | | 4 | 3 | | | | 7 | 7 | 34.90 | 52.50 | 7 50– 7 99 |
| 8 00– 8 99 | | | 3 | 3 | | | | | | | 7 | 9 | 2 | 4 | 6 | | | | 21 | 13 | 45.40 | 61.50 | 8 00– 8 99 |
| 9 00– 9 99 | | | 4 | 4 | | 2 | 1 | | | | 3 | 14 | 2 | 6 | 2 | | | | 17 | 21 | 54.00 | 76.20 | 9 00– 9 99 |
| 10 00–10 99 | | | 5 | 1 | | 1 | 2 | 2 | | | 4 | 14 | | 3 | 1 | | | | 14 | 19 | 61.00 | 89.50 | 10 00–10 99 |
| 11 00–11 99 | | 1 | 7 | 1 | | 1 | | 1 | | | 4 | 5 | | | 1 | | 1 | | 16 | 6 | 69.30 | 93.70 | 11 00–11 99 |
| 12 00–12 99 | | | 5 | | | 1 | | 1 | | | 3 | 6 | | | | | | | 10 | 6 | 74.50 | 97.90 | 12 00–12 99 |
| 13 00–13 99 | 2 | | 5 | | | | | | | | 4 | 1 | | | | | | | 11 | 1 | 80.00 | 98.60 | 13 00–13 99 |
| 14 00–14 99 | 1 | | 1 | | | | | | | | 1 | | | | 1 | | | | 4 | | 82.00 | | 14 00–14 99 |
| 15 00–15 99 | 1 | | 1 | 4 | | | | | | | 6 | | 1 | | 1 | | | | 14 | | 89.30 | | 15 00–15 99 |
| 16 00–17 99 | 2 | | 2 | 2 | | | | | | | 2 | 2 | | | | | | | 8 | 2 | 93.40 | 100.00 | 16 00–17 99 |
| 18 00–19 99 | 1 | | | | | | | | | | 1 | | | | | | | | 2 | | 94.60 | | 18 00–19 99 |
| 20 00–24 99 | 5 | | 4 | | | | | | | | | | | | | | | | 9 | | 99.00 | | 20 00–24 99 |
| 25 00–29 99 | 1 | | | | | | | | | | | | | | | | | | 1 | | 99.50 | | 25 00–29 99 |
| 30 00–34 99 | 1 | | | | | | | | | | | | | | | | | | 1 | | 100.00 | | 30 00–34 99 |
| Total | 14 | 1 | 41 | 35 | 1 | 5 | 9 | 4 | 20 | 32 | 41 | 73 | 5 | 23 | 26 | 3 | 5 | 1 | 196 | 143 | | | Total |

www.ingramcontent.com/pod-product-compliance
Lightning Source LLC
LaVergne TN
LVHW010520100826
845148LV00001B/50